MW00786182

The Oxford Handbook of Suicide and Self-Injury

OXFORD LIBRARY OF PSYCHOLOGY

EDITOR-IN-CHIEF

Peter E. Nathan

AREA EDITORS:

Clinical Psychology
David H. Barlow

Cognitive Neuroscience
Kevin N. Ochsner and Stephen M. Kosslyn

Cognitive Psychology
Daniel Reisberg

Counseling Psychology
Elizabeth M. Altmaier and Jo-Ida C. Hansen

Developmental Psychology
Philip David Zelazo

Health Psychology
Howard S. Friedman

History of Psychology
David B. Baker

Methods and Measurement
Todd D. Little

Neuropsychology
Kenneth M. Adams

Organizational Psychology
Steve W. J. Kozlowski

Personality and Social Psychology
Kay Deaux and Mark Snyder

OXFORD LIBRARY OF PSYCHOLOGY

Editor in Chief PETER E. NATHAN

The Oxford Handbook of Suicide and Self-Injury

Edited by

Matthew K. Nock

UNIVERSITY PRESS

OXFORD
UNIVERSITY PRESS

Oxford University Press is a department of the University of
Oxford. It furthers the University's objective of excellence in research,
scholarship, and education by publishing worldwide.

Oxford   New York
Auckland   Cape Town   Dar es Salaam   Hong Kong   Karachi
Kuala Lumpur   Madrid   Melbourne   Mexico City   Nairobi
New Delhi   Shanghai   Taipei   Toronto

With offices in
Argentina   Austria   Brazil   Chile   Czech Republic   France   Greece
Guatemala   Hungary   Italy   Japan   Poland   Portugal   Singapore
South Korea   Switzerland   Thailand   Turkey   Ukraine   Vietnam

Oxford is a registered trademark of Oxford University Press
in the UK and certain other countries.

Published in the United States of America by
Oxford University Press
198 Madison Avenue, New York, NY 10016

© Oxford University Press 2014

First issued as an Oxford University Press paperback, 2017

All rights reserved. No part of this publication may be reproduced, stored in
a retrieval system, or transmitted, in any form or by any means, without the prior
permission in writing of Oxford University Press, or as expressly permitted by law,
by license, or under terms agreed with the appropriate reproduction rights organization.
Inquiries concerning reproduction outside the scope of the above should be sent to the
Rights Department, Oxford University Press, at the address above.

You must not circulate this work in any other form
and you must impose this same condition on any acquirer.

Library of Congress Cataloging-in-Publication Data
The Oxford handbook of suicide and self-injury / edited by Matthew K. Nock.
pages cm — (Oxford library of psychology)
ISBN: 978–0–19–538856–5 (hardcover); 978–0–19–066938–6 (paperback)
1. Suicide.   2. Suicide—Psychology.   3. Self-injurious behavior.   I. Nock, Matthew. K
HV6545.O9394 2013
362.28—dc23
2012050013

SHORT CONTENTS

The *Oxford Library of Psychology*, a landmark series of handbooks, is published by Oxford University Press, one of the world's oldest and most highly respected publishers, with a tradition of publishing significant books in psychology. The ambitious goal of the *Oxford Library of Psychology* is nothing less than to span a vibrant, wide-ranging field and, in so doing, to fill a clear market need.

Encompassing a comprehensive set of handbooks, organized hierarchically, the *Library* incorporates volumes at different levels, each designed to meet a distinct need. At one level are a set of handbooks designed broadly to survey the major subfields of psychology; at another are numerous handbooks that cover important current focal research and scholarly areas of psychology in depth and detail. Planned as a reflection of the dynamism of psychology, the *Library* will grow and expand as psychology itself develops, thereby highlighting significant new research that will impact on the field. Adding to its accessibility and ease of use, the *Library* will be published in print and, later on, electronically.

The *Library* surveys psychology's principal subfields with a set of handbooks that capture the current status and future prospects of those major subdisciplines. This initial set includes handbooks of social and personality psychology, clinical psychology, counseling psychology, school psychology, educational psychology, industrial and organizational psychology, cognitive psychology, cognitive neuroscience, methods and measurements, history, neuropsychology, personality assessment, developmental psychology, and more. Each handbook undertakes to review one of psychology's major subdisciplines with breadth, comprehensiveness, and exemplary scholarship. In addition to these broadly conceived volumes, the *Library* also includes a large number of handbooks designed to explore in depth more specialized areas of scholarship and research, such as stress, health and coping, anxiety and related disorders, cognitive development, or child and adolescent assessment. In contrast to the broad coverage of the subfield handbooks, each of these latter volumes focuses on an especially productive, more highly focused line of scholarship and research. Whether at the broadest or most specific level, however, all of the *Library* handbooks offer synthetic coverage that reviews and evaluates the relevant past and present research and anticipates research in the future. Each handbook in the *Library* includes introductory and concluding chapters written by its editor to provide a roadmap to the handbook's table of contents and to offer informed anticipations of significant future developments in that field.

An undertaking of this scope calls for handbook editors and chapter authors who are established scholars in the areas about which they write. Many of the nation's and world's most productive and best-respected psychologists have agreed to edit *Library* handbooks or write authoritative chapters in their areas of expertise.

For whom has the *Oxford Library of Psychology* been written? Because of its breadth, depth, and accessibility, the *Library* serves a diverse audience, including graduate students in psychology and their faculty mentors, scholars, researchers, and practitioners in psychology and related fields. Each will find in the *Library* the information they seek on the subfield or focal area of psychology in which they work or are interested.

Befitting its commitment to accessibility, each handbook includes a comprehensive index, as well as extensive references to help guide research. And because the *Library* was designed from its inception as an online as well as a print resource, its structure and contents will be readily and rationally searchable online. Further, once the *Library* is released online, the handbooks will be regularly and thoroughly updated.

In summary, the *Oxford Library of Psychology* will grow organically to provide a thoroughly informed perspective on the field of psychology, one that reflects both psychology's dynamism and its increasing interdisciplinarity. Once published electronically, the *Library* is also destined to become a uniquely valuable interactive tool, with extended search and browsing capabilities. As you begin to consult this handbook, we sincerely hope you will share our enthusiasm for the more than 500-year tradition of Oxford University Press for excellence, innovation, and quality, as exemplified by the *Oxford Library of Psychology*.

Peter E. Nathan
Editor-in-Chief
Oxford Library of Psychology

ABOUT THE EDITOR

Matthew K. Nock

Matthew K. Nock, PhD, is a professor of psychology and director of the Laboratory for Clinical and Developmental Research in the Department of Psychology at Harvard University. Professor Nock received his PhD in psychology from Yale University (2003) and completed his clinical internship at Bellevue Hospital and the New York University Child Study Center (2003). Nock's research is aimed at advancing the understanding of why people behave in ways that are harmful to themselves, with an emphasis on suicide and other forms of self-harm. His research is multidisciplinary in nature and uses a range of methodological approaches (e.g., epidemiologic surveys, laboratory-based experiments, and clinic-based studies) to better understand how these behaviors develop, how to predict them, and how to prevent their occurrence. This work is funded by grants from the National Institutes of Health and several private foundations, has been published in over 100 scientific papers and book chapters. Nock's work has been recognized through the receipt of four early-career awards from the American Psychological Association, the Association for Behavioral and Cognitive Therapies, and the American Association of Suicidology; and in 2011 he was named a MacArthur Fellow. In addition to conducting research, Nock has been a consultant/scientific advisor to the National Institutes of Health, the World Health Organization's World Mental Health Survey Initiative, the American Psychological Association, and the American Psychiatric Association DSM-5 Childhood and Adolescent Disorder Work Group. At Harvard, Professor Nock teaches courses on statistics, research methods, self-destructive behaviors, developmental psychopathology, and cultural diversity—for which he has received several teaching awards, including the Roslyn Abramson Teaching Award and the Petra Shattuck Prize.

CONTRIBUTORS

Kristen Batejan
Department of Psychiatry and Behavioral Sciences
Duke University School of Medicine
Durham, NC

Theodore P. Beauchaine
Department of Psychology
The Ohio State University
Columbus, OH

José Manoel Bertolote
Department of Neurology, Psychology and
  Psychiatry
Botucatu Medical School—UNESP
  Botucatu, Brazil
Australian Institute for Suicide Research and
  Prevention
Griffith University
Brisbane, Australia

Beth Brodsky
Department of Psychiatry
College of Physicians and Surgeons
Columbia University
New York, NY

Jacqueline Buchanan
Center for Suicide Risk Assessment
New York State Psychiatric Institute
Columbia University
New York, NY

Katie A. Busch
Private practice
Sante Fe, NM

Sheila E. Crowell
Department of Psychology
University of Utah
Salt Lake City, UT

Christina M. Derbidge
Department of Psychology
VA Salt Lake City Health Care System
Salt Lake City, UT

Barbara D'Orio
Department of Psychiatry and Behavioral Sciences
Emory University
Atlanta, GA

Paul R. Duberstein
Center for the Study and Prevention
  of Suicide
Department of Psychiatry
University of Rochester
Rochester, NY

Carl Ernst
McGill Group for Suicide Studies
Douglas Mental Health University Institute
McGill University
Montreal, Quebec, Canada

Christianne Esposito-Smythers
Department of Psychology
George Mason University
Fairfax, VA

Jan Fawcett
Department of Psychiatry
University of New Mexico
School of Medicine
Albuquerque, NM

Virginia Fineran
Department of Psychiatry
Columbia University College of Physicians &
  Surgeons
New York, NY

Laura M. Fiori
McGill Group for Suicide Studies
Douglas Mental Health University Institute
McGill University
Montreal, Quebec, Canada

Joseph C. Franklin
Department of Psychology
Harvard University
Cambridge, MA

Mark J. Goldblatt
Department of Psychiatry
Harvard Medical School
Cambridge, MA

John D. Guerry
Department of Psychiatry
Columbia University
New York, NY

Nancy L. Heath
Department of Educational and Counselling
Psychology
McGill University
Montreal, Quebec, Canada

Nicole Heilbron
Department of Psychiatry and Behavioral
Sciences
Duke University School of Medicine
Durham, NC

Marnin J. Heisel
Center for the Study and Prevention of Suicide
Department of Psychiatry
University of Rochester
Rochester, NY
Departments of Psychiatry and Epidemiology
and Biostatistics
Schulich School of Medicine and Dentistry
The University of Western Ontario
Lawson Health Research Institute
London, Ontario, Canada

Marc Hillbrand
Department of Psychiatry
Yale University School of Medicine
New Haven, CT

Jill M. Hooley
Department of Psychology
Harvard University
Cambridge, MA

Colleen M. Jacobson
Department of Psychology
Iona University
New Rochelle, NY

Stephanie Gantt Johnson
Department of Psychiatry and Behavioral
Sciences
Emory University
Atlanta, GA

Thomas E. Joiner, Jr.
Department of Psychology
Florida State University
Tallahassee, FL

Nadine J. Kaslow
Department of Psychiatry and Behavioral
Sciences
Emory University
Atlanta, GA

E. David Klonsky
Department of Psychology
University of British Columbia
Vancouver, British Columbia, Canada

Stephen P. Lewis
Department of Psychology
University of Guelph
Guelph, Ontario, Canada

Gerhard Libal
Private practice
Ulm, Germany

Marsha M. Linehan
Behavioral Research and Therapy
Clinics
Department of Psychology
University of Washington
Seattle, WA

Shannon-Dell MacPhee
Department of Educational and Counselling
Psychology
McGill University
Montreal, Quebec, Canada

John Mann
Department of Psychiatry
Columbia University
New York, NY

Eve K. Mościcki
American Psychiatric Institute for Research
and Education
Arlington, VA

Jennifer J. Muehlenkamp
Department of Psychology
University of Wisconsin-Eau Claire
Eau Claire, WI

Matthew K. Nock
Department of Psychology
Harvard University
Cambridge, MA

Holly Parker
Department of Psychology
Harvard University
Cambridge, MA
and
Edith Nourse Rogers Memorial Hospital
Bedford, MA

Paul L. Plener
Department of Child and Adolescent
Psychiatry and Psychotherapy
University of Ulm
Ulm, Germany

Kelly Posner
Department of Psychiatry
Columbia University
New York, NY

Mitchell J. Prinstein
Department of Psychology
University of North Carolina at Chapel Hill
Chapel Hill, NC

Miesha N. Rhodes
School of Medicine
Emory University
Atlanta, GA

Jessica D. Ribeiro
Department of Psychology
Florida State University
Tallahassee, FL

M. David Rudd
Department of Psychology
University of Memphis
Memphis, TN

Edward A. Selby
Department of Psychology
Rutgers, The State University of New Jersey
New Brunswick, NJ

Matthew D. Selekman
Partners for Collaborative Solutions
Evanston, IL

Regina M. Sherman
Department of Psychiatry and Behavioral
    Science
Emory University
Atlanta, GA

Anthony Spirito
Center for Alcohol and Addiction Studies
Department of Psychiatry and Human
    Behavior
Warren Alpert Medical School
Brown University
Providence, RI

Megan Spokas
University of Pennsylvania
La Salle University
Philadelphia, PA

Sarah A. St. Germain
Department of Psychology
Harvard University
Cambridge, MA

Barbara Stanley
Department of Psychiatry
Columbia University College of
    Physicians & Surgeons
New York, NY

Jessica R. Toste
Department of Special Education
The University of Texas at Austin
Austin, TX

Ellen Townsend
Department of Special Education
The University of Texas at Austin
Austin, TX

Gustavo Turecki
Douglas Institute
McGill University
Montreal, Quebec, Canada

Agnes van der Heide
Department of Public Health
Erasmus MC, University Medical Centre
    Rotterdam
Rotterdam, The Netherlands

Erin F. Ward-Ciesielski
Behavioral Research and Therapy Clinics
Department of Psychology
University of Washington
Seattle, WA

Julie Weismoore
Department of Psychology
George Mason University
Fairfax, VA

Amy Wenzel
Perelman School of Medicine
University of Pennsylvania
Philadelphia, PA

Janis Whitlock
College of Human Ecology
Cornell University
Ithaca, NY

Kseniya Yershova
New York State Psychiatric Institute
Columbia University
New York, NY

Rupa P. Zimmermann
Department of Psychiatry and Human
    Behavior
Warren Alpert Medical School
Brown University
Providence, RI

CONTENTS

Introduction to the Handbook

Matthew K. Nock

Abstract

This introduction provides an outline of the *Oxford Handbook of Suicide and Self-Injury.* It describes the purpose of this Handbook and describes the six primary sections of this volume, which focus on: (I) Classification, (II) Phenomenology and Epidemiology, (III) Approaches to the understanding of self-harm, (IV) Assessment, (V) Prevention and Intervention, and (VI) Special Issues.

Key Words: suicide, self-injury, self-harm, classification, phenomenology, epidemiology, assessment, prevention, intervention

Self-injurious behaviors are among the most alarming and perplexing of all human behaviors. Most of what we do as humans is aimed at keeping ourselves alive and passing on our genes. We eat, sleep, work, cooperate with others, procreate, and sacrifice for our offspring all in the service of survival. So why, then, in some instances do some people act in complete opposition to this innate and ever-present drive for self-preservation? Why do some people cut or burn their skin, and at the most extreme end of the continuum, intentionally end their own lives? These are questions that have remained unanswered for thousands of years, and as a result, self-injurious behaviors continue to be one of the leading causes of death worldwide.

The purpose of this book is to provide a comprehensive overview of the state of the science on self-injurious behaviors, including both suicidal and nonsuicidal self-injury. The authors of the chapters that appear in this volume include the world's leading experts on these topics, resulting in a final product that is authoritative and forward looking. The chapters are written for a broad audience with the hopes that this volume will be accessible to researchers, clinicians, teachers, and the general public.

This volume is organized into six different sections containing a total of 29 chapters. Part I of the book focuses on the classification of self-injurious behaviors. There has been a great deal of debate about what "counts" as self-injurious behavior as well as about how to distinguish among different forms of self-injurious thoughts and behaviors. In Chapter 2, Kelly Posner and colleagues provide a comprehensive review of the current state of the art in classifying and defining different forms of self-injurious behaviors. In Chapter 3, Jennifer Muehlenkamp tackles the important question of how to distinguish between suicidal forms of self-injury, in which a person has some intention of dying from his or her behavior, and nonsuicidal self-injury, in which people have no desire to die. Jill Hooley and Sarah St. Germain conclude Part I with Chapter 4, which includes an interesting discussion of whether and how the conceptualization of self-injurious behavior might be expanded to include indirect forms of self-injury. Should behaviors such as excessive drinking and smoking, repeatedly engaging in abusive relationships, and so on be considered self-injurious? Where should we draw the line?

Part II focuses on the phenomenology and epidemiology of self-injurious behaviors. The vast majority of research on self-injurious behaviors has focused on suicidal, rather than nonsuicidal, self-injury, and the content of this volume reflects that difference. As research on suicide has developed, we have learned that there are important differences in the manifestation, prediction, and prevention of suicidal behaviors across the life span. For instance, the prevalence of suicidal behavior is low in childhood, increases dramatically during adolescence, and then levels off for most groups during adulthood except for White males, who see a second dramatic increase in suicide risk after age 65 years. In addition, although there is now some evidence for the effectiveness of treatments for suicidal thoughts and behaviors among adults, there is very limited evidence for children and adolescents. In fact, some evidence even suggests that certain treatments may actually *increase* the risk of suicidal thoughts and behaviors among youth. Chapter 5 (Christianne Esposito-Smythers and colleagues), Chapter 6 (Eve Mościcki), and Chapter 7 (Paul Duberstein and Marnin Heisel) review what is currently known about suicidal behaviors among children and adolescents, adults, and the elderly, respectively. Finally, in Chapter 8, Janis Whitlock and Matthew Selekman synthesize what is currently known about how nonsuicidal self-injury differs across the life span—an important but understudied issue.

Part III is aimed at providing a better understanding of *why* people engage in self-injurious behaviors. We are fortunate that some of the best and brightest minds in the field, each working from a slightly different perspective, contributed to chapters aimed at presenting the most up-to-date thinking and evidence regarding why people do things to purposely harm themselves. As with the previous section, most of these chapters focus on suicidal behavior, which reflects the fact that much more research has been conducted on this type of behavior. The chapters in this section review recent advances in the understanding of suicidal behavior from the perspectives of genetics and neurobiology (Chapter 9; Gustavo Tureki and colleagues), developmental psychopathology (Chapter 10; Ted Beauchaine and colleagues), social and ecological models (Chapter 11; Mitch Prinstein and colleagues), cognitive and information processing models (Chapter 12; Amy Wenzel and Megan Spokas), and psychodynamic models (Chapter 13; Mark Goldblatt). Chapter 14, by Nadine Kaslow and colleagues, provides an important review of

how factors related to race/ethnicity, spirituality/religion, and sexual orientation may influence the occurrence of suicidal behaviors. Finally, the concluding chapters in this section attempt to pull this all together by outlining comprehensive theoretical models of suicidal behavior (Chapter 15; Edward Selby, Thomas Joiner, and Jessica Ribeiro) and nonsuicidal self-injury (Chapter 16; Colleen Jacobson and Kristen Batejan).

Part IV focuses on the assessment of self-injurious behaviors—a tricky issue that has received increased attention in recent years, as more and more work has highlighted the importance of both distinguishing between suicidal and nonsuicidal self-injury, and in assessing more subtle suicidal behaviors such as suicide gestures and aborted suicide attempts. In Chapter 17, David Rudd reviews the current standards in the assessment and management of suicidal behaviors in both scientific and clinical settings. In Chapter 18, David Klonsky and Stephen Lewis review recent advances in the assessment of nonsuicidal self-injury.

Part V of this volume covers one of the most important, yet challenging, issues in this area of scientific and clinical work: the prevention and treatment of suicidal and nonsuicidal self-injury. Despite the scope and seriousness of these problems, the field has struggled to develop and identify effective prevention and intervention strategies for self-injurious behaviors. However, over the past decade, we have seen some exciting advances and promising leads. Focusing first on suicidal behaviors, programs aimed at prevention, psychological interventions, and pharmacological interventions are reviewed in Chapter 19 (José Bertolote), Chapter 20 (Erin F. Ward-Ciesielski and Marsha Linehan), and Chapter 21 (Jan Fawcett and Katie Busch), respectively. Subsequently, the prevention, psychological treatment, and pharmacological treatment of nonsuicidal self-injury are reviewed in Chapter 22 (Nancy Heath and colleagues), Chapter 23 (Barbara Stanley and colleagues), and Chapter 24 (Paul Plenar and Gerhard Libal), respectively.

Part VI reviews several topics not typically covered in books on self-injurious behaviors, but ones that I think are understudied and important for us to consider. Chapter 25, by Marc Hillbrand, reviews what is currently known about the overlap between self-injurious and violent behaviors. This is a link that has been known for decades but remains poorly understood. Understanding why these behaviors often co-occur can open up new insights in the development and treatment of both types of behaviors. Chapter 26, written by Ellen Townsend, reviews the state of the science on suicide terrorism. Many scholars view suicide terrorism (also referred to as suicide bombings) as completely different from suicidal behavior in which there is no intent to harm another person. This chapter is included here for two reasons. First, although such acts do include homicidal intent, they also include intentional self-inflicted death. Second, such behaviors appear to be on the rise, and so it is important that we understand them and develop ways to predict and prevent them. Prior research on suicidal (and homicidal) behavior may inform such efforts—and work on suicide terrorism may also inform these other areas. Chapter 27, written by Agnes van der Heide, reviews assisted suicide and euthanasia. This, too, is a topic that many distinguish from suicidal behavior in which there is no assistance in dying. And this, too, is a topic that I believe is useful for scholars of suicide and self-injury to consider and ultimately address. Finally, Chapter 28,

by Holly Parker, reviews what is known about survivors of suicide—those who have lost a loved one to this devastating problem. Millions of people lose a loved one to suicide each year, yet the effects of such loss are not well understood, as surprisingly little research has attempted to understand this aspect of the problem. Parker's chapter highlights what we have learned in this area, and it outlines the most important next steps for future research.

I am grateful to all of the contributors to this volume for writing the thoughtful and thorough chapters that follow. Although many long-standing questions remain about these truly devastating problems, it is clear that we have learned a great deal in the past few years and we are excited to be able to present these advances in one comprehensive volume. I learned a great deal reading the chapters that follow, finding them immensely helpful in advancing my own understanding of these problems, and I hope you do as well.

PART 1

Classification of Self-Injurious Behaviors

The Classification of Suicidal Behavior

Kelly Posner, Beth Brodsky, Kseniya Yershova, Jacqueline Buchanan, *and* John Mann

Abstract

Consistent definitions of suicide and the full spectrum of suicidal phenomena are critical for suicide prevention and the advancement of knowledge across disciplines. Historically, the absences of conceptual clarity, uniform nomenclature, and standardized assessment methods have blended definitional boundaries between suicidal and nonsuicidal self-injurious behavior and suicidal ideation. The range of suicidal behavior was restricted to suicide and suicide attempts, and it did not include or distinguish between these and other types of suicidal behavior now known to be related to suicide. The most significant advancement in the classification of suicide includes partial or "nonzero" intent to die as both a sufficient and necessary criterion, which may be stated or inferred from the self-injury lethality or surrounding circumstances. These key developments should inform the adoption of an internationally accepted diagnostic system for naming and classifying suicidal behavior and ideation, which in turn should guide medical, legal, and scientific communication.

Key Words: suicide, nomenclature, classification, suicidal behavior, suicidal ideation, self-injurious behavior, nonsuicidal self-injurious behavior, diagnostic systems

Reinforcing its status as one of the world's greatest public health crises, suicide has become the leading cause of injury mortality in the Unites States (Rockett et al., 2012), as well as in other countries (Even, 2011; Stone et al., 2006), surpassing motor vehicle crashes. Suicide prevention efforts are thus critical and depend upon appropriate identification. Clinical understanding, prediction, and prevention of suicide are contingent upon adequate assessment. However, medicine has been challenged by a lack of conceptual clarity, consistent nomenclature, and standardized approaches when assessing suicidal and nonsuicidal self-injurious behavior and suicidal ideation. These difficulties encumber interpretation of suicidal occurrences and, consequently, precise communication, on an individual and population basis. The United States Centers for Disease Control (CDC) characterized the variability in suicide terminology as having far-reaching consequences,

rendering comparison of international prevalence rates difficult and hampering prevention efforts (Crosby, Ortega, & Melanson, 2011).

The Institute of Medicine of the United States National Academies also identified inconsistency in classification and nomenclature as a major impediment to suicide prevention: "research on suicide is plagued by many methodological problems... definitions lack uniformity... [and] reporting of suicide is inaccurate," hence "a common language or set of terms in describing suicidal phenomena [is needed]" (Goldsmith, Pellmar, Kleinman, & Bunney, 2002). Widespread variation in typology and nomenclature has manifested in imprecise information dissemination about suicidal phenomena in research settings, the impact of which is especially apparent in cases where incidence rates of the target behavior are low. Such is the case with deaths by suicide, as findings are inconsistent across epidemiological studies

(Gibbons, Hur, Brown, & Mann, 2009). Moreover, low base rates of suicide hinder prediction efforts (Brown, Beck, Steer, & Grisham, 2000; Pokorny, 1993). The dearth of a unified nomenclature and classification system is a fundamental impediment to the prediction of suicidal behavior across clinical and research settings (Silverman, Berman, Sanddal, O'Carroll, & Joiner, 2007). Additionally, international drug regulators were challenged by a lack of consistent classification and standardized terminology in addressing medication safety concerns arising from suicidal adverse events. The nonuniformity of data imposed methodological limitations, compromising their interpretability and subsequently hampering scientific evaluation of medication safety (Meyer et al., 2010; Posner, Oquendo, Gould, Stanley, & Davies, 2007). This obstacle was a major impetus for the implementation of meaningful common language in describing suicidal phenomena, now adopted by the US Centers for Disease Control, the US Food and Drug Administration, and branches of the US Military.

The impact of suicide classification on suicide prevention, research, and clinical care cannot be overestimated. This chapter summarizes the evolution of suicide-related nomenclature and the history of classification, and details current approaches to global uniformity in the field.

Evolution of Suicide Nomenclature and Classification

Nomenclature and classification of suicidal behavior are critical issues for research and practice (Silverman, 2006). O'Carroll et al. (1996) distinguished between nomenclature and classification. Nomenclature is a "set of commonly understood, logically defined terms," while classification is defined as "several elements that go beyond a mere nomenclature, including comprehensiveness; a systematic arrangement of items in groups or categories... [with] scientific validity,...accuracy sufficient for research or clinical practice...and an unambiguous set of rules for assigning items to a single place..." (O'Carroll et al., 1996, p. 240). Nomenclature provides the language for classification, which in turn provides the organization of conceptual relationships.

Historically, the origin of the term "suicide" (from the Latin *sui–*, of oneself, and—*caedere,* to kill) dates back to Sir Thomas Browne's memoir, *Religio Medici* (1642), which spurred debate in the coming centuries as to the morality of suicide. The focus of suicide later shifted toward its study

(Barraclough, & Shepherd, 1994; Goldsmith et al., 2002). Emile Durkheim (1858–1917), French sociologist, is credited with the first influential study of suicide. In his classical sociological work, *Le Suicide* (1897), Durkheim suggests that "suicide is applied to all cases of death resulting directly or indirectly from a positive or negative act by the victim himself, which he knows will produce the result" (Durkheim, 1951, p. 59; Goldsmith et al., 2002). Durkheim's characterization of suicide influenced subsequent definitions, and the sociological risk factors outlined in *Le Suicide* presage current knowledge and pitfalls of suicide risk assessment, such as the difficulty in categorizing suicidal occurrences.

Definitions of suicide have been inconsistent regarding "intent" to die (Ivanoff, 1989; Mayo, 1992). Despite the broad similarity of these definitions, there have long been calls for full and precise concordance in nomenclature and classification. In the 1970s, the National Institute of Mental Health (NIMH) in the United States held a conference on suicide prevention. NIMH's Committee on Classification and Nomenclature, chaired by Aaron Beck, highlighted the need for a universal nomenclature and a method for distributing this information (Beck et al., 1972). The Committee proposed the division of suicidal phenomena into three classes: (1) suicide, (2) suicide attempt, and (3) suicidal ideas. Each type of suicidal event was further characterized by (i) certainty of the rater (1%–100%); (ii) potential lethality, or the objective medical danger to life if the act were to have been or was in fact carried out; (iii) zero, low, medium, or high level of intent to die inferred from present or past behavior using clinical judgment; (iv) mitigating circumstances without which the suicidal event might not have occurred (e.g., intoxication); and (v) the type of self-harm method, which in turn bears on determination of intent and lethality (Beck & Greenberg, 1971). This nomenclature and classification system were very influential; however, they did not account for the full range of suicidal behavior or distinguish between suicide attempts and other types of suicidal behavior, including preparatory acts or behavior (e.g., writing a suicide note).

In the United States, coroners and medical examiners have often been assigned the roles of decision makers in determining whether a death is listed as a suicide. To address misclassification and inconsistency due to lack of explicit criteria for classifying death by suicide, in the 1980s, a group of coroners, medical examiners, public health agencies, and statisticians gathered under the auspices of the CDC to develop Operational Criteria for the Determination of Suicide (OCDS) (Rosenberg et al., 1988).

The OCDS defined suicide as "death arising from an act inflicted upon oneself with the intent to kill oneself" (Rosenberg et al., 1988) and, more specifically, as "death from injury, poisoning, or suffocation where there is evidence (either explicit or implicit) that the injury was self-inflicted and that the decedent intended to kill himself/herself" (O'Carroll et al., 1996, p. 244). The CDC adopted the OCDS definition of suicide in their nomenclature; however, the definition was criticized on the grounds that it required subjective judgment. It was inherent in the definition that subjective judgment was required to evaluate the difference between suicide and death from other causes, as well as whether an act was intentionally or unintentionally self-inflicted.

In the same decade, the World Health Organization Regional Office for Europe (WHO/EURO) as part of their Multicentre Study of Parasuicide adopted a definition of suicide as "an act with a fatal outcome which the deceased, knowing or expecting a fatal outcome had initiated and carried out with the purpose of provoking the changes he desired" (De Leo, Burgis, Bertolote, Kerkhof, & Bille-Brahe, 2006, p. 8). The definition of intent to "provoke [desired] changes" was not limited to intent to die, but rather could include changes in relationships such as obtaining sympathy from others (Bille-Brahe et al., 1995).

Components of Suicide: Agency, Intent, and Outcome

Authors of the WHO/EURO Multicentre Study subsequently identified and proposed unifying terminology for universal components within previous definitions of suicide, yielding a typology for suicidal behavior as a function of agency, intent, and outcome (De Leo et al., 2006). Intent, agency, and outcome continue to pervade the most current nomenclature and classification systems and efforts to assess and define suicidal behavior more uniformly and reliably.

AGENCY

An act of suicide must be self-instigated or self-initiated but not necessarily self-inflicted. Agency must account for any outcome in which the victim is directly or indirectly responsible, even if not necessarily the agent of the fatal act (De Leo et al., 2004). For example, "suicide by cop" occurs when one acts in such a way as to induce police officers to fire at him or her (Mohandie & Meloy, 2000). Furthermore, agency does not necessarily require active involvement but may rather be a passive act. As in the situations of passive refusal to live (e.g., rejecting food or a life-saving medicine), the perceived severity of a self-injurious act does not mitigate classification of this behavior as suicidal. As Durkheim remarked, "refusal to take food is as suicidal as self-destruction by a dagger or fire-arm" (Durkheim, 1951, p. 42).

INTENT

Intent to die has been a long-standing, critical, and controversial component of the definition of suicide. Intent is the desire for a certain outcome, which is often confused with the motivation for the desire or the factors that "motivate" or result in the desire (Hjelmeland & Ostamo, 1997). Intent has been difficult to measure due to (1) varying degree of definitiveness of intent; (2) the rarity of a single intent or a desire for a single outcome accompanying an action, just as an action may have multiple motivations driving a particular desire; and (3) the lack of inherent interpretability of intent, as it is usually unobservable (Andriessen, 2006; Egel, 1999; Mayo, 1992). Despite the lack of objectivity in the assessment of intent, intent must nevertheless be determined in order to distinguish suicidal behavior from other self-harming behaviors (Allen, 2000). Without intent, it becomes difficult to evaluate any action as different from an accident or other forms of self-injurious behavior that are nonsuicidal, such as cutting oneself with the intent to release intense feelings but without wanting to end one's life (Allen, 2000; Andriessen, 2006; Linehan, 1997). Omission of the assessment of intent can lead to "unacceptable levels of heterogeneity amongst subjects" regarding the classification and subclassifications of self-injurious behavior (Linehan, 1997).

OUTCOME

Suicide must have death as an outcome. A suicide attempt must at least have the actual or believed potential for death as an outcome. However, without intent, suicide or nonfatal suicide attempt cannot be distinguished from homicide or an accident. Outcome and intent are linked but "not perfectly associated" (De Leo et al., 2004).

The degree of medical injury resulting from an attempt is not directly correlated with the intent to die (Silverman & Maris, 1995), and only modestly correlated with degree of intent. Moreover, in the case of someone who expresses no intent to die but engages in a behavior to that end, outcome by itself cannot be used to determine suicide (O'Carroll et al., 1996).

Psychiatric Classification Systems (ICD-10 and DSM)

Until the *DSM-5*, the two widely used medical classification systems, the *Diagnostic and Statistical Manual of Mental Disorders* (*DSM-IV-TR*) and the *International Classification of Disease* (*ICD-10*) lodged suicide within the diagnoses of major depressive episode and borderline personality disorder (American Psychiatric Association [APA], 1994; World Health Organization [WHO], 2000). The *ICD-10* included suicide as an external cause of morbidity and mortality (WHO, 2000). Two categories were included—namely, suicide and intentionally self-inflicted poisoning or injury, both of which can be further classified by the type of method. However, no definitions accompanied this terminology and the "self-inflicted injury" class did not distinguish between suicidal behavior and nonsuicidal self-injurious behavior, both of which limited the utility of this system.

Furthermore, unlike criteria for psychiatric disorders, the *DSM* (Oquendo, Baca-García, Mann, & Giner, 2008) and *ICD* (WHO, 2000) systems did not include reliable rules for determining suicidal behavior. As a consequence, suicidal behavior in high-risk patients with other disorders (e.g., in posttraumatic stress disorder or alcohol dependence) and/or those with a past history of suicidal behavior who deny present risk on the mental status exam may not have been identified with prior diagnostic algorithms. Suicidologists recommended the inclusion of suicidal behavior as a separate diagnostic category on a sixth axis of the *DSM* (Oquendo et al., 2008), and the *DSM-5* includes a suicidal behavior disorder, along with a nonsuicidal self-injury disorder (APA, 2012). This issue illustrates the necessity of a universally implemented classification system, as well as the deleterious effects of the absence of such an approach.

Classification of Suicidal Behavior

Historically, multiple broad terms, such as "deliberate self-harm" and "parasuicide," have encompassed all nonfatal self-injurious acts, regardless of whether suicidal intent was associated with the behavior. For example, "self-mutilation" involves self-injurious

behavior for reasons other than intended death. Use of these broader terms perpetuates imprecision in classification (O'Carroll et al., 1996). Suicidal intent can be reliably obtained (Jeglic, Brown, & Henriques, 2006), and assessment of intent is critical to classifying suicidal ideation and behavior (Linehan, 1997). Moreover, there is extensive empirical support for the use of a more restricted, intent-based definition of suicidal behavior (Joe, 2004; O'Carroll et al., 1996; Satcher, 1999). This definition allows for clearer distinctions between types of suicidal behavior. The classification of suicidal behavior is necessary for accurate risk assessment and the assignment of further clinical interventions.

Trends in the Development of Suicide Risk Classification Systems in the United States

In the last decade, the US Food and Drug Administration (FDA) and the CDC adopted a classification system that was utilized, in part, to address international controversies over a critical safety question regarding the relationship between medications and suicidal ideation and behavior. Regulators were faced with variability in the classification of suicidal ideation and behavior, which significantly undermined interpretability of data (Meyer et al., 2010). Classification errors resulted in both over- and underclassification of possible suicidal events and included instances of a patient slapping herself in the face being labeled a "suicide attempt"; a patient with schizophrenia hitting his head against the wall and explaining his thoughts were "about to explode" being labeled a "suicide attempt"; a patient having thoughts of killing herself but having no intention of acting on the thoughts being labeled a "suicide attempt"; a patient attempting to hang himself with a rope after a dispute with his father being labeled a "personality disorder"; a patient with intentional overdose not labeled a suicide attempt; and suicidal ideation labeled a suicide attempt (Posner et al., 2007). In contrast, application of the improved classification algorithm developed under the auspices of the US FDA led to increased precision relative to prior customary unsystematic classification, and it further reinforced the importance of classification for scientific findings and the public health.

Self-Injurious Behavior

The first necessary element to establish suicidal or nonsuicidal behavior is the presence of deliberate self-injurious behavior, in which one intentionally tries to hurt oneself. Thus, an essential condition of self-injurious behavior is that the self-harm or potential for self-harm itself is a deliberate consequence of the behavior. This initial necessary element is distinct from acts that are dangerous but not undertaken with the motivation to inflict harm on oneself (e.g., driving fast, drinking excessively), as the potential lethality of the self-harming behavior must be an intended consequence of the act. The CDC adopts the term *self-directed violence* and states that it is akin to self-injurious behavior (Crosby et al., 2011), denoting that these terms are essentially interchangeable (Fig. 2.2).

It is important to note that self-injurious behavior, not self-injury, is the accurate term. In self-injurious behavior, whether suicidal or nonsuicidal, neither physical harm nor the potential for physical harm is required. Rather, any behavior for which the end goal is to inflict harm to oneself is classified as self-injurious behavior (Fig. 2.1). Whether physical injury is realized has been one of the significant areas of confusion in the field. Examples include an individual pulling the trigger of a loaded gun directed at his head and the gun fails to fire, or a person walking into the middle of a road who is rescued by a third party before being hit by oncoming traffic. Relatedly, the lethality of the act also does not determine the classification of self-injurious behavior (e.g., as soon as the first pill has been swallowed or a scratch has been made and the potential for harm has been established), ultimately leading to either suicidal or nonsuicidal classification.

DISTINCTION BETWEEN SUICIDAL AND NONSUICIDAL SELF-INJURIOUS BEHAVIOR

The distinction between suicidal and nonsuicidal self-injurious behavior hinges upon intent to die. Self-injurious behavior is classified as suicidal as opposed to nonsuicidal if any nonzero stated or inferred intent to die is a reason for the behavior. The importance of the inclusion of any nonzero intent to die is readily recognizable in clinical practice; when individuals feel suicidal, they often have several motives. Within the context of a suicide risk assessment, one may be asked, "Did you want to kill yourself?," the answer may be "No" due to the presence of mixed motives, and the behavior may be misclassified. If, instead, one was asked, "Did any part of you want to end your life when you engaged in this behavior?," the answer may be very different and be indicative of some intent. Thus, the understanding that the presence

of any nonzero intent to die is sufficient to classify a behavior as suicidal is of critical importance. Conversely, for an act to be classified as nonsuicidal self-injurious behavior, the individual must have engaged in the act entirely for reasons other than to end one's life.

Death as a result of suicidal self-injurious behavior is classified as suicide. Nonfatal suicidal self-injurious behavior can take the form of *suicide attempt, interrupted attempt, self-interrupted/aborted attempt,* and *preparatory acts or behavior* toward suicide (Fig. 2.1).

Suicide

Suicide is defined as death resulting from intentional self-injurious behavior, associated with any intent to die as a result of the behavior. Importantly, intent can either be stated explicitly by the individual (as in a suicide note or report of communication to someone) or inferred. For those who do not leave a suicide note, intent can be determined by talking to family or friends or by taking into account circumstantial evidence of a self-inflicted fatal act, inferred from the method or circumstance. If the only reasonable intent for the lethal act was suicide (such as when shooting oneself in the head or jumping from a high story), then intent can be inferred.

Definitions of Suicide Attempt

Identification of suicide attempts is essential, with an extensive body of literature evidencing suicide attempts as predictive of deaths by suicide (Brown et al., 2000; Dorpat & Ripley, 1967; Nordstrom, Samuelsson, & Asberg, 1995; Oquendo et al., 2004). In the 1960s, Stengel introduced the term "suicide attempt" to distinguish two clinical groups: those with fatal from those with nonfatal outcomes from acts with the intent to die (Stengel, 1962). However, pointing to the ambivalence of many suicide attempters, Kreitman et al. (1969) argued that "the great majority of patients so designated are not in fact attempting suicide" and proposed "parasuicide" to account for self-injurious behavior without intent to die (Kreitman, Philip, Greer, & Bagley, 1969).

As a result of their Multicentre Study, WHO/EURO defined parasuicide as "an act with a non-fatal outcome, in which an individual deliberately initiates a non-habitual behavior that, without interventions from others, will cause self-harm, or deliberately ingests a substance in excess of the prescribed or generally recognized

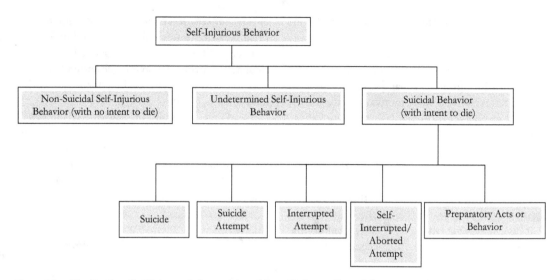

Figure 2.1a. Classification of self-injurious behavior (adapted from CDC surveillance definitions; Crosby et al., 2011).

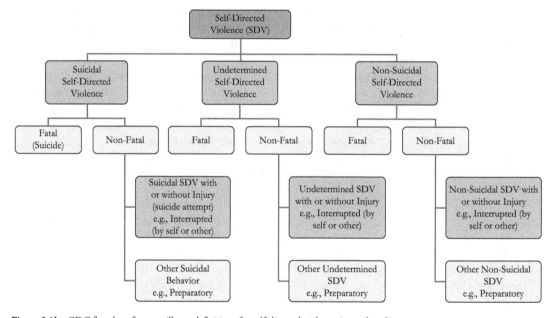

Figure 2.1b. CDC flowchart for surveillance definitions for self-directed violence (reproduced).

therapeutic dosage, and which is aimed at realizing changes which the subject desired, via the actual or expected physical consequences" (Platt et al., 1992, p. 99). This definition was to be included in the *ICD-10* Classification of Mental and Behavioral Disorders in order to (1) include acts that are interrupted before self-harm occurs; (2) exclude those in which a person does not understand the consequences (e.g., mental retardation or severe mental illness); and (3) exclude acts of nonsuicidal self-injurious behavior (also considered habitual acts) (Mohandie & Meloy,

2000). However, by 1999, the WHO/EURO adopted an outcome-based orientation toward defining self-injurious behavior, moving toward the terms "fatal" and "nonfatal" suicidal behavior with an understanding that intent is not always ascertainable (De Leo, Bertolote, Schmidtke, Bille-Brahe, & Kerkhof, 1999). Parasuicide is now included in the CDC's list of unacceptable terms (Fig. 2.3), as it obscures the boundary between suicide attempt and nonsuicidal self-injurious behavior by failing to categorize behavior with respect to intent to die.

Definitions

Self-directed violence (analogous to self-injurious behavior)

Behavior that is self-directed and deliberately results in injury or the potential for injury to oneself.

This does not include behaviors such as parachuting, gambling, substance abuse, tobacco use or other risk taking activities, such as excessive speeding in motor vehicles. These are complex behaviors some of which are risk factors for SDV but are defined as behavior that while likely to be life-threatening is not recognized by the individual as behavior intended to destroy or injure the self. (Farberow, N. L. (Ed.) (1980). The Many Faces of Suicide. New York: McGraw-Hill Book Company). These behaviors may have a high probability of injury or death as an outcome but the injury or death is usually considered unintentional. Hanzlick R, Hunsaker JC, Davis GJ. *Guide for Manner of Death Classification*. National Association of Medical Examiners. Available at: http://www.charlydmiller.com/LIB03/2002NAMEmannerofdeath.pdf. Accessed 1 Sept 2009.

Self-directed violence is categorized into the following:

Non-suicidal (as defined below)

Suicidal (as defined below).

Non-suicidal self-directed violence

Behavior that is self-directed and deliberately results in injury or the potential for injury to oneself.

There is no evidence, whether implicit or explicit, of suicidal intent. Please see appendix for definition of implicit and explicit.

Suicidal self-directed violence

Behavior that is self-directed and deliberately results in injury or the potential for injury to oneself.

There is evidence, whether implicit or explicit, of suicidal intent.

Suicide attempt

A non-fatal self-directed potentially injurious behavior with any intent to die as a result of the behavior.

A suicide attempt may or may not result in injury.

Interrupted self-directed violence – by self or by other

By other - A person takes steps to injure self but is stopped by another person prior to fatal injury. The interruption can occur at any point during the act such as after the initial thought or after onset of behavior.

By self (in other documents may be termed "aborted" suicidal behavior) - A person takes steps to injure self but is stopped by self prior to fatal injury.

Source: Posner K, Oquendo MA, Gould M, Stanley B, Davies M. Columbia Classification Algorithm of Suicide Assessment (C-CASA): Classification of Suicidal Events in the FDA's Pediatric Suicidal Risk Analysis of Antidepressants. Am J Psychiatry. 2007; 164:1035-1043. http://cssrs.columbia.edu/

Other suicidal behavior including preparatory acts

Acts or preparation towards making a suicide attempt, but before potential for harm has begun. This can include anything beyond a verbalization or thought, such as assembling a method (e.g., buying a gun, collecting pills) or preparing for one's death by suicide (e.g., writing a suicide note, giving things away). Posner et al, 2007.

Suicide

Death caused by self-directed injurious behavior with any intent to die as a result of the behavior.

Figure 2.2. CDC definitions of self-directed violence (reproduced).

> **Unacceptable Terms**
>
> The panel felt the following terms are unacceptable for describing self-directed violence:
>
> - Completed suicide - This terminology implies achieving a desired outcome whereas those involved in the mission of "reducing disease, premature death, and discomfort and disability" (J. Last, Dictionary of Epidemiology 1988) would view this event as undesirable. Alternate term: suicide
> - Failed attempt - This terminology gives a negative impression of the person's action, implying an unsuccessful effort aimed at achieving death. Alternate terms: suicide attempt or suicidal self-directed violence.
> - Nonfatal suicide – This terminology portrays a contradiction. "Suicide" indicates a death while "nonfatal" indicates that no death occurred. Alternate term: suicide attempt
> - Parasuicide – Formally used to refer to a person's self-directed violence whether or not the individual had an intent to die. However, the World Health Organization is now favoring the term suicide attempt. Alternate terms: non-suicidal self-directed violence or suicidal self-directed violence.
> - Successful suicide – This term also implies achieving a desired outcome whereas those involved in the mission of "reducing disease, premature death, and discomfort and disability" would view this event as undesirable. Alternate term: suicide.
> - Suicidality - This terminology is often used to refer simultaneously to suicidal thoughts and suicidal behavior. These phenomena are vastly different in occurrence, associated factors, consequences and interventions so should be addressed separately. Alternate terms: suicidal thoughts and suicidal behavior.
> - Suicide gesture, Manipulative act, and Suicide threat – Each of these terms gives a value judgment with a pejorative or negative impression of the person's intent. They are usually used to describe an episode of nonfatal, self-directed violence. A more objective description of the event is preferable such as non-suicidal self-directed violence or suicidal self-directed violence.

Figure 2.3. CDC definitions of unacceptable terms (reproduced).

The CDC currently defines "suicide attempt" as a potentially self-injurious act committed with at least some intent to die, as a result of the act (Crosby et al., 2011; Posner et al., 2007). This definition of a "suicide attempt" makes it clear that (1) the outcome does not need to involve self-injury, but rather the potential for self-injury; (2) any nonzero intent to die qualifies a self-injurious act as suicidal; and (3) the intent to die and the behavior must be causally linked, that is, self-injury or potential for it occurs as a result of at least a partial intent to die. In other words, the individual engaged in that particular behavior, at least in part, as the means or way to end his or her life.

Suicide attempt survivors often report they are ambivalent in making an attempt, and the gravity of an attempt cannot be discounted when intent to die is less than 100%. The prevailing definition of intent as any "nonzero" wish to die originally proposed by O'Carroll and colleagues (1996) acknowledges the ambivalence often experienced by those who engage in suicidal behavior and accounts for the multiple motivations often involved. For example, a man may attempt suicide after wanting to escape the emotional pain of a large financial loss, but at the same time a part of him may not want to die because he would leave his children behind without a father. Due to this man's nonzero intent, his act would be classified as suicidal. The intent

and the behavior must be linked. This means that a self-injurious behavior can only be classified as a suicide attempt if there was at least partial intent to die *as a result of the act*. Under certain circumstances ascertaining intent to die directly from the person may be difficult. For example, one may deny having intent to die due to shame and embarrassment over having made a suicide attempt.

Another important component of this definition of suicide attempt is the distinction between self-injurious behavior and self-injury (i.e., actual self-injury is not required, just the potential for harm). For instance, if a person places a loaded gun to his head and pulls the trigger, but the gun fails to fire, this act would be labeled a "suicide attempt"—and became so as soon as the trigger was pulled—despite the lack of medical damage. Despite the actual outcome, the intent (or inferred intent) was sufficient to classify this instance as a suicide attempt. Additionally, if a person engages in an act that has almost no potential of death (e.g., takes three low-dose tablets of a mild analgesic), it is still labeled a suicide attempt if the person had some intent to die as a result of this action. Thus, a classifier's preconceived notions as to lethal potential should not influence a classification. With seemingly low-lethality methods, the critical factor is what the person believed when he or she engaged in that behavior (i.e., intent of the act)—whether the behavior was enacted, at least in part, as a method or means to end his or her life.

Stated or Inferred Intent

Importantly, intent may be stated or inferred, though the field has been riddled with misunderstandings that intent derives only from what the person reports about his or her own intent. Inference of intent can come via psychological assessment and input from other informants such as friends and family (O'Carroll, 1989) or from the clinical circumstances. Intent may be inferred in two ways: (1) the individual's own perception of the potential lethality of an act, that is, denying intent to die but admitting the possibility of death from own actions; and (2) acts of impressive circumstances, that is, action explainable by no other potential intent than intent to die (De Leo et al., 2004; Posner et al., 2007). For example, inference of intent to die can come from potentially highly lethal behavior, such as trying to shoot oneself in the head or jumping from a high floor of a building—circumstances in which no other intent but suicide can be inferred. Conversely, inference about a lack of intent to die cannot be inferred from a nonlethal method used in connection with intent to die. If a person engages in an act that has almost no potential of death (e.g., takes three low-dose tablets of an analgesic), the act is labeled a suicide attempt if the person had some intent to die as a result of this action. Additionally, the circumstances involving what was done, for example, where on the body the person tried to injure himself or herself, can be utilized to infer intent or lack thereof. For example, if an individual cut his or her leg or hand, this is not typically indicative of suicidal intent. Other sources of information can also be of critical assistance in inferring intent, such as information from family members or hospital records. Even if inferred intent is not always reliable (Linehan, 1997), there is evidence that a potential attempter's or an observer's perception of lethality of a suicidal act is directly related to the individual's actual suicidal intent (Beck, Beck, & Kovacs, 1975) (Fig. 2.1 and Table 2.1). Awareness and understanding of the potential for death are necessary and may affect diagnosis of suicide in those with intellectual disability or those with psychosis. For example, if an individual engages in behavior that can be fatal without realizing it (e.g., jumping from a lethal height as a result of a delusional belief that one can fly, as opposed to having a suicidal command hallucination), then intent cannot be inferred (Beck & Greenberg, 1971).

When Intent Cannot Be Inferred

In circumstances when intent is not ascertainable and cannot be inferred, a classification of undetermined self-injurious behavior (or undetermined self-directed violence) is indicated (Fig. 2.1a). Reliability for this undetermined classification has been established in the FDA-commissioned classification algorithm for suicide assessment (Posner et al., 2007).

NONSUICIDAL SELF-INJURIOUS BEHAVIOR

To predict suicide risk accurately and make clinically sound decisions regarding treatment and hospitalization, it is essential to understand the distinction between an episode of nonsuicidal self-injurious behavior (NSSIB) and a suicide attempt. While most patients who engage in both self-injurious behaviors can describe the difference in the intent of their behaviors, some patients report a vague understanding of their intent when engaging in self-injurious behaviors. Issues in classifying intent in complex cases like these pose difficulty in developing a widely accepted classification system for nonsuicidal self-injurious behaviors.

The term "nonsuicidal self-injurious behavior" has replaced other terms and has been used to classify self-injurious behaviors characterized by the occurrence of self-inflicted and deliberate bodily harm with no intent to die. Most common examples of NSSIB include nonlethal lacerations, burns, or head banging (Favazza, 1989a, 1989b; Gunderson & Hoffman, 2005). Although suicide attempts and NSSIB share self-injury as the outcome, they are fundamentally different in intent, method, medical lethality, and pattern (i.e., repeated stereotypical episodes for NSSIB versus single or intermittent events for suicide attempts) and are subjectively perceived by the actor as quite distinct (Favazza, 1998). While not a suicidal behavior, NSSIB, however, is associated with an increased risk of suicide attempts and therefore should be both assessed and distinguished from suicide attempts. Approximately 55% to 85% of individuals who engage in NSSIB have a history of at least one suicide attempt and individuals who self-injure are at increased risk for suicide (Brent et al., 2002).

Substance abuse and eating disorders are not considered examples of NSSIB because the bodily harm *itself* is not deliberate (i.e., an intended consequence of the behavior). Furthermore, to distinguish NSSIB from other deliberate self-injurious behaviors such as tattooing, scarification, and body piercing, the behavior must be outside the realm of socially sanctioned forms of self-injury that are regarded as expressions of individuality, cultural identity, and creativity (Favazza, 1998).

The importance of distinguishing NSSIB from suicidal behavior is reflected in the classification of nonsuicidal self-injury and suicidal behavior as distinct disorders in the *DSM-5*. The characterization of NSSIB as a syndrome is based on a prominent pattern of age of onset, symptoms, precipitants and course, and greater impairment (Linehan, 1997; Muehlenkamp, 2005),

Nonsuicidal self-injurious behaviors are primarily distinguished from suicides and suicide attempts in that they are performed with the intent to self-injure but without intent to die. The phenomenon of nonsuicidal self-injury (NSSIB) is becoming a focus of increasing clinical concern, intervention, and research.

As with suicide and suicidal behavior, consistent definitions of NSSIB are necessary to evaluate the effectiveness of clinical interventions, as well as to compare research findings across different studies. Although the term NSSIB has become more consistently used in the literature over the past 5 years, there are many other terms used to describe behaviors that appear to be intentional efforts to self-injure in the absence of any intent to die. Historically, Menninger, in his 1938 book *Man Against Himself*, first described self-injury as a coping mechanism to avoid suicide. The term "self-mutilation" was used to describe behaviors such as wrist cutting, head banging, trichotillomania, and self-castration (Lester & Perdue, 1972).

Any classification of NSSIB must attempt to ascertain the intent or purpose of the behavior. The following are the functions of NSSIB that are most commonly reported by patients (Gunderson & Hoffman, 2005, pp. 49–50): (1) affect regulation: "to make the individual feel better by reducing emotional tension" and reestablishing a sense of emotional control over a prior state of dysregulation; (2) distraction from emotional pain; (3) self-punishment: "Gunderson & Ridolfi (2001) [report] from their clinical experience that cutting mostly serves the function of self-punishment, 'providing relief from a poorly articulated but intolerable state involving intense shame, remorse, and convictions of badness and alienation' (p. 63)"; (4) concrete proof of emotional distress: a scar or bruise can provide concrete evidence of an emotional state that allows the individual to self-validate; (5) alleviation of numbness and depersonalization: "Favazza (1989) calls this function 'return to reality,'" where

individuals report that self-injury provides immediate relief from intolerable feelings of numbness; and (6) release of anger: "acting on angry feelings through self-harm seems safer and less guilt producing than to express anger toward others (Favazza, 1989)."

Further research on the phenomenology, intent, and function of NSSIB as an attempt to cope with and regulate emotional distress is needed to distinguish an episode of NSSIB from a suicide attempt. However, currently there is agreement regarding the clinical value of recognizing both the distinction as well as the increased risk for morbidity by suicide attempts in individuals who engage in NSSIB.

The Full Range of Suicidal Behavior and Its Importance

Historically, a suicide risk assessment or screening queried solely about lifetime or recent suicide attempts, which resulted in the omission of other types of significant suicidal behaviors (e.g., buying a gun in preparation to kill oneself; giving away possessions; writing a will; putting a noose around one's neck and changing one's mind; poising to jump and someone else preventing the jump). Thus, in addition to suicide attempt, the full range of suicidal behavior includes interrupted attempt, self-interrupted/aborted attempt, and preparatory acts or behavior toward an attempt. Extant literature has shown that those who report any lifetime suicidal behaviors are more likely to engage in future suicidal behaviors and therefore all of these behaviors are important to include in the classification of the entire spectrum of suicidal behavior. *Preparatory acts or behavior* signify increased risk for future suicide attempts and deaths by suicide (Beck, Brown, Steer, Dahlsgaard, & Grisham, 1999; Marzuk, Tardiff, Leon, Portera, & Weiner, 1997; Steer, Beck, Garrison, & Lester, 1988). In a longitudinal study individuals who engage in preparatory behaviors are 8–10 times more likely to die by suicide (Beck & Brown, unpublished data). Individuals with a history of *an interrupted attempt* have been found to be three times more likely to die by suicide than nonattempters over 5 to 10 years after their interrupted attempt (Steer et al., 1988; Steer & Beck, 1988). A history of *self-interrupted/aborted attempts* is also associated with subsequent suicide attempts. For example, inpatient aborted attempters have been found to be more likely to have made a suicide attempt compared to inpatients with no history of an aborted attempt (Barber, Marzuk, Leon, & Portera, 1998; Marzuk et al., 1997). Moreover, behaviors, not typically assessed routinely account for the majority of suicidal behaviors. For example, in a large sample of patients studied in clinical trials, only 12% of their reported suicidal behaviors during trial were suicide attempts; the remaining 88% consisted of the other three types of behaviors (Mundt, Posner, Greist, & Federico, 2011). Furthermore, each one of these other lifetime behaviors significantly predicted subsequent suicidal behavior over a relatively short-term follow-up, all were similarly predictive, and the total number of different suicidal behaviors increased risk (Posner, 2012).

Interrupted Attempt, Self-Interrupted/Aborted Attempt, Preparatory Acts or Behavior

Interrupted attempt is defined as a behavior toward an imminent suicide attempt that is stopped by an outside circumstance before any potential for harm occurs. In the absence of interruption, a suicide attempt would have occurred (see Table 2.1). *Self-interrupted/aborted attempt* is a potentially self-injurious behavior toward an imminent suicide attempt where the individual stops himself or herself instead of being stopped by external circumstances or another person. Once harm or the potential for harm occurred, that behavior is classified as a suicide attempt (Barber et al., 1998; Marzuk et al., 1997). As such, once the individual makes the first cut on the skin or swallows the first pill, regardless of whether he or she stopped any further self-harm, the event is considered a suicide attempt. *Preparatory act or behavior* toward suicide refers to any act or preparation toward imminently making a suicide attempt. These behaviors include preparations for one's death (e.g., writing a suicide note, giving things away, checking an insurance policy, revising a will) or assembling a specific method (e.g., buying a gun, collecting pills).

Toward a Meaningful Common Language

Across disciplines and geographical locations, a multitude of terms have been used to describe the same potentially self-injurious event (e.g., the same event is labeled a suicide attempt, not a suicide attempt, a gesture, etc.). Furthermore, some of these terms hold pejorative connotations (e.g., "threat," "manipulative," "hostile") (Goldston, 2003; O'Carroll et al., 1996). In an effort to eliminate redundant, pejorative, imprecise, or biasing terminology and move toward meaningful, common language, the CDC surveillance definitions for self-directed violence, based on recommendations

from a panel of expert suicidologists, specified that certain terms be removed from the suicide nomenclature, including *completed suicide, failed attempt, nonfatal suicide, parasuicide, successful suicide, suicidality, suicide gesture, manipulative act,* and *suicide threat* (Fig. 2.3) (Crosby et al., 2011). While implementation of these recommendations is far from complete, the narrowing of terminology is a useful means of facilitating the transition to a uniform nomenclature and classification system.

To attain objectively descriptive nomenclature, terms that connote value judgments are to be avoided, such as *completed suicide,* which ascribes positive qualities to suicide; "completing a suicide" is akin to "completing a task." *Failed attempt* similarly connotes a value judgment in which the unrealized suicide is depicted as an error. Furthermore, terms that imply that the suicidal behavior is nonsuicidal in nature obfuscate the boundaries between suicidal behavior and other types of self-injurious behavior. For example, *suicide gesture* may indicate that the intent of the behavior is to provoke reactions from others rather than to die, in which case the behavior is not suicidal. Alternately, the term may indicate that the behavior falls short of a suicide attempt; however, whether the behavior is suicidal remains ambiguous because it is unclear whether intent to die is a necessary condition of a *suicide gesture.* Finally, terms such as *manipulative act,* aside from confounding the presence of intent to die, carry negative value judgments, thereby undermining objectivity within a classification system.

Importance of Classification of Suicidal Ideation and Its Distinction From Suicidal Behavior

When Dr. Aaron Beck began developing a suicide ideation scale in the 1970s, the definition of suicidal ideation overlapped with that of suicidal behavior. Beck et al. (1972) described "suicide ideas" as including behaviors that are directly observed or inferred. He offered the example of a person taking barbiturates out of a bottle and then returning them to the bottle before engaging in the lethal act and categorized it as a form of suicidal ideation, suggesting that one may infer ideation from this behavior. Overlap in the definition of ideation and behavior was also evident in the FDA analysis of adverse event labels. For example, ideation was labeled as behavior when a patient with thoughts of killing himself or herself was labeled a suicide attempt (Posner et al., 2007).

Accurate classification of suicidal behavior necessitates its clearer delineation from suicidal ideation

Table 2.1 Classification of Suicidal and Nonsuicidal Self-Injurious Behavior

Behavior Type and Definition	Key Components of Definitions	Examples
Suicide: Death resulting from intentional self-injurious behavior, associated with any intent to die as a result of the behavior	• The outcome of the behavior is death. • Nonzero intent to die: If there is *any* intent/desire to die associated with the act, then the act is a suicide. • Intent can either be stated explicitly by the individual or inferred.	• Person died by hanging himself and left a note stating intent to die. • Person died of shooting self in the head; intent is inferred from the impressive circumstance. • Person died of swallowing pills and family members state he expressed a desire to die.
Suicide Attempt: A nonfatal self-directed potentially injurious behavior with any intent to die as a result of the behavior	• Evidence may be explicit or implicitly inferred. • Nonzero: If there is *any* intent/desire to die associated with the act, then the act is a suicide attempt. • There does not have to be any injury or harm, only the potential for injury or harm.	• Person swallows four pills because wanted to die (stated intent). • Person pulls trigger; gun failed to fire (no injury necessary, intent is inferred). • Person shoots self in face; survives and verbalizes no intent to die (inferred by impressive clinical circumstances).
Interrupted Attempt: A person takes steps toward making a suicide attempt but is stopped by another person prior to any injury or potential injury.	• If not for the interruption, actual attempt would have occurred. • No injury occurs. • However, once they ingest any pills, pull the trigger (even if the gun fails to fire), or make the first scratch, it becomes an attempt rather than an interrupted attempt.	• Person has pills in hand but is stopped from ingesting (*once person swallows any pills, this becomes an attempt*) • Person has gun pointed toward self, gun is grabbed away by someone else, or is somehow prevented from pulling trigger (*once person pulls trigger, even if the gun fails to fire, it is an attempt*). • Person is poised to jump but is grabbed and taken down from the ledge. • Person has noose around neck but has not yet started to hang—is stopped from doing so.
Self-Interrupted/Aborted Attempt: A person takes steps to injure self but stops self prior to any injury or potential for injury.	• If not for the interruption, actual attempt would have occurred. • No injury occurs. • However, as soon as the first pill is swallowed or the first scratch is made, it becomes a suicide attempt.	• Person takes out pills to make an attempt; changes mind and does not swallow any. • Person goes to the top of a building to jump; changes mind and turns around. • Person begins to drive at high speed toward a cliff; changes mind and drives home.
Preparatory Acts or Behavior: Acts or preparation toward making a suicide attempt	• Preparatory behavior, beyond a verbalization or thought • Assembling the method to kill oneself • Preparing for one's death by suicide	• Giving away valuable possessions • Writing a suicide note • Buying or collecting pills • Purchasing a gun • Writing a will
Nonsuicidal Self-Injurious Behavior: Behavior that is self-directed and deliberately results in injury or the potential for injury to oneself	• There is no evidence, whether implicit or explicit, of suicidal intent. • The behavior must be outside the realm of socially sanctioned forms of self-injury regarded as expressions of individuality and creativity such as tattooing and piercing.	• Person cuts self in order to distract from emotional pain. • Person carves on self to gain attention from parents. • Person burns self to feel alive. • Person scratches wounds to bleed as self-punishment.

due to the historical trend of conflating the two, as is seen in some of the dimensional approaches to suicide risk assessment. Suicidal ideation is more common than suicidal behavior; however, because a majority of ideators never engage in overt self-injurious behavior, ideation has proven difficult to utilize as an indicator for subsequent suicidal behavior (McAuliffe, 2002). Increasingly, however, research has demonstrated the utility of suicidal ideation in predicting attempts (Kessler, Borges, & Walters, 1999; Posner et al., 2011), broadening the scope of predictors, which traditionally focused on the utility of past suicide attempts as a general predictor for subsequent suicide attempts and deaths by suicide (Lewinsohn, Rohde, & Seeley, 1996; Rudd, Joiner, & Rajab, 1996).

Severe or pervasive ideation has been shown to predict future attempts (Brent et al., 1993; Fergusson et al., 2005; Lewinsohn, Rohde, & Seeley, 1994; Pfeffer et al., 1993; Wichstrom, 2000) and deaths by suicide (Brown et al., 2000) in adolescent and adult populations. Passive ideation, such as a wish to die, has been identified as a risk factor for death by suicide (Brown, Steer, Henriques, & Beck, 2005), with those reporting a wish to die being approximately 5 to 6 times more likely to end their life (Brown et al., 2005). Moreover, although several different terms have been used to refer to passive ideation (e.g., "better off dead," "thoughts of my own death"), it is only a "wish to die" that has been consistently associated with significantly increased risk, therefore eliminating other types of passive thoughts from the spectrum of suicidal ideation.

Furthermore, subsequent research found only ideation to be predictive of a future attempt (past or recent suicide attempt did not predict) in an adolescent emergency department follow-up study (King, Gipson, Agarwala, & Opperman, 2012), clearly emphasizing the need to appropriately assess and classify ideation as distinct from suicidal behavior. Another reason for distinguishing ideation from behavior is to disabuse the false notion that ideation always co-occurs with behavior. While suicidal behavior is almost always reported accompanying suicidal ideation, it is possible for an individual to admit suicidal behavior without accompanying suicidal ideation (Fawcett, 1992). Therefore, suicidal behavior should be assessed even if ideation is denied, and the assessment and classification of suicidal ideation are equally important as that of suicidal behavior.

A more precise delineation of discrete types of suicidal ideation and their associated definitions was reinforced by research findings that specific types of ideation are associated with elevated risk for subsequent suicidal behavior. In contrast, the dimensional approach to suicidal ideation did not show prediction, underscoring the need to classify types of suicidal thoughts with respect to intent to die and intent to act (Posner et al., 2011). The NIMH Suicide Research Centers Project offered an expert consensus on the definition of suicidal ideation and included wish to die, thoughts of killing oneself, and intent to kill oneself.

In the 1970s, the definition of suicidal ideation included intent to act or any intent to act on suicidal thoughts or carry out suicidal plans. Suicidal ideation was described as "having thoughts, ideas, and intentions about suicide" (Bagley, 1975, p. 201) and "plans and wishes to commit suicide" (Beck, Kovacs, & Weissman, 1979, p. 344). In these definitions, intent to act was a necessary component of suicidal ideation and as such was largely unacknowledged as a separate entity. However, there has been increasingly international convergence that intent is critical for delineating types of ideation (Hawton, 1987). Suicidal ideation was divided into active and passive suicidal ideation (Beck et al., 1979). Beck et al. (1979) defined passive ideation as a "desire" rather than a plan, elicited by questions such as the following: "Would [you] take precautions to save [your] life?," "Would [you] leave life/death to chance?," and "Would [you] avoid steps necessary to save or maintain [your] life?" (p. 346). Active ideation was defined as a "desire to make an active suicide attempt" (p. 346).

The classification of suicidal ideation into passive and active ideation has been incorporated into current classification systems, and it illustrates how their distinction may help rank these categories in order of severity, with active ideation considered more severe than passive ideation. The categorization by severity has also been incorporated into current classification systems by means of discriminating between ideation with and without intent to act (Posner et al., 2011). When intent and ideation are not distinguished, ideation not characterized by intent to act is unrecognized. Current classification systems distinguish intent to act from suicidal ideation, and thoughts or plans about suicide without any intent to act are still considered suicidal ideation (Brown et al., 2005), though a less severe form (Posner et al., 2011; Silverman et al., 2007). It is important to note that *intent to act* and *intent to die* are different concepts. Intent to die is a necessary condition for a behavior to be classified as suicidal. Intent to act demarcates less and more severe types of suicidal ideation. Ideation is a cognitive occurrence separate from, but predictive of, suicidal behavior (Posner et al., 2011).

Conclusion

Professionals in different fields, from health care facilities to the military, need to acquire a better understanding of suicidal behavior and self-injury, which will ultimately improve risk assessment, prediction, and prevention of suicidal behavior. Yet without objective definitions of suicidal behavior and clear criteria for distinguishing suicidal ideation and suicidal behavior, suicidal ideation and suicidal intent, suicidal and nonsuicidal self-injurious behavior, the task remains elusive and so does our ability to care for persons at risk. The history of the conceptualization of suicidal behavior illustrates the need for a continued and concerted effort to develop a well-defined standardized terminology and a comprehensive classification system that would be adopted by the World Health Organization and the international diagnostic systems.

Because our knowledge of suicidal phenomena is evolving, development of a comprehensive classification system will be an iterative process: Any such system will be refined and revised with accumulation of empirical evidence regarding the reliability, validity, and, especially, predictive utility of an evolving system (Maris, 1992; O'Carroll et al., 1996). However, adoption of clear guidelines for classifying suicidal ideation and behavior by the US regulatory bodies and agencies, as well as the inclusion of suicidal behavior and nonsuicidal self-injury in the *DSM-5*, demonstrate that the classification of suicidal behavior is moving in the direction of uniformity in classification of suicidal behavior. The next challenge for the field would be to coordinate a comprehensive effort to disseminate a uniform classification system across multiple health professions, community services, government organizations, and educational settings. A widely accepted and utilized standardized nomenclature and classification system is essential for the study of suicidal behavior and the development, evaluation of interventions for the treatment, and prevention of suicidal behavior.

References

Allen, F. (2000). Suicide: What is to be done? *Australian Psychologist, 2000*(35), 29–31.

American Psychiatric Association. (1994). *Diagnostic and statistical manual of mental disorders* (4th ed., Text rev.) Washington, DC: American Psychiatric Association.

American Psychiatric Association. (2012). American Psychiatric Association board of trustees approves DSM-5: Diagnostic manual passes major milestone before May 2013 publication [Press release].

Andriessen, K. (2006). On "intention" in the definition of suicide. *Suicide and Life-Threatening Behavior, 36*(5), 533–538.

Bagley, C. R. (1975). Suicidal behavior and suicidal ideation in adolescents: Problem for counselors in education. *British Journal of Guidance and Counselling, 3*(2), 190–208.

Barber, M. E., Marzuk, P. M., Leon, A. C., & Portera, L. (1998). Aborted suicide attempts: A new classification of suicidal behavior. *American Journal of Psychiatry, 155*(3), 385–389.

Barraclough, B., & Shepherd, D. (1994). A necessary neologism: The origin and uses of suicide. *Suicide and Life-Threatening Behavior, 24*(2), 113–126.

Beck, A. T., Beck, R., & Kovacs, M. (1975). Classification of suicidal behaviors: I. Quantifying intent and medical lethality. *American Journal of Psychiatry, 132*(3), 285–287.

Beck, A. T., Brown, G. K., Steer, R. A., Dahlsgaard, K. K., & Grisham, J. R. (1999). Suicide ideation at its worst point: A predictor of eventual suicide in psychiatric outpatients. *Suicide and Life-Threatening Behavior, 29*, 1–9.

Beck, A., Davis, J., Frederick, C., Perlin, S., Pokorny, A., Schulman, R.,...& Wittlin, B. (1972). Classification and nomenclature. In A. Beck et al. (Eds.), *Suicide prevention in the seventies* (pp. 7–12). Washington, DC: US Government Printing Office.

Beck, A., & Greenberg, R. (1971). The nosology of suicidal phenomena: Past and future perspectives. *Bulletin of Suicidology, 8*, 10–17.

Beck, A. T., Kovacs, M., & Weissman, A. (1979). Assessment of suicidal intention: The Scale for Suicide Ideation. *Journal of Consulting and Clinical Psychology, 47*(2), 343–352.

Bille-Brahe, U., Schmidtke, A., Kerkhof, A. J., De Leo, D., Lönnqvist, J., Platt, S., & Sampaio Faria, J. (1995). Background and introduction to the WHO/EURO Multicentre Study on Parasuicide. *Crisis, 16*(2), 72–78, 84.

Brent, D. A., Perper, J. A., Moritz, G., Allman, C., Friend, A., Roth, C.,...Baugher, M. (1993). Psychiatric risk factors for adolescent suicide: A case-control study. *Journal of the American Academy of Child and Adolescent Psychiatry, 32*(3), 521–529.

Brent, D. A., Oquendo, M., Birmaher, B., Greenhill, L., Kolko, D., Stanley, B.,...Mann, J. J. (2002). Familial pathways to early-onset suicide attempt: Risk for suicidal behavior in offspring of mood-disordered suicide attempters. *Archives of General Psychiatry, 59*(9), 801–807.

Brown, G. K., Beck, A. T., Steer, R. A., & Grisham, J. R. (2000). Risk factors for suicide in psychiatric outpatients: A 20-year prospective study. *Journal of Consulting and Clinical Psychology, 68*(3), 371–7.

Brown, G. K., Steer, R. A., Henriques, G. R., & Beck, A. T. (2005). The internal struggle between the wish to die and the wish to live: A risk factor for suicide. *American Journal of Psychiatry, 162*(10), 1977–1979.

Crosby, A., Ortega, L., & Melanson, C. (2011). *Self-directed violence: Uniform definitions and recommended data elements* (Version 1.0). Atlanta, GA: Centers for Disease Control and Prevention.

De Leo, D., Bertolote, J., Schmidtke, A., Bille-Brahe, U., & Kerkhof, A. (1999). Definitions in suicidology: The evidence-based and the public health approach. In *20th World Congress of the International Association for Suicide Prevention, Athens, Proceedings book* (p. 194).

De Leo, D., Burgis, S., Bertolote, J., Kerkhof, A., Bille-Brahe, U., (2004). Definitions of suicidal behaviour. In D. De Leo, U. Bille-Brahe, A. Kerkhof, A. Schmidtke (Eds.), *Suicidal behaviour: Theories and research findings* (pp. 17–39). Gottingen, Germany: Hogrefe & Huber Publishers.

De Leo, D., Burgis, S., Bertolote, J. M., Kerkhof, A. J., & Bille-Brahe, U. (2006). Definitions of suicidal behavior: Lessons learned from the WHO/EURO Multicentre Study. *Crisis: The Journal of Crisis Intervention and Suicide Prevention, 27*(1), 4–15.

Dorpat, T., & Ripley, H. (1967). The relationship between attempted suicide and committed suicide. *Comprehensive Psychiatry, 8*(2), 74–79.

Durkheim, E. (1951). *Suicide: A study in sociology.* New York, NY: Free Press.

Egel, L. (1999). On the need for a new term for suicide. *Suicide and Life-Threatening Behavior, 29*(4), 2.

Even, D. (2011, December 6). After success in three cities, new suicide prevention program could expand nationwide. *Haaretz.* Retrieved August 2013, from http://www.haaretz.com/print-edition/news/after-success-in-three-cities-new-suicide-prevention-program-could-expand-nationwide-1.399734.

Favazza, A. R. (1998). The coming of age of self-mutilation. *Journal of Nervous and Mental Disease, 186*(5), 259–268.

Fawcett, J. (1992). Suicide risk factors in depressive disorders and in panic disorder. *Journal of Clinical Psychiatry, 53*(Suppl.), 9–13.

Fergusson, D., Doucette, S., Glass, K. C., Shapiro, S., Healy, D., Hebert, P., & Hutton, B. (2005). Association between suicide attempts and selective serotonin reuptake inhibitors: Systematic review of randomised controlled trials. *British Medical Journal, 330*(7488), 396.

Gibbons, R. D., Hur, K., Brown, C. H., & Mann, J. J. (2009). Relationship between antiepileptic drugs and suicide attempts in patients with bipolar disorder. *Archives of General Psychiatry, 66*(12), 1354–1360.

Goldsmith, S. K., Pellmar, T. C., Kleinman, A. M., & Bunney, W. E. (Eds.). (2002). *Reducing suicide.* Washington, DC: The National Academics Press.

Goldston, D. B. (Ed.). (2003). *Measuring suicidal behavior and risk in children and adolescents.* Washington, DC: American Psychological Association.

Gunderson, J. G., & Hoffman, P. D. (Eds.). (2005). *Understanding and treating borderline personality disorder: A guide for professionals and families.* American Psychiatric Pub.

Hawton, K. (1987). Assessment of suicide risk. *British Journal of Psychiatry, 150,* 145–153.

Hjelmeland, H., & Ostamo, A. (1997). WHO/EURO Multicentre Study on Parasuicide. *Crisis, 18*(3), 140–141.

Ivanoff, A. (1989). Identifying psychological correlates of suicidal behavior in jail and detention facilities. *Psychiatric Quarterly, 60*(1), 73–84.

Jeglic, E., Brown, G., & Henriques, G. (2006). Cognition, cognitive therapy, and suicidality. In T. Ellis (Ed.), *Cognition and suicide: Theory, research, and therapy* (pp. 53–75). Washington, DC: American Psychological Association.

Joe, S. (2004, April). *Self-directed violence definitions: a review of the scientific literature.* Paper presented at the Uniform Definitions of Self-Injury conference, the National Center for Injury Prevention and Control, Centers for Disease Control and Prevention. Miami, FL.

Kessler, R. C., Borges, G., & Walters, E. E. (1999). Prevalence of and risk factors for lifetime suicide attempts in the National Comorbidity Survey. *Archives of General Psychiatry, 56*(7), 617–626.

King, C., Gipson, P., Agarwala, P., & Opperman, K. (2012). *Using the C-SSRS to Assess Adolescents in Psychiatric Emergency Settings: Predictive Validity Across a One-Year Period.* 52nd Annual NCDEU Meeting, Phoenix, AZ.

Kreitman, N., Philip, A. E., Greer, S., & Bagley, C. R. (1969). Parasuicide. *British Journal of Psychiatry, 115*(523), 746–747.

Lester, D., & Perdue, W. C. (1972). Suicide, homicide, and color-shading response on the Rorschach. *Perceptual and Motor Skills, 35*(2), 562.

Lewinsohn, P. M., Rohde, P., & Seeley, J. R. (1994). Psychosocial risk factors for future adolescent suicide attempts. *Journal of Consulting and Clinical Psychology, 62*(2), 297–305.

Lewinsohn, P. M., Rohde, P., & Seeley, R. (1996). Adolescent suicidal ideation and attempts: Prevalence risk factors, and clinical implications. *Clinical Psychology: Science and Practice, 3*(1), 25–46.

Linehan, M. M. (1997). Behavioral treatments of suicidal behaviors. Definitional obfuscation and treatment outcomes. *Annals of the New York Academy of Sciences, 836,* 302–328.

Maris, R. W. (1992). How are suicides different? In R. W. Maris, A. L. Berman, J. T. Maltsberger, & R. I. Yufit (Eds.). *Assessment of prediction of suicide* (pp. 65–87). New York, NY: Guildford Press.

Marzuk, P. M., Tardiff, K., Leon, A. C., Portera, L., & Weiner, C. (1997). The prevalence of aborted suicide attempts among psychiatric in-patients. *Acta Psychiatrica Scandinavica, 96*(6), 492–496.

Mayo, D. J. (1992). What is being predicted?: The definition of "suicide." In R. W. Maris, J. T. Maltsberger, & R. I. Yufit (Eds.), *Assessment of prediction of suicide* (pp. 88–101). New York, NY: Guilford Press.

McAuliffe, C. M. (Ed.). (2002). *Suicidal ideation as an articulation of intent: A focus for suicide prevention?* (Vol. 6). Cork, Ireland: Brunner-Routledge.

Menninger, K. A. (1938). *Man against himself.* New York, NY: Harcourt, Brace.

Meyer, R. E., Salzman, C., Youngstrom, E. A., Clayton, P. J., Goodwin, F. K., Mann, J. J.,…Sheehan, D. V. (2010). Suicidality and risk of suicide—definition, drug safety concerns, and a necessary target for drug development: A consensus statement. *Journal of Clinical Psychiatry, 71*(8), e1–e21.

Mohandie, K., & Meloy, J. R. (2000). Clinical and forensic indicators of "suicide by cop". *Journal of Forensic Sciences, 45*(2), 6.

Muehlenkamp, J. J. (2005). Self-injurious behavior as a separate clinical syndrome. *American Journal of Orthopsychiatry, 75*(2), 324–333.

Mundt, J., Posner, K., Greist, J., & Federico, M. (2011, October 3-4) *eC-SSRS assessments of lifetime ideation and behavior are predictive of suicidal behaviors occurring during trial participation.* Poster session presented at the ISCTM 2011 Autumn Conference, Amelia Island, FL.

Nordstrom, P., Samuelsson, M., & Asberg, M. (1995). Survival analysis of suicide risk after attempted suicide. *Acta Psychiatrica Scandinavica, 91*(5), 336–340.

O'Carrol, P. W. (1989). A consideration of the validity and reliability of suicide mortality data. *Suicide and Life-Threatening Behavior, 19*(1), 16.

O'Carroll, P. W., Berman, A. L., Maris, R. W., Moscicki, E. K., Tanney, B. L., & Silverman, M. M. (1996). Beyond the Tower of Babel: A nomenclature for suicidology. *Suicide and Life-Threatening Behavior, 26*(3), 237–252.

Oquendo, M. A., Baca-García, E., Mann, J. J., & Giner, J. (2008). Issues for DSM-V: Suicidal behavior as a separate diagnosis on a separate axis. *American Journal of Psychiatry*, *165*(11), 1383–1384.

Oquendo, M., Galfalvy, H., Russo, S., Ellis, S. P., Grunebaum, M. F., Burke, A., & Mann, J. J. (2004). Prospective study of clinical predictors of suicidal acts after a major depressive episode in patients with major depressive disorder or bipolar disorder. *American Journal of Psychiatry*, *161*(8), 1433–1441.

Pfeffer, C. R., Klerman, G. L., Hurt, S. W., Kakuma, T., Peskin, J. R., & Siefker, C. A. (1993). Suicidal children grow up: Rates and psychosocial risk factors for suicide attempts during follow-up. *Journal of the American Academy of Child and Adolescent Psychiatry*, *32*(1), 106–113.

Platt, S., Bille-Brahe, U., Kerkhof, A. J. F. M., Schmidtke, A., Bjerke, T., Crepet, P., ... & Faria, J. S. (1992). Parasuicide in Europe: the WHO/EURO multicentre study on parasuicide. I. Introduction and preliminary analysis for 1989. *Acta Psychiatrica Scandinavica*, *85*(2), 97–104.

Pokorny, A. D. (1993). Suicide prediction revisited. *Suicide and Life-Threatening Behavior*, *23*(1), 1–10.

Posner, K. (2012, May 29–June 1). *Prediction of suicidal behavior in clinical trials using the C-SSRS*. Paper presented at the *52nd Annual NCDEU Meeting*, Phoenix, AZ.

Posner, K., Brown, G. K., Stanley, B., Brent, D. A., Yershova, K. V., Oquendo, M. A.,...Mann, J. J. (2011). The Columbia-Suicide Severity Rating Scale: Initial validity and internal consistency findings from three multisite studies with adolescents and adults. *American Journal of Psychiatry*, *168*(12), 1266–1277.

Posner, K., Oquendo, M. A., Gould, M., Stanley, B., & Davies, M. (2007). Columbia classification algorithm of suicide assessment (C-CASA): Classification of suicidal events in the FDA's pediatric suicidal risk analysis of antidepressants. *American Journal of Psychiatry*, *164*(7), 1035–1043.

Rockett, I. R. H., Regier, M. D., Kapusta, N. D., Coben, J. H., Miller, T. R., Hanzlick, R. L.,...Smith, G. S. (2012). Leading causes of unintentional and intentional injury mortality: United States, 2000–2009. *American Journal of Public Health*, *102*(11), e84–e92.

Rosenberg, M. L., Davidson, L. E., Smith, J. C., Berman, A. L., Buzbee, H., Gantner, G.,...Murray, D. (1988). Operational criteria for the determination of suicide. *Journal of Forensic Sciences*, *33*(6), 1445–1456.

Rudd, M. D., Joiner, T. E., & Rajab, M. H. (1996). Relationships among suicide ideators, attempters, and multiple attempts in a young-adult sample. *Journal of Abnormal Psychology*, *105*(4), 541–550.

Satcher, D. (1999). *The Surgeon General's call to action to prevent suicide*. Washington, DC: US P.H.S. Department of Health and Human Services.

Silverman, M. M. (2006). The language of suicidology. *Suicide and Life-Threatening Behavior*, *36*(5), 519–532.

Silverman, M. M., & Maris, R. W. (1995). The prevention of suicidal behaviors: An overview. *Suicide and Life-Threatening Behavior*, *25*(1), 10–21.

Silverman, M. M., Berman, A. L., Sanddal, N. D., O'Carroll, P. W., & Joiner, T. E. (2007). Rebuilding the Tower of Babel: A revised nomenclature for the study of suicide and suicidal behaviors. Part 1: Background, rationale and methodology. *Suicide and Life-Threatening Behavior*, *37*(3), 248–263.

Steer, R. A., & Beck, A. (1988). Use of the Beck Depression Inventory, Hopelessness Scale, Scale for Suicidal Ideation, and Suicidal Intent Scale with Adolescents. *Advances in Adolescent Mental Health*, *3*, 219–231.

Steer, R. A., Beck, A. T., Garrison, B., & Lester, D. (1988). Eventual suicide in interrupted and uninterrupted attempters: A challenge to the cry-for-help hypothesis. *Suicide and Life-Threatening Behavior*, *18*(2), 119–128.

Stengel, E. (1962). Recent research into suicide and attempted suicide. *American Journal of Psychiatry*, *118*, 725–727.

Stone, D. H., Jeffrey, S., Dessypris, N., Kyllekidis, S., Chishti, P., Papadopoulos, F. C., & Petridou, E. T. (2006). Intentional injury mortality in the European Union: how many more lives could be saved? *Injury Prevention*, *12*(5), 327–332.

Wichstrom, L. (2000). Predictors of adolescent suicide attempts: a nationally representative longitudinal study of Norwegian adolescents. *Journal of the American Academy of Child and Adolescent Psychiatry*, *39*(5), 603–610.

World Health Organization. (2000). *International statistical classification of diseases and health related problems*. Geneva, Switzerland: Author.

Distinguishing Between Suicidal and Nonsuicidal Self-Injury

Jennifer J. Muehlenkamp

Abstract

Suicide and nonsuicidal self-injury (NSSI) continue to be significant behavioral health concerns for adolescents and adults. Research is progressing with regard to understanding these two behaviors and the connection they share. However, a number of questions remain. Complicating current understanding of either behavior is the high co-occurrence between suicide and NSSI, the degree of risk correlates shared, and blurred definitional guidelines. This chapter provides a comprehensive review of the existing literature in an effort to synthesize the current knowledge about what constitutes NSSI versus suicidal behavior, and how the two behaviors truly differ from each other across a number of descriptive features, demographic characteristics, and psychosocial variables. The chapter concludes with a discussion of the relationship between NSSI and suicide attempts, offering directions for future research in this area.

Key Words: suicide, nonsuicidal self-injury, differences, characteristics, intent, psychopathology

Researchers and clinicians have argued that there is an important distinction between suicidal and nonsuicidal self-injurious (NSSI) behaviors for some time (e.g., Favazza, 1996; Linehan, 2000; Muehlenkamp, 2005; Walsh & Rosen, 1988), and it is now largely accepted that NSSI is different from suicidal behavior. However, the field continues to face significant challenges in understanding what constitutes NSSI versus suicidal behavior, how they truly differ, and how best to clearly define these behaviors in an effort to promote a precise scientific study of them. Recent efforts have been made to improve existing nomenclatures that make clear the distinction between suicide and self-injury (Claes & Vandereycken, 2007; O'Carroll et al., 1996; Silverman, Berman, Sanddal, O'Carroll, & Joiner, 2007b), but these taxonomies have not been widely adopted and at times conflict with prevailing definitions and terms used by researchers and professionals around the world (DeLeo et al., 2006; Hawton & van Heeringen, 2009; ISSS, 2007; Nock & Favazza, 2009; Silverman et al., 2007a; Walsh, 2006). The proposed diagnostic criteria for a NSSI disorder by the *Diagnostic and Statistical Manual of Mental Disorders*, fifth edition (*DSM-5*; American Psychiatric Association, 2013) should help improve nosological difficulties as well as improve the precision of research in this area.

Further complicating matters is the fact that there is a high degree of co-occurrence between suicidal ideation, suicide attempts, and self-injury. There also are a number of similarities in the known risk factors and correlates of suicide attempts and NSSI (see Andover, Morris, Wren, & Bruzzese, 2012; Skegg, 2005), although the degree, pattern, course, and treatment responses of these relationships appear to vary (e.g., Brown et al., 2005; Kessler, Berglund, et al., 2005; Muehlenkamp, 2006; Linehan et al., 2006; Nock & Kazdin, 2002; Taliaferro et al., 2012). In addition, recent studies have identified subclasses of self-injurers that have differential relationships to suicidal behaviors

(Klonsky & Olino, 2008; Taliaferro, Thullen, & Muehlenkamp, unpublished data; Whitlock, Muehlenkamp, & Eckenrode, 2008), suggesting there may be important variations in the relationship between NSSI and suicide. Consequently, some have argued for conceptualizing these behaviors along a general continuum of self-harm (Linehan, 2000; Stanley et al., 1992) that can range from mild, indirect self-harm such as occasional binge drinking, to moderate direct self-harm such as bruising or burning, to severe self-harm (e.g., cutting), ending with lethal self-harm (Nock, Cha, & Dour, 2011; Skegg, 2005; Walsh, 2006). This conceptualization recognizes that behaviors along the continuum can co-occur, share some common features and correlates of risk, and is recognized as having validity for understanding potential progressions from lesser forms of self-harm to suicide (Joiner, 2005; St. Germain & Hooley, 2012). However, there remains a need to tease apart potentially meaningful differences between self-harm behaviors. Doing so would facilitate the development of accurate theoretical models for understanding the interrelationships among them, as well as to inform the design of appropriate prevention and treatment programs. Consistent with this initiative, and due to the historical obfuscation of suicide and NSSI, this chapter will focus on elucidating known differences between these two behaviors.

Construct Definition—Intent and Function

As noted in the definitions offered by Posner and colleagues (see Chapter 2), the prevailing method for differentiating NSSI from suicide attempts is whether the person acknowledges an intent to die as a result of engaging in the behavior. Using intent to die to discriminate NSSI from suicidal self-injury has been supported conceptually (Hjelmeland & Groholt, 2005; O'Carroll et al., 1996; Silverman et al., 2007a). Data also support the notion that intent to die is critical to differentiating NSSI from suicide. Using data from the National Comorbidity Survey, Nock and Kessler (2006) identified a number of differences between self-injurers and suicide attempters, but they found intent to die to be the strongest differentiating variable. This finding has been replicated by others (Jacobson et al., 2008; Larsson & Sund, 2008), suggesting that intent to die is indeed an important and reliable differentiating variable. Furthermore, studies that have assessed implicit suicidal cognitions show that individuals who have stronger implicit associations with suicide/

death are significantly more likely to attempt suicide in the future than those with weak implicit suicide cognitions (Nock et al., 2010; Randall, Rowe, Dong, Nock, & Colman, 2013).

Indirect evidence also exists, with studies of community adolescents and young adults showing that self-injuring persons who also attempted suicide are more likely to report higher levels of suicidal ideation, fewer reasons for living, and greater repulsion by life/less attraction to life than those only engaged in NSSI (Brausch & Gutierrez, 2010; Muehlenkamp & Gutierrez, 2007; Whitlock & Knox, 2007). In an earlier study, Muehlenkamp and Gutierrez (2004) found that self-injuring adolescents were less repulsed by life than were suicidal adolescents and that having a positive attraction to life discriminated NSSI and suicide attempt groups, indicating that self-injurers are interested in living. In addition, research has shown that individuals who engage in NSSI do not perceive death to be a likely outcome of their NSSI (Favazza & Rosenthal, 1998; Muehlenkamp, 2005; Patton et al., 1997; Stanley et al., 2001). In contrast, persons reporting intent to die tend to engage in more lethal acts (Andover & Gib, 2010; Brown et al., 2004; Douglas, Cooper, Amos et al., 2004; Harriss & Hawton, 2005), be more accurate in estimating the lethality of their behavior, and tend to avoid discovery (Cooper et al., 2005; Douglas et al., 2004; Stanley et al., 2002). They are also more likely to die by suicide (Harriss, Hawton, & Zahl, 2005; Groholt et al., 2000; Nock & Kessler, 2006). Therefore, the data are consistent with the theoretical notion that suicide attempts are behaviors designed to terminate consciousness (Shneidman, 1985; Walsh, 2006), whereas acts of NSSI are intended to modify conscious experience, potentially in an effort to continue living (Walsh, 2006; Wenzel & Beck, 2008), lending validity to utilizing intent as a primary method for differentiating NSSI from suicide attempts.

However, the use of lethal intent to distinguish the behaviors is not without problems. Despite many researchers relying upon the "non-zero" rule of intent to die (O'Carroll et al., 1996) to establish whether a behavior is classified as NSSI or a suicide attempt, research shows that intent to die is a fluid cognitive state that demonstrates great temporal variability and frequent changes in severity (Daigle & Cote, 2006; King et al., 1995; Prinstein, 2008; Rodham, Hawton, & Evans, 2004). As pointed out by Hooley (2008) in her review of NSSI, using intent to discriminate behaviors requires a person to have accurate insight into motivations for a behavior during a time of significant distress, which is not always possible (see also Rudd, 2006). Many assessments of both NSSI and suicide attempts include retrospective self-reports, which possess many problems, including recall, hindsight, and informant biases (Miller, Rathus, & Linehan, 2007; Silverman et al., 2007a; Velting, Rathus, & Asnis, 1998). The concerns raised around using intent to die as the primary differentiating feature of NSSI and suicide attempts are legitimate, particularly because requiring intent to die has been demonstrated to affect prevalence rates (Hawton & vanHeeringen, 2009; Nock & Kessler, 2006), results in difficulties comparing findings (Jenkins & Singh, 2000; Nock et al., 2007; Westefeld et al., 2000), and may suggest different standards of care for responding and treatment (Groholt et al., 2000; Jobes & Drozd, 2004; Klonsky, Muehlenkamp, Lewis, & Walsh, 2011; Linehan, 1993; Muehlenkamp, 2006; Muehlenkamp, Ertelt, & Azure, 2008; Simon & Hales, 2006; Wenzel & Beck, 2008).

Despite the difficulties with assessing suicidal intent, recent research examining the motivations, or reasons, reported for engaging in NSSI and suicide attempts can also aid in differentiating the behaviors. While much of the existing research refers to the *functions* of NSSI or suicide (e.g., Klonsky, 2007; Nock 2009), it is important not to confuse a behavioral understanding of the term *function* (i.e., the relation between a behavior and its consequences) from the colloquial definition of *function* as "the reason for or purpose of a behavior" (see Lloyd-Richardson et al., 2009, p. 32), the latter being synonymous with the definition of intent. Hence, the research on the functions of NSSI and suicidal behavior can lend further understanding to differentiating NSSI from suicide on the basis of the general intent underlying the behavior.

There is consensus within the research that both NSSI and suicide attempts are overdetermined, being motivated by multiple reasons per episode. Researchers have documented that persons engaging in NSSI report an average of 4.1 reasons underlying the behavior (Whitlock, Muehlenkamp, et al., 2008), but this can range up to 13 different reasons (Brown et al., 2002; Klonsky & Glenn, 2009; Laye-Gindhu & Schonert-Reichl, 2005; Nixon et al., 2002). Similarly, research on the number of reasons endorsed for attempting suicide averages three but ranges up to eight (Brown et al., 2002; Hawton & Rodham, 2006; Madge et al., 2008). Also of importance are findings that NSSI and suicide attempts tend to be motivated by very

similar reasons that broadly involve the regulation of intrapersonal states and interpersonal environments (Baetens, Claes, Muehlenkamp, Grietens, & Onghena, 2011; Brown et al., 2002; Hjelmeland & Groholt, 2005; Nock & Cha, 2009; Nock & Prinstein, 2004; Muehlenkamp, Brausch, Quigley, & Whitlock, 2013). However, the pattern of associations and primary motivations endorsed significantly differ and can therefore help to distinguish between the behaviors.

Research on the reasons for engaging in NSSI consistently finds that while multiply determined (e.g., Klonsky, 2009, Messer & Fremouw, 2007), the most commonly reported intent is to regulate an aversive internal state. Specifically, both adults and adolescents self-report that NSSI is used primarily to reduce the experience of intolerable negative emotional or cognitive states, to self-punish, or to generate some type of feeling (Anderson & Sansone, 2003; Chapman, Gratz, & Brown, 2006; Gratz, 2003; Haas & Popp, 2006; Klonsky & Glenn, 2009; Kumar, Pepe, & Steer, 2004; Lloyd-Richardson, Perrine, Dierker, & Kelley, 2007; Nixon et al., 2002; Nock & Prinstein, 2004; Rodham et al., 2004; Whitlock, Eckenrode, & Silverman, 2006). Recent studies of adolescents and young adults with a history of NSSI confirmed these top functions and demonstrated that the specific functions of NSSI were uniquely associated with different skills deficits, personality characteristics, and risk behaviors (Turner, Chapman, & Layden, 2012; Zetterqvist, Lundh, & Svedin, 2013), lending further evidence to the multidetermined nature of NSSI. Many retrospective self-report studies have documented that individuals report increasing negative affect prior to the act of NSSI, which is subsequently followed by a significant reduction in negative affect and/or an increase in positive affect, most often relief (Claes, Klonsky et al., 2010; Claes & Vandereycken, 2007; Kamphuis et al., 2007; Laye-Gindhu & Schonert-Reichl, 2005). These retrospective studies were recently confirmed in three prospective, electronic diary studies of emotional experiences prior to and following unique episodes of NSSI (Armey, Crowther, & Miller, 2011; Muehlenkamp, Engel, et al., 2009; Nock, Prinstein, & Sterba, 2009).

Studies examining the physiological reactions of persons who engage in NSSI corroborate these self-reported reasons for NSSI. For example, Nock and Mendes (2008) found that adolescents with a history of NSSI demonstrated significantly increased physiological reactivity to distressing laboratory tasks relative to controls, and a study by Haines and colleagues (1995) found that imagining NSSI acts led to a significant reduction in physiological arousal within those reporting a history of NSSI behavior. These findings were recently replicated by Welch and colleagues (2008), who found a significant reduction in physiological arousal, and self-reported emotional arousal, immediately after imagining self-injury. This result was in contrast to the finding of increased physiological arousal following imagery of an accidental injury, thus lending support to the notion that acts of NSSI may modify aversive physiological arousal.

Suicide attempts have also been documented to be motivated by a desire to modulate aversive psychological states and obtain relief (Brown et al., 2002; Hjelmeland & Hawton, 2004; Linehan, 1993; Shneidman, 1985); however, research has shown that suicide attempts tend to be primarily motivated by an intensely strong desire to escape/die or to unburden others (Baetens et al., 2011; Baumeister, 1990; Brown et al., 2002; Hawton & Rodham, 2006; Hjelmeland & Hawton, 2004; Joiner, 2005; Van Orden et al., 2006). Yet a recent study among active duty soldiers found that suicide attempts were most strongly associated with the reported function of alleviating emotional distress (Bryan, Rudd, & Wertenberger, 2013), and multiple functions, including social reasons, were also endorsed. This study suggests the functions underlying suicide attempts may not be that different from NSSI. Recent data also support interpersonal reasons for acts of NSSI (Heath, Ross, et al., 2009; Klonsky & Glenn, 2009; Lloyd-Richardson et al., 2009; Muehlenkamp et al., 2013; Zetterqvist et al., 2013), but these intents tend to be secondary to affect regulation. There have been very few studies directly comparing the reasons for engaging in suicide attempts relative to NSSI. Of those that exist, most find few differences in the overall number of reasons for engaging in these behaviors, and the secondary intents tend not to differ between the groups (Baetens et al., 2009; Hawton & Rodham, 2006; Hjelmeland & Groholt, 2005). However, there is a consistent finding that the dominant intent for either behavior does significantly differ. Suicide attempts are more likely to be motivated by reasons of wanting to die and making others better off, whereas NSSI is primarily motivated by desires to regulate emotions or self-punish (Baetens et al., 2009; Brown et al., 2002; Haas & Popp, 2006; Hawton & Rodham, 2006; Klonsky & Glenn,

2009; Madge et al., 2008). In addition, there is evidence that some persons report using NSSI to prevent, or avert, suicidal impulses (Klonsky, 2007; Laye-Gindhu & Schonert-Reichl, 2005; Nixon et al., 2002; Nock, 2009), which is antithetical to making a suicide attempt. This reason should alarm providers to possible increased risk for a suicide attempt, but nonetheless it offers further evidence that these two behaviors are distinct. Therefore, the collective research on the motivation, or reasons, underlying either NSSI or suicide attempts appears to collectively support efforts to differentiate these behaviors on the basis of intent.

Descriptive Characteristics

As noted earlier, the primary method for differentiating NSSI and suicide attempts has been on the basis of intent. There remain a number of other important distinctions between these two behaviors with regards to the primary characteristics and demographics, as well as on key psychiatric, personality, and cognitive variables. Knowing these different features can help to inform the assessment, classification, and differentiation of a behavior as NSSI or a suicide attempt.

Course and Prevalence Rates

Both suicide attempts and NSSI exhibit a similar developmental course in that both tend to peak in prevalence during adolescence and young adulthood (CDC, 2010; Kessler et al., 1999; Klonsky & Muehlenkamp, 2007; Lewinsohn et al., 2001; Muehlenkamp, 2005; Rodham & Hawton, 2009; Whitlock et al., 2006), but it appears that NSSI may have a slightly earlier age of onset (age 13) than suicide attempts (age 16) (Hilt, Cha, & Nolen-Hoeksema, 2008; Jacobson & Gould, 2007; Miller & Smith, 2008; Nock, Borges et al., 2008; Sourander et al., 2006; Wichstrom, 2009). Of note is that rates of NSSI appear to decrease with age after one enters middle age (Favazza, 2009; Hawton & Harriss, 2008; Walsh, 2006; Zanarini, Frankenburg et al., 2005); although longitudinal studies are needed to empirically verify this observation. In contrast, age is positively correlated with suicide in most countries (Horton, 2006; Pearson & Conwell, 1995), although this is not always the case in the United States, where bimodal distributions and ethnic variations are noted (CDC, 2010; Conwell & Heisel, 2006; Horton, 2006; Lewinsohn et al., 2001). So, despite a similar pattern of peak onset, there appear to be notable differences in the lifetime course of NSSI relative to suicidal behavior.

Differences also exist with regard to the prevalence rates of both behaviors. Establishing accurate prevalence rates of NSSI has been difficult because there are few true epidemiological studies. However, emerging data from large samples of adolescent and young adult populations permit reasonable estimates of prevalence rates for NSSI. Overall, NSSI appears to be more common than suicide attempts, with lifetime prevalence rates of NSSI among community adolescents averaging between 13% and 28% worldwide (Brunner et al., 2013; Heath, Schaub, Holly, & Nixon, 2009; Lloyd-Richardson et al., 2007; Muehlenkamp, Williams et al., 2009; Muehlenkamp, Claes, Havertape, & Plener, 2012; Rodham & Hawton, 2009; Wedig & Nock, 2007). Estimates of lifetime prevalence of NSSI among college students ranges from 12% to 37% (Glenn & Klonsky, 2009; Gratz, 2006; Heath et al., 2008; Heath et al., 2007; Muehlenkamp, Hoff, et al., 2008; Whitlock et al., 2006), and lifetime rates among adults range up to 21% (Klonsky, Oltmanns, & Turkheimer, 2003). Rates tend to be much higher among clinical samples, with some noting lifetime rates as high as 80% (e.g., Claes, Vandereycken, & Vertommen, 2005; Heath et al., 2009). These rates fall substantially for 1-year prevalence, which results in an average yearly prevalence around 9.0% for community samples (Baetens et al., 2009; Hilt, Nock, et al., 2008; Madge et al., 2008; Muehlenkamp et al., 2012; Patton et al., 1997; Hawton & Rodham, 2006; Taliaferro et al., 2012), and up to 59% for inpatients (Guertin et al., 2001; Kirkcaldy et al., 2007; Nock, Holmberg, et al., 2007). When averaged across studies and populations, the lifetime prevalence of NSSI approximates 18% and a yearly prevalence of 9%, although rates differ substantially depending on the type of assessment used and population (Muehlenkamp et al., 2012).

Contrary to the high rates for NSSI, the lifetime and yearly prevalence rates of reported suicide attempts are substantially lower. For example, in a study of over 500,000 adolescents, Evans et al. (2005) reported an average yearly rate of suicide attempts to be 6.4% (95% CI, 5.4–7.5) across 128 studies from North American and European countries and Australia/New Zealand. Numerous studies in the United States and Europe report yearly suicide attempt rates in adolescents to be around 8.5% (CDC, 2010, 2012; Grunbaum et al., 2004; Kessler et al., 2005; Madge et al., 2008; McKeown et al., 2006). However, one study estimated the lifetime prevalence of suicide attempts worldwide, including adolescents and adults, to be 2.7% (Nock, Borges,

et al., 2008). Suicide death rates for those ages 15 to 19 years are estimated to range between 7.4 to 9.9 (per 100,000) and drop to 1.2 per 100,000 for those aged 10 to 14 years (Anderson & Smith, 2005; McKeown et al., 2006). Across all age groups, the CDC (2010) reports a crude rate of 11.2 (per 100,000) for deaths by suicide, and it is estimated that there are approximately 25 suicide attempts per death. Thus, the prevalence of suicide attempts and deaths, while of great concern, is significantly lower than those reported for NSSI.

Also of importance is the consistency of the NSSI lifetime and yearly prevalence rates reported internationally and across regions in the United States (Brunner et al., 2007; Claes et al., 2005; Evren, Kural, & Cakmak, 2006; Fliege et al., 2006; Hawton & Rodham, 2006; Izutsu et al., 2006; Laukkanen et al., 2008; Madge et al., 2008; Muehlenkamp et al., 2012; Nada-Raja et al., 2003; O'Connor et al., 2009; Plener et al., 2009; Resch et al., 2008; Zoroglu et al., 2003). In contrast, suicide prevalence rates tend to vary significantly around the world and within regions of a country (Bridges & Kunselman, 2003; Hawton & van Heeringen, 2009; Liu, 2009; McKeown et al., 2006; Terao, Soeda, Yoshimura et al., 2002). For example, China has some of the highest rates of suicide deaths (Phillips et al., 2002; Wasserman, Cheng, & Jiang, 2005), whereas suicide deaths are quite low in countries such as Iran, Egypt, and Greece (Hawton & van Heeringen, 2009). The considerable variability in suicide rates represents another point of disparity between NSSI and suicide, suggesting that suicide attempts may be influenced by cultural variables to a greater extent than is NSSI (see also Range et al., 1999; Walker, Alabi, Roberts, & Obasi, 2010). In sum, it appears NSSI is differentiated from suicide on the basis of the lifetime course, prevalence, and relative international or regional stability of the behavior.

Methods, Lethality, and Frequency

In addition to establishing the intent underlying the behavior, NSSI and suicide appear to be clearly differentiated by the methods used to inflict injury (Claes & Vandereycken, 2007; Muehlenkamp, 2005; Skegg, 2005; Walsh, 2006). People who attempt suicide tend to use highly lethal methods (Berman et al., 2006; Hawton & van Heeringen, 2009), whereas most NSSI involves low-lethality behaviors that result in minimal damage (Skegg, 2005; Walsh, 2006). This difference remains true across community and inpatient settings (Nock & Prinstein, 2005; Rodham et al., 2004; Whitlock et al., 2006). The most common methods of suicide attempts worldwide are hanging and ingestion of toxic substance (Berman et al., 2006). Within the United States, the three most frequent methods of suicide attempts in order are firearms (including for women; see Brent 2001; Canetto, 2001), suffocation, and poisoning/overdose (Baker, Hu, Wilcox, & Baker, 2013; Berman et al., 2006; CDC, 2010). Cutting is among the *least* common method of documented suicide attempts and accounts for less than 1.4% of all deaths in the United States (CDC, 2010; Maris et al., 2000). When cutting does result in death, it tends to be due to the location where the cuts are made such as on the jugular vein or carotid artery (Berman et al., 2006; Douglas et al., 2004; Maris et al., 2000).

In contrast, cutting is the most commonly reported method used for NSSI (Gratz & Chapman, 2007; Lloyd-Richardson et al., 2007; Madge et al., 2008; Muehlenkamp, 2005; Nixon et al., 2008; Rodham & Hawton, 2009; Trepal & Wester, 2007; Whitlock et al., 2006; Zoroglu et al., 2003) and is usually performed on areas of the body associated with very low lethality such as the forearms and upper legs (Csorba et al., 2009; Laye-Gindhu & Schonert-Reichl, 2005; Nixon et al., 2002; Whitlock, Muehlenkamp, et al., 2011). Other common methods of NSSI, which hold even lower lethality ratings than cutting (see Skegg, 2005), include skin abrading, interfering with wound healing, banging/self-hitting, and burning (Jacobson & Gould, 2007; Klonsky & Muehlenkamp, 2007). Among studies of deliberate self-harm, which often include self-injuries with suicidal intent, significant differences across numerous variables are frequently found between self-poisoners and self-cutters that are comparable to those found between suicide attempters and NSSI-only groups (e.g., Lilley et al., 2008; Madge et al., 2008; Rodham et al., 2004), further supporting the distinctions between behaviors representing a suicide attempt and NSSI.

Another important distinction between suicide attempts and NSSI includes the number of methods used. Most people endorsing repeated NSSI report using more than one method for their self-injury (Laye-Gindhu & Schonert-Reichl, 2005; Lloyd-Richardson et al., 2007; Madge et al., 2008; Muehlenkamp & Gutierrez, 2004; Nixon et al., 2002; Nock & Mendes, 2008). Aggregated across studies, it appears that repeat self-injurers use an average of four different methods for their

NSSI (Glenn & Klonsky, 2009; Klonsky, 2009; Lloyd-Richardson et al., 2007; Muehlenkamp & Gutierrez, 2004, 2007; Nixon et al., 2002; Whitlock et al., 2006) and the number of methods used is positively correlated with frequency of the NSSI (Whitlock et al., 2011). In opposition, many people endorsing repeated suicide attempts tend to use the same method (Bergen, Hawton, Waters, Ness, et al., 2012; Berman et al., 2006; Runeson, Tidemalm, Dahlin, Lichtenstein, & Langstrom, 2010), although they increase the potential lethality of the method with subsequent attempts (Miller et al., 2013). Among those engaging in NSSI who also attempt suicide, the suicide attempt method tends to be different from the methods used for NSSI and is most frequently an overdose (Bergen et al., 2012; Cloutier et al., 2010; Nock, Joiner et al., 2006; Stanley et al., 2001).

Lastly, there also are key differences in the frequency of the two behaviors. Although approximately 25% of community-based youth report engaging in only one or two acts of NSSI (refer to Chapter 10), a majority report a more chronic history of NSSI and endorse a high frequency of repetitive NSSI that ranges over 100 separate episodes (Heath et al., 2008; Laye-Gindhu & Schonert-Reichl, 2005; Whitlock et al., 2006, 2011). Despite this high frequency of NSSI, very few report seeking or requiring medical help for injuries (Evans et al., 2005; Fortune, Sinclair, & Hawton, 2008; Madge et al., 2008; Nixon et al., 2002; Whitlock et al., 2006, 2011). The lack of a need for medical attention highlights the low-lethality nature of NSSI and is in opposition to suicide attempts. The frequency of suicide attempts across the lifetime tends to be comparatively low (Lilley et al., 2008). Yet repetition of NSSI is very common and the likelihood of engaging in repeat episodes of NSSI is larger than suicide repetition rates (Lilley et al., 2008; Nock, Holmberg et al., 2007). Although many suicide attempts go undetected, more individuals who attempt suicide seek help or require medical attention (Baetens et al., 2009; Evans et al., 2005; Fortune et al., 2008; Larsson & Sund, 2008; Nixon et al., 2002) than those who engage in NSSI. Therefore, the existing data strongly support differentiating NSSI from suicide attempts on the basis of the method used, body locations injured, frequency of the behavior, and overall severity/lethality.

Race/Ethnicity/Socioeconomic Status

Most of the existing studies on NSSI have only documented the relative prevalence of NSSI acts across different racial/ethnic groups and have not examined variables associated with race/ethnicity that may impact risk for and rates of NSSI. Although some studies have noted that NSSI tends to be reported more frequently by Caucasians than other minority groups (Bhugra, Singh et al., 2002; Borrill, Fox, & Roger, 2011; Lloyd-Richardson et al., 2007; Sansone, Sellborn, Chang, & Jewell, 2012), others have found similar rates between all ethnic/racial groups regardless of the severity of NSSI (Whitlock et al., 2006, 2008), whereas others have found variations across select ethnic groups (Cwik et al., 2011; Gratz, Latzman, et al., 2012). The lack of research on racial/ethnic variation is a serious limitation of the extant research and may explain the equivocal findings. However, the patterns noted appear to be somewhat similar to those found for suicide attempts. Epidemiological data suggest that Caucasians attempt suicide at higher rates than other racial/ethnic groups (CDC, 2010; Horton, 2006; Kessler et al., 1999; Oquendo et al., 2004); however, some studies report that Hispanic adolescents and Asian American college students have the highest rates of suicide attempts relative to other racial/ethnic groups (Grunbaum, 2004; Kisch, Leino, & Silverman, 2005; Tortolero & Roberts, 2001). Additionally, deaths from suicide tend to be highest among indigenous people worldwide, including Native Americans in the United States (Anderson, 2002; CDC, 2010; Fortune & Hawton, 2007; Wissow et al., 2001; Yuen et al., 2000). It is important to note that race/ethnicity often interacts with gender, age, socioeconomic status, cultural values, and acculturative stressors to influence rates and risk for suicide attempts and deaths (Colucci & Martin, 2007; Goldston et al., 2008; Gomez, Miranda, & Polanco, 2011; Purselle et al., 2009). Similar relationships may be found for NSSI but research has yet to examine them so it is premature to suggest that there are variations between suicide attempts and NSSI on the basis of race/ethnicity.

With regard to socioeconomic status (SES), research continuously supports findings that low socioeconomic status is strongly associated with suicide attempts (Berman et al., 2006; Horton, 2006). Studies of economic climate and employment rates frequently find higher suicide rates among unemployed and lower SES persons (Milner, Page, & LaMontagne, 2013; Purselle et al., 2009; Solano et al., 2012), as well as during times of economic deprivation (Hawton et al., 2001; Stack, 2000; Ying & Chang, 2009). However, some studies suggest that this may not always be the case (Shah & Bhandarkar, 2008) and may vary based on the general income level of the country (Noh, 2009). In contrast to suicide and SES, very little data are available regarding NSSI and socioeconomic status. Of the few studies reporting on the SES of the participants, most have reported that SES does not vary between those who do and do not engage in NSSI (Whitlock et al., 2006, 2008; Wong et al., 2007); however, a recent study of 500 randomly selected youth did find a significant difference between the groups with lower SES youth reporting more engagement in NSSI (Nixon et al., 2008). High rates of NSSI also have been independently reported within samples of privileged youth (Yates, Tracy et al., 2008) and among low SES groups (Nada-Raja et al., 2004; Tyler et al., 2003). There may be some SES differences between NSSI and suicide attempts, but the lack of data for NSSI makes drawing firm conclusions premature.

Sexual Orientation and Gender

There are no clear differences between NSSI and suicide attempts on the basis of sexual orientation. Both NSSI and suicide attempts are common among homosexual and bisexual persons, often with rates being higher than among heterosexuals (Marshal, Dietz, Friedman, Stall, Smith, et al., 2011; O'Connor et al., 2009; Russell & Joyner, 2001; Whitlock et al., 2006; Whitlock & Knox, 2007). Risk for both NSSI and suicide attempts is believed to peak during the coming-out process (Blosnich & Bossarte, 2012; Remafedi et al., 1993; Whitlock et al., 2006), and the risk may be more pronounced for males than females (Garofalo et al., 1999; Remafedi et al., 1998; Russell & Toomey, 2013). However, there have been no known longitudinal studies of NSSI within gay, lesbian, bisexual, and transgender groups to determine risk trajectories.

It is well established that females attempt suicide at significantly higher rates than males (Canetto & Lester, 1995; Gold, 2006; Gould et al., 2003; Madge et al., 2008), yet males are more likely to die from suicide (Cooper et al., 2005; Gold, 2006; Maris et al., 2000). One exception is China, where females are more likely to attempt and die by suicide than are males (Phillips et al., 2002). The gender distribution of NSSI is less clear. Many studies report that females are more likely to engage in NSSI than are males (Brunner et al., 2007; Jacobson et al., 2008; Laye-Gindhu & Schonert-Reichl, 2005; Muehlenkamp & Gutierrez, 2007; Muehlenkamp,

Williams et al., 2009; Nixon et al., 2008; Rodham et al., 2004; Whitlock et al., 2006, 2011). However, just as many studies also find that males and females are equally likely to engage in NSSI (Baetens et al., 2009; Gratz, 2001; Izutsu et al., 2006; Klonsky et al., 2003; Muehlenkamp & Gutierrez, 2004; Nixon et al., 2002; Nock, Joiner et al., 2006; Tyler et al., 2003; Zoroglu et al., 2003). The equivocal results are likely due to variations in the samples, definitions used, methods included as NSSI, time frame assessed, or type of assessment tool used (Heath et al., 2009). For example, Hawton and Rodham (2006) found that females were more likely to report lifetime acts of NSSI than were males, but there was no gender difference in the percent of males and females reporting repetitive NSSI; this finding has not been replicated (see Brunner et al., 2007; Whitlock et al., 2011). Gender was also found to vary across different subclasses of NSSI in young adults, with females being overrepresented within high-severity groups (Klonsky & Olino, 2008; Whitlock et al., 2008). Recent studies suggest that males and females differ in the types of NSSI methods used (Claes, Vandereycken, & Vertommen, 2007; Heath, Toste, Nedecheva, & Charlebois, 2008; Izutsu et al., 2006; Whitlock, Eckenrode et al., 2006; Whitlock et al., 2011), which mirrors findings that suicide attempt methods vary between genders (Berman et al., 2006; Maris et al., 2000; Skegg, 2005). Collectively, the research appears to remain equivocal about the influence of gender in reliably differentiating NSSI from suicide.

Psychosocial Differences

One of the complicating factors in differentiating NSSI from suicide attempts is that they appear to share similar risk factors in terms of psychiatric profiles, abuse histories/family environments, personality, and cognitive features. In reviewing the literature, it becomes clear that many of the distal risk factors identified for suicide and NSSI are the same (e.g., Jacobson & Gould, 2009; Joiner, 2005; Nock, 2009; Nock et al., 2013; Skegg, 2005). Although there are few studies directly comparing NSSI and suicide attempts on these variables, a close inspection of the research reveals that there are reliable, albeit small, differences across the distal variables. It looks like NSSI and suicide can generally be differentiated by the severity of the pathology/dysfunction, but the global group differences noted in the studies reviewed may not always be applicable to an individual client.

Psychiatric Diagnoses

Both suicide attempts and NSSI are associated with a number of diagnostic categories and the presence of any diagnosis is associated with increased risk for self-harm in general (Kessler et al., 1999; Resch et al., 2008). However, NSSI appears to be particularly heterogeneous with regard to the diagnoses represented (Jacobson et al., 2008; Klonsky et al., 2003; Lofthouse et al., 2009; Trepal & Wester, 2007), but it tends to be associated with lower amounts of psychiatric morbidity compared to suicide. For example, research has noted that approximately 94% to 98% of persons worldwide who attempt or die from suicide meet criteria for at least one psychiatric disorder (Bertolote, Fleischmann et al., 2004; Cavanagh et al., 2003); however, more recent studies indicate that 66% of suicide attempters across 21 different countries have a preexisting Axis I disorder (Nock et al., 2009). Among individuals attempting suicide who do not meet full criteria, many still experience significant psychiatric symptoms, leading experts to conclude that it is quite rare for suicidal behavior to occur in the absence of significant psychopathology (Ernst et al., 2004; Hawton & van Heeringen, 2009). On the contrary, research examining pathology in NSSI suggests that only 22% to 40% of those in community samples (Klonsky & Olino, 2008; Whitlock et al., 2006, 2008) and up to 87% of inpatient adolescents (Nock, Joiner et al., 2006) meet criteria for at least one disorder. A recent study reported that the presence of NSSI was not associated with specific psychiatric diagnoses among a sample of inpatient adolescents (Warzocha, Pawelczyk, & Gmitrowicz, 2010). These studies indicate that a meaningful portion of persons with NSSI will not exhibit clinically significant levels of psychiatric dysfunction (Institute of Medicine, 2002). However, similar to suicide attempts, individuals endorsing even one lifetime act of NSSI tend to show elevated levels of psychopathology compared to no self-harm controls (Andover et al., 2005; Brunner et al., 2013; Claes et al., 2007; Hasking et al., 2008; Hawton, Rodham, Evans, & Harriss, 2009; Kirkcaldy et al., 2007; Larsson & Sund, 2008; Muehlenkamp & Gutierrez, 2004; Nixon et al., 2008; Penn et al., 2003; Sampson et al., 2004; Swenson et al., 2008; Wong et al., 2007).

With regard to specific diagnostic profiles, research with adolescents and adults shows that depression, substance use disorders, mania, anxiety, conduct disorder, and borderline and antisocial personality disorders are the most common diagnoses among suicide attempters (Brent et al., 1993; Cooper et al., 2005; Douglas et al., 2004; Goldston et al., 2006; Haw et al., 2001; Nock & Kessler, 2006), although people diagnosed with anorexia nervosa have some of the highest suicide attempt and mortality rates (Bulik et al., 2008; Holm-Denoma et al., 2008; Pompili et al., 2004). These same disorders are found within persons reporting NSSI but exhibit weaker associations (Brunner et al., 2007; 2013; Claes et al., 2007; Csorba et al., 2009; Favaro et al., 2008; Jacobson et al., 2008; Kirkcaldy et al., 2007; Lofthouse et al., 2009; Nock, Joiner et al., 2006; Ross & Heath, 2003; Swenson et al., 2008). For example, research indicates that the presence of substance use or abuse is particularly critical to elevating suicide risk (Arsenault-Lapierre et al., 2004; Berman et al., 2006; Cooper et al., 2005; Csorba et al., 2009; Marttunen et al., 1991; Wong et al., 2007); yet substance use and abuse is much less common and exhibits a weak relationship to NSSI (Brunner et al., 2007; Madge et al., 2008; Nixon et al., 2002; Nock, Holmberg et al., 2007; Whitlock et al., 2006). Relatedly, borderline personality disorder is particularly associated with suicide attempts (Krysinska et al., 2006; Linehan, 1993; Verona et al., 2004) and studies comparing NSSI groups to no-NSSI controls find that those with NSSI have elevated symptoms of this disorder (Andover et al., 2005; Jacobson et al., 2008; Nock, Joiner et al., 2006). However, many who engage in NSSI do not meet full criteria for borderline personality disorder (Muehlenkamp, Ertelt et al., 2011; Nock, Joiner et al., 2006; Selby, Bender, Gordon, Nock, & Joiner, 2012). Lastly, in the couple of studies directly comparing diagnostic profiles of NSSI and suicide attempters, results indicate that a diagnosis of major depressive disorder, posttraumatic stress disorder, and/or substance use disorder are predictive of suicide attempts relative to NSSI (Csorba et al., 2008; Dougherty et al., 2009; Jacobson et al., 2008; Nock & Kazdin, 2002, 2006; Prinstein et al., 2008; Taliaferro et al., 2012). It appears that suicide is characterized to a greater degree by the presence and severity of mood and substance use disorders than is NSSI, but it is important to highlight the great paucity of studies directly comparing the diagnostic profiles of these two groups. Therefore, differentiating the two behaviors on only their diagnostic correlates would be unwise until additional data are available.

Abuse/Family Environment

It is well established that childhood abuse, particularly sexual abuse, is a significant risk factor for suicide (see Brodsky & Stanley, 2008 for a review) and similar ideas have been proposed for NSSI (Low et al., 2000; Yates, 2004, 2009). Sexual abuse, specifically, has demonstrated a relatively robust relationship to suicide even when other important environmental and psychiatric variables are controlled (Enns et al., 2006; Horesch et al., 2009; Isohookana et al., 2013; Joiner et al., 2007; Martin et al., 2004; Taliaferro et al., 2012; Wherry et al., 2013) and appears to relate to an earlier age of onset for a first suicide attempt (Slama et al., 2009). Despite beliefs that sexual abuse is very common in individuals who engage in NSSI, a recent review of the empirical literature found that sexual abuse had a small-to-medium (phi = .23) association with NSSI (Klonsky & Moyer, 2008), and a study of over 700 college students found no difference in abuse histories between NSSI and controls (Heath et al., 2008). In fact, a number of studies have documented that the association between childhood sexual abuse and NSSI tends to be mediated by other clinical and psychosocial variables (Glassman et al., 2007; Gratz, 2006; Paivio & McCulloch, 2004; Swannell et al., 2012; Weierich & Nock, 2008). Yet physical abuse retains a significant direct relationship to NSSI when such variables are controlled (Evren & Evren, 2005; Gratz, Conrad, & Roemer, 2002; Klonsky & Moyer, 2008; Swannell et al., 2012). It appears that physical abuse is more important to, and a stronger predictor of, NSSI (Gratz & Chapman, 2007; Klonsky & Moyer, 2008; Muehlenkamp, Kerr et al., 2010; Whitlock et al., 2008; Yates, Carlson, & Egeland, 2008), whereas sexual abuse remains minimally associated with NSSI in some samples and tends to be more predictive of repetitive, chronic NSSI than intermittent NSSI (Isohookana et al., 2013; Klonsky & Moyer, 2008; Tyler et al. 2003; Whitlock et al., 2006; Yates, Carlson, et al., 2008; Zoroglu et al., 2003). Thus, sexual abuse may be a marker for more severe NSSI. In a handful of studies comparing abuse histories between NSSI and suicide attempt groups, results also support the notion that physical abuse is more prevalent and strongly associated with NSSI, whereas sexual abuse is more strongly linked to suicide attempts (Brodsky & Stanley, 2008; Hawton & van Heeringen, 2009; Horesh et al., 2009; Nock & Kessler, 2006; O'Connor et al., 2009; Stanley et al., 2001; Zorogulu et al., 2003), particularly among women diagnosed with borderline personality disorder (Soloff, Lynch, & Kelly, 2002; Zanarini, 2000).

Along with abuse experiences, research has suggested that a negative, chaotic family environment can also place a person at increased risk for suicide and NSSI (Gould et al., 2003; Klonsky & Glenn, 2009; Linehan, 1993; Miller, Rathus, & Linehan, 2007; Warzocha et al., 2010). Research has demonstrated that poor family functioning, including conflicts, lack of cohesiveness, poor bonding/attachment, and parental psychopathology, are risk factors for suicidal behavior (Dunkley & Grilo, 2007; Evans, Hawton, & Rodham, 2004; Fergusson et al., 2000; Hsu, Chen, & Lung, 2013; Lowenstein, 2005; Muehlenkamp & Gutierrez, 2007). Consistent with these findings, research has demonstrated similar relationships between poor and conflicted relationships with parents, family violence, parental criticism, and NSSI (Brunner et al., 2013; Crowell et al., 2008; Di Pierro et al., 2012; Glassman et al., 2007; Gratz et al., 2002; Heath et al., 2008; Hoff & Muehlenkamp, 2009; Kaess et al., 2013; Tulloch et al., 1997; Yates, Tracy et al., 2008). The data seem to indicate that parental criticism may be particularly salient to understanding pathways to NSSI among adolescents (see Wedig & Nock, 2007; Yates, Tracy et al., 2008), and interestingly, Hilt, Nock, and colleagues (2008) found that family relationships improved following acts of NSSI. Data are equivocal regarding the composition of families, with some research demonstrating elevated risk for either NSSI or suicide among nonintact families (Rubenstein et al., 1998; Sourander et al., 2006). Based upon the existing research, it appears that both behaviors are influenced by a negative and invalidating family environment.

Impulsivity and Aggression

While both NSSI and suicide attempts demonstrate strong relationships with impulsivity and aggression (Di Pierro et al., 2012; Fazaa & Page, 2009; Giegling et al., 2009; Laye-Gindhu & Schonert-Reichl, 2005; Nock & Kessler, 2006; Ross & Heath, 2003; Ross, Heath, & Toste, 2009; Skegg, 2005), the current research indicates that these personality traits may have a stronger association with NSSI than with suicide. For example, in their sample of adult women with borderline personality disorder, Stanley et al. (2001) found that NSSI acts were significantly different from suicide attempts on the basis of aggression scores, and research in samples of nonborderline persons show that those who engaged in NSSI scored significantly higher on aggression measures than controls (Claes, Muehlenkamp et al., 2010; Kirkcaldy et al., 2007; Laye-Gindhu & Schonert-Reichl, 2005; Nixon et al., 2008; Ross & Heath, 2003).

In regard to impulsivity, suicide attempts associated with planning and premeditation are associated with greater lethality (Douglas et al., 2004; Witte et al., 2008), whereas acts of NSSI are more likely to involve little planning or premeditation. Researchers commonly observe that persons engaging in NSSI report doing so within 1 hour or less of experiencing an urge (Csorba et al., 2008; Lloyd-Richardson et al., 2007; Madge et al., 2008; Nixon et al., 2002; Nock & Prinstein, 2005), despite documentation that many do attempt to resist urges (Klonsky & Glenn, 2008) and that around 25% report planning and specific routines for NSSI (Csorba, 2009; Whitlock et al., 2006, 2008). Further, studies directly comparing NSSI to suicide attempts have found that persons reporting NSSI exhibit significantly greater levels of impulsivity than suicide attempters (Cloutier et al., 2009; Klonsky & Olino, 2008; Nixon et al., 2002, 2008). Although Nock and Kessler (2006) reported that suicide attempters were distinguished from suicide gesturers by higher levels of impulsive and aggressive symptoms, a recent study of over 11,600 adolescents found that those who planned and attempted suicide were *more* impulsive than those who attempted without a plan. Additionally, Baca-Garcia et al. (2005) reported that impulsivity was negatively related to lethality of suicide attempts and suicide attempt status was not associated with trait impulsivity. Yet these results are not without controversy; a recent study comparing individuals reporting NSSI only to those reporting both NSSI and suicide attempts found that the NSSI plus suicide group scored significantly higher on self-report and behavioral measures of impulsivity (Dougherty et al., 2009), and this difference was maintained at a 6-week follow-up. These results contrast with those reported by Janis and Nock (2009) in which no difference between NSSI and controls were found on multiple behavioral tests of impulsiveness (see also Di Pierro et al., 2012); yet McCloskey and colleagues (2012) found congruence between self-report and behavioral indices of impulsivity in predicting NSSI. In a longitudinal study of over 4,700 adolescents, You and Leung (2012) found that impulsivity traits prospectively predicted both the occurrence and repetition of NSSI. Additionally, Wu et al. (2009) reported that impulsivity was significantly higher among suicide attempters than controls, but results were inconsistent across the self-report and behavioral measures and did not compare to NSSI groups.

Research has also recently attempted to examine the concept of impulsivity in a more precise manner, drawing upon the four-factor conceptu-alization of Whiteside and Lynam (2001). Studies examining the relative contributions of negative urgency, lack of premeditation, lack of persever-ance, and sensation seeking have found differential associations between these facets of impulsivity and both suicidal and NSSI behaviors. For example, a study of 76 inpatient drug/alcohol residents found that an interaction between negative urgency and lack of premeditation was significantly predictive of both suicidal and NSSI behaviors (Lynam et al., 2011). Those who scored high on negative urgency and low on premeditation were most likely to engage in either behavior. There did not appear to be significant differences between NSSI and suicidal acts. Other studies have also demonstrated that neg-ative urgency appears to be most salient to NSSI acts (Glenn & Klonsky, 2010; Taylor, Peterson, & Fischer, 2012), particularly when faced with a negative affective state (Bresin, Carter, & Gordon, 2013). However, Glenn and Klonsky (2010) found that in addition to negative urgency differentiat-ing self-injurers from controls, lack of perseverance predicted more recent and frequent NSSI. A simi-lar finding was reported by Dvorak and colleagues (2013) with regard to suicidal behavior among a large sample of college students. Collectively, the current research appears to indicate that impulsivity and aggression are related to both NSSI and sui-cide but that impulsivity (in the form of negative urgency) may be a more proximal risk for NSSI than for suicide. This is consistent with Joiner's (2005) theory suggesting that impulsivity is a distal predictor for suicide via impulsive risk taking such as NSSI, which results in an acquired capacity for suicide. However, the inconsistent results across studies suggest there is no definitive answer regard-ing the role of impulsivity and additional research in this area is needed.

Cognitive Features
Problem Solving

An extensive body of research has shown that suicidal individuals exhibit significant deficits in problem solving (Linda, Marroquin, & Miranda, 2012; Pollock & Williams, 1998; Williams et al., 2005). Among adult populations, suicidal persons are found to generate fewer and less adaptive or effective problem-solving strategies (McLaughlin et al., 1996; Pollock & Williams, 2001) and be less flexible in their thinking (Jollant et al., 2005). Although problem-solving deficits are also consis-tently found within suicidal adolescents compared

to controls, the differences are significantly attenu-ated when depressive symptoms and hopelessness are controlled (Speckens & Hawton, 2005), sug-gesting that problem-solving difficulties may result from other problematic cognitions (e.g., hopeless-ness). Of note, a study of over 700 community ado-lescents found that while problem-solving deficits and passive coping were associated with suicidal behavior, hopelessness was more predictive for females whereas poor/avoidant problem solving was most predictive of suicidality among males (Labelle et al., 2013). Regardless, the research largely sup-ports the idea that suicidal persons experience con-stricted cognitions that hinder abilities to generate and implement effective problem-solving strategies (Skegg, 2005; Speckens & Hawton, 2005).

There is a slightly different pattern noted among those reporting NSSI. While deficits in problem solving have been noted (Andrews, Martin, & Hasking, 2012; Herpertz, Sass, & Favazza, 1997; McAuliffe et al., 2006), they tend to be more nuanced than for suicidal persons. In contrast to the research with suicidal persons, data with NSSI adults and adolescents show that they are as capa-ble as controls in generating numerous adaptive solutions (Andover et al., 2007; Nock & Mendes, 2008). Variations are noted, however, in NSSI per-sons' ability to choose and believe they can imple-ment the adaptive strategies relative to controls (Nock & Mendes, 2008; Oldershaw et al., 2009). Furthermore, Andover and colleagues (2007) reported that although NSSI and control groups did not differ in the use of problem-solving-based cop-ing, NSSI participants were significantly less likely to utilize social support strategies and more likely to utilize avoidant methods (see also Claes et al., 2010; Hasking et al., 2008). Although there are no known studies directly comparing problem-solving skills between NSSI and suicide attempt groups, it seems that the primary difference in problem-solving dif-ficulties between NSSI and suicide is in the ability to generate solutions, with suicidal persons being less able. If held to be true, this subtle difference between groups may largely result from associated cognitive obstacles linked to the suicidal mindset, such as hopelessness.

Hopelessness

As aptly observed and noted by Walsh (2006), NSSI and suicidal behavior can be clearly differ-entiated on the level of hopelessness experienced. Hopelessness is identified as a critical risk factor for suicidal behavior (Brown et al., 2000; Rudd, 2006;

Thompson et al., 2009), but it is less commonly found among NSSI groups. The relatively lower levels of hopelessness observed between those with NSSI and suicide attempts are likely due to the conceptual distinction wherein persons who are suicidal think dichotomously and believe their pain cannot be relieved so suicide becomes the final answer (Baumeister, 1990; Shneidman, 1985; Wenzel & Beck, 2008). Supporting this notion are studies documenting that deficits in positive future thinking evidence a stronger relationship to suicide than to global hopelessness (O'Connor & Cassidy, 2007; O'Connor et al., 2008). In contrast, the cognitions of NSSI persons are comparably less pessimistic because they perceive choices and feel capable of changing their situation or modifying their pain and therefore are not hopeless about alleviating their distress. As Walsh (2006) notes, NSSI offers a sense of control over the distressing situation, and this perceived control is in direct opposition to the experience of hopelessness. This conceptual distinction has been supported by studies comparing individuals engaged in NSSI to those who also attempted suicide, finding that the NSSI-only group exhibited significantly greater attractions to life, reasons for living, future-orientated thinking, and less hopelessness (Brausch & Gutierrez, 2009; Claes et al., 2010; Muehlenkamp & Gutierrez, 2004, 2007; Taliaferro et al., 2012; Whitlock & Knox, 2007). As these results reveal, if hopelessness begins to increase substantially for a person who is engaged in NSSI, concerns about suicidality should be triggered and a thorough risk assessment be undertaken.

Relationship Between Nonsuicidal Self-Injury and Suicide Attempts

Although the focus of this chapter has been on differentiating NSSI from suicide attempts, it is essential to offer a discussion of how NSSI and suicide do relate to each other. As noted earlier, while these two behaviors are distinct from one another in a number of ways, they also share similarities in their proximal risk factors (Andover et al., 2012; Gould et al., 2003; Guerry & Prinstein, 2010; Skegg, 2005; Wichstrom, 2009) and are inextricably linked to each other. Prevailing etiological models and theories of suicidal behavior (e.g., Joiner, 2005; Linehan, 1993; Williams et al., 2005) and NSSI (Chapman et al., 2006; Nock, 2009; Nock & Cha, 2009), as well as treatment paradigms (Gratz, 2007; Klonsky, Muehlenkamp, Lewis, & Walsh, 2011; Miller et al., 2007; Walsh, 2006), pay special attention to and attempt to account for the

relation between these behaviors. Therefore, it is important to understand how these two behaviors are associated.

It is estimated that up to 85% of persons attempting suicide have a history of NSSI (Stanley et al., 1992) and from another perspective, researchers estimate that as many as 70% of individuals with a history of NSSI will attempt suicide at some point in their lives (Dulit et al., 1994; Nixon et al., 2002; Nock, Joiner et al., 2006). Yet interestingly, the rates of suicide attempts within college student samples with a history of NSSI tend to be less than 40% (Whitlock et al., 2006, 2011; Whitlock & Knox, 2007). Regardless of the exact percentage of those with NSSI histories attempting suicide, it has been found that merely the presence of a history of NSSI significantly increases the risk for both suicide attempts and death by suicide even after other known suicide risk factors like ideation and depression are controlled (Andover & Gib, 2010; Brent, 2011; Claes, Muehlenkamp et al., 2010; Hawton & vanHeeringen, 2009; Swenson et al., 2008; Whitlock et al., 2008, 2013). For example, Klonsky and Olino (2008) found that college students with the presence of NSSI history were eight times more likely to consider suicide and 25 times more likely to have attempted suicide compared to no-NSSI controls. This result is similar to Cooper et al.'s (2005) finding that adults with a history of deliberate self-harm (including NSSI and/or a prior suicide attempt) had a 34-fold increase in risk of death by suicide. Whitlock and Knox (2007) compared odds ratios for suicidal behavior between persons with NSSI and those reporting only suicidal ideation, finding that the sole presence of NSSI history was associated with 5.6-fold increase in risk of generating a suicide plan and almost a 10-fold increase in risk of attempting suicide compared to those reporting only suicidal ideation. Lastly, Klonsky and colleagues (2013) found that NSSI had a significant association to suicidal behavior that was greater than the associations between suicide and symptoms of borderline personality disorder, depression, anxiety, and impulsivity across four unique samples; only NSSI history and suicidal ideation significantly predicted attempted suicide.

Because many of the studies examining the relationship between NSSI and suicide are cross-sectional, the temporal ordering of the two behaviors is unclear. However, there is growing evidence to suggest that NSSI may be a precursor for suicidal behavior. First, research has documented that people who engage in NSSI tend to be younger than those who attempt suicide (Claes, Muehlenkamp et al., 2010; Cloutier et al., 2009; Klonsky & Olino, 2008), with the age of onset for suicide attempts in adolescents being 6 months to a year later than the age of onset for NSSI (Nock, Holmberg, et al., 2007). In addition, repetitive acts of NSSI show a particularly strong link to suicide attempts and completed suicide (Cooper et al., 2005; Hawton & Harriss, 2008; Whitlock et al., 2013; Zahl & Hawton, 2004). Recently, a handful of longitudinal studies have demonstrated that a history of NSSI prospectively predicts suicide attempts more strongly than other known risk factors, including prior suicide attempts (Asarnow et al., 2011; Guan, Fox, & Prinstein, 2012; Whitlock et al., 2013; Wilkinson et al., 2011). These findings have been supported across short (24–28 weeks) and long (2.5 years) follow-up periods as well as across gender, ethnicity, and age (Asarnow et al., 2011; Guan et al., 2012; Tang et al., 2011). Of note, some of these studies also demonstrated that suicide attempts were poor predictors of future NSSI (Prinstein et al., 2008; Whitlock et al., 2013; Wilkinson et al., 2011), suggesting that NSSI confers unique risk for future suicidal thoughts and behavior.

However, it remains unclear what features of NSSI contribute to the incremental risk for suicide posed by engaging in NSSI. Numerous studies have documented that as the frequency and severity of NSSI increase, risk for suicide attempts also significantly increase (Andover & Gib, 2010; Klonsky & Olino, 2008; Prinstein et al., 2008; Whitlock & Knox, 2007). Nock and colleagues (2006) found that engaging in NSSI for a greater number of years, using a greater number of methods, and lacking physical pain during NSSI were all features of NSSI significantly associated with suicide attempts (see also Orbach et al., 1996). Whitlock and colleagues (2008) offer additional support for these findings. In their latent class analysis of self-injuring college students, Whitlock et al. found that the most "severe" group of self-injurers was characterized by a high frequency of NSSI and use of a greater number of NSSI methods, and that this group also evidenced the most suicidality. In their longitudinal study of over 1,400 college students, Whitlock and colleagues (2013) found a dose–response relationship between NSSI frequency and suicidality such that those with five or more NSSI acts were four times more likely to have reported suicidal thoughts and/or behavior at the 2-year follow-up assessment compared to those with four or fewer acts of NSSI.

Despite these findings, some contradictory results have also been reported. In their longitudinal study of adolescents, Prinstein and colleagues (2008) found that while frequency of NSSI was associated with baseline suicidal ideation and a slower remission of suicidal ideation over time, NSSI frequency was not significantly associated with repeated suicide attempts at 9- and 18-month follow-ups. Similarly, within a sample of 2,900 adolescents, Wichstrom (2009) found that NSSI did not increase risk of future suicide attempts over a 5-year time period. Further, Nock et al. (2006) also reported finding that frequency of NSSI was not associated with suicide attempts. Thus, it appears that frequency may not be the critical indicator of suicide risk, but instead, markers pertaining to the severity of NSSI are important. For example, recent studies have noted that frequency of cutting is particularly salient to increased suicide risk (Cooper et al., 2005; Glenn & Klonsky, 2009), whereas other methods of NSSI exhibit weak or no relationship with suicide risk. Whitlock and colleagues (Whitlock et al., 2006, 2008) have presented data suggesting that as frequency of NSSI increases, markers of severity such as the number and type of methods used and amount of tissue damage incurred also increase. Also reported were findings that as the frequency of NSSI increased, participants were more likely to report injuring more severely than intended and that NSSI interfered with different aspects of their life. These results are consistent with reports from adolescent and young adult samples that NSSI has addictive properties, requiring increasingly severe injury to produce the same effects (Buser & Buser, 2013; Csorba et al., 2007; Haas & Popp, 2006; Klonsky, 2009; Nixon et al., 2002).

The potentially addictive nature of NSSI is particularly alarming when considering risk for suicide. Joiner (2005, Joiner et al., 2012) has proposed that repeated exposure to painful and provocative experiences, such as NSSI, can lead to increased habituation to pain over time. This habituation then contributes to an increased ability to engage in potentially lethal acts of self-harm. There is support for this idea (Orbach et al., 1996; van Orden et al., 2008), as well as evidence presented earlier that individuals with chronic NSSI underestimate the potential severity or lethality of their self-injurious behaviors (Stanley et al., 2001). The severity of NSSI is also likely to be higher among individuals who self-injure alone and among those who self-injure for regulation of internal states (Glenn & Klonsky, 2009; Klonsky & Olino, 2008), both of which have also been associated with significantly increased likelihood of suicide attempts (Glenn & Klonsky, 2009; Nock & Prinstein, 2005). While Whitlock et al. (2013) found that 20 or more acts of NSSI were prospectively associated with suicidal behavior among college students with a history of NSSI, the extant research appears to support the notion that crude frequency of NSSI is less important to understanding suicide risk than are variables such as the severity, number and types of methods used, and experience (or lack) of pain during NSSI. Regardless, NSSI and suicide maintain a tenacious relationship and it is imperative that research continues to examine the similarities and unique variants between these two behaviors. While evidence suggests that not all persons who engage in NSSI are at risk for suicide and therefore may not require immediate intervention (Walsh, 2009), potential risk for suicide should remain a concern for anyone with a history of NSSI.

Concluding Comments

Suicide and NSSI are significant health concerns worldwide, particularly among adolescents and young adults but also into later adulthood. While the two behaviors are conceptually distinct, they share many phenomenological features and appear to be closely entwined. Unfortunately, research specifically examining the unique and shared characteristics and risk factors for both NSSI and suicide is lacking. Research in both domains is growing substantially, advancing understanding of suicidal processes and NSSI pathogenesis, but research in each field is occurring relatively independent from the other. Studies that do examine both NSSI and suicide are largely cross-sectional, prohibiting advanced knowledge of the interactive nature between NSSI and suicidal behavior. It is imperative that the field begin to move beyond basic descriptive, cross-sectional studies of the primary characteristics of NSSI and suicide and begin to examine more complex symptom-based profiles, interactive models, and longitudinal and developmental trajectories of these behaviors so their nuanced relationship and differences can be better understood. For example, it would be worthwhile for longitudinal studies to examine the unique contribution of psychosocial variables to the emergence of NSSI relative to suicidal behavior and to examine these relationships between genders and across ethnicities. Studies on resilience or protective factors among those deemed vulnerable or at risk for NSSI/suicide are also greatly needed. On a related vein of inquiry, very little is known about the true course of NSSI behaviors across the age span, nor *how* NSSI actually contributes to risk for suicidal behavior. Additional studies on the course of suicidal behaviors would also benefit the field. It is also unclear how similar or different inpatient samples are from community samples with regard to risk and protective features of either NSSI or suicide. Epidemiological studies representing numerous countries and areas of the world are also needed to provide a more solid estimation of the true prevalence and incidence of NSSI across age groups so that comparisons can be made to suicidal behavior. Finally, studies examining the course and interrelationship between NSSI and suicidal thoughts and behaviors over time and across age groups, ethnicities, and genders would begin to advance current knowledge about the intricacies of the NSSI–suicide relationship. While it remains important to ensure researchers clearly define their concepts of NSSI and suicide to ensure their distinction within the data collected; minimizing the potential severity of NSSI in relation to risk for suicide would be irresponsible. The field must continue to examine NSSI and suicidal thoughts/behaviors so that comprehensive etiological models can advance our understanding, treatment, and prevention of both self-destructive behaviors.

References

American Psychiatric Association. (2013). *Diagnostic and statistical manual of mental disorders* (5th ed.). Arlington, VA: American Psychiatric Publishing.

Anderson, R. N. (2002). Deaths: Leading causes for 2000. *National Vital Statistics Reports, 50,* Retrieved from http://www.cdc.gov/nchs/data/nvsr/nvsr50/nvsr50_16.pdf.

Anderson, M., & Sansone, R. (2003). Tattooing as a means of acute affect. *Clinical Psychology & Psychotherapy, 10,* 316–318.

Anderson, R. N., & Smith, B. L. (2005). Deaths: leading causes for 2002. *National vital statistics reports, 53,* 67–70.

Andover, M. S., & Gibb, B. E. (2010). Non-suicidal self-injury, attempted suicide, and suicidal intent among psychiatric inpatients. *Psychiatry Research, 178*(1), 101–105.

Andover, M. S., Morris, B. W., Wren, A., & Bruzzese, M. E. (2012). The co-occurrence of non- suicidal self-injury and attempted suicide among adolescents: Distinguishing risk factors and psychosocial correlates. *Child and Adolescent Psychiatry and Mental Health, 6,* 11.

Andover, M. S., Pepper, C. M., & Gibb, B. E. (2007). Self-mutilation and coping strategies in a college sample. *Suicide and Life-Threatening Behavior, 37,* 238–243.

Andover, M. S., Pepper, C. M., Ryabchenko, K. A., Orrico, E. G., & Gibb, B. E. (2005). Self-mutilation and symptoms of depression, anxiety, and borderline personality disorder. *Suicide and Life-Threatening Behavior, 35,* 581–591.

Andrews, T., Martin, G., & Hasking, P. (2012). Differential and common correlates of non- suicidal self-injury and alcohol use among community-based adolescents. *Advances in Mental Health, 11*(1), 55–66.

Armey, M., Crowther, J., & Miller, I. (2011). Changes in ecological momentary assessment reported affect associated with episodes of nonsuicidal self-injury. *Behavior Therapy, 42*(4), 579–588.

Arsenault-Lapierre, G., Kim, C., & Turecki, G. (2004). Psychiatric diagnoses in 3275 suicides: A meta-analysis. *BMC Psychiatry, 4,* 37.

Asarnow, J. R., Porta, G., Spirito, A., Emslie, G., Calrke, G., Wagner, K. D.,...Brent, D. A. (2011). Suicide attempts and nonsuicidal self-injury in the treatment of resistant depression in adolescents: Findings from the TORDIA study. *Journal of the American Academy of Child Psychology, 50,* 772–781.

Baca-Garcia, E., Diaz-Sastre, C., Resa, E. G., Blasco, H., Conesa, D. B., Oquendo, M. A.,...de Leon, J. (2005). Suicide attempts and impulsivity. *European Archives of Psychiatry and Clinical Neuroscience, 255,* 152–156.

Baetens, I., Claes, L., Muehlenkamp, J., Grietens, H., & Onghena, P. (2011). Non-suicidal and suicidal self-injurious behavior among Flemish adolescents: A web-survey. *Archives of Suicide Research, 15,* 56–67.

Baetens, I., Claes, L., Muehlenkamp, J. J., Grietens, H., & Onghena, P. (2009, June). *Why do people hurt themselves? Functions of self-injurious behavior in the picture.* Paper presented at the annual International Society for the Study of Self-injury conference, Stony Brook, NY.

Baker, S. P., Hu, G., Wilcox, H. C., & Baker, T. D. (2013). Increase in suicide by hanging/suffocation in the U.S., 2000–2010. *American Journal of Preventive Medicine, 44,* 146–149.

Baumeister, R. F. (1990). Suicide as escape from self. *Psychological Review, 97,* 90–113.

Bergen, H., Hawton, K., Waters, K., Ness, J., Cooper, J.,...Kapur, N. (2012). How do methods of non-fatal self-harm relate to eventual suicide? *Journal of Affective Disorders, 136*(3), 526–533.

Berman, A. L., Jobes, D. A., & Silverman, M. M. (2006). *Adolescent suicide: Assessment and intervention* (2nd ed.). Washington, DC: American Psychological Association.

Bertolote, J. M., Fleischmann, A., De Leo, D., & Wasserman, D. (2004). Psychiatric diagnoses and suicide: Revisiting the evidence. *Crisis, 25,* 147–155.

Bhugra, D., Singh, J., Fellow Smith, E., & Bayliss, C. (2002). Deliberate self-harm in adolescents: A case study among two ethnic groups. *European Journal of Psychiatry, 16,* 145–151.

Blosnich, J., & Bossarte, R. (2012). Drivers of disparity: Differences in socially based risk factors of self-injurious and suicidal behaviors among sexual minority college students. *Journal of American College Health, 60*(2), 141–149.

Borrill, J., Fox, P., & Roger, D. (2011). Religion, ethnicity, coping style, and self-reported self-harm in a diverse non-clinical UK population. *Mental Health, Religion and Culture, 14*(3), 259–269.

Brausch, A. M., & Gutierrez, P. M. (2010). Differences in non-suicidal self-injury and suicide attempts in adolescents. *Journal of Youth and Adolescence, 39,* 233–242.

Brausch, A. M., & Gutierrez, P. M. (2009). The role of body image and disordered eating as risk factors for depression and suicidal ideation in adolescents. *Suicide and Life-Threatening Behavior, 39,* 58–71.

Brent, D. A. (2001), Firearms and suicide. *Annals of the New York Academy of Sciences, 932,* 225–240.

Brent, D. (2011). Nonsuicidal self-injury as a predictor of suicidal behavior in depressed adolescents. *American Journal of Psychiatry, 168,* 452–454.

Brent, D., Perper, J., Moritz, G., Allman, C., Friend, A., Roth, C.,...Baugher, M. (1993). Psychiatric risk factors for adolescent suicide: a case-control study. *Journal of the American Academy of Child and Adolescent Psychiatry, 32,* 521–529.

Bresin, K., Carter, D., & Gordon, K. (2013). The relationship between trait impulsivity, negative affective states, and urge for nonsuicidal self-injury: A daily diary study. *Psychiatry Research, 205*(3), 227–231.

Bridges, F. S., & Kunselman, J. C. (2003). Rates of suicide in the world: 2002 update. *North American Journal of Psychology, 5,* 479–484.

Brodsky, B., & Stanley, B. (2008). Adverse childhood experiences and suicidal behavior. *Psychiatric Clinics of North America, 31,* 223–235.

Brown, G., Beck, A. T., Steer, R., & Grisham, J. (2000). Risk factors for suicide in psychiatric outpatients: A 20-year prospective study. *Journal of Consulting and Clinical Psychology, 68,* 371–377.

Brown, G. K., Ten Have, T., Henriques, G. R., Xie, S. X., Hollander, J. E., & Beck, A. T. (2005). Cognitive therapy for the prevention of suicide attempts: A randomized controlled trial. *Journal of the American Medical Association, 294,* 563–570.

Brown, M. Z., Comtois, K. A., & Linehan, M. M. (2002). Reasons for suicide attempts and nonsuicidal self-injury in women with borderline personality disorder. *Journal of Abnormal Psychology, 111,* 198–202.

Brown, M. Z., Henriques, G. R., Sosdjan, D., & Beck, A. T. (2004). Suicide intent and accurate expectations of lethality: Predictors of medical lethality of suicide attempts. *Journal of Consulting and Clinical Psychology, 72,* 1170–1174.

Brunner, R., Kaess, M., Parzer, P., Fischer, G., Resch, F., Carli, V., et al. (2013). Characteristics of non-suicidal self-injury and suicide attempts among adolescents in Europe: Results from the European Research Consortium seyle. *European Psychiatry, 28,* 1.

Brunner, R., Parzer, P., Hafner, J., Steen, R., Roos, J., Klett, M., & Resch, F. (2007). Prevalence and psychological correlates of occasional and repetitive deliberate self-harm in adolescents. *Archives of Pediatric and Adolescent Medicine, 161,* 641 649.

Bryan, C., Rudd, M., & Wertenberger, E. (2013). Reasons for suicide attempts in a clinical sample of active duty soldiers. *Journal of Affective Disorders, 144*(1-2), 148–152.

Bulik, C. M., Thornton, L., Pinheiro, K., Klump, K. L., Brandt, H., Crawford, S.,...Kay, W. H. (2008). Suicide attempts in anorexia nervosa. *Journal of Psychosomatic Medicine, 70*(3), 378–383.

Buser, T., & Buser, J. (2013). Conceptualizing nonsuicidal self-injury as a process addiction: Review of research and implications for counselor training and practice. *Journal of Addictions & Offender Counseling, 34*(1), 16–29.

Canetto, S. S. (2001). Girls and suicidal behavior. In M. Forman-Brunell (Ed.), *Girlhood in America: An encyclopedia* (vol. 2, pp. 616–621).

Canetto, S. S., & Lester, D. (1995). Gender and the primary prevention of suicide mortality. *Suicide and Life-Threatening Behavior, 25,* 58–69.

Cavanagh, J. T., Carson, A. J., Sharpe, M., & Lawrie, S. M. (2003). Psychological autopsy studies of suicide: A systematic review. *Psychological Medicine, 33,* 395–405.

Centers for Disease Control and Prevention. (2010). *Web-based injury statistics query and reporting system (WISQARS)*. Retrieved from http://www.cdc.gov/ncipc/wisqars/default.htm.

Centers for Disease Control and Prevention. (2012). *Trends in the prevalence of suicide-related behaviors, National YRBS: 1991–2011*. Retrieved from http://www.cdc.gov/healthyyouth/yrbs.

Chapman, A. L., Gratz, K. L., & Brown, M. B. (2006). Solving the puzzle of deliberate self-harm: The experiential avoidance model. *Behavior Research and Therapy, 44*, 371–394.

Claes, L., Klonsky, E. D., Muehlenkamp, J., Kuppens, P., & Vandereycken, W. (2010). The affect-regulation function of nonsuicidal self-injury in eating disordered patients: Which affect states are regulated? *Comprehensive Psychiatry, 51*, 386–392.

Claes, L., Muehlenkamp, J. J., Vandereycken, W., Hamelinck, L., Martens, H., & Claes, S. (2010). Comparison of non-suicidal self-injurious behavior and suicide attempts in patients admitted to a psychiatric crisis unit. *Personality and Individual Differences, 48*, 83–87.

Claes, L., & Vandereycken, W. (2007). Self-injurious behavior: Differential diagnosis and functional differentiation. *Comprehensive Psychiatry, 48*, 137–144.

Claes, L., Vandereycken, W., & Vertommen, H. (2007). Self-injury in female versus male psychiatric patients: A comparison of characteristics, psychopathology, and aggression regulation. *Personality and Individual Differences, 42*, 611–621.

Claes, L., Vandereycken, W., & Vertommen, H. (2005). Self-care versus self-harm: Piercing, tattooing, and self-injuring in eating disorders. *European Eating Disorders Review, 13*, 11–18.

Cloutier, P., & Humphreys, L. (2009). Measurement of nonsuicidal self-injury in adolescents. *Self-injury in youth: The essential guide to assessment and intervention*, 115–142.

Cloutier, P., Martin, J., Kennedy, A., Nixon, M. K., & Muehlenkamp, J. J. (2010). Characteristics and co-occurrence of adolescent non-suicidal self-injury and suicidal behaviours in pediatric emergency crisis services. *Journal of Youth and Adolescence, 39*(3), 259–269.

Colucci, E., & Martin, G. (2007). Ethnocultural aspects of suicide in young people: A systematic literature review part 1: Rates and methods of youth suicide. *Suicide and Life-Threatening Behavior, 37*, 197–221.

Conwell, Y., & Heisel, M. (2006). The elderly. In R. I. Simon & R. E. Hales (Eds.), *American psychiatric textbook of suicide assessment and management*. Arington,VA: American Psychiatric Publishing.

Cooper, J., Kapur, N., Webb, R. Lawlor, M., Guthrie, E., Mackway-Jones, K., & Appleby, L. (2005). Suicide after deliberate self-harm: A 4-year cohort study. *American Journal of Psychiatry, 162*, 297–303.

Crowell, S. E., Beauchaine, T. P., McCauley, E., Smith, C. J., Vasilev, C. A., & Stevens, A. L. (2008). Parent-child interactions, peripheral serotonin, and self-inflicted injury in adolescents. *Journal of Consulting and Clinical Psychology, 76*, 15–21.

Csorba, J., Dinya, E., Plener, P., Nagy, E., & Páli, E. (2009). Clinical diagnoses, characteristics of risk behaviour, differences between suicidal and non-suicidal subgroups of Hungarian adolescent outpatients practising self-injury. *European Child & Adolescent Psychiatry, 18*, 309–320.

Csorba, J., Sorfoso, Z., Steiner, P., Ficsor, B., Harkany, E., Babrik, Z., Pali, E., & Solymossy, M. (2007). Maladaptive strategies, dysfunctional attitudes and negative life events among adolescents treated for the diagnosis of "suicidal behaviour.". *Psychiatria Hungarica, 22*, 200–211.

Cwik, M. F., Barlow, A., Tingey, L., Larzelere-Hinton, F., Goklish, N., & Walkup, J. T. (2011). Nonsuicidal self-injury in an American Indian Reservation Community: Results from the White Mountain Apache Surveillance System, 2007-2008. *Journal of the American Academy of Child and Adolescent Psychiatry, 50*, 860–869.

Daigle, M. S., & Cote, G. (2006). Nonfatal suicide-related behavior among inmates: Testing for gender and type differences. *Suicide and Life-Threatening Behavior, 36*, 670–681.

DeLeo, D., Burgis, S., Bertolote, J. M., Kerkhof, A. J. F. M., & Bille-Brahe, M. (2006). Definition of suicidal behavior: Lessons learned from the WHO/EURO Multicentre Study. *Crisis, 27*, 4–15.

Di Pierro, R., Sarno, I., Perego, S., Gallucci, M., & Madeddu, F. (2012). Adolescent nonsuicidal self-injury: The effects of personality traits, family relationships and maltreatment on the presence and severity of behaviours. *European Child & Adolescent Psychiatry, 21*(9), 511–520.

Dougherty, D. M., Mathias, C. W., Marsh-Richard, D. M., Prevette, K. N., Dawes, M. A., Hatzis, E. S.,… Nouvion, S. O. (2009). Impulsivity and clinical symptoms among adolescents with non-suicidal self-injury with or without attempted suicide. *Psychiatry Research, 169*, 22–27.

Douglas, J., Cooper, J., Amos, T., Webb, R., Guthrie, E., & Appleby, L. (2004). "Near-fatal" deliberate self-harm: Characteristics, prevention and implications for the prevention of suicide. *Journal of Affective Disorders, 79*, 263–268.

Dulit, R. A., Fyer, M. R., Leon, A. C., Brodsky, B. S., & Frances, A. J. (1994). Clinical correlates of self-mutilation in borderline personality disorder. *American Journal of Psychiatry, 151*, 1305–1311.

Dunkley, D. M., & Grilo, C. M. (2007). Self-criticism, low self-esteem, depressive symptoms, and over-evaluation of shape and weight in binge eating disorder patients. *Behavior Research and Therapy, 45*, 139–149.

Dvorak, R., Lamis, D., & Malone, P. (2013). Alcohol use, depressive symptoms, and impulsivity as risk factors for suicide proneness among college students. *Journal of Affective Disorders, 149*(1–3), 326–334.

Enns, M., Cox, B., Afifi, T., De Graaf, R., Ten Have, M., & Sareen, J. (2006). Childhood adversities and risk for suicidal ideation and attempts: a longitudinal population-based study. *Psychological Medicine, 36*, 1769–1778.

Ernst, C., Lalovic, A., Lesage, A., Seguin, M., Tousignant, M., & Turecki, G. (2004). Suicide and no Axis I psychopathology. *BMC Psychiatry, 4*, 7.

Evans, E., Hawton, K., & Rodham, K. (2004). Factors associated with suicidal phenomena in adolescents: A systematic review of population-based studies. *Clinical Psychology Review, 24*, 957–979.

Evans, E., Hawton, K., Rodham, K., & Deeks, J. (2005). The prevalence of suicidal phenomena in adolescents: A systematic review of population based studies. *Suicide and Life-Threatening Behavior, 35*, 239–250.

Evren, C., & Evren, B. (2005). Self-mutilation in substance-dependent patients and relationship with childhood abuse and neglect, alexithymia, and temperament and character dimensions of personality. *Drug and Alcohol Dependence, 80*, 15–22.

Evren, C., Kural, S., & Cakmak, D. (2006). Clinical correlates of self-mutilation in Turkish male substance-dependent inpatients. *Psychopathology, 39*, 248–254.

Favaro, A., Santonastaso, P., Monteleone, P., Bellodi, L., Mauri, M., Rotondo, A., …Maj, M. (2008). Self-injurious behavior and attempted suicide in purging bulimia nervosa: Associations with psychiatric comorbidity. *Journal of Affective Disorders,105*, 285–289.

Favazza, A. R. (1996). *Bodies under siege: Self-mutilation and body modification in culture and psychiatry (2nd ed.).* Baltimore, MD: Johns Hopkins University Press.

Favazza, A. R. (2009). A cultural understanding of nonsuicidal self-injury. In M. K. Nock (Ed.), *Understanding nonsuicidal self-injury: Origins, assessment, and treatment* (pp. 19–35). Washington, DC: American Psychological Association.

Favazza, A. R., & Rosenthal, R. J. (1998). The coming of age of self-mutilation. *Journal of Nervous and Mental Disease, 186*, 259–268.

Fazaa, N., & Page, S. (2009). Personality style and impulsivity as determinants of suicidal subgroups. *Archives of Suicide Research, 13*, 31–45.

Fergusson, D. M., Woodward, L. J., & Horwood, L. J. (2000). Risk factors and life processes associated with the onset of suicidal behavior during adolescence and early adulthood. *Psychological Medicine, 30*, 23–39.

Fliege, H., Kocalevent, T. D., Walter, O. B., Beck, S., & Gratz, K. L. (2006). Three assessment tools for deliberate self-harm and suicide behavior: Evaluation and psychopathological correlates. *Journal of Psychosomatic Research, 61*, 113–121.

Fortuna, L. R., Perez, D. J., Canino, G., Sribney, W., & Alegria, M. (2007). Prevalence and correlates of lifetime suicidal ideation and suicide attempts among Latino subgroups in the United States. *Journal of Clinical Psychiatry, 68*, 572–581.

Fortune, S., & Hawton, K. (2007). Suicide and deliberate self-harm in children and adolescents. *Paediatrics and Child Health, 17*, 443–447.

Fortune, S., Sinclair, J., & Hawton, K. (2008). Adolescents' views on preventing self-harm. *Social Psychiatry & Psychiatric Epidemiology, 43*, 96–104.

Garofalo, R., Wolf, R. C., Wissow, L. S., Woods, E. R., & Goodman, E. (1999). Sexual orientation and risk of suicide attempts among a representative sample of youth. *Archives of Pediatrics and Adolescent Medicine, 153*, 487–493.

Giegling, I., Olgiati, P., Hartmann, A. M., Calati, R., Moller, H. J., Rujescu, D., & Serretti, A. (2009). Personality and attempted suicide: Analysis of anger, aggression and impulsivity. *Journal of Psychiatric Research, 43*, 1262–1271.

Glassman, L. H., Weierich, M. R., Holley, J. M., Deliberto, T. L., & Nock, M. K. (2007). Child maltreatment, nonsuicidal self-injury, and the mediating role of self-criticism. *Behavior Research and Therapy, 45*, 2483–2490.

Glenn, C., & Klonsky, E. (2010). A multimethod analysis of impulsivity in nonsuicidal self- injury. *Personality Disorders: Theory, Research, and Treatment, 1*(1), 67–75.

Glenn, C. R., & Klonsky, E. D. (2009). Social context during non-suicidal self-injury indicates suicide risk. *Personality and Individual Differences, 46*, 25–29.

Gold, L. H. (2006). Suicide and gender. In R. L Simon, & R. E. Hales (Eds.), *Textbook of suicide assessment and management* (pp. 77–106). Washington, DC: American Psychiatric Publishing.

Goldston, D. B., Molock, S. D., Whitbeck, L. B., Murakami, J. L., Zayas, L. H., & Hall, G. C. N. (2008). Cultural considerations in adolescent suicide prevention and psychosocial treatment. *American Psychologist, 63*, 14–31.

Goldston, D. B., Reboussin, B. A., & Daniel, S. S. (2006). Predictors of suicide attempts: State and trait components. *Journal of Abnormal Psychology, 115*, 842–849.

Gomez, J., Miranda, R., & Polanco, L. (2011). Acculturative stress, perceived discrimination, and vulnerability to suicide attempts among emerging adults. *Journal of Youth and Adolescence, 40*(11), 1465–1476.

Gould, M. S., Greenberg, T., Velting, D. M., & Shaffer, D. (2003). Youth suicide risk and preventative interventions: A review of the past 10 years. *Journal of the American Academy of Child and Adolescent Psychiatry, 42*, 386–405.

Gratz, K. L. (2007). Targeting emotion dysregulation in the treatment of self-injury. *Journal of Clinical Psychology, 63*, 1091–1103.

Gratz, K. (2006). Risk factors for deliberate self-harm among female college students: The role and interaction of childhood maltreatment, emotional inexpressivity, and affect intensity/reactivity. *American Journal of Orthopsychiatry, 76*, 238–250.

Gratz, K. L. (2003). Risk factors for and functions of deliberate self-harm: An empirical and conceptual review. *Clinical Psychology: Science and Practice, 10*, 192–205.

Gratz, K. L. (2001). Measurement of deliberate self-harm: Preliminary data on the Deliberate Self-Harm Inventory. *Journal of Psychopathology and Behavioral Assessment, 23*, 253–263.

Gratz, K. L., & Chapman, A. L. (2007). The role of emotional responding and childhood maltreatment in the development and maintenance of deliberate self-harm among male undergraduates. *Psychology of Men and Masculinity, 8*, 1–14.

Gratz, K. L., Conrad, S. D., & Roemer, L. (2002). Risk factors for deliberate self-harm among college students. *American Journal of Orthopsychiatry, 72*, 128–140.

Gratz, K. L., Latzman, R., Young, J., Heiden, L., Damon, J., Hight, T., & Tull, M.bT. (2012). Deliberate self-harm among underserved adolescents: The moderating roles of gender, race, and school-level and association with borderline personality features. *Personality Disorders: Theory, Research, and Treatment, 3*(1), 39 54.

Groholt, B., Ekeberg, O., Wichstrom, L., & Haldorsen, T. (2000). Young suicide attempters: A comparison between a clinical and an epidemiological sample. *Journal of the American Academy of Child and Adolescent Psychiatry, 39*, 868–875.

Grunbaum, J.A., Kann, L., Kinchen, S., Ross, J., Hawkins, J., Lowry, R., et al. (2004). Youth risk behavior surveillance—United States, 2003. *MMWR Surveillance Summaries: Morbidity and Mortality Weekly Report Surveillance Summaries/CDC, 53*, 1–96.

Guan, K., Fox, K. R., & Prinstein, M. J. (2012). Nonsuicidal self-injury as a time-invariant predictor of adolescent suicide ideation and attempts in a diverse community sample. *Journal of Consulting and Clinical Psychology, 80*, 842–849.

Guerry, J. D., & Prinstein, M. J. (2010). Longitudinal prediction of adolescent nonsuicidal self-injury: Examination of a cognitive vulnerability-stress model. *Journal of Clinical Child and Adolescent Psychology, 39*, 77–89.

Guertin, T., Lloyd-Richardson, E., Spirito, A., Donaldson, D., & Boergers, J. (2001). Self-mutilative behavior in adolescents who attempt suicide by overdose. *Journal of the American Academy of Child and Adolescent Psychiatry, 40,* 1062–1069.

Haas, B., & Popp, F. (2006). Why do people injure themselves? *Psychopathology, 39,* 10–18.

Haines, J., Williams, C. L., Brain, K. L., & Wilson, G. V. (1995). The psychophysiology of self-mutilation. *Journal of Abnormal Psychology, 104,* 471–489.

Harriss, L., & Hawton, K. (2005). Suicidal intent in deliberate self-harm and the risk of suicide: The predictive power of the Suicide Intent Scale. *Journal of Affective Disorders, 86,* 225–233.

Harriss, L., Hawton, K., & Zahl, D. (2005). Value of measuring suicidal intent in the assessment of people attending hospital following self-poisoning or self-injury. *British Journal of Psychiatry, 186,* 60–66.

Hasking, P., Momeni, R., Swannell, S., & Chia, S. (2008). The nature and extent of non-suicidal self-injury in a non-clinical sample of young adults. *Archives of Suicide Research, 12,* 208–218.

Haw, C., Hawton, K., Houston, K., Townsend, E. (2001). Psychiatric and personality disorders in deliberate self-harm patients. *British Journal of Psychiatry, 178,* 48–54.

Hawton, K., Clements, A., Sakarovitch, C., Simkin, S., & Deeks, J. J. (2001). Suicide in doctors: a study of risk according to gender, seniority and specialty in medical practitioners in England and Wales, 1979–1995. *Journal of Epidemiology and Community Health, 55,* 296–300.

Hawton, K., & Harriss, L. (2008). How often does deliberate self-harm occur relative to each suicide? A study of variations by gender and age. *Suicide and Life-Threatening Behavior, 38,* 650–660.

Hawton, K., & Rodham, K. (2006). *By their own young hand: Deliberate self-harm and suicidal ideas in adolescents.* London, UK: Jessica Kingsley.

Hawton, K., Rodham, K., Evans, E., & Harriss, L. (2009). Adolescents who self harm: A comparison of those who go to hospital and those who do not. *Child and Adolescent Mental Health, 14,* 24–30.

Hawton, K., & van Heeringen, K. (2009). Suicide. *Lancet, 373,* 1372–1381.

Heath, N. L., Ross, S., Toste, J. R., Charlebois, A., & Nedecheva, T. (2009). Retrospective analysis of social factors and nonsuicidal self-injury among young adults. *Canadian Journal of Behavioural Science, 41,* 180–186.

Heath, N. L., Schaub, K., Holly, S., & Nixon, M. K. (2009). Self-injury today: Review of population and clinical studies in adolescents. In M. K. Nixon & N. L. Heath (Eds.), *Self-injury in youth: The essential guide to assessment and intervention* (pp. 9–27). New York, NY: Routledge.

Heath, N. L., Toste, J. R., & Beettam, E. L. (2007). "I am not well-equipped" High school teachers' perception of self-injury. *Canadian Journal of School Psychology, 21,* 73–92.

Heath, N., Toste, J., Nedecheva, T., & Charlebois, A. (2008). An examination of nonsuicidal self-injury among college students. *Journal of Mental Health Counseling, 30,* 137–156.

Herpertz, S., Sass, H., & Favazza, A. (1997). Impulsivity in self-mutilative behavior: psychometric and biological findings. *Journal of Psychiatric Research, 31,* 451–465.

Hilt, L. M., Cha, C. B., & Nolen-Hoeksema, S. (2008). Nonsuicidal self-injury in young adolescent girls: Moderators of the distress-function relationship. *Journal of Consulting and Clinical Psychology, 76,* 63–71.

Hilt, L. M., Nock, M. K., Lloyd-Richardson, E. E., & Prinstein, M. J. (2008). Longitudinal study of non-suicidal self-injury among young adolescents: Rates, correlates, and preliminary test of an interpersonal model. *Journal of Early Adolescence, 28,* 455–469.

Hjelmeland, H., & Groholt, B. (2005). A comparative study of young and adult deliberate self-harm patients. *Crisis, 26,* 64–72.

Hjelmeland, H., & Hawton, K. (2004). International aspects of non-fatal suicidal behavior. In D. De Leo, U. Bille-Brahe, A. Kerkhof, & A. Schmidtke (Eds.), *Suicidal behavior: Theories and research findings* (pp. 67–78). Cambridge, MA: Hogrefe & Huber.

Hoff, E. R., & Muehlenkamp, J. J. (2009). Non-suicidal self-injury in college students: The role of perfectionism and rumination. *Suicide and Life-Threatening Behavior, 39,* 576–587.

Holm-Denoma, J. M., Witte, T. K., Gordon, K. G., Herzog, D. B., Franko, D. L., Fichter, M., ... Joiner, T. E., Jr. (2008). Death by suicide among individuals with anorexia as arbiters between explanations of the anorexia-suicide link. *Journal of Affective Disorders, 107*(1-3), 231–236.

Hooley, J. M. (2008). Self-harming behavior: Introduction to the special series on non-suicidal self-injury and suicide. *Applied and Preventive Psychology, 12,* 155–158.

Horesch, N., Nachshoni, T., Wolmer, L., & Toren, P. (2009). A comparison of life events in suicidal and nonsuicidal adolescents and young adults with major depression and borderline personality disorder. *Comprehensive Psychiatry, 50,* 496–502.

Horton, L. (2006). Social, cultural, and demographic factors in suicide. In R. L. Simon & R. E. Hales (Eds.), *Textbook of suicide assessment and management* (pp. 107–137). Washington, DC: American Psychiatric Publishing.

Hsu, Y., Chen, P., & Lung, F. (2013). Parental bonding and personality characteristics of first episode intention to suicide or deliberate self-harm without a history of mental disorders. *BMC Public Health, 13*(1), 1–8.

Institute of Medicine. (2002). *Reducing suicide: A national imperative.* Washington, DC: National Academy Press.

International Society for the Study of Self-injury. (2007, June). *Definitional issues surrounding our understanding of self-injury.* Conference proceedings from the Annual Meeting.

Isohookana, R., Riala, K., Hakko, H., & Rasanen, P. (2013). Adverse childhood experiences and suicidal behavior of adolescent psychiatric inpatients. *European Child and Adolescent Psychiatry, 22*(1), 13–22.

Izutsu, T., Shimotsu, S., Matsumoto, T., Okada, T., Kikuchi, A., Kojimoto, M., ... Yoshikawa, K. (2006). Deliberate self-harm and childhood hyperactivity in junior high school students. *European Child and Adolescent Psychiatry, 14,* 1–5.

Jacobson, C. M., & Gould, M. (2007). The epidemiology and phenomenology of non-suicidal self-injurious behavior among adolescents: A critical review of the literature. *Archives of Suicide Research, 11,* 129–147.

Jacobson, C. M., & Gould, M. (2009). Suicide and nonsuicidal self-injurious behaviors among youth: Risk and protective factors. In S. Nolen-Hoeksema, L. M. Hilt (Eds.), *Handbook of depression in adolescents* (pp. 207–235). New York, NY: Routledge/Taylor & Francis.

Jacobson, C. M., Muehlenkamp, J. J., Miller, A. L., & Turner, J. B. (2008). Psychiatric impairment among adolescents engaging in different types of deliberate self-harm. *Journal of Clinical Child and Adolescent Psychology, 37,* 363–375.

Janis, I. B., & Nock, M. K. (2009). Are self-injurers impulsive?: Results from two behavioral laboratory studies. *Psychiatry Research*, *169*, 261–267.

Jenkins, R., & Singh, B. (2000). General population strategies of suicide prevention. In K. Hawton & K. van Heeringen (Eds.), *International handbook of suicide and attempted suicide* (pp. 631–644). Chichester, England: John Wiley & Sons.

Jobes, D. A., & Drozd, J. F. (2004). The CAMS approach to working with suicidal patients. *Journal of Contemporary Psychotherapy*, *34*, 73–85.

Joiner, T. E. (2005). *Why people die by suicide*. Cambridge, MA: Harvard University Press.

Joiner, T. E., Ribeiro, J., & Silva, C. (2012). Nonsuicidal self-injury, suicidal behavior, and their co-occurrence as viewed through the lens of the interpersonal theory of suicide. *Current Directions in Psychological Science*, *21*, 342–347.

Joiner, T. E., Sachs-Ericsson, N. J., Wingate, L. R., Brown, J. S., Anestis, M. D., & Selby, E. A. (2007). Childhood physical and sexual abuse and lifetime number of suicide attempts: A persistent and theoretically important relationship. *Behaviour Research and Therapy*, *45*, 539–547.

Jollant, F., Bellivier, F., Leboyer, M. (2005). Impaired decision making in suicide attempters. *American Journal of Psychiatry*, *162*, 304–310.

Kaess, M., Parzer, P., Mattern, M., Plener, P., Bifulco, A., Resch, F., & Brunner, R. (2013). Adverse childhood experiences and their impact on frequency, severity, and the individual function of nonsuicidal self-injury in youth. *Psychiatry Research*, *206*(2/3), 265–272.

Kamphuis, J. H., Ruyling, S. B., & Reijntjes, A. H. (2007). Testing the emotion regulation hypothesis among self-injuring females: Evidence for differences across mood states. *Journal of Nervous and Mental Disease*, *195*, 912–918.

Kessler, R. C., Berglund, P., Borges, G., Nock, M., & Wang, P. S. (2005). Trends in suicide ideation, plans, gestures, and attempts in the United States, 1990-1992 to 2001-2003. *Journal of the American Medical Association*, *293*, 2487–2495.

Kessler, R. C., Borges, G., & Walters, E. E. (1999). Prevalence of and risk factors for lifetime suicide attempts in the National Comorbidity Survey. *Archives of General Psychiatry*, *56*, 617–626.

King, C. A., Segal, H., Kaminiski, K., Naylor, M., Ghaziuddin, N., & Radpour, L. (1995). A prospective study of adolescent suicidal behavior following hospitalization. *Suicide and Life-Threatening Behavior*, *25*, 327–338.

Kirkcaldy, B. D., Brown, J. M., & Siefen, G. R. (2007). Profiling adolescents attempting suicide and self-injurious behavior. *International Journal on Disability and Human Development*, *6*, 75–86.

Kisch, J., Leino, E., & Silverman, M. (2005). Aspects of suicidal behavior, depression, and treatment in college students: Results from the spring 2000 national college health assessment survey. *Suicide and Life-threatening Behavior*, *35*, 3–13.

Klonsky, E. D. (2007). The functions of deliberate self-injury: A review of the evidence. *Clinical Psychology Review*, *27*, 226–239.

Klonsky, E. D. (2009). The functions of self-injury in young adults who cut themselves: Clarifying the evidence for affect-regulation. *Psychiatry Research*, *166*, 260–268.

Klonsky, E. D., & Glenn, C. R. (2009). Psychosocial risk and protective factors. In M. K. Nixon & N. L. Heath (Eds.), *Self-injury in youth: The essential guide to assessment and intervention* (pp. 45–58). New York, NY: Routledge.

Klonsky, E. D., & Glenn, C. R. (2008). Resisting urges to self-injure. *Behavioral and Cognitive Psychotherapy*, *36*, 211–220.

Klonsky, E. D., May, A. M., & Glenn, C. R. (2013). The relationship between nonsuicidal self-injury and attempted suicide: Converging evidence from four samples. *Journal of Abnormal Psychology*, *122*, 231–237.

Klonsky, E. D., & Moyer, A. (2008). Childhood sexual abuse and non-suicidal self-injury: Meta-analysis. *British Journal of Psychiatry*, *192*, 166–170.

Klonsky, E. D., & Muehlenkamp, J. J. (2007). Non-suicidal self-injury: A research review for the practitioner. *Journal of Clinical Psychology/In Session*, *63*, 1045–1056.

Klonsky, E. D., Muehlenkamp, J. J., Lewis, S., & Walsh, B.W. (2011). *Advances in psychotherapy: Nonsuicidal self-injury*. Cambridge, MA: Hogrefe Press.

Klonsky, E. D., & Olino, T. M. (2008). Identifying clinically distinct subgroups of self-injurers among young adults: A latent class analysis. *Journal of Consulting and Clinical Psychology*, *76*, 22–27.

Klonsky, E. D., Oltmanns, T. F., & Turkheimer, E. (2003). Deliberate self-harm in a nonclinical population: Prevalence and psychological correlates. *American Journal of Psychiatry*, *160*, 1501–1508.

Krysinska, K., Heller, T. S., & De Leo, D. (2006). Suicide and deliberate self-harm in personality disorders. *Current Opinion in Psychiatry*, *19*, 95–101.

Kumar, G., Pepe, D, & Steer, R. A. (2004). Adolescent psychiatric inpatients' self-reported reasons for cutting themselves. *Journal of Nervous and Mental Disease*, *192*, 830–836.

Labelle, R., Breton, J., Pouliot, L., Dufresne, M., & Berthiaume, C. (2013). Cognitive correlates of serious suicidal ideation in a community sample of adolescents. *Journal of Affective Disorders*, *145*(3), 370–377.

Larsson, B., & Sund, A. M. (2008). Prevalence, course, incidence, and 1-year prediction of deliberate self-harm and suicide attempts in early Norwegian school adolescents. *Suicide and Life-Threatening Behavior*, *38*, 152–165.

Laukkanen, E., Rissanen, M.-L., Honkalampi, K., Kylmä, J., Tolmunen, T., & Hintikka, J. (2009). The prevalence of self-cutting and other self-harm among 13- to 18-year-old Finnish adolescents. *Social Psychiatry and Psychiatric Epidemiology*, *44*, 23–28.

Laye-Gindhu, A., & Schonert-Reichl, K. (2005). Nonsuicidal self-harm among community adolescents: Understanding the "whats" and "whys" of self-harm. *Journal of Youth and Adolescence*, *34*, 447–457.

Lewinsohn, P. M., Rhode, P., Seeley, J. R., & Baldwin, C. L. (2001). Gender differences in suicide attempts from adolescence to young adulthood. *Journal of the American Academy of Child and Adolescent Psychiatry*, *40*, 427–434.

Lilley, R., Owens, D., Horrocks, J., House, A., Noble, R., Bergen, H., et al. (2008). Hospital care and repetition following self-harm: Multicentre comparison of self-poisoning and self-injury. *The British Journal of Psychiatry*, *192*, 440–445.

Linda, W., Marroquin, B., & Miranda, R. (2012). Active and passive problem solving as moderators of the relation between negative life event stress and suicidal ideation among suicide attempters and non-attempters. *Archives of Suicide Research*, *16*(3), 183–197.

Linehan, M. M. (1993). *Cognitive-behavioral treatment of borderline personality disorder*. New York, NY: Guilford Press.

Linehan, M. M. (2000). Behavioral treatments of suicidal behaviors: Definitional obfuscation and treatment outcomes. In R. W. Maris, S. S., Cannetto, J. L. McIntosh, & M. M. Silverman (Eds.), *Review of suicidology* (pp. 84–111). New York, NY: Guilford Press.

Linehan, M. M., Comtois, K. A., Murray, A. M., Gallop, R. J., Korslund, K. E., Reynolds, S. K.,…Lindenboim, N. (2006). Two-year randomized controlled trial and follow-up of dialectical behavior therapy vs therapy by experts for suicidal behaviors and borderline personality disorder. *Archives of General Psychiatry, 63,* 757–766.

Liu, K. (2009). Suicide rates in the world: 1950–2004. *Suicide and Life-Threatening Behavior, 39,* 204–213.

Lloyd-Richardson, E. E., Nock, M. K., & Prinstein, M. J. (2009). Functions of adolescent nonsuicidal self-injury. In M. K. Nixon & N. L. Heath (Eds.), *Self-injury in youth: The essential guide to assessment and intervention* (pp. 29–41). New York, NY: Routledge.

Lloyd-Richardson, E. E., Perrine, N., Dierker, L., & Kelley, M. L. (2007). Characteristics and functions of non-suicidal self-injury in a community sample of adolescents. *Psychological Medicine, 37,* 1183–1192.

Lofthouse, N., Muehlenkamp, J. J., & Adler, R. (2009). Nonsuicidal self-injury and co-occurrence. In M. K. Nixon & N. L. Heath (Eds.), *Self-injury in youth: The essential guide to assessment and intervention* (pp. 59–78). New York, NY: Routledge.

Low, G., Jones, D., MacLeod, A., Power, M., & Duggan, C. (2000). Childhood trauma, dissociation, and self-harming behavior: A pilot study. *British Journal of Medical Psychology, 73,* 269–278.

Lowenstein, L. F. (2005). Youths who intentionally practice self-harm: Review of the recent research 2001-2004. *International Journal of Adolescent Medical Health, 17,* 225–230.

Lynam, D. R., Miller, J. D., Miller, D. J., Bornovalova, M. A., & Lejuez, C. W. (2011). Testing the relations between impulsivity-related traits, suicidality, and nonsuicidal self-injury: A test of the incremental validity of the UPPS model. *Personality Disorders: Theory, Research, and Treatment, 2,* 151–160.

Madge, N., Hewitt, A., Hawton, K., Jan de Wilde, E., Corcoran, P., Fekete, S.,…Ystgaard, M. (2008). Deliberate self-harm within an international community sample of young people: Comparative findings from the Child & Adolescent Self-harm in Europe (CASE) study. *Journal of Child Psychology and Psychiatry, 49,* 667–677.

Maris, R., Berman, A., & Silverman, M. (2000). *Comprehensive textbook of suicidology.* New York, NY: Guilford Press.

Marshal, M., Dietz, L., Friedman, M., Stall, R., Smith, H., D'Augelli, A. R., & Brent, D. A. (2011). Suicidality and depression disparities between sexual minority and heterosexual youth: A meta-analytic review. *Journal of Adolescent Health, 49*(2), 115–123.

Martin, G., Bergen, H. A., Richardson, A. S., Allison, S., & Roeger, L. (2004). Sexual abuse and suicidality: Gender differences in a large community sample of adolescents. *Child Abuse and Neglect, 28,* 491–503.

Marttunen, M. J., Aro, H. M., Henriksson, M. M., & Lonnqvist, J. K. (1991). Mental disorders in adolescent suicide: DSM-III-R axes I and II diagnoses in suicides among 13-to 19-year-olds in Finland. *Archives of General Psychiatry, 48*(9), 834.

McAuliffe, C., Corcoran, P., Keeley, H. S., Arensman, E., Bille-Brahe, U., De Leo, D.,…Wasserman, D. (2006). Problem-solving ability and repetition of deliberate self-harm: A multicenter study. *Psychological Medicine, 36,* 45–55.

McCloskey, M., Look, A., Chen, E., Pajoumand, G., & Berman, M. (2012). Nonsuicidal self-injury: Relationship to behavioral and self-rating measures of impulsivity and self-aggression. *Suicide and Life-Threatening Behavior, 42*(2), 197–209.

McKeown, R. E., Cuffe, S. P., & Schulz, R. M. (2006). US suicide rates by age group, 1970-2002: An examination of recent trends. *American Journal of Public Health, 96,* 1744–1751.

McLaughlin, J. A., Miller, P., & Warwick, H. (1996). Deliberate self-harm in adolescents: hopelessness, depression, problems and problem-solving. *Journal of Adolescence, 19,* 523–532.

Messer, J. M., & Fremouw, W. J. (2007). A critical review of explanatory models for self-mutilating behaviors in adolescents. *Clinical Psychology Review, 28,* 162–178.

Miller, M., Hempstead, K., Nguyen, T., Barber, C., Rosenberg-Wohl, S., & Azrael, D. (2013). Method choice in nonfatal self-harm as a predictor of subsequent episodes of self-harm and suicide: Implications for clinical practice. *American Journal of Public Health, 103*(6). doi: 10.2105/AJPH.2013.301326.

Miller, A. L., Rathus, J. H., & Linehan, M. M. (2007). *Dialectical behavior therapy with suicidal adolescents.* New York, NY: Guilford Press.

Miller, A. L., & Smith, H. L. (2008). Adolescent non-suicidal self-injurious behavior: The latest epidemic to assess and treat. *Applied and Preventive Psychology, 12,* 178–188.

Milner, A., Page, A., & LaMontagne, A. (2013). Long-term unemployment and suicide: A systematic review and meta-analysis. *PLoS One, 8*(1), 1–6.

Muehlenkamp, J. J. (2005). Self-injurious behavior as a separate clinical syndrome. *American Journal of Orthopsychiatry, 75,* 324–333.

Muehlenkamp, J. J. (2006). Empirically supported treatments and general therapy guidelines for non-suicidal self-injury. *Journal of Mental Health Counseling, 28,* 166–185.

Muehlenkamp, J. J., Brausch, A., Quigley, K., & Whitlock, J. (2013). Interpersonal features and functions of non-suicidal self-injury. *Suicide and Life-Threatening Behavior, 43*(1), 67–80.

Muehlenkamp, J. J., Claes, L., Havertape, L., & Plener, P.L. (2012). International prevalence of adolescent non-suicidal self-injury and deliberate self-harm. *Child and Adolescent Psychiatry and Mental Health, 6,* 1–9.

Muehlenkamp, J. J., Engel, S. G., Crosby, R. D., Wonderlich, S. A., Simonich, H., & Mitchell, J. E. (2009). Emotional states preceding and following acts of non-suicidal self-injury in bulimia nervosa patients. *Behavior Research and Therapy, 47,* 83–87.

Muehlenkamp, J. J., Ertelt, T. W., & Azure, J. A. (2008). Treating outpatient suicidal adolescents: Guidelines from the empirical literature. *Journal of Mental Health Counseling, 30,* 105–120.

Muehlenkamp, J. J., Ertelt, T., Claes, L., & Miller, A. L. (2011). Borderline personality features differentiate non-suicidal and suicidal self-injury in adolescent outpatients. *Journal of Child Psychology and Psychiatry, 52,* 148–155.

Muehlenkamp, J. J., & Gutierrez, P. M. (2004). An investigation of differences between self-injurious behavior and suicide attempts in a sample of adolescents. *Suicide and Life Threatening Behavior, 34,* 12–23.

Muehlenkamp, J. J., & Gutierrez, P. M. (2007). Risk for suicide attempts among adolescents who engage in non-suicidal self-injury. *Archives of Suicide Research, 11,* 69–82.

Muehlenkamp, J. J., Hoff, E. R., Licht, J.G., Azure, J.A., & Hasenzahl, S. J. (2008). Rates of non-suicidal self-injury: A cross-sectional analysis of exposure. *Current Psychology, 4,* 234–241.

Muehlenkamp, J. J., Kerr, P., Bradley, A., Adams Larsen, M. (2010). Abuse subtypes and non-suicidal self-injury: Preliminary evidence of complex emotion regulation patterns. *Journal of Nervous and Mental Disease, 4,* 258–263.

Muehlenkamp, J. J., Williams, K. L., Gutierrez, P. M., & Claes, L. (2009). Cohort differences in lifetime non-suicidal self-injury among high school students across 5 years. *Archives of Suicide Research, 13,* 317–329.

Nada-Raja, S., Morrison, D., & Skegg, K. (2003). A population-based study of help-seeking for self-harm in young adults. *Australian and New Zealand Journal of Psychiatry, 37,* 600–605.

Nada-Raja, S., Skegg, K., Langley, J., Morrison, D., & Sowerby, P. (2004). Self-harmful behaviors in a population based sample of young adults. *Suicide and Life-Threatening Behavior, 34,* 177–186.

Nixon, M. K., Cloutier, P. F., & Aggarwal, S. (2002). Affect regulation and addictive aspects of repetitive self-injury in hospitalized adolescents. *Journal of the American Academy of Child and Adolescent Psychiatry, 41,* 1333–1341.

Nixon, M. K., Coutier, P., & Jansson, S. M. (2008). Nonsuicidal self-harm in youth: A population-based survey. *Canadian Medical Association Journal, 178,* 306–312.

Nock, M. K. (2009). Why do people hurt themselves? New insights into the nature and functions of self-injury. *Current Directions in Psychological Science, 18,* 78–83.

Nock, M. K., Borges, G., Bromet, E. J., Alonso, J., Angermeyer, M., Beautrais, A.,…Williams, D. (2008). Cross-national prevalence and risk factors for suicidal ideation, plans, and attempts. *British Journal of Psychiatry, 192,* 98–105.

Nock, M. K., & Cha, C. B. (2009). Psychological models of non-suicidal self-injury. In M. K. Nock (Ed.), *Understanding nonsuicidal self-injury: Origins, assessment, and treatment* (pp. 65–77). Washington, DC: American Psychological Association.

Nock, M. K., Cha, C. B., & Dour, H. (2011). Disorders of impulse-control and self-harm. In D. H. Barlow (Ed.), *Oxford handbook of clinical psychology* (pp. 504–529). New York, NY: Oxford University Press.

Nock, M. K., Deming, C., Fullerton, C., Gilman, S., Goldenberg, M., Kessler, R. C.,…Ursano, R. J. (2013). Suicide among soldiers: A review of psychosocial risk and protective factors. *Psychiatry, 76*(2), 97–125.

Nock, M. K., & Favazza, A. R. (2009). Nonsuicidal self-injury: Definition and classification. In M. K. Nock (Ed.), *Understanding nonsuicidal self-injury: Origins, assessment, and treatment* (pp. 9–18). Washington, DC: American Psychological Association.

Nock, M. K., Holmberg, E. B., Photos, V. I., & Michel, B. D. (2007). Self-injurious thoughts and behaviors interview: Development, reliability, and validity in an adolescent sample. *Psychological Assessment, 19,* 309–317.

Nock, M. K., Hwang, I., Sampson, N., Kessler, R. C., Angermeyer, M., Beautrais, A.,…Williams, D. R. (2009). Cross-national analysis of the associations among mental disorders and suicidal behavior: Findings from the WHO World Mental Health Surveys. *PLOS Medicine, 6,* e1000123.

Nock, M. K., Joiner, T. E., Gordon, K. H., Lloyd-Richardson, E., & Prinstein, M. J. (2006). Non-suicidal self-injury among adolescents: Diagnostic correlates and relation to suicide attempts. *Psychiatry Research, 144,* 65–72.

Nock, M. K., & Kazdin, A. E. (2002). Examination of affective, cognitive, and behavioral factors and suicide-related outcomes in children and young adolescents. *Journal of Clinical Child and Adolescent Psychology, 31,* 48–58.

Nock, M. K., & Kessler, R. C. (2006). Prevalence of and risk factors for suicide attempts vs. suicide gestures: Analysis of the national comorbidity survey. *Journal of Abnormal Psychology, 115,* 616–623.

Nock, M. K., & Mendes, W. B. (2008). Physiological arousal, distress tolerance, and social problem-solving deficits among adolescent self-injurers. *Journal of Consulting and Clinical Psychology, 76,* 28–38.

Nock, M., Park, J., Finn, C., Deliberto, T., Dour, H., & Banaji, M. R. (2010). Measuring the suicidal mind: Implicit cognition predicts suicidal behavior. *Psychological Science, 21*(4), 511–517.

Nock, M. K., & Prinstein, M. J. (2004). A functional approach to the assessment of self-mutilative behavior. *Journal of Consulting and Clinical Psychology, 72,* 885–890.

Nock, M. K., & Prinstein, M. J. (2005). Contextual features and behavioral functions of self-mutilation among adolescents. *Journal of Abnormal Psychology, 114,* 140–146.

Nock, M. K., Prinstein, M. J., & Sterba, S. (2009). Revealing the form and function of self-injurious thoughts and behaviors: A real-time ecological assessment study among adolescents and young adults. *Journal of Abnormal Psychology, 118,* 816–827.

Noh, Y. H. (2009). Does unemployment increase suicide rates? The OECD panel evidence. *Journal of Economic Psychology, 30,* 575–582.

O'Carroll, P. W., Berman, A. L., Maris, R. W., Moscicki, E. K., Tanney, B. L., & Silverman, M. M. (1996). Beyond the tower of Babel: A nomenclature for suicidology. *Suicide and Life-Threatening Behavior, 26,* 237–252.

O'Connor, R. C., & Cassidy, C. (2007). Predicting hopelessness: The interaction between optimism/pessimism and specific future expectancies. *Cognition and Emotion, 21,* 596–613.

O'Connor, R. C., Fraser, L., Whyte, M.-C., MacHale, S., & Masterton, G. (2008). A comparison of specific positive future expectancies and global hopelessness as predictors of suicidal ideation in a prospective study of repeat self-harmers. *Journal of Affective Disorders, 110,* 207–214.

O'Connor, R. C., Rasmussen, S., Miles, J., & Hawton, K. (2009). Self-harm in adolescents: self-report survey in schools in Scotland. *The British Journal of Psychiatry, 194,* 68–72.

Oldershaw, A., Grima, E., Jollant, F., Richards, C., Simic, M., Taylor, L., & Schmidt, U. (2009). Decision making and problem solving in adolescents who deliberately self-harm. *Psychological Medicine, 39,* 95–104.

Orbach, I., Stein, D., Palgi, Y., Asherov, J., Har-Even, D., & Elizur, A. (1996). Perception of physical pain in accident and suicide attempt patients: Self-preservation vs. self-destruction. *Journal of Psychiatric Research, 30,* 307–320.

Oquendo, M. A., Lizardi, D., Greenwald, S., Weissman, M. M., & Mann, J. J. (2004). Rates of lifetime suicide attempt and rates of lifetime major depression in different ethnic groups in the United States. *Acta Psychiatrica Scandinavica, 110,* 446–451.

Paivio, S. C., & McCulloch, C. R. (2004). Alexithymia as a mediator between childhood trauma and self-injurious behaviors. *Child Abuse and Neglect, 28,* 339–354.

Patton, G. C., Harris, R., Carlin, J. B., Hibbert, M. E., Coffey, C., Schwartz, M., & Bowes, G. (1997). Adolescent suicidal behaviors: A population-based study of risk. *Psychological Medicine, 37*, 715–724.

Pearson, J., & Conwell, Y. (1995). Suicide in late life: challenges and opportunities for research. *International Psychogeriatrics, 7*, 131–136.

Penn, J. V., Esposito, C. L., Schaeffer, L. E., Fritz, G. K., & Spirito, A. (2003). Suicide attempts and self-mutilative behavior in a juvenile correctional facility. *Journal of the American Academy of Child and Adolescent Psychiatry, 42*, 762–769.

Phillips, M. R., Li, X., & Zhang, Y. (2002). Suicide rates in China, 1995-1999. *Lancet, 359*, 835–840.

Plener, P., Libal, G., Keller, F., Fegert, J.M., & Muehlenkamp, J. J. (2009). An international comparison of adolescent non-suicidal self-injury (NSSI) and suicide attempts: Germany and U.S. *Psychological Medicine, 39*, 1549–1558.

Pollock, L. R., & Williams, J. M. (1998). Problem solving and suicidal behavior. *Suicide and Life-Threatening Behavior, 28*, 375–387.

Pollock, L. R., & Williams, J. M. (2001). Effective problem solving in suicide attempters depends on specific autobiographical recall. *Suicide and Life-Threatening Behavior, 31*, 386–396.

Pompili, M., Mancinelli, I. Girardi, P. Ruberto, A., & Tatareli, R. (2004). Suicide in anorexia nervosa: A meta-analysis. *International Journal of Eating Disorders, 36*(1), 99–103.

Prinstein, M. J. (2008). Introduction to the special section on suicide and nonsuicidal self-injury: A review of unique challenges and important directions for self-injury science. *Journal of Consulting and Clinical Psychology, 76*, 1–8.

Prinstein, M. J., Nock, M. K., Simon, V., Aikins, J. W., Cheah, C. S. L., & Spirito, A. (2008). Longitudinal trajectories and predictors of adolescent suicidal ideation and attempts following inpatient hospitalization. *Journal of Consulting and Clinical Psychology, 76*, 92–103.

Purselle, D., Heninger, M., Hanzlick, R., & Garlow, S. (2009). Differential association of socioeconomic status in ethnic and age defined suicides. *Psychiatry Research, 167*, 258–265.

Randall, J. R., Rowe, B. H., Dong, K. A., Nock, M. K., & Colman, I. (2013). Assessment of self-harm risk using implicit thoughts. *Psychological Assessment*, e-pub ahead of print. doi: 10.1037/a0032391.

Range, L., Leach, M., McIntyre, D., Posey-Deters, P., Marion, M., Kobac, S.H., …Vigil, J. (1999). Multicultural perspectives on suicide. *Aggression and Violent Behavior, 4*(4), 413–430.

Remafedi, G., Farrow, J. A., & Deisher, R. W. (1993). Risk factors for attempted suicide in gay and bisexual youth. In L. D. Garnets, D. C. Kimmel (Eds.), *Psychological perspectives on lesbian and gay male experiences* (pp. 486–499). New York, NY: Columbia University Press.

Remafedi, G., French, S., Story, M., Resnick, M. D., & Blum, R. (1998). The relationship between suicide risk and sexual orientation: Results of a population-based study. *American Journal of Public Health, 88*, 57–60.

Resch, F., Parzer, P., Brunner, R., & BELLA Study Group. (2008). Self-mutilation and suicidal behavior in children and adolescents: Prevalence and psychosocial correlates: Results of the BELLA study. *European Child and Adolescent Psychiatry, 17*(Suppl. 1), 92–98.

Rodham, K., & Hawton, K. (2009). Epidemiology and phenomenology of nonsuicidal self-injury. In M. K. Nock (Ed.), *Understanding nonsuicidal self-injury: Origins, assessment, and treatment* (pp. 37–63). Washington, DC: American Psychological Association.

Rodham, K., Hawton, K., & Evans, E. (2004). Reasons for deliberate self-harm: Comparison of self-poisoners and self-cutters in a community sample of adolescents. *Journal of the American Academy of Child and Adolescent Psychiatry, 43*, 80–87.

Ross, S., & Heath, N. (2003). Two models of adolescent self-mutilation. *Suicide and Life-Threatening Behavior, 33*, 277–287.

Ross, S., Heath, N. L., & Toste, J. R. (2009). Non-suicidal self-injury and eating pathology in high school students. *American Journal of Orthopsychiatry, 79*, 83–92.

Rubenstein, J. L., Halton, A., Kasten, L., Rubin, C., & Stechler, G. (1998). Suicidal behavior in adolescents. *American Journal of Orthopsychiatry, 68*, 274–284.

Rudd, M. D. (2006). *The assessment and management of suicidology*. Sarasota, FL: Professional Resources Press.

Runeson, B., Tidemalm, D., Dahlin, M., Lichtenstein, P., & Langstrom, N. (2010). Method of attempted suicide as predictor of subsequent successful suicide: National long term cohort study. *British Medical Journal, 341*(7765), 8138.

Russell, S. T., & Joyner, K. (2001). Adolescent sexual orientation and suicide risk: Evidence from a national survey. *American Journal of Public Health, 91*, 1276–1281.

Russell, S., & Toomey, R. (2013). Risk and protective factors for suicidal thoughts among sexual minority youth: Evidence from the add health study. *Journal of Gay and Lesbian Mental Health, 17*(2), 132–149.

Sampson, E., Mukherjee, S., Ukoumunne, O. C., Mullan, N., & Bullock, T. (2004). History of deliberate self-harm and its association with mood fluctuation. *Journal of affective disorders, 79*, 223–227.

Sansone, R., Sellbom, M., Chang, J., & Jewell, B. (2012). An examination of racial differences in self-harm behavior. *Psychiatry Research, 200*(1), 49–51.

Selby, E. A., Bender, T. W., Gordon, K. H., Nock, M. K., & Joiner, T. E. (2012). Non-suicidal self-injury (NSSI) disorder: A preliminary study. *Personality Disorders: Theory, Research, and Treatment, 3*, 167–173.

Shah, A., & Bhandarkar, R. (2008). Cross-national study of the correlation of general population suicide rates with unemployment rates. *Psychological Reports, 103*, 793–796.

Shneidman, E. S. (1985). *Definition of suicide*. New York: Wiley.

Silverman, M. M., Berman, A. L., Sanddal, N. D., O'Carroll, P. W., & Joiner, T. E., Jr. (2007a). Rebuilding the tower of Babel: A revised nomenclature for the study of suicide and suicide behaviors Part 1: Background, rationale, and methodology. *Suicide and Life-Threatening Behavior, 37*, 248–263.

Silverman, M. M., Berman, A. L., Sanddal, N. D., O'Carroll, P. W., & Joiner, T. E., Jr. (2007b). Rebuilding the tower of Babel: A revised nomenclature for the study of suicide and suicide behaviors Part 2: Suicide-related ideations, communications, and behaviors. *Suicide and Life-Threatening Behavior, 37*, 264–277.

Simon, R. I., & Hales, R. E. (2006). *Textbook of suicide assessment and management*. Washington, DC: American Psychiatric Publishing.

Skegg, K. (2005). Self-harm. *Lancet, 366*, 1471–1483.

Slama, F., Courtet, P., Golmard, J., Mathieu, F., Guillaume, S., Yon, L., Jollant, F., Misson, H., Jaussent, I., Leboyer, M., &

Bellivier, F. (2009). Admixture analysis of age at first suicide attempt. *Journal of Psychiatric Research, 43*, 895–900.

Solano, P., Pizzorno, E., Gallina, A., Mattei, C., Gabrielli, F., & Kayman, J. (2012). Employment status, inflation and suicidal behaviour: An analysis of a stratified sample in Italy. *International Journal of Social Psychiatry, 58*(5), 477–484.

Soloff, P. H., Lynch, K. G., & Kelly, T. M. (2002). Childhood abuse as a risk factor for suicidal behavior in borderline personality disorder. *Journal of Personality Disorders, 16*, 201–214.

Sourander, A., Aromaa, A., Pihlakoski, L, Haavisto, A., Rautava, P., Helenius, H., & Sillanpää, M. (2006). Early predictors of deliberate self-harm among adolescents: A prospective follow-up study from age 3 to age 15. *Journal of Affective Disorders, 93*, 87–96.

Speckens, A. E., & Hawton, K. (2005). Social problem solving in adolescents with suicidal behavior: A systematic review. *Suicide and Life-Threatening Behavior, 35*, 365–387.

Stack, S. (2000). Suicide: a 15-year review of the sociological literature part I: cultural and economic factors. *Suicide and Life-Threatening Behavior, 30*, 145–162.

Stanley, B., Gameroff, M. J., Michalsen, V., & Mann, J. J. (2001). Are suicide attempters who self-mutilate a unique population? *American Journal of Psychiatry, 158*, 427–432.

Stanley, B., Wincehl, R., Molcho, A., Simeon, D., & Stanley, M. (1992). Suicide and the self- harm continuum: Phenomenological and biochemical evidence. *International Review of Psychiatry, 4*, 149–155.

St. Germain, S., & Hooley, J. (2012). Direct and indirect forms of non-suicidal self-injury: Evidence for a distinction. *Psychiatry Research, 197*(1/2), 78–84.

Swannell, S., Martin, G., Page, A., Hasking, P., Hazell, P., Taylor, A., & Protani, M. (2012). Child maltreatment, subsequent non-suicidal self-injury and the mediating roles of dissociation, alexithymia and self-blame. *Child Abuse and Neglect, 36*(7-8), 572–584.

Swenson, L. P., Spirito, A., Dyl, J., Kittler, J., & Hunt, J. I. (2008). Pyschiatric correlates of nonsuicidal cutting behaviors in an adolescent inpatient sample. *Child Psychiatry and Human Development, 39*, 427–438.

Taliaferro, L. A., Muehlenkamp, J. J., Borowsky, I. W., McMorris, B. J., & Kugler, K. C. (2012). Risk factors, protective factors, and co-occurring health behaviors distinguishing self- harm groups: A population-based sample of adolescents. *Academic Pediatrics, 12*, 205–213.

Tang, J., Yu, Y., Wu, Y., Ma, Y., Zhu, H., Zhang, P., & Liu, Z. (2011). Association between non-suicidal self-injuries and suicide attempts in Chinese adolescents and college students: A cross-section study. *PloS One, 6*, e17977.

Taylor, J., Peterson, C., & Fischer, S. (2012). Motivations for self-injury, affect, and impulsivity: A comparison of individuals with current self-injury to individuals with a history of self-injury. *Suicide and Life-Threatening Behavior, 42*(6), 602–613.

Terao, T., Soeda, S., Yoshimura, R., Nakamura, J., & Iwata, N. (2002). Effect of latitude on suicide rates in Japan. *The Lancet, 360*, 1892.

Thompson, M., Kuruwita, C., & Foster, E. M. (2009). Transitions in suicide risk in a nationally representative sample of adolescents. *Journal of Adolescent Health, 44*, 458–463.

Tortolero, S. R., & Roberts, R. E. (2001). Differences in nonfatal suicide behaviors among Mexican and European American middle school children. *Suicide and Life-Threatening Behavior, 31*, 214–223.

Trepal, H. C., & Wester, K. L. (2007). Self-injurious behaviors, diagnoses, and treatment methods: What mental health professionals are reporting. *Journal of Mental Health Counseling, 29*, 363–375.

Tulloch, A. L., Blizzard, L., & Pinkus, Z. (1997). Adolescent-parent communication in self-harm. *Journal of Adolescent Health, 21*, 267–275.

Turner, B., Chapman, A., & Layden, B. (2012). Intrapersonal and interpersonal functions of non suicidal self-injury: Associations with emotional and social functioning. *Suicide and Life-Threatening Behavior, 42*(1), 36–55.

Tyler, K. A., Whitbeck, L. B., Hoyt, D. R., & Johnson, K. D. (2003). Self-mutilation and homeless youth: The role of family abuse, street experiences, and mental disorders. *Journal of Research on Adolescence, 13*, 457–474.

Van Orden, K. A., Lynam, M. E., Hollar, D., & Joiner, T. E. (2006). Perceived burdensomeness as an indicator of suicidal symptoms. *Cognitive Therapy and Research, 30*, 457–467.

Van Orden, K. A., Witte, T. K., Gordon, K. H., Bender, T. W., & Joiner, T. E. (2008). Suicidal desire and the capability for suicide: Tests of the interpersonal-psychological theory of suicidal behavior among adults. *Journal of Consulting and Clinical Psychology, 76*, 72–83.

Velting, D. M., Rathus, J. H. and Asnis, G. M. (1998), Asking adolescents to explain discrepancies in self-reported suicidality. *Suicide and Life-Threatening Behavior, 28*, 187–196.

Verona, E., Sachs-Ericsson, N., & Joiner, T. E. (2004). Suicide attempts associated with externalizing psychopathology in an epidemiological sample. *American Journal of Psychiatry, 161*, 444–451.

Walker, R., Alabi, D., Roberts, J., & Obasi, E. (2010). Ethnic group differences in reasons for living and the moderating role of cultural worldview. *Cultural Diversity and Ethnic Minority Psychology, 16*(3), 372–378.

Walsh, B. W. (2006). *Treating self-injury: A practical guide.* New York, NY: Guilford Press.

Walsh, B. W. (2009). Strategies for responding to self-injury: When does the duty to protect apply? In J. L. Werth, E. R. Welfel, & G. A. H. Benjamin (Eds.), *The duty to protect: Ethical, legal and professional considerations for mental health professionals* (pp. 181–193). Washington, DC: American Psychological Association.

Walsh, B. W., & Rosen, P. (1988). *Self-mutilation. Theory, research, and treatment.* New York, NY: Guilford Press.

Warzocha, D., Pawelczyk, T., & Gmitrowicz, A. (2010). Associations between deliberate self- harm episodes in psychiatrically hospitalised youth and the type of mental disorders and selected environmental factors. *Archives of Psychiatry and Psychotherapy, 12*(2), 23–29.

Wasserman, D., Chenge, Q., & Jiang, G–X. (2005). Global suicide rates among young people aged 15-19. *World Psychiatry, 4*, 114–120.

Wedig, M. M., & Nock, M. K. (2007). Parental expressed emotion and adolescent self-injury. *Journal of the American Academy of Child and Adolescent Psychiatry, 46*, 1171–1178.

Weierich, M. R., & Nock, M. K. (2008). Posttraumatic stress symptoms mediate the relation between childhood sexual abuse and non-suicidal self-injury. *Journal of Consulting and Clinical Psychology, 76*, 39–44.

Welch, S. S., Linehan, M. M., Sylvers, P., Chittams, J., & Rizvi, S. L. (2008). Emotional responses to self-injury imagery in borderline personality disorder. *Journal of Consulting and Clinical Psychology, 76*, 45–51.

Wenzel, A., & Beck, A. T. (2008). A cognitive model of suicidal behavior: Theory and treatment. *Applied and Preventive Psychology, 12*, 189–201.

Westefeld, J. S., Range, L. M., Rogers, J. R., Maples, M. R., Bromley, J. L., & Alcorn, J. (2000). Suicide: An overview. *The Counseling Psychologist, 28*, 445–510.

Wherry, J., Baldwin, S., Junco, K., & Floyd, B. (2013). Suicidal thoughts/behaviors in sexually abused children. *Journal of Child Sexual Abuse, 22*(5), 534–551.

Whiteside, S. P., & Lynam, D. R. (2001). The five-factor model and impulsivity: Using a structural model of personality to understand impulsivity. *Personality and Individual Differences, 30*, 669–689.

Whitlock, J., Eckenrode, J., & Silverman, D. (2006). Self-injurious behaviors in a college population. *Pediatrics, 117*, 1939–1948.

Whitlock, J., & Knox, K. (2007). The relationship between self-injurious behavior and suicide in a young adult population. *Archives of Pediatric and Adolescent Medicine, 161*, 634–640.

Whitlock, J., Muehlenkamp, J., & Eckenrode, J. (2008). Variation in nonsuicidal self-injury: Identification and features of latent classes in a college population of emerging adults. *Journal of Clinical Child and Adolescent Psychology, 37*, 725–735.

Whitlock, J., Muehlenkamp, J., Eckenrode, J., Purington, A., Adams, G.B., Barreira, P., & Kress, V. (2013). Nonsuicidal self-injury as gateway to suicide in young adults. *Journal of Adolescent Health, 52*, 486–492.

Whitlock, J., Muehlenkamp, J., Purington, A., Eckenrode, J., Barreira, P., Baral Abrams, G.,...Knox, K. (2011). Nonsuicidal self-injury in a college population: General trends and sex differences. *Journal of American College Health, 59*(8), 691–698.

Wichstrom, L. (2009). Predictors of non-suicidal self-injury versus attempted suicide: Similar or different? *Archives of Suicide Research, 13*, 105–122.

Wilkinson, P., Kelvin, R., Roberts, C., Dubicka, B., & Goodyer, I. (2011). Clinical and psychosocial predictors of suicide attempts and nonsuicidal self-injury in the Adolescent Depression Antidepressants and Psychotherapy Trial (ADAPT). *American Journal of Psychiatry, 168*, 495–501.

Williams, J. M., Barnhofer, T., Crane, C., & Beck, A. T. (2005). Problem solving deteriorates following mood challenge in formerly depressed patients with a history of suicidal ideation. *Journal of Abnormal Psychology, 114*, 421–431.

Wisslow, L., Walkup, J., Barlow, A., Reid, R., & Kane, S. (2001). Cluster and regional influences on suicide in a Southwestern American Indian tribe. *Social Science and Medicine, 53*, 1115–1124.

Witte, T. K., Merrill, K. A., Stellrecht, N. E., Bernert, R. A., Hollar, D. L., Schatschneider, C., & Joiner, T. (2008). "Impulsive" youth suicide attempters are not necessarily all that impulsive. *Journal of Affective Disorders, 107*, 107–116.

Wong, J. P., Stewart, S. M., Ho, S. Y., & Lam, T. H. (2007). Risk factors associated with suicide attempts and other self-injury among Hong Kong adolescents. *Suicide and Life-Threatening Behavior, 37*, 453–466.

Wu, C–S., Liao, S. C., Lin, K. M., Tseng, M. M. C., Wu, E. C., & Liu, S. K. (2009). Multidimensional assessments of impulsivity in subjects with history of suicidal attempts. *Comprehensive Psychiatry, 50*, 315–321.

Yates, T. M. (2004). The developmental psychopathology of self-injurious behavior: Compensatory regulation in post-traumatic adaptation. *Clinical Psychology Review, 24*, 35–74.

Yates, T. M. (2009). Developmental pathways from child maltreatment to nonsuicidal self-injury. In M. K. Nock (Ed.), *Understanding nonsuicidal self-injury: Origins, assessment, and treatment* (pp. 117–138). Washington, DC: American Psychological Association.

Yates, T. M., Carlson, E. A., & Egeland, B. (2008). A prospective study of child maltreatment and self-injurious behavior in a community sample. *Development and Psychopathology, 20*, 651–671.

Yates, T. M., Tracy, A. J., & Luthar, S. S. (2008). Nonsuicidal self-injury among "privileged" youths: Longitudinal and cross-sectional approaches to developmental process. *Journal of Consulting and Clinical Psychology, 76*, 52–62.

Ying, Y. H., & Chang, K. (2009). A study of suicide and socioeconomic factors. *Suicide and Life-Threatening Behavior, 39*(2), 214–226.

You, J., & Leung, F. (2012). The role of depressive symptoms, family invalidation and behavioral impulsivity in the occurrence and repetition of non-suicidal self-injury in Chinese adolescents: A 2-year follow-up study. *Journal of Adolescence, 35*(2), 389–395.

Yuen, N. Y., Nahulu, L. B., Hishinuma, E. S., & Miyamoto, R. H. (2000). Cultural identification and attempted suicide in Native Hawaiian adolescents. *Journal of the American Academy of Child and Adolescent Psychiatry, 39*, 360–367.

Zahl, D. L., & Hawton, K. (2004). Repetition of deliberate self-harm and subsequent suicide risk: long-term follow-up study of 11 583 patients. *The British Journal of Psychiatry, 185*, 70–75.

Zanarini, M. C. (2000). Childhood experiences associated with the development of borderline personality disorder. *Psychiatric Clinics of North America, 23*, 89–101.

Zanarini, M. C., Frankenburg, G. R., Hennen, J., Reich, B., & Silk, K. R. (2005). The McLean study of adult development (MSAD): Overview and implications of the first six years of prospective follow-up. *Journal of Personality Disorders, 19*, 505–523.

Zetterqvist, M., Lundh, L., & Svedin, C. (2013). A comparison of adolescents engaging in self-injurious behaviors with and without suicidal intent: Self-reported experiences of adverse life events and trauma symptoms. *Journal of Youth and Adolescence, 42*, 1257-1272.

Zetterqvist, M., Lundh, L., Dahlstrom, O., & Svedin, C. (2013). Prevalence and function of non-suicidal self-injury (NSSI) in a community sample of adolescents, using suggested DSM-5 criteria for a potential NSSI disorder. *Journal of Abnormal Child Psychology, 41*(5), 759–773.

Zoroglu, S. S., Tuzun, W., Sar, V., Tutkun, H., Savacs, H. A., Ozturk, M.,...Kora, M. E. (2003). Suicide attempt and self-mutilation among Turkish high school students in relation with abuse, neglect and dissociation. *Psychiatry and Clinical Neuroscience, 57*, 119–126.

Should We Expand the Conceptualization of Self-Injurious Behavior? Rationale, Review, and Recommendations

Jill M. Hooley *and* Sarah A. St. Germain

Abstract

Self-injurious behavior typically involves deliberate acts that directly damage the body but are performed in the absence of suicidal intent. The most common examples of direct self-injury are cutting and burning. Yet there are other ways that people may mistreat or abuse themselves without altering bodily tissue directly. Such "indirect" methods of self-injury might include substance abuse, eating-disordered behavior, risky or reckless behavior, and involvement in abusive relationships. In this chapter we consider the possibility that the conceptualization of self-injurious behavior should be expanded to include indirect forms of self-injury. We also present data that bear on this issue. Consideration of the boundaries of self-injury is especially important now that nonsuicidal self-injury disorder has been identified in *DSM-5* as a condition in need of further study.

Key Words: nonsuicidal self-injury, *DSM-5*, substance use disorders, eating disorders, abusive relationships, health risk behaviors, suicide, self-criticism

Instances of self-injurious behavior (SIB) have been reported throughout history. However, rates of self-injury appear to be increasing in recent years (Nock, 2009). It should therefore come as little surprise that the study of self-harming behavior is now a focus of much empirical attention.

One impediment to progress with regard to the understanding and treatment of self-injurious behavior has been the lack of consistency in how these behaviors are conceptualized, defined, and classified. This can be seen in the wide array of terms that are commonly used to refer to self-injurious acts (see Hooley, 2008; Nock & Favazza, 2009). These include deliberate self-harm, self-mutilation, self-cutting, and parasuicide. With the publication of the *Diagnostic and Statistical Manual of Mental Disorders*, fifth edition (*DSM-5*; APA, 2013) proposed criteria for nonsuicidal self-injury (NSSI) disorder are now available. However, as its placement in Section III of *DSM-5* attests, NSSI disorder is currently regarded as a clinical condition in need of additional study.

One particular problem concerns the apparent heterogeneity of self-harming behaviors. In the current literature the terms "self-injury" and "self-harm" are typically used to describe visible forms of direct self-injury such as cutting or burning. However, these are not the only behaviors that people can use to cause damage to their bodies. It is possible that prevailing definitions of self-injurious behavior might be too narrow (Turp, 2002). That is, other behaviors that involve people mistreating or abusing themselves may have much in common with more direct forms of self-injurious behavior. Many researchers and clinicians in the field have raised the question of whether and how these behaviors may be related to less direct forms of self-destruction, and whether such behaviors should be included in the study of self-injurious behavior. It is not known whether those who engage in more indirect forms of self-injury share common clinical characteristics with those who engage in direct self-injurious behaviors. This issue is of interest insofar as such "indirect" forms of self-injury might warrant consideration as part of a spectrum of self-harming behaviors. Identifying any such commonalities would seem to be a sensible research target, especially in light of the clinical severity of these behaviors as well as the relative lack of comprehensive theoretical models that can inform treatment.

In this chapter we describe "indirect" forms of self-injury, outlining the types of behaviors that might be subsumed into this category. We then consider the possibility that these might warrant consideration as part of a broader spectrum of self-injurious behaviors. We begin by describing the types of behaviors that might be considered to reflect indirect forms of self-injury. We then review what is known about these behaviors and about their links to more direct forms of self-injury. This is followed by a discussion of findings from new research that compares those who engage in more indirect forms of self-injury with those who engage in direct forms. Many researchers have suggested that direct self-injury is best represented as its own clinical syndrome (Favazza & Rosenthal, 1993; Muehlenkamp, 2005; Oquendo, Baca-Garcia, Mann, & Giner, 2008). Our conclusions speak to this issue. They also have implications for the conceptualization of NSSI in *DSM-5* and beyond.

Direct and Indirect Forms of Self-Harm

Self-harming behavior generally involves deliberate actions that are directly harmful to the self (Nock, Cha, & Dour, 2010; Nock, Wedig, Holmberg, & Hooley, 2008). Direct self-injury is considered "direct" because actual physical harm occurs without any "intervening steps" (Nock, Cha, et al., 2009). The prototypical example is skin cutting. After the act of cutting, the harmful result (the actual wound and associated bleeding) is immediately visible. This direct and deliberate destruction of body tissue in the absence of any intent to die is what is referred to as NSSI (see Nock, Joiner, Gordon, Lloyd-Richardson, & Prinstein, 2006).

Of course, it is immediately apparent that direct forms of self-injury are not the only ways that people can engage in self-destructive or self-damaging behaviors. Consider the person with chronic alcohol abuse who, over time, sustains liver damage or develops a vitamin B12 deficiency. Or the person with an eating disorder who restricts food intake

and, in so doing, deprives the body of essential nutrients that will later result in heart problems or cognitive issues (e.g., "starvation syndrome"). To what extent should these more "indirect" forms of self-harm be considered and included in studies of self-injury? To what extent do these forms of self-harming behavior warrant special consideration within our classification system?

Indirect self-injurious behavior involves behavior that is clearly damaging to the self but does not involve the deliberate and direct alteration of bodily tissue. Indirect SIB is considered "indirect" in that any associated physical harm occurs with intervening steps and is not always immediately externally visible. For our purposes, indirect SIB is defined as purposeful behavior that is a source of concern for clinicians or family members, occurs in repetitive patterns (i.e., not sporadic or context dependent), and which, in indirect ways, has the potential to compromise physical integrity and be harmful to one's body. According to this definition, individuals who abuse drugs (including alcohol) or who engage in severe eating-disordered behaviors (e.g., restriction, purging) would be classified as engaging in indirect SIB. Additionally, this broadened class of SIB also includes individuals who repeatedly engage in abusive relationships, as well as those who habitually and deliberately engage in risky or reckless behaviors. This conceptualization also recognizes that a number of types of self-harm may occur "by omission" in the form of inadequate self-care behaviors (Turp, 2002).

But where should we draw a limit? As others have noted (see Skegg, 2005), it is not always easy to determine the line between self-injurious and other potentially harmful behaviors. Many people skip meals occasionally or get less sleep than they know is good for them. Many people procrastinate, smoke, or fail to get enough exercise. Should these behaviors, then, be considered forms of indirect self-injury? What makes something "bad enough" to reflect indirect SIB?

Common sense dictates that statistically frequent or normative behaviors (even those with known negative health consequences such as cigarette smoking) should not automatically be viewed as indirect forms of self-harm. Occasional or sporadic behaviors (drinking too much at a party) also would not be included. Rather than see any deviation from optimal living as evidence of pathology, we would suggest that indirect SIB must (a) be repeated or persistent, (b) be clinically significant (ideally indicated by established diagnostic criteria or previously validated cutoffs on clinical assessments), (c) represent a source of serious concern to either the person or others, and (d) have the potential to lead to marked and lasting physical damage over time. Examples of behaviors that would and would not "count" as indirect forms of self-injury are outlined in Table 4.1.

We also note that there are a few prominent examples of behaviors that may *look* like forms of indirect self-injury but that do not fit the definition. Consider, for example, the individual suffering from a major depressive episode. Part of the clinical picture may involve such symptoms as not eating, resulting in weight loss. However, this behavior is not deliberate or purposeful but is instead part of the syndrome of depression. It is not a specific treatment target and the eating disturbance is expected to remit if the depression is successfully treated. In a related vein, some might regard the extreme hand washing of a patient with obsessive-compulsive disorder to be an example of self-damaging behavior to the extent that the skin on the hands becomes painful and raw. Again, however, a key distinction is the lack of purposefulness or volition. By definition, compulsions are not free acts. The excessive hand washing of the patient with obsessive-compulsive disorder is ritualized and it is not a deliberate act performed to harm the physical self. Repeated hand washing is also not an essential aspect of obsessive-compulsive disorder, which may instead be characterized by excessive cleaning, checking, or counting rituals.

Measuring Indirect Forms of Self-Injury

Incorporating the concept of clinical significance into any definition of indirect self-injury permits the use of existing reference points or statistical cutoffs in many cases. For example, in Table 4.1, clinically significant substance abuse is considered to be an example of indirect self-injurious behavior, whereas normalized college drinking (which is usually context dependent and sporadic) is not. Clinically significant substance abuse is often measured by structured diagnostic interviews such as the SCID (First, Spitzer, Gibbon, & Williams, 1996). Other self-report instruments such as the Michigan Alcohol Screening Test (MAST; Mischke & Venneri, 1987) or the Drug Abuse Screening Test (DAST; Gavin, Ross, & Skinner, 1989) also are in routine use. From a research standpoint, those who meet diagnostic criteria for substance use disorder or who score above conventional cutoffs on well-validated screening instruments can therefore conveniently be considered to be engaging in indirect forms of self-injurious behavior.

In a related vein, we would suggest that for disordered eating to reflect indirect self-injury it would be necessary for a given individual to either meet *DSM* criteria for an eating disorder (such as anorexia nervosa, bulimia nervosa, or binge eating disorder) or score above the accepted clinical cutoff on an instrument assessing eating pathology such as the Eating Disorder Examination Questionnaire (Fairburn & Beglin, 1994). As noted earlier, the occasional skipping of meals (while probably not

Table 4.1 Examples of Indirect Self-Injurious Behaviors

Counts: Examples of Indirect Self-Injurious Behaviors	Does Not Count as Indirect Self-Injurious Behavior
Clinically significant substance abuse	Occasional drinking
Clinically significant eating-disordered behaviors	Skipping meals occasionally
Pattern of (2+) abusive relationships, meeting criteria for interpersonal violence	Having one abusive relationship and leaving that person
Risky/reckless behavior: persistent promiscuity with physical/psychological effects	Fewer than two "random hook-ups" with no notable physical/psychological consequences
Risky/reckless behavior: careless driving (driving around rotaries the wrong way)	Driving consistently 5–10 mph above the speed limit
Risky/reckless behavior: deliberately not taking medication (asthma/insulin)	Not taking medication because of cost or access
Risky/reckless behavior: excessive spending on unnecessary items while not fulfilling the basic needs of life	Occasionally splurging on a luxury item

beneficial) is not an example of indirect self-injury because it is not purposeful, repetitive, and potentially harmful to the body. However, a person who regularly avoids eating to engage in some form of volitional self-starvation would be considered to be engaging in indirect self-injurious behavior.

In considering eating disorders or substance use problems as forms of indirect self-harm, we can rely on previously established clinical cutoffs or diagnostic criteria. However, other forms of indirect harm may not map on to formal disorders or syndromes within the current diagnostic nomenclature. In such cases it is important again to consider the criteria we outlined earlier. Accordingly, an individual who repeatedly gets involved in physically, emotionally, or sexually abusive relationships may be considered to be engaging in indirect self-injury. This is because such behavior has the potential to compromise physical integrity, occurs in a repetitive pattern, and is likely to present a source of concern to informed friends and family as well as to clinical professionals. However, it is also important that the individual have some autonomy with regard to entering into or remaining in the relationship. A woman who remains in an abusive relationship solely out of fear that her children would be hurt if she left should not be considered to be engaging in an indirect form of self-harm.

The Link Between Direct and Indirect Forms of Self-Injury

Clinicians have long been comfortable with the idea that behaviors that look very different in terms of their surface characteristics might result from similar underlying functions, motivations, or conflicts (Turp, 2002). To date, however, formal research exploring the relationship between direct and indirect forms of self-injury is still very limited. Examination of the available literature does suggest that people who engage in direct self-injury are also likely to engage in indirect forms of self-injurious behavior. In the following sections we provide a brief review of some of this evidence. It is important to emphasize, however, that just because two clinical conditions co-occur does not provide strong evidence that they are related and represent different manifestations of the same underlying latent trait or construct. On the other hand, absence of clinical comorbidity between direct and indirect forms of self-injury would provide strong evidence that they should be viewed as distinct and unrelated clinical constructs.

Direct Self-Injury and Substance Use

There is no shortage of evidence supporting a link between self-injurious behavior and substance abuse. In one large epidemiological study, self-injurious adolescents in the United Kingdom listed problems with alcohol as one of their main concerns. More specifically, alcohol abuse was found in 7% of the total sample (Hawton, Fagg, Simkin, Bale, & Bond, 2000). In a later investigation of 89 inpatient adolescents who engaged in self-injury, Nock et al. (2006) reported that 59.6% met criteria for a substance use disorder. Although some of this comorbidity was attributable to nicotine dependence, marijuana abuse (12.6%) and dependence (29.5%) as well as alcohol abuse (18%) and dependence (16.8%) were also commonly noted.

Several other studies have reported high rates of comorbidity between direct self-injury and substance use disorders (Beutrais et al., 1996; Gupta & Trzepacz, 1997; Hilt, Nock, Lloyd-Richardson, & Prinstein, 2008; Kessler, Borges, & Walters, 1999; Putnins, 1995). Hilt and colleagues (2008) found that participants who engaged in direct self-injurious behavior were significantly more likely to have engaged in hard drug use than those who did not engage in direct self-injury. Of the participants who self-injured, 46.7% reported using drugs, compared to only 4.4% of those who did not. Data collected from real-time assessments also show that thoughts of self-injury often co-occur with thoughts of using drugs or alcohol or thoughts of binging and purging (Nock, Prinstein, & Sterba, 2009).

Direct Self-Injury and Eating Disorders

The results of many research studies clearly indicate that direct self-injurious behavior and eating disorders co-occur (Dohm et al., 2002; Favaro & Santonastaso, 2000; Favazza, DeRosear, & Conterio, 1989; Paul et al., 2002; Sansone & Levitt, 2002; Stein, Lilenfeld, Wildman, & Marcus, 2004; Winchel & Stanley, 1991; Wonderlich et al., 2001). Most research assessing comorbidity between direct SIB and eating pathology is localized to specific populations, and thus several studies have investigated the frequency of direct SIB in patients with diagnosed eating disorders. For example, Fahy and Eisler (1993) reported that approximately one-quarter of patients with bulimia nervosa and one-quarter of patients with anorexia nervosa reported deliberate acts of self-harm within the past year. Additionally, Solano and colleagues (2005) showed that 32% of outpatients with eating disorders reported at least one lifetime act of direct SIB. Not surprisingly, comorbidity between direct SIB and eating pathology also exists in inpatient populations—one study found that 44% of females on an eating disorder unit reported having engaged in direct SIB (Claes, Vandereycken, & Vertommen, 2001).

Researchers have also investigated a possible relationship between eating pathology and direct SIB in community samples. Specifically, several studies have shown that approximately 50%–80% of self-injurers also qualify for an eating disorder diagnosis (Claes, Vandereycken, & Vertommen, 2004, 2005; Conterio & Lader, 1998; Favazza & Favazza, 1987; Ross, Heath, & Toste, 2009; Sansone, & Levitt, 2002; Walsh & Rosen, 1988). For example, Favazza, DeRosear, and Conterio (1989) reported that 38% of university students who engaged in SIB also reported having an eating disorder diagnosis. Similarly, college students who engaged in SIB were more likely to report more than one symptom of an eating disorder than those students who did not engage in SIB (Whitlock, Eckenrode, & Silverman, 2006). Ross and colleagues (2009), using standardized measures in an adolescent community sample, reported that participants in the NSSI group had significantly higher scores on several subscales of eating pathology. Specifically, direct self-injurers scored higher than controls on subscales assessing desire for thinness, bulimic behaviors, body dissatisfaction, feelings of ineffectiveness, increased distrust of other people, difficulty identifying moods, difficulty regulating impulses, and social insecurity.

Two other recent studies merit mention. Brausch and Gutierrez (2010) found that high school students who engaged in direct SIB reported less body satisfaction and more disordered eating than those who had never engaged in direct self-injurious behavior. Furthermore, MacLaren and Best (2010) noted that college students with higher rates of NSSI (defined as 10 or more incidents of NSSI), as well as those who engaged in NSSI less frequently than this, both reported higher rates of food starving (45% and 29%, respectively) than healthy controls (10%) did. Lastly, in a study using ecological momentary assessment methods to assess self-injurious thoughts in real time, adolescents and young adults reported that 15%–20% of the time thoughts of engaging in direct SIB were accompanied by thoughts of binging or purging (Nock, Prinstein, & Sterba, 2009).

Most of the research on self-injurious behavior and eating disorders has documented only their high comorbidity. However, a few researchers have begun to speculate about the potential conceptual, functional, and etiological links between direct self-injury and eating disorders. Some have suggested that direct self-injurious behavior should be listed as a symptom of eating disorders (Alderman, 1997; Cross, 1993; Favaro & Santonastaso, 2000; Favazza et al., 1989). These researchers believe that eating-disordered behavior and direct self-injury might be better viewed as "interchangeable coping strategies" rather than as simply comorbid conditions (Muehlenkamp, 2005). Support for this idea also comes from clinicians, who have noted that when one behavior ceases (self-injury or the eating disorder) the other behavior sometimes becomes manifest (Alderman, 1997; Favaro & Santonastaso, 2000; Favazza et al., 1989; Favazza & Favazza, 1996). Some theorists have further suggested that eating disorders and self-injurious behaviors may have similar origins (e.g., body dissatisfaction or extreme negative affectivity) and may both function to provide a sense of control (Cross, 1993). Another possible explanation is articulated by Lader (2006), who asserts that body-focused behaviors like eating pathology or direct SIB may represent a "fragmentation" where an individual sees herself as separate from others. The body ostensibly serves as the boundary between self and other, and it can also serve as a canvas to convey information about feeling states.

Direct Self-Injury and Continued Involvement in Abusive Relationships

The possible link between direct self-injury and a tendency to be involved in emotionally, sexually, or physically abusive relationships has not yet been adequately researched. Most of what we know comes from the research literature on intimate partner violence (IPV). IPV is defined as a pattern of sexual, physical, or emotional violence by an intimate partner in the context of coercive control (Ford-Gilboe et al., 2009; Tjaden & Thoennes, 2000). In addition to its obvious psychological and emotional effects, IPV has also been found to be associated with increased physical health problems, such as physical injury, chronic pain, gynecological problems, sexually transmitted diseases, and gastrointestinal problems (Campbell, 2002).

Very few studies have examined the specific relationship between IPV and self-injurious behaviors. A landmark study by Sansone et al. (2007) found that the experience of intimate partner physical and psychological violence in adulthood was linked with direct self-injurious behaviors in female psychiatric inpatients. Additionally, Levesque et al. (2010) reported that the experience of IPV (physical, psychological, and sexual) was a significant predictor of recent direct SIB in both female and male university students.

Another area of relevant research examines the impact of relationship violence on other health risk behaviors and suicide. Berenson et al. (2001) investigated the occurrence of SIB in adolescents who either witnessed or experienced violence, broadly defined. They reported that adolescents who had both witnessed *and* experienced violence showed the highest rates of adverse health behaviors. Adolescents in this group reported engaging in direct self-injurious behavior approximately six times more often than those who had neither witnessed nor experienced violence. Additionally, adolescents who witnessed and experienced violence showed increased frequencies of a variety of other risky behaviors. In particular, they were two to four times more likely than those who did not witness or experience violence to engage in substance use, consider suicide, attempt suicide, have an early age of first sexual intercourse, or have a sexual partner who had multiple other sexual partners. It should be noted, however, that violence in this study included robbery, physical assault, threatened or completed rape, and threats to a person's life. The researchers did not specifically measure relationship violence.

It also warrants mention that women with a history of relationship violence show increased health risk behaviors. These include smoking, alcohol, and drug abuse (Golding, 1999; Weaver & Resnick, 2004). Importantly, IPV has also been linked to increased rates of suicidal ideation and suicide attempts (Golding, 1999).

Self-Injury and Risky or Reckless Behaviors

Individuals who make conscious decisions to engage in risky and reckless behaviors that are clearly self-damaging have been little studied. However, one area of research that may be relevant here concerns health risk behaviors. Health risk behaviors are defined as those behaviors that place an individual at increased risk of serious health problems that contribute to death, disability, or social problems (Centers for Disease Control and Prevention, 1997). Research suggests that health risk behaviors such as alcohol and drug use, aggression, early sexual intercourse, not regularly using contraception, and delinquency tend to "cluster together" (Fortenberry, Costa, Jessor, & Donovan, 1997).

There also is evidence linking risky sexual practices in adolescents with direct self-injurious behavior (Brown, Houck, Grossman, Lescano, & Frenkel, 2008; Brown, Houck, Hadley, & Lescano, 2005; DiClemente, Ponton, & Hartley, 1991). Brown and colleagues (2005) reported a unique association between sexual risk behaviors such as infrequent condom use and direct self-injurious behavior. This relationship existed even when psychological and social factors such as impulsivity and sexual abuse history were statistically controlled. Additionally, recent research has noted that the frequency of direct self-injurious behavior may be related to risky sexual behaviors. In a recent study, Brown et al. (2008) found that individuals who had engaged in direct self-injury more than three times during their lives were significantly more likely to have had sex and significantly less likely to use condoms than individuals who had engaged in direct self-injury less frequently than this. Lastly, Hilt and colleagues (2008) reported that adolescents who engaged in direct SIB were significantly more likely to have used substances while engaging in sexual intercourse (i.e., risky sexual behavior) in the past year compared to those who did not engage in direct SIB.

How Might Direct and Indirect Self-injury Be Related?

As is clear from our brief review, indirect forms of self-injury often co-occur with direct self-injury. However, any informed decision about whether the definition of self-injurious behavior should be broadened to include indirect methods of self-harm cannot be based on comorbidity data alone. Bad things often cluster together. Moreover, depression is highly comorbid with direct self-injury (see Nock et al., 2006; Ross & Heath, 2002) as is posttraumatic stress disorder (Favazza & Favazza, 1996; Greenspan & Samuel, 1989; Pitman, 1990). Yet these are not clinical conditions that we would argue are forms of indirect self-injury. Comorbidity data, therefore, only take us so far. They suggest that direct and indirect forms of self-injury are found together. However, they provide no information about why this might be the case.

If forms of direct and indirect self-injury do tend to co-occur, why might this be so? One possibility is that those with an inclination toward self-injury may be drawn to a variety of methods, both direct and indirect. If this is the case, direct and indirect self-injury could be viewed as alternate forms of self-destructive behavior, with the choice of method selected being based on personal preferences, needs, or convenience. If this *alternate behaviors model* is correct, we would anticipate that people who engage in direct and indirect forms of self-injury would score differently from controls on a variety of relevant measures and yet not be significantly different from each other on the same variables.

Another possibility is that direct and indirect forms of self-injury are related behaviors that lie at different points on a severity continuum, with direct self-injury representing a more extreme and severe form of self-harm (*severity model*). To the extent that this is true, we would anticipate that, on all relevant variables of interest, people who engage in direct forms of self-injury would score higher than those who engaged only in indirect forms of self-injury and that both groups would score significantly higher than controls.

Yet another possibility is that direct self-injury represents not only a more severe variant but also a variant with its own distinct psychological characteristics (*distinct condition model*). To the extent that this is true, we might expect that there might be specific variables that would distinguish people who engage in direct forms of self-injury from both healthy controls *and* people who engage in indirect forms of self-injury.

Comparing Direct and Indirect Self-Injury

In an initial effort to explore these different models of association, we examined the similarities and differences between people who engaged in direct self-injurious behavior and people who engaged in only indirect self-injurious behaviors. These included continued involvement in abusive relationships, substance abuse, eating disorders, and reckless or risky behaviors. Although such indirect self-injurious behaviors may be accepted under a very broad definition of self-injurious behavior (see Turp, 2002), there is currently *no* empirical research that compares characteristics of those who only engage in indirect versus direct methods of self-injury.

Our research was designed to explore the following questions. Do individuals who engage *only* in indirect forms of self-injury have clinical characteristics in common with those who engage in direct forms of self-injury? Are people who engage in only indirect self-injury less severe in terms of their general psychopathology than people who engage in direct self-injury? Are there ways in which those who engage in direct forms of self-injury are different from those who engage only in indirect forms of self-injury?

To this end, we recruited a community sample of 156 participants. Of these, 50 participants were currently engaging in direct forms of self-injurious behavior and another 38 reported indirect forms of self-injury. We also recruited a sample of controls (*n* = 68) who reported no history of either direct or indirect self-injury. All participants then completed a battery of self-report measures designed to tap various aspects of psychopathology. These measures included the Beck Depression Inventory (BDI-2; Beck, Steer, & Brown, 1996), a measure of self-criticism (see Hooley, Ho, Slater, & Lockshin, 2010), the Schedule for Non-adaptive and Adaptive Personality (SNAP; Clark, 1993), the Positive and Negative Affect Scales Questionnaire (PANAS; Watson, Clark, & Tellegen, 1988), and the Dissociative Experiences Scale 2 (DES2; Bernstein & Putnam, 1986).

To be included in the study, participants assigned to the direct self-injury group were required to have cut or burned themselves at least twice in the previous 2 months. Case Example 1 provides an illustration of direct self-injury. Indirect forms of self-injury included clinically significant eating disordered behavior, substance use, and risky/reckless behavior. Indirect self-injury is illustrated in Case Example 2.

However, what was notable during participant recruitment was the link between direct and indirect forms of self-injury. With only one exception, *all* of the participants who engaged in direct forms of self-injury also engaged in indirect forms of self-injury. This suggests that direct self-injury rarely occurs in isolation from other forms of self-injurious behaviors. Moreover, what this means for our comparison of direct and indirect self-injuring participants is that the levels of indirect self-harming behaviors are essentially the same across the two groups. More specifically, the only way in which the direct self-injury group differed from the indirect self-injury group was that the former group contained people who cut and burned, whereas the other group did not. Case Example 3 highlights this overlap between direct and indirect self-injury in one of our participants.

The specific details of our findings are described in full elsewhere (see St. Germain & Hooley, 2012). Overall, when the direct and the indirect self-injury groups were compared, the pattern of findings indicated a high degree of similarity between the groups. On a large number of the measures, participants in the direct and indirect self-injury groups had mean scores that were significantly elevated relative to

> ### Case Example 1: Direct Self-Injurious Behavior
>
> Patricia is a 25-year-old female who has been cutting herself since she was 15 years old. When she first started cutting, she cut several times a day for several weeks. Currently, Patricia estimates that she cuts about twice a week. Recently, she cut her left wrist so deep as to sever her radial artery. She reports always feeling pain when she cuts. However, she states that this pain is "really a combination of pain and relief—so each cancels the other out." Patricia reports that she cuts when she is under a lot of stress, angry with herself, or when she feels that she is not in control of things around her. Patricia says that cutting makes her feel more balanced, and that by cutting her focus goes to something else. Recently she has been cutting in front of her boyfriend during interpersonal conflicts, which she reports doing so that someone else feels guilty when they hurt her. Patricia reports that the function of her direct self-injury has changed with time. When she started, it was to feel anything. Later, cutting behavior served as more of a release. In this way, when she was caught up in the moment and something happened, the cutting was "the calm in the middle of the storm." Currently, she views cutting as a way to punish herself for being "defective." Tellingly, Patricia describes cutting as a "good friend that became an enemy."

controls but that were not significantly different from each other. Comparisons of the direct and the indirect self-injury groups revealed no significant differences on measures of dissociation, aggression, impulsivity, self-esteem, negative temperament, depressive symptoms, and borderline personality disorder.

Even in the absence of significant between-group differences, scores for the direct self-injury group were always higher than scores for those in the indirect self-injury group. This might incline us to view direct and indirect self-injury as fundamentally similar constructs with direct self-injury simply being the more severe variant. However, there were also some important (and significant) differences between individuals who engaged in direct self-injury and those who engaged only in indirect methods of self-injurious behavior. The nature and clinical importance of these differences provides support for the distinct condition model described earlier. More specifically, compared with participants in the indirect self-injury group, those who used direct forms of self-injury made more highly negative self-evaluations on a measure of self-criticism (see Glassman, Weierich, Hooley, Deliberto, & Nock, 2007; Hooley, Ho, Slater, & Lockshin, 2010). They also scored significantly higher on the SNAP subscale that measured suicide proneness, and they reported a history of more suicide attempts.

Taken together, these findings suggest that people who engage in indirect and direct forms

> ### Case Example 2: Indirect Self-Injurious Behavior
>
> Alan is a 31-year-old male with a history of anxiety and depression who has been involved in various methods of indirect self-injurious behavior over the past 10 years. First, Alan reports drinking anywhere from two to seven times per week. When he drinks, he "drinks to oblivion"; in other words, he drinks until he loses consciousness. Accordingly, Alan maintains that "there is no in-between with me." He also uses cocaine whenever he can afford it. When he can buy the drug, he uses constantly until the money runs out. Alan also tends to drive when he is under the influence, because he doesn't care what happens to him. Alan reports that he has lost many friends and ruined several relationships because of drinking and drugging. He says that he does not really know why he engages in these behaviors but that he knows that he "makes bad decisions." He does notice that he is more likely to use substances after an argument or when he is experiencing a lot of stress. Lastly, he engages in high-risk sexual encounters. Alan says that "it's not something that I'd like to do or would want to do, but I do it anyways." He has been diagnosed with numerous sexually transmitted diseases as a result of these encounters. He states that when something is due or he is really "stressed out," he looks for these encounters and uses this behavior to avoid more important things. Sadly, Alan believes that he's "not going to be any good" and "just doesn't have good coping skills."

Case Example 3: Direct and Indirect Self-Injurious Behavior

Annette is a 23-year-old single female who has engaged in direct as well as indirect self-injurious behaviors since she was a freshman in high school. She reports that there is "no coping method that is as effective as burning." She prefers to cut or burn instead of engage in other behaviors because she can do it alone. Annette reports that she always feels pain at the start, but once she begins to bleed or blister, she doesn't feel pain anymore. She likes to see how long she can take the pain, so she waits for skin to heal over and then she burns again. Annette reports that it "hurts when I want it to. It releases pain and stress—it's like a literal purging." In terms of indirect self-injury, Annette drinks five times a week until she passes out. She recently stated that eating-disordered behaviors such as restricting her food intake and purging through vomiting were "her new bad idea." In addition, Annette puts herself into risky situations. For example, she went to New York City around 3 a.m. one day with no money and no place to go. She ended up staying with people she had met 2 days earlier via the Internet. Annette resorts to self-injury when she is feeling "any overwhelming emotion," specifically helplessness, guilt, or the urge to punish herself. She says that her motivation to engage in these behaviors is to reflect the fact that she "sucks at life" and "messes up everything."

of self-injury have much in common. Relative to non-self-injuring controls, they show high levels of dispositional negative affect, depression, aggression, impulsivity, and low self-esteem. Dissociative tendencies were also high in both groups. However, there were also some notable differences. Individuals who engaged in direct forms of self-injury viewed themselves in a much more self-critical way than did people who engaged only in indirect forms of self-injury. These individuals also had a much higher potential for suicide (assessed using the SNAP) and also reported having made more suicide attempts in the past.

Conclusion

Self-damaging behaviors that do not deliberately alter bodily tissue have much in common with more direct forms of self-injury. Examples of such "indirect" methods of self-injury include involvement in abusive relationships, substance abuse, reckless behavior, or eating-disordered behavior. Empirical data suggest that there are many similarities between direct self-injurers and those who engage in only indirect methods of self-injury. For example, compared to non-self-injuring controls, those who engaged in direct *or* indirect forms of self-injury are more impulsive, experience more problems with negative emotions (negative temperament, depression), have more problems with aggression, tend to be more undercontrolled in their behavior (disinhibition), and have lower levels of self-esteem. They also have more dissociative experiences and report more symptoms of borderline personality disorder than control participants do. However, despite being very different from the controls on all of

these measures, there were no significant differences between the direct SIB and indirect SIB groups on all of the measures just described. This suggests that although these behaviors appear very different in terms of execution, they may actually belong on a broader continuum of self-injurious behavior.

There are, however, some important differences between people who engage in direct forms of self-injury and those who use more indirect methods. First, those who engage in direct SIB are much more self-critical than people who engage only in indirect forms of self-injury. They also have a higher potential for suicide. This was evident from both the group scores on a measure of suicide proneness and was further supported by the higher number of past suicide attempts (frequency count) that individuals in the direct SIB group reported.

Across all the variables examined, the means for people in the direct group were always higher than the means for those in the indirect group (although both groups generally scored in the clinical range). Nonetheless, direct self-injurers consistently reported somewhat higher levels of psychopathology and impairment than people in the indirect group did, and we were unable to identify any characteristics that were uniquely elevated in the indirect group.

What are the implications of these findings? First, our data provide very little support for the idea that direct and indirect forms of self-injury are simply alternative manifestations of a common underlying set of characteristics or latent construct. On many measures the direct and indirect self-injurious participants scored higher than the non-self-harming controls. However, in every case, mean scores for the direct self-injury group were always higher than the mean scores for the indirect self-injury group. Although these differences were not always statistically significant, it is noteworthy that people in the direct self-injury group invariably showed higher levels of pathology and impairment than people in the indirect self-injury group did. This suggests that, relative to indirect self-injury, direct self-injury represents a more severe form of self-harm.

There were also several measures on which people in the direct self-harm group scored significantly higher than both controls and those in the indirect self-injury group. Individuals who cut or burn themselves hate themselves more than those who engage in more indirect forms of self-injury do. They are also at higher suicide risk. This combination of high self-hatred and elevated suicide proneness may represent a cluster of variables that are particularly important for understanding direct (as opposed to indirect) self-injury.

In conclusion, our data provide no support for regarding direct and indirect forms of self-harm as interchangeable behaviors. Rather, our preliminary findings are more consistent with the distinct condition model. As such, they provide support for current recommendations to conceptualize direct self-injurious behavior as a distinct and independent syndrome (APA, 2013; Muehlenkamp, 2005; Oquendo et al., 2008). The increased suicide potential of people who engage in direct self-injury represents a factor that, even considered alone, provides an important reason for retaining a distinction between direct and indirect self-injurious behavior. If the conceptualization of self-injurious behavior were to be expanded to include indirect forms of self-injury, researchers and clinicians might be in danger of failing to identify those high-risk individuals who are most self-critical and most at risk for suicide. Therefore, expanding the conceptualization of self-injury to include indirect methods of self-injury does not appear to be warranted at this time.

Future Directions: Belief About the Self as a Risk Factor for Nonsuicidal Self-Injury

The role of self-hatred warrants increased attention in the study of direct self-injury. Our data suggest that this is a variable that distinguishes those who engage in direct self-injurious behavior from those who engage in other, more indirect forms of self-injury. Elsewhere, we have also shown that levels of self-hatred are higher in people who engage

in direct self-injury relative to healthy controls, and that beliefs about being bad or defective are associated with increased willingness to endure physical pain (see Hooley et al., 2010). In a study involving ecological momentary assessment, Nock and colleagues (2009) have also reported that self-hatred is a trigger for self-injury in those who already engage in the behavior.

Although beyond the scope of the present chapter, we believe that highly negative core schemas about the self may play a causal role in the development of direct self-injurious behavior. More specifically, they may provide an avenue to understanding why one person chooses to respond to intense negative affect by cutting or burning his or her skin when another person in a similar situation might head to a bar, punch a pillow, go out for a run, or call a friend. People who hold core beliefs about being bad, flawed, or defective (defective self-model; see Hooley et al., 2010) may be less inclined to value (and so protect) their bodies. This may lead these individuals to have less psychological resistance to the idea of direct self-injury than people who have self-schemas that are more benign. Now that direct self-injury (NSSI) is being recognized as an independent disorder, it is incumbent on clinical researchers to learn more about the factors that place individuals at high risk for the development of self-injurious behaviors. We also need to develop effective treatments for NSSI. Cognitive models of the self may represent a productive avenue of inquiry with the potential to facilitate a better understanding of the etiology and treatment of direct self-injurious behavior.

References

Alderman, T. A. (1997). *The scarred soul: Understanding and ending self-inflicted violence.* Oakland, CA: New Harbinger.

American Psychiatric Association. (2013). *Diagnostic and statistical manual of mental disorders* (5th ed.). Washington, DC: Author.

Beck, A. T., Steer, R. A., & Brown, G. K. (1996). *Manual for the Beck Depression Inventory-II.* San Antonio, TX: Psychological Corporation.

Berenson, A. B., Wiemann, C. M., & McCombs, S. (2001). Exposure to violence and associated health risk behaviors among adolescent girls. *Archives of Pediatrics and Adolescent Medicine, 155,* 1238–1242.

Bernstein, E. M., & Putnam, F. W. (1986). Development, reliability, and validity of a dissociation scale. *Journal of Nervous and Mental Disease, 174*(12), 727–735.

Beutrais, A., Joyce, P., Mulder, R., Fergusson, D., Deavoll, B., & Nightingale, S. (1996). Prevalence and comorbidity of mental disorders in persons making serious suicide attempts: A case-control study. *American Journal of Psychiatry, 153,* 1009–1014.

Brausch, A. M., & Gutierrez, P. M. (2010). Differences in non-suicidal self-injury and suicide attempts in adolescents. *Journal of Youth and Adolescence, 39*, 233–242.

Brown, L. K., Houck, C. D., Grossman, C. I., Lescano, C. M., & Frenkel, J. L. (2008). Frequency of adolescent self-cutting as a predictor of HIV risk. *Journal of Developmental and Behavioral Pediatrics, 29*(3), 161–165.

Brown, L. K., Houck, C. D., Hadley, W. S., & Lescano, C. M. (2005). Self-cutting and sexual risk among adolescents in intensive psychiatric treatment. *Psychiatric Services, 56*, 216–218.

Campbell, J. (2002). Health consequences of intimate partner violence. *Lancet, 359*, 1331–1336.

Centers for Disease Control and Prevention (CDC). (1997). Youth risk behavior surveillance: National college health risk behavior survey. *Morbidity and Mortality Weekly Report, 46*(SS-6), 1–54.

Claes, L., Vandereycken, W., & Vertommen, H. (2001). Self-injurious behaviors in eating-disordered patients. *Eating Behaviors, 2*, 263–272.

Claes, L., Vandereycken, W., & Vertommen, H. (2004). Personality traits in eating disordered patients with and without self-injurious behaviors. *Journal of Personality Disorders, 18*, 399–404.

Claes, L., Vandereycken, W., & Vertommen, H. (2005). Self-care versus self-harm: Piercing, tattooing, and self-injuring in eating disorders. *European Eating Disorders Review, 13*, 11–18.

Clark, L. A. (1993). *Schedule for nonadaptive and adaptive personality (SNAP): Manual for administration, scoring, and interpretation.* Minneapolis: University of Minnesota Press.

Conterio, K., & Lader, W. (1998). *Bodily harm: The breakthrough treatment program for self-injurers.* New York, NY: Hyperion.

Cross, L. W. (1993). Body and self in feminine development: Implications for eating disorders and delicate self-mutilation. *Bulletin of the Menninger Clinic, 57*, 41–69.

DiClemente, R. J., Ponton, L. E., & Hartley, D. (1991). Prevalence and correlates of cutting behavior: Risk for HIV transmission. *Journal of the American Academy of Child and Adolescent Psychiatry, 30*, 733–739.

Dohm, F., Striegel-Moore, R., Wilfley, D., Pike, K., Hook, J., & Fairburn, C. (2002). Self-harm and substance abuse in a community sample of black and white women with binge eating disorder or bulimia. *International Journal of Eating Disorders, 32*, 389–400.

Fahy, T., & Eisler, I. (1993). Impulsivity in eating disorders. *British Journal of Psychiatry, 161*, 643–647.

Fairburn, C. G., & Beglin, S. (1994). Assessment of eating disorders: Interview or self-report questionnaire? *International Journal of Eating Disorders, 16*, 363–370.

Favaro, A., & Santonastaso, P. (2000). Self-injurious behaviors in anorexia nervosa. *Journal of Nervous and Mental Disease, 188*, 537–542.

Favazza, A. R., DeRosear, L., & Conterio, K. (1989). Self-mutilation and eating disorders. *Suicide and Life Threatening Behavior, 19*(4), 352–361.

Favazza, A. R., & Favazza, B. (1987). *Bodies under siege: Self-mutilation in culture and psychiatry.* Baltimore, MD: Johns Hopkins University Press.

Favazza, A. R., & Favazza, B. (1996). *Bodies under siege: Self-mutilation in culture and psychiatry* (2nd ed.). Baltimore, MD: Johns Hopkins University Press.

Favazza, A. R., & Rosenthal, R. (1993). Diagnostic issues in self-mutilation. *Hospital and Community Psychiatry, 44*, 134–140.

First, M. B., Spitzer, R. L., Gibbon, M., & Williams, J. B. W. (1996). *Structured clinical interview for DSM-IV axis I disorders, clinician version* (SCID-CV). Washington, DC: American Psychiatric Press.

Ford-Gilboe, M., Wuest, J., Varcoe, C., Davies, L., Merritt-Gray, M., Campbell, J., & Wilk, P. (2009). Modelling the effects of intimate partner violence and access to resources on women's health in the early years after leaving an abusive partner. *Social Science and Medicine, 68*, 1021–1029.

Fortenberry, J., Costa, F., Jessor, R., & Donovan, J. (1997). Contraceptive behavior and adolescent lifestyles: A structural modeling approach. *Journal of Research on Adolescence, 7*, 307–329.

Gavin, D., Ross, H., & Skinner, H. (1989). Diagnostic validity of the drug abuse screening test in the assessment of DSM III drug disorders. *British Journal of Addiction, 84*, 301–307.

Glassman, L. H., Weierich, M. R., Hooley, J. M., Deliberto, T. L., & Nock, M. K. (2007). Child maltreatment, non-suicidal self-injury, and the mediating role of self-criticism. *Behavior Research and Therapy, 45*, 2483–2490.

Golding, J. M. (1999). Intimate partner violence as a risk factor for mental disorders. *Journal of Family Violence, 6*, 81–95.

Greenspan, G. C., & Samuel, S. E. (1989). Self-cutting after rape. *American Journal of Psychiatry, 146*, 789–790.

Gupta, B., & Trzepacz, P. (1997). Serious overdosers admitted to a general hospital: Comparison with nonoverdose self-injuries and mentally ill patients with suicidal ideation. *General Hospital Psychiatry, 19*, 209–215.

Hawton, K., Fagg, J., Simkin, S., Bale, E., & Bond, A. (2000). Deliberate self-harm in adolescents in Oxford, 1985-1995. *Journal of Adolescence, 23*(1), 47–55.

Hilt, L. M., Cha, C. B., & Nolen-Hoeksema, S. (2008). Nonsuicidal self-injury in young adolescent girls: Moderators of the distress-function relationship. *Journal of Consulting and Clinical Psychology, 76*, 63–71.

Hilt, L. M., Nock, M., Lloyd-Richardson, E., & Prinstein, M. (2008). Longitudinal study of non-suicidal self-injury among young adolescents: Rates, correlates, and preliminary test of an interpersonal model. *Journal of Early Adolescence, 28*, 455–469.

Hooley, J. M. (2008). Self-harming behavior: Introduction to the special series on non-suicidal self-injury and suicide. *Journal of Applied and Preventative Psychology, 12*, 155–158.

Hooley, J. M., Ho, D. T., Slater, J., & Lockshin, A. (2010). Pain perception and non-suicidal self-injury: A laboratory investigation. *Personality Disorders: Theory, Research and Treatment, 1*, 170–179. .

Kessler, R., Borges, G., & Walters, E. (1999). Prevalence of and risk factors for lifetime suicide attempts in the National Comorbidity Survey Replication. *Archives of General Psychiatry, 56*, 617–626.

Lader, W. (2006). A look at the increase in body focused behaviors. *Paradigm, 11*, 14–18.

Levesque, C., Lafontaine, M.-F., Bureau, J-F., Cloutier, P., & Dandurand, C. (2010). The influence of romantic attachment and intimate partner violence on non-suicidal self-injury in young adults. *Journal of Youth and Adolescence, 39*, 474–483.

MacLaren, V. V., & Best, L. A. (2010). Nonsuicidal self-injury, potentially addictive behaviors, and the Five Factor Model in undergraduates. *Personality and Individual Differences, 29,* 521–525.

Mischke, H., & Venneri, R. (1987). Reliability and validity of the MAST, Mortimer-Filkins Questionnaire and CAGE in DWI assessment. *Journal of Studies on Alcohol, 48,* 492–501.

Muehlenkamp, J. J. (2005). Self-injurious behavior as a separate clinical syndrome. *American Journal of Orthopsychiatry, 75,* 324–333.

Nock, M. N. (2009). Why do people hurt themselves? New insights into the nature and fucntions of self-injury. *Current Directions in Psychological Science, 18,* 78–783.

Nock, M., Cha, C. B., & Dour, H. J. (2010). Disorders of impulse-control and self-harm. In D. H. Barlow (Ed.), *Oxford handbook of clinical psychology* (pp. 504–529). New York: Oxford University Press.

Nock, M. K., & Favazza, A. R. (2009). Non-suicidal self-injury: Definition and classification. In M. K. Nock (Ed.), *Understanding nonsuicidal self-injury* (pp. 9–18). Washington, DC: American Psychological Association.

Nock, M., Joiner, T., Gordon, K., Lloyd-Richardson, E., & Prinstein, M. (2006). Non-suicidal self-injury among adolescents: Diagnostic correlates and relation to suicide attempts. *Psychiatry Research, 144*(1), 65–72.

Nock, M., Prinstein, M., & Sterba, S. (2009). Revealing the form and function of self-injurious thoughts and behaviors: A real-time ecological assessment study among adolescents and young adults. *Journal of Abnormal Psychology, 118*(4), 816–827.

Nock, M., Wedig, M., Holmberg, E., & Hooley, J. M. (2008). Emotion Reactivity Scale: Psychometric evaluation and relation to self-injurious thoughts and behaviors. *Behavior Therapy, 39,* 107–116.

Oquendo, M., Baca-Garcia, E., Mann, J., & Giner, J. (2008). Issues for DSM-V: Suicidal behavior as a separate diagnosis on a separate axis. *American Journal of Psychiatry, 165,* 1383–1384.

Paul, T., Schroeter, K., Dahme, B., & Nutzinger, D. (2002). Self-injurious behavior in women with eating disorders. *American Journal of Psychiatry, 159,* 408–411.

Pitman, R. K. (1990). Self-mutilation in combat related post-traumatic stress disorder. *American Journal of Psychiatry, 147,* 123–124.

Putnins, A. (1995). Recent drug use and suicidal behavior among young offenders. *Drug and Alcohol Review, 14,* 151–158.

Ross, S., & Heath, N. (2002). A study of the frequency of self-mutilation in a community sample of adolescents. *Journal of Youth and Adolescence, 31,* 67–77.

Ross, S., Heath, N. L., & Toste, J. R. (2009). Non-suicidal self-injury and eating pathology in high school students. *American Journal of Orthopsychiatry, 79,* 83–92.

Sansone, R., & Levitt, J. L. (2002). Self-harm behaviors among those with eating disorders: An overview. *Eating Disorders, 10,* 205–213.

Sansone, R. A., Chu, J., & Wiederman, M. W. (2007). Self-inflicted bodily harm among victims of intimate-partner violence. *Clinical Psychology and Psychotherapy, 14,* 352–357.

Skegg, K. (2005). Self-harm. *Lancet, 366,* 1471–1483.

Solano, R., Fernandez-Aranda, F., Aitken, A., Lopez, C., & Vallejo, J. (2005). Self-injurious behavior in people with eating disorders. *European Eating Disorders Review, 13,* 3–10.

St. Germain, S. A., & Hooley, J. M. (2012). Direct and indirect forms of non-sucidal self-injury: Evidence for a distinction. *Psychiatry Research, 197,* 78–84.

Stein, D., Lilenfeld, L. R., Wildman, P. C., & Marcus, M. D. (2004). Attempted suicide and self-injury in patients diagnosed with eating disorders. *Comprehensive Psychiatry, 45,* 447–451.

Tjaden, P., & Thoennes, N. (2000). *Extent, nature and consequences of intimate partner violence: Findings from the National Violence against Women Survey.* Washington, D.C.: National Institute of Justice and the Center for Disease Control and Prevention.

Turp, M. (2002). The many faces of self-harm. *Psychodynamic Practice, 8,* 197–217.

Walsh, B. W., & Rosen, P. M. (1988). Self-mutilation: Theory, research, and treatment. New York, NY: Guilford Press.

Watson, D., Clark, L. A., & Tellegen, A. (1988). Development and validation of brief measures of positive and negative affect: The PANAS scales. *Journal of Personality and Social Psychology, 54*(6), 1063–1070.

Weaver, T., & Resnick, H. (2004). Toward developing complex multivariate models for examining intimate partner violence-physical health relationship. *Journal of Interpersonal Violence, 19*(11), 1342–1349.

Whitlock, J., Eckenrode, J., & Silverman, D. (2006). Self-injurious behaviors in a college population. *Pediatrics, 117,* 1939–1948.

Winchel, R., & Stanley, M. (1991). Self-injurious behavior: A review of the behavior and biology of self-mutilation. *American Journal of Psychiatry, 148,* 306–317.

Wonderlich, S., Crosby, R., Mitchell, J., Thompson, K., Redlin, J., Demuth, G., Smyth, J., &, .. Haseltine, B. (2001). Eating disturbance and sexual trauma in childhood and adulthood. *International Journal of Eating Disorders, 30,* 401–412.

PART 2

Phenomenology and Epidemiology

Suicidal Behaviors Among Children and Adolescents

Christianne Esposito-Smythers, Julie Weismoore, Rupa P. Zimmermann, *and* Anthony Spirito

Abstract

This chapter examines the prevalence of suicidal ideation and behavior in children and adolescents as well as a number of risk factors that contribute to suicidal behavior. Depression, disruptive behavior disorders, and substance use disorders place adolescents at high risk for suicidal behavior, with comorbidity further increasing risk. Cognitive factors, especially hopelessness and poor problem solving, have also been related to suicidal behavior among adolescents. A prior suicide attempt is one of the best predictors of both a repeat attempt and eventual completed suicide. Research on families indicates that suicidal behavior is transmitted through families. Although abnormalities in the serotonergic system have not been consistently linked to suicidal behavior, genetic and neurobiologic studies suggest that impulsive aggression may be the mechanism through which decreased serotonergic activity is related to suicidal behavior. Findings from intervention studies are modest and indicate the need for substantially more theory-driven treatment research.

Key Words: children, adolescents, suicidal behavior, risk factors, familial transmission, genetics, treatment

Suicidal behavior increases in frequency as children transition from preadolescence through adolescence. This chapter begins with an overview of the prevalence of suicidal ideation and attempts in children and adolescents. The main focus of the chapter is on the risk factors that increase the likelihood of suicidal behavior in adolescents, with an emphasis in emotional, behavioral, and cognitive factors. Genetic and neurobiological contributions to suicidal behavior are also described briefly. The chapter concludes with a review of the literature on the treatment of adolescents who attempt suicide.

Epidemiology
Completed Suicide

Suicide completion was the third leading cause of death among 15- to 24-year-olds in the United States in 2006 (Heron et al., 2009). Suicide incidence increases markedly in the late teenage years

and continues to rise until the early twenties. Among the 15–24 age group, data collected between 1950 and 2004 indicated a peak in death rates for suicide in 1990 (13.2 per 100,000). The increase in the rate of suicide from the 1970s through the late 1990s has been attributed to rising rates of depression, an increase in substance abuse, and the increased availability of firearms among adolescents (Commission on Adolescent Suicide Prevention, 2005). According to the Centers for Disease Control and Prevention (CDC, 2004), death by firearms (49%) is the leading cause of death for persons between 10 and 19 years of age, followed by suffocation (mostly hanging; 38%) and poisoning (7%).

It is only in the past decade that the suicide rate among the 15–24 age group has begun to decrease. In 2000, suicide rates decreased (10.2 per 100,000), and rates did not significantly vary through 2004 (US Department of Health & Human Services, [US

DHHS], 2006). Most recently, the rate of suicide in 2006 among 15- to 24-year-olds was 9.9 per 100,000 (Heron et al., 2009). It is unclear why this decrease occurred. Olfson and colleagues (2002) note there was more than a three-fold increase in antidepressant use by adolescents between 1987 and 1996, which might account for the decrease in suicide. In addition, suicide awareness programs were introduced into high schools during the mid-1980s.

When the 15- to 19-year-old age group is considered, a different pattern emerges. Specifically, the suicide rate increased 18% from 2003 to 2004 (CDC, 2007). Bridge, Greenhouse, Weldon, Campo, and Kelleher (2008) found that the suicide rate in this age group decreased 5.3% between 2004 and 2005 but note that the rates in both 2004 and 2005 were still significantly higher than the rates that would be expected based on the 1996–2003 trends. Bridge et al. (2008) suggest a range of factors that could account for these increases, including an increase in known risk factors, higher rates of untreated depression due to the black box warnings on selective serotonin reuptake inhibitors, an increase in the use of Internet social networking, and an increase in suicide among US soldiers.

Suicide Ideation and Attempt

Based on US data from the 2007 Youth Risk Behavior Surveillance (YRBS) data, 14.5% of teenagers seriously consider attempting suicide and 11.3% of youth develop a suicide plan. Additionally, 6.9% of teenagers attempt suicide one or more times (Eaton et al., 2008). Further, 2.0% of teenagers make a suicide attempt that results in an injury, poisoning, or overdose that has to be treated by a doctor or nurse (Eaton et al., 2008).

Gender

Differences by gender in completed suicide among 15- to 29-year-olds are pronounced (US DHHS, 2006): 16.8 per 100,000 for males and 3.6 for females in 2004. Death rates for suicide among females peaked in 1980 (4.3) and in 1994 for males (23.0). However, in males the trend increased steadily from 1950 (6.5) to its peak in 1994 (23.0) and began decreasing thereafter to 17.1 per 100,000 in 2004. For females, the trend in suicide rates is much more stable: 2.6 per 100,000 in 1950, and 3.6 in 2004.

Gender differences also exist in nonlethal suicidal behaviors. Results from the 2007 YRBS of high school students show that the prevalence of having seriously considered attempting suicide was higher among female (18.7%) than male (10.3%) students (Eaton et al., 2008). Similarly, the prevalence of having developed a suicide plan was higher among female (13.4%) than male (9.2%) students as were suicide attempts, females (9.3%) compared to males (4.6%) and suicide attempts that had to be treated by a doctor or nurse, females (2.4%) compared to males (1.5%).

Why is this gender difference so pronounced? Psychological factors and sex-related method preferences are considered to contribute to the pattern of gender differences (Shaffer & Hicks, 1994). The gender difference in youth suicide is most likely due to the greater likelihood of males having multiple risk factors for suicide such as comorbid mood and alcohol abuse disorders, greater levels of aggression, and choice of more lethal suicide attempt methods, which make them more likely than females to make a lethal suicide attempt (Brent, Baugher, Bridge, Chen, & Chiapetta, 1999; Gould, Fisher, Parides, Flory, & Shaffer, 1996; Shaffer & Pfeffer, 2001).

Race/Ethnicity

In the United States, rates of death by suicide were highest among 15- to 24-year-old Native American males, with a rate of 30.7 per 100,000 in 2004, followed by White (not Hispanic or Latino) males with a rate of 19.0 and White (includes those of Hispanic and non-Hispanic origin) males with a rate of 17.9 (US DHHS, 2006). Asian and Pacific Islanders had the lowest suicide rate (females, 2.8; males, 9.3) among youth (US DHHS, 2006). As noted earlier, Native Americans report the highest rates of attempted suicide during adolescence. The National American Indian Adolescent Health Survey (Borowsky, Resnick, Ireland, & Blum, 1999) sampled more than 11,000 Native American students in schools on reservations in eight Indian Health Service areas. The overall rate of lifetime suicide attempts was 16.8%, and the rate for girls was 21.8%. However, the rates varied considerably across tribes. The high rates among Native Americans have been related to low social integration, access to firearms, and substance abuse (Middlebrook, LeMaster, Beals, Novins, & Manson, 2001).

White youth traditionally have had higher suicide rates than non-White youth, but the gap has been narrowing due to an increase in youth suicide among African American males (Centers for Disease Control and Prevention, 2005). In recent years, suicide and nonfatal suicidal behavior have emerged as crucial health issues for African American youth (Goldsmith, Pellmar, Kleinman, & Bunny, 2002).

Although African American youth have historically had lower suicide rates than have White youth, during 1980 to 1995 the suicide rate increased 233% among 10- to 14-year-old African Americans compared to a 120% increase among White youth in this age group, and increased 126% among 15- to 19-year-old African Americans compared with a 19% increase among White youth in this age group (Borowsky, Ireland, & Resnick, 2001; CDC, 1998).

According to the 2007 YRBS data (Eaton et al., 2008), Hispanic adolescents seriously considered attempting suicide in the prior year at higher rates than White or Black adolescents (see Table 5.1). The prevalence of having made a suicide plan in the prior year was also higher among Hispanic adolescents (12.8%) than White (10.8%) and Black (9.5%) adolescents. Hispanic adolescents consistently report higher rates of suicide attempts than other groups, especially among females. Suicide attempts that required medical attention were also higher among Hispanic (2.9%) than White (1.5%) adolescents.

Age of Onset and Course

Suicide is uncommon in childhood and early adolescence. Among the 10- to 14-year-old group, most suicides occur between ages 12 and 14 years. After puberty, rates of suicide increase with age until they stabilize in young adulthood. In 2006, there were 219 suicides in the United States among children between the ages of 5 and 14 years as compared to 4,189 suicides among youth aged 15 to 24 years (Heron et al., 2009). Some possible explanations for why suicide rates consistently increase from childhood to adolescence include the greater prevalence of psychopathology that emerges during adolescence, particularly combinations of mood disorder and substance abuse (Brent et al., 1999; Groholt, Ekeberg, Wichstrom, & Haldorsen, 1998; Shaffer, Gould, Fisher, & Trautman, 1996). Moreover, adolescents possess further developed cognitive skills than younger children and are thus more capable of planning and executing a lethal suicide attempt (Brent et al., 1999; Groholt et al., 1998). In addition, older adolescents have more autonomy and less parental supervision and social support, which may increase the likelihood for disconnection and make recognition of imminent risk less likely.

According to Lewinsohn and colleagues (1996), longitudinal studies provide evidence indicating that the more severe (high intent or planning) and persistent (high frequency or duration) the suicidal ideation, the more likely it is that suicidal ideation may eventuate in an attempt. Suicide attempters who demonstrate persistent suicidal ideation, particularly with a plan or high intent to commit suicide, or both, are at increased risk for making another suicide attempt (Goldston et al., 1999; Lewinsohn, Rohde, & Seeley, 1996). Suicidal behavior tends to reoccur and may be a warning of suicide completion (Bridge, Goldstein, & Brent, 2006). A prior suicide attempt is the single most significant risk factor for youth suicide in both case-control and prospective studies, increasing the risk of a subsequent completion 10–60 fold (Brent et al., 1999; Shaffer et al., 1996). The risk for repetition is highest in the first 3–6 months after a suicide attempt but remains substantially elevated from the general population for at least 2 years (Goldston et al., 1999; Lewinsohn et al., 1996). The risk of suicidal behavior reoccurring is estimated to range from 10% upon a 6-month follow-up to 42% upon a 21-month follow-up, with a median recurrence rate of 5%–15% per year (Goldston et al., 1999; Hawton, Zahl, & Weatherall, 2003). Among suicide attempters, the rates of subsequent completed suicide are 0.5%–1.0% per year; these rates are considerably elevated compared to the general population (Hawton et al., 2003).

Primary Individual Risk Factors

In this section, we review selected emotional, behavioral, and cognitive risk factors for attempted

Table 5.1 Rates of Seriously Considering and Actual Attempting Suicide in the Prior Year Among Adolescents by Race and Gender

	Seriously Considered Attempting Suicide in Prior Year (%)	Attempted Suicide in Prior Year (%)
Hispanic		
Male	10.7	6.3
Female	21.1	14.0
Black		
Male	8.5	5.5
Female	18.0	9.9
White		
Male	10.2	3.4
Female	17.8	7.7

Source: From the 2007 Youth Risk Behavior Surveillance Survey (Eaton et al., 2008).

and completed suicide among adolescents. We draw upon thorough comprehensive reviews, cited in each respective area, when coming to conclusions. We begin each section with a brief overview of a specific risk factor followed by a few representative studies, with an emphasis given to recent prospective research. Particular attention is paid to cognitive processes found to underlie risk factors, particularly emotional and behavioral states. The neurobiology of suicide is reviewed later in this volume (see also Chapter 11). It is also important to note that this review focuses on studies conducted with adolescents, primarily between the ages of 13 to 18 years. For a comprehensive review of risk factors associated with completed suicide in children and younger adolescents (ages < 14 years), see Dervic, Brent, and Oquendo (2008).

Emotional States and Disorders

A number of emotional states have been associated with adolescent suicidal behavior, with the primary states including depressed mood, anxiety, and anger (Evans, Hawton, & Rodham, 2004; Wolfsdorf, Freeman, D'Eramo, Overholser, & Spirito, 2003). Though most research has examined the link between depressed mood and suicidality, anxiety and anger may be equally important when explaining suicidal behavior. Next we review studies on the symptoms of each emotional state followed by research on the psychiatric disorder typically found to accompany each state.

DEPRESSED MOOD AND MOOD DISORDERS

Numerous studies have documented a strong and consistent association between depressed mood and adolescent suicidal behavior across clinical and community-based samples (Evans et al., 2004). For example, Goldston, Reboussin, and Daniel (2006) followed a sample of 180 adolescents discharged from a psychiatric inpatient unit for a median of 11 years (range of 6 months to 13 years). They found that self-reported depressive symptoms predicted future suicide attempts. There also exists evidence to suggest that specific depressive symptoms may be more strongly associated with suicidal behavior than other symptoms (Wolfsdorf et al., 2003). Nrugham, Larsson, and Sund (2008) followed a representative sample of 2,464 high school students and found that the depressive symptoms of disturbed concentration, middle insomnia, and hopelessness were correlated with suicide attempts but only worthlessness, assessed at age 15, was prospectively found to predict suicide attempts between

15 to 20 years of age. Greater severity of depressed mood has been associated with slower remission of suicidal ideation among previously hospitalized adolescents (Prinstein et al., 2008).

Research also suggests that the association between severity of depressed mood and adolescent suicidality may vary as a function of suicide history. Esposito, Spirito, Boergers, and Donaldson (2003) found that adolescents with a history of more than one suicide attempt (repeat suicide attempters) reported more severe depressive symptoms than first-time attempters. In a similar study, Goldston, Daniel, Reboussin, and Kelley (1996) found that repeat suicide attempters but not first-time attempters (all of whom made an attempt within the last 2 weeks) reported more severe depressive symptoms than adolescents with no suicide attempt history. These results suggest that a severe depressed mood may be a particularly salient risk factor for repeat suicide attempters, but other mood states, as well as cognitive and behavioral factors, may play a greater role for recent first-time adolescent attempters.

Similar to research on depressive mood states, depressive disorders have consistently been associated with completed and attempted suicide among adolescents (Evans et al., 2004; Gould, Greenberg, Velting, & Shaffer, 2003). In a review conducted by Gould et al. (2003), rates of depressive disorders among adolescent suicide victims were found to range from 49% to 64%. Further, the odds ratios of completed suicide among adolescents with mood disorders ranged from 11 to as high as 27. In contrast, findings regarding rates of bipolar disorders among suicide victims have been mixed with some reporting high and others low rates (Gould et al., 2003).

A formal diagnosis of major depression disorder (MDD) also is common in attempted suicide. In a naturalistic prospective study conducted by Goldston et al. (2009), 180 adolescents discharged from an adolescent psychiatric inpatient unit were followed and repeatedly assessed for up to 13 years. After controlling for demographic variables and prehospitalization suicide attempts, MDD and dysthymic disorder were found to be associated with increased risk for suicide attempts. MDD, in particular, was associated with more than a five-fold increase in risk for suicide attempts, with this relationship strengthening as adolescents grew older. Further, MDD and dysthymia were found to be more common among repeat than first-time attempters. Nrugham et al. (2008) also found an association between mood disorders and suicide attempts in a large community-based sample of 2,464 high school students. However, in their study, MDD and depressive disorder not otherwise specified (MDDNOS) were found to correlate with suicide attempts among adolescents, while only dysthymia diagnosed at age 15 was found to prospectively predict suicide attempts between 15 to 20 years of age, even after controlling for depressive symptoms. Research has also begun to examine the association between pediatric bipolar disorder and suicide attempts among adolescents. In a large clinical sample of 405 children and adolescents, ages 7–17 years, approximately one-third of youth reported a history of suicide attempts (Goldstein et al., 2005).

The association between mood disorders and suicidal behavior may be explained, in part, through cognitive processes associated with depression. Research conducted to date suggests that cognitive errors (e.g., overgeneralization, catastrophizing, selective abstraction), the cognitive triad (i.e., negative views of self, world, and future), and depressive automatic thoughts (e.g., "I don't deserve to be loved") are associated with depression in youth (Jacobs, Reinecke, Gollan, & Kane, 2008; Shirk, Boergers, Eason, & Van Horn, 1998). These cognitive processes occur with high frequency and are difficult to control. Automatic thoughts, in particular, are believed to pervade streams of consciousness and occur almost involuntarily. With repeated negative behavioral events, these dysfunctional cognitions become more stable and pervasive, especially if left untreated. It is at this point that suicidal behavior may be contemplated. Indeed, cognitive errors and components of the cognitive triad (e.g., hopelessness and worthlessness) have been associated with suicidality among adolescents (Brent, Kolko, Allan, & Brown, 1990; Kingsbury, Hawton, Steinhardt, & James, 1999).

ANXIETY SYMPTOMS AND DISORDERS

Similar to research in the area of depressed mood, an ample amount of research suggests that adolescent suicide attempters report elevated levels of anxiety. Generally, research in this area suggests that adolescent suicide attempters report higher levels of anxiety than those without an attempt history, though results are not always consistent (Evans et al., 1994). Goldston et al. (1999, 2006) found that self-reported symptoms of anxiety, particularly trait anxiety, predicted future suicide attempts in adolescents over shorter (5 years) and longer term (median of 11 years) follow-up. Brezo et al. (2008) followed a representative randomly selected community sample of 2,000 children (ages 6–12 years) into early adulthood (ages 19–24 years). They found that high-risk anxiousness trajectories, relative to low risk, were associated with a 60% increase in the likelihood of attempted suicide, though this finding was reduced to a trend level when covariates were controlled. Similar to depressed mood, there also exists evidence to suggest that anxiety may be increased with repetitive suicidal behavior (Goldston et al., 1996).

Research also suggests that a formal diagnosis of an anxiety disorder is associated with adolescent suicidal behavior (Evans et al., 2004), though results have been somewhat mixed. Goldston et al. (2009) found that generalized anxiety disorder and panic disorder predicted future suicide attempts, though only panic disorder remained significant in a multivariate model. Generalized anxiety and panic disorder were also found to be more common among repeat in comparison to first-time attempters. In contrast, in a large epidemiologic sample of children and adolescents ages 9 to 16 years, although anxiety disorders were found to predict suicidality (ideation, plans, and/or attempts) over the course of 3-month follow-up in univariate analyses, this association was reduced to a trend level after adjusting for other disorders and covariates. However, follow-up analyses suggested that generalized anxiety disorder did predict suicidality when comorbid with major depressive disorder (Foley, Goldston, Costello, & Angold, 2006).

Similar to mood disorders, anxiety disorders may also be associated with suicidality through associated cognitive distortions. Research has shown that adolescents with anxiety disorders have a lower threshold for perceived threat, underestimate their competency in dealing with perceived threat, expect negative outcomes in threatening situations, and experience higher levels of anxious automatic thoughts in comparison to youth without anxiety disorders (Barrett, Rapee, Dadds, & Ryan, 1996; Bögels & Zigterman, 2000). Over time, such anxious thoughts may become overwhelming, especially when combined with depression-related cognitive distortions (see comorbidity), as anxiety and depressive disorders often co-occur. Under such conditions, suicidal behavior may be considered as a means of escape. Further, research suggests that a combination of internalizing and externalizing disorders may pose a particularly high risk for suicidal behavior among adolescents (Foley et al., 2006; Goldston et al., 2009).

ANGER

Research suggests that the association between anger and suicidality varies as a function of suicide history. In an adolescent inpatient sample, Stein, Apter, Ratzoni, Har-Even, and Avidan (1998) found that repeat attempters, first-time attempters, and nonsuicidal inpatient controls, reported more trait anger than community controls, but only repeat suicide attempters reported more anger than nonsuicidal inpatients. Esposito, Spirito, Boerger, and Donaldson (2003) found evidence to suggest that repeat adolescent suicide attempters report higher levels of trait anger than first-time attempters in an emergency room adolescent sample. In a third study that took recency of suicidal behavior into account, Goldston et al. (1996) found higher levels of self-reported trait anger among previous (but not current) suicide attempters than among adolescents who recently made a repeat attempt, those who recently made a first suicide attempt, and those who never made a suicide attempt in a sample of inpatients. When level of state anger was examined, no differences were found across groups. Cumulatively, results suggest that when recency of suicidal behavior is *not* taken into account, adolescents with more significant suicide histories appear to report particularly high levels of trait anger. However, the work of Goldston et al. (1996) suggests that recent suicidal behavior may have a cathartic effect with respect to anger.

In line with Goldston's work, research suggests that some adolescents may engage in suicidal behavior as a means of permanently ending or coping with unresolved anger. This may be particularly true for adolescents who endorse "a wish to die" as a motivation for their suicide attempt (Boergers, Spirito, & Donaldson, 1998). Research also suggests that a suicide attempt effectively reduces anger-related emotional arousal for some adolescents and/or temporarily suspends situations that provoke intense anger. Negron, Piacentini, Graae, Davies, and Shaffer (1997) conducted a study that examined self-reported levels of anger before and after a suicidal crisis that was precipitated by a significant stressor. Anger was found to increase from the time of the precipitant stressor to the time of the suicidal crisis for all adolescents. However, those who carried through with an attempt during the suicidal crisis reported a greater decrease in anger than those with only suicidal ideation.

Behavioral Factors and Disorders

Prior suicidal behavior, nonsuicidal self-injury, impulsivity, and aggression are among some of the most well-studied behavioral factors associated with suicidality among adolescents (Esposito, Spirito, & Overholser, 2003). Impulsivity and aggression are often manifest in adolescents diagnosed with externalizing disorders, such as disruptive behavior and substance use disorders, which have also been linked with completed and attempted suicide among adolescents (Esposito-Smythers & Spirito, 2004; Evans et al., 2004; Gould et al., 2003a). Further, research suggests that a combination of internalizing and externalizing disorders may pose a particularly high risk for suicidal behavior among adolescents (Foley et al., 2006; Goldston et al., 2009).

PRIOR SUICIDAL BEHAVIOR

A prior suicide attempt is one of the best predictors of eventual completed suicide (Shaffer et al., 1996) as well as future suicide attempts (Goldston et al., 2009; Prinstein et al., 2008) among adolescents. Prior suicide attempts are estimated to occur in 25% to 33% of all completed suicides (Shaffer et al., 1996). Hawton et al. (2003) followed a sample of 5,414 adolescents and young adults (ages 10 to 24 years) who presented to a hospital following an act of deliberate self-harm (defined as intentional self-poisoning or self-injury regardless of motivation) and found that the risk of completed suicide over the course of 1 year among this group was 35 times the annual population risk in males and 75 times the annual population risk in females. In a study conducted by Goldston et al. (1999), the number of prior attempts was found to be the strongest predictor of a posthospitalization suicide attempt (Goldston et al., 1999). Groholt, Ekeberg, and Haldorsen (2006) followed 106 adolescents who were hospitalized for a suicide attempt and found that approximately 64% of these adolescents reported a repeat attempt within 24 months.

Theories of suicidal behavior suggest that prior suicidal experiences sensitize the individual to suicide-related thoughts and behaviors (Beck, 1996; Joiner 2005). Relatedly, Joiner (2005) emphasizes that a capacity to engage in lethal self-injury must be acquired over time. This acquisition can happen in a number of ways. The most straightforward method is repeated suicide attempts that slowly increase in severity. However, the experience of extreme injury and pain (or threat thereof) over time can also lead individuals to lose their innate fear of pain, thus allowing them to engage in lethal self-injurious acts (Joiner, 2005; Van Orden, Witte, Gordon, Bender, & Joiner, 2008). Joiner (2005) suggests that people become capable of suicidal behavior only after they have habituated to dangerous behavior. Therefore, it is possible that prior suicidal behavior lowers the threshold of stress needed to precipitate future suicidal behavior. Given that repetitive suicidal behavior has also been associated with more severe psychiatric disturbance (Esposito, Spirito, Boergers, & Donaldson, 2003; Goldston et al., 1996, 2009; Stein et al., 1998), the combination of the repetitive sensitization of the suicidal experience, severe psychiatric disturbance, and associated cognitive distortion may place repeat attempters at particularly high risk for completed suicide.

NONSUICIDAL SELF-INJURY

Self-harm without suicidal intent, referred to as nonsuicidal self-injury (NSSI), is associated with adolescent suicidal behavior. Joiner (2005) suggests that both suicidal injury and NSSI may lead an individual to habituate to pain, which in turn, increases the probability of future suicidal acts. In line with this theory, NSSI has been found to be highly prevalent among adolescent suicide attempters and to differentiate repeat from first-time attempters. Nock, Joiner, Gordon, Lloyd-Richardson, and Prinstein (2006) found that 70% of psychiatrically hospitalized adolescents with a history of NSSI reported a lifetime history of a suicide attempt and 55% reported a history of multiple suicide attempts. Esposito, Spirito, Boergers, and Donaldson (2003) found greater severity of NSSI among multiple than first-time adolescent suicide attempters. Further, Prinstein et al. (2008) found greater frequency of NSSI to be associated with slower remission of suicidal ideation among previously hospitalized adolescents, suggesting that NSSI may also be associated with a poor outcome among suicidal youth.

IMPULSIVE AND AGGRESSIVE BEHAVIORS

Impulsivity and aggression are two behaviors that have been studied in relation to adolescent suicidality. In a review of related literature, Turecki (2005) concluded that adolescent suicide completers and attempters exhibit higher levels of impulsivity than both nonsuicidal adolescents and older suicidal adults. However, Tureki (2005) notes that findings have been somewhat mixed, which may, in part, be due to the use of different methods to assess impulsivity (e.g., self-report versus performance-based tasks), differences in the manner in which impulsivity is defined across studies, and limitations associated with current measurement approaches. McGirr et al. (2008) used behavioral and personality trait self-report assessments to examine impulsivity in a

sample of 645 suicide completers (ages 11–87 years). Impulsivity was found to be negatively associated with age of suicide, even after controlling for major psychopathology. Sanislow, Grilo, Fehon, Axelrod, and McGlashan (2003) examined impulsivity as a correlate of suicide risk (ideation and/or behavior) in a sample of 81 psychiatrically hospitalized adolescents and 81 adolescents detained in a juvenile detention facility. After controlling for depressive symptoms, impulsivity predicted suicidality for the juvenile offenders, but not for the psychiatrically hospitalized adolescents. Thus, the association between impulsivity and suicidality may vary as a function of the sample characteristics (i.e., impulsivity is associated with suicide in adolescent and young adult samples rather than older persons) and samples with higher levels of conduct/externalizing problems.

Research also suggests that there is a connection between aggressive and suicidal behaviors for some adolescents (see also Chapter 27). Similar to the impulsivity literature, aggression is often measured and defined differently across studies, which may contribute to discrepant findings. Renaud, Berlim, McGirr, Tousignant, and Turecki (2008) compared informant reports of aggressive behaviors in a sample of 55 child and adolescent suicide victims to a community control sample of 55 nonsuicidal adolescents. History of aggressive behavior was found to be significantly greater among adolescent suicide completers than community controls. However, in a multivariate model controlling for psychiatric factors, the relation between aggression and suicide was reduced to nonsignificance. In a psychiatrically hospitalized sample of 270 adolescents, Kerr et al. (2007) failed to find a difference in self- or parent-report of aggression between those with and without a history of a suicide attempt (past month or lifetime) in the sample as a whole. However, youth self-report of aggression was found to be associated with suicidal behavior among youth with internalizing symptoms. In another study, O'Donnell, Stueve, and Wilson-Simmons (2005) followed a community sample of 769 African American and Latino adolescents over the course of 3 years. Aggressive behaviors reported by adolescents in the 8th grade (i.e., fighting, carrying a weapon, use of a weapon) were found to predict suicidality (ideation, plan, and/or attempt) in the 11th grade for females but not for males.

Beyond trait-level assessment of aggression, the association between more relational forms of aggression, such as bullying, and adolescent suicidality has also been examined. A recent review conducted by Kim and Leventhal (2008) suggests that adolescent perpetrators and victims of bullying are at increased risk for suicidal behavior. In a sample of 208 Swedish adolescents, Ivarsson, Broberg, Arvidsson, and Gillberg (2005) found that involvement in any kind of bullying (victim, perpetrator, both) was associated with a history of suicide attempts. Likewise, Kim, Leventhal, Koh, and Boyce (2009) prospectively used a peer nomination design to study bullying and risk for suicide in a sample of 1,655 Korean 7th and 8th graders. Results indicated that adolescent perpetrators and victims of bullying were at increased risk for suicidal ideation and attempts compared to adolescents not involved in any form of bullying.

Though impulsivity and aggression have been examined independently in the adolescent suicide literature, more recent research has focused on impulsive aggression (i.e., quickly responding with heightened levels of hostility/anger to frustration or confrontation). Recent research suggests that impulsive aggression may be genetically transmitted (Brent & Melhem, 2008; Bronisch & Lieb, 2008). A number of family studies (see the "Family Risk Factors" section for a more detailed review) suggest that impulsive aggression in adolescent offspring (Melhem et al., 2007) or both parent and adolescent offspring (Brent et al., 2002) increases risk of an adolescent suicide attempt. Brent et al. (2003) found that impulsive aggression among adolescent offspring was the most powerful predictor of the transmission of suicidal behavior from parent to child.

DISRUPTIVE BEHAVIOR DISORDERS

Research suggests that an association exists between disruptive behavior disorders and completed and attempted suicide among adolescents, particularly in the presence of comorbid mood disorders (Evans et al., 2004; Gould et al., 2003). In studies of completed suicide, approximately one-third of male suicide victims were found to have had a conduct disorder diagnosis (see Gould et al., 2003). Goldston et al. (2009) found that conduct disorder and attention-deficit/hyperactivity disorder predicted future suicide attempts, though only conduct disorder remained significant in a multivariate model. Further, follow-up analyses suggested that conduct disorder primarily conferred risk for attempted suicide in the presence of major depressive disorder. In a large epidemiologic sample of 1,420 children and adolescents ages 9 to 16 years,

disruptive behavior disorders were found to predict suicidality (ideation, plans, and/or attempts) over the course of 3-month follow-up, even after adjusting for other disorders and covariates (Foley et al., 2006). There is a particularly strong association between disruptive behavior disorders and repetitive suicidal behavior (Esposito, Spirito, & Overholser, 2003).

Aggression is one behavior found to underlie disruptive behavior disorders such as oppositional defiant and conduct disorders. An association between aggression and the tendency to attribute hostile intention to others, referred to as "hostile attribution bias," has been well documented (Dodge, 2006). This cognitive distortion may play a role in the association between disruptive behavior disorders and adolescent suicidality. Adolescents who consistently misperceive hostility in interactions with others may feel persecuted and victimized. Further, they may lose their affiliations with healthy peers by responding to their distorted perceptions of hostility with aggression. Aggressive responding in ambiguous situations, when considered unwarranted by peers, can bring about peer rejection (Dodge, 2006). Over time, misperceptions of hostility and related negative feedback may become increasingly overwhelming for adolescents at which point suicide may be considered as a viable option for escape, especially when adolescents also have concurrent problem-solving deficiencies (see the section on "Problem Solving").

SUBSTANCE USE DISORDERS

Substance use disorders (SUDs) have been associated with both completed and attempted suicide among adolescents. In a review conducted by Esposito-Smythers and Spirito (2004), rates of any SUD among adolescent suicide completers were found to range from 27% to 50%, alcohol use disorder ranged from 22% to 27%, and rates of illicit drug use disorders ranged from 13% to 25%. Compared to matched community controls, adolescent suicide completers were 6 to 8.5 times more likely to be diagnosed with any SUD, eight times more likely to have an alcohol use disorder, and almost nine times more likely to have an illicit drug use disorder (Esposito-Smythers & Spirito, 2004)

A relationship also has been found between SUDs and suicide attempts, particularly in the presence of comorbid disorders. Esposito-Smythers and Spirito (2004) also reviewed the suicide attempt literature and concluded that adolescent suicide attempters exhibit elevated rates of SUDs. Rates of alcohol and/or cannabis use disorders were found to range from 27% to 50% among suicide attempters. Across studies reviewed, the presence of an alcohol use disorder and/or an SUDs was associated with a three- to six-fold increase in suicide attempts. Variation in rates can be explained in part by the sample (inpatient, outpatient), method of diagnostic assessment (research diagnostic interview vs. clinical interview), and the age of the sample (Esposito-Smythers & Spirito, 2004).

Results of more recent longitudinal research conducted with community samples yield consistent findings. In a naturalistic longitudinal study in which 180 adolescents were followed for up to 13 years post psychiatric hospitalization, Goldston et al. (2009) found that SUDs predicted future suicide attempts in univariate analyses and that the relation between SUDs and suicidality strengthened as adolescents grew older. However, this association was nonsignificant in multivariate analyses, suggesting SUDs primarily confer risk for suicidal behavior in the presence of other mental health disorders. Similar results were found in a large epidemiologic sample of 1,420 children and adolescents ages 9 to 16 years. SUDs only predicted suicidality (ideation, plans, and/or attempts) in the presence of other mental health disorders, particularly depression, over the course of 3-month follow-up (Foley et al., 2006). Additionally, some research suggests that rates of alcohol and cannabis use disorders increase with repetitive suicidal behavior (D'Eramo, Prinstein, Freeman, Grapentine, & Spirito, 2004).

In a recent review, Bagge and Sher (2008) provide an empirically based conceptual framework for understanding the complex relation between alcohol use and suicidal behavior, much of which can also be applied to substances other than alcohol. Bagge and Sher (2008) explore the empirical basis for two dimensions of this association—directionality (i.e., alcohol leads to suicidal behavior, suicidal behavior leads to alcohol use, or a spurious relation) and temporality (proximal versus distal effects of alcohol use and suicidal behavior). For example, one model offered by Hufford (2001) suggests that alcohol increases risk for suicidal behavior in a proximal as well as distal manner. The acute effects of intoxication may heighten psychological distress, increase aggressiveness (toward self and others), enhance suicide-specific alcohol expectancies (e.g., "alcohol will give me the courage to make a suicide attempt"), and inhibit the generation and implementation of adaptive coping strategies. Among individuals contemplating suicide, this concurrent increase in

psychological distress, aggressiveness, and cognitive distortion may be sufficient to propel suicidal thoughts into action. When examined distally, alcohol use disorders may be associated with increases in stress and co-occurring psychopathology, which, in turn, increases risk for suicidal behavior. Over time, stress resulting from substance-related social, academic, and/or legal problems, when combined with depressive symptoms, may reach a level where a suicide attempt is viewed as a means to cope with perceived insurmountable difficulties and emotions. Bagge and Sher (2008) conclude that the association between alcohol and suicidal behavior is complex, and not fully understood.

CO-OCCURRING MOOD AND BEHAVIOR RISK FACTORS/DISORDERS

Studies that have examined psychiatric risk factors for adolescent suicidal behavior concur that various combinations of comorbidity, within and across internalizing and externalizing diagnoses, increase risk for completed and attempted suicide. Goldston et al. (2009) found that the likelihood of adolescent suicide attempts increased by 250% with each additional psychiatric disorder. The majority of research suggests that mood disorders, in combination with anxiety, disruptive behavior, and/or SUDs, is associated with increased risk for suicide completion and attempts.

Studies of suicide victims suggest that mood disorders in combination with a conduct or substance use disorder (Brent et al., 1993; Shaffer et al., 1996) increase risk for completed suicide. Results are similar for studies with suicide attempters. Goldston et al. (2009) found that comorbid diagnoses of major depression and conduct disorder contributed unique risk for suicide attempts. Foley et al. (2006) found that risk for suicidality (ideation, plans, and/or attempts) was greatest for adolescents when MDD was found to be comorbid with general anxiety disorder or oppositional-defiant disorder.

Adolescents with comorbid conditions may experience cognitive distortions associated with each independent diagnosis. Indeed, Ronan and Kendall (1997) found that depressed/anxious adolescents reported more distorted cognitive processes than depressed-only and control groups. Similarly, Epkins (2000) found that comorbid (aggressive/delinquent and depressed/anxious) and internalizing groups of adolescents reported similar levels of cognitive distortions, which were higher than those in both externalizing and control groups. This increase in cognitive dysfunction associated with internalizing disorders may be responsible for the increased risk of suicidal behavior found in both internalizing and comorbid conditions.

Cognitive Factors

Earlier we reviewed cognitive factors associated with emotional and behavioral risk, including distorted cognitive processing. Here we review hopelessness and problem solving, two additional cognitive factors that have received significant empirical investigation in the adolescent suicide literature.

HOPELESSNESS

Hopelessness is a cognitive state that often accompanies depression and is reported by many adolescents who attempt suicide. Hopelessness entails a lowered expectation of obtaining certain goals and is accompanied by feelings of personal futility, loss of motivation, and the expectation that the future will yield negative personal consequences. Groholt et al. (2006) followed 92 adolescent suicide attempters over the course of 9 years and found that higher baseline levels of hopelessness independently predicted future suicide attempts in a multivariate model that included a wide range of potentially confounding factors. Stewart et al. (2005) examined hopelessness in a sample of 2,044 adolescents from Hong Kong and the United States, and found that hopelessness predicted suicidal ideation, even after controlling for depressive symptoms.

Although numerous studies have demonstrated a relation between hopelessness and adolescent suicidal behavior, hopelessness does not consistently predict suicidality once depression is controlled (see Esposito, Johnson, Spirito, & Overholser, 2003). Such findings suggest that hopelessness may only place adolescents at risk for suicidal behavior for a time-limited period during a depressive episode (Dori & Overholser, 1999). Goldston et al. (2006) partitioned hopelessness into state and trait variants and found that a significant portion of the variance in hopelessness scores was comprised of time-limited state-like feelings, though both trait and state components of hopelessness were found to predict future suicide attempts.

PROBLEM SOLVING

Results of two reviews yield evidence to suggest a relationship between problem solving and suicidality, though the nature of this relationship is unclear (see Esposito, Johnson, Spirito, & Overholser, 2003; Speckens & Hawton, 2005). The literature in this area is mixed due in part to a number of methodological differences and limitations across studies. For example, problem-solving measures employed across studies vary in type (e.g., self-report, performance based), problem focus (e.g., problem precipitating the suicidal act, major problem experienced in past month, real-life problems in general, hypothetical problems), instruction (e.g., ask participants to indicate what they would do, what they have done, what the effect was), and aspect of problem solving assessed (e.g., perception versus actual problem-solving skills). Further, the majority of studies are cross-sectional, employ self-report measures, and do not control for important confounding variables such as depression and hopelessness (Esposito, Johnson, Spirito, & Overholser, 2003; Speckens & Hawton, 2005).

Generally, it is believed that suicidal behavior is enacted by many adolescents as a means to resolve problems. This maladaptive coping strategy may result from an inability to generate effective solutions to problems, selection of ineffective problem-solving alternatives when faced with problems, and/or a general lack of confidence in one's problem-solving ability. Indeed, McLaughlin, Miller, and Warwick (1996) found that most adolescents (68%) who attempted suicide in their study expected that it would positively influence their problems, by leading to death, temporary relief from problems, or communicating their level of pain to others. Another 38% reported that they were unable to think of anything else to do to solve their problems. Beliefs that problems are irresolvable (Orbach, Mikulincer, Blumenson, Mester, & Stein, 1999) and that problem solving is a threatening task (Orbach et al., 2007) also have been associated with adolescent suicidal behavior. Hawton, Kingsbury, Steinhardt, James, and Fagg (1999) followed a sample of adolescents admitted to a general hospital for a suicide attempt over the course of 1 year. Those who made a repeat suicide attempt during the follow-up, in comparison to nonrepeaters, generated fewer and less effective problem-solving responses. However, this relationship was reduced to a statistical trend level after controlling for depression severity.

Conversely, confidence in problem solving has been found to be a strong *protective* factor against suicidality among adolescents. In a longitudinal study conducted with 180 psychiatrically hospitalized adolescents followed for up to 6 years, Goldston et al. (2001) found that strong survival and coping beliefs were associated with decreased risk for future suicide attempts among previously suicidal youth.

Therefore, problem solving may function as both a risk factor for and/or a protective factor against suicidality in adolescents.

Family Risk Factors

Wagner, Silverman, and Martin (2003) published a comprehensive review of familial risk factors associated with adolescent suicidality. Low-cohesion, high-conflict, and unsatisfying parent–adolescent relationships, in particular, were more frequently observed in the families of adolescents who attempt and/or complete suicide than controls. Yet the relation between such family variables and adolescent suicidal behavior is often lessened or reduced to nonsignificance when other related factors, such as adolescent or parental psychopathology, are taken into account (Brent & Melhem, 2008; Evans et al., 2004; Gould et al., 2003). Here, we focus on studies that examine the familial transmission of suicidal behavior. This section concludes with a general review of research on the relation between childhood physical and sexual abuse and adolescent suicidality, as abuse is relatively prevalent in families with a suicidal adolescent and has been shown to be strongly related to suicidal behavior.

Familial Transmission of Suicidal Behavior

Results from adoption studies, twin studies, and family studies all provide evidence to suggest that suicidal behavior is transmitted from parent to child (see Bronisch & Lieb, 2008 and Brent & Melhem, 2008 for comprehensive reviews). Chapter 11 of this volume also contains a comprehensive review on this topic. Here we will present just a few key points.

Overall, results of adoption, twin, and family studies suggest that the transmission of suicidality from parent to child is due in part to genetics and may be mediated by intermediate phenotypes such as impulsive aggression. Parental mental health disorders such as mood, anxiety, alcohol use, and personality disorders, may also increase risk for adolescent suicidal behavior among predisposed youth, though familial transmission of suicidality appears to occur independent of these problems (Brent et al., 1996, 2002; Melham et al., 2007). Brent and Mann (2006) offer a stress-diathesis model in which child and parent psychopathology, suboptimal family environment, childhood abuse, the presence of impulsive aggression or neurocognitive deficits, and life stress convene to facilitate the transmission of suicidality from parent to child. However, as suggested by Brent and Mann (2006), great individual variation exists in the risk factors and processes that lead to suicide. Future research is needed to improve the understanding of the sequence and nature of the relation between salient factors associated with the transmission of suicidality from parent to child.

Childhood Physical and Sexual Abuse

Research generally supports a link between childhood abuse and the development of suicidal behavior among adolescents. However, as noted in a review by Brodsky and Stanley (2008), substantive conclusions about this relationship are hampered by many methodological limitations of research conducted in this area. For example, much of the research on childhood abuse is correlational, based on retrospective report, differs in the measurement of abuse (e.g., standardized measures, clinical interviews), differs in the definition of abuse (e.g., age difference between victim and perpetrator, relation to perpetrator), and differs in the type of abuse examined (e.g., sexual abuse, physical abuse, neglect, or various combinations).

With these limitations in mind, King and Merchant (2008) conducted a comprehensive review of studies that examine the association between childhood abuse (sexual, physical, and/or neglect) and adolescent suicidality and concluded that the large majority of studies suggest that childhood abuse predicts suicidal thoughts and behavior among adolescents. For example, Eisenberg, Ackard, and Resnick (2007) examined the relation between sexual abuse and suicidality in a large high school sample of 131,862 American adolescents. More than half of the adolescents with a history of sexual abuse reported a lifetime history of suicide attempt. Likewise, Fergusson, Beautrais, and Horwood (2003) examined the relationship between childhood sexual abuse and suicide attempts in 1,063 adolescents and young adults from New Zealand (ages of 14–21 years). Results indicated that adolescent victims of childhood sexual abuse had elevated rates of suicidal ideation and attempts compared to nonvictims. Similarly, Martin, Bergen, Richardson, Roeger, and Allison (2004) longitudinally examined the relationship between childhood sexual abuse and suicidality in an Australian sample of 2,485 high school students. Results indicated that sexually abused adolescents were more likely to report suicidal ideation, plans, threats, and attempts than nonabused adolescents. Further, for male adolescents, the risk of suicide attempts was 15 times greater for victims of sexual abuse, after controlling for depressive symptoms, hopelessness, and family functioning. In contrast, for female adolescents, sexual abuse did not predict suicide attempts when depressive symptoms, hopelessness, and family functioning were controlled. Thus, there may be different pathways through which childhood sexual abuse leads to suicidality among males and females.

The relationship between sexual abuse and suicidal behavior is likely moderated by factors such as gender, age at the time of detection, and number of perpetrators (Evans et al., 2004). There also is evidence that abuse may influence suicidal behavior through an association with impulsivity and aggression (Baud, 2005; Brodsky & Stanley, 2008) or by negatively impacting neurobiological development (see Chapter 11 of this volume for more detail on the neurobiology of suicidal behavior). Further, as suggested in the family studies reviewed earlier, sexual abuse is common in the parents of sexually abused children, and these parents often have histories of psychiatric disorders and suicidal behavior themselves. In these distressed families, both the environment and genetic factors likely increase risk for offspring suicidal behavior.

Environmental Risk Factors

Although a number of environmental factors (e.g., firearm availability) have been related to attempted and completed suicide during adolescence, in this section we focus on two prominent environmental risk factors: exposure to suicidal behavior and stressful life events.

Exposure to Suicidal Behavior

Social learning theory suggests that most human behavior is learned through modeling. Therefore, exposure to suicidal behavior, whether it is indirectly through the media or directly through contact with a suicidal individual, may lead to imitation of suicidal behavior in some individuals. Research examining the effects of cluster suicides (excessive number of suicides that occur in close temporal and geographical proximity), media influence, and personal exposure to the suicidal behavior of adolescent peers on subsequent suicidal behavior is reviewed next.

In a comprehensive review that examined the impact of modeling on adolescent suicidal behavior, Insel and Gould (2008) concluded that there is ample empirical evidence to support the existence of cluster suicides, though this phenomenon appears to be unique to adolescents and young adults, and does not account for the majority of adolescent suicides. The media also has a significant influence on suicidal behavior among adolescents and adults alike, though results are more consistent in studies that examine the effects of nonfictional descriptions of suicides (e.g., newspaper and television reports) as opposed to fictional portrayals of suicides on television or in movies (Insel & Gould, 2008). Research has also begun to explore the effects of exposure to suicide via the Internet, which has given rise to the phenomena of cybersuicide pacts (suicide pacts among strangers who meet over the Internet (see Insel & Gould, 2008).

When examining the relation between exposure to the suicidal behavior of friends and peers on personal suicidal behavior, social modeling is one potential vehicle for transmission but assertive pairing (i.e., youth with mental illness may be more likely to choose peers with similar problems) also may play a role. Therefore, the possibility exists that youth who are vulnerable to suicidality may belong to a group of like-minded peers prior to any suicidal acts. Regardless of the mechanism, in their review, Insel and Gould (2008) conclude that the majority of studies provide significant support for an association between exposure to the suicidal behavior of adolescent peers and adolescent suicide attempts. Factors such as temporal proximity of the exposure and emotional closeness to the suicide model may impact this relationship.

Cerel, Roberts, and Nilsen (2005) assessed a sample of 5,852 high school students and found that adolescents exposed to a peer who made a nonlethal suicide attempt were 3.5 times more likely to report suicidal ideation, 3.6 times more likely to report a suicide attempt, and 1.8 times more likely to inflict injuries requiring medical attention in the next year than adolescents without this exposure history. Further, adolescents exposed to a peer who completed suicide were 5.4 times more likely to report suicidal ideation, 9.4 times more likely to report a suicide attempt, and 3.1 times more likely to inflict injuries requiring medical attention in the next year than adolescents who were not exposed to a peer who completed suicide. In contrast, Watkins and Gutierrez (2003) compared 27 high school students exposed to the completed suicide of a peer suicide to 27 matched controls without this exposure history. No significant differences in suicidal ideation or suicidal behaviors were found. A study conducted by Mercy et al. (2001) suggests that factors such as emotional closeness to the suicide attempter/victim and time since exposure may play a role in discrepant findings. Mercy et al. (2001) compared 153 suicide attempters treated in an emergency department to 513 controls, ages 13–34 years. Exposure to the attempted and/or completed suicide of a friend or acquaintance was actually associated with a *reduced* risk of suicide attempts, though this was only found for those exposed to suicidal behavior more than 1 year prior to the interview and those who did not feel emotionally close to the friend or acquaintance. The authors suggest that greater temporal and emotional distance between adolescents and a suicide model may allow adolescents time to more accurately process the negative consequences of suicide. Further research is needed to reconcile findings regarding suicide risk among peers of adolescents who attempt or commit suicide.

Stressful Life Events

There is equivocal evidence that suicidal adolescents experience more negative life events than their nonsuicidal counterparts, though prevalence and type of stressors may vary by age (e.g., greater prevalence of parent–child conflict in younger adolescents versus romantic conflict in older adolescents) and co-occurring diagnoses (see Gould et al., 2003). For example, Portzky, Audenaert, and van Heeringen (2005) interviewed relatives of 19 Belgium adolescent suicide completers who died between the ages of 15 and 19 years. Results indicated that the majority of adolescent suicide completers experienced multiple, significant, negative life events within a year or less of completed suicide. Similarly, Liu and Tein (2005) assessed a sample of 1,362 Chinese high school students and found that adolescents who had attempted suicide reported more negative life events in the past year than did suicide ideators and nonsuicidal youth. Suicide ideators also reported more negative life events than nonsuicidal youth. In a sample of 3,005 adolescents from Mexico City, Borges et al. (2008) found that the experience of any traumatic event (i.e., serious injury, serious illness, victim of violence, witness to domestic violence) increased the likelihood of making a suicide plan five-fold and making an attempt six-fold. Further, those who experienced three or more traumatic events were 13.7 times more likely to report a suicide attempt than those who did not experience any traumatic events.

Intervention Studies

Suicidal ideation is often assessed in treatment studies as a secondary outcome, particularly in studies of depression, and also has been examined as a moderator of treatment outcome. For example, in a clinical trial comparing cognitive-behavioral, systemic behavioral family, and nondirective supportive therapies for depressed adolescents (Barbe, Bridge, Birmaher, Kolko, & Brent, 2004), suicidal depressed adolescents were more likely to be depressed at the end of the trial than nonsuicidal depressed adolescents. To date, however, interventions specifically for children and adolescents with suicidal ideation have not been reported in the literature. Adolescents who attempt suicide have been the focus of treatment outcome studies. Next we review current community treatment approaches, quasi-experimental studies, and randomized trials with adolescent suicide attempters. Only psychosocial studies are reviewed because studies of pharmacologic treatments specifically designed to reduce suicidal behavior have not been reported in children and adolescents (see Chapter 23 for studies among adults).

Community Treatment of Adolescents Who Attempt Suicide

Our group has published the only study, to our knowledge, of typical psychotherapy received by adolescent suicide attempters (Spirito, Stanton, Donaldson, & Boergers, 2002). Sixty-three adolescents who had made a suicide attempt which required treatment in an emergency department (ED) and were discharged to outpatient care were followed for 3 months after their attempt. Their therapists were questioned about their treatment. Therapists treating these patients were primarily masters-level social workers (63.0%) but also included masters-level marriage and family therapists (9.3%), doctoral-level psychologists (20.4%), clinical nurse specialists (1.9%), and psychiatrists (5.6%). Thirty-four percent of these adolescents received individual therapy, and 66% of the adolescents received some combination of individual plus parent/adolescent sessions. The therapists reported that 58% of the families dropped out of therapy against medical advice. Attendance ranged from 0 to 22 with an average of 7.0 sessions. Fifty-two percent of the adolescents attended six or fewer sessions. Supportive psychotherapy techniques were reported by three-fourths of the sample, psychodynamic and cognitive techniques by one-half of the sample, and behavioral techniques by one-third of the sample.

Seven years later, in a second study, we followed suicidal adolescents, most but not all were attempters, after discharge from an inpatient psychiatric unit (Spirito et al., 2011). Data regarding community psychotherapy received by these adolescents after discharge were obtained by mail from a subsample of therapists (*n*= 84). The therapists consisted primarily of masters-level social workers (44%), masters-level marriage and family therapists (19%), and doctoral-level psychologists (25%). Individual therapy, with portions of a session devoted to parent/adolescent conjoint treatment, was reported by 76.5% of therapists as their treatment approach. The median number of sessions attended was 10 and the mean was 13. The adolescent or adolescent's family canceled or failed to attend anywhere from one to nine appointments. Fifteen of the 84 cases (18%) terminated within the first 3 months of treatment. Nine of these terminations were unplanned.

In treating their adolescent clients, the most commonly used therapy techniques included trying to enhance the adolescent's cognitive or affective perspective-taking skills; encouraging expression of feeling; and monitoring suicidal thoughts, feelings, or behaviors. Cognitive-behavioral therapy (CBT) techniques were used most often by all disciplines—psychiatrists, psychologists, and social workers.

Our two studies indicate that a substantial portion of adolescents who attempt suicide will not receive an adequate course of outpatient mental health care, although this number appears to have decreased over time. Nonetheless, community-based clinicians identify inconsistent patient attendance and difficulties in engagement as considerable challenges in providing effective care to families (Quinn, Epstein, & Cumblad, 1995). The data from our second study suggest a shift in techniques such that therapists are now reporting greater use of cognitive and behavioral techniques when working with suicidal adolescents than they did in the same community roughly 7 years earlier. These findings also suggest that research protocols testing cognitive-behavioral approaches might eventually find their way into community care.

Individual Psychotherapy

Three individual therapy trials with suicide attempters have been reported. Rathus and Miller (2002), using a quasi-experimental design, compared the treatment efficacy of dialectical behavioral therapy (DBT; *n* = 29) to standard care for 82 suicidal adolescents (one-third were attempters) with borderline features. Adolescents in both groups attended approximately 24 sessions over 3 months.

The DBT group, which had more severe symptoms than the treatment as usual (TAU) group at baseline, had fewer psychiatric hospitalizations and higher rates of treatment completion than the standard care group. About 40% reattempted suicide over the course of treatment, but no differences in rates of repeat suicide attempts were found.

A recently conducted National Institute of Mental Health (NIMH)-funded multisite study, Treatment of Adolescent Suicide Attempters (TASA), was a feasibility study comparing three conditions: an individual CBT, a selective serotonin reuptake inhibitor (SSRI) medication algorithm, and a combined CBT/SSRI group (Brent et al., 2009). Adolescents with unipolar depression and a history of a suicide attempt within the past 90 days were enrolled. The TASA investigators discovered early on that families of adolescents who had attempted suicide would not accept randomization. Therefore, a patient choice design was used in an open trial. Of the 124 adolescents enrolled, 22 were randomized and the remainder chose CBT alone (*n* = 17), medication alone (*n* = 14), or the combination (*n* = 93). At 6-month follow-up, 19% of the sample had experienced a suicidal event, that is, completed suicide, attempted suicide, preparatory events toward suicidal behavior, or suicidal ideation. Suicide attempts occurred in 12% of these events with the mean time to a repeat attempt being about 45 days. Based on those findings, the investigators concluded that the CBT protocol used in this study was worth further investigation. In addition, Brent et al. (2009) recommended that more sessions in the first 4 weeks, with safety planning, might be needed to reduce the occurrence of suicidal events that occur in the first month.

Donaldson, Spirito, and Esposito-Smythers (2005) completed the only randomized trial of individual therapy with adolescent suicide attempters. More than half of the sample were multiple attempters. Both treatments were delivered in an individual format with conjoint parent–adolescent sessions. Adolescents who had attempted suicide were randomized to either 10 sessions of a skills-based cognitive-behavioral treatment (*n* = 18) or a supportive relationship treatment (*n* = 17). In the skills-based treatment, the adolescents were taught both problem-solving and affect management skills in a structured fashion. The supportive therapy was unstructured and used nondirective techniques to address the symptoms and problems which the patient volunteered. Seven different therapists provided both treatments to control for therapist effects. Participants in both conditions improved on suicidal ideation and depression at 3- and 6-month follow-ups, but there were no between-group differences.

Family Therapy

One quasi-experimental study and one experimental study of family therapy have been published in the literature. A six-session outpatient family therapy program called "SNAP" (Successful Negotiation/Acting Positively) was conducted with 140 female minority adolescent suicide attempters (Rotheram-Borus, Piacentini, Miller, Grae, & Castro-Blanco, 1994). Problem-solving skills were taught in SNAP and were practiced using role playing, modeling, and feedback. Negotiating, active listening skills, and strategies for managing affective arousal were also taught. Although a randomized trial was not conducted, SNAP reduced overall symptom levels.

Harrington et al. (1998) provided family therapy to 162 adolescents who had attempted suicide by overdose. Patients were randomly assigned to either routine care or routine care plus, a four-session home-based family intervention. The family sessions focused on discussion of the suicide attempt, communication skills, problem solving, and psychoeducation on adolescent development. The additional home-based family intervention resulted in reduced suicidal ideation at 6-month follow-up compared to routine care, but only for adolescents without major depression. There were no differences in rate of suicide reattempts.

Group Therapy

One study of group therapy in Great Britain (Wood, Trainor, Rothwell, Moore, & Harrington, 2001) randomized 63 adolescents who had deliberately harmed themselves on at least two occasions within a year, to group therapy plus routine care or routine care alone. The intervention included attendance at six "acute" group sessions, which focused on specific topics and utilized CBT and DBT techniques, followed by weekly process-oriented long-term group therapy, which could continue until the patient felt ready to terminate the sessions. Adolescents in routine care attended a median of four sessions. Adolescents who received group therapy were less likely to make more than one repeat suicide attempt than adolescents who had routine care (2/32 versus 10/31). More sessions of routine care were associated with a worse outcome but more sessions of group therapy were associated

with a better outcome. The Wood et al. (2001) study was the first study to demonstrate a reduction in repeat suicide attempts. However, Hazell et al. (2009) replicated the study in Australia and did not find many differences between groups at 6- and 12-month follow-up, with the exception that the experimental group reported a greater improvement over time in global symptom ratings. Surprisingly, adolescents receiving group therapy had significantly higher rates of suicidal behavior at 6-month follow-up than adolescents receiving routine care (88% versus 68%).

Comprehensive Treatment Programs

Katz, Cox, Gunasekara, and Miller (2004) compared the effects of an inpatient psychiatric hospital unit based on DBT to a traditional, psychodynamically oriented unit. Both units resulted in a significant reduction in suicidal ideation and behavior at 1-year follow-up, but there was no difference between units. Two randomized studies have tested comprehensive treatment programs with suicide attempters. Rudd et al. (1996) devised a 2-week day treatment program for older adolescents and young adults (58% attempters). Group therapy occurred throughout the day and focused on psychoeducation, problem-solving, and traditional experiential-affective techniques. The experimental program resulted in improvements in suicidal ideation and behavior. However, the comparison group, which received standard care in the community, had comparable improvement. Patients with comorbid symptoms experienced the most improvement with the experimental treatment (Joiner, Voelz, & Rudd, 2001).

Huey et al. (2004) randomized adolescents presenting with psychiatric emergencies to either psychiatric hospitalization or multisystemic therapy (MST), a family-focused home-based intervention that addresses home, school, and community factors related to youth difficulties with a particular emphasis on parenting skills. A variety of behavioral interventions are typically delivered in MST. Caseloads are low for each therapist and they receive frequent supervision. At 1-year follow-up, the MST group had significantly lower rates of suicide attempts than the hospitalized adolescents.

Adjunctive Treatment Programs

King et al. (2006) tested whether the addition of a social network support team would improve outcomes for psychiatrically hospitalized suicide attempters after discharge. Youth-nominated support persons were asked to maintain weekly supportive contacts with the adolescents. Interventionists in turn contacted the support persons to help provide guidance. When compared to standard care, the intervention resulted in a decrease in suicidal ideation at follow-up for girls but not for boys. There were no differences across groups in suicidal behavior.

Treatment Issues With Adolescent Suicide Attempters: Implications for Future Research

There are several issues pertinent to treatment of suicidality in adolescents. First, adolescent suicide attempters who follow through with a psychotherapy referral often fail to receive an adequate course of treatment (Spirito et al., 2002, 2011). Treatment adherence has been found to vary as a function of type of outpatient treatment. King, Hovey, Brand, and Wilson (1997) studied adolescent suicide attempters and ideators following a psychiatric hospitalization and found that the patients were most compliant with their outpatient medication visits (67%), followed by individual therapy (51%), and then family therapy (33%). However, treatment attendance is not just a function of patient/family commitment. Often service barriers (e.g., placing patients on waiting lists and transferring patients from one therapist to another) can play a role in impeding families' access to treatment (Spirito et al., 2002).

One factor that undoubtedly affects treatment attendance is that families who enter into treatment often have multiple sources of stress in their lives that make participation in treatment a burden. Thus, efforts must be made early on to problem-solve through obstacles to treatment participation. Specific steps to encourage families to come to counseling regularly and complete the full treatment program have been tested with some success by Spirito, Boergers, Donaldson, Bishop, and Lewander (2001).

Second, suicidal behavior rarely occurs in the absence of psychopathology (Shaffer et al., 1996), and further adolescent suicide attempters possess great diagnostic heterogeneity. For example, D'Eramo et al. (2004) studied 104 psychiatrically hospitalized adolescents and found that multiple attempters were more likely to be diagnosed with at least one externalizing disorder, especially SUDs, and to have more than one comorbid diagnosis than adolescents with no suicidal behavior or just suicidal ideation. Thus, treatment of suicidal behavior must by necessity address the symptomatology associated with the accompanying psychiatric disorder.

Third, there exists evidence for at least two distinct types of suicide attempters: impulsive suicide attempters with predominant externalizing symptoms and nonimpulsive suicide attempters with predominant internalizing symptoms. Relative to impulsive attempters, nonimpulsive attempters have been found to have higher levels of depression and hopelessness and a trend toward greater suicidal ideation (Brown, Overholser, Spirito, & Fritz, 1991). Thus, treatment must be flexible enough to address these different presentations.

Fourth, parental psychopathology is related to adolescent dysfunction in general, including suicidality (Brent et al., 1993). Several studies have found that parent psychopathology in general is related to poor functioning among adolescent suicide attempters (Fergusson, Woodward, & Horwood, 2000; Klimes-Dougan, Free, & Ronsaville, 1999). There are several pathways by which parental psychopathology may relate significantly to adolescent suicidality. Genetic transmission of suicidal behavior may be the mechanism by which parents affect adolescent suicidal behavior. Parents with a history of suicidality may model suicidality for their adolescent. Parents may make statements about life not being with worth living in response to an adolescent's behavior or other family conflict, or actually attempt suicide. Alternatively, family processes in these families may inadvertently reinforce suicidal behavior via attention (Wagner et al., 2003). Parents may differentially reinforce suicidal behavior rather than more adaptive behavior in their adolescent. Another possibility is that the adolescent may use threats to engage in suicidal behavior instrumentally (i.e., to control his or her environment and to terminate aversive family relationship patterns). Similarly, some adolescents express suicidality in order to decrease conflict in their home or as a means of escape from school and other problems.

Fifth, when enrolled in trials immediately following a suicide attempt, many of these adolescents will be on one or more medications. Consequently, it is difficult to test the effectiveness of psychotherapeutic or psychosocial treatments alone. Thus, combined psychotherapeutic or psychosocial/psychopharmacologic treatments, with a standard algorithm guiding medication use, may be the research designs best suited to address the clinical and ethical realities of studying such a high-risk population. Sixth, identifying subclinical levels of sadness or pessimism that can be managed before they reach crisis proportions, via individual efforts or booster sessions, is a priority. Therefore, research protocols may need to include both scheduled and as needed booster sessions over a 4- to 6-month period, which complicates the research design and follow-up.

Finally, the treatment outcome literature on adolescent suicide attempters is small. Investigator concerns about liability in clinical trials with such high-risk patients have also affected new trial initiation (Pearson, Stanley, King, & Fisher, 2001). Additionally, adolescents with a history of suicidal behavior are vulnerable to a sudden resurgence of suicidal feelings during treatment (Beck, 1996). If this occurs during a research protocol, it often results in patients being removed from clinical trials. Under such conditions, a substantial percentage of suicidal adolescents may never complete treatment trials, making it difficult to accrue knowledge. Thus, it is important to keep suicidal adolescents in research protocols so that the results of these studies will be more relevant to community care. Recent recommendations on how to manage these high-risk patients in clinical protocols (Oquendo, Stanley, Ellis, & Mann, 2004) may encourage more research.

Future Directions

Many of the strongest known risk factors for child and adolescent suicidal behavior were reviewed in this chapter. Future research will need to disentangle how individual traits, such as impulsive aggression, interact with genetic factors, neurobiology, and stressful family environments to result in suicidal behavior in adolescents. Also important to investigate will be the protective factors that keep adolescents with high-risk profiles from progressing to suicidal behavior.

The precise link between genes, serotoninergic activity, personality characteristics (e.g., impulsive aggression, psychiatric disorders), and suicidal behavior will be difficult to elucidate given the complex nature of both the genotype and phenotype. Underlying traits and behavioral dimensions such as impulsivity may be more precisely measured than Axis I or Axis II psychiatric disorders and thus may prove easier to examine in relation to genetic factors and serotoninergic dysfunction (Baud, 2005). Precise definitions of suicidal behavior also are necessary to accurately and consistently classify adolescents into groups.

The treatment outcome literature on suicide attempters is quite small. Only two psychosocial studies to date have found an effect on continued suicidal behavior and one has failed to replicate. There is a clear need for additional studies to determine the best approaches to reducing repetitive suicidal behavior. The neurobiology of suicide suggests that pharmacologic treatments may be useful in the treatment of adolescents who attempt suicide, particularly multiple attempters. The complicated psychosocial factors associated with adolescent suicidal behavior will require that psychotherapy accompany any medication treatment. Understanding individual genetic and neurobiologic vulnerabilities will eventually lead to tailored interventions that have the greatest likelihood of affecting suicidal behavior.

References

Bagge, C. L., & Sher, K. J. (2008). Adolescent alcohol involvement and suicide attempts: Toward the development of a conceptual framework. *Clinical Psychology Review*, *28*, 1283–1296.

Barbe, R. P., Bridge, J., Birhamer, B., Kolko, D., & Brent, D. A. (2004). Suicidality and its relationship to treatment outcome in depressed adolescents. *Suicide and Life-Threatening Behavior*, *34*, 44–55.

Barrett, P. M., Rapee, R. M., Dadds, M. M., & Ryan, S. M. (1996). Family enhancement of cognitive style in anxious and aggressive children. *Journal of Abnormal Child Psychology*, *24*, 187–199.

Baud, P. (2005). Personality traits as intermediary phenotypes in suicidal behavior: Genetic issues. *American Journal of Medical Genetics Part C: Seminars in Medical Genetics*, *133C*, 34–42.

Beck, A. T. (1996). Beyond belief: A theory of modes, personality, and psychopathology. In P. Salkovskis (Ed.), *Frontiers of cognitive therapy* (pp. 1–25). New York, NY: Guilford Press.

Boergers, J., Spirito, A., & Donaldson, D. (1998). Reasons for adolescent suicide attempts: Associations with psychological functioning. *Journal of the American Academy of Child and Adolescent Psychiatry*, *37*, 1287–1293.

Bögels, S. M., & Zigterman, D. (2000). Dysfunctional cognitions in children with social phobia, separation anxiety disorder, and generalized anxiety disorder. *Journal of Abnormal Child Psychology*, *28*, 205–211.

Borges, G., Benjet, C., Medina-Mora, M. E., Orozco, R., Molnar, B. E., & Nock, M. K. (2008). Traumatic events and suicide-related outcomes among Mexico City adolescents. *Journal of Child Psychology and Psychiatry*, *49*, 654–666.

Borowsky, I., Resnick, M., Ireland, M., & Blum, R. (1999). Suicide attempts among American Indian and Alaska Native youth. *Archives of Pediatric and Adolescent Medicine*, *153*, 573–580.

Borowsky, I. W., Ireland, M., & Resnick, M. D. (2001). Adolescent suicide attempts: Risk and protectors. *Pediatrics*, *107*, 485–493.

Brent, D., Greenhill, L., Compton, S., Emshe, G., Wells, K., Walker, J.,…Turner, J. B. (2009). The Treatment of Adolescent Suicide Attempter Study (TASA): Predictors of suicidal events in an open trial. *Journal of the American Academy of Child and Adolescent Psychiatry*, *48*, 987–996.

Brent, D. A., Baugher, M., Bridge, J., Chen, T., & Chiapetta, L. (1999). Age- and sex-related risk factors for adolescent suicide.

Journal of the American Academy of Child and Adolescent Psychiatry, 38, 1497–1505.

Brent, D. A., Bridge, J., Johnson, J., & Connolly, J. (1996). Suicidal behavior runs in families: A controlled family study of adolescent suicide victims. *Archives of General Psychiatry, 53*, 1145–1152.

Brent, D. A., Kolko, D. J., Allan, M. J., & Brown, R. V. (1990). Suicidality in affectively disordered adolescent inpatients. *Journal of the American Academy of Child and Adolescent Psychiatry, 29*, 586–593.

Brent, D. A., & Mann, J. J. (2006). Familial pathways to suicidal behavior: Understanding and preventing suicide among adolescents. *New England Journal of Medicine, 355*, 2719–2721.

Brent, D. A., & Melhem, N. (2008). Familial transmission of suicidal behavior. *Psychiatric Clinics of North America, 31*, 157–177.

Brent, D. A., Oquendo, M., Birmaher, B., Greenhill, L., Kolko, D., Stanley B., et al. (2002). Familial pathways to early-onset suicide attempt: Risk for suicidal behavior in offspring of mood-disordered suicide attempters. *Archives of General Psychiatry, 59*, 801–807.

Brent, D. A., Oquendo, M., Birmaher, B., Greenhill, L., Kolko, D., Stanley B., et al. (2003). Peripubertal suicide attempts in offspring of suicide attempters with siblings concordant for suicidal behavior. *American Journal of Psychiatry, 160*, 1468–1493.

Brent, D. A., Perper, J.A., Moritz, G., Allman, C., Roth, C., Schweers, J. et al. (1993). Psychiatric risk factors for adolescent suicide: A case-control study. *Journal of the American Academy of Child and Adolescent Psychiatry, 32*, 521–529.

Brezo, J., Barker, E. D., Paris, J., Hebert, M., Vitaro, F., Tremblay, R. E., & Tureki, G. (2008). Childhood trajectories of anxiousness and disruptiveness as predictors of suicide attempts. *Archives of Pediatric and Adolescent Medicine, 162*, 1015–1021.

Bridge, J. A., Goldstein, T. R., & Brent, D. A. (2006). Adolescent suicide and suicidal behavior. *Journal of Child Psychology and Psychiatry, 47*, 372–394.

Bridge, J. A., Greenhouse, J., Weldon, A., Campo, J., & Kelleher, K (2008). Suicide trends among youths aged 10 to 19 years in the United States, 1996–2005. *Journal of the American Medical Association, 300*, 1025–1026.

Brodsky, B. S., & Stanley, B. (2008). Adverse childhood experiences and suicidal behavior. *Psychiatric Clinics of North America, 31*, 223–235.

Bronisch, T., & Lieb, R.L. (2008). Maternal suicidality and suicide risk in offspring. *Psychiatric Clinics of North America, 31*, 213–221.

Brown, L. K., Overholser, J., Spirito, A., & Fritz, G. K. (1991). The correlates of planning in adolescent suicide attempts. *Journal of the American Academy of Child and Adolescent Psychiatry, 30*, 95–99.

Center for Disease Control and Prevention. (1998). Suicide among black youths: United States, 1980-1995. *Morbidity and Mortality Weekly Report, 47*, 193–196.

Centers for Disease Control and Prevention. (2004). Youth risk behavior surveillance—United States, 2003. *Morbidity and Mortality Weekly Report, 53*(SS-2), 1–96.

Centers for Disease Control and Prevention. (2005). *Compressed mortality file. Underlying cause-of-death*. Retrieved July 2013, from http://wonder.cdc.gov/mortSQL.html.

Centers for Disease Control and Prevention. (2007). Suicide trends among youths and young adults aged 10-24 years: United States, 1990–2004. *Morbidity and Mortality Weekly Report, 56*, 905–908.

Cerel, J., Roberts, T. A., & Nilsen, W. J. (2005). Peer suicidal behavior and adolescent risk behavior. *Journal of Nervous and Mental Disease, 193*, 237–243.

Commission on Adolescent Suicide Prevention. (2005). Youth suicide. In D. L. Evans, E. B. Foa, R. E. Gur, H. Hendin, C. P. O'Brien, M. E. P. Seligman, & B. T. Walsh (Eds.), *Treating and preventing adolescent mental health problems: What we know and what we don't know* (pp. 434–443). New York, NY: Oxford University Press.

D'Eramo, K., Prinstein, M., Freeman, J., Grapentine, W., & Spirito, A. (2004). Psychiatric diagnoses and comorbidity in relation to suicidal behavior among psychiatrically hospitalized adolescents. *Child Psychiatry and Human Development, 35*, 35–41.

Dervic, K., Brent, D. D., & Oquendo, M. A. (2008). Completed suicide in childhood. *Psychiatric Clinics of North America, 31*, 271–291.

Dodge, K. (2006). Translational science in action: Hostile attributional style and the development of aggressive behavior. *Development and Psychopathology, 18*, 791–814.

Donaldson, D., Spirito, A., & Esposito-Smythers, C. (2005). Treatment for adolescents following a suicide attempt: Results of a pilot trial. *Journal of the American Academy of Child and Adolescent Psychiatry, 44*, 113–120.

Dori, G. A., & Overholser, J. C. (1999). Depression, hopelessness, and self-esteem: Accounting for suicidality in adolescent psychiatric inpatients. *Suicide and Life-Threatening Behavior, 29*, 309–318.

Eaton, D. K., Kann, L., Kinchen, S., Shanklin, S., Ross, J., Hawkins, J., ... Wechsler, H. (2008). Youth risk behavior surveillance: United States, 2007. *MMWR Surveillance Summary, 57*(4), 1–131.

Eisenberg, M. E., Ackard, D. M., & Resnick, M. D. (2007). Protective factors and suicide risk in adolescents with a history of sexual abuse. *Journal of Pediatrics, 151*, 482–487.

Epkins, C. C. (2000). Cognitive specificity in internalizing and externalizing problems in community and clinic-referred children. *Journal of Clinical Child Psychology, 29*, 199–208.

Esposito, C., Spirito, A., Boergers, J., & Donaldson, D. (2003). Affective, behavioral, and cognitive functioning in adolescents with multiple suicide attempts. *Suicide and Life-Threatening Behavior, 33*, 389–399.

Esposito, C., Johnson, B., Spirito, A., & Overholser, J. (2003). Cognitive factors: Hopelessness, coping, problem-solving, self-esteem. In A. Spirito & J. Overholser (Eds.), *Evaluating and Treating Adolescent Suicide Attempters: From Research to Practice*. San Diego, CA: Academic Press.

Esposito, C., Spirito, A., & Overholser, J. (2003). Behavioral factors: Impulsive and aggressive behavior. In A. Spirito & J. Overholser (Eds.), *Evaluating and treating adolescent suicide attempters: From research to practice* (pp.147–157). San Diego, CA: Academic Press.

Esposito-Smythers, C., & Spirito, A. (2004). Adolescent suicidal behavior and substance use: A review with implications for treatment research. *Alcoholism: Clinical and Experimental Research, 28*(Suppl.), 77S–88S.

Evans, E., Hawton, K., & Rodham, K. (2004). Factors associated with suicidal phenomena in adolescents: A systematic review of population-based studies. *Clinical Psychology Review, 24*, 957–979.

Fergusson, D. M., Beautrais, A. L., & Horwood, L. J. (2003). Vulnerability and resiliency to suicidal behaviors among young people. *Psychological Medicine, 33*, 61–73.

Fergusson, D. M., Woodward, L. J., & Horwood, L. J. (2000). Risk factors and life processes associated with the onset of suicidal behaviour during adolescence and early adulthood. *Psychological Medicine, 30*, 23–39.

Foley, D. L., Goldston, D. B., Costello, E. J., & Angold, A. (2006). Proximal psychiatric risk factors for suicidality in youth: The Great Smoky Mountains Study. *Archives of General Psychiatry, 63*, 1017–1024.

Goldsmith, S. K., Pellmar, T. C., Kleinman, A. M, & Bunney, W. E., (2002). *Reducing suicide: A national imperative.* Washington, DC: Institute of Medicine, National Academies Press.

Goldstein, T. R., Birmaher, B., Axelson, D., Ryan, N., Strober, M., Gill, M. K., …Keller, M. (2005). History of suicide attempts in pediatric bipolar disorder: Factors associated with increased risk. *Bipolar Disorders, 7*, 525–535.

Goldston, D. B., Daniel, S. S., Erkanli, A., Reboussin, B. A., Mayfield, A., Frazier, P. H., & Treadway, S. L. (2009). Psychiatric diagnoses as contemporaneous risk factors for suicide attempts among adolescents and young adults: Developmental changes. *Journal of Consulting and Clinical Psychology, 77*, 281–290.

Goldston, D. B., Daniel, S., Reboussin, D. M., & Kelley, A. (1996). First-time suicide attempters, repeat attempters and previous attempters on an adolescent inpatient psychiatry unit. *Journal of the American Academy of Child and Adolescent Psychiatry, 35*, 631–639.

Goldston, D. B., Daniel, S. S., Reboussin, B. A., Reboussin, D. M., Frazier, P. H., & Harris, A. E. (2001). Cognitive risk factors and suicide attempts among formerly hospitalized adolescents: A prospective naturalistic study. *Journal of the American Academy of Child and Adolescent Psychiatry, 40*, 91–99.

Goldston, D. B., Daniel, S. S., Reboussin, D. M., Reboussin, B. A., Frazier, P. H., & Kelley, A. E. (1999). Suicide attempts among formerly hospitalized adolescents: A prospective naturalistic study of risk during the first 5 years after discharge. *Journal of the American Academy of Child and Adolescent Psychiatry, 38*, 660–671.

Goldston, D. B., Reboussin, B. A., & Daniel, S. S. (2006). Predictors of suicide attempts: State and trait components. *Journal of Abnormal Psychology, 115*, 842–849.

Gould, M. S., Fisher, P., Parides, M., Flory, M., & Shaffer, D. (1996). Psychosocial risk factors of child and adolescent completed suicide. *Archives of General Psychiatry, 53*, 1155–1162.

Gould, M. S., Greenberg, T., Velting, D. M., & Shaffer, D. (2003). Youth suicide risk and preventive interventions: A review of the past 10 years. *Journal of the American Academy of Child and Adolescent Psychiatry, 42*, 386–405.

Groholt, B., Ekeberg, O., & Haldorsen, T. (2006). Adolescent suicide attempters: What predicts future suicidal acts? *Suicide and Life-Threatening Behavior, 36*, 638–650.

Groholt, B., Ekeberg, O., Wichstrom, L., & Haldorsen, T. (1998). Suicide among children and younger and older adolescents in Norway: A comparative study. *Journal of the American Academy of Child and Adolescent Psychiatry, 37*, 473–481.

Harrington, R., Kerfoot, M., Dyer, E., McNiven, F., Gill, J., Harrington, V., …Byford, S. (1998). Randomized trial of a home-based family intervention for children who have

deliberately poisoned themselves. *Journal of the American Academy of Child and Adolescent Psychiatry, 37*, 512–518.

Hawton, K., Kingsbury, S., Steinhardt, K., James, A., & Fagg, J. (1999). Repetition of deliberate self-harm by adolescents: The role of psychological factors. *Journal of Adolescence, 22*, 369–378.

Hawton, K., Zahl, D., & Weatherall, R. (2003). Suicide following deliberate self-harm: Long-term follow-up of patients who presented to a general hospital. *British Journal of Psychiatry, 182*, 537–542.

Hazell, P., Martin, G., McGill, K., Kay, T., Wood, A., Trainor, G., & Harrington, R. (2009). Group therapy for repeated deliberate self-harm in adolescents: Failure of replication of a randomized trial. *Journal of the American Academy of Child and Adolescent Psychiatry, 48*, 662–670.

Heron, M. P., Hoyert, D. L., Murphy, S. L., Xu, J. Q., Kochanek, K. D., & Tejada-Vera, B. (2009). *Deaths: Final data 2006. National vital statistics reports* (Vol. 57). Hyattsville, MD: National Center for Health Statistics.

Hufford, M. R. (2001). Alcohol and suicidal behavior. *Clinical Psychology Review, 21*, 797–811.

Huey, S., Henggeler, S. W., Rowland, M. D., Halliday-Boykins, C. A., Cunningham, P. B., Pickrel, S. G., & Edwards, J. (2004). Multisystemic therapy effects on attempted suicide by youths presenting psychiatric emergencies. *Journal of the American Academy of Child and Adolescent Psychiatry, 43*, 183–190.

Insel, B. J., & Gould, M. S. (2008). Impact of modeling on adolescent suicidal behavior. *Psychiatric Clinics of North America, 31*, 293–316.

Ivarsson, T., Broberg, A. G., Arvidsson, T., & Gillberg, C. (2005). Bullying in adolescence: Psychiatric problems in victims and bullies as measured by the Youth Self Report (YSR) and the Depression Rating Scale (DSRS). *Nordic Journal of Psychiatry, 59*, 365–373.

Jacobs, R. H., Reinecke, M. A., Gollab, J. K., & Kane, P. (2008). Empirical evidence of cognitive vulnerability for depression among children and adolescents: A cognitive science and developmental perspective. *Clinical Psychology Review, 28*, 759–783.

Joiner, T. (2005). *Why people die by suicide.* Cambridge, MA: Harvard University Press.

Joiner, T., Voelz, Z., & Rudd, M. D. (2001). For suicidal young adults with comorbid depression and anxiety disorders, problem-solving treatment may be better than treatment as usual. *Professional Psychology: Research and Practice, 32*, 278–282.

Katz, L., Cox, B., Gunasekara, S., & Miller, A. (2004). Feasibility of dialectical behavior therapy for suicidal adolescent inpatients. *Journal of the American Academy of Child and Adolescent Psychiatry, 43*, 276–282.

Kerr, D. C., Washburn, J. J., Feingold, A., Kramer, A. C., Ivey, A. Z., & King, C. A. (2007). Sequelae of aggression in acutely suicidal adolescents. *Journal of Abnormal Child Psychology, 35*, 817–830.

Kim, Y. S., & Leventhal, B. (2008). Bullying and suicide: A review. *International Journal of Adolescent Medicine and Health, 20*, 133–154.

Kim, Y. S., Leventhal, B. L., Koh, Y., & Boyce, W. T. (2009). Bullying increased suicide risk: Prospective study of Korean adolescents. *Archives of Suicide Research, 13*, 15–30.

King, C., Hovey, J., Brand, E., & Wilson, R. (1997). Suicidal adolescents after hospitalization: Parent and family impacts on treatment follow-through. *Journal of the American Academy of Child and Adolescent Psychiatry, 36*, 85–93.

King, C., & Merchant, C. (2008). Social and interpersonal factors relating to adolescent suicidality: A review of the literature. *Archives of Suicide Research, 12*, 181–196.

King, C. A., Kramer, A., Preuss, L., Kerr, D. C. R., Weisse, L., & Venkataraman, S. (2006). Youth-nominated support team for suicidal adolescents (version 1): A randomized controlled trial. *Journal of Consulting and Clinical Psychology, 74*, 199–206.

Kingsbury, S., Hawton, K., Steinhardt, K., & James, A. (1999). Do adolescents who take overdoses have specific psychological characteristics? A comparative study with psychiatric and community controls. *Journal of the American Academy of Child and Adolescent Psychiatry, 38*, 1125–1131.

Klimes-Dougan, B., Free, K., & Ronsaville, D. (1999). Suicidal ideation and attempts: A longitudinal investigation of children of depressed and well mothers. *Journal of the American Academy of Child and Adolescent Psychiatry, 38*, 651–659.

Lewinsohn, P. M., Rohde, P., & Seeley, J. R. (1996). Adolescent suicidal ideation and attempts: Prevalence, risk factors, and clinical implications. *Clinical Psychology: Science and Practice, 3*, 25–46.

Liu, X., & Tein, J. (2005). Life events, psychopathology, and suicidal behavior in Chinese adolescents. *Journal of Affective Disorders, 86*, 195–203.

Martin, G., Bergen, H. A., Richardson, A. S., Roeger, L., & Allison, S. (2004). Sexual abuse and suicidality: Gender differences in a large community sample of adolescents. *Child Abuse and Neglect, 28*, 491–503.

McGirr, A., Renaud, A., Bureau, A., Seguin, M., Lesage, A., & Turecki, G. (2008). Impulsive-aggressive behaviours and completed suicide across the life cycle: A predisposition for younger age of suicide. *Psychological Medicine, 38*, 407–417.

McLaughlin, J. A., Miller, P., & Warwick, H. (1996). Deliberate self-harm in adolescents: Hopelessness, depression, problems, and problem-solving. *Journal of Adolescence, 19*, 523–532.

Melhem, N. M., Brent, D. A., Ziegler, M., Iyengar, S., Kolko, D. J., Oquendo, M. et al. (2007). Familial pathways to early-onset suicidal behavior: Familial and individual antecedents of suicidal behavior. *American Journal of Psychiatry, 164*, 1364–1370.

Mercy, J. A., Kresnow, M. J., O'Carroll, P. W., Lee, R. K., Powell, K. E., Potter, L. B., ... Bayer, T. L. (2001). Is suicide contagious? A study of the relation between exposure to the suicidal behavior of others and nearly lethal suicide attempts. *American Journal of Epidemiology, 154*, 120–127.

Middlebrook, D. L., LeMaster, P. L., Beals, J., Novins, D. K., & Manson, S. M. (2001). Suicide prevention in American Indian and Alaska Native communities: A critical review of programs. *Suicide and Life Threatening Behavior, 31*, 132–149.

Negron, R., Piacentini, J., Graae, F., Davies, M., & Shaffer, D. (1997). Microanalysis of adolescent suicide attempters and ideators during the acute suicidal episode. *Journal of the American Academy of Child and Adolescent Psychiatry, 36*, 1512–1519.

Nock, M., Joiner, T., Gordon, K., Lloyd-Richardson, E., & Prinstein, M. (2006). Non-suicidal self-injury among adolescents: Diagnostic correlates and relation to suicide attempts. *Psychiatry Research, 144*, 65–72.

Nrugham, L., Larsson, B., & Sund, A. M. (2008). Specific depressive symptoms and disorders as associates and predictors of suicidal acts across adolescence. *Journal of Affective Disorders, 111*, 83–93.

O'Donnell, L., Stueve, A., & Wilson-Simmons, R. (2005). Aggressive behaviors in early adolescence and subsequent suicidality among urban youths. *Journal of Adolescent Health, 37*, 517.e15–517.e25.

Olfson, M., Marcus, S. C., Weissman, M. M., & Jensen, P. S. (2002). National trends in the use of psychotropic medications by children. *Journal of the American Academy of Child and Adolescent Psychiatry, 41*, 514–521.

Oquendo, M., Stanley, B., Ellis, S., & Mann, J. J. (2004). Protection of human subjects in intervention research for suicidal behavior. *American Journal of Psychiatry, 161*, 1558–1563.

Orbach, I., Blomenson, R., Mikulincer, M., Gilboa-Schechtman, E., Rogolsky, M., & Retzoni, G. (2007). Perceiving a problem-solving task as a threat and suicidal behavior in adolescents. *Journal of Social and Clinical Psychology, 26*, 1010–1034.

Orbach, I., Mikulincer, M., Blumenson, R., Mester, R., & Stein, D. (1999). The subjective experience of problem irresolvability and suicidal behavior: Dynamics and measurement. *Suicide and Life-Threatening Behavior, 29*, 150–164.

Pearson, J., Stanley, B., King, C., & Fisher, C. (2001). Intervention research with persons at high risk for suicidality: Safety and ethical considerations. *Journal of Clinical Psychiatry, 62*, 17–26.

Portzky, G., Audenaert, K., & van Heeringen, K. (2005). Suicide among adolescents: A psychological autopsy study of psychiatric, psychosocial and personality-related risk factors. *Social Psychiatry and Psychiatric Epidemiology, 40*, 922–930.

Prinstein, M. J., Nock, M. K., Simon, V., Aikins, J. W., Cheah, C. S. L., & Spirito, A. (2008). Longitudinal trajectories and predictors of adolescent suicidal ideation and attempts following inpatient hospitalization. *Journal of Consulting and Clinical Psychology, 76*, 92–103.

Quinn, K., Epstein, M., & Cumblad, C. (1995). Developing comprehensive, individualized community-based services for children and youth with emotional and behavioral disorders: Direct service providers' perspectives. *Journal of Child and Family Studies, 4*, 19–42.

Rathus, J., & Miller, A. (2002). Dialectical behavior therapy adapted for suicidal adolescents. *Suicide and Life-Threatening Behavior, 32*, 146–157.

Renaud, J., Berlim, M.T., McGirr, A., Tousignant, M., & Turecki, G. (2008). Current psychiatric morbidity, aggression/impulsivity, and personality dimensions in child and adolescent suicide: A case control study. *Journal of Affective Disorders, 105*, 221–228.

Ronan, K. R., & Kendall, P. C. (1997). Self-talk in distressed youth: States-of-mind and content specificity. *Journal of Clinical Child Psychology, 26*, 330–337.

Rotheram-Borus, M. J., Piacentini, J., Miller, S., Graae, F., & Castro-Blanco, D. (1994). Brief cognitive-behavioral treatment for adolescent suicide attempters and their families. *Journal of the American Academy of Child and Adolescent Psychiatry, 33*, 508–517.

Rudd, M. D., Rajab, M. H., Orman, D. T., Stulman, D. A., Joiner, T., & Dixon, W. (1996). Effectiveness of an outpatient intervention targeting suicidal young adults: Preliminary results. *Journal of Consulting and Clinical Psychology, 64*, 179–190.

Sanislow, C. A., Grilo, C. M., Fehon, D. C., Axelrod, S. R., & McGlashan, T. H. (2003). Correlates of suicide risk in juvenile detainees and adolescent inpatients. *Journal of the American Academy of Child and Adolescent Psychiatry, 42*, 234–240.

Shaffer, D., Gould, M. S., Fisher, P., & Trautman, P. (1996). Psychiatric diagnosis in child and adolescent suicide. *Archives of General Psychiatry, 53*, 339–348.

Shaffer, D., & Hicks, R. (1994). Suicide. In I. B. Pless (Ed.), *The epidemiology of childhood disorders* (pp. 339–365). New York, NY: Oxford University Press.

Shaffer, D., & Pfeffer, C. (2001). Practice parameter for the assessment and treatment of children and adolescents with suicidal behavior. *American Academy of Child and Adolescent Psychiatry, 40*, 24S–51S.

Shirk, S. R., Boergers, J., Eason, A., & Van Horn, M. (1998). Dysphoric interpersonal schemata and preadolescents' sensitization to negative events. *Journal of Clinical Child Psychology, 27*, 54–68.

Speckens, E. M., & Hawton, K. (2005). Social problem-solving in adolescents with suicidal behavior: A systematic review. *Suicide and Life-Threatening Behavior, 35*, 365–387.

Spirito, A., Boergers, J., Donaldson, D., Bishop, D., & Lewander, W. (2001). An intervention trial to improve adherence to community treatment by adolescents after a suicide attempt. *Journal of the American Academy of Child and Adolescent Psychiatry, 41*, 435–442.

Spirito, A., Simon, V., Cancilliere, M. K., Stein, R, Norcutt, R., Loranger,K., & Prinstein, M. J. (2011). *Outpatient psychotherapy practice with suicidal adolescents following psychiatric hospitalization for suicide ideation or a suicide attempt. Clinical Child Psychology and Psychiatry, 16*, 53–64.

Spirito, A., Stanton, C., Donaldson, D., & Boergers, J. (2002). Treatment-as-usual for adolescent suicide attempters: Implications for the choice of comparison groups in psychotherapy research. *Journal of Clinical Child Psychology, 31*, 41–47.

Stein, D., Apter, A., Ratzoni, G., Har-Even, D., & Avidan, G. (1998). Association between multiple suicide attempts and negative affects in adolescents. *Journal of the American Academy of Child & Adolescent Psychiatry, 37*, 488–494.

Stewart, S. M., Kennard, B. D., Lee, P. W., Mayes, T., Hughes, C., & Emslie, G. (2005). Hopelessness and suicidal ideation among adolescents in two cultures. *Journal of Child Psychology and Psychiatry, 46*, 364–372.

Tureki, G. (2005). Dissecting the suicide phenotype: The role of impulsive-aggressive behaviors. *Journal of Psychiatric Neuroscience, 30*, 398–408.

US Department of Health & Human Services. (2006). *Health, United States, 2006 with chartbook on trends in the health of Americans.* Hyattsville, MD: National Center for Health Statistics.

Van Orden, K. A., Witte, T. K., Gordon, K. H., Bender, T. W., & Joiner, T. E. (2008). Suicidal desire and the capability for suicide: Tests of the interpersonal-psychological theory of suicidal behavior among adults. *Journal of Consulting and Clinical Psychology, 76*, 72–83.

Wagner, B. M., Silverman, M. A. C., & Martin, C. E. (2003). Family factors in youth suicidal behaviors. *American Behavioral Scientist: Suicide in Youth, 46*, 1171–1191.

Watkins, R. L., & Gutierrez, P. M. (2003). The relationship between exposure to adolescent suicide and subsequent suicide risk. *Suicide and Life-Threatening Behavior, 33*, 21–32.

Wolfsdorf, B. A., Freeman, J., D'Eramo, K., Overholser, J., & Spirito, A. (2003). Mood states: Depression, anger, and anxiety. In A. Spirito & J. Overholser (Eds.), *Evaluating and treating adolescent suicide attempters: From research to practice* (pp. 53–88). San Diego, CA: Academic Press.

Wood, A., Trainor, G., Rothwell, J., Moore, A., & Harrington, R. (2001). Randomized trial of group therapy for repeated deliberate self harm in adolescents. *Journal of the American Academy of Child and Adolescent Psychiatry, 40*, 1246–1253.

Suicidal Behaviors Among Adults

Eve K. Mościcki

Abstract

Suicidal behaviors are fatal or nonfatal outcomes of complex, dynamic trajectories of risk and protection. This chapter describes the epidemiology of fatal and nonfatal suicide events among adults in the United States. It discusses sources of data on suicide mortality and morbidity, and methodological challenges associated with obtaining reliable and valid information. Recent data on incidence of suicide fatalities among US adults, prevalence and incidence of nonfatal suicidal behaviors, mechanism of injury, sociodemographic characteristics, onset, and course are presented. Key distal and proximal risk processes for suicide mortality and morbidity in adults are discussed from an individual and environmental perspective. The chapter concludes with a brief overview of how an understanding of the complex trajectories that contribute to suicidal behaviors may be leveraged to identify potential opportunities for preventive intervention and promising directions for future research.

Key Words: suicidal behaviors, fatal, nonfatal, incidence, prevalence, adults, sociodemographic, age of onset, risk, protection

Suicide conveys a significant disease burden, which the World Health Organization (WHO) estimates to be 1.3% of the total global burden of disease (WHO, 2008). Worldwide, the number of persons estimated to have died by suicide in 2004, approximately 844,000 (WHO, 2008), is equivalent to the population of the state of Delaware. The consequences of suicide are especially grim for low-income countries, where suicide ranks as the third leading cause of death among persons 15–44 years of age, disproportionately affecting young people and adults during what could be their most productive years (WHO, 2001).

Suicide mortality is the tip of a broad-based pyramid. The emotional consequences of suicide can be devastating to families, and the additional societal burden of injury associated with nonfatal suicidal behaviors is large. It includes reported and unreported events that are not medically treated,

emergency department visits, and, in a substantial proportion of cases, hospitalization costs. In 2007, 395,320 people were treated in emergency departments for self-inflicted injuries; 165,997 people were hospitalized due to self-inflicted injury (CDC, 2009). By 2011, the number of people treated in emergency departments for self-inflicted injuries had grown to 487,700 (CDC, 2012). The direct costs associated with suicide mortality and morbidity, which include costs of autopsies and investigations, expenses associated with emergency intervention and medical treatment, and hospital and inpatient physician costs, have been estimated to total $68 million for suicide fatalities and $581 million for attempted suicides, or a total of $0.7 billion (Palmer, Revicki, Halpern, & Hatziandreu, 1995). Total indirect costs, which include premature mortality and years of potential life lost for suicide fatalities, lost earnings and productivity due to suicide attempt–related disability, and lost productivity of loved ones grieving a suicide death, have been estimated to range between $11.8 billion (Goldsmith, Pellmar, Kleinman, & Bunney, 2002) and $34.6 billion (CDC, 2012), staggering amounts even in today's economy.

Suicidal behaviors are highly complex. Both fatal and nonfatal suicide events result from the interplay of dynamic trajectories of risk and protection. Despite the challenges presented by this complexity, beginning with Durkheim's first systematic observations in 1897 (Durkheim, 1951), the study of suicide has generated a rich and growing scientific knowledge base that today allows us to identify opportunities for preventive intervention. This chapter reviews the epidemiology of fatal and nonfatal suicide events among adults in the United States. Sources of population-based data on suicide mortality and morbidity are discussed briefly, and methodological challenges associated with obtaining reliable and valid information are considered. Recent data on incidence of suicide fatalities among US adults, prevalence and incidence of nonfatal suicidal behaviors, mechanism of injury, sociodemographic characteristics, onset, and course are presented. Key distal and proximal risk processes for suicide mortality and morbidity in adults are discussed from an individual and environmental perspective. The chapter concludes with a brief overview of how an understanding of the complex interplay of trajectories that contribute to suicidal behaviors may be leveraged to identify potential opportunities for preventive intervention and promising directions for future research.

Suicide Mortality

The Institute of Medicine defines suicide as a "fatal, self-inflicted destructive act with explicit or inferred intent to die" (Goldsmith et al., 2002, p. 27). This definition encompasses the three key criteria that distinguish suicidal from other injurious acts: (1) the act must be self-inflicted; (2) the act must be intentional; and (3) the objective of the act is death. This section discusses the epidemiology of fatal suicidal behaviors in adults. Sources of data and methodological challenges are considered, and the most recent available data on incidence, mechanism of death, and sociodemographic correlates are presented.

Suicide Mortality: Sources of Data

The primary source of data on suicide fatalities in the United States is the National Vital Statistics System (NVSS) in the National Center for Health Statistics (NCHS), Centers for Disease Control and Prevention (CDC) (CDC, 2013). Records of deaths in each calendar year are compiled by state vital statistics offices and submitted to NCHS. US mortality data are currently coded using the *International Classification of Diseases*, Tenth Revision (*ICD-10*) (WHO, 2007), which codes a fatal suicide event as Intentional Self Harm, X60-X84.

Operational criteria for classification of suicide deaths were developed and published in 1988 (Rosenberg et al., 1988), but they are not uniformly applied in all jurisdictions. While national-level mortality data are reported from a single source at NCHS, there is no uniform infrastructure in the United States for reporting mortality data at the state or county level. Official reporting of deaths varies depending on the composition of the medicolegal system in each state. Eleven states use a coroner system, 22 use a medical examiner system, and 18 use a mixed medicolegal system in which some jurisdictions have a coroner while others in the same state have a medical examiner (Committee for the Workshop on the Medicolegal Death Investigation System, 2003). A coroner is typically an elected or appointed official who usually serves a single county and often is not required to be a physician or to have medical training. For example, in Georgia, an individual can be a coroner if he or she is a registered voter, at least 25 years of age, does not have any felony convictions, has earned a high school diploma or the equivalent, and receives annual training of 1 week's duration. In contrast, a medical examiner is typically a physician, pathologist, or forensic pathologist with medical expertise and may have jurisdiction over a county, district, or an entire state. For example, in one Pennsylvania county, the medical examiner has fully staffed laboratory facilities and a university faculty appointment. Because of the continuing societal stigma that surrounds suicide death, and the great variability in state-level required training and preparation for the individual who signs the death certificate, the organization of a state's death reporting system may have nontrivial implications for the accurate classification of suicide deaths.

Each state requires that deaths occurring under unusual, suspicious, or violent circumstances undergo medicolegal investigation that may include an autopsy (Committee for the Workshop on the Medicolegal Death Investigation System, 2003; Hoyert, Kung, & Xu, 2007). Suicide deaths fall into this category. While the overall autopsy rate in the

United States declined more than 50% from 1972 to 2007, the rate for external causes, including suicide deaths, increased. In 2007 the rate of suicide fatalities referred for investigation to medical examiners or coroners was 59.9% (Hoyert, 2011).

Suicide Mortality: Incidence and Trends

At the time of this writing, the most recent available data at the national level were the Final Data for 2010 (Murphy, Xu, & Kochanek, 2013), which represent the final reported numbers for deaths from all causes. As previously stated, death classification is according to the *ICD-10* (WHO, 2007). It should be noted that all overall suicide death rates reported in this chapter are age-adjusted rates unless specifically indicated otherwise. The rates are adjusted to the US Standard Year 2000 population (Anderson & Rosenberg, 1998; Murphy et al., 2013). Age-adjusted mortality data from 2010 are reported here when they are available; other data are from available years.

In 2010, intentional self-harm (suicide) was the tenth leading cause of death in the United States, accounting for about 1.6% of total deaths. The age-adjusted rate was 12.1/100,000, representing a 2.5% increase over the age-adjusted rate for 2009 (Murphy et al., 2013). The age-adjusted suicide rate had been relatively flat since the *ICD-10* was implemented in 1999, hovering between 10.4/100,000 in 2000 and 10.9/100,000 in 2002, 2004, 2005, and 2006, but began to increase in 2007.

For most of the latter half of the 20th century, suicide ranked eighth among the leading causes of death in the United States. With the implementation of *ICD-10* in 1999, suicide dropped from the eighth leading cause of death to the eleventh (Hoyert, Arias, Smith, Murphy, & Kochanek, 2001). Changes in the classification and coding rules for selecting the underlying cause of death associated with new versions of the *ICD*, however, do not account entirely for suicide's change in the rank order among the leading causes of death. Suicide rates had already begun a slow but consistent decline during the years of *ICD-9* coding (Fig. 6.1). Since 1933, when the NVSS first began reporting mortality data from all states in the United States,[1] the age-adjusted rate has ranged from 14.3/100,000 in 1940 and 13.7/100,000 in 1977 to 10.5/100,000 in 1999 and 10.4/100,000 in 2000. Total population suicide rates were generally below 12/100,000 in the 1950s and began to increase to over 12/100,000 throughout the 1960s. During the decade of the 1970s, annual rates were generally higher than 13/100,000, but they began declining again in the late 1980s through the 1990s (Grove & Hetzel, 1968; Heron et al., 2009; Kung, Hoyert, Xu, & Murphy, 2008; Linder & Grove, 1947). The suicide rates in the first years of the new millennium were the lowest in 60 years but began to increase with the uptick in 2007.

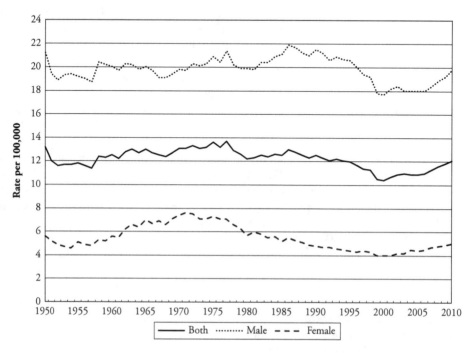

Figure 6.1. Suicide rates per 100,000, total population and by sex, United States, 1950–2010. NCHS: http://www.cdc.gov/nchsdeaths.htm

It may be useful to put these figures into some perspective. Compared with the leading cause of death in the United States, diseases of the heart, intentional self-harm is a relatively rare event. In 2010, the age-adjusted death rate from diseases of the heart was 179.1/100,000, continuing a long-term decreasing trend. The number of deaths from this leading cause was 597,689, more than 15 times the number of deaths from suicide, which in 2010 was 38,364 (Murphy et al., 2013).

There is wide geographic variation in suicide rates, with consistently higher rates reported in Western and Mountain states. In 2010, the state-specific age-adjusted rates reflected the typical historical pattern, ranging from 6.9/100,000 in the District of Columbia, 7.7/100,000 in New Jersey and New York, to 21.8 in Montana, 22.4/100,000 in Wyoming, and 22.8/100,000 in Alaska (Murphy et al., 2013).

Suicide Mortality: Mechanism of Death

Multiple studies have documented that the US suicide rate is largely driven by the firearm suicide rate (Boyd, 1983; Boyd & Mościcki, 1986; Goldsmith et al., 2002; Hu, Wilcox, Wissow, & Baker, 2008; Kaplan, Adamek, & Johnson, 1994; Miller, Azrael, Hepburn, Hemenway, & Lippman, 2006), which in 2010 was 6.1/100,000. Boyd (1983) showed that the documented increase in suicide rates from 1953 to 1978 was largely accounted for by an increase in firearm suicide rates; rates for suicide by means other than firearms did not change during that time period. A follow-up ecological analysis showed that the increase in firearm suicide rates paralleled an increase in the domestic production of civilian firearms (Boyd & Mościcki, 1986). Seventy percent of suicide deaths occur in the home, the majority of which are firearm suicides (Kellerman et al., 1992). Analyses of household firearm ownership data from the General Social Survey and mortality data from the NVSS indicated a significant decline in firearm suicide rates for every 10% decrease in household firearm ownership from 1981 to 2002 (Miller et al., 2006).

An encouraging recent trend is the general decline in the annual proportion of suicides by means of firearms. Firearm suicides accounted for 59% of all suicide deaths in 1996. This proportion has declined slowly to 56% in 2000, 52% in 2005 and 2006, and 51% in 2010.

The nonfirearm suicide rate for 2010 was 6.0/100,000 (Murphy et al., 2013). Suffocation was the second-highest ranking means of suicide death, with an age-adjusted rate of 3.1/100,000, followed by poisoning (2.1/100,0000), and fall (0.3/100,000) (Murphy et al., 2013).

Suicide Mortality: Sociodemographic Patterns

Selected sociodemographic characteristics are associated with an increased risk for suicide death. Although technically they are associated with the increased probability of the outcome of interest and do precede it (Kraemer et al., 1997; Last, 1988; Mrazek & Haggerty, 1994), they should not be confused with causal risk or protective factors. Consistent with the typology proposed by Kraemer et al. (1997), sociodemographic characteristics such as sex, age, race/ethnicity, or educational achievement are considered to be fixed or variable markers and are here termed "correlates."

SUICIDE MORTALITY: SEX

Both numbers and rates of suicide fatalities in the United States are consistently higher among men than among women, regardless of race, ethnicity, or age, and among older persons (Fig. 6.2) (US DHHS, 2010a). Non-Hispanic White men account for the largest proportion of suicides in the United States; the overall population suicide rate is dominated by the rate for this sociodemographic group. In 2010, the age-adjusted rate for White men was 22.0/100,000, compared with 9.1/100,000 for Black men, 5.6/100,000 for White women, and 1.8/100,000 for Black women (Murphy et al., 2013). The annual male-to-female ratio is approximately four suicide deaths among men to every one among women (Heron et al., 2009; Kung et al., 2008; Murphy et al., 2013). For both men and women, suicide rates are more than 2 times higher among Whites than Blacks; the 2010 ratio was 2.5 (Murphy et al., 2013).

SUICIDE MORTALITY: AGE AND BIRTH COHORT

Overall suicide mortality rates are higher for older age groups, although the increase with age is accounted for by the rates for older White men. As can be seen in Figure 6.2, the typical age distribution pattern is not uniform across the major US racial and ethnic groups, suggesting that differential risk and protective processes are at work. Among Black men, the highest suicide rates occur in the 20- to 34-year age group. Unlike White men, among whom rates are highest in the oldest age groups, the highest rates for both White and Black women occur between ages 30 and 60 years. Historically,

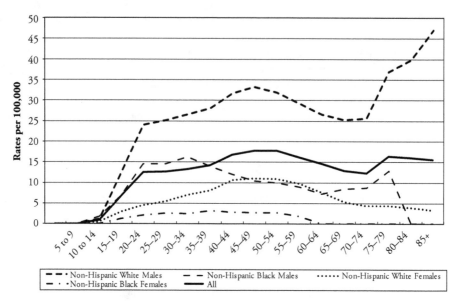

Figure 6.2. Suicide Rates per 100,000 by Age, Sex, and Race, United States, 2007. NCHS: http://www.cdc.gov/nchs/data/dvs/MortFinal2007_WorktableOrig291R.pdf.

Black women have had lower rates of suicide death than any other racial or ethnic group. In 2007, age-specific rates for Black women ages 10–14 and 60 years and higher were not estimated because the number of deaths (less than 20 in each 5-year age group) was too low to provide a reliable estimate (Kung et al., 2008). This sociodemographic group merits more careful study to identify potential protective processes (Mościcki, 1994).

Manton et al. (1987) examined cohort effects on suicide rates from 1968 to 1981 among White and non-White men and White and non-White women, controlling for age and period effects. They found few differences between race and sex groups but identified higher rates of suicide for two birth cohorts. One was the cohort born before World War I, the "oldest old" during the 1980s. The other was the cohort born after World War II, the "baby boomers," who moved into middle age at the beginning of the millennium. This trend has continued. A recent detailed analysis by Hu et al. (2008) noted changes from 1999 to 2005 in suicide fatality rates within selected age and sex groups. During this time period, the annual increase in suicide rates for Whites 40–64 years of age, the age group which includes the baby boom cohort born between 1945 and 1965, was 2.7% for men and 3.9% for women, respectively.

SUICIDE MORTALITY: ETHNICITY AND RACE

Suicide fatality rates are higher for non-Hispanic groups than for Hispanic groups. Suicide mortality data within specific Hispanic groups, for example,

Mexican Americans, Puerto Ricans, Cuban Americans, are not available, but suicide does not rank as a leading cause of death among Hispanic groups (Heron, 2010; Kung et al., 2008; Murphy et al., 2013). In 2010, the age-adjusted suicide rate for non-Hispanics was 13.1/100,000 compared with 5.9/100,000 for Hispanics; the ratio was 2.2 (Murphy et al., 2013).

Within both Hispanic and non-Hispanic groups, rates for Whites and Blacks reflect the general age, race, and sex trends previously noted. Rates are highest for non-Hispanic White men (24.2/100,000) and lowest for non-Hispanic Black women (1.9/100,000) (Murphy et al., 2013).

Historically, the major US racial ethnic group with the highest suicide rates has been the American Indian/Alaska Native (AI/AN) population. In 2006, although suicide was the eleventh ranking cause of death in the United States, it was the eighth leading cause of death in the AI/AN population and accounted for 2.8% of all AI/AN deaths (Heron, 2010). The most recently available data indicate that there were 469 suicide deaths in 2010, with an age-adjusted rate of 10.8/100,000 (Murphy et al., 2013). It is encouraging to see that in recent years rates among AI/AN groups have been lower than rates from previous decades, which in some years the Indian Health Service (IHS) estimated to be more than twice as high as suicide rates for non-AI/AN groups (Day & Lanier, 2003; US DHHS, 2009). The ratio of suicide deaths in AI/AN groups compared with Whites was 0.8 in 2010 (Murphy et al., 2013). The age distribution patterns are similar to those seen for Black men, with the highest suicide rates for both AI/AN men and women occurring in younger, rather than older, age groups (Hlady & Middaugh, 1988; US DHHS, 2009). In 2006, suicide was the second leading cause of death in young AI/AN men 10–34 years of age, the leading cause of death among AI/AN women 10–14 years of age (based on 18 deaths), and the second leading cause of death in AI/AN women 15–24 years of age (Heron, 2010).

National-level data on suicide rates for Asian Americans or Pacific Islanders (API) have not been routinely reported in previous years, partly because of small numbers and partly because of the great ethnic and racial diversity represented in this population group. Based on 2006 data, however, suicide was the ninth leading cause of death in all API groups and accounted for 1.8% of all API deaths (Heron, 2010). Data from 2010 indicate that there were 1,061 suicides, with an age-adjusted rate of 6.2/100,000. The ratio of suicide deaths in API groups compared with Whites, the group most highly affected by suicide, was 0.5 (Murphy et al., 2013).

SUICIDE MORTALITY: MARITAL STATUS

Considerably higher suicide rates have been reported for separated/divorced and widowed persons than for those married or never married (Kposowa, 2000; Luoma & Pearson, 2002; Smith, Mercy, & Conn, 1988). The rates appear to be particularly high for young adults 20–34 years of age regardless of race, with the highest rates occurring among young White men (Luoma & Pearson, 2002).

Suicide Morbidity

This section discusses the epidemiology of non-fatal suicidal behaviors in adults, with a primary focus on attempted suicide. Sources of data and methodological challenges are considered, and the most recent available data on prevalence, incidence, mechanism of injury, and sociodemographic correlates are presented.

The Institute of Medicine report on suicide defines attempted suicide as "a non-fatal, self-inflicted destructive act with explicit or inferred intent to die" (Goldsmith et al., 2002, p. 27). As with fatal suicidal behavior, there are essential constructs that are reflected in this basic definition. They are (1) the act must be self-directed; (2) there is an intent to die, that is, the act includes a desire to die at some nonzero level, and the expectation that death will result from action; and (3) there is an element of lethality, that is, there is potential for harm or death associated with the mechanism of injury, which may be moderated by the accurate expectation of dying.

Suicide Morbidity: Sources of Data and Methodological Challenges

Unlike data for suicide mortality, for which there is a consistent and relatively standardized reporting process, there is no single national or primary source of data on the occurrence and risk factors for suicide morbidity among adults. There are instead multiple avenues for obtaining information on suicide morbidity, including surveillance systems, hospital discharge data, and periodic population-based surveys. Most data on suicidal behaviors come from self-report surveys, but there are also some studies that have used hospital discharge data and External Cause of Injury Codes (E-codes)[2] to examine the prevalence of attempted suicide. Each approach has its strengths and limitations.

The National Electronic Injury Surveillance System (NEISS) (US Consumer Product Safety Commission, 2013) collects data from a national probability sample of hospitals in the United States and its territories on an ongoing basis. The NEISS is an Internet-based resource of the US Consumer Products Safety Commission and contains data on hospital visits involving injuries associated with consumer products. NEISS data can be used to estimate the number of medically injurious self-injuries presenting in emergency departments. A major advantage of this resource is that the injury data are objective; that is, unlike most other sources of information on suicide morbidity, NEISS data are not based on self-reports. Two major disadvantages, however, are that NEISS data do not distinguish between suicidal and nonsuicidal self-injury, and they do not capture self-injuries that are not treated in emergency departments or hospitals. Due to these important shortcomings, the generalizability of NEISS data is limited.

Another source of information on adult self-injuries is E-codes from hospital discharge data such as those available through the National Hospital Discharge Survey (NHDS) (Buie, Owings, DeFrances, & Golosinskiy, 2010; Palmer et al., 1995; Spicer & Miller, 2000). The NHDS, which is conducted by the National Center for Health Statistics (CDC, 2013), uses a national sample of approximately 500 hospitals to collect annual data from sampled inpatient records. While a strength is that the NHDS, like the NEISS, does not rely on self-report, it has the same important limitation in not being able to report on cases that are not admitted to the hospital. Another potential limitation comes from the quality of coding that may be found in hospital records. It is not clear whether these data distinguish between suicidal and nonsuicidal self-injuries. Rhodes et al. (2008) examined the accuracy of hospital separation E-codes for classifying self-poisoning as suicidal behavior and concluded that these were not consistently applied. They also found less consistent documentation for elderly self-poisonings than for younger age groups.

The majority of reports on the occurrence and risk factors for suicidal behaviors in the adult population are based on data that come from population-based, epidemiologic surveys in small geographic areas and, more recently, at the national level (Borges et al., 2009; Fortuna, Perez, Canino, Sribney, & Alegría, 2007; Garroutte et al., 2003; Ialongo et al., 2002; Joe, Baser, Breeden, Neighbors, & Jackson, 2006; Kessler, Borges, & Walter, 1999; Kessler, Berglund, Borges, Nock, & Wang, 2005; Mościcki et al., 1988; Nock & Kessler, 2006; Paykel, Myers, Lindenthal, & Tanner, 1974; Schwab, Warheit, & Holzer, 1972; Sorenson & Golding, 1988; Verona, Sachs-Ericsson, & Joiner, 2004). A notable advantage that epidemiologic surveys have over surveillance systems and hospital discharge data is that they are able to capture information on cases outside of the hospital setting. Further, because they are based on probability samples, findings can be generalized to the populations represented by the samples. One disadvantage, however, is that the surveys rely on self-reports.

Early epidemiologic surveys that generated data on suicidal behaviors in US adults include the 1969 New Haven Study (Paykel et al., 1974), a 1971 survey in a northern Florida county (Schwab et al., 1972), and the National Institute of Mental Health Epidemiologic Catchment Area Study (ECA) conducted in the early 1980s (Mościcki et al., 1988; Regier et al., 1984). More current data are available at the national level and come from the first National Comorbidity Survey (NCS) from 1990 to 1992 (Kessler et al., 1999) and the NCS Replication (NCS-R) conducted a decade later, from 2001 to 2003 (Kessler et al., 2005). Both the NCS and NCS-R were nationally representative household surveys of adults 18–54 years of age. Two other national-level psychiatric epidemiology surveys, the National Survey of American Life (NSAL) (Jackson et al., 2004; Joe et al., 2006) and the National

Latino and Asian American Survey (NLAAS) (Alegría et al., 2004, 2007; Fortuna et al., 2007; Takeuchi, Zane, et al., 2007), provide data on nonfatal suicidal behaviors among African Americans, Caribbean Blacks, Latino groups, and Asian Americans. Analyses of data from the Collaborative Psychiatric Epidemiology Surveys (CPES) (Borges et al., 2009) have also generated estimates of nonfatal suicidal behaviors among Mexican American adults.

In addition to the long-standing need for a comprehensive national system to document the scope of nonfatal suicidal behaviors, the study of suicide morbidity faces other methodological challenges. Foremost among these is the lack of a standardized nomenclature: There are no clear, operational definitions that have been uniformly applied for collection of data on nonfatal suicidal behaviors. This has presented a major barrier to reliable research.

Multiple terms have been used to describe the complex concept of suicidal behavior. With a few notable exceptions (e.g., Goldsmith et al., 2002; Nock & Kessler, 2006; O'Carroll et al., 1996), most are poorly defined but have been liberally applied throughout the literature. Previously used terms include, for example, suicide attempt, suicidal behavior, parasuicide, intentional self-harm, self-injurious behavior, suicide gesture, and suicide threat. The inconsistent and interchangeable use of multiple terms to describe behaviors that may or may not be truly suicidal has resulted in unnecessary confusion in the scientific literature and findings that are difficult to interpret. For example, the term "intentional self-harm" has sometimes been used to describe attempted suicide. However, "intentional self-harm" is equally applicable as a descriptor of nonsuicidal self-injury, which may be motivated by an intense need to relieve tension rather than a desire to die, and therefore is not considered suicidal behavior. The consequences of failing to establish a clear and consistent nomenclature are not trivial. Besides the potential to overestimate prevalence of attempted suicide (Nock & Kessler, 2006; O'Carroll et al., 1996), misclassification and misinterpretation of self-injurious thoughts or behaviors may lead to an inappropriate diagnosis or etiology or, worse, the wrong preventive or treatment intervention. On the other hand, accurate case identification may have great potential for a better understanding of which specific self-injurious behaviors might represent subtypes with potentially distinct underlying pathophysiology.

The CDC's National Center for Injury Prevention and Control has recently taken the lead in developing uniform definitions for surveillance of suicidal behaviors based on the key constructs of self-inflicted behavior, intent, and desire to die (Crosby, Ortega, & Melanson, 2011). This nomenclature fills a huge gap in the field by providing a set of clear definitions to distinguish nonsuicidal from suicidal self-directed behaviors. Such definitions will be useful for both surveillance and research purposes. It is hoped that the nomenclature also will be a major step in discouraging the use of appealing, but less than rigorous, descriptors that may have been considered adequate in the past but are no longer acceptable for contemporary scientific investigation and public health policy.

Suicide Morbidity: Prevalence and Incidence

Most reports of the occurrence of nonfatal suicidal behaviors in the population are prevalence estimates of attempted suicide based on self-reports from cross-sectional surveys. Selected key surveys that have generated prevalence data on suicidal behaviors among adults in the overall US population and in selected ethnic and age groups are shown in Table 6.1. Many of the estimates are from population-based surveys in small geographic areas, but two sets of estimates at the national level, separated by a decade, come from the NCS (Kessler et al., 1999; Nock & Kessler, 2006) and NCS-R (Kessler et al., 2005; Nock & Kessler, 2006). In addition, national estimates are now available for selected ethnic groups in the United States through data generated by the NSAL (Joe et al., 2006), NLAAS (Fortuna et al., 2007), and CPES (Borges et al., 2009).

Overall lifetime prevalence of suicidal ideation in the general adult population ranges from 2.6% in the earliest survey from 1969 (Paykel et al., 1974) to 15.6% in the NCS-R (Nock et al., 2008a). Overall lifetime prevalence of suicide plans was ascertained in the NCS, NCS-R, and CPES. The estimate is 3.9% from the NCS (Kessler et al., 1999); 4.3% from the CPES (Borges et al., 2009); and 5.4% from the NCS-R (Nock et al., 2008a). Overall lifetime prevalence of suicide attempts in the population ranges from 1.1% in New Haven (Paykel et al., 1974) to 5.0% in the NCS-R (Nock et al., 2008a). It is not clear whether the higher estimates from more recent studies reflect a true increase in lifetime prevalence, or improved ascertainment methods.

Estimates of 12-month prevalence of suicidal ideation, plans, and attempts among adults are available from a small number of surveys and are shown in Table 6.2. The range for 12-month suicidal ideation in the general population is 1.5% (Paykel et al., 1974) to 3.3% (Kessler et al., 2005). Only two estimates of 12-month prevalence of suicide plans are available for the general adult population, both from the NCS studies. Twelve-month prevalence of suicide plans in the NCS was 0.7% (Kessler et al., 2005) and 1.0% in the NCS-R (Kessler et al., 2005). Barrios et al. (2000) reported a higher estimate for suicide plans, 7.9%, among college students 18–24 years of age. Twelve-month prevalence estimates for suicide attempts range from 0.2% to 1.7% (Barrios, Everett, Simon, & Brener, 2000; Ialongo et al., 2002; Joe et al. 2006; Kessler et al., 2005; Nock & Kessler, 2006; Paykel et al., 1974; Petronis, Samuels, Mościcki, & Anthony, 1990).

Only three studies have reported incidence of nonfatal suicidal behaviors among adults, one from a population-based study in Great Britain, and two based on data from the Baltimore ECA site (Table 6.2). Gunnell et al. (2004) collected data on suicidal thoughts at two time points, 18 months apart, and estimated overall annual incidence of suicidal ideation to be 2.3% (Gunnell, Harbord, Singleton, Jenkins, & Lewis, 2004). Petronis et al. (1990) estimated a 1-year suicide attempt incidence rate of 190/100,000 person-years. This rate was based on two waves of data, baseline plus a 1-year follow-up, collected in the early 1980s. A third wave of data collection was completed during a 13-year follow-up. Kuo et al. (2001) estimated cumulative 13-year and annual incidence rates for both suicidal ideation and attempts, shown in Table 6.2. The cumulative incidence for suicide attempts was 1.9%; the annual rate was 149/100,000 person-years. Estimates for suicidal ideation were a 13-year cumulative incidence of 5.6% and an annual incidence of 416/100,000 person-years (Kuo, Gallo, & Tien, 2001).

SUICIDE MORBIDITY: INTENT

Among the key population-based surveys that collected data on nonfatal suicidal behaviors, only the NCS, NCS-R, NLAAS, and NSAL included questions about intent, one of the fundamental criteria for suicidal self-injuries. In these surveys, if respondents reported that they had attempted suicide, they were then asked which of the following statements most accurately described their attempt: (1) "I made a serious attempt to kill myself and it was only luck that I did not succeed,"

Table 6.1 Lifetime Prevalence of Non-Fatal Suicidal Behaviors Among Adults From Selected Population-Based Community Surveys, United States

Study Site, Study Dates, Reference[a]	Sample Characteristics		Suicidal Ideation	Suicide Plan	Suicide Attempt
New Haven, CT 1969 Paykel et al., 1974	720 adults, ≥ 18 years White Black	88% 12%	2.6		1.1
Northern Florida county 1971 Schwab et al., 1972	1,645 adults, mean age = 41 White Black	78% 22%			2.7
Epidemiologic Catchment Area Study (ECA), all sites 1981–1985 Mościcki et al., 1988	18,571 adults, ≥ 18 years Non-Black/Non-Hispanic Black Hispanic	69% 23% 8%			2.9[b] 3.0[b] 2.3[b] 3.3[b]
ECA, New Haven, CT	5,034 adults ≥ 18 years Non-Black/Non-Hispanic Black Hispanic	90% 8% 1%			2.4
ECA, Baltimore, MD	3,481 adults ≥ 18 years Non-Black/Non-Hispanic Black Hispanic	65% 34% 1%			3.4
ECA, St. Louis, MO	3,004 adults ≥ 18 years Non-Black/Non-Hispanic Black Hispanic	61% 38% <1%			3.1
ECA, Piedmont area, NC	3,921 adults ≥ 18 years Non-Black/Non-Hispanic Black Hispanic	64% 36% <1%			1.5
ECA, Los Angeles, CA	3,131 adults ≥ 18 years Non-Black/Non-Hispanic Black Hispanic	51% 5% 44%			4.3
ECA, Los Angeles, CA 1981–1985 Sorenson & Golding, 1988	3,125 adults ≥ 18 years Non-Hispanic White Hispanic	42% 46%	18.9 8.8		5.1 3.2
Colorado Social Health Survey 1985–1986 Verona et al., 2004	4,745 adults, mean age = 43 Non-Hispanic White Hispanic African American Other	84% 10% 4% 2%			3.7
National Comorbidity Survey 1990–1992 Kessler et al., 1999 Nock & Kessler, 2006	5,877 respondents, ages 15–54 Non-Hispanic White Non-Hispanic Black Hispanic Other	78% 12% 9% <1%	13.5	3.9	4.6 "Gesture"[c] 1.9 Attempt 2.7

Table 6.1 Continued

Study Site, Study Dates, Reference[a]	Sample Characteristics		Suicidal Ideation	Suicide Plan	Suicide Attempt
American Indian Services Utilization, Psychiatric Epidemiology, Risk and Protective Factors Project (AI-SUPERPFP) 1997–1999 Garroutte et al., 2003	1,456 American Indian Northern Plains tribal members, ages 15–57				
	Males	49%			6.4
	Females	51%			10.8
Baltimore, MD 1999–2000 Ialongo et al., 2002	1,157 African American young adults ages 19–22		14.3		5.3
	Males	44%			
	Females	56%			
National Survey of American Life 2001–2003 Joe et al., 2006	5,181 adults ≥ 18 years		11.7		4.1
	African American	69%	11.7		4.0
	Caribbean Black	31%	12.3		5.1
National Latino and Asian American Study 2002–2003 Fortuna et al., 2007	2,554 Latino adults ≥ 18 years		10.1		4.4
	Puerto Rican	10%	14.2		6.9
	Cuban	5%	7.0		2.9
	Mexican	57%	9.8		3.9
	Other Latino	29%	9.9		4.9
Collaborative Psychiatric Epidemiologic Surveys (CPES), 2001–2003 Borges et al., 2009	1,284 Mexican Americans		13.8	4.3	6.3
	Mexican born	44%	7.8	2.0	2.0
	US born	56%	18.6	6.2	8.9
National Comorbidity Survey Replication (NCS-R) 2001–2003 Nock et al., 2008a	9,282 adults ≥ 18 years		15.6	5.4	5.0
	Non-Hispanic White	70%			
	Non-Hispanic Black	13%			
	Hispanic	12%			
	Other	5%			

[a]In chronological order by survey date.
[b]Weighted by age, sex, and race/ethnicity to standardize the combined ECA 5-site population to the 1980 US household population (Mościcki et al., 1988).
[c]Defined by endorsement of the statement, "My attempt was a cry for help. I did not intend to die" (Kessler et al., 2005).

(2) "I tried to kill myself, but I knew the method was not foolproof," or (3) "My attempt was a cry for help, I did not want to die" (Fortuna et al., 2007; Joe et al., 2006; Kessler et al., 1999, 2005). Respondents who endorsed either the first or the second statement were considered to have made a suicide attempt; respondents who endorsed the third ("cry for help") statement were considered to have made a suicide "gesture." Among lifetime attempters in the NCS, 53% endorsed the first (39.3%) or the second (13.3%) statement; 47% endorsed the third statement (Kessler et al., 1999). These proportions are strikingly similar to those observed in the NSAL, where 55.4% of respondents endorsed the first (41.7%) or the second (13.7%)

statement and 44.6% endorsed the third (Joe et al., 2006). In the NLAAS, a remarkably similar proportion of respondents, 41%, endorsed the first statement about a serious attempt; proportions for the second and third statements have not been reported (Fortuna et al., 2007). Lifetime prevalence rates for nonsuicidal self-injurious behaviors (i.e., "gestures") and attempts appear in Table 6.1; 12-month prevalence rates are shown in Table 6.2. Both lifetime and 12-month estimates imply that true attempts may be more common than nonsuicidal self-injurious behaviors, although the proportion of persons in the population who report the latter is nontrivial and clearly of concern. There appear to be important differences between attempters and "gesturers"

Table 6.2 Twelve-Month Prevalence and Incidence[a] of Non-Fatal Suicidal Behaviors Among Adults From Selected Population-Based Community Surveys, United States

Study Site, Study Dates, Reference[b]	Sample Characteristics		Suicidal Ideation	Suicide Plan	Suicide Attempt
New Haven, CT 1969 Paykel et al., 1974	720 adults, ≥ 18 years		12-month prevalence[c] 1.5		12-month prevalence 0.6
	White	88%			
	Black	12%			
Northern Florida county 1971 Schwab et al., 1972	1,645 adults, mean age = 41		Current[d] 15.9		
	White	78%			
	Black	22%			
ECA Wave 2, Baltimore, MD 1982 Petronis et al., 1990	3,481 adults ≥ 18 years				12-month prevalence 0.22
					1-year incidence: 190/100,000 person-years
	Non-Black/ Non-Hispanic	65%			
	Black	34%			
	Hispanic	1%			
National Comorbidity Survey 1990–1992 Kessler et al., 1999 Nock & Kessler, 2006	5,877 respondents, ages 15–54		12-month prevalence 2.8	12-month prevalence 0.7	12-month prevalence: "Gesture"[d] 0.3 Attempt 0.4
	Non-Hispanic White	78%			
	Non-Hispanic Black	12%			
	Hispanic	9%			
	Other	1%			
ECA 13-year follow-up, Baltimore, MD 1993–1996 Kuo et al., 2001	1,920 adults alive and interviewed at follow-up		13-year cumulative incidence 5.6		13-year cumulative incidence 0.19
			Annual incidence: 415.9/100,000 person-years		Annual incidence: 148.8/100,000 person-years
College Health Risk Behavior Survey 1999 Barrios et al., 2000	2,857 college undergraduates 18–24 years of age		12-month prevalence 11.4	12-month prevalence 7.9	12-month prevalence, all attempts 1.7
					12-month prevalence, medically injurious attempts 0.4
	White	71%			
	Black	11%			
	Hispanic	7%			
Baltimore, MD 1999–2000 Ialongo et al., 2002	1,157 African American young adults ages 19–22		6-month prevalence 1.9		12-month prevalence 1.2
					6-month prevalence 0.4
	Males	44%			
	Females	56%			

Table 6.2 Continued

Study Site, Study Dates, Reference[b]	Sample Characteristics		Suicidal Ideation	Suicide Plan	Suicide Attempt
National Survey of Psychiatric Morbidity 2000–2001 Gunnell et al., 2004	2,404 adults ages 16–74 Males Females	42% 58%	Annual incidence 2.3		
National Comorbidity Survey Replication (NCS-R) 2001–2003 Nock et al., 2008a	4,320 respondents ages 15–54 Non-Hispanic White Non-Hispanic Black Hispanic Other	70% 13% 12% 5%	12-month prevalence 3.3	12-month prevalence 1.0	12-month prevalence: "Gesture"[e] 0.2 Attempt 0.6
National Survey of American Life 2001–2003 Joe et al., 2006	5,181 adults ≥ 18 years African American Caribbean Black	69% 31%	12-month prevalence 2.1		12-month prevalence 0.2

[a]Prevalence and incidence are per 100 unless otherwise noted.
[b]In chronological order by survey date.
[c]Defined by affirmative response to "Have you thought of taking your life, even if you would not really do it?" (Paykel et al., 1974).
[d]Defined by endorsement of any one of the following responses to "How often do you think about suicide?": seldom, sometimes, often, all of the time (Schwab et al., 1972).
[e]Non-suicidal self-injurious behavior, defined by endorsement of the statement, "My attempt was a cry for help. I did not intend to die" (Kessler et al., 2005).

that may represent differential risk and etiological pathways, and perhaps underlying pathophysiology (Keilp et al., 2006; Nock & Kessler, 2006).

Suicide Morbidity: Mechanism of Injury

While population-based epidemiologic surveys have generated rich data for the study of nonfatal suicidal behaviors, there is very little information from these sources on mechanisms of self-inflicted injury. Hospital-based data are the primary source of information in this area. Available information from infrequent reports consistently shows that self-poisoning/ingestion accounts for the vast majority of self-injuries seen in the hospital, estimated to be approximately 70% or more of all cases (McCaig & Nawar, 2006; Pitts, Niska, Xu, & Burt, 2008; Weissman, 1974); recent evidence suggests that the majority of self-poisonings are deliberate (Rhodes et al., 2008). Cutting and stabbing account for approximately 10%–14% of self-injuries seen in hospital emergency departments (Spicer & Miller, 2000; Weissman, 1974). As discussed earlier, hospital data are limited because cases not seen in hospitals cannot be ascertained. There may also be definitional issues associated with suicidal intent and possible failure to appropriately distinguish between suicidal and nonsuicidal self-injury.

Suicide Morbidity: Sociodemographic Patterns
SUICIDE MORBIDITY: SEX

In general, and in contrast to suicide deaths, prevalence rates of both lifetime and 12-month nonfatal suicidal behaviors are higher among women than among men, regardless of age or race/ethnicity (Ialongo et al., 2002; Joe et al., 2006; Nock et al., 2008b; Nock & Kessler, 2006; Mościcki, 1994; Mościcki et al., 1988; Paykel et al., 1974; Schwab et al., 1972; Verona et al., 2004; Weissman, 1974). This well-known and consistent observation has generated a great deal of discussion in the literature, and several plausible explanations have been proposed (Mościcki, 1994). A common explanation is the fact that men are more likely to use more lethal means for self-injury, such as firearms. Another explanation is that of recall bias, as women are known to be better reporters of health events and health history than are men. Recent findings indicate that there are sex differences in the intent behind a self-injurious act, and they underscore the importance of ascertaining this key criterion in all studies of suicidal behavior. Nock and Kessler's examination of "gesture" and attempt data from the NCS indicated that, although the prevalence of lifetime attempts was higher among women than among men, the proportion of women was significantly higher among respondents reporting nonsuicidal "gestures" than among those reporting attempts (Nock & Kessler, 2006).

Available data from studies conducted over three different time periods suggest that there are no significant sex differences in recent or incident suicidal ideation or behaviors (Table 6.2). Petronis et al. (1990) first reported no differences between men and women in incidence of suicide attempts from 1-year follow-up data in the Baltimore ECA. In the 13-year follow-up of the same cohort, Kuo et al. (2001) reported no significant sex differences in incidence of either ideation or attempts. Gunnell et al. (2004) also found no significant differences between men and women in annual incidence of suicidal ideation. Analyses of pooled data from the NCS and NCS-R (Kessler et al., 2005) indicated that there were no significant differences by sex for suicide plans, gestures, or attempts, but there was a weak association of female sex with 12-month prevalence of suicidal ideation. Given the timeframe, it is possible that this finding can be explained by women's better recall of their health history.

SUICIDE MORBIDITY: AGE AND BIRTH COHORT

Unlike suicide mortality rates, which are higher in older age groups, both lifetime and recent rates for nonfatal suicidal behaviors are higher in younger age groups. Higher rates of suicidal behaviors among adolescents than among adults have been consistently observed (e.g., Beautrais et al., 1996; Kessler et al., 1999; Mościcki, 1994; Rhodes et al., 2008). Even within adult developmental periods, however, the rates are higher in younger age groups. For example, ECA data indicate that suicidal behaviors are approximately three times higher among young adults 18–25 years than they are among persons over 65 years of age (Mościcki et al., 1988). In the Baltimore ECA follow-up, Kuo et al. (2001) found that younger women 18–44 years of age at baseline had higher risk for new-onset ideation and attempts than did women in older age groups. Data from the NCS showed higher risk for younger cohorts; the cohort born during 1966–1975 had a six times higher risk for both suicidal ideation and attempts than did the cohort born during 1936–1945 (Kessler et al., 1999). Pooled data from both the NCS and NCS-R indicate that the highest risk for any nonfatal suicidal behaviors among adults occurs in persons 18–24 years (Kessler et al., 2005).

SUICIDE MORBIDITY: ETHNICITY AND RACE

There are no clear patterns of nonfatal suicidal behaviors by race/ethnicity (Table 6.1). Analyses of ECA data indicated that risk was higher among non-Hispanic Whites than among Blacks and Hispanics for lifetime suicidal behaviors (Mościcki et al., 1988; Sorenson & Golding, 1988), but not for incident behaviors (Kuo et al., 2001; Petronis et al., 1990). The NCS found that risk for lifetime suicide attempts, but not ideation, was significantly lower among non-Hispanic Blacks than among Whites (Kessler et al., 1999). Pooled 12-month data for the NCS and NCS-R, however, showed no significant differences in either suicidal ideation or attempts by race/ethnicity (Kessler et al., 2005). NLAAS data, which included Puerto Rican, Cuban, and other Latino samples, show no significant differences in lifetime ideation and attempts between any Latino groups (Fortuna et al., 2007). Analyses of data from the NSAL found significant differences by both ethnicity and sex, with prevalence rates of lifetime suicide attempts significantly higher among African American women and Caribbean Black men, but not among African American men or Caribbean Black women (Joe et al., 2006). Even within a single ethnic group, migration patterns, age at migration, and place of birth are associated with differential risks for suicidal behaviors (Borges et al., 2009). Findings from such large studies of specific racial and ethnic groups in the US population underscore the importance of taking into account race, ethnicity, culture, and migration patterns to better understand highly complex behaviors (Alegría et al., 2004; Takeuchi, Alegría, et al., 2007). Besides giving emphasis to the complexity of suicidality, they suggest that ethnicity and race are likely markers, moderators, or confounders for other risk processes; they also indicate that culture must be taken into account if we are to better understand and prevent suicidal behaviors.

SUICIDE MORBIDITY: SOCIOECONOMIC STATUS AND EDUCATION

There is evidence suggesting that lower socioeconomic status (SES) and lower educational attainment may increase risk for suicidal behaviors among non-Hispanic White adults; the patterns in other race/ethnic groups are not consistent. Analyses of lifetime data from the ECA showed higher odds ratios among persons in the lowest SES categories (Mościcki et al., 1988). Analyses of lifetime data from the NCS (Kessler et al., 1999) and NSAL (Joe et al., 2006), and of pooled 12-month data from the NCS and NCS-R (Kessler et al., 2005; Nock & Kessler, 2006), indicated that adults with lower educational attainment had higher odds ratios for both suicidal ideation and suicide attempts. Consistent with these findings, Kuo et al. found a significant association between lower SES and 13-year incident suicide attempts but not incident suicidal ideation (Kuo et al., 2001). Sorenson and Golding (1988) found a similar pattern among non-Hispanic Whites in the Los Angeles ECA, with higher prevalence of lifetime suicide attempts among those with less than median education. The opposite was true, however, among Hispanics, with higher prevalence among Hispanics with higher than median education (Sorenson & Golding, 1988). Data from the more recently completed NLAAS indicated significantly lower odds of lifetime suicidal ideation, but not suicide attempts, for Latino adults with 16 or more years of education (Fortuna et al., 2007).

SUICIDE MORBIDITY: MARITAL STATUS

There is consistent evidence from studies covering various timeframes that persons who have been previously married are at higher risk for suicidal thinking and behaviors (Gunnell et al., 2004; Kessler et al., 1999, 2005; Kuo et al., 2001; Petronis et al., 1990). This finding has been reported most frequently for persons who are separated or divorced, but there is some evidence that widowed adults may also be at higher risk (Kuo et al., 2001). While it is possible that the actual event of divorce or separation may act as a precipitant to suicidal thinking and behavior, it is more likely that persons who are separated or divorced carry a greater burden of risk antecedent to marriage and may be more likely to end up in unstable relationships. This sociodemographic correlate may be a marker for other risk processes.

Suicide Mortality and Morbidity: Onset and Course

Both nonfatal and fatal suicidal behaviors first emerge during the adolescent years. As shown in Figure 6.2, suicide deaths are extremely rare in children. There is a general belief that young children are incapable of suicidal intent; indeed, from a developmental perspective, it is clear that young children do not have a genuine understanding of the concept of death. The National Center for Health Statistics does not include intentional self-harm as a potential cause of death in children below the age of 5 years. In 2007 there were 4 suicide deaths recorded in children ages 5–9 years, compared with 180 deaths among 10- to 14-year-olds and 1,481 in 15- to 19-year-olds (US DHHS, 2010b). Suicide mortality rates increase rapidly during adolescence in all the major race/ethnic groups and, as previously noted, continue to increase with age for White men.

Findings from retrospective and prospective data indicate that nonfatal suicidal behaviors also have their onset during the developmentally turbulent period of adolescence. Ialongo et al. (2002), in their follow-up of young, urban, African American adults, found that the onset of a first suicide attempt occurred between the ages of 11 and 15 years. In the NLAAS, 62% of adult Latino attempters reported their first attempt occurred when they were under age 18 (Fortuna et al., 2007). Suicide morbidity age-of-onset curves from the NCS (Kessler et al., 1999) and NSAL (Joe et al., 2006) are remarkably similar to suicide mortality curves among males in all race/ethnicity groups except non-Hispanic Whites. There is general agreement that the teens and early 20s represent the period of greatest risk for first onset of suicidal ideation, plan, and attempt, with a probable peak in the mid-to-late teens and elevated, but decreasing risk into young adulthood (Gunnell et al., 2004; Joe et al., 2006; Kessler et al., 1999; Lewinsohn, Rohde, & Seeley, 1996; Nock et al., 2008b). The risk for first attempt appears to be higher than the risk for a suicide plan during this period, with nonplanned, impulsive attempts more common than planned attempts (Joe et al., 2006; Kessler et al., 1999).

These behavioral observations from epidemiologic studies are consistent with what is now known about brain maturation from longitudinal imaging studies of children, adolescents and young adults, with differential maturation of cortical structures occurring in a roughly back-to-front progression. The prefrontal cortex, which is associated with higher order executive functions and emotional control, continues to mature into the mid-20s (Gogtay et al., 2004; Steinberg, 2008). Developmental trajectories of brain maturation occur at different rates in males and females, with females peaking earlier than males (Lenroot et al., 2007; Wilke,

Krägeloh-Mann, & Holland, 2007). From a developmental and social neuroscience perspective, it is during this period that enormous physiological, hormonal, social, and contextual changes also occur. There is also evidence that risk taking increases from childhood to adolescence and decreases from adolescence to adulthood (Steinberg, 2008). This process parallels dramatic structural and functional cortical changes that may be manifested behaviorally as extreme emotional lability; impulsivity; experimentation with alcohol, nicotine, and other substances; or first onset of a mental disorder and/or suicidal behavior in vulnerable individuals. The observed decreasing risk of first onset of suicidal ideation, plan, and attempt beyond adolescence is again consistent with increased myelination and connectivity of white matter in the prefrontal cortex in late adolescence, a process that continues into the mid-20s (Gogtay et al., 2004; Steinberg, 2008).

The fact that the prevalence of suicidal ideation is consistently higher than that of suicide attempts indicates that not all ideators make plans and that not all those who think about suicide progress to suicidal behaviors. The majority of adults in the general population who report suicidal ideation do not make a plan or attempt suicide. Based on available evidence from retrospective studies, it appears that approximately one-third of lifetime or 12-month ideators transition to making a plan, and about one-fourth of ideators make an impulsive or unplanned attempt (Joe et al., 2006; Kessler et al., 1999, 2005). Among ideators who do make a plan, however, the risk of attempting suicide is high (Joe et al., 2006; Kessler et al., 1999, 2005). The period of transition from ideation to action is approximately 1 year for both planned and unplanned attempts; the risk of progression from ideation to plan to attempt is highest in the first year (Kessler et al., 1999; Nock et al., 2008b). Ninety percent of impulsive attempts, that is, suicidal behaviors among ideators without a plan, and 60% of planned attempts, occur within 1 year of onset of ideation (Joe et al., 2006; Kessler et al., 1999, 2005). From a public health perspective, these transitions present multiple opportunities for preventive and/or treatment intervention.

Risk and Protective Processes

This section discusses what is known about risk processes that contribute to suicidal behaviors among adults. Potential protective processes also are considered. Risk and protection are discussed within a general framework that highlights distal and proximal, and individual and environmental processes.

Risk and Protective Processes: General Considerations

Risk and protection are not static entities; they should be thought of as complex, dynamic processes internal and external to the individual that change over time and interact with each other to increase or decrease risk for nonfatal and fatal suicidal behaviors. The potential for suicidal behavior increases with an individual's burden of risk (Juurlink, Herrmann, Szalai, Kopp, & Redelmeier, 2004; Kessler et al., 1999; Scott et al., 2010). In considering risk, it is important to remember that suicide is rarely, if ever, an outcome of a single risk process.

Risk processes can be distal or proximal, individual or environmental, fixed or malleable (Mann et al., 2005; Mościcki, 2001). Distal risk represents potential underlying biological, interpersonal, and/or contextual vulnerability and is necessary but not sufficient for suicidal behavior. The major distal risk processes that are significantly associated with suicidal behaviors include psychopathology, comorbidity, selected endophenotypes, and familial contribution to risk (Mann et el., 2009; Mościcki et al., 1988; Mościcki, 1994, 1997, 2001; Rich, Young, & Fowler, 1986). Proximal risk processes, on the other hand, are more closely associated with suicidal events and, in the context of increased distal risk, may act as stressors or precipitants to potentially fatal actions. Proximal processes are neither necessary nor sufficient for suicidal behavior (Mościcki, 1994, 1997, 2001). Proximal processes that have been associated with suicidal behaviors include access to firearms, stressful life events or loss, intoxication, contagion, incarceration, physical illness, and prescription medications. No single distal or proximal risk process is unique to suicidal behaviors: Many persons without a history of suicidal behavior can be and have been exposed to them. It is their co-occurrence and interaction with distal processes that can lead to the necessary and sufficient conditions that result in a fatal or nonfatal suicide event. While this complexity calls for complicated and intricate causal models, it also provides multiple opportunities to alleviate an individual's suffering by highlighting potential points of intervention (Mann et al., 2005; Mościcki, 2001).

Most known risk and protective processes for suicidal behaviors have been identified at the individual or, less often, the interpersonal level. From a public health perspective, however, it is also useful to consider potential risk and protective processes that may exist at the environmental or contextual levels. Organizing our understanding of risk and protection for suicidal behaviors into broad categories or classes makes it possible to more readily develop plausible strategies for preventive and treatment interventions (Mann et al., 2005; Mościcki, 2001).

It is important to distinguish between fixed, immutable correlates or markers such as age and sex (Kraemer et al., 1997) and potentially causal processes that are malleable and thus may become possible targets for preventive interventions (Kraemer et al., 1997; Mościcki, 2001). An awareness of fixed markers such as sociodemographic correlates is nonetheless useful, as they may be indicators of possible risk processes in specific populations. For example, trend data such as the recent increase in suicide deaths among middle-aged, non-Hispanic Whites, or the frequently noted low rates among Black women, indicate opportunities to more closely examine risk and protective processes within defined population groups. More generally, maintaining an awareness of and distinction between a fixed marker and causal risk process is critical for developing appropriate intervention strategies (Kraemer et al., 1997; Mościcki, 2001).

Most epidemiologic evidence on risk for suicidal behaviors comes from population-based psychological autopsy studies. These are retrospective, intensive investigations of consecutive suicide deaths occurring within a defined time period and geographic area (Mościcki, 1997, 2001). The psychological autopsy process involves conducting interviews with individuals who were close to the decedent, most often members of the family, and combining these interview data with available corroborating evidence from hospital, medical examiner, and justice system records to develop a comprehensive profile of the deceased (Beskow, Runeson, & Åsgård, 1990; Cavanagh, Carson, Sharpe, & Lawrie, 2003). The strongest psychological autopsy studies have used case-control designs with appropriate comparison groups (Cavanagh et al., 2003). Other sources of information on risk and protection include case-control studies of serious suicide attempters, and population-based surveys.

Risk and Protective Processes: Distal Risk Processes

RISK AND PROTECTIVE PROCESSES: PSYCHOPATHOLOGY

Strong and consistent evidence from both national and international studies indicates that suicide is a complication of psychiatric illness (Conwell et al., 1996; Henriksson et al., 1993, 1995; Lesage et al., 1994; Mann, 2003; Mann et al., 2005; Rich, Young, & Fowler, 1986). Over 90% of adult suicide deaths are associated with psychiatric disorders (Conwell et al., 1996; Henriksson et al., 1993, 1995; Lesage et al., 1994; Rich, Young, & Fowler, 1986). In addition to the strong link with suicide fatalities, psychiatric disorders are also found in the large majority of persons who make serious suicide attempts (Beautrais et al., 1996; Beautrais, 2001; Ialongo et al., 2002; Joe et al., 2006; Kessler et al., 1999, 2005; Mościcki et al., 1988). Psychiatric illness is a necessary condition for suicidal behaviors (Mościcki, 2001; Rich, Young, & Fowler, 1986). The mental disorders most frequently found in psychological autopsy investigations of suicide deaths include mood/depressive disorders, substance use disorders, and personality disorders.

Mood disorders, principally major depression and bipolar disorder, are associated with approximately 50% to 60% of suicide fatalities among adult men and women (Conwell et al., 1996; Henriksson et al., 1993; Mann, 2003; Rich, Young, & Fowler, 1986; Rich, Fowler, Fogarty, & Young, 1988) and represent the largest proportion of diagnoses among adults with nonfatal suicidal behaviors (Beautrais et al., 1996; Beautrais, 2001; Kessler et al., 2005). Mood disorders are found in a higher proportion of female than male suicides, even though suicide rates and numbers of suicide deaths are much lower among women than men (Rich, Fowler, et al., 1988). Although the strong association of major depression with nonfatal and fatal suicidal behaviors is consistent across all age groups, the proportion of persons with depression is higher among elderly suicides than among younger adults (Conwell & Brent, 1995; Henriksson et al., 1993, 1995; Rich, Young, & Fowler, 1986). The link with depression is maintained, or even strengthened, when the death/suicide cluster is removed from the diagnostic algorithm for depression (Ialongo et al., 2002; Kessler et al., 1999; Mościcki et al., 1988; Nock & Kessler, 2006; Wilcox, Storr, & Breslau, 2009). Paradoxically, however, objective severity of depression does not appear to be a reliable predictor of suicide. Rather, it is the subjective perception of depression's impact, in the presence of hopelessness, increased suicidal ideation, and co-occurring disorders, that appears to be a more reliable predictor of suicidal behavior (Beck, Steer, Kovacs, & Garrison, 1985; Dumais et al., 2005; Mann et al., 1999).

Substance use disorders, especially alcohol abuse or dependence, are generally the second most frequent disorders found among adults who die by suicide (Henriksson et al., 1995; Rich, Young, & Fowler, 1986), although in one psychological autopsy study in a New York county, substance use disorders were more frequent than mood disorders (Conwell et al., 1996). Substance use disorders have been found in approximately equal frequency among both men and women who die by suicide (Dumais et al., 2005; Ialongo et al., 2002; Nock & Kessler, 2006; Rich, Fowler, et al., 1988), but there are differences by age, with higher frequencies among younger adults who die by suicide (Conwell et al., 1996; Rich, Young, & Fowler, 1986) or attempt suicide (Beautrais et al., 1996; Beautrais, 2001; Kessler et al., 2005; Kuo et al., 2001; Nock & Kessler, 2006; Petronis et al., 1990). Both alcohol and drug dependence convey substantially greater, independent risk for subsequent nonfatal suicidal behaviors than do alcohol and drug abuse without dependence, with primary effects on suicidal ideation and suicide attempts without a plan (Borges et al., 2000). Alcohol is the most frequently noted substance of abuse, although studies also have investigated selected illegal drugs such as cocaine (Marzuk, Tardiff, et al., 1992). Recent clinical and community studies have included nicotine dependence as well and have found a strong cross-sectional association between current smoking and risk for suicidal thoughts or behaviors (Breslau et al., 2005; Hemmingsson & Kriebel, 2003; Malone et al., 2003; Oquendo et al., 2004). Limited prospective work in a community sample of young adults suggests that nicotine dependence, as indicated by current smoking, may independently increase risk for suicidal thoughts and attempts even when alcohol use disorders and other psychiatric diagnoses are controlled for (Breslau et al., 2005). The number of substances contributing to risk appears to be more important than the type of substance of use, abuse, or dependence; risk for suicidal behaviors increases in a dose–response relationship with the number of substances reported (Borges et al., 2000).

Other diagnoses more commonly found in higher proportions among younger adult suicide attempters and fatalities include disorders characterized by behavioral dysregulation and aggression, such as oppositional-defiant disorder, borderline personality disorder, or antisocial personality disorder (Dumais et al., 2005; Hawton, Houston, Haw, Townsend, & Harriss, 2003; Henriksson et al., 1993; Ialongo et al., 2002; Keilp et al., 2006; Kuo et al., 2001; Nock & Kessler, 2006; Rich, Young, & Fowler, 1986).

Only a handful of psychological autopsy studies have reported any anxiety disorders among suicide fatalities, with frequencies ranging from 0.0% to 11% (Conwell et al., 1996; Henriksson et al., 1993, 1996; Lesage et al., 1994). On the other hand, population-based epidemiologic surveys have examined suicidal ideation and attempts among adults with various anxiety disorders and have reported significantly elevated lifetime or incident risk associated with most. Adjusted lifetime risk estimates range from 1.5% to 5.6% for specific anxiety disorders, and from 2.5% to 6.0% for any anxiety disorder (Joe et al., 2006; Kessler et al., 1999, 2005; Sareen et al., 2005). Sareen et al. (2005) found that risk for incident suicidal ideation was significantly associated with any anxiety disorder and specifically with social phobia, generalized anxiety disorder, and obsessive-compulsive disorder. Risk for incident suicide attempts was significantly associated with any anxiety disorder and with simple phobia, but not with other specific anxiety disorders.

Attention has increasingly turned to the potential role of posttraumatic stress disorder (PTSD) in fatal and nonfatal suicidal behavior. PTSD has only recently been recognized as a valid psychiatric diagnosis; it was not until 1980 that it was added to the nomenclature with the publication of the third edition of the *Diagnostic and Statistical Manual of Mental Disorders* (*DSM*) (APA, 1980; Nemeroff et al., 2006). Possibly because of its recency as a diagnosis, only one report on PTSD in a population-based sample of adult suicide deaths has been published. Gradus et al. (2010) examined mortality data from Danish health registries covering a period from 1994 to 2006. They found that those with a diagnosis of PTSD had 5.3 times the rate of suicide death compared with those without PTSD, adjusted for depression and selected sociodemographic characteristics as potential confounders. Further, the rate of suicide was substantially higher for those with a history of both PTSD and depression than from either diagnosis alone (Gradus et al., 2010). In the few epidemiologic studies of suicide morbidity that have included PTSD, significantly elevated risk for lifetime suicidal behaviors ranged from 4.0% to 6.0% (Joe et al., 2006; Kessler et al., 1999). There is evidence suggesting that the nature of the traumatic exposure may be related to the development of PTSD and associated suicidal behavior. In a follow-up study of young urban adults who had previously participated in a large, community-based, randomized prevention trial, Wilcox et al. (2009) found a significant and independent association of PTSD and subsequent suicide attempts (RR = 2.7). Of note, they also found that PTSD associated with exposure to assaultive violence significantly increased the risk for subsequent suicide attempt, but that exposure to a nonassaultive traumatic event did not (Wilcox et al., 2009). This is consistent with Nock and Kessler's report that increased risk for suicidal self-injurious behavior was associated with a history of multiple incidents of rape, sexual abuse, and physical assault (Nock & Kessler, 2006).

Although suicidal behaviors associated with schizophrenia and schizoaffective disorder are of great concern in clinical patients (Bourgeois et al., 2004; Caldwell & Gottesman, 1990; Hawton et al., 2005; Palmer et al., 2005; Tsuang et al., 1980), information on psychotic disorders from population-based studies of suicide is rare. Available findings indicate that the prevalence of suicidal behaviors and suicide deaths associated with psychotic disorders in the population is considerably smaller than that from mood and substance use disorders. In the general population, lifetime diagnoses of psychotic disorders have been found in less than 20% of suicide fatalities (Heila, Isometsä, Henriksson, Marttunen, & Lönnqvist, 1997; Rich, Motooka, Fowler, & Young, 1988; Robins, 1986), and in less than 6% of nonfatal suicidal behaviors (Joe et al., 2006; Kessler et al., 1999; Nock & Kessler, 2006; Sorenson & Golding, 1988). The adjusted risk for nonfatal suicidal behavior does not appear to be significantly higher for persons with a history of psychotic disorders, which suggests that mood and substance use disorders that are comorbid with a psychotic disorder are more likely to increase suicide risk than psychotic disorders alone (Joe et al., 2006; Kessler et al., 1999, 2005; Kuo et al., 2001; Nock & Kessler, 2006).

RISK AND PROTECTIVE PROCESSES: CO-OCCURRING DISORDERS

There is increasing recognition by researchers that co-occurrence of psychiatric disorders is the rule rather than the exception (Boyd et al., 1984; Helzer et al., 2008; Regier et al., 1990), and consistent evidence that co-occurrence of psychiatric disorders is a key contributor to elevated risk for both fatal and nonfatal suicide behaviors. In the few psychological autopsy studies that have investigated this variable, co-occurring mental, substance use, and/or physical disorders were found in approximately 70% to 80% of individuals who died by suicide (Lesage et al., 1994; Rich, Young, & Fowler,

1986). Both clinical and epidemiologic studies of nonfatal suicidal behaviors have also found greatly elevated risk among adults with more than one diagnosis (Beautrais et al., 1996; Fortuna et al., 2007; Hawton et al., 2003, 2005; Ialongo et al., 2002; Joe et al., 2006; Kessler et al., 1999; Kuo et al., 2001; Mościcki, 1994; Sareen et al., 2005). Occurrence of comorbid disorders may increase risk for multiple attempts (Forman, Berk, Henriques, Brown, & Beck, 2004; Hawton et al., 2003, 2005). For example, the link between increased suicide risk and awareness of disease in newly diagnosed schizophrenia patients appears to be mediated by depression and hopelessness (Bourgeois et al., 2004; Hawton et al., 2005); similarly, risk for incident suicidal ideation and attempts is increased with co-occurrence of mood and anxiety disorders (Sareen et al., 2005). Compelling evidence from epidemiologic studies of different populations points to a dose–response relationship, with risk for both suicidal ideation and attempts increasing with the number of diagnoses (Beautrais et al., 1996; Ialongo et al., 2002; Joe et al., 2006; Kessler et al., 1999; Mościcki, 1994; Sareen et al., 2005). These findings suggest that suicidal behaviors are more likely to be associated with more severe forms of mental illness and may be a necessary condition for suicidality. Mood and substance use disorders, and mood and personality disorders, are the most frequently identified co-occurring conditions (Beautrais et al., 1996; Dumais et al., 2005; Fortuna et al., 2007; Henriksson et al., 1993; Rich, Young, et al., 1986). The risk for suicidal behavior associated with a diagnosis of depression is increased with a history of lifetime aggression, impulsivity, substance abuse, and a family history of suicide (Dumais ct al., 2005; Mann, 2003).

RISK AND PROTECTIVE PROCESSES: HISTORY OF SUICIDE ATTEMPTS

A history of previous suicide attempts has consistently been shown to increase risk for both subsequent attempts and suicide death, especially in the context of bipolar illness, depression, or schizophrenia; the population attributable fraction has been estimated to range from 4.0 to 9.3 (Gunnell et al., 2008; Robins et al., 1959; Tidemalm et al., 2008). Although previous suicide attempts are not clinically reliable in identifying individuals at imminent risk for death (Beck et al., 1990; Pokorny, 1993), more recent efforts at constructing a risk index using population-based data appear promising (Borges et al., 2006). Recent findings also indicate that a history of multiple attempts may be a behavioral marker for severe psychopathology (Forman et al., 2004). Multiple attempters are more likely to have comorbid disorders, more feelings of hopelessness, and poorer global functioning (Forman et al., 2004).

RISK AND PROTECTIVE PROCESSES: NEUROCHEMICAL CORRELATES AND ENDOPHENOTYPES

Recent rapid advances in neuroscience, brain imaging technology, mapping of the human genome, and increasing understanding of endophenotypes and gene–environment interactions have opened highly promising avenues of investigation into the pathophysiology of suicidal behaviors and provided unprecedented opportunities for new insights into the biological underpinnings of behavioral components of suicide vulnerability. An understanding of the pathophysiology of such components can lead to identification of suicide endophenotypes, the genes responsible for them, and development of targeted preventive or treatment interventions.

An endophenotype is an internal phenotype between gene and disease, which must meet five criteria. These include (1) an association with illness in the population; (2) heritability of 20% or greater; (3) primarily state independent; (4) cosegregation of illness and endophenotype within families; and (5) a higher frequency in nonaffected family members than in the general population (Gottesman & Gould, 2003).

Early neurochemical investigations in suicide attempters and studies of postmortem brain tissue of suicide fatalities focused on the serotonergic system, a neuroendocrine system that plays a key role in the pathophysiology of depression. Initial studies found that levels of cerebral spinal fluid (CSF) 5HIAA (5-hydroxyindole acetic acid) were deficient in the brains of adult violent suicide attempters and suicide fatalities (see Mann, 2003 for a review). Serotonergic system alterations play a role in clinical features that have been linked to suicidal behaviors, including hopelessness and pessimism. Suicide attempters feel more hopeless and pessimistic than other patients in the face of equivalent psychiatric illness or adverse life events (Mann, 2003; Oquendo et al., 2004). Serotonergic dysfunction is now known to be independently associated with aggression as well as depression, and it may also be associated with disinhibition and hopelessness (Mann, 2003; Mann et al., 2009); both are associated with increased risk for nonfatal and fatal suicidal behavior (Dumais et al., 2005; Mann, 2003) and are heritable (Mann,

2003; Mann et al., 2009). Serotonergic function also is involved in the regulation of satiety and hunger. While the exact mechanism is not clear, the shared link between satiety, mood, and impulsivity or aggression may help explain epidemiologic and clinical observations of increased risk for nonfatal and fatal suicidal behaviors associated with lower body mass index and lower levels of total plasma cholesterol (Favaro, Caregaro, di Pascoli, Brambilla, & Santonastaso, 2004; Freedman et al., 1995; Jacobs, Muldoon, & Rastam, 1995; Kaplan et al., 1997; Kim & Myint, 2004; Magnusson, Rasmussen, Lawlor, Tynelius, & Gunnell, 2006). More work is needed, however, to determine whether CSF 5HIAA deficiency can be considered to be an endophenotype (Mann et al., 2009).

Endophenotypes for which there is now sufficient evidence of a significant association with suicidal behaviors, and which meet the Gottesman and Gould criteria, include impulsive-aggressive traits, early onset of major depression, neurocognitive function, and heightened cortisol response to social stress (Mann et al., 2009). Proposed candidate endophenotypes, which meet some, but not all, of the Gottesman and Gould criteria include altered serotonergic system function (e.g., CSF 5HIAA deficiency), altered brain glucose metabolism, dysfunction in interpersonal reactivity, and affect dysregulation (Mann et al., 2009).

RISK AND PROTECTIVE PROCESSES: FAMILIAL FACTORS

Familial factors represent biological, interpersonal, and environmental risk and their interaction. Individuals at elevated risk for nonfatal and fatal suicidal behaviors are more likely to come from families with a history of suicide or mental and substance use disorders (Borges et al., 2006; Egeland & Sussex, 1985; Hawton et al., 2005; Lesage et al., 1994; Mann, 2003; Mann et al., 2009; Melhem et al., 2007; Runeson & Åsberg, 2003). The heritability, or genetic contribution, of a broad suicide phenotype, which includes ideation, plans, and attempts, is estimated to be approximately 30% to 50% (Mann et al., 2009). Aggression and impulsivity are transmitted in families and have biological correlates (Mann et al., 2009)

In addition to the biological vulnerabilities represented by endophenotypes and mental and substance use disorders, a disrupted and toxic family environment may also contribute to elevated risk. Suicide risk increases in domestic environments characterized by family conflict, a disrupted marital relationship, and physical or sexual abuse (Briere & Zaidi, 1989; Luoma & Pearson, 2002; Roustit et al., 2009; Smith et al., 1988). A history of sexual abuse, especially in women, significantly increases risk for suicidal behaviors in adults (Briere & Zaidi, 1989; Roustit et al., 2009). There may be a dose–response relationship between history of sexual or physical abuse and subsequent suicide attempts; multiple abuse events are associated with increased risk (Nock & Kessler, 2006). Based on our current understanding of endophenotypes, stress, and gene–environment interplay (Caspi et al., 2002; Mann et al., 2009; Moffitt et al., 2006), it is likely, for example, that a biologically vulnerable individual may be at higher risk than a nonvulnerable individual in the context of an abusive family environment. The nature of the environment may aggravate biological vulnerability, which in turn may increase the risk for adverse mental health outcomes, including suicidal behaviors.

Risk and Protective Processes: Proximal Risk Processes

RISK AND PROTECTIVE PROCESSES: STRESSFUL LIFE EVENTS AND LOSS

The occurrence of stressful life events that precede a nonfatal or fatal suicide event has been consistently documented in both the news media (e.g., Kelly, 2008) and in the scholarly literature (Henriksson et al., 1993; Rich, Fowler, et al., 1988; Rich, Ricketts, Fowler, & Young, 1988; Rich, Young, et al., 1986; Rich, Warstadt, Nemiroff, Fowler, & Young, 1991). Although anecdotal accounts in the popular press in particular often initiate speculation about whether the event "caused" the suicidal behavior, evidence from well-designed studies indicates that, while stressful life events can indeed increase the risk for suicidal behavior, they are not in and of themselves directly causal. Specific negative life events are likely to differ with age. For young adults, stressors may include such things as a fight with a romantic partner or parents, a humiliating experience, failure of an exam or class, peer rejection, or exposure to interpersonal violence. For older adults, job loss, the death of a spouse, suspicion of terminal illness, perceived loss of independence, exposure to disaster, or sudden disability may be more salient stressors.

Like all proximal risk processes, stressful life events are neither necessary nor sufficient for suicidal behaviors. With few exceptions, there is

nothing unique about most of the life events that may precede suicide, since most individuals experience similar events and do not attempt or die by suicide. Rather, it is the personal perception of the impact of the event that increases risk for nonfatal and fatal suicidal behaviors (Mann, 2003; Mann et al., 2009; Rich et al., 1991; Wilcox et al., 2009), suggesting that the psychiatric response to the stressor must be taken into account. This is consistent with previous observations from clinical studies that it is the impact of depression or other disease on the individual rather than its severity, or impact of the stressor rather than its nature, that may be the salient element in suicide risk (Mann, 2003; Rich et al., 1991). There is also some evidence that the type of stressor or event may be less important than the number of stressors; higher risk for suicidal thinking and behaviors is associated with a greater number of stressors (Gunnell et al., 2004; Juurlink et al., 2004; Kessler et al., 1999; Scott et al., 2010).

The specific life events of unemployment and job loss have received attention recently in the context of the worldwide economic recession. Evidence for a direct link with suicidal behaviors is ambiguous, however, and confounded by the fact that both unemployment and suicidal behaviors may share common antecedent risk, since persons with psychiatric illness are more likely to be unemployed or at higher risk of becoming unemployed (Agerbo, 2005; Beautrais et al., 1998; Blakely, Collings, & Atkinson, 2003). Recent longitudinal work suggests that there may be an indirect link, as unemployment and financial strain as stressors may have a causal influence on depression and suicidal thinking and behaviors, particularly in individuals who may have underlying biological vulnerabilities (Blakely et al., 2003; Gunnell et al., 2004).

RISK AND PROTECTIVE PROCESSES: ACCESS TO LETHAL MEANS

Evidence from ecological analyses suggests that suicide rates may be driven in part by availability of specific methods for fatal injury (Boyd & Mościcki, 1986; Markush & Bartolucci, 1984; Marzuk, Leon, et al., 1992). As previously noted, firearms are the most frequent mechanism employed among suicide fatalities in the United States, followed by suffocation, poisoning, and falls (Murphy et al., 2013). Poisoning is the most common mechanism employed by adults who attempt suicide (McCaig & Nawar, 2006; Pitts et al., 2008; Weissman, 1974), followed by cutting and stabbing (Spicer & Miller, 2000; Weissman, 1974).

The proportion of suicide deaths accounted for by firearms has been slowly declining since 1990, although the reasons for this are not entirely clear. Nonetheless, this trend is encouraging, since from a public health perspective a decrease in the leading mechanism of death can in turn result in a decrease in the overall suicide rate.

RISK AND PROTECTIVE PROCESSES: INTOXICATION

Psychological autopsy studies have found that approximately 25% to 50% of adults who die by suicide are intoxicated at the time of death, with higher proportions among younger suicides (Ford, Rushforth, Rushforth, Hirsch, & Adelson, 1979; Goldsmith et al., 2002; Hlady & Middaugh, 1988; May et al., 2002; Rich, Young, et al., 1986). Alcohol is the primary intoxicating substance, but other drugs also can play a role, as well as intoxication with multiple substances (Borges & Rosovsky, 1996; Marzuk, Tardiff, et al., 1992). Intoxication has been linked with increased impulsivity and disinhibition (Beautrais et al., 1996; Henriksson et al., 1993; Kessler et al., 1999; Lesage et al., 1994; Petronis et al., 1990; Rich, Young, et al., 1986). Ethanol is known to have a disinhibitory effect on individuals with existing social and psychological problems (Goldsmith et al., 2002), and current drug use can increase risk of unplanned (impulsive) attempted suicide among ideators (Borges & Rosovsky, 1996; Borges et al., 2000). Available evidence suggests that increased risk for suicidal behaviors is linked with current substance use rather than a history of substance use (Borges & Rosovsky, 1996; Borges et al., 2000; Marzuk, Tardiff, et al., 1992). Intoxication can take on greater potency in combination with other proximal risk processes such as a stressful life event and ready access to a lethal mechanism of death, especially a firearm (Hlady & Middaugh, 1988). An example of a particularly lethal risk constellation may include a major depressive episode and comorbid substance use disorder, relationship loss, intoxication, and availability of a firearm.

RISK AND PROTECTIVE PROCESSES: CONTAGION

There is a great deal of evidence from ecological studies on the influence of the media on suicidal behaviors (Gould & Shaffer, 1986; Hawton & Williams, 2002; Phillips & Carstersen, 1986; Schmidtke & Häfner, 1988). Both print and broadcast media have the potential to have an effect on vulnerable individuals, whether the death being reported on is fact or fiction. Media impact is most likely when the mechanism of death is portrayed in detail or when a story is reported in a dramatic or sensationalized manner (Hawton & Williams, 2002). Youth and young adults are more vulnerable than older persons, which, from a developmental perspective, is consistent with the intense peer orientation of youth and recent understanding of cortical development and executive function continuing into the mid-20s (Gogtay et al., 2004; Steinberg, 2008). Recognition of the media's potential influence on suicidal behaviors has prompted the development of media guidelines for the responsible reporting of suicides in the United States and other nations (American Foundation for Suicide Prevention et al., 2011; O'Carroll & Potter, 1994).

RISK AND PROTECTIVE PROCESSES: INCARCERATION

Suicide rates among prisoners are substantially higher than in the general population (Fazel & Benning, 2009; Patterson & Hughes, 2008; Salive, Smith, & Brewer, 1989), and suicide fatalities rank among the leading causes of death in jails and lockups (Hayes, 1989; Patterson & Hughes, 2008; Salive et al., 1989; US DHHS, 1999). It is not clear whether incarceration independently increases risk for suicidal behaviors, since, as in unemployment, the incarcerated population shares overlapping distal risks for multiple serious outcomes, including suicidal behaviors (Fazel & Benning, 2009; Patterson & Hughes, 2008). Persons with mental and/or substance use disorders are more likely to be unemployed and/or homeless, at higher risk for criminal behavior or victimization, and more likely to be arrested and detained (Coldwell & Bender, 2007; US DHHS, 1999; West et al., 2009).

RISK AND PROTECTIVE PROCESSES: NONPSYCHIATRIC ILLNESS

Selected nonpsychiatric illnesses have been associated with elevated risk for suicide, the most commonly identified being HIV/AIDS, Huntington disease, and malignant neoplasms (Harris & Barraclough, 1994; Marzuk, 1994). Careful investigation, however, has found that patients with chronic, and especially terminal, illness exhibit characteristics that are known to be independent risk processes for suicidal behaviors (Harris & Barraclough, 1994; Marzuk, 1994). The effect of nonpsychiatric illness on suicide is thought to be mediated by depression, substance use disorders, and other suicide risk processes (Conwell, Duberstein, & Caine, 2001; Harris & Barraclough, 1994; Marzuk, 1994). For example, the previously reported strong association with HIV/AIDS has since been shown to be much weaker than initially believed, and likely accounted for by other risk processes for suicide (Marzuk et al., 1988, 1997) such as substance use disorders.

Recent work has found epilepsy, cancer, and heart attack or stroke to be independently associated with planned suicide attempts, and a greater number of physical conditions to be associated with suicidal outcomes (Scott et al., 2010). Further, moderate to severe pain in the context of nonpsychiatric illness has been found to independently increase risk for suicide death among the elderly (Juurlink et al., 2004), and arthritis, headache, and other chronic pain independently increase risk for lifetime suicidal ideation and suicide attempts (Scott et al., 2010). The relationship between physical conditions and suicidality may be stronger in younger age groups (Scott et al., 2010).

RISK AND PROTECTIVE
PROCESSES: PHARMACEUTICALS

People with serious medical conditions are more likely to be exposed to multiple powerful pharmaceuticals, which in turn may contribute to the development of depression (Sorenson, 1991). The role of polypharmacy has not been systematically examined in controlled studies. Recent medical and public attention has turned to selected serotonin reuptake inhibitors (SSRIs) as potential precipitants of suicidal thinking and behaviors in patients being treated for depression. This scrutiny was initiated when data from efficacy trials of SSRIs raised concerns about increases in suicidal thinking and behaviors in youth, prompting the Food and Drug Administration (FDA) in 2004 to issue a strong public health advisory about the safety of SSRIs (US DHHS, 2004). This "black box" warning conveyed the highest level of urgency and was initially focused on risk associated with antidepressant use in adolescent patients. It was later extended to include adult patients, amid continuing scientific controversy and uncertainty (Barbui, Esposito, & Cipriani, 2009; US DHHS, 2005).

Rigorous observational studies and meta-analyses have found no evidence that SSRIs or antidepressants increase risk for suicide in adults, and conversely they have found consistent evidence that they may save lives (Barbui et al., 2009; Gibbons, Hur, Bhaumik, & Mann, 2005; Isacsson, Holmgren, Ösby, & Ahlner, 2009; Simon, Savarino, Operskalski, & Wang, 2006). An ecological, county-level analysis of antidepressant prescriptions and suicide death rates from 1996 to 1998 found that US counties with higher prescription rates of newer antidepressants, including both SSRIs and non-SSRIs, had lower suicide rates than counties with higher use rates of tricyclic antidepressants (Gibbons et al., 2005). Simon et al. (2006) analyzed data on acute-phase antidepressant treatment in patients enrolled in a large group health plan. They linked computerized records with hospital discharge data and state and national death certificate information and also found no evidence of increased risk for medically injurious suicide attempts or suicide death after starting antidepressant medication, and no increased risk associated with newer antidepressants. They did find that risk for a serious attempt requiring hospitalization was highest in the month before the start of treatment. The risk fell by more than one-half in the first month following the start of treatment, then declined progressively over the next 5 months. Isacsson et al. (2009), in a case-control study that examined toxicology data from suicide and nonsuicide deaths in Sweden, concluded that antidepressant use reduced the risk of suicide death by 43%. Furthermore, a recently published meta-analysis confirmed that SSRIs convey a protective effect in adults, although there appears to be an increased risk among adolescents (Barbui et al., 2009).

The FDA revised the black box warning again to acknowledge the protective effect of SSRIs for adults and elderly (US DHHS, 2007). The warning about higher risk among adolescents remained, as did the warning of higher risk among young adults ages 18–24 years. A serious unintended public health consequence of these well-intended policy decisions may be an increase in suicide rates as patients (or parents) reject effective and potentially life-saving psychopharmacological treatments. This effect has already been documented for youth suicides (Gibbons et al., 2007).

RISK AND PROTECTIVE PROCESSES: SEXUAL
ORIENTATION

The scientific evidence for a link between suicidal behaviors and sexual orientation continues to be inconsistent, although some work suggests that there may be increased risk for attempted suicide in gay, lesbian, bisexual, and/or transgender (GLBT) populations (King et al., 2008). Consistent findings from studies that have controlled for mental disorders and other distal risk processes associated with suicidal thinking and behaviors have documented elevated risk for nonfatal suicidal behaviors among young gay and bisexual males (Cochran & Mays, 2000; Goldsmith et al., 2002; Herrell et al., 1999; McDaniel et al., 2001). Evidence for independent risk of sexual orientation for suicide death, however, is lacking; two psychological autopsy studies that ascertained sexual orientation of the decedents did not find that sexual orientation independently increased risk, once mental and substance use disorders had been controlled for (Rich, Fowler, Young, & Blenkush, 1986; Shaffer, Fisher, Hicks, Parides, & Gould, 1995). Investigators have called for more research in this area, as GLBT populations, and young people in particular, may be more vulnerable to the known risk processes for suicidal behaviors, including mental disorders (King et al., 2008; McDaniel et al., 2001; Mościcki, Potter, & Muehrer, 1995; Working Groups, 1995).

Protective Processes

There has been very little systematic research on beneficial exposures that may protect vulnerable individuals against suicidal behaviors (Mann et al., 2005). What is known has primarily come from ecological studies, limited treatment trials, or has been inferred from studies of risk. For example, existing evidence indicates that as many as 80% of suicide decedents with mental illness may be untreated at the time of death, suggesting that timely identification and appropriate treatment of mental disorders can potentially save lives. Recent reports suggest that this may indeed be the case, as appropriate treatment for major depressive disorder and bipolar illness, the mood disorders responsible for the largest proportion of suicide deaths, has a protective effect against suicidal behavior (Barbui et al., 2009; Gibbons et al., 2005; Goodwin et al., 2003; Isacsson et al., 2009). Lithium in particular has been shown to reduce risk for suicidal behaviors among adults with bipolar disorder (Collins & McFarland, 2008; Goodwin et al., 2003), but there is also limited evidence that clozapine may protect against suicide attempts among schizophrenic and schizoaffective patients (Meltzer et al., 2003). Most findings of this nature come from pharmacological trials, but there is also strong evidence that cognitive-behavioral therapy and dialectical behavioral therapy, both evidence-based nonpharmacological interventions, can protect against suicidal behaviors (Brown et al., 2005; Linehan et al., 2006).

Studies at the ecological and contextual level suggest several promising, albeit long-term, preventive approaches that may protect against suicidal behavior in adults. Universally offered preventive interventions to reduce aggressive behaviors among children in the early elementary grades in high-risk schools may delay or prevent onset of suicidal behaviors in young adulthood (Wilcox et al., 2008). Culturally influenced coping strategies, such as values reflecting strong moral objections to suicide, and family support, are associated with lower occurrence of suicidal ideation and attempts among Latinos (Fortuna et al., 2007); reduction of proximal risk such as intoxication (Pridemore & Snowden, 2009; Smart & Mann, 1990) or means restriction, such as limiting access to potentially lethal pharmaceuticals by changing packaging (Hawton, 2002), or to firearms by, for example, regulations or safe storage (Ludwig & Cook, 2000; Shenassa, Rogers, Spalding, & Roberts, 2004; Sloan, Rivara, Reay, Ferris, & Kellermann, 1990), are all promising strategies for reducing suicide rates. Another promising approach is provider or gatekeeper education, as has been demonstrated in the Götland study in Sweden (Rutz, von Knorring, & Wålinder, 1992) and the US Air Force suicide prevention program (Knox, Litts, Talcott, Feig, & Caine, 2003; Knox et al., 2010). Finally, there is the intriguing possibility that very low levels of lithium in drinking water may be associated with lower suicide rates in exposed communities (Ohgami, Terao, Shiotsuki, Ishii, & Iwata, 2009).

All of these vastly differing, but promising, approaches underscore the complexity of suicidal behaviors. Just as it is highly unlikely that exposure to a single risk process will lead to suicidal behaviors, it is also unlikely that any one preventive approach will protect all vulnerable individuals against suicide injury or death. A combination of culturally and developmentally sensitive environmental-level and individual-level interventions is more likely to be successful in preventing suicide.

Conclusion

Our understanding of the interplay of risk and protective processes for suicide has grown tremendously in recent decades and can become the basis for preventive strategies that can be developed and delivered from a variety of perspectives. Since preventive approaches are likely to differ depending on the type of risk or protection that is targeted, Table 6.3 illustrates one potential approach for organizing our understanding of what we already know

Table 6.3 Risk and Protective Processes for Fatal and Nonfatal Suicide Events in Adults

Context	Distal Risk	Proximal Risk	Protection
Individual	Mental disorder Substance use/abuse disorder Comorbidity Neurochemical vulnerability/ selected endophenotypes Family history of mental disorder/suicidality History of abuse Previous suicide attempt Sexual orientation?	Intensely stressful life event/ loss, e.g., death of loved one, personal failure/humiliation, incarceration, perceived loss of independence Hopelessness Intoxication Access to lethal means Pain?	Appropriate treatment for mental/ substance use disorder, e.g., lithium Tx for bipolar disorder, SSRIs for major depression Emotional well-being Specific behavioral intervention for suicidality, e.g., cognitive-behavioral therapy, dialectical behavioural therapy Early identification of mental disorder?
Environment	Disruptive/dysfunctional family environment Easy availability of firearms Environment with few protective factors Dangerous neighborhood? Cultural depression/cultural grief?	Contagion Firearm in home	Community-wide approach (e.g., Air Force program) Improved screening for depression/ appropriate training for primary care providers (e.g., Götland study) Preventive interventions in childhood? Social support/cultural values? Access to mental health, substance abuse services? Responsible firearm storage/means restriction?

about suicide risk and protection; areas requiring more investigation are indicated by question marks.

Suicide is preventable. Despite the gaps in the knowledge base and the need for more information and more accurate data on risk and protection, we know enough now so that we can begin to apply our understanding to reduce risk and increase protection of vulnerable individuals, alleviate suffering, and save lives.

Future Directions

Table 6.3 highlights current gaps in the scientific knowledge base and opportunities for future epidemiologic research. First, while there is solid evidence on multiple, individual-level, distal and proximal risk processes such as mental and substance use disorders, family history, and access to lethal means, much remains to be learned about potential protective processes at both the individual and environmental levels. Second, information is needed on the distribution of endophenotypes in the population. Future epidemiologic studies must be in a position to take advantage of what is now known about endophenotypes for suicidal behaviors, and to collect biological data in addition to behavioral data. Even when collection of biological specimens

is not feasible, epidemiologic studies should be able to ascertain information on behavioral endophenotypes with biological underpinnings, such as aggression and impulsivity. More accurate information in this area will lead to more precise models and better prediction of imminent risk. Third, it is critical that an appropriate nomenclature be used in all studies of nonfatal suicidal behaviors. Intent must be rigorously ascertained in order to accurately distinguish between suicidal and nonsuicidal self-injury. Careful attention to these important issues will do much to move the field forward and will have a meaningful impact on the prevention of suicide morbidity and mortality.

Notes

1. The National Vital Statistics System first began reporting mortality data from all states in the United States in 1933. Rates and trends prior to that date are not generalizable to the entire US population (Linder & Grove, 1947).
2. External Cause of Injury Codes, or E-codes, were developed as a component of the *ICD* and are used for uniform coding of mortality and morbidity from unintentional and intentional injuries. For more information, see http://www.who.int/classifications/icd/adaptations/iceci/en/index.html and Centers for Disease Control and Prevention, Recommended framework for presenting injury mortality data. MMWR 1997; 46 (No. RR-14).

References

Agerbo, A. (2005). Effect of psychiatric illness and labour market status on suicide: A healthy worker effect? *Journal of Epidemiology and Community Health, 59,* 598–602.

Alegría, M., Mulvaney-Day, N., Torres, M., Polo, A., Cao, Z., & Canino, G. (2007). Prevalence of psychiatric disorders across Latino subgroups in the United States. *American Journal of Public Health, 97,* 68–75.

Alegría, M., Vila, D., Woo, M., Canino, G., Takeuchi, D., Vera, M., ... Shrout, P. (2004). Cultural relevance and equivalence in the NLAAS instrument: Integrating etic and emic in the development of cross-cultural measures for a psychiatric epidemiology and services study of Latinos. *International Journal of Methods in Psychiatric Research, 13,* 270–288.

American Foundation for Suicide Prevention, Annenberg Public Policy Center, Columbia University Department of Psychiatry, National Alliance on Mental Illness - New Hampshire, Substance Abuse and Mental Health Services Administration, Suicide Awareness Voices of Education et al. (2011). *Recommendations for Reporting on Suicide.* Retrieved October 2013 from http://reportingonsuicide.org/.

American Psychiatric Association. (1980). *Diagnostic and statistical manual of mental disorders* (3rd ed.). Washington, DC: Author.

Anderson, R. N., & Rosenberg, H. M. (1998). Age standardization of death rates: Implementation of the year 2000 standard. *National Vital Statistics Reports, 47*(3), 1–16, 20.

Barbui, C., Esposito, E., & Cipriani, A. (2009). Selective serotonin reuptake inhibitors and risk of suicide: A systematic review of observational studies. *Canadian Medical Association Journal, 180,* 291–297.

Barrios, L. C., Everett, S. A., Simon, T. R., & Brener, N. D. (2000). Suicide ideation among US college students: Associations with other risk behaviors. *Journal of American College Health, 48,* 229–233.

Beautrais, A. (2001). Suicides and serious suicide attempts: Two populations or one? *Psychological Medicine, 31,* 837–845.

Beautrais, A. L., Joyce, P. R., & Mulder, R. T. (1998). Unemployment and serious suicide attempts. *Psychological Medicine, 28,* 209–218.

Beautrais, A. L., Joyce, P. R., Mulder, R. T., Fergusson, D. M., Deavoll, B. J., & Nightingale, S. K. (1996). Prevalence and comorbidity of mental disorders in persons making serious suicide attempts: A case-control study. *American Journal of Psychiatry, 153,* 1009–1014.

Beck, A. T., Brown, G., & Berchik, R. J. (1990). Relationship between hopelessness and ultimate suicide: A replication with psychiatric outpatients. *American Journal of Psychiatry, 147,* 190–195.

Beck, A. T., Steer, R. A., Kovacs, M., & Garrison, B. (1985). Hopelessness and eventual suicide: A 10-year prospective study of patients hospitalized with suicidal ideation. *American Journal of Psychiatry, 142,* 559–563.

Beskow, J., Runeson, B., & Åsgård, U. (1990). Psychological autopsies: Methods and ethics. *Suicide and Life-Threatening Behavior, 20,* 307–323.

Blakely, T. A., Collings, S. C. D., & Atkinson, J. (2003). Unemployment and suicide: Evidence for a causal association? *Journal of Epidemiology and Community Health, 57,* 594–600.

Borges, G., Angst, J., Nock, M. K., Ruscia, A. M., Walters, E. E., & Kessler, R. C. (2006). A risk index for 12-month suicide attempts in the National Comorbidity Survey Replication (NCS-R). *Psychological Medicine, 36,* 1747–1757.

Borges, G., Breslau, J., Su, M., Miller, M., Medina-Mora, M. E., & Aguílar-Gaxìola, S. (2009). Immigration and suicidal behavior among Mexicans and Mexican Americans. *American Journal of Public Health, 99,* 728–733.

Borges, G., & Rosovsky, H. (1996). Suicide attempts and alcohol consumption in an emergency room sample. *Journal of Studies on Alcohol, 57,* 543–548.

Borges, G., Walters, E. E., & Kessler, R. C. (2000). Associations of substance use, abuse, and dependence with subsequent suicidal behavior. *American Journal of Epidemiology, 151,* 781–789.

Bourgeois, M., Swendsen, J. Young, F., Zmador, X., Pini, S., Cassano, G. B., ... InterSePT Study Group. (2004). Awareness of disorder and suicide risk in the treatment of schizophrenia: Results of the International Suicide Prevention Trial. *American Journal of Psychiatry, 161,* 1494–1496.

Boyd, J. H. (1983). The increasing rate of suicide by firearms. *New England Journal of Medicine, 308,* 872–874.

Boyd, J. H., Burke, J. D., Gruenberg, E., Holzer, C. E., Rae, D. S., George, L. K., ... Nestadt, G. (1984). Exclusion criteria of DSM-III: A study of co-occurrence of hierarchy-free syndromes. *Archives of General Psychiatry, 41,* 983–989.

Boyd, J. H., & Mościcki, E. K. (1986). Firearms and youth suicide. *American Journal of Public Health, 76,* 1240–1242.

Breslau, N., Schultz, L. R., Johnson, E. O., Peterson, E. L., & Davis, G. C. (2005). Smoking and the risk of suicidal behavior: A prospective study of a community sample. *Archives of General Psychiatry, 62,* 328–334.

Briere, J., & Zaidi, L. Y. (1989). Sexual abuse histories and sequelae in female psychiatric emergency room patients. *American Journal of Psychiatry, 146,* 1602–1606.

Brown, G. K., Ten Have, T., Henriques, G. R., Xie, S. X., Hollander, J. E., & Beck, A. T. (2005). Cognitive therapy for the prevention of suicide attempts. *Journal of the American Medical Association, 294,* 563–570.

Buie, V.C., Owings, M.F., DeFrances, C.J., Golosinskiy. A (2010). National Hospital Discharge Survey: 2006 summary. National Center for Health Statistics. Vital Health Stat 13(168). 2010. Retrieved October 2013 from http://www.cdc.gov/nchs/data/series/sr_13/sr13_168.pdf.

Caldwell, C. B., & Gottesman, I. I. (1990). Schizophrenics kill themselves too: A review of risk factors for suicide. *Schizophrenia Bulletin, 16,* 571–589.

Caspi, A., McClay, J., Moffitt, T. E., Mill, J., Martin, J., Craig, I. W., ... Poulton, R. (2002). Role of genotype in the cycle of violence in maltreated children. *Science, 297,* 851–854.

Cavanagh, J. T., Carson, A. J., Sharpe, M., & Lawrie, S. M. (2003). Psychological autopsy studies of suicide: A systematic review. *Psychological Medicine, 33,* 395–405.

Centers for Disease Control and Prevention, National Center for Health Statistics, National Hospital Discharge Survey. (2013). Retrieved June 2013, from http://www.cdc.gov/nchs/nhds.htm.

Centers for Disease Control and Prevention. (2009). *Suicide facts at a glance, Summer 2009.* Retrieved October 2013 from http://www.dstc.cc.al.us/Uploads/files/Suicide.pdf.

Centers for Disease Control and Prevention. (2012). *Suicide facts at a glance 2012.* Retrieved June 2013, from http://www.cdc.gov/ViolencePrevention/pdf/Suicide_DataSheet-a.pdf.

Centers for Disease Control and Prevention. (2013). *National vital statistics system.* Retrieved June 2013, from http://www.cdc.gov/nchs/nvss.htm.

Cochran, S. D., & Mays, V. M. (2000). Lifetime prevalence of suicide symptoms and affective disorders among men reporting same-sex sexual partners: Results from NHANES-III. *American Journal of Public Health, 90,* 573–578.

Coldwell, C. M., & Bender, W. S. (2007). The effectiveness of assertive community treatment for homeless populations with severe mental illness: A meta-analysis. *American Journal of Psychiatry, 164,* 393–399.

Collins, J. C., & McFarland, B. H. (2008). Divalproex, lithium and suicide among Medicaid Patients with bipolar disorders. *Journal of Affective Disorder, 107,* 23–28.

Committee for the Workshop on the Medicolegal Death Investigation System. (2003). *Medicolegal death investigation system: Workshop summary.* Washington, DC: National Academies Press.

Conwell, Y., & Brent, D. (1995). Suicide and aging: Patterns of psychiatric diagnosis. *International Psychogeriatrics, 7,* 149–164.

Conwell, Y., Duberstein, P. R., & Caine, E. D. (2001). Risk factors for suicide in later life. *Biological Psychiatry, 52,* 193–204.

Conwell, Y., Duberstein, P. R., Cox, C., Herrmann, J. H., Forbes, N. T., & Caine, E. D. (1996). Relationships of age and axis, I diagnoses in victims of completed suicide: A psychological autopsy study. *American Journal of Psychiatry, 153,* 1001–1008.

Crosby, A. E., Ortega, L., & Melanson, C. (2011). *Self-directed violence surveillance: Uniform definitions and recommended data elements. Version 1.0.* Atlanta, GA: Centers for Disease Control and Prevention, National Center for Injury Prevention and Control. Retrieved August 2013, from http://www.cdc.gov/violenceprevention/pub/selfdirected_violence.html.

Day, G. E., & Lanier, A. P. (2003). Alaska Native mortality, 1979-1998. *Public Health Reports, 118,* 518–530.

Dumais, A., Lesage, A. D., Alda, M., Roleau, G., Dumont, M., Chawky, N.,...Turecki, G. (2005). Risk factors for suicide completion in major depression: A case-control study of impulsive and aggressive behaviors in men. *American Journal of Psychiatry, 162,* 2116–2124.

Durkheim, E. (1951). *Suicide: A study in sociology.* J. A. Spaulding & G. Simpson, Trans. New York, NY: Free Press.

Egeland, J. A., & Sussex, J. N. (1985). Suicide and family loading for affective disorders. *Journal of the American Medical Association, 254,* 915–918.

Favaro, A., Caregaro, L., di Pascoli, L., Brambilla, F., & Santonastaso, P. (2004). Total serum cholesterol and suicidality in anorexia nervosa. *Psychosomatic Medicine, 66,* 548–552.

Fazel, S., & Benning, R. (2009). Suicides in female prisoner in England and Wales, 1978–2004. *British Journal of Psychiatry, 194,* 183–184.

Ford, A. B., Rushforth, N. B., Rushforth, N., Hirsch, C. S., & Adelson, L. (1979). Violent death in a metropolitan county: II. Changing patterns in suicides (1959-1974). *American Journal of Public Health, 69,* 459–464.

Forman, E. M., Berk, M. S., Henriques, G. R., Brown, G. K., & Beck, A. T. (2004). History of multiple suicide attempts as a behavioral marker of severe psychopathology. *American Journal of Psychiatry, 161,* 437–443.

Fortuna, L., Perez, D., Canino, G., Sribney, W., & Alegría, M. (2007). Prevalence and correlates of lifetime suicidal ideation and suicide attempts among Latino subgroups in the United States. *Journal of Clinical Psychiatry, 68,* 572–581.

Freedman, D. S., Byers, T., Barrett, D. H., Stroup, N. E., Eaker, E., & Monroe-Blum, H. (1995). Plasma lipid levels and psychological characteristics in men. *American Journal of Epidemiology, 141,* 507–517.

Garroutte, E. M., Goldberg, J., Beals, J., Herrell, R., Manson, S. M., & AI-SUPERPFP Team. (2003). Spirituality and attempted suicide among American Indians. *Social Science and Medicine, 56,* 1571–1579.

Gibbons, R. D., Brown, C. H., Hur, K., Marcus, S. M., Bhaumik, D. K., Erkens, J. A.,...Mann, J. J. (2007). Early evidence on the effects of regulators' suicidality warnings on SSRI prescriptions and suicide in children and adolescents. *American Journal of Psychiatry, 164,* 1356–1363.

Gibbons, R. D., Hur, K., Bhaumik, D. K., & Mann, J. J. (2005). The relationship between antidepressant medication use and rate of suicide. *Archives of General Psychiatry, 62,* 165–172.

Gogtay, N., Giedd, J. N., Lusk, L., Hayashi, K. M., Greenstein, D., Vaituzis, A. C.,...Thompson, P. M. (2004). Dynamic mapping of human cortical development during childhood through early adulthood. *Proceedings of the National Academy of Sciences USA, 101,* 8174–8179.

Goldsmith, S. K., Pellmar, T. C., Kleinman, A. M., & Bunney, W. E. (Eds.). (2002). *Reducing suicide: A national imperative.* Washington, DC: National Academies Press.

Goodwin, F. K., Fireman, B., Simon, G. E., Hunkeler, E. M., Lee, J., & Revicki, D. (2003). Suicide risk in bipolar disorder during treatment with lithium and divalproex. *Journal of the American Medical Association, 290,* 1467–1473.

Gottesman, I. I., & Gould, T. D. (2003). The endophenotype concept in psychiatry: Etymology and strategic intentions. *American Journal of Psychiatry, 160,* 636–645.

Gould, M. S., & Shaffer, D. (1986). The impact of suicide in television movies. *New England Journal of Medicine, 315,* 690–694.

Gradus, J. L., Qin, P., Lincoln, A. K., Miller, M., Lawler, E., Sørenson, H. T., & Lash, T. L. (2010). Posttraumatic stress disorder and completed suicide. *American Journal of Epidemiology, 171,* 721–727.

Grove, R. D., & Hetzel, A. M. (1968). *Vital statistics rates in the United States, 1940-1960.* Washington, DC: USGPO.

Gunnell, D., Harbord, R., Singleton, N., Jenkins, R., & Lewis, G. (2004). Factors influencing the development and amelioration of suicidal thoughts in the general population. *British Journal of Psychiatry, 185,* 385–93.

Gunnell, D., Hawton, K., Ho, D., Evans, J., O'Connor, S., Potokar, J.,...Kapur, N. (2008). Hospital admissions for self-harm after discharge from psychiatric inpatient care: Cohort study. *British Journal of Psychiatry, 337,* a2278.

Harris, E. C., & Barraclough, B. M. (1994). Suicide as an outcome for medical disorders. *Medicine, 73,* 281–296.

Hawton, K. (2002). United Kingdom legislation on pack sizes of analgesics: Background, rationale, and effects on suicide and deliberate self-harm. *Suicide and Life-Threatening Behavior, 32,* 223–229.

Hawton, K., Houston, K., Haw, C., Townsend, E., & Harriss, L. (2003). Comorbidity of Axis I and Axis II disorders inpatients who attempted suicide. *American Journal of Psychiatry, 160,* 1494–1500.

Hawton, K., Sutton, L., Haw, C., Sinclair, J., & Deeks, J. J. (2005). Schizophrenia and suicide: Systematic review of risk factors. *British Journal of Psychiatry, 187,* 9–20.

Hawton, K., & Williams, K. (2002). Influences of the media on suicide. *British Medical Journal, 325,* 1374–1375.

Hayes, L. M. (1989). Jail suicide update *2*:(2).

Heila, H., Isometsä, E. T., Henriksson, M. M., Marttunen, M. J., & Lönnqvist, J. K. (1997). Suicide and schizophrenia: A nationwide psychological autopsy study on age- and sex-specific clinical characteristics of 92 suicide victims with schizophrenia. *American Journal of Psychiatry*, *154*, 1235–1242.

Helzer, J. E., Kraemer, H. C., Krueger, R. F., Wittchen, H-U., Sirovatka, P. J., & Regier, D. A. (Eds.). (2008). *Dimensional approaches in diagnostic classification: Refining the research agenda for DSM-V*. Arlington, VA: American Psychiatric Association.

Hemmingsson, T., & Kriebel, D. (2003). Smoking at age 18-20 and suicide during 26 years of follow-up—how can the association be explained? *International Journal of Epidemiology*, *32*, 1000–1005.

Henriksson, M. M., Aro, H. M., Marttunen, M. J., Heikkinen, M. E., Isometsä, E. T., Kuoppasalmi, K. I., & Lönnqvist, J. K. (1993). Mental disorders and comorbidity in suicide. *American Journal of Psychiatry*, *150*, 935–940.

Henriksson, M. M., Isometsä, E. T., Kuoppasalmi, K. I., Heikkinen, M. E., Marttunen, M. J., & Lönnqvist, J. K. (1996). Panic disorder in completed suicide. *Journal of Clinical Psychiatry*, *57*, 275–281.

Henriksson, M. M., Marttunen, M. J., Isometsä, E. T., Heikkinen, M. E., Hillevi, M. A., Kuoppasalmi, K. I., & Lönnqvist, J. K. (1995). Mental disorders in elderly suicide. *International Psychogeriatrics*, *7*, 275–286.

Heron, M. (2010). Deaths: Leading causes for 2006. *National Vital Statistics Reports*, *58*(14). Retrieved May, 2010 from http://www.cdc.gov/nchs/data/nvsr/nvsr58/nvsr58_14.pdf.

Heron, M. P., Hoyert, D. L., Murphy, S. L., Xu, J. Q., Kochanek, K. D., & Tejada-Vera, B. (2009). Deaths: Final data for 2006. *National Vital Statistics Reports*, *57*(14). Retrieved July 2009, from http://www.cdc.gov/nchs/data/nvsr57/nvsr57_14.pdf.

Herrell, R., Goldberg, J., True, W. R., Ramakrishnan, V., Lyons, M., Eisen, S., & Tsuang, M. T. (1999). Sexual orientation and suicidality: A co-twin control study in adult men. *Archives of General Psychiatry*, *56*, 867–874.

Hlady, W. G., & Middaugh, J. P. (1988). Suicides in Alaska: Firearms and alcohol. *American Journal of Public Health*, *78*, 179–180.

Hoyert, D. L. (2011). *The changing profile of autopsied deaths in the United States, 1972-2007*. [NCHS Data Brief No. 67]. Hyattsville, MD: National Center for Health Statistics.

Hoyert, D. L., Arias, E., Smith, B. L., Murphy, S. L., & Kochanek, K. D. (2001). Deaths: Final data for 1999. *National Vital Statistics Reports*, *4*(8). Retrieved July 2009, from http://www.cdc.gov/nchs/data/nvsr/nvsr49/nvsr49_08.pdf.

Hoyert, D. L., Kung, H. C., & Xu, J. (2007). Autopsy patterns in 2003. *Vital Health Statistics*, *20*(32). Retrieved July 2009, from http://www.cdc.gov/nchs/data/series/sr_20/sr20_032.pdf.

Hu, G., Wilcox, H. C., Wissow, L., & Baker, S. P. (2008). Mid-life suicide: An increasing problem in US whites, 1999-2005. *American Journal of Preventive Medicine*, *35*, 589–593.

Ialongo, N., McCreary, B. K., Pearson, J. L., Koenig, A. L., Wagner, B. M., Schmidt, N. B.,...Kellam, S. G. (2002). Suicidal behavior among urban, African American young adults. *Suicide and Life-Threatening Behavior*, *32*, 256–271.

Isacsson, G., Holmgren, A., Ösby, U., & Ahlner, J. (2009). Decrease in suicide among the individuals treated with antidepressants: A controlled study of antidepressant in suicide, Sweden 1995-2005. *Acta Psychiatrica Scandinavica*, *120*, 1–8.

Jackson, J. S., Torres, M., Caldwell, C. H., Neighbors, H. W., Nesse, R. M., Taylor, R. J.,...Williams, D. R. (2004). The National Survey of American Life: A study of racial, ethnic and cultural influences on mental disorders and mental health. *International Journal of Methods in Psychiatric Research*, *13*, 196–207.

Jacobs, D. R., Muldoon, M. F., & Rastam, L. (1995). Invited commentary: Low blood cholesterol, nonillness mortality, and other nonatherosclerotic disease mortality: A search for causes and confounders. *American Journal of Epidemiology*, *141*, 518–522.

Joe, S., Baser, R. E., Breeden, G., Neighbors, H. W., & Jackson, J. S. (2006). Prevalence of and risk factors for lifetime suicide attempts among blacks in the United States. *Journal of the American Medical Association*, *296*, 2112–2123.

Juurlink, D. N., Herrmann, N., Szalai, J. P., Kopp, A., & Redelmeier, D. A. (2004). Medical illness and the risk of suicide in the elderly. *Archives of Internal Medicine*, *164*, 1179–1184.

Kaplan, J. R., Muldoon, M. F., Manuck, S. B., & Mann, J. J. (1997). Assessing the observed relationship between low cholesterol and violence-related mortality. In D. M. Stoff & J. J. Mann (Eds.), *The neurobiology of suicide: From the bench to the clinic* (pp. 57–80). New York, NY: New York Academy of Sciences.

Kaplan, M. S., Adamek, M. E., & Johnson, S. (1994). Trends in firearm suicide among older American males: 1979-1988. *Gerontologist*, *34*, 59–65.

Keilp, J. G., Gorlyn, M., Oquendo, M. A., Brodsky, B., Ellis, S. P., Stanley, B., & John Mann, J. (2006). Aggressiveness, not impulsiveness or hostility, distinguishes suicide attempters with major depression. *Psychological Medicine*, *36*, 1779–1788.

Kellerman, A. L., Rivara, F. P., Somes, G., Reay, D. T., Francisco, J., Banton, J. G.,...Hackman, B. B. (1992). Suicide in the home in relation to gun ownership. *New England Journal of Medicine*, *327*, 467–472.

Kelly, K. (2008, November 6). His job at Bear gone, Mr. Fox chose suicide. *Wall Street Journal*. Retrieved November 2008, from http://www.theaustralian.com.au/business/news/the-hidden-toll-on-wall-street/story-e6frg90f-1111117963056.

Kessler, R. C., Berglund, P., Borges, G., Nock, M., & Wang, P. S. (2005). Trends in suicide ideation, plans, gestures, and attempts in the United States, 1990-1992 to 2001-2003. *Journal of the American Medical Association*, *293*, 2487–2495.

Kessler, R. C., Borges, G., & Walters, E. E. (1999). Prevalence of and risk factors for lifetime suicide attempts in the National Comorbidity Survey. *Archives of General Psychiatry*, *56*, 617–626.

Kim, Y. K., & Myint, A. M. (2004). Clinical application of low serum cholesterol as an indicator for suicide risk in major depression. *Journal of Affective Disorders*, *81*, 161–166.

King, M., Semlyen, J., Tai, S. S., Killaspy, H., Osborn, D., Popelyuk, D., et al. (2008). A systematic review of mental disorder, suicide, and deliberate self-harm in lesbian, gay and bisexual people. *BMC Psychiatry*, *8*, 70.

Knox, K. L., Litts, D. A., Talcott, G. W., Feig, J. C., & Caine, E. D. (2003). Risk of suicide and related adverse outcomes after exposure to a suicide prevention programme in the US Air Force: Cohort study. *British Medical Journal*, *327*, 1376–1378.

Knox, K. L., Pflanz, S., Talcott, G. W., Campise, R. L., Lavigne, J. E., Bajorska, A., ...Caine, E. D. (2010). The US Air Force suicide prevention program: implications for public health policy. *American Journal of Public Health, 100*(12), 2457–2463.

Kposowa, A. (2000). Marital status and suicide in the National Longitudinal Mortality Study. *Journal of Epidemiology and Community Health, 54*, 254–261.

Kraemer, H. C., Kazdin, A. E., Offord, D. R., Kessler, R. C., Jensen, P. S., & Kupfer, D. J. (1997). Coming to terms with the terms of risk. *Archives of General Psychiatry, 54*, 337–343.

Kung, H. C., Hoyert, D. L., Xu, J. Q., & Murphy, S. L. (2008). Deaths: Final data for 2005. *National Vital Statistics Reports, 56*(10). Retrieved July 2009, from http://www.cdc.gov/nchs/data/nvsr/nvsr56/nvsr56_10.pdf.

Kuo, W. H., Gallo, J. J., & Tien, A. Y. (2001). Incidence of suicide ideation and attempts in adults: The 13-year follow-up of a community sample in Baltimore, Maryland. *Psychological Medicine, 31*, 1181–1191.

Last, J. M. (1988). *A dictionary of epidemiology* (2nd ed.). New York, NY: Oxford University Press.

Lenroot, R. K., Gogtay, N., Greenstein, D. K., Wells, E. M., Wallace, G. L., Clasen, L. S., ...Giedd, J. N. (2007). Sexual dimorphism of brain developmental trajectories during childhood and adolescence. *Neuroimage, 36*, 1065–1073.

Lesage, A. D., Boyer, R., Grunberg, F., Vanier, C., Morissette, R., Ménard-Buteau, C., & Loyer, M. (1994). Suicide and mental disorders: A case-control study of young men. *American Journal of Psychiatry, 151*, 1063–1068.

Lewinsohn, P. M., Rohde, P., & Seeley, J. R. (1996). Adolescent suicidal ideation and attempts: Prevalence, risk factors, and clinical implications. *Clinical Psychology: Science and Practice, 3*, 25–46.

Linder, F. E., & Grove, R. D. (1947). *Vital statistics rates in the United States 1900-1940.* Washington, DC: US Government Printing Office.

Linehan, M. M., Comtois, K. A., Murray, A. M., Brown, M. Z., Gallop, R. J., Heard, H. L., ...Lindenboim, N. (2006). Two-year randomized controlled trial and follow-up of dialectical behavior therapy vs therapy by experts for suicidal behaviors and borderline personality disorder. *Archives of General Psychiatry, 63*, 757–766.

Ludwig, J., & Cook, P. J. (2000). Homicide and suicide rates associated with implementation of the Brady Handgun Violence Prevention Act. *Journal of the American Medical Association, 284*, 585–591.

Luoma, J. B., & Pearson, J. L. (2002). Suicide and marital status in the United States, 1991-1996: is widowhood a risk factor? *American Journal of Public Health, 92*, 1518–22.

Magnusson, P. K., Rasmussen, F., Lawlor, D. A., Tynelius, P., & Gunnell, D. (2006). Association of body mass index with suicide mortality: A prospective cohort study of more than one million men. *American Journal of Epidemiology, 163*(1), 1–8.

Malone, K. M., Waternaux, C., Haas, G. L., Cooper, T. B., Li, S., & Mann, J. J. (2003). Cigarette smoking, suicidal behavior, and serotonin function in major psychiatric disorders. *American Journal of Psychiatry, 160*, 773–779.

Mann, J. J. (2003). Neurobiology of suicidal behaviour. *Nature Reviews Neuroscience, 4*, 819–828.

Mann, J. J., Apter, A., Bertolote, J., Beautrais, A., Currier, D., Haas, A., ...Hendin, H. (2005). Suicide prevention strategies: A systematic review. *Journal of the American Medical Association, 294*, 2064–2074.

Mann, J. J., Arango, V. A., Avenevoli, S., Brent, D. A., Champagne, F. A., Clayton, P., ...Wenzel, A. (2009). Candidate endophenotypes for genetic studies of suicidal behavior. *Biological Psychiatry, 65*, 556–563.

Mann, J. J., Waternaux, C., Haas, G. L., & Malone, K. M. (1999). Toward a clinical model of suicidal behavior in psychiatric patients. *American Journal of Psychiatry, 156*,181–189.

Manton, K. G., Blazer, D. G., & Woodbury, M. A. (1987). Suicide in middle age and later life: Sex and race specific life table and cohort analysis. *Journal of Gerontology, 42*, 219–227.

Markush, R. E., & Bartolucci, A. A. (1984). Firearms and suicide in the United States. *American Journal of Public Health, 74*, 123–127.

Marzuk, P. M. (1994). Suicide and terminal illness. *Death Studies, 18*, 497–512.

Marzuk, P. M., Leon, A. C., Tardiff, K., Morgan, E. B., Stajic, M., & Mann, J. J. (1992). The effect of access to lethal methods of injury on suicide rates. *Archives of General Psychiatry, 49*, 451–458.

Marzuk, P. M., Tardiff, K., Leon, A. C., Hirsch, C. S., Hartwell, N., Portera, L., ...Iqbal, M. I. (1997). HIV seroprevalence among suicide victims in New York City, 1991-1993. *American Journal of Psychiatry, 154*, 1720–1725.

Marzuk, P. M., Tardiff, K., Leon, A. C., Stajic, M., Morgan, E. B., & Mann, J. J. (1992). Prevalence of cocaine use among resident of New York City who committed suicide during a one-year period. *American Journal of Psychiatry, 149*, 371–375.

Marzuk, P. M., Tierney, H., Tardiff, K., Gross, E. M., Morgan, E. B., Hsu, M. A, & Mann, J. J. (1988). Increased risk of suicide in persons with AIDS. *Journal of the American Medical Association, 259*,1333–1337.

May, P. A., Van Winkle, N. W., Williams, M. B., McFeeley, P. J., DeBruyn, L. M., & Serna, P. (2002). Alcohol and suicide death among American Indians of New Mexico: 1980-1998. *Suicide and Life-Threatening Behavior, 32*, 240–254.

McCaig, L. F., & Nawar, E. N. (2006). National Hospital Ambulatory Medical Care Survey: 2004 emergency department summary. *Advance Data from Vital and Health Statistics, 372*, 1–29.

McDaniel, J. S., Purcell, D., & D'Augelli, A. R. (2001). The relationship between sexual orientation and risk for suicide: Research findings and future directions for research and prevention. *Suicide and Life-Threatening Behavior, 31*, 84–105.

Melhem, N. M., Brent, D. A., Ziegler, M., Iyengar, S., Kolko, D., Oquendo, M., ...Mann, J. J. (2007). Familial pathways to early-onset suicidal behavior: Familial and individual antecedents of suicidal behavior. *American Journal of Psychiatry, 164*, 1364–1370.

Meltzer, H. Y., Alphs, L., Green, A. I., Altamura, C., Anand, R., Bertoldi, A., ...International Suicide Prevention Trial Study Group. (2003). Clozapine treatment for suicidality in schizophrenia. *Archives of General Psychiatry, 60*, 82–91.

Miller, M., Azrael, D., Hepburn, L., Hemenway, D., & Lippman, S. J. (2006). The association between changes in household firearm ownership and rates of suicide in the United States, 1981-2002. *Injury Prevention, 12*, 178–182.

Moffitt, T. E., Caspi, A., & Rutter, M. (2006). Measured gene-environment interactions in psychopathology concepts, research strategies, and implications for research, intervention, and public understanding of genetics. *Perspectives on Psychological Science, 1*, 5–27.

Mościcki, E. K. (1994). Gender differences in completed and attempted suicides. *Annals of Epidemiology, 4*, 152–158.

Mościcki, E. K. (1997). Identification of suicide risk factors using epidemiologic studies. *Psychiatric Clinics of North America, 20*, 499–517.

Mościcki, E. K. (2001). Epidemiology of completed and attempted suicide: Toward a framework for prevention. *Clinical Neuroscience Research, 1*, 310–323.

Mościcki, E. K., O'Carroll, P., Rae, D. S., Locke, B. Z., Roy, A., & Regier, D. A. (1988). Suicide attempts in the Epidemiologic Catchment Area Study. *Yale Journal of Biology and Medicine, 61*, 259–268.

Mościcki, E. K., Potter, L., & Muehrer, P. (1995). Research issues in suicide and sexual orientation. *Suicide and Life-Threatening Behavior,* 25(Suppl.), 1–3.

Mrazek, P. J., & Haggerty, R. J., (Eds.). (1994). *Reducing risks for mental disorders: Frontiers for preventive intervention research.* Washington, DC: National Academies Press.

Murphy, S. L., Xu, J., & Kochanek, K. D. (2013). Deaths: Final data for 2010. *National Vital Statistics Reports, 61*(4). Retrieved June 2013, from http://www.cdc.gov/nchs/data/nvsr/nvsr61/nvsr61_04.pdf.

Nemeroff, C. B., Bremmer, J. D., Foa, E. B., Mayberg, H. S., North, C. S., & Stein, M. B. (2006). Posttraumatic stress disorder: A state-of-the-science review. *Journal of Psychiatric Research, 40*, 1–21.

Nock, M. K., Borges, G., Bromet, E. K., Alonso, J., Angermeyer, M., Beautrais, A.,...Williams, D. (2008a). Cross-national prevalence and risk factors for suicidal ideation, plans and attempts. *British Journal of Psychiatry, 192*, 98–105.

Nock, M. K., Borges, G., Bromet, E. K., Cha, C. B., Kessler, R. C., & Lee, S. (2008b). Suicide and suicidal behavior. *Epidemiologic Reviews, 30*,133–154.

Nock, M. K., & Kessler, R. C. (2006). Prevalence of and risk factors for suicide attempts versus suicide gestures: Analysis of the National Comorbidity Survey. *Journal of Abnormal Psychology, 115*, 616–623.

O'Carroll, P. W., Berman, A. L., Maris, R. W., Mościcki, E. K., Tanney, B. L., & Silverman, M. (1996). Beyond the Tower of Babel: A nomenclature for suicidology. *Suicide and Life-Threatening Behavior, 26*, 237–252.

O'Carroll, P. W., & Potter, L. B.(1994). Suicide contagion and the reporting of suicide: Recommendations from a national workshop. *MMWR Recommendations and Reports, 43*(RR-6), 9–17.

Ohgami, H., Terao, T., Shiotsuki, I., Ishii, N., & Iwata, N. (2009). Lithium levels in drinking water and risk of suicide. *British Journal of Psychiatry, 194*, 464–465.

Oquendo, M. A., Galfalby, H., Russo, S., Ellis, S. P., Grunebaum, M. F., Burke, A., & Mann, J. J. (2004). Prospective study of clinical predictors of suicidal acts after a major depressive episode in patients with major depressive disorder or bipolar disorder. *American Journal of Psychiatry, 161*, 1433–1441.

Palmer, B. A., Pankratz, S., & Bostwick, J. M. (2005). The lifetime risk of suicide in schizophrenia. *Archives of General Psychiatry, 62*, 247–253.

Palmer, C. S., Revicki, D. A., Halpern, M. T., & Hatziandreu, E. J. (1995). The cost of suicide and suicide attempts in the United States. *Clinical Neuropharmacology, 18*, S25–S33.

Patterson, R. F., & Hughes, K. (2008). Review of completed suicides in the California Department of Corrections and Rehabilitation, 1999-2004. *Psychiatric Services, 59*, 676–682.

Paykel, E. S., Myers, J. K., Lindenthal, J. J., & Tanner, J. (1974). Suicidal feelings in the general population: A prevalence study. *British Journal of Psychiatry, 124*, 460–469.

Petronis, K. R., Samuels, J. F., Mościcki, E. K., & Anthony, J. C. (1990). An epidemiologic investigation of potential risk factors for suicide attempts. *Social Psychiatry and Psychiatric Epidemiology, 25*, 193–199.

Phillips, D. P., & Carstensen, M. S. (1986). Clustering of teen-age suicides after television news stories about suicide. *New England Journal of Medicine, 315*, 685–689.

Pitts, S. R., Niska, R. W., Xu, J., & Burt, C. W. (2008). National Hospital Ambulatory Medical Care Survey: 2006 emergency department summary. *National Health Statistics Reports, 7*, 1–38.

Pokorny, A. D. (1993). Suicide prediction revisited. *Suicide and Life-Threatening Behavior, 23*, 1–10.

Pridemore, W. A., & Snowden, A. J. (2009). Reduction in suicide mortality following a new national alcohol policy in Slovenia: An interrupted time-series analysis. *American Journal of Public Health, 99*, 915–920.

Regier, D. A., Farmer, M. E., Rae, D. S., Locke, B. Z., Keith, S. J., Judd, L. L., & Goodwin, F. K. (1990). Comorbidity of mental disorders with alcohol and other drug abuse. Results from the Epidemiologic Catchment Area (ECA) study. *Journal of the American Medical Association, 264*, 2511–2518.

Regier, D. A., Myers, J. K., Kramer, M., Robins, L. N., Blazer, D. G., Hough, R. L.,...Locke, B. Z. (1984). The NIMH Epidemiologic Catchment Area program: Historical context, major objectives, and study population characteristics. *Archives of General Psychiatry, 41*, 934–941.

Rhodes, A. E., Bethell, J., Spence, J., Links, P. S., Streiner, D. L., & Jaakkimainen, R. L. (2008). Age-sex differences in medicinal self-poisonings: A population-based study of deliberate intent and medical severity. *Social Psychiatry Psychiatric Epidemiology, 43*, 462–652.

Rich, C. L., Fowler, R. C., Fogarty, L. A., & Young, D. (1988). San Diego suicide study. III. Relationships between diagnoses and stressors. *Archives of General Psychiatry, 45*, 589–592.

Rich, C. L., Fowler, R. C., Young, D., & Blenkush, M. (1986). San Diego suicide study: Comparison of gay to straight males. *Suicide and Life-Threatening Behavior, 16*, 448–457.

Rich, C. L., Motooka, M. S., Fowler, R. C., & Young, D. (1988). Suicide by psychotics. *Biological Psychiatry, 23*, 595–601.

Rich, C. L., Ricketts, J. E., Fowler, R. C., & Young, D. (1988). Some differences between men and women who commit suicide. *American Journal of Psychiatry, 145*, 718–722.

Rich, C. L., Warstadt, G. M., Nemiroff, R. A., Fowler, R. C., & Young, D. (1991). Suicide, stressors, and the life cycle. *American Journal of Psychiatry, 148*, 524–527.

Rich, C. L., Young, D., & Fowler, R. C. (1986). San Diego suicide study. I. Young vs old subjects. *Archives of General Psychiatry, 43*, 577–582.

Robins, E. (1986). Psychosis and suicide. *Biological Psychiatry, 21*, 665–672.

Robins, E., Murphy, G. E., Wilkinson, R. H., Seymour, G., & Kayes, J. (1959). Some clinical considerations in the prevention of suicide based on a study of 134 successful suicides. *American Journal of Public Health, 49*, 888–899.

Rosenberg, M. L., Davidson, L. E., Smith, J. C., Berman, A. L., Buzbee, H., Gantner, G.,...Murray, D. (1988). Operational criteria for the determination of suicide. *Journal of Forensic Science, 33*, 1445–1456.

Roustit, C., Renahy, E., Guernec, G., Lesieur, S., Prizot, I., & Chauvin, P. (2009). Exposure to interparental violence and psychosocial maladjustment in the adult life course: Advocacy for early prevention. *Journal of Epidemiology Community Health, 63*, 563–568.

Runeson, B., & Åsberg, M. (2003). Family history of suicide among suicide victims. *American Journal of Psychiatry, 160,* 1525–1526.

Rutz, W., von Knorring, L., & Wålinder, J. (1992). Long-term effects of an educational program for general practitioners given by the Swedish Committee for the Prevention and Treatment of Depression. *Acta Psychiatrica Scandinavica, 85,* 83–88.

Salive, M. E., Smith, G. S., & Brewer, T. F. (1989). Suicide mortality in the Maryland state prison system, 1979 through 1987. *Journal of the American Medical Association, 262,* 365–369.

Sareen, J., Cox, B. J., Afifi, T. O., de Graaf, R., Asmundson, G. J., Ten Have, M., & Stein, M. B. (2005). Anxiety disorders and risk for suicidal ideation and suicide attempts. A population-based longitudinal study of adults. *Archives of General Psychiatry, 62,* 1249–1257.

Schmidtke, A., & Häfner, H. (1988). The Werther effect after television films: New evidence for an old hypothesis. *Psychological Medicine, 18,* 665–676.

Schwab, J. J., Warheit, G. J., & Holzer, C. E., III. (1972). Suicidal ideation and behavior in a general population. *Diseases of the Nervous System, 33,* 745–748.

Scott, K. M., Hwang, I., Wai-Tat Chiu, A. M., Kessler, R. C., Sampson, N. A., Angermeyer, M., ...Nock, M. K. Chronic physical conditions and their association with first onset of suicidal behavior in the world mental health surveys. *Psychosomatic Medicine, 72*(7), 712–719.

Shaffer, D., Fisher, P., Hicks, R. H., Parides, M., & Gould, M. (1995). Sexual orientation in adolescents who commit suicide. *Suicide and Life-Threatening Behavior, 25,* 64–71.

Shenassa, E. D., Rogers, M. L., Spalding, K. L., & Roberts, M. B. (2004). Safer storage of firearms at home and risk of suicide: A study of protective factors in a nationally representative sample. *Journal of Epidemiology and Community Health, 58,* 841–848.

Simon, G. E., Savarino, J., Operskalski, B., & Wang, P. S. (2006). Suicide risk during antidepressant treatment. *American Journal of Psychiatry, 163,* 41–47.

Sloan, J. H., Rivara, F. P., Reay, D. T., Ferris, J. A., & Kellermann, A. L. (1990). Firearm regulations and rates of suicide: A comparison of two metropolitan areas. *New England Journal of Medicine, 322,* 369–373.

Smart, R. G., & Mann, R. E. (1990). Changes in suicide rates after reductions in alcohol consumption and problems in Ontario, 1975-1983. *British Journal of Addiction, 85,* 463–468.

Smith, J. C., Mercy, J. A., & Conn, J. M. (1988). Marital status and the risk of suicide. *American Journal of Public Health, 78,* 78–80.

Sorenson, S. B. (1991). Suicide among the elderly: Issues facing public health. *American Journal of Public Health, 81,* 1109–1110.

Sorenson, S. B., & Golding, J. M. (1988). Suicide ideation and attempts in Hispanics and non-Hispanic whites: Demographic and psychiatric disorder issues. *Suicide and Life-Threatening Behavior, 18,* 205–218.

Spicer, R. S., & Miller, T. R. (2000). Suicide acts in 8 states: Incidence and case fatality rates by demographics and method. *American Journal of Public Health, 90,* 1885–1891.

Steinberg, L. (2008). A social neuroscience perspective on adolescent risk-taking. *Developmental Review, 28,* 78–106.

Takeuchi, D., Alegría, M., Jackson, J., & Williams, D. (2007). Immigration and mental health: Diverse findings in Asian, Black, and Latino populations. *American Journal of Public Health, 97,* 11–12.

Takeuchi, D., Zane, N., Hong, S., Chae, D., Gong, F., Gee, G.C., ...Alegría, M. (2007). Immigration-related factors and mental disorders among Asian Americans. *American Journal of Public Health, 97,* 84–90.

Tidemalm, D., Långström, N., Lichtenstein, P., & Runeson, B. (2008). Risk of suicide after suicide attempt according to coexisting psychiatric disorder: Swedish cohort study with long term follow-up. *British Medical Journal, 33,* a2205.

Tsuang, M. T., Woolson, R. F., & Fleming, J. A. (1980). Premature deaths in schizophrenia and affective disorders: An analysis of survival curves and variables affecting shortened survival. *Archives of General Psychiatry, 37,* 979–983.

US Consumer Product Safety Commission. (2013). *National electronic injury surveillance system (NEISS).* Retrieved October 2013, from http://www.cpsc.gov/en/Research--Statistics/NEISS-Injury-Data/.

US Department of Health and Human Services. (1999). *Mental health: A report of the Surgeon General.* Rockville, MD: US Department of Health and Human Services, Substance Abuse and Mental Health Services Administration, Center for Mental Health Services, National Institutes of Health, National Institute of Mental Health.

US Department of Health and Human Services, Centers for Disease Control and Prevention, National Center for Health Statistics, Data Warehouse. (2010a). *Death rates for 113 selected causes, by 5-year age groups, race, and sex: United States, 1999-2007.* Retrieved June 2013, from http://www.cdc.gov/nchs/data/dvs/MortFinal2007_WorktableOrig291R.pdf.

US Department of Health and Human Services, Centers for Disease Control and Prevention, National Center for Health Statistics, Data Warehouse. (2010b). *Deaths from 113 selected causes, by 5-year age groups, race, and sex: United States, 1999-2007.* Retrieved June 2013, from http://www.cdc.gov/nchs/data/dvs/MortFinal2007_WorkTable291F.pdf.

US Department of Health and Human Services, Food and Drug Administration, Center for Drug Evaluation and Research. (2004). *Worsening depression and suicidality in patients being treated with antidepressant medications.* Retrieved October 2013, from http://www.fda.gov/Drugs/DrugSafety/PostmarketDrugSafetyInformationforPatientsandProviders/DrugSafetyInformationforHeathcareProfessionals/PublicHealthAdvisories/ucm161696.htm.

US Department of Health and Human Services, Food and Drug Administration, Center for Drug Evaluation and Research. (2005). *Suicidality in adults being treated with antidepressant medications.* Retrieved October 2013, from http://www.fda.gov/Drugs/DrugSafety/PostmarketDrugSafetyInformationforPatientsandProviders/DrugSafetyInformationforHeathcareProfessionals/PublicHealthAdvisories/ucm053169.htm.

US Department of Health and Human Services, Food and Drug Administration, Center for Drug Evaluation and Research. (2007). *Antidepressant use in children, adolescents, and adults.* Retrieved June 2010, from http://www.fda.gov/Drugs/DrugSafety/InformationbyDrugClass/UCM096273.

US Department of Health and Human Services, Indian Health Service. (2009). *Trends in Indian health, 2002-2003 Edition.* Washington, DC: US Government Printing Office.

Verona, E., Sachs-Ericsson, N., & Joiner, T. E. (2004). Suicide attempts associated with externalizing psychopathology in an epidemiological sample. *American Journal of Psychiatry, 161,* 444–451.

Weissman, M. M. (1974). The epidemiology of suicide attempts 1960 to 1971. *Archives of General Psychiatry, 30,* 737–746.

West, J. C., Wilk, J. E., Rae, D. S., Muszynski, I. S., Rubio Stipec, M., Alter, C. L.,...Regier, D. A. (2009). Medicaid prescription drug policies and medication access and continuity: Findings from ten states. *Psychiatric Services, 60,* 601–610.

Wilcox, H. C., Kellam, S. G., Brown, H., Poduska, J. M., Ialongo, N. S., Wang, W., & Anthony, J. C. (2008). The impact of two universal randomized first- and second-grade classroom interventions on young adult suicide ideation and attempts. *Drug and Alcohol Dependence, 95*(Suppl.), S60–S73.

Wilcox, H. C., Storr, C. L., & Breslau, N. (2009). Posttraumatic stress disorder and suicide attempts in a community sample of urban American young adults. *Archives of General Psychiatry, 66,* 305–311.

Wilke, M., Krägeloh-Mann, I., & Holland, S. K. (2007). Global and local development of gray and white matter volume in normal children and adolescents. *Experimental Brain Research, 178,* 296–307.

Working Groups, Workshop on Suicide and Sexual Orientation. (1995). Recommendations for a research agenda on suicide and sexual orientation. *Suicide and Life-Threatening Behavior, 25,* 82–94.

World Health Organization. (2001.) *Mental health: New understanding, new hope.* Retrieved July 2009, from http://www.who.int/whr/2001/en/.

World Health Organization. (2007). International statistical classification of diseases and health related problems (10th rev.). Retrieved July 2009, from http://www.who.int/classifications/apps/icd/icd10online/.

World Health Organization. (2008). *The global burden of disease: 2004 update.* Retrieved July 2009, from http://www.who.int/healthinfo/global_burden_disease/GBD_report_2004update_full.pdf.

Person-Centered Prevention of Suicide Among Older Adults

Paul R. Duberstein *and* Marnin J. Heisel

Abstract

This chapter reviews the clinical risk factors for suicide in older adults and offers a person-centered approach to prevention, one that focuses less on biomedical concepts such as "disease" and more on decision-making concepts related to personologic and motivational processes, such as risk detection, treatment seeking, and treatment adherence. Person-centered approaches to primary prevention are theorized to succeed when they are perceived as posing little threat to self-determination. Person-centered approaches to secondary prevention are theorized to succeed when they are perceived as enhancing the autonomous decision making of at-risk individuals, their family members, and the individual(s) from whom help is sought. A person-centered framework could advance suicidology and complement rapidly developing research in basic and applied decision making.

Key Words: decision making, depression, humanistic, older adults, personality, prevention, public health, public policy, suicide

Hostility, aggression, and emotional dysregulation have been emphasized in clinical theories of suicidal behavior for more than seven decades (Buie & Maltsberger, 1989; Hendin, 1991; Zilboorg, 1937). Yet these constructs are of dubious relevance for understanding suicide mortality in older adulthood (Duberstein, Seidlitz, & Conwell, 1996). Age differences in the clinical characteristics of people who die by suicide have been extensively documented (Conner, Duberstein, & Conwell, 1999; Conwell, Duberstein, Cox, & Herrmann, 1996; Conwell et al., 1998; Duberstein, Conwell, & Caine, 1994; McGirr et al., 2008), and older adults who die by suicide can be distinguished from those who engage in nonsuicidal self-injury (Tsoh et al., 2005; Useda et al., 2007). Just as conclusions about the cause of cancer in older adults cannot be drawn from research on younger adults, knowledge about suicide mortality in older adults cannot be

gleaned solely from research on younger people who contemplate suicide. Given the questionable utility of surrogate endpoints (Links, Heisel, & Quastel, 2005; Wortzel, Gutierrez, Homaifar, Breshears, & Harwood, 2010), this chapter focuses nearly exclusively on suicide mortality.

In the first two sections, we summarize the current state of knowledge on demographic and clinical risk markers for suicide in older adults. We then review published research on the role of person variables in late-life suicide mortality and argue for integrating personology (Krueger, Caspi, & Moffitt, 2000; Millon, 2003) in suicide prevention efforts. In the fourth section, we summarize the standard prevention approaches, behaviorally oriented primary prevention and biomedically oriented secondary prevention (Kaplan, 2000). Next, in the chapter's centerpiece, we offer a vision of *person-centered prevention* and contrast it to the current standards. Like the term "client-centered" (Rogers, 1951), the term "person-centered" is used to orient attention to the missing element in most prevention models: the person.

The core propositions of person-centered prevention are outlined in Table 7.1 and elaborated on later in the chapter. Suicide is typically conceptualized as an individual act of personal volition, one catalyzed in part by the failure of deeply distressed individuals to seek or be receptive to effective treatment or support. Yet it is inadequate, from a public health perspective, to consider suicide as an act of a lone individual. Rather, suicide is an act that also is facilitated by organizational and political decision-making processes (Douglas, 1986; Oliver, 2006). These decision-making processes lead to the development of suicide prevention initiatives that, for example, unwittingly ignore fundamental human desires and motives, particularly the need for self-determination (Ryan & Deci, 2000). To redress this problem, our person-centered approach holds that the success of all interventions—be they clinical encounters with individual patients or families, broader community-wide interventions, or public policy initiatives—depends on the extent to which fundamental human needs for autonomy, competence, and relatedness have been accommodated. We theorize that person-centered approaches to primary prevention will succeed to the extent that they are perceived as posing little threat to self-determination (Moller, Ryan, & Deci, 2006). Similarly, person-centered approaches to secondary prevention are theorized to succeed to the extent that they enhance autonomous decision making (Ryan & Deci, 2000) on the part of all stakeholders (Oliver, 2006), particularly at-risk individuals, their family members, and the individual(s) from whom help is sought. It is vital to acknowledge the needs of patients and clinicians alike for autonomy.

Caveat Emptor

Three qualifiers must be considered. First, generalizations about suicide among "older people" should be made with caution. The age at which one is considered to be "older" varies across cultures and from one era to the next. Researchers often use 65 years of age as a cutoff, corresponding to the retirement age established by the Committee on Economic Security, which launched the American Social Security system in 1935. People 65 years of age and older are heterogeneous socially, culturally, spiritually, and in terms of physical and mental health. It is possible that risk factors for suicide in a 65-year-old and an 85-year-old may differ, but there are few data on this issue (Chochinov et al., 1995; Erlangsen, Bille-Brahe, & Jeune, 2003; Waern, Rubenowitz, & Wilhelmson, 2003). In this chapter, the term "older" refers to individuals 65 years of age and older.

Second, it is often assumed that suicide is rare in the absence of a diagnosable mental disorder (Chochinov et al., 1995), but the conceptualization and measurement of mental disorders and suicide (Bostwick & Cohen, 2009; Leeman, 2009) in individuals with chronic physical illness, neurodegenerative diseases, and acute life-threatening illness remain ambiguous, and there are ethical debates as to when and how to intervene in these diverse contexts. This chapter rests on the assumption that thoughts of suicide and a wish for hastened death

Table 7.1 Core Propositions of Person-Centered Suicide Prevention

- Whereas standard approaches to prevention are based on a biomedical or behavioral model, the person-centered approach is based on a humanistic model.

- The success of any intervention depends on the extent to which fundamental human needs for autonomy, competence, and relatedness (Ryan & Deci, 2000) have been accommodated.

- Primary prevention efforts fail if they are perceived as potentially interfering with the fundamental desire for self-determination, particularly the need for autonomy.

- Secondary prevention efforts fail if they are perceived as potentially interfering with the fundamental desire for self-determination, particularly the needs for autonomy and competence.

- Person-centered primary prevention efforts succeed by being invisible or unintrusive.

- Person-centered secondary prevention efforts can succeed in a multitude of ways. There is no single path to success. Some will succeed by promoting competence; others will succeed by promoting autonomy, and still others will succeed by promoting relatedness.

are appropriate targets for intervention even in the absence of a major mental disorder.

Third, risk factors tend to be context specific. Risk factors that appear robust in some clinical, social, cultural, and historical contexts might be associated with lower risk in others (Neeleman, 2002). Some societal forces may amplify risk in some demographic groups, while having little influence or even leading to declines in risk in other groups (Gunnell, Middleton, Whitley, Dorling, & Frankel, 2003). These caveats all point to the need for sensitivity to context and frank humility in considering the available literature.

Demographic Risk Markers
Age, Gender, Race, National, and Regional Differences

Suicide rates for men in the United States increase with age, but women's rates peak in midlife and remain stable or decline slightly thereafter. Suicide rates among White men 85 years and older are almost six times the nation's age-adjusted rate. Among individuals 65 years of age and older in the United States, the ratio of suicide for men:women approaches 7:1; but in most other countries, the ratio is closer to 3:1. In the United States, Whites have higher suicide rates than Blacks across the life span, and patterns of risk differ with age.

Regional differences in suicide rates have been observed since the early 19th century (Durkheim, 1951). Countries in Northern Europe (e.g., Sweden, Finland, Denmark, Norway, and Iceland) have higher rates than those in Southern Europe (e.g., Italy and Spain). In the United States, the more densely populated states in the Middle Atlantic region (e.g., New York and New Jersey) and New England (e.g., Massachusetts, Rhode Island, and Connecticut) have lower rates than the Mountain States (e.g., Nevada, Wyoming, Montana, and Arizona). Acknowledging minor annual variations, the crude rates in the Mountain States are nearly twice those of the Middle Atlantic region. For reasons that remain unexplained, some states have relatively high suicide rates among older adults and relatively low rates among 15- to 24-year-olds (e.g., Vermont), although in other states (e.g., North Dakota), the reverse is true. In most cases, the relative rates in the two age groups are roughly comparable in each state. For example, Massachusetts has the lowest rate of suicide among older adults and the second lowest rate of suicide among 15- to 24-year olds.

Significant geographic variability in rates of mental disorders have been reported in postmortem samples of suicide (Arsenault-Lapierre, Kim, & Turecki, 2004; Duberstein & Witte, 2009). Alcohol dependence may be a more potent risk factor in Sweden than in France (Norstrom, 1995) or in one region of the United States compared to another. These differences are real and cannot be explained away as reporting artifacts (Duberstein & Witte, 2009). Consequently, macro-level prevention strategies require a deep understanding of location-specific risk indices, yet relevant data are rarely available. Prevention programs can be implemented targeting specific risk indices in specific populations and communities after regionally and socioculturally specific risk indices have been identified.

Marital Status and Living Arrangements

Durkheim (1951) established that suicide rates for people who are single, divorced, or widowed are higher than those for married people. Suicide risk after widowhood is highest in the immediate aftermath, and the increased risk appears to be highest 4 years within the first few years. In one study, those who took their lives within 4 years of the loss were more likely to have a history of early loss than those who died after a longer period of widowhood (Duberstein, Conwell, & Cox, 1998).

The data examining suicide risk in relation to living arrangements are mixed (Beautrais, 2002; Duberstein et al., 2004; Rubenowitz, Waern, Wilhelmson, & Allebeck, 2001; Tsoh et al., 2005), probably reflecting the fact that residential choice is determined by local rather than universal conditions, such as cultural and subcultural norms, housing prices, and population density. Our research, conducted in the United States, showed that people who died by suicide were less likely to live with family; they also were less likely to have children and be married (Duberstein et al., 2004).

Socioeconomic Status

Consistent with research on mixed-aged samples (Brown, Beck, Steer, & Grisham, 2000), older adults who have less education (Conwell et al., 2000) and lower incomes (Duberstein, Conwell, Conner, Eberly, & Caine, 2004) are at elevated suicide risk. These findings are consistent with the expanding literature on socioeconomic status and health (Phelan, Link, & Tehranifar, 2010). Across virtually all health indicators outcomes, lower SES is associated with worse outcomes. Why would there be an association between socioeconomic status and suicide? Health care providers might be less likely to assess and treat mental disorders in patients with less education or income due to implicit bias (van Ryn & Fu, 2003). Also, because these patients may have more medical comorbidity, health care providers may be less attentive to their mental health needs (Klinkman, 1997; Rost et al., 2000). Patients themselves may have lower levels of mental health literacy (Howard, Sentell, & Gazmararian, 2006) and more stigmatized attitudes toward the receipt of mental health care.

Moving beyond the doctor–patient relationship, socioeconomic status is often tied to neighborhood contextual influences (Phelan et al., 2010), which increases the likelihood of exposure to a range of adversities (Kubzansky et al., 2005), including stressors that have been shown to increase suicide risk in older adults, such as financial strains, employment changes, and family discord (Beautrais, 2002; Duberstein et al., 2004; Rubenowitz et al., 2001). People living in disadvantaged neighborhoods are more likely to have been exposed chronically to neurotoxins (Krieger, 2008; Schell, 1998), which may play a role in suicide.

Clinical Risk Markers

To paraphrase Barraclough (1971), studying the living is hard enough, and studying the dead is nearly impossible. Yet hundreds of postmortem studies of suicide have appeared worldwide since the psychological autopsy (PA) method was invented in the 1930s in response to New York City Mayor Fiorello LaGuardia's call for deeper understanding of a spate of police suicides (Friedman, 1967; Heiman, 1975). Despite its limitations, the PA is the most efficient approach to the identification of suicide risk markers, particularly the clinical features that are present in the days, weeks, and months prior to death (Duberstein & Conwell, 1997; Duberstein & Witte, 2009). The pace of PA research in the United States has lagged over the past decade, but interest in the methods continues to surge elsewhere. From 1997 to 2006, 11 PA studies on personality disorders and suicide mortality were conducted—all outside the United States (Duberstein & Witte, 2009). Although few PA studies have provided the comprehensive covariate coverage required to conclude that any single clinical condition is truly an "independent" risk marker for suicide, the emerging literature points to the significance of mental disorders as well as physical illness and functional impairment.

Clinically Significant Symptoms of Emotional Distress

More than 75% of older adults who die by suicide have clinically significant mood symptoms at the time of death. In industrialized countries, it is the rare older adult who dies by suicide without a diagnosable (but frequently undiagnosed) mood disorder (Ernst et al., 2004). This is true in community samples of those who died by suicide (Beautrais, 2002; Chiu et al., 2004; Harwood, Hawton, Hope, & Jacoby, 2001; Waern et al., 2002) as well as in suicidal deaths occurring in nursing homes (Suominen et al., 2003), and in patients hospitalized on medical units (Suominen, Isometsä, Heila, Lönnqvist, & Henriksson, 2002). Risk is not confined to major depression; minor depressive disorder and dysthymia also confer increased risk (Waern et al., 2002), as does bipolar disorder and adjustment disorder (Chiu et al., 2004). Active or remitted substance misuse (Conner et al., 2000; Kölves, Varnik, Tooding, & Wasserman, 2006; Waern et al., 2002) also are important considerations.

Physical Illness, Functional Impairment, and Pain

Physical illness, notably cancer and lung disease, appears to increase suicide risk in older adults, even after controlling for mental disorders (Grabbe, Demi, Camann, & Potter, 1997; Llorente et al., 2005; Quan, Arboleda-Florez, Fick, Stuart, & Love, 2002; Tsoh et al., 2005; Waern et al., 2002). Cancer and chronic pulmonary disease conferred suicide risk in a cohort of 822 suicides among individuals 55 years of age and older (Quan et al., 2002) and chronic lung disease was independently associated with death by suicide in a study of adults 66 years and older (Juurlink, Herrmann, Szalai, Kopp, & Redelmeier, 2004). Studies have also suggested that suicide risk is elevated among patients suffering from chronic obstructive pulmonary disease (Horton-Deutsch, Clark, & Farran, 1992; Suominen et al., 2002).

Why might there be a relationship between physical illness and suicide? *Biological* interpretations posit that there are pathophysiological influences on brain function that increase suicide risk. For instance, some tumors could have specific effects on the central nervous system, increasing risk for depression and subsequent suicide. A *health systems and medical decision-making* interpretation posits that overburdened primary care or specialty physicians may underappreciate their patients' mental health needs (Klinkman, 1997), not inquire about thoughts of suicide (Feldman et al., 2007), or not know how to respond to disclosures of suicide ideation (Vannoy, Tai-Seale, Duberstein, Eaton, & Cook, 2011). Patients themselves may discount their mental symptoms and default to focusing on physical health concerns because of perceptions about limited physician interest, time, and expertise. As older patients who die by suicide are far more likely to be seen by a primary care provider than by a specialty mental health provider (Luoma, Martin, & Pearson, 2002), interactions between patients and primary care providers (Epstein et al., 2005) should be considered in theoretical models of suicide.

From a *psychological* perspective, the meaning and experience of the disease, as derived from social norms as well as one's personal experiences, can lead to a loss of perceived control and feelings of burdensomeness. For example, pulmonary problems may be linked with suicide risk due to the terror of suffocation and associated feelings of being out of control. Growing infirm in a body that robs one's independence along with a deteriorating capacity to care for one's activities of daily living (e.g., toileting, bathing) could lead to existential malaise and feelings of psychological burdensomeness (Joiner, 2005; Wilson, Curran, & McPherson, 2005). Even the expectation of physical pain or disability may be sufficient to increase risk in some. With respect to macro-level considerations, we hypothesize that psychological burdensomeness may be particularly problematic among individuals residing in societies that devalue help seeking and place a high premium on autonomy or "independence." Similarly, feelings of economic burdensomeness (Emanuel, Fairclough, Slutsman, & Emanuel, 2000) are hypothesized to be particularly acute among residents of regions with inadequate health care financing or approaches to end-of-life care.

Moving Beyond Clinical Risk Markers: Epidemiologic Personology

Many older people who die by suicide had an active mood disorder, physical illness, or functional impairment, but few people in such circumstances even seriously contemplate taking their own lives, let alone take action. Identification of other risk markers that could be targeted prior to the development of mental disorders or age-related health problems or during the routine course of patient care for these conditions is necessary. Risk markers exist at multiple levels of analysis and unfold over different timeframes (Krieger, 2008). There is a need to move beyond temporally proximal risk markers (mood disorders, physical illness), mainly because these interventions are often too little, too late.

Our focus is on individual-level, temporally distal person variables (Magnusson, 1990), the study

of which has been designated *personology* (Krueger et al., 2000; Millon, 2003; Murray, 1962). The term encompasses not only traits, processes, disorders, motives, and goals but also attitudes, beliefs, values, styles of communication, and styles of decision making along with other psychological phenomena that Millon (2003) noted may be "partitioned conceptually for pragmatic or scientific purposes, but...are segments of an inseparable biopsychosocial entity" (p. 951). Attempts to alter the course of patients' developmental trajectories before they develop potentially malignant disorders could decrease risk (individual-level prevention) and lower the suicide rate (population-level prevention).

Calling for closer ties between personality psychologists and prevention scientists, Krueger et al. (2000) coined the term *epidemiologic personology*. The ultimate success of such an endeavor remains to be seen, but its failure to gain traction prior to the 21st century certainly represents a casualty of specialization (Kushner, 1991), a product of bureaucratization (Weber, 1946) and consequent partitioning of the institutions designed to support science (Douglas, 1986). In the United States, the institutions themselves are inherently fragmented, a consequence of the dispersal of power envisioned by the founders (Oliver, 2006). In this section, we explain why it is important to move beyond partitioned proximal risk markers, provide a conceptual rationale for integrating personology in suicide prevention efforts, and review the evidence for the role of person variables in late-life suicide mortality. In the subsequent section, we explain how a person-centered approach to prevention could inform (not replace) contemporary primary and secondary prevention approaches.

Rationale for Integrating Personology in Suicide Prevention Efforts

The central reason for focusing on person variables is that they drive developmental trajectories and decision-making processes that affect all realms of life tied to suicide risk, including mental and physical health, social relations, and interaction with health care providers and health care "systems," including risk detection, treatment seeking, and treatment adherence. Person variables increase risk for the mental disorders that drive risk (Duberstein, Pálsson, Waern, & Skoog, 2008; Weiss et al., 2009) and significantly influence other risk markers, including overall medical illness burden (Chapman, Lyness, & Duberstein, 2007), poor physical function (Chapman, Duberstein, & Lyness, 2007;

Duberstein et al., 2003; K. R. Krueger, Wilson, Shah, Tang, & Bennett, 2006), and pain (Calabrese, Lyness, Sörensen, & Duberstein, 2006).

Person variables also influence how individuals become aware of and respond to the physical and emotional conditions that confer suicide risk. There is a long tradition in medical sociology (Pescosolido, 1992) and health services research (Safer, Tharps, Jackson, & Leventhal, 1979) of attempting to understand why people in need of treatment do not seek care promptly or adhere to treatment. More recently, researchers have examined the influence of person variables on decisions to seek mental health treatment (Goodwin, Hoven, Lyons, & Stein, 2002) or utilize other health services (Chapman et al., 2009). In a qualitative study (Epstein et al., 2010), participants who described themselves as "always very dark" reported being so accustomed to their "gloom" that it was difficult for them and those in their social networks to appreciate their descent into depression. In contrast, those who described themselves as a "people person" or "life of the party" were unaccustomed to the experiences of gloominess or moodiness. They were not attuned to the nuances of their own moods and found it difficult to reconcile their self-image as an "outgoing likeable person" with the experience of depression. This also made it more difficult for family members and friends to perceive that they were depressed.

The idea that some mood disorders might be more difficult to detect in relatively extraverted individuals has received support in at least one study (Duberstein et al., 2011). Other research has shown that traits could undermine treatment by rupturing alliances (Zuroff et al., 2000) or by leading to missed appointments (Ciechanowski et al., 2006) and nonadherence (Jerant, Chapman, Duberstein, Robbins, & Franks, 2011). For example, secondary analyses of a large multisite study showed that perfectionism undermined the therapeutic alliance and, in turn, was associated with poorer outcomes (Zuroff et al., 2000).

Evidence for the Role of Person Variables in Late-Life Suicide Mortality

Numerous prospective studies have been conducted on younger cohorts (Brezo, Paris, & Turecki, 2006; Conner, Duberstein, Conwell, Seidlitz, & Caine, 2001), but we are aware of only one relevant prospective study of an older cohort that has examined the influence of person variables on suicide

risk (Tsoh, Chiu, Duberstein, Chan, & Conwell, unpublished data). Notwithstanding its small sample size ($n = 66$) and the relatively few suicides ($n = 5$) over the 6-year follow-up period, survival analyses showed that people who were low in trait Agreeableness were at elevated risk. The authors noted that the decedents tended to be distrustful and suspicious of others and saw themselves as selfish, competitive, manipulative, and calculating.

Three postmortem studies have examined whether person variables are independently associated with suicide risk (Harwood et al., 2001; Tsoh et al., 2005; Useda et al., 2007), two of which compared those who survived a suicide attempt with those who died (Tsoh et al., 2005; Useda et al., 2007). Although these studies were conducted in vastly different settings, Hong Kong and Western New York, the consistency in findings is remarkable.

The Hong Kong study showed that, compared to people who survived a suicide attempt, those who died were lower in neuroticism, more conscientious, less open to new experiences, and more agreeable (Tsoh et al., 2005). The Western New York study similarly showed that people who died by suicide were lower in neuroticism, more achievement oriented (higher in conscientiousness), and lower in facets of openness to fantasy and aesthetics (Useda et al., 2007). In both studies, people who died by suicide appeared to be somewhat psychologically healthier than those who survived suicide attempts, but we should hasten to add that individuals dying by suicide did not score in the "normal" range of psychological health. The findings from Hong Kong and Western New York suggest that older adults who die by suicide might appear to be relatively well adjusted, particularly when compared to those with a history of suicide attempts. A qualitative investigation of people who died by suicide without seeking any medical advice in the United Kingdom (Harwood et al., 2001; Owens, Lambert, Donovan, & Lloyd, 2005) amplifies the findings from Hong Kong and Western New York and provides important clues to clinicians and preventionists alike. The UK researchers described:

> Stoical individuals who were determined to soldier on unaided... (they) were portrayed as habitual nonconfiders or as having practiced deliberate deception, artfully concealing the true nature and extent of their troubles from those around them. (Owens, Lambert, Donovan, & Lloyd, 2005, p. 506)

Viewing the personality data from a public health perspective, we maintain that older people who die by suicide following their first suicide attempt possess personal characteristics that diminish the likelihood of their suicide risk being detected by social supports and professional care providers. Their shy reclusiveness and avoidance of novelty might explain why so few had sought appropriate mental health treatment prior to death by suicide (Duberstein, 2001). In contrast, those who made at least one suicide attempt prior to their fatal one may be characterized by a different pattern of treatment rejection (Tyrer, Mitchard, Methuen, & Ranger, 2003), one marked by suspicion and lack of trust (Tsoh et al., unpublished data).

Two caveats and directions for future research are offered. First, it is clear that person variables confer suicide risk, but direct evidence for the mediating role of decision-making processes involved in symptom detection, help seeking, treatment initiation, or treatment adherence is needed. Second, personology requires the examination of intraindividual differences, changes within an individual over time, and within-person patterns of traits. Virtually all personologic research in suicide has been conducted within the standard individual differences framework, despite Lester's (1972) speculation, four decades ago, that "although the suicidal person does not possess unique traits, there occurs in the suicidal person a unique combination of traits" (p. 321). More creative approaches to data analyses would be useful.

Prevention Science

Controversy abounds concerning the labels used to designate prevention research and program implementation. Several typologies have been proposed (Kaplan, 2000; Knox, Conwell, & Caine, 2004; National Institute of Mental Health, 1998; Rose, 1992). Distinctions have been drawn between high-risk and population-based approaches (Kaplan, 2000; Rose, 1992) and between universal, targeted, selective, and indicated approaches (Knox et al., 2004; National Institute of Mental Health, 1998). For our purposes, the critical issue is whether programs target populations on the basis of a clinical risk factor, such as suicide ideation or depression. For this reason, the distinction between primary prevention and secondary prevention (Kaplan, 2000) is more useful.

Primary Prevention

Guided by a behavioral (vs. biomedical) model of health, the main targets of primary prevention programs are health behavior and decision making (Kaplan, 2000): alcohol, tobacco, drug use, maintenance of a healthful diet, exercise, and safety with regard to sex, food, medication, transportation, firearms, and so on. Although not focused on suicide (or any other single cause of death), primary prevention programs are still likely to affect population-level suicide rates. Those of greatest professional and media attention include legislation and policy restricting access to firearms or bridges as well as mandates concerning carbon monoxide emissions as well as the manufacturing, packaging, and distribution of medications (Hawton, 2002; Hawton et al., 2009; Mann et al., 2005).

Medication mandates have been successful (Hawton, 2002), illustrating the potential of applying libertarian paternalism (Thaler & Sunstein, 2008) to questions of health policy. Blister packs make it difficult to take a large number of pain relievers in a short period of time, decreasing the risk of suicide by overdose (Hawton, 2002). The mandate is "paternalistic" in the sense that the government intervenes to shape citizen behavior. (As an aside, the sexist nature of this designation speaks to the need for a different term. Parentalism might be a better choice.) It is "libertarian" in the sense that liberty (Berlin, 1969) or autonomous (Ryan & Deci, 2000) decision-making processes are not unduly restricted. People are "nudged" to behave more healthfully and are not inconvenienced in the process. Person-centered primary prevention efforts succeed by being invisible. Some laws, policies, mandates, or advertising campaigns have the potential to affect public safety and thus decrease the likelihood of apparently impulsive (Conner, 2004) suicide acts. Moreover, primary prevention initiatives could enhance quality of life by modifying attitudes about aging, shifting cultural norms concerning the acceptability of suicide in older adulthood, and increasing rates of healthful behaviors. Each new law, regulation, or public education campaign (e.g., to enhance lay response to distress [Owens et al., 2009]), provides an opportunity for an enterprising scholar to examine its effect on suicide rates. Typically, economists and those with training in public health have been more likely than psychologists to seize these opportunities for data analyses, but this should change as psychologists begin to expand their focus from individuals to communities (Sarason, 1981) and to public health.

Shifts in laws, policy, and public education are just a few components of primary prevention. There are others. An initiative was mounted in 1983 and 1984 to train all 18 primary care physicians on the Swedish island of Gotland (population 58,000) in detecting and treating depression (Rutz, 2001). Two years into the study, the number of suicides had decreased by 60%, presumably due to increases in the prescription of antidepressants and lithium. Notably, the suicide rate declined in women, but not men. In addition to demonstrating the potential value of a public health approach to suicide prevention, this study teaches of the dangers of discontinuing effective clinical education programs absent a plan for sustainability. Deaths by suicide increased following program discontinuation.

In Japan, researchers used a quasi-experimental design to conduct a 10-year program of community mental health presentations, depression screenings, and mental health outreach to community-residing older adults living in a small rural town (Oyama, Koida, Sakashita, & Kudo, 2004). During the study's intervention stage, a 73% reduced risk of death by suicide was observed for men 65 years of age or older, and a 76% reduced risk was observed for women; risk remained low through the study's maintenance phase. Caution is warranted, as a decrease in one or two deaths by suicide in a region of the size examined (population 7,010) could have greatly affected the suicide rates. Subsequent reports of similar reductions in rates of suicide among older women in other small Japanese towns employing a similar methodology (Oyama et al., 2005, 2006; Oyama, Fujita, Goto, Shibuya, & Sakashita, 2006) suggest that the findings are relatively robust (Oyama et al., 2008), albeit sex-specific.

In Italy, a telephone distress and outreach service called TeleHelp-TeleCheck reduced late-life suicide risk (De Leo, Carollo, & Dello Buono, 1995; De Leo, Dello Buono, & Dwyer, 2002). Physicians typically referred older patients to this social support service outfitting at-risk individuals with personal alarm buttons linked to a response network (TeleHelp) that additionally provided telephonic support calls twice weekly and/or as needed (TeleCheck). Over the 11-year period of study, there was a significant reduction in risk for suicide among women but not for men. Again, caution is warranted, as rates of suicide among TeleHelp-TeleCheck users were compared with estimates based on regional suicide rates, rather than with controls.

The efforts in Japan and Italy exemplify the potential effectiveness of primary prevention interventions for older women. They have had little or no impact on the suicide rates of older men,

perhaps because they have not addressed fundamental barriers to help seeking in men (Addis & Mahalik, 2003). Primary prevention programs can potentially save more lives than interventions targeting high-risk groups, because more suicides will be observed in large populations at relatively low risk than in small, high-risk population. Clearly, suicide prevention requires researchers and clinicians to focus on the treatment of mood disordered patients with comorbid physical illness hospitalized for a suicide attempt, but it is just as important, and potentially more cost-effective, to identify at-risk patients long before they develop a mood disorder, let alone a suicidal crisis. Whereas clinical initiatives might be most effective with patients who are already engaged with the health care delivery system, primary prevention programs are needed to reach those who are not engaged or who are treatment rejecting.

STANDARD CRITIQUES OF PRIMARY PREVENTION

The most damaging critiques are often the most insidious and difficult to grasp (Douglas, 1986; Sarason, 1981). Culture and politics shape the way societies conceptualize and label the institutions built to meet its needs (Douglas, 1986). In the case of suicide prevention, the institutions of interest include the procedure- and disease-specific entities involved in health care training, payment, and research funding. Not a single federal agency is devoted to primary prevention. Of the 28 institutes, offices, and centers that constitute the National Institutes of Health in the United States, many refer to different disease classes (e.g., "cancer," "stroke," "digestive disease") not prevention per se. A similar observation holds for the ways in which most university departments are arrayed. In order for primary prevention to gain traction, there will need to be a reconceptualization and reorganization of the institutions that help shape the day-to-day activities of scientists, scholars, and clinicians. As this would entail an inherently political process (Oliver, 2006), change is unlikely to happen soon: "Incrementalism pervades nearly every area of public health policy" (Oliver, 2006, p. 203).

Numerous obstacles to primary prevention exist. Some reflect deeply rooted, core ideological leanings. Values placed on liberty (Berlin, 1969) and individualism (Bellah, Madsen, Sullivan, Swidler, & Tipton, 1991) lead many to scoff at social engineering and view with skepticism efforts to cajole people to behave more healthfully. As the commentator

Peggy Noonan (2009) put it in an op-ed piece about the American health care debate of 2009:

> We are living in a time in which educated people who are at the top of American life feel they have the right to make very public criticisms of…let's call it the private, pleasurable but health-related choices of others. They shame smokers and the overweight. Drinking will be next.…Americans in the most personal, daily ways feels they are less free than they used to be. And they are right, they are less free. Who wants more of that? (p. A13)

Primary prevention initiatives will continue to be paralyzed by the failure to reach consensus on competing values, particularly the value of individual freedoms and responsibility versus the value of public or collective health. This is an ongoing refrain in debates about public health initiatives, not only in the United States but in many industrialized nations (Cappelen & Norheim, 2005).

Primary prevention has little intuitive appeal. Although the human brain evolved mechanisms to make rapid and correct judgments about complex issues (Gigerenzer, 2007), making decisions to engage proactively in the ever-expanding list of health-promoting behaviors is not instinctual, in any sense of the term (Graham & Martin, 2012).

Behaviorally oriented primary prevention programs may be viewed as unjust (Rawls, 1958) if they ignore fundamental structural or socioeconomic causes (Krieger, 2008; Phelan et al., 2010) of suicide. From the perspective of social justice, if primary prevention programs cannot address powerful structural determinants of suicide, they may inadvertently increase risk. Of course, primary prevention programs addressing structural inequality could be designed.

Finally, it has been suggested that even so-called universal interventions will not reach many at-risk people (Neeleman, 2002), and this is particularly true of those interventions that require the at-risk individual to make an active decision to "opt-in," as opposed to those programs espoused by libertarian paternalists that require little active decision making (Thaler & Sunstein, 2008). In a study designed to decrease social isolation among seniors 75 years of age or older who lived alone, half the experimental group declined repeated offers of help (Clarke, Clarke, & Jagger, 1992). Research on the characteristics of older patients entering research studies suggests that patients 80 years or older and those with lower levels of education are less willing to participate in research (Gallo et al., 2005). Their needs

are thus more likely to go unrecognized. This phenomenon is not specific to research on depression or social isolation. In research on dementia prevention, for example, "[r]isk factors and clinical trial participation are currently at odds…patients at highest risk…are least likely to participate in clinical trials" (Cummings, Doody, & Clark, 2007, p. 1624).

To the extent that primary prevention programs require people to make an active decision to enhance their quality of life, they will need to actively engage the disenfranchised. Primary prevention programs that do not require active decision making may hold greater promise. A distinguished group of British researchers concluded that reducing access to lethal means and crafting economic policies that reduce unemployment may decrease the suicide rate; treating people is a less promising strategy (Lewis, Hawton, & Jones, 1997).

Secondary Prevention

Guided by a biomedical (vs. behavioral) model of health (Kaplan, 2000), the main targets in secondary prevention are the clinical conditions and diseases known to confer suicide risk (e.g., major depression). Many believe that, ideally, secondary prevention programs should involve determining whether an evidence-based treatment offered to patients with a particular clinical condition leads to fewer suicides over a follow-up period than a control treatment. Yet two pragmatic considerations pose challenges to the design and implementation of this ideal study. First, the proscription against withholding potentially effective treatment for those at risk for suicide creates an ethical barrier to mounting randomized clinical trials. Second, the low base rate of deaths by suicide makes it all but impossible to conduct rigorous efficacy or effectiveness research (Pokorny, 1993). As one group (Borges, Anthony, & Garrison, 1995) stated, "truly monumental segments of person-time are needed to achieve adequate statistical power" (p. 229). Not surprisingly, a review of 208 articles yielded no studies that examined whether a treatment reduced death by suicide (Links, Heisel, & Quastel, 2005).

At the beginning of this chapter, we noted we would focus *nearly* exclusively on suicide mortality. In the absence of secondary prevention data on suicide mortality, we have chosen to mention a few secondary prevention studies on suicidal ideation, a surrogate endpoint of arguable utility (Wortzel et al., 2010). The Prevention of Suicide in Primary Care Elderly-Collaborative Trial (Bruce et al., 2004) was designed to determine whether a treatment algorithm reduced depression and suicide ideation among primary care patients over the age of 60 years. In a comparison of the effects of antidepressant medication and/or interpersonal psychotherapy versus usual care, patients receiving the study intervention showed a greater decrease in prevalence of suicidal ideation by the end of the intervention (Bruce et al., 2004). Follow-up analyses revealed that in those that were randomly assigned to the intervention, depressed patients had a higher response rate over 24 months than patients in practices providing usual care. Specifically, they experienced a greater decline in suicidal ideation and had lower levels of depressive symptoms. The reason for this difference could be explained by the fact that patients in the intervention group were more likely to be treated for depression than were patients receiving usual care (Alexopoulos et al., 2009).

Similar findings were reported in another study of collaborative care (Unützer et al., 2006). Outside of primary care contexts, studies of psychotherapies, including dialectical behavior therapy (Lynch, Morse, Mendelson, & Robins, 2003; Lynch et al., 2007) and interpersonal psychotherapy (Heisel, Duberstein, Talbot, King, & Tu, 2009) have shown promise.

STANDARD CRITIQUES OF SECONDARY PREVENTION

Even if we discard the idealized vision of secondary prevention and accept the idea of surrogate endpoints, secondary prevention programs are still vulnerable to damaging critiques. Few at-risk patients, particularly men (Addis & Mahalik, 2003) and those of lower socioeconomic status, will avail themselves of treatment, due in part to their reluctance to seek help. Many patients cannot afford mental health treatment, and high-quality services are not readily available in this country (and elsewhere). Barry Lebowitz (2004), who had worked as a Branch Chief at the National Institute of Mental Health, predicted that it was unlikely that successful multicomponent interventions (Bruce et al., 2004; Unützer et al., 2006) could feasibly be implemented in real-world settings, at least in the United States.

Beyond these practical critiques, core features of secondary prevention programs, including the use of screening instruments and manualized treatments, have come under attack. Treatments are typically not tailored to patients' preferences and life circumstances (Gum et al., 2006; Pyne et al., 2005; Raue, Schulberg, Heo, Klimstra, & Bruce,

2009), which could lead to poor levels of treatment adherence and high levels of dropout. But an even deeper problem concerns not the patients but health care providers themselves. Some have argued that manualized treatments have "reduc[ed] the clinician to a research assistant who can run subjects in a relatively uniform...way" (Westen, Novotny, & Thomson-Brenner, 2004, p. 639) and "produced a literature that often seems to be lacking something. What is missing is what we initially sought in our professional lives—our patients' voices" (Gabbard & Freedman, 2006, p. 184).

Moving Beyond Primary and Secondary Prevention: Person-Centered Prevention

Whereas some primary prevention programs have been critiqued as too costly or intrusive, secondary prevention programs have been decried as offering "one-size-fits-all" solutions to problems that require tailored, preference-sensitive (Gum et al., 2006; Pyne et al., 2005; Raue et al., 2009) solutions and depriving clinicians of their professional identity (Leydon et al., 2011; Westen, Novotny, & Thompson-Brenner, 2004) and their patients' voices (Gabbard & Freedman, 2006). Whether the critique is offered by conservative commentators (Noonan, 2009), psychotherapists (Gabbard & Freedman, 2006; Westen et al., 2004), or primary care physicians (Baik et al., 2010; Dowrick et al., 2009; Leydon et al., 2011), the message is similar. At the risk of oversimplification, we maintain that standard prevention approaches have not yet been implemented in a manner that is sensitive to the needs for self-determination (Ryan & Deci, 2000), particularly the need for autonomy (Table 7.1). Too often primary prevention initiatives with unfavorable cost-benefit ratios have been implemented without acknowledging the presence of options that are just as effective yet less restrictive of freedoms. Similarly, some of the tools of secondary prevention—screening instruments and manualized treatments—present challenges to the autonomy of the provider–patient relationship. Health care providers, be they psychotherapists or primary care providers, desire latitude to exercise professional judgment and offer tailored, personalized solutions to their patients' presenting problems with minimal interference from third parties. When providers sense a challenge to their autonomy, patients are likely to suffer. Whereas a person-centered approach to primary prevention is theorized to succeed if it cannot be reasonably perceived as threatening the desire for self-determination, a person-centered approach to secondary prevention is theorized to succeed if it enhances the autonomy of both the at-risk individual and the individual(s) from whom help is sought.

Person-Centered Critique of Primary Prevention

A major problem with primary prevention is that it targets behaviors pertaining to health (e.g., smoking, exercise, eating, vaccines) and safety (e.g., firearms, seatbelts) without addressing the fundamental, affect-laden need for autonomous self-determination (Moller et al., 2006; Ryan & Deci, 2000). Some primary prevention initiatives, particularly those concerning firearms, have been easy targets for critics not because they are inherently wrong or misguided but because preventionists have often failed to craft a compelling narrative (Oliver, 2006) that anticipates and responds to the affectively charged environment. Attempts to push through legislation, policy, or mandates are repeatedly stymied. It is true that rational and persuasive arguments could be made for expending precious and finite resources on firearms legislation and policy (Mann et al., 2005; Sorenson & Miller, 2006). Still, these initiatives inevitably involve taking something away from someone in a manner that is likely to generate considerable emotion. Liberty, property, and self-defense are all perceived to be at stake. Until such initiatives could be presented as conferring a significant benefit—one that clearly outweighs the costs (Oliver, 2006)—they will likely meet with much opposition.

Person-centered prevention must depart from the classic humanistic conceptualization of nondirective client centeredness (Rogers, 1951) by adopting a more directive stance. It could not be otherwise: Nondirective public policy is an oxymoron. By definition, the primary prevention directives offered by libertarian paternalists are not affectively charged. Few people become emotional about prying a pain relief tablet from a blister pack as opposed to emptying it from a bottle. If there is a "pill bottle" lobby, it is not very powerful. As there is little emotion involved in medication-packaging decisions, they are unimpeachable from the perspective of person-centered prevention. At the same time, they are probably not as potent as initiatives that involve more emotion and effort, such as restricting firearm access. Between the anodyne initiatives proffered by the libertarian paternalists and the threats to the autonomy of the firearm lobby and defenders of the Second Amendment to the US Constitution, there

is a lot of gray. Many proposals and pieces of legislation remain in limbo, largely because they are perceived by their proponents to be benign but are apparently not as unthreatening as blister packs.

Consider proposals to place barriers on bridges. Anyone who thinks it is difficult to get emotional about metal or mesh to prevent people from jumping might be surprised to learn that considerable sums are spent annually on court proceedings to settle lawsuits from advocacy groups. *Friends of the Bridge*, a Santa Barbara, California–based community group, is dedicated not to the prevention of suicide but to the prevention of the construction of a metal barrier on a bridge because it is seen to be a waste of money (Foster, 2010). Failure to anticipate and address concerns from community groups such as *Friends of the Bridge* exacts considerable opportunity costs. In the face of such opposition, primary preventionists would be well advised to retreat and search for a more benign intervention. But in some local contexts, there is no reasonable alternative. In these scenarios, primary prevention efforts must anticipate counterarguments, particularly those concerning freedom and self-determination, and use marketing and communication strategies to disarm potential critics and marshal public support (Beautrais, Gould, & Caine, 2010).

Person-Centered Critique of Secondary Prevention

Secondary prevention initiatives cannot be shown to be effective without also demonstrating that at-risk individuals have been identified and enrolled in the treatment. Few at-risk older adults, particularly men, self-refer for specialty mental health treatment. The vital task of risk identification is currently allocated de facto to older patients' primary care providers, who have been encouraged to solve the problem of inadequate risk identification by using screening instruments, typically depression scales. Beyond the well-established problems with depression screening (Gilbody, Sheldon, & Wessely, 2006; Gilbody, Richards, Brealey, & Hewitt, 2007; Palmer & Coyne, 2003) a person-centered perspective offers three additional critiques and a potential solution.

First, responses to screening instruments are influenced by person variables. Personality affects reports of physical symptoms (Chapman, Duberstein, Sörensen, Lyness, & Emery, 2006; Duberstein et al., 2003; Jerant, Chapman, Duberstein, & Franks, 2010), mood symptoms (Duberstein & Heisel, 2007), and suicidal ideation (Heisel et al.,

2006). Some patients, on account of their personality traits, may underreport symptoms. The habitual nonconfiders of the sort described by Owens and colleagues (2005) may have spuriously low scores on screening instruments, misleading the primary care provider, and eventuating in what may be termed *risk-detection decisional failure*. The patient's suicide risk is undetected. Second, responses to screening instruments also are influenced by motivation and conscious intention. People lie, equivocate, minimize, and dissemble, particularly when truth telling is disincentivized. Third, although depression screening questionnaires are well received by many patients (Dowrick et al., 2009; Epstein et al., 2010), physicians tend to be more skeptical (Baik et al., 2010; Dowrick et al., 2009; Leydon et al., 2011) and are concerned that their autonomy is being slowly eroded by third-party intruders, including screening instruments.

A person-centered approach to secondary prevention thus invites consideration of the development of screens that might be more personal, less likely to incentivize a particular response, and less of a threat to the patient–provider relationship. The assessment of psychosocial characteristics that are associated with suicide risk (Duberstein, Conwell, Conner, Eberly, & Caine, 2004; Rubenowitz et al., 2001; Tsoh et al., 2005; Useda et al., 2007) and with health beliefs represents a person-centered alternative to depression screening that could improve suicide risk-detection and risk management in primary care. Interactive multimedia computer programs and tailored communication strategies (Rimer & Kreuter, 2006) have been used to educate patients about an array of preventive health behaviors (Wofford, Smith, & Miller, 2005) and to help patients make decisions about depression treatment (Kravitz et al., 2013). Properly deployed, they could also be used to persuade older adults to talk with their health care providers about their thoughts of suicide.

As discussed elsewhere (Chapman et al., 2011), psychosocial assessments in primary care settings might confer a host of benefits beyond the mitigation of suicide risk. It could improve the provision of patient-centered care (Epstein et al., 2005) by offering a structured means for doctors to get to know and relate to their patients, and potentially increase the patient's sense of autonomy and competence. The mere presence of these assessment tools in primary care waiting rooms would convey to patients that the provision of high-quality personalized health care is not solely about ordering laboratory tests, arriving at the correct diagnosis, and prescribing appropriate treatments. It is also about expressing concern and empathy, understanding the patient's perspective, and enhancing the motivation of patients to take care of themselves (Williams, Lynch, & Glasgow, 2007). We believe these activities could be facilitated by tailored psychosocial assessments .

Computerized, tailored psychosocial assessments in primary care would require substantial investment in infrastructure, but the cost offsets are likely to be favorable. Even without a radical reorganization of the care delivery system, a person-centered approach could improve the current practice of depression screening. Item response theory (Yang, Tommet, & Jones, 2009) could be applied to identify items on depression or suicide screening instruments that are influenced by traits. Depression screening instruments could then be calibrated to individual traits or trait configurations. In this manner, depression screening instruments could account for personality-linked "overreporting" or "underreporting." Gender differences have been observed in the screening properties (e.g., sensitivity, specificity, cut scores) of depression scales (Allen-Burge, Storandt, Kinscherf, & Rubin, 1994; Heisel, Duberstein, Lyness, & Feldman, 2010; Yang et al., 2009), and it would be surprising if person variables did not influence these properties.

Advice for the Practicing Clinician: Reaching and Responding to the Disengaged

Concerns with assessing suicide risk include false positives, incorrectly judging an older adult to be at risk of death by suicide, and false negatives, incorrectly judging a suicidal older adult to be at no or low risk of suicide. False positives can lead to unnecessary treatments, treatment side effects, and other expenses, including costs to society and payers. These errors are more likely to occur with patients who are conflictually engaged with the mental health care delivery system; we have discussed risk management strategies elsewhere (Duberstein & Heisel, 2008). In keeping with our focus in this chapter on the disengaged and disenfranchised, we will confine the remainder of our discussion to false negatives. Health care providers must be proactive in seeking opportunities to intervene with these individuals. In addition to asking, *what characteristics of this patient may increase the likelihood of suicide?* other questions should be considered. These are shown in Table 7.2.

Table 7.2 Reaching and Responding to the Disengaged: Questions to Consider

In the Clinic

- How might this patient's personal characteristics (e.g., traits) lead me to miss indicators of suicide risk or undermine treatment engagement?

- Is there anything about this patient that might make it difficult for him or her to seek help?

- How can I support this patient's needs for autonomy, competence, and relatedness?

- Is there anything about this patient that might make it difficult for me to respond to his or her signals?

- What can I do to enhance the likelihood that a suicidal patient will tell me that he or she is feeling suicidal?

- Am I attentive and responsive to my patient's values and treatment preferences?

- If not, what is preventing my attending fully to my patient?

Out in the Community

- How can I reach out to people in need who have never seen a mental health provider?

- What can I do to bring a public health perspective to my clinical work and engage patients more effectively?

- How can I partner with primary health care providers, specialty health care providers, home health services, community agencies, aging service agencies, or faith communities?

- How can I engage community partners and people in need of services without threatening their autonomy or competence?

False negatives can lead to serious physical injury and/or death. People who are believed to be at no or low risk may still be at heightened risk for suicide by virtue of the presence of other risk factors. False negatives are more likely to occur with patients who seek to evade intervention, do not like a provider, have little or no history with the mental health care delivery system, or attribute their distress to aging, medical issues, or life events. Even seasoned clinicians will struggle to elicit good clinical information from some at-risk patients (Allen-Burge et al., 1994; O'Connor, Rosewarne, & Bruce, 2001), given the tendency to minimize or underreport depressive symptoms (Eaton, Neufeld, Chen, & Cai, 2000; Gallo, Rabins, & Anthony, 1999; Lyness et al., 1995). As a consequence, mood disorders and related symptoms are less likely to be treated. Patients may be at risk if they do not have a prior history of suicide attempt and even if they do not report sadness or dysphoria. They may steadfastly deny feeling sad, but they may admit to feeling blue, irritable, disgusted, frustrated, angry, annoyed, or worried about feelings of burdensomeness.

Somatic complaints may be common. Some patients will work hard to avoid reporting sadness even when they are feeling miserable; clinicians need to explore a range of negative emotions and experiment with new ways of connecting with patients. Even if patients deny sadness or other negative emotions, clinicians must still inquire about thoughts and plans for suicide. An excellent book on the art of eliciting suicidal ideation is available (Shea, 1999). Clinical training tools have recently been developed by a Canadian group devoted to enhancing late-life suicide prevention (Canadian Coalition for Seniors' Mental Health, 2008).

It is important to conceptualize the "difficult to reach" patient in a broader systems perspective, and it is vital to gather collateral information from other care providers (McDaniel, Campbell, Hepworth, & Lorenz, 2005), relatives, friends, and acquaintances. At the same time, cases of suicide have been documented in which family members had been forewarned prior to the suicide but declined to intervene (Miller, 1978). Some family members and physicians may be too preoccupied managing an older adult's multiple medical problems to think about his or her mental health, a phenomenon known as "competing demands" (Klinkman, 1997). Moreover, mental health providers must recognize that collateral contacts may not provide useful information about the patient's condition as a consequence of ageism, stigma, or conflict with the patient (Sher, McGinn, Sirey, & Meyers, 2005; Sirey et al., 2001). Physicians who hold ageist or stigmatized beliefs may be less likely to have keen insight into the emotional status of at-risk older adults (Uncapher & Areán, 2000). The same may be true of family members.

Much has been written about the "ability" of primary care physicians to inquire about suicide (Feldman et al., 2007; Vannoy et al., 2011; Vannoy et al., 2010). Yet there is considerable variability in the behavior of primary care physicians with respect to mental health assessments and referrals. Sources of the individual variations have been investigated (Chapman, Duberstein, Epstein, Fiscella, & Kravitz, 2008; Duberstein, Chapman, Epstein,

McCollumn, & Kravitz, 2008; Kravitz et al., 2006), but not in a sample of physicians caring for older patients. A series of secondary analyses of data collected in a clinical trial showed that primary care physicians who had personal experiences with psychotherapy (Kravitz et al., 2006) and those who were more emotionally vulnerable and dutiful (Duberstein et al., 2008) were more likely to assess for depression, document its presence, and make a referral. Findings documenting the importance of physicians' personal characteristics in mental health assessments point to the potential importance of the personal characteristics of psychotherapists and other health care providers who are entrusted with the care of older at-risk individuals.

Any discussion of the difficult-to-reach patient would be incomplete without some mention of sociodemographic considerations. For reasons that remain poorly understood, physicians are less likely to recognize and diagnose mood disorders in men than in women (Callahan et al., 1997; Stoppe, Sandholzer, Huppertz, Duwe, & Staedt, 1999). Whether family members, friends, or psychotherapists are less likely to detect mood disorders in older men than in older women is unknown. Communication (Johnson, Roter, Powe, & Cooper, 2004; van Ryn & Fu, 2003) and the detection and diagnosis of mood symptoms and disorders (Comino, Silove, Manicavasagar, Harris, & Harris, 2001) might be more difficult when primary care physicians and patients are of different races or ethnic backgrounds. It is unknown whether a similar phenomenon is observed with psychotherapists, friends, or family members.

Conclusion

Only recently has suicide emerged from the shadows of religion and the law as a topic of legitimate inquiry in clinical science. With the advent of biomedical understanding, disease, disorder, and illness became the lingua franca of Western suicidology. Treatment, particularly of depressive disorders, is now considered a vital component of efforts to prevent older adults from taking their own lives. Although marked increases are expected in the number of older people requiring and entering mental health treatment, many at-risk patients will not avail themselves of services. Mental illnesses and health-related existential angst are not inexorably fatal, but the failure to seek and receive adequate treatment and support just might be.

Creative methods must be developed and tested to enhance risk detection, treatment initiation,

and adherence. At the same time, suicide prevention resources might be misdirected (Krieger, 2008; Sarason, 1981) if too much explanatory power is granted to the mental disorders and physical illnesses that are present in the days, weeks, or months prior to death. Such a focus may lead researchers, clinicians, and policy makers to underestimate the role of risk markers at other levels of analysis (Krieger, 2008) that unfold over longer periods of time. It is thus essential to develop and disseminate prevention programs that target risk markers long before the development of acute suicide risk. Whereas secondary prevention programs might be most effective with patients that are already engaged with the health care delivery system, primary prevention programs are needed to reach those who are disengaged or outside the system.

Reasons why people do not show up with alacrity in the offices of mental health practitioners are numerous. Some are treatment rejecting, others lack the needed financial resources, and still others hold attitudes about mental health conditions and treatments that will prevent them from getting help. Ethical considerations and data compel the creation of person-centered approaches that meet the needs of all, not just those who happen to appear in our offices. These approaches require tools, techniques, and resources to decrease suicide risk at the population level and redress the at-risk individual's failure to seek and receive adequate treatment or support.

To accomplish this, basic marketing tools must be incorporated into the preventionist toolbox. Primary preventionists must be more mindful of the political narratives that have heretofore stymied their efforts (Oliver, 2006). Secondary preventionists need to develop powerful, tailored interventions to reluctant help-seekers get the help they need ensure that. This will require relating to all stakeholders—particularly at-risk individuals, family members, and health care providers—in a manner that promotes their autonomy and does not undermine their perceived competence.

Future Directions

1. Data from mental health services and from self-reports consistently indicate that women more frequently engage in suicidal behavior and yet mortality data indicate that men more frequently die by suicide. Theoretical and empirical effort is needed to address this apparent paradox.

2. Community-level research programs have demonstrated success in identifying older adults at

risk for suicide, bringing those at risk for suicide into clinical care or bringing effective clinical care to them, and effectively reducing risk for death by suicide. However, these programs have tended to work for women, not men. Why?

3. It has been argued that screening instruments, treatment algorithms, and manualized treatments have served to diminish the autonomy of health care providers. How can we produce an evidence base that addresses these important critiques?

4. Most older men who die by suicide had never received mental health treatment, either from a primary care provider or specialty mental health provider. Advances in communication and information technology could be used to increase the identification of at-risk individuals in primary care. The electronic re-design of primary care offices could feature interactive multimedia computer programs that are tailored to persuade patients to talk with their doctor about their personal concerns. What patient characteristics (traits, needs, etc.) might make some individuals particularly well suited for this type of intervention? How else could we take advantage of advances in communication and information technology, such as social networking Web sites or telecare support, to reach the disengaged or the disenfranchised?

Further Reading

Duberstein, P. R., & Heisel, M.J. (2008). Assessment and treatment of suicidal behaviour in later life. In K. Laidlaw & B. Knight (Eds.), *Handbook of emotional disorders in later life: Assessment and treatment* (pp. 311–344). New York: Oxford University Press.

Duberstein, P., & Witte, T. (2009). Suicide risk in personality disorders: An argument for a public health perspective. In P. Kleespies (Ed.), *Evaluating and managing behavioral emergencies: An evidence-based resource for the mental health practitioner* (pp. 257–286). Washington, D.C.: APA.

Joiner, T. (2005). *Why people die by suicide.* Cambridge, MA: Harvard University Press.

Kaplan, R. M. (2000). Two pathways to prevention. *American Psychologist, 55,* 382–396.

Krueger, R. F., Caspi, A., & Moffitt, T. E. (2000). Epidemiological personology: The unifying role of personality in population-based research on problem behaviors. *Journal of Personality, 68,* 967–998.

References

Addis, M. E., & Mahalik, J. R. (2003). Men, masculinity, and the contexts of help seeking. *American Psychologist, 58*(1), 5–14.

Alexopoulos, G. S., Reynolds, C. F., 3rd., Bruce, M. L., Katz, I. R., Raue, P. J., Mulsant, B. H.,...The PROSPECT Group. (2009). Reducing suicidal ideation and depression

in older primary care patients: 24-month outcomes of the PROSPECT study. *The American Journal of Psychiatry, 166*(8), 882–890.

Allen-Burge, R., Storandt, M., Kinscherf, D. A., & Rubin, E. H. (1994). Sex differences in the sensitivity of two self-report depression scales in older depressed inpatients. *Psychology and Aging, 9*(3), 443–445.

Arsenault-Lapierre, G., Kim, C., & Turecki, G. (2004). Psychiatric diagnoses in 3275 suicides: A meta-analysis. *BMC Psychiatry, 4,* 37.

Baik, S. Y., Gonzales, J. J., Bowers, B. J., Anthony, J. S., Tidjani, B., & Susman, J. L. (2010). Reinvention of depression instruments by primary care clinicians. *Annals of Family Medicine, 8*(3), 224–230.

Barraclough, B. M. (1971). Suicide in the elderly: Recent developments in psychogeriatrics. *British Journal of Psychiatry,* Supplement, 6, 87–97.

Beautrais, A. L. (2002). A case control study of suicide and attempted suicide in older adults. *Suicide and Life-Threatening Behavior, 32*(1), 1–9.

Beautrais, A. L., Gould, M. S., & Caine, E. D. (July 2010). Preventing suicide by jumping from bridges owned by the city of Ithaca and by Cornell University: Consultation to Cornell University. Available at http://meansrestrictionstudy.fs.cornell.edu/studyDocs.cfm.

Bellah, R. N., Madsen, R., Sullivan, W. M., Swidler, A., & Tipton, S. M. (1991). *The good society.* New York, NY: Random House.

Berlin, I. (1969). *Four essays on liberty.* New York, NY: Oxford University Press.

Borges, G., Anthony, J. C., & Garrison, C. Z. (1995). Methodological issues relevant to epidemiologic investigations of suicidal behaviors of adolescents. *Epidemiologic Reviews, 17*(1), 228–239.

Bostwick, J. M., & Cohen, L. M. (2009). Differentiating suicide from life-ending acts and end-of-life decisions: A model based on chronic kidney disease and dialysis. *Psychosomatics, 50*(1), 1–7.

Brezo, J., Paris, J., & Turecki, G. (2006). Personality traits as correlates of suicidal ideation, suicide attempts, and suicide completions: A systematic review. *Acta Psychiatrica Scandinavica, 113*(3), 180–206.

Brown, G. K., Beck, A. T., Steer, R. A., & Grisham, J. R. (2000). Risk factors for suicide in psychiatric outpatients: A 20-year prospective study. *Journal of Consulting and Clinical Psychology, 68*(3), 371–377.

Bruce, M. L., Ten Have, T. R., Reynolds, C. F., 3rd., Katz, I. I., Schulberg, H. C., Mulsant, B. H.,...Alexopoulos, G. S. (2004). Reducing suicidal ideation and depressive symptoms in depressed older primary care patients: A randomized controlled trial. *JAMA: Journal of the American Medical Association, 291*(9), 1081–1091.

Buie, D. H., & Maltsberger, J. T. (1989). The psychological vulnerability to suicide. In D. Jacobs & H. N. Brown (Eds.), *Suicide: Understanding and responding: Harvard Medical School perspectives* (pp. 59–71). Madison, CT: International Universities Press.

Calabrese, S. K., Lyness, J. M., Sörensen, S., & Duberstein, P. R. (2006). Personality and the association of pain and depression. *American Journal of Geriatric Psychiatry, 14*(6), 546–549.

Callahan, E. J., Bertakis, K. D., Azari, R., Helms, L. J., Robbins, J., & Miller, J. (1997). Depression in primary care: Patient factors that influence recognition. *Family Medicine, 29*(3), 172–176.

Canadian Coalition for Seniors' Mental Health. (2008). *Canadian Coalition for Seniors' Mental Health national guidelines: The assessment of suicide risk and prevention of suicide.* Toronto, ON: Canadian Coalition for Seniors' Mental Health.

Cappelen, A. W., & Norheim, O. F. (2005). Responsibility in health care: A liberal egalitarian approach. *Journal of Medical Ethics, 31*(8), 476–480.

Chapman, B., Duberstein, P., & Lyness, J. M. (2007). Personality traits, education, and health-related quality of life among older adult primary care patients. *Journals of Gerontology: Series B: Psychological Sciences and Social Sciences, 62B*(6), P343–P352.

Chapman, B. P., Duberstein, P. R., Epstein, R. M., Fiscella, K., & Kravitz, R. L. (2008). Patient-centered communication during primary care visits for depressive symptoms: What is the role of physician personality? *Medical Care, 46*(8), 806–812.

Chapman, B. P., Duberstein, P. R., Sörensen, S., & Lyness, J. M. (2006). Personality and perceived health in older adults: The five factor model in primary care. *Journals of Gerontology: Series B: Psychological Sciences and Social Sciences, 61B*(6), P362–P365.

Chapman, B. P., Lyness, J. M., & Duberstein, P. (2007). Personality and medical illness burden among older adults in primary care. *Psychosomatic Medicine, 69*(3), 277–282.

Chapman, B. P., Roberts, B. W., & Duberstein, P. R. (2011). Personality and longevity: Knowns, unknowns, and implications for public health and personalized medicine. *Journal of Aging Research, 2011*, 759170.

Chapman, B. P., Shah, M., Friedman, B., Drayer, R., Duberstein, P. R., & Lyness, J. M. (2009). Personality traits predict emergency department utilization over 3 years in older patients. *American Journal of Geriatric Psychiatry, 17*(6), 526–535.

Chiu, H. F., Yip, P. S., Chi, I., Chan, S., Tsoh, J., Kwan, C. W., . . . Caine, E. (2004). Elderly suicide in Hong Kong—a case-controlled psychological autopsy study. *Acta Psychiatrica Scandinavica, 109*(4), 299–305.

Chochinov, H. M., Wilson, K. G., Enns, M., Mowchun, N., Lander, S., Levitt, M., & Clinch, J. J. (1995). Desire for death in the terminally ill. *American Journal of Psychiatry, 152*(8), 1185–1191.

Ciechanowski, P., Russo, J., Katon, W., Simon, G., Ludman, E., Von Korff, M., . . . Lin, E. (2006). Where is the patient? the association of psychosocial factors and missed primary care appointments in patients with diabetes. *General Hospital Psychiatry, 28*(1), 9–17.

Clarke, M., Clarke, S. J., & Jagger, C. (1992). Social intervention and the elderly: A randomized controlled trial. *American Journal of Epidemiology, 136*(12), 1517–1523.

Comino, E. J., Silove, D., Manicavasagar, V., Harris, E., & Harris, M. F. (2001). Agreement in symptoms of anxiety and depression between patients and GPs: The influence of ethnicity. *Family Practice, 18*(1), 71–77.

Conner, K. R. (2004). A call for research on planned vs. unplanned suicidal behavior. *Suicide and Life-Threatening Behavior, 34*(2), 89–98.

Conner, K. R., Duberstein, P. R., & Conwell, Y. (1999). Age-related patterns of factors associated with completed suicide in men with alcohol dependence. *American Journal on Addictions, 8*, 312–318.

Conner, K. R., Duberstein, P. R., Conwell, Y., Herrmann, J. H. J., Cox, C., Barrington, D., & Caine, E. D. (2000). After the drinking stops: Completed suicide in individuals with remitted alcohol use disorders. *Journal of Psychoactive Drugs, 32*(3), 333–337.

Conner, K. R., Duberstein, P. R., Conwell, Y., Seidlitz, L., & Caine, E. D. (2001). Psychological vulnerability to completed suicide: A review of empirical studies. *Suicide and Life-Threatening Behavior, 31*(4), 367–385.

Conwell, Y., Duberstein, P. R., Cox, C., & Herrmann, J. H. (1996). Relationship of age and axis I diagnoses in victims of completed suicide: A psychological autopsy study. *American Journal of Psychiatry, 153*(8), 1001–1008.

Conwell, Y., Duberstein, P. R., Cox, C., Herrmann, J., Forbes, N., & Caine, E. D. (1998). Age differences in behaviors leading to completed suicide. *American Journal of Geriatric Psychiatry, 6*(2), 122–126.

Conwell, Y., Lyness, J. M., Duberstein, P., Cox, C., Seidlitz, L., DiGiorgio, A., & Caine, E. D. (2000). Completed suicide among older patients in primary care practices: A controlled study. *Journal of the American Geriatrics Society, 48*(1), 23–29.

Cummings, J. L., Doody, R., & Clark, C. (2007). Disease-modifying therapies for Alzheimer disease: Challenges to early intervention. *Neurology, 69*(16), 1622–1634.

De Leo, D., Carollo, G., & Dello Buono, M. (1995). Lower suicide rates associated with a Tele-Help/Tele-check service for the elderly at home. *American Journal of Psychiatry, 152*, 632–634.

De Leo, D., Dello Buono, M., & Dwyer, J. (2002). Suicide among the elderly: The long-term impact of a telephone support and assessment intervention in Northern Italy. *British Journal of Psychiatry, 181*, 226–229.

Douglas, M. (1986). *How institutions think.* Syracuse, NY: Syracuse University Press.

Dowrick, C., Leydon, G. M., McBride, A., Howe, A., Burgess, H., Clarke, P., . . . Kendrick, T. (2009). Patients' and doctors' views on depression severity questionnaires incentivised in UK quality and outcomes framework: Qualitative study. *BMJ (Clinical Research ed.), 338*, b663.

Duberstein, P. R. (2001). Are closed-minded people more open to the idea of killing themselves? *Suicide and Life-Threatening Behavior, 31*(1), 9–14.

Duberstein, P. R., Chapman, B. P., Epstein, R. M., McCollumn, K. R., & Kravitz, R. L. (2008). Physician personality characteristics and inquiry about mood symptoms in primary care. *Journal of General Internal Medicine, 23*(11), 1791–1795.

Duberstein, P. R., & Conwell, Y. (1997). Personality disorders and completed suicide: A methodological and conceptual review. *Clinical Psychology: Science and Practice, 4*(4), 359–376.

Duberstein, P. R., Conwell, Y., & Caine, E. D. (1994). Age differences in the personality characteristics of suicide completers: Preliminary findings from a psychological autopsy study. *Psychiatry: Interpersonal and Biological Processes, 57*(3), 213–224.

Duberstein, P. R., Conwell, Y., Conner, K. R., Eberly, S., & Caine, E. D. (2004). Suicide at 50 years of age and older: Perceived physical illness, family discord and financial strain. *Psychological Medicine, 34*(1), 137–146.

Duberstein, P. R., Conwell, Y., Conner, K. R., Eberly, S., Evinger, J. S., & Caine, E. D. (2004). Poor social integration and suicide: Fact or artifact? A case-control study. *Psychological Medicine, 34*(7), 1331–1337.

Duberstein, P. R., Conwell, Y., & Cox, C. (1998). Suicide in widowed persons: A psychological autopsy comparison of recently and remotely bereaved older subjects. *American Journal of Geriatric Psychiatry*, 6(4), 328–334.

Duberstein, P. R., & Heisel, M. J. (2007). Personality traits and the reporting of affective disorder symptoms in depressed patients. *Journal of Affective Disorders*, 103(1–3), 165–171.

Duberstein, P. R., & Heisel, M. J. (2008). Assessment and treatment of suicidal behaviour in later life. In K. Laidlaw & B. Knight (Eds.), *Handbook of emotional disorders in later life: Assessment and treatment* (pp. 311–344). New York, NY: Oxford University Press.

Duberstein, P. R., Ma, Y., Chapman, B. P., Conwell, Y., McGriff, J., Coyne, J. C., ... Lyness, J. M. (2011). Detection of depression in older adults by family and friends: Distinguishing mood disorder signals from the noise of personality and everyday life. *International Psychogeriatrics*, 23(4), 634–643.

Duberstein, P. R., Pálsson, S. P., Waern, M., & Skoog, I. (2008). Personality and risk for depression in a birth cohort of 70-year-olds followed for 15 years. *Psychological Medicine*, 38(5), 663–671.

Duberstein, P. R., Seidlitz, L., & Conwell, Y. (1996). Reconsidering the role of hostility in completed suicide: A life-course perspective. In J. M. Masling & R. F. Bornstein (Eds.), *Psychoanalytic perspectives on developmental psychology* (pp. 257–323). Washington, DC: American Psychological Association.

Duberstein, P. R., Sörensen, S., Lyness, J. M., King, D. A., Conwell, Y., Seidlitz, L., & Caine, E. D. (2003). Personality is associated with perceived health and functional status in older primary care patients. *Psychology and Aging*, 18(1), 25–37.

Duberstein, P., & Witte, T. K. (2009). Suicide risk in personality disorders: An argument for a public health perspective. In P. M. Kleespies (Ed.), *Behavioral emergencies: An evidence-based resource for evaluating and managing risk of suicide, violence, and victimization* (pp. 257–286). Washington, DC: American Psychological Association.

Durkheim, E. (1951). *Suicide: A study in sociology*. New York, NY: Free Press.

Eaton, W. W., Neufeld, K., Chen, L. S., & Cai, G. (2000). A comparison of self-report and clinical diagnostic interviews for depression: Diagnostic interview schedule and schedules for clinical assessment in neuropsychiatry in the Baltimore Epidemiologic Catchment Area follow-up. *Archives of General Psychiatry*, 57(3), 217–222.

Emanuel, E. J., Fairclough, D. L., Slutsman, J., & Emanuel, L. L. (2000). Understanding economic and other burdens of terminal illness: The experience of patients and their caregivers. *Annals of Internal Medicine*, 132(6), 451–459.

Epstein, R. M., Duberstein, P. R., Feldman, M. D., Rochlen, A. B., Bell, R. A., Kravitz, R. L., ... Paterniti, D. A. (2010). "I didn't know what was wrong:" How people with undiagnosed depression recognize, name and explain their distress. *Journal of General Internal Medicine*, 25(9), 954–961.

Epstein, R. M., Franks, P., Fiscella, K., Shields, G. C., Meldrum, S. C., Kravitz, R. L., & Duberstein, P. R. (2005). Measuring patient-centered communication in patient-physician consultations: Theoretical and practical issues. *Social Science and Medicine*, 61(7), 1516–1528.

Erlangsen, A., Bille-Brahe, U., & Jeune, B. (2003). Differences in suicide between the old and the oldest old. *Journals of Gerontology: Series B, Psychological Sciences and Social Sciences*, 58(5), S314–22.

Ernst, C., Lalovic, A., Lesage, A., Seguin, M., Tousignant, M., & Turecki, G. (2004). Suicide and no Axis I psychopathology. *BMC Psychiatry*, 4, 7.

Feldman, M. D., Franks, P., Duberstein, P. R., Vannoy, S., Epstein, R., & Kravitz, R. L. (2007). Let's not talk about it: Suicide inquiry in primary care. *Annals of Family Medicine*, 5(5), 412–418.

Foster, J. (2010, January 7). New tactic by opponents of bridge suicide barrier. Available at: http://www.svjournal.com/archive/8/1/5718/. Retrieved November 26, 2013.

Friedman, P. (1967). Suicide among police: A study of 93 suicides among New York City policemen, 1934-1940. In E. S. Shneidman (Ed.), *Essays in self-destruction* (pp. 414–449). New York, NY: Science House.

Gabbard, G. O., & Freedman, R. (2006). Psychotherapy in The Journal: What's missing? *American Journal of Psychiatry*, 163(2), 182–184.

Gallo, J. J., Bogner, H. R., Straton, J. B., Margo, K., Lesho, P., Rabins, P. V., & Ford, D. E. (2005). Patient characteristics associated with participation in a practice-based study of depression in late life: The Spectrum Study. *International Journal of Psychiatry in Medicine*, 35(1), 41–57.

Gallo, J. J., Rabins, P. V., & Anthony, J. C. (1999). Sadness in older persons: 13-year follow-up of a community sample in Baltimore, Maryland. *Psychological Medicine*, 29(2), 341–350.

Gigerenzer, G. (2007). *Gut feelings: The intelligence of the unconscious*. New York, NY: Penguin.

Gilbody, S., Richards, D., Brealey, S., & Hewitt, C. (2007). Screening for depression in medical settings with the patient health questionnaire (PHQ): A diagnostic meta-analysis. *Journal of General Internal Medicine*, 22(11), 1596–1602.

Gilbody, S., Sheldon, T., & Wessely, S. (2006). Should we screen for depression? *BMJ (Clinical Research ed.)*, 332(7548), 1027–1030.

Goodwin, R. D., Hoven, C. W., Lyons, J. S., & Stein, M. B. (2002). Mental health service utilization in the United States. the role of personality factors. *Social Psychiatry and Psychiatric Epidemiology*, 37(12), 561–566.

Grabbe, L., Demi, A., Camann, M. A., & Potter, L. (1997). The health status of elderly persons in the last year of life: A comparison of deaths by suicide, injury, and natural causes. *American Journal of Public Health*, 87(3), 434–437.

Graham, R. G., & Martin, G. I. (2012). Health behavior: A Darwinian reconceptualization. *American Journal of Preventive Medicine*, 43(4), 451–455.

Gum, A. M., Areán, P. A., Hunkeler, E., Tang, L., Katon, W., Hitchcock, P., ... Unützer, J. (2006). Depression treatment preferences in older primary care patients. *The Gerontologist*, 46(1), 14–22.

Gunnell, D., Middleton, N., Whitley, E., Dorling, D., & Frankel, S. (2003). Why are suicide rates rising in young men but falling in the elderly?—A time-series analysis of trends in England and Wales 1950-1998. *Social Science and Medicine*, 57(4), 595–611.

Harwood, D., Hawton, K., Hope, T., & Jacoby, R. (2001). Psychiatric disorder and personality factors associated with suicide in older people: A descriptive and case-control study. *International Journal of Geriatric Psychiatry*, 16(2), 155–165.

Hawton, K. (2002). United Kingdom legislation on pack sizes of analgesics: Background, rationale, and effects on suicide and deliberate self-harm. *Suicide and Life-Threatening Behavior*, 32(3), 223–229.

Hawton, K., Bergen, H., Simkin, S., Brock, A., Griffiths, C., Romeri, E., ... Gunnell, D. (2009). Effect of withdrawal of co-proxamol on prescribing and deaths from drug poisoning in England and Wales: Time series analysis. *BMJ (Clinical Research ed.)*, *338*, b2270.

Heiman, M. F. (1975). Police suicides revisited. *Suicide*, *5*(1), 5–20.

Heisel, M. J., Duberstein, P. R., Conner, K. R., Franus, N., Beckman, A., & Conwell, Y. (2006). Personality and reports of suicide ideation among depressed adults 50 years of age or older. *Journal of Affective Disorders*, *90*(2–3), 175–180.

Heisel, M. J., Duberstein, P. R., Lyness, J. M., & Feldman, M. D. (2010). Screening for suicide ideation among older primary care patients. *Journal of the American Board of Family Medicine*, *23*(2), 260–269.

Heisel, M. J., Duberstein, P. R., Talbot, N. L., King, D. A., & Tu, X. M. (2009). Adapting interpersonal psychotherapy for older adults at risk for suicide: Preliminary findings. *Professional Psychology: Research and Practice*, *40*(2), 156–164.

Hendin, H. (1991). Psychodynamics of suicide, with particular reference to the young. *American Journal of Psychiatry*, *148*(9), 1150–1158.

Horton-Deutsch, S. L., Clark, D. C., & Farran, C. J. (1992). Chronic dyspnea and suicide in elderly men. *Hospital and Community Psychiatry*, *43*(12), 1198–1203.

Howard, D. H., Sentell, T., & Gazmararian, J. A. (2006). Impact of health literacy on socioeconomic and racial differences in health in an elderly population. *Journal of General Internal Medicine*, *21*(8), 857–861.

Jerant, A., Chapman, B., Duberstein, P., & Franks, P. (2010). Effects of personality on self-rated health in a 1-year randomized controlled trial of chronic illness self-management. *British Journal of Health Psychology*, *15*(2), 321–335.

Jerant, A., Chapman, B., Duberstein, P., Robbins, J., & Franks, P. (2011). Personality and medication non-adherence among older adults enrolled in a six-year trial. *British Journal of Health Psychology*, *16*(1), 151–169.

Johnson, R. L., Roter, D., Powe, N. R., & Cooper, L. A. (2004). Patient race/ethnicity and quality of patient-physician communication during medical visits. *American Journal of Public Health*, *94*(12), 2084–2090.

Joiner, T. (2005). *Why people die by suicide*. Cambridge, MA: Harvard University Press.

Juurlink, D. N., Herrmann, N., Szalai, J. P., Kopp, A., & Redelmeier, D. A. (2004). Medical illness and the risk of suicide in the elderly. *Archives of Internal Medicine*, *164*(11), 1179–1184.

Kaplan, R. M. (2000). Two pathways to prevention. *American Psychologist*, *55*(4), 382–396.

Klinkman, M. S. (1997). Competing demands in psychosocial care. A model for the identification and treatment of depressive disorders in primary care. *General Hospital Psychiatry*, *19*(2), 98–111.

Knox, K. L., Conwell, Y., & Caine, E. D. (2004). If suicide is a public health problem, what are we doing to prevent it? *American Journal of Public Health*, *94*(1), 37–45.

Kölves, K., Varnik, A., Tooding, L. M., & Wasserman, D. (2006). The role of alcohol in suicide: A case-control psychological autopsy study. *Psychological Medicine*, *36*(7), 923–930.

Kravitz, R. L., Franks, P., Feldman, M., Meredith, L. S., Hinton, L., Franz, C.,...Epstein, R. M. (2006). What drives referral from primary care physicians to mental health specialists? A randomized trial using actors portraying depressive symptoms. *Journal of General Internal Medicine*, *21*(6), 584–589.

Kravitz, R. L., Franks, P., Feldman, M. D., Tancredi, D. J., Slee, C. A., Epstein, R. M.,...Jerant, A. (2013). Patient

engagement programs for recognition and initial treatment of depression in primary care: A randomized trial. *Journal of the American Medical Association*, *310*(17), 1818–1828.

Krieger, N. (2008). Proximal, distal, and the politics of causation: What's level got to do with it? *American Journal of Public Health*, *98*(2), 221–230.

Krueger, K. R., Wilson, R. S., Shah, R. C., Tang, Y., & Bennett, D. A. (2006). Personality and incident disability in older persons. *Age and Ageing*, *35*(4), 428–433.

Krueger, R. F., Caspi, A., & Moffitt, T. E. (2000). Epidemiological personology: The unifying role of personality in population-based research on problem behaviors. *Journal of Personality*, *68*(6), 967–998.

Kubzansky, L. D., Subramanian, S. V., Kawachi, I., Fay, M. E., Soobader, M. J., & Berkman, L. F. (2005). Neighborhood contextual influences on depressive symptoms in the elderly. *American Journal of Epidemiology*, *162*(3), 253–260.

Kushner, H. I. (1991). *American suicide: A psychocultural exploration*. New Brunswick, NJ: Rutgers University Press.

Lebowitz, B. D. (2004). Clinical trials in late life: New science in old paradigms. *The Gerontologist*, *44*(4), 452–458.

Leeman, C. P. (2009). Distinguishing among irrational suicide and other forms of hastened death: Implications for clinical practice. *Psychosomatics*, *50*(3), 185–191

Lester, D. (1972). *Why people kill themselves: A summary of research findings on suicidal behavior*. Springfield, IL: Charles Thomas.

Lewis, G., Hawton, K., & Jones, P. (1997). Strategies for preventing suicide. *British Journal of Psychiatry*, *171*, 351–354.

Leydon, G. M., Dowrick, C. F., McBride, A. S., Burgess, H. J., Howe, A. C., Clarke, P. D.,...QOF Depression Study Team. (2011). Questionnaire severity measures for depression: A threat to the doctor-patient relationship? *British Journal of General Practice*, *61*(583), 117–123.

Links, P. S., Heisel, M. J., & Quastel, A. (2005). Is suicide ideation a surrogate endpoint for geriatric suicide? *Suicide and Life-Threatening Behavior*, *35*(2), 193–205.

Llorente, M. D., Burke, M., Gregory, G. R., Bosworth, H. B., Grambow, S. C., Horner, R. D.,...Olsen, E. J. (2005). Prostate cancer: A significant risk factor for late-life suicide. *American Journal of Geriatric Psychiatry*, *13*(3), 195–201.

Luoma, J. B., Martin, C. E., & Pearson, J. L. (2002). Contact with mental health and primary care providers before suicide: A review of the evidence. *American Journal of Psychiatry*, *159*(6), 909–916.

Lynch, T. R., Cheavens, J. S., Cukrowicz, K. C., Thorp, S. R., Bronner, L., & Beyer, J. (2007). Treatment of older adults with co-morbid personality disorder and depression: A dialectical behavior therapy approach. *International Journal of Geriatric Psychiatry*, *22*(2), 131–143.

Lynch, T. R., Morse, J. Q., Mendelson, T., & Robins, C. J. (2003). Dialectical behavior therapy for depressed older adults: A randomized pilot study. *American Journal of Geriatric Psychiatry*, *11*(1), 33–45.

Lyness, J. M., Cox, C., Curry, J., Conwell, Y., King, D. A., & Caine, E. D. (1995). Older age and the underreporting of depressive symptoms. *Journal of the American Geriatrics Society*, *43*(3), 216–221.

Magnusson, D. (1990). Personality development from an interactional perspective. In L. A. Pervin (Ed.), *Handbook of personality theory and research* (pp. 193–222). New York, NY: Guilford Press.

Mann, J. J., Apter, A., Bertolote, J., Beautrais, A., Currier, D., Haas, A.,...Hendin, H. (2005). Suicide prevention strategies: A systematic review. *Journal of the American Medical Association*, *294*(16), 2064–2074.

McDaniel, S. H., Campbell, T. L., Hepworth, J., & Lorenz, A. (2005). *Family-oriented primary care (2nd ed.).* New York, NY: Springer.

McGirr, A., Renaud, J., Bureau, A., Seguin, M., Lesage, A., & Turecki, G. (2008). Impulsive-aggressive behaviours and completed suicide across the life cycle: A predisposition for younger age of suicide. *Psychological Medicine*, *38*(3), 407–417.

Miller, M. (1978). Geriatric suicide: The Arizona study. *The Gerontologist*, *18*(5, Pt. 1), 488–495.

Millon, T. (2003). It's time to rework the blueprints: Building a science for clinical psychology. *American Psychologist*, *58*(11), 949–961.

Moller, A. C., Ryan, R. M., & Deci, E. L. (2006). Self-determination theory and public policy: Improving the quality of consumer decisions without using coercion. *Journal of Public Policy and Marketing*, *25*(1), 104–116.

Murray, H. (1962). *Explorations in personality: A clinical and experimental study of fifty men of college age by the workers at the Harvard Psychological Clinic.* New York, NY: Science Editions.

National Institute of Mental Health. (1998). *Priorities for prevention research at NIMH: A report of the National Advisory Mental Health Council workgroup on mental disorders prevention research.* [NIH publication 98–4321]. Bethesda, MD: NIMH.

Neeleman, J. (2002). Beyond risk theory: Suicidal behavior in its social and epidemiological context. *Crisis*, *23*(3), 114–120.

Noonan, P. (2009, July 25–26). Common sense may sink ObamaCare. *Wall Street Journal*, p. A13.

Norstrom, T. (1995). Alcohol and suicide: A comparative analysis of France and Sweden. *Addiction*, *90*(11), 1463–1469.

O'Connor, D. W., Rosewarne, R., & Bruce, A. (2001). Depression in primary care. 1: Elderly patients' disclosure of depressive symptoms to their doctors. *International Psychogeriatrics*, *13*(3), 359–365.

Oliver, T. R. (2006). The politics of public health policy. *Annual Review of Public Health*, *27*, 195–233.

Owens, C., Lambert, H., Donovan, J., & Lloyd, K. R. (2005). A qualitative study of help seeking and primary care consultation prior to suicide. *British Journal of General Practice*, *55*(516), 503–509.

Owens, C., Owen, G., Lambert, H., Donovan, J., Belam, J., Rapport, F., & Lloyd, K. (2009). Public involvement in suicide prevention: Understanding and strengthening lay responses to distress. *BMC Public Health*, *9*, 308.

Oyama, H., Fujita, M., Goto, M., Shibuya, H., & Sakashita, T. (2006). Outcomes of community-based screening for depression and suicide prevention among Japanese elders. *The Gerontologist*, *46*(6), 821–826.

Oyama, H., Koida, J., Sakashita, T., & Kudo, K. (2004). Community-based prevention for suicide in elderly by depression screening and follow-up. *Community Mental Health Journal*, *40*(3), 249–263.

Oyama, H., Ono, Y., Watanabe, N., Tanaka, E., Kudoh, S., Sakashita, T.,...Yoshimura, K. (2006). Local community intervention through depression screening and group activity for elderly suicide prevention. *Psychiatry and Clinical Neurosciences*, *60*(1), 110–114.

Oyama, H., Sakashita, T., Ono, Y., Goto, M., Fujita, M., & Koida, J. (2008). Effect of community-based intervention using depression screening on elderly suicide risk: A meta-analysis of the evidence from Japan. *Community Mental Health Journal*, *44*(5), 311–320.

Oyama, H., Watanabe, N., Ono, Y., Sakashita, T., Takenoshita, Y., Taguchi, M.,...Kumagai, K. (2005). Community-based suicide prevention through group activity for the elderly successfully reduced the high suicide rate for females. *Psychiatry and Clinical Neurosciences*, *59*(3), 337–344.

Palmer, S. C., & Coyne, J. C. (2003). Screening for depression in medical care: Pitfalls, alternatives, and revised priorities. *Journal of Psychosomatic Research*, *54*(4), 279–287.

Pescosolido, B. A. (1992). Beyond rational choice: The social dynamics of how people seek help. *American Journal of Sociology*, *97*(4), 1096–1138.

Phelan, J. C., Link, B. G., & Tehranifar, P. (2010). Social conditions as fundamental causes of health inequalities: Theory, evidence, and policy implications. *Journal of Health and Social Behavior*, *51*(1, Suppl.), S28–S40.

Pokorny, A. D. (1993). Suicide prediction revisited. *Suicide and Life-Threatening Behavior*, *23*(1), 1–10.

Pyne, J. M., Rost, K. M., Farahati, F., Tripathi, S. P., Smith, J., Williams, D. K.,...Coyne, J. C. (2005). One size fits some: The impact of patient treatment attitudes on the cost-effectiveness of a depression primary-care intervention. *Psychological Medicine*, *35*(6), 839–854.

Quan, H., Arboleda-Florez, J., Fick, G. H., Stuart, H. L., & Love, E. J. (2002). Association between physical illness and suicide among the elderly. *Social Psychiatry and Psychiatric Epidemiology*, *37*(4), 190–197.

Raue, P. J., Schulberg, H. C., Heo, M., Klimstra, S., & Bruce, M. L. (2009). Patients' depression treatment preferences and initiation, adherence, and outcome: A randomized primary care study. *Psychiatric Services*, *60*(3), 337–343.

Rawls, J. (1958). Justice as fairness. *Philosophical Review*, *67*, 164–194.

Rimer, B. K., & Kreuter, M. W. (2006). Advancing tailored health communication: A persuasion and message effects perspective. *Journal of Communication*, *56*(Suppl. 1), S184–S201.

Rogers, C. (1951). *Client-centered therapy: Its current practice, implications and theory.* London, UK: Constable.

Rose, G. (1992). *The strategy of prevention medicine.* Oxford, UK: Oxford University Press.

Rost, K., Nutting, P., Smith, J., Coyne, J. C., Cooper-Patrick, L., & Rubenstein, L. (2000). The role of competing demands in the treatment provided primary care patients with major depression. *Archives of Family Medicine*, *9*(2), 150–154.

Rubenowitz, E., Waern, M., Wilhelmson, K., & Allebeck, P. (2001). Life events and psychosocial factors in elderly suicides—a case-control study. *Psychological Medicine*, *31*(7), 1193–1202.

Rutz, W. (2001). Preventing suicide and premature death by education and treatment. *Journal of Affective Disorders*, *62*(1–2), 123–129.

Ryan, R. M., & Deci, E. L. (2000). Self-determination theory and the facilitation of intrinsic motivation, social development, and well-being. *American Psychologist*, *55*(1), 68–78.

Safer, M. A., Tharps, Q. J., Jackson, T. C., & Leventhal, H. (1979). Determinants of three stages of delay in seeking care at a medical clinic. *Medical Care*, *17*(1), 11–29.

Sarason, S. B. (1981). An asocial psychology and a misdirected clinical psychology. *American Psychologist*, *36*(8), 827–836.

Schell, L. M. (1998). Culture as a stressor: A revised model of biocultural interaction. *American Journal of Physical Anthropology, 102,* 67–77.

Shea, S. C. (1999). *The practical art of suicide assessment: A guide for mental health professionals and substance abuse counselors.* Hoboken, NJ: Wiley.

Sher, I., McGinn, L., Sirey, J. A., & Meyers, B. (2005). Effects of caregivers' perceived stigma and causal beliefs on patients' adherence to antidepressant treatment. *Psychiatric Services, 56*(5), 564–569.

Sirey, J. A., Bruce, M. L., Alexopoulos, G. S., Perlick, D. A., Raue, P., Friedman, S. J., & Meyers, B. S. (2001). Perceived stigma as a predictor of treatment discontinuation in young and older outpatients with depression. *American Journal of Psychiatry, 158*(3), 479–481.

Sorenson, S. B., & Miller, M. (2006). Incomplete priorities: Ignoring the role of firearms in us suicides. *American Journal of Public Health, 96*(7), 1149; author reply 1149–1150.

Stoppe, G., Sandholzer, H., Huppertz, C., Duwe, H., & Staedt, J. (1999). Gender differences in the recognition of depression in old age. *Maturitas, 32*(3), 205–212.

Suominen, K., Henriksson, M., Isometsä, E., Conwell, Y., Heila, H., & Lönnqvist, J. (2003). Nursing home suicides: A psychological autopsy study. *International Journal of Geriatric Psychiatry, 18*(12), 1095–1101.

Suominen, K., Isometsä, E., Heila, H., Lönnqvist, J., & Henriksson, M. (2002). General hospital suicides—a psychological autopsy study in Finland. *General Hospital Psychiatry, 24*(6), 412–416.

Thaler, R. H., & Sunstein, C. R. (2008). *Nudge: Improving decisions about health, wealth, and happiness.* New Haven, CT: Yale University Press

Tsoh, J., Chiu, H. F. K., Duberstein, P. R., Chan, S. S. M., Chi, I., Yip, P. S. F., & Conwell, Y. (2005). Attempted suicide in elderly Chinese persons: A multi-group, controlled study. *American Journal of Geriatric Psychiatry, 13*(7), 562–571.

Tyrer, P., Mitchard, S., Methuen, C., & Ranger, M. (2003). Treatment rejecting and treatment seeking personality disorders: Type R and type S. *Journal of Personality Disorders, 17*(3), 263–268.

Uncapher, H., & Areán, P. A. (2000). Physicians are less willing to treat suicidal ideation in older patients. *Journal of the American Geriatrics Society, 48*(2), 188–192.

Unützer, J., Tang, L., Oishi, S., Katon, W., Williams, J. W., Jr, Hunkeler, E.,...for the IMPACT Investigators. (2006). Reducing suicidal ideation in depressed older primary care patients. *Journal of the American Geriatrics Society, 54*(10), 1550–1556.

Useda, J. D., Duberstein, P. R., Conner, K. R., Beckman, A., Franus, N., Tu, X., & Conwell, Y. (2007). Personality differences in attempted suicide versus suicide in adults 50 years of age or older. *Journal of Consulting and Clinical Psychology, 75*(1), 126–133.

van Ryn, M., & Fu, S. S. (2003). Paved with good intentions: Do public health and human service providers contribute to racial/ethnic disparities in health? *American Journal of Public Health, 93*(2), 248–255.

Vannoy, S., Tai-Seale, M., Duberstein, P., Eaton, L., & Cook, M. A. (2011). Now what should I do?—physician responses to suicide ideation in late-life primary care. *Journal of General Internal Medicine, 26,* 1005–1011.

Vannoy, S. D., Fancher, T., Meltvedt, C., Unützer, J., Duberstein, P., & Kravitz, R. L. (2010). Suicide inquiry in primary care: Creating context, inquiring, and following up. *Annals of Family Medicine, 8*(1), 33–39.

Waern, M., Rubenowitz, E., Runeson, B., Skoog, I., Wilhelmson, K., & Allebeck, P. (2002). Burden of illness and suicide in elderly people: Case-control study. *BMJ (Clinical Research ed.), 324*(7350), 1355.

Waern, M., Rubenowitz, E., & Wilhelmson, K. (2003). Predictors of suicide in the old elderly. *Gerontology, 49*(5), 328–334.

Waern, M., Runeson, B. S., Allebeck, P., Beskow, J., Rubenowitz, E., Skoog, I., & Wilhelmsson, K. (2002). Mental disorder in elderly suicides: A case-control study. *American Journal of Psychiatry, 159*(3), 450–455.

Weber, M. (1946). Bureaucracy. In Wright Mills (Ed.) & H. H. Gerth (Trans.)., *From Max Weber: Essays in sociology* (pp. 196–244). New York, NY: Oxford University Press.

Weiss, A., Sutin, A. R., Duberstein, P. R., Friedman, B., Bagby, R. M., & Costa, P. T. J. (2009). The personality domains and styles of the five-factor model are related to incident depression in Medicare recipients aged 65 to 100. *American Journal of Geriatric Psychiatry, 17*(7), 591–601.

Westen, D., Novotny, C. M., & Thompson-Brenner, H. (2004). The empirical status of empirically supported psychotherapies: Assumptions, findings, and reporting in controlled clinical trials. *Psychological Bulletin, 130*(4), 631–663.

Williams, G. C., Lynch, M., & Glasgow, R. E. (2007). Computer-assisted intervention improves patient-centered diabetes care by increasing autonomy support. *Health Psychology, 26*(6), 728–734.

Wilson, K. G., Curran, D., & McPherson, C. J. (2005). A burden to others: A common source of distress for the terminally ill. *Cognitive Behaviour Therapy, 34*(2), 115–123.

Wofford, J. L., Smith, E. D., & Miller, D. P. (2005). The multimedia computer for office-based patient education: A systematic review. *Patient Education and Counseling, 59*(2), 148–157.

Wortzel, H. S., Gutierrez, P. M., Homaifar, B. Y., Breshears, R. E., & Harwood, J. E. (2010). Surrogate endpoints in suicide research. *Suicide and Life-Threatening Behavior, 40*(5), 500–505.

Yang, F. M., Tommet, D., & Jones, R. N. (2009). Disparities in self-reported geriatric depressive symptoms due to sociodemographic differences: An extension of the bi-factor item response theory model for use in differential item functioning. *Journal of Psychiatric Research, 43*(12), 1025–1035.

Zilboorg, G. (1937). Considerations on suicide, with particular reference to the young. *American Journal of Orthopsychiatry, 7,* 15–31.

Zuroff, D. C., Blatt, S. J., Sotsky, S. M., Krupnick, J. L., Martin, D. J., Sanislow, C. A.,3rd, & Simmens, S. (2000). Relation of therapeutic alliance and perfectionism to outcome in brief outpatient treatment of depression. *Journal of Consulting and Clinical Psychology, 68*(1), 114–124.

Nonsuicidal Self-Injury Across the Life Span

Janis Whitlock *and* Matthew D. Selekman

Abstract

Although increasingly well documented and understood in adolescence, the study of nonsuicidal self-injury (NSSI) in children, adults, and the elderly is thin and gives rise to far more questions than answers. This chapter is intended to summarize what is known about NSSI etiology, risk and protective factors, consequences, trajectory, and treatment in three distinct developmental stages: childhood, adolescence, and adulthood. Because of the general paucity of research about NSSI in childhood and adulthood, there exists noticeable unevenness across sections that also serves to highlight need for knowledge. It concludes that better understanding of the ways in which elemental NSSI characteristics change over time is essential. Some of the core areas for study are variation in NSSI experience, consequences, treatment strategies, and recovery processes with regard to age of onset and duration.

Key Words: childhood, adolescence, adults, elderly, life span, development, nonsuicidal self-injury, NSSI

Understanding nonsuicidal self-injury (NSSI) across the life span requires comprehension of the interaction between developmental periods and self-injury behaviors. Such interactions are, however, woefully understudied to date. Although increasingly well documented and understood in adolescence, the study of NSSI in children, adults, and the elderly is thin and gives rise to far more questions than answers. This chapter is intended to summarize what is known about NSSI etiology, risk and protective factors, consequences, trajectory, and treatment in three distinct developmental stages: childhood, adolescence, and adulthood. Because the extant NSSI-related research seldom accounts for developmental variation within studies and because of the general paucity of research about NSSI in childhood and adulthood, dividing the chapter into these developmental areas will result in noticeable unevenness across sections that also serve to highlight need for knowledge. The chapter is generally organized by developmental period

and includes a brief description of all developmental period–specific information available to date. Where there is no developmentally specific information available, as is true for treatment approaches and NSSI consequences, a general review is provided at the end of the chapter.

Were developmental period the only factor in understanding NSSI trajectories, the research road map might be quite straightforward. However, as Nock and Favazza (2009) have so aptly pointed out, understanding of NSSI is complicated by the fact that what exactly constitutes NSSI (a) is sometimes murky; (b) is often but not always associated with a variety of other psychiatric issues, some of which may be quite pronounced; and (c) appears in a variety of forms that vary by severity and periodicity. Because of this, identifying the contribution of developmental stage to NSSI trajectories is anything but clear. For the purpose of this review, we adopt the taxonomy first articulated by Favazza and Simeon (1995) and more recently updated by Nock and Favazza

(2009). In this taxonomy, the vast majority of those who engage in NSSI practice what is termed *common* NSSI. This form of self-injury includes individuals for whom NSSI is (a) compulsive (i.e., ritualistic and rarely premeditated, such as hair pulling or trichotillomania), (b) episodic (i.e., every so often and with no identification as someone who self-injures), and (c) repetitive (i.e., performed on a regular basis and with identification as someone who self-injures). They further specify that self-injury among those who perform it repetitively can be mild, moderate, or severe depending on the lethality of the injuries. Although common NSSI can and does co-occur with other *Diagnostic and Statistical Manual of Mental Disorders* (*DSM*) classifiable mental illnesses, such as depression or anxiety, it is also increasingly evident in individuals with no other mental illness. Indeed, in a recent study of NSSI in college populations, 44% of those reporting NSSI did not show symptoms of *DSM-IV* classifiable disorders (Gollust, Eisenberg, & Golberstein, 2008).

In addition to common NSSI, Favazza and Nock (2009) identify two other categories: *stereotypic* and *major* NSSI. *Stereotypic* NSSI refers to high-frequency repetitive self-injury often without implements and most frequently among individuals with developmental disabilities or neuropsychiatric disorders. It typically results in only minor physical injury (e.g., head banging or self-biting). *Major* NSSI refers to self-injury performed very infrequently (perhaps even once) but with very serious physical consequences (e.g., eye enucleating or castration). Major NSSI occurs most often among individuals with psychotic disorders or as a result of serious drug- or alcohol-induced psychological impairment. This chapter is focused primarily on common NSSI. Where the literature is focused on stereotypic or major NSSI, this will be indicated.

Nonsuicidal Self-Injury in Children
PREVALENCE AND ETIOLOGY

NSSI in children is most often identified in those with existing psychiatric disorders such as schizophrenia (Green, 1967, 1968), Tourette's syndrome (Mathews et al., 2004; Robertson, 1992), and Lesch-Nyhan syndrome (Anderson & Ernst, 1994; Hall, Oliver, & Murphy 2001; Putnam & Stein, 1985; Simpson & Porter, 1981). Prevalence rates of NSSI within each of these specific populations are unknown. Though rare in infancy, self-injury does sometimes occur in infants and toddlers with severe mental retardation and/or autism. The most severe forms occur in children who cannot speak and have

been theorized to be attributable to "self-offensive" acts that result from tension related to a child's experiences of his or her internal and external worlds (Shentoub & Soulairac, 1961).

Estimates for prevalence rates of NSSI among community populations of children below the age of 12 are virtually nonexistent. When prevalence rates of NSSI for children are provided, they are most often reported within the broader context of "self-harm," which includes suicide-related thoughts or behaviors as well. Only two studies identified for this review included prevalence data for children below the ages of 11 years and both of these use the broader self-harm definition or are limited by a methodology likely to distort the actual prevalence rate. One of these studies is based on results of a survey of over 10,000 children, parents, and teachers and is documented in a report on the prevalence and characteristics of self-harm in the United Kingdom published by the Social Care Institute of Excellence (Meltzer, Gatward, Goodman, & Ford, 2001). This study found a self-harm prevalence rate among children ages 5–10 years to be 1.3%. More specifically, it was 0.8% among children with no known mental health difficulties, 6.2% among children with a diagnosed anxiety disorder, and 7.5% in cases where children had been diagnosed with chronic mental distress (e.g., conduct or hyperkinetic disorders). The lowest rate (0.4%) was among 5- to 7-year-old girls and the highest (2.1%) was among 8- to 10-year-old boys. In a report issued by ChildLine (Dow, 2004) based on demographic analyses of calls coming into a helpline about self-harm (suicidal intent is not differentiated), only 2% of the calls were from children between the ages of 5 and 11 years. Unfortunately, while informative, this study is limited by the bias built into the sample and thus is unlikely to provide any meaningful estimate of prevalence (Dow, 2004).

Although estimates of NSSI prevalence in child populations are unavailable, studies among older populations which document age of onset find that 5.1%–24% of self-injurious respondents report initiating NSSI under the age of 11 years (Heath, Toste, & Beetam, 2006; Ross & Heath, 2002; Whitlock, Eckenrode, & Silverman, 2006). Studies of school faculty and staff also suggest that a significant number of children engage in NSSI—some starting as early as kindergarten (Heath et al., 2006; Purington, Whitlock, & Pochtar, 2009).

DEVELOPMENTAL CONSIDERATIONS

Unfortunately, other than age of onset, very little data exist to inform the understanding of how

NSSI characteristics in otherwise normally developing children might differ from those of adolescents or adults. The study of self-harm (inclusive of suicidality) in the United Kingdom cited earlier (Meltzer et al., 2001) did explore risk factors for child self-harm and found that risk was heightened by (a) increases in the number of stressful life events experienced, (b) presence of poor parental mental health, (c) presence of family discord and dysfunction, and (d) presence of frequent punishment. Although this list bears strong similarity to the list of risk factors for adolescents and adults, the short- and long-term emotional, mental, behavioral, and social impact of accumulating risk and later NSSI may be different from one age group to another because of differences in developmental capacity, tasks, and processes. For example, because children generally are not capable of sophisticated abstract thinking, planning, and long-term perspective (Piaget, 1964) and because they tend to overattribute external events to themselves (Shaw, 2000), they are typically more emotionally reactive to early childhood trauma and adversity than they would be to similar events had they occurred later in life. Children also tend to overestimate the role they play in causing external events to happen (Shaw, 2000). Negative events, particularly as they accumulate, are processed by an amygdala (responsible for emotion identification and response) not yet in full dialogue with the cerebral cortex (responsible for higher order cognitive processing). As a result, children are likely to look for a concrete cause for negative events and to identify themselves as key causal agents. In addition, they often lack the experience needed to appreciate that the pain, which they and those they love may be experiencing as a result of difficult or traumatic life events or transitions, will pass with time. These developmental differences may lead to a behavioral response, such as NSSI, disproportionate to that evidenced by adolescents or adults faced with similar contextual stimuli.

Although existing evidence suggests that, as in adolescence and adulthood, self-injury in children is likely used as a means of expressing and mitigating emotional distress, there are no studies of NSSI function in normally developing children. Since NSSI is relatively uncommon in childhood, even among children experiencing severe or multiple risk factors, early adoption and utilization of NSSI as a coping mechanism suggests that physiological vulnerabilities and/or early exposure to NSSI may also play a role in age of onset. It is not yet known whether early-onset NSSI has characteristics and

trajectories that differ from NSSI that has its onset during adolescence or adulthood. It seems reasonable to hypothesize, for example, that early NSSI onset may lead to more severe and intransigent forms of NSSI over time and might be comorbid with more severe or numerous mental health issues than in adolescent or adult NSSI trajectories.

Nonsuicidal Self-Injury in Adolescents and Young Adults
PREVALENCE AND ETIOLOGY

Because NSSI is believed to be most common among adolescents and young adults, most NSSI research is conducted among these groups—primarily with youth in secondary schools and college settings. For example, the small but steadily growing body of NSSI scholarship consistently shows an average age of onset between 11 and 15 years, depending on the sample parameters such as current age of sample population (Jacobson & Gould, 2007; Klonsky & Muehlenkamp, 2007; Kumar, Pepe, & Steer, 2004; Muehlenkamp & Gutierrez, 2004; Nixon, Cloutier, & Aggarwal, 2002; Nock & Prinstein, 2004). Variation in age of onset tends to be normally distributed with about 25% indicating starting between the ages of 10 and 14 years, 27% between 15 and 16 years, and 38.6% between 17 and 24 years (Whitlock, Eckenrode, et al., 2006). Duration of NSSI is understudied, but where it has been studied tends to vary by population and age of onset (Heath, Toste, Nedecheva, & Charlebois, 2008). For example, in their study of college students, Whitlock and colleagues (2006) found that among individuals with repeat NSSI who reported no NSSI in the past year and no intention of practicing NSSI again, the majority (79.8%) reported stopping NSSI within 5 years of starting and 40% reporting stopping within 1 year of starting.

Lifetime prevalence of NSSI ranges from 12% to 37.2% in secondary school populations (see Jacobson & Gould, 2007 and Rodham & Hawton, 2009 for reviews) and 12% to 38% in young adult populations (Gratz, Conrad, & Roemer, 2002; Heath et al., 2008; Polk & Liss, 2007; Whitlock, Eckenrode, et al., 2006). Studies typically find that about 6%–7% of adolescents and young adults who report current NSSI (NSSI in the past year/6 months) (Gollust et al., 2008; Jacobson & Gould, 2007; Whitlock, Eckenrode, et al., 2006) and that of all youth reporting any NSSI, over three-quarters report repeat NSSI (>1 episode), about half report between two and ten lifetime incidents, and 20%–25% report more than ten lifetime incidents. Overall, about a quarter of all adolescents and young adults with NSSI history report practicing NSSI only once in their lives (Heath et al., 2008; Whitlock, Eckenrode, et al., 2006). However, at least one study has shown even a single NSSI episode to be significantly correlated with a history of abuse and with comorbid conditions such as suicidality and psychiatric distress (Whitlock, Eckenrode, et al., 2006), suggesting that there may be a group of adolescents in which a single incident of NSSI serves as a risk indicator for other risk behaviors or pathology.

The most common NSSI forms reported by adolescents and young adults include scratching, cutting, punching or banging objects with the conscious intention of self-injury, punching or banging oneself, biting, ripping or tearing the skin, carving on the self, and burning oneself (Briere & Gil, 1998; Heath et al., 2008; Klonsky, 2007a, 2007b; Laye-Gindu & Schonert-Reichl, 2005; Whitlock, Eckenrode, et al., 2006). While these forms are those most commonly reported, they are not the only forms of NSSI practiced among adolescents and young adults. Studies of NSSI forms used in adolescent and young adult populations indicate that a wide range of forms are used, including trichotillomania, wound interference, embedding, bone breaking (or attempted bone breaking), and ingesting caustic substances (Klonsky, 2007a, 2007b; Laye-Gindu & Schonert-Reichl, 2005; Lloyd-Richardson, Perrine, Dierker, & Kelley, 2007; Nock & Prinstein, 2004; Walsh, 2006; Whitlock, Eckenrode, et al., 2006). The majority of young people reporting repeat self-injury also report using multiple methods to injure. In one study of those who reported repeat NSSI, 70% reported using multiple methods, with about half reporting using two to four methods. Further, those reporting repeat NSSI also were more likely to report injuring multiple body locations (Whitlock, Eckenrode, et al., 2006).

NSSI practices can be highly variable depending on the nature and degree of engagement in NSSI (i.e., compulsive, episodic, or repetitive) and on the context within which it is performed. For example, in a recent study of college students, most of those who practice NSSI (63.7%) report injuring in private, 10.2% indicate preferring a particular room or place, and 8.8% report injuring in the presence of others and another 18% report ever having self-injured while under the influence of drugs or alcohol (Whitlock et al., 2011). Notably, in one study of 30 adolescents and young adults asked to provide real-time data on NSSI and suicide thoughts and actions over a 2-week period reported thinking about NSSI in conjunction with drugs or alcohol 15%–20% of the time but actually engaging in NSSI in conjunction with drugs and/or alcohol only 3% of the time (Nock, Prinstein, & Sterba, 2009). The Whitlock et.al (2011) study also found significant gender variation in NSSI patterns with males being significantly more likely than females to report injuring in the presence of others, letting others cause injuries, injuring another person as part of an NSSI routine, and injuring while intoxicated. Males also were more likely than females to report intoxication during an instance when they injured themselves more severely than intended (Whitlock et al., 2011). In a similar vein, a survey of NSSI trends in secondary schools with school counselors, social workers, and nurses as respondents suggested that there may be various contexts in which NSSI is initiated and maintained. For example, while most of the respondents (81.5%) indicated being aware of students conforming to the individuals who fit the profile of the private individual injurer who tells few people if anyone at all, 69.4% of the respondents indicated awareness of individuals who injured and openly shared this fact with others. Another 25.9 % indicated having observed youth who injure alone but who show or tell others about their injuries share their injuries as a means of being part of a group, and another 17.2% reported that their school contained groups of youth who injure together as a part of group membership (Purington et al., 2009).

Similarly, the extent of body damage incurred as a result of NSSI practices varies considerably. In one study, 21% of all young people with NSSI experience reported injuring themselves more severely than intended, and 47% of these reported multiple episodes of injuring themselves more severely than intended. Over a third (35.3%) of those with NSSI experience in this study indicated that they should have been seen by a medical professional for their injury, but only 6.5% reported actually seeking medical attention (Whitlock, Eckenrode, et al., 2006). Similar findings have been reported in a large study of secondary school student self-harm in the United Kingdom, where 12.6% of adolescents reporting any self-harming behavior reported seeking medical attention (Hawton, Rodham, Evans, & Weatherall, 2002). A better understanding of the severity and associated lethality of NSSI based on clinical assessment of presenting NSSI characteristics would be immensely helpful in medical, psychiatric, and community settings, where quick assessment of safety and treatment needs is warranted.

Empirical study of primary NSSI characteristics suggests that NSSI can be grouped or classified by clinical features in ways that may predict risk for other psychiatric disorders, risk behaviors, and suicidality. For example, using latent class analysis techniques, Klonsky and Olino (2008) identified four classes differentiated by NSSI form, function, and descriptive feature (e.g., time elapsed from consideration to execution of NSSI, pain, and whether one injures alone or with a group). They found that when compared to other classes, the class with the greatest comorbidity with suicidality was characterized by forms capable of causing more serious physical damage (e.g., cutting), a later age of onset, and primarily composed of females who injure with some degree of premeditation, in private, and who do so primarily to regulate negative affect. The other most severe class was characterized by forms capable of causing serious physical damage, though through a greater variety of forms than the former class, and for social reasons as much as with the intention of regulating negative affect. Also using a latent class analysis approach to classification of NSSI characteristics in relation to psychological distress, suicidality, and disordered eating, Whitlock, Muehlenkamp, and Eckenrode (2008) identified three classes differentiated by four basic NSSI characteristics: lifetime NSSI frequency, the type of form used, the number of forms employed, and gender. Like Klonksy and Olino (2008), they found that the highest severity class (i.e., that most likely to report suicidality, disordered eating, and psychological distress) were composed primarily of females using multiple NSSI forms capable of causing a high degree of tissue damage, and who reported over 11 lifetime NSSI incidents. They also found that, compared to the other two groups, this group was more likely to report having inflicted more damage than intended, having friends who self-injured, perceiving that NSSI interferes with their life, and possessing a history of sexual, emotional, or physical abuse. Although more study of how presenting NSSI characteristics can be employed to quickly assess risk for physical damage as a result of NSSI and of risk for suicidality and other psychiatric disorders is warranted, these two studies do support clinical contention that there are important clinical differences in NSSI meaning, lethality, and effective treatment approaches (Conterio & Lader, 1998; Muehlenkamp, 2005; Walsh, 2006).

The study of initial motivation for NSSI adoption is important in light of the widespread belief that NSSI has increased in prevalence and has spread into populations within which it was previously undocumented or in which it was believed to occur at very low frequency. Perhaps reflective of the shifting set of dominant contributors to NSSI, studies of initial motivation are not consistent in their findings about why people initiate NSSI. For example, in a study of Canadian college students, Heath and colleagues (2009) find that social motivations were common in NSSI initiation and maintenance. Similarly, a UK-based study of adolescent self-harm in school-based populations found that being associated with the "Goth" subgroup (youth identifying with "gothic" style dress and comportment) was significantly associated with adoption of self-injurious behavior in the study population (Rutledge, Rimer, & Scott, 2008; Young, Sweeting, & West, 2006). Even when social influences are present, however, studies also find a majority of respondents (adolescent, secondary school, and college) identify "accidental discovery" or an impulsive response to overwhelming negative affect as the primary reason for initiating NSSI (Heath, Ross, Toste, Charlebois, & Nedecheva, 2009; Whitlock, Eckenrode, et al., 2006).

Although an important means of testing the practice-based observation that NSSI may be spreading into community populations through exposure to media and friendship groups, asking respondents to consciously identify causes for NSSI adoption is limited by a variety of methodological issues and biases. In other words, it often is difficult for individuals to consciously link possible external exposure (e.g., through media or general knowledge that NSSI is practiced by peer groups) to the personal motivation for adopting the practice. Studies of contagion among adolescents in clinical settings, however, demonstrate the tendency for NSSI to spread. For example, in an empirical study of social contagion in clinical settings, Walsh and Deorfler (2009) found that NSSI occurs in statistically significant clusters, can be triggered by staff departures in residential settings, and can be mapped using a sociogram across adolescents in a special education school. They also identified promising approaches for preventing social contagion in group settings, including encouraging youth to discuss NSSI with adults but not with peers and requiring the covering of wounds to prevent triggering the behavior in others (Walsh & Doerfler, 2009).

Variation in reported sources of inspiration for initiating NSSI also may be linked to the possibility that important, and dynamic, variations in the social meaning and practice of NSSI exist—particularly among middle and high school populations (Prinstein, Guerry, Browne, & Rancourt, 2009). Although a life course approach to the study of NSSI acknowledges potentially important variation in individual NSSI trajectories, similar study of variation in social forms of NSSI is warranted. For example, while studies of NSSI on college campuses often identify individuals who practice NSSI in private and primarily as a means of regulating negative affect or dissociation, some studies are surfacing different NSSI forms. For example, Young and colleagues' (2006) study of self-harm in Goth populations suggests that, for youth who identify with Goth (or "emo") subgroups, self-injury may be practiced as a form of social bonding or membership. This self-injury may or may not conform to the epidemiological characteristics in NSSI form, frequency, and function associated with the profile of someone engaging in NSSI alone. Similarly, in a study of NSSI in secondary school settings as observed by New York State secondary school nurses, social workers, and counselors, respondents identify Goth subgroups as a common group to evidence NSSI (Purington et al., 2009). Because of the difference in primary NSSI function and rituals among these groups, it is quite likely that variation in detection, prevention, and treatment approaches will also be warranted. Indeed, in his description of protocols likely to be effective in secondary school settings, Walsh (2006) indicates that assessing for group involvement is an important step of intervention protocols. Such a focus is needed as NSSI may carry fundamentally different risks for individuals participating in NSSI for social versus individual emotion regulation purposes, and effective intervention is likely to vary based on level of group involvement.

In contrast to research on NSSI initiation, research on NSSI function is far more consistent. In general, function models of NSSI break down into three basic categories: psychological, social, and biological. Psychological models are typically described using the four-function model first identified by Nock and Prinstein (2004) as *automatic positive reinforcement* (i.e., NSSI is motivated by the desire to feel something in the wake of dissociation or to generate a rush of energy), *automatic negative reinforcement* (i.e., NSSI is motivated by the desire to escape negative affect reinforced by negative internal states such as anger or grief), *social positive reinforcement* (i.e., NSSI is motivated by the desire to gain attention or access to resources), and *social negative reinforcement* (i.e., NSSI is motivated

by the desire to avoid punishment from others). While not all researchers conceptualize or describe psychological function using these four categories (see Klonksy for a review, 2007a), a broad base of empirical evidence suggests that one of the primary functions of NSSI is to avoid psychological pain, to express psychological distress, and to refocus one's attention away from negative stimulus (Hawton & Rodham, 2006; Klonksy, 2007a; Nock & Prinstein, 2004, 2005; Rodham, Hawton, & Evans, 2004; Selekman, 2006a, 2006b, 2009; Selekman & Shulem, unpublished data; Walsh, 2007). In keeping with this, Andover, Pepper, and Gibb (2007) found that individuals with an NSSI history tend to utilize avoidant coping strategies significantly more often than their non-self-injurious peers and that female, but not male, self-mutilators endorsed using problem-solving and social support–seeking strategies less often than those without an NSSI history. This is particularly resonant with adolescents' responses to function questions who tend to cite reasons directly linked to emotion regulation, an area of concentrated development during adolescence. Such responses include "to cope with negative feelings," "to relieve stress," "to deal with frustration," "to relieve pain," "to feel something," "to change emotional pain into physical pain," and "to get a rush or surge of energy" (Chapman, Gratz, & Brown, 2006; Jacobson & Gould, 2007; Klonsky, 2007a; Laye-Gindhu & Schonert-Reichl, 2005; Nixon et al., 2002; Nock & Prinstein, 2004; Whitlock et al., 2011).

The fact that adolescents, with whom most NSSI function studies have been conducted, also tend to indicate reasons for NSSI such as "so someone would pay attention" and "to get a rush or surge of energy" underscore the role of both social and biological roles in maintaining NSSI. Social function models point to the importance of viewing NSSI as a behavior undertaken to fulfill multiple functions simultaneously, many of which are fundamentally interpersonal in nature. In addition to being identified as factors that predispose or place at risk adolescents who ultimately adopt NSSI as an outlet for negative emotion (Prinstein et al., 2009; Yates, 2004), research finds interpersonal factors also make significant contributions to NSSI maintenance (Favazza, 1998; Nock & Prinstein, 2004; Prinstein et al., 2009; Yates, 2004).

Lastly, biological models of function tend to focus primarily on the role of NSSI in the regulation of endogenous opioids. The homeostasis model of NSSI, for example, suggests that people who self-injure may have chronically low levels of endogenous opioids. In this model, NSSI is fundamentally remedial—it represents an attempt to restore opioids to normal levels. Low levels of opioids may result from a history of abuse, trauma, or neglect or may be biologically endowed through other processes (Sher & Stanley, 2008). These models are helpful in deepening understanding about how and why NSSI becomes addictive (Nixon et al., 2002; Winchel & Stanley, 1991).

Although current function models are silent on the alchemic particularities of psychological, social, and biological models in promoting and maintaining NSSI, there does exist broad agreement that NSSI likely fulfills multiple functions simultaneously and serves as an outlet behavior for a variety of psychiatric conditions such as depression and posttraumatic stress disorder (Briere & Gil, 1998; Brown, Comtois, & Linehan, 2002; Chapman et al., 2006; Claes, Vandereychen, & Vertommen, 2006; Figueroa, 1988; Himber, 1994; Klonsky, 2007a; Laye-Gindhu & Schonert-Reichl, 2005; Nixon et al., 2002; Nock & Prinstein, 2004, 2005; Osuch, Noll, & Putnam, 1999).

DEMOGRAPHIC PREDICTORS OF NONSUICIDAL SELF-INJURY IN ADOLESCENTS AND YOUNG ADULTS

Perhaps the most salient theme to emerge from existing literature is that there is no one "self-injurer" profile. Difficulty identifying a profile may be due partly to the widely varied motivations reported for initiating and engaging in NSSI. Within clinical populations, those who self-injure tend to possess high levels of depression and anxiety and comparatively few coping mechanisms (Haines & Williams, 2003). However, as Strong (1998) notes, those who self-injure are also found in "the best neighborhoods and private schools, in colleges and in the workplace" and are "often bright, talented and creative achievers—perfectionists who push themselves beyond all human bounds, people-pleasers who cover their pain with a happy face" (p. 18). She suggests it is more common than assumed for someone engaging in NSSI to be high functioning and to go undetected by the service system.

Although most research finds adolescent and young adult females to be 1.5–3.0 times more likely to self-injure than their male peers (Conterio & Lader, 1998; Favazza, 1999; Purington et al., 2009; Whitlock, Eckenrode, et al., 2006), other empirical research suggests that the gender gap may be narrower than assumed (Briere & Gil, 1998; Deiter,

Nicholls, & Pearlman, 2000; Dulit, Fyer, Leon, Brodsky, & Frances, 1994; Galley, 2003; Heath et al., 2008; Martin, Rozanes, Pearce, & Allison, 1995). The difficulty in accurately assessing the sex distribution of NSSI may arise from the variation in which males and females engaging in NSSI are found, how they self-injure, and how likely they are to seek treatment (Alderman, 1997; Connors, 2000). The fact that no gender differences were found in individuals reporting a single NSSI incident (Whitlock, Eckenrode, et al., 2006) and that gender differences emerge in class analyses of NSSI (Klonsky & Olino, 2008; Whitlock et al., 2008) and in rituals and practices (Whitlock et al., 2011) suggests that while a gender gap may exist in NSSI prevalence, there may also exist important differences in the forms and contexts within which NSSI is practiced (Purington et al., 2009). In light of the gendered patterns evident in disorders similar to NSSI, such as suicidal behavior and disordered eating (Lewinsohn, Rohde, Seeley, & Baldwin, 2001; Lewinsohn, Seeley, Moerk, & Striegel-Moore, 2002), it is likely that analysis of gender differences in NSSI will surface gender-related distinctions with implications for clinical detection and treatment and prevention approaches.

Findings on the association between NSSI and ethnicity in adolescents and young adults are inconclusive. Although a small number of studies comparing Caucasian to non-Caucasian youth show significantly higher rates among the former (Muehlenkamp & Gutierrez, 2004, 2007; Whitlock, Eckenrode, et al., 2006; Whitlock, Purington, Eells, & Cummings, 2009), other studies show similarly high rates in minority samples (Favazza, 1999; Laye-Gindhu & Schonert-Reichl, 2005; Whitlock & Knox, 2007) or only modest differences between Caucasians and Asian students (Whitlock, Eckenrode, et al., 2006). Although parallels between NSSI and eating disorders have led some to speculate that NSSI is likely to be most prevalent among middle- and upper-income individuals, no existing research supports this contention. Indeed, other researchers have reported NSSI to exist in low-income populations (Nixon, Cloutier, & Jansson, 2008; Whitlock, Eckenrode, et al., 2006). Further, studies of NSSI in college students have revealed no socioeconomic (SES) differences (Whitlock, Eckenrode, et al., 2006; Whitlock et al., 2011). There is some evidence linking NSSI to sexual orientation such that incidence of NSSI is elevated among those who report exclusive homosexual attraction and some same-sex attraction

(Whitlock, Eckenrode, et al., 2006) and particularly prevalent among those with bisexual or questioning sexual orientation statuses (Whitlock, Eckenrode, et al., 2006; Whitlock et al., 2011).

RISK AND PROTECTIVE FACTORS

Risk factors are conditions that increase the likelihood of a negative outcome. In this case, these are conditions that precede and directly or indirectly contribute to the onset and maintenance of NSSI. Protective factors are conditions that effectively buffer people from a negative outcome. Like risk factors, protective factors may precede or co-occur with NSSI and may directly or indirectly influence development or continuation of NSSI. Although relatively easy to identify general contributors to NSSI, discerning the nature of the particular relationship between risk and protective factors and NSSI is more art than science; it is far easier to identify salient contributors to any given outcome in retrospect than it is to predict an outcome given a potential set of contributors. This is largely due to the complex interaction between environment, personality, and developmental processes (typically broken into discrete though related domains: physiological, social, emotional, moral, cognitive, and spiritual).

Understanding of the origins and evolution of common forms of NSSI in adolescence is also complicated by the fact that NSSI is increasingly regarded as both a potential indicator of mental illness, when present at clinical levels (which have yet to be agreed upon), as well as one of several possible expressions of what could be regarded as normative adolescent risk taking and culture (Clarke & Whittaker, 1998; Favazza, 1996; Young et al., 2006). Indeed, the complexity, multitude, and rapidity of developmental changes during adolescence provide a uniquely fertile environment for the dynamic interplay between risk and protection—with behavior results not always predictable at the outset. In a thorough and recent review of the literature, Klonsky and Glenn (2009) synthesized and shared what is known about NSSI psychosocial risk and protective factors. As they note, extant literature generally centers on four broad categories of risk to date: emotion disregulation (e.g., negative emotionality, dissociate experiences, and alexithymia), self-derogation, childhood adversity (e.g., familial neglect, child abuse, attachment difficult), and comorbid or antecedent psychiatric disorders (e.g., borderline personality disorder, anxiety, depression, eating disorder, and substance abuse) (see Klonsky & Glenn, 2009, for a review).

Within these categories, individual-level risk factors (temperament, comorbid mental illness, and physiological vulnerability) have commanded the greatest empirical attention. Exploration of environmental contributors to NSSI tend to focus on the role of family dynamics and functioning and of childhood experiences of abuse (particularly sexual abuse), neglect, and trauma, and there exists little controversy about the contributions of these to later development of NSSI (typically in adolescence though sometimes earlier or later) (see Yates, 2004 and Jacobson & Gould, 2007 for a thorough review of this literature). Exploration of the role that emotion reactivity and management play in NSSI has also proven fruitful. Though nascent, extant studies confirm theoretical suppositions that poor emotion regulation skills in conjunction with higher levels of emotional reactivity may be a risk factor for engagement in NSSI (Linehan, 1993; Najmi, Wegner, & Nock, 2007; Nock, Wedig, Holmberg, & Hooley 2008).

Outside of these broad areas, there exists a smattering of research on the contributions of various external settings and processes to the onset and continuation of adolescent NSSI. Though limited, studies of peer groups (Heath et al., 2009; Prinstein et al., 2009; Yip, Ngan, & Lam, 2002; Young et al., 2006), media and Internet influence (Murray & Fox, 2006; Murray, Warm, & Fox, 2005; Whitlock, Powers, & Eckenrode, 2006; Whitlock, Purington, & Gershkovich, 2009), and social and cultural trends and pressures related to body modification and objectification (Favazza, 1996; Stirn & Hinz, 2008; Young et al., 2006) all find positive and significant associations with NSSI.

Studies of the link between NSSI and other mental health–related disorders suggest that the presence of an existing mental illness or risk condition (e.g. excessive alcohol use or disordered eating) may heighten the risk of NSSI onset among adolescents. Studies of NSSI comorbidity show strong positive correlations to major depressive disorder, borderline personality disorder, alexithymia, anxiety disorder, substance use disorders, posttraumatic stress disorder, smoking, antisocial behavior, and disordered eating (Alderman, 1997; Claes, Vandereycken, & Vertommen, 2001; Connors, 2000; Conterio & Lader, 1998; Favazza, DeRosear, & Conterio, 1989; Holmes & Nadelson, 2000; Jacobs & Isaacs, 1986; Jacobson, Muehlenkamp, & Miller, 2009; Kumar et al., 2004; Nock, Joiner, Gordon, Lloyd-Richardson, & Prinstein, 2006; Ross, Heath, & Toste, 2009; Sansone & Levitt, 2002; Tantam &

Whittaker, 1993). Although much of this research reflects comorbidity in clinical populations, more recent studies of these relationships in community populations of youth document similar patterns, though at lower levels of association (Gollust et al., 2008; Ogle & Clements, 2008; Whitlock, Eckenrode, et al., 2006).

In many ways, the stage of life we identify as adolescence is, in and of itself, a risk factor for NSSI. Indeed, the study of NSSI risk and protective factors in adolescence is incomplete without adequate reckoning of the role development plays in making NSSI an attractive option for adolescents. This also is important since adolescence is the most common period of onset for most major mental disorders (Kessler et al., 2005). Adolescence, regardless of its exact boundaries, is a distinct stage of life from both childhood and adulthood. It is the life period in which childhood gives way to focus on development of the capacities required for adulthood (Erickson, 1968; Havighurst, 1972), and it is the only period to rival early childhood in the complexity and rapidity of change. Unlike early childhood, in which the extent of growth is obvious, much of the development occurring in the adolescent years occurs within the seemingly invisible domains associated with psychological, social, moral, cognitive, sexual, and spiritual maturity. Not only does full maturity mandate robust development in each of these areas, it requires integration between them. Maladaptive behaviors, such as NSSI, may arise during this time as individuals use a variety of strategies for reaching and maintaining emotional equilibrium. This may help to explain the relatively short duration of NSSI activity among otherwise well-functioning individuals (Whitlock, Eckenrode, et al., 2006).

Moreover, since development is neither linear nor simply concurrent, asynchronistic development during the adolescent years, when brains, bodies, and sense of self are undergoing profound change, is more the norm than not. For example, lab studies of decision making consistently show few age differences in cognitive processes relevant to risk taking and decision making between adolescents and adults in laboratory settings (Steinberg & Cauffman, 1996). These similarities, however, dissipate in neurological studies, which do show significant variation in underlying biological substrates associated with neurological processing of risk by age (Casey, Getz, & Galvin, 2008; Hare et al., 2008) and in real-life settings when intense contextual stimuli influence self-regulation processes—all of which are still undergoing development in the adolescent period.

When novelty and sensation-seeking impulses, both of which increase dramatically at puberty, are coupled with low self-regulatory competence, which does not fully mature until early adulthood, there exists psychologically fertile ground for seemingly aberrant behavior (Steinberg, 2004). When these conditions are accompanied by psychosocial factors that frustrate or delay healthy developmental processes, such as early childhood trauma, biological imbalances or difficult temperamental dispositions, overly demanding or challenging environments, and/or persistent inconsistency in the nature of the demands of various social environments (e.g., family, peers, school, community), there are likely to be detrimental consequences (Lerner & Steinberg, 2004). Thus, the brain–behavior–social context interactions that occur during this period have profound implications for emotion and motivation (Dahl, Spear, Kelley, Shaikh, & Clayton, 2004) and often give rise to behaviors that appear highly clinically significant but which may be time limited and/or part of a normal developmental trajectory.

It is during this period that less than healthy methods of coping, such as self-injury, emerge. As Conterio and Lader (1998) so aptly point out, self-injury may serve as an outlet for the "growing pains" of adolescence through its capacity to give form and expression to discomfort with physical changes and sexual impulses, confusion about the twin need for autonomy and connection, the need to perform perfectly in all social situations, and the need for psychological validation. NSSI may also be, as Favazza (1996, 2009) has so beautifully articulated, a physical and metaphorical attempt to integrate spirit, body, and psyche. An NSSI episode may be thus experienced by some as a transcendental act, one capable of conferring authenticity and— even if fleetingly—physical, mental, emotional, and spiritual equilibrium. Its particular attractiveness to adolescents, then, may lie in its capacity to serve as a vehicle for simultaneous expression of pain and a striving toward wholeness—both of which are abundant during the adolescent period.

Nonsuicidal Self-Injury in Adults

Although popularly branded as the "newest teen epidemic" (Welsh, 2004), NSSI is neither new nor unique to the adolescent years. Some of the earliest NSSI cases appeared in the 18th century (Brumberg, 2006; Favazza, 1996) and often involved adults (largely women in their 20s or 30s) or male war veterans ("Whittaker Found Guilty," 1880). Cases of "delicate self-cutting" were documented in the 1960s and were most commonly identified among young women, primarily in their 20s (Pao, 1969). Although seemingly rare, NSSI also has been documented in elderly populations (Parks & Feldman, 2006).

Despite its long-standing origins, empirical understanding of NSSI in adults is sorely lacking. What literature does exist on adult NSSI often is conducted on small or specialized populations, limiting generalizability. As a result, estimates of primary NSSI characteristics, such as prevalence, frequency, and form, are unavailable. Since so much of the adolescent NSSI literature includes young adults, it is not clear precisely what age group constitutes "adult"-onset NSSI. However, since the literature in general is so thin, this section will include studies in which the sample is 18+ years and is not drawn from a community sample of college students.

Although reasonable to assume that NSSI in adulthood would share important features with NSSI in adolescence, such as function, comorbidity with other disorders, contextual risk factors, consequences, and treatment approaches, there may be important distinctions. For example, in light of the developmental integration and stability afforded adults in comparison to children and adolescents, where NSSI may serve as a coping mechanism in normally developing young people with transient deficits in emotion regulation, it seems likely that adults who employ NSSI may suffer from emotional and mental imbalances not linked to natural developmental processes. If so, NSSI in adults may signal comorbid mental illness and may be more difficult to effectively treat.

Very few studies report prevalence rates of NSSI in adults. One of the earliest studies, conducted by Briere and Gil (1998), reports on the results of two studies: one undertaken as part of a nationally representative study of trauma and its effects and the other as part of study of victimization history and trauma symptoms in multiple clinical samples. Using an NSSI item intended to assess a 6-month prevalence, they found that 4% of the general population sample reported ever engaging in NSSI and 0.3% reported often engaging in NSSI. Although they found no gender differences in the NSSI sample, they did find a link between any NSSI in the previous 6 months and childhood abuse. Among the clinical adult sample, 21% indicated at least occasional self-injury in the past 6 months, while the corresponding figure for frequent NSSI was 8%. Similar to the community sample finding, a history of sexual abuse predicted NSSI, though not other trauma history. There were no significant gender differences in NSSI history, though younger age predicted NSSI in both samples. Similar to adolescent studies, individuals in clinical samples reporting any NSSI were also more likely to report concomitant diagnoses of posttraumatic stress disorder, dissociative disorder, or borderline personality disorder. In line with this, a study of NSSI prevalence rates among a sample of military recruits by Klonsky and colleagues (2003) found a 4% prevalence rate. The same study found that anxiety played a major role in adult NSSI.

In contrast to these US-based studies, a recent community sample study of Australian adults aged 18–30 years documented a prevalence rate of 40.8% (Hasking, Momeni, Swannell, & Chia, 2008). They found that over one-third of those who engaged in NSSI used one (37.5%) or two methods of NSSI (29.2%). The majority reported engaging in NSSI within the last year (36.0%), with a significant number reporting NSSI within the last month (15.2%).

Information on other NSSI characteristics in adult samples also is scarce. In the Briere and Gil (1998) study noted earlier, they found cutting, biting, scratching, and punching to be the most commonly employed NSSI forms (endorsed by over 40% of the self-injurious sample). Hasking et al. (2008) found scratching and cutting to be the most common forms. Briere and Gil (1998) also found that rather than merely representing a psychological symptom, NSSI was most commonly undertaken as a means of regulating negative affect and dissociation. Similar to the function literature identified for adolescents, they conclude that NSSI may be best understood as a coping mechanism and best treated through use of strategies aimed at increasing and enhancing adaptive coping skills. Similarly, in a study of NSSI motivation in a clinical sample of adult inpatients at a freestanding tertiary care psychiatric hospital, Osuch, Noll, and Putnam (1999) found cutting, scratching, hitting, and burning to be the most common NSSI forms reported. Like studies conducted with adolescents, they found the primary motivation for NSSI to be related to affect regulation.

In another study based on a survey of individuals watching a daytime television program on NSSI and who responded to an invitation to complete a survey about their NSSI experience, Favazza and Conterio (1989) found NSSI to be common among women in their mid- to late 20s who first deliberately harmed themselves in early adolescence. Consistent with the severe class NSSI category identified by Whitlock and colleagues (2008), they found that the majority of the respondents who exhibited high lifetime NSSI frequency (>50 occasions) used cutting as the dominant NSSI form. These respondents also reported using multiple, potentially damaging forms such as burning and self-hitting. Also consistent was their finding that many of these women reported comorbid disorders, such as disordered eating, alcohol abuse, and suicidal behavior.

Studies of NSSI in elderly populations are virtually nonexistent. Although there are studies of "self-harm" in the elderly, these are almost always focused primarily on suicide (Dennis, Wakefield, Molloy, Andrews, & Friedman, 2007; Hawton & Harriss, 2006; Pierce, 1987). In the one review article of NSSI in the elderly, Parks and Feldman (2006) identify the great need for research in this area. Once done, Parks and Feldman (2006) predict that studies are likely to find that although NSSI is uncommon in the elderly, risk factors such as dementia, depressive disorders, physical illness, and loss of a spouse all may contribute to NSSI onset. They further hypothesize that in contrast to adolescents and adults, NSSI function in elderly populations may stem from frustration and from deficits in the ability to communicate effectively with others—similar to the role NSSI is hypothesized to play in children with developmental difficulties that affect communication skills.

Consequences of Nonsuicidal Self-Injury: A Life Course Perspective

Studies of the consequences of NSSI are rare, largely because it is fundamentally longitudinal and, as of the time of this writing, there exists no published study designed to test the longitudinal trajectories of NSSI. One exception is a 6-year longitudinal study of individuals diagnosed with borderline personality disorder in which NSSI was measured at each time point. The McLean Study of Adult Development followed 299 participants, aged 18 to 35 years with a BPD diagnosis, and found a 65% decrease in NSSI behaviors from baseline. At baseline, 81% of the participants reported engaging in NSSI within the previous 2 years, while only 26% of the participants reported engaging in NSSI at a 6-year follow-up (Zanarini, Frankenburg, Hennen, Reich, & Silk, 2005). Whether this decrease in NSSI is unique to the population studied, regression to the mean following study entry, or represents

a natural developmental decline in NSSI tendency is unknown but suggests that future inquiry along these lines may be fruitful.

Despite the limited evidence available to illuminate NSSI consequences, we do know that NSSI is correlated with a variety of adverse mental health conditions (see the "Risk and Protective Factors" section earlier in this chapter) and that the magnitude and duration of these associations vary by population studied (e.g., they tend to be stronger in clinical populations than in community population studies). Of these, the relationship between NSSI and suicide-related behavior is, perhaps, the most speculated about consequence to consider. That NSSI and suicidal behaviors are related is well documented and not in question at this point (Gardner & Cowdry, 1985; Muehlenkamp & Guiterrez, 2004; Walsh, 2006; Walsh & Rosen, 1988; Whitlock & Knox, 2007), but the nature of the relationship remains somewhat ambiguous. Most NSSI treatment specialists and scholars agree that in the vast majority of cases NSSI is utilized to temporarily alleviate distress rather than to signal the intention to end one's life (Favazza, 1996; Tantam & Whitaker, 1992; Walsh & Rosen, 1988). Indeed, some see it as a highly functional alternative to suicide (Alderman, 1997; Strong, 1998). Thus, in its relation to suicide, NSSI possesses an ambiguous, seemingly paradoxical, status as both a functional, albeit worrisome, means of sustaining life by decreasing strong negative affect while simultaneously serving as a potential harbinger for suicidal intent and attempts. This dual status suggests that efforts to discern variations in motivation and intent may be the most productive means of generating information useful in tailoring treatment guidelines, materials, and services. Although Walsh (2006) has argued that NSSI and suicide are entirely distinct psychological and behavioral phenomena, Joiner (2006) theorizes that some suicidal individuals acquire the capacity to engage in high-lethality behavior (i.e., suicide) by engaging in increasingly severe NSSI over time. Assuming that suicidal behavior is a *consequence* of NSSI supposes a temporal relationship that has yet to be documented. If this assumption proves true, then the data would suggest that for some, NSSI serves as a harbinger of distress that, if left unmitigated, may lead people to consider or attempt suicide.

Although it is consistently documented that people with NSSI history are at a heightened risk for suicide-related behaviors, it also is true that in at least two studies, the majority of those who engage in NSSI do not exhibit any suicidal behavior at all (Muehlenkamp & Guiterrez, 2004; Whitlock & Knox, 2007). Similarly, although NSSI is comorbid with a variety of other mental health–related disorders, it also is true that a significant number of people report NSSI as a stand-alone behavior (Gollust et al., 2008). This fact suggests that there may be a variety of NSSI trajectories in which long-term consequences range from insignificant to highly lethal, depending on factors that have yet to be identified. Since mental disorders in childhood and adolescence are significant predictors of important social and health outcomes in adulthood, including educational attainment (Breslau, Lane, Sampson, & Kessler, 2008), financial earnings (Kessler et al., 2008), marital instability (Kessler, Walters, & Forthofer, 1998), and substance use (Merikangas, et al., 1998), better understanding the particular contributions of NSSI to subsequent mental health status is important.

Treatment of Nonsuicidal Self-Injury Across the Life Span

Research on NSSI treatment, though an area of considerable importance, is still in its infancy. And, like much of the literature cited earlier, what little NSSI treatment study does exist is focused largely in adolescents (primarily clinical populations with higher NSSI severity than might be found in community populations). In a review of NSSI-focused treatment strategies, Muehlenkamp (2006) summarized promising strategies based on the inclusion of NSSI in some suicide-focused treatment models and its dominant function as an emotion regulation mechanism. She concludes that approaches utilizing largely cognitive-behavioral therapy (CBT)–based techniques are likely to prove most efficacious in NSSI treatment. Because of the time-limited and structured coping skill–building nature of the technique, she specifically identifies problem-solving therapy and dialectical behavioral therapy as the most promising CBT-based candidates. Her review of studies utilizing each of these strategies with people with suicide and NSSI-related behavior suggests that both may be efficacious under the right treatment conditions, but that neither has yet shown relative efficacy.

Review of the components likely to serve as the primary levers of change suggests that viewing the client as a partner in treatment, providing a structured treatment plan in a well-defined time frame, focusing on development and applied practice of coping skills (behavioral interventions), and addressing cognitive distortion and negative core beliefs (cognitive restructuring) may be primary ingredients of change. However, as Muehlenkamp (2006) points out, one of the major shortcomings with the studies on which these conclusions are based is that it is hard to determine how effective these treatment approaches are specifically with nonsuicidal self-injurious clients. This difficulty arises from the fact that findings are seldom specific to NSSI and are not differentiated by age (most include adolescents and adults or only adults).

Using strategies aimed at integrating CBT-based approaches with ecological and systems approaches, Miller, Rathus, and Linehan (2007) and Santisteban, Muir, Mena, and Mitriani (2003) have developed an NSSI and suicidality treatment framework based on integrative family systems-oriented approaches and salient elements of dialectical behavior therapy. Largely based on work with adolescents, these approaches expand beyond the individual level and remedial focus of CBT-based treatments to address systemic and contextual factors that serve as positive and negative reinforcements of the behavior. For example, Miller and his colleagues' (2007) treatment model includes a psychoeducational concurrent group approach for parents and adolescents, where coping capacity of both parents and adolescents is regarded as a treatment focus. Although promising, evaluation of this approach has yet to be conducted.

Similarly, Santisteban and his colleagues' (2003) integrative borderline family therapy approach integrates key elements of structural family therapy (Minuchin, 1974; Minuchin & Fishman, 1981), brief strategic family therapy (Szapocznik, Hervis, & Schwartz, 2003), multidimensional family therapy (Liddle et al., 2000), motivational-enhancement therapy (Miller & Rollnick, 2002), and the therapeutic ideas developed at the Oregon Social Learning Research Center for antisocial and conduct disorder children and adolescents (Chamberlain & Rosicky, 1995; Patterson, Reid, & Dishion, 1992). The primary aims of the integrative borderline family therapy approach are to stabilize the adolescent's self-harming and suicidal behaviors, strengthen parent–adolescent relationships, and improve family communications and conflict resolution skills. In a study of the efficacy of this approach on NSSI and suicidality, researchers found that seven out of the ten families in their project reported high satisfaction with their treatment experiences and having strong alliances with their therapists (Santisteban et al., 2003).

Although NSSI treatment trials are scarce, development and implementation models of NSSI treatment have been in use for many years. Developed and articulated by practitioners with substantial experience in treating NSSI, practitioners and consumers of these approaches often report significant success. For example, Conterio and Lader (1998) use an integrative multifaceted treatment model that incorporates psychodynamic principles and cognitive-behavioral strategies in individual and group work. In other words, the program has an "insight" component, aimed at helping the client understand him or herself better, as well as a "coping" component, in which healthier modes of relating and problem solving are learned. In this way, the impulses to injure are viewed as "clues" to underlying feelings, motives, and communications that the client cannot organize or cope with effectively. Using strategies such as the impulse log, where the client records a daily account of his or her struggles with urges to injure, the emphasis immediately is on breaking the direct path from impulse to injury and having the client reflect and manage the underlying dynamics that are driving the behavior. The program seeks to substitute delay, reflection, and healthy coping for the previous destructive cycle of self-injurious behavior. To better accommodate variation in client developmental stage at the time of entry, Lader and Conterio's (1998) approach develops unique individualized plans based on common presenting factors (e.g., family of origin issues, trauma, and loss) and unique factors related to developmental stage, emotional maturity, psychosocial history, and gender. In preliminary three time point evaluation of program effectiveness, Lader, Hertzbach, and Nock (unpublished data) found a significant decrease in medical hospitalization due to self-injury and an increase in the use of more adaptive coping strategies. Treatment effects were maintained at 12-month follow-up.

Similarly, NSSI treatment veteran Barent Walsh (2006; Walsh & Rosen, 1988) describes a cognitive-behavioral approach for treating NSSI in both adolescents and adults. He emphasizes a micro-detailed assessment that focuses on environmental, cognitive, affective, and behavioral antecedents and consequences. His treatment approach emphasizes responding to NSSI with "a low-key dispassionate demeanor" and "respectful curiosity." His interventions are skills focused in a manner derived from dialectical behavioral therapy (DBT) and other mindfulness-based therapies. He also discusses the role of body alienation in NSSI for trauma-surviving clients. He describes in detail (Walsh, 2006) the evidence-based practice of prolonged exposure (Foa, Chrestman & Gilboa-Schectman, 2009; Foa, Keane, & Friedman, 2000) for the treatment of trauma-derived NSSI and the mechanisms behind social contagion of self-injury (Walsh, 2006; Walsh & Doerfler, 2009; Walsh & Rosen, 1985). As with other commonly utilized approaches, evaluation of this approach is promising, but lacking in rigor and detail. Walsh and Doerfler (2009) described an application of DBT in a group home setting for adolescents that was successful in reducing psychiatric hospitalizations, suicidal behavior, and NSSI. Their study found that clients who remained in treatment longer (12 months or more) did better than those who left early in treatment (the mean was 4 months). Their interpretation of these results was that those who received two or more rounds of DBT skills training and individual therapy had better outcomes because they had ample time to learn, practice, and implement their DBT skills.

Selekman (2005, 2006a, 2006b, 2008, 2009) adds a unique twist to DBT-based ecological approaches to NSSI and other self-harming behaviors by focusing on utilizing strength-based approaches to engaging clients in development of treatment plans and means for utilizing competencies to overcome barriers to desired change. He underscores the importance of including and collaborating with key referent others in the ecological system, including but not limited to parents, peers, key members from the adolescent and family's social networks, as well as with involved helping professionals from larger systems. His framework focuses on the importance of transcending deficit-based theoretical frameworks in which therapists chart treatment plans and approaches and using what he calls a "collaborative strengths-based brief therapy" approach (Selekman, 2005, 2006a, 2006b, 2008, 2009). Multiple ecological levels are targeted for intervention and engagement and areas of the clients life so commonly overlooked (e.g., gender power imbalances, cultural issues, social injustice issues, incorporating spiritual dimension of clients' lives, and wider societal factors). As part of this approach, Selekman encourages self-injurious clients to identify and employ characteristics of what he calls the "spaces in between"—characteristics of the moments when clients are not self-harming or engaging in equivalent behaviors. In this way, he seeks to capitalize on the steps clients and their support system have already taken toward resolving their difficulties and preventing their situations from getting much worse.

Similar to the aforementioned models, no comprehensive evaluation of this model exists. In a small study, Selekman and Shulem (unpublished data) conducted a qualitative and process-focused study with 20 high-school-aged self-harming adolescents and their families. In this study, "self-harm" was broadly defined and included NSSI, bulimia, substance abuse, and sexually risky behavior. Most had already experienced multiple treatment experiences. All of the participants expressed high satisfaction with the collaborative strengths-based brief therapy approach and appreciate the strength-focused approach. To help assess the staying power of their positive treatment experiences, Shulem met with each family at 6 months, 1 year, and 2 years post treatment. All 20 families reported doing well and there was no return of self-harming and equivalent behavioral difficulties. The adolescents had also made improvement academically and behaviorally in school.

The paucity of well-controlled empirically validated treatment models for self-harming difficulties across all age groups has led to innovative development of a variety of promising approaches. Grounded largely in DBT (Linehan, 2000; Linehan, Heard, & Armstrong, 1993; Shearin & Linehan, 1994) and CBT (Evans et al., 1999), these approaches have yet to be systematically evaluated with NSSI and across a variety of ages.

Research Implications

Although nascent, the study of NSSI across the life span is important because it allows for consideration of developmental and contextual features in the expression and recovery process of NSSI. Such an approach has proven immensely useful in the understanding and treatment of similar conditions such as depression (Hankin et al., 1998; Rao, Hammen, & Daley, 1999) and disordered eating (Patton, Selzer, Coffey, Carlinm, & Wolfe, 1999). Using a life-span study approach mandates assessment of the extent to which NSSI characteristics vary meaningfully across developmental stages. As such, we might expect variation in a multitude of NSSI characteristics, including but not limited to, age of onset and cessation, lifetime prevalence, NSSI forms used, reasons for initiating the behavior, psychological function of the behavior, frequency and duration of the behavior, the particularities of rituals and practices used when injuring, extent and nature of association with other risk behaviors (e.g., disordered eating, drug/alcohol use, and risky sexual activity), risk and protective factors, subjective

meaning, recovery processes, and effective treatment approaches. A life span approach to the study of NSSI also assumes that the unfolding and particularities of the behavior might vary meaningfully depending on what developmental states one traverses during the periods in which NSSI is initiated, practiced, and ceased. Such a process assumes that time and developmental stages interact in ways that create particular trajectories with meaningful variation in NSSI characteristics.

As a guide for needed research, these expectations are useful. Particularly in combination with the obvious gaps in knowledge evidenced in the aforementioned review, they point to several elemental questions in need of address.

NONSUICIDAL SELF-INJURY IN CHILDREN

As evident from the brevity of the section on children earlier in this chapter, there are large gaps in knowledge about how NSSI manifests in children and with what consequences. Research aimed at understanding the epidemiology of NSSI in children, as a general population and among subpopulations, would deepen knowledge considerably. Although the general paucity of information renders germane any contribution in knowledge, we regard the following as central:

- Does "common" NSSI occur in children (i.e., does it occur in children not already exhibiting significant psychiatric conditions)? If so, how are the basic epidemiological characteristics (form, frequency, function, initial motivation, rituals and practices, risk and protective factors, comorbidity) similar to (or different from) adolescent- and adult-onset NSSI?
- Do the consequences of childhood onset NSSI differ from those of adolescents and adults? Do the subjective meanings of NSSI differ by age group?
- How are the treatment approaches and recovery processes different in childhood-onset NSSI compared to adolescent- and adult-onset NSSI? How do each of these categories vary by subgroups (e.g., demographic characteristics, psychiatric characteristics, familial characteristics, etc.)?

NONSUICIDAL SELF-INJURY IN ADOLESCENCE

Although it is clear that understanding of NSSI in adolescence is the most robust of all developmental groups considered, much remains to be learned. Fortunately, future research efforts will benefit from the small but significant body of work already accumulated and is likely to advance basic understanding of NSSI relevance to all developmental groups. The three general adolescent-specific areas that merit attention include the following:

- Is there variation in basic NSSI epidemiological characteristics among subgroups of youth (e.g., by demographic profile, family and living status, and geographic region)?
- What is the role of NSSI in normative and nonnormative adolescent developmental trajectories? Given that it is well established that the first symptoms of adult psychiatric disorders can appear very early in life and that psychiatric trajectories from childhood to adulthood can show both homotypic and heterotypic continuities, it seems plausible to theorize that even low-frequency or short-duration NSSI may serve as an indication of subclinical emotional disorders that may or may not originate from and evolve into more serious conditions. While it is quite likely that NSSI will present in more severe forms and to directly and indirectly contribute to more serious adverse outcomes when preceded and/or accompanied by risk-laden events (which may be biological, temperamental, or contextual in nature), extant research prohibits validation of this assumption and warrants additional investigation.
- What is the mechanism through which NSSI spreads in community and clinical populations? More important, what are promising means for intervention and prevention of contagion?

NONSUICIDAL SELF-INJURY IN ADULTS

Knowledge about the presentation of NSSI in adults is similarly lacking. Since adults are assumed to have accomplished many of the core developmental tasks regarded as contributors to development of NSSI in childhood and adolescence, it would be particularly useful to understand the developmental origin of adult-onset NSSI. Understanding and addressing areas where adults evidence some degree of developmental arrest may be useful in formulating treatment approaches. As with children, research aimed at understanding the epidemiology of NSSI in adults, as a general population and among subpopulations, would add much to our knowledge base.

NONSUICIDAL SELF-INJURY ACROSS THE LIFE COURSE

Better understanding of the ways in which elemental NSSI characteristics change over time is essential. Some of the core areas for study are variation in NSSI experience, consequences, treatment strategies, and recovery processes with regard to age of onset and duration. For example, future studies will ideally elucidate the following: How does developmental stage affect NSSI initiation and function, form and severity, trajectory and recovery? And how does NSSI affect the capacity to thrive or the likelihood of developing comorbid conditions? Related to this, it also is important to understand the role that developmental processes, capacities, tasks, and timing play in moderating NSSI epidemiology and trajectories. The tendency for NSSI to peak in adolescence suggests a significant interaction between development and behavior—very little of which has been explored theoretically or empirically (the one exception to this is a brief but helpful consideration of NSSI and adolescent development covered by Conterio and Lader, 1998). In light of the growing body of research that suggests that for some individuals, indicators of mental and emotional imbalance may be both subclinical and heterotypic (i.e., one of several possible manifestations of distress or disorder) (Kessler, Costello, Ries Merikangas, & Bedirhan Ustun, 2000; Pine, Cohen, Cohen, & Brook, 1999), understanding the relationship and the evolution of NSSI in relation to other mental disorders, risk behaviors, and in reference to external contexts will help to locate the particular role NSSI plays in normative and nonnormative development.

References

Alderman, T. (1997). *The scarred soul: Understanding and ending self-inflicted violence.* Oakland, CA: New Harbinger.

Anderson, L. T., & Ernst, M. (1994). Self-injury in lesch nyhan disease. *Journal of Autism and Developmental Disorders, 24,* 67–81.

Andover, M. S., Pepper, C. M., & Gibb, B. E. (2007). Self-mutilation and coping strategies in a college sample. *Suicide and Life-Threatening Behavior, 37,* 238–243.

Breslau, J., Lane, M., Sampson, N., & Kessler, R. C. (2008). Mental disorders and subsequent educational attainment in a US national sample. *Journal of Psychiatric Research, 42,* 708–716.

Briere, J., & Gil, E. (1998). Self-mutilation in clinical and general population samples: Prevalence, correlates, and functions. *American Journal of Orthopsychiatry, 68,* 609–620.

Brown, M. Z., Comtois, K. A., & Linehan, M. M. (2002). Reasons for suicide attempts and nonsuicidal self-injury in women with borderline personality disorder. *Journal of Abnormal Psychology, 111,* 198–202.

Brumberg, J. J. (2006). Are we facing an epidemic of self-injury? *Chronicle of Higher Education, 53*(16), B6.

Casey, B. J., Getz, S., & Galvan, A. (2008). The adolescent brain. *Developmental Review, 28,* 62–77.

Chamberlain, P., & Rosicky, J. G. (1995). The effectiveness of family therapy in the treatment of adolescents with conduct disorders and delinquency. *Journal of Marital and Family Therapy, 21,* 441–459.

Chapman, A. L., Gratz, K. L., & Brown, M. Z. (2006). Solving the puzzle of deliberate self-harm: The experiential avoidance model. *Behavior Research and Therapy, 44*, 371–394.

Claes, L., Vandereycken, W., & Vertommen, H. (2001). Self-injurious behaviors in eating-disordered patients. *Eating Behaviors, 2*, 263–272.

Claes, L., Vandereycken, W., & Vertommen, H. (2006). Self-injury in female versus male psychiatric patients: A comparison of characteristics, psychopathology and aggression regulation. *Personality and Individual Differences, 42*, 611–621.

Clarke, L., & Whittaker, M. (1998). Self-mutilation: Culture, contexts, and nursing responses. *Journal of Clinical Nursing, 7*, 129–137.

Connors, R. (2000). *Self-injury: Psychotherapy with people who engage in self-inflicted violence.* Northvale, NJ: Jason Aronson.

Conterio, K., & Lader, W. (1998). *Bodily harm: The breakthrough healing program for self injurers.* New York, NY: Hyperion Press.

Dahl, R., Spear, L. P., Kelley, A., Shaikh, R., & Clayton, R. (2004). *Adolescent brain development: Vulnerabilities and opportunities.* New York, NY: New York Academy of Sciences.

Deiter, P. J., Nicholls, S. S., & Pearlman, L. A. (2000). Self-injury and self capacities: Assisting an individual in crisis. *Journal of Clinical Psychology, 56*, 1173–1191.

Dennis, M. S., Wakefield, P., Molloy, C., Andrews, H., & Friedman, T. (2007). A study of self-harm in older people: Mental disorder, social factors and motives. *Aging and Mental Health, 11*, 520–525.

Dow, P. (2004). *"I feel like I'm invisible" children talking to ChildLine about self-harm.* [No. 0800-1111]. Camelot Foundation/Mental Health Foundation.

Dulit, R. A., Fyer, M. R., Leon, A. C., Brodsky, B. S., & Frances, A. J. (1994). Clinical correlates of self-mutilation in borderline personality disorder. *American Journal of Psychiatry, 151*, 1305–1311.

Evans, K., Tyrer, P., Catalan, J., Schmidt, U., Davidson, K., Dent, J.,…Thompson, S. (1999). Manual-assisted cognitive-behaviour therapy (MACT): A randomized controlled trial of a brief intervention with bibliotherapy in the treatment of recurrent deliberate self-harm. *Psychological Medicine, 29*, 19–25.

Favazza, A. R. (1998). The coming of age of self-mutilation. *Journal of Nervous and Mental Disease, 186*, 259–268.

Favazza, A. R. (1996). *Bodies under siege: Self-mutilation and body modification in culture and psychiatry* (2nd ed.). Baltimore, MD: Johns Hopkins University Press.

Favazza, A. R. (1999). Self mutilation. In D. G. Jacobs (Ed.), *The Harvard Medical School guide to suicide assessment and intervention* (pp. 125–145). San Francisco, CA: Jossey-Bass.

Favazza, A. R. (2009). A cultural understanding of nonsuicidal self-injury. In M. K. Nock (Ed.), *Understanding nonsuicidal self-injury: Origins, assessment, and treatment* (pp. 19–35). Washington, DC: American Psychological Association.

Favazza, A. R., & Conterio, K. (1989). Female habitual self-mutilators. *Acta Psychiatrica Scandinavia, 79*, 283–289.

Favazza, A. R., DeRosear, L., & Conterio, K. (1989). Self-mutilation and eating disorders. *Suicide and Life-Threatening Behavior, 19*, 352–361.

Favazza, A. R., & Simeon, D. (1995). Self-mutilation. In E. Hollander, & D. Stein (Eds.), *Impulsivity and aggression* (pp. 185–200). New York, NY: Wiley.

Figueroa, M. D. (1988). A dynamic taxonomy of self-destructive behavior. *Psychotherapy: Theory, Research, Practice, Training, 25*, 280–287.

Foa, E. B., Chrestman, K. R., & Gilboa-Schectman, E. (2009). *Prolonged exposure therapy for adolescents with PTSD.* New York, NY: Oxford University Press.

Foa, E. B., Keane, T. M., & Friedman, M. J. (2000). *Effective treatments for PTSD.* New York, NY: Guildford Press.

Galley, M. (2003, December 3). Student self-harm: Silent school crisis. *Education Week*, p. 2.

Gardner, D. L., & Cowdry, R. W. (1985). Suicidal and parasuicidial behavior in borderline personality disorder. *Psychiatric Clinics of North America, 8*, 389–403.

Gollust, S. E., Eisenberg, D., & Golberstein, E. (2008). Prevalence and correlates of self-injury among university students. *Journal of American College Health, 56*, 491–498.

Gratz, K. L., Conrad, S. D., & Roemer, L. (2002). Risk factors for deliberate self-harm among college students. *American Journal of Orthopsychiatry, 72*, 128–140.

Green, A. H. (1967). Self-mutilation in schizophrenic children. *Archives of General Psychiatry, 17*, 234–244.

Green, A. H. (1968). Self-destructive behavior in physically abused schizophrenic children: Report of cases. *Archives of General Psychiatry, 19*, 171–179.

Haines, J., & Williams, C. L. (2003). Coping and problem solving of self-mutilators. *Journal of Clinical Psychology, 59*, 1097–1106.

Hall, S., Oliver, C., & Murphy, G. (2001). Self-injurious behaviour in young children with lesch nyhan syndrome. *Developmental Medicine and Child Neurology, 43*, 745–749.

Hankin, B. L., Abramson, L. Y., Moffitt, T. E., Silva, P. A., McGee, R., & Angell, K. E. (1998). Development of depression from preadolescence to young adulthood: Emerging gender differences in a 10-year longitudinal study. *Journal of Abnormal Psychology, 107*, 128–140.

Hare, T. A., Tottenham, N., Galvan, A., Voss, H. U., Glover, G. H., & Casey, B. J. (2008). Biological substrates of emotional reactivity and regulation in adolescence during an emotional go-nogo task. *Biological Psychiatry, 63(10)*, 927–934.

Hasking, P., Momeni, R., Swannell, S., & Chia, S. (2008). The nature and extent of non-suicidal self-injury in a non-clinical sample of young adults. *Archives of Suicide Research, 12*, 208–218.

Havighurst, R. J. (1972). *Developmental tasks and education.* New York, NY: David McKay.

Hawton, K., & Harriss, L. (2006). Deliberate self-harm in people aged 60 years and over: Characteristics and outcome of a 20-year cohort study. *International Journal of Geriatric Psychiatry, 21*, 572–581.

Hawton, K., & Rodham, K. (2006). *By their own young hand: Deliberate self-harm and suicidal ideas in adolescents.* London, UK: Jessica Kingsley.

Hawton, K., Rodham, K., Evans, E., & Weatherall, R. (2002). Deliberate self harm in adolescents: Self report survey in schools in England. *British Medical Journal, 325*, 1207–1211.

Heath, N., Toste, J., & Beettam, E. (2006). "I am not well-equipped": High school teachers' perceptions of self-injury. *Canadian Journal of School Psychology, 21*, 73–92.

Heath, N. L., Ross, S., Toste, J. R., Charlebois, A., & Nedecheva, T. (2009). Retrospective analysis of social factors and nonsuicidal self-injury among young adults. *Canadian Journal of Behavioral Sciences, 41*, 180–186.

Heath, N. L., Toste, J. R., Nedecheva, T., & Charlebois, A. (2008). An examination of nonsuicidal self-injury among college students. *Journal of Mental Health Counseling, 30,* 137–156.

Himber, J. (1994). Blood rituals: Self-cutting in female psychiatric inpatients. *Psychotherapy: Theory, Research, Practice, Training, 31,* 620–631.

Holmes, A., & Nadelson, C. A. (Eds.). (2000). *Cutting the pain away: Understanding self mutilation.* Philadelphia, PA: Chelsea House.

Jacobs, B. W., & Isaacs, S. (1986). Pre-pubertal anorexia nervosa: A retrospective controlled study. *Journal of Child Psychology and Psychiatry, 27,* 237–250.

Jacobson, C. M., & Gould, M. (2007). The epidemiology and phenomenology of non-suicidal self-injurious behavior among adolescents: A critical review of the literature. *Archives of Suicide Research, 11,* 129–147.

Joiner, T. E. (2006). *Why people die by suicide.* Cambridge, MA: Harvard University Press.

Kessler, R. C., Berglund, P., Demler, O., Jin, R., Merikangas, K. R., & Walters, E. E. (2005). Lifetime prevalence and age-of-onset distributions of DSM-IV disorders in the national comorbidity survey replication. *Archives of General Psychiatry, 62,* 593–602.

Kessler, R. C., Costello, E. J., Ries Merikangas, K., & Bedirhan Ustun, T. (2000). *Psychiatric epidemiology: Recent advances and future directions.* [No. 01-3537]. Washington, DC: Mental Health.

Kessler, R. C., Heeringa, S., Lakoma, M. D., Petukhova, M., Rupp, A. E., Wang, P. S.,...Zaslavsky, A. M. (2008). Individual and societal effects of mental disorders on earnings in the United States: Results from the national comorbidity survey replication. *American Journal of Psychiatry, 165,* 703–711.

Kessler, R. C., Walters, E. E., & Forthofer, M. S. (1998). The social consequences of psychiatric disorders, III: Probability of marital stability. *American Journal of Psychiatry, 155,* 1092–1096.

Klonsky, E. D. (2007a). The functions of deliberate self-injury: A review of the empirical evidence. *Clinical Psychology Review, 27,* 226–239.

Klonsky, E. D. (2007b). Non-suicidal self-injury: An introduction. *Journal of Clinical Psychology, 63,* 1039–1043.

Klonsky, E. D., & Glenn, C. R. (2009). Assessing the functions of non-suicidal self-injury: Psychometric properties of the inventory of statements about self-injury (ISAS). *Journal of Psychopathology and Behavioral Assessment, 31,* 215–219.

Klonsky, E. D., & Muehlenkamp, J. J. (2007). Self-injury: A research review for the practitioner. *Journal of Clinical Psychology, 63,* 1045–1056.

Klonsky, E. D., & Olino, T. M. (2008). Identifying clinically distinct subgroups of self-injurers among young adults: A latent class analysis. *Journal of Consulting and Clinical Psychology, 76,* 22–27.

Klonsky, E. D., Oltmanns, T. F., & Turkheimer, E. (2003). Deliberate self-harm in a nonclinical population: Prevalence and psychological correlates. *American Journal of Psychiatry, 160,* 1501–1508.

Kumar, G., Pepe, D., & Steer, R. A. (2004). Adolescent psychiatric inpatients' self-reported reasons for cutting themselves. *Journal of Nervous and Mental Disease, 192,* 830–836.

Laye-Gindhu, A., & Schonert-Reichl, K. A. (2005). Nonsuicidal self-harm among community adolescents: Understanding the "whats" and "whys" of self-harm. *Journal of Youth and Adolescence, 34,* 447–457.

Lerner, R. M., & Steinberg, L. (Eds.). (2004). *Handbook of adolescent psychology* (2nd ed.). Hoboken, NJ: Wiley.

Lewinsohn, P. M., Rohde, P., Seeley, J. R., & Baldwin, C. L. (2001). Gender differences in suicide attempts from adolescence to young adulthood. *Journal of the American Academy of Adolescent Psychiatry, 40,* 427–434.

Lewinsohn, P. M., Seeley, J. R., Moerk, K. C., & Striegel-Moore, R. H. (2002). Gender differences in eating disorder symptoms in young adults. *International Journal of Eating Disorders, 32,* 426–440.

Liddle, H. A., Rowe, C., Diamond, G. M., Sessa, F. M., Schmidt, S., & Ettinger, D. (2000). Toward a developmental family therapy: The clinical utility of research on adolescence. *Journal of Marital and Family Therapy, 26,* 485–500.

Linehan, M. M. (1993). *Cognitive-behavioral treatment with borderline personality disorder.* New York, NY: Guilford Press.

Linehan, M. M. (2000). The empirical basis of dialectical behavior therapy: Development of new treatments versus evaluation of existing treatments. *Clinical Psychology: Science and Practice, 7,* 113–119.

Linehan, M. M., Heard, H. L., & Armstrong, H. E. (1993). Naturalistic follow-up of a behavioral treatment for chronically parasuicidal borderline patients. *Archives of General Psychiatry, 50,* 971–974.

Lloyd-Richardson, E. E., Perrine, N., Dierker, L., & Kelley, M. L. (2007). Characteristics and functions of non-suicidal self-injury in a community sample of adolescents. *Psychological Medicine, 37,* 1183–1192.

Martin, G., Rozanes, P., Pearce, C., & Allison, S. (1995). Adolescent suicide, depression and family dysfunction. *Acta Psychiatrica Scandinavica, 92,* 336–344.

Mathews, C. A., Waller, J., Glidden, D. V., Lowe, T. L., Herrera, L. D., Budman, C. L.,...Reus, V. I. (2004). Self injurious behaviour in tourette syndrome: Correlates with impulsivity and impulse control. *Journal of Neurology, Neurosurgery and Psychiatry, 75,* 1149–1155.

Meltzer, H., Gatward, R., Goodman, R., & Ford, T. (2001). *Children and adolescents who try to harm, hurt or kill themselves. A report of further analysis from the national survey of the mental health of children and adolescents in Great Britain in 1999.* London, UK: Office for National Statistics.

Merikangas, K. R., Mehta, R. L., Molnar, B. E., Walters, E. E., Swendsen, J. D., Aguilar-Gaziola, S.,...Kessler, R. C. (1998). Comorbidity of substance use disorders with mood and anxiety disorders: Results of the international consortium in psychiatric epidemiology. *Addictive Behaviors, 23,* 893–907.

Miller, A. L., Rathus, J. H., & Linehan, M. (2007). *Dialectical behavior therapy for suicidal adolescents.* New York, NY: Guilford Press.

Miller, W. R., & Rollnick, S. (2002). *Motivational interviewing* (2nd ed.). New York, NY: Guilford Press.

Minuchin, S. (1974). *Families and family therapy.* Cambridge, MA: Harvard University Press.

Minuchin, S., & Fishman, H. C. (1981). *Family therapy techniques.* Cambridge, MA: Harvard University Press.

Muehlenkamp, J. J. (2005). Self-injurious behavior as a separate clinical syndrome. *American Journal of Orthopsychiatry, 75,* 324–333.

Muehlenkamp, J. (2006). Empirically supported treatments and general therapy guidelines for non-suicidal self-injury. *Journal of Mental Health Counseling, 28,* 166–185.

Muehlenkamp, J. J., & Gutierrez, P. M. (2004). An investigation of differences between self-injurious behavior and suicide attempts in a sample of adolescents. *Suicide and Life-Threatening Behavior, 34*, 12–24.

Muehlenkamp, J., & Gutierrez, P. M. (2007). Risk for suicide attempts among adolescents who engage in non-suicidal self-injury. *Archives of Suicide Research, 11*, 69–82.

Murray, C. D., & Fox, J. (2006). Do internet self-harm discussion groups alleviate or exacerbate self-harming behaviour? *Australian e-Journal for the Advancement of Mental Health, 5*(3), 1–9.

Murray, C. D., Warm, A., & Fox, J. (2005). The internet, self-harm, and adolescents. *Australian e-Journal for the Advancement of Mental Health, 4*(1), 1–9.

Najmi, S., Wegner, D. M., & Nock, M. K. (2007). Thought suppression and self-injurious thoughts and behaviors. *Behaviour Research and Therapy, 45*, 1957–1965.

Nixon, M. K., Cloutier, P., & Jansson, S. M. (2008). Nonsuicidal self-harm in youth: A population-based survey. *Canadian Medical Association Journal, 178*, 306–312.

Nixon, M. K., Cloutier, P. F., & Aggarwal, S. (2002). Affect regulation and addictive aspects of repetitive self-injury in hospitalized adolescents. *Journal of the American Academy of Child and Adolescent Psychiatry, 41*, 1333–1341.

Nock, M., & Favazza, A. R. (2009). Non-suicidal self-injury: Definition and classification. In M. K. Nock (Ed.), *Understanding non-suicidal self-injury: Origins, assessment, and treatment* (pp. 9–18). Washington, DC: American Psychological Association.

Nock, M. K., Joiner, T. E., Gordon, K. H., Lloyd-Richardson, E., & Prinstein, M. J. (2006). Non-suicidal self-injury among adolescents: Diagnostic correlates and relation to suicide attempts. *Psychiatry Research, 144*, 65–72.

Nock, M. K., & Prinstein, M. J. (2004). A functional approach to the assessment of self-mutilative behavior. *Journal of Consulting and Clinical Psychology, 72*, 885–890.

Nock, M. K., & Prinstein, M. J. (2005). Contextual features and behavioral functions of self-mutilation among adolescents. *Journal of Abnormal Psychology, 114*, 140–146.

Nock, M. K., Prinstein, M. J., & Sterba, S. K. (2009). Revealing the form and function of self-injurious thoughts and behaviors: A real-time ecological assessment study among adolescents and young adults. *Journal of Abnormal Psychology, 118*(4), 816.

Nock, M. K., Wedig, M. M., Holmberg, E. B., & Hooley, J. M. (2008). The Emotion Reactivity Scale: Development, evaluation, and relation to self-injurious thoughts and behaviors. *Behavior Therapy, 39*, 107–116.

Ogle, R. L., & Clements, C. M. (2008). Deliberate self-harm and alcohol involvement in college-aged females: A controlled comparison in a nonclinical sample. *American Journal of Orthopsychiatry, 78*, 442–448.

Osuch, E. A., Noll, J. G., & Putnam, F. W. (1999). The motivations for self-injury in psychiatric inpatients. *Psychiatry, 62*, 334–346.

Pao, P. N. (1969). The syndrome of delicate self-cutting. *British Journal of Medical Psychology, 42*, 195–206.

Parks, S. M., & Feldman, S. M. (2006). Self-injurious behavior in the elderly. *Consultant Pharmacist, 21*(11), 905–910.

Patterson, G. R., Reid, J. B., & Dishion, T. J. (1992). *Antisocial boys: A social interactional approach* (Vol. 4). Eugene, OR: Castalia.

Patton, G. C., Selzer, R., Coffe, C., Carlin, J. B., & Wolfe, R. (1999). Onset of adolescent eating disorders: Population based cohort study over 3 years. *British Medical Journal, 318*, 765–768.

Piaget, J. (1964). Part 1 cognitive development in children: Piaget. Development and learning. *Journal of Research in Science Teaching, 2*, 176–186.

Pierce, D. (1987). Deliberate self-harm in the elderly. *International Journal of Geriatric Psychiatry, 2*, 105–110.

Pine, D. S., Cohen, E., Cohen, P., & Brook, J. (1999). Adolescent depressive symptoms as predictors of adult depression: Moodiness or mood disorder? *American Journal of Psychiatry, 156*, 133–135.

Polk, E., & Liss, M. (2007). Psychological characteristics of self-injurious behavior. *Personality and Individual Differences, 43*, 567–577.

Prinstein, M. J., Guerry, J. D., Browne, C. B., & Rancourt, D. (2009). Interpersonal models of nonsuicidal self-injury. In M. K. Nock (Ed.), *Understanding nonsuicidal self-injury: Origins, assessment, and treatment* (pp. 79–98). Washington, DC: American Psychological Association.

Purington, A., Whitlock, J., & Pochtar, R. (2009). Non-suicidal self-injury in secondary schools: A descriptive study of prevalence, characteristics, and interventions. *Manuscript Submitted for Publication,*

Putnam, N., & Stein, M. (1985). Self-inflicted injuries in childhood. A review and diagnostic approach. *Clinical Pediatrics, 24*, 514–518.

Rao, U., Hammen, C., & Daley, S. E. (1999). Continuity of depression during the transition to adulthood: A 5-year longitudinal study of young women. *American Academy of Child and Adolescent Psychiatry, 38*, 908–915.

Robertson, M. M. (Ed.). (1992). *Self-injurious behavior and Tourette syndrome.* New York: Raven Press.

Rodham, K., & Hawton, K. (2009). Epidemiology and phenomenology of nonsuicidal self-injury. In M. K. Nock (Ed.), *Understanding nonsuicidal self-injury: Origins, assessment, and treatment* (pp. 37–62). Washington, DC: American Psychological Association.

Rodham, K., Hawton, K., & Evans, E. (2004). Reasons for deliberate self-harm: Comparison of self-poisoners and self-cutters in a community sample of adolescents. *Journal of the American Academy of Adolescent Psychiatry, 43*, 80–87.

Ross, S., Heath, N., & Toste, J. (2009). Non-suicidal self-injury and eating pathology in high school students. *American Journal of Orthopsychiatry, 29*, 83–92.

Ross, S., & Heath, N. (2002). A study of the frequency of self-mutilation in a community sample of adolescents. *Journal of Youth and Adolescence, 31*, 66–77.

Rutledge, C. M., Rimer, D., & Scott, M. (2008). Vulnerable goth teens: The role of schools in this psychosocial high-risk culture. *Journal of School Health, 78*, 459.

Sansone, R. A., & Levitt, J. L. (2002). Self-harm behaviors among those with eating disorders: An overview. *Eating Disorders, 10*, 205–213.

Santisteban, D. A., Muir, J. A., Mena, M. P., & Mitrani, V. B. (2003). Integrated adolescent with BPD features family therapy: Meeting the challenges of treating adolescent with BPD features. *Psychotherapy: Theory, Research, Practice, Training, 40*, 251–264.

Selekman, M. D. (2005). *Pathways to change: Brief therapy with difficult adolescents* (2nd ed.). New York, NY: Guilford Press.

Selekman, M. D. (2006a). Co-authoring solution-determined stories with self-harming adolescents. *Context, 87*, 34–40.

Selekman, M. D. (2006b). *Working with self-harming adolescents: A collaborative strengths-based approach*. New York, NY: W. W. Norton.

Selekman, M. D. (2008). Mission possible: The art of engaging tough teens. *Psychotherapy Networker, 32*, 23–24.

Selekman, M. D. (2009). *The adolescent and young adult self-harming treatment manual: A collaborative strengths-based brief therapy approach*. New York, NY: W. W. Norton.

Shaw, J. A. (2000). Children, adolescents, and trauma. *Psychiatric Quarterly, 71*, 227–243.

Shearin, E. N., & Linehan, M. M. (1994). Dialectical behavior therapy for borderline personality disorder: Theoretical and empirical foundations. *Acta Psychiatrica Scandinavica, Supplementum, 379*, 61–68.

Shentoub, S. A., & Soulairac, A. (1961). L'enfant automutilateur. *Psychiatrie De l'Enfant, 3*, 111–145.

Sher, L., & Stanley, B. H. (2008). The role of endogenous opioids in the pathophysiology of self-injurious and suicidal behavior. *Archives of Suicide Research, 12*, 299–308.

Simpson, C. A., & Porter, G. L. (1981). Self-mutilation in children and adolescents. *Bulletin of the Meninger Clinic, 45*, 428–438.

Steinberg, L. (2004). Risk taking in adolescence: What changes, and why? *Annals New York Academy of Sciences, 1021*, 51–58.

Steinberg, L., & Cauffman, E. (1996). Maturity of judgment in adolescence: Psychosocial factors in adolescent decision-making. *Law and Human Behavior, 20*, 249–272.

Stirn, A., & Hinz, A. (2008). Tattoos, body piercings, and self-injury: Is there a connection? investigations on a core group of participants practicing body modification. *Psychotherapy Research, 18*, 326–333.

Strong, M. (1998). *A bright red scream: Self-mutilation and the language of pain*. New York, NY: Viking.

Szapocznik, J., Hervis, O., & Schwartz, S. (2003). *Brief strategic family therapy for adolescent drug abuse*. [NIH Pub. No. 03-4751]. Bethesda, MD: National Institute on Drug Abuse.

Tantam, D., & Wittaker, J. (1992). Personality disorder and self-wounding. *British Journal of Psychiatry, 161*, 451–464.

Tantam, D., & Whittaker, J. (1993). Self-wounding and personality disorder. In P. Tyrer & G. Stein (Eds.), *Personality disorder reviewed* (pp. 191–224). London, UK: American Psychiatric Press.

Walsh, B. (2006). *Treating self-injury: A practical guide*. New York, NY: Guilford Press.

Walsh, B. (2007). Clinical assessment of self-injury: A practical guide. *Journal of Clinical Psychology, 63*, 1057–1068.

Walsh, B., & Doerfler, L. A. (2009). Residential treatment of self-injury. In M. K. Nock (Ed.), *Understanding non-suicidal self-injury: Origins, assessment, and treatment* (pp. 271–290). Washington, DC: American Psychological Association.

Walsh, B., & Rosen, P. (1985). Self-mutilation and contagion: An empirical test. *American Journal of Psychiatry, 142*, 119–120.

Walsh, B., & Rosen, P. (1988). *Self-mutilation: Theory, research and treatment*. New York, NY: Guilford Press.

Welsh, P. (2004). Students' scars point to emotional pain. *USA Today*, p. 11A.

Whitlock, J. (2009, June). *NSSI in a college population: Trends and emergent findings from the 8 college study*. Presentation at the Annual Meeting of the International Society for the Study of Self-Injury, Long Island, NY.

Whitlock, J., Eckenrode, J., & Silverman, D. (2006). Self-injurious behaviors in a college population. *Pediatrics, 117*, 1939–1948.

Whitlock, J., Muehlenkamp, J., Purington, A., Eckenrode, J., Barreira, P., Baral-Abrahms, G., ...Knox, K. (2011). Non-suicidal self-injury in a college population: General trends and gender differences. *Journal of the American College of Health, 59*(8), 691–698.

Whitlock, J., Purington, A., Eells, G., & Cummings, N. (2009). Self-injurious behavior in college populations: Perceptions and experiences of college mental health providers. *Journal of College Student Psychotherapy, 23*, 172–183.

Whitlock, J., Purington, A., & Gershkovich, M. (2009). Media, the internet, and nonsuicidal self-injury. In M. K. Nock (Ed.), *Understanding nonsuicidal self-injury: Origins, assessment, and treatment* (pp. 139–155). Washington, DC: American Psychological Association.

Whitlock, J. L., & Knox, K. (2007). The relationship between suicide and self-injury in a young adult population. *Archives of Pediatrics and Adolescent Medicine, 161*, 634–640.

Whitlock, J. L., Muehlenkamp, J., & Eckenrode, J. (2008). Variation in non-suicidal self-injury: Identification of latent classes in a community population of young adults. *Journal of Clinical Child and Adolescent Psychology, 37*, 725–735.

Whitlock, J. L., Powers, J. L., & Eckenrode, J. (2006). The cutting edge: The internet and adolescent self-injury. *Developmental Psychology, 42*, 407–17.

Whittaker found guilty. (1880, May 30). *New York Times*, p. 2.

Wichstrom, L. (2009). Predictors of non-suicidal self-injury versus attempted suicide: Similar or different? *Archives of Suicide Research, 13*, 105–122.

Winchel, R. M., & Stanley, M. (1991). Self-injurious behavior: A review of the behavior and biology of self-mutilation. *American Journal of Psychiatry, 148*, 306–317.

Yates, T. M. (2004). The developmental psychopathology of self-injurious behavior: Compensatory regulation in posttraumatic adaptation. *Clinical Psychological Review, 24*, 35–74.

Yates, T. M., Luthar, S. S., & Tracy, A. J. (2008). Nonsuicidal self-injury among "privileged" youths: Longitudinal and cross-sectional approaches to developmental process. *Journal of Consulting and Clinical Psychology, 76*, 52–62.

Yip, K., Ngan, M., & Lam, I. (2002). An explorative study of peer influence and response to adolescent self-cutting behavior in Hong Kong. *Smith Studies in Social Work, 72*, 379–401.

Young, R., Sweeting, H., & West, P. (2006). Prevalence of deliberate self harm and attempted suicide within contemporary goth youth subculture: Longitudinal cohort study. *British Medical Journal, 332*, 1058–1061.

Zanarini, M. C., Frankenburg, F. R., Hennen, J., Reich, B., & Silk, K. R. (2005). The Mclean study of adult development (MSAD): Overview and implications of the first six years of prospective follow-up. *Journal of Personality Disorders, 19*, 505–523.

PART 3

Approaches to Understanding Self-Injurious Behaviors

Genetic and Neurobiological Approaches to Understanding Suicidal Behaviors

Laura M. Fiori, Carl Ernst, *and* Gustavo Turecki

Abstract

Historically, societal views on suicidal behaviors have largely revolved around the religious and moral implications of ending one's life. These views have differed greatly across cultures and time, and only recently has it become recognized that suicidal behaviors often reflect underlying mental illnesses and are not simply matters of conscience. This understanding led to the awareness that suicide could be empirically studied: a fundamental idea that has ultimately given rise to the current state of suicide research. This chapter focuses on studies investigating neurobiological processes associated with suicide. We first examine evidence implicating genetic factors in the susceptibility to suicidal behaviors, and subsequently, we discuss molecular, neurochemical, and other biological approaches used by studies investigating this complex phenotype.

Key Words: suicide, suicidal behavior, association studies, gene expression, neurobiology, neurotransmitter systems

Over the past century, myriad studies have provided recognition and insight into the presence and role of hereditary factors in relation to suicidal behaviors, and they have played a crucial role in directing future studies to understanding the development and clinical presentation of these behaviors. Arising from this, examination of the most basic of inherited factors, the genetic code, became a logical step in uncovering molecular mechanisms involved in suicide. In parallel, neurobiological studies have provided evidence for the presence of specific biological alterations which are functionally associated with suicidal behaviors. Through the integration of genetic and neurobiological findings, the identification of the biological substrates of suicide and the characterization of the mechanisms by which these act and interact will eventually allow us to develop improved methods by which to treat and prevent suicidal behaviors. While historically there has been a separation between epidemiological, psychosocial,

genetic, and neurobiological studies, these fields have begun to merge in recent decades as it has become increasingly evident that there is a strong interplay between each of these factors. As such, although the focus of this chapter is on the genetic and neurobiological aspects of suicidal behavior, most of the studies incorporate many additional variables, which may eventually allow us to develop an integrated understanding of the biological and environmental factors involved in the etiology and pathology of suicidal behaviors. This chapter first reviews research into the genetic epidemiology and neurochemistry of suicide, then examines how genetic and molecular studies will be instrumental in gaining important insight into neurobiological factors underlying the suicide process.

Genetics

The idea that hereditary factors played a role in suicidal behavior is not new and has been noted by many researchers over time, as early as 1790, when Charles Moore, in his book entitled *A Full Enquiry Into the Subject of Suicide*, noted that suicide tended to cluster in families. In the centuries following this publication, case reports of twins concordant for suicide began to emerge, pointing the way toward the understanding that suicidal behaviors may possess what today we interpret as a genetic component. In 1949, Franz Kallman and colleagues noted that "suicide is likely to be conceded as the least disputable example of a trait determined largely by heredity, while accidental death is often found to be the favorite choice of a condition attributed to strictly environmental influences" (Kallmann, De Porte, De Porte, & Feingold, 1949, p. 113).

The idea that suicide possessed a neurobiological basis also began to emerge in the 1900s. In a set of papers published in the 1930s, Nolan Lewis reviewed many of the demographic, social, and medical factors associated with suicide and attempted suicide, and noted the importance of biology, particularly in terms of "adaptation" for suicidal behaviors (Lewis, 1933, 1934). A series of studies followed that progressively helped in the recognition that suicidal behavior had a biological basis. Progressively, researchers became interested in the investigation of the genetic epidemiology of suicide and, more recently, on the study of molecular factors conferring susceptibility to suicidal behavior and underlying the suicide process. This section first examines studies that support the existence of heritable factors in suicidal behavior, then examines methods by which these genetic factors have been studied.

Whereas case-report studies played an important role in first demonstrating the potential for the involvement of heritable factors in suicidality, these types of studies have an inherent risk of representing chance findings and lack the power to properly assess genetic and environmental effects that may be involved in the transmission of suicidal behavior. In the last few decades, numerous family, twin, and adoption studies have provided the necessary statistical evidence to support the role of genetic factors in the transmission of suicidal behavior and have allowed researchers to identify specific clinical and behavioral components which are associated with the familial transmission of suicidality. In addition, these studies have suggested that genetic factors accounting for the transmission of suicidal behavior are distinct from those influencing the transmission of other psychiatric disorders.

Family Studies

Family studies allow us to test the hypothesis that a trait aggregates (clusters) in families, as well as to investigate patterns of transmission and other factors, such as cotransmitted conditions, that may help to explain familial aggregation. One of the first studies to quantify the magnitude of familial aggregation of suicide completion was the seminal psychological autopsy study conducted by Eli Robins and colleagues in 1959, which found that between 6% and 31% of first-degree and second-degree relatives of suicide probands had a history of suicidal behavior, depending on the psychiatric diagnosis of the proband. A series of subsequent studies has supported this observation in different populations (Barraclough, Bunch, Nelson, & Sainsbury, 1974; Murphy & Wetzel, 1982; Roy, 1983; Woodruff, Clayton, & Guze, 1972) using primarily a family-history design, that is, asking the proband or an informant about familial recurrence of suicidal behavior.

Family-history studies are limited by several biases and cannot properly investigate familial aggregation. One of the central questions puzzling researchers investigating familial transmission of suicidal behavior has been whether familial aggregation of suicide was explained by familial aggregation of psychiatric disorders, which frequently cosegregate in suicidal families. Properly designed family studies can address this type of question. One of the first studies to suggest that suicidal behavior was transmitted independently from psychiatric illnesses was the family study by Tsuang in 1983, who examined, by means of a combination of direct interviews and medical charts, relatives of patients with schizophrenia, bipolar disorder, and depression, of whom a subset had completed suicide (Tsuang, 1983). This study identified different rates of risk for suicide in the relatives of suicides, nonsuicides, and nonpsychiatric controls, suggesting that transmission of psychopathology and suicide were not identical.

Greater proof for the independent transmission of psychiatric disorders and suicide came from the study by Egeland and Sussex, who examined mood disorders and suicide in the Old Order Amish, an isolated religious community in Pennsylvania (Egeland & Sussex, 1985). Using the extensive medical and genealogical records kept by this community over the past century, they identified 26 suicide completers, all clustered in four families in which mood disorders also displayed familial aggregation. No suicides occurred in other families who also displayed aggregation of similar mood disorders, strongly suggesting that genetic factors which increase the predisposition to suicide completion are distinct from those affecting the predisposition to other psychiatric disorders. However, as no suicides were found among families without mood disorders, it also seemed clear that transmission of suicidal behavior was conditional on the liability for psychopathology.

The first study to properly measure the familial aggregation of suicide, while adjusting for the role of psychopathology, was the study conducted by Brent and colleagues, which focused on adolescent suicide completers. They found higher recurrence in families of suicide completers compared to those of controls, an effect that remained significant after controlling for the increased rates of psychopathology in the probands and their families (Brent, Bridge, Johnson, & Connolly, 1996). Specifically, they found adjusted recurrence risks of 5.2 and 2.4, respectively, for first- and second-degree relatives of suicide completers. This study also found that probands with high levels of Cluster B traits had higher familial loadings of suicide than other probands, an observation that is consistent with the notion that part of the familial aggregation of suicidal behavior could be attributed to cosegregation with impulsive-aggressive traits. Similar results were found in a study conducted by our group in families of adult suicide completers and population controls (Kim et al., 2005). We found that relatives of suicide completers were over 10 times more likely than relatives of comparison subjects to attempt or complete suicide after controlling for psychopathology. While relatives of suicide completers were not more likely to exhibit suicidal ideation, they had more severe suicidal ideation than relatives of comparison subjects. Similarly to the observations made by Brent et al. (1996), we found that familial aggregation was stronger for the suicide completers diagnosed with Cluster B personality disorders (Kim et al., 2005).

As these studies were only able to control statistically for the effects of psychopathology, our group more recently conducted a study using a three-group design. More specifically, we conducted direct and blind assessments of a total of 718 relatives from 51 families of depressed suicide probands, 34 families of living depressed probands without histories of suicidal behavior, and 35 families of psychiatrically normal community controls. We found clear evidence that familial transmission of suicide and major depression are distinct, while partially overlapping. In addition, using this design we could

demonstrate that histories of aggression and Cluster B personality disorders function as endophenotypes of suicide; in other words, they account for familial recurrence of suicidal behavior (McGirr et al., 2009).

Twin Studies

Compared to family studies, twin studies can separate environmental from genetic effects, as monozygotic (MZ) twins and dizygotic (DZ) twins share, respectively, 100% and an average of 50% of the genomic variants, while both twin types equally share the environment. The first case report of suicide concordance among MZ twins was made almost two centuries ago, and since that time numerous other case reports and twin studies have emerged, of which the majority have found support for a higher concordance of suicidal behavior among MZ compared to DZ twins (Turecki, 2001).

The three largest studies examining suicidal behavior in twins used twin pairs recruited through twin registries and examined only suicide attempts or suicidal ideation. The largest study was performed by Statham and colleagues using an Australian sample and found that the history of suicidal behavior in one twin was a predictor for suicidal behavior in MZ but not DZ twins (Statham et al., 1998). This study also found that genetic factors explained approximately 45% of the variance in these behaviors and 55% of the heritability for serious suicide attempts. Following this study, Glowinski and colleagues examined a sample of female adolescent twins from the United States and found higher rates of suicide attempts in MZ twins, with genetic influences explaining 35%–75% of the variance in risk (Glowinski et al., 2001). Thirdly, using the Vietnam Era Twin Registry from the United States, Fu and colleagues examined suicidal ideation and suicide attempts in men and found that after controlling for psychiatric disorders, the heritability for ideation was 36%, and the heritability for suicide attempts was 17% (Fu et al., 2002).

Given the infrequent nature of suicide completion, studies examining concordance rates for suicide completion have been forced to use much smaller sample sizes. Roy and colleagues examined 176 twin pairs in which at least one twin had committed suicide and found that the concordance for suicide completion was 11.3% in the MZ twins and 1.8% in the DZ twins (Roy, Segal, Centerwall, & Robinette, 1991). Roy and colleagues also examined rates of suicide attempts in surviving cotwins and found that 10 of 26 surviving MZ cotwins had attempted suicide compared to 0 of 9 surviving DZ cotwins (Roy, Segal, & Sarchiapone, 1995). In order to determine whether this elevated risk was due to factors associated with grief, rather than a shared inheritance for suicidality, Segal and Roy examined suicide attempts in surviving cotwins whose twin died by means other than suicide. They found no differences between rates of suicide attempts between MZ and DZ twins, supporting the hypothesis that the higher rates of concordance were specifically due to the inheritance of risk factors for suicide (Segal & Roy, 1995).

Adoption Studies

Similar to twin studies, adoption studies can also differentiate between genetic and environmental factors by comparing the rates of suicidality or other psychiatric disorders between the biological and adoptive relatives of adoptees.

The first study to specifically examine the relationship between suicide completion in adoptees and suicide completion among their adopted and biological families was carried out by Schulsinger and colleagues 30 years ago (Schulsinger, Kety, Rosenthal, & Wender, 1979). This study compared rates of familial (biological and adopted) suicides between 57 adoptees who committed suicide and 57 living adoptees, identified using the Danish population registry. Among the 269 biological relatives of suicide completers, 12 had committed suicide, compared to 2 biological relatives of the control adoptees. Additionally, they found no incidents of suicide among the adoptive families of the suicide completers or controls, highlighting the important role of genetic, rather than environmental influences.

A second adoption study was performed by Wender and colleagues using a larger sample from the Danish population registry, comprised of 71 adoptees with affective disorders and 71 healthy adopted controls (Wender et al., 1986). They identified increases in both attempted and completed suicides among biological relatives of adoptees with affective disorders compared to the biological relatives of controls. Rates of suicide completions were particularly elevated and displayed a 15-fold higher prevalence in the biological relatives of the cases. They found no differences in suicide attempts or completion among the adoptive relatives, again demonstrating the importance of heritable factors. Interestingly, results showed only an eight-fold increase in unipolar depression, which provides additional support for the independent heritability

for factors related to suicide and other psychiatric disorders. Indeed, they found that affect regulation was a greater indicator than depression for suicidal behavior, and they proposed that impulse control may play an important role in suicide.

Third, and most recently, a study using a large sample from the National Swedish Register identified greater rates of suicidal behavior in adoptees compared to nonadopted controls and observed that psychiatric morbidity in the biological parents accounted for a third of the increased risk (von Borczyskowski, Hjern, Lindblad, & Vinnerljung, 2006).

Identification of Genetic Loci

The results of the family, twin, and adoption studies have made it clear that heritable factors play a role in suicidal behaviors and, in doing so, point toward a role for genetic factors in the etiology and psychopathology of suicide. Next is a summary of studies conducted attempting to map and/or identify molecular genetic factors implicated in suicidal behavior.

ASSOCIATION AND LINKAGE STUDIES

Linkage studies investigate cosegregation between a phenotype and genetic markers, and they have been typically non–hypothesis driven, as they have tested markers spanning the entire genome. Relatively few linkage studies have been conducted with suicidal behavior compared to studies investigating different psychiatric phenotypes. In part, this is related to the challenges associated with having access to biological material from affected relatives, some of whom may have died by suicide. As such, only three linkage studies have been conducted investigating loci segregating with suicidal behavior. One study examined suicidality among families with alcohol-dependent probands and found that suicide attempts and suicidality were linked with regions on chromosomes 1, 2, and 3 (Hesselbrock et al., 2004). Another study using probands with recurrent early-onset major depressive disorder identified a number of chromosomal regions linked with suicide attempts, including 2p, 5q, 6q, 8p, 11q, and Xq (Zubenko et al., 2004). A third study, performed in a large bipolar pedigree, identified regions linked with either suicide completions (2q, 4p, 6q) or suicide attempts (10q) (Cheng et al., 2006). As seen for other phenotypes, there has been a decrease in the level of enthusiasm for linkage studies, at least as conducted until now, as they are seen as not having yielded meaningful and consistent results.

Unlike linkage studies, association studies do not investigate cosegregation but instead compare genetic variability between all cases and controls. Numerous association studies have been performed to investigate polymorphisms in candidate genes, many of which will be discussed in later sections. Many of these studies also examined the relationship between these polymorphisms and clinical correlates of suicidality, such as comorbid psychiatric disorders, as well as impulsive-aggression and Cluster B personality disorders. Our group maintains a database of these studies, which may be accessed through our Web page (http://www.douglasrecherche.qc.ca/suicide). As with linkage studies, there has also been a significant decrease in the enthusiasm associated with studies using a candidate gene approach. However, the availability of dense single-nucleotide polymorphism (SNP) panels now allows researchers to instead conduct exploratory, genome-wide studies, investigating large samples of unrelated individuals. These studies, usually referred to as genome-wide association studies (GWASs), are currently being conducted in several psychiatric phenotypes, including suicidal behavior.

To date, however, only one non–candidate gene association study has been performed. This study, conducted by our group, examined the relationship between markers on the X chromosome and suicide completion in a French Canadian sample (Fiori, Zouk, Himmelman, & Turecki, 2011). This study identified several regions displaying high evidence of association with suicide, as well as loci which were specifically associated with suicide in individuals with comorbid depressive disorders.

GENE EXPRESSION STUDIES

Gene expression studies provide us with gene functional information. By comparing brain tissue from individuals who died by suicide with tissue from controls, we can obtain valuable information on the functional profile of the brain prior to death. The use of microarray technology allows us to screen genes in parallel and virtually obtain a snapshot of brain gene activity in the moments before death and, as such, gain valuable insight into biological processes underlying suicide. To date, 13 microarray studies have been performed which specifically examined gene expression differences between suicide completers and nonsuicide controls. All of these studies have examined postmortem brain tissues and have mainly focused on the prefrontal cortex (Brodmann areas [BA] 8, 9, 10, 11, 44, 45, 46,

and 47) or the limbic area (amygdala, hippocampus, BA 24, and BA 29). Two more recent studies by our group have examined additional brain regions in order to obtain a broader view of gene expression changes occurring in the brain (Ernst, Deleva, et al., 2009; Sequeira et al., 2009).

All but one study (Sibille et al., 2004) identified multiple genes that displayed differential expression in suicide completers. As these studies generate large amounts of data, and the reporting of significant findings is often at the discretion of the researcher, the tendency to focus upon genes within known and potentially relevant pathways can make it difficult to identify trends in "nontraditional" genes which are highly differentially expressed but were not reported. Nonetheless, several pathways have been consistently implicated in these studies, including the glutamatergic and γ-amino-butyric acid (GABA)-ergic neurotransmitter systems, as well as the polyamine system, which will be discussed in later sections of this chapter. Although these large data sets have the potential to generate many false-positive results, the consistency of findings in these pathways provides strong evidence to support the notion that differential gene expression is an important factor in suicidality.

Interestingly, microarray studies have only produced minimal evidence for dysregulation of genes involved in the more traditional neurotransmitter pathways. This is in contradiction to the results of many studies that have specifically implicated these pathways in suicide. The reason for this discrepancy is not clear.

EPIGENETICS

Epigenetics refers to processes that alter gene expression without changing DNA sequences. Two important epigenetic processes are DNA methylation and posttranslational histone modifications. Evidence suggests that environmental factors can influence epigenetic processes (Weaver et al., 2004), and as such, epigenetic factors are excellent mechanisms to investigate in suicide and other psychiatric conditions where the environment is thought to play an important etiological role.

DNA methylation is a covalent modification at the 5' position of cytosine, occurring at CG dinucleotides. This modification can prevent the binding of proteins to DNA, and it has typically has been associated with gene repression when located in promoter regions (Rollins et al., 2006), although increased gene expression also could occur if methylation prevented the binding of repressive elements. Altered levels of DNA methylation have been observed in the promoter regions of several genes in suicide completers. The first study to examine this was performed by our group using DNA extracted from the hippocampus of suicide completers with a history of early childhood neglect or abuse, and it identified increased methylation in the promoter regions of the ribosomal RNA genes which was associated with decreased gene expression (McGowan et al., 2008). Following this, Poulter and colleagues identified altered levels of DNA methyltransferase activities in several brain regions of suicide completers as well as alterations in DNA methylation in the promoter region of the $GABA_A$ α1 subunit, which was associated with levels of a particular isoform of DNA methyltransferase (Poulter et al., 2008). Another study examined the role of allele-specific methylation of the serotonin 2A receptor (HTR2A) and found that methylation of the C allele of the T102C polymorphism was significantly different in white blood cells obtained from suicide attempters diagnosed with schizophrenia, but not in attempters diagnosed with bipolar disorder, nor was it differentially methylated in brain tissues of suicide completers (De Luca, Viggiano, Dhoot, Kennedy, & Wong, 2009). Two other studies conducted by our group examining methylation patterns of gene promoters should be mentioned. The first study examined the promoter region of the tropomyosin-related kinase B T1 variant (TrkB.T1) in brains of suicide completers and found that methylation at specific sites was correlated with gene expression, which was associated with the decreased brain expression of this gene in a subset of suicide completers (Ernst, Deleva, et al., 2009). The other study focused on the hippocampus glucocorticoid receptor and translated to humans results previously found in animal models of early environmental influences (McGowan et al., 2009). This study highlighted the importance of early environmental adversity on the regulation of the hypothalamic-pituitary-adrenal (HPA) axis, a system that is important in stress response.

Histones are the core proteins involved in the packaging of DNA into nucleosomes and can be covalently modified at specific residues by acetylation, methylation, phosphorylation, SUMOylation, and ubiquitinylation (Berger, 2007). The effect of these modifications on gene expression depends upon the histone protein (H2A, H2B, H3, H4), amino acid residue, modification, and positioning within the gene. Alterations in histone modifications have been examined in a number of psychiatric disorders, including suicide (Akbarian et al., 2005; Ernst, Chen, & Turecki, 2009; Huang & Akbarian, 2007). Our group examined the tri-methyl modification of lysine 27 in histone 3 (H3K27me3) and found increased levels of this modification in the promoter region of TrkB.T1, which were associated with decreased expression of this gene in BA 10 (Ernst, Chen, et al., 2009). On the other hand, we conducted another study examining the H3K27me3 modification in the promoter region of two polyamine genes, spermine synthase (SMS) and spermine oxidase (SMOX), and found no association between levels of modified H3K27 and suicide completion or expression of these genes in BA 8/9.

PROTEOMICS

Although alterations in mRNA levels are often indicators for alterations in protein expression, this is not always the case. As the levels of the various proteins comprising the proteome theoretically represent the endpoint for gene expression changes, measurement of their levels should conceivably reveal a more accurate picture of the mechanisms involved in suicidal behavior. However, the field of proteomics has lagged behind that of high throughput genetic research, largely due to a lack of suitable experimental techniques. To date, only two studies have been performed investigating proteome alterations in suicidal behavior. The first study was performed by Brunner and colleagues, who investigated the cerebrospinal fluid (CSF) of unmedicated, depressed suicide attempters and nonattempter controls (Brunner et al., 2005). Using two-dimensional gel electrophoresis, they identified one protein which was found at much lower concentrations in the suicide attempters. However, they were unable to determine the identity of this protein due to the limited amount of material. The second proteomic study was performed by Schlicht and colleagues using prefrontal cortex tissues obtained from suicide completers and healthy controls (Schlicht et al., 2007). Using two-dimensional gel electrophoresis and mass spectrometry, they identified five proteins which differed in intensity between the two groups, and they were able to identify three of these: crystallin chain B, glial fibrillary acidic protein (GFAP), and manganese superoxide dismutase.

Neurotransmitter Systems

Synaptic transmission in the central nervous system (CNS) underlies much of what makes us who we are. It is also the main site of the action of the psychopharmaceutical agents currently in use, and it is therefore not surprising that the role of the neurotransmitter systems represents one of the most commonly studied facets of suicidal behaviors. Classically, these pathways have been examined through measurements of the levels of the neurotransmitters and their metabolites, as well as the binding properties of their receptors, in the blood, urine, CSF, or brains of suicide completers. This early work has now been complemented with numerous molecular studies to examine many aspects of gene transcription, as well as more detailed analyses of the metabolic and downstream signaling pathways. This section will focus on the main neurotransmitter systems investigated in suicide to date, summarizing results from neurochemical studies, as well as those using complementary approaches.

Serotonin

The serotonin (5-HT) system is the most studied neurotransmitter in suicide research, and studies focusing on this system have a long history, dating back a few decades. 5-HT neurons originate in the dorsal raphe nucleus of the brainstem, where 5-HT is synthesized from tryptophan by the actions of tryptophan hydroxylase (TPH) and aromatic L-amino acid decarboxylase. Metabolism occurs mainly by monoamine oxidase (MAO) and aldehyde dehydrogenase to produce 5-hydroxyindoleacetic acid (5-HIAA). At least 14 mammalian 5-HT receptors are known, and all are G protein–coupled receptors (GPCR) except HTR3, a ligand-gated ion channel (Nichols & Nichols, 2008).

Alterations in serotonergic function related to suicidal behavior have been found using techniques aimed at assessing various markers of serotonin in living humans and in postmortem brain tissue. The findings from these studies point to a net reduction in serotonergic neurotransmission as the neurobiological alteration associated with suicidality. However, not all studies have obtained these results, and it has been recognized that these compounds are highly influenced by postmortem and antemortem factors not associated with suicide (Arango, Underwood, & Mann, 1997).

Numerous studies also have examined the expression and function of genes involved in 5-HT neurotransmission, of which the most well characterized are the 5-HT transporter (SERT, SLC6A4) and the receptors HTR1A and HTR2A. Many studies have examined the levels of SERT in the frontal cortex by measuring the binding of ligands such as [^{3}H]-paroxetine or [^{3}H]-imipramine. As this protein is found on axons of 5-HT neurons, these measurements are interpreted to indicate the integrity of 5-HT innervation. Overall, results have been mixed and although the general trend appears to be for decreased binding in suicide completers, studies have also found increases or no changes (refer to Purselle & Nemeroff, 2003, for a review). HTR1A also has been studied in suicide completers; however, postmortem binding studies have been fairly inconsistent. Several studies have found decreases in HTR1A binding in the brainstem (Arango et al., 2001; Boldrini, Underwood, Mann, & Arango, 2008), and increases have been seen in the prefrontal cortex of suicide completers in some (Arango, Underwood, Gubbi, & Mann, 1995; Huang et al., 2004), but not all studies (Arranz, Eriksson, Mellerup, Plenge, & Marcusson, 1994; Matsubara, Arora, & Meltzer, 1991). Interestingly, alterations in downstream signaling pathways following HTR1A activation have also been observed in suicide completers (Hsiung et al., 2003). Greater support has been found for the involvement of HTR2A than HTR1A. Several studies have found increased binding in postmortem samples using either [^{3}H]-ketanserin or [^{125}I]-lysergic acid diethylamide (Arango et al., 1990; Hrdina, Demeter, Vu, Sotonyi, & Palkovits, 1993; Mann, Stanley, McBride, & McEwen, 1986; Pandey et al., 2002), and increased protein and mRNA expression have also been observed (Escriba, Ozaita, & Garcia-Sevilla, 2004; Pandey et al., 2002). However, as with SERT and HTR1A, there have been inconsistent findings (Arranz et al., 1994; Cheetham, Crompton, Katona, & Horton, 1988; Klempan, Sequeira, et al., 2009; Lowther, De Paermentier, Crompton, Katona, & Horton, 1994). Interestingly, imaging studies of suicide attempters have found decreases in HTR2A binding in anxious and depressed individuals, which was negatively correlated with personality measures of hopelessness (Audenaert et al., 2001; van Heeringen et al., 2003). As with HTR1A, alterations in downstream signaling pathways involved in HTR2A signaling have been observed in some brain regions of suicide completers (Rosel et al., 2004).

Expression studies have assessed the role of genes involved in 5-HT metabolism, particularly the TPH genes (1 and 2) and MAO genes (A and B). Several studies have examined the expression of TPH2 in the dorsal raphe nucleus of suicide completers and have found elevated levels of mRNA, protein, and TPH immunoreactivity in suicide completers (Bach-Mizrachi et al., 2006, 2008; Boldrini, Underwood, Mann, & Arango, 2005). As this finding is counter to the idea that low 5-HT transmission is involved in suicide, it was suggested that these increases may reflect a compensatory mechanism in the brainstem. MAO-A and MAO-B are involved in the metabolism of 5-HT as well as the catecholamines and have also been implicated in suicidal behavior. However, most studies have focused on genetic polymorphisms rather than expression or function of these genes. There is some evidence for increased expression of MAO-A, although this was found only in the hypothalamus of suicide completers (Sherif, Marcusson, & Oreland, 1991). Although results for the involvement of MAO-B have been typically negative, a recent study found increased density of MAO-B in the frontal cortex of suicide completers (Ballesteros, Maeztu, Callado, Meana, & Gutierrez, 2008).

Numerous genetic association studies have been performed in serotonergic genes, including SERT, HTR1A, HTR1B, HTR2A, MAO-A, TPH1, and TPH2 (refer to Anguelova, Benkelfat, & Turecki, 2003; Arango, Huang, Underwood, & Mann, 2003; Brezo, Klempan, & Turecki, 2008, for reviews). The most convincing association has been with a functional promoter insertion/deletion in SERT. A recent meta-analysis found that the short allele, which is associated with decreased gene expression, was overrepresented in those with suicide attempts and violent suicides (Anguelova et al., 2003). Although positive associations have been seen with the majority of other serotonergic genes examined, many conflicting results have also been obtained, and there has been no overwhelming evidence to support the involvement of genetic polymorphisms in any of these genes in suicidal behavior.

Catecholamines

The catecholamines comprise dopamine (DA), norepinephrine (NE), and epinephrine (Epi). The role of DA in psychiatry has been best studied in schizophrenia, where it is the main target of the antipsychotics. NE plays many roles in the sympathetic nervous system, while Epi is a hormone released by the adrenal gland into the bloodstream (Berecek & Brody, 1982). DA is synthesized from tyrosine through the sequential actions of tyrosine hydroxylase and aromatic L-amino acid decarboxylase. DA is then converted to NE by dopamine-β-hydroxylase, and NE is acted upon by phenylethanolamine N-methyltransferase to produce Epi. Catecholamine metabolism occurs through the actions of MAO

and catechol-O-methyltransferase (COMT). There are five DA receptors, which are all GPCRs, and are classified as D1-like (DRD1 and DRD5) and D2-like (DRD2, DRD3, and DRD4), which differ in their localization and downstream signaling effects (Missale, Nash, Robinson, Jaber, & Caron, 1998). Both NE and Epi activate two forms of GPCRs, the α- and β-adrenoceptors, each of which have several subtypes and are associated with specific second messenger systems (Summers & McMartin, 1993).

Studies examining DA and its metabolites have focused largely on levels of its metabolites, homovanillic acid (HVA) and dihydroxyphenylacetic acid (DOPAC), in the CSF or urine of suicide attempters. Although several studies identified decreased levels of metabolites in suicide attempters (Banki, Arato, & Kilts, 1986; Engstrom, Alling, Blennow, Regnell, & Traskman-Bendz, 1999; Roy et al., 1986; Roy, Karoum, & Pollack, 1992; Sher et al., 2006) and completers (Bowden et al., 1997b), this has not been found in all studies (Placidi et al., 2001; Roy et al., 1985; Tripodianakis, Markianos, Sarantidis, & Agouridaki, 2002). Inconsistent results have also been obtained when assessing the relationship between CSF HVA levels and behavioral correlates of suicidal behavior (Jokinen, Nordstrom, & Nordstrom, 2007; Mann & Currier, 2007). Similar conflicting findings have been found by researchers measuring NE and its metabolite 3-methoxy-4-hydroxyphenylglycol (MHPG) in urine or CSF samples from suicide attempters, as well as in postmortem tissues of suicide completers. Some studies have found elevated levels of NE and MHPG (Arango, Ernsberger, Sved, & Mann, 1993; Brown, Goodwin, Ballenger, Goyer, & Major, 1979; Tripodianakis et al., 2002), whereas others have found decreased levels (Secunda et al., 1986) or no differences (Arranz, Blennow, Eriksson, Mansson, & Marcusson, 1997; Beskow, Gottfries, Roos, & Winblad, 1976; Placidi et al., 2001; Roy, Pickar, De Jong, Karoum, & Linnoila, 1989).

Receptor binding studies have assessed the properties of DRD1 and DRD2 in suicide completers. One study examined the basal ganglia of depressed suicide completers and found no differences in numbers or affinities of DRD1 and DRD2 in antidepressant-free suicides, but increased numbers and decreased affinity of DRD2, and increased DRD1 in antidepressant-treated suicides, suggesting that differences were related to treatment rather than suicide (Bowden, Theodorou, et al., 1997). Another study investigating DRD2 in the caudate of depressed suicide completers also found no significant differences in number or affinity (Allard & Norlen, 2001). However, several studies by Pitchot and colleagues assessing downstream effects of DRD2 activation found significant differences between suicide attempters and controls, with suicide attempters demonstrating reduced growth hormone responses after treatment with a DRD2 agonist (Pitchot, Hansenne, et al., 2001; Pitchot, Hansenne, Gonzalez Moreno, & Ansseau, 1992; Pitchot, Reggers, et al., 2001). Two studies examined DA uptake sites in several brain regions of depressed suicide completers and found no significant differences in either numbers or affinities (Allard & Norlen, 1997; Bowden et al., 1997a).

The adrenoceptors also have been examined in suicide completers. Arango and colleagues examined α1 and α2 receptors in the prefrontal and temporal cortices of suicide completers and found an increase in α1 binding sites in the prefrontal cortex, with no alterations in the temporal cortex and no differences in α2 receptors in either region (Arango et al., 1993). The opposite trend was observed by three studies which found decreased α1 binding in the prefrontal cortex, temporal cortex, and caudate of suicide completers (Gross-Isseroff, Dillon, Fieldust, & Biegon, 1990), the hippocampus of antidepressant-treated suicide completers (Crow et al., 1984), and the prefrontal cortex of alcoholic suicide completers (Underwood, Mann, & Arango, 2004). Another study found no differences in numbers of α1 receptors in suicide completers but increased α2 binding in the temporal cortex and decreased numbers of α2 receptors in the occipital cortex, hippocampus, caudate, and amygdala (De Paermentier et al., 1997). Several other groups have investigated α2 binding and protein levels and have found increased amounts of α2 receptors in the high-affinity state (Callado et al., 1998; Meana & Garcia-Sevilla, 1987; Ordway, Widdowson, Smith, & Halaris, 1994), increased α2 numbers in the hippocampus and frontal cortex (Gonzalez et al., 1994), and elevated α2 protein levels and mRNA expression in the prefrontal cortex (Escriba et al., 2004; Garcia-Sevilla et al., 1999). However, one study found decreased α2 binding in the frontal cortex of alcoholic suicide completers (Underwood et al., 2004), and a recent microarray study found decreased mRNA expression of α2A receptors in depressed suicide completers (Klempan, Sequeira, et al., 2009). Many researchers also have investigated the β receptors in suicide completers, with differing results. Several groups

found increased β receptor binding in the frontal cortex (Mann et al., 1986) and temporal cortex (Arango et al., 1990) of suicide completers, whereas others have found decreases in these same regions (De Paermentier, Cheetham, Crompton, Katona, & Horton, 1990; Little, Clark, Ranc, & Duncan, 1993). In the same vein, although one study found an increased risk for suicide in individuals taking β-blocking medication for cardiovascular diseases (Sorensen, Mellemkjaer, & Olsen, 2001), this was not confirmed in another study (Callreus, Agerskov, Hallas, & Andersen, 2007).

Several association studies have investigated catecholamine receptors and their metabolism in suicidal behavior. Two studies investigated an exon III polymorphism in DRD4 and found no significant differences between suicide attempters and controls (Persson et al., 1999; Zalsman et al., 2004). Two studies have found positive associations with suicide attempts and polymorphisms in DRD2 (Johann, Putzhammer, Eichhammer, & Wodarz, 2005; Suda et al., 2009). Several association studies have also examined polymorphisms in the α2A receptor, and while one study from our group found a weak association with the functional Asn251Lys polymorphism in male French-Canadian suicide completers (Sequeira et al., 2004), this was not found in other populations (Fukutake et al., 2008; Martin-Guerrero et al., 2006). Interestingly, another study found an association of a promoter polymorphism with suicide completion in Japanese females, but not males (Fukutake et al., 2008), which was also not significantly associated in the all-male sample used in our study (Sequeira et al., 2004). Recently, another α2A polymorphism was identified to be associated with increased suicidal ideation during antidepressant treatment (Perroud et al., 2009). The relationship between COMT and suicidal behavior has been extensively studied, in particular the Val158Met polymorphism. The Met allele of this enzyme is associated with decreased activity (Lachman et al., 1996), and a recent meta-analysis of association studies supported its involvement in suicidal behavior (Kia-Keating, Glatt, & Tsuang, 2007).

Overall, the results for the catecholamine systems are highly diverse, but several trends have emerged. Measurements in postmortem and peripheral samples point toward a decrease in levels of DA and its metabolites, as well as decreased activity of DRD2 receptors. There also appears to be an increase in NE and its metabolites, as well as increased expression of the α2 and β2 receptors, in the brains of suicide completers (Pandey & Dwivedi, 2007).

However, it is clear that additional studies will be required in order to gain a consensus on the role of these systems in suicidal behavior.

Other Systems
GLUTAMATE AND GABA

Glutamate and GABA are the primary excitatory and inhibitory neurotransmitters in the brain, respectively. Glutamate is synthesized either from glucose obtained from the tricarboxylic acid (TCA) cycle, or from glutamine, which is synthesized by glial cells and taken up by neurons (Daikhin & Yudkoff, 2000). Glutamate transmission is terminated by reuptake into neurons or astrocytes, which then convert it to glutamine to be resynthesized into glutamate by glutaminase (GLS) (Daikhin et al., 2000). The metabolism of GABA is intricately tied to that of glutamate, which is the precursor for GABA synthesis by glutamic acid decarboxylase (GAD). Additionally, following its release into synapses, GABA is transported into astrocytes and converted to glutamine (Bak, Schousboe, & Waagepetersen, 2006).

Glutamate acts on four classes of receptors: the ionotropic α-amino-3-hydroxy-5- hydroxy-5-methyl-4- isoxazolepropionate (AMPA), kainate, and N-methyl-D-aspartate (NMDA) receptors, as well as the metabotropic glutamate receptors (Conn & Pin, 1997; Dingledine, Borges, Bowie, & Traynelis, 1999). Several protein studies have assessed the ionotropic receptors in suicide. Two studies examining NMDA receptors in the brain found no differences in antagonist binding between suicide completers and controls (Holemans et al., 1993; Noga et al., 1997). However, another study found a decrease in high-affinity, glycine displaceable binding in suicide completers, although no changes to the potency or efficacy of glycine to inhibit this binding, as well as no differences in antagonist binding (Nowak, Ordway, & Paul, 1995). Another study examined modulatory sites of the NMDA receptor and found no alterations in the frontal and parietal cortices of suicide completers (Palmer, Burns, Arango, & Mann, 1994), but significant differences in the hippocampus, suggesting region-specific alterations in NMDA receptor functioning (Nowak et al., 2003). Two studies examining AMPA receptors found increased binding in the caudate (Freed, Dillon-Carter, & Kleinman, 1993; Noga et al., 1997), although no differences in the putamen or nucleus accumbens (Noga et al., 1997). Another study found no differences in kainate receptor binding in the striatum or nucleus accumbens (Noga et al., 1997).

Microarray studies have identified alterations in the levels of several glutamate receptors, including subunits for NMDA, AMPA, and kainite receptors, as well as the metabotropic glutamate receptor 3 (Klempan, Sequeira, et al., 2009; Sequeira et al., 2009; Thalmeier et al., 2008). Additionally, downregulated expression has been observed for GLS, glutamate-ammonia ligase (glutamine synthetase) (GLUL), and glial high-affinity glutamate transporters SLC1A2 and SLC1A3 (Kim, Choi, Baykiz, & Gershenfeld, 2007; Klempan, Sequeira, et al., 2009; Sequeira et al., 2009). The involvement of AMPA receptor 3 (GRIA3) is particularly interesting as it has been associated with a number of psychiatric conditions, including bipolar disorder, schizophrenia, and citalopram treatment-emergent suicidal ideation (Gécz et al., 1999; O'Connor, Muly, Arnold, & Hemby, 2007; Laje et al., 2007; Magri et al., 2008). Treatment-emergent suicidal ideation has also been associated with polymorphisms in kainite receptor 2 (GRIK2) (Laje et al., 2007; Menke et al., 2008). Interestingly, several of these glutamatergic genes are localized to glia, which lends support for the involvement of dysregulated astroglial functioning in psychiatric disorders.

The relationship of GABA levels to suicide was assessed by Korpi and colleagues, who measured GABA concentrations in several brain regions of suicide completers and controls, and found no significant differences in any region, although there was a trend for increased levels in the hypothalamus (Korpi, Kleinman, & Wyatt, 1988). Another study measured GABA concentrations in the CSF of suicide attempters with personality disorders and found increased levels which were highly related to impulsivity in these individuals (Lee, Petty, & Coccaro, 2009).

GABA acts upon two classes of receptors: ionotropic $GABA_A$ receptors and metabotropic $GABA_B$ receptors. Measurements of benzodiazepine binding sites, reflecting quantities of the $GABA_A$ receptors, have been performed by several groups. Manchon and colleagues reported an increased number of type I binding sites in the hippocampus with a slightly increased binding affinity in suicide completers (Manchon et al., 1987). A later study by the same group found no differences in receptor density but increased affinity of $GABA_A$ receptors in the hippocampus of violent suicide completers (Rochet et al., 1992). Pandey and colleagues found significantly increased receptor density in the prefrontal cortex, particularly in violent suicide completers, although no alterations in ligand affinity (Pandey et al., 1997). Other studies have found an increased number of sites in the frontal cortex of suicide completers, with no differences in the temporal cortex, amygdala, hippocampus, or locus coeruleus (Cheetham, Crompton, Katona, Parker, & Horton, 1988; Stocks, Cheetham, Crompton, Katona, & Horton, 1990; Zhu et al., 2006). Only two receptor binding studies have examined $GABA_B$ receptors in brains of suicide completers and have been mainly negative, with the exception of a slight increase in binding affinity in the temporal cortex of drug-free suicide completers (Arranz, Cowburn, Eriksson, Vestling, & Marcusson, 1992; Cross, Cheetham, Crompton, Katona, & Horton, 1988). Other protein studies examining proteins such as GABA aminotransferase (Sherif et al., 1991), GAD (Cheetham et al., 1988), and GABA transporter-1 (Sundman-Eriksson & Allard, 2002) have also been negative. Finally, a recent neuroanatomical study investigating GAD-immunoreactivity found significantly increased reactivity in the hippocampus of suicide completers (Gos et al., 2009), which may indicate alterations in the levels of GABAergic neurons in suicide completers.

Despite the conflicting results from protein studies, expression studies have now observed dysregulated expression of many GABAergic genes in suicide completers. Altered expression of numerous $GABA_A$ and $GABA_B$ receptor subunits was observed across prefrontal and limbic brain regions, as well as $GABA_A$ receptor-associated protein like 1, and a GABA transporter (SLC6A1) (Choudary et al., 2005; Kim et al., 2007; Klempan, Sequeira, et al., 2009; Merali et al., 2004; Sequeira et al., 2007, 2009). Moreover, a study from our group found that 16% and 36% of the probesets annotated to be involved in GABAergic signaling were significantly differentially expressed in BA 44 and 46, respectively (Klempan, Sequeira, et al., 2009). There also is evidence for the involvement of epigenetic processes in the alteration of GABAergic transmission in suicide, as a recent study by Poulter and colleagues found a hypermethylation of the promoter region of $GABA_A$ α1 in the prefrontal cortex of suicide completers, which was associated with decreased expression (Poulter et al., 2008). This effect was not found in the α5 subunit, indicating gene specificity.

In sum, although studies investigating glutamate and GABA have yielded some conflicting results, the evidence for their involvement in suicide is overwhelming. Although the traditional focus on suicide research has been the 5-HT system, it seems clear that these two systems show considerable

promise for investigating the neurobiological basis of suicide as well as being potential sites for pharmaceutical treatments.

OTHER

Acetylcholine (ACh) is a key neurotransmitter in both the parasympathetic and sympathetic components of the autonomic nervous system, and it plays an important role in the control of attention, learning, and memory in the CNS (Fine et al., 1997; Hasselmo, Anderson, & Bower, 1992; Sarter, Bruno, & Turchi, 1999). The two major classes of ACh receptors are the metabotropic GPCR muscarinic receptors (mAChR) and the ionotropic nicotinic receptors (nAChR) (Lucas-Meunier, Fossier, Baux, & Amar, 2003).

The role of cholinergic neurotransmission in suicide has been examined in several binding studies. Meyerson and colleagues found increased mAChR densities in the cerebral cortex of suicide completers (Meyerson et al., 1982); however, no differences were observed by two studies in the frontal cortex, hypothalamus, or pons (Kaufmann et al., 1984; Stanley, 1984). Downstream signaling through mAChR was examined by measuring [^{35}S]GTPγS binding following receptor stimulation in the prefrontal cortex and was not found to be significantly different in suicide completers (Gonzalez-Maeso, Rodriguez-Puertas, Meana, Garcia-Sevilla, & Guimon, 2002). Interestingly, a more recent study investigating M1 and M4 mAChR found higher binding in the anterior cingulate cortex of suicide completers, particularly in those with schizophrenia (Zavitsanou, Katsifis, Mattner, & Huang, 2004), which may indicate a role for specific receptor types in suicide.

On another note, suicide by ingestion of organophosphate pesticides, which irreversibly inhibit the breakdown of ACh in the synapse, is an increasingly recognized problem in developing countries. And while this reflects the availability of a highly effective means of committing suicide, it has also been suggested that long-term exposure to organophosphates may play a causal role in suicidal behavior (Jaga & Dharmani, 2007; London, Flisher, Wesseling, Mergler, & Kromhout, 2005). It also has been recently proposed that ACh may be involved in suicidality through its effects on other neurotransmitter systems (Niederhofer, 2008). Overall, there is some evidence for increased AChR or ACh signaling in suicide; however, more studies will be needed to confirm these findings and to investigate the possible relationship between organophosphates and suicide.

Endogenous opioids are a class of short peptides, including the enkephalins, dynorphins, endorphins, endomorphins, and nociceptin, which have important roles in mood and nociception. Opioids bind with differing affinities to the four major types of opioid receptors, which are all GPCRs, and display different anatomical distributions (Corbett, Henderson, McKnight, & Paterson, 2006). Although the effects of opioids on mood are well known and opioids have been suggested as candidates for new antidepressants (Berrocoso, Sanchez-Blazquez, Garzon, & Mico, 2009), relatively few studies have examined the opioid system in suicide. Three studies have examined μ-opioid receptor density and affinity in brains of suicide completers, although the results have not been consistent. Two studies observed elevated receptor density in several brain regions of suicide completers, with no significant changes in receptor affinity (Gabilondo, Meana, & Garcia-Sevilla, 1995; Gross-Isseroff, Dillon, Israeli, & Biegon, 1990), while another study found no alterations in receptor density but higher affinity ligand binding in suicide completers (Zalsman et al., 2005). Another study assessed signaling through μ-opioid receptors and found no significant differences between the groups (Gonzalez-Maeso et al., 2002). Finally, one study investigated the mRNA expression of μ-opioid receptors and found it to be upregulated in the prefrontal cortex of suicide completers (Escriba et al., 2004). Overall, there is only minimal and conflicting evidence for the involvement of the opioids in the psychopathology of suicide, with results suggesting increased binding affinities and/or expression of μ-opioid receptors. However, given that this system is still not fully understood, further studies are warranted to confirm these findings and to investigate the role of other opioid receptors.

Stress Systems

One of the most widely used models to conceptualize risk for mental disorders, which has also been adopted in suicide research, is based on the notion of a stress-diathesis interaction. In the case of suicidal behavior, this model assumes that suicide results from the combination of stressors and predisposing factors. The systems discussed in this section may be involved in both stress and predisposition, as they represent sites at which the first effects resulting from stress may be apparent. Any factors influencing their capacities to respond to these stressors can have numerous long-term consequences. The two traditional stress systems in humans include the sympathetic nervous system, in which the catecholamines described earlier play essential roles, and the HPA axis system. A third stress response system whose role in psychiatric disorders has been less studied is the polyamine system.

Hypothalamic-Pituitary-Adrenal Axis

The HPA axis plays an essential role in adaptation to biological and behavioral homeostatic stressors. Activation of the HPA system involves the release of corticotrophin-releasing hormone (CRH) from the paraventricular nucleus of the hypothalamus, which stimulates the pituitary gland to release adrenocorticotropic hormone (ACTH), resulting in the release of glucocorticoids from the adrenal gland (Herman et al., 2003). These hormones travel systemically and act to increase the expression of genes involved in metabolism and inflammatory responses, and produce numerous effects in the CNS.

Dysregulation of the HPA system has been proposed for several psychiatric conditions, including depressive disorders (McIsaac & Young, 2009), psychotic disorders (Bennett Ao, 2008), and posttraumatic stress disorder (Yehuda, 1997). One of the earliest studies to implicate the HPA axis in suicide was by Bunney and Fawcett in 1965, with the identification of high levels of 17-hydroxycorticosteroids in depressed suicidal patients (Bunney & Fawcett, 1965). Following this, studies identified elevated levels of CRH in the CSF (Arato, Banki, Bissette, & Nemeroff, 1989) and frontal cortex (Nemeroff, Owens, Bissette, Andorn, & Stanley, 1988) of suicide completers, indicative of increased activation of the HPA axis in suicide. One of the most common methods to examine the functioning of the HPA axis is the dexamethasone suppression test, with dexamethasone nonsuppression being indicative of elevated HPA activity. Early studies identified increased nonsuppression among suicidal adolescents (Robbins & Alessi, 1985), and suicide attempters who later died by suicide demonstrated a greater rate of nonsuppression compared to suicide attempters and nonattempters who did not go on to commit suicide (Norman, Brown, Miller, Keitner, & Overholser, 1990). Similar results continue to be seen, supporting good predictive power of dexamethasone nonsuppression for suicidal behavior (Coryell & Schlesser, 2001; Jokinen et al., 2007). Gene expression differences have also been found in suicide completers, including a decreased expression of the glucocorticoid receptor in the hippocampus of suicide completers with a history of childhood abuse (McGowan et al., 2009), and elevated expression of the CRH1 receptor (CRHR1) in the prefrontal cortex of suicide completers (Merali et al., 2004).

Relatively few genetic association studies have been performed for HPA axis genes. Of note are the studies focusing on the CRHR1, which was found to be associated with suicide attempts, but not in individuals exposed to high levels of lifetime stress (Wasserman, Sokolowski, Rozanov, & Wasserman, 2008; Wasserman, Wasserman, Rozanov, & Sokolowski, 2009). Another study found that genotypes in CRHR1 and the CRH binding protein (CRHBP) influenced suicide attempts and severity of suicidal behaviors in individuals with schizophrenia (De Luca et al., 2010), and the same group found a small association between suicidal behaviors and CRH receptor 2 (CRHR2) in those with bipolar disorder (De Luca, Tharmalingam, & Kennedy, 2007). Although there is only minor evidence regarding the role of heritable factors in HPA dysfunction, recent findings have indicated that first-degree relatives of suicide completers also display blunted cortisol responses under stress, indicating that alterations in HPA functioning are partially due to heritable factors.

Overall, there is strong support for a disturbance in HPA axis functioning in suicidal behavior, although the biological mechanisms linking the two are not yet known. One popular theory regarding the role of the HPA system in depression postulates that long-term activation of the HPA axis, and the resulting elevated glucocorticoid levels, have toxic effects on neurons in the hippocampus (McKinnon, Yucel, Nazarov, & MacQueen, 2009). As hippocampal neurogenesis is an important mechanism involved in antidepressant and stress responses (Dranovsky & Hen, 2006), this chronic overactivity may also be relevant to suicidal behavior.

Polyamines

The polyamines are ubiquitous aliphatic molecules comprising putrescine, spermidine, and spermine, which contain two, three, and four amino groups, respectively, and which are positively charged at physiological pH. In addition, the guanidino-amine agmatine, whose presence in mammalian brains was discovered much more recently than the other polyamines (Li et al., 1994), may also be considered among this group (Moinard, Cynober, & de Bandt, 2005). The polyamine system has been identified in all organisms and plays an important role in numerous essential cellular functions, including growth, division, and

signaling cascades (Gilad & Gilad, 2003; Minguet, Vera-Sirera, Marina, Carbonell, & Blazquez, 2008; Seiler & Raul, 2005; Tabor & Tabor, 1984). In addition, evidence supports its involvement in stress responses at both cellular and behavioral levels (Gilad et al., 2003; Rhee, Kim, & Lee, 2007). Interestingly, the polyamine stress response (PSR) appears to be developmentally regulated, and the emergence of the adult PSR is correlated with the cessation of the hyporesponsive period of the HPA system (Gilad, Gilad, Eliyayev, & Rabey, 1998).

Alterations of the polyamine system have been observed in several pathological conditions, including cancer (Tabor et al., 1984), ischemia (Gilad & Gilad, 1991), Alzheimer's disease (Morrison, Bergeron, & Kish, 1993), and mental disorders (Fiori & Turecki, 2008). Although the involvement of the polyamine system in schizophrenia, depression, and anxiety disorders has been studied for over two decades, its role in suicide had not been suspected prior to a study by our group which found consistent decreases in levels of spermidine/spermine N-1 acetyltransferase (SAT1) across several brain regions obtained from French Canadian suicide completers both with and without major depression. Further, our study identified an SNP (rs6526342) in the promoter region, which was significantly associated with suicide completion (Sequeira et al., 2006). Since this initial study, decreased expression of SAT1 has been observed in other brain regions and populations (Guipponi et al., 2009; Klempan, Rujescu, et al., 2009; Klempan, Sequeira, et al., 2009; Sequeira et al., 2007). Dysregulated expression of additional polyamine related genes, including SMS, SMOX, and ornithine aminotransferase-like 1 (OATL1), has also been identified (Klempan, Sequeira, et al., 2009; Sequeira et al., 2007).

We recently characterized the haplotype structure of the promoter region of SAT1 and identified three polymorphisms, including rs6526342, which played a role in determining the expression of SAT1 in the brain and in vitro (Fiori, Mechawar, & Turecki, 2009). The most interesting results were found with a variable-length tandem adenine repeat in the promoter region, whose length was sufficient to determine the expression of reporter gene constructs, and which was found to be significantly associated with suicide completion among individuals with depressive disorders (Fiori & Turecki, 2010). Additional studies by our group have identified elevated levels of putrescine and spermidine in the brains of suicide completers, which may be a consequence of the decreased activity of SAT1 (Chen et al., 2010).

Although the mechanism by which altered polyamine levels can influence risk for suicide or other psychiatric disorders is not yet clear, several mechanisms have been proposed. First, the polyamines have been shown to influence transmission through several neurotransmitter systems, including the catecholamines (Bastida et al., 2007; Bo, Giorgetti, Camana, & Savoldi, 1990; Hirsch et al., 1987; Ritz, Mantione, & London, 1994), glutamate (Williams, 1997), GABA (Brackley, Goodnow, Nakanishi, Sudan, & Usherwood, 1990; Gilad, Gilad, & Wyatt, 1992; Morgan & Stone, 1983), and nitric oxide (Galea, Regunathan, Eliopoulos, Feinstein, & Reis, 1996), each of which may be involved in psychiatric disorders. Agmatine itself is believed to act as a neurotransmitter through imidazoline receptors, α2-adrenoceptors, nAChR, and HTR3 receptors; this theory is supported by its storage in synaptic vesicles and capacity to be released upon depolarization (Reis & Regunathan, 2000). Second, polyamines interact with several transmembrane channels, including inward-rectifying K^+ channels, ionotropic glutamate receptors, and L-type Ca^{2+} channels, and thus can influence the properties of excitable cells (Doyle, Kirby, Murphy, & Shaw, 2005; Williams, 1997). Finally, both agmatine and putrescine demonstrate anxiolytic and antidepressant effects in animal studies (Gong et al., 2006; Lavinsky, Arteni, & Netto, 2003; Zeidan, Zomkowski, Rosa, Rodrigues, & Gabilan, 2007; Zomkowski et al., 2002, 2004; Zomkowski, Santos, & Rodrigues, 2005, 2006), which could be particularly relevant for suicide completers with comorbid mood or anxiety disorders.

Cell Signaling

The main function of cell signaling pathways is to transduce messages from outside the cell to produce specific alterations within the cell. This section will focus specifically on signal transduction pathways that result in changes in gene expression. The two mechanisms by which these effects occur are through receptors located at the cell surface, whose effects on gene transcription occur through second messenger systems, and nuclear receptors, whose inactive forms reside primarily in the cytoplasm and which become activated when bound by their membrane-permeable ligands. These receptors then pass through the nuclear pore to the nucleus, where they act directly upon the DNA by binding to specific recognition sites within gene promoter regions.

Cell surface receptors typically possess extracellular, transmembrane, and intracellular domains. Following binding of a ligand to the extracellular domain, conformational changes are induced which can alter its ability to interact with intracellular molecules or activate the enzymatic activity of the receptor itself. Based upon the type of receptor and the nature of the ligand being bound, different intracellular signaling pathways are activated or repressed.

Many of the neurotransmitter receptors are GPCRs, for which ligand binding allows the intracellular domain to interact with various G-proteins to activate second messenger signaling pathways, mainly those involving cyclic AMP (cAMP) or 1,4,5-inositoltriphosphate (IP3). As discussed earlier, many of these receptors have already been implicated in suicidal behavior, and alterations in downstream signaling pathways have also been observed in suicide completers. Although the trend has been for impaired signaling through various components of the cAMP and IP3 pathways in postmortem brain tissues of suicide completers (Dwivedi et al., 2008; Dwivedi, Rao, et al., 2003; Hsiung et al., 2003; Pacheco et al., 1996; Shimon, Agam, Belmaker, Hyde, & Kleinman, 1997; Shimon et al., 1998), some studies have either found no change, or evidence for increased signaling (Lowther, Crompton, Katona, & Horton, 1996; Lowther, Katona, Crompton, & Horton, 1997). These differences may be due to differing regulation of second messenger signaling across the brain (Rosel et al., 2000), use of antidepressants (Lowther et al., 1997), or the presence of other psychiatric disorders (Dwivedi et al., 2002).

Growth factor receptors are another important class of cell surface receptors, and following binding of their ligands, the receptors dimerize and activate the tyrosine kinase activity of their intracellular domain, resulting in autophosphorylation that allows the intracellular domains to interact with proteins involved in various second messenger systems (Pawson, 1994). The neurotrophins are a class of peptide growth factors secreted by specific cells to increase the growth and survival of neurons, and include nerve growth factor (NGF), neurotrophin 3 (NT-3), neurotrophin 4 (NT-4), and brain-derived neurotrophic factor (BDNF). Among this group, only signaling by BDNF, and its receptor TrkB, have been implicated in suicide. While microarray studies have failed to identify differences in the expression of BDNF itself, decreased protein levels of BDNF and expression of TrkB have been observed in several postmortem studies of suicide completers (Dwivedi, Rizavi, et al., 2003; Ernst, Deleva, et al., 2009; Pandey et al., 2008), supporting a role for a downregulation of BDNF/TrkB signaling. One of these studies determined that downregulated TrkB expression was due to the decreased expression of one specific TrkB isoform, TrkB.T1, which is expressed exclusively in astrocytes (Ernst, Deleva, et al., 2009). Many association studies have examined the Val66Met polymorphism of BDNF in suicidal behavior, although results have been mixed, and associations generally appear not to be with suicide completion, but rather with other aspects of suicidal behavior (Iga et al., 2007; Perroud et al., 2008; Sarchiapone et al., 2008; Zarrilli et al., 2009). Although the mechanism by which decreased BDNF/TrkB signaling plays a role in suicide is not yet known, several studies have implicated this pathway in depression. Antidepressant use has been shown to increase the expression of BDNF in both the periphery (Sen, Duman, & Sanacora, 2008) and the brain (Chen, Dowlatshahi, MacQueen, Wang, & Young, 2001), which has been associated with improvement of depressive symptoms (Brunoni, Lopes, & Fregni, 2008). Interestingly, a recent study found that SNPs in BDNF and the neurotrophin tyrosine kinase receptor 2 (NTRK2) were associated with antidepressant treatment-emergent suicidal ideation (Perroud et al., 2009).

Fibroblast growth factor (FGF) is another growth factor which has been implicated in suicide. This growth factor is involved in cell proliferation and differentiation in development, and it has essential roles in neuronal signal transduction in adults (Ornitz & Itoh, 2001). Several microarray studies have identified downregulated expression of proteins involved in FGF signaling in brains of suicide completers (Kim et al., 2007; Tochigi et al., 2008). Similar to BDNF, FGF has also been shown to be upregulated following antidepressant treatment (Bachis, Mallei, Cruz, Wellstein, & Mocchetti, 2008).

As discussed earlier, there is some evidence for dysregulated function of the glucocorticoid receptor in suicide, but there have been few studies on the role of other nuclear receptors in suicidal behavior. Estrogen has been implicated in depression and schizophrenia (Ostlund, Keller, & Hurd, 2003), and several studies have examined polymorphisms in estrogen receptors in suicidal behavior, none of which were found to be significantly associated (Giegling et al., 2008, 2009; Tsai, Wang, Hong, & Chiu, 2003). Low levels of testosterone, which acts at the androgen receptor, have been observed in suicide attempters, although the relationship with violence of the attempts has not been consistent (Gustavsson, Traskman-Bendz, Higley, & Westrin, 2003; Tripodianakis, Markianos, Rouvali, & Istikoglou, 2007). Whether there are defects in androgen receptor functioning in suicidal behavior remains unknown.

Cholesterol and Lipid Metabolism

Lipids and their metabolites are involved in numerous biological processes, including energy metabolism, immune function, and second messenger signaling, as well as being essential components of cellular membranes. Cholesterol metabolism appears to be particularly important in psychiatric disorders, and beyond its essential role in determining membrane fluidity and localization of proteins in lipid bilayers, is required for the synthesis of steroid hormones and fat-soluble vitamins.

The interest in cholesterol as a possible biological correlate of suicide and related behaviors dates as far back as 1979, when Virkkunen demonstrated that male subjects with antisocial personality disorder—a high-risk group prone to violence and suicide—had lower levels of serum cholesterol than the control group of male patients with other personality disorders (Virkkunen, 1979). It was only after concerns were raised over the safety of using cholesterol-lowering medications that particular attention was paid to the seeming relationship between cholesterol and violent behavior. In particular, two large randomized, double-blind lipid-lowering trials revealed that although decreasing serum cholesterol with lipid-lowering medications was effective in reducing mortality from coronary heart disease, the overall mortality rate was not significantly different (Frick et al., 1987; Lipid Research Clinics Program, 1984). The reduction in cardiac-related deaths appeared to be offset by an increase in violence-related deaths, including suicide, accidents, and homicide. To examine the issue more globally, Muldoon and colleagues combined the results of primary prevention trials using meta-analytic techniques and concluded that there was a significant increase in non-illness-related mortality (i.e., deaths from accidents, suicide, or violence) in groups receiving treatment to lower cholesterol concentrations compared with controls (Muldoon, Manuck, & Matthews, 1990). Although nonsignificant results have been observed among more recent meta-analyses, this may reflect the modification of inclusion criteria in these trials to exclude individuals with histories of psychiatric illnesses and substance abuse (Muldoon, Manuck, Mendelsohn, Kaplan, & Belle, 2001). Support for a relationship between cholesterol metabolism and suicide has also been found in large epidemiological studies in which low serum cholesterol levels have been frequently associated with suicidal behavior (Ellison & Morrison, 2001; Neaton et al., 1992; Partonen, Haukka, Virtamo, Taylor, & Lonnqvist, 1999; Zhang et al., 2005; Zureik, Courbon, & Ducimetiere, 1996). Although gender-specific effects have been observed (Lindberg, Rastam, Gullberg, & Eklund, 1992; Zhang et al., 2005), this has not been the case in all studies (Ellison et al., 2001). Although a relationship between low serum cholesterol levels and suicide has not been described in all studies (Iribarren, Reed, Wergowske, Burchfiel, & Dwyer, 1995), the overall evidence strongly supports the involvement of cholesterol in suicidal behavior.

There also has been some evidence supporting a relationship between suicide attempts and low serum levels of cholesterol, as well as other lipids, from studies in psychiatric populations (Atmaca, Kuloglu, Tezcan, Ustundag, & Bayik, 2002; Diaz-Sastre et al., 2007; Lee & Kim, 2003; Marcinko et al., 2007, 2008; Perez-Rodriguez et al., 2008; Vuksan-Cusa, Marcinko, Nad, & Jakovljevic, 2009). Clinical studies, however, have not been as consistent as epidemiological studies. Nevertheless, intriguingly, many studies have identified low cholesterol levels to be a specific marker for violent suicide methods, such that lower serum cholesterol levels have been observed in violent compared to nonviolent suicide attempters (Alvarez et al., 2000; Atmaca, Kuloglu, Tezcan, & Ustundag, 2003, 2008; Marcinko, Martinac, Karlovic, & Loncar, 2004; Vevera, Zukov, Morcinek, & Papezova, 2003), as well as in the brain tissues of violent suicide completers (Lalovic et al., 2007b). As with the epidemiological studies, gender-specific differences have sometimes been observed, with greater effects being found in male compared to female suicide attempters (Diaz-Sastre et al., 2007; Perez-Rodriguez et al., 2008). The relationship between suicidal behavior and the levels of other lipids, such as fatty acids and triglycerides, has been difficult to interpret, as some studies have described decreased levels in the serum of suicide attempters (Huan et al., 2004; Sublette, Hibbeln, Galfalvy, Oquendo, & Mann, 2006; Vuksan-Cusa et al., 2009), which has not been observed in the brains of suicide completers (Lalovic et al., 2007a; McNamara et al., 2009). As

the relationship between peripheral and brain levels of cholesterol and other lipids remains unclear (Dietschy & Turley, 2001), these discrepant results could suggest differing roles for lipid metabolism in suicidal behavior between the two systems, or alternatively, alterations in lipid metabolism may be specific to suicide attempters.

In addition to altered levels of the lipids themselves, evidence for a dysregulation in lipid metabolism in suicidal behavior also has emerged from gene expression studies. Recent microarray studies have identified altered expression of several lipid-related genes in the brains of suicide completers, including the low-density lipoprotein receptor (LDL-R) (Kim et al., 2007), chemokine-like factor superfamily 5 (CKLFSF5), erbb2 interacting protein (ERBB2IP), fatty acid desaturase 1 (FADS1), gremlin 1, cysteine knot superfamily (GREM1), interferon gamma-inducible protein 16 (IFI16), leptin receptor (LEPR), myotubularin related protein 10 (MTMR10), Notch homolog 1 (NOTCH1), phosphoinositide-3-kinase (class 2 alpha; PIK3C2A), phosphatidylinositol 3,4,5-trisphosphate-dependent RAC exchanger 1 (PREX1), S100 calcium binding protein beta (S100B), and stearoyl-CoA desaturase (SCD) (Lalovic, Klempan, Sequeira, Luheshi, & Turecki, 2010). The ability of long-term alterations in the expression of cholesterol metabolic genes to confer risk for suicidal behavior has been observed in carriers of a mutation involved in Smith-Lemli-Opitz (SLO) syndrome, an autosomal recessive disorder resulting from mutations in the gene coding for 7-dehydrocholesterol reductase (DHCR7), an enzyme involved in cholesterol biosynthesis. While carriers of this mutation are phenotypically normal, they display low levels of cholesterol and display suicidal behavior (Lalovic et al., 2004).

Several mechanisms have been proposed to explain the role of altered lipid and cholesterol metabolism in suicide and other psychiatric disorders. Many of these theories propose a relationship between cholesterol and 5-HT neurotransmission resulting from alterations in membrane fluidity (Diebold et al., 1998; Engelberg, 1992). Although unlikely, this mechanism is partly supported by experimental studies confirming a relationship between cholesterol and 5-HT in humans (Buydens-Branchey, Branchey, Hudson, & Fergeson, 2000). Secondly, altered immune responses, in which lipids play an essential role, have been implicated in other psychiatric disorders (Sperner-Unterweger, 2005), and some studies have suggested that the role of lipid metabolism in suicide may be due to a relationship between increased levels of pro-inflammatory cytokines and the levels of cholesterol and fatty acids (Maes et al., 1997; Penttinen, 1995). A more recent explanation is associated with the role cholesterol plays in the development and function of neural synapses (Chattopadhyay & Paila, 2007; Mauch et al., 2001). Regardless of the molecular mechanisms that may mediate this relationship, a possible behavioral link may be through impulsive-aggressive traits. Accordingly, it seems reasonable to posit that a relationship should exist between our dietary needs and our behaviors. As such, when in need of dietary intake, our behavior should naturally become more aggressive, which in turn, may increase suicide risk in individuals at risk.

Other Systems

As research into the neurobiological basis of suicidal behavior continues, new biological pathways continue to emerge as potential sites harboring factors involved in this complex trait. While a discussion of all known pathways which have been implicated in suicide is beyond the scope of this chapter, several of the newer findings will be discussed in this section.

As well as being involved in intracellular signaling pathways through its conversion to cAMP, adenosine triphosphate (ATP) is an essential component of cellular energy metabolism. Altered expression of several ATP-related genes has been observed in two microarray studies. One study observed down-regulated expression of the Na+/K+-ATPase alpha 3 subunit (ATP1A3) in the prefrontal cortex of suicide completers with depression, bipolar disorder, and schizophrenia (Tochigi et al., 2008). Another study found that TCA cycle and ATP-related genes were significantly associated with gene expression differences between depressed and nondepressed suicide completers, and suggested that these defects may be markers for suicidal behavior in the context of depression (Klempan, Sequeira, et al., 2009). Mitochondria are the organelles in which much of the cellular energy metabolism occurs, and it is of interest that altered expression of genes encoded by mitochondrial DNA has also been observed in suicide and other psychiatric disorders (Iwamoto & Kato, 2006; Rezin, Amboni, Zugno, Quevedo, & Streck, 2009).

Nitric oxide (NO) is a gaseous signaling molecule with important roles in cardiovascular, muscular, immune, and nervous system functions. NO is synthesized from L-arginine by several NO synthases (NOS), which differ in both their tissue and cellular distributions. NO has been implicated in several psychiatric conditions, including depression, and appears to play an important role in learning and memory (Zhou & Zhu, 2009). Several studies have now investigated the role of NO function in suicide. Two studies found elevated plasma levels of NO in depressed suicide attempters (Kim et al., 2006; Lee et al., 2006). Two studies have also examined polymorphisms in NOS genes, and while one study found that genotypes within NOS1 and NOS3 were associated with aspects of suicidal behavior (Rujescu et al., 2008), another group found no association between NOS3 polymorphisms and suicide attempts (Saiz et al., 2007). Clearly additional work will be required to clarify the role of NO in suicidal behavior, although there is some evidence that its involvement may be through increasing impulsive behaviors (Reif et al., 2009).

In addition to many of the factors described in previous sections, synaptic transmission is also highly regulated by presynaptic factors controlling the vesicle-mediated release of neurotransmitters. Considerable evidence is now emerging implicating altered function of this system in suicide. One study identified a decreased ratio of synapsin/synaptophysin in suicide completers (Vawter et al., 2002), while another group observed alterations in syntaxin and synaptosomal-associated protein (25 kDa) (SNAP25) levels in the SNARE complex (Honer et al., 2002). Alterations in the expression of numerous other related genes have been found in microarray studies of suicide completers, including vesicle-associated membrane protein 3 (VAMP3), synaptotagmin XIII (SYT13), synaptophysin-like protein (SYPL), synapsin II (SYN2), synaptosomal-associated protein (23 kDa) SNAP23, SNAP25, and synaptosomal-associated protein (29 kDa) (SNAP29) (Klempan, Sequeira, et al., 2009; Sequeira et al., 2009). Finally, variants in vesicle-associated membrane protein 4 (VAMP4) were associated with suicide attempts in one study (Wasserman, Geijer, Rozanov, & Wasserman, 2005).

Future Studies

Although the understanding of the role of neurobiological factors in suicide has vastly increased within the last few decades, we are far from developing an integrated picture of how specific alterations at the levels of DNA, mRNA, protein, or neuroactive molecules interact to confer risk for suicidal behaviors. Additionally, we remain far from understanding how this knowledge can be used to chemically treat these behaviors. The majority of studies performed to date have focused on genes and proteins of interest, and while these studies continue to be important, they are not sufficient to address these issues. Microarrays have played an essential role in highlighting new molecular pathways involved in suicidal behavior, and in the future more high throughput methods should be used to study this complex trait.

GWASs have become a popular tool to investigate complex diseases and have been performed in several psychiatric disorders, including depression, bipolar disorder, schizophrenia, and attention-deficit/hyperactivity disorder. A GWAS has not yet been performed in suicide completers, although efforts to do so are currently under way. Along with identifying SNPs associated with suicide, these studies can be used to examine copy number variations, large segments of chromosomal deletions and amplifications, which have been observed in other psychiatric conditions, most notably bipolar disorder, schizophrenia, and autism (Cook & Scherer, 2008).

The majority of microarray studies in suicide performed to date have used 3' expression arrays, which typically probe only the 3' end of mRNAs. Newer arrays have now been developed which can specifically probe the expression of each exon within a gene. Importantly, this will allow for the identification of proteins which show specific splicing differences among suicide completers, and which may improve our understanding of how these genes function in suicide.

While gene expression studies have typically focused on mRNA, the importance of other classes of RNA molecules has become increasingly recognized. MicroRNAs are short, single-stranded RNA molecules which bind to specific mRNA molecules and target them for degradation (Carthew & Sontheimer, 2009). Recent studies have examined the role of altered microRNA levels and functions in other psychiatric conditions (Abu-Elneel et al., 2008; Chen, Wang, Burmeister, & McInnis, 2009; Hansen et al., 2007), and microRNAs are currently under investigation for their role in suicide.

Finally, the epigenetic studies of suicide to date have only focused on genes of interest. Examination of alterations in CpG methylation at a larger scale is now possible using comparative hybridization arrays (Wilson et al., 2006) and very soon through large-scale, genome-based deep sequencing. Histone modifications can also be examined at a higher throughput level using ChIP-based methods. These large-scale studies will open the door to the systematic investigation of epigenetic effects that may be involved in suicide risk. As epigenetic markings are potentially reversed, this is an exciting area of investigation that creates the opportunity for eventual intervention and future avenues for risk modification.

References

Abu-Elneel, K., Liu, T., Gazzaniga, F. S., Nishimura, Y., Wall, D. P., Geschwind, D. H., … Kosik, K. S. (2008). Heterogeneous dysregulation of microRNAs across the autism spectrum. *Neurogenetics, 9*, 153–161.

Akbarian, S., Ruehl, M. G., Bliven, E., Luiz, L. A., Peranelli, A. C., Baker, S. P., Guo, Y. (2005). Chromatin alterations associated with down-regulated metabolic gene expression in the prefrontal cortex of subjects with schizophrenia. *Archives of General Psychiatry, 62*, 829–840.

Allard, P., & Norlen, M. (1997). Unchanged density of caudate nucleus dopamine uptake sites in depressed suicide victims. *Journal of Neural Transmission, 104*, 1353–1360.

Allard, P., & Norlen, M. (2001). Caudate nucleus dopamine D(2) receptors in depressed suicide victims. *Neuropsychobiology, 44*, 70–73.

Alvarez, J. C., Cremniter, D., Gluck, N., Quintin, P., Leboyer, M., Berlin, I., … Spreux-Varoquaux, O. (2000). Low serum cholesterol in violent but not in non-violent suicide attempters. *Psychiatry Research, 95*, 103–108.

Anguelova, M., Benkelfat, C., & Turecki, G. (2003). A systematic review of association studies investigating genes coding for serotonin receptors and the serotonin transporter: II. Suicidal behavior. *Molecular Psychiatry, 8*, 646–653.

Arango, V., Ernsberger, P., Marzuk, P. M., Chen, J. S., Tierney, H., Stanley, M., … Mann, J. J. (1990). Autoradiographic demonstration of increased serotonin 5-HT2 and beta-adrenergic receptor binding sites in the brain of suicide victims. *Archives of General Psychiatry, 47*, 1038–1047.

Arango, V., Ernsberger, P., Sved, A. F., & Mann, J. J. (1993). Quantitative autoradiography of alpha 1- and alpha 2-adrenergic receptors in the cerebral cortex of controls and suicide victims. *Brain Research, 630*, 271–282.

Arango, V., Huang, Y. Y., Underwood, M. D., & Mann, J. J. (2003). Genetics of the serotonergic system in suicidal behavior. *Journal of Psychiatric Research, 37*, 375–386.

Arango, V., Underwood, M. D., Boldrini, M., Tamir, H., Kassir, S. A., Hsiung, S., … Mann, J. J. (2001). Serotonin 1A receptors, serotonin transporter binding and serotonin transporter mRNA expression in the brainstem of depressed suicide victims. *Neuropsychopharmacology, 25*, 892–903.

Arango, V., Underwood, M. D., Gubbi, A. V., & Mann, J. J. (1995). Localized alterations in pre- and postsynaptic serotonin binding sites in the ventrolateral prefrontal cortex of suicide victims. *Brain Research, 688*, 121–133.

Arango, V., Underwood, M. D., & Mann, J. J. (1997). Postmortem findings in suicide victims. Implications for in vivo imaging studies. *Annals of the New York Academy of Science, 836*, 269–287.

Arato, M., Banki, C. M., Bissette, G., & Nemeroff, C. B. (1989). Elevated CSF CRF in suicide victims. *Biological Psychiatry, 25*, 355–359.

Arranz, B., Blennow, K., Eriksson, A., Mansson, J. E., & Marcusson, J. (1997). Serotonergic, noradrenergic, and dopaminergic measures in suicide brains. *Biological Psychiatry, 41,* 1000–1009.

Arranz, B., Cowburn, R., Eriksson, A., Vestling, M., & Marcusson, J. (1992). Gamma-aminobutyric acid-B (GABAB) binding sites in postmortem suicide brains. *Neuropsychobiology, 26,* 33–36.

Arranz, B., Eriksson, A., Mellerup, E., Plenge, P., & Marcusson, J. (1994). Brain 5-HT1A, 5-HT1D, and 5-HT2 receptors in suicide victims. *Biological Psychiatry, 35,* 457–463.

Atmaca, M., Kuloglu, M., Tezcan, E., & Ustundag, B. (2003). Serum leptin and cholesterol levels in schizophrenic patients with and without suicide attempts. *Acta Psychiatrica Scandinavica, 108,* 208–214.

Atmaca, M., Kuloglu, M., Tezcan, E., & Ustundag, B. (2008). Serum leptin and cholesterol values in violent and non-violent suicide attempters. *Psychiatry Research, 158,* 87–91.

Atmaca, M., Kuloglu, M., Tezcan, E., Ustundag, B., & Bayik, Y. (2002). Serum leptin and cholesterol levels in patients with bipolar disorder. *Neuropsychobiology, 46,* 176–179.

Audenaert, K., Van Laere, K., Dumont, F., Slegers, G., Mertens, J., van Heeringen, C., & Dierckx, R. A. (2001). Decreased frontal serotonin 5-HT 2a receptor binding index in deliberate self-harm patients. *European Journal of Nuclear Medicine, 28,* 175–182.

Bach-Mizrachi, H., Underwood, M. D., Kassir, S. A., Bakalian, M. J., Sibille, E., Tamir, H., . . . Arango, V. (2006). Neuronal tryptophan hydroxylase mRNA expression in the human dorsal and median raphe nuclei: Major depression and suicide. *Neuropsychopharmacology, 31,* 814–824.

Bach-Mizrachi, H., Underwood, M. D., Tin, A., Ellis, S. P., Mann, J. J., & Arango, V. (2008). Elevated expression of tryptophan hydroxylase-2 mRNA at the neuronal level in the dorsal and median raphe nuclei of depressed suicides. *Molecular Psychiatry, 13,* 507–13, 465.

Bachis, A., Mallei, A., Cruz, M. I., Wellstein, A., & Mocchetti, I. (2008). Chronic antidepressant treatments increase basic fibroblast growth factor and fibroblast growth factor-binding protein in neurons. *Neuropharmacology, 55,* 1114–1120.

Bak, L. K., Schousboe, A., & Waagepetersen, H. S. (2006). The glutamate/GABA-glutamine cycle: Aspects of transport, neurotransmitter homeostasis and ammonia transfer. *Journal of Neurochemistry, 98,* 641–653.

Ballesteros, J., Maeztu, A. I., Callado, L. F., Meana, J. J., & Gutierrez, M. (2008). Specific binding of [3H]Ro 19-6327 (lazabemide) to monoamine oxidase B is increased in frontal cortex of suicide victims after controlling for age at death. *European Neuropsychopharmacology, 18,* 55–61.

Banki, C. M., Arato, M., & Kilts, C. D. (1986). Aminergic studies and cerebrospinal fluid cations in suicide. *Annals of the New York Academy of Science, 487,* 221–230.

Barraclough, B., Bunch, J., Nelson, B., & Sainsbury, P. (1974). A hundred cases of suicide: Clinical aspects. *British Journal of Psychiatry, 125,* 355–373.

Bastida, C. M., Cremades, A., Castells, M. T., Lopez-Contreras, A. J., Lopez-Garcia, C., Sanchez-Mas, J., & Peñafiel, R. (2007). Sexual dimorphism of ornithine decarboxylase in the mouse adrenal: Influence of polyamine deprivation on catecholamine and corticoid levels. *American Journal of Physiology-Endocrinology and Metabolism, 292,* E1010–E1017.

Bennett Ao, M. R. (2008). Stress and anxiety in schizophrenia and depression: Glucocorticoids, corticotropin-releasing hormone and synapse regression. *Australian and New Zealand Journal of Psychiatry, 42,* 995–1002.

Berecek, K. H., & Brody, M. J. (1982). Evidence for a neurotransmitter role for epinephrine derived from the adrenal medulla. *American Journal of Physiology, 242,* H593–H601.

Berger, S. L. (2007). The complex language of chromatin regulation during transcription. *Nature, 447,* 407–412.

Berrocoso, E., Sanchez-Blazquez, P., Garzon, J., & Mico, J. A. (2009). Opiates as antidepressants. *Current Pharmaceutical Design, 15,* 1612–1622.

Beskow, J., Gottfries, C. G., Roos, B. E., & Winblad, B. (1976). Determination of monoamine and monoamine metabolites in the human brain: Post mortem studies in a group of suicides and in a control group. *Acta Psychiatrica Scandinavica, 53,* 7–20.

Bo, P., Giorgetti, A., Camana, C., & Savoldi, F. (1990). EEG and behavioural effects of polyamines (spermine and spermidine) on rabbits. *Pharmacological Research, 22,* 481–491.

Boldrini, M., Underwood, M. D., Mann, J. J., & Arango, V. (2005). More tryptophan hydroxylase in the brainstem dorsal raphe nucleus in depressed suicides. *Brain Research, 1041,* 19–28.

Boldrini, M., Underwood, M. D., Mann, J. J., & Arango, V. (2008). Serotonin-1A autoreceptor binding in the dorsal raphe nucleus of depressed suicides. *Journal of Psychiatric Research, 42,* 433–442.

Bowden, C., Cheetham, S. C., Lowther, S., Katona, C. L., Crompton, M. R., & Horton, R. W. (1997a). Dopamine uptake sites, labelled with [3H]GBR12935, in brain samples from depressed suicides and controls. *European Neuropsychopharmacology, 7,* 247–252.

Bowden, C., Cheetham, S. C., Lowther, S., Katona, C. L., Crompton, M. R., & Horton, R. W. (1997b). Reduced dopamine turnover in the basal ganglia of depressed suicides. *Brain Research, 769,* 135–140.

Bowden, C., Theodorou, A. E., Cheetham, S. C., Lowther, S., Katona, C. L., Crompton, M. R., & Horton, R. W. (1997). Dopamine D1 and D2 receptor binding sites in brain samples from depressed suicides and controls. *Brain Research, 752,* 227–233.

Brackley, P., Goodnow, R., Jr., Nakanishi, K., Sudan, H. L., & Usherwood, P. N. (1990). Spermine and philanthotoxin potentiate excitatory amino acid responses of Xenopus oocytes injected with rat and chick brain RNA. *Neuroscience Letters, 114,* 51–56.

Brent, D. A., Bridge, J., Johnson, B. A., & Connolly, J. (1996). Suicidal behavior runs in families. A controlled family study of adolescent suicide victims. *Archives of General Psychiatry, 53,* 1145–1152.

Brezo, J., Klempan, T., & Turecki, G. (2008). The genetics of suicide: A critical review of molecular studies. *Psychiatric Clinics of North America, 31,* 179–203.

Brown, G. L., Goodwin, F. K., Ballenger, J. C., Goyer, P. F., & Major, L. F. (1979). Aggression in humans correlates with cerebrospinal fluid amine metabolites. *Psychiatry Research, 1,* 131–139.

Brunner, J., Bronisch, T., Uhr, M., Ising, M., Binder, E., Holsboer, F., & Turck, C. W. (2005). Proteomic analysis of the CSF in unmedicated patients with major depressive disorder reveals alterations in suicide attempters. *European Archives of Psychiatry and Clinical Neuroscience, 255,* 438–440.

Brunoni, A. R., Lopes, M., & Fregni, F. (2008). A systematic review and meta-analysis of clinical studies on major depression and BDNF levels: Implications for the role of neuroplasticity in depression. *International Journal of Neuropsychopharmacology, 11,* 1169–1180.

Bunney, W. E., & Fawcett, J. A. (1965). Possibility of a biochemical test for suicidal potential: An analysis of endocrine findings prior to three suicides. *Archives of General Psychiatry, 13,* 232–239.

Buydens-Branchey, L., Branchey, M., Hudson, J., & Fergeson, P. (2000). Low HDL cholesterol, aggression and altered central serotonergic activity. *Psychiatry Research, 93,* 93–102.

Callado, L. F., Meana, J. J., Grijalba, B., Pazos, A., Sastre, M., & Garcia-Sevilla, J. A. (1998). Selective increase of alpha2A-adrenoceptor agonist binding sites in brains of depressed suicide victims. *Journal of Neurochemistry, 70,* 1114–1123.

Callreus, T., Agerskov, A. U., Hallas, J., & Andersen, M. (2007). Cardiovascular drugs and the risk of suicide: A nested case-control study. *European Journal of Clinical Pharmacology, 63,* 591–596.

Carthew, R. W., & Sontheimer, E. J. (2009). Origins and mechanisms of miRNAs and siRNAs. *Cell, 136,* 642–655.

Chattopadhyay, A., & Paila, Y. D. (2007). Lipid-protein interactions, regulation and dysfunction of brain cholesterol. *Biochemical and Biophysical Research Communications, 354,* 627–633.

Cheetham, S. C., Crompton, M. R., Katona, C. L., & Horton, R. W. (1988). Brain 5-HT2 receptor binding sites in depressed suicide victims. *Brain Research, 443,* 272–280.

Cheetham, S. C., Crompton, M. R., Katona, C. L., Parker, S. J., & Horton, R. W. (1988). Brain GABAA/benzodiazepine binding sites and glutamic acid decarboxylase activity in depressed suicide victims. *Brain Research, 460,* 114–123.

Chen, B., Dowlatshahi, D., MacQueen, G. M., Wang, J. F., & Young, L. T. (2001). Increased hippocampal BDNF immunoreactivity in subjects treated with antidepressant medication. *Biological Psychiatry, 50,* 260–265.

Chen, G. G., Fiori, L. M., Moquin, L., Gratton, A., Mamer, O., Mechawar, N., & Turecki G. (2010). Evidence of altered polyamine concentrations in cerebral cortex of suicide completers. *Neuropsychopharmacology, 35*(7), 1477–1484.

Chen, H., Wang, N., Burmeister, M., & McInnis, M. G. (2009). MicroRNA expression changes in lymphoblastoid cell lines in response to lithium treatment. *International Journal of Neuropsychopharmacology, 2,* 1–7.

Cheng, R., Juo, S. H., Loth, J. E., Nee, J., Iossifov, I., Blumenthal, R.,...Baron, M. (2006). Genome-wide linkage scan in a large bipolar disorder sample from the National Institute of Mental Health genetics initiative suggests putative loci for bipolar disorder, psychosis, suicide, and panic disorder. *Molecular Psychiatry, 11,* 252–260.

Choudary, P. V., Molnar, M., Evans, S. J., Tomita, H., Li, J. Z., Vawter, M. P.,...Jones, E. G. (2005). Altered cortical glutamatergic and GABAergic signal transmission with glial involvement in depression. *Proceedings of the National Academy of Sciences USA, 102,* 15653–15658.

Conn, P. J., & Pin, J. P. (1997). Pharmacology and functions of metabotropic glutamate receptors. *Annual Review of Pharmacology and Toxicology, 37,* 205–237.

Cook, E. H., & Scherer, S. W. (2008). Copy-number variations associated with neuropsychiatric conditions. *Nature, 455,* 919–923.

Corbett, A. D., Henderson, G., McKnight, A. T., & Paterson, S. J. (2006). 75 years of opioid research: The exciting but vain quest for the Holy Grail. *British Journal of Pharmacology, 147*(Suppl. 1), S153–S162.

Coryell, W., & Schlesser, M. (2001). The dexamethasone suppression test and suicide prediction. *American Journal of Psychiatry, 158,* 748–753.

Cross, J. A., Cheetham, S. C., Crompton, M. R., Katona, C. L., & Horton, R. W. (1988). Brain GABAB binding sites in depressed suicide victims. *Psychiatry Research, 26,* 119–129.

Crow, T. J., Cross, A. J., Cooper, S. J., Deakin, J. F., Ferrier, I. N., Johnson, J. A.,...Lofthouse, R. (1984). Neurotransmitter receptors and monoamine metabolites in the brains of patients with Alzheimer-type dementia and depression, and suicides. *Neuropharmacology, 23,* 1561–1569.

Daikhin, Y., & Yudkoff, M. (2000). Compartmentation of brain glutamate metabolism in neurons and glia. *Journal of Nutrition, 130,* 1026S-1031S.

De Luca, V., Tharmalingam, S., & Kennedy, J. L. (2007). Association study between the corticotropin-releasing hormone receptor 2 gene and suicidality in bipolar disorder. *European psychiatry, 22,* 282–287.

De Luca, V., Tharmalingam, S., Zai, C., Potapova, N., Strauss, J., Vincent, J., & Kennedy, J. L. (2010). Association of HPA axis genes with suicidal behaviour in schizophrenia. *Journal of Psychopharmacology, 24*(5), 677–682.

De Luca, V., Viggiano, E., Dhoot, R., Kennedy, J. L., & Wong, A. H. (2009). Methylation and QTDT analysis of the 5-HT2A receptor 102C allele: Analysis of suicidality in major psychosis. *Journal of Psychiatric Research, 43,* 532–537.

De Paermentier, F., Cheetham, S. C., Crompton, M. R., Katona, C. L., & Horton, R. W. (1990). Brain beta-adrenoceptor binding sites in antidepressant-free depressed suicide victims. *Brain Research, 525,* 71–77.

De Paermentier, F., Mauger, J. M., Lowther, S., Crompton, M. R., Katona, C. L., & Horton, R. W. (1997). Brain alpha-adrenoceptors in depressed suicides. *Brain Research, 757,* 60–68.

Diaz-Sastre, C., Baca-Garcia, E., Perez-Rodriguez, M. M., Garcia-Resa, E., Ceverino, A., Saiz-Ruiz, J.,...de Leon, J. (2007). Low plasma cholesterol levels in suicidal males: A gender- and body mass index-matched case-control study of suicide attempters and nonattempters. *Progress in Neuro-Psychopharmacology and Biological Psychiatry, 31,* 901–905.

Diebold, K., Michel, G., Schweizer, J., Diebold-Dorsam, M., Fiehn, W., & Kohl, B. (1998). Are psychoactive-drug-induced changes in plasma lipid and lipoprotein levels of significance for clinical remission in psychiatric disorders? *Pharmacopsychiatry, 31,* 60–67.

Dietschy, J. M., & Turley, S. D. (2001). Cholesterol metabolism in the brain. *Current Opinion Iin Lipidology, 12,* 105–112.

Dingledine, R., Borges, K., Bowie, D., & Traynelis, S. F. (1999). The glutamate receptor ion channels. *Pharmacological Reviews, 51,* 7–61.

Doyle, K. M., Kirby, B. P., Murphy, D., & Shaw, G. G. (2005). Effect of L-type calcium channel antagonists on spermine-induced CNS excitation in vivo. *Neuroscience Letters, 380,* 247–251.

Dranovsky, A., & Hen, R. (2006). Hippocampal neurogenesis: Regulation by stress and antidepressants. *Biological Psychiatry, 59,* 1136–1143.

Dwivedi, Y., Rao, J. S., Rizavi, H. S., Kotowski, J., Conley, R. R., Roberts, R. C.,...Pandey, G. N. (2003). Abnormal expression and functional characteristics of cyclic adenosine monophosphate response element binding protein in postmortem brain of suicide subjects. *Archives of General Psychiatry, 60,* 273–282.

Dwivedi, Y., Rizavi, H. S., Conley, R. R., Roberts, R. C., Tamminga, C. A., & Pandey, G. N. (2002). mRNA and protein expression of selective alpha subunits of G proteins are abnormal in prefrontal cortex of suicide victims. *Neuropsychopharmacology, 27*, 499–517.

Dwivedi, Y., Rizavi, H. S., Conley, R. R., Roberts, R. C., Tamminga, C. A., & Pandey, G. N. (2003). Altered gene expression of brain-derived neurotrophic factor and receptor tyrosine kinase B in postmortem brain of suicide subjects. *Archives of General Psychiatry, 60*, 804–815.

Dwivedi, Y., Rizavi, H. S., Teppen, T., Zhang, H., Mondal, A., Roberts, R. C., ... Pandey, G. N. (2008). Lower phosphoinositide 3-kinase (PI 3-kinase) activity and differential expression levels of selective catalytic and regulatory PI 3-kinase subunit isoforms in prefrontal cortex and hippocampus of suicide subjects. *Neuropsychopharmacology, 33*, 2324–2340.

Egeland, J. A., & Sussex, J. N. (1985). Suicide and family loading for affective disorders. *Journal of the American Medical Association, 254*, 915–918.

Ellison, L. F., & Morrison, H. I. (2001). Low serum cholesterol concentration and risk of suicide. *Epidemiology, 12*, 168–172.

Engelberg, H. (1992). Low serum cholesterol and suicide. *Lancet, 339*, 727–729.

Engstrom, G., Alling, C., Blennow, K., Regnell, G., & Traskman-Bendz, L. (1999). Reduced cerebrospinal HVA concentrations and HVA/5-HIAA ratios in suicide attempters. Monoamine metabolites in 120 suicide attempters and 47 controls. *European Neuropsychopharmacology, 9*, 399–405.

Ernst, C., Chen, E. S., & Turecki, G. (2009). Histone methylation and decreased expression of TrkB.T1 in orbital frontal cortex of suicide completers. *Molecular Psychiatry, 14*, 830–832.

Ernst, C., Deleva, V., Deng, X., Sequeira, A., Pomarenski, A., Klempan, T., ... Turecki, G. (2009). Alternative splicing, methylation state, and expression profile of tropomyosin-related kinase B in the frontal cortex of suicide completers. *Archives of General Psychiatry, 66*, 22–32.

Escriba, P. V., Ozaita, A., & Garcia-Sevilla, J. A. (2004). Increased mRNA expression of alpha2A-adrenoceptors, serotonin receptors and mu-opioid receptors in the brains of suicide victims. *Neuropsychopharmacology, 29*, 1512–1521.

Fine, A., Hoyle, C., Maclean, C. J., Levatte, T. L., Baker, H. F., & Ridley, R. M. (1997). Learning impairments following injection of a selective cholinergic immunotoxin, ME20.4 IgG-saporin, into the basal nucleus of Meynert in monkeys. *Neuroscience, 81*, 331–343.

Fiori, L. M., Mechawar, N., & Turecki, G. (2009). Identification and characterization of SAT1 promoter variants in suicide completers. *Biological Psychiatry, 66*, 460–467.

Fiori, L. M., & Turecki, G. (2008). Implication of the polyamine system in mental disorders. *Journal of Psychiatry and Neuroscience, 33*, 102–110.

Fiori, L. M., & Turecki, G. (2010). Association of the SAT1 In/del polymorphism with suicide completion. *American Journal of Medical Genetics B. Neuropsychiatric Genetics, 153B*, 825–829.

Fiori, L. M., Zouk, H., Himmelman, C., & Turecki, G. (2011). X chromosome and suicide. *Molecular Psychiatry, 16*(2), 216–226.

Freed, W. J., Dillon-Carter, O., & Kleinman, J. E. (1993). Properties of [3H]AMPA binding in postmortem human brain from psychotic subjects and controls: Increases in caudate nucleus associated with suicide. *Experimental Neurology, 121*, 48–56.

Frick, M. H., Elo, O., Haapa, K., Heinonen, O. P., Heinsalmi, P., Helo, P. et al. (1987). Helsinki Heart Study: Primary-prevention trial with gemfibrozil in middle-aged men with dyslipidemia. Safety of treatment, changes in risk factors, and incidence of coronary heart disease. *New England Journal of Medicine, 317*, 1237–1245.

Fu, Q., Heath, A. C., Bucholz, K. K., Nelson, E. C., Glowinski, A. L., Goldberg, J., ... Manninen, V. (2002). A twin study of genetic and environmental influences on suicidality in men. *Psychological Medicine, 32*, 11–24.

Fukutake, M., Hishimoto, A., Nishiguchi, N., Nushida, H., Ueno, Y., Shirakawa, O., & Maeda, K. (2008). Association of alpha2A-adrenergic receptor gene polymorphism with susceptibility to suicide in Japanese females. *Progress in Neuro-Psychopharmacology and Biological Psychiatry, 32*, 1428–1433.

Gabilondo, A. M., Meana, J. J., & Garcia-Sevilla, J. A. (1995). Increased density of mu-opioid receptors in the postmortem brain of suicide victims. *Brain Research, 682*, 245–250.

Galea, E., Regunathan, S., Eliopoulos, V., Feinstein, D. L., & Reis, D. J. (1996). Inhibition of mammalian nitric oxide synthases by agmatine, an endogenous polyamine formed by decarboxylation of arginine. *Biochemical Journal, 316*(Pt. 1), 247–249.

Garcia-Sevilla, J. A., Escriba, P. V., Ozaita, A., La Harpe, R., Walzer, C., Eytan, A., & Guimón, J. (1999). Up-regulation of immunolabeled alpha2A-adrenoceptors, Gi coupling proteins, and regulatory receptor kinases in the prefrontal cortex of depressed suicides. *Journal of Neurochemistry, 72*, 282–291.

Gécz, J., Barnett, S., Liu, J., Hollway, G., Donnelly, A., Eyre, H., ... Mulley, J. C. (1999). Characterization of the human glutamate receptor subunit 3 gene (GRIA3), a candidate for bipolar disorder and nonspecific X-linked mental retardation. *Genomics, 62*, 356–368.

Giegling, I., Chiesa, A., Calati, R., Hartmann, A. M., Moller, H. J., De Ronchi, D., ... Serretti, A. (2009). Do the estrogen receptors 1 gene variants influence the temperament and character inventory scores in suicidal attempters and healthy subjects? *American Journal of Medical Genetics B. Neuropsychiatric Genetics, 150B*, 434–438.

Giegling, I., Rujescu, D., Mandelli, L., Schneider, B., Hartmann, A. M., Schnabel, A, ... Serretti, A. (2008). Estrogen receptor gene 1 variants are not associated with suicidal behavior. *Psychiatry Research, 160*, 1–7.

Gilad, G. M., & Gilad, V. H. (1991). Polyamines can protect against ischemia-induced nerve cell death in gerbil forebrain. *Experimental Neurology, 111*, 349–355.

Gilad, G. M., & Gilad, V. H. (2003). Overview of the brain polyamine-stress-response: Regulation, development, and modulation by lithium and role in cell survival. *Cellular and Molecular Neurobiology, 23*, 637–649.

Gilad, G. M., Gilad, V. H., Eliyayev, Y., & Rabey, J. M. (1998). Developmental regulation of the brain polyamine-stress-response. *International Journal of Developmental Neuroscience, 16*, 271–278.

Gilad, G. M., Gilad, V. H., & Wyatt, R. J. (1992). Polyamines modulate the binding of GABAA-benzodiazepine receptor ligands in membranes from the rat forebrain. *Neuropharmacology, 31*, 895–898.

Glowinski, A. L., Bucholz, K. K., Nelson, E. C., Fu, Q., Madden, P. A., Reich, W., & Health, A. C. (2001). Suicide attempts in an adolescent female twin sample. *Journal of the American Academy of Child and Adolescent Psychiatry, 40*, 1300–1307.

Gong, Z. H., Li, Y. F., Zhao, N., Yang, H. J., Su, R. B., Luo, Z. P., & Li, J. (2006). Anxiolytic effect of agmatine in rats and mice. *European Journal of Pharmacology, 550*, 112–116.

Gonzalez, A. M., Pascual, J., Meana, J. J., Barturen, F., del Arco, C., Pazos, A., & García-Sevilla, J. A. (1994). Autoradiographic demonstration of increased alpha 2-adrenoceptor agonist binding sites in the hippocampus and frontal cortex of depressed suicide victims. *Journal of Neurochemistry, 63*, 256–265.

Gonzalez-Maeso, J., Rodriguez-Puertas, R., Meana, J. J., Garcia-Sevilla, J. A., & Guimon, J. (2002). Neurotransmitter receptor-mediated activation of G-proteins in brains of suicide victims with mood disorders: Selective supersensitivity of alpha(2A)-adrenoceptors. *Molecular Psychiatry, 7*, 755–767.

Gos, T., Gunther, K., Bielau, H., Dobrowolny, H., Mawrin, C., Trubner, K.,...Bogerts, B. (2009). Suicide and depression in the quantitative analysis of glutamic acid decarboxylase-Immunoreactive neuropil. *Journal of Affective Disorders, 113*, 45–55.

Gross-Isseroff, R., Dillon, K. A., Fieldust, S. J., & Biegon, A. (1990). Autoradiographic analysis of alpha 1-noradrenergic receptors in the human brain postmortem. Effect of suicide. *Archives of General Psychiatry, 47*, 1049–1053.

Gross-Isseroff, R., Dillon, K. A., Israeli, M., & Biegon, A. (1990). Regionally selective increases in mu opioid receptor density in the brains of suicide victims. *Brain Research, 530*, 312–316.

Guipponi, M., Deutsch, S., Kohler, K., Perroud, N., Le Gal, F., Vessaz, M.,...Malafosse, A. (2009). Genetic and epigenetic analysis of SSAT gene dysregulation in suicidal behavior. *American Journal of Medical Genetics B. Neuropsychiatric Genetics, 150B*, 799–807.

Gustavsson, G., Traskman-Bendz, L., Higley, J. D., & Westrin, A. (2003). CSF testosterone in 43 male suicide attempters. *European Neuropsychopharmacology, 13*, 105–109.

Hansen, T., Olsen, L., Lindow, M., Jakobsen, K. D., Ullum, H., Jonsson, E.,...Werge, T. (2007). Brain expressed microRNAs implicated in schizophrenia etiology. *PLoS ONE, 2*, e873.

Hasselmo, M. E., Anderson, B. P., & Bower, J. M. (1992). Cholinergic modulation of cortical associative memory function. *Journal of Neurophysiology, 67*, 1230–1246.

Herman, J. P., Figueiredo, H., Mueller, N. K., Ulrich-Lai, Y., Ostrander, M. M., Choi, D. C., & Cullinan, W. E. (2003). Central mechanisms of stress integration: Hierarchical circuitry controlling hypothalamo-pituitary-adrenocortical responsiveness. *Frontiers in Neuroendocrinology, 24*, 151–180.

Hesselbrock, V., Dick, D., Hesselbrock, M., Foroud, T., Schuckit, M., Edenberg, H.,...Nurnberger, J. I., Jr. (2004). The search for genetic risk factors associated with suicidal behavior. *Alcoholism: Clinical and Experimental Research, 28*, 70S–76S.

Hirsch, S. R., Richardson-Andrews, R., Costall, B., Kelly, M. E., de Belleroche, J., & Naylor, R. J. (1987). The effects of some polyamines on putative behavioural indices of mesolimbic versus striatal dopaminergic function. *Psychopharmacology (Berl), 93*, 101–104.

Holemans, S., De Paermentier, F., Horton, R. W., Crompton, M. R., Katona, C. L., & Maloteaux, J. M. (1993). NMDA glutamatergic receptors, labelled with [3H]MK-801, in brain samples from drug-free depressed suicides. *Brain Research, 616*, 138–143.

Honer, W. G., Falkai, P., Bayer, T. A., Xie, J., Hu, L., Li, H. Y.,...Trimble, W. S. (2002). Abnormalities of SNARE mechanism proteins in anterior frontal cortex in severe mental illness. *Cerebral Cortex, 12*, 349–356.

Hrdina, P. D., Demeter, E., Vu, T. B., Sotonyi, P., & Palkovits, M. (1993). 5-HT uptake sites and 5-HT2 receptors in brain of antidepressant-free suicide victims/depressives: Increase in 5-HT2 sites in cortex and amygdala. *Brain Research, 614*, 37–44.

Hsiung, S. C., Adlersberg, M., Arango, V., Mann, J. J., Tamir, H., & Liu, K. P. (2003). Attenuated 5-HT1A receptor signaling in brains of suicide victims: Involvement of adenylyl cyclase, phosphatidylinositol 3-kinase, Akt and mitogen-activated protein kinase. *Journal of Neurochemistry, 87*, 182–194.

Huan, M., Hamazaki, K., Sun, Y., Itomura, M., Liu, H., Kang, W.,...Hamazaki, T. (2004). Suicide attempt and n-3 fatty acid levels in red blood cells: A case control study in China. *Biological Psychiatry, 56*, 490–496.

Huang, H. S., & Akbarian, S. (2007). GAD1 mRNA expression and DNA methylation in prefrontal cortex of subjects with schizophrenia. *PLoS ONE, 2*, e809.

Huang, Y. Y., Battistuzzi, C., Oquendo, M. A., Harkavy-Friedman, J., Greenhill, L., Zalsman, G.,...Mann, J. J. (2004). Human 5-HT1A receptor C(-1019)G polymorphism and psychopathology. *International Journal of Neuropsychopharmacology, 7*, 441–451.

Iga, J., Ueno, S., Yamauchi, K., Numata, S., Tayoshi-Shibuya, S., Kinouchi, S.,...Ohmori, T. (2007). The Val66Met polymorphism of the brain-derived neurotrophic factor gene is associated with psychotic feature and suicidal behavior in Japanese major depressive patients. *American Journal of Medical Genetics B. Neuropsychiatric Genetics, 144B*, 1003–1006.

Iribarren, C., Reed, D. M., Wergowske, G., Burchfiel, C. M., & Dwyer, J. H. (1995). Serum cholesterol level and mortality due to suicide and trauma in the Honolulu Heart Program. *Archives of Internal Medicine, 155*, 695–700.

Iwamoto, K., & Kato, T. (2006). Gene expression profiling in schizophrenia and related mental disorders. *Neuroscientist, 12*, 349–361.

Jaga, K., & Dharmani, C. (2007). The interrelation between organophosphate toxicity and the epidemiology of depression and suicide. *Reviews on Environmental Health, 22*, 57–73.

Johann, M., Putzhammer, A., Eichhammer, P., & Wodarz, N. (2005). Association of the -141C Del variant of the dopamine D2 receptor (DRD2) with positive family history and suicidality in German alcoholics. *American Journal of Medical Genetics B. Neuropsychiatric Genetics, 132B*, 46–49.

Jokinen, J., Carlborg, A., Martensson, B., Forslund, K., Nordstrom, A. L., & Nordstrom, P. (2007). DST non-suppression predicts suicide after attempted suicide. *Psychiatry Research, 150*, 297–303.

Jokinen, J., Nordstrom, A. L., & Nordstrom, P. (2007). The relationship between CSF HVA/5-HIAA ratio and suicide intent in suicide attempters. *Archives of Suicide Research, 11*, 187–192.

Kallmann, F. J., De Porte, J., De Porte, E., & Feingold, L. (1949). Suicide in twins and only children. *American Journal of Human Genetics, 1*, 113–126.

Kaufmann, C. A., Gillin, J. C., Hill, B., O'Laughlin, T., Phillips, I., Kleinman, J. E., & Wyatt, R. J. (1984). Muscarinic binding in suicides. *Psychiatry Research, 12*, 47–55.

Kia-Keating, B. M., Glatt, S. J., & Tsuang, M. T. (2007). Meta-analyses suggest association between COMT, but not HTR1B, alleles, and suicidal behavior. *American Journal of Medical Genetics B. Neuropsychiatric Genetics, 144,* 1048–1053.

Kim, C. D., Seguin, M., Therrien, N., Riopel, G., Chawky, N., Lesage, A. D., & Turecki, G. (2005). Familial aggregation of suicidal behavior: A family study of male suicide completers from the general population. *American Journal of Psychiatry, 162,* 1017–1019.

Kim, S., Choi, K. H., Baykiz, A. F., & Gershenfeld, H. K. (2007). Suicide candidate genes associated with bipolar disorder and schizophrenia: An exploratory gene expression profiling analysis of post-mortem prefrontal cortex. *BMC Genomics, 8,* 413.

Kim, Y. K., Paik, J. W., Lee, S. W., Yoon, D., Han, C., & Lee, B. H. (2006). Increased plasma nitric oxide level associated with suicide attempt in depressive patients. *Progress in Neuro-Psychopharmacology and Biological Psychiatry, 30,* 1091–1096.

Klempan, T. A., Rujescu, D., Merette, C., Himmelman, C., Sequeira, A., Canetti, L., ... Turecki, G. (2009). Profiling brain expression of the spermidine/spermine N(1)-acetyltransferase 1 (SAT1) gene in suicide. *American Journal of Medical Genetics B. Neuropsychiatric Genetics, 150B,* 934–943.

Klempan, T. A., Sequeira, A., Canetti, L., Lalovic, A., Ernst, C., Ffrench-Mullen, J., & Turecki, G. (2009). Altered expression of genes involved in ATP biosynthesis and GABAergic neurotransmission in the ventral prefrontal cortex of suicides with and without major depression. *Molecular Psychiatry, 14,* 175–189.

Korpi, E. R., Kleinman, J. E., & Wyatt, R. J. (1988). GABA concentrations in forebrain areas of suicide victims. *Biological Psychiatry, 23,* 109–114.

Lachman, H. M., Papolos, D. F., Saito, T., Yu, Y. M., Szumlanski, C. L., & Weinshilboum, R. M. (1996). Human catechol-O-methyltransferase pharmacogenetics: Description of a functional polymorphism and its potential application to neuropsychiatric disorders. *Pharmacogenetics, 6,* 243–250.

Laje, G., Paddock, S., Manji, H., Rush, A. J., Wilson, A. F., Charney, D., & McMahon, F. J. (2007). Genetic markers of suicidal ideation emerging during citalopram treatment of major depression. *American Journal of Psychiatry, 164,* 1530–1538.

Lalovic, A., Klempan, T., Sequeira, A., Luheshi, G., & Turecki, G. (2010). Altered expression of lipid metabolism and immune response genes in the frontal cortex of suicide completers. *Journal of Affective Disorders, 120,* 24–31.

Lalovic, A., Levy, E., Canetti, L., Sequeira, A., Montoudis, A., & Turecki, G. (2007a). Fatty acid composition in postmortem brains of people who completed suicide. *Journal of Psychiatry and Neuroscience, 32,* 363–370.

Lalovic, A., Levy, E., Luheshi, G., Canetti, L., Grenier, E., Sequeira, A., & Turecki, G. (2007b). Cholesterol content in brains of suicide completers. *International Journal of Neuropsychopharmacology, 10,* 159–166.

Lalovic, A., Merkens, L., Russell, L., Arsenault-Lapierre, G., Nowaczyk, M. J., Porter, F. D., ... Turecki G. (2004). Cholesterol metabolism and suicidality in Smith-Lemli-Opitz syndrome carriers. *American Journal of Psychiatry, 161,* 2123–2126.

Lavinsky, D., Arteni, N. S., & Netto, C. A. (2003). Agmatine induces anxiolysis in the elevated plus maze task in adult rats. *Behavioural Brain Research, 141,* 19–24.

Lee, B. H., Lee, S. W., Yoon, D., Lee, H. J., Yang, J. C., Shim, S. H., ... Kim, Y. K. (2006). Increased plasma nitric oxide metabolites in suicide attempters. *Neuropsychobiology, 53,* 127–132.

Lee, H. J., & Kim, Y. K. (2003). Serum lipid levels and suicide attempts. *Acta Psychiatrica Scandinavica, 108,* 215–221.

Lee, R., Petty, F., & Coccaro, E. F. (2009). Cerebrospinal fluid GABA concentration: Relationship with impulsivity and history of suicidal behavior, but not aggression, in human subjects. *Journal of Psychiatric Research, 43,* 353–359.

Lewis, N. D. (1933). Studies on suicide: 1. Preliminary survey of some significant aspects of suicide. *Psychoanalytic Review, 20,* 241–273.

Lewis, N. D. (1934). Studies on suicide: II. Some comments on the biological aspects of suicide. *Psychoanalytic Review, 21,* 146–153.

Li, G., Regunathan, S., Barrow, C. J., Eshraghi, J., Cooper, R., & Reis, D. J. (1994). Agmatine: An endogenous clonidine-displacing substance in the brain. *Science, 263,* 966–969.

Lindberg, G., Rastam, L., Gullberg, B., & Eklund, G. A. (1992). Low serum cholesterol concentration and short term mortality from injuries in men and women. *British Medical Journal, 305,* 277–279.

Lipid Research Clinics Program. (1984). The Lipid Research Clinics Coronary Primary Prevention Trial results. I. Reduction in incidence of coronary heart disease. *Journal of the American Medical Association, 251,* 351–364.

Little, K. Y., Clark, T. B., Ranc, J., & Duncan, G. E. (1993). Beta-adrenergic receptor binding in frontal cortex from suicide victims. *Biological Psychiatry, 34,* 596–605.

London, L., Flisher, A. J., Wesseling, C., Mergler, D., & Kromhout, H. (2005). Suicide and exposure to organophosphate insecticides: Cause or effect? *American Journal of Industrial Medicine, 47,* 308–321.

Lowther, S., Crompton, M. R., Katona, C. L., & Horton, R. W. (1996). GTP gamma S and forskolin-stimulated adenylyl cyclase activity in post-mortem brain from depressed suicides and controls. *Molecular Psychiatry, 1,* 470–477.

Lowther, S., De Paermentier, F., Crompton, M. R., Katona, C. L., & Horton, R. W. (1994). Brain 5-HT2 receptors in suicide victims: Violence of death, depression and effects of antidepressant treatment. *Brain Research, 642,* 281–289.

Lowther, S., Katona, C. L., Crompton, M. R., & Horton, R. W. (1997). Brain [3H]cAMP binding sites are unaltered in depressed suicides, but decreased by antidepressants. *Brain Research, 758,* 223–228.

Lucas-Meunier, E., Fossier, P., Baux, G., & Amar, M. (2003). Cholinergic modulation of the cortical neuronal network. *Pflugers Archiv, 446,* 17–29.

Maes, M., Smith, R., Christophe, A., Vandoolaeghe, E., Van Gastel, A., Neels, H., ... Meltzer, H. Y. (1997). Lower serum high-density lipoprotein cholesterol (HDL-C) in major depression and in depressed men with serious suicidal attempts: Relationship with immune-inflammatory markers. *Acta Psychiatrica Scandinavica, 95,* 212–221.

Magri, C., Gardella, R., Valsecchi, P., Barlati, S. D., Guizzetti, L., Imperadori, L., ... Barlati, S. (2008). Study on GRIA2, GRIA3 and GRIA4 genes highlights a positive association between schizophrenia and GRIA3 in female patients. *American Journal of Medical Genetics B. Neuropsychiatric Genetics, 147B,* 745–753.

Manchon, M., Kopp, N., Rouzioux, J. J., Lecestre, D., Deluermoz, S., & Miachon, S. (1987). Benzodiazepine receptor and neurotransmitter studies in the brain of sui-cides. *Life Science, 41*, 2623–2630.

Mann, J. J., & Currier, D. (2007). A review of prospective stud-ies of biologic predictors of suicidal behavior in mood disor-ders. *Archives of Suicide Research, 11*, 3–16.

Mann, J. J., Stanley, M., McBride, P. A., & McEwen, B. S. (1986). Increased serotonin2 and beta-adrenergic receptor binding in the frontal cortices of suicide victims. *Archives of General Psychiatry, 43*, 954–959.

Marcinko, D., Marcinko, V., Karlovic, D., Marcinko, A., Martinac, M., Begic, D., & Jakovljević, M. (2008). Serum lipid levels and suicidality among male patients with schizoaf-fective disorder. *Progress in Neuro-Psychopharmacology and Biological Psychiatry, 32*, 193–196.

Marcinko, D., Martinac, M., Karlovic, D., & Loncar, C. (2004). Cholesterol serum levels in violent and non-violent young male schizophrenic suicide attempters. *Psychiatria Danubina, 16*, 161–164.

Marcinko, D., Pivac, N., Martinac, M., Jakovljevic, M., Mihaljevic-Peles, A., & Muck-Seler, D. (2007). Platelet sero-tonin and serum cholesterol concentrations in suicidal and non-suicidal male patients with a first episode of psychosis. *Psychiatry Research, 150*, 105–108.

Martin-Guerrero, I., Callado, L. F., Saitua, K., Rivero, G., Garcia-Orad, A., & Meana, J. J. (2006). The N251K func-tional polymorphism in the alpha(2A)-adrenoceptor gene is not associated with depression: A study in suicide com-pleters. *Psychopharmacology (Berl), 184*, 82–86.

Matsubara, S., Arora, R. C., & Meltzer, H. Y. (1991). Serotonergic measures in suicide brain: 5-HT1A binding sites in frontal cortex of suicide victims. *Journal of Neural Transmission. General Section, 85*, 181–194.

Mauch, D. H., Nagler, K., Schumacher, S., Goritz, C., Muller, E. C., Otto, A., & Pfrieger, F. W. (2001). CNS synaptogenesis promoted by glia-derived cholesterol. *Science, 294*, 1354–1357.

McGirr, A., Alda, M., Seguin, M., Cabot, S., Lesage, A., & Turecki, G. (2009). Familial aggregation of suicide explained by cluster B traits: A three-group family study of suicide con-trolling for major depressive disorder. *American Journal of Psychiatry, 166*, 1124–1134.

McGowan, P. O., Sasaki, A., D'Alessio, A. C., Dymov, S., Labonte, B., Szyf, M., & Meaney, M. J. (2009). Epigenetic regulation of the glucocorticoid receptor in human brain associates with childhood abuse. *Nature Neuroscience, 12*, 342–348.

McGowan, P. O., Sasaki, A., Huang, T. C., Unterberger, A., Suderman, M., Ernst, C., … Szyf, M. (2008). Promoter-wide hypermethylation of the ribosomal RNA gene promoter in the suicide brain. *PLoS ONE, 3*, e2085.

McIsaac, S. A., & Young, A. H. (2009). The role of hypothalamic pituitary-adrenal axis dysfunction in the etiology of depres-sive disorders. *Drugs of Today (Barcelona), 45*, 127–133.

McKinnon, M. C., Yucel, K., Nazarov, A., & MacQueen, G. M. (2009). A meta-analysis examining clinical predictors of hip-pocampal volume in patients with major depressive disorder. *Journal of Psychiatry and Neuroscience, 34*, 41–54.

McNamara, R. K., Jandacek, R., Rider, T., Tso, P., Dwivedi, Y., Roberts, R. C., … Pandey, G. N. (2009). Fatty acid composi-tion of the postmortem prefrontal cortex of adolescent male and female suicide victims. *Prostaglandins, Leukotrienes, and Essential Fatty Acids, 80*, 19–26.

Meana, J. J., & Garcia-Sevilla, J. A. (1987). Increased alpha 2-adrenoceptor density in the frontal cortex of depressed suicide victims. *Journal of Neural Transmission, 70*, 377–381.

Menke, A., Lucae, S., Kloiber, S., Horstmann, S., Bettecken, T., Uhr, M., … Binder, E. B. (2008). Genetic markers within glutamate receptors associated with antidepressant treatment-emergent suicidal ideation. *American Journal of Psychiatry, 165*, 917–918.

Merali, Z., Du, L., Hrdina, P., Palkovits, M., Faludi, G., Poulter, M. O., & Anisman, H. (2004). Dysregulation in the sui-cide brain: mRNA expression of corticotropin-releasing hormone receptors and GABA(A) receptor subunits in frontal cortical brain region. *Journal of Neuroscience, 24*, 1478–1485.

Meyerson, L. R., Wennogle, L. P., Abel, M. S., Coupet, J., Lippa, A. S., Rauh, C. E., & Beer, B. (1982). Human brain recep-tor alterations in suicide victims. *Pharmacology, Biochemistry, and Behavior, 17*, 159–163.

Minguet, E. G., Vera-Sirera, F., Marina, A., Carbonell, J., & Blazquez, M. A. (2008). Evolutionary diversification in polyamine biosynthesis. *Molecular Biology and Evolution, 25*, 2119–2128.

Missale, C., Nash, S. R., Robinson, S. W., Jaber, M., & Caron, M. G. (1998). Dopamine receptors: From structure to func-tion. *Physiological Reviews, 78*, 189–225.

Moinard, C., Cynober, L., & de Bandt, J. P. (2005). Polyamines: Metabolism and implications in human dis-eases. *Clinical Nutrition, 24*, 184–197.

Morgan, P. F., & Stone, T. W. (1983). Structure-activity studies on the potentiation of benzodiazepine receptor binding by ethylenediamine analogues and derivatives. *British Journal of Pharmacology, 79*, 973–977.

Morrison, L. D., Bergeron, C., & Kish, S. J. (1993). Brain S-adenosylmethionine decarboxylase activity is increased in Alzheimer's disease. *Neuroscience Letters, 154*, 141–144.

Muldoon, M. F., Manuck, S. B., & Matthews, K. A. (1990). Lowering cholesterol concentrations and mortality: A quan-titative review of primary prevention trials. *British Medical Journal, 301*, 309–314.

Muldoon, M. F., Manuck, S. B., Mendelsohn, A. B., Kaplan, J. R., & Belle, S. H. (2001). Cholesterol reduction and non-illness mortality: Meta-analysis of randomised clinical trials. *British Medical Journal, 322*, 11–15.

Murphy, G. E., & Wetzel, R. D. (1982). Family history of sui-cidal behavior among suicide attempters. *Journal of Nervous and Mental Disease, 170*, 86–90.

Neaton, J. D., Blackburn, H., Jacobs, D., Kuller, L., Lee, D. J., Sherwin, R., … Wentworth, D. (1992). Serum choles-terol level and mortality findings for men screened in the Multiple Risk Factor Intervention Trial. Multiple Risk Factor Intervention Trial Research Group. *Archives of Internal Medicine, 152*, 1490–1500.

Nemeroff, C. B., Owens, M. J., Bissette, G., Andorn, A. C., & Stanley, M. (1988). Reduced corticotropin releasing factor binding sites in the frontal cortex of suicide victims. *Archives of General Psychiatry, 45*, 577–579.

Nichols, D. E., & Nichols, C. D. (2008). Serotonin receptors. *Chemical Reviews, 108*, 1614–1641.

Niederhofer, H. (2008). Is suicidality associated with acetylcho-line? *International Psychogeriatrics, 20*, 1291.

Noga, J. T., Hyde, T. M., Herman, M. M., Spurney, C. F., Bigelow, L. B., Weinberger, D. R., & Kleinman, J. E. (1997). Glutamate receptors in the postmortem striatum of schizo-phrenic, suicide, and control brains. *Synapse, 27*, 168–176.

Norman, W. H., Brown, W. A., Miller, I. W., Keitner, G. I., & Overholser, J. C. (1990). The dexamethasone suppression test and completed suicide. *Acta Psychiatrica Scandinavica*, *81*, 120–125.

Nowak, G., Ordway, G. A., & Paul, I. A. (1995). Alterations in the N-methyl-D-aspartate (NMDA) receptor complex in the frontal cortex of suicide victims. *Brain Research, 675*, 157–164.

Nowak, G., Szewczyk, B., Sadlik, K., Piekoszewski, W., Trela, F., Florek, E., & Pilc, A. (2003). Reduced potency of zinc to interact with NMDA receptors in hippocampal tissue of suicide victims. *Polish Journal of Pharmacology, 55*, 455–459.

O'Connor, J. A., Muly, E. C., Arnold S.E., & Hemby, S. E. (2007). AMPA receptor subunit and splice variant expression in the DLPFC of schizophrenic subjects and rhesus monkeys chronically administered antipsychotic drugs. *Schizophrenia Research, 90*, 28–40.

Ordway, G. A., Widdowson, P. S., Smith, K. S., & Halaris, A. (1994). Agonist binding to alpha 2-adrenoceptors is elevated in the locus coeruleus from victims of suicide. *Journal of Neurochemistry, 63*, 617–624.

Ornitz, D. M., & Itoh, N. (2001). Fibroblast growth factors. *Genome Biology, 2*, REVIEWS3005.

Ostlund, H., Keller, E., & Hurd, Y. (2003). Estrogen receptor gene expression in relation to neuropsychiatric disorders. *Annals of the New York Academy of Science, 1007*, 54–63.

Pacheco, M. A., Stockmeier, C., Meltzer, H. Y., Overholser, J. C., Dilley, G. E., & Jope, R. S. (1996). Alterations in phosphoinositide signaling and G-protein levels in depressed suicide brain. *Brain Research, 723*, 37–45.

Palmer, A. M., Burns, M. A., Arango, V., & Mann, J. J. (1994). Similar effects of glycine, zinc and an oxidizing agent on [3H]dizocilpine binding to the N-methyl-D-aspartate receptor in neocortical tissue from suicide victims and controls. *Journal of Neural Transmission. General Section, 96*, 1–8.

Pandey, G. N., Conley, R. R., Pandey, S. C., Goel, S., Roberts, R. C., Tamminga, C. A.,...Smialek, J. (1997). Benzodiazepine receptors in the post-mortem brain of suicide victims and schizophrenic subjects. *Psychiatry Research, 71*, 137–149.

Pandey, G. N., & Dwivedi, Y. (2007). Noradrenergic function in suicide. *Archives of Suicide Research, 11*, 235–246.

Pandey, G. N., Dwivedi, Y., Rizavi, H. S., Ren, X., Pandey, S. C., Pesold, C.,...Tamminga, C. A. (2002). Higher expression of serotonin 5-HT(2A) receptors in the postmortem brains of teenage suicide victims. *American Journal of Psychiatry, 159*, 419–429.

Pandey, G. N., Ren, X., Rizavi, H. S., Conley, R. R., Roberts, R. C., & Dwivedi, Y. (2008). Brain-derived neurotrophic factor and tyrosine kinase B receptor signalling in post-mortem brain of teenage suicide victims. *International Journal of Neuropsychopharmacology, 11*, 1047–1061.

Partonen, T., Haukka, J., Virtamo, J., Taylor, P. R., & Lonnqvist, J. (1999). Association of low serum total cholesterol with major depression and suicide. *British Journal of Psychiatry, 175*, 259–262.

Pawson, T. (1994). Tyrosine kinase signalling pathways. *Princess Takamatsu Symposia, 24*, 303–322.

Penttinen, J. (1995). Hypothesis: Low serum cholesterol, suicide, and interleukin-2. *American Journal of Epidemiology, 141*, 716–718.

Perez-Rodriguez, M. M., Baca-Garcia, E., Diaz-Sastre, C., Garcia-Resa, E., Ceverino, A., Saiz-Ruiz, J.,...de Leon, J. (2008). Low serum cholesterol may be associated with suicide attempt history. *Journal of Clinical Psychiatry, 69*, 1920–1927.

Perroud, N., Aitchison, K. J., Uher, R., Smith, R., Huezo-Diaz, P., Marusic, A.,...Craig, I. (2009). Genetic predictors of increase in suicidal ideation during antidepressant treatment in the GENDEP project. *Neuropsychopharmacology, 34*, 2517–2528.

Perroud, N., Courtet, P., Vincze, I., Jaussent, I., Jollant, F., Bellivier, F.,...Malafosse, A. (2008). Interaction between BDNF Val66Met and childhood trauma on adult's violent suicide attempt. *Genes, Brain, and Behavior, 7*, 314–322.

Persson, M. L., Geijer, T., Wasserman, D., Rockah, R., Frisch, A., Michaelovsky, E.,...Weizman, A. (1999). Lack of association between suicide attempt and a polymorphism at the dopamine receptor D4 locus. *Psychiatric Genetics, 9*, 97–100.

Pitchot, W., Hansenne, M., Gonzalez, M. A., Pinto, E., Reggers, J., Fuchs, S.,...Ansseau, M. (2001). Reduced dopamine function in depressed patients is related to suicidal behavior but not its lethality. *Psychoneuroendocrinology, 26*, 689–696.

Pitchot, W., Reggers, J., Pinto, E., Hansenne, M., Fuchs, S., Pirard, S., & Ansseau, M. (2001). Reduced dopaminergic activity in depressed suicides. *Psychoneuroendocrinology, 26*, 331–335.

Pitchot, W., Hansenne, M., Gonzalez Moreno, A., & Ansseau, M. (1992). Suicidal behavior and growth hormone response to apomorphine test. *Biological Psychiatry, 31*, 1213–1219.

Placidi, G. P., Oquendo, M. A., Malone, K. M., Huang, Y. Y., Ellis, S. P., & Mann, J. J. (2001). Aggressivity, suicide attempts, and depression: Relationship to cerebrospinal fluid monoamine metabolite levels. *Biological Psychiatry, 50*, 783–791.

Poulter, M. O., Du, L., Weaver, I. C., Palkovits, M., Faludi, G., Merali, Z.,...Anisman, H. (2008). GABAA receptor promoter hypermethylation in suicide brain: Implications for the involvement of epigenetic processes. *Biological Psychiatry, 64*, 645–652.

Purselle, D. C., & Nemeroff, C. B. (2003). Serotonin transporter: A potential substrate in the biology of suicide. *Neuropsychopharmacology, 28*, 613–619.

Reif, A., Jacob, C. P., Rujescu, D., Herterich, S., Lang, S., Gutknecht, L.,...Lesch, K. P. (2009). Influence of functional variant of neuronal nitric oxide synthase on impulsive behaviors in humans. *Archives of General Psychiatry, 66*, 41–50.

Reis, D. J., & Regunathan, S. (2000). Is agmatine a novel neurotransmitter in brain? *Trends in Pharmacological Sciences, 21*, 187–193.

Rezin, G. T., Amboni, G., Zugno, A. I., Quevedo, J., & Streck, E. L. (2009). Mitochondrial dysfunction and psychiatric disorders. *Neurochemical Research, 34*, 1021–1029.

Rhee, H. J., Kim, E. J., & Lee, J. K. (2007). Physiological polyamines: Simple primordial stress molecules. *Journal of Cellular and Molecular Medicine, 11*, 685–703.

Ritz, M. C., Mantione, C. R., & London, E. D. (1994). Spermine interacts with cocaine binding sites on dopamine transporters. *Psychopharmacology (Berl), 114*, 47–52.

Robbins, D. R., & Alessi, N. E. (1985). Suicide and the dexamethasone suppression test in adolescence. *Biological Psychiatry, 20*, 107–110.

Rochet, T., Kopp, N., Vedrinne, J., Deluermoz, S., Debilly, G., & Miachon, S. (1992). Benzodiazepine binding sites and their modulators in hippocampus of violent suicide victims. *Biological Psychiatry, 32*, 922–931.

Rollins, R. A., Haghighi, F., Edwards, J. R., Das, R., Zhang, M. Q., Ju, J., & Bestor, T. H. (2006). Large-scale structure of genomic methylation patterns. *Genome Research, 16,* 157–163.

Rosel, P., Arranz, B., San, L., Vallejo, J., Crespo, J. M., Urretavizcaya, M., & Navarro, M. A. (2000). Altered 5-HT(2A) binding sites and second messenger inositol trisphosphate (IP(3)) levels in hippocampus but not in frontal cortex from depressed suicide victims. *Psychiatry Research, 99,* 173–181.

Rosel, P., Arranz, B., Urretavizcaya, M., Oros, M., San, L., & Navarro, M. A. (2004). Altered 5-HT2A and 5-HT4 postsynaptic receptors and their intracellular signalling systems IP3 and cAMP in brains from depressed violent suicide victims. *Neuropsychobiology, 49,* 189–195.

Roy, A. (1983). Family history of suicide. *Archives of General Psychiatry, 40,* 971–974.

Roy, A., Agren, H., Pickar, D., Linnoila, M., Doran, A. R., Cutler, N. R., & Paul, S. M. (1986). Reduced CSF concentrations of homovanillic acid and homovanillic acid to 5-hydroxyindoleacetic acid ratios in depressed patients: Relationship to suicidal behavior and dexamethasone nonsuppression. *American Journal of Psychiatry, 143,* 1539–1545.

Roy, A., Karoum, F., & Pollack, S. (1992). Marked reduction in indexes of dopamine metabolism among patients with depression who attempt suicide. *Archives of General Psychiatry, 49,* 447–450.

Roy, A., Ninan, P., Mazonson, A., Pickar, D., Van Kammen, D., Linnoila, M., & Paul, S. M. (1985). CSF monoamine metabolites in chronic schizophrenic patients who attempt suicide. *Psychological Medicine, 15,* 335–340.

Roy, A., Pickar, D., De Jong, J., Karoum, F., & Linnoila, M. (1989). Suicidal behavior in depression: Relationship to noradrenergic function. *Biological Psychiatry, 25,* 341–350.

Roy, A., Segal, N. L., Centerwall, B. S., & Robinette, C. D. (1991). Suicide in twins. *Archives of General Psychiatry, 48,* 29–32.

Roy, A., Segal, N. L., & Sarchiapone, M. (1995). Attempted suicide among living co-twins of twin suicide victims. *American Journal of Psychiatry, 152,* 1075–1076.

Rujescu, D., Giegling, I., Mandelli, L., Schneider, B., Hartmann, A. M., Schnabel, A.,...Serretti, A. (2008). NOS-I and -III gene variants are differentially associated with facets of suicidal behavior and aggression-related traits. *American Journal of Medical Genetics B. Neuropsychiatric Genetics, 147B,* 42–48.

Saiz, P. A., Garcia-Portilla, M. P., Paredes, B., Arango, C., Morales, B., Alvarez, V.,...Bobes, J. (2007). Lack of association between endothelial nitric oxide synthase (NOS3) gene polymorphisms and suicide attempts. *Behavioral and Brain Functions, 3,* 32.

Sarchiapone, M., Carli, V., Roy, A., Iacoviello, L., Cuomo, C., Latella, M. C.,...Janal, M. N. (2008). Association of polymorphism (Val66Met) of brain-derived neurotrophic factor with suicide attempts in depressed patients. *Neuropsychobiology, 57,* 139–145.

Sarter, M., Bruno, J. P., & Turchi, J. (1999). Basal forebrain afferent projections modulating cortical acetylcholine, attention, and implications for neuropsychiatric disorders. *Annals of the New York Academy of Science, 877,* 368–382.

Schlicht, K., Buttner, A., Siedler, F., Scheffer, B., Zill, P., Eisenmenger, W.,...Bondy, B. (2007). Comparative proteomic analysis with postmortem prefrontal cortex tissues of suicide victims versus controls. *Journal of Psychiatric Research, 41,* 493–501.

Schulsinger, F., Kety, S. S., Rosenthal, D., & Wender, P. H. (1979). A family study of suicide. In M. Schou & E. Stromgren (Eds.), *Origin, prevention and treatment of affective disorders* (pp. 277–287). London, UK: Academic Press.

Secunda, S. K., Cross, C. K., Koslow, S., Katz, M. M., Kocsis, J., Maas, J. W., & Landis, H. (1986). Biochemistry and suicidal behavior in depressed patients. *Biological Psychiatry, 21,* 756–767.

Segal, N. L., & Roy, A. (1995). Suicide attempts in twins whose co-twins' deaths were non-suicides. *Personality and Individual Differences, 19,* 937–940.

Seiler, N., & Raul, F. (2005). Polyamines and apoptosis. *Journal of Cellular and Molecular Medicine, 9,* 623–642.

Sen, S., Duman, R., & Sanacora, G. (2008). Serum brain-derived neurotrophic factor, depression, and antidepressant medications: Meta-analyses and implications. *Biological Psychiatry, 64,* 527–532.

Sequeira, A., Mamdani, F., Ernst, C., Vawter, M. P., Bunney, W. E., Klempan, T.,...Turecki, G. (2009). Global brain gene expression analysis links glutamatergic and GABAergic alterations to suicide and major depression. *PLoS ONE, 4,* e6585.

Sequeira, A., Gwadry, F. G., Ffrench-Mullen, J. M., Canetti, L., Gingras, Y., Casero, R. A., Jr.,...Turecki, G. (2006). Implication of SSAT by gene expression and genetic variation in suicide and major depression. *Archives of General Psychiatry, 63,* 35–48.

Sequeira, A., Klempan, T., Canetti, L., Ffrench-Mullen, J., Benkelfat, C., Rouleau, G. A., & Turecki, G. (2007). Patterns of gene expression in the limbic system of suicides with and without major depression. *Molecular Psychiatry, 12,* 640–655.

Sequeira, A., Mamdani, F., Lalovic, A., Anguelova, M., Lesage, A., Seguin, M.,...Turecki, G. (2004). Alpha 2A adrenergic receptor gene and suicide. *Psychiatry Research, 125,* 87–93.

Sher, L., Mann, J. J., Traskman-Bendz, L., Winchel, R., Huang, Y. Y., Fertuck, E., & Stanley, B. H. (2006). Lower cerebrospinal fluid homovanillic acid levels in depressed suicide attempters. *Journal of Affective Disorders, 90,* 83–89.

Sherif, F., Marcusson, J., & Oreland, L. (1991). Brain gamma-aminobutyrate transaminase and monoamine oxidase activities in suicide victims. *European Archives of Psychiatry and Clinical Neuroscience, 241,* 139–144.

Shimon, H., Agam, G., Belmaker, R. H., Hyde, T. M., & Kleinman, J. E. (1997). Reduced frontal cortex inositol levels in postmortem brain of suicide victims and patients with bipolar disorder. *American Journal of Psychiatry, 154,* 1148–1150.

Shimon, H., Sobolev, Y., Davidson, M., Haroutunian, V., Belmaker, R. H., & Agam, G. (1998). Inositol levels are decreased in postmortem brain of schizophrenic patients. *Biological Psychiatry, 44,* 428–432.

Sibille, E., Arango, V., Galfavy, H. C., Pavlidis, P., Erraji-Benchekroun, L., Ellis, S. P., & John Mann, J. (2004). Gene expression profiling of depression and suicide in human prefrontal cortex. *Neuropsychopharmacology, 29,* 351–361.

Sorensen, H. T., Mellemkjaer, L., & Olsen, J. H. (2001). Risk of suicide in users of beta-adrenoceptor blockers, calcium channel blockers and angiotensin converting enzyme inhibitors. *British Journal of Clinical Pharmacology, 52,* 313–318.

Sperner-Unterweger, B. (2005). Immunological aetiology of major psychiatric disorders: Evidence and therapeutic implications. *Drugs, 65,* 1493–1520.

Stanley, M. (1984). Cholinergic receptor binding in the frontal cortex of suicide victims. *American Journal of Psychiatry, 141,* 1432–1436.

Statham, D. J., Heath, A. C., Madden, P. A., Bucholz, K. K., Bierut, L., Dinwiddie, S. H.,...Martin, N. G. (1998). Suicidal behaviour: An epidemiological and genetic study. *Psychological Medicine, 28,* 839–855.

Stocks, G. M., Cheetham, S. C., Crompton, M. R., Katona, C. L., & Horton, R. W. (1990). Benzodiazepine binding sites in amygdala and hippocampus of depressed suicide victims. *Journal of Affective Disorders, 18,* 11–15.

Sublette, M. E., Hibbeln, J. R., Galfalvy, H., Oquendo, M. A., & Mann, J. J. (2006). Omega-3 polyunsaturated essential fatty acid status as a predictor of future suicide risk. *American Journal of Psychiatry, 163,* 1100–1102.

Suda, A., Kawanishi, C., Kishida, I., Sato, R., Yamada, T., Nakagawa, M.,...Hirayasu, Y. (2009). Dopamine D2 receptor gene polymorphisms are associated with suicide attempt in the Japanese population. *Neuropsychobiology, 59,* 130–134.

Summers, R. J., & McMartin, L. R. (1993). Adrenoceptors and their second messenger systems. *Journal of Neurochemistry, 60,* 10–23.

Sundman-Eriksson, I., & Allard, P. (2002). [(3)H]Tiagabine binding to GABA transporter-1 (GAT-1) in suicidal depression. *Journal of Affective Disorders, 71,* 29–33.

Tabor, C. W., & Tabor, H. (1984). Polyamines. *Annual Review of Biochemistry, 53,* 749–790.

Thalmeier, A., Dickmann, M., Giegling, I., Schneider, B., Hartmann, M., Maurer, K.,...Rujescu, D. (2008). Gene expression profiling of post-mortem orbitofrontal cortex in violent suicide victims. *International Journal of Neuropsychopharmacology, 11,* 217–228.

Tochigi, M., Iwamoto, K., Bundo, M., Sasaki, T., Kato, N., & Kato, T. (2008). Gene expression profiling of major depression and suicide in the prefrontal cortex of postmortem brains. *Neuroscience Research, 60,* 184–191.

Tripodianakis, J., Markianos, M., Rouvali, O., & Istikoglou, C. (2007). Gonadal axis hormones in psychiatric male patients after a suicide attempt. *European Archives of Psychiatry and Clinical Neuroscience, 257,* 135–139.

Tripodianakis, J., Markianos, M., Sarantidis, D., & Agouridaki, M. (2002). Biogenic amine turnover and serum cholesterol in suicide attempt. *European Archives of Psychiatry and Clinical Neuroscience, 252,* 38–43.

Tsai, S. J., Wang, Y. C., Hong, C. J., & Chiu, H. J. (2003). Association study of oestrogen receptor alpha gene polymorphism and suicidal behaviours in major depressive disorder. *Psychiatric Genetics, 13,* 19–22.

Tsuang, M. T. (1983). Risk of suicide in the relatives of schizophrenics, manics, depressives, and controls. *Journal of Clinical Psychiatry, 44,* 396–400.

Turecki, G. (2001). Suicidal behavior: Is there a genetic predisposition? *Bipolar Disorders, 3,* 335–349.

Underwood, M. D., Mann, J. J., & Arango, V. (2004). Serotonergic and noradrenergic neurobiology of alcoholic suicide. *Alcoholism: Clinical and Experimental Research, 28,* 57S–69S.

van Heeringen, C., Audenaert, K., Van Laere, K., Dumont, F., Slegers, G., Mertens, J., & Dierckx, R. A. (2003). Prefrontal 5-HT2a receptor binding index, hopelessness and personality characteristics in attempted suicide. *Journal of Affective Disorders, 74,* 149–158.

Vawter, M. P., Thatcher, L., Usen, N., Hyde, T. M., Kleinman, J. E., & Freed, W. J. (2002). Reduction of synapsin in the hippocampus of patients with bipolar disorder and schizophrenia. *Molecular Psychiatry, 7,* 571–578.

Vevera, J., Zukov, I., Morcinek, T., & Papezova, H. (2003). Cholesterol concentrations in violent and non-violent women suicide attempters. *European Psychiatry, 18,* 23–27.

Virkkunen, M. (1979). Serum cholesterol in antisocial personality. *Neuropsychobiology, 5,* 27–30.

von Borczyskowski, A., Hjern, A., Lindblad, F., & Vinnerljung, B. (2006). Suicidal behaviour in national and international adult adoptees: A Swedish cohort study. *Social Psychiatry and Psychiatric Epidemiology, 41,* 95–102.

Vuksan-Cusa, B., Marcinko, D., Nad, S., & Jakovljevic, M. (2009). Differences in cholesterol and metabolic syndrome between bipolar disorder men with and without suicide attempts. *Progress in Neuro-Psychopharmacology and Biological Psychiatry, 33,* 109–112.

Wasserman, D., Geijer, T., Rozanov, V., & Wasserman, J. (2005). Suicide attempt and basic mechanisms in neural conduction: Relationships to the SCN8A and VAMP4 genes. *American Journal of Medical Genetics B. Neuropsychiatric Genetics, 133B,* 116–119.

Wasserman, D., Sokolowski, M., Rozanov, V., & Wasserman, J. (2008). The CRHR1 gene: A marker for suicidality in depressed males exposed to low stress. *Genes, Brain, and Behavior, 7,* 14–19.

Wasserman, D., Wasserman, J., Rozanov, V., & Sokolowski, M. (2009). Depression in suicidal males: Genetic risk variants in the CRHR1 gene. *Genes, Brain, and Behavior, 8,* 72–79.

Weaver, I. C., Cervoni, N., Champagne, F. A., D'Alessio, A. C., Sharma, S., Seckl, J. R.,...Meaney, M. J. (2004). Epigenetic programming by maternal behavior. *Nature Neuroscience, 7,* 847–854.

Wender, P. H., Kety, S. S., Rosenthal, D., Schulsinger, F., Ortmann, J., & Lunde, I. (1986). Psychiatric disorders in the biological and adoptive families of adopted individuals with affective disorders. *Archives of General Psychiatry, 43,* 923–929.

Williams, K. (1997). Modulation and block of ion channels: A new biology of polyamines. *Cellular Signalling, 9,* 1–13.

Wilson, I. M., Davies, J. J., Weber, M., Brown, C. J., Alvarez, C. E., MacAulay, C.,...Lam, L. W. (2006). Epigenomics: Mapping the methylome. *Cell Cycle, 5,* 155–158.

Woodruff, R. A., Clayton, P. J., & Guze, S. B. (1972). Suicide attempts and psychiatric diagnosis. *Diseases of the Nervous System, 33,* 617–621.

Yehuda, R. (1997). Sensitization of the hypothalamic-pituitary-adrenal axis in posttraumatic stress disorder. *Annals of the New York Academy of Science, 821,* 57–75.

Zalsman, G., Frisch, A., Lewis, R., Michaelovsky, E., Hermesh, H., Sher, L.,...Weizman, A. (2004). DRD4 receptor gene exon III polymorphism in inpatient suicidal adolescents. *Journal of Neural Transmission, 111,* 1593–1603.

Zalsman, G., Molcho, A., Huang, Y., Dwork, A., Li, S., & Mann, J. J. (2005). Postmortem mu-opioid receptor binding in suicide victims and controls. *Journal of Neural Transmission, 112,* 949–954.

Zarrilli, F., Angiolillo, A., Castaldo, G., Chiariotti, L., Keller, S., Sacchetti, S.,...Sarchiapone, M. (2009). Brain derived neurotrophic factor (BDNF) genetic polymorphism (Val66Met) in suicide: A study of 512 cases. *American Journal of Medical Genetics B. Neuropsychiatric Genetics, 150B,* 599–600.

Zavitsanou, K., Katsifis, A., Mattner, F., & Huang, X. F. (2004). Investigation of m1/m4 muscarinic receptors in the anterior cingulate cortex in schizophrenia, bipolar disorder, and major depression disorder. *Neuropsychopharmacology, 29,* 619–625.

Zeidan, M. P., Zomkowski, A. D., Rosa, A. O., Rodrigues, A. L., & Gabilan, N. H. (2007). Evidence for imidazoline receptors involvement in the agmatine antidepressant-like effect in the forced swimming test. *European Journal of Pharmacology, 565,* 125–131.

Zhang, J., McKeown, R. E., Hussey, J. R., Thompson, S. J., Woods, J. R., & Ainsworth, B. E. (2005). Low HDL cholesterol is associated with suicide attempt among young healthy women: The Third National Health and Nutrition Examination Survey. *Journal of Affective Disorders, 89,* 25–33.

Zhou, L., & Zhu, D. Y. (2009). Neuronal nitric oxide synthase: Structure, subcellular localization, regulation, and clinical implications. *Nitric Oxide, 20,* 223–230.

Zhu, H., Karolewicz, B., Nail, E., Stockmeier, C. A., Szebeni, K., & Ordway, G. A. (2006). Normal [3H]flunitrazepam binding to GABAA receptors in the locus coeruleus in major depression and suicide. *Brain Research, 1125,* 138–146.

Zomkowski, A. D., Hammes, L., Lin, J., Calixto, J. B., Santos, A. R., & Rodrigues, A. L. (2002). Agmatine produces antidepressant-like effects in two models of depression in mice. *Neuroreport, 13,* 387–391.

Zomkowski, A. D., Rosa, A. O., Lin, J., Santos, A. R., Calixto, J. B., & Rodrigues, A. L. (2004). Evidence for serotonin receptor subtypes involvement in agmatine antidepressant like-effect in the mouse forced swimming test. *Brain Research, 1023,* 253–263.

Zomkowski, A. D., Santos, A. R., & Rodrigues, A. L. (2005). Evidence for the involvement of the opioid system in the agmatine antidepressant-like effect in the forced swimming test. *Neuroscience Letters, 381,* 279–283.

Zomkowski, A. D., Santos, A. R., & Rodrigues, A. L. (2006). Putrescine produces antidepressant-like effects in the forced swimming test and in the tail suspension test in mice. *Progress in Neuro-Psychopharmacology and Biological Psychiatry, 30,* 1419–1425.

Zubenko, G. S., Maher, B. S., Hughes, H. B., III, Zubenko, W. N., Scott, S. J., & Marazita, M. L. (2004). Genome-wide linkage survey for genetic loci that affect the risk of suicide attempts in families with recurrent, early-onset, major depression. *American Journal of Medical Genetics B. Neuropsychiatric Genetics, 129,* 47–54.

Zureik, M., Courbon, D., & Ducimetiere, P. (1996). Serum cholesterol concentration and death from suicide in men: Paris prospective study I. *British Medical Journal, 313,* 649–651.

Developmental Approaches to Understanding Suicidal and Self-Injurious Behaviors

Sheila E. Crowell, Christina M. Derbidge, *and* Theodore P. Beauchaine

Abstract

Suicidal behaviors are observed across most of the life span, beginning in late childhood. At present, however, few life span developmental studies of suicide risk have appeared in the literature. Rather, almost all research on suicide and related behaviors has been conducted with samples circumscribed by age (e.g., adolescents, elderly). Moreover, until recently most of this work was conducted among those with depression or borderline personality disorder, of whom only subsets manifest suicidal behaviors. In this chapter, we review existing research on suicide and suicide risk from a developmental psychopathology perspective. Although precipitating events leading to suicide and suicide attempts vary widely across the life span, core functions of the behaviors are remarkably similar. Indeed, common psychological and interpersonal processes may heighten risk for suicide, regardless of age. We explore how specific biological vulnerabilities interact with such processes across time to promote ineffective coping, risk for suicide, and the emergence of multiple forms of psychopathology among adolescents and young adults. We conclude by offering several developmental hypotheses of suicide risk into adulthood and later life.

Key Words: self-injury, suicidal behavior, suicide, self-injurious thoughts and behaviors, developmental psychopathology, life span, biological vulnerability, psychosocial risk

In almost all Western cultures, age is a strong marker of suicide risk (World Health Organization [WHO], 2002). In the United States, for example, 35.7 per 100,000 males over age 75 commit suicide—higher than any other demographic group (National Center for Injury Prevention and Control, 2006). Despite strong prediction by age, however, suicide is also a leading cause of death in younger demographic groups. In fact, it is the second leading cause of death among young adults ages 25–34 years (eclipsed only by unintentional injury), the fourth leading cause of death among 10- to 14-year-olds, and the third leading cause of death among 15- to 24-year-olds (National Center for Injury Prevention and Control, 2006). Both males and females of all racial/ethnic backgrounds are affected.

Although such statistics are alarming, the number of people who engage in nonlethal self-injury is far greater. In the United States, over 395,000 people are treated in emergency rooms annually for self-inflicted injuries (National Center for Injury Prevention and Control, 2009), which may represent as few as 30% of those who self-injure (Crosby, Cheltenham, & Sacks, 1999). Many researchers conceptualize suicide as one end of a spectrum of related thoughts and behaviors, including ideation, nonsuicidal self-injury (NSSI), and suicide attempts (Brent et al., 1988; Stanley, Winchel, Molcho, Simeon, & Stanley, 1992). However, relations among such behaviors may be more complex than assumed previously (Nock, Joiner, Gordon, Lloyd-Richardson, & Prinstein, 2006). For example, NSSI often serves a different emotional function

(Brown, Comtois, & Linehan, 2002). Nevertheless, studying suicide risk behaviors together has conceptual advantages. Most important, any self-inflicted injury is the single best predictor of eventual suicide (Joiner et al., 2005). There is also substantial overlap in biological vulnerabilities and psychosocial risk factors associated with nonsuicidal and suicidal self-injury and, to a lesser degree, suicidal ideation. Furthermore, many individuals follow a developmental progression that begins with ideation and progresses to behaviors that increase in lethality and degree of suicidal intent. Accordingly, identifying individuals on this high-risk trajectory is an urgent public health priority (Crowell, Beauchaine, & Linehan, 2009; Derbidge & Beauchaine, in press).

Developmental/life span conceptualizations of suicide are not new (see Blumenthal & Kupfer, 1990; Leenaars, 1991; Stillion & McDowell, 1996). However, there are limitations to the existing literature. First, most developmental models focus on adolescents and young adults, thereby neglecting important processes that continue into later life (e.g., Portes, Sandhu, & Longwell-Grice, 2002). Second, many models are based on clinical impressions and have not been tested rigorously in prospective longitudinal studies (Linehan, 1993; Perelberg, 1999). Third, existing models have weighted either environmental or biological factors as etiologically dominant, rarely examining interactions between the two (e.g., Baumeister, 1990; deCatanzaro, 1980). Fourth, most life span approaches have identified correlates of suicide at different ages, but few have attended to underlying mechanisms of risk (Stillion & McDowell, 1996). Finally, hypotheses on the development of suicide are often extrapolated from studies of mood or personality disorders (Rao, Weissman, Martin, & Hammond, 1993; Yen et al., 2003), which may or may not always be relevant for suicidal populations.

Because no studies of suicide risk have followed individuals from infancy into old age, a fully integrated life span model is premature (for extensive follow-up periods, see Dunedin, Minnesota, and Terman studies; Caspi, 2000; Krueger et al., 2002; Tomlinson-Keasey, Warren, & Elliott, 1986). Indeed, in a review of depression across the life span, Hammen, Garber, and Ingram (2010) noted that "investigators of child/adolescent depression and adult depression have pursued separate paths," resulting in "critical gaps in both fields that are in part attributable to this typical age-related division of labor and its usual designs and methods" (p. 282). The same can be said of suicide research.

Despite these limitations, more integrative developmental models of suicide and related behaviors have begun to emerge (e.g., Beauchaine, Klein, Crowell, Derbidge, & Gatzke-Kopp, 2009; Crowell, Kaufman, & Lenzenweger, 2013; Crowell, Beauchaine, & Lenzenweger, 2008; Crowell et al., 2009; Derbidge & Beauchaine, in press). Such models, and the literature from which they derive, paint a complicated picture of suicidality and its emergence across the life span. Moreover, developmental approaches may provide insight into a critically important question: Why now? Indeed, risk for suicide peaks at a unique time for each person based upon the intersection of biological vulnerabilities, psychosocial risk factors, and developmental processes, among other possible factors. Prior to articulating a developmental model, we provide an overview of relevant definitions and concepts.

Definitions and Concepts
Defining Suicidal and Self-Injurious Behaviors

Causes of suicide have been examined and debated for centuries (see Durkheim, 1897, for a review). What might be considered modern studies of suicide and self-injury, characterized by use of the scientific method, emerged between the 1930s and 1950s (e.g., Mason, 1954; Offer & Barglow, 1960; Simpson, 1950; Zilboorg, 1936). Despite this established tradition, however, defining and conceptualizing suicidal behaviors remains challenging (Linehan, Comtois, Brown, Heard, & Wagner, 2006; O'Carroll et al., 1996; Silverman, Berman, Sanddal, O'Carroll, & Joiner, 2007a, 2007b). For example, ascertaining whether a suicide occurred can be difficult, and current data may vastly underestimate the number of such deaths. The range of nonlethal suicide-related thoughts and behaviors is even more difficult to define, and no nomenclature has received universal acceptance (see Nock, 2010). Although the extensive debate on the definition of suicidal behaviors exceeds the scope of this chapter, interested readers are referred to Chapter 2 of this volume.

Disagreement notwithstanding, several key principles have widespread support (Linehan, Comtois, et al., 2006). These include (1) categorizing self-injurious behaviors into relevant subtypes based on intent, lethality of method, and physical consequence to the individual; (2) using familiar and readily defined terms (e.g., common terms, such as "suicide attempt," should be maintained); (3) promoting clarity by abandoning use of ambiguous terms (e.g., self-harm, which is often used to describe harmful but nonsuicidal behaviors such as binge drinking or decorative body piercing); and (4) encouraging consistency of terminology across settings (e.g., research, epidemiology, clinical practice, medical records, coroner's reports).

We conceptualize self-injurious thoughts and behaviors (SITBs) as the broadest category, of which suicide attempts are only a subset. Self-inflicted injury includes all deliberate acts of self-injury with intent to cause bodily harm or death. Such behaviors can be subdivided into (1) suicidal behaviors (SBs), where there is ambivalent or definite suicidal intent, and (2) nonsuicidal self-injury (NSSI), which includes all purposeful acts of bodily harm without suicidal intent. Within this framework, suicidal ideation is conceptualized separately because it is a cognitive process rather than a behavior. In this review, we emphasize studies of SB and repetitive NSSI. Whenever possible, we use the terminology most appropriate to the study being reviewed. In many cases, the broad label of SITB is most appropriate, since many who engage in repetitive NSSI also attempt suicide (see Nock, 2010; Nock et al., 2006).

Suicidal and Nonsuicidal Self-Injury in *the* Diagnostic and Statistical Manual of Mental Disorders

Suicidal behavior and NSSI are usually associated with clinically significant psychopathology (Brent, Johnson, et al., 1994; Brent et al., 1988; Renaud, Berlim, McGirr, Tousignant, & Turecki, 2008; Shaffer et al., 1996). Postsuicide family interviews confirm that about 90% of suicide completers meet criteria for one or more disorders outlined in the *Diagnostic and Statistical Manual of Mental Disorders*, fourth edition (*DSM-IV*; American Psychiatric Association [APA], 2000). However, relations between suicidality and psychopathology are complex and have been discussed extensively elsewhere (see, e.g., Beauchaine et al., 2009; Crowell et al., 2008, 2009, 2013; Derbidge & Beauchaine, in press; Chapter 5, this volume). As noted in these reviews, suicide-related diagnostic criteria are common to both depression and borderline personality disorder (APA, 2000). However, observed rates of suicidal ideation, SB, and NSSI are also elevated among those with substance use disorders, other personality disorders (e.g., avoidant, antisocial), externalizing behavior disorders (e.g., oppositional defiant disorder, conduct disorder), anxiety disorders (e.g., generalized anxiety disorder,

posttraumatic stress disorder, social phobia), eating disorders, and psychotic disorders, among others (APA, 2006). Moreover, longitudinal studies indicate that suicidality is often chronic, sometimes extending beyond remission of acute psychiatric disturbance (Mehlum, Friis, Vaglum, & Karterud, 1994). There has been ongoing effort to list SITB within the *DSM* as its own diagnostic entity (Kahan & Pattison, 1984). Indeed, the *DSM-5* now includes two distinct suicide-related disorders in the section devoted to "conditions for further study": *suicidal behavior disorder* and *nonsuicidal self-injury*.

In our view, suicide-related behaviors and NSSI are multidetermined phenomena that (a) should not be defined as discrete disorders based solely on specific behaviors, *and* (b) are better understood by focusing on stable underlying individual differences (i.e., traits) that give rise to broad classes of behavior, which eventuate in SB only among some individuals. Similar trait-based conceptualizations of mental illness have been espoused by others (see Beauchaine & McNulty, 2013), have several advantages over identifying disorders strictly by behaviors (e.g., Clark, 2005; Watson, Clark, & Chmielewski, 2008), and undergird the dimensional Research Domain Criteria approach to classification and assessment of psychopathology currently being developed by the National Institute of Mental Health (for extended discussion, see Beauchaine, Klein, Erickson, & Norris, 2013). One advantage of a dimensional approach is the accommodation of topographical changes in behavior across development. For example, impulsive and emotionally dysregulated behaviors that emerge from stable individual differences rarely result in SB among young children yet may develop into such behaviors by adolescence or adulthood, especially when they interact with high-risk environments (see later). Our current diagnostic system usually specifies different disorders based on topographic, developmental changes in behavior, even when those behaviors are better explained by coherent vulnerability traits. This obscures considerable continuity in risk for psychopathology, with adverse consequences for etiological models and prediction of later psychiatric distress (for extended discussion, see Beauchaine, Hinshaw, & Pang, 2010; Beauchaine & McNulty, 2013). For this reason alone, there are limitations to creating a new diagnostic category defined simply by a single behavior.

With this caveat in mind, self-injury appears to result from a confluence of (1) trait impulsivity, a highly heritable behavioral predisposition;

(2) emotion dysregulation, a largely socialized trait that emerges later in development in high-risk familial and peer contexts (see Beauchaine et al., 2009; Crowell et al., 2009, 2013; Derbidge & Beauchaine, in press; Linehan, 1993); and other predisposing risk factors, including (3) cognitive dysfunction (e.g., inability to evaluate environmental stressors and their likely consequences due to loneliness, hopelessness, low self-worth, etc.; see Nock & Kazdin, 2002); and (4) interpersonal distress (e.g., problematic interpersonal relationships). Importantly, none of these factors in isolation accounts for much variance in suicide-related thoughts and behaviors. Thus, no diagnostic category or single etiological pathway captures the diversity inherent to suicide risk.

Life Span Approaches to Understanding Risk
The History of Life Span Approaches to Suicide

As noted earlier, life span research on suicide is sparse. However, there are several noteworthy attempts at conceptualizing suicide and self-injury across development (see Blumenthal & Kupfer, 1990; Crowell et al., 2008, 2009, 2013; Derbidge & Beauchaine, in press; Leenaars, 1991; Stillion & McDowell, 1996). Until quite recently, many such accounts maintained existing age-related divisions between children, adolescents, adults, and the elderly. In such cases, suicide is often understood as an interaction between vulnerabilities and risks that are common across individuals, and those that are specific to a particular cohort (see Stillion & McDowell, 1996). The cohort perspective is uniquely suited to understanding the history and stressors experienced by groups of individuals. However, it requires constant updating as specific cohorts move through different developmental epochs. For example, the so-called baby boomers showed a rise in adolescent suicide, which has continued unabated in subsequent cohorts (Berman, Jobes, & Silverman, 2006). The boom generation is often described as more "self-focused" and "career driven" than prior cohorts (Stillion & McDowell, 1996)—characteristics that figure into theoretical accounts of increased depression and suicide among its members. For example, the recent spike in midlife suicide rates, particularly among women, may be attributed partially to stressors this generation faces during physical and career-related decline. Data-based projections predict that suicide rates will increase by as much as 50% when this cohort moves into late life (Mathers & Loncar, 2006). This exemplifies the cohort-based approach to life span research—generation membership may interact adversely with cohort-specific developmental stressors.

A variety of more specific etiological approaches have also emerged. These perspectives tend to describe suicide in terms that are either biologically (e.g., Mann, 2003), contextually (e.g., Dube et al., 2001), or psychologically focused (e.g., Shneidman, 1985, 1991). An example of the psychological approach is exemplified by the work of Shneidman, who proposed 10 commonalities of suicide. Shneidman asserts that the psychological commonalities of suicide are shared by those of all backgrounds and ages. Even though there are biological and physiological concomitants to suicide, the act itself is one "of volition and frustrated psychological needs, and … [is] always related to overwhelming psychological pain" (Shneidman, 1991, p. 39). Thus, the urge and will to stop this pain are assumed to be at the core of all suicidal acts. These 10 commonalities have been quite influential to modern suicide prevention efforts (see Berman et al., 2006; Bongar, 2002). For example, treatments targeting emotion dysregulation are based on the belief that SITBs emerge from intolerable psychological distress (Linehan, 1993).

Because Shneidman's (1985) 10 commonalities have been so important to current life span formulations of suicide, we list them here: (1) a common *purpose* is to seek a solution to psychological pain (suicide is not random, pointless, or purposeless, but is the only conceivable solution to an unsolvable problem); (2) a common *goal* is cessation of consciousness (a form of approach or movement toward death that occurs when an individual experiences high levels of cognitive constriction, elevated perturbation, and has access to high-lethality means); (3) a common *stimulus* is intolerable psychological pain (suicide is an act of escape from intolerable emotion, unendurable suffering, and unacceptable anguish); (4) a common *stressor* is frustrated psychological needs (e.g., achievement, affiliation, harm avoidance, play, and understanding among others [Murray, 1938]; when such needs are thwarted, psychological pain increases); (5) a common *emotion* is hopelessness/helplessness (an overwhelming sense that there are no solutions; note that this contrasts with early formulations of suicide as an act of frustrated aggression or misdirected hostility); (6) a common *cognitive state* is ambivalence (both like and dislike for the idea of death); (7) a common *perceptual state* is constriction (a transient psychological narrowing of options when in a state of panic or crisis); (8) a common *action* is escape (a form of active avoidance, departure, or a need to stop pain); (9) a common *interpersonal act* is communication (not necessarily a "cry for help;" instead, an expression of unfulfilled needs that were not expressed successfully prior to suicide); and (10) a common *consistency* is lifelong coping patterns (i.e., reactions to stressors are largely consistent across the life span; therefore, even though the act of suicide is novel, by definition, emotions and coping strategies that manifested during earlier distress are consistent with the later suicidal act).

The life span approach described by Shneidman (1991) can be conceptualized as a cube where risk for suicide increases at the peak of (a) high psychosocial pressures (press); (b) intolerable psychological distress (pain); and (c) cognitive constriction and/or the self-destructive tendency toward "precipitous or ill-advised action" (perturbation, p. 47). These three factors continue to be foci of suicide research, although terminology has evolved to fit within broader psychological and neuroscience literatures. Shneidman defines pain and perturbation in a manner similar to current conceptualizations of emotion dysregulation and impulsivity, respectively. There is considerable research suggesting that biological vulnerabilities for emotion dysregulation and impulsivity interact with psychosocial stressors (similar to Shneidman's "press") to potentiate suicide risk (see Beauchaine et al., 2009; Crowell et al., 2009, 2013).

Vulnerability Across the Life Span

More recently, interest in understanding *vulnerability* to psychopathology across the life span has burgeoned (see, e.g., Beauchaine & McNulty, 2013; Beauchaine et al., 2008; Ingram & Price, 2010). The notion of vulnerability has been discussed most often by developmental psychopathologists, as many who study adults subscribe to the view that adult psychological adjustment represents an endpoint of developmental processes, including biological maturity, mastery of key life skills, and consolidation of personality traits (see Rutter & Sroufe, 2000; Sroufe, 2009, for how the developmental psychopathology approach differs). The extension of vulnerability research beyond childhood follows from recognition that coherence in behavioral patterns may emerge by adulthood, yet development continues across the life span. Moreover, a number of psychiatric disorders manifest initially in adulthood, which suggests that some vulnerabilities may not lead to psychopathology until later in life.

Although the concept of vulnerability has been applied inconsistently in the literature (for reviews, see Luthar, Cicchetti, & Becker, 2000; Shannon, Beauchaine, Brenner, Neuhaus, & Gatzke-Kopp, 2007), consistency has begun to emerge. Traditionally, the term has been used to describe stable and enduring personality and behavioral traits that confer susceptibility to psychopathology (see Ingram & Price, 2010; Meehl, 1962). More recently, a distinction has been made between vulnerabilities as preexisting biological traits and risk factors as environmental potentiators of vulnerability (see Shannon et al., 2007). Biological vulnerabilities are often highly heritable temperamental predispositions. Examples include behavioral inhibition (Kagan, 2008) and trait impulsivity (Neuhaus & Beauchaine, 2013), which predispose to internalizing and externalizing psychopathology, respectively, especially in high-risk environments. Importantly, however, biological vulnerabilities may be conferred through allostatic and epigenetic as well as genetic mechanisms (see Beauchaine, Neuhaus, Zalewski, Crowell, & Potapova, 2011). For example, prenatal nicotine exposure and traumatic brain injury each confer vulnerability to externalizing behavior (Gatzke-Kopp & Beauchaine, 2007; Gatzke-Kopp & Shannon, 2008) and fetal hypoxia may confer vulnerability to schizophrenia (Asarnow & Kernan, 2008). Biological vulnerabilities are exacerbated by environmental risk, further affecting already compromised biological systems. For instance, drugs of abuse—particularly strong stimulants—down-regulate the dopaminergic pathways implicated in reward responding (see, e.g., Beauchaine et al., 2011; Mead, Beauchaine, & Shannon, 2010). Thus, vulnerability cannot be defined independent of environmental risk, and vice-versa. Similarly, development of suicidality is a dynamic process, shaped by reciprocal transactions between central nervous system functions and contextual risk factors. Both must be understood if we wish to articulate why stressful life events potentiate suicide among some individuals and not others.

A Developmental Psychopathology Perspective

As noted earlier, suicide affects individuals of nearly all ages. However, age has been accounted for differently in existing models. Cohort-based approaches examine the unique stressors of each developmental stage, emphasizing differences across life phases (see earlier). In contrast, common factors approaches (e.g., Shneidman, 1985, 1991) emphasize commonalties. The developmental psychopathology (DP) perspective takes both approaches. Accordingly, psychological distress is understood in terms of both continuities and discontinuities across development (Rutter & Sroufe, 2000; Sroufe & Rutter, 1984). Dysfunctional behaviors are presumed to emerge in part through repeated struggles to navigate normative developmental challenges (e.g., Sroufe, 1990, 2009). If a person navigates such challenges successfully at one stage of development, his or her ability to cope with subsequent challenges is improved. If not, continuity in psychological distress is more likely.

As alluded to by the aforementioned discussion, the study of developmental continuities and discontinuities in SB and NSSI is uncommon. Rather, researchers have historically studied correlates and putative causal events, which can be categorized into those addressing *intra*personal or *inter*personal processes. Broadly speaking, *intra*personal processes include constructs such as psychiatric disorders, personality characteristics, or maladaptive cognitions (e.g., hopelessness). In contrast, *inter*personal processes include family context, environmental risks, or high-conflict relationships. This approach often assumes static characteristics of individuals or contexts, which is incongruent with transactional, life span developmental approaches (Baltes, 1980; Cicchetti & Rogosch, 1996). Indeed, at every stage of life, individuals are influenced by environmental factors spanning many levels of analysis, including family, close relationships, neighborhoods/communities, and political/economic climates. At the same time, individuals act on their environments to evoke particular responses. Early in life, children affect their environments through biologically based temperamental predispositions. Over time, children apply increasingly complex behavioral and psychological responses within the environment, ideally increasing the chances of navigating developmental challenges successfully. However, in extremely high-risk environments, such as those characterized by violence, behavioral repertoires that are adaptive in one setting (e.g., staying quiet around an abusive caregiver) can become maladaptive in others (e.g., school), conferring lifelong risk for psychopathology (see Mead et al., 2010, for a review).

Researchers studying suicidality are only beginning to hypothesize similar dynamic processes, including developmental trajectories and risk for suicide (Beauchaine et al., 2009; Crowell et al.,

2008, 2009, 2013; Derbidge & Beauchaine, in press). We therefore draw from a related literature for an example of such continuities. It is well known that antisocial behavior is highly stable over the life span. Thus, individuals who are highly aggressive at one developmental stage tend to remain so at later points, although the topography of aggression changes. These trajectories are therefore described as heterotypic in nature—progressing along a pathway characterized by behavioral differences across development: preschool hyperactivity → early oppositionality → grade school physical aggression → adolescent delinquency → adult criminal involvement (see Beauchaine & McNulty, 2013; Beauchaine et al., 2010). Continuities have also been outlined for anxiety and mood disorders, although the pathways are typically described as homotypic (e.g., Cicchetti & Toth, 1998), with similar behavioral manifestations across development (e.g., worry, withdrawal). In contrast, continuities in SB and NSSI are not well understood. However, strategies marked by active avoidance of psychological distress are common among those who ultimately commit suicide. Such strategies include attempted suicide, NSSI, substance use, and binge eating, among others. Key *questions* include how these problematic strategies emerge, how they are activated under acute stress, and how they contribute to suicide risk.

Although there are many possible answers to these questions, the following hypotheses are consistent with a developmental psychopathology approach (see Beauchaine et al., 2009; Beauchaine & McNulty, 2013; Crowell et al., 2009): (1) impulse control deficits—a core predisposing vulnerability—derive from heritable compromises in central serotonergic and dopaminergic function, conferring broad risk for behavioral dyscontrol and psychopathology; (2) emotion dysregulation—a far less heritable trait—is shaped and maintained via interactions between biologically vulnerable (i.e., impulsive) children and high-risk familial and peer contexts, which canalize emotional lability through repeated operant reinforcement of negative affect; (3) over time, this canalization of emotional lability leads to pervasive *intra*personal deficits, including extreme emotion dysregulation, poor behavioral control, and maladaptive cognitions, as well as *inter*personal deficits, such as difficulties with conflict resolution and social withdrawal; and (4) convergence of these vulnerabilities and risk factors increases probability of suicide when life stressors exceed, either repeatedly or acutely, a person's ability to cope, thereby limiting perceived alternatives. We examine each of these four points in turn.

Impulsivity and Vulnerability to Suicidal Behaviors

We hypothesize that *impulse control deficits derive from heritable compromises in central serotonergic and dopaminergic function, which confer broad rather than specific risk for psychopathology* (Beauchaine et al., 2009; Neuhaus & Beauchaine, 2013). Although some degree of impulsivity is common among young children, those manifesting extreme disinhibition are vulnerable to a wide range of psychopathological sequelae (Beauchaine et al., 2010; Hinshaw et al., 2012). As noted earlier, early-life impulsivity is often the first stage of a heterotypically continuous trajectory leading from attention-deficit/hyperactivity disorder (ADHD) to later oppositionality, conduct problems, delinquency, and antisocial personality development (Beauchaine, Gatzke-Kopp, & Mead, 2007; Patterson, Degarmo, & Knutson, 2000). Accordingly, and consistent with behavioral genetics findings (Krueger et al., 2002; Tuvblad, Zheng, Raine, & Baker, 2009; Young, Stallings, Corley, Krauter, & Hewitt, 2000), trait impulsivity is a core predisposing vulnerability to externalizing disorders (see Beauchaine & McNulty, 2013). Although less often acknowledged, impulsivity also confers vulnerability to later mood disorders and heterotypic comorbidity of internalizing and externalizing psychopathology (see, e.g., Hirshfeld-Becker et al., 2002; Sauder, Beauchaine, Gatzke-Kopp, Shannon, & Aylward, 2012).

Defining and Conceptualizing Impulsivity

Numerous definitions of impulsivity have been proposed, most of which capture overlapping facets of the construct (Neuhaus & Beauchaine, 2013). Among these alternatives, we prefer a behavioral description of impulsivity, defined as an action that is "socially inappropriate or maladaptive and is quickly emitted without forethought" (Oas, 1985, p. 142). By this definition, SITBs can often be viewed as an impulsive act, since it is almost always maladaptive and is usually committed without full consideration of its physical, emotional, or interpersonal effects. At other times, however, SITBs are planned meticulously with great attention to the range of potential consequences.

In order to understand how impulsivity may be linked to SITBs, we differentiate between *behavioral* impulsivity, which comprises observable actions, and *trait* impulsivity, a highly heritable and enduring component of personality (see Krueger et al., 2002). Behavioral genetics studies have provided rich information about the heritability of trait impulsivity and how it interacts with environments to potentiate externalizing psychopathology. Even though impulsivity consistently yields heritability coefficients (h^2) of around .80, the trait interacts strongly with environmental risk factors in the pathogenesis of different externalizing syndromes (see Beauchaine & McNulty, 2013; Krueger, Markon, Patrick, Benning, & Kramer, 2007). An accumulating literature places SB and NSSI with other externalizing behaviors based on familial patterns of heritability, as well as shared biological vulnerabilities, psychosocial risk factors, and developmental trajectories (see, e.g., Beauchaine et al., 2009; Crowell et al., 2009, 2013; Thorell, 2009). For example, girls diagnosed with ADHD in childhood are at heightened risk for engaging in NSSI as adolescents (Hinshaw et al., 2012). This does not suggest, however, that suicidality results solely from trait impulsivity. Rather, trait impulsivity may be a necessary but insufficient etiological agent, increasing risk for SB and NSSI only in combination with other high-risk traits, particularly emotion dysregulation (see earlier; Sauder, Derbidge, & Beauchaine, unpublished data; Lenzenweger & Castro, 2005).

Heritability of Suicidal Behaviors and Trait Impulsivity

Family and twin studies indicate that suicidality is between 30% and 55% heritable (Voracek & Loibl, 2007) and is transmitted largely independent of specific psychiatric disorders (see also Brent et al., 2003; Currier & Mann, 2008; Glowinski et al., 2001; Roy, Rylander, & Sarchiapone, 1997). Relatives of self-injuring individuals are at three-fold higher risk of self-injury in general, and at five-fold higher risk for attempted and completed suicide (Baldessarini & Hennen, 2004). Additionally, twin studies consistently find increased risk among monozygotic (MZ) relative to dizygotic (DZ) twins (see Spirito & Esposito-Smythers, 2006 for a review). For example, among 3,372 twins in the Vietnam Era Twin Registry, a heritability coefficient of .42 was reported for suicide attempts (Fu et al., 2002). However, even though impulsivity is largely heritable (see also Eysenck, 1993; Krueger et al., 2002; Tuvblad, Zheng, Raine, & Baker, 2009), behavioral genetics studies do not indicate specific genes involved. Recently, researchers have sought to identify the biological and environmental mechanisms that underlie familial transmission of SITB (see Joiner, Brown, & Wingate, 2005).

Biology of Impulsivity and Vulnerability to Suicidal Behaviors

The neural substrates of trait impulsivity and appetitive motivation are well understood. According to most models, impulsivity derives largely from either or both of two central nervous system networks (see Beauchaine, 2001; Beauchaine et al., 2007; Crowell et al., 2005; Depue & Lenzenweger, 2005; Gray & McNaughton, 2000). The first is the central serotonin (5-HT) system. Serotonergic neurons project from the dorsal raphe nucleus to the septohippocampal system, amygdala, and frontal cortex. The septo-hippocampal system exerts inhibitory effects on behavior in the face of conflicting motivational goals (Gray & McNaughton, 2000). These inhibitory effects produce anxiety, which is expressed behaviorally as passive avoidance. Those with deficient septo-hippocampal functioning are less likely to halt prepotent behaviors when environmental cues indicate safer alternatives. Among rats, lesions to the raphe nuclei result in stronger preference for reward (Bizot, Le Bihan, Puech, Hamon, & Thiébot, 1999), whereas 5-HT agonists promote self-controlled choice (Evenden & Ryan, 1996).

A second source of impulsivity derives from the mesolimbic (striatal) and mesocortical (anterior and prefrontal cortices) dopamine (DA) systems (for reviews see Gatzke-Kopp, 2011; Gatzke-Kopp & Beauchaine, 2007). Hypoactivation within these pathways predisposes to ADHD and related impulsive behaviors, including sensation seeking, and risk for aggression and substance use disorders (for reviews, see Beauchaine & Gatzke-Kopp, 2012; Gatzke-Kopp et al., 2009). Projections from the ventral tegmental area to the nucleus accumbens are activated during all approach behaviors, including those that are impulsive (see Berridge & Robinson, 2003; Gray & McNaughton, 2000; Sagvolden, Johansen, Aase, & Russell, 2005). Although early work hypothesized overactivation of the central DA system (e.g., Fowles, 1988; Quay, 1993), accumulating evidence now implicates underactivation of the mesolimbic and mesocortical pathways among those who are impulsive (Berridge & Robinson, 2003; Bush et al., 1999; Vaidya et al., 1998; Volkow et al., 2009). Several findings link deficits within the 5-HT and DA systems to SB, NSSI, and completed suicide, providing further evidence for the role of impulsivity in self-injurious behaviors (see Beauchaine et al., 2009; Crowell et al., 2009). Importantly, both the structure and function of these systems can be altered by exposure to chronic stress, substance use, traumatic brain injury, and so

on, further compromising impulse control abilities among vulnerable individuals (see Beauchaine et al., 2011; Gatzke-Kopp & Shannon, 2008; Mead et al., 2010).

SEROTONIN AND SELF-INJURIOUS THOUGHTS AND BEHAVIORS

Consistent with the notion that SITBs are often impulsive, neurobiological and postmortem studies of suicide reveal 5-HT dysfunction in the prefrontal cortex (PFC). This includes decreased presynaptic serotonin transporter (5-HTT) binding sites and increased postsynaptic 5-HT receptor sites (see Mann, Brent, & Arango, 2001). Suicide attempters also perform poorly on cognitive performance tasks that depend on the PFC (Jollant et al., 2005; Keilp et al., 2001). In a positron emission tomography (PET) study, depressed bipolar (BP) patients with histories of SB exhibit reduced 5-HTT binding in the midbrain and increased 5-HTT binding in the anterior cingulate cortex (ACC) compared with depressed BP patients with no history of SB (Cannon et al., 2006). Depressed suicide attempters also have reduced 5-HT2A receptor binding in the PFC compared with healthy controls (Audenaert et al., 2001).

There are several 5-HT candidate genes for SITB, most of which were selected on the basis of established biological correlates of suicide (see Mann et al., 2009). These include 5-HTR1A, 5-HTR2A, TPH1, TPH2, and 5-HTTLPR genes among others. The 5-HTR1A and 5-HTR2A genes code for specific serotonin receptors. Postmortem studies of suicide victims reveal increased 5-HT1A and 5-HT2A receptors in the prefrontal cortex, suggesting compensatory neuronal proliferation due to chronically depleted 5-HT levels (Bondy, Buettner, & Zill, 2006). However, research on the 5-HT1A and 2A receptor genes has produced conflicting results (Currier & Mann, 2008). Similarly, genes coding for tryptophan hydroxylase (TPH1 and TPH2), a rate-limiting enzyme for 5-HT production, have been linked to suicide, albeit inconclusively. In one meta-analysis, an association between the A-allele of the TPH1 gene and SB was found among Caucasians (Bondy et al., 2006). Another study linked an intronic polymorphism of the TPH2 gene with suicide in depression (Zill et al., 2004). However, a later study associated the same polymorphism with depression only (Haghighi et al., 2008). Inconsistent findings such as these have plagued almost all areas of psychiatric genetics in the last decade (for a discussion, see Beauchaine &

Gatzke-Kopp, 2013), often as a result of small sample sizes and differently ascertained phenotypes (see Bosker et al., 2011). Nevertheless, larger studies with clear phenotypes confirm genetic vulnerabilities to suicide that are distinct from those for depression. Brezo and colleagues (2010) followed over 1,200 participants and found that a variation of the TPH1 gene was relevant only to the diathesis of suicide attempts and not depression. Moreover, three different variants of the 5HTR2A genes predicted suicidal behavior in interaction with childhood sexual or physical abuse assessed 22 years prior. These were different genes than those that interacted with abuse to predict depression (Brezo et al., 2010).

In addition to these findings, the gene coding for the serotonin transporter has received considerable attention in research on depression. The 5-HTTLPR gene affects synaptic 5-HT levels, a target of most modern antidepressants. Genetic studies suggest that the short allele on the promoter region of the 5-HTT gene (5-HTTLPR) confers risk for psychopathology and SITB, especially following adverse life experiences (see Currier & Mann, 2008; Mead et al., 2010). The 5-HTTLPR gene has two common allelic variations (short and long), which results in three genotypes: homozygous long (ll), homozygous short (ss), and heterozygous (sl) (e.g., Greenberg et al., 1999). Carriers of the short allele are at higher risk for a number of negative outcomes, including bipolar disorder, alcohol abuse, and violent suicide attempts, among those with major depression (Baca-Garcia et al., 2002; Bellivier et al., 2000; Kaufman et al., 2004; McHugh, Hofmann, Asnaani, Sawyer, & Otto; Sander et al., 1998). Such outcomes are most likely among individuals who were exposed to early adversity (e.g., Caspi et al., 2003). Thus, the 5-HTTLPR gene likely confers broad vulnerability to psychopathology, which is potentiated by environmental risk (for a review, see Mead et al., 2010). Indeed, several developmental studies confirm that risk for suicide results from such gene × environment interactions. In particular, extreme childhood adversity, such as sexual abuse and other forms of trauma, interact with serotonin genes to predict SITB both cross-sectionally and longitudinally (e.g., Cicchetti, Rogosch, Sturge-Apple, & Toth, 2010; Gibb, McGeary, Beevers, & Miller, 2006; Roy, Hu, Janal, & Goldman, 2007).

DOPAMINE AND SELF-INJURIOUS THOUGHTS AND BEHAVIORS

Relative to serotonin, associations between dopaminergic function and suicidality have only begun to emerge (Sher et al., 2006). As noted earlier, low DA function has been related consistently to trait impulsivity and associated forms of psychopathology among children, adolescents, and adults (see Beauchaine & McNulty, 2013; Bush et al., 1999; Rubia, 2011; Sauder et al., unpublished data; Vaidya et al., 1998). As might be expected given the predisposing role of impulsivity to SITB, low central DA function has also been linked to SB and NSSI. Decreased peripheral markers of DA have been found among suicide attempters (Roy, Karoum, & Pollack, 1992). Reduced DA turnover is also observed in the basal ganglia of suicide attempters (Bowden et al., 1997). Furthermore, in DA challenge tests, decreased responding is observed among suicide attempters and victims, independent of depression (Pitchot, Hansenne, & Ansseau, 2001; Pitchot, Hansenne, Moreno, & Ansseau, 1992; Pitchot, Reggers, et al., 2001), and low DA binding in mesolimbic structures predicts individual differences in negative affectivity and irritability (Laakso et al., 2003). Finally, functional imaging studies indicate reduced striatal responding to monetary incentives among self-injuring adolescents (Sauder et al., unpublished data). Once again, however, such findings have not been fully consistent, with some studies indicating no relation between DA and suicide, and no differences in the affinity or number of DA receptors (see Currier & Mann, 2008). Nevertheless, across several studies, biological vulnerabilities that give rise to trait impulsivity are observed among self-injuring samples (Crowell et al., 2013). Moreover, family studies of suicide suggest that trait impulsivity is a likely candidate for familial transmission, given its exceedingly high heritability and the intergenerational transmission of impulsive personality traits and behaviors (e.g., Brook, Whiteman, & Zheng, 2004).

SEROTONIN, DOPAMINE, AND NEGATIVE AFFECTIVITY

In addition to impulse control disorders, familial aggregation of mood disorders is also observed among relatives of self-injuring adolescents and adults (Brent & Mann, 2005; Brent, Perper, et al., 1994; White, Gunderson, Zanarini, & Hudson, 2003). At first glance the co-occurrence of impulse control and mood disorders among self-injurers and their first-degree relatives may seem perplexing. However, common neurobiological substrates may account for some of the phenotypic overlap. Indeed, both impulse and mood disorders are characterized by irritability, low positive affectivity, and emotional lability, which have all been linked with deficiencies of 5-HT and/or DA. For example, impulsive aggression toward the self or others in the face of provocation or frustration (Coccaro, Bergeman, Kavoussi, & Seroczynski, 1997; Coccaro, Bergeman, & McClearn, 1993) is linked to decreased 5-HT function, especially among males (see Carver & Miller, 2006). This trait has been identified as a risk factor for SITB in several studies and is often related to violent attempts (Brent & Mann, 2005). In one large high-risk sample, familial impulsive aggression mediated the transmission of early-onset SITB (Brent et al., 2003). Similarly, a neural substrate common to both impulsivity and depression is deficient responding to reward in the mesolimbic DA system (e.g., Forbes, Shaw, & Dahl, 2007; Gatzke-Kopp et al., 2009; Sauder et al., unpublished data). As noted earlier, positron emission tomography studies indicate that low mesolimbic DA functioning is experienced as aversive, predisposing one to irritability and negative affectivity (e.g., Laakso et al., 2003). Animal models suggest that physical aggression activates dopaminergic circuits and is likely experienced as rewarding. Indeed, mice exhibit extracellular increases in nucleus accumbens DA during and following conflict (Couppis & Kennedy, 2008). Importantly, the reward pathway, including the nucleus accumbens, is implicated in addiction (Berridge & Robinson, 2003), and many hypothesize that self-injury becomes addictive over time (e.g., Nixon, Cloutier, & Aggarwal, 2002). Taken together, these studies suggest a developmental trajectory in which 5-HT and DA vulnerabilities interact with environmental contexts across development to facilitate increasingly risky behaviors including SITB.

Emotion Dysregulation, Developmental Context, and Suicidal Behaviors

These studies reveal that 5-HT and DA dysfunction confer vulnerability to psychopathology, which is expressed behaviorally as impulsivity, negative affectivity, irritability, and sensation seeking. As noted earlier, however, impulsivity is a necessary but insufficient predisposition to SITB. This observation leads to our second hypothesis, that *extreme emotion dysregulation, although neurobiologically mediated, is shaped and maintained via interactions between biologically vulnerable (i.e., impulsive) children and high-risk familial and peer contexts, which canalize emotional lability through repeated operant reinforcement of negative affect.*

By the time suicidal behaviors emerge, most individuals report extreme psychological distress. Adolescents and adults who self-injure are more anxious, depressed, and hostile than both clinical and typical controls (Darche, 1990; Ross & Heath, 2003). Moreover, emotion dysregulation is a core precipitant of SITB among self-injuring adolescents and adults with borderline personality disorder (Klonsky, 2007; Linehan, Rizvi, Welch, & Page, 2008; Nixon et al., 2002; Zlotnick, Donaldson, Spirito, & Pearlstein, 1997). Affective instability— a term that is often used interchangeably with emotion dysregulation—is a highly stable criterion among adults diagnosed with borderline personality disorder (McGlashan et al., 2005). Emotion dysregulation underlies diverse forms of psychopathology (see Beauchaine, 2001; Beauchaine et al., 2007), and there is a long tradition of exploring the development of emotional lability among impulsive youth (Patterson, Chamberlain, & Reid, 1982; Patterson, DeBaryshe, & Ramsey, 1989; Patterson et al., 2000). However, there are a number of unresolved issues, which we describe briefly next.

Defining and Conceptualizing Emotion Dysregulation

Emotions are evolutionarily shaped response tendencies that promote behaviors necessary for survival (Ekman, 1992). Many emotional responses are automated and therefore rapid and dynamic, allowing a person to act quickly to salient information (e.g., Cole, Martin, & Dennis, 2004; Ekman & Friesen, 1976; Gross, 1998). Although understanding emotional processes is important in the study of psychopathology given that so many disorders are characterized by poor modulation of affect (Beauchaine, 2001; Beauchaine et al., 2007), assessing *regulation* of emotion presents both conceptual and measurement challenges. Foremost among these are the difficulties encountered in quantifying the construct objectively, since many emotion regulatory processes are internal and therefore unobservable directly. In contrast, emotion *dysregulation* is often reflected in observable behaviors. Accordingly, we focus on emotion dysregulation, which captures "patterns of emotion regulation that have acquired a maladaptive quality, such that emotions seem to interfere with functioning" (Cole & Hall, 2008, p. 266).

Recently, there has been a rapid proliferation of research on emotion regulation and dysregulation. However, there are inconsistencies across studies in terminology, measurement, and levels of analysis (e.g., behavioral, physiological, psychological). Given space constraints, we cannot review this literature here. Rather, readers are referred to other articles for a thorough consideration of these and other issues (e.g., Cole, Hall, & Hajal, 2013; Cole et al., 2004; Goldsmith & Davidson, 2004; Gross, 2007). Nevertheless, it is important to operationalize emotion dysregulation for subsequent sections. According to Cole et al. (2013), dysregulated emotion can be distinguished from normal emotional responses by four key characteristics. First, dysregulated emotions endure, and regulatory attempts are usually ineffective. Prolonged irritability, generalized anxiety, depressed mood, and trait hostility/explosive anger are mood states that are unresponsive to efforts at modulation among those with certain psychiatric disorders. By this definition, self-injury is a maladaptive attempt at modulating prolonged negative affect. Although often effective in the short run, distraction from psychological distress via self-injury does not provide sustained relief from negative mood, and it may have devastating long-term consequences. Second, dysregulated emotions interfere with appropriate social and goal-directed behaviors. Third, dysregulated emotions are often expressed in inappropriate social contexts, when the type of emotion is unshared by others. Finally, the onset of dysregulated emotions is often too abrupt and recovery is often too slow. Poor recovery (e.g., dysphoria that does not respond to situational changes) and/or lability (e.g., unpredictable and quick changes of mood) are common among individuals who engage in SITB (see Kuo & Linehan, 2009).

Emotion dysregulation encompasses a number of more specific emotion constructs, including negative affectivity, irritability, neuroticism, emotional lability, emotional sensitivity, emotional instability, and emotional reactivity. Although each of these constructs captures specific manifestations of negative mood, there are also elements common among them. Moreover, topographically different emotional difficulties across the life span may emerge from a common underlying trait, as discussed earlier. For example, Caspi (2000) reported that children who were "restless, negativistic, distractible, and labile" or "fearful and easily upset by strangers" (p. 160) were far more likely to meet criteria for psychological disorders in young adulthood than temperamentally well-adjusted children. Moreover, undercontrolled children attempted suicide at a far greater rate than both inhibited and well-adjusted children. Thus, conceptualizing emotion dysregulation across development necessitates a flexible application of related terms in order to understand continuities from early childhood to later in life.

Further Biological Correlates of Emotion Dysregulation and Suicidal Behaviors

NOREPINEPHRINE AND EMOTION DYSREGULATION

In addition to 5-HT and DA (reviewed earlier), the noradrenergic system (NE) has been implicated in mood regulation, social affiliation, irritability, and stress reactivity (see Beauchaine et al., 2011; Cloninger, 2000; Gurvits, Koenigsberg, & Siever, 2000; Skodol et al., 2002). Norepinephrine is released centrally from the locus coeruleus, which projects to the neocortex, limbic regions, the thalamus, and the cerebellum. Importantly, NE is synthesized from DA by DA-β-hydroxylase (DBH), which oxidizes DA into NE. Thus, these neurotransmitter systems are interdependent. Disrupted NE functioning is observed among adult suicide attempters, and adult suicide victims exhibit fewer NE neurons in the locus coeruleus (Arango, Underwood, & Mann, 1996). Postmortem studies indicate that the brains of depressed suicide victims have heightened sensitivity in NE receptors in the frontal cortex and brainstem, which is likely due to chronic NE deficits (González-Maeso, Rodríguez-Puertas, Meana, García-Sevilla, & Guimón, 2002; Ordway, Widdowson, Smith, & Halaris, 1994). Furthermore, increased activity of tyrosine hydroxylase, a rate-limiting enzyme in the synthesis of NE, is also observed among suicide victims (Zhu et al., 1999). Several studies indicate that early life stress modifies NE system functioning in adulthood (e.g., Heim & Nemeroff, 2001; Melia et al., 1992). Indeed, the locus coeruleus serves both general arousal and social affiliative functions. Acute stress triggers corticotrophin-releasing factor from the hypothalamic-pituitary-adrenal (HPA) axis to the locus coeruleus (Pardon, Ma, & Morilak, 2003). This leads to a cascade of biological responses, including increased heart rate, loss of appetite, amygdala activation, and inhibited executive control (Charney, 2004; Porges, 1995; Tsigos & Chrousos, 2002). In turn, social affiliation is inhibited. In animal studies, repeated exposure to stress leads to NE facilitation of HPA reactivity. Young rats exposed repeatedly to dominant males experience lasting alterations to the NE system (see Gould & Tanapat, 1999).

HYPOTHALAMIC-PITUITARY-ADRENAL AXIS

Not surprisingly, reactivity of the HPA axis is linked with suicidal behavior. Evidence in support of this comes from studies using the dexamethasone suppression test (DST), a cortisol challenge paradigm. Cortisol nonsuppression indexes HPA hyperactivity and predicts later suicide across impressively long periods of time (Lester, 1992). In one study, Coryell and Schlesser (2001) followed a group of depressed adults 15 years after psychiatric hospitalization and found that cortisol nonsuppressors on the DST were at 14-fold greater risk of death by suicide. Adolescent inpatients who later commit suicide are more likely to be dexamethasone nonsuppressors than other inpatient suicide attempters and nonattempters (Norman, Brown, Miller, Keitner, & Overholser, 1990). Although cross-sectional results on the DST have been conflicting (see Jokinen et al., 2007 for a review), a recent meta-analysis indicated that nonsuppressors are at four-fold greater risk of later suicide compared with nonsuppressors (Mann et al., 2006). Thus, HPA axis hyperactivity is a biomarker of heightened stress reactivity and risk for later suicide among those who have made a prior attempt.

AUTONOMIC NERVOUS SYSTEM FUNCTIONING

There is an extensive literature linking autonomic measures to emotion dysregulation and psychopathology (see, e.g., Beauchaine, 2001, 2012; Beauchaine & Gatzke-Kopp; 2012; Beauchaine, Katkin, Strassberg, & Snarr, 2001; El-Sheikh et al., 2009; Porges, 1995, 2007). For example, respiratory sinus arrhythmia (RSA) is a well-established index of emotion regulation capabilities when assessed under appropriate stimulus conditions. Within an acceptable respiratory band (see Ritz, 2009), RSA captures vagal efference to the heart (Berntson et al., 1997). In general, low RSA and excessive RSA reactivity (i.e., withdrawal) to emotion evocation confer vulnerability to psychopathology, whereas high RSA confers protection (see Beauchaine, 2012; Katz & Gottman, 1997; Shannon et al., 2007). As with all biomarkers, reduced RSA is not specific to suicidality and is observed across psychiatric disorders characterized by emotion dysregulation, including severe conduct problems (Beauchaine et al., 2001), trait hostility (Sloan et al., 1994), and both depression and anxiety disorders (Lyonfelds, Borkovec, & Thayer, 1995; Rechlin, Weis, Spitzer, & Kaschka, 1994; Thayer, Friedman, & Borkovec, 1996; Yeragani et al., 1993), among others. Nevertheless, self-injuring adolescent females show reduced RSA at baseline, and RSA withdrawal in response to sad emotion induction (Crowell et al., 2005).

The Developmental Context of Emotion Dysregulation

As outlined earlier, emotion dysregulation and RSA are socialized largely within families, are sensitive to additional environmental inputs, and therefore emerge as predictors of psychopathology later in development than more heritable behavioral traits such as impulsivity (Calkins, 1997; Shipman & Zeman, 2001). For example, group differences in RSA are observed among impulsive middle school children and adolescents, but not among impulsive preschoolers (Beauchaine et al., 2007). Presumably, poor emotion regulation and associated deficiencies in RSA emerge over time among vulnerable children, through mechanisms outlined later.

Consistent with our developmental model, the literature on biological correlates of emotion dysregulation suggests that heritable traits—including impulsivity—interact with environmentally shaped emotional lability to potentiate suicidal tendencies and behaviors (e.g., Hinshaw et al., 2012). Inherited compromises in serotonergic and dopaminergic function confer vulnerability, expressed as trait impulsivity, emotion dysregulation, and irritability. These traits affect responses to acute stressors, and their functioning may be altered permanently as a result (Mead et al., 2010). This highlights the importance of both environmental risk factors and biology × environment interactions in shaping psychopathology. Contextual risk for SITB can be understood at multiple levels of analysis. To date, the vast majority of research on SB and NSSI has focused on broad contextual factors, with a much smaller number of studies examining family processes that potentiate risk.

The Developmental Context and Risk for Suicidal Behaviors

It is well known that certain contextual factors, including family interaction patterns, increase risk for negative health outcomes among children. For example, children raised in high-risk neighborhoods may develop behavior problems due to exposure to violence or deviant peer group affiliations (Dishion, McCord, & Poulin, 1999; Ingoldsby & Shaw, 2002). Nevertheless, even when families are matched on socioeconomic status (SES), and when variables such as family income are controlled statistically, high-risk family processes still predict increased emotional and behavioral dysregulation among impulsive youth (see Ingoldsby & Shaw, 2002; Lynch & Cicchetti, 2002; Shields & Cicchetti, 1994). According to our developmental model, high-risk family environments potentiate impulsive behaviors through repeated conflict escalation where operant processes reinforce emotional lability. This hypothesis is based on extensive data demonstrating that negative reinforcement of emotional lability and arousal shapes and maintains antisocial behaviors within families (Patterson et al., 1982, 1989, 2000). According to this formulation, emotion dysregulation emerges from the interaction between the child's temperamental vulnerability (i.e., impulsivity) and familial-contextual factors that intermittently reinforce emotional lability, anger, and/or rigid emotional inhibition.

Previous developmental models of SITB emphasized similar contextual factors. Linehan (1993) suggested that risk for self-injury emerges in part from *invalidating developmental contexts*. There are three specific components to her theory. First, youth at risk for SITB are likely to be emotionally vulnerable. This is defined as high baseline sensitivity to emotion evocation, an intense response to emotional stimuli, and a slow return to emotional baseline (see also Kuo & Linehan, 2009). Second, invalidating caregivers eschew and/or reject children's emotional expressions, which are frequent, intense, and at times overwhelming. Consequently, the emotional needs of such children may exceed the environmental capacity to provide consistent support and validation. Finally, invalidating environments are characterized by intermittent reinforcement of extreme negative affect, which functions to elicit intermittent support during emotional distress. Recent work provides empirical support for this model among self-injuring adolescents. In one study, high levels of observed family conflict and low peripheral serotonin interacted to predict self-injurious behaviors (Crowell, Beauchaine, McCauley et al., 2008), accounting for 64% of the variance in SITB. Furthermore, in dyadic conflict interactions between self-injuring teens and their mothers, (1) maternal invalidation is associated with adolescent anger and opposition/defiance, and (2) self-injuring dyads are more likely to escalate conflict than control dyads (Crowell et al., 2013). Thus, family environments characterized by rejection, invalidation, and conflict are associated with self-injury. However, further research is needed to test developmental models of emotion dysregulation and SITB among impulsive youth more broadly.

Research on family processes is important because a majority of behavioral interventions target individuals and families. Moreover, families can potentially buffer children and adolescents from community stress by modeling effective coping skills, providing emotional support, and through appropriate parental supervision. In contrast, when stability and/or safety levels of a home are compromised, a child's odds of adaptational success decrease markedly (Richters & Martinez, 1993). Thus, even if families do not cause psychopathology, NSSI, or suicide directly, family stress and ineffective conflict resolution may lead to early adaptational failures, including academic difficulties and poor social problem solving. Although such outcomes are not inevitable, adversities and pressures within the broader community often heighten risk for instability in the home. To our knowledge, no research has characterized self-injuring adolescents within the context of multiple social systems (see Szapocznik & Kurtines, 1993). However, in one study, maternal physical punishment mediated the relation between poverty and youth depression assessed 2 years later (Eamon, 2002). In turn, child abuse increases risk for borderline personality development and suicidal behaviors (Brown, Cohen, Johnson, & Smailes, 1999; Lyons-Ruth, 2008).

Since relations among broad contextual risk, family conflict, and later suicide have not been well articulated, we draw upon the larger body of suicide-related risk factors to explore possible links. For example, suicide-related behaviors increase in response to unemployment, poverty, and loneliness (see Crawford & Prince, 1999). These factors likely correlate with other risk factors for suicide, including substance use, neighborhood SES, rural living, child abuse, and hopelessness (Berman et al., 2006; Bongar, 2002; Sampson & Mrazek, 2001), especially among those for whom multiple concurrent and historical risks converge (see Aguirre & Watts, 2010). Statistics dating to the 1920s indicate disproportionalites in health-related problems across communities, with low SES neighborhoods exhibiting higher rates of infant mortality, crime, mental and physical illness, physical abuse, homicide, and suicide (Sampson, Morenoff, & Gannon-Rowley, 2002). Moreover, when individuals are selected randomly to move away from such environments, as in the Moving to Opportunity (MTO) study, mental and physical health risks decline (Leventhal & Brooks-Gunn, 2003; US Department of Housing and Urban Development, 2003). Although suicide outcomes are not discussed in the MTO reports, associated risks for suicide were affected by the change of residence. Such changes likely result from reduced exposure to crime and violence, and an improved sense of safety, both of which have important implications for concurrent and future suicide risk.

The Development of Intra- and Interpersonal Risk for Suicide

Research on externalizing psychopathology suggests that impulsive youth who are reared in poor neighborhoods are at greater risk for juvenile delinquency (Lynam et al., 2000). Moreover, family processes often mediate relations between poverty and child maladjustment, such as when economic pressures lead to parental depression, demoralization, conflict, and disruptions in skillful parenting (see Conger et al., 1992). As described earlier, these family processes are often characterized by repeated, high-conflict interactions where operant processes shape and maintain emotionally labile patterns of interacting (Patterson et al., 1989, 2000). This leads to our hypothesis that *over time, negative reinforcement of emotional lability and aggression leads to pervasive intrapersonal deficits, including extreme emotion dysregulation, poor behavioral control, and maladaptive cognitions, as well as interpersonal deficits, such as difficulties with conflict resolution and social withdrawal.*

Nearly all research on suicide, SB, and NSSI confirms these intra- and interpersonal correlates of suicidality (Berman et al., 2006; Bongar, 2002). Independently, however, no single factor causes suicide. Indeed, there are few mental or physical health outcomes that can be understood adequately by identifying correlates or proximal causal events. To borrow an example from medicine, myocardial infarction occurs proximally when a large clot obstructs blood flow to the heart. Yet heart attacks are etiologically complex and multidetermined, with risk factors that can often be traced to both genes and environment, including early childhood risk factors. This example highlights the importance of adopting a life span approach to any health outcome, including suicide. In seminal work on life span developmental psychology, Baltes argues that "a developmental orientation is needed whenever the behavior identified involves a change process and is better understood if placed in the context of chains and patterns of antecedent and subsequent events" (Baltes, 1980, p. 66).

An Integrated Approach to Suicidal and Self-Injurious Behaviors

The earlier described review suggests a trajectory leading from early temperamental vulnerabilities to exposure to environmental risk factors to later suicide risk. By young adulthood there is considerable consolidation of personality, behavior, and coping strategies. Thus, many risk factors for suicide are likely present by this time. However, most vulnerable individuals—even those who experience vulnerability and chronic risk—do not develop suicide-related behaviors (see Dube et al., 2001). Thus, our final hypothesis is that *vulnerabilities and risks increase the probability of suicide only when life stressors exceed, either repeatedly or acutely, a person's ability to cope, thereby limiting perceived alternatives.*

At present, theories of suicide suggest that people choose to end their life due to intolerable psychological pain (see Shneidman, 2001). However, this broad conceptualization leaves several questions unanswered, such as why many individuals do not commit suicide in the face of unbearable life circumstances, how a person comes to develop such an extreme emotional response pattern, and why certain stages of life are associated with increased risk compared with others. As emphasized throughout this review, the developmental psychopathology perspective examines continuities across development. A central continuity seen among those who engage in self-injury is problematic coping strategies characterized by both active and passive avoidance of emotional distress. We have suggested that such coping strategies emerge among vulnerable individuals, particularly those raised in high-risk environments.

There is a rich literature examining coping strategies among those who attempt suicide. Common strategies include social withdrawal (Spirito, Overholser, & Stark, 1989), use of maladaptive behaviors (Wilson et al., 1995), emotion suppression, and blame (Horesh et al., 1996). Suicidal adolescents also use fewer cognitive strategies for coping with stressful life events (Asarnow, Carlson, & Guthrie, 1987). Coping strategies are relatively stable over time, across a wide range of psychological and physical conditions. For example, coping strategies predict psychological adjustment 10 years following traumatic spinal cord injury and are the most stable predictor of later distress (Pollard & Kennedy, 2007). Furthermore, among the criteria for major depression, suicidal behavior/ideation is the most stable symptom (Lewinsohn, Petit, Joiner, & Seeley, 2003; Oquendo et al., 2004; Williams, Crane, Barnhofer, Van der Does, & Segal, 2006). Nearly all accounts of SB and NSSI hypothesize that self-injurious acts are a maladaptive means of coping with intense psychological distress (see Crowell et al., 2005).

According to one recent hypothesis, the probability of depressive relapse is higher among those who quickly reactivate problematic cognitions, including suicide ideation, in response to small changes in mood (Williams, Van der Does, Barnhofer, Crane, & Segal, 2008). In a study of depressed adults, suicide attempters were more likely to activate cognitions related to guilt, hopelessness, and suicidality in response to minor mood fluctuations (Antypa, Van der Does, & Penninx, 2009). The authors hypothesized that suicidal individuals may regularly experience thoughts of guilt about the past and hopelessness about the future, and are therefore quicker to identify suicide as a solution. Although further studies are needed, cognitive reactivity of suicide ideation may be one factor that accounts for the stability of suicidal behaviors across extended periods of time. Implicit associations between death and self-referential words (e.g., I, me) may be one behavioral marker of this cognitive process (see Nock et al., 2010).

Consistent with the broader developmental literature, the developmental psychopathology approach emphasizes biology × environment interactions, continuities and discontinuities across development, and unique challenges and opportunities associated with each developmental stage (Cicchetti, 2008). Development is understood as an active and lifelong process. Accordingly, chronological age alone is not considered an organizing variable for life span research (Baltes, 1980). We have emphasized interacting processes that likely contribute to suicide risk at any stage of life. However, rates of suicide fluctuate across the life span, suggesting that unique stressors may potentiate risk among a larger number of vulnerable individuals during particular developmental stages. Before the age of 10 years, for example, suicide is exceptionally uncommon and is often related to profound psychopathology or intellectual impairment (see Hawton, 1982). After age 10, suicide rates begin to rise relative to other causes of death (National Center for Injury Prevention and Control, 2009). For females, suicide rates are highest between females ages 45–54 (rate of 8.4 per 100,000), whereas for males, rates are highest above age 75 (rate of 35.7 per 100,000).

Early in development young children are protected from suicide by virtue of their age and its correlates (lack of exposure to and knowledge of suicide, fewer episodes of psychological distress, lack of opportunity to engage in risky behaviors, etc.). Conversely, unique demands of other life stages may increase suicide risk for certain individuals. For example Erikson (1973) defined the developmental challenge of young adulthood (ages 18–35) as one of strengthening intimacy and solidarity or, if the stage is not successfully navigated, isolation and social distance. If one subscribes to this perspective, it may not be surprising that suicide is the second leading cause of death among 24- to 35-year-old males who are unmarried and isolated socially (National Center for Injury Prevention and Control, 2006). In addition, aging is associated with many physical and cognitive changes that may contribute to risk among vulnerable individuals. For example, menopause may contribute to suicide risk among middle-aged women (Shah, 2007). Loneliness and a decline of physical and cognitive health are believed to contribute substantially to risk for suicide among older males (Alpass & Neville, 2003). Therefore, developmental expectations and life challenges should also be considered in any conceptualization of suicide risk.

Concluding Remarks

Suicide is an individualized choice that occurs relatively infrequently. Thus, anticipating and preventing suicide is as difficult as predicting any low base-rate behavior. In an effort to identify those who are at highest risk, researchers have reported numerous correlates of suicide, SB, and NSSI but have often studied similar phenomena with different names. We have focused on some of the contributing factors to suicide, highlighting converging literatures and examining vulnerabilities, risks, and continuities across development. We propose that genetic and neural vulnerabilities for impulsivity and emotion dysregulation interact with environmental rejection, invalidation, and conflict. Across time, repeated transactions between a vulnerable youth and a high-risk environment contribute to psychopathology, poor coping strategies, rejection sensitivity, and social withdrawal, among other negative outcomes. Indeed, these same interacting factors likely confer risk for many problematic, multifinal outcomes—not just suicide.

Reducing risk for suicidal and nonsuicidal self-injury is an urgent public health priority (US Public Health Service, 1999). Currently, some prevention strategies show promise among individuals who have expressed ideation or have self-injured previously (Gould, Greenberg, Velting, & Shaffer, 2003; Linehan, 1993). It is well known, however, that many who commit suicide never visit a mental health professional, communicate their intent, or attempt suicide previously (Isometsa et al.,

1995; Rihmer, Barsi, Arató, & Demeter, 1990). Thus, prevention programs need to be offered early—well before a first and potentially lethal self-injurious event.

In the future, suicide research should reach beyond identification of diagnostic, psychosocial, and biological correlates of self-injury. Though such descriptive approaches are necessary in characterizing psychiatric syndromes, they are less useful for predicting human behavior, including complex health outcomes. To date, most research has emphasized main effects of either biology or environment, yet biology × environment interaction effects often account for far more variance in adverse outcomes than main effects (Beauchaine, Neuhaus, Brenner, & Gatzke-Kopp, 2008; Crowell, Beauchaine, McCauley et al., 2008). Accordingly, contemporary models of psychopathology emphasize the importance of both neurobiological and contextual influences on behavior. Although there is much to learn, studying relevant biology × environment interactions on developing suicidal behavior will increase our understanding of etiology, which usually translates onto more effective interventions (see e.g., Beauchaine & Marsh, 2006; Beauchaine et al., 2008).

References

Aguirre, R. T. P., & Watts, T. D. (2010). Suicide and alcohol use among American Indians: Toward a transactional-ecological framework. *Journal of Comparative Social Welfare*, 26, 3–11.

Alpass, F. M., & Neville, S. (2003). Loneliness, health and depression in older males. *Aging and Mental Health*, 7, 212–216.

American Psychiatric Association. (2000). *Diagnostic and statistical manual of mental disorders* (4h ed., text rev.). Washington, DC: Author.

American Psychiatric Association. (2006). *Practice guidelines for the treatment of psychiatric disorders: Compendium.* Arlington, VA: Author.

Antypa, N., Van der Does, A. J. W., & Penninx, B. W. J. H. (2009). Cognitive reactivity: Investigation of a potentially treatable marker of suicide risk in depression. *Journal of Affective Disorders*, 122, 46–52.

Arango, V., Underwood, M. D., & Mann, J. J. (1996). Fewer pigmented locus coeruleus neurons in suicide victims: Preliminary results. *Biological Psychiatry*, 39, 112–120.

Asarnow, J. R., Carlson, G. A., & Guthrie, D. (1987). Coping strategies, self-perceptions, hopelessness, and perceived family environments in depressed and suicidal children. *Journal of Consulting and Clinical Psychology*, 55, 361–366.

Asarnow, R. F., & Kernan, C. L. (2008). Childhood schizophrenia. In T. P. Beauchaine & S. P. Hinshaw (Eds.), *Child and adolescent psychopathology* (pp. 614–642). Hoboken, NJ: Wiley.

Audenaert, K., Van Laere, K., Dumont, F., Slegers, G., Mertens, J., van Heeringen, C., & Diercx, R. A. (2001). Decreased frontal serotonin 5-HT2a receptor binding index in deliberate self-harm patients. *European Journal of Nuclear Medicine and Molecular Imaging*, 28, 175–182.

Baca-Garcia, E., Vaquero, C., Diaz-Sastre, C., Saiz-Ruiz, J., Fernandez-Piqueras, J., & de Leon, J. (2002). A gender-specific association between the serotonin transporter gene and suicide attempts. *Neuropsychopharamcology*, 26, 692–695.

Baldessarini, R., & Hennen, J. (2004). Genetics of suicide: An overview. *Harvard Review of Psychiatry*, 12, 1–13.

Baltes, P. B. (1980). Life-span developmental psychology. *Annual Review of Psychology*, 31, 65–110.

Baumeister, R. F. (1990). Suicide as escape from self. *Psychological Review*, 97, 90–113.

Beauchaine, T. P. (2001). Vagal tone, development, and Gray's motivational theory: Toward an integrated model of autonomic nervous system functioning in psychopathology. *Development and Psychopathology*, 13, 183–214.

Beauchaine, T. P. (2012). Physiological markers of emotion and behavior dysregulation in externalizing psychopathology. *Monographs of the Society for Research in Child Development*, 77, 79–86

Beauchaine, T. P., & Gatzke-Kopp, L. M. (2012). Instantiating the multiple levels of analysis perspective in a program of study on externalizing behavior. *Development and Psychopathology*, 24, 1003–1018.

Beauchaine, T. P., & Gatzke-Kopp, L. M. (2013). Genetic and environmental influences on behavior. In T. P. Beauchaine & S. P. Hinshaw (Eds.), *Child and adolescent psychopathology* (2nd ed., pp. 111–140). Hoboken, NJ: Wiley.

Beauchaine, T. P., Gatzke-Kopp, L., & Mead, H. K. (2007). Polyvagal theory and developmental psychopathology: Emotion dysregulation and conduct problems from preschool to adolescence. *Biological Psychology*, 74, 174–184.

Beauchaine, T. P., Hinshaw, S., & Pang, K. C. (2010). Comorbidity of attention-deficit/hyperactivity disorder and early onset conduct disorder: Biological, environmental, and developmental mechanisms. *Clinical Psychology Science and Practice*, 17, 327–336.

Beauchaine, T. P., Katkin, E. S., Strassberg, Z., & Snarr, J. (2001). Disinhibitory psychopathology in male adolescents: Discriminating conduct disorder from attention-deficit/hyperactivity disorder through concurrent assessment of multiple autonomic states. *Journal of Abnormal Psychology*, 110, 610–624.

Beauchaine, T. P., Klein, D. N., Crowell, S. E., Derbidge, C., & Gatzke-Kopp, L. M. (2009). Multifinality in the development of personality disorders: A biology × sex × environment interaction model of antisocial and borderline traits. *Development and Psychopathology*, 21, 735–770.

Beauchaine, T. P., Klein, D. N., Erickson, N. L., & Norris, A. L. (2013). Developmental psychopathology and the Diagnostic and statistical manual of mental disorders. In T. P. Beauchaine & S. P. Hinshaw (Eds.), *Child and adolescent psychopathology* (2nd ed., pp. 29–110). Hoboken, NJ: Wiley

Beauchaine, T. P., & Marsh, P. (2006). Taxometric methods: Enhancing early detection and prevention of psychopathology by identifying latent vulnerability traits. In D. Cicchetti & D. Cohen (Eds.) *Developmental psychopathology* (2nd ed., pp. 931–967). Hoboken, NJ: Wiley.

Beauchaine, T. P., & McNulty, T. (2013). Comorbidities and continuities as ontogenic processes: Toward developmental spectrum model of externalizing psychopathology. *Development and Psychopathology*, 25, 1505–1527.

Beauchaine, T. P., Neuhaus, E., Brenner, S., & Gatzke-Kopp, L. (2008). Ten good reasons to consider biological processes in prevention and intervention research. *Development and Psychopathology, 20*, 745–774.

Beauchaine, T. P., Neuhaus, E., Zalewski, M., Crowell, S. E., & Potapova, N. (2011). The effects of allostatic load on neural systems subserving motivation, mood regulation, and social affiliation. *Development and Psychopathology, 23*, 975–999.

Bellivier, F., Szöke, A., Henry, C., Lacoste, J., Bottos, C., Nosten-Bertrand, M.,...Leboyer, M. (2000). Possible association between serotonin transporter gene polymorphism and violent suicidal behavior in mood disorders. *Biological Psychiatry, 48*, 319–322.

Berman, A. L., Jobes, D. A., & Silverman, M. M. (2006). *Adolescent suicide: Assessment and intervention* (2nd ed.). Washington, DC: American Psychological Association.

Berntson, G. G., Bigger, T. J., Eckberg, D. L., Grossman, P., Kaufmann, P. G., Malik, M.,...van der Molen, M. W. (1997). Heart rate variability: Origins, methods, and interpretive caveats. *Psychophysiology, 34*, 623–648.

Berridge, K. C., & Robinson, T. E. (2003). Parsing reward. *Trends in Neurosciences, 26*, 507–513.

Bizot, J. C., Le Bihan, C., Puech, A. J., Hamon, M., & Thiébot, M. H. (1999). Serotonin and tolerance to delay of reward in rats. *Psychopharmacology, 146*, 400–412.

Blumenthal, S. J., & Kupfer, D. J. (Eds.). (1990). *Suicide over the life cycle.* Washington, DC: American Psychiatric Press.

Bondy, B., Buettner, A., & Zill, P. (2006). Genetics of suicide. *Molecular Psychiatry, 11*, 336–351.

Bongar, B. (2002). *The suicidal patient: Clinical and legal standards of care* (2nd ed.). Washington, DC: American Psychological Association.

Bosker, F. J., Hartman, C. A., Nolte, I. M., Prins, B. P., Terpstra, P., Posthuma, D.,...Nolen, W. A. (2011). Poor replication of candidate genes for major depressive disorder using genome-wide association data. *Molecular Psychiatry, 16*, 516–532.

Bowden, C., Cheetham, S. C., Lowther, S., Katona, C. L. E., Crompton, M. R., & Horton, R. W. (1997). Reduced dopamine turnover in the basal ganglia of depressed suicides. *Brain Research, 769*, 135–140.

Brent, D. A., Johnson, B. A., Perper, J., Connolly, J., Bridge, J., Bartle, S., & Rather, C. (1994). Personality disorder, personality traits, impulsive violence, and completed suicide in adolescents. *Journal of the American Academy of Child and Adolescent Psychiatry, 32*, 69–75.

Brent, D. A., & Mann, J. J. (2005). Family genetic studies, suicide, and suicidal behavior. *American Journal of Medical Genetics Part C: Seminars in Medical Genetics, 133C*, 13–24.

Brent, D. A., Oquendo, M., Birmaher, B., Greenhill, L., Kolko, D., Stanley, B.,...Mann, J. (2003). Peripubertal suicide attempts in offspring of suicide attempters with siblings concordant for suicidal behavior. *American Journal of Psychiatry, 160*, 1486–1493.

Brent, D. A., Perper, J. A., Goldstein, C. E., Kolko, D., Allan, M., Allman, C., & Zelenak, J. P. (1988). Risk factors for adolescent suicide: A comparison of adolescent suicide victims with suicidal inpatients. *Archives of General Psychiatry, 45*, 581–588.

Brent, D. A., Perper, J. A., Moritz, G., Liotus, L., Schweers, J., Balach, L., & Roth, C. (1994). Familial risk factors for adolescent suicide: A case-control study. *Acta Psychiactra Scandinavica, 89*, 52–58.

Brezo, J., Bureau, A., Merette, C., Jomphe, V., Barker, E. D., Vitaro, F., & Turecki, G. (2010). Differences and similarities in the serotonergic diathesis for suicide attempts and mood disorders: A 22-year longitudinal gene-environment study. *Molecular Psychiatry, 15*, 831–843.

Brook, J. S., Whiteman, M., & Zheng, L. (2004). Intergenerational transmission of risks for problem behavior. *Journal of Abnormal Child Psychology, 30*, 65–76.

Brown, J., Cohen, P., Johnson, J. G., & Smailes, E. M. (1999). Childhood abuse and neglect: Specificity of effects on adolescent and young adult depression and suicidality. *Journal of the American Academy of Child and Adolescent Psychiatry, 38*, 1490–1496.

Brown, M. Z., Comtois, K. A., & Linehan, M. M. (2002). Reasons for suicide attempts and nonsuicidal self-injury in women with borderline personality disorder. *Journal of Abnormal Psychology, 111*, 198–202.

Bush, G., Frazier, J. A., Rauch, S. L., Seidman, L. J., Whalen, P. J., Jenike, M. A.,...Biederman, J. (1999). Anterior cingulate cortex dysfunction in attention-deficit/hyperactivity disorder revealed by fMRI and the counting stroop. *Biological Psychiatry, 45*, 1542–1552.

Calkins, S. D. (1997). Cardiac vagal tone indices of temperamental reactivity and behavioral regulation in young children. *Developmental Psychobiology, 31*, 125–135.

Cannon, D. M., Ichise, M., Fromm, S. J., Nugent, A. C., Rollis, D., Gandhi, S. K.,...Drevets, W. C. (2006). Serotonin transporter binding in bipolar disorder assessed using [11C]DASB and positron emission tomography. *Biological Psychiatry, 60*, 207–217.

Carver, C. S., & Miller, C. J. (2006). Relations of serotonin function to personality: Current views and a key methodological issue. *Psychiatry Research, 144*, 1–15.

Caspi, A. (2000). The child is the father of the man: Personality continuities from childhood to adulthood. *Journal of Personality and Social Psychology, 78*, 158–172.

Caspi, A., Sugden, K., Moffitt, T. E., Taylor, A., Craig, I. W., Harrington, H.,...Poulton, R. (2003). Influence of life stress on depression: Moderation by a polymorphism in the 5-HTT gene. *Science, 301*, 386–389.

Charney, D. S. (2004). Psychobiological mechanisms of resilience and vulnerability: Implications for successful adaptation to extreme stress. *Focus, 2*, 368–391.

Cicchetti, D. (2008). A multiple-levels-of-analysis perspective on research in developmental psychopathology. In T. P. Beauchaine & S. P. Hinshaw (Eds.), *Child and adolescent psychopathology* (pp. 27–57). Hoboken, NJ: Wiley.

Cicchetti, D., & Rogosch, F. A. (Eds.). (1996). Developmental pathways: Diversity in process and outcome [Special Issue]. *Development and Psychopathology, 8*, 597–666.

Cicchetti, D., Rogosch, F. A., Sturge-Apple, M., & Toth, S. L. (2010). Interactions of child maltreatment and 5-HTT polymorphisms: Suicidal ideation among children from low-SES backgrounds. *Journal of Pediatric Psychology, 35*, 536–546.

Cicchetti, D., & Toth, S. L. (1998). The development of depression in children and adolescents. *American Psychologist, 53*, 221–241.

Clark, L. A. (2005). Temperament as a unifying basis for personality and psychopathology *Journal of Abnormal Psychology, 114*, 505–521.

Cloninger, C. R. (2000). Biology of personality dimensions. *Current Opinion in Psychiatry, 13*, 611–616.

Coccaro, E. F., Bergeman, C. S., Kavoussi, R. J., & Seroczynski, A. D. (1997). Heritability of aggression and irritability: A twin study of the Buss-Durkee Aggression Scales in adult male subjects. *Biological Psychiatry, 41,* 273–284.

Coccaro, E. F., Bergeman, C. S., & McClearn, G. E. (1993). Heritability of irritable impulsiveness: A study of twins reared together and apart. *Psychiatry Research, 48,* 229–242.

Cole, P. M., & Hall, S. E. (2008). Emotion dysregulation as a risk factor for psychopathology. In T. P. Beauchaine & S. P. Hinshaw (Eds.), *Child and adolescent psychopathology* (pp. 265–299). Hoboken, NJ: Wiley.

Cole, P. M., Hall, S. E., & Hajal, N. J. (2013). Emotion dysregulation as a risk factor for psychopathology. In T. P. Beauchaine & S. P. Hinshaw (Eds.), *Child and adolescent psychopathology* (2nd ed., pp. 341–373). Hoboken, NJ: Wiley.

Cole, P. M., Martin, S. E., & Dennis, T. A. (2004). Emotion regulation as a scientific construct: Methodological challenges and directions for child development research. *Child Development, 75,* 317–333.

Conger, R. D., Conger, K. J., Jr., G. H. E., Lorenz, F. O., Simons, R. L., & Whitbeck, L. B. (1992). A family process model of economic hardship and adjustment of early adolescent boys. *Child Development, 63,* 526–541.

Coryell, W., & Schlesser, M. (2001). The dexamethasone suppression test and suicide prediction. *American Journal of Psychiatry, 158,* 748–753.

Couppis, M., & Kennedy, C. (2008). The rewarding effect of aggression is reduced by nucleus accumbens dopamine receptor antagonism in mice. *Psychopharmacology, 197,* 449–456.

Crawford, M. J., & Prince, M. (1999). Increasing rates of suicide in young men in England during the 1980s: The importance of social context. *Social Science and Medicine, 49,* 1419–1423.

Crosby, A. E., Cheltenham, M. P., & Sacks, J. J. (1999). Incidence of suicidal ideation and behavior in the United States, 1994. *Suicide and Life-Threatening Behavior, 30,* 177–179.

Crowell, S. E., Baucom, B. R., McCauley, E., Potapova, N. V., Fitelson, M., Barth, H.,...Beauchaine, T. P. (2013). Mechanisms of contextual risk for adolescent self-injury: Invalidation and conflict escalation in mother-child interactions. *Journal of Clinical Child and Adolescent Psychology, 42,* 467–480.

Crowell, S. E., Beauchaine, T. P., & Lenzenweger, M. F. (2008). The development of borderline personality and self-injurious behavior. In T. P. Beauchaine & S. P. Hinshaw (Eds.), *Child and adolescent psychopathology* (pp. 510–539). Hoboken, NJ: Wiley.

Crowell, S. E., Beauchaine, T. P., & Linehan, M. M. (2009). A biosocial developmental model of borderline personality: Elaborating and extending Linehan's theory. *Psychological Bulletin, 135,* 495–510.

Crowell, S. E., Beauchaine, T. P., McCauley, E., Smith, C., Stevens, A. L., & Sylvers, P. D. (2005). Psychological, physiological, and serotonergic correlates of parasuicidal behavior among adolescent girls. *Development and Psychopathology, 17,* 1105–1127.

Crowell, S. E., Beauchaine, T. P., McCauley, E., Smith, C., Vasilev, C., & Stevens, A. L. (2008). Parent-child interactions, peripheral serotonin, and intentional self-injury in adolescents. *Journal of Consulting and Clinical Psychology, 76,* 15–21.

Crowell, S. E., Kaufman, E. A., & Lenzeweger, M. F. (2013). The development of borderline personality and self-inflicted injury. In T. P. Beauchaine & S. P. Hinshaw (Eds.), *Child and adolescent psychopathology* (2nd ed., pp. 577–609). Hoboken, NJ: Wiley.

Currier, D., & Mann, J. J. (2008). Stress, genes and the biology of suicidal behavior. *Psychiatric Clinics of North America, 31,* 247–269.

Darche, M. A. (1990). Psychological factors differentiating self-mutilating and non-self-mutilating adolescent inpatient females. *Psychiatric Hospital, 21,* 31–35.

deCatanzaro, D. (1980). Human suicide: A biological perspective. *Behavioral and Brain Sciences, 3,* 265–272.

Depue, R. A., & Lenzenweger, M. F. (2005). A neurobehavioral dimensional model of personality disturbance. In M. F. Lenzenweger & J. F. Clarkin (Eds.), *Major theories of personality disorder* (2nd ed., pp. 391–454). New York, NY: Guilford Press.

Derbidge, C., & Beauchaine, T. P. (in press). A developmental model of self-inflicted injury, borderline personality, and suicide risk. In M. Lewis & K. Rudolph (Eds.), *Handbook of developmental psychopathology* (3rd ed.). New York, NY: Springer.

Dishion, T. J., McCord, J., & Poulin, F. (1999). When interventions harm: Peer groups and problem behavior. *American Psychologist, 54,* 755–764.

Dube, S. R., Anda, R. F., Felitti, V. J., Chapman, D. P., Williamson, D. F., & Giles, W. H. (2001). Childhood abuse, household dysfunction, and the risk of attempted suicide throughout the life span: Findings from the Adverse Childhood Experiences Study. *Journal of the American Medical Association, 286,* 3089–3096.

Durkheim, E. (1897). *Suicide,* (Trans. W. D. Halls). New York, NY: The Free Press.

Eamon, M. K. (2002). Influences and mediators of the effect of poverty on young adolescent depressive symptoms. *Journal of Youth and Adolescence, 31,* 231–242.

Ekman, P. (1992). An argument for basic emotions. *Cognition and Emotion, 6,* 169–200.

Ekman, P., & Friesen, W. V. (1976). Measuring facial movement. *Environmental Psychology and Nonverbal Behavior, 1,* 56–75.

El-Sheikh, M., Kouros, C. D., Erath, S., Keller, P., Cummings, E. M., & Staton, L. (2009). Marital conflict and children's externalizing behavior: Interactions between parasympathetic and sympathetic nervous system activity. *Monographs of the Society for Research in Child Development, 74*(1, Serial No. 292).

Erikson, E. H. (1973). Growth and crisis. In T. Millon (Ed.), *Theories of psychopathology and personality* (pp. 136–156). Philadelphia, PA: W. B. Saunders.

Evenden, J. L., & Ryan, C. N. (1996). The pharmacology of impulsive behaviour in rats: The effects of drugs on response choice with varying delays of reinforcement. *Psychopharmacology, 128,* 161–170.

Eysenck, H. J. (1993). The nature of impulsivity. In W. G. McCown, J. L. Johnson, & M. B. Shure (Eds.), *The impulsive client: Theory, research, and treatment* (pp. 57–69). Washington, DC: American Psychological Association.

Forbes, E. E., Shaw, D. S., & Dahl, R. E. (2007). Alterations in reward-related decision making in boys with recent and future depression. *Biological Psychiatry, 61,* 633–639.

Fowles, D. C. (1988). Psychophysiology and psychopathology: A motivational approach. *Psychophysiology, 25,* 373–391.

Fu, Q., Heath, A. C., Bucholz, K. K., Nelson, E., Glowinski, A. L., Goldberg, J.,...Eisen, S. A. (2002). A twin study of genetic and environmental influences on suicidality in men. *Psychological Medicine, 32*, 11–24.

Gatzke-Kopp, L. M. (2011). Canary in the coalmine: Sensitivity of mesolimbic dopamine to environmental adversity during development. *Neuroscience and Biobehavioral Reviews, 35*, 794–803.

Gatzke-Kopp, L. M., & Beauchaine, T. P. (2007). Central nervous system substrates of impulsivity: Implications for the development of attention-deficit/hyperactivity disorder and conduct disorder. In D. Coch, G. Dawson, & K. Fischer (Eds.), *Human behavior, learning, and the developing brain: Atypical development* (pp. 239–263). New York, NY: Guilford Press.

Gatzke-Kopp, L. M., Beauchaine, T. P., Shannon, K. E., Chipman-Chacon, J., Fleming, A. P., Crowell, S. E., … Johnson, L. C. (2009). Neurological correlates of reward responding in adolescents with and without externalizing behavior disorders. *Journal of Abnormal Psychology, 118*, 203–213.

Gatzke-Kopp, L. M., & Shannon, K. E. (2008). Brain injury as a risk factor for psychopathology. In T. P. Beauchaine & S. P. Hinshaw (Eds.), *Child and adolescent psychopathology* (pp. 208–233). Hoboken, NJ: Wiley.

Gibb, B. E., McGeary, J. E., Beevers, C. G., & Miller, I. W. (2006). Serotonin transporter (5-HTTLPER) genotype, childhood abuse, and suicide attempts in adult psychiatric inpatients. *Suicide and Life Threatening Behavior, 36*, 687–693.

Glowinski, A. L., Bucholz, K. K., Nelson, E. C., Fu, Q., Madden, P. A. F., Reich, W., & Heath, A. C. (2001). Suicide attempts in an adolescent female twin sample. *Journal of the American Academy of Child and Adolescent Psychiatry, 40*, 1300–1307.

Goldsmith, H. H., & Davidson, R. J. (2004). Disambiguating the components of emotion regulation. *Child Development, 75*, 361–365.

González-Maeso, J., Rodríguez-Puertas, R., Meana, J. J., García-Sevilla, J. A., & Guimón, J. (2002). Neurotransmitter receptor-mediated activation of G-proteins in brains of suicide victims with mood disorders: Selective supersensitivity of 2A-adrenoceptors. *Molecular Psychiatry, 7*, 755–767.

Gould, E., & Tanapat, P. (1999). Stress and hippocampal neurogenesis. *Biological Psychiatry, 46*, 1472–1479.

Gould, M. S., Greenberg, T., Velting, D. M., & Shaffer, D. (2003). Youth suicide risk and preventive interventions: A review of the past 10 years. *Journal of the American Academy of Child and Adolescent Psychiatry, 42*, 386–405.

Gray, J. A., & McNaughton, N. (2000). *The neuropsychology of anxiety: An enquiry in to the functions of the septo-hippocampal system* (2nd ed.). Oxford, UK: Oxford University Press.

Greenberg, B. D., Tolliver, T. J., Huang, S-J., Li, Q., Bengel, D., & Murphy, D. L. (1999). Genetic variation in the serotonin transporter promoter region affects serotonin uptake in human blood platelets. *American Journal of Medical Genetics, 88*, 83–87.

Gross, J. J. (1998). The emerging field of emotion regulation: An integrative review. *Review of General Psychology, 2*, 271–299.

Gross, J. J. (2007). *Handbook of emotion regulation*. New York, NY: Guilford Press.

Gurvits, I. G., Koenigsberg, H. W., & Siever, L. (2000). Neurotransmitter dysfunction in patients with borderline personality disorder. *Psychiatric Clinics of North America, 23*, 27–40.

Haghighi, F., Bach-Mizrachi, H., Huang, Y. Y., Arango, V., Shi, S., Dwork, A. J., … Mann, J. J. (2008). Genetic architecture of the human tryptophan hydroxylase 2 gene: Existence

of neural isoforms and relevance for major depression. *Molecular Psychiatry, 13*, 813–820.

Hammen, C. L., Garber, J., & Ingram, R. E. (2010). Vulnerability to depression across the lifespan. In R. E. Ingram & J. M. Price (Eds.), *Vulnerability to psychopathology: Risk across the lifespan* (2nd ed., pp. 282–287). New York, NY: Guilford Press.

Hawton, K. (1982). Attempted suicide in children and adolescents. *Journal of Child Psychology and Psychiatry, 23*, 497–503.

Heim, C., & Nemeroff, C. B. (2001). The role of childhood trauma in the neurobiology of mood and anxiety disorders: Preclinical and clinical studies. *Biological Psychiatry, 49*, 1023–1039.

Hinshaw, S. P., Owens, E. B., Zalecki, C., Huggins, S. P., Montenegro-Nevado, A., Schrodek, E., & Swanson, E. N. (2012). Prospective follow-up of girls with attention-deficit/hyper-activity disorder into young adulthood: Continuing impairment includes elevated risk for suicide attempts and self-injury. *Journal of Consulting and Clinical Psychology, 80*, 1041–1051.

Hirshfeld-Becker, D. R., Biederman, J., Faraone, S. V., Violette, H., Wrightsman, J., & Rosenbaum, J. F. (2002). Temperamental correlates of disruptive behavior disorders in young children: Preliminary findings. *Biological Psychiatry, 51*, 563–574.

Horesh, N., Rolnick, T., Iancu, I., Dannon, P., Lepkifker, E., Apter, A., & Kotler, M. (1996). Coping styles and suicide risk. *Acta Psychiatrica Scandinavica, 93*, 489–493.

Ingoldsby, E. M., & Shaw, D. S. (2002). Neighborhood contextual factors and early-starting antisocial pathways. *Clinical Child and Family Psychology Review, 5*, 21–55.

Ingram, R. E., & Price, J. M. (Eds.). (2010). *Vulnerability to psychopathology: Risk across the lifespan* (2nd ed.). New York, NY: Guilford Press.

Isometsa, E., Heikkinen, M., Marttunen, M., Henriksson, M., Aro, H., & Lonnqvist, J. (1995). The last appointment before suicide: Is suicide intent communicated? *American Journal of Psychiatry, 152*, 919–922.

Joiner, T. E., Brown, J. S., & Wingate, L. R. (2005). The psychology and neurobiology of suicidal behavior. *Annual Review of Psychology, 56*, 287–314.

Joiner, T. E., Y., C., Fitzpatrick, K. K., Witte, T. K., Schmidt, N. B., Berlim, M. T., … Rudd, M. D. (2005). Four studies on how past and current suicidality relate even when "everything but the kitchen sink" is covaried. *Journal of Abnormal Psychology, 114*, 291–303.

Jokinen, J., Carlborg, A., Mårtensson, B., Forslund, K., Nordström, A-L., & Nordström, P. (2007). DST non-suppression predicts suicide after attempted suicide. *Psychiatry Research, 150*, 297–303.

Jollant, F., Bellivier, F., Leboyer, M., Astruc, B., Torres, S., Verdier, R., … Courtet, P. (2005). Impaired decision making in suicide attempters. *American Journal of Psychiatry, 162*, 304–310.

Kagan, J. (2008). Behavioral inhibition as a risk factor for psychopathology. In T. P. Beauchaine & S. P. Hinshaw (Eds.), *Child and adolescent psychopathology* (pp. 157–179). Hoboken, NJ: Wiley.

Kahan, J., & Pattison, E. M. (1984). Proposal for a distinctive diagnosis: The deliberate self-harm syndrome (DSH). *Suicide and Life-Threatening Behavior, 14*, 17–35.

Katz, L. F., & Gottman, J. M. (1997). Buffering children from marital conflict and dissolution. *Journal of Clinical Child Psychology, 26*, 157–171.

Kaufman, J., Yang, B-Z., Douglas-Palumberi, H., Houshyar, S., Lipschitz, D., Krystal, J. H., & Gelernter, J. (2004). Social supports and serotonin transporter gene moderate depression in maltreated children. *Proceedings of the National Academy of Sciences USA, 101*, 17316–17321.

Keilp, J. G., Sackeim, H. A., Brodsky, B. S., Oquendo, M. A., Malone, K. M., & Mann, J. J. (2001). Neuropsychological dysfunction in depressed suicide attempters. *American Journal of Psychiatry, 158*, 735–741.

Klonsky, E. D. (2007). The functions of deliberate self-injury: A review of the evidence. *Clinical Psychology Review, 27*, 226–239.

Krueger, R. F., Hicks, B. M., Patrick, C. J., Carlson, S. R., Iacono, W. G., & McGue, M. (2002). Etiologic connections among substance dependence, antisocial behavior, and personality: Modeling the externalizing spectrum. *Journal of Abnormal Psychology, 111*, 411–424.

Krueger, R. F., Markon, K. E., Patrick, C. J., Benning, S. D., & Kramer, M. D. (2007). Linking antisocial behavior, substance use, and personality: An integrative quantitative model of the adult externalizing spectrum. *Journal of Abnormal Psychology, 116*, 645–666.

Kuo, J. R., & Linehan, M. M. (2009). Disentangling emotion processes in borderline personality disorder: Physiological and self-reported assessment of biological vulnerability, baseline intensity, and reactivity to emotionally evocative stimuli. *Journal of Abnormal Psychology, 118*, 531–544.

Laakso, A., Wallius, E., Kajander, J., Bergman, J., Eskola, O., Solin, O., ... Hietala, J. (2003). Personality traits and striatal dopamine synthesis capacity in healthy subjects. *American Journal of Psychiatry, 160*, 904–910.

Leenaars, A. A. (Ed.). (1991). *Life span perspectives of suicide: Timelines in the suicide process.* New York, NY: Plenum Press.

Lenzenweger, M. F., & Castro, D. D. (2005). Predicting change in borderline personality: Using neurobehavioral systems indicators within an individual growth curve framework. *Development and Psychopathology, 17*, 1207–1237.

Lester, D. (1992). The dexamethasone suppression test as an indicator of suicide: A meta-analysis. *Pharmacopsychiatry, 25*, 265–270.

Leventhal, T., & Brooks-Gunn, J. (2003). Moving to opportunity: An experimental study of neighborhood effects on mental health. *American Journal of Public Health, 93*, 1576–1582.

Lewinsohn, P. M., Petit, J. W., Joiner, T. E., & Seeley, J. R. (2003). The symptomatic expression of major depressive disorder in adolescents and young adults. *Journal of Abnormal Psychology, 112*, 244–252.

Linehan, M. M. (1993). *Cognitive-behavioral treatment of borderline personality disorder.* New York, NY: Guilford Press.

Linehan, M. M., Comtois, K. A., Brown, M. Z., Heard, H. L., & Wagner, A. W. (2006). Suicide attempt self-injury interview (SASII): Development, reliability, and validity of a scale to assess suicide attempts and intentional self-injury. *Psychological Assessment, 18*, 303–312.

Linehan, M. M., Rizvi, S. L., Welch, S. S., & Page, B. (2008). Psychiatric aspects of suicidal behaviour: Personality disorders. In K. Hawton & K. van Heeringen (Eds.), *The International Handbook of Suicide and Attempted Suicide* (pp. 147–178): John Wiley & Sons.

Luthar, S. S., Cicchetti, D., & Becker, B. (2000). The construct of resilience: A critical evaluation and guidelines for future work. *Child Development, 71*, 543–562.

Lynam, D., Caspi, A., Moffitt, T. E., Wikström, P. O. H., Loeber, R., & Novak, S. (2000). The interaction between impulsivity and neighborhood context on offending: The effects of impulsivity are stronger in poorer neighborhoods. *Journal of Abnormal Psychology, 109*, 563–574.

Lynch, M., & Cicchetti, D. (2002). Links between community violence and the family system: Evidence from Children's feelings of relatedness and perceptions of parent behavior. *Family Processes, 41*, 519–532.

Lyonfelds, J. D., Borkovec, T. D., & Thayer, J. F. (1995). Vagal tone in generalized anxiety disorder and the effects of aversive imagery and worrisome thinking. *Behavior Therapy, 26*, 457–466.

Lyons-Ruth, K. (2008). Contributions of the mother-infant relationship to dissociative, borderline, and conduct symptoms in young adulthood. *Infant Mental Health Journal, 29*, 203–218.

Mann, J. J. (2003). Neurobiology of suicidal behaviour. *Nature Reviews Neuroscience, 4*, 819–828.

Mann, J. J., Arango, V. A., Avenevoli, S., Brent, D. A., Champagne, F. A., Clayton, P., ... Wenzel, A. (2009). Candidate endophenotypes for genetic studies of suicidal behavior. *Biological Psychiatry, 65*, 556–563.

Mann, J. J., Brent, D. A., & Arango, V. (2001). The neurobiology and genetics of suicide and attempted suicide: A focus on the serotonergic system. *Neuropsychopharamcology, 24*, 467–477.

Mann, J. J., Currier, D., Stanley, B., Oquendo, M. A., Amsel, L. V., & Ellis, S. P. (2006). Can biological tests assist prediction of suicide in mood disorders? *International Journal of Neuropsychopharmacology, 9*, 465–474.

Mason, P. (1954). Suicide in adolescents. *Psychoanalytic Review, 41*, 48–54.

Mathers, C. D., & Loncar, D. (2006). Projections of global mortality and burden of disease from 2002 to 2030. *PLoS Medicine, 3*, e442.

McGlashan, T. H., Grilo, C. M., Sanislow, C. A., Ralevski, E., Morey, L. C., Gunderson, J. G., ... Pagano, M. (2005). Two-year prevalence and stability of individual DSM-IV criteria for schizotypal, borderline, avoidant, and obsessive-compulsive personality disorders: Toward a hybrid model of Axis II disorders. *American Journal of Psychiatry, 162*, 883–889.

Mead, H. K., Beauchaine, T. P., & Shannon, K. E. (2010). Neurobiological adaptations to violence across development. *Development and Psychopathology, 22*, 1–22.

Meehl, P. E. (1962). Schizotaxia, schizotypy, schizophrenia. *American Psychologist, 17*, 827–838.

Mehlum, L., Friis, S., Vaglum, P., & Karterud, S. (1994). The longitudinal pattern of suicidal behaviour in borderline personality disorder: A prospective follow-up study. *Acta Psychiatrica Scandinavica, 90*, 124–130.

Melia, K. R., Rasmussen, K., Terwilliger, R. Z., Haycock, J. W., Nestler, E. J., & Duman, R. S. (1992). Coordinate regulation of the cyclic AMP system with firing rate and expression of tyrosine hydroxylase in the rat locus coeruleus: Effects of chronic stress and drug treatments. *Journal of Neurochemistry, 58*, 494–502.

National Center for Injury Prevention and Control. (2006). *CDC injury fact book.* Atlanta, GA: Centers for Disease Control and Prevention.

National Center for Injury Prevention and Control. (2009). *CDC injury research agenda, 2009-2018.* Retrieved August

2013, from http://www.cdc.gov/injury/ResearchAgenda/index.html.

Neuhaus, E., & Beauchaine, T. P. (2013). Impulsivity and vulnerability to psychopathology. In T. P. Beauchaine & S. P. Hinshaw (Eds.), *Child and adolescent psychopathology* (2nd ed., pp. 197–226). Hoboken, NJ: Wiley.

Nixon, M. K., Cloutier, P. F., & Aggarwal, S. (2002). Affect regulation and addictive aspects of repetitive self-injury in hospitalized adolescents. *Journal of the American Academy of Child and Adolescent Psychiatry, 41*, 1333–1341.

Nock, M. K. (2010). Self-injury. *Annual Review of Clinical Psychology, 6*, 339–363.

Nock, M. K., Joiner, T. E., Gordon, K. H., Lloyd-Richardson, E., & Prinstein, M. J. (2006). Non-suicidal self-injury among adolescents: Diagnostic correlates and relation to suicide attempts. *Psychiatry Research, 144*, 65–72.

Nock, M. K., & Kazdin, A. E. (2002). Examination of affective, cognitive, and behavioral factors and suicide-related outcomes in children and young adolescents. *Journal of Clinical Child and Adolescent Psychology, 31*, 48–58.

Nock, M. K., Park, J. M., Finn, C. T., Deliberto, T. L., Dour, H. J., & Banaji, M. R. (2010). Measuring the suicidal mind. *Psychological Science, 21*, 511–517.

Norman, W. H., Brown, W. A., Miller, I. W., Keitner, G. I., & Overholser, J. C. (1990). The dexamethasone suppression test and completed suicide. *Acta Psychiatrica Scandinavica, 81*, 120–125.

O'Carroll, P. W., Berman, A. L., Maris, R. W., Moscicki, E. K., Tanney, B. L., & Silverman, M. M. (1996). Beyond the Tower of Babel: A nomenclature for suicidology. *Suicide and Life-Threatening Behavior, 26*, 237–252.

Oas, P. (1985). The psychological assessment of impulsivity: A review. *Journal of Psychoeducational Assessment, 3*, 141–156.

Offer, D., & Barglow, P. (1960). Adolescent and young adult self-mutilation incidents in a general psychiatric hospital. *Archives of General Psychiatry, 3*, 194–204.

Oquendo, M. A., Barrera, A., Ellis, S. P., Li, S., Burke, A. K., Grunebaum, M.,...Mann, J. (2004). Instability of symptoms in recurrent major depression: A prospective study. *American Journal of Psychiatry, 161*, 255–261.

Ordway, G. A., Widdowson, P. S., Smith, K. S., & Halaris, A. (1994). Agonist binding to a2-adrenoceptors is elevated in the locus coeruleus from victims of suicide. *Journal of Neurochemistry, 63*, 617–624.

Pardon, M-C., Ma, S., & Morilak, D. A. (2003). Chronic cold stress sensitizes brain noradrenergic reactivity and noradrenergic facilitation of the HPA stress response in Wistar Kyoto rats. *Brain Research, 971*, 55–65.

Patterson, G. R., Chamberlain, P., & Reid, J. B. (1982). A comparative evaluation of a parent-training program. *Behavior Therapy, 13*, 638–650.

Patterson, G. R., DeBaryshe, B. D., & Ramsey, E. (1989). A developmental perspective on antisocial behavior. *American Psychologist, 44*, 329–335.

Patterson, G. R., Degarmo, D. S., & Knutson, N. (2000). Hyperactive and antisocial behaviors: Comorbid or two points in the same process? *Development and Psychopathology, 12*, 91–106.

Perelberg, R. J. (Ed.). (1999). *Psychoanalytic understanding of violence and suicide.* New York, NY: Routledge.

Pitchot, W., Hansenne, M., & Ansseau, M. (2001). Role of dopamine in non-depressed patients with a history of suicide attempts. *European Psychiatry, 16*, 424–427.

Pitchot, W., Hansenne, M., Moreno, A. G., & Ansseau, M. (1992). Suicidal behavior and growth hormone response to apomorphine test. *Biological Psychiatry, 15*, 1213–1219.

Pitchot, W., Reggers, J., Pinto, E., Hansenne, M., Fuchs, S., Pirard, S., & Ansseau, M. (2001). Reduced dopaminergic activity in depressed suicides. *Psychoneuroendocrinology, 26*, 331–335.

Pollard, C., & Kennedy, P. (2007). A longitudinal analysis of emotional impact, coping strategies and post-traumatic psychological growth following spinal cord injury: A 10-year review. *British Journal of Health Psychology, 12*, 347–362.

Porges, S. W. (1995). Orienting in a defensive world: Mammalian modifications of our evolutionary heritage. A polyvagal theory. *Psychophysiology, 32*, 301–318.

Porges, S. W. (2007). The polyvagal perspective. *Biological Psychiatry, 74*, 116–143.

Portes, P. R., Sandhu, D. S., & Longwell-Grice, R. (2002). Understanding adolescent suicide: A psychosocial interpretation of developmental and contextual factors. *Adolescence, 37*, 1–5.

Quay, H. C. (1993). The psychobiology of undersocialized aggressive conduct disorder: A theoretical perspective. *Development and Psychopathology, 5*, 165–180.

Rao, U., Weissman, M. M., Martin, J. A., & Hammond, R. W. (1993). Childhood depression and risk of suicide: A preliminary report of a longitudinal study. *Journal of the American Academy of Child and Adolescent Psychiatry, 32*, 21–27.

Rechlin, T., Weis, M., Spitzer, A., & Kaschka, W. P. (1994). Are affective disorders associated with alterations of heart rate variability? *Journal of Affective Disorders, 32*, 271–275.

Renaud, J., Berlim, M. T., McGirr, A., Tousignant, M., & Turecki, G. (2008). Current psychiatric morbidity, aggression/impulsivity, and personality dimensions in child and adolescent suicide: A case-control study. *Journal of Affective Disorders, 105*, 221–228.

Richters, J. E., & Martinez, P. E. (1993). Violent communities, family choices, and children's chances: An algorithm for improving the odds. *Development and Psychopathology, 5*, 609–627.

Rihmer, Z., Barsi, J., Arató, M., & Demeter, E. (1990). Suicide in subtypes of primary major depression. *Journal of Affective Disorders, 18*, 221–225.

Ritz, T. (2009). Studying noninvasive indices of vagal control: The need for respiratory control and the problem of target specificity. *Biological Psychology, 80*, 158–168.

Ross, S., & Heath, N. L. (2003). Two models of adolescent self-mutilation. *Suicide and Life-Threatening Behavior, 33*, 277–287.

Roy, A., Karoum, F., & Pollack, S. (1992). Marked reduction in indexes of dopamine metabolism among patients with depression who attempt suicide. *Archives of General Psychiatry, 49*, 447–450.

Roy, A., Rylander, G., & Sarchiapone, M. (1997). Genetics of suicide. *Annals of the New York Academy of Sciences, 836*, 135–157.

Roy, A. Hu, X-Z., Janal, M. N., Goldman, D. (2007). Interaction between childhood trauma and serotonin transporter gene variation in suicide. *Neuropsychopharmacology, 32*, 2046–2052.

Rubia, K. (2011). "Cool" inferior frontostriatal dysfunction in attention-deficit/hyperactivity disorder versus "hot" ventromedial orbitofrontal-limbic dysfunction in conduct disorder: a review. *Biological Psychiatry, 69*, e69–e87.

Rutter, M., & Sroufe, L. A. (2000). Developmental psychopathology: Concepts and challenges. *Development and Psychopathology, 12*, 265–296.

Sagvolden, T., Russell, V. A., Aase, H., Johansen, E. B., & Farshbaf, M. (2005). Rodent models of attention-deficit/hyperactivity disorder. *Biological Psychiatry, 57*, 1239–1247.

Sampson, R. J., Morenoff, J. D., & Gannon-Rowley, T. (2002). Assessing neighborhood effects: Social processes and new directions in research. *Annual Review of Sociology, 28*, 443–478.

Sampson, S. M., & Mrazek, D. A. (2001). Depression in adolescence. *Current Opinion in Pediatrics, 13*, 586–590.

Sander, T., Harms, H., Dufeu, P., Kuhn, S., Hoehe, M., Lesch, K-P.,...Schmidt, L. G. (1998). Serotonin transporter gene variants in alcohol-dependent subjects with dissocial personality disorder. *Biological Psychiatry, 43*, 908–912.

Sauder, C., Beauchaine, T. P., Gatzke-Kopp, L. M., Shannon, K. E., & Aylward, E. (2012). Neuroanatomical correlates of heterotypic comorbidity in externalizing male adolescents. *Journal of Clinical Child and Adolescent Psychology, 41*, 346–352.

Shaffer, D., Gould, M. S., Fisher, P., Trautman, P., Moreau, D., Kleinman, M., & Flory, M. (1996). Psychiatric diagnosis in child and adolescent suicide. *Archives of General Psychiatry, 53*, 339–348.

Shah, A. (2007). The relationship between suicide rates and age: An analysis of multinational data from the World Health Organization. *International Psychogeriatrics, 19*, 1141–1152.

Shannon, K. E., Beauchaine, T. P., Brenner, S. L., Neuhaus, E., & Gatzke-Kopp, L. (2007). Familial and temperamental predictors of resilience in children at risk for conduct disorder and depression. *Development and Psychopathology, 19*, 701–727.

Sher, L., Mann, J. J., Traskman-Bendz, L., Winchel, R., Huang, Y., Fertuck, E. & Stanley, F. E. (2006). Lower cerebrospinal fluid homovanillic acid levels in depressed suicide attempters. *Journal of Affective Disorders, 90*, 83–89.

Shields, A. M., & Cicchetti, D. (1994). The development of emotional and behavioral self-regulation and social competence among maltreated school-age children. *Development and Psychopathology, 6*, 57–75.

Shipman, K. L., & Zeman, J. (2001). Socialization of children's emotion regulation in mother-child dyads: A developmental psychopathology perspective. *Development and Psychopathology, 13*, 317–336.

Shneidman, E. S. (1985). *Definition of suicide*. New York, NY: Wiley.

Shneidman, E. S. (1991). The commonalities of suicide across the life span. In A. A. Leenaars (Ed.), *Life span perspectives of suicide: Timelines in the suicide process* (pp. 39–52). New York, NY: Plenum Press.

Shneidman, E. S. (2001). *Comprehending suicide: Landmarks in 20th-century suicidology*. Washington, DC: American Psychological Association.

Silverman, M. M., Berman, A. L., Sanddal, N. D., O'Carroll, P. W., & Joiner, T. E. (2007a). Rebuilding the Tower of Babel: A revised nomenclature for the study of suicide and suicidal behaviors. Part 1: Background, rationale, and methodology. *Suicide and Life-Threatening Behavior, 37*, 264–277.

Silverman, M. M., Berman, A. L., Sanddal, N. D., O'Carroll, P. W., & Joiner, T. E. (2007b). Rebuilding the Tower of Babel: A revised nomenclature for the study of suicide and suicidal behaviors. Part 2: Suicide-related ideations,

communications, and behaviors. *Suicide and Life-Threatening Behavior, 37*, 264–277.

Simpson, G. (1950). Methodological problems in determining the aetiology of suicide. *American Sociological Review, 15*, 658–663.

Skodol, A. E., Siever, L. J., Livesley, W. J., Gunderson, J. G., Pfohl, B., & Widiger, T. A. (2002). The borderline diagnosis II: Biology, genetics, and clinical course. *Biological Psychiatry, 51*, 951–963.

Sloan, R. P., Shapiro, P. A., Bigger, J. T., Bagiella, M., Steinman, R. C., & Gorman, J. M. (1994). Cardiac autonomic control and hostility in healthy subjects. *American Journal of Cardiology, 74*, 298–300.

Spirito, A., & Esposito-Smythers, C. (2006). Attempted and completed suicide in adolescence. *Annual Review of Clinical Psychology, 2*, 237–266.

Spirito, A., Overholser, J., & Stark, L. J. (1989). Common problems and coping strategies II: Findings with adolescent suicide attempters. *Journal of Abnormal Child Psychology, 17*, 213–221.

Sroufe, L. A. (1990). Considering normal and abnormal together: The essence of developmental psychopathology. *Development and Psychopathology, 2*, 335–347.

Sroufe, L. A. (2009). The concept of development in developmental psychopathology. *Child Development Perspectives, 3*, 178–183.

Sroufe, L. A., & Rutter, M. (1984). The domain of developmental psychopathology. *Child Development, 55*, 17–29.

Stanley, B., Winchel, R., Molcho, A., Simeon, D., & Stanley, M. (1992). Suicide and the self-harm continuum: Phenomenological and biochemical evidence. *International Review of Psychiatry, 4*, 149–155.

Stillion, J. M., & McDowell, E. E. (1996). *Suicide across the life span*. Washington, DC: Taylor & Francis.

Szapocznik, J., & Kurtines, W. M. (1993). Family psychology and cultural diversity: Opportunities for theory, research, and application. *American Psychologist, 48*, 400–407.

Thayer, J. F., Friedman, B. H., & Borkovec, T. D. (1996). Autonomic characteristics of generalized anxiety disorder and worry. *Biological Psychiatry, 39*, 255–266.

Thorell, L. H. (2009). Valid electrodermal hyporeactivity for depressive suicidal propensity offers links to cognitive theory. *Acta Psychiatrica Scandinavica, 119*, 338–349.

Tomlinson-Keasey, C., Warren, L. W., & Elliott, J. E. (1986). Suicide among gifted women: A prospective study. *Journal of Abnormal Psychology, 95*, 123–130.

Tsigos, C., & Chrousos, G. P. (2002). Hypothalamic-pituitary-adrenal axis, neuroendocrine factors and stress. *Journal of Psychosomatic Research, 53*, 865–871.

Tuvblad, C., Zheng, M., Raine, A., & Baker, L. (2009). A common genetic factor explains the covariation among ADHD ODD and CD symptoms in 9–10 year old boys and girls. *Journal of Abnormal Child Psychology, 37*, 153–167.

US Department of Housing and Urban Development. (2003). *Moving to opportunity: Interim impacts evaluation*. Retrieved August 2013, from http://www.abtassociates.com/reports/2003302754569_71451.pdf.

U.S. Public Health Service. (1999). *The surgeon general's call to action to prevent suicide*, Washington, DC: United States Public Health Service.

Vaidya, C. J., Austin, G., Kirkorian, G., Ridlehuber, H. W., Desmond, J. E., Glover, G. H., & Gabrieli, J. D. E. (1998). Selective effects of methylphenidate in attention deficit hyperactivity disorders: A functional magnetic resonance study. *Proceedings of the National Academy of Sciences USA, 95*, 14494–14499.

Volkow, N. D., Wang, G. J., Kollins, S. H., Wigal, T. L., Newcorn, J. H., Telang, F.,...Swanson, J. M. (2009). Evaluating dopamine reward pathway in ADHD: Clinical implications. *Journal of the American Medical Association, 302*, 1084–1091.

Voracek, M., & Loibl, L. M. (2007). Genetics of suicide: A systematic review of twin studies. *Wiener Klinische Wochenschrift, 119*, 463–475.

Watson, D., Clark, L. A., & Chmielewski, M. (2008). Structures of personality and their relevance to psychopathology: II. Further articulation of a comprehensive unified trait structure. *Journal of Personality, 76*, 1485–1522.

White, C. N., Gunderson, J. G., Zanarini, M. C., & Hudson, J. I. (2003). Family studies of borderline personality disorder: A review. *Harvard Review of Psychiatry, 11*, 8–19.

Williams, J., Van der Does, A., Barnhofer, T., Crane, C., & Segal, Z. (2008). Cognitive reactivity, suicidal ideation and future fluency: Preliminary investigation of a differential activation theory of hopelessness/suicidality. *Cognitive Therapy and Research, 32*, 83–104.

Williams, J. M. G., Crane, C., Barnhofer, T., Van der Does, A. J. W., & Segal, Z. V. (2006). Recurrence of suicidal ideation across depressive episodes. *Journal of Affective Disorders, 91*, 189–194.

Wilson, K. G., Stelzer, J., Bergman, J. N., Kral, M. J., Inayatulla, M., & Elliott, C. A. (1995). Problem solving, stress, and coping in adolescent suicide attempts. *Suicide and Life-Threatening Behavior, 25*, 241–252.

World Health Organization. (2002). *World report on violence and health*, Geneva, Switzerland: Author.

Yen, S., Shea, M. T., Pagano, M., Sanislow, C. A., Grilo, C. M., McGlashan, T. H., & Morey, L. C. (2003). Axis I and axis II disorders as predictors of prospective suicide attempts: Findings from the collaborative longitudinal personality disorders study. *Journal of Abnormal Psychology, 112*, 375–381.

Yeragani, V. K., Pohl, R., Berger, R., Balon, R., Ramersh, C., Glitz, D.,...Weinberg, P. (1993). Decreased heart rate variability in panic disorder patients: A study of power-spectral analysis of heart rate. *Psychiatry Research, 46*, 89–103.

Young, S. E., Stallings, M. C., Corley, R. P., Krauter, K. S., & Hewitt, J. K. (2000). Genetic and environmental influences on behavioral disinhibition. *American Journal of Medical Genetics, 96*, 684–695.

Zhu, M-Y., Klimek, V., Dilley, G. E., Haycock, J. W., Stockmeier, C., Overholser, J. C.,...Ordway, G. A. (1999). Elevated levels of tyrosine hydroxylase in the locus coeruleus in major depression. *Biological Psychiatry, 46*, 1275–1286.

Zilboorg, G. (1936). Differential diagnostic types of suicide. *Archives of General Psychiatry, 35*, 270–291.

Zill, P., Buttner, A., Eisenmenger, W., Moller, H-J., Bondy, B., & Ackenheil, M. (2004). Single nucleotide polymorphism and haplotype analysis of a novel tryptophan hydroxylase Isoform (TPH2) gene in suicide victims. *Biological Psychiatry, 56*, 581–586.

Zlotnick, C., Donaldson, D., Spirito, A., & Pearlstein, T. (1997). Affect regulation and suicide attempts in adolescent inpatients. *Journal of the American Academy of Child and Adolescent Psychiatry, 36*, 793–798.

Social and Ecological Approaches to Understanding Suicidal Behaviors and Nonsuicidal Self-Injury

Nicole Heilbron, Joseph C. Franklin, John D. Guerry, *and* Mitchell J. Prinstein

Abstract

This chapter reviews current theoretical models and empirical findings related to social and ecological influences on the development of self-injurious thoughts and behaviors (SITBs). Specifically, distal factors related to peer (i.e., peer status and victimization, friendship and social support, peer influence), family (i.e., family communication and problem solving, relationship quality, child maltreatment), and neighborhood contexts are examined. A novel conceptualization that integrates biological and psychological factors with social and ecological contextual variables is presented. This theoretical model proposes that social priming and pain offset relief represent two specific mediators of the links between general social influence mechanisms and SITBs. Future directions for studying the influence of social and ecological contexts on the emergence and maintenance of suicidal behaviors and nonsuicidal self-injury are discussed.

Key Words: social influence, peer relations, family functioning, neighborhood, social priming, distal factors, ecological model

In recent years, researchers have made significant progress toward identifying psychological and psychiatric factors that portend risk of suicidal behavior (i.e., suicidal ideation, suicide attempts) and nonsuicidal self-injury (NSSI). Although studies of individual personality and mental health variables have offered important insights into the correlates and predictors of self-injurious thoughts and behaviors (SITBs), research aimed at understanding the interactive effects of intrapersonal factors and social and ecological contextual variables is sorely needed. Indeed, theoretically driven studies designed to examine the nature of interdependent associations among individual (e.g., psychiatric disorder), social (e.g., peer and family support), and environmental (e.g., neighborhood) factors are of critical importance in formulating a comprehensive understanding of the etiology of suicidality and NSSI. Moreover, consistent with Bronfenbrenner's (1977,

1979) ecological model, the study of peer, family, and neighborhood contexts in research on SITBs is crucial for informing effective preventative efforts and clinical intervention strategies.

The primary focus of this chapter is the role of social and ecological factors in the *development* of suicide-related behaviors and NSSI. Our conceptualization of the domains of peers, family, and neighborhood is informed largely by the integration of developmental psychopathology and systems theory perspectives. In light of recent calls for greater integration of these approaches (e.g., Davies & Cicchetti, 2004), the first aim of this chapter is to provide an overview of empirical findings related to how peer, family, and neighborhood systems may be implicated in the development of SITBs. Consistent with the basic tenets of both developmental psychopathology and systems approaches, the development of these behaviors is reflected in the principles of equifinality (i.e., multiple causes may result in a particular outcome) and multifinality (i.e., multiple outcomes may originate from a single factor or mechanism) (Cicchetti, 1990; Cicchetti & Rogosch, 1996; Nichols, 1999; Sroufe, 1989). For example, individual (e.g., attributional style, depression), family (e.g., quality of parent–child/adolescent communication, exposure to interparental conflict), and broader environmental factors (e.g., neighborhood context, peer experiences) may serve different roles and functions in the development of SITBs. Thus, the first aim of this chapter is primarily focused on a review of distal factors that may create intra- and interpersonal vulnerabilities to engaging in SITBs. The second aim is to propose a theoretical model that conceptualizes how social experiences, including social influence, may be implicated as specific risk factors for engaging in SITBs. This conceptualization follows from Nock's (2009) general theoretical model of NSSI in that the proposed model merges biological and psychological factors with social and ecological contextual factors. This model is intended to provide the impetus for novel testable hypotheses regarding the influence of social and ecological contexts on the emergence and maintenance of suicide-related behaviors and NSSI.

Definitions of Terms

In this chapter, the terminology used is generally aligned with the nomenclature devised by Silverman, Berman, Sanddal, O'Carroll, and Joiner (2007). Specifically, references to suicide-related behavior include suicide-related ideation, suicide-related communication (e.g., suicide threat), and suicide attempts. Suicidality refers to the broad class of suicide-related behaviors. The use of the term NSSI is one notable departure from the terms presented by Silverman and colleagues (2007). We have adopted the term NSSI to refer to the direct and deliberate destruction of an individual's own body tissue in the absence of intent to die (Nock & Favazza, 2009; Prinstein, 2008). Because the chapter includes a review of literature related to both suicide-related behaviors and NSSI, we also apply the term self-injurious thoughts and behaviors (SITBs) to refer to the general class of self-harm behaviors that may be suicidal or nonsuicidal (see Nock & Favazza, 2009, for additional discussion).

Theoretical Models of Social and Ecological Factors

Although contemporary research on suicide generally has focused on the study of individual psychiatric and psychological characteristics as distal risk factors, the inception of empirical research on suicidology has placed a much greater emphasis on society-level factors (e.g., economic conditions) (see Maris, Berman, & Silverman, 2000, for a review of the empirical foundations of suicidology). Indeed, the salience of social and ecological variables in the study of suicide risk is central to Durkheim's seminal sociological work on suicide (Durkheim, 1897, 1951). In brief, Durkheim (1897, 1951) proposed that the suicide rate represents a marker of social solidarity within the greater society. More specifically, he contended that social relationships, which connect and regulate individual behavior, are of vital importance in understanding how social forces affect the suicide rate. In his theoretical conceptualization, Durkheim (1897, 1951) conceived of four distinct forms of suicide: egoism, altruism, anomie, and fatalism. These differing types of suicidal behavior reflect a unique pattern of problematic social integration and moral regulation. For example, egoistic suicide is defined as suicidal acts committed by individuals who are not strongly supported by membership in a cohesive social network, whereas anomic suicide is defined as suicidal acts committed during times of crisis or rapid societal change when individuals may be more likely to feel disconnected and aimless. Although Durkheim's theories and methods were not without critique (e.g., Kushner & Sterk, 2005), they provided the first example of a comprehensive, empirical theory of suicidology that emphasized suicidal behavior as an outcome of external, social factors rather than focusing primarily on individual psychopathology.

The legacy of Durkheim's work is apparent in a more recent theory of suicide articulated by Joiner (2005). Whereas Durkheim posited a curvilinear association between an individual's degree of social integration and suicide rates (i.e., too much and too little social integration conferred the greatest risk of suicide), Joiner's (2005) interpersonal-psychological theory draws attention to two key interpersonally relevant constructs: perceived burdensomeness and failed belongingness. Perceived burdensomeness refers to a state of mind characterized by feelings that a person's life presents a burden to family, friends, and/or the broader society (Joiner, 2005). Similar to the Durkheimian emphasis on low integration, failed belongingness represents a state of mind in which an individual feels alienated from other people and experiences him/herself as failing to be an integral member of family, friends, or valuable social group (Joiner, 2005). Joiner (2005) theorizes that when combined with the acquired capacity to self-injure, the experience of perceiving oneself as a burden and of feeling a lack of belonging create a potent risk for death by suicide. This compelling theoretical conceptualization has been the subject of a rapidly growing research base and has found preliminary support in numerous research studies with adults (e.g., Nademin et al., 2008; Van Orden, Witte, Gordon, Bender, & Joiner, 2008; Van Orden, Witte, James, et al., 2008). Joiner's theory is discussed in greater detail later in the chapter.

With respect to a more explicitly developmental focus, several other researchers have presented theoretical models that include an emphasis on putative risk and protective factors in the study of social and ecological influences and SITBs. For example, Bridge, Goldstein, and Brent (2006) detailed a developmental-transactional model of suicidal behavior in adolescents. In this model, identifiable precursors to suicidality are highlighted with an initial focus on parental variables (e.g., parental mood disorder, impulsive aggression, suicide attempt) as distal risk factors for youth suicidal behavior. Bridge and colleagues (2006) suggest a variant of a diathesis-stress model whereby adolescent suicidal ideation may lead to suicide attempt in the presence of acute stressors (e.g., interpersonal loss, conflict) and in the absence of protective factors (e.g., strong family, school connections). This conceptualization is similar to the "stress-buffer" hypothesis proposed by Cohen and Wills (1985), in that it predicts that social support may be protective in the face of stressful conditions.

In sum, the science of suicidology found its beginnings in the empirical work of Durkheim (1897, 1951), with a primary focus on society-level variables as the impetus for changes in suicide rates. As research has evolved, greater emphasis has been placed on explicating the direct, indirect, and interactive effects of social and ecological factors on SITBs. Although there remain many unanswered questions regarding the mechanisms underlying observed associations, contemporary theories have begun to integrate various facets of intra- and interpersonal functioning into biopsychosocial models of suicide risk (e.g., King & Merchant, 2008; Linehan, 1993). The remainder of this chapter reviews research findings on distal risk factors related to peer, family, and neighborhood contexts, followed by a novel conceptualization of social mechanisms specific to SITBs that are required to produce SITBs as compared to other, functionally equivalent, health risk behaviors.

Peer Functioning and Self-Injurious Thoughts and Behaviors

The study of peer factors in the developmental psychopathology of suicidality and NSSI has been a topic of growing interest in recent years (see King & Merchant, 2008; Prinstein, 2003, for reviews). The increasing emphasis on peer functioning is further underscored by the fact that adolescents frequently cite interpersonal problems, including peer rejection/victimization, social isolation, and peer relationship conflict, as precipitants of suicidal behavior (e.g., Berman & Schwartz, 1990; Brent et al., 1993; Brent, Baugher, Bridge, Chen, & Chiappetta, 1999; Gould, Fisher, Parides, Flory, & Shaffer, 1996; Hawton, Fagg, & Simkin, 1996) and engagement in NSSI (e.g., see Hawton & Harriss, 2006). Given the heightened importance of peer relationships during adolescence, it follows that this developmental period represents a particularly critical time for understanding the role of peers in youth SITB. Moreover, recent findings have documented significant increases in the rate of engagement in SITBs, including NSSI, at the transition from childhood to adolescence (Centers for Disease Control [CDC], 2004; Gould, Greenberg, Velting, & Shaffer, 2003; Kessler, Berglund, Borges, Nock, & Wang, 2005; World Health Organization [WHO], 2005). Accordingly, the following section is focused on adolescent peer functioning in the development of suicidality and NSSI. The empirical literature related to three central peer constructs is reviewed, namely, (1) peer status/victimization, (2) friendship and perceived social support, and (3) peer influence. This conceptualization of peer functioning is based on the work of Hartup (1996), which was adapted by Prinstein (2003). Clinical implications and avenues for future research directions are discussed.

Peer Status and Victimization

The extent to which children and adolescents are liked by their peers represents a clear starting point for considering the role of peers in the development of youth suicidality. There is a long-standing tradition of research on links between measures of likeability (i.e., peer sociometric status; popular, average, neglected, controversial, rejected) and psychological adjustment (see Kupersmidt, Coie, & Dodge, 1990; Kupersmidt & Dodge, 2004; Parker & Asher, 1987, for reviews). More recently, a reputation-based construct has been introduced in order to distinguish between being liked/disliked by peers and being viewed as popular and having reputational status in the social hierarchy (Parkhurst & Hopmeyer,

1998). Together, these markers of peer status (i.e., preference- and reputation-based popularity) represent important avenues for explicating the role peer functioning may play in the emergence of suicidal behaviors and NSSI. Unfortunately, studies linking these measures of peer status and SITB are quite rare.

Results drawn from a recent longitudinal study conducted in our laboratory provided support for the importance of peer-nominated measures of peer status (preference- and reputation-based popularity) as predictors of change in suicidal ideation over a 2-year period (Heilbron & Prinstein, in press). Specifically, findings drawn from a latent growth curve analysis suggested that low levels of preference-based popularity were associated with increases in suicidal ideation over time in a community sample. This study presents the first evidence of longitudinal associations between peer rejection and increases in suicidal ideation, thereby adding to prior work that has documented concurrent associations (e.g., Prinstein, Boergers, Spirito, Little, & Grapentine, 2000). Interestingly, with respect to NSSI, positive concurrent associations were revealed between NSSI and both peer status constructs, controlling for depressive symptoms. It is possible that this finding reflects a growing belief among adolescents that NSSI represents a marker of social status or membership in a valued subculture. This possibility is bolstered by the fact that the links between NSSI and peer status held despite controlling for depressive symptoms, suggesting that a general orientation toward risk-taking behaviors may be a contributing factor. This is consistent with preliminary evidence that adolescents who engage in NSSI also are at greater risk of engaging in other health risk behaviors (e.g., tobacco use, substance use, disordered eating) (Hilt, Cha, & Nolen-Hoeksema, 2008). Thus, it may be that adolescents who self-injure are perceived by peers as more popular and well liked because they are engaging in behaviors that are socially valued and command respect within a particular adolescent peer context. Note that this proposition may account, in part, for the initiation of the behavior, but it does not provide a particularly compelling rationale for why the behaviors may be maintained outside of the peer context. For example, it may be that initially an individual is more likely to engage in SITBs if the imagined reward of increased social status outweighs the punishment of painful (or not so painful) self-injury. The latter part of this chapter addresses mechanisms through which SITB becomes associated with other potential rewards, thus explaining the maintenance of this behavior.

In a parallel line of peer research, there has been growing interest in the role of peer victimization as a possible precipitant of SITB. Several recent high-profile cases reported in the media have generated considerable speculation that being victimized by peers is a direct cause of suicide. The term "bullycide" has emerged to describe this apparent phenomenon (e.g., Marr & Field, 2001). There also are numerous news reports of parents who, after losing a child to suicide, have taken legal action against school officials for failing to take adequate steps to prevent their child's victimization (e.g., James, 2009). Although it seems reasonable to conclude that engaging in any number of self-harm behaviors represents a foreseeable consequence of peer victimization or bullying, there is a limited research base that has tested *causal* associations between problematic peer experiences and suicide-related behaviors. It certainly is true that peer victimization has been linked to a host of concurrent (e.g., Hawker & Boulton, 2000) and longitudinal adjustment difficulties (see Juvonen & Graham, 2001); however, there remain many untested questions regarding the specific role of perceptions of peer experiences in the development of SITB.

To date, research aimed at testing links between peer victimization experiences and SITBs has been plagued by several significant methodological shortcomings. Specifically, the vast majority of studies have employed cross-sectional designs (e.g., Ivarsson, Broberg, Arvidsson, & Gillberg, 2005; Kaltiala-Heino, Rimpelä, Marttunen, Rimpelä, & Räntanen, 1999; Klomek, Marrocco, Kleinman, Schonfeld, & Gould, 2007; Mills, Guerin, Lynch, Daly, & Fitzpatrick, 2004), making it impossible to test hypotheses related to causality or yield temporally based conclusions regarding victimization as an antecedent or consequence to self-injurious thoughts. Findings from two known longitudinal studies were decidedly mixed. Klomek and colleagues (2008) reported no evidence of a predictive association between boys' childhood peer victimization at age 8 and their self-reported suicidal ideation at age 18. In our recent longitudinal research, findings were indicative of a direct link between overt forms of peer victimization (e.g., verbal threats) and increasing trajectories of suicidal ideation; however, this effect was only true for girls (Heilbron & Prinstein, in press).

A second major limitation of previous work on peer victimization and SITBs relates to the measurement of the primary constructs of interest. For example, with several exceptions (e.g., Heilbron & Prinstein, in press; Kim, Koh, & Leventhal, 2004; Rigby & Slee, 1999), few studies have examined peer victimization using traditional sociometric assessment measures, which are believed to be the most valid indicators of peer status (Coie & Dodge, 1983). In addition, many studies have obtained self-report measures of both the predictor and criterion variables, leading to problems associated with common method variance. Finally, studies linking peer victimization and SITB often have failed to control for depressive symptoms, which limits conclusions as to whether peer victimization experiences are independently predictive of SITB or may merely serve as a proxy for negative affect (see Kim & Leventhal, 2008 for additional discussion).

In sum, given the growing number of cases for which peer victimization is identified as the "cause" of adolescent suicide, it is imperative that researchers systematically address this theorized link using well-validated measures and methods. As noted by Kochenderfer-Ladd and colleagues (2001), there is heterogeneity in children's responses to peer victimization and corresponding effects on individual adjustment, such that intervention and prevention efforts should be informed by an understanding of the differing pathways of adaptation and maladaptation. In addition, the question of whether peer victimization is a cause, a consequence, or possibly both a cause and consequence of psychopathology has been raised by numerous researchers (e.g., Kim, Leventhal, Koh, Hubbard, & Boyce, 2006; Klomek et al., 2008). There also is an emergent literature suggesting that both victims and bullies are at greater risk for suicide, and that the combination of both being a bully and being a victim may represent a particularly heightened risk of SITB (e.g., Klomek et al., 2007). As such, informing the interpretation of empirical findings with a sound theoretical rationale may be especially important for advancing knowledge of the role of peers in the developmental psychopathology of suicide-related behaviors and NSSI.

Based on an examination of current findings and developmental theory, the associations in question may be conceptualized from a variety of theoretical perspectives, including incidental (i.e., concomitant) and causal models, or an integration of both perspectives (Parker & Asher, 1987). Note that because research in this area typically uses correlational methods, "causal" models represent heuristic conceptualizations of links between peer functioning and adjustment but rarely are examined in a manner that can confirm true causality.

With respect to incidental models, two theoretical models are proposed. First, suicide-related outcomes and NSSI may result from the dynamic interplay between psychopathology and peer experiences (e.g., rejection, victimization) over time, whereby the same underlying psychopathology may be expressed differently at different stages of development (i.e., heterotypic continuity). For example, it may be that the bidirectional influences of rudimentary psychopathology on peer victimization experiences manifest in developing psychopathology that ultimately takes the form of suicide-related behaviors and/or NSSI. This transactional model suggests that the onset of psychopathology increases vulnerability to negative peer experiences and vice versa, and that continuity over time may be represented in different behavioral manifestations or symptom presentations (e.g., depression, anxiety, externalizing symptoms, suicidality).

A second incidental model suggests that the association between problematic peer experiences, psychopathology, and suicide-related behaviors may be mediated by other peer factors. For instance, it may be that peer victimization is related to other peer constructs that are more closely associated with suicidality. One such peer construct is deviant peer affiliation. Peer victimization has been identified as a risk factor for a variety of externalizing behaviors, including aggression, substance use, and delinquency (e.g., Khatri, Kupersmidt, & Patterson, 2000; Sullivan, Farrell, & Kliewer, 2006). Deviant peer affiliation also has been associated with externalizing symptoms, substance use, health risk behaviors, internalizing symptoms, and suicide-related behaviors (Andrews, Tildesley, Hops, & Li, 2002; Christakis & Fowler, 2007; Dishion, 2000; Keenan, Loeber, Zhang, Stouthamer-Loeber, & Van Kammen, 1995; Prinstein, 2007; Prinstein, Boergers, & Spirito, 2001; Stevens & Prinstein, 2005). The potential role of peer influence is discussed in greater detail later.

In contrast to incidental theoretical models, two causal models are proposed. First, negative peer experiences may represent a moderator of the association between psychopathology and suicidality. For example, consistent with a diathesis-stress model, experiences of peer victimization may trigger a vulnerability to suicide-related behaviors. It may be that the stress associated with being victimized by peers potentiates the link between depressogenic attributions and suicidal ideation. Conversely, perhaps peer victimization mediates the association between psychopathology and suicidality such that the link might be partly explained by the experience of peer victimization.

Taken together, the study of peer status and victimization represents an important avenue for future investigations of the etiology of SITB. Indeed, it has been contended that negative peer status may represent an antecedent to peer victimization, such that being victimized by peers may be central to the process of peer rejection (see Boivin, Hymel, & Hodges, 2001 for a review). For example, in a heuristic model of paths linking peer rejection to adolescent SITB, Prinstein (2003) proposed several co-occurring mechanisms whereby peer rejection may lead to heightened peer victimization, which may in turn represent an interpersonal stressor that directly precipitates suicidal behavior. It follows that future research aimed at testing such theorized mechanisms will provide an extremely important contribution toward understanding how peer status may be implicated in the development of adolescent SITB.

Friendship and Perceived Social Support

In addition to the consideration of broader peer status variables (e.g., popularity, victimization), the study of peer functioning requires an examination of the role of friendship in psychological adjustment. Previous studies have demonstrated that among adolescents, the lack of a close, supportive dyadic friendship presents an increased risk of difficulties in social and psychological adaptation (Newcomb & Bagwell, 1995), including problems coping with stressful life events (Cohen & Wills, 1985). Studies on SITB examining friendship predictors are relatively rare; yet relevant findings can be found in literatures on friendship quality, perceived social support from friends, and on social network predictors. Each is discussed briefly next.

Relatively few studies have examined how the number and quality of friendships are implicated in the development of suicide-related thoughts and behaviors. There is some evidence that the support received from friendships may compensate for poor family support in adolescent adjustment (e.g., Gauze, Bukowski, Aquan-Assee, & Sippola, 1996); however, this has not been closely examined in longitudinal studies of SITB outcomes. Similarly, Prinstein and colleagues (2000) reported evidence of an independent, direct pathway between lower levels of support within close friendships and higher levels of suicidal ideation

among an inpatient sample of adolescents who had been hospitalized for concerns related to suicidality. Yet Kerr, Preuss, and King (2006) found that for adolescent boys, perceived support from friends was positively associated with levels of suicidal ideation, perhaps because these friends may have been active in risk-taking behavior. In terms of NSSI specifically, the importance of close friendship has been examined in several studies. For instance, Hilt and colleagues (2008) observed that adolescent girls who self-reported lower quality communication with close friends were likely to engage in NSSI for social reinforcement (e.g., to gain attention from others, to avoid interpersonal task demands) when they were experiencing higher levels of self-reported peer victimization.

In addition to work examining direct effects of friendship support on SITB, a host of studies has compared support from peers and family members as competing predictors of SITB (e.g., Harter, Marold, & Whitesell, 1992; Kerr et al., 2006; Kidd et al., 2006). Data drawn from community and clinical samples have been relatively consistent in demonstrating that greater interpersonal problems, social isolation, and a lack of peer support are especially predictive of higher rates of suicide-related behaviors, as well as death by suicide (e.g., Berman & Schwartz, 1990; Johnson et al., 2002; Lewinsohn, Rohde, & Seeley, 1996; Lewinsohn, Rohde, Seeley, & Baldwin, 2001; Mazza & Reynolds, 1998; Perkins & Hartless, 2002; Prinstein et al., 2000). It is perhaps not surprising that supportive peer relationships may serve as a buffer against SITB, and indeed these findings are consistent with the core themes underlying the theories posited by Joiner (2005) and Durkheim (1897, 1951).

Several other interesting findings have emerged regarding the role of social network variables and youth SITB. For example, using data from the National Longitudinal Study of Adolescent Health (Add Health), Bearman and Moody (2004) found that for girls only, being socially isolated from peers and having intransitive friendships (i.e., having a friendship network spanning numerous disconnected peers) increased the odds of suicidal ideation over the course of a 1-year span. With respect to boys, Bearman and Moody (2004) reported that membership in a tightly networked school community, for which there was a high relative density of friendship connections, served as a protective factor against suicide attempts. In a sociological analysis, Haynie, South, and Bose (2006) found evidence of gender differences in the effects of residential mobility on rates of attempted suicide among adolescents who participated in the Add Health study. Specifically, Haynie and colleagues reported that adolescent girls had a heightened risk of attempting suicide during a 1-year period following a residential move, whereas no effect was observed for boys. Preliminary evidence suggested that the effect for girls appeared to be mediated, at least in part, by higher rates of social isolation, victimization, delinquency, and lower school attachment (Haynie et al., 2006).

In sum, these preliminary findings highlight the importance of exploring how friendship experiences may contribute to the initiation and maintenance of SITBs. Importantly, findings offer support for the reciprocal, distal influences between people and their friendship contexts. Results do not offer an explanation of the specific mechanisms underlying how and why such friendship qualities may contribute to the exacerbation or attenuation of self-injurious acts. Several hypotheses will be discussed later in the section on specific social influences on SITBs.

Peer Influence

The role of peer influence on SITBs has garnered significant interest in the psychological research community in recent years. The increased prevalence of SITBs among adolescents has many parents, educators, and clinicians concerned that a "peer contagion" effect may be contributing to the apparent rise. These concerns are not without merit. In terms of suicidal behaviors, previous studies have examined the presence of suicide clusters, which refers to the presence of an unusually high number of suicides or suicide attempts occurring in close temporal or geographic proximity (e.g., Gould, 1990; Insel & Gould, 2008). The notion of clusters is distinct from a "contagion effect" in that contagion relates to the actual process of influence whereby suicidal behavior increases the occurrence of subsequent suicidal behavior (Insel & Gould, 2008). With respect to social influence and suicidality, Prinstein and colleagues (2001) found that in a community sample, adolescents' suicidal behavior was associated with their friends' suicidal behavior, and that this was even more pronounced in the context of high levels of depression and family dysfunction.

With respect to NSSI, there is indeed some evidence from the clinical literature to suggest that for people receiving care in a treatment facility (e.g., psychiatric inpatient unit), one patient's engagement in NSSI is associated with other patients' engagement in NSSI, even among individuals who have no previous history of engaging in NSSI behaviors (Ghaziuddin, Tsai, Naylor, & Ghaziuddin, 1992; Rada & James, 1982; Raine, 1982; Rosen & Walsh, 1989; Taiminen, Kallio-Soukainen, Nokso-Koivisto, Kaljonen, & Kelenius, 1998; Walsh & Rosen, 1985). There also is a growing research base suggesting that discussions of NSSI (i.e., methods, associated feelings) have become quite common on the Internet, including in forums that are believed to be frequented by adolescents (Whitlock, Powers, & Eckenrode, 2006).

The study of possible influence mechanisms requires careful attention to two tenets of "homophily" that may account for similarity between an adolescent and his/her friends' attitudes or behaviors (Kandel, 1978). First, similarities between adolescents and their peers may be explained by adolescents' tendency to befriend individuals whom they perceive to be most similar to themselves (i.e., "selection effects"). Second, peers' engagement in specific behaviors, or the expression of specific attitudes, may increase the likelihood of similar behaviors and attitudes among others (i.e., "socialization effects"). To date, most studies of peer influence of SITBs have focused on documenting the presence of clusters and, to a much lesser extent, on identifying and disentangling selection and socialization effects (Joiner, 2003). Accordingly, there has been remarkably limited emphasis on specifying mechanisms that may underlie these effects, including possible "contagion effects" (Joiner, 1999). Moreover, it is important to note that the co-occurrence of SITBs among a group of individuals is not sufficient evidence of an influence mechanism. It may be that stressors shared among a group of individuals (i.e., "third variables") may account for clustered increases in SITBs.

These questions were addressed directly in a recent study from our laboratory. Prinstein and colleagues (2010) found preliminary support for selection and socialization effects of NSSI in two longitudinal studies within community-based and clinically referred samples. In a clinically referred sample, adolescents' self-reported NSSI was longitudinally associated with increases in self-injurious behavior (i.e., NSSI, suicidality) among their closest friends (i.e., selection effects). Also, friends' reports of self-injurious behavior longitudinally predicted increases in the adolescents' NSSI (i.e., socialization effects; Prinstein et al., 2010). Socialization effects also were revealed in a community sample of youth.

Adolescents' best friends' reports of their engagement in NSSI were prospectively associated with increasing levels of target adolescents' NSSI over a 2-year period (Prinstein et al., 2010). In both studies, selection and socialization effects were revealed after controlling for depressive symptoms as a predictor of NSSI. Both studies also revealed moderation effects for gender; effects were revealed only for girls. It may be that the high levels of self-disclosure, reliance, and the overall quality of girls' friendships create a context in which the effects of social influence are likely to be especially potent.

In terms of NSSI, behavioral and social psychological theories provide a conceptual basis for the processes underlying peer influence effects (Heilbron & Prinstein, 2008). For example, it may be that those adolescents who believe that their close friends or high-status peers endorse NSSI as an adaptive and appropriate behavior are particularly likely to emulate that behavior. Consistent with the theorized social functions of NSSI (see Nock & Prinstein, 2004, 2005), the endorsement of NSSI behavior may be conducted in a public manner that will be observed by those who will confer rewards (e.g., discussing NSSI with peers). The physical scars often associated with NSSI also may serve as markers of social status within a peer group that supports such behaviors. In other words, the ability to tolerate self-inflicted pain may be related to high levels of status among peers who have positive regard for NSSI behaviors. The opposite effect may be true in peer groups that do not promote NSSI, meaning that discussion of NSSI and physical scarring that is suggestive of engagement in self-injuring behaviors may represent shameful acts that compromise an individual's status in the group.

As a complement to behavioral perspectives, social psychological theories (e.g., Blanton & Christie, 2003; Fishbein & Azjen, 1975; Gibbons, Gerrard, & Lane, 2003) provide varying conceptualizations of how and why individuals tend to emulate or model the attitudes and behaviors of their peers. Much of this research literature has been predicated on identity-based theories for understanding peer influence, which share several basic assumptions with proposed behavioral mechanisms (e.g., conformity to peers to elicit rewards). For instance, behavioral theories emphasize social rewards, whereas identity-based theories contend that conformity is primarily motivated by internal needs and self-evaluation. Moreover, social psychological theories are generally founded on the assumption that individuals tend to engage in behaviors that serve to establish or maintain a positive sense of self-concept (e.g., Markus & Wurf, 1987; Schlenker, 1985). As such, individuals engage in the process of social comparison to evaluate themselves in reference to their perceptions of others' attitudes/behavior (i.e., social norms), and they adapt their behavior in such a way that will confirm a favorable sense of self.

Among adolescents, it seems plausible that peers provide an informational source for exploring NSSI, as well as serving a role in setting social norms that adolescents use to evaluate their decision to engage in NSSI behavior. For example, adolescents who have difficulties regulating negative emotions may learn from peers that NSSI represents a potential strategy for emotion regulation. If engaging in NSSI as an emotional regulation strategy is associated with peers who project a desired identity (i.e., exhibited by high-status peers, close friends, or a subgroup of peers with whom an adolescent identifies), it follows that adolescents may choose NSSI as a behavior that will help them to both cope with negative emotions and achieve a desired self-image. Application of an identity-based model therefore suggests that peer influence may not be relevant to the emotional conditions that precipitate the desire to engage in NSSI, but rather for the selection of NSSI as a behavioral strategy to regulate emotions.

In sum, a developmental psychopathology perspective on the etiology of SITB behaviors must consider the dynamic nature of peer influence effects on the initiation and maintenance of the behaviors. For example, it is possible that conforming to perceived social norms serves as a primary motivation for engaging in SITB, but that the behavior may persist based largely on other sources of reinforcement. At the most simplistic level, it may be that individuals initiate self-injurious behavior in response to peer pressure or with the goal of conforming to social norms yet ultimately maintain the behavior as a means of regulating emotional distress or reducing negative affect. Indeed, NSSI serves multiple functions that may change over time and may reflect numerous psychological difficulties (Klonsky, 2007; Lloyd-Richardson, Nock, & Prinstein, 2008; Nock & Prinstein, 2004, 2005; Suyemoto, 1998). In addition, there also may be considerable intraindividual variability in the functions of NSSI such that different functions may motivate engagement in different NSSI behaviors (e.g., skin cutting, burning) across different episodes, or at different points in development. These possibilities are discussed in greater detail next as part of the integrative biopsychosocial model of specific social influences on SITB.

Summary of Peer Functioning and Self-Injurious Thoughts and Behaviors

The study of peer functioning has much to contribute to understanding risk factors and contingencies that may motivate, reinforce, or prevent adolescents' engagement in SITBs. Indeed, in light of the salience of peer relationships in adolescence, it follows that research aimed at clarifying the mechanisms whereby peer experiences, including rejection and victimization, may be implicated in the emergence and maintenance of SITBs is of critical importance. Similarly, prospective investigations designed to more rigorously examine the selection and socialization effects that may underlie peer influence processes are urgently needed.

Family Functioning and Self-Injurious Thoughts and Behaviors

Based on the results of adoption, twin, and family studies, a fairly extensive empirical literature has emerged documenting genetic explanations for familial aggregation of suicidality, including possible intermediate phenotypes (i.e., impulsive aggression, neuroticism) (e.g., Brent & Melhem, 2008; Brent et al., 2004; Mann, Waternaux, Haas, & Malone, 1999). These studies demonstrate that although there is a strong genetic component in explaining the familial transmission of suicidal behavior, there remains much to be learned about the social and ecological bases of how particular family experiences may translate into risk of SITB. Indeed, recent calls for research aimed at examining possible psychological mediators (e.g., communication patterns, relationship quality) of the family transmission of SITBs highlight the importance of generating a knowledge base that could inform clinical practice guidelines for the assessment and treatment of suicidality and NSSI in the family context (Lizardi et al., 2009). Several comprehensive literature reviews have summarized how various family factors such as problematic communication, caregiver loss, and parental psychopathology may be related to adolescent suicidality (see Gould et al., 2003; Wagner, 1997; Wagner, Silverman, & Martin, 2003 for reviews). Although the literature is fairly consistent in documenting links between family discord and adolescent suicide and suicide attempts (e.g., Asarnow & Carlson, 1988; Brent et al., 1994; Fergusson & Lynskey, 1995; Gould et al., 1996;

Kosky, Silburn, & Zubrick, 1990), less attention has been paid to examining *how* particular family dynamics or characteristics of family functioning may be implicated in SITB. The following section will briefly discuss empirical findings related to key family factors (i.e., communication and problem solving, perceived support and parent–child/adolescent relationship quality, child maltreatment) and the etiology of SITBs.

Family Communication and Problem Solving

In a detailed review of the empirical literature, Wagner (1997) found limited evidence to support problematic family communication or problem-solving skills as a risk factor for youth suicidality. In addition, he noted that methodological constraints hampered the ability to draw conclusions regarding the role of family communication in SITBs (Wagner, 1997). For example, much of the research has been based on correlational designs and involved self-reports of dyadic and whole-family functioning, and there also was little known about the temporal nature of observed associations. With respect to available prospective studies, Wagner (1997) reported some support for theorized associations between whole-family and parent–child relationship functioning as predictors of suicidal ideation and suicide attempts, controlling for depressive symptoms; however, he noted that there was no evidence to support links between these predictors and completed suicides.

In a subsequent review, Wagner and colleagues (2003) suggested that although evidence from cross-sectional studies of family functioning is inconsistent, findings generally point to family cohesion, support, and family conflict as factors that reliably discriminate between suicidal adolescents and both clinical and nonclinical control groups (e.g., Cetin, 2001; Perkins & Hartless, 2002; Rubenstein, Halton, Kasten, Rubin, & Stechler, 1998). With respect to more recent research, longitudinal studies have begun to shed light on the nature of associations between dysfunctional family communication, problem solving, and SITB. For example, in a clinical sample of adolescents, Prinstein and colleagues (2000) observed an indirect association between adolescent reports of global family dysfunction and increased suicidal ideation over time. Specifically, findings suggested that high levels of family dysfunction predicted increases in adolescent oppositionality and conduct problems, which were in turn associated with increases in depressive symptoms and suicidal ideation. Thus, consistent with Wagner's (1997) review, there was little evidence that after accounting for theorized mediating variables, difficulties with communication or problem solving in the family had a direct effect on changes in adolescent suicidality over time.

Recent research aimed at understanding how emotionality is expressed within the family context has yielded interesting results. Sim and colleagues (2009) theorized that the emotional environment of the family may have important implications for how adolescents develop emotion regulation skills and, consequently, whether they are at risk of engaging in NSSI. This hypothesis is predicated on the conceptual model proposed by Linehan (1993), wherein it is suggested that the interaction of a biologically based vulnerability and invalidation of emotion may compromise an individual's ability to acquire adaptive emotion regulation strategies. Results indicated that girls' emotion regulation skills partially mediated the association between an invalidating emotional climate in the family and their engagement in NSSI. These authors reported that the apparent gender difference may have been an artifact of a small sample size of boys; however, they did note that findings were consistent with a body of literature documenting gender differences in research on emotion and psychopathology (Zeman, Cassano, Perry-Parrish, & Stegall, 2006).

In a study of parental expressed emotion (EE), Wedig and Nock (2007) examined several potential mediators and moderators of the association between EE and SITB. This work draws on a well-developed literature linking high levels of EE in the family to various manifestations of psychopathology (see Hooley, 2007). Families high in EE are characterized by the dimensions of hostility, emotional overinvolvement, and critical comments directed toward a particular family member. Wedig and Nock (2007) found that among adolescents, parental EE was significantly associated with several forms of SITBs (i.e., suicidal ideation, plans, attempts, NSSI). With respect to specific pathways, Wedig and Nock (2007) observed that high levels of parental criticism were associated with increases in SITBs, even when controlling for other forms of psychopathology. No associations were reported for parental emotional overinvolvement. In more detailed analyses of self- and parental criticism, findings further suggested that adolescent self-criticism moderated links between parental criticism and SITBs. Specifically, results indicated that for SITBs, the effects of parental criticism are

especially pernicious when combined with high levels of self-criticism (Wedig & Nock, 2007).

Family Support and Relationship Quality

In addition to an empirical literature documenting associations between SITBs and the quality of family communication and problem solving, there is a sizeable research base examining family social support and relationship quality variables (see King & Merchant, 2008 for a comprehensive review). Although many of these studies have similar limitations to what was noted in the peer support literature (e.g., cross-sectional designs, reliance on self-report measures), there are many intriguing findings that can be gleaned from the existing studies.

In terms of perceived support from family members, Wagner (1997) noted that based on correlational findings from cross-sectional studies, links between low family support and suicide attempts were evident when comparing suicide attempters with a nonequated normal control group; however, evidence of such links was notably absent when comparing clinical control groups equated for psychopathology. Interestingly, in a subsequent review, Wagner et al. (2003) suggest that there may be important differences between the nature of suicidal behavior and links to family functioning. For example, they contend that there is fairly consistent empirical support linking suicide-related thoughts and behaviors (both fatal and nonfatal) to problematic parent-child relationship quality (e.g., relationships characterized by high conflict and low closeness), whereas findings suggest that associations between family systems problems (e.g., low cohesion, low adaptability) and insecure parent-child attachments are stronger for nonfatal suicidal behaviors (i.e., suicidal ideation, suicide attempts) than for completed suicide.

With respect to prospective studies, work by Lewinsohn and colleagues (1994) examined family support as a predictor of later suicide attempts using a prospective design. Results suggested that after controlling for a history of prior suicide attempts, family support did not predict later attempts. In a later study of the same cohort, low family support predicted suicide attempts into young adulthood for females; however, for males low friend support was a significant predictor (Lewinsohn et al., 2001). In contrast, Fergusson and Lynskey (1995) examined parent-child relationship quality in a community sample and observed that lower maternal emotional responsiveness and greater parental harsh disciplinary practices were prospectively associated with a higher likelihood of suicide attempts.

Several longitudinal studies also have highlighted that family support and parent-child relationship quality may be implicated in future SITBs (Fergusson, Woodward, & Horwood, 2000; Garber, Little, Hilsman, & Weaver, 1998; Johnson et al., 2002); however, with few exceptions, findings are based on self-reported information. For example, Connor and Rueter (2006) reported that the association between observed parental warmth and later adolescent SITBs (a composite measure of suicidal ideation, suicide plans, and suicide attempts) was mediated by adolescent emotional distress. Moreover, observed maternal warmth predicted adolescent suicidality but did not predict emotional distress (Connor & Rueter, 2006). Results of this study highlight the importance of examining individual and parent variables, and also the value of using multiple forms of measurement (i.e., observation, self-report) to address the problems associated with shared method variance. Moreover, whereas results of cross-sectional studies have stressed the importance of the father–child relationship (e.g., Gould et al., 1996; Tousignant, Bastien, & Hamel, 1993), it is imperative that prospective studies be conducted to further test the nature of theoretically driven hypotheses related to qualities of the parent–child relationship as predictors of SITBs. In addition, Wagner et al. (2003) concluded that problematic parent–teen relationships, especially with fathers, are predictive of completed suicide, whereas the same is not true of low family cohesion and high conflict in families. These results suggest that there may be important differences in the pattern of associations among differing types of SITBs that should be carefully addressed in future longitudinal studies.

In sum, it is important to consider direct associations between measures of family functioning and SITBs, as well as possible indirect associations. For example, it may be that there are critical mediators of these associations that have yet to be fully tested (e.g., negative qualities of the parent–child relationship, depression). Moreover, consistent with a developmental systems perspective, several studies have examined how family relationships, including perceived support, may interact with peer variables to heighten or mitigate risk of SITBs (e.g., Kidd et al., 2006; Prinstein et al., 2000). Indeed, in light of preliminary findings that social context variables may exert an additive effect on SITBs (e.g., Perkins & Hartless, 2002), Kidd and colleagues (2006) contended that theoretically guided research examining

interactive effects between and among the various social domains (i.e., peer, family, community/neighborhood) is clearly needed. Kidd et al. (2006) also suggest that results of such studies could provide important insights for informing clinical practice.

Child Maltreatment

Over the past 15 years, a considerable empirical literature has evolved documenting links between different forms of child maltreatment (i.e., physical abuse, sexual abuse, emotional abuse, neglect) and SITB. Numerous studies have observed relatively robust associations between childhood abuse and both suicide and suicide attempts (e.g., Borowsky, Ireland, & Resnick, 2001; Christoffersen, Poulsen, & Nielsen, 2003; Fergusson, Horwood, & Lynskey, 1996; Kosky et al., 1990; Salzinger, Rosario, Feldman, & Ng-Mak, 2007). Findings regarding associations between suicidal ideation and a history of childhood abuse are more inconsistent (see Wagner et al., 2003). Childhood abuse also has been linked to later NSSI in clinical and community populations (e.g., Low, Jones, MacLeod, Power, & Duggan, 2000; van der Kolk, Perry, & Herman, 1991; Wiederman, Sansone, & Sansone, 1999; Yates, Carlson, & Egeland, 2008). In light of evidence that childhood traumatic experiences are highly prevalent among individuals at elevated risk of SITBs, the Institute of Medicine (2002) has identified the interdisciplinary study of the physiological and psychological effects of childhood trauma as a critical area for future research on the developmental psychopathology of suicide.

In addition to identifying childhood abuse experiences as a distal risk factor for SITBs, researchers have begun to examine whether specific types of abuse or neglect are differentially associated with the development of suicidal behaviors or NSSI. For example, there is preliminary evidence that sexual abuse may present a particularly significant risk of suicide attempts (e.g., Brown, Cohen, Johnson, & Smailes, 1999; Fergusson et al., 1996; Johnson et al., 2002; Rosenberg et al., 2005). Similarly, there is some evidence that childhood sexual abuse is associated with recurrent NSSI, whereas physical abuse is more closely linked to intermittent NSSI (Yates et al., 2008). Taken together, these efforts represent an important contribution in the evolution of this literature; however, it is imperative that childhood maltreatment be considered in the context of other relevant covariates and contextual factors. Yates (2004, 2009) described how an organizational theory of development which reflects the basic tenets of a developmental psychopathology approach can offer a useful perspective for conceptualizing links between childhood traumatic experiences and the development of self-injurious behaviors. This theoretical model offers an excellent rationale for why applying the principles of developmental theory may be particularly relevant to clarifying pathways linking maltreatment and NSSI and resolving apparent discrepant findings (see Yates, 2004, 2009).

Summary of Family Functioning and Self-Injurious Thoughts and Behaviors

In conclusion, although it is clear that family functioning is relevant to the development of SITBs, there remain many important avenues for future research to elucidate the mechanisms underlying observed associations. Indeed, Wagner and colleagues (2003) emphasized that many conclusions that have been drawn related to family factors and SITBs are unfounded because the results are based on research that is unable to establish the temporal sequence of the theorized family-based risk factors of interest and SITBs. Wagner et al. (2003) further stressed that prospective studies, informed by the principles of developmental psychopathology (namely multi- and equifinality), represent a fruitful direction for future research efforts aimed at testing theorized pathways between characteristics of the family context and SITBs.

Neighborhood Factors

In stark contrast to the relatively large body of research that has examined individual or micro-level predictors of suicidal behaviors, very little work has begun to explore neighborhood and community-level risk factors. This omission is somewhat surprising given the clear, long-standing imperative to expand the study of self-injury to include complex transactions between individuals and their broader social contexts (e.g., Durkheim, 1897, 1951). Indeed, it has been recognized recently that "an understanding of the collective characteristics of communities that may confer risk, at the individual level, for suicide and a whole family of outcomes has not advanced significantly since Durkheim's work in the 19th Century" (Knox, Conwell, & Caine, 2004, p. 38). Nevertheless, important inroads have begun to emerge from preliminary work in this area.

The majority of research to date has examined simple cross-sectional associations among various neighborhood or other community-level variables

and regional rates of nonsuicidal self-injury, suicidal self-injury, or completed suicides (e.g., Ayton, Rasool, & Cottrell, 2003; Congdon, 1996; Hawton, Harriss, Hodder, Simkin, & Gunnell, 2001). The methodology employed by research of this kind generally involves collecting patient data from hospital emergency room admissions and using demographic data to link individual cases of self-injury to their respective geographic locales or "catchment" areas. Then, current census data typically are utilized to calculate variables of interest for each referent catchment area. In these studies, the most commonly examined theoretically based predictor variables include area measures of socioeconomic deprivation and social fragmentation (or "anomie"), the latter of which has been derived from Durkheim's (1897, 1951) hypothesized concept of social integration. It should initially be cautioned that much of this extant research—either due to certain limitations inherent to archival or large-scale epidemiological data analysis or to inadequate, a priori attention paid to the definition of self-injury constructs—has been limited by a failure to make a critical distinction between suicidal and nonsuicidal self-injury.

A study by Hawton et al. (2001) is representative of such nascent cross-sectional research into neighborhood risk factors for self-injury. This study utilized an inclusive sample of all adolescent and adult patients presenting to a local hospital for incidents of "deliberate self-harm" (presumably including both suicidal and nonsuicidal self-injury) over a 10-year period, as well as public records of completed suicides from the same geographic area and time period. Two census-derived indices were computed: (1) a composite index of social fragmentation based on rates of population turnover, proportion of single-person households, and proportion of nonmarried adults; and (2) the Townsend Index, a commonly used measure of community socioeconomic deprivation. Results suggested that, after controlling for district social fragmentation, higher levels of socioeconomic deprivation were associated with increased area rates of deliberate self-injury. Interestingly, however, the converse association was reportedly not observed. That is, the strong, positive association between district social fragmentation and rates of self-injury and suicide ceased to be significant after accounting for socioeconomic factors. Hawton and colleagues (2001) also presented a parallel pattern of findings regarding district rates of completed suicides. That is, although significant associations were revealed between greater district socioeconomic deprivation and higher suicide rates, this association was only true for males and did not hold after controlling for the social fragmentation variable. No correlation was found, on the other hand, between district social fragmentation and corresponding local rates of suicide.

Similar associations have been found between community rates of child and adolescent self-injury and community impoverishment. Ayton et al. (2003) analyzed computer records of all pediatric patients (i.e., those under the age of 18 years) presenting to a local emergency room over a 2-year period for deliberate self-poisoning, cutting, or illicit drug and alcohol poisoning. (As noted earlier, it was apparently not possible to explicitly determine the suicidal intent of these incidences.) In a procedure nearly identical to that of Hawton and colleagues (2001), Ayton et al. (2003) used 61 postal codes as the ecological units of analysis. Greater levels of community socioeconomic deprivation (i.e., Townsend scores) were again found to correlate with higher local rates of child/adolescent self-injury, above and beyond the shared associations with such aggregate community measures of social fragmentation (i.e., proportion of single-parent households, moving households with children, and adult long-term sickness). Indeed, such research findings seem to converge with the larger body of literature which supports an inverse relationship between small geographic area rates of completed suicides and/or self-injury and neighborhood or community-level socioeconomic characteristics (e.g., Congdon, 1996; Gunnell, Peters, Kammerling, & Brooks, 1995; see Rehkopf & Buka, 2006, for a review). Further, preliminary evidence suggests that measures of community socioeconomic hardship may serve as a more consistent, concurrent predictor of self-injury and suicide than those of social fragmentation (at least based on the present operationalization of these constructs).

A more nuanced picture of the apparent association between community socioeconomic factors and self-injury can be gleaned from the scarce number of cross-sectional studies that have taken advantage of more advanced, multilevel modeling approaches. Importantly, the overall goal of such research has been to differentiate between various sources of individual risk for self-injury and broader community or societal sources of risk. More specifically, much of this work has attempted to determine the relative or incremental contribution of certain suicide risk factors embedded within a broadly defined social or ecological context, as compared to parallel measures collected at the individual level. For instance, in a rare case-controlled ecological study, Miller and colleagues (2005) collected data for all recorded deaths by suicide as well as deaths resulting from accidents occurring in New York City during a 1-year period. In multilevel models controlling for important individual characteristics such as age, race, gender, and per capita income, results revealed that cases of suicide were significantly more likely than accidental death controls to live in neighborhoods with higher levels of income inequality (operationalized both as the percent of total income earned by the lowest earning 70% of households within each district or as the similarly derived "Gini coefficient").

Another cross-sectional, multilevel modeling study conducted by Cubbin, LeClere, and Smith (2000) offers further insight into the relative and independent contributions of neighborhood and individual socioeconomic factors to self-injury. Utilizing a national epidemiological sample of injury-related deaths among adults, these investigators were able to simultaneously examine whether a wide range of individual and neighborhood factors were associated with rates of completed suicides. A number of important findings were revealed. First, although the risk of suicide was found to be statistically unrelated to measures of socioeconomic status at the *individual* level, a number of *neighborhood*-level variables emerged as significant predictors, including higher poverty/lower community socioeconomic status, residential mobility, a higher proportion of racial/ethnic minority residents, and a greater proportion of poor, female-headed households. Impressively, these associations held after controlling for a number of individual demographic (i.e., age, gender, race, marital status) and socioeconomic characteristics (i.e., income needs, educational attainment, employment, occupational status). To directly quantify the nature of these associations, Cubbin et al. (2000) reported a 50% increased risk of suicide mortality for individuals living in neighborhoods characterized by low socioeconomic status, high concentrations of racial minorities, and high residential and family instability.

Complementing the growing research literature that has focused on concurrent community/neighborhood predictors of self-injury, a small number of studies have begun to examine risk factors for other outcomes hypothesized to be relevant to self-injury. Perez-Smith, Spirito, and Boergers (2002), examining a sample of adolescents presenting to a pediatric emergency room after a recent suicide attempt, found that a census-derived composite measure of neighborhood social networks predicted adolescent hopelessness. More specifically, after controlling for individuals' depressive symptoms and family socioeconomic status, adolescents living in neighborhoods characterized by greater concentrations of males and adults (and comparably fewer females and children) were associated concurrently with individual measures of adolescent hopelessness. Interestingly, measures of neighborhood impoverishment were not found to predict hopelessness. Similarly, Ross (2000) examined neighborhood risk factors and their association to local rates of depression. Using multilevel data and adjusting for such individual-level variables as race, ethnicity, sex, age, education, employment, and income, Ross (2000) found that residents who lived in neighborhoods characterized by a high percentage of poor, single mother–led households had higher reported levels of depression than residents of more advantaged neighborhoods. This effect was completely mediated by the perceived breakdown of neighborhood social order (e.g., crime, vandalism, substance use).

Overall, the consistent findings of these studies, however preliminary, strongly suggest that characteristics of communities, neighborhoods, or other socially integrated geographic areas are not simply proxies for individual characteristics. However, much more research must be conducted to identify and further explicate the nature of broader social or ecological risk factors for self-injury alongside traditionally defined, individual-level risk factors. Indeed, a variety of social hardships and inequalities measured at both individual and community levels likely confer overlapping, as well as distinctive risk for self-injury. As such, a particularly promising area for future research might include a closer examination into certain community-level risk factors for self-injury that appear to have dissonant or even inverse associations as compared to parallel individual measures. For example, Hawton et al. (2001) found that financial problems in males were associated with higher rates of deliberate self-harm only in the context of more affluent communities (i.e., lower rates of deliberate self-harm were found among less economically advantaged men living in poorer neighborhoods). Equally as provocative, Neeleman and Wessely (1999) found that suicide rates among ethnic minority neighborhood residents were higher in areas where minority groups were smaller. Thus, it is possible that the strength and even the direction of various individual-level correlates of self-injury can vary depending on the broader ecological and social context. As a more nuanced picture of community and neighborhood factors relevant to self-injury begins to emerge, research into potential mediators and moderators of these associations will be critical.

Mechanisms of Social Influence That Are Specific to Self-Injurious Thoughts and Behaviors

In the preceding sections we have reviewed studies demonstrating that social factors are nonspecifically related to SITBs, but so far there has been little discussion in this literature as to why or how social factors are specific to SITBs. Much of the extant research indicates that social factors confer nonspecific risks for self-injurious behaviors. This literature has suggested that the association between SITBs and such factors as social isolation, conflicts with peers and family, and stressful neighborhood and community environments are mediated by factors such as increased stressful life events, emotion dysregulation, and psychopathology. Although increases in these mediating factors are associated with increased SITBs, they also are associated with increases in other maladaptive behaviors that are functionally equivalent to self-injury, such as substance abuse or risky sexual behavior (e.g., Prinstein, Guerry, Browne, & Rancourt, 2009). This literature has provided crucial information about SITBs, but there remains a crucial gap in knowledge about social influences that are specific to SITBs and how they transact with other aspects of SITBs (e.g., biological, cognitive, and behavioral factors).

Whereas the peer, family, and neighborhood factors confer an increased vulnerability for health risk behaviors, including SITBs (reviewed earlier), in the following sections we posit that social mechanisms specific to SITBs are required to produce SITBs instead of other, functionally equivalent, health risk behaviors. The model presented is similar to those of other health risk behaviors such as adolescent smoking. In these models, more distal and nonspecific factors such as emotion dysregulation might confer increased vulnerability for substance use more generally, but more proximal and specific factors such as social modeling of smoking in movies may be required to specifically produce tobacco use instead of alcohol, heroin, or cocaine use (Heatherton & Sargent, 2009). Indeed, as Figure 11.1 (and this chapter as whole) suggests, social factors are among the most important in the study of SITBs because they serve at least three roles in the development of SITBs: (1) peer, family, and neighborhood factors

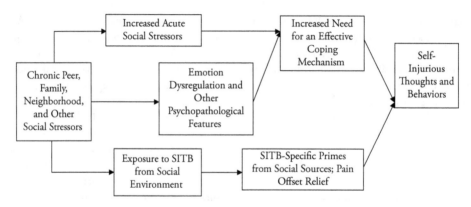

Figure 11.1. Heuristic model of three mechanisms linking social factors to self-injurious thoughts and behaviors. (Reciprocal associations are hypothesized but not depicted, to retain clarity of this figure.)

confer an increased risk for emotion dysregulation and psychopathology; (2) particularly potent, acute, social stressors (e.g., fights with friends or parents) instantiate the need for effective coping mechanisms; and (3) social mechanisms prime individuals to specifically engage in SITBs. Whereas previous sections of this chapter reviewed the literature relevant to the first two roles, the following sections will propose new models for the third role.

To this end, the primary purposes of the following sections are to employ an ecological perspective to (1) articulate *why* social factors may specifically influence SITBs and make the case that these factors are among the most important in the study of self-injury; (2) discuss general social influence mechanisms that may explain *how* social factors may influence SITBs specifically; (3) introduce a new model for how social influence directly and specifically impacts SITBs: the social priming hypothesis; (4) propose how social priming and pain offset relief may transact; and (5) analyze the degree to which social priming and pain offset relief are consistent with social, biological, and behavioral data on SITBs.

Social Influence

From an evolutionary perspective, the ability to learn socially confers an adaptive advantage because it is generally more efficient to "do as others are doing" than to develop all behaviors based solely on one's own experiences (Zentall, 2006). This is because others' behavior presumably has already been shaped by environmental consequences, thus "doing as the group does" serves to pool the experiences of each group member, thereby decreasing the number of costly trial-and-error experiences for each organism. For example, if the normal food

supply of a group of rabbits has disappeared, many of them likely will perish due to hunger and eating novel, but unfortunately poisonous, foods. To maximize chances of group survival, it would be helpful if, when a subset of these rabbits has discovered a viable new food source, the other rabbits copy their behavior instead of ignoring it and continuing to try other, potentially dangerous, foods. Indeed, research on animal behavior has shown that when one animal observes another's behavior being reinforced, the observer acquires that behavior more quickly; conversely, when the other animal's behavior is not reinforced, the observer acquires that behavior more slowly (Akins & Zentall, 1998; Groesbeck & Duerfeldt, 1971; Heyes, Jaldow, & Dawson, 1994). Exploring the general mechanisms of this social learning, Mineka and Cook (1988) determined that when one monkey observed the fearful reaction of another monkey to a snake (which this second monkey had been conditioned to fear), the fearful reaction of the other monkey acted as an unconditioned stimulus paired with the snake (a neutral stimulus). This caused the snake to become a conditioned stimulus that was associated with fear for the observing monkey. In other words, the observer monkey learned to fear the snake by observing the fearful reaction of the other monkey to the snake.

Similar general processes have been shown to occur in humans. This includes processes such as socialization effects of homophily (Prinstein et al., 2009), where individuals adopt the beliefs and behaviors of their peer group. These effects are often explained through more specific mechanisms such as peer deviancy training (Granic & Dishion, 2003). In this phenomenon, deviant behaviors such as substance use or breaking rules are positively reinforced by peers (e.g., via laughing during descriptions of such behavior), whereas more normative or prosocial behaviors are extinguished (e.g., no response is given to descriptions of these behaviors). Supporting such findings, evidence from the persuasion literature indicates that social context alters beliefs and, moreover, that these beliefs are maintained in the absence of social context (see Wood, 2000). For instance, Lundgren and Prislin (1998) conducted a study in which participants in three different conditions generated arguments on an issue along the following lines: (1) a group that was motivated to make an accurate argument; (2) a group that was motivated to defend its own position; and (3) a group that was motivated to make a favorable impression on an interaction partner. Results showed that the accurate group presented balanced arguments, the defense group presented polarized arguments, and the impression group made arguments that were congruent with their interaction partner's apparent position. Importantly, this study controlled for possible social desirability bias (which was a possibility because these initial results were gathered publicly) by showing that these results held when participants were asked to make their arguments privately (Lundgren & Prislin, 1998; Prinstein & Cohen, 2006). Consistent with these findings, social identity theory (Tajfel, 1982; Turner, 1991) suggests that when individuals view themselves as part of an ingroup (e.g., jocks), this group serves as a reference for social comparison. As a result, individuals adopt prototypic ingroup attitudes and beliefs as their own (e.g., being athletic is important; I must play football) (Prinstein & Cohen, 2006). From these and similar lines of evidence, it clear that social context has a strong influence on beliefs and subsequent behaviors.

This argument for social learning seems to be consistent with patently adaptive behaviors such as avoiding snakes, eating nutritious foods, and even obtaining short-term rewards through unlawful means (i.e., some deviant behaviors). However, the application of this argument to things that would seem to qualify as punishing unconditioned stimuli (e.g., self-injury) is less intuitive (Heilbron & Prinstein, 2008). Such counterintuitive effects are substantiated by evidence that individuals will acquire and maintain beliefs that are clearly and objectively incorrect if they are socially influenced to do so. For example, Asch (1951) famously conducted an experiment where participants, embedded in a group of confederates, were asked to judge the relative length of three lines (with the correct judgments being obvious). Results revealed that that when the confederates gave a wrong answer, approximately 75% of the participants would agree with this incorrect judgment. One might assume that this is the result of superficial social conformity, but in a meta-analysis of 97 Asch-type experiments, Bond and Smith (1996) found that these obviously incorrect beliefs were maintained even when privately assessed. Echoing such findings, it may be that social factors influence beliefs about SITBs and that despite the apparently incorrect nature of these beliefs (e.g., hurting yourself will make you feel better) such ways of thinking are acquired socially and maintained even in private. As detailed later, these beliefs may be self-fulfilling as they may actually lead to an experience of SITBs as less painful and more relieving.

In accordance with these findings in support of general social influence, the following sections will focus on two possible mechanisms through which social factors may specifically influence SITBs: (1) social priming and (2) pain offset relief. In doing so, a tentative answer to Nock's (2009) question of "why choose self-injury to regulate affect?" is provided because social priming has a strong influence on which of many functionally equivalent behaviors to regulate affect are chosen. Given that social primes relevant to SITBs are common (see later), social mechanisms are absolutely crucial to understanding and preventing self-injurious behaviors. Because this is the first time that these specific mechanisms have been proposed, there are few direct empirical tests of this model. It is hoped that this presentation of the model will generate testable hypotheses that will allow for a greater understanding of SITBs.

Priming: The Situated Inference Model

One of the central questions in self-injury research is how people so greatly overcome the instinct to avoid pain that they intentionally self-administer it (cf. Joiner, 2005). For nonsuicidal self-injury research, a second central question is how people obtain emotional relief from intentionally self-administering pain. One possibility is that self-injurers are somehow biologically wired to enjoy pain; however, although self-injury is associated with increased pain threshold and tolerance, self-injurers still feel pain and report that it is aversive (e.g., Franklin, Aaron, Arthur, Shorkey, & Prinstein, 2012). Based on social psychology priming research, another possibility is that self-injurers have been primed with information that SITB is relatively painless, relieving, or otherwise beneficial. Such priming may then influence the thoughts, behaviors, and goals of individuals, thereby generating SITB.

According to the Situated Inference Model of priming (Loersch & Payne, 2011), there are three major components to priming. First, individuals must be exposed to a prime. Primes can occur in any modality (e.g., sounds, words, images) and do not require awareness to have an effect. The prime works by making prime-relevant content more psychologically accessible. For example, being primed with words such as "punch" or "fight" would make the concept of hostility more accessible. Second, primes are most effective when the concepts associated with the prime are misattributed as one's own natural response to some aspect of a situation. For example, after a hostility prime, an individual may misattribute hostility to a person with whom he or she interacts rather than attributing hostility to the prime. Third, depending on what Loersch and Payne (2011) call the "afforded questions" of a given situation, the prime may have a wide range of effects on the perception of a given object or person, behaviors, and goal striving. For instance, Loersch and Payne (2011) reviewed empirical literature showing that hostility primes can influence semantic priming by increasing the speed of identifying a gun; construal priming by increasing the perception of another individual as hostile or leading oneself to act with more hostility; and goal priming by motivating an individual to seek out situations in which he or she can aggress toward an object or person. The effect of the prime—whether on semantics, construals, behaviors, or goals—depends on the nature of the situation. If the situation evokes the question "Who/what is that?," then construal priming may occur; if the situation evokes the question "What will I do?," then behavior priming may occur; and if the situation evokes the question "What do I want?," then goal priming may occur (Loersch & Payne, 2011).

Based on this model, if an individual were primed with information that a painful stimulus was not, in fact, very painful, then construal priming may occur such that the individual perceives the stimulus as relatively painless. This priming may be partially responsible for a phenomenon known as placebo analgesia, where certain expectations about a painful stimulus reduce the painfulness of that stimulus (e.g., Millan, 2002; Montgomery & Kirsch, 1997; Price et al., 1999; Rainville, 2002;

Staats, Hekmat, & Staats, 1998). Similarly, if an individual were primed with information that a given stimulus has relieving effects, then construal priming may occur such that the individual feels relieved even if the stimulus itself actually had no effects. Such priming may be largely responsible for the effectiveness of most antidepressants, particularly selective serotonin reuptake inhibitors (see Kirsch, 2009). Indeed, drugs that *reduce* serotonin in the synaptic cleft are just as effective at relieving depressive symptoms as popular drugs that increase serotonin availability (Kasper & McEwen, 2008). This suggests that priming about drug effects—rather than the chemical ingredients of the drug—accounts for the antidepressant effect.

Similar powerful priming effects could conceivably play a role in SITBs. A prime that indicated that self-injury was relatively painless may lead to a real reduction in the perceived painfulness of a self-injurious behavior. This might reduce an important barrier to such behaviors—pain—thereby increasing the likelihood of self-injury. Depending on the situation, a prime that suggested that self-injury was emotionally relieving may have a wide range of effects. Consistent with semantic priming, this may contribute to stronger implicit associations with or attentional biases toward self-injury (cf. Cha et al., 2010; Nock et al., 2010). Other situations may generate construal priming, where an individual displays a positive attitude toward self-injury and is more easily able to entertain self-injurious thoughts. Still other situations may engender behavior and goal priming, where an individual actively seeks out or takes an opportunity to engage in self-injury.

Social Stimuli as Self-Injurious Thought and Behavior Primes

The previous section described how it is possible that primes could have a strong and specific effect on SITBs. This raises an important question: What might act as SITB primes? One likely culprit is the social milieu—the media, Internet, and peers. This is consistent with empirical evidence that media, Internet, and peer influence may engender NSSI.

The potential increase in NSSI over the last decade may be due in part to increased attention on, and depictions of, NSSI in the media (see Whitlock, Purington, & Gershkovich, 2009). Whitlock, Powers, and Eckenrode (2006) posited that this effect might be similar to the social contagion of anorexia nervosa in the 1980s and 1990s. Supporting this possibility, the rates of NSSI references in songs, movies, and news articles have increased dramatically in recent years (Whitlock, Purrington, & Gershkovich, 2009). Whereas only four movies and one song between 1966 and 1985 had references to NSSI, researchers found in the years 2001–2005 alone, 23 movies and 38 songs with references to self-injury were released (Whitlock et al., 2009). Furthermore, Whitlock et al. (2009) found that the self-injurers depicted in movies were typically strong characters with high appeal, which likely adds to the attractiveness of NSSI. A similar increase has been observed on the Internet: Whitlock et al. (2006) found that in the 5 years preceding their study, hundreds of new NSSI message boards emerged. However, it is difficult to determine causality within these associations because it is also possible that an increased NSSI prevalence would lead to more media references and Internet sites about NSSI.

The evidence for peer influence on NSSI is more direct. First, studies demonstrate that many individuals are aware that their peers engage in NSSI. Nock and Prinstein (2005) found that 82% of an adolescent psychiatric inpatient sample reported that one of their friends had engaged in NSSI in the past year. Similarly, Muehlenkamp, Hoff, Licht, Azure, and Hasenzahl (2008) found that 64% of 1,965 undergraduates knew someone who had engaged in NSSI. Likewise, Heath et al. (2009) found that 65% of an undergraduate sample with a history of NSSI talked to their friends about their NSSI. Moreover, several studies have also shown that individuals often engage in NSSI in groups. Klonsky and Olino (2008) found that only 47% of their NSSI sample engaged in NSSI exclusively when alone, and Heath et al. (2009) found that 17.4% of their NSSI group had self-injured in front of friends. Similar clinical reports indicate the NSSI often occurs in dyads or groups on psychiatric inpatient units (Rosen & Walsh, 1988; Taiminen, Kallio-Soukainen, Nokso-Koivisto, Kaljonen, & Helenius, 1998; Walsh & Rosen, 1985).

Second, studies suggest that peer influence contributes to the development of NSSI in others. Heath et al. (2009) found that 58.8% of their NSSI group reported that they knew of a friend who engaged in NSSI before they began the behavior. Similarly, Muehlenkamp et al. (2008) found that individuals who knew someone that engaged in NSSI were more likely to engage in NSSI themselves. By analyzing the specific pattern of NSSI incidents on inpatient units, two clinical studies determined that the majority of instances in their samples were the result of contagion (Taiminen et al., 1998; Walsh & Rosen, 1985). In both community-based and clinically referred samples, Prinstein et al. (2010) found that, for girls, the perception of a best friend's engagement in NSSI at baseline longitudinally predicted their own engagement in NSSI 18 months later. Taken together, this growing literature provides strong support for the hypothesis that social influence has a strong impact on NSSI.

Consistent with the Situated Inference Model (Loersch & Payne, 2011), the media, Internet, and peers may increase the accessibility of certain concepts (e.g., cutting yourself makes you feel better; suicide is a good way to escape your anguish), become misattributed as originating from the individual or a given situation (e.g., acute stress), and lead to various SITBs depending on the "afforded questions" of the situation. This suggests that social factors may have a powerful—and preventable—effect on the development, maintenance, and experience of SITBs.

How the Social Priming Hypothesis Fits With Biological Models of Self-Injurious Thoughts and Behaviors

Although the social priming hypothesis is consistent with social and cognitive perspectives on self-injury, how well does this model match biological data on self-injury? Despite excellent work from several teams of researchers, the neurobiology of self-injury remains poorly understood, in part because of the logistical and ethical difficulties inherent in studying this topic. Such studies are difficult to conduct on suicidal self-injury. Neurobiological research on suicidal self-injury primarily has focused on abnormalities in the serotonergic system—from genes to central and peripheral levels of serotonin, with a few lines of research focusing on other neurotransmitter and hormonal systems (see Joiner, Brown, & Wingate, 2005, for a review). Unfortunately, such abnormalities are not specific to suicide (e.g., low serotonin is indicative of various mood, anxiety, impulse-control, autism spectrum, psychotic disorders) and for ethical reasons there are no experimental studies on the neurobiology of suicide. Accordingly, it currently is impossible to empirically determine how relevant priming is to suicidal self-injury on a neurobiological level. Fortunately, NSSI does lend itself to experimental laboratory research with biological measures. As detailed later, preliminary laboratory research indicates that priming can produce some of the biological correlates of NSSI in individuals with no NSSI history.

Although the social priming hypothesis is consistent with the majority of neurobiological data on NSSI, it seems to be mostly inconsistent with opioid-related models, such as the Opioid Homeostasis Model (e.g., Favazza & Conterio, 1989; Richardson & Zaleski, 1986; Sher & Stanley, 2009), which are perhaps the most formally articulated neurobiological models of NSSI. Accordingly, we will attempt to examine the validity of such models before determining how the social priming hypothesis compares to models that are not opioid focused.

Versions of the Opioid Homeostasis Model have been around for at least two decades (e.g., Favazza & Conterio, 1989; Richardson & Zaleski, 1986). Recently, this model has been articulated more specifically in terms of newer definitions of NSSI (Sher & Stanley, 2009; Stanley et al., 2010). This model has two major tenets: (1) people who engage in NSSI have low baseline levels of opioids, possibly due to chronic stress; and (2) the function of NSSI is to bring opioid levels back to homeostasis (Sher & Stanley, 2009). This is an intuitive model that has face validity because of the well-known association between pain and endorphins; it is also laudable in that it is clear and testable. As reviewed later, however, some aspects of this model do not appear to stand up well to empirical evidence.

Although there is no direct support for the tenet that NSSI is associated with lower baseline levels of opioids, indirect evidence is generally consistent with this hypothesis. Chronic stress is associated with low baseline opioids levels (e.g., Bremner, 2003) and NSSI is associated with chronic stress (see Klonsky, 2007). More directly, Stanley et al. (2010) found that inpatients with a history of both suicide and NSSI displayed lower levels of two opioid metabolites than inpatients with a history of suicide attempts alone. However, consistent with other investigations (e.g., Andover & Gibb, 2010), the suicide plus NSSI group in this study displayed significantly higher levels of depression, hopelessness, and overall psychopathology than the suicide-only group. Metabolite comparisons did not control for these variables. This leaves open the possibility that these variables—rather than NSSI status—accounted for group differences in opioid metabolites.

Additionally, although Stanley et al. (2010) did not find significant group differences in serotoninergic or dopaminergic metabolites, this was likely due to low power as the total sample size of the study was 29. Indeed, there were moderate effect sizes for group differences in both serotonergic ($d = .49$) and dopaminergic ($d = .66$) metabolites. This latter finding suggests that other major neurotransmitters may vary at baseline in individuals with a history of NSSI. This indicates that nonopioid mechanisms may also be important correlates of NSSI, casting doubt on an opioid-specific mechanism for NSSI. Supporting at least some role for nonopioid mechanisms, Russ et al. (1994) found that the opioid antagonist naltrexone did not affect pain perception in patients with a history of NSSI. Taken together, there is some supporting evidence for the hypothesis that NSSI is associated with lower opioids at baseline, but more studies are necessary to more definitively test this possibility.

There are several lines of evidence against the tenet that NSSI functions to bring opioid levels to a homeostatic level. The first is a challenge to the process of homeostasis: It is unclear why the body would want to maintain a certain (homeostatic) level of opioids. Berridge (2004) argued that the concept of homeostasis in behavioral neuroscience is illusory. Because many processes and behaviors seem to hold near a constant level, it is natural to make the teleological assumption that these near-constant levels are maintained for a reason (i.e., homeostasis). But Berridge (2004) pointed out that homeostatic mechanisms would require specific set points and error detection mechanisms, and there is little evidence for the existence of such mechanisms. Settling-point regulation is a more likely explanation for what is often assumed to be homeostatic regulation. Settling points are relatively stable states caused by a balance of opposing forces in the absence of error detection. For example, numerous opposing forces created a constant sea level for centuries, resulting in a specific definition for sea level—8,850 m below the peak of Mt. Everest (Berridge, 2004). One of the forces contributing to this balance is global temperature; thus, as global temperature has increased, sea level has increased over the last century. Similarly, there are no specific set points or error detection mechanisms for body weight or hunger (Berridge, 2004; Bolles, 1981). Body weight is more effectively explained as a setting point influenced by factors like activity level and the availability of calorie-rich foods. As these forces have changed over the last few decades, average body weight has increased. Correspondingly, the balance of a wide range of genetic, biological, affective, cognitive, social, and environmental forces may determine opioid levels. There is no evidence for a preferred set point of opioids in the body or for an error detection mechanism that initiates NSSI as a result of opioid levels.

The second line of evidence comes from work suggesting that NSSI may occur in the presence of abnormally *increased* opioids rather than abnormally low opioids. This is because acute stress almost always occurs directly before NSSI (Klonsky, 2007) and acute stress is associated with increased opioids (Butler & Finn, 2009). Because opioids would already be abnormally increased when NSSI begins, it seems unlikely that the function of NSSI would be to increase opioids. NSSI may further increase opioid levels due to pain-induced opioids; however, by this point a NSSI-stimulated opioid increase would be relatively unimportant because opioid levels would already be elevated. Of note, at least one study has found that chronic life stress was associated with a relatively small peak level of plasma concentrations of beta endorphins during a mental arithmetic task (Pike et al., 1997). This suggests that stress may not increase opioids in individuals who engage in NSSI (and are chronically stressed), meaning that opioids would still be low when NSSI began for a subset of individuals. It should be noted, however, that Pike et al. (1997) did not control for baseline levels of opioids. The proportion of change from baseline in the two groups was similar (~25% for the chronic stress group; ~30% for the control group; p. 453), indicating that opioid reactivity was similar across groups. In any case, if the stressors that typically elicit NSSI (e.g., fights with parents) were insufficient to elicit opioid reactivity in people who engage in NSSI, it may be that the moderate self-injury indicative of NSSI would be similarly insufficient.

Third, evidence that naltrexone decreases self-injury in pervasive developmental disorder populations is sometimes cited as evidence that NSSI is regulated by opioids (e.g., Sher & Stanley, 2009). Yet this would seem to provide direct falsification evidence against the Opioid Homeostasis Model. Naltrexone is an opioid antagonist, meaning that it blocks opioid activity. The Opioid Homeostasis Model would accordingly predict that naltrexone should cause higher levels of self-injury in an attempt to increase opioids; nonetheless, the opposite pattern is typically observed. Fourth and finally, it is unclear how the Opioid Homeostasis Model would explain evidence that NSSI-proxy scripts are sufficient to induce autonomic regulation in people with a history of NSSI (Brain et al., 1998; Haines et al., 1995; Welch et al., 2008). These studies demonstrate that top-down factors are sufficient

to generate NSSI-relevant regulation, meaning that bottom-up factors such as opioids induced by pain are not necessary.

Overall, there appears to be substantial falsification evidence against the Opioid Homeostasis Model and relatively little corroborating evidence. Opioids likely play a role in NSSI, but the nature of this role remains unclear.

The social priming hypothesis does, however, appear to be consistent with several NSSI laboratory studies that have examined the biological correlates of NSSI. These studies have shown that NSSI proxies (i.e., stimuli designed to mimic NSSI in the laboratory, such as painful stimuli) generate the biological correlates of cognitive-affective regulation. Three studies have employed NSSI imagery scripts as NSSI proxies and measured physiological arousal (Brain et al., 1998; Haines et al., 1995; Welch et al., 2008). Each study found that the NSSI proxies led to reduced physiological arousal in participants with a history of NSSI. Schmahl et al. (2006) used painful stimuli as an NSSI proxy and functional magnetic resonance imaging (fMRI) of the brain as their dependent variable. In self-injurers, results revealed that pain led to the neural correlates of both cognitive regulation (increased dorsolateral prefrontal cortex activity) and emotion regulation (decreased amygdala activity). In a follow-up study, Niedtfeld et al. (2010) obtained similar emotion regulation correlate results in both self-injurers and healthy controls. Echoing these findings, Franklin et al. (2010) found that a painful NSSI proxy led to the psychophysiological correlates of cognitive regulation (increased prepulse inhibition) in NSSI participants. Results also revealed that the NSSI proxy generated the psychophysiological correlates of emotion regulation (diminished startle eyeblink reactivity) in both healthy controls and NSSI participants.

A follow-up study to Franklin et al. (2010) provides preliminary evidence for the connection between social priming and the biological correlates of NSSI. Franklin et al. (2011) replicated this study in three groups of healthy control participants. Each group was primed with a different paragraph of information about the NSSI proxy, the cold pressor task (i.e., painful ice water). Participants were not informed about the true purpose of the study; they were told that it was a memory study. At the beginning of the study, they were asked to memorize the paragraph about the cold pressor task and they were told that they would have to write as much of the paragraph as they could remember at the end of the study. One group read a priming paragraph that described the cold pressor task as very painful (Painful Group); another read a priming paragraph that described the equipment used in the cold pressor task (Neutral Group); and a final group read a priming paragraph that described the cold pressor task as relaxing and relieving (Relaxing Group). The Painful and Neutral Groups showed biological response patterns after the NSSI proxy that were identical to those of the healthy control group in Franklin et al. (2011). In contrast, the Relaxing Group displayed biological response patterns that were identical to those of the NSSI group in Franklin et al. (2010). This demonstrated that a subtle prime suggesting that a painful stimulus has relieving effects is sufficient to generate biological response patterns to painful stimuli that mimic those of NSSI participants. These results suggest that more powerful primes from the media, Internet, and peers could strongly influence self-injury.

Relevance of Social Priming to Behavioral Models of Self-Injury

Substantial evidence indicates that self-injury leads to affect regulation (e.g., Baumeister, 1990; Klonsky, 2007), which may positively and negatively reinforce self-injury. Moreover, a growing literature suggests that the removal of an acutely painful stimulus leads to affect regulations for both self-injurers and noninjurers (e.g., Franklin et al., 2010; Leknes, Brooks, Wiech, & Tracey, 2008). Next we propose that this "pain offset relief" is one of the primary mechanisms through which self-injury generates affect regulation and we explain how social priming may interact with this phenomenon.

Pain Offset Relief

Pain has been defined as the unpleasant sensory and emotional experience associated with actual or potential tissue damage (International Association for the Study of Pain Task Force on Taxonomy, 1994). It seems counterintuitive that pain could be associated with anything other than increased negative affect, punishment, or avoidance. This sometimes leads families, friends, and even mental health care professionals to assume that people who engage in SITBs have a morbid love of pain or that they are "wired differently" to process pain as pleasure. These assumptions are at odds with empirical evidence that people who engage in SITBs feel pain and process it as aversive—though they do tend to display moderately higher pain thresholds and pain endurance levels (e.g., Franklin et al., 2012). So how

can SITBs lead to affect regulation? Consistent with the ideas touched on in recent studies (e.g., Bresin & Gordon, 2011; Franklin et al., 2010, 2012), we propose that relief caused by pain offset (i.e., the removal or reduction of a painful stimulus) is the primary (but not sole) mechanism of affect regulation in self-injury.

The removal of a painful stimulus does not return emotions to a "neutral" or prepain state; rather, it seems to generate a pleasant emotional state. People who engage in SITBs may unintentionally (or intentionally in some cases) tap into this pain offset relief phenomenon in order to reduce stress or increase good feelings. This phenomenon is consistent with the opponent process theory of acquired motivation (Solomon, 1980; also see Joiner [2005] for an application of this theory to suicidal self-injury). The opponent process theory proposes that in response to every stimulus there are two major reactions: a primary process and an opponent process. The primary process reaches maximum intensity soon after stimulus onset and diminishes completely soon after the stimulus offset. Conversely, the opponent process reaches maximum intensity slowly and lingers long after the offset of the stimulus. Across repeated presentations of a given stimulus, the primary process remains the same, but the opponent process increases in intensity. At any given time, the state of an organism is determined by taking the absolute value of the difference between the intensity of the primary process and the opponent process. As such, the primary process is most salient immediately after the onset of a stimulus, whereas the opponent process is most salient after the offset of a stimulus. For SITB, the primary process is pain and the opponent process is relief. According to the opponent process theory, relief should be most salient soon after pain offset. The opponent process theory would also make two other predictions about pain offset relief: Relief should be more intense when pain is more intense, and relief should become more intense across repeated pain administrations (cf. Solomon, 1980).

Several studies indirectly support the existence of pain offset relief. Becerra and Borsook (2008) found that the onset of pain was associated with a negative change in functional magnetic resonance imaging signal in an area of the brain associated with reward, the nucleus accumbens. The offset of pain was associated with a positive signal change in the nucleus accumbens, suggesting that pain offset is rewarding. Leknes et al. (2008) found that pain offset relief was more intense when pain intensity was more intense. Similarly, Bresin et al. (2010) found that self-reported diminished negative affect after pain offset was more intense for individuals high in trait emotional reactivity. Likewise, Bresin and Gordon (2011) found self-reported diminished negative affect after pain offset in individuals with and without a history of NSSI. For both NSSI and non-NSSI groups, Franklin et al. (2010) showed that pain offset decreased negative affect as assessed by startle eyeblink reactivity.

One potential problem with this pain offset relief hypothesis is that pain may not completely offset during an episode of NSSI. For example, wounds from cutting or burning may hurt for days after the episode. Interestingly, basic pain studies suggest that complete pain offset may not be necessary to generate relief. Grill and Coghill (2002) found that a one degree increase in the intensity of a painful heat stimulus (e.g., from 49 to 50 degrees) led to a one unit increase in perceived pain intensity (on a 1–10 scale). Strikingly, a one degree decrease (e.g., from 50 to 49 degrees) led to a 3.5 unit decrease in perceived pain intensity. The authors concluded that pain intensity reduction activates powerful analgesic mechanisms that serve to "amplify awareness of stimulus offset and to reinforce escape behaviors" (p. 2205); this may represent the evolutionary function of pain offset relief. In other words, pain may be punishing because it decreases survival, whereas the removal of pain may be rewarding because it increases survival. Neurobiological studies have supported these findings (Derbyshire & Osborn, 2009), with Derbyshire and Osborn (2008) showing that this effect increases in intensity across repeated painful stimuli (cf. opponent process theory; Solomon, 1980). Although these studies measured pain relief instead of emotional relief, DeWall et al. (2010) recently demonstrated that there is a large degree of overlap between physical pain relief and emotional pain relief. Results showed that acetaminophen reduced both physical and emotional pain as assessed by both psychological and neurological measures. This indicates that the pain offset analgesia findings described earlier may apply to pain offset relief, but studies are needed to directly examine this possibility.

These studies suggest that an individual may induce several instances of pain offset relief (even if the offset is not complete) during a single self-injury session. For example, an individual may cut herself several times over the course of 1 minute and feel intense pain throughout much of that minute. Yet, because of small variations in pain intensity during that minute (e.g., variations in how the knife is cutting through the skin, removal of the knife for a few seconds), the individual may experience numerous instances of relief that increase in intensity and reinforce self-injury. Moreover, the intensity of pain offset relief may increase after repeated self-injury episodes (cf. Derbyshire & Osborn, 2008; Joiner, 2005; Solomon, 1980).

Social priming may contribute to pain offset relief during self-injury in at least two ways. First, social priming may be key to getting individuals to attempt self-injury for the first time. During this first episode, individuals would experience pain offset relief, thereby behaviorally reinforcing self-injury. Through opponent processes, after repeated episodes of self-injury, relief may become stronger and painfulness may become diminished. In other words, some individuals may start engaging in self-injury because of social priming but continue engaging in self-injury because of reinforcement from pain offset relief. Second, social priming may affect the experience of self-injury itself, making it less painful or more relieving. For example, consistent with placebo analgesia, certain primes may reduce the painfulness of self-injury, thereby reducing perhaps the most effective barrier to self-injury (cf. Joiner, 2005). Similarly, certain primes may accentuate the relief associated with self-injury.

In summary, social priming may play a central role in self-injury. As described earlier, social priming may influence both the biological and behavioral mechanisms that reinforce self-injury. Most important, however, social priming may help to explain why self-injury is often chosen when several functionally equivalent behaviors are available. Given that it may play a central role in self-injury, social priming may also represent an important target for self-injury prevention and treatment.

Conclusions and Future Research Directions

Findings from prior research on adolescent suicidality and NSSI underscore the challenges inherent in studying how and why social and ecological factors may be implicated in the emergence and maintenance of SITB. Although considerable gains have been made toward advancing our understanding of SITB, many questions remain unanswered regarding mechanisms through which these behaviors influence, and are influenced by, affective and social experiences. Nock's (2009) general theoretical model provides an important framework for conceptualizing how distal factors may create intra- and interpersonal vulnerabilities to engaging in SITB. As described in this chapter, there are social, behavioral, cognitive, and biological components to self-injury; however, until we can effectively link these domains together in a way that provides a more complete picture of both the distal, nonspecific factors and the proximal, specific factors that influence self-injury, this important topic will remain inscrutable. Moreover, understanding causal links between risk factors and SITBs is imperative for informing effective prevention and intervention programs. Accordingly, future research imperatives aimed at explicating and rigorously testing such theorized causal mechanisms are sorely needed to inform the development of effective prevention and intervention programs.

References

Andover, M. S., & Gibb, B. E. (2010). Non-suicidal self-injury, attempted suicide, and suicidal intent among psychiatric inpatients. *Psychiatry Research, 178*, 101–105.

Akins, C. K., & Zentall, T. R. (1998). Imitation in Japanese quail: The role of reinforcement of demonstrator responding. *Psychonomic Bulletin and Review, 5*, 694–697.

Andrews, J. A., Tildesley, E., Hops, H., & Li, F. (2002). The influence of peers on young adult substance use. *Health Psychology, 21*, 349–357.

Asarnow, J. R., & Carlson, G. (1988). Suicide attempts in preadolescent child psychiatry inpatients. *Suicide and Life-Threatening Behavior, 18*, 129–136.

Asch, S. E. (1951). Effects of group pressure on the modification and distortion of judgments. In H. Guetzkow (Ed.), *Groups, leadership and men* (pp. 177–190). Pittsburgh, PA: Carnegie Press.

Ayton, A., Rasool, H., & Cottrell, D. (2003). Deliberate self-harm in children and adolescents: Association with social deprivation. *European Child and Adolescent Psychiatry, 12*, 303–307.

Baumeister, R. F. (1990). Suicide as escape from self. *Psychological Review, 97*, 90–113.

Bearman, P. S., & Moody, J. (2004). Suicide and friendships among American adolescents. *American Journal of Public Health, 94*, 89–95.

Becerra, L. & Borsook, D. (2008). Signal valence in the nucleus accumbens to pain onset and offset. *European Journal of Pain, 12*, 866–869.

Berman, A. L., & Schwartz, R. H. (1990). Suicide attempts among adolescent drug users. *American Journal of Diseases of Children, 144*, 310–314.

Berridge, K. C. (2004). Motivation concepts in behavioral neuroscience. *Physiology and Behavior, 81*, 179–209.

Blanton, H. B., & Christie, C. (2003). Deviance regulation: A theory of action and identity. *Review of General Psychology, 7*, 115–149.

Boivin, M., Hymel, S., & Hodges, E. V. E. (2001). Toward a process view of peer rejection and harassment. In J. Juvonen & S. Graham (Eds.), *School-based peer harassment: The plight of the vulnerable and victimized* (pp. 265–289). New York, NY: Guilford Press.

Bolles, R.C. (1981). Some functionalist thoughts about regulation. In F. Toates & T. W. Halliday (Eds.), Analysis of motivational processes (pp. 63–75). New York, NY: Academic Press.

Bond, R., & Smith, P. B. (1996). Culture and conformity: A meta-analysis of studies using Asch's (1952b, 1956) line judgment task. *Psychological Bulletin, 119*, 111–137.

Borowsky, I. W., Ireland, M., & Resnick, M. D. (2001). Adolescent suicide attempts: Risks and protectors. *Pediatrics, 107*, 485–493.

Brain, K. L., Haines, J., & Williams, C. L. (1998). The psychophysiology of self-mutilation: Evidence of tension reduction. *Archives of Suicide Research, 4*, 227–242.

Bremner, J.D. (2003). Long-term effects of childhood abuse on brain and neurobiology. *Child and Adolescent Psychiatric Clinical of North America, 12*, 271–292.

Brent, D. A., Baugher, M., & Bridge, J., Chen, T., & Chiappetta, L. (1999). Age- and sex-related risk factors for adolescent suicide. *Journal of the American Academy of Child and Adolescent Psychiatry, 38*, 1497–1505.

Brent, D. A., & Melhem, N. (2008). Familial transmission of suicidal behavior. *Psychiatric Clinics of North America, 31*, 157–177.

Brent, D. A., Oquendo, M., Birmaher, B., Greenhill, L., Kolko, D., Stanley, B., ... Mann, J. J. (2004). Familial transmission of mood disorders: Convergence and divergence with transmission of suicidal behavior. *Journal of the American Academy of Child and Adolescent Psychiatry, 43*, 1259–1266.

Brent, D. A., Perper, J. A., Moritz, G., Allman, C., Friend, A., Roth, C., ... Baugher, M. (1993). Psychiatric risk factors for adolescent suicide: A case-control study. *Journal of the American Academy of Child and Adolescent Psychiatry, 32*, 521–529.

Brent, D. A., Perper, J. A., Moritz, G., Liotus, L., Schweers, J., Balach, L., & Roth, C. (1994). Familial risk factors for adolescent suicide: A case-control study. *Acta Psychiatrica Scandinavica, 89*, 52–58.

Bresin, K., Gordon, K. H., Bender, T. W., Gordon, L. J., & Joiner, T. E. (2010). No pain, no change: Reductions in prior negative affect following physical pain. *Motivation and Emotion, 34*, 280–287.

Bresin, K., & Gordon, K. H. (2011). Changes in negative affect following pain (vs. nonpainful) stimulation in individuals with and without a history of nonsuicidal self-injury. *Personality Disorders: Theory, Research, and Treatment, 4*(1), 62–66

Bridge, J. A., Goldstein, T. R., & Brent, D. A. (2006). Adolescent suicide and suicidal behavior. *Journal of Child Psychology and Psychiatry, 47*, 372–394.

Bronfenbrenner, U. (1977). Toward an experimental ecology of human development. *American Psychologist, 32*, 513–531.

Bronfenbrenner, U. (1979). *The ecology of human development*. Cambridge, MA: Harvard University Press.

Brown, J., Cohen, P., Johnson, J. G., & Smailes, E. M. (1999). Childhood abuse and neglect: Specificity and effects on adolescent and young adult depression and suicidality. *Journal of the American Academy of Child and Adolescent Psychiatry, 38*, 1490–1496.

Butler, R. K., & Finn, D. P. (2009). Stress-induced analgesia. *Progress in Neurobiology, 88*, 184–202.

Centers for Disease Control. (2004). Youth risk behavior surveillance—United States 2003. *Morbidity and Mortality Weekly Report, 53*, 1–29.

Cetin, F. C. (2001). Suicide attempts and self-image among Turkish adolescents. *Journal of Youth and Adolescence, 30*, 641–651.

Cha, C. B., Najmi, S., Park, J. M., Finn, C. T., & Nock, M. K. (2010). Attentional bias toward suicide-related stimuli predicts suicidal behavior. *Journal of Abnormal Psychology, 119*, 616–622.

Christakis, N. A., & Fowler, J. H. (2007). The spread of obesity in a large social network over 32 years. *New England Journal of Medicine, 357*, 370–379.

Christoffersen, M. N., Poulsen, H. D., & Nielsen, A. (2003). Attempted suicide among young people: Risk factors in a prospective register based study of Danish children born in 1966. *Acta Psychiatrica Scandinavica, 108*, 350–358.

Cicchetti, D. (1990). A historical perspective on the discipline of developmental psychopathology. In J. Rolf, A. Masten, D. Cicchetti, K. Nuechterlein, & S. Weintraub (Eds.), *Risk and protective factors in the development of psychopathology* (pp. 2–28). New York, NY: Cambridge University Press.

Cicchetti, D., & Rogosch, F. A. (1996). Equifinality and multifinality in developmental psychopathology. *Development and Psychopathology, 8*, 597–600.

Congdon, P. (1996). Suicide and parasuicide in London: A small area-study. *Urban Studies, 33*, 137–158.

Cohen, S., & Wills, T. A. (1985). Stress, social support, and the buffering hypothesis. *Psychological Bulletin, 98*, 310–357.

Coie, J. D., & Dodge, K. A. (1983). Continuities and changes in children's social status: A five-year longitudinal study. *Merrill-Palmer Quarterly, 29*, 261–282.

Connor, J. J., & Rueter, M. A. (2006). Parent-child relationships as systems of support or risk for adolescent suicidality. *Journal of Family Psychology, 20*, 143–155.

Cubbin, C., LeClere, F. B., & Smith, G. S. (2000). Socioeconomic status and injury mortality: Individual and neighborhood determinants. *Journal of Epidemiology and Community Health, 54*, 517–524.

Davies, P. T., & Cicchetti, D. (2004). Toward an integration of family systems and developmental psychopathology approaches. *Development and Psychopathology, 16*, 477–481.

Derbyshire, S. W. G., & Osborn, J. (2008). Enhancement of offset analgesia during sequential testing. *European Journal of Pain, 12*, 980–989.

Derbyshire, S. W. G., & Osborn, J. (2009). Offset analgesia is mediated by activation in the region of the periaquedectual grey and rostral ventromedial medulla. *Neuroimage, 47*, 1002–1006.

Dewall, C. N., MacDonald, G., Webster, G. D., Masten, C. L., Baumeister, R. F. ... Eisenberger, N. I. (2010). Acetaminophen reduces social pain: Behavioral and neutral evidence. *Psychological Science, 27*, 931–937.

Dishion, T. (2000). Cross-setting consistency in early adolescent psychopathology: Deviant friendships and problem behavior sequelae. *Journal of Personality, 68*, 1109–1126.

Durkheim, E. (1897). *Suicide.* New York, NY: Free Press.

Durkheim, E. (1951). *Suicide: A study in sociology.* (J. A. Spaulding & G. Simpson, Trans.). New York, NY: Free Press.

Favazza, A. R., & Conterio, K. (1989). Female habitual self-mutilators. *Acta Psychiatrica Scandinavica, 79*, 283–289.

Fergusson, D. M., Horwood, L. J., & Lynskey, M. T. (1996). Childhood sexual abuse and psychiatric disorder in young adulthood: II. Psychiatric outcomes of childhood sexual abuse. *Journal of the American Academy of Child and Adolescent Psychiatry, 35*, 1365–1374.

Fergusson, D. M., & Lynskey, M. T. (1995). Suicide attempts and suicidal ideation in a birth cohort of 16-year-old New Zealanders. *Journal of the American Academy of Child and Adolescent Psychiatry, 34*, 1308–1317.

Fergusson, D. M., Woodward, L. J., & Horwood, L. J. (2000). Risk factors and life processes associated with the onset of suicidal behaviour during adolescence and early adulthood. *Psychological Medicine, 30*, 23–39.

Fishbein, M., & Ajzen, I. (1975). *Belief, attitude, intention, and behavior: An introduction to theory and research.* Reading, MA: Addison-Wesley.

Franklin, J. C., Aaron, R. V., Arthur, M. S., Shorkey, S. P., & Prinstein, M. J. (2012). Nonsuicidal self-injury and diminished pain perception: The role of emotion dysregulation. *Comprehensive Psychiatry, 53*(6), 691–700.

Franklin, J. C., Aaron, R. V., Shorkey, S. P., Arthur, M. S., Lane, S. T., Puzia, M. E., ... Prinstein, M. J. (2011, November). *Placebo regulation and pain relief may partially explain why nonsuicidal self-injury is reinforcing: Experimental and psychophysiological evidence.* Poster presented at the meeting of the Association for Behavioral and Cognitive Therapies, Toronto, ON.

Franklin, J. C., Hessel, E. T., Aaron, R. V., Arthur, M. S., Heilbron, N., & Prinstein, M. J. (2010). The function of nonsuicidal self-injury: Support for cognitive-affective regulation and opponent processes from a novel psychophysiological paradigm. *Journal of Abnormal Psychology, 119*, 850–862.

Garber, J., Little, S., Hilsman, R., & Weaver, K. R. (1998). Family predictors of suicidal symptoms in young adolescents. *Journal of Adolescence, 21*, 445–457.

Gauze, C., Bukowski, W. M., Aquan-Assee, J., & Sippola, L. K. (1996). Interactions between family environment and friendship and associations with self-perceived well-being during adolescence. *Child Development, 67*, 2201–2216.

Ghaziuddin, M., Tsai, L. Y., Naylor, M. W., & Ghaziuddin, N. (1992). Mood disorder in a group of self-cutting adolescents. *Acta Paedopsychiatrica, 55*, 103–105.

Gibbons, F. X., Gerrard, M., & Lane, D. J. (2003). A social reaction model of adolescent health risk. In J. M. Suls & K. Wallston (Eds.), *Social psychological foundations of health and illness* (pp.107–136). Oxford, UK: Wiley-Blackwell.

Gould, M. S. (1990). Suicide clusters and media exposure. In S. J. Blumenthal & D. J. Kupfer (Eds.), *Suicide over the life cycle: Risk factors, assessment, and treatment of suicidal patients* (pp. 517–532). Washington, DC: American Psychiatric Association.

Gould, M. S., Fisher, P., Parides, M., Flory, M., & Shaffer, D. (1996). Psychosocial risk factors of child and adolescent completed suicide. *Archives of General Psychiatry, 53*, 1155–1162.

Gould, M. S., Greenberg, T., Velting, D. M., & Shaffer, D. (2003). Youth suicide risk and preventive interventions: A review of the past 10 years. *Journal of the American Academy of Child and Adolescent Psychiatry, 42*, 386–405.

Gould, M. S., Jamieson, P., & Romer, D. (2003). Media contagion and suicide among the young. *American Behavioral Scientist, 46*, 1269–1284.

Granic, I., & Dishion, T. J. (2003). Deviant talk in adolescent friendships: A step toward measuring a pathogenic attractor process. *Social Development, 12*, 314–334.

Grill, J. D., & Coghill, R. C. (2002). Transient analgesia evoked by noxious stimulus offset. *Journal of Neurophysiology, 87*, 2205–2208.

Groesbeck, R. W., & Duerfeldt, P. H. (1971). Some relevant variables in observational learning of the rat. *Psychonomic Science, 22*, 41–43.

Gunnell, D., Peters, T., Kammerling, R., & Brooks, J. (1995). Relation between parasuicide, suicide, psychiatric admissions, and socio-economic deprivation. *British Medical Journal, 311*, 226–230.

Haines, J., Williams, C. L., Brain, K. L., & Wilson, G. V. (1995). The psychophysiology of self-mutilation. *Journal of Abnormal Psychology, 104*, 471–489.

Harter, S., Marold, D. B., & Whitesell, N. R. (1992). Model of psychosocial risk factors leading to suicidal ideation in young adolescents. *Development and Psychopathology, 4*, 167–188.

Hartup, W. W. (1996). The company they keep: Friendships and their developmental significance. *Child Development, 67*, 1–13.

Hawker, D. S. J., & Boulton, M. J. (2000). Twenty years' research on peer victimization and psychosocial maladjustment: A meta-analytic review of cross-sectional studies. *Journal of Child Psychology and Psychiatry, 41*, 441–455.

Hawton, K., Fagg, J., & Simkin, S. (1996). Deliberate self-poisoning and self-injury in children and adolescents under 16 years of age in Oxford, 1976-1993. *British Journal of Psychiatry, 169*, 202–208.

Hawton, K., & Harriss, L. (2006). Deliberate self-harm in people aged 60 years and over: Characteristics and outcome of a 20-year cohort. *International Journal of Geriatric Psychiatry, 21*, 572–581.

Hawton, K., Harriss, L., Hodder, K., Simkin, S., & Gunnell, D. (2001). The influence of economic and social environment on deliberate self-harm and suicide: An ecological and person-based study. *Psychological Medicine, 31*, 827–836.

Haynie, D. L., South, S. J., & Bose, S. (2006). Residential mobility and attempted suicide among adolescents: An individual-level analysis. *Sociological Quarterly, 47*, 693–721.

Heath, N. L., Ross, S., Toste, J. R., Charlebois, A., & Nedecheva, T. (2009). Retrospective analysis of social factors and nonsuicidal self-injury among young adults. *Canadian Journal of Behavioural Science, 41*, 180–186.

Heatherton, T. F., & Sargent, J. D. (2009). Does watching smoking in movies promote teenage smoking? *Current Directions in Psychological Science, 18*, 63–68.

Heilbron, N., & Prinstein, M. J. (2010). Adolescent peer victimization, peer status, & suicide-related thoughts and behaviors: Examining concurrent and longitudinal associations. *Merrill-Palmer Quarterly, 56*, 388–420.

Heilbron, N., & Prinstein, M. J. (2008). Peer influence and adolescent nonsuicidal self-injury: A theoretical review of mechanisms and moderators. *Applied and Preventive Psychology, 12*, 169–177.

Heyes, C. M., Jaldow, E., & Dawson, G. R. (1994). Imitation in rats: Conditions of occurrence in a bidirectional control procedure. *Learning and Motivation, 25*, 276–287.

Hilt, L. M., Cha, C. B., & Nolen-Hoeksema, S. (2008). Nonsuicidal self-injury in young adolescent girls: Moderators of the distress-function relationship. *Journal of Consulting and Clinical Psychology, 76*, 63–71.

Hooley, J. M. (2007). Expressed emotion and relapse of psychopathology. *Annual Review of Clinical Psychology, 3*, 329–352.

Insel, B. J., & Gould, M. S. (2008). Impact of modeling on adolescent suicidal behavior. *Psychiatric Clinics of North America, 31*, 293–216.

Institute of Medicine. (2002). *Reducing suicide: A national imperative*. Washington, DC: National Academy Press.

International Association for the Study of Pain Task Force on Taxonomy. (1994). *Classification of chronic pain syndromes and definition of pain terms* (2nd ed.). Seattle, WA: IASP Press.

Ivarsson, T., Broberg, A. G., Arvidsson, T., & Gillberg, C. (2005). Bullying in adolescents: Psychiatric problems in victims and bullies as measured by the Youth Self Report (YSR) and the Depression Self-Rating Scale (DSRS). *Nordic Journal of Psychiatry, 59*, 365–373.

James, S. D. (April 2, 2009). Teen commits suicide due to bullying: Parents sue school for son's death. *ABC News*. Retrieved June 2009, from http://abcnews.go.com/Health/MindMoodNews/story?id=7228335&page=1.

Johnson, J. G., Cohen, P., Gould, M. S., Kasen, S., Brown, J., & Brook, J. S. (2002). Childhood adversities, interpersonal difficulties, and risk for suicide attempts during late adolescence and early adulthood. *Archives of General Psychiatry, 59*, 741–749.

Joiner, T. E. (1999). The clustering and contagion of suicide. *Current Directions in Psychological Science, 8*, 89–92.

Joiner, T. E. (2003). "Contagion" of suicidal symptoms as a function of assortative relating and shared relationship stress in college roommates. *Journal of Adolescence, 26*, 495–504.

Joiner, T. E. (2005). *Why people die by suicide*. Cambridge, MA: Harvard University Press.

Joiner, T. E., Brown, J. S., & Wingate, L. R. (2005). The psychology and neurobiology of suicidal behavior. *Annual Review of Psychology, 56*, 287–314.

Juvonen, J., & Graham, S. (Eds.). (2001). *Peer harassment in schools: The plight of the vulnerable and victimized*. New York, NY: Guilford Press.

Kaltiala-Heino, R., Rimpelä, M., Marttunen, M., Rimpelä, A., & Räntanen, P. (1999). Bullying, depression, and suicidal ideation in Finnish adolescents: School survey. *British Medical Journal, 319*, 348–351.

Kandel, D. B. (1978). Homophily, selection, and socialization in adolescent friendships. *American Journal of Sociology, 84*, 427–436.

Kasper, S., & McEwen, B. S. (2008). Neurobiological and clinical effects of the antidepressant tianeptine. *CNS Drugs, 22*, 15–26.

Keenan, K., Loeber, R., Zhang, Q., Stouthamer-Loeber, M., & Van Kammen, W. (1995). Influence of deviant peers on the development of boys' disruptive and delinquent behavior: A temporal analysis. *Development and Psychopathology, 7*, 715–726.

Kerr, D. C., Preuss, L. J., & King, C. A. (2006). Suicidal adolescents' social support from family and peers: Gender-specific associations with psychopathology. *Journal of Abnormal Child Psychology, 34*, 103–114.

Kessler, R. C., Berglund, P., Borges, G., Nock, M., & Wang, P. S. (2005). Trends in suicide ideation, plans, gestures, and attempts in the United States 1990-92 to 2001-2003. *Journal of the American Medical Association, 293*, 2487–2495.

Khatri, P., Kupersmidt, J. B., & Patterson, C. (2000). Aggression and peer victimization as predictors of self-reported behavioral and emotional adjustment. *Aggressive Behavior, 26*, 345–358.

Kidd, S., Henrich, C. C., Brookmeyer, K. A., Davidson, L., King, R. A., & Shahar, G. (2006). The social context of adolescent suicide attempts: Interactive effects of parent, peer, and school social relations. *Suicide and Life-Threatening Behavior, 36*, 386–395.

Kim, Y. S., Koh, Y. J., & Leventhal, B. L. (2004). Prevalence of school bullying in Korean middle school students. *Archives of Pediatrics and Adolescent Medicine, 158,* 737–741.

Kim, Y. S., & Leventhal, B. L. (2008). Bullying and suicide: A review. *International Journal of Adolescent Medicine and Health, 20,* 133–154.

Kim, Y. S., Leventhal, B. L., Koh, Y., Hubbard, A., & Boyce, W. T. (2006). School bullying and youth violence: Causes or consequences of psychopathologic behavior? *Archives of General Psychiatry, 63,* 1035–1041.

King, C. A., & Merchant, C. R. (2008). Social and interpersonal factors relating to adolescent suicidality: A review of the literature. *Archives of Suicide Research, 12,* 181–196.

Kirsch, I. (2009). *The emperor's new drugs: Exploding the antidepressant myth.* New York, NY: Bodley Head.

Klomek, A. B., Marrocco, F., Kleinman, M., Schonfeld, I. S., & Gould, M. S. (2007). Bullying, depression, and suicidality in adolescents. *Journal of the American Academy of Child and Adolescent Psychiatry, 46,* 40–49.

Klomek, A. B., Sourander, A., Kumpulainen, K., Piha, J., Tamminen, T., Moilanen, I., …Gould, M. S. (2008). Childhood bullying as a risk for later depression and suicidal ideation among Finnish males. *Journal of Affective Disorders, 109,* 47–55.

Klonsky, E. D. (2007). The functions of deliberate self-injury: A review of the evidence. *Clinical Psychology Review, 27*(2), 226–239.

Klonsky, E. D., & Olino, T. M. (2008). Identify clinically distinct subgroups of self-injurers among young adults: A latent class analysis. *Journal of Consulting and Clinical Psychology, 76,* 22–27.

Knox, K. L., Conwell, Y., & Caine, E. D. (2004). If suicide is a public health problem, what are we doing to prevent it? *American Journal of Public Health, 94,* 37–45.

Kochenderfer-Ladd, B., & Ladd, G. W. (2001). Variations in peer victimization: Relations to children's maladjustment. In J. Juvonen & S. Graham (Eds.), *Peer harassment in school: The plight of the vulnerable and victimized* (pp. 25–48). New York, NY: Guilford Press.

Kosky, R., Silburn, S., & Zubrick, S. R. (1990). Are children and adolescents who have suicidal thoughts different from those who attempt suicide? *Journal of Nervous and Mental Disease, 178,* 38–43.

Kupersmidt, J. B., Coie, J. D., & Dodge, K. A. (1990). The role of poor peer relationships in the development of disorder. In S. R. Asher & J. D. Coie (Eds.), *Peer rejection in childhood* (pp. 274–305). New York, NY: Cambridge University Press.

Kupersmidt, J. B., & Dodge, K. A. (2004). *Children's peer relations: From development to intervention.* Washington, DC: American Psychological Association.

Kushner, H. I., & Sterk, C. E. (2005). The limits of social capital: Durkheim, suicide, and social cohesion. *American Journal of Public Health, 95,* 1139–1143.

Leknes, S., Brooks, J. C. W., Wiech, K., & Tracey, I. (2008). Pain relief as an opponent process: a psychophysical investigation. *European Journal of Neuroscience, 28,* 794–801.

Lewinsohn, P. M., Rohde, P., & Seeley, J. R. (1994). Psychosocial risk factors for future adolescent suicide attempts. *Journal of Consulting and Clinical Psychology, 62,* 297–305.

Lewinsohn, P. M., Rohde, P., & Seeley, J. R. (1996). Adolescent suicidal ideation and attempts: Prevalence, risk factors, and clinical implications. *Clinical Psychology: Science and Practice, 3,* 25–46.

Lewinsohn, P. M., Rohde, P., Seeley, J. R., & Baldwin, C. L. (2001). Gender differences in suicide attempts from adolescence to young adulthood. *Journal of the American Academy of Child and Adolescent Psychiatry, 40,* 427–434.

Linehan, M. M. (1993). *Cognitive-behavioral treatment of borderline personality disorder.* New York, NY: Guilford Press.

Lizardi, D., Sher, L., Sullivan, G. M., Stanley, B., Burke, A., & Oquendo, M. A. (2009). Association between familial suicidal behavior and frequency of attempts among depressed suicide attempters. *Acta Psychiatrica Scandinavica, 119,* 406–410.

Lloyd-Richardson, E. E., Nock, M. K. & Prinstein, M. K. (2008). Functions of adolescent non-suicidal self-injury. In M. K. Nixon & N. Heath (Eds.), *Self-injury in youth: Essential guide to assessment and intervention* (pp. 29–41). New York, NY: Routledge.

Loersch, C., & Payne, B.K. (2011). The situated interference model: An integrative account of the effects of primes on perception, behavior, and motivation. *Perspectives of Psychological Science, 6,* 234–252.

Low, G., Jones, D., MacLeod, A., Power, M., & Duggan, C. (2000). Childhood trauma, dissociation and self-harming behaviour: A pilot study. *British Journal of Medical Psychology, 73,* 269–278.

Lundgren, S. R., & Prislin, R. (1998). Motivated cognitive processing and attitude change. *Personality and Social Psychology Bulletin, 24,* 715–726.

Mann, J. J., Waternaux, C., Haas, G. L., & Malone, K. M. (1999). Toward a clinical model of suicidal behavior in psychiatric patients. *American Journal of Psychiatry, 156,* 181–189.

Maris, R. W., Berman, A. L., & Silverman, M. M. (2000). *Comprehensive textbook of suicidology.* New York, NY: Guilford Press.

Markus, H., & Wurf, E. (1987). The dynamic self-concept: A social psychological perspective. *Annual Review of Psychology, 38,* 299–337.

Marr, N., & Field, T. (2001). *Bullycide: Death at playtime, an exposé of child suicide caused by bullying.* Oxfordshire, UK: Success Unlimited.

Mazza, J. J., & Reynolds, W. M. (1998). A longitudinal investigation of depression, hopelessness, social support, and major and minor life events and their relation to suicidal ideation in adolescents. *Suicide and Life-Threatening Behavior, 28,* 358–374.

Millan, M. J. (2002). Descending control of pain. *Progress in Neurobiology, 66,* 355–474.

Miller, J. R., Piper, T. M., Ahern, J., Tracy, M., Tardiff, K. J., Vlahov, D., & Galea, S. (2005). Income inequality and risk of suicide in New York City neighborhoods: A multilevel case-control study. *Suicide and Life-Threatening Behavior, 35,* 448–459.

Mills, C., Guerin, S., Lynch, F., Daly, I., & Fitzpatrick, C. (2004). The relationship between bullying, depression, and suicidal thoughts/behaviour in Irish adolescents. *Irish Journal of Psychological Medicine, 21,* 112–116.

Mineka, S., & Cook, M. (1988). Social learning and the acquisition of snake fear in monkeys. In T. R. Zentall & B. G. Galef (Eds.), *Social learning: Psychological and biological perspectives* (pp. 51–73). Hillsdale, NJ: Erlbaum.

Montgomery, G. H., & Kirsch, I. (1997). Classical conditioning and the placebo effect. *Pain, 72,* 107–113.

Muehlenkamp, J. J., Hoff, E. R., Licht, J., Azure, J. A., & Hasenzahl, S. J. (2008). Rates of non-suicidal self-injury: A cross-sectional analysis of exposure. *Current Psychology, 27,* 234–241.

Nademin, E., Jobes, D. A., Pflanz, S. E., Jacoby, A. M., Ghahramanlou-Holloway, M., Campise, R., …Johnson, L. (2008). An investigation of interpersonal-psychological variables in air force suicides: A controlled-comparison study. *Archives of Suicide Research, 12,* 309–326.

Neeleman, J., & Wessely, S. (1999). Ethnic minority suicide: A small area geographical study in south London. *Psychological Medicine, 29,* 429–436.

Newcomb, A. F., & Bagwell, C. L. (1995). Children's friendship relations: A meta-analytic review. *Psychological Bulletin, 117,* 306–347.

Nichols, W. C. (1999). Family systems therapy. In S. W. Russ & T. H. Ollendick (Eds.), *Handbook of psychotherapies with children and families* (pp. 137–151). New York, NY: Kluwer Academic/Plenum.

Niedtfeld, I., Schulze, L., Kirsch, P., Herpertz, S. C., Bohus, M., & Schmahl, C. (2010). Affect regulation and pain in borderline personality disorder: A possible link to the understanding of self-injury. *Biological Psychiatry, 68,* 383–391.

Nock, M. K. (2009). Why do people hurt themselves? New insights into the nature and functions of self-injury. *Current Directions in Psychological Science, 18,* 78–83.

Nock, M. K., & Favazza, A. R. (2009). Nonsuicidal self-injury: Definition and classification. In M. K. Nock (Ed.), *Understanding nonsuicidal self-injury: Origins, assessment, and treatment* (pp. 9–18). Washington, DC: American Psychological Association.

Nock, M. K., Park, J. M., Finn, C. T., Deliberto, T. L., Dour, H. J., & Banaji, M. R. (2010). Measuring the suicidal mind: Implicit cognition predicts suicidal behavior. *Psychological Science, 21,* 511–517.

Nock, M. K., & Prinstein, M. J. (2004). A functional approach to the assessment of self-mutilative behavior. *Journal of Consulting and Clinical Psychology, 72,* 885–890.

Nock, M. K., & Prinstein, M. J. (2005). Contextual features and behavioral functions of self-mutilation among adolescents. *Journal of Abnormal Psychology, 114,* 140–146.

Parker, J. G., & Asher, S. R. (1987). Peer relations and later personal adjustment: Are low-accepted children at risk? *Psychological Bulletin, 102,* 357–389.

Parkhurst, J. T., & Hopmeyer, A. (1998). Sociometric popularity and peer-perceived popularity: Two distinct dimensions of peer status. *Journal of Early Adolescence, 18,* 125–144.

Perez-Smith, A., Spirito, A., & Boergers, J. (2002). Neighborhood predictors of hopelessness among adolescent suicide attempters: Preliminary investigation. *Suicide and Life-Threatening Behavior, 32,* 139–145.

Perkins, D. F., & Hartless, G. (2002). An ecological risk-factor examination of suicide ideation and behavior of adolescents. *Journal of Adolescent Research, 17,* 3–26.

Pike, J. L., Smith, T. L., Hauger, R. L., Nicassio, P. M., Patterson, T. L., McClintick, J.,…Irwin, M. R. (1997). Chronic life stress alters sympathetic, neuroendocrine, and immune responsivity to an acute psychological stressor in humans. *Psychosomatic Medicine, 59,* 447–457.

Price, D. D., Milling, L. S., Kirsch, I., Duff, A., Montgomery, G. H., & Nicholls, S. S. (1999). An analysis of factors that contribute to the magnitude of placebo analgesia in an experimental paradigm. *Pain, 83,* 147–156.

Prinstein, M. J. (2003). Social factors: Peer relationships. In A. Spirito & J. C. Overholser (Eds.), *Evaluating and treating adolescent suicide attempters: From research to practice* (pp. 193–209). New York, NY: Academic Press.

Prinstein, M. J. (2007). Moderators of peer contagion: A longitudinal examination of depression socialization between adolescents and their best friends. *Journal of Clinical Child and Adolescent Psychology, 36,* 159–170.

Prinstein, M. J. (2008). Introduction to the special section on suicide and nonsuicidal self-injury: A review of unique challenges and important directions for self-injury science. *Journal of Consulting and Clinical Psychology, 76,* 1–8.

Prinstein, M. J., Boergers, J., & Spirito, A. (2001). Adolescents' and their friends' health-risk behavior: Factors that alter or add to peer influence. *Journal of Pediatric Psychology, 26,* 287–298.

Prinstein, M. J., Boergers, J., Spirito, A., Little, T. D., & Grapentine, W. L. (2000). Peer functioning, family dysfunction, and psychological symptoms in a risk factor model for adolescent inpatients' suicidal ideation severity. *Journal of Clinical Child Psychology, 29,* 392–405.

Prinstein, M. J. & Cohen, G. L. (2006, April). *A social norm framework for understanding peer contagion effects.* In M. J. Prinstein & J. K. Kupersmidt (Co-Chairs), Paper presented at the Annual Conference of the Society for Research on Adolescence, San Francisco, CA.

Prinstein, M. J., Guerry, J. D., Browne, C. B., & Rancourt, D. (2009). Interpersonal models of nonsuicidal self-injury. In M. K. Nock (Ed.), *Understanding nonsuicidal self-injury: Origins, assessment, and treatment* (pp. 79–98). Washington, DC: American Psychological Association.

Prinstein, M. J., Heilbron, N., Guerry, J. D., Franklin, J. C., Rancourt, D., Simon, V., & Spirito, A. (2010). Peer influence and nonsuicidal self injury: Longitudinal results in community and clinically-referred adolescent samples. *Journal of Abnormal Child Psychology, 38*(5), 669–682.

Rada, R. T., & James, W. (1982). Urethral insertion of foreign bodies: A report of contagious self-mutilation in a maximum-security hospital. *Archives of General Psychiatry, 39,* 423–429.

Raine, W. J. B. (1982). Self-mutilation. *Journal of Adolescence, 5,* 1–13.

Rainville, P. (2002). Brain mechanisms of pain affect and pain modulation. *Current Opinion in Neurobiology, 12,* 195–204.

Rehkopf, D. H., & Buka, S. L. (2006). The association between suicide and the socio-economic characteristics of geographic areas: A systematic review. *Psychological Medicine, 36,* 145–157.

Richardson, J. S, & Zaleski, W. A. (1986). Endogenous opiates and self-mutilation. *American Journal of Psychiatry, 140,* 867–872.

Rigby, K., & Slee, P. T. (1999). Suicidal ideation among adolescent school children, involvement in bully/victim problems and perceived low social support. *Suicide and Life-Threatening Behavior, 29,* 119–130.

Rosen, P. M., & Walsh, B. W. (1989). Patterns of contagion in self-mutilation epidemics. *American Journal of Psychiatry, 146,* 656–658.

Rosenberg, H. J., Jankowski, M. K., Sengupta, A., Wolfe, R. S., Wolford, G. L., & Rosenberg, S. D. (2005). Single and multiple suicide attempts and associated health risk factors in New Hampshire adolescents. *Suicide and Life-Threatening Behavior, 35,* 547–557.

Ross, C. E. (2000). Neighborhood disadvantage and adult depression. *Journal of Health and Social Behavior, 41*, 177–187.

Rubenstein, J. L., Halton, A., Kasten, L., Rubin, C., & Stechler, G. (1998). Suicidal behavior in adolescents: Stress and protection in different family contexts. *American Journal of Orthopsychiatry, 68*, 274–284.

Russ, M. J., Roth, S. D., Kakuma, T., Harrison, K., & Hull, J. W. (1994). Pain perception in self-injurious borderline patients: Naloxone effects. *Biological Psychiatry, 35*, 207–209.

Salzinger, S., Rosario, M., Feldman, R. S., & Ng-Mak, D. S. (2007). Adolescent suicidal behavior: Associations with preadolescent physical abuse and selected risk and protective factors. *Journal of the American Academy of Child and Adolescent Psychiatry, 46*, 859–866.

Schlenker, B. R. (1985). *The self and social life*. New York, NY: McGraw-Hill.

Schmahl, C., Bohus, M., Esposito, F., Treede, R. D., Di Salle, F., Greffrath, W., ... Seifritz, E. (2006) Neural correlates of antinociception in borderline personality disorder. *Archives of General Psychiatry, 63*, 659–667.

Sher, L., & Stanley, B. (2009). Biological models of nonsuicidal self-injury. In M. K. Nock (Ed.), *Understanding nonsuicidal self-injury: Origins, assessment, and treatment* (pp. 99–116). Washington, DC: American Psychological Association.

Silverman, M. M., Berman, A. L., Sanddal, N. D., O'Carroll, P. W., & Joiner, T. E. (2007). Rebuilding the Tower of Babel: A revised nomenclature for the study of suicide and suicidal behaviors. Part II: Suicide-related ideations, communications and behaviors. *Suicide and Life-Threatening Behavior, 37*, 264–277.

Sim, L., Adrian, M., Zeman, J., Cassano, M., & Friedrich, W. N. (2009). Adolescent deliberate self-harm: Linkages to emotion regulation and family emotional climate. *Journal of Research on Adolescence, 19*, 75–91.

Solomon, R. L. (1980). The opponent-process theory of acquired motivation: The costs of pleasure and the benefits of pain. *American Psychologist, 35*, 691–712.

Sroufe, L. A. (1989). Pathways to adaptation and maladaptation: Psychopathology as developmental deviation. In D. Cicchetti (Ed.), *Rochester symposium on developmental psychopathology: The emergence of a discipline* (pp. 13–40). Hillsdale, NJ: Erlbaum.

Staats, P., Hekmat, H., & Staats, A. (1998). Suggestion/placebo effects on pain: Negative as well as positive. *Journal of Pain and Symptom Management, 15*, 235–243.

Stanley, B., Sher, L., Wilson, S., Ekman, R., Huang, Y., & Mann, J. J. (2010). Non-suicidal self-injurious behavior, endogenous opioids and monoamine neurotransmitters. *Journal of Affect Disorders, 124*, 134–140.

Stevens, E. A., & Prinstein, M. J. (2005). Peer contagion of depressogenic attributional styles among adolescents: A longitudinal study. *Journal of Abnormal Child Psychology, 33*, 25–37.

Sullivan, T. N., Farrell, A. D., & Kliewer, W. (2006). Peer victimization in early adolescence: Association between physical and relational victimization and drug use, aggression, and delinquent behaviors among urban middle school students. *Development and Psychopathology, 18*, 119–137.

Suyemoto, K. L. (1998). The functions of self-mutilation. *Clinical Psychology Review, 18*, 531–554.

Taiminen, T. J., Kallio-Soukainen, K., Nokso-Koivisto, H., Kaljonen, A., & Kelenius, H. (1998). Contagion of deliberate self-harm among adolescent inpatients. *Journal of the American Academy of Child and Adolescent Psychiatry, 37*, 211–217.

Tajfel, H. (1982). Social psychology of intergroup relations. *Annual Review of Psychology, 33*, 1–39.

Tousignant, M., Bastien, M. F., & Hamel, S. (1993). Suicidal attempts and ideations among adolescents and young adults: The contribution of the father's and mother's care and of parental separation. *Social Psychiatry and Psychiatric Epidemiology, 28*, 256–261.

Turner, J. C. (1991). *Social influence*. Belmont, CA: Thomson Brooks/Cole.

van der Kolk, B. A., Perry, J. C., & Herman, J. L. (1991). Childhood origins of self-destructive behavior. *American Journal of Psychiatry, 148*, 1665–1671.

Van Orden, K. A., Witte, T. K., Gordon, K. H., Bender, T. W., & Joiner, T. E. (2008). Suicidal desire and the capability for suicide: Tests of the interpersonal-psychological theory of suicidal behavior among adults. *Journal of Consulting and Clinical Psychology, 76*, 72–83.

Van Orden, K. A., Witte, T. K., James, L. M., Castro, Y., Gordon, K. H., Braithwaite, S. R., ... Joiner, T. E. (2008). Suicidal ideation in college students varies across semesters: The mediating role of belongingness. *Suicide and Life-Threatening Behavior, 38*, 427–435.

Wagner, B. M. (1997). Family risk factors for child and adolescent suicidal behavior. *Psychological Bulletin, 121*, 246–298.

Wagner, B., Silverman, M. A. C., & Martin, A. E. (2003). Family factors in youth suicidal behaviors. *American Behavioral Scientist, 46*, 1171–1191.

Walsh, B. W., & Rosen, P. (1985). Self-mutilation and contagion: An empirical test. *American Journal of Psychiatry, 142*, 119–120.

Wedig, M. M., & Nock, M. K. (2007). Parental expressed emotion and adolescent self-injury. *Journal of the American Academy of Child and Adolescent Psychiatry, 46*, 1171–1178.

Welch, S. S., Linehan, M. M., Sylvers, P., Chittams, J., & Rizvi, S. L. (2008). Emotional responses to self-injury imagery among adults with borderline personality disorder. *Journal of Consulting and Clinical Psychology, 76*, 45–51.

Whitlock, J. L., Powers, J. L., & Eckenrode, J. (2006). The virtual cutting edge: The internet and adolescent self-injury. *Developmental Psychology, 42*, 407–417.

Whitlock, J., Purington, A., & Gershkovich, M. (2009). Media, the internet, and nonsuicidal self-injury. In In M. K. Nock (Ed.), *Understanding nonsuicidal self-injury: Origins, assessment, and treatment* (pp. 139–155). Washington, DC: American Psychological Association.

Wiederman, M. W., Sansone, R. A., & Sansone, L. A. (1999). Bodily self-harm and its relationship to childhood abuse among women in a primary care setting. *Violence Against Women, 5*, 155–163.

Wood, W. (2000). Attitude change: Persuasion and social influence. *Annual Review of Psychology, 51*, 539–570.

World Health Organization. (2005). *Suicide prevention*. Retrieved October 2005, from http://www.who.int/mental_health/prevention/suicide/suicideprevent/en/.

Yates, T. M. (2004). The developmental psychopathology of self-injurious behavior: Compensatory regulation in posttraumatic adaptation. *Clinical Psychology Review, 24*, 35–74.

Yates, T. M. (2009). Developmental pathways from child maltreatment to nonsuicidal self-injury. In M. K. Nock (Ed.), *Understanding nonsuicidal self-injury: Origins, assessment, and treatment* (pp. 117–137). Washington, DC: American Psychological Association.

Yates, T. M., Carlson, E. A., & Egeland, B. (2008). A prospective study of child maltreatment and self-injurious behavior in a community sample. *Development and Psychopathology, 20*, 651–671.

Zeman, J., Cassano, M., Perry-Parrish, C., & Stegall, S. (2006). Emotion regulation in children and adolescents. *Journal of Developmental and Behavioral Pediatrics, 27*, 155–168.

Zentall, T. R. (2006). Imitation: Definitions, evidence, and mechanisms. *Animal Cognition, 9*, 335–353.

Cognitive and Information Processing Approaches to Understanding Suicidal Behaviors

Amy Wenzel *and* Megan Spokas

Abstract

Cognitive and information processing variables have the potential to account for the mechanisms that lead up to and operate during a suicidal crisis. This chapter evaluates the empirical research on suicide-relevant cognitive content variables (i.e., hopelessness, perfectionism, burdensomeness, low belongingness, unbearability) and information processing variables (i.e., problem-solving deficits, overgeneral memory, future thinking, attentional biases, implicit associations). It is concluded that many of these variables interact with one another during suicidal crises and can serve as both distal and proximal risk factors for suicidal behavior. In addition, five contemporary cognitive models of suicidal behavior are presented, and the manner in which they might operate at different stages in the onset of suicidal crises is considered.

Key Words: cognition, information processing, distortions, biases, hopelessness

An array of demographic (e.g., age, ethnicity), psychiatric (e.g., depression), and psychosocial (e.g., social isolation) variables have been investigated as correlates and predictors of suicidal behavior. Prospective research has demonstrated that many of these variables indeed predict suicide attempts and death by suicide (see Joiner, Brown, & Wingate, 2005; Mościcki, 1999; Oquendo, Currier, & Mann, 2006; Wenzel, Brown, & Beck, 2009, for reviews). However, when these variables are incorporated into complex algorithms and used prospectively to identify people who ultimately take their own lives, they fail to account for even one death (e.g., Goldstein, Black, Nasrallah, & Winokur, 1991). Moreover, the vast majority of people characterized by any one of these risk factors do not engage in suicidal behavior. Thus, it is incumbent upon scholars to identify characteristics of suicidal individuals that have the potential to be more targeted in understanding, explaining, and eventually predicting their harmful behavior.

Variables relevant to the cognition and information processing of suicidal individuals have promise in shedding light on the psychological processes that set the stage for these self destructive acts. In fact, over 20 years ago, Charles Neuringer (1988) wrote, "There exists a group of suicidologists who believe that the key to understanding and predicting suicide resides in the analysis of self-destructive individuals' patterns of organizing their thought processes" (p. 43). Thus, an investigation of cognitive variables that explain or predict suicidal behavior might not only yield another, and perhaps a more specific, class of characteristics that distinguish suicidal from nonsuicidal individuals, but they might also provide clues about the mechanisms at work that lead up to and operate during a suicidal crisis.

Cognition is a broad construct that generally refers to mental activity. There are two aspects of cognition that have been linked to psychiatric symptoms and disordered behavior (cf. Ingram & Kendall, 1986). *Cognitive content* refers to thoughts, beliefs, assumptions, attitudes, and images. In other words, cognitive content is relevant to *what* people are thinking. In contrast, *information processing* refers to the manner in which people perceive, attend to, encode, consolidate, store, and retrieve information that they encounter in their daily lives. Information processing is relevant to *how* people are thinking. In this chapter, we propose that suicidal individuals are characterized by distinct patterns in their cognitive content as well as disruption and biases in the manner in which they process information.

We suggest that distortions in cognitive content and information processing are important in understanding suicidal behavior from two perspectives. First, suicidal individuals are characterized by *distal* cognitive variables that have the potential to increase risk for the onset or exacerbation of psychiatric symptoms and for the emergence of additional life stressors. These cognitive variables put individuals at risk for developing an array of factors that, in turn, increase the risk that a person might engage in suicidal behavior. For example, people who have poor problem-solving skills might have an increased likelihood of experiencing psychiatric symptoms (e.g., depression) and unnecessary life stress when faced with a problem that they have difficulty handling, which can in turn increase the risk of engaging in suicidal behavior. In such individuals, problem-solving deficits are associated with suicidal behavior through indirect means. Second, suicidal individuals are characterized by *proximal* cognitive variables that are activated and at work immediately preceding and during a suicidal crisis. For example, people who have poor problem-solving skills might have difficulty identifying a solution other than suicide to relieve their current level of distress. In these individuals, impaired problem solving is associated with suicidal behavior through direct means. In this chapter, we consider the distal and proximal risk posed by suicide-relevant patterns of cognitive content and information processing. In addition, we highlight similarities and differences among cognitively based psychological theories of suicidal behavior. We end the chapter with suggestions of directions for future research.

Cognitive Content

Empirical research and clinical observation have identified several themes in the cognitive contents of suicidal individuals, including (a) hopelessness, (b) perfectionism, (c) burdensomeness, (d) low belongingness, and (e) unbearability. The common feature among these themes is that they are

the individual's *perceptions*. In line with cognitive models of psychopathology (e.g., Beck, 1970), many suicidologists propose that negative interpretations or appraisals of one's situation or life events, rather than the events themselves, are most closely associated with psychological distress and suicidal ideation. The following sections describe and evaluate the research that has been conducted on each of these five content areas.

Hopelessness

Hopelessness, or negative expectations for the future, is the cognitive variable most extensively studied by suicidologists. Almost half a century ago, Beck (1963) noted that "suicide preoccupations...seemed related to the patient's conceptualization of his situation as untenable or hopeless" (p. 328). Today, countless studies have confirmed that hopelessness is associated with a broad array of variables relevant to suicidal behavior. For example, hopelessness is associated with increased suicidal ideation and intent even after controlling for the effects of depression (e.g., Beck, Steer, & Brown, 1993; Minkoff, Bergman, Beck, & Beck, 1973). Furthermore, hopelessness plays a crucial role in explaining the association between suicidal ideation and other suicide risk factors, including rumination (Smith, Alloy, & Abramson, 2006), life stress (Rudd, 1990), childhood sexual abuse (Meadows & Kaslow, 2002; Spokas, Wenzel, Stirman, Brown, & Beck, 2009), and childhood maltreatment (Gibb et al., 2001). Collectively, these findings suggest that hopelessness can largely explain the associations between an array of risk factors and suicidal ideation. That is, these risk factors are associated with an increase in hopelessness, which in turn is associated with an increase in suicidal thoughts.

Moreover, prospective studies have illustrated that hopelessness is a robust risk factor for eventual suicide, in many cases several years later. For example, studies have demonstrated that hopelessness predicts eventual suicide in clinical samples, including a 5- to 10-year follow-up of patients who had been hospitalized for suicidal ideation (e.g., Beck, Brown, & Steer, 1989; Beck, Steer, Kovacs, & Garrison, 1985) and a 3-year follow-up of psychiatric outpatients (e.g., Beck, Brown, Berchick, Stewart, & Steer, 1990). In their meta-analysis of the Beck Hopelessness Scale (BHS; Beck, Weissman, Lester, & Trexler, 1974) as a predictor of eventual suicide in high-risk patients, McMillan, Gilbody, Beresford, and Neilly (2007) found that people who exceeded a standard cutoff score (i.e., BHS score of

9 or greater) were over four times more likely than people who scored below the cutoff to die by suicide. Hopelessness also predicts suicide in nonclinical samples, as Wen-Hung, Gallo, and Eaton (2004) determined that adults in their community epidemiological study who reported hopelessness at their baseline assessment were 11 times more likely to die by suicide in a 13-year follow-up period than those who denied hopelessness.

Overall, a large body of research supports hopelessness as a key cognitive factor associated with increased suicide risk. In short, people are at risk for suicidal behavior when they have pessimistic views of their future. Chronic hopelessness can serve as a distal risk factor for suicidal behavior. Moreover, scholars also have proposed that increases in state-like hopelessness can serve as a proximal risk factor, in that it likely contributes to the activation of the acute suicidal crisis (Wenzel et al., 2009; Young et al., 1996). Hopelessness is a more potent variable than depression in accounting for suicidal behavior, and it explains the association between a number of established risk factors and suicidal behavior. The support for the relations between hopelessness and suicide-relevant variables is so well established that it is essential for researchers to account for its effects when investigating other cognitive variables that have the potential to be important in explaining suicidal behavior.

Perfectionism

The association between perfectionism and suicidal thoughts and behaviors is another widely studied area of inquiry, with the idea that perfectionism generates stress and exacerbates the degree to which suicidal individuals experience stress as aversive (Hewitt, Flett, Sherry, & Caelian, 2006). Perfectionism is best conceptualized as a multidimensional construct. For instance, Hewitt and Flett (1991) defined two components of perfectionism: *self-oriented perfectionism*, which reflects the tendency to set high goals and standards for oneself, and *socially prescribed perfectionism*, which reflects the tendency to be overly critical of one's behaviors and excessively concerned about others' expectations. Many researchers have argued that it is excessive self-critical evaluative concerns, rather than setting high standards for oneself, that increases a person's vulnerability to psychiatric distress, including suicidal behavior (Dunkley, Blankstein, Masheb, & Grilo, 2006; Klibert, Langhinrichsen-Rohling, & Saito, 2005).

A recent comprehensive review of suicide and perfectionism suggests that socially prescribed perfectionism correlates positively with suicidal ideation (R. C. O'Connor, 2007). In several studies, socially prescribed perfectionism predicted the severity of suicidal ideation even when accounting for the effects of hopelessness and/or depression (Hewitt, Flett, & Turnbull-Donovan, 1992; Hewitt, Flett, & Weber, 1994; R. C. O'Connor et al., 2007). Empirical research suggests that resulting stress (Chang, Watkins, & Banks, 2004), hopelessness (Dean & Range, 1999; Dean, Range, & Groggin, 1996), rumination (D. B. O'Connor, O'Connor, & Marshall, 2007), and intense psychological pain (Flamenbaum & Holden, 2007) may explain the association between socially prescribed perfectionism and suicidal ideation and intent. That is, self-critical evaluative concerns create stress, hopelessness, rumination, and psychological pain for people, which in turn increase suicidal ideation. In addition, individuals who are high in socially prescribed perfectionism display interpersonal hostility (Haring, Hewitt, & Flett, 2003) and report high levels of interpersonal sensitivity (Hewitt & Flett, 1991), both of which have the potential to prompt perceptions of social rejection and, in turn, suicidal ideation. Less research has examined the association between perfectionism and suicide attempts, rather than ideation, but the few studies in this area suggest that socially prescribed perfectionism is more characteristic of attempters than nonattempters (e.g., Hewitt, Norton, Flett, Callender, & Cowan, 1998).

Only a few studies have prospectively investigated the association between perfectionism and suicide-related outcomes, and the findings from these studies are mixed. In two studies, measures of perfectionism failed to predict suicidal ideation over a period ranging from 20 days to 6 months (Enns, Cox, & Inayatulla, 2003; Enns, Cox, Sareen, & Freeman, 2001). In contrast, Chang (1998) found that higher levels of self-critical evaluative concerns predicted higher levels of suicidal ideation among Caucasian undergraduate students 4 weeks after initial testing. Furthermore, Beevers and Miller (2004) found that perfectionism, as measured by the Dysfunctional Attitudes Scale (Imber et al., 1990), endorsed by people hospitalized for depression, predicted suicidal ideation 6 months later independently of hopelessness.

In sum, empirical evidence suggests that people with suicidal ideation and those who have made a suicide attempt report being overly critical of themselves and having excessive concern about others' expectations for them. Some empirical research suggests that self-critical evaluative concerns predict the severity of future suicidal ideation. Overall, we view socially prescribed perfectionism as a distal risk factor for suicidal behavior, in that it provides a context for the activation of some of the other cognitive variables described in this chapter in the time immediately preceding a suicidal crisis. Thus, it will be important for future research to identify the precise mechanism by which socially prescribed perfectionism exacerbates suicidal ideation. On the basis of the research conducted to date, candidate mechanisms include stress, hopelessness, rumination, psychological pain, interpersonal hostility, and interpersonal sensitivity. It also is possible that self-evaluative critical concerns feed into the cognitive contents described in the next two sections (i.e., perceived burdensomeness and low belongingness).

Burdensomeness

According to Joiner (2005), a particularly salient cognitive content variable contributing to the desire to die is the perception that one is a burden on others. It is not simply a perception that one is incompetent or ineffective but, specifically, that one's incompetence negatively affects others. This perspective was informed by evolutionary theory, which suggests that being a burden on one's kin can decrease one's self-preservation instincts (DeCatanzaro, 1991). However, Joiner's theory emphasizes the perception of being a burden, rather than the objective measurement of burdensomeness, which makes this construct another cognitive content variable, like hopelessness and perfectionism, that is subject to mood-congruent distortion.

The association between perceived burdensomeness and suicide-relevant variables has received an increasing amount of empirical support. Perceived burdensomeness is associated with suicidal ideation in samples of nonclinical undergraduate participants (Brown, Dahlen, Mills, Rick, & Biblarz, 1999), nonclinical community participants (DeCatanzaro, 1995), psychiatric patients (DeCatanzaro, 1995; Van Orden, Lynam, Hollar, & Joiner, 2006), and combat veterans (Brenner et al., 2008). In addition, it is associated with a lifetime history of suicide attempts in psychiatric outpatients (Van Orden et al., 2006) and in patients receiving methadone maintenance treatment (Conner, Britton, Sworts, & Joiner, 2007) after controlling for variables such as depression, hopelessness, demographic variables, drug use, and aggression. Joiner et al. (2002) compared suicide notes written by those who committed suicide with notes written by those who attempted suicide but survived and found that perceived

burdensomeness was the only characteristic that differentiated between the two groups. In addition, perceived burdensomeness was also the only dimension associated with the lethality of the suicidal act, such that a greater level of perceived burdensomeness was associated with a greater degree of lethality.

Overall, this growing body of research suggests that perceived burdensomeness is commonly experienced by suicidal individuals and that it accounts for unique variance in suicidal thoughts and behaviors above and beyond many variables that also increase risk of suicide. Although we agree with Joiner and his colleagues in viewing perceived burdensomeness as a proximal risk factor (Van Orden, Witte, Gordon, Bender, & Joiner, 2008), we also view this construct as a distal risk factor that can exacerbate other variables that create the context for a suicidal crisis to emerge. To investigate this possibility, we encourage future researchers to determine the manner in which perceived burdensomeness interacts with depression and hopelessness in order to explain the pathway that leads to suicidal acts. Although perceived burdensomeness accounts for unique variance in predicting suicide-relevant constructs, it also overlaps substantially with these variables ($r = .61$ with depression; $r = .68$ with hopelessness; Joiner at al., 2009). It is possible that these three constructs contribute to a negative feedback cycle in which the intensity of distorted perceptions of one's life circumstances and associated mood disturbance exacerbate one another in a bidirectional manner. It also will be important to examine the association between socially prescribed perfectionism and perceived burdensomeness, as it is logical to hypothesize that perceptions of failure in living up to the expectations of others could feed into a sense of burdensomeness.

Low Belongingness

Joiner (2005) proposed a second cognitive content variable related to increased risk of suicidal behavior: low belongingness. Low belongingness refers to the perception that one is alienated from others or is not an important member of a group, such as a family or circle of friends (Joiner et al., 2009). The notion that low belongingness is related to suicide has its earliest roots in the writings of Émile Durkheim (1897, 1951), who theorized that individuals who are well integrated into social relationships are unlikely to kill themselves, whereas "un-integrated" individuals are at risk for suicide. Indeed, a large amount of research confirms that social isolation is common in people who report suicidal ideation (e.g., Bonner & Rich, 1987; Roberts, Roberts, & Chen, 1998) as well as in those who die by suicide (see Trout, 1980 for a review). Interestingly, Joiner has observed that suicide rates decrease during times in which people "pull together," such as times of celebration (Joiner, Hollar, & Van Orden, 2006) or times of tragedy (Biller, 1977). These findings raise the possibility that some societal events function to decrease people's sense of social isolation and alienation.

The reader may note that low belongingness could be better characterized as a life circumstance or social functioning rather than as distorted cognitive content. Indeed, empirical research indicates that demographic variables such as living alone (Conner, Duberstein, & Conwell, 1999) and being of unmarried status (Kposowa, 2000) are associated with increased rates of suicide. However, the associations between these demographic variables and suicide rates tell us little about the mechanism by which suicidal crises are activated in individuals who fall into these demographic categories. They also do not explain suicidal ideation in individuals who do not meet this demographic profile yet feel disconnected from others. Van Orden, Witte, James, et al. (2008) suggested that a key factor in understanding suicidal behavior is loneliness associated with a perception of thwarted belonging. As was seen in previous sections of this chapter, the central characteristic is, again, the perception of the individual. Empirical research indicates that greater endorsement of low belongingness is associated with increased suicidal ideation (Van Orden, Witte, Gordon, et al., 2008; Van Orden, Witte, James, et al., 2008) and a higher probability of a lifetime suicide attempt after controlling for demographic and psychological variables that also are associated with suicidal behavior (Conner et al., 2007). In fact, it even accounts for the tendency of college students to report increased suicidal ideation during the summer months, when the college campus is less active (Van Orden, Witte, James, et al., 2008).

Low belongingness is another promising cognitive candidate for explaining the mechanism underlying suicidal behavior. As with perceived burdensomeness, it is likely that this construct can serve as both a distal and proximal risk factor for suicidal ideation and behavior. Also like perceived burdensomeness, low belongingness correlates highly with standard measures of depression and hopelessness (rs = .65 and .63, respectively; Joiner et al., 2009). Therefore, it will be important to identify the paths by which these variables interact and exacerbate one

another to prompt a suicidal crisis. In addition, low belongingness is another variable that will be important to examine in the context of socially prescribed perfectionism, as the interpersonal consequences of this cognitive style (i.e., interpersonal hostility, interpersonal sensitivity) could alienate others and contribute to the perception of low belongingness (Hewitt et al., 2006). Additional research, particularly in clinical populations, is necessary to better determine the degree to which one's subjective sense of belongingness can predict suicide attempts and/or death by suicide.

Unbearability

Edwin Shneidman's theory of suicidal behavior emphasizes the instrumental roles of (a) experiencing intense psychological pain and (b) viewing suicide as an escape from such pain (Shneidman, 1993). Shneidman used the term *psychache* to describe psychological and emotional pain that becomes intolerable and increases the risk of suicide. To date, the relation between psychache and suicide-related variables has not been subject to much empirical investigation. However, clinical experience and some initial research suggests that individuals who attempt suicide often view suicide as the only escape from an unbearable situation. For example, in a study of adults recently making a suicide attempt, almost all of the participants indicated that the motive for their attempt was to escape from unbearable situations or thoughts (Michel, Valach, & Waeber, 1994). Similarly, in a study of adolescent suicide attempters, 80% of the participants reported that the reason for attempting suicide was that "the situation was so unbearable that I had to do something, and I didn't know what else to do" (Kienhorst, De Wilde, Diekstra, & Wolters, 1995). Finally, elderly individuals who made a suicide attempt most commonly reported that the reason for their self-injurious behavior was "to gain relief from an unbearable state of mind" (Dennis, Wakefield, Molloy, Andrews, & Friedman, 2007).

Thus, preliminary evidence suggests that the perception of unbearability is central in understanding suicidal behavior. Our research group has suggested that the perception of unbearability is the major cognitive content domain that characterizes individuals who make impulsive suicide attempts (Wenzel et al., 2009), as there is evidence that those who make impulsive attempts are less hopeless and depressed than those who make planned attempts (Simon et al., 2001). It is possible that the perception of unbearability exerts greater proximal than distal effects, as these perceptions tend to arise suddenly and with great intensity during times of emotion dysregulation. It will be important for future research to identify the degree to which these cognitive content domains characterize different subgroups of suicidal individuals, as our research group has speculated that hopelessness characterizes people who are chronically suicidal, whereas the perception of unbearability characterizes people who engage in impulsive self-injurious acts (Wenzel et al., 2009).

Summary

Suicidologists have identified many domains of cognitive content associated with suicidal behavior. Hopelessness is the most well-documented (and quite possibly the most central) domain, but other domains also help to shed light into the thoughts and beliefs that characterize suicidal individuals, including perfectionism, burdensomeness, low belongingness, and unbearability. As stated previously, all of these content areas reflect perceptions by the suicidal individual. However, not everyone who endorses one or more of these domains will consider or attempt suicide. In fact, it is likely that it is the combination between these cognitive content areas and unhelpful patterns of information processing that culminate in a suicidal act. We suggest that many of the information processing impairments and biases described in the next section serve to make these perceptions especially rigid and inflexible, impervious to information to the contrary that might signal hope or relief. It is likely that suicidal individuals engage in a circular process of attending to information that confirms beliefs in these domains, while overlooking information that is inconsistent with these beliefs but that could very well provide a glimmer of hope or the beginnings of a solution to their life problems.

Information Processing

Two types of information processing patterns have been examined in samples of suicidal individuals. First, there is evidence that some suicidal individuals exhibit general impairment in particular aspects of information processing. That is, regardless of the content of the information to which they are attending, they exhibit performance deficits. In this section, we describe empirical research that speaks to three types of information processing impairment often observed in suicidal individuals: (a) problem-solving deficits, (b) overgeneral memory, and (c) dichotomous thinking. Second, there is evidence that suicidal individuals exhibit

biases when they are processing particular types of information. That is, they demonstrate the ability to process some types of information in a similar manner as nonsuicidal individuals, but they process other types of information, usually information that is relevant to suicide, in a different manner. In this section, we describe biases in (a) future thinking, (b) attentional allocation, and (c) implicit associations.

Impairment in Information Processing
PROBLEM-SOLVING DEFICITS

Several theorists have conceptualized suicidal behavior as a failure to generate alternative solutions to suicide, suggesting that suicidal individuals are characterized by deficits in their problem-solving abilities (e.g., Patsiokas, Clum, & Luscomb, 1979; Reinecke, 2006; Schotte & Clum, 1982, 1987). Overall, most studies find a significant association between problem-solving deficits and increased suicidal ideation. Several investigations use the Means-Ends Problem-Solving Test (MEPS; Platt & Spivack, 1972) to assess problem solving. This test provides respondents with a series of interpersonal situations, along with a stated need and desired outcome for each situation. Respondents are asked to provide a response outlining the manner in which each of the outcomes can be achieved. Responses are then coded in several ways, the most common outcome of interest being the number of provided "relevant means" to achieve the outcome and the effectiveness of the identified solutions. Using this test, several studies have shown that suicide ideators and attempters have deficits in generating effective solutions to achieving their desired outcomes (Evans, Williams, O'Loughlin, & Howells, 1992; Pollock & Williams, 2001, 2004; Priester & Clum, 1993; Schotte & Clum, 1982).

Some scholars have studied self-appraisals of problem-solving abilities and conceptualize problem-solving deficits as low confidence in one's problem-solving abilities. Results from these studies indicate that suicidal ideation is associated with lower perceptions of one's problem-solving abilities, both among college students (Dixon, Heppner, & Anderson, 1991) and patients who have made suicide attempts or who endorse suicidal ideation (Rudd, Rajab, & Dahm, 1994). Jeglic, Sharp, Chapman, Brown, and Beck (2005) found that a negative outlook on one's ability to solve difficult problems was associated with a family history of suicide attempts and a history of making multiple suicide attempts in a sample of people who had recently attempted suicide. In fact, this negative problem-solving orientation mediated the association between family history of suicide and multiple-attempt status, suggesting that expecting problem-solving efforts to fail, and therefore viewing suicide as a viable solution, may be partly learned through the family environment.

Problem-solving deficits also can be conceptualized as an avoidance of solving problems. Several studies have found that suicidal patients demonstrate greater avoidance and passivity in attempts to solve problems than nonsuicidal psychiatric controls (Linehan, Camper, Chiles, Strosahl, & Shearin, 1987; Orbach, Bar-Joseph, & Dror, 1990). Extending this area of research, Orbach et al. (2007) found, in a combined sample of adolescent psychiatric inpatients and nonclinical control group participants, that the tendency to appraise problem-solving tasks as threatening was associated with increased suicidal ideation, whereas the tendency to appraise problem-solving tasks as challenging was associated with lower suicidal ideation.

Very few studies have examined the relation between problem solving and suicidality in prospective studies. In one exception, Priester and Clum (1993) examined the role of problem-solving deficits in predicting adjustment following a stressor (i.e., a failed college exam). Those college students who experienced the stressor and also displayed problem-solving deficits (i.e., difficulty generating solutions to problems, greater perceptions of negative consequences for their generated solutions) experienced the highest levels of suicidal ideation several days following the exam. In addition, Dieserud, Roysmab, Braverman, Dalgard, and Ekeberg (2003) found, in a sample of recent suicide attempters, that lower expectations of one's problem-solving abilities were associated with making a repeat suicide attempt in an 18-month follow-up period. Results such as these need further replication in various types of samples, particularly clinical samples of high-risk patients. Yet these initial prospective studies of problem-solving deficits among suicide attempters suggest that difficulty generating solutions to problems and low self-appraised problem-solving capacity may be predictive of future suicidal behavior.

Most researchers conceptualize the association between problem-solving deficits and suicidal ideation within a diathesis-stress model. Deficits in problem solving act as a distal risk factor exacerbating the effects of stressful events, thereby increasing hopelessness and suicide risk (Schotte &

Clum, 1982; Wenzel et al., 2009). In fact, hopelessness has been shown to mediate the association between problem-solving appraisals and suicidal ideation (Dixon, Heppner, & Rudd, 1994), as well as the association between threatening appraisals of problem-solving tasks and suicidal ideation (Orbach et al., 2007). However, it also has been proposed that problem-solving deficits influence suicidal behavior in a proximal manner, as individuals with poor problem-solving skills often report having difficulty identifying any solution to their distress other than suicide when they are in the midst of a suicidal crisis (Reinecke, 2006).

Overall, research suggests that problem-solving deficits contribute to suicidal ideation and to suicidal behavior. Individuals reporting suicidal ideation and/or a history of suicide attempts report low confidence in their problem-solving capacities, demonstrate avoidance of problem solving, and have difficulty generating effective solutions to potential interpersonal problems. Such deficits in problem solving are likely to increase hopelessness when faced with a stressful problem, which in turn increases the focus on suicide as a potential solution to the crisis. Preliminary studies indicate that such deficits are predictive of future suicidal ideation and behavior, but more prospective studies are needed to confirm problem-solving deficits as predictors of suicidal acts. Furthermore, additional research is needed to examine the manner in which problem-solving deficits interact with the cognitive content domains described earlier in this chapter. For example, Chang (2002) found that especially high levels of suicidal ideation were reported by college students characterized by poor problem-solving ability and socially prescribed perfectionism. We also speculate that problem-solving deficits have the potential to be especially lethal in combination with a cognitive orientation of perceived unbearability.

OVERGENERAL MEMORY

Autobiographical memories are personal memories that form our life history and contribute to our sense of self (Williams, Barnhoffer, Crane, & Duggan, 2006; Williams et al., 2007). Over 20 years ago, it was observed that when suicidal patients were cued with single words and instructed to retrieve one particular autobiographical memory, on about half of the trials they made a general response that summarized a category of activities (e.g., "when I go to my family reunion each summer"; Williams & Broadbent, 1986a). This response style is indicative of a phenomenon called *overgeneral memory*, which occurs when people truncate the iterative process of searching for memories that match the specificity of the task that is being asked of them. Subsequent research has confirmed that people who have made recent suicide attempts or who have engaged in recent self-injurious behavior are particularly likely to retrieve overgeneral memories on cueing tasks and take longer to retrieve specific memories, even when they are no longer suicidal (Evans et al., 1992; Kaviani, Rahimi-Darabad, & Naghavi, 2005; Pollock & Williams, 2001; Sinclair, Crane, Hawton, & Williams, 2007; Williams & Dritschel, 1988; Williams et al., 1996). This cognitive pattern characterizes suicidal patients regardless of whether they are diagnosed with an affective disorder (Leibetseder, Rohrer, Mackinger, & Fartacek, 2006). Although early studies suggested that suicidal patients demonstrated the most pronounced overgeneral memory when presented with positive cues, which presumably cued them to retrieve a pleasant memory, most research suggests that the tendency to retrieve overgeneral memories occurs regardless of the valence of the cue (Williams et al., 2007).

Williams and his colleagues (Williams, 2006; Williams et al., 2007) have recently developed a cognitive model of autobiographical memory deficits associated with emotional disorders that identifies three processes at work in this type of information processing impairment (i.e., CaRFAX: *ca*pture and *ru*mination, *f*unctional *a*voidance, and e*x*ecutive control). First, when asked to identify a specific memory, people who exhibit an overgeneral memory style truncate their search at a level characterized by only general information. This truncated search is an example of functional avoidance of painful memories associated with negative affect (cf. Conway & Pleydell-Pearce, 2000). Second, most of the cues used in studies of autobiographical memory are emotion words; it is likely that these emotion words activate negative and dysfunctional cognitive filters, which in turn "capture" the attention of people with an overgeneral memory style and make it more difficult for them to retrieve specific memories. Over time, this cognitive style feeds into a cognitive pattern of *mnemonic interlock*, in which the associations between these nonspecific descriptions are elaborated and are more likely to be identified in subsequent instances in which the person is called upon to retrieve an autobiographical memory (Williams, 1996). "Capture" at this level of information is particularly likely in people who engage in excessive rumination (e.g., Watkins & Teasdale, 2001). Third, both of these cognitive

styles interact with reduced executive capacity, which is particularly characteristic of patients who report depression or a history of trauma. According to Williams et al. (2007), people with reduced executive capacity are easily distracted by rumination over associations in memory that are prompted by word cues, which decreases the likelihood that they can maintain a focus on the task at hand—to generate a specific personal memory. Together, these three factors maintain the overgeneral memory style, the longer term consequences of which include deficits in problem solving (e.g., Arie, Apter, Prbach, Yefet, & Zalzman, 2008; Evans et al., 1992; Pollock & Williams, 2001; Sidley, Whitaker, Calam, & Wells, 1997), an inability to imagine future events (e.g., Williams et al., 1996), and a longer course of affective illness (Peeters, Wessel, Merckelbach, & Boon-Vermeeren, 2002).

The CaRFAX model was developed to explain overgeneral memory in patients who most often exhibit this retrieval style, which includes suicidal patients as well as those who are depressed but not suicidal and who have reported a previous trauma. Williams et al. (2006) elaborated more specifically upon the manner in which overgeneral memory exacerbates suicidal thoughts and behaviors in suicidal patients. They suggested that, in hopelessness-driven suicidal behavior, overgeneral memory facilitates suicidal crises by prolonging affective disturbance, disrupting problem solving, and reducing the individual's ability to engage in specific, future-oriented thinking. In these instances, the difficulty retrieving specific personal memories prevents the individual from accessing memories of similar experiences that could provide useful information to inform decisions made during the current crisis. However, there is another subset of suicidal patients for whom the pattern of autobiographical memory retrieval is problematic in the other direction, such that they have a tendency to retrieve very specific and painful memories (e.g., patients with borderline personality disorder). If one regards overgeneral memory as an affective gating mechanism, which protects people from painful memories, then people who engage in suicidal behavior as an emotion regulation strategy might have a deficit in retrieving general, rather than specific, personal memories (Startup et al., 2001). Williams et al. (2006) speculated that optimal psychological well-being is achieved when people have access to both general and specific memories and can navigate their hierarchy of memories with ease in order to retrieve memories that are appropriate for the situation for which the memories are needed.

Like many of the variables described in this chapter, we propose that overgeneral memory can serve as both a distal and proximal risk factor for suicidal behavior. From a distal perspective, overgeneral memory has the potential to increase risk for suicidal behavior because (a) it reduces one's ability to solve problems effectively, which could exacerbate life stress and affective disturbance; (b) it reduces one's ability to think specifically about the future, which could provide a context for chronic hopelessness to develop; and (c) it exacerbates the course of affective disturbance, which in and of itself increases the risk for suicidal behavior. Preliminary research raises the possibility that it also might interact with the cognitive content variables described previously in the chapter (e.g., socially prescribed perfectionism) to put individuals at an especially high risk for suicidal behavior (cf. Rasmussen, O'Connor, & Brodie, 2008). However, it is also likely that an overgeneral memory style plays an important proximal role in exacerbating suicidal crises, as it prevents suicidal individuals from accessing specific memories of past problems that could provide clues of how to solve their current problems (cf. Williams & Dritschel, 1988). Indeed, recent evidence suggests that the problem-solving abilities of formerly suicidal patients with an overgeneral memory style are especially reactive to a negative mood induction (Williams, Barnhofer, Crane, & Beck, 2005), which raises the possibility that these individuals will be ineffective in addressing their life problems when in a high level of distress. In addition, an inability to think specifically about the future could reinforce cognitions associated with hopelessness.

DICHOTOMOUS THINKING

Dichotomous thinking refers to the tendency to make extreme, polarized judgments, with little consideration given to information or evidence that might lead to a more balanced appraisal. Dichotomous thinking is reflected in instances in which an individual views his or her circumstances as "all good" or "all bad," ignoring the "shades of gray" in between (Neuringer, 1961). Neuringer (1961, 1967) raised the possibility that dichotomous thinking could increase suicide risk by limiting a person's ability to attend to evidence that does not support the view that one's future is hopeless or unbearable.

To test the notion that suicidal individuals are characterized by dichotomous thinking, Neuringer conducted a series of studies in which he compared suicidal patients, psychiatric control patients, and healthy volunteers in their performance on the Semantic Differential Task (Osgood, 1957). In this task, participants were presented with 18 provocative concepts (e.g., God, communism, shame, hate) and were instructed to rate the concepts along several scales reflecting Evaluation (e.g., good-bad, worthless-valuable), Activity (e.g., passive-active, fast-slow), and Potency (e.g., strong-weak, cold-hot). Participants received higher scores for responses that reflected the extreme ends of the poles. When making evaluative judgments, suicidal patients demonstrated a similar tendency as psychiatric controls to respond in an extreme manner, with both groups making more extreme judgments than healthy volunteers (e.g., Neuringer, 1961). However, when making judgments on the Activity and Potency scales, the ratings of suicidal patients were more extreme than those of both groups (e.g., Neuringer, 1967). Neuringer and Lettieri (1971) found that patients who were at the greatest risk for eventual suicide demonstrated more pronounced dichotomous thinking than patients who were at moderate and low risk for eventual suicide. Moreover, among the patients with the highest suicide risk, the degree of dichotomous thinking correlated positively with self-reported suicidal ideation. The tendency to engage in dichotomous thinking was demonstrated again over 20 years later, as Litinsky and Haslam (1998) found that suicidal patients exhibited higher rates of dichotomous thinking than nonsuicidal patients on the Thematic Apperception Test (Murray, 1943).

Overall, the results from these studies provide moderate evidence to support the notion that dichotomous thinking is particularly evident in suicidal individuals. It is likely that dichotomous thinking is not independent from impairment in problem solving, as dichotomous thinking has the potential to limit suicidal individuals from identifying and accurately evaluating multiple solutions to their life problems. We view dichotomous thinking as both a distal and proximal risk factor for suicidal behavior—distal in that it likely contributes to difficulties in solving life's problems and to the development of dysfunctional attitudes and beliefs; and proximal in that it could facilitate a fixation on suicide as the only option in the midst of severe distress.

Biases in Information Processing
FUTURE THINKING

Beginning in the 1990s, research was conducted to determine the precise components of hopelessness that are associated with suicidal ideation and recent suicidal behavior. Specifically, researchers were interested in determining whether people who experience high levels of hopelessness have excessively negative expectations for the future, lack positive expectations for the future, or both. To investigate this issue, A. K. MacLeod and Byrne (1996) developed the Future Thinking Task (FTT), in which participants were given 1 minute to generate as many positive future experiences as possible (i.e., experiences to which they were looking forward) and another minute to generate as many negative future experiences as possible (i.e., experiences to which they were not looking forward). Participants completed this task with three time frames in mind: the next week, including today; the next year; and the next 5–10 years. Scores on this task are the total number of responses in each condition, and scores can be aggregated to obtain a total score for positive future thinking and for negative future thinking. Although the FFT can be regarded as a measure of cognitive content, it is included in this section on information processing because the dependent variables represent the fluency with which future events are identified.

Studies that used this task with suicidal patients yielded remarkably consistent results. Relative to psychiatric controls and healthy controls, suicidal patients demonstrated impairment in generating positive expectations for the future; however, they did not differ from controls when generating negative expectations for the future (e.g., Conaghan & Davidson, 2002; A. K. MacLeod, Pankhanai, Lee, & Mitchell, 1997; A. K. MacLeod et al., 1998). This body of research demonstrates that positive future thinking, but not negative future thinking, is significantly associated with hopelessness (R. C. O'Connor, O'Connor, O'Connor, Smallwood, & Miles, 2004) and suicidal ideation (R. C. O'Connor et al., 2007). In fact, it shows that positive future thinking is a better predictor of suicidal ideation than hopelessness over a short follow-up period (i.e., 2 months; R. C. O'Connor, Fraser, Whyte, MacHale, & Masterson, 2008). The relation between positive future thinking and suicide potential is particularly strong in people who report high levels of life stress (R. C. O'Connor et al., 2004) and in those who endorse high levels of socially prescribed perfectionism (R. C. O'Connor et al., 2004; R. C. O'Connor et al., 2007). When suicidal individuals do identify positive expectancies for the future, such as goals, these expectancies are often nonspecific and associated with a host of

reasons why they will not be achieved (Vincent, Boddana, & MacLeod, 2004). Recent research suggests that impairments in future positive thinking are related to difficulties in generating positive expectancies for the self, but not for others (A. K. MacLeod & Conway, 2007), and may vary as a function of cognitive reactivity to minor changes in depressed mood (Williams, Van der Does, Barnhoffer, Crane, & Segal, 2008).

Like many of the constructs described in this chapter, we view deficits in positive future thinking as having both distal and proximal relevance in explaining suicidal behavior. People who have difficulty identifying positive events that they expect to occur in the future are likely to be at risk for developing other risk factors for suicidal behavior, such as a perception of hopelessness. However, in the midst of a suicidal crisis, we expect that those who have difficulty identifying positive future events would be at a particularly high risk for attempting suicide because they see few reasons for living or future events to which they can look forward.

ATTENTIONAL ALLOCATION

Attentional biases are observed when people direct their attention toward certain categories of stimuli at the expense of other categories of stimuli. This type of cognitive bias is theorized to maintain and exacerbate emotional distress because it activates cognitive structures that are unique to the pathology underlying the emotional distress (Becker, Strohbach, & Rinck, 1999). Three teams of investigators have used the Emotional Stroop Task to examine attentional biases toward suicide-relevant stimuli in suicidal and nonsuicidal patients (Becker et al., 1999; Cha, Sajmi, Park, Finn, & Nock, 2010; Williams & Broadbent, 1986b). In the Emotional Stroop Task, participants are presented with a variety of stimuli written in varying ink colors, and they are instructed to ignore the content of the stimulus and instead name the ink color. When participants with psychopathology demonstrate slowed color naming in response to stimuli consistent with their pathology, it is assumed that the content of the stimuli captured their attention away from the color-naming task at hand (C. M. MacLeod, 2005).

Results from all three of these studies indicated that suicidal patients (i.e., patients who had recently made a suicide attempt or who had made a suicide attempt at some point in their lives) demonstrated interference when naming the colors of suicide-relevant stimuli, such that suicidal patients took longer to name the ink colors of suicide-relevant words than to name the ink colors of neutral stimuli. This pattern of interference was not observed with generally negative stimuli. These results suggest that, once a person has made a suicide attempt, he or she is at an increased likelihood to detect suicide-relevant stimuli and to become distracted by them. Moreover, results from Cha et al. (2010) raise the possibility that the presence of an attentional bias toward suicide-relevant stimuli predicts suicide attempts above and beyond standard clinical predictors, such as a history of multiple attempts and severity of suicidal ideation.

The research described in this section characterizes attentional biases as a distal risk factor, as the patients in these studies were not necessarily in a suicidal crisis when they were completing the experimental task. They had either been in a suicidal crisis in the days and hours leading up to the experiment but were stabilized at the time of testing, or they had made a suicide attempt at some point in their lives but were not necessarily receiving treatment aimed at reducing their suicide risk. However, we also conceptualize attentional biases as a proximal risk factor that could facilitate a suicide act in times of acute distress (Wenzel et al., 2009).

IMPLICIT ASSOCIATIONS

The Implicit Association Test (IAT; Greenwald, McGhee, & Schwartz, 1998) is a computerized, reaction-time test to assess people's cognitions about sensitive topics that are not always captured adequately by self-report. Participants are oriented to two categories, each with bipolar anchors. One category is related to the construct of interest (e.g., life–death), and the other category is related to a judgment or attitude about the construct of interest (e.g., me–not me). During the task, participants are presented with stimuli that fall into one of these four domains (i.e., life, death, me, not me) and are asked to make a key press as quickly as possible to categorize the stimuli. Using this example, in one test block, participants would press the same key for both "death" and "me" (death = me) stimuli, and a different key for "life" and "not me" (life = not me) stimuli. In the second test block, the pairings are reversed, such that "death" and "not me" (death = not me) use the same key press, and "life" and "me" (life = me) use the same key press. According to Nock and Banaji (2007), "the IAT rests on the assumption that it should be easier to make the same behavioral response (i.e., a key press) to concepts that are strongly associated relative to concepts that are weakly associated" (p. 709). That

is, it would be expected that suicidal participants would more quickly classify suicide-relevant stimuli when they would have to press the key that is associated with "me" than when they would have to press the key that is associated with "not me." Such findings would provide evidence that suicidal individuals have strong cognitive associations between indicators of the self and indicators of suicidality.

Several studies have demonstrated that this pattern of results indeed emerges. Nock and Banaji (2007) used an IAT that included images of self-injury and neutral images (e.g., pictures of non-injured skin) and self-relevant and other-relevant words (i.e., me–not me). They found that adolescents who had made a suicide attempt in the past year demonstrated a strong positive association between self-injury and themselves; that adolescents reporting suicidal ideation in the past year demonstrated a small positive association between self-injury and themselves; and that nonsuicidal adolescents demonstrated a strong negative association between self-injury and themselves. Moreover, performance in this IAT predicted suicidal ideation and attempts in the past year as well as suicidal ideation 6 months later above and beyond established demographic (e.g., age) and psychiatric (e.g., presence of a mood disorder, prior ideation, or attempt) variables. In a subsequent study, Price, Nock, Charney, and Mathew (2009) found that patients with treatment-resistant depression exhibited a reduction in the strength of escape = me associations after being given a dose of intravenous ketamine (i.e., a glutamate-modulating agent that substantially reduces depressive symptoms approximately 24 hours after intravenous administration) and that reductions in the escape = me associations correlated with reductions in self-report measures of suicidal ideation. Moreover, Nock et al. (2010) reported that death = me associations were more pronounced among a sample of suicide attempters who were admitted to the emergency department than among people who presented to the emergency department for other reasons. The presence of implicit associations with death predicted reattempts 6 months later above and beyond variables such as the presence of a depressive disorder, a history of multiple attempts, suicidal ideation reported at baseline, and the clinician's and patient's predictions of reattempt.

This small body of literature provides convincing evidence that identification with suicide-relevant variables, such as self-injury, escape, and death, is an objective marker of suicidal behavior. Suicidal individuals have a strong cognitive network of associations between their self-representation and suicidal stimuli, which means that they are more likely than nonsuicidal individuals to call these associations from memory and direct their attention toward them. It is possible that these implicit associations increase the likelihood that (and the speed at which) a person experiences suicidal ideation when he or she experiences emotional distress. Although the research on suicide-relevant implicit associations to date suggests that they are a distal risk factor for suicidal behavior, it is likely that they serve as proximal risk factors for suicidal behavior when they are activated in the midst of emotional distress.

Summary

People who have engaged in suicidal behavior or who have received treatment for suicidal ideation demonstrate a tendency to engage in dichotomous thinking, an impaired ability to retrieve specific personal memories, the inability to identify positive future experiences, a bias in the direction of their attentional allocation, and self-identification with suicide-relevant stimuli. It is likely that many of these information processing distortions and biases contribute to the inability to solve problems effectively. It will be important for future research to determine the manner in which these information processing biases work in conjunction with the cognitive variables described earlier in the chapter to explain suicidal thoughts and behaviors. Some research shows that hopelessness mediates the association between problem-solving deficits and suicidal ideation (Dixon et al., 1994; Orbach et al., 2007), which raises the possibility that some of the suicide-relevant cognitive contents are activated in response to information processing impairments and the stress that they cause. Other research shows that some of the information processing distortions and biases are especially pronounced in people with socially prescribed perfectionism (e.g., R. C. O'Connor et al., 2007; Rasmussen et al., 2008), and that the combination of this cognitive content variable with the information processing distortions are associated with the greatest risk of suicidal ideation. Future research must disentangle whether the influences of these cognitive variables are additive, whether they affect one another in a bidirectional manner, and whether these variables co-occur because of a third factor (e.g., depression).

The research described in this section supports the conceptualization of these information processing impairments and biases as distal risk factors for suicidal behavior, as most patients exhibited them when they were not currently in a suicidal crisis. It is possible that these impairments and biases exert their distal effects by increasing the likelihood that suicide-relevant cognitive contents are activated. However, as we stated in each individual section, we also view these variables as proximal risk factors for the engagement in suicidal behavior during times of acute distress. It is not difficult to imagine that problem-solving impairments, dichotomous thinking, overgeneral memory style, difficulty in identifying positive future events, attentional biases toward suicide-relevant cues, and the rapid association of the self with suicide-relevant constructs would make it difficult for suicidal individuals to see solutions other than self-injury to their problems and emotional pain.

These information processing variables are valuable because they shed light on the cognitive mechanisms that lead to suicidal behavior. In conjunction with the cognitive content variables, they have the potential to provide a rich conceptualization of the clinical presentations of suicidal patients. However, to date, most of these variables have been examined cross-sectionally, such that suicidal patients or individuals at high risk for suicide are compared with nonsuicidal patients or individuals at lower risk for suicide. Prospective research, like that conducted by Nock and his colleagues (Cha et al., 2010; Nock & Banaji, 2007; Nock et al., 2010), is needed to verify that these variables predict future suicidal acts independently of established risk factors, such as depression, and identify the precise amount of variance for which they can account in explaining suicidal behavior.

Cognitive Theories of Suicidal Behavior

A number of recent cognitive theories of suicidal behavior have recently been proposed, all of which incorporate a subset of the cognitive content domains and information processing variables described in this chapter. In this section, we highlight four of these cognitive models: (a) Joiner's (2005) interpersonal-psychological theory, (b) William's (2001) cry of pain model, (c) Rudd's (2006) fluid vulnerability mode, and (d) Wenzel et al.'s (2009) cognitive model of suicidal acts.

Interpersonal-Psychological Theory of Suicidal Behavior

Joiner's (2005) elegant interpersonal-psychological theory indicates that people will engage in suicidal behavior when they have the desire to die as well as the ability to enact lethal self-harm. Joiner conceptualized the desire to die as consisting of two of the cognitive content areas described earlier in the chapter: perceived burdensomeness and a low sense of belonging. The capacity to enact lethal self-harm is acquired over time when a person has repeated experiences involving pain and injury, thereby eroding the self-preservation instinct. The most direct way a person acquires the ability to enact lethal self-harm is by previous self-injurious behavior; however, this capacity also can be acquired by experiencing accidental injuries, combat experience, and having repeated exposure to pain and injury (e.g., as a medical professional).

Joiner's research group has conducted systematic empirical research on this model, and data supporting its main tenets are rapidly accumulating. For instance, Van Orden, Witte, Gordon, et al. (2008) found that the interaction between perceived burdensomeness and low belongingness predicted suicidal ideation in undergraduate research participants above and beyond depression. Joiner et al. (2009) replicated this finding among a larger, more diverse community sample of young adults, although it should be acknowledged that they used proxy measures of perceived burdensomeness and low belongingness (i.e., a self-report measure of the manner in which respondents think others feel about them, a self-report measure of family social support). Van Orden, Witte, Gordon, et al. (2008) also verified that a lifetime history of suicide attempts and engaging in painful, provocative, and impulsive behaviors was associated with a higher capacity to engage in lethal self-harm and that perceived burdensomeness interacted with the acquired capacity to engage in lethal self-harm to predict clinician-rated suicide risk. The measure of the ability to engage in lethal self-harm did not, in itself, predict clinician-rated suicide risk; it only exerted its effect in the context of a strong desire to die, as represented by perceived burdensomeness. This finding verifies Joiner's (2005) assertion that it is the confluence of these factors, rather than any factor alone, that increases the probability that a person will engage in suicidal behavior.

The critical test of the model was conducted by Joiner et al. (2009), who examined whether a three-way interaction between perceived burdensomeness, low belongingness, and a lifetime number of suicide attempts predicted suicide attempt status in a sample of participants who were referred for a recent attempt or for severe suicidal ideation. The expected three-way interaction was observed, even while controlling for a host of demographic variables (e.g., age, gender), family history of suicide, current and past diagnoses of depression and bipolar disorder, depressive symptoms, hopelessness, and features of borderline personality disorder. Joiner's (2005) theory holds significant clinical implications, as it points to three concrete variables that can be assessed by clinicians as they are conducting suicide risk assessments.

Cry of Pain Model

The cry of pain (CoP) model (Williams, 2001) was developed to extend Baumeister's (1990) widely cited escape theory of suicide by including other key components to explain suicidal behavior. According to the CoP model, there is an increased likelihood of suicidal behavior when people experience stressful or negative life events associated with four psychological characteristics. First, the individual experiences a sense of defeat and loss. Second, the individual cannot escape the situation, oftentimes because of poor problem solving. As a result, the person views himself or herself as trapped. Third, the person has little hope for rescue, which further reinforces the perception of entrapment. Variables associated with rescue include a strong social support network and the ability to engage in positive future thinking. Fourth, the perception of entrapment induces learned helplessness, which promotes beliefs that the person will not be able to change his or her life experiences. The "cry" is the suicidal act in which the person engages as a reaction to his or her painful life circumstances and psychological state (Williams & Pollock, 2001). Thus, the CoP model incorporates both cognitive content variables (e.g., perceptions of entrapment) as well as information processing variables (e.g., problem-solving deficits, impairment in positive future thinking).

Like Joiner's (2005) model, the CoP model is attractive because of its parsimony and the increasing amount of data in its support. For example, R. C. O'Connor (2003) indicated that patients hospitalized for parasuicide endorsed higher levels of defeat, lower levels of escapability, lower levels of emotional/informational social support, and lower levels of positive social interaction as compared to a matched group of patients who were hospitalized for physical problems. A logistic regression, including depression, hopelessness, and the CoP variables (i.e., defeat, escape potential, social support), correctly classified 90% of the patients. In fact, defeat, social support, and the interaction of escape potential and social support were the only significant variables in the regression, suggesting that they were more important than depression and hopelessness in differentiating between parasuicidal patients and hospital controls. Subsequently, Rasmussen et al. (2010) determined that the CoP variables discriminated between first-time versus repeat self-harm patients. Moreover, there is experimental evidence to suggest that experiencing a defeating event increases self-reports of defeat and in turn impairs episodic memory (Johnson, Tarrier, & Gooding, 2008). This finding raises the possibility of an association between the CoP variables and an overgeneral memory style in the genesis of suicidal behavior.

Fluid Vulnerability Theory

Rudd's (2006) fluid vulnerability theory (FVT) was developed to explain the risk for and process of suicidal crises in individual suicidal acts and the manner in which they relate to future suicidal acts. At the heart of this theory is the activation of the *suicidal mode*, which is defined as interwoven suicide-relevant beliefs, physiological symptoms, emotions, behaviors, and motivations (Rudd, 2000). According to Rudd, suicidal episodes occur when the suicidal mode is activated, which results in expressions such as core cognitive contents (i.e., unlovability, helplessness, poor distress tolerance, perceived burdensomeness), acute dysphoria, physiological arousal, and suicide-relevant behaviors. Future suicidal episodes are triggered when one or more of these aspects of the suicidal mode are activated by what Rudd calls an "aggravating event," which is essentially an internal or external stressor. When the aggravating event has resolved, the suicidal mode is deactivated, and acute risk subsides. The key prediction from this model is that people who are at risk of repeat suicide attempts have higher baseline risk levels, and aspects of their suicidal mode are triggered more easily than in people who are not at risk to engage in repeat suicide attempts.

Although we know of no research that has been conducted specifically to test the FVT, several of its tenets have a basis in cognitive theory (e.g., Beck, 1996). Moreover, a great deal of empirical research supports the notion that multiple attempters more easily enter into suicidal crises and are characterized by more suicide-relevant risk factors than single attempters and nonattempters (Joiner & Rudd, 2000; Rudd, Joiner, & Rajab, 1996). As described earlier in the chapter, research on many of the core cognitive content domains identified in FVT is well established. It will be important for future research

to characterize empirically the precise nature of the affective and behavioral domains and the manner in which they interact with the cognitive domain to facilitate suicidal behavior.

Cognitive Model of Suicidal Acts

Our research group developed a cognitive model of suicidal acts to reflect the facts that (a) several psychological variables have been documented in the empirical literature to increase the risk of suicidal behavior; (b) the vast majority of suicidal individuals are diagnosed with a psychiatric disorder, and there are important cognitive processes associated with psychiatric disorders that have the potential to increase the risk of suicidal behavior; and (c) there are likely several cognitive variables at work during suicidal crises that contribute to the actual decision to make a suicide attempt (Wenzel & Beck, 2008; Wenzel et al., 2009). First, we regard the psychological variables demonstrated in the literature to increase the risk of suicidal behavior as *dispositional vulnerability factors*. In most cases, these variables are insufficient to prompt suicidal crises in and of themselves. However, we propose that they increase the risk of suicidal behavior in three ways: (a) by exacerbating psychiatric symptoms, (b) by creating unnecessary life stress, and (c) by distorting cognitive processes at work during suicidal crises. All of the cognitive constructs described in this chapter can be regarded as dispositional vulnerability factors. Second, any cognitive model of suicidal behavior must account for the fact that 90% or more of people who attempt or die by suicide are diagnosed with at least one psychiatric disorder (Beautrais et al., 1996; Bertolote, Fleischmann, De Leo, & Wasserman, 2003; Suominen et al., 1996). There is a long history of research suggesting that psychiatric disorders are characterized by maladaptive *schemas*, or cognitive structures that influence the cognitive contents and biases in the information processing of people who suffer from these disorders. We propose that when maladaptive schemas gain sufficient strength (e.g., in the instance of a severe Axis I disorder or comorbid Axis I or Axis II disorders), there is an increased likelihood that a schema associated with suicidal thoughts and behaviors will be activated. When people who engage in suicidal behavior are not diagnosed with a psychiatric disorder, it is likely that they have an especially high loading on several dispositional vulnerability factors (see R. C. O'Connor, 2009, for a similar conceptualization).

Thus, we propose that a suicide schema can be activated when (a) maladaptive schemas associated with psychiatric disorders gain sufficient strength, (b) one or more dispositional vulnerability factors are particularly pronounced and cause substantial life stress, or (c) both. When a suicide schema is activated, there is a high likelihood that a person will enter into a suicidal crisis when he or she faces additional life stress or disappointment. Cognitive processes at work during a suicidal crisis include (a) a state of hopelessness, unbearability, or desperation; (b) attentional biases toward suicide-relevant cues; (c) difficulty disengaging from suicide-relevant cues; (d) narrowed attentional focus on suicide as the only option (i.e., attentional fixation); and (e) acute suicidal ideation. The individual makes a suicide attempt when the confluence of these cognitive processes passes a critical threshold, called the *threshold of tolerance*. The threshold varies between individuals and even changes at different periods in a person's life, depending on one's previous history of self-injurious behavior, the acquisition of strategies to tolerate distress, and social support.

As is described in this chapter, much empirical research supports the notion that dispositional vulnerability factors increase the risk of suicidal behavior. There is also a great deal of research supporting the notion that psychiatric disorders are associated with increased risk of suicidal behavior, although the cognitive mechanism by which this occurs has not yet been subject to empirical scrutiny. In contrast, there is a paucity of research that has identified the psychological mechanisms that lead to suicide attempts in the midst of acute distress or suicidal crises. Thus, a strength of this model is that it incorporates well-documented constructs that are known to increase the risk of suicidal behavior. However the model's weakness is that the precise mechanisms at work during suicidal crises are largely theoretical at this time.

Summary

All four of the models of suicidal behavior reviewed in this section advance our understanding of cognitive events associated with suicidal acts. We do not view these theories as mutually exclusive, but rather as explaining important aspects of a multifaceted behavioral expression. Joiner's (2005) interpersonal-psychological theory of suicidal behavior and Williams's (2001) CoP model are the most parsimonious models, have the most empirical support for their core tenets, and include constructs that are the most targeted toward suicidal behavior, rather than psychiatric disorders in general. Rudd's (2006) FVT acknowledges the accumulation of

risk factors and the ease by which suicidal crises are activated as a function of these risk factors. The cognitive model developed by our research group (Wenzel et al., 2009) accounts for psychological factors associated with increased risk that have been identified in the empirical literature, conceptualizes increased risk in light of the presence of psychiatric disorders, and speculates about the cognitive processes that take place in the midst of a suicidal crisis.

One might regard the three constructs in Joiner's (2005) model—perceived burdensomeness, low belongingness, and the acquired ability to enact lethal self-harm—as the three most specific dispositional vulnerability factors that serve as distal risk factors for suicidal behavior. In addition, the constructs in Williams's (2001) CoP model have the potential to characterize the mechanism through which distal risk factors activate Rudd's (2006) suicidal mode. That is, it is possible that a person characterized by perceived burdensomeness, low belongingness, and the acquired ability to enact lethal self-harm is especially sensitive to perceptions of defeat, entrapment, and learned helplessness in the context of stressful or disappointing negative life events. These psychological constructs have the potential to activate a suicidal mode, at which point the cognitive processes that our group proposed to characterize suicidal behavior (e.g., attentional fixation) are put into action. Empirical research is needed to test this notion. Nevertheless, we raise the possibility that there are different levels of constructs that contribute to suicidal behavior—those that pose distal risk, those that form an intermediate level between distal risk and a suicidal crisis, and those that pose proximal risk in the context of acute distress—and that the constructs associated with the theories described in this section fall into one or more of these tiers and work in combination to put people at risk for suicidal behavior.

Conclusion and Future Directions

The literature on cognitive variables associated with suicidal behavior originated with the foresight of Charles Neuringer and has expanded profusely over the past decade. We now know that suicidal individuals are particularly likely to have perceptions of hopelessness, socially prescribed perfectionism, burdensomeness, low belongingness, and unbearability. We also know that many suicidal individuals have difficulty generating solutions to problems, low confidence in their problem-solving abilities, an overgeneral memory style, a tendency to engage in dichotomous thinking, difficulty generating positive events that they expect to occur in the future, attentional biases toward suicide-relevant stimuli, and implicit associations between suicide-relevant concepts and their self-identity. Research is beginning to show that these cognitive constructs do not exist in isolation; for example, people with an overgeneral memory style exhibit problem-solving deficits and difficulty identifying positive future events. More research is needed to (a) identify the interactions between and causal effects of these variables in order to determine more precisely the mechanism that underlies suicidal behavior, (b) identify the specific distal and proximal functions associated with these variables, and (c) determine the longitudinal course of these variables and the manner in which they predict suicidal behavior. Moreover, research is sorely needed to identify the sequence of psychological events that underlie acute suicidal crises. For example, research by Fawcett and colleagues has shown that people who attempt suicide while they are hospitalized exhibited agitation in the 7 days preceding the attempt (Busch, Clark, & Fawcett, 1993; Busch, Fawcett, & Jacobs, 2003). That is, it is possible that agitation could be the affective-behavioral expression of cognitive processes at work in acute suicidal crises.

Investigations of the risk factors for suicidal behavior have been conducted for the past half century. Nevertheless, the prediction of suicide remains elusive, and clinicians and survivors alike are often at a loss to answer the question of why a particular person engages in suicidal behavior. The cognitive variables and models described in this chapter have the potential to provide a richer understanding of suicidal behavior than we have had in the past, as they not only distinguish between suicidal and non-suicidal individuals, but they also capture aspects of the internal psychological processes of suicidal individuals. Moreover, unlike variables relevant to the demographic profiles and psychiatric histories of suicidal individuals, cognitive variables are amenable to modification through treatment. Thus, continued investigation into the cognitive characteristics of suicidal individuals has the potential to provide clinicians and families with a meaningful psychological profile of their patients or loved ones and specific points for prevention and intervention.

References

Arie, M., Apter, A., Orbach, I., Yefet, Y., & Zalman, G. (2008). Autobiographical memory, interpersonal problem solving, and suicidal behavior in adolescent inpatients. *Comprehensive Psychiatry, 49*, 22–29.

Baumeister, R. F. (1990). Suicide as escape from self. *Psychological Review, 97*, 90–113.

Beautais, A. L., Joyce, P. R., Mulder, R. T., Fergusson, D. M., Deavoll, B. J., & Nightengale, S. K. (1996). Prevalence and comorbidity of mental disorders in persons making serious suicide attempts: A case-control study. *American Journal of Psychiatry, 153*, 1009–1014.

Beck, A. T. (1963). Thinking and depression: I. Idiosyncratic content and cognitive distortions. *Archives of General Psychiatry, 9*, 324–333.

Beck, A. T. (1970). *Depression: Causes and treatment.* Philadelphia: University of Pennsylvania Press.

Beck, A. T. (1996). Beyond belief: A theory of modes, personality, and psychopathology. In P. Salkovskis (Ed.), *Frontiers of cognitive therapy* (pp. 1–25). New York, NY: Guilford Press.

Beck, A. T., Brown, G., Berchick, R. J., Stewart, B. L., & Steer, R. A. (1990). Relationship between hopelessness and ultimate suicide: A replication with psychiatric outpatients. *American Journal of Psychiatry, 147*, 190–195.

Beck, A. T., Brown, G., & Steer, R. A. (1989). Prediction of eventual suicide in psychiatric inpatients by clinical ratings of hopelessness. *Journal of Consulting and Clinical Psychology, 57*, 309–310.

Beck, A. T., Steer, R. A., & Brown, G. (1993). Dysfunctional attitudes and suicidal ideation in psychiatric outpatients. *Suicide and Life-Threatening Behavior, 23*, 11–20.

Beck, A. T., Steer, R. A., Kovacs, M., & Garrison, B. (1985). Hopelessness and eventual suicide: A 10-year prospective study of patients hospitalized with suicidal ideation. *American Journal of Psychiatry, 142*, 559–563.

Beck, A. T., Weissman, A., Lester, D., & Trexler, L. (1974). The measurement of pessimism: The Hopelessness Scale. *Journal of Consulting and Clinical Psychology, 42*, 861–865.

Becker, E. S., Strohbach, D., & Rinck, M. (1999). A specific attentional bias in suicide attempters. *Journal of Nervous and Mental Disease, 187*, 730–735.

Beevers, C. G., & Miller, I. W. (2004). Perfectionism, cognitive bias, and hopelessness as prospective predictors of suicidal ideation. *Suicide and Life-Threatening Behavior, 34*, 126–137.

Bertolote, J. M., Fleischmann, A., De Leo, D., & Wasserman, D. (2003). Suicide and mental disorders: Do we know enough? *British Journal of Psychiatry, 183*, 382–383.

Biller, O. A. (1977). Suicide related to the assassination of the President John F. Kennedy. *Suicide and Life-Threatening Behavior, 7*, 40–44.

Bonner, R. L., & Rich, A. R. (1987). Toward a predictive model of suicidal ideation and behavior: Some preliminary data in college students. *Suicide and Life-Threatening Behavior, 17*, 50–63.

Brenner, L. A., Gutierrez, P. M., Cornette, M. M., Betthauser, L. M., Bahraini, N., & Staves, P. J. (2008). A qualitative study of potential suicide risk factors in returning combat veterans. *Journal of Mental Health Counseling, 30*, 211–225.

Brown, R. M., Dahlen, E., Mills, C., Rick, J., & Biblarz, A. (1999). Evaluation of an evolutionary model of self-preservation and self-destruction. *Suicide and Life-Threatening Behavior, 29*, 58–71.

Busch, K. A., Clark, D. C., & Fawcett, J. (1993). Clinical features of inpatient suicide. *Psychiatric Annals, 23*, 256–262.

Busch, K. A., Fawcett, J., & Jacobs, D. G. (2003). Clinical correlates of inpatient suicide. *Journal of Clinical Psychiatry, 64*, 14–19.

Cha, C. B., Najmi, S., Park, J. M., Finn, C. T., & Nock, M. K. (2010). Attentional bias toward suicide-related stimuli predicts suicidal behavior. *Journal of Abnormal Psychology, 119,* 616–622.

Chang, E. C. (1998). Cultural differences, perfectionism, and suicidal risk in a college population: Does social problem solving still matter? *Cognitive Therapy and Research, 22,* 237–254.

Chang, E. C. (2002). Examining the link between perfectionism and psychological maladjustment: Social problem solving as a buffer. *Cognitive Therapy and Research, 26,* 581–595.

Chang, E. C., Watkins, A., & Banks, K. H. (2004). How adaptive and maladaptive perfectionism relate to positive and negative psychological functioning: Testing a stress-mediation model in black and white female college students. *Journal of Counseling Psychology, 51,* 93–102.

Conaghan, S., & Davidson, K. M. (2002). Hopelessness and the anticipation of positive and negative future experiences in older parasuicidal adults. *British Journal of Clinical Psychology, 41,* 233–242.

Conner, K. R., Britton, P. C., Sworts, L. M., & Joiner, T. E., Jr. (2007). Suicide attempts among individuals with opiate dependence: The critical role of belonging. *Addictive Behaviors, 32,* 1395–1404.

Conner, K. R., Duberstein, P. R., & Conwell, Y. (1999). Age-related patterns of factors associated with completed suicide in men with alcohol dependence. *American Journal on Addictions, 8,* 312–318.

Conway, M. A., & Pleydell-Pearce, C. W. (2000). The construction of autobiographical memories in the self-memory system. *Psychological Review, 107,* 261–288.

DeCatanzaro, D. (1991). Evolutionary limits to self-preservation. *Ethology and Sociobiology, 12,* 13–28.

DeCatanzaro, D. (1995). Reproductive status, family interactions, and suicidal ideation: Surveys of the general public and high-risk groups. *Ethology and Sociobiology, 16,* 385–394.

Dean, P. J., & Range, L. M. (1999). Testing the escape theory of suicide in an outpatient clinical population. *Cognitive Therapy and Research, 23,* 561–572.

Dean, P. J., Range, L. M., & Groggin, W. C. (1996). The escape theory of suicide in college students: Testing a model that includes perfectionism. *Suicide and Life-Threatening Behavior, 26,* 181–186.

Dennis, M. S., Wakefield, P., Molloy, C., Andrews, H., & Friedman, T. (2007). A study of self-harm in older people: Mental disorder, social factors and motives. *Aging and Mental Health, 11,* 520–525.

Dieserud, G., Roysamb, E., Braverman, M. T., Dalgard, O. S., & Ekeberg, O. (2003). Predicting repetition of suicide attempt: A prospective study of 50 suicide attempters. *Archives of Suicide Research, 7,* 1–15.

Dixon, W. A., Heppner, P. P., & Anderson, W. P. (1991). Problem-solving appraisal, stress, hopelessness, and suicide ideation in a college population. *Journal of Counseling Psychology, 38,* 51–56.

Dixon, W. A., Heppner, P. P., & Rudd, M. D. (1994). Problem-solving appraisal, hopelessness, and suicide ideation: Evidence for a mediational model. *Journal of Counseling Psychology, 41,* 91–98.

Dunkley, D. M., Blankstein, K. R., Masheb, R. M., & Grilo, C. M. (2006). Personal standards and evaluative concerns dimensions of "clinical" perfectionism: A reply to Safren et al. (2002, 2003) and Hewitt et al. (2003). *Behaviour Research and Therapy, 44,* 63–84.

Durkheim, E. (1951). *Suicide.* New York, NY: Free Press.

Enns, M. W., Cox, B. J., & Inayatulla, M. (2003). Personality predictors of outcome for adolescents hospitalized for suicidal ideation. *Journal of the American Academy of Child and Adolescent Psychiatry, 42,* 720–727.

Enns, M. W., Cox, B. J., Sareen, J., & Freeman, P. (2001). Adaptive and maladaptive perfectionism in medical students: A longitudinal investigation. *Medical Education, 35,* 1034–1042.

Evans, J., Williams, J. M., O'Loughlin, S., & Howells, K. (1992). Autobiographical memory and problem-solving strategies of parasuicide patients. *Psychological Medicine, 22,* 399–405.

Flamenbaum, R., & Holden, R. R. (2007). Psychache as a mediator in the relationship between perfectionism and suicidality. *Journal of Counseling Psychology, 54,* 51–61.

Gibb, B. E., Alloy, L. B., Abramson, L. Y., Rose, D. T., Whitehouse, W. G., & Hogan, M. E. (2001). Childhood maltreatment and college students' current suicidal ideation: A test of the hopelessness theory. *Suicide and Life-Threatening Behavior, 31,* 405–415.

Goldstein, R. B., Black, D. W., Nasrallah, A., & Winokur, G. (1991). The prediction of suicide: Sensitivity, specificity, and predictive value of a multivariate model applied to suicide among 1906 patients with affective disorders. *Archives of General Psychiatry, 48,* 418–422.

Greenwald, A. G., McGhee, D. E., & Schwartz,, J. L. (1998). Measuring individual differences in implicit cognition: The implicit association test. *Journal of Personality and Social Psychology, 74,* 1464–1480.

Haring, M., Hewitt, P. L., & Flett, G. L. (2003). Perfectionism and the quality of intimate relationships. *Journal of Marriage and the Family, 65,* 143–158.

Hewitt, P. L., & Flett, G. L. (1991). Perfectionism in the self and social contexts: Conceptualization, assessment, and association with psychopathology. *Journal of Personality and Social Psychology, 60,* 456–470.

Hewitt, P. L., Flett, G. L., Sherry, S. B., & Caelian, C. (2006). Trait perfectionism dimensions and suicidal behavior. In T. E. Ellis (Ed.), *Cognition and suicide: Theory, research, and therapy* (pp. 215–235). Washington, DC: APA Books.

Hewitt, P. L., Flett, G. L., & Turnbull-Donovan, W. (1992). Perfectionism and suicide potential. *British Journal of Clinical Psychology, 31,* 181–190.

Hewitt, P. L., Flett, G. L., & Weber, C. (1994). Perfectionism, hopelessness, and suicide ideation. *Cognitive Therapy and Research, 18,* 439–460.

Hewitt, P. L., Norton, G. R., Flett, G. L., Callender, L., & Cowan, T. (1998). Dimensions of perfectionism, hopelessness, and attempted suicide in a sample of adolescents. *Suicide and Life-Threatening Behavior, 28,* 395–406.

Imber, S. D., Pilkonis, P. A., Sotsky, S. M., Elkin, I., Watkins, J. T., Collins, J. F., ... Glass, D. R. (1990). Mode-specific effects among three treatments for depression. *Journal of Consulting and Clinical Psychology, 58,* 352–359.

Ingram, R. E., & Kendall, P. C. (1986). Cognitive clinical psychology: Implications of an information processing perspective. In R. E. Ingram (Ed.), *Information processing approaches to clinical psychology* (pp. 3–21). San Diego, CA: Academic Press.

Jeglic, E. L., Sharp, I. R., Chapman, J. E., Brown, G. K., & Beck, A. T. (2005). History of family suicide behaviors and negative problem solving in multiple suicide attempters. *Archives of Suicide Research, 9,* 135–146.

Johnson, J., Tarrier, N., & Gooding, P. (2008). An investigation of aspects of the cry of pain model of suicide risk: The role of defeat in impairing memory. *Behaviour Research and Therapy*, *46*, 968–975.

Joiner, T. (2005). *Why people die by suicide*. Cambridge, MA: Harvard University Press.

Joiner, T. E., Brown, J. S., & Wingate, L. R. (2005). The psychology and neurobiology of suicidal behavior. *Annual Review of Psychology*, *56*, 287–314.

Joiner, T. E., Jr., Hollar, D., & Van Orden, K. A. (2006). On Buckeyes, Gators, Super Bowl Sunday, and the Miracle on Ice: "Pulling together" is associated with lower suicide rates. *Journal of Social and Clinical Psychology*, *25*, 180–196.

Joiner, T. E., Pettit, J. W., Walker, R. L., Voelz, Z. R., Cruz, J., Rudd, M. D., & Lester, D. (2002). Perceived burdensomeness and suicidality: Two studies on the suicide notes of those attempting and those completing suicide. *Journal of Social and Clinical Psychology*, *21*, 531–545.

Joiner, T. E., Jr., & Rudd, M. D. (2000). Intensity and duration of suicidal crises vary as a function of previous suicide attempts and negative life events. *Journal of Consulting and Clinical Psychology*, *68*, 909–916.

Joiner, T. E., Jr., Van Orden, K. A., Witte, T. K., Selby, E. A., Riberio, J. D., Lewis, R., & Rudd, M. D. (2009). Main predictions of the interpersonal-psychological theory of suicidal behavior: Empirical tests in two samples of young adults. *Journal of Abnormal Psychology*, *118*, 634–646.

Kaviani, H., Rahmimi-Darabad, P., & Naghavi, H. R. (2005). Autobiographical memory retrieval and problem solving deficits of Iranian depressed patients attempting suicide. *Journal of Psychopathology and Behavioral Assessment*, *27*, 39–44.

Kienhorst, I. C. W. M., De Wilde, E. J., Diekstra, R. F. W., & Wolters, W. H. G. (1995). Adolescents' image of their suicide attempt. *Journal of the American Academy of Child and Adolescent Psychiatry*, *34*, 623–628.

Klibert, J. J., Langhinrichsen-Rohling, J., & Saito, M. (2005). Adaptive and maladaptive aspects of self-oriented versus socially prescribed perfectionism. *Journal of College Student Development*, *46*, 141–156.

Kposowa, A. J. (2000). Marital status and suicide in the National Longitudinal Mortality Study. *Journal of Epidemiology and Community Health*, *54*, 254–261.

Leibetseder, M. M., Rohrer, R. R., Mackinger, H. F., & Fartacek, R. R. (2006). Suicide attempts: Patients with and without an affective disorder show impaired autobiographical memory specificity. *Cognition and Emotion*, *20*, 516–526.

Linehan, M. M., Camper, P., Chiles, J. A., Strosahl, K., & Shearin, E. N. (1987). Interpersonal problem solving and parasuicide. *Cognitive Therapy and Research*, *11*, 1–12.

Litinsky, A. M., & Haslam, N. (1998). Dichotomous thinking as a sign of suicide risk on the TAT. *Journal of Personality Assessment*, *71*, 368–378.

MacLeod, A. K., & Byrne, A. (1996). Anxiety, depression, and the anticipation of future positive and negative experiences. *Journal of Abnormal Psychology*, *105*, 286–289.

MacLeod, A. K., & Conway, C. (2007). Well-being and positive future thinking for the self versus others. *Cognition and Emotion*, *21*, 1114–1124.

MacLeod, A. K., Pankhania, B., Lee, M., & Mitchell, D. (1997). Parasuicide, depression and the anticipation of positive and negative future experiences. *Psychological Medicine*, *27*, 973–977.

MacLeod, A. K., Tata, P., Evans, K., Tyrer, P., Schmidt, U., Davidson, K., . . . Catalan, J. (1998). Recovery of positive future thinking within a high-risk parasuicide group: Results from a pilot randomized controlled trial. *British Journal of Clinical Psychology*, *37*, 371–379.

MacLeod, C. M. (2005). The Stroop task in cognitive research. In A. Wenzel & D. C. Rubin (Eds.), *Cognitive methods and their application to clinical research* (pp. 17–40). Washington, DC: APA Books.

McMillan, D., Gilbody, S., Beresford, E., & Neilly, L. (2007). Can we predict suicide and non-fatal self-harm with the Beck Hopelessness Scale? A meta-analysis. *Psychological Medicine*, *37*, 769–778.

Meadows, L. A., & Kaslow, N. J. (2002). Hopelessness as mediator of the link between reports of a history of child maltreatment and suicidality in African American women. *Cognitive Therapy and Research*, *26*, 657–674.

Michel, K., Valach, L., & Waeber, V. (1994). Understanding deliberate self-harm: The patients' views. *Crisis*, *15*, 172–178, 186.

Minkoff, K., Bergman, E., Beck, A. T., & Beck, R. (1973). Hopelessness, depression, and attempted suicide. *American Journal of Psychiatry*, *130*, 455–459.

Mościcki, E. K. (1999). Epidemiology of suicide. In D. G. Jacobs (Ed.), *The Harvard Medical School guide to suicide assessment intervention* (pp. 40–51). San Francisco, CA: Jossey-Bass.

Murray, H. A. (1943). *Thematic apperception test*. Cambridge, MA: Harvard University Press.

Neuringer, C. (1961). Dichotomous evaluations in suicidal individuals. *Journal of Consulting Psychology*, *25*, 445–449.

Neuringer, C. (1967). The cognitive organization of meaning in suicidal individuals. *Journal of General Psychology*, *76*, 91–100.

Neuringer, C. (1988). The thinking processes in suicidal women. In D. Lester (Ed.), *Why women kill themselves* (pp. 43–52). Springfield, IL: Charles C. Thomas.

Neuringer, C., & Lettieri, D. L. (1971). Cognition, attitude, and affect in suicidal individuals. *Life-Threatening Behavior*, *1*, 106–124.

Nock, M. K., & Banaji, M. R. (2007). Prediction of suicide ideation and attempts among adolescents using a brief performance-based test. *Journal of Consulting and Clinical Psychology*, *75*, 707–715.

Nock, M. K., Park, J. L., Finn, C. T., Deliberto, T. L., Dour, H. J., & Banaji, M. R. (2010). Measuring the "suicidal mind:" Implicit cognition predicts suicidal behavior. *Psychological Science*, *21*, 511–517.

O'Connor, D. B., O'Connor, R. C., & Marshall, R. (2007). Perfectionism and psychological distress: Evidence of the mediating effects of rumination. *European Journal of Personality*, *21*, 429–452.

O'Connor, R. C. (2003). Suicidal behavior as a cry of pain: Test of a psychological model. *Archives of Suicide Research*, *7*, 297–308.

O'Connor, R. C. (2007). The relations between perfectionism and suicidality: A systematic review. *Suicide and Life-Threatening Behavior*, *37*, 698–714.

O'Connor, R. C. (2009). Psychological perspectives on suicidal behaviour. In U. Kumar & M. K. Mandal (Eds.), *Suicidal behaviour: Assessment of people at risk* (pp. 3–19). Thousand Oaks, CA: Sage.

O'Connor, R. C., Fraser, L., Whyte, M-C., MacHale, S., & Masterson, G. (2008). A comparison of specific positive future expectancies and global hopelessness as predictors of suicidal ideation in a prospective study of repeat self-harmers. *Journal of Affective Disorders, 110,* 207–214.

O'Connor, R. C., O'Connor, D. B., O'Connor, S. M., Smallwood, J., & Miles, J. (2004). Hopelessness, stress, and perfectionism: The moderating effects of future thinking. *Cognition and Emotion, 18,* 1099–1120.

O'Connor, R. C., Whyte, M-C., Fraser, L., Masterton, G., Miles, J., & MacHale, S. (2007). Predicting short-term outcome in well-being following suicidal behaviour: The conjoint effects of social perfectionism and positive future thinking. *Behaviour Research and Therapy, 45,* 1543–1555.

Oquendo, M. A., Currier, D., & Mann, J. J. (2006). Prospective studies of suicidal behavior in major depressive and bipolar disorders: What is the evidence for predictive risk factors? *Acta Psychiatrica Scandinavia, 114,* 151–158.

Orbach, I., Bar-Joseph, H., & Dror, N. (1990). Styles of problem solving in suicidal individuals. *Suicide and Life-Threatening Behavior, 20,* 56–64.

Orbach, I., Blomenson, R., Mikulincer, M., Gilboa-Schechtman, E., Rogolsky, M., & Retzoni, G. (2007). Perceiving a problem-solving task as a threat and suicidal behavior in adolescents. *Journal of Social and Clinical Psychology, 26,* 1010–1034.

Osgood, C. (1957). *The measurement of meaning.* Urbana: University of Illinois Press.

Patsiokas, A. T., Clum, G. A., & Luscomb, R. L. (1979). Cognitive characteristics of suicide attempters. *Journal of Consulting and Clinical Psychology, 47,* 478–484.

Peeters, F., Wessel, I., Merckelbach, H., & Boon-Vermeeren, M. (2002). Autobiographical memory specificity and the course of major depressive disorder. *Comprehensive Psychiatry, 43,* 344–350.

Platt, J. J., & Spivack, G. (1972). Problem-solving thinking of psychiatric patients. *Journal of Consulting and Clinical Psychology, 39,* 148–151.

Pollock, L. R., & Williams, J. M. G. (2001). Effective problem solving in suicide attempters depends on specific autobiographical recall. *Suicide and Life-Threatening Behavior, 31,* 386–396.

Pollock, L. R., & Williams, J. M. G. (2004). Problem-solving in suicide attempters. *Psychological Medicine, 34,* 163–167.

Price, R. B., Nock, M. K., Charney, D. S., & Mathew, S. J. (2009). Effects of intravenous ketamine on explicit and implicit measures of suicidality in treatment-resistant depression. *Biological Psychiatry, 66,* 522–526.

Priester, M. J., & Clum, G. A. (1993). The problem-solving diathesis in depression, hopelessness, and suicide ideation: A longitudinal analysis. *Journal of Psychopathology and Behavioral Assessment, 15,* 239–254.

Rasmussen, S., Fraser, L., Gotz, M., MacHale, S., Mackie, R., Masterton, G.,…O'Connor, R. C. (2010). Elaborating the cry of pain model of suicidality: Testing a psychological model of first-time and repeat self-harm patients. *British Journal of Clinical Psychology, 49,* 15–30.

Rasmussen, S. A., O'Connor, R. C., & Brodie, D. (2008). The role of perfectionism and autobiographical memory in a sample of parasuicide patients: An exploratory study. *Crisis, 29,* 64–72.

Reinecke, M. A. (2006). Problem solving: A conceptual approach to suicidality and psychotherapy. In T. E. Ellis (Ed.), *Cognition and suicide: Theory, research, and therapy* (pp. 237–260). Washington, DC: APA Books.

Roberts, R. E., Roberts, C. R., & Chen, Y. R. (1998). Suicidal thinking among adolescents with a history of attempted suicide. *Journal of the Academy of Child and Adolescent Psychiatry, 37,* 1294–1300.

Rudd, M. D. (1990). An integrative model of suicidal ideation. *Suicide and Life-Threatening Behavior, 20,* 16–30.

Rudd, M. D. (2000). The suicidal mode: A cognitive behavioral model of suicidality. *Suicide and Life-Threatening Behavior, 30,* 18–33.

Rudd, M. D. (2006). Fluid vulnerability theory: A cognitive approach to understanding the process of acute and chronic suicide risk. In T. E. Ellis (Ed.), *Cognition and suicide: Theory, research, and therapy* (pp. 355–368). Washington, DC: APA Books.

Rudd, M. D., Joiner, T., & Rajab, M. H. (1996). Relationships among suicide ideators, attempters, and multiple attempters in a young adult sample. *Journal of Abnormal Psychology, 105,* 541–550.

Rudd, M. D., Rajab, M. H., & Dahm, P. F. (1994). Problem-solving appraisal in suicide ideators and attempters. *American Journal of Orthopsychiatry, 64,* 136–149.

Schotte, D. E., & Clum, G. A. (1982). Suicide ideation in a college population: A test of a model. *Journal of Consulting and Clinical Psychology, 50,* 690–696.

Schotte, D. E., & Clum, G. A. (1987). Problem-solving skills in suicidal psychiatric patients. *Journal of Consulting and Clinical Psychology, 55,* 49–54.

Shneidman, E. S. (1993). *Suicide as psychache: A clinical approach to self-destructive behavior.* Lanham, MD: Jason Aronson.

Sidley, G. L., Whitaker, K., Calam, R. M., & Wells, A. (1997). The relationship between problem-solving and autobiographical memory in parasuicide patients. *Behavioural and Cognitive Psychotherapy, 25,* 195–202.

Sinclair, J. M. A., Crane, C., Hawton, K., & Williams, J. M. G. (2007). The role of autobiographical memory specificity in deliberate self-harm. *Journal of Affective Disorders, 102,* 11–18.

Simon, T. R., Swann, A. C., Powell, K. E., Potter, L. B., Kresnow, M., & O'Carroll, P. W. (2001). Characteristics of impulsive suicide attempts and attempters. *Suicide and Life-Threatening Behavior, 32,* 49–59.

Smith, J. M., Alloy, L. B., & Abramson, L. Y. (2006). Cognitive vulnerability to depression, rumination, hopelessness, and suicidal ideation: Multiple pathways to self-injurious thinking. *Suicide and Life-Threatening Behavior, 36,* 443–454.

Spokas, M., Wenzel, A., Stirman, S. W., Brown, G. K., & Beck, A. T. (2009). Suicide risk factors and mediators between childhood sexual abuse and suicide ideation among male and female suicide attempters. *Journal of Traumatic Stress, 22,* 467–470.

Startup, M., Heard, H., Swales, M., Jones, B., Williams, J. M. G., & Jones, R. S. P. (2001). Autobiographical memory and parasuicide in borderline personality disorder. *British Journal of Clinical Psychology, 40,* 113–120.

Suominen, K., Henriksson, M., Suokas, J., Isometsä, E., Ostamo, A., & Lönnqvist, J. (1996). Mental disorders and comorbidity in attempted suicide. *Acta Psychiatrica Scandinavia, 94,* 234–240.

Trout, D. L. (1980). The role of social isolation in suicide. *Suicide and Life-Threatening Behavior, 10,* 10–23.

Van Orden, K. A., Lynam, M. E., Hollar, D., & Joiner, T. E., Jr. (2006). Perceived burdensomeness as an indicator of suicidal symptoms. *Cognitive Therapy and Research, 30,* 457–467.

Van Orden, K. A., Witte, T. K., Gordon, K. H., Bender, T. W., & Joiner, T. E., Jr. (2008). Suicidal desire and the capability for suicide: Tests of the interpersonal-psychological theory of suicidal behavior among adults. *Journal of Consulting and Clinical Psychology, 76*, 72–83.

Van Orden, K. A., Witte, T. K., James, L. M., Castro, Y., Gordon, K. H., Braithwaite, S. R., ... Joiner, T. E., Jr. (2008). Suicidal ideation in college students varies across semesters: The mediating role of belongingness. *Suicide and Life-Threatening Behavior, 38*, 427–435.

Vincent, P. J., Boddana, P., & MacLeod, A. K. (2004). Positive life goals and plans in parasuicide. *Clinical Psychology and Psychotherapy, 11*, 90–99.

Watkins, E., & Teasdale, J. D. (2001). Rumination and overgeneral memory in depression: Effects of self-focus and analytic thinking. *Journal of Abnormal Psychology, 110*, 353–357.

Wen-Hung, K., Gallo, J. J., & Eaton, W. W. (2004). Hopelessness, depression, substance disorder, and suicidality: A 13-year community-based study. *Social Psychiatry and Psychiatric Epidemiology, 39*, 497–501.

Wenzel, A., & Beck, A. T. (2008). A cognitive model of suicidal behavior: Theory and treatment. *Applied and Preventive Psychology, 12*, 189–201.

Wenzel, A., Brown, G. K., & Beck, A. T. (2009). *Cognitive therapy for suicidal patients: Scientific and clinical applications.* Washington, DC: APA Books.

Williams, J. M. G. (1996). Depression and the specificity of autobiographical memory. In D. C. Rubin (Ed.), *Remembering our past: Studies in autobiographical memory* (pp. 244–267). Cambridge, UK: Cambridge University Press.

Williams, J. M. G. (2001). *The cry of pain.* London, UK: Penguin.

Williams, J. M. G. (2006). Capture and rumination, functional avoidance, and executive control (CaRFAX): Three processes that underlie overgeneral memory. *Cognition and Emotion, 20*, 548–568.

Williams, J. M. G., Barnhofer, T., Crane, C., & Beck, A. T. (2005). Problem solving deteriorates following mood challenge in formerly depressed patients with a history of suicidal ideation. *Journal of Abnormal Psychology, 114*, 421–431.

Williams, J. M. G., Barnhoffer, T., Crane, C., & Duggan, D. S. (2006). The role of overgeneral memory in suicidality. In T. E. Ellis (Ed.), *Cognition and suicide: Theory, research, and therapy* (pp. 173–192). Washington, DC: APA Books.

Williams, J. M. G., Barnhofer, T., Crane, C., Hermans, D., Raes, F., Watkins, E., & Dalgleish, T. (2007). Autobiographical memory specificity and emotional disorder. *Psychological Bulletin, 133*, 122–148.

Williams, J. M. G., & Broadbent, K. (1986a). Autobiographical memory in suicide attempters. *Journal of Abnormal Psychology, 95*, 144–149.

Williams, J. M. G., & Broadbent, K. (1986b). Distraction by emotional stimuli: Use of a Stroop task with suicide attempters. *British Journal of Clinical Psychology, 25*, 101–110.

Williams, J. M., & Dritschel, B. H. (1988). Emotional disturbance and the specificity of autobiographical memory. *Cognition and Emotion. 2*, 221–234.

Williams, J. M. G., Ellis, N. C., Tyers, C., Healy, H., Rose, G., & MacLeod, A. K. (1996). The specificity of autobiographical memory and imageability of the future. *Memory and Cognition, 24*, 116–125.

Williams, J. M. G., & Pollock, L. R. (2001). Psychological aspects of the suicidal process. In K. van Heeringen (Eds.), *Understanding suicidal behaviour* (pp. 76–93). Chichester, UK: John Wiley.

Williams, J. M. G., Van der Does, A. J. W., Barnhofer, T., Crane, C., & Segal, Z. (2008). Cognitive reactivity, suicidal ideation, and future thinking: Preliminary investigation of a differential activation theory of hopelessness/suicidality. *Cognitive Therapy and Research, 32*, 83–104.

Young, M., Fogg, L., Scheftner, W., Fawcett, J., Akiskal, H., & Maser, J. (1996). Stable trait components of hopelessness: Baseline and severity to depression. *Journal of Abnormal Psychology, 105*, 155–165.

Psychodynamics of Suicide

Mark J. Goldblatt

Abstract

Suicidal behavior is complex and difficult to understand. Theories of self-destruction have evolved along with the field of psychoanalysis to include models of the mind from all theoretical branches. This chapter explores theories of suicide beginning with Freud's early work on melancholia and the splitting of the ego that enables self-attack. Later contributions emphasize the protective role of ego functioning and its collapse in suicidal distress. This chapter provides an overview of suicide dynamics from a broadened perspective of psychoanalytic thinking about affects, coping mechanisms, and relationships in the patient's internal and external world.

Key Words: psychodynamics of suicide, affective states, ego disintegration, object relations, narcissistic rage

The psychodynamics of suicide initially were rooted in Freud's observations of melancholia and arose out of drive theory and the topographical model of the mind (1917). As psychoanalysis evolved to include Freud's structural theory (1923), more emphasis was given toward a psychological understanding of the ego and conflicts between the ego and the superego. Significant contributions to the dynamics of suicide have developed as psychoanalytic theory has grown. American ego psychology has underscored the relevance of innate qualities that protect the self unless overwhelmed by unbearable affect leading to ego breakdown and suicidal collapse. The work of Melanie Klein and contemporary Kleinian analysts has expanded our understanding of issues such as envy and projective identification, which are often central to the survival of suicidal patients. Object relations theories, emphasizing the importance of conflicts between internalized aspects of the self; self psychology with its contributions on narcissism and shame; and contemporary relational theories have contributed in significant ways to

understanding issues relating to suicide. This chapter provides an overview of suicide dynamics from a broadened perspective of psychoanalytic thinking about affects, coping mechanisms, and relationships in the patient's internal and external world.

Psychodynamic Models of Suicide

Contemporary models of the suicidal mind have developed from clinical data and emerging psychoanalytic theory. Hendin (1991) suggested that the psychodynamic meaning of suicide is understood by observing both its affective and cognitive components. Affective states that become intolerable are considered to be suicide inviting. Cognitive components help clarify the affective constituent states by adding meaning to affects and perceptions.

Several studies have pointed to a range of affects that play a role in suicidality. However, these studies have limitations based on sample size and methodology. Freud's (1917) seminal thesis on hostility turned inward lays the groundwork for hate as a suicide-inviting affect. Studies link suicide with rage (Hendin, 1969; Plutchik & van Praag, 1990; Weissman, Fox, & Klerman, 1973); guilt (Hendin & Haas, 1991); hopelessness (Beck, Steer, Kovaks, & Garrison, 1985; Fawcett et al., 1987; Minkoff, Begman, Beck, & Besck, 1973); desperation (Hendin, 1991; Hendin, Maltsberger, Haas, Szanto, & Rabinowicz, 2004); and anxiety (Fawcett et al., 1990). Maltsberger (1988) described potentially lethal affects of aloneness, self-contempt, and murderous rage as intolerable psychic states that are suicide inviting. Adler and Buie (1979) identified intolerable aloneness as central to the pathology of patients with borderline personality disorder. More recently, a variety of intense, unpleasant affect states have been identified that are suicide inviting, including feelings of abandonment, self-hatred, rage, and anguish of intense degree (Hendin, Maltsberger, & Szanto, 2007). In addition to anxiety and hopelessness, and particularly in severe or malignant narcissistic personalities, aggression and rage can be the primary underlying propellants to suicide (Kernberg, 1992).

Cognitive components clarify affective states. Conscious and unconscious fantasies about death add meaning to these states for the suicidal person. Bell (2008) underscores the importance of fantasies that underlie all attempts at suicide. These fantasies are usually unconscious and relate to the self and the body. Common fantasies about suicide include death as a means for rebirth (Hendin, 1963; Jones, 1911; Maltsberger & Buie, 1980; Zilboorg, 1938); death as reunion; death as revenge, self-punishment, or atonement (Haim, 1974); death as escape (Furst & Ostow, 1979; Grinker, 1967; Kilpatrick, 1948); and death as assassination (Hale, 2008). Fantasies of suicide can represent revenge, retaliation, or triumph and serve to regulate and control intense sadistic impulses, hatred, rage, or shame. Daydreams of punishing, retaliating against, or destroying somebody by committing suicide can paradoxically be an effective incentive that makes it possible to continue to stay alive (Maltsberger, Ronningstam, Weinberg, Schechter, & Goldblatt, 2010). However, under certain stressful circumstances such as unbearable depression, psychosis, or alcohol and drug intoxication, these daydreams may take a malignant turn and lead to suicide.

More recently, an empirical study of the mental processes accompanying suicide evaluated psychodynamic constructs in nonschizophrenic suicidal psychiatric patients (Kaslow et al., 1998). These authors evaluated four psychodynamic concepts of suicidal behavior: self-directed aggression, object loss producing unresolved grief, ego functioning disturbance, and pathological object relations. Their findings suggested strong support for impaired object relations in suicide attempters, who viewed relationships more negatively and more likely to produce malevolence or pain. They found that the intrapsychic structure of these patients was consistent with borderline pathology, showing a predominance of primitive defenses such as splitting, projection, and projective identification. The experience of loss appeared to play a crucial role, first in terms of childhood experience, and later in light of recent adult losses. In this study there was little support for the hypothesis of self-directed aggression and no support for the hypothesis of impaired ego functioning. The authors concede that this study is limited by several factors, including the study instruments, the patients involved (suicide attempters versus suicide completers), and the inability to measure the role of unconscious factors.

Freud's Drive Theory

Self-directed aggression in suicide was originally described in Freud's *Mourning and Melancholia* (1917) and has been elaborated by Menninger (1933), Hendin (1951), and Sifneos and McCourt (1962). Freud's drive theory involved conscious and unconscious libidinal and aggressive urges that had to be defended against, leading to symptoms and suffering. In *Mourning and Melancholia* (1917), he suggested that in melancholia, where there is ambivalence toward a lost object, the ego splits, and part of the ego becomes identified with the abandoned object so that hostility related to the object continues and is directed toward the patient's own ego. In this way the patient is able to attack the self and kill himself in the process of killing the ambivalently held object.

Some years later, in *The Ego and the Id* (1923) Freud described a second mechanism for suicide where the superego becomes so harsh in its attack on the ego that it abandons the ego and leaves it to die. Fenichel (1932) elaborated this further, describing the anxiety that arises in depression as a fear "by the ego lest the superego abandon it" (p. 580), and suggested that this formulation was "of fundamental importance in the psychology of suicide" (p. 580). Echoing Menninger (1933), Fenichel (1934) wrote:

> Indeed, the psychogenesis of depressions, as it has just been described, appears to corroborate the thesis that every suicide corresponds to a wish to kill, which has been deflected on to the ego. But what seems to

be of more importance, and to be correlated with the great tendency to suicide in depressions, is the complete loss of self-regard that is forced on the ego through the wrath of the super-ego. (p. 106)

Menninger (1933) elaborated on Freud's formulation of introjection of the lost object with displacement of the feelings that were initially directed toward the object now experienced in relation to the self. He emphasized primitive oral fantasies in formulating a suicidal triad consisting of three unconscious wishes: the wish to kill, the wish to be killed, and the wish to die. These wishes related to the three areas of mental functioning, the id, ego, and superego, and were thought to arise from the oral phase of development, relating to aspects of taking in and spitting out aggressive feelings. The implication is that the presence of all three components, the wish to kill (seen as an ego function), the wish to be killed (punishment from the superego), and the wish to die (the death instinct) resulted in the fatal outcome.

Ego Psychology
Following Freud's two seminal descriptions of the suicidal mind, the psychoanalytic literature on suicide concentrated somewhat narrowly on the disturbed relationship between the superego and the ego. The development of American ego psychology described suicide as a phenomenon accompanied by more extensive disturbance in ego functioning. This was noted at least since Glover wrote, "although primarily the result of destructive forces directed through the super-ego, [suicide] could not come about without a regression of the ego to primitive animistic levels and the adoption of primitive autoplastic methods of dealing with tension based on the processes of primary identification" (Glover, 1930/1956, p. 121). He saw suicide as developing in individuals with an impaired psychic structure. Severe self-criticism arising from that part of the psychic structure dealing with self-judgment (i.e., the superego) would normally be neutralized by the defensive actions of the ego. However, suicide could result in those individuals whose protective ego was impaired such that it functioned at an archaic level and was inadequate to deal with the destructive onslaught from the superego. Harsh self-attack was in and of itself difficult for the individual to tolerate, but suicide came about because of inadequacies in coping mechanisms.

The psychological significance of the ego has evolved extensively. Anna Freud (1936) described defense mechanisms that are utilized to deal with underlying conflicts, and compromises that are forged to satisfy critical self-attack and control of unacceptable infantile impulses. The manner of functioning of the ego leads to character style, which enables functioning or collapse in times of distress. She emphasizes the self-critical superego in depressed suicidal patients, balanced by the protective efforts of the ego, which are accessible to therapeutic intervention.

Hartmann (1939/2008, 1950) emphasized the adaptive functioning of the ego with reciprocity between the individual and the environment leading to an enhanced ability to deal with areas of conflictual and adaptive functioning. These abilities often break down during a suicidal regression. Disturbances in the capacity for affect regulation, thinking, failures in the synthetic function of the ego (self-object differentiation), reality testing, and the mechanisms of defense are crucial for survival and indicate self breakup during a suicidal crisis (Maltsberger, 2004). Under extremes of stress, associated with desperation, dissociative phenomena, and deterioration in work and social functioning, the failing ego is unable to sustain itself and suicidal actions often ensue (Hendin et al., 2004). The treatment implications that arise from this work suggest that although the patient's self-sustaining ability may be threatened through overwhelming depression or hopeless self-attack, engagement with an informed, caring therapist can function as an external sustaining ego, lending strength and providing hope through difficult times.

Jacobson's work (1964, 1971) has led to a greater understanding of problems relating to separation and individuation. Incomplete psychological separation resulting in confusion of self and object representations increases suicide vulnerability (Maltsberger, 1993).

Mahler and colleagues (Mahler, Pine, & Bergman, 1975) described the process of maturation and the phases of psychic development. Her work on how the infant separates emotionally from the mother and develops his own life has important implications for the development of borderline psychopathology. The affective lability of borderline patients has been attributed to problems in this phase of development, leading to an inability to self-soothe and a propensity to hopeless disintegration of the self. Kernberg (1970) described different levels of ego functioning based on internalization of object relationships that differentiated overall functioning and ability to cope with life stressors.

Arlow and Brenner (1964) reviewed ego malfunctions observable in the psychoses. They suggested that the analyst recognize which ego and superego functions are involved in the defensive regression of psychosis. In treatment, the therapist works "to reduce the patient's overwhelming anxiety sufficiently to make life livable. When the psychopathology of the psychoses is viewed from this frame of reference it may be possible to mitigate the intensity of the intrapsychic conflict and to enhance the ego's function of integration and adaptation" (Arlow & Brenner, 1969, p. 12). The ego failures in suicide appear to parallel their description of its functioning during periods of psychoses.

SPECIFIC EGO FUNCTIONING IMPAIRMENT ASSOCIATED WITH SELF-BREAKUP AND EGO REGRESSION IN SUICIDE

Affect Regulation

The capacity for regulating and modulating affect is severely impaired in a suicidal state. Suicide can be understood as a desperate defensive effort to take flight from an intolerable internal affective environment. Affective desperation, often compounded by other intense emotions of hopelessness, rage, feelings of abandonment, self-hatred, anxiety, and loneliness, breaks through the defenses that normally serve to contain such overwhelming feeling states. These states threaten to overwhelm the patient by thrusting him or her into a regression-inviting state of traumatic anxiety (Hendin et al., 2004).

Impaired Cognition

In suicidal states the ego functions for thinking, language (especially symbolic and abstracting capacities), and cognitive organization are frequently disturbed. Shneidman (1985) pointed the suicidal persons' cognition; he referred to dichotomous thinking, "all or nothing," "either-or" perspectives. He wrote that suicidal people suffer from "tunnel vision," where they are unable to appreciate nuances and shades of meaning, implying that when suicide looms, time loses meaning and life becomes arrested in a moment that feels like eternal agony.

Intolerable subjective states are commonly followed by a shift to less meaningful, integrative forms of thought and awareness, which Baumeister (1990) referred to as *cognitive deconstruction*. When cognition is deconstructed, he argues, awareness of self and action becomes concrete and short term. Awareness is limited to proximal, immediate tasks and goals. "Higher meanings" are removed from

awareness. In "deconstructed" states personal identity fades and self-awareness is limited to a primitive sense of the body, mostly experiencing only sensations and movements. There is an ongoing struggle to stop time and to avoid meaning; in deconstruction the patient alternates between emotionally dead emptiness and bursts of negative affect when deconstruction fails. There is no hope, no connectedness, and no time. Baumeister appeared to argue that these cognitive changes are at once defensive and regressive in nature. When severe emotional strain reaches a certain level of intensity, the individual's ability to think and plan normally is impaired. Changes in cognition serve to cope with overwhelming affect, through archaic mechanisms that lead to withdrawal and isolation, but paradoxically leave the patient even more vulnerable due to interpersonal and intrapsychic remoteness.

The higher levels of thinking are more typical of patients whose egos have matured so they are capable of using fantasy as trial action in thought. These are not possible as long as inner and outer worlds are isomorphic. For these patients, the ability to imagine is lost. Their inner world is felt to be so awful that they are not able to imagine anything other than their suffering and therefore cannot see a way out of their utter desperation (Baumeister, 1990).

Bateman and Fonagy (2004) describe a hierarchy of thought processing whereby "experiencing a thought as only a thought is a developmental achievement" (p. 68) that patients with borderline personality disorder struggle to attain. They use the term "*psychic equivalence*" to portray an experience of the external world that is invariably "isomorphic with the internal" (p. 69) world. They use the term *pretend mode* for a level of functioning in which experiences in fantasy are not equated to what transpires in the outer world. In pretend mode, a daydream or masturbation fantasy is subjectively experienced as really happening, but not really happening in the outer world, and not having any implications for it. The pretend mode therefore implies the capacity for fantasy and the capacity for a time to suspend disbelief. In mentalization, the highest level of thinking, development has gone a step further. Defined as "the capacity to think about mental states as separate from, yet potentially causing actions," mentalization arises "as part of an integration of the pretend and psychic equivalent modes of functioning" (p. 70). Pretend mode implies more self-development than psychic equivalence mode, and mentalization more developmental achievement than pretend mode. When suicidal, certain patients think in a restricted manner that limits their outlook and endangers their safety. Suicidal patients appear to think in a way that patients with borderline personality disorder usually think. This regression in cognition increases the risk for suicidal behavior.

Thoughts and feelings can be experienced as representations of objects and self taking their place on the stage of the inner world, where fantasy can portray trial action in thought, the self remaining aware that to think and to feel are not to do (Sandler & Rosenblatt, 1962). These internal psychic representations are a way of conceptualizing how the mind conceives and manages experience.

Bateman and Fonagy held that suicide occurs in psychic equivalence mode and intends to destroy a detached component of the self, the "alien self." Patients decouple their reality sense from reality when attempting suicide (moving thereby to the pretend mode of subjectivity), behaving as though acting on their fantasy has no implications for the outer world. In this state suicidal patients are able to suspend reality testing to a certain extent and act in a way that suggests they do not actually believe in the physical principles of life that we normally take for granted, for example, that death is permanent.

Synthetic Functioning Fails

The synthetic function of the ego, the integrating and harmonizing function of the ego, fails in suicidal crises. Self-cohesion loosens. Patients cannot maintain adequate capacity for self and object differentiation (self and object representations become confused and the self breaks up). The "self" may be understood as an integrated ego representational construction in which the body-self, the mental-self, the feeling-self, and the relational-self are all coordinated and continuous across time. This harmonization fails in true suicidal crises. The subjective experience of a patient whose self is disintegrating is very different from that of one who feels some pleasure in and experiences relief from surrendering to the reverie of a sustaining suicidal fantasy (Maltsberger, 2004; Maltsberger et al., 2010). The patient who experiences himself as a whole real person is able to think and feel, even difficult or painful feelings. When the self is experienced as fragmented, the patient is unable to face the world and feels like he, or the world, is falling apart.

Maltsberger (1993) postulates a spectrum of body-self disturbances in suicidal states ranging from mild experiences of bodily illness in hypochondriasis to the delusions of body pathology in body dysmorphic disorders, which contribute to suicidal breakdown. The body-self boundary is less than solid and may erode, leading to body representational splits, which may contribute to suicide (Stolorow, 1975). Self and object representations are necessary ego aspects for coping with the vicissitudes of development and stressors of trauma (Sandler & Rosenblatt, 1962). Impairments in stable body representation and confusion of self and object-representations make patients vulnerable to suicide.

In suicidal states the self-representation fissures into separate fragments. Subjectively it seems to the patient that intolerable affects arise from the alienated body. The body-representation, formerly part of the self-representation, now assumes the characteristics of an object representation. With disturbed reality testing, killing forces may then turn against the body-as-object. Absent a body-representation, it appears to the fractured, mutilated self that suicide would not result in self-annihilation, but rather protect it. The split-off, evil and intolerable body-self alone would be jettisoned in suicide; the rest of the self would survive (Maltsberger, 2004).

The functioning of the ego worsens in suicidal states. Loss of an observing ego deprives the patient of the ability to recognize emotional distress and institute recovery mechanisms. Descriptions of suicidal crises (Hendin, Maltsberger, Lipschitz, Haas, & Kyle, 2001) include deterioration in social or occupational functioning as a marker of a suicidal crisis.

Impaired Reality Testing

Fantasies that may have been pleasurable or comforting can turn into goals for action. Functionally at least, many suicidal patients are, under the press of intense mental pain, deluded. Under the force of false beliefs (*viz.,* that suicide leads to survival and a better life in the hereafter) they may go into action. Many patients, in the painful intensity of the moment, abandon any belief that others care for them, or that their deaths will lead to the suffering of others left behind. Some become delusionally convinced that family and friends would be better off without them, or that others (including their therapists) secretly want them dead. Others yet may be utterly convinced that they are so evil they must be killed to put a stop to the evil they inflict on others (Maltsberger & Buie, 1980).

Many suicidal patients regress to the level of psychotic defensive operations. This may be seen in psychological testing where the connection between abandonment or loss of self-esteem is associated with impaired reality testing (Marcus, 1988). There is a predominance of more primitive defense mechanism such as dissociation (in which split-off feelings are separated from conscious awareness), projection, distortion, and denial (Laufer & Laufer, 1989). In a more recent elaboration of Anna Freud's (1936) description of the ego, Apter et al. (1989) have described the defense mechanisms that were observable in an empirical study of suicidal patients. These authors found that aggression was either directed inward on the self or outward toward others depending on the form of internal defense mechanism. Aggression was turned inward through the use of repression, for regressed suicidal patients, while nonsuicidal patients directed aggression outwardly through the mechanism of denial. In their study, the use of displacement differentiated violent from nonviolent patients.

Melanie Klein

Defenses of splitting, projection, and projective identification are important concepts that were elaborated to a great degree by Melanie Klein and her followers, and they are highly relevant to understanding the suicidal patient. Klein emphasized the hope for union with good internal objects, which are preserved, in the suicidal fantasy.

> According to the findings of Abraham and James Glover, a suicide is directed against the introjected object. But, while in committing suicide, the ego intends to murder its bad objects, in my view at the same time it also always aims at saving its loved objects, internal and external. To put it shortly: in some cases the phantasies underlying suicide aim at preserving the internalized good objects, and that part of the ego which is identified with good objects, and also at destroying the other part of the ego which is identified with the bad objects and the id. Thus the ego is enabled to become united with its loved objects.
>
> In other cases suicide seems to be determined by the same type of phantasies, but here they related to the external world and real objects, partly as substitutes for the internalized ones. As already stated, the subject hates not only his "bad" objects, but his id as well and that vehemently.
>
> At bottom we perceive in such a step his reaction to his own sadistic attacks on his mother's body, which to a little child is the first representative of the outside world. Hatred and revenge against the real

(good) objects also always plays an important part in such a step, but it is precisely the incontrollable dangerous hatred, which is perpetually welling up in him, from which the real melancholic by his suicide is in part struggling to preserve his real objects. (Klein, 1935, pp. 276–277)

Echoing Freud's earlier formulation of suicide resulting from an overly cruel superego attack (1923), Klein also recognized that "too harsh a conscience gives rise to worry and unhappiness" and that "the strain of such phantasies of internal warfare and the fears connected with it are at the bottom of what we recognize as a vindictive conscience...expressed in deep mental disturbance and lead to suicide" (Klein, 1935, p. 340).

Bion extended Klein's contributions on projective identification and envy, through his description of the attack on linking (Bion, 1959). Emotion that is too intense to be contained by the immature psyche causes an attack on all that links the infant to the breast. The internal object is considered to worsen the situation. Envy produces an attack by the mind on itself, in order to protect the self by destroying its link to the object. Seen in this light, suicide is an action energized by the dynamics of the treatment and is seen as an acting out of the transference. According to Bion, suicidal actions represent behaviors that relate to feelings toward the therapist. These feelings may be unconscious but play a very important role in suicide.

> Attacks on the link, therefore, are synonymous with attacks on the analyst's, and originally the mother's, peace of mind. The capacity to introject is transformed by the patient's envy and hate into greed devouring the patient's psyche; similarly, peace of mind becomes hostile indifference. At this point analytic problems arise through the patient's employment (to destroy the peace of mind that is so much envied) of acting out, delinquent acts and threats of suicide.. (p. 314)

More recently Kernberg (2007, 2009) underscored the role of envy in suicide. Envy (Kite, 2001, cited by Cairo-Chiarandini, 2001, p. 1391) may be defined as "a hostile feeling, culminating in ill will and malice, that stems from the perception of superiority or advantage held by another." In an effort to control unbearable feelings (in particular, envy), the body is to be killed in an effort to save the internal objects and protect the self. This is taken up more directly by the object relations theorists.

Object Relations Theorists

Winnicott (1960) emphasized conflicts between different internalized aspects of the self and saw suicide as an attack on bad internal objects or unwanted aspects of the self:

> In the child's management of his inner world and in the attempt to preserve in it what is felt to be benign, there are moments when he feels that all would be well if a unit of malign influence could be eliminated. (This is equivalent to the scapegoat idea.) Clinically there appears a dramatization of ejection of badness (kicking, passage of flatus, spitting, etc.). Alternatively the child is accident-prone, or there is a suicide attempt—with the aim to destroy the bad within the self; in the total fantasy of the suicide there is to be a survival, with the bad elements destroyed, but survival may not occur. (Winnicott, 1975, p. 209)

Winnicott's concept of the false self (1965) as a defensive function to protect the true self also plays a role in some patients' suicide. He saw the ego as defensively forming a structure known as the false self to care for the central or true self that was the container of psychic reality. Suicide may occur under two separate formulations: In more severe cases, where the false self takes over to such an extent that the true self is "under threat of annihilation" (p. 133), suicide may be seen as a "reassertion of the true self" (p. 133). In this formulation, suicide is viewed as a last ditch attempt to break away from the dominance of the false self, a final attempt of expression by the true self. In less extreme pathology, suicide falls under the purview of the false self, as a protection of the true self from further assault.

> More towards health: The False Self has as its main concern a search for conditions which will make it possible for the True Self to come into its own. If conditions cannot be found then there must be reorganized a new defense against exploitation of the True Self, and if there be doubt then the clinical result is suicide. Suicide in this context is the destruction of the total self in avoidance of annihilation of the True Self. When suicide is the only defense left against betrayal of the True Self, then it becomes the lot of the False Self to organize the suicide. This, of course, involves its own destruction, but at the same time eliminates the need for its continued existence, since its function is the protection of the True Self from insult. (p. 143)

Kilpatrick (1948) emphasized overwhelming self-hate, hopelessness, and alienation in suicidal patients for whom suicide acts toward restoring self-esteem. She points out that the unconscious idealized self-image is often accompanied by its counterpart, a despised self-image. "When we understand narcissism not as love for the self, but as love of the idealized image of the self, we become aware of the gravity of self-hate and alienation which needs to be present" (p. 19). This view is maintained in contemporary object relations theory, which formulates suicide as an attempt by the superego, with which the good self is identified, to eliminate the bad self (Hendin, 1991).

Suicide has been viewed by several authors as representing reunion with the lost object (Fenichel, 1945; Hendin, 1991). Asch (1980) took up the role of pathological internal objects, which are projected and interacted with. He suggested that in response to object loss, the patient enlists another in the role of executioner. He emphasizes the double aim in suicide, "of first cleansing the self, and then uniting (actually re-uniting) with an omnipotent love object" (p. 52).

Self Psychology

Pathology developing from the lack of a nurturing maternal figure during childhood results in disturbances in self-esteem and identity formation with an inability to develop soothing interjects and comfort oneself during times of distress/loss (Kohut, 1971). Narcissistic injuries lead to a breakup in self-cohesion and result in aggressive responses, which can be self-directed (Kohut, 1977). When these patients experience object loss/distress, they feel it as a narcissistic attack that can lead to depression and anxiety about disintegration. Some patients who experience loss and are unable to turn to others for support develop a deep feeling of isolating, paralyzing loneliness, similar to separation anxiety, which is suicide inviting (Buie & Maltsberger, 1989). Kohut (1984) described this anxiety as "the deepest anxiety man can experience" (p. 16), leading to suicidal despair.

> Fragile selves react with narcissistic rage for the sake of their assertiveness because they don't have self-righting mechanisms at their disposal. The lack of selfobject experiences, then, can lead to a state of extreme helplessness, fragmentation, and narcissistic rage. Suicidal behavior is the result of a final attempt to evoke a reaction of the selfobject, to experience one's own efficacy, and to regulate the self-state. In a fantasy of archaic grandiosity, the body and the personal world may be destroyed, and in this act the

sense of one's own agency is rescued. (Hartmann & Milch, 2000, p. 88)

Narcissistic rage associated with functional regression, lack of control, irrationality, and an archaic perception of reality can lead to suicide if turned against the self (Baumeister, 1990; Kohut, 1972).

Shame and aggression are closely related, as feelings of shame can motivate anger, rage, or humiliated fury (Lewis, 1971) and be directed toward the self in suicide (Baumeister, 1990). Shameful feelings are usually triggered when facing failure, rejection, and loss of support, or when experiencing threats to the sense of internal or external control. Shame is associated with failure to maintain or reach ideals, or achieve important aspirations and goals. It indicates incompetence—an inability to control or understand (Broucek, 1982). Certain patients attack themselves following narcissistic injuries that leave them feeling isolated, fearful, and enraged. In this state of narcissistic rage, they may turn their aggression on themselves.

Mental Disorders and Suicide

BORDERLINE PERSONALITY DISORDER

Patients with borderline personality disorder are often defined by their affective lability and potential to regress into suicidal states as a way of coping with their inner turmoil and hopelessness. Early intrapsychic conflicts produce a susceptibility to splitting in the patient's self-representation in times of stress, resulting in the development of borderline pathology. Perry (1989) described three psychodynamic conflicts associated with suicide: separation-abandonment, object hunger and conflict over emotional needs, and anger. In these patients, suicide may be seen as the patient's identifying with the good self and punishing the bad (Kernberg, 1970). Other definitions of borderline pathology have emphasized an inner sense of badness, with poor ego control (Gunderson, 1984); aloneness (Adler & Buie, 1979); aloneness, self-hatred, and murderous rage Maltsberger (1986); and shame-panic (Jacobs, 1992).

TRAUMA

Fenichel (1934) noted the association between trauma and suicide, and formulated a description of superego attack that grows out of Freud's (1923) description of the role of the superego in suicide:

Among the traumatic neuroses, too, there are narcissistic cases in which the trauma is perceived as a punishment meted out by the super-ego to the ego. This personification of fate as a parental imago, which harbors good or bad intentions toward the ego, is again an expression of an infantile narcissistic attitude. In depressions, this surrender is brought about by the person's own super-ego, whose entry into the field of action is merely dreaded in the traumatic neuroses; the super-ego actually destroys the depressive patient's joy in life. For to have a "desire to live" evidently means that one feels supported by one's super-ego. When this feeling vanishes, all the helplessness of a deserted babe reappears. The suicide that is undertaken by the ego, in the final analysis, must correspond to the illusion of regaining the lost parental imagos and their protection. (Fenichel, 1934, p. 106)

Studies of suicide in veterans with posttraumatic stress disorder (PTSD) showed that veterans with intense combat-related guilt were at increased risk for suicide (Hendin & Haas, 1991). In veterans with chronic PTSD, suicidal behavior was associated with paternal inconsistency of love, and PTSD symptoms of survivor guilt and crying (Hyer, McCranie, Woods, & Boudewyns, 1990). More recent literature (Kotler, Iancu, Efroni, & Amir, 2001) suggests that PTSD patients are at increased risk for suicide, which may be due to impulsivity and decreased with social support. Suicide attempts themselves have been seen as traumatic and suicide inviting (Maltsberger, Goldblatt, Ronningstam, Weinberg, & Schechter, 2011).

Conclusion

The dynamic understanding of the suicidal mind has evolved as psychoanalytic thinking has progressed. Psychoanalytic theory of suicide has sought to provide a concept of self-destruction consistent with a theory of mind. The importance of drives and aggression, including superego attack, initially dominated, consistent with the psychoanalytic model of the time. Later, the sustaining functions of the ego were acknowledged, and the role of introjected objects became more clearly defined. In this chapter the psychodynamic meaning of suicide has been explored from the perspective of the major analytic theorists. The role of affects as suicide inviting is prominently featured. The need to contain overwhelming affective states through ego defense mechanisms leads to concepts of internalization of objects and their ability to sustain or punish the self. Conscious and unconscious fantasies have been usefully elaborated to clarify meaning of self-destructive actions. Psychodynamics of suicide have evolved to include theories from all branches of psychoanalytic thinking, ultimately aimed at explaining this complex concept of destruction of the self, and thereby extending hope of providing therapeutic intervention.

Acknowledgments

The section of this chapter entitled "Specific Ego Functioning Impairment Associated With Self-Breakup and Ego Regression in Suicide" was developed in discussion with the Boston Suicide Study Group, whose members are Terry Maltsberger, Mark Goldblatt, Elsa Ronningstam, and Mark Schechter.

References

Adler, G., & Buie, D. H. (1979). Aloneness and borderline psychopathology: The possible relevance of childhood developmental issues. *International Journal of Psycho-Analysis, 60*, 83–96.

Apter, A., Plutchik, R., Sevy, S., Korn, M., Brown, S., & van Praag, H. (1989). Defense mechanisms in risk of suicide and risk of violence. *American Journal of Psychiatry, 146*, 1027–1031.

Arlow, J. A., & Brenner, C. (1964). The psychopathology of the psychoses. In J. A. Brenner & C. Arlow (Eds.), *Psychoanalytic concepts and the structural theory* (pp. 144–185). New York, NY: International Universities Press.

Arlow, J. A., & Brenner, C. (1969). The psychopathology of the psychoses: A proposed revision. *International Journal of Psycho-Analysis, 50*, 5–14.

Asch, S. S. (1980). Suicide and the hidden executioner. *International Review of Psycho-Analysis, 7*, 51–60.

Bateman, A., & Fonagy, P. (2004). *Psychotherapy for borderline personality disorder*. Oxford, UK: Oxford University Press.

Baumeister, R. F. (1990). Suicide as escape from self. *Psychological Review, 97*, 90–223.

Beck, A. T., Steer, R. A., Kovacs, M., & Garrison, B. (1985). Hopelessness and eventual suicide: A 10-year prospective study of patients hospitalized with suicidal ideation. *American Journal of Psychiatry, 142*, 559–563.

Bell, D. (2008). Who is killing what or whom. Some note on the internal phenomenology of suicide. In S. Briggs, A. Lemma, & W. Crouch (Eds.), *Relating to self-harm and suicide* (pp. 45–60). New York, NY: Routledge.

Bion, W. R (1959). Attacks on linking. *International Journal of Psycho-Analysis, 40*, 308–315.

Boston Suicide Study Group. (2011). Personal communication.

Broucek, F. J. (1982). Shame and its relationship to early narcissistic developments. *International Journal of Psycho-Analysis, 63*, 369–378.

Buie, D. H., & Maltsberger, J. T. (1989). The psychological vulnerability to suicide. In D. Jacobs & H. Brown (Eds.), *Suicide: Understanding and responding* (pp. 59–72). Madison, CT: International Universities Press.

Cairo-Chiarandini, I. (2001). To have and have not: Clinical uses of envy. *Journal of the American Psychoanalytic Association, 49*, 1391–1404.

Fawcett, J., Scheftner, W., Clark, D., Hedeker, D., Gibbons, R., & Coryell, W. (1987). Clinical predictors of suicide in patients with major affective disorders: A controlled prospective study. *American Journal of Psychiatry, 144*, 35–40.

Fawcett, J., Scheftner, W. A., Fogg, L., Clark, D. C., Young, M. A., Hedeker, D., & Gibbons, R. (1990). Time-related predictors of suicide in major affective disorder. *American Journal of Psychiatry, 147*, 1189–1194.

Fenichel, O. (1932). Outline of clinical psychoanalysis. *Psychoanalysis Quarterly, 1*, 545–652.

Fenichel, O. (1934). Outline of clinical psychoanalysis. *Psychoanalysis Quarterly, 3*, 42–127.

Fenichel, O. (1945). *The psychoanalytic theory of neurosis*. New York, NY: Norton.

Freud, S. (1917). *Mourning and melancholia*. London, UK: Hogarth Press.

Freud, S. (1923). *The ego and the id*. London, UK: Hogarth Press.

Freud, A. (1936). *The ego and the mechanisms of defense*. London, UK: Hogarth Press.

Furst, S. S., & Ostow, M. (1979). The psychodynamics of suicide. In L. D. Hankoff & B. Einsidler (Eds.), *Suicide: Theory and clinical aspects* (pp 165–178). Littleton, MA: PSG.

Glover, E. (1956). Grades of ego-differentiation. In E. Glover, *On the early development of mind* (pp. 112–129). London, UK: Imago. (original work published 1930)

Grinker, R. R. (1967). The psychodynamics of suicide and attempted suicide. In L. Yochelson (Ed.), *Symposium on suicide* (pp 67–70). Washington, DC: George Washington University.

Gunderson, J. G. (1984). *Borderline personality disorder*. Washington, DC: American Psychiatric Press.

Haim, A. (1974). *Adolescent suicide*. New York, NY: International Universities Press.

Hale, R. (2008). Psychoanalysis and suicide: process and typology. In S. Briggs, A. Lemma, & W. Crouch (Eds.), *Relating to self-harm and suicide* (pp. 13–24). New York, NY: Routledge.

Hartmann, H. (2008). *Ego psychology and the problem of adaptation*. New York, NY: International Universities Press. (original work published 1939).

Hartmann H. (1939). Psycho-analysis and the concept of health. *International Journal of Psycho-Analysis, 20*, 308–321.

Hartmann, H. (1950). Comments on the psychoanalytic theory of the ego. *Psychoanalytic Study of the Child, 5*, 74–96.

Hartmann, H., & Milch, W. E. (2000). The need for efficacy in the transference of suicidal patients: Transference and countertransference issues. *Progress in Self Psychology, 16*, 87–101.

Hendin, H. (1963). The psychodynamics of suicide. *Journal of Nervous and Mental Disorders, 136*, 236–244.

Hendin, H. (1969). *Black suicide*. New York, NY: Basic Books.

Hendin, H. (1991). Psychodynamics of suicide, with particular reference to the young. *American Journal of Psychiatry, 148*, 1150–1158.

Hendin, H., & Haas, A. P. (1991). Suicide and guilt as manifestations of PTSD in Vietnam combat veterans. *American Journal of Psychiatry, 148*, 586–591.

Hendin, H., Maltsberger, J. T., Haas, A. P., Szanto, K., & Rabinowicz, H. (2004). Desperation and other affective states in suicidal patients. *Suicide and Life-Threatening Behavior, 34*, 386–394.

Hendin, H., Maltsberger, J. T., Lipschitz, A., Haas, A., & Kyle, J. (2001). Recognizing and responding to a suicide crisis. *Suicide and Life Threatening Behavior, 31*, 115–128.

Hendin, H., Maltsberger, J. T., & Szanto, K. (2007). The role of intense affective states in signaling a suicide crisis. *Journal of Nervous and Mental Disease, 195*, 363–368.

Jacobs, D. (1992). Evaluating and treating suicidal behavior in the borderline patient. In D. Jacobs (Ed.), *Suicide and clinical practice* (pp. 115–130). Washington, DC: American Psychiatric Press.

Jacobson, E. (1964). *The self and object world.* New York, NY: International Universities Press.

Jacobson, E. (1971). *Depression.* Madison, CT: International Universities Press.

Jones, E. (1911). On "dying together"—with special reference to Heinrich Van Kleist's suicide. In *Essays on applied psychoanalysis* (Vol. 1, pp. 9–15). New York, NY: International Universities Press.

Kaslow, N. J., Reviere, S. L., Chance, S. E., Rogers, J. H., Hatcher, C. A., Wasserman, F., …Seelig, B. (1998). An empirical study of the psychodynamics of suicide. *Journal of the American Psychoanalytic Association, 46*, 777–796.

Kernberg, O. (1970). A psychoanalytic classification of character pathology. *Journal of the American Psychoanalytic Association, 18*, 800–822.

Kernberg, O. (1992). *Aggression in personality disorders and perversions.* New Haven, CT: Yale University Press.

Kernberg, O. (2007). The almost untreatable narcissistic patient. *Journal of American Psychoanalytic Association, 55*(2), 503–539.

Kernberg, O. (2009). The concept of the death drive: A clinical perspective. *International Journal of Psychoanalysis, 90*, 1009–1023.

Kilpatrick, E. (1948). A psychoanalytic understanding of suicide. *American Journal of Psychoanalysis, 8*, 13–23.

Klein, M. (1935). A contribution to the psychogenesis of manic depressive states. In *Love, guilt and reparation & other works: 1921-1945* (pp. 276–277). New York, NY: Delacorte Press.

Kohut, H. (1971). *The analysis of the self.* New York, NY: International Universities Press.

Kohut, H. (1977). *The restoration of the self.* New York, NY: International Universities Press.

Kohut, H. (1984). *How does analysis cure?* (A. Goldberg & P. Stepansky, Eds.). Chicago, IL: University of Chicago Press.

Kotler, M., Iancu, I., Efroni, R., & Amir, M. (2001). Anger, impulsivity, social support, and suicide risk in patients with posttraumatic stress disorder. *Journal of Nervous and Mental Disease, 189*(3), 162–167.

Laufer, M., & Laufer, M. E. (1989). *Developmental breakdown and psychoanalytic treatment in adolescence: Clinical studies.* New Haven, CT: Yale University Press.

Lewis, H. B. (1971). Shame and guilt in neurosis. *Psychoanalytic Review, 58*, 419–438.

Maltsberger, J. T. (1988). Suicide danger: Clinical estimation and decision. *Suicide and Life-Threatening Behavior, 18*, 47–54.

Maltsberger, J. T. (1993). Confusions of the body, the self and others in suicidal states. In A. Leenaars (Ed.), *Suicidology: Essays in honor of Edwin Shneidman* (pp. 148–171). NJ: Jason Aronson.

Maltsberger, J. T. (2004). The descent into suicide. *International Journal of Psychoanalysis, 85*, 653–658.

Maltsberger, J. T., & Buie, D. H. (1980). The devices of suicide: Revenge, riddance, and rebirth. *International Review of Psychoanalysis, 7*, 61–72.

Maltsberger, J. T., Goldblatt, M. J. Ronningstam, E., Weinberg, I., & Schechter, M. (2011). Traumatic subjective experiences invite suicide. *Journal of the Academy of Psychoanalysis and Dynamic Psychiatry, 39*(4), 671–693.

Maltsberger, J. T., Ronningstam, E., Weinberg, I., Schechter, M., & Goldblatt, M. J. (2010). Suicide fantasy as a life-sustaining recourse. *Journal of the American Academy of Psychoanalysis and Dynamic Psychiatry, 38*(4), 611–624.

Mahler, M., Pine, F., & Bergman, A. (1975). *The psychological birth of the human infant.* New York, NY: Basic Book.

Marcus, B. (1988). Cognitive regression and dynamic factors in suicide: An integrative approach. In H. D. Lerner & P. M. Lerner (Eds.), *Primitive mental states and the Rorschach* (pp. 155–174). Madison, CT: International Universities Press.

Menninger, K. A. (1933). Psychoanalytic aspects of suicide. *International Journal of Psychoanalysis, 14*, 376–390.

Minkoff, K., Begman, E., Beck, A. T., & Besck, R. (1973). Hopelessness, depression and attempted suicide. *American Journal of Psychiatry, 130*, 455–459.

Perry, J. C. (1989). Personality disorders, suicide and self-destructive behavior. In D. Jacobs & H. M. Brown (Eds.), *Suicide: Understanding and responding. Harvard Medical School Perspectives* (pp. 157–170). Madison, CT: International Universities Press.

Plutchik, R., & van Praag, H. M. (1990). Psychosocial correlates of suicide and violence risk. In H. M. van Praag, R. Plutchik, & A. Apter (Eds.), *Violence and sociality: Perspectives in clinical and psychological research* (p. 256). New York, NY: Brunner Mazel.

Sandler, J., & Rosenblatt, B. (1962). The concept of the representational world. *Psychoanalytic Study of the Child, 17*, 128–145.

Shneidman, E. (1985). *Definition of suicide.* New York, NY: Wiley.

Sifneos, P. E., & McCourt, W. F. (1962). Wishes for life and death of some patients who attempted suicide. *Mental Hygiene, 46*, 543–552.

Stolorow, R. D. (1975). Toward a functional definition of narcissism. *International Journal of Psycho-Analysis, 56*, 179–185.

Weissman, M., & Fox Klerman, G. L. (1973). Hostility and depression associated with suicide attempts. *American Journal of Psychiatry, 130*, 450–455.

Winnicott, D. W. (1960). The theory of the parent-infant relationship. In *Maturational processes and the facilitating environment* (pp. 37–55). New York, NY: Basic Books.

Winnicott, D. W. (1965). *The maturational processes and the facilitating environment: Studies in the theory of emotional development. The International Psycho-Analytical Library* (Vol. 64, pp. 1–276). London, UK: Hogarth Press and the Institute of Psycho-Analysis.

Winnicott, D. W. (1975). Through paediatrics to psycho-analysis. The International Psycho-Analytical Library (Vol. 100, pp. 1–325). London, UK: The Hogarth Press and the Institute of Psycho-Analysis.

Zilboorg, G. (1938). The sense of immortality. *Psychoanalytic Quarterly, 7*, 171–199.

Racial/Ethnic, Spiritual/Religious, and Sexual Orientation Influences on Suicidal Behaviors

Regina M. Sherman, Barbara D'Orio, Miesha N. Rhodes, Stephanie Gantt Johnson, *and* Nadine J. Kaslow

Abstract

Race/ethnicity, spirituality/religious affiliation, and sexual orientation increasingly are being examined as related to mental health. This chapter focuses our attention on the link between these key cultural factors and suicidal ideation, attempts, and completions. Particular attention is given to intrapersonal, social and situational, and cultural and environmental risk and protective factors associated with suicidal behavior among African Americans, Hispanics/Latinos, Asian Americans/Pacific Islanders, and Native Americans/Alaska Natives, as well as the association between both spirituality/religiosity and sexual orientation and suicide risk and the expressions of suicidal behavior. The last section reviews the implications of these cultural factors for prevention and intervention efforts with suicidal persons and offers recommendations for future research.

Key Words: culture, race/ethnicity, spirituality/religion, sexual orientation, suicidal behavior

The past decade has witnessed burgeoning attention to the ways in which culture influences suicide (Goldston et al., 2008; Leach, 2006; Leong & Leach, 2008). Recently, there have been calls for greater appreciation of the cultural context of suicidal behaviors, as well as for culturally competent interventions for these behaviors (Goldsmith, Pellmar, Kleinman, & Bunney, 2002). This focus reflects the racial/ethnic diversity of our nation, the awareness of the role that spirituality and religion play in the mental health of many people, and the mounting empirical support suggesting that there are stressors unique to sexual minorities that impact psychological well-being.

The representation of people of color in the United States has grown steadily during the past several decades, a trend expected to continue as we move through the 21st century. Racial and ethnic minorities currently comprise one-third of the US population, but by the year 2050, they are projected to comprise 54% of the US population

(US Census Bureau, 2008). Race/ethnicity are key determinants of mental health outcomes, including suicidal behavior (ideation, attempts, and completions) (Brener, Hassan, & Barrios, 1999; Morrison & Downey, 2000). Across cultures, there is marked variability in terms of rates of suicidal behaviors and beliefs and attitudes regarding such behaviors (Goldston et al., 2008). Understanding race/ethnicity as related to intrapersonal, social and situational, and cultural and environmental risk and protective factors for suicidal behavior is necessary in order to develop prevention programs and to adequately treat ethnic minority populations presenting to treatment (Centers for Disease Control and Prevention, 2009).

Another set of pertinent cultural variables to consider with regard to suicidal behavior is spirituality and religiosity. There is significant, yet not consistent, evidence that religious factors are associated with lower levels of suicidal ideation, attempts, and completions, as well as with more negative attitudes regarding suicidal behavior (Colucci & Martin, 2008). Spirituality/religion may prevent suicidal behavior through religious doctrines that prohibit suicide and through the meaning, comfort, and support that spiritual/religious communities provide (Koenig, 2009). Models need to be developed for suicidal persons that address various aspects of spirituality, religion, and meanings in life.

There is mounting empirical support for the fact that same-gender sexual orientation and bisexuality exerts an independent influence on suicidal ideation, attempts, and completions, particularly for adolescents and young adults (Silenzio, Pena, Duberstein, Cerel, & Knox, 2007). A meta-analysis yielded a two-fold increase in suicide attempts in lesbian, gay, and bisexual (LGB) people (King et al., 2008). There is nascent evidence that transgender youth also are at elevated risk for seriously contemplating and attempting suicide (Grossman & D'Augelli, 2007).

The increasing diversification of the US population demands that mental health professionals consider racial/ethnic, spiritual/religious affiliation, and sexual orientation when understanding mental health concerns and, more specifically, suicidal behaviors. Indeed, attention to common risk and protective factors for suicide in different racial/ethnic groups, spiritual/religious influences on suicidal behavior, and sexual orientation variables as related to suicide risk and the expressions of suicidal behavior are essential for understanding suicidal behavior and its manifestations, making clinical estimates of suicide risk, and implementing strategies to reduce suicide risk (American Psychiatric Association, 2003).

This chapter reviews suicide epidemiology and intrapersonal, social and situational, and cultural and environmental risk and protective factors among the four most populous minority sociopolitical groups in the United States (African American, Hispanic/Latino, Native American/Alaska Native [NA/AN], Asian American/Pacific Islander [AA/PI]). In addition, the relationship between spirituality/religion and suicidal behaviors is explored. This chapter also includes a section on suicidal behavior within the lesbian, gay, bisexual, and transgender (LGBT) population. Finally, concluding comments are offered with regard to the prevention and intervention implications of these cultural influences and directions for future research.

Race/Ethnicity
Epidemiology

In 2006, suicide was ranked as a top 10 leading cause of death among persons ages 10–64 years,

accounting for 33,289 deaths (http://www.cdc.gov/injury/wisqars/index.html). It was the 8th, 9th, 10th, 13th, and 16th leading cause of death for NA/AN, AA/PI, Non-Hispanic Whites, Hispanics/Latinos, and African Americans, respectively. During 2002–2006, the highest suicide rates were among NA/AN males with 26.18 suicides per 100,000 and Non-Hispanic White males with 24.69 suicides per 100,000. Of all female race/ethnicity groups, the NA/AN and Non-Hispanic Whites had the highest rates with 6.70 and 6.15 suicides per 100,000, respectively. AA/PIs had the lowest suicide rates among males, while African Americans had the lowest suicide rate among females (http://www.cdc.gov/injury/wisqars/index.html).

During 2002–2006, among adolescents and young adults, the greatest percentage of suicides occurred by firearm and suffocation for all race/ethnicity groups, with suffocation being more common in the NA/AN population and firearm death in the African American population as compared to other racial/ethnic groups. Among adults, most suicides occurred by firearm, suffocation, and poisoning for all racial/ethnic groups, with suffocation being the most common among AA/PIs and firearms and poisonings being the most frequently employed mode of suicide among non-Hispanic Whites. NA/ANs were also more likely than their ethnic minority counterparts to die by poisoning. Among older adults, across virtually all racial/ethnic groups, the greatest percentage of suicides occurred by firearm. The exception to this was the AA/PI group, for whom suffocation accounted for the highest percentage of suicides (http://www.cdc.gov/injury/wisqars/index.html).

African Americans
DEMOGRAPHICS

There are 38.9 million African Americans in the United States, 12.6% of the total population (US Census Bureau, 2011a). The large majority of African Americans live in the eastern part of the country, with particularly high numbers residing in the southeastern states.

EPIDEMIOLOGY

In 2006, 1,953 African Americans completed suicide in the United States. Suicide was the third leading cause of death among African American youth (15- to 24-year-olds), sixth leading cause for 25- to 34-year-olds, and eighth leading cause for 35- to 44-year-olds. It was not a top ten leading cause of death for African Americans 45 years and older. Among African Americans who died by suicide, 1,668 (85%) were males and 285 (15%) were females. Among African Americans, firearms were the predominant method of suicide (52.1%), followed by suffocation (24.4%) and poisoning (11.2%) (http://www.cdc.gov/injury/wisqars/index.html).

African American youth suicide rates were generally low until the beginning of the 1980s when rates started to increase radically, particularly for young African American males (Centers for Disease Control and Prevention, 1998). Between 1981 and 1994, the rate increased 78%. Since then, the rate has decreased, from 11.48 in 1994 to 6.25 in 2006 for 15- to 24-year-olds. The increased rates of suicide among young African American males appear to be attributable in large part to greater use of firearms (Joe & Kaplan, 2002). Not only have young African American males had an increase in their rates of suicide completions but also in rates of suicide attempts (Joe & Marcus, 2003). Although non-Hispanic White youth were twice as likely as African American youth to complete suicide, the rate of suicide grew faster in this time period among African American males than among non-Hispanic White males. African American male youth have the highest risk among all racial/ethnic and gender groups for attempted suicide and suicide attempts that require medical attention (Centers for Disease Control and Prevention, 2004). African Americans end their lives at a younger age than other individuals who commit suicide (Garlow, Purselle, & Heninger, 2005).

RISK FACTORS

For African Americans, intrapersonal risk factors for suicidal behavior include younger age; aggression; hopelessness; low levels of life satisfaction and self-efficacy; maladaptive coping; self-directed religious coping; psychiatric history; psychological symptoms and disorders; substance abuse; and low levels of religiosity, spirituality, and ethnic identity (Anglin, Gabriel, & Kaslow, 2005; Cook, Pearson, Thompson, Black, & Rabins, 2002; Joe, Baser, Breeden, Neighbors, & Jackson, 2006; Kaslow et al., 1998, 2002, 2004; Kaslow, Thompson, Meadows, et al., 2000; Molock, Puri, Matlin, & Barksdale, 2006; Reviere et al., 2007; Thompson, Kaslow, Bradshaw, & Kingree, 2000; Thompson, Kaslow, & Kingree, 2002; Thompson et al., 1999; Willis, Coombs, Drentea, & Cockerham, 2003). For African American youth, intrapersonal risk factors for suicidal ideation and attempts include being

female, having basic needs unmet (e.g., not having shelter or adequate food), risk-taking behavior, and depression (Ialongo et al., 2004; O'Donnell, O'Donnell, Wardlaw, & Stueve, 2004; Price, Dake, & Kucharewski, 2001). These are similar to the risk factors noted among other ethnic/racial groups.

Social and situational risk factors include numerous and/or severe negative life events, being divorced or widowed, relationship discord, intimate partner violence, threatening others with violence, low levels of family adaptability and cohesion, childhood maltreatment, exposure to substance abuse and intimate partner violence in one's family of origin, social dysfunction, poor interpersonal conflict resolution skills, low levels of social support, and in some studies a collectivist worldview (Compton, Thompson, & Kaslow, 2005; Cook et al., 2002; Harris & Molock, 2000; Kaslow, Thompson, Brooks, & Twomey, 2000; Kaslow, Thompson, Meadows, et al., 1998, 2000, 2002; Ragin et al., 2002; Thompson, Kaslow, Short, & Wyckoff, 2002; Thompson, Kaslow, Bradshaw, et al., 2000; Thompson et al., 1999, 2002; Thompson, Kaslow, Kingree, et al., 2000; Twomey, Kaslow, & Croft, 2000; Vanderwerker et al., 2007). For youth, risk factors within this rubric also include same-gender sexual relationships (O'Donnell et al., 2004). Further, multiple suicide attempts among African Americans are linked to higher levels of social engagement and investment in interpersonal relationships (Merchant, Kramer, Joe, Venkataraman, & King, 2009).

Cultural and environmental risk factors include geographic location, deindustrialization in inner cities, low levels of education and economic resources, residing in areas with high rates of income inequality, access to firearms, and a limited sense of community belonging (Burr, Hartman, & Matteson, 1999; Clarke, Colantonio, Rhodes, & Escobar, 2008; Cook et al., 2002; Joe et al., 2006; Kaslow et al., 1998, 2002, 2005; Kubrin, Wadsworth, & DiPietro, 2006; Thompson et al., 2002; Willis et al., 2003). One cultural and environmental risk factor that deserves particular attention is acculturation. Acculturation has been proposed as an explanation for the increased suicide deaths among African American men (Walker, 2007). As a result of African Americans' efforts to fit in with mainstream culture, factors that traditionally protected them from suicidal behavior (e.g., strong religious and spiritual values, extended family networks/kinships) cease to serve as adequate preventative measures, and environmental pressures to assimilate may amplify psychological distress. In the face of social and economic stressors and environmental pressures to assimilate, acculturated African Americans who lack traditional modes of coping (e.g., religious ties, familial support) may experience more psychological distress and be at greater risk for suicidal behaviors, as such behaviors are more prevalent in the majority culture (Walker, 2007). Moreover, African Americans may be at increased risk for suicide when they experience continuous alienation from mainstream and/or African American culture. In addition, as African Americans become more acculturated, suicidal behavior may no longer be shunned.

PROTECTIVE FACTORS

Intrapersonal protective factors for African Americans include older age, hope, self-efficacy, adaptive coping, collaborative religious coping, religious well-being and a strong religious belief system, a belief that God is responsible for life, and positive ethnic identity (Gibbs, 1997; Kaslow et al., 2002, 2004; Meadows, Kaslow, Thompson, & Jurkovic, 2005; Molock et al., 2006). Being married and family cohesion are salient situational and social protective factors (Walker, 2007). However, the social and situational protective factor that has received the greatest support among African Americans is social support (Gibbs, 1997; Kaslow et al., 1998, 2005; Meadows, Kaslow, Thompson, & Jurkovic, 2005; Nisbet, 1996; Willis et al., 2003). It has been suggested, for example, that the extended family and friendship networks that help African Americans with financial stressors and child rearing in addition to providing emotional support may account for a lower rate of fatal suicide attempts by African American women (Nisbet, 1996). Consistent with this, for African American youth, family closeness is a key resilience factor with regard to suicidal ideation and attempts (O'Donnell et al., 2004).

Cultural and environmental protective factors include southern residence, cultural views that suicide is unacceptable, effectiveness at attaining resources, institutional ties, and engagement in religious activities (Anglin et al., 2005; Kaslow et al., 2002, 2004; Walker, Lester, & Joe, 2006; Walker, Utsey, Bolden, & Williams, 2005). It may be the case that the mechanisms by which protective factors function may be related to belief systems (i.e., suicide as unacceptable) or thwarted attempts (i.e., family intervention/interruption of an attempt) (Walker, 2007). Further, there are countless culture-based strengths (e.g., psychological and

emotional hardiness, spiritually based coping, strong kinship bonds, flexible family roles, broad social support networks, positive ethnic group identity, collectivism) that are associated with lower rates among African Americans as a community (Utsey, Hook, & Stanard, 2007).

Hispanic/Latinos
DEMOGRAPHICS

There are 50.5 million Latinos in the United States, 16.3% of the total population (US Census Bureau, 2011a). Hispanics/Latinos account for one-half of the nation's total population growth. Hispanics/Latinos are a diverse population representing many nationalities (e.g., Mexican, Puerto Rican, Central American, South American, Cuban, Dominican), each with its own social structures that can vary across gender, age, and class (Canino & Roberts, 2001). Hispanic/Latino subgroups vary with regard to the likelihood of being born in America, length of time in America, income and level of education, migration status, and prevailing social attitudes (Alegria et al., 2007; Canino & Roberts, 2001). Hispanics/Latinos share common characteristics such as the Spanish language, *familismo* (family-centered values), and spirituality and beliefs, which have been shaped by a history of colonization and conquest (Garcia-Preto, 2005).

EPIDEMIOLOGY

In 2006, 2,177 Hispanics/Latinos completed suicide in the United States. Suicide was the sixth leading cause of death among Hispanic/Latino youth between the ages of 10–14 years, the third leading cause of death for 15- to 24-year-olds, the fourth leading cause of death for 24- to 34-year-olds, the seventh leading cause of death for 35- to 44-year-olds, and the ninth leading cause of death for 45- to 54-year-olds. It was not a top ten leading cause of death for Hispanic/Latinos 55 years and older (http://www.cdc.gov/injury/wisqars/index. html). Among Hispanic/Latinos who died by suicide, 1,813 were males (83%) and 364 were female (17%). Suffocation (38.5%) and firearms (37.5%) were the most common methods of suicide followed by poisoning (11.3%) (http://www.cdc.gov/ injury/wisqars/index.html).

Ten percent of Hispanic/Latinos report a history of suicidal ideation and 4.4% have made a suicide attempt; 62% of these suicide attempts were made prior to the age of 18 years (Fortuna, Perez, Canino, Sribney, & Alegria, 2007). Hispanics/Latinos born in the United States are two times more likely to have made an attempt than those who are not (Fortuna et al., 2007). Second-generation Hispanics/Latinos are 2.9 times more likely to make an attempt than foreign-born Hispanics/Latinos. Second-generation Hispanics/Latinos are also more likely to abuse alcohol and marijuana (Peña et al., 2008).

Hispanic/Latino youth are half as likely to complete suicide as non-Hispanic Whites; there are, however, significantly higher rates of suicidal ideation and suicide attempts in young Hispanics/Latinos at high school (McKenzie, Serfaty, & Crawford, 2003). Female Hispanic/Latino youth have the highest rates of suicide contemplation (24.2%), planning for a suicide attempt (18.5%), and suicide attempts (14.9%) compared to all ethnic/racial counterparts (Centers for Disease Control and Prevention, 2009).

RISK FACTORS

The following are key intrapersonal risk factors for suicidal behavior in the Hispanic/Latino community: younger age, mixed ethnicity, low self-esteem resulting from internalizing familial conflict, feeling that basic and emotional needs are not being met, depression, alcohol use disorders, and legal problems (Centers for Disease Control and Prevention, 2009; Cuellar & Curry, 2007; Fortuna et al., 2007; Garcia, Skay, Sieving, Naughton, & Bearinger, 2008; O'Donnell et al., 2004; Smokowski & Bacallao, 2006). The culture bound syndrome of *ataques de nervios*, which is characterized by loss of control and dissociation, also plays a role in Hispanic/Latino suicide among female youth (Zayas, Bright, Alvarez-Sanchez, & Cabassa, 2009; Zayas, Lester, Cabassa, & Fortuna, 2005).

Myriad social and situational risk factors for suicide in this population have been noted, including childhood history of emotional and sexual abuse, mother who abuses alcohol, sexual relationship with a member of the same sex, marital dissolution, intimate partner violence, family stress, and social role changes (Cuellar & Curry, 2007; Krishnan, Hilbert, & VanLeeuwen, 2001; Locke & Newcomb, 2005; O'Donnell et al., 2004; Smokowski & Bacallao, 2006; Tillman & Weiss, 2009; Wadsworth & Kubrin, 2007). Among youth, a history of emotional and sexual abuse, separations from parents, perceived family dysfunction, parent–child conflict due to varying degrees of acculturation, poor mother–daughter communication, expectations of obligation to the family, and romantic relationship difficulties are significant predictors of suicidal behavior (Fortuna et al., 2007; Goldston et al.,

2008; Hovey & King, 1996; Santisteban & Mena, 2009; Zayas et al., 2005, 2009). It is unclear which of these factors are unique to this ethnic/racial group and which are true across cultures.

The following have been found to be cultural and environmental risk factors for suicide behavior for Hispanics/Latinos: being a native of the United States, smaller immigrant communities, inequality and discrimination, cultural assimilation, acculturative stress, and higher degree of acculturation (Fortuna et al., 2007; Kaestner, Pearson, Keene, & Geronimus, 2009; Peña et al., 2008; Wadsworth & Kubrin, 2007; Zayas et al., 2005). Foreign-born Hispanics/Latinos commit suicide at a higher rate than their US-born counterparts at statistically significant levels, indicating that the stress of immigration may create higher suicide rates for foreign-born populations (Wadsworth & Kubrin, 2007). Related are the findings that suicide counts are higher when Hispanics/Latinos are more culturally assimilated (Wadsworth & Kubrin, 2007). Among immigrant and second-generation Hispanic/Latino adolescents, acculturative stress and traumatic immigration are positively correlated with suicidal ideation (Hovey & King, 1996; Santisteban & Mena, 2009). Some of these cultural and environmental risk factors may be understood in the context of cultural influences on gender roles. *Marianismo*, for example, is the expectation that females be dependent and focused on family, which may be in contrast with mainstream American society, thereby increasing the acculturative stress experienced by Hispanic/Latino women, which in turn may increase a Hispanic/Latino woman's risk for suicide (Goldston et al., 2008).

PROTECTIVE FACTORS

No intrapersonal protective factors have been found for adults in this population. However, a key intrapersonal protective factor among youth is confidence in one's own ability to problem solve (Locke & Newcomb, 2005). A significant social and situational variable that serves a protective function among Hispanics/Latinos is closeness to family (Fortuna et al., 2007; O'Donnell, O'Donnell, Wardlaw, & Stueve, 2004). This variable plus good relations with parents are social and situational protective factors among Latino adolescents (Locke & Newcomb, 2005). The cultural and environmental factors that play a protective role are higher levels of education, affluence, mobility, and church attendance and involvement (Fortuna et al., 2007; Locke & Newcomb, 2005). In terms of acculturation, the presence of other foreign-born Hispanics/Latinos is a protective factor in Hispanic/Latino immigrant populations, possibly because immigrant populations have an easier time developing social networks in geographic areas more densely populated with immigrants (Wadsworth & Kubrin, 2007). Moreover, suicide rates are lower in geographic areas where there were lower levels of linguistic, educational, residential, and other types of assimilation into mainstream culture (Wadsworth & Kubrin, 2007).

Asian American/Pacific Islanders

DEMOGRAPHICS

There are over 15 million AA/PIs in the United States, approximately 5% of the US population. The AA/PI racial/ethnic group is expected to double in the next 25 years, making it the most rapidly growing racial/ethnic group in the United States (US Census Bureau, 2011a). The majority of the AA/PI population lives in western states (predominantly California and Hawaii). Comprising approximately 43 different ethnic groups, the AA/PI category is extremely diverse. The majority of AA/PIs were born outside of the United States. A large proportion of Chinese and Japanese Americans, however, are fourth- and fifth-generation Americans. AA/PIs speak over 100 languages and dialects, and about 35% of the AA/PI population lives in households where there is limited English proficiency in household members over age 13. The ethnic groups with the most limited English proficiency in the household include Hmong American (61%), Cambodian American (56%), Laotian American (52%), Vietnamese American (44%), Korean American (41%), and Chinese American (40%) (http://mentalhealth.samhsa.gov/cre/fact2.asp).

EPIDEMIOLOGY

In 2006, 810 AA/PIs completed suicide in the United States. Suicide was the seventh leading cause of death among 10- to 14-year-old AA/PIs, the second leading cause of death among AA/PI youth (15–24 years old), third leading cause of death for 25- to 34-year-old AA/PIs, the fourth leading cause of death for 35- to 44-year-olds, the fifth leading cause of death for 45- to 54-year-olds, and the ninth leading cause of death for AA/PIs between the ages of 55 and 64 years. It was not a top ten leading cause of death for AA/PIs 65 years and older (http://www.cdc.gov/injury/wisqars/dataandstats.html). AA/PIs over the age of 65 years in primary care settings, however, reported the greatest amount of suicidal

ideation when compared with other ethnic groups (Bartels et al., 2002).

Among the AA/PIs who killed themselves in 2006, 560 (69%) were males and 250 (31%) were females. The gender differences in rates of suicide for adolescents in this population are not as significant as those in other ethnic groups, largely due to the low rates of suicide among the males. Suffocation (44%) was the predominant method of suicide among AA/PIs, followed by firearms (21.6%), poisoning (14.2%), and falls (7.2%). Japanese Americans have been found to have completed suicide at a proportional rate slightly higher than Chinese Americans, whereas Filipino Americans are significantly lower than either Japanese or Chinese Americans (Lester, 1994). Among adolescents, suicide has been found to be the leading cause of death among South Asians ages 15–24 years residing in the United States (Hovey & King, 1996).

Among youth, Native Hawaiian girls between grades 9 and 12 have significantly higher rates for seriously considering attempting suicide in the past year and have made more plans about suicide in the past year relative to other AA/PI and non-Hispanic White girls (Nishimura, Goebert, Ramisetty-Mikler, & Caetano, 2005). However, non-Hispanic White boys have higher rates of suicide attempts within the past year in comparison with other AA/PI and Native Hawaiian boys. AA/PI girls are more likely than their male counterparts to seriously consider attempting suicide, make plans about suicide, attempt suicide, and require treatment for a suicide attempt (Nishimura et al., 2005). Regarding college-age young adults, AA/PIs are more likely to seriously consider suicide and are more likely to attempt suicide than their non-Hispanic White counterparts (Kisch, Leino, & Silverman, 2005).

RISK FACTORS

The following are key intrapersonal risk factors for suicidal behavior in the AA/PI racial/ethnic group: age, hopelessness, poor sense of self-worth, deficient coping mechanisms, depression, substance abuse/dependence, and religious orientation (Chung, 2003; Clarke et al., 2008; Lau, Jernewall, Zane, & Myers, 2002; Leong, Leach, Yeh, & Chou, 2007; Noh, 2007). For youth, internalizing symptoms, depression and dysthymia, and binge drinking are key intrapersonal risk factors (Lau et al., 2002; Nishimura et al., 2005).

Social and situational risk factors found among AA/PIs include death in the family, sexual orientation, emotional deprivation and abuse from parents, parent–child conflict, varying levels of acculturation between parents and children, negative interactions with significant others, dissatisfying romantic relationships, relationship breakups, social isolation and immersion in academic studies, lack of support and direction in life, racism, sexism, and job loss (Choi, Rogers, & Werth, 2009; Chung, 2003; Lau et al., 2002; Leong et al., 2007; Noh, 2007). In terms of social and situational risk factors for young people, youth with high parent–child conflict are 30 times more likely to evidence suicidal behavior (Lau et al., 2002). For youth with parent–child conflict, there is a stronger association between parent–child conflict and suicidal behaviors for less acculturated youth than for highly acculturated youth; less acculturated AA/PI youth may hold more collectivistic values, including the importance of *filial piety*, relationship harmony, and avoiding confrontation and conflict, making the risk factor of parent–child conflict especially relevant for traditional AA/PI families (Lau et al., 2002). In addition, AA/PI youth who experience intense pressure to succeed from their families, coupled with self-identity problems (e.g., being considered a "model minority"), may experience increased suicidal ideation and attempts (Leong et al., 2007).

Cultural and environmental risk factors among AA/PIs include job loss and low socioeconomic status, sexism and racism, a weak sense of community belonging, lower levels of acculturation, and higher levels of acculturative stress (Chung, 2003; Clarke et al., 2008; Leong et al., 2007; Yeh, McCabe, Hough, Dupuis, & Hazen, 2003). With regard to acculturation, of particular note are findings that AA/PIs who immigrate at the age of 10 years or older have a higher risk for suicide than those who immigrate at ages younger than 10 years; this may be associated with cultural traits, incomplete integration, the challenge of having to adjust to a different culture, and traumatic immigration experiences (Aubert, Daigle, & Daigle, 2004). In addition, greater identification with one's culture of origin shows some connection with suicidal ideation, but not attempts, in AA/PI college students (Kennedy, Parhar, Samra, & Gorzalka, 2005). In a related vein, suicidal youth are more likely than their nonsuicidal peers to have been born outside the United States, a finding that may reflect the fact that less acculturated young people may espouse a more collectivist attitude and become more psychologically distressed in the face of family conflict and challenges to group harmony (Lau et al., 2002). Consistent with this, for youth, the transition to both high school and college is a cultural/environmental risk factor for suicidal behavior, which again is a reflection of the link between assimilation and suicidal behavior risk in this population (Nishimura et al., 2005).

PROTECTIVE FACTORS

There is a dearth of information on protective factors within this population, with regard to both youth and adults. No intrapersonal protective factors for AA/PIs could be found in the literature. Social and situational protective factors include having an intact family and a supportive social network (Clarke et al., 2008; Leong et al., 2007). In addition, fulfilling academic obligations may offer young Asian American women a familiar focus in their lives, which may provide a sense of validation of self-worth, thereby protecting them from suicidal thoughts and behaviors (Chung, 2003). Cultural and environmental protective factors include greater levels of biculturalism and a strong sense of community belonging (Clarke et al., 2008; Leong et al., 2007).

Native American/Alaska Natives
DEMOGRAPHICS

There are 2.9 million NA/ANs in the United States, 0.9% of the total population (US Census Bureau, 2011a). Of NA/ANs, 49% identify as NA/AN only, and 51% identify as NA/AN in combination with one or more other races (US Census Bureau, 2011a). Eighty percent of NA/ANs speak only English at home; of the 20% who speak a language other than English at home, 6% speak English less than "very well." Navajo had the highest percentage who spoke a language other than English at home (US Census Bureau, 2011b). More than 64% of NA/ANs who speak a language other than English live in an "American Indian or Alaskan Native area", which are federally recognized (US Census Bureau, 2011b). Approximately 34% of the NA/AN population live in Native American areas, 2% in Alaska Native village areas, and 64% outside of tribal areas (US Census Bureau, 2011a). Approximately 30% of the NA/AN population is under age 18, compared with 24% of the total US population, whereas 8.3% of NA/AN adults were 65 years or older, compared with 13.7% of the total population of the same age (US Census Bureau, 2011a).

EPIDEMIOLOGY

In 2006, 395 NA/ANs completed suicide in the United States. Suicide was the second leading cause of death among NA/ANs between the ages of 10 and 34 years, the fifth leading cause of death for 35- to 44-year-olds, and the seventh leading cause of death for 45- to 54-year-olds. Suicide was not a top ten leading cause of death for NA/ANs 55 years or older. Among NA/ANs who killed themselves, 309 (78%) were males and 86 (22%) were females. Suffocation (41.3%) was the predominant method of suicide among NA/ANs followed by firearms (39.0%) and poisoning (13.2%) (http://www.cdc.gov/injury/wisqars/index.html). Between 2002 and 2006, the highest suicide rates were among NA/AN males (26.18 suicides per 100,000), compared to non-Hispanic White males (24.69/100,000).

Suicide deaths account for nearly one in five deaths among NA/AN 15- to 19-year-olds, a much higher proportion of deaths than occurs in other ethnic groups in this same age range. Gender differences in this age group are less pronounced than in other ethnic groups, in large part due to the relatively higher rate of suicide among the females (a rate almost triple that of females in the general population). Among NA/AN youth attending Bureau of Indian Affairs schools in 2001, 16% had attempted suicide within the previous year (Shaughnessy, Doshi, & Jones, 2004). Female high school students made more suicide attempts than males and ninth graders were more likely than those in any other high school grades to make a suicide attempt.

RISK FACTORS

The literature, particularly with NA/AN adults, is quite limited with regard to information about relevant risk factors for suicidal behavior. The following are key intrapersonal risk factors for suicidal behavior among NA/ANs (youth and adults): somatic symptoms (e.g., headaches and stomach problems), having health concerns, engaging in self-harming and other-directed violent behaviors, engaging in sexual risk behaviors, learning difficulties, depression, conduct disorder, alcohol and drugs abuse/dependence, intoxication, cigarette smoking, and history of being treated for emotional problems (Borowsky, Resnick, Ireland, & Blum, 1999; Clarke et al., 2008; Freedenthal & Stiffman, 2004; Grossman, Milligam, & Deyo, 1991; Middlebrook, LeMaster, Beals, Novins, & Manson, 2001; Shaughnessy et al., 2004).

Relatively few social and situational risk factors for suicide among adults in this population have been identified; those that have been identified include recent and severe stressful life events,

marrying outside one's tribal group, and separation from family (Middlebrook et al., 2001; Paproski, 1997). Among youth, social and situational risk factors are as follows: a history of sexual or physical abuse, a family history of suicide attempt/completion or substance abuse, alienation from one's family, gang involvement, and having a friend attempt or complete suicide (Borowsky et al., 1999; Freedenthal & Stiffman, 2004; Grossman et al., 1991). This latter finding is consistent with research on "cluster" suicides, or groupings of suicides that have been reported in several NA/AN communities in both the United States and Canada, which have also been identified as risk factors in NA/AN adolescent populations (Borowsky et al., 1999; Freedenthal & Stiffman, 2004). There is mounting evidence that NA/AN youth may be particularly vulnerable to suicide contagion (Wissow, Walkup, Barlow, Reid, & Kane, 2001), a finding that may reflect the intense social networks for youth residing on rural reservations. Because of the high rates of suicide on some reservations, NA/AN youth may have increased exposure to suicidal behavior among their family members and friends. Such experiences are associated with trauma and loss, which in turn increases their vulnerability to engaging in suicidal behavior.

The following have been found to be cultural and environmental risk factors for suicide behavior: disadvantages in income and low social class, disadvantages in education, access to firearms, a limited sense of community belonging, and separation from culture (Clarke et al., 2008; Middlebrook et al., 2001; Paproski, 1997). Attention also has been given to acculturation as a relevant cultural and environmental risk factor. Acculturation into the US mainstream is relevant when discussing risk factors for suicide given that NA/AN tribal communities experience higher rates of suicide in times of high acculturation (Middlebrook et al., 2001). The lower rates of suicide among the Navajo may be partially explained by protection from acculturative stresses given their relatively remote homeland. In addition, Navajo traditional beliefs about death, which prevail today, including condemnation against any behavior that might invite death, may serve a protective function (Middlebrook et al., 2001). Among NA/AN youth, community isolation is a key cultural and environmental risk factor (Grossman et al., 1991). Additional cultural and environmental risk factors for suicidal ideation and attempts among NA/AN youth are attending a boarding school, living on a reservation, and perceived discrimination due to being of native descent (Freedenthal & Stiffman, 2004; Middlebrook et al., 2001).

PROTECTIVE FACTORS

Once again, the literature on protective factors is limited, particularly with adults. Intrapersonal protective factors for NA/AN youth include being in good emotional health, academic success, a cultural spiritual orientation, and a strong cultural identity (Borowsky et al., 1999; Freedenthal & Stiffman, 2004; Garroutte et al., 2003). For these youth, the ability to discuss problems with family or friends, feeling connected to family, family satisfaction, and social support are relevant social and situational protective factors (Borowsky et al., 1999; Freedenthal & Stiffman, 2004). Among NA/ANs, a strong sense of community belonging is the only cultural and environmental factor that appears to buffer adults from suicidal behavior (Clarke et al., 2008). For youth, being in a school with a nurse or a clinic reduces their risk for suicidal behavior (Borowsky et al., 1999).

Spirituality and Religion

Spirituality is considered to be personal; it is an experience that individuals define for themselves that is largely free from the institutions and rules associated with religion (Koenig, 2009). Religion, on the other hand, involves beliefs, practices, and rituals related to God, or in Eastern traditions, the Ultimate Truth or Reality. Religion has its roots in traditions maintained by a group of people with common beliefs and practices regarding the sacred. It usually has specific beliefs about life after death and rules about conduct that guide social groups or communities (Koenig, 2009).

Traditionally, spirituality and religion have offered an individual a collective source of meaning, hope, comfort, deliverance in the face of hardship and difficult life experiences, and have been shown to positively influence beliefs, practices, and outcomes related to mental and physical health (Dash, Jackson, & Rasor, 1997; Newlin, Knafl, & Melkus, 2002). Spirituality and religion have been used as coping tools by promoting a positive worldview that is optimistic and hopeful; providing examples and role models that help one to accept suffering; giving individuals a sense of indirect control (e.g., God has a plan); offering support (both community and divine); and providing access regardless of financial, emotional, physical, or social circumstances (Koenig, 2009).

Regarding suicide specifically, spirituality and religion have been identified as cultural factors that act as a buffer against suicidal ideation, attempts, and completion in ethnic minorities (Garlow et al., 2005; Greening & Stoppelbein, 2002; Harris & Molock, 2000; Marion & Range, 2003), as well as within the general population (Molock et al., 2006). This is supported by the finding that those who identify as more religious have 84% lower rates of suicide (Koenig & Larson, 2001). One explanation for this is that the act of suicide has been historically condemned in most major religious traditions (Gearing & Lizardi, 2009). Indeed, religions commonly espouse moral objections toward suicide, thereby decreasing pro-suicide ideology (Dervic et al., 2004; Stack & Wasserman, 1995).

Contrary to the studies that have identified spirituality/religion as a protective factor, other studies have found that spirituality/religion and suicide are not associated (Dervic et al., 2004; Eshun, 2003; Kamal & Lowenthal, 2002) and that spirituality is a risk factor for suicide, specifically when individuals are struggling with spiritual/religious concerns (Chatters, 2000; Exline, Yali, & Sanderson, 2000; Johnson & Hayes, 2003). The beliefs that one has committed a sin too big to be forgiven, will not be viewed favorably by God, or will be punished harshly for his or her sins have been identified as salient risk factors as well (Chatters, 2000; Exline et al., 2000).

Religions

CHRISTIANITY

In the United States, 78.4% of adults identify as Christian, which is comprised of Protestant, Catholic, Mormon, Catholic, Jehovah's Witness, and Orthodox (Russian, Greek). Taking into account the total US population, non-Hispanic Whites make up the majority of those in the United States who identify as Christian. When looking at racial/ethnic groups individually, however, Christianity is the most predominant religion among African Americans and Hispanics/Latinos (Pew Forum on Religion & Public Life, 2008). With respect to suicide, Christianity has historically taught that suicide would fate an individual to eternal damnation (Vandecreek & Mottram, 2008) and responded by denying individuals religious burial rites (Gearing & Lizardi, 2009). There are, however, no specific biblical statements about the eternal destiny following a completed suicide (Vandecreek & Mottram, 2008).

JUDAISM

Among adults living in the United States, 1.7% identify as Jewish, 95% of whom are White (Pew

Forum on Religion & Public Life, 2008). Similar to Christianity, Jewish traditions also have condemned suicide and have viewed suicide as one of the most serious sins (Ventegodt & Merrick, 2005). Jews are forbidden from intentionally causing harm to their bodies, and especially from taking their own lives. These teachings are reinforced by the denial of burial rites to individuals who have completed suicide (Gearing & Lizardi, 2009). Of note, there are three specific cases in which suicide is not forbidden under Jewish law: if one is being forced by someone to commit murder, forced to commit an act of idolatry, or forced to commit adultery or incest (Ventegodt & Merrick, 2005).

ISLAM

In 2008, 0.7% of adults living in the United States identified as Muslim. Islam is the most racially diverse religion in the United States, comprised of 37% non-Hispanic Whites, 24% African Americans, 20% AA/PIs, and 19% individuals of other races (Pew Forum on Religion & Public Life, 2008). In Islamic tradition, the Koran explicitly forbids individuals from killing themselves and maintains that suicide excludes an individual from heaven and condemns him or her to perpetual hell (Kamal & Lowenthal, 2002). There is a dearth of literature examining the relationship between Islam and suicidal behaviors in the United States. In the United Kingdom, compared to Hindus, Muslims endorse more moral (including spiritual/religious) reasons for living and have more overall reasons for living (Kamal & Lowenthal, 2002). From an international perspective, there is some suggestion that suicide completion rates are lower in Muslims than in those of other religions, even in countries that have populations that espouse several different religious persuasions (Lester, 2006). However, suicide attempt rates are not lower in Muslims as compared to non-Muslims (Lester, 2006).

BUDDHISM

In 2008, 0.6% of adults living in the United States identified as Buddhist, 32% of whom are AA/PI and 53% of who are non-Hispanic Whites (Pew Forum on Religion & Public Life, 2008). Suicide is contrary to basic Buddhist values (Keown, 1996, 1998). In the Buddhist tradition, self-harm is considered wrong, and killing oneself is seen as an offensive act toward ancestors (Leong et al., 2007). Buddhism encourages contemplation of death and suffering; at the same time it discourages disruption of the natural processes or order, and views suicide

as an individual's interference with the life cycle (Leong et al., 2007). Moreover, when an individual dies by suicide, the belief is that he or she did not have sufficient time to prepare for death and did not enter death with the appropriate mindset, which may result in difficulty during reincarnation (Kamal & Lowenthal, 2002; Vandecreek & Mottram, 2008). In addition, Buddhism views suicide as negative due to its selfishness and its impact on family and community (Leong et al., 2007).

HINDUISM

In 2008, 0.4% of adults living in the United States identified as Hindu, 88% of whom are AA/PI (Pew Forum on Religion & Public Life, 2008). Hindus have a fairly high rate of suicide completions (Leach, 2006). Hindu males attempt suicide more frequently than females, which is contrary to rates seen in Christianity (Leong et al., 2007). In addition, Hindus who attempt suicide are typically not under the influence of alcohol or drugs. In Hinduism, suicide is neither actively deterred nor condoned (Leong et al., 2007). Similar to Buddhism, in Hinduism there does not appear to be a threat of eternal damnation following a suicide, as seen in Christianity; however, difficulties that may result during reincarnation are considered a deterrent (Kamal & Lowenthal, 2002; Vandecreek & Mottram, 2008). Furthermore, for many Hindus, suicide is considered a "bad" death and some believe that the spirit of the individual who completed suicide will return to haunt the living (Leong et al., 2007).

Racial/Ethnic Groups

AFRICAN AMERICANS

Of all the major racial and ethnic groups in the United States, African American adults are the most likely to report a formal religious affiliation; 85% of African American adults identify as Christian, and 1% as Muslim. Twelve percent of African American adults are not affiliated with a religion, but of them, 70% state that religion is important in their lives. Only 1% of African American adults identify as atheist or agnostic (Pew Forum on Religion & Public Life, 2008).

As previously noted, religious affiliation and high levels of religiosity, orthodoxy, and devotion have been identified as protective factors against suicide among African Americans (Anglin et al., 2005; Chance, Kaslow, Summerville, & Wood, 1998; Gibbs, 1997; Greening & Stoppelbein, 2002; Leong & Leach, 2008; Willis, Coombs, Cockerham, &

Frison, 2002). In considering spirituality/religion, it is important to note that one's orientation toward spirituality/religion, or the manner in which spirituality/religion is used as a coping mechanism, may influence its effects. For example, the freedom to resolve one's own problems has been related to more suicide attempts, whereas individuals who have an active and cooperative relationship with God identify more reasons for living (Molock et al., 2006).

HISPANIC/LATINO

Among Hispanic/Latino adults, 84% identify as Christian and 14% report being unaffiliated with a religious denomination. When compared with all other ethnic groups in the United States, Hispanic/Latinos are most identified with Catholicism; 58% of Hispanic/Latinos identify as Catholic (Pew Forum on Religion & Public Life, 2008).

Spirituality/religion has been found to be a suicide buffer among Hispanic/Latino Americans (Range et al.,1999). Hispanic/Latino heritage identifies with a concept known as *fatalismo*, which is associated with Catholicism and suggests that one cannot change the unchangeable and that life should be lived without attempting to control one's environment (Hovey & King, 1996; Range et al., 1999). In addition, Catholicism teaches that taking a life in any circumstance is a sin. Therefore, for Hispanic/Latinos who firmly believe in and practice their faith, these beliefs may serve as buffers against suicide (Range et al., 1999).

ASIAN AMERICAN/PACIFIC ISLANDER

In the United States, AA/PI adults are the ethnic group least likely to be affiliated with a religion. Among AA/PI adults, 45% identify as Christian, 14% as Hindu, 9% as Buddhist, 4% as Muslim, and 7% as atheist or agnostic (3% and 4%, respectively) (Pew Forum on Religion & Public Life, 2008). Among AA/PIs, attitudes and beliefs about spirituality/religion are generally derived from Buddhism, Confucianism, Taoism, and Hinduism. However, compared to mainstream religions, AA/PIs hold beliefs from a mixture of faiths and vary widely within faiths consistent with Christianity, Islam, and Judaism (Leong et al., 2007).

Research exploring the association between spirituality/religion in AA/PIs is scarce given that the majority of studies focus on Christianity. What has been identified is that Buddhism can act as a buffer against suicide among AA/PIs when an individual identifies with the sense of reverence for the larger cycle of life (Leong et al., 2007). It is useful to consider that Eastern faiths may act as deterrents to suicide in AA/PIs, but they also may provide an acceptable rationale for completing suicide (Leong et al., 2007).

NATIVE AMERICAN/ALASKA NATIVE

Within the NA/AN community, neither commitment to cultural spirituality nor to Christianity is associated with suicide attempts (Garroutte et al., 2003). However, a commitment to cultural spirituality does appear to buffer individuals from attempting suicide (Garroutte et al., 2003). Spirituality/religion, however, may help NA/ANs recover from a history of suicide attempts. Research has found that the process of healing from a suicide attempt is facilitated by one's connection to native spirituality as expressed through prayer, singing, drumming, awareness of the Creator, being in nature, engaging in rituals, and sharing spiritual experiences with others (Paproski, 1997).

Lesbian, Gay, Bisexual, and Transgender
Demographics

In 2010, there were 605,472 same sex couples identified by the US Census (2011a) with California, New York, Texas, and Florida leading the country in total number of same-sex unmarried partner households. The Human Rights Campaign suggests that historically (i.e., the 2000 US Census) the count of lesbian and gay families could be undercounted by as much as 62% (http://www.hrc.org). Prevalence data on homosexuality vary considerably. The Healthy People 2010 Companion Document for Lesbian, Gay, Bisexual and Transgender Health suggests that US homosexual prevalence ranges between 1.4% and 6% for women and 2.8% to 10% for men (Gay and Lesbian Medical Association and LGBT Health Experts, 2001). Approximately 7.5% of survey samples admit to same-sex desire, while 9.8% of men and 5% of women report at least one episode of same-gender sexual activity.

Little data exist on the prevalence of transgender individuals in the United States. Rates have been estimated to be between 1 in 10,000 and 1 in 40,000 natal males and between 1 in 30,000 and 1 in 100,000 natal females (Cohen-Kettenis, 2004). Activists place the prevalence between 1 in 500 and 1 in 2,500 for both males and females (http://ai.eecs.umich.edu/people/conway/TS/TSprevalence.html).

It is important to consider that lesbian, gay, bisexual, and transgender (LGBT) prevalence data vary significantly due to sexuality and transgender identity frequently being excluded from most national surveys. If sexuality and transgender identity are included in surveys, there would be considerable variation in prevalence estimates based on the factors that are being measured (e.g., any prior same-sex behaviors, same-sex behaviors in the recent past, same-sex desire and self-identification as being part of the LGBT community).

Epidemiology

There are no accurate data regarding completed suicides in the LGBT population. Medical examiners do not collect data on LGBT suicides as surviving family members may not be aware of their loved one's sexual orientation or transgender identity, or they may feel too ashamed to disclose this information. Research, however, has found that the LGBT population has higher rates of suicide attempts and suicidal ideation when compared with the general population (Gay and Lesbian Medical Association and LGBT Health Experts, 2001). Among lesbians, 18% report a history of at least one suicide attempt and more than half endorse a history of suicidal ideation (Bradford, Ryan, & Rothblum, 1994). Similarly, among gay men, 12% report having made at least one suicide attempt, and 21% endorse having made suicide plans in the past (Paul et al., 2002). Male to female (MTF) transgender individuals report a 32.4% suicide attempt rate and female to male (FTM) individuals report a 26.2% suicide attempt rate (Kenegay, 2005).

No data can be located specifically about differential rates in suicide completions between LGB and heterosexual youth. However, studies comparing rates of suicide behavior among LGB and heterosexual youth show significantly higher rates for the former group, with LGB youth being two to four times more likely to have suicidal thoughts and attempts (Botempo & D'Augelli, 2002; Eisenberg & Resnick, 2006; Russell & Joyner, 2001; Saewye et al., 2007; Suicide Prevention Resource Center, 2008). These attempts are most likely to occur during adolescence and young adulthood. It has been postulated that the elevated rates of suicide attempts may be a result of the myriad psychosocial stressors that often accompany being LGB, such as gay-related stress, gender nonconformity, dropping out of school, psychiatric disorders and substance abuse, family problems, lack of social support, suicide attempts by acquaintances, homelessness, and victimization (Bontempo, 2002; Kitts, 2005).

Risk Factors

Intrapersonal risk factors for suicide associated within the LGB population include younger age (i.e., adolescence), precocious sexual development, gender nonconformity, early self-identification as LGB, psychological stress associated with "coming out," sexual activity at a younger age, a dearth of sexual activity in adulthood, psychological distress, depression, anxiety, and substance abuse (Cochran, Mays, Alegria, Ortega, & Takeuchi, 2007; Cochran, Mays, & Sullivan, 2003; Diaz, Ayala, Bein, Henne, & Marin, 2001; Jesdale & Zierler, 2002; King et al., 2008; Mays & Cochran, 2001; McDaniel, Purcell, & D'Augelli, 2001; Sandfort, Melendez, & Diaz, 2007). There is some suggestion that gender nonconformity accounts for almost all of the variation in suicidal behavior between LGB and heterosexual persons (Fitzpatrick, Euton, Jones, & Schmidt, 2005). Among the transgender population, 75% of MTF individuals report being transgender as the reason for prior attempts, while 52.9% of FTM individuals report being transgender as a prime motivation to attempt suicide (Kenegay, 2005). Additional intrapersonal risk factors for this group include younger age and depression (Clements-Nolle, Marx, & Katz, 2006). Among LGB youth, sexual risk-taking behaviors, depression, and substance abuse are salient intrapersonal risk factors for suicidal behavior (Epstein & Spirito, 2009; Fergusson, Horwood, & Beautrais, 2009). Of note, however, not all studies have found depression or substance use to be risk factors for suicidal ideation or attempts in LGB youth and have found them to be less salient risk factors than among heterosexual youth (Silenzio et al., 2007). The challenges posed by developing sexual and/or gender identity in LGBT youth are also believed to increase their risk for suicide attempts (Lesbon, 2002). Negative body image and negative assumptions about how others view their bodies elevate risk in transgender youth (Grossman & D'Augelli, 2007).

Social and situational risk factors for LGB individuals include early disclosure of self-identification to others and victimization (McDaniel et al., 2001), whereas forced sex and victimization have been found for transgender individuals (Clements-Nolle et al., 2006). For LGB youth, abuse within the family (physical, sexual, emotional), early openness about their sexuality with family members, being classified as gender atypical by parents, parents' discouragement of gender atypical behaviors, family rejection, a recent attempt by a friend or family member, and victimization all are relevant variables in this domain (D'Augelli et al., 2005; McBee-Strayer & Rogers, 2002; Russell & Joyner, 2001; Ryan, Huebner, Diaz, & Sanchez, 2009). With regard to the latter, LGBT youth are 9 to10 times more likely to report repeated episodes of victimization than their heterosexual peers.

For the LGB population, cultural and environmental risk factors include exposure to homophobia and discrimination (Diaz et al., 2001; Jesdale & Zierler, 2002; Mays & Cochran, 2001; McDaniel et al., 2001; Sandfort et al., 2007). This is further supported by the finding that between 1990 and 1999, the suicide attempt rate differential between LGB and heterosexual non-Hispanic White adolescent males decreased in states that enacted antidiscrimination employment laws based on sexual orientation (Jesdale & Zierler, 2002). Discrimination is also a cultural and environmental risk factor for transgender individuals (Clements-Nolle et al., 2006). In addition, LGB youth who are members of ethnic groups with strong prohibitions against same-gender sexual relationships are at increased risk for suicidal ideation (Balsam, Huang, Fieland, Simoni, & Walters, 2004; Kulkin, Chauvin, & Percle, 2000).

Protective Factors

There is a striking lack of data about factors that protect LGBT individuals from engaging in suicidal behavior. The only intrapersonal protective factor identified for adults is self-efficacy (Carrico et al., 2007). For youth, a few social and situational variables buffer them from suicidal ideation and attempts, such as family connectedness and support and adult caring (Eisenberg & Resnick, 2006; Kidd et al., 2006). For LGB youth, one cultural and environmental protective factor is school safety (Eisenberg & Resnick, 2006).

Concluding Comments

Understanding racial/ethnic, spiritual/religious, and sexual orientation differences in the pathways to suicidal behavior is essential for suicide prevention efforts and treatment interventions for diverse populations. The myriad biological, psychological, social, and cultural factors that have direct and/or indirect effects on developing pathways to suicidal behavior within different racial/ethnic groups must be considered. For example, more attention needs to be paid to the ways in which ethnic identity, level of acculturation, LGBT identity, social class factors, group's social position, discrimination, and stigma interact to influence the presentation and treatment

of suicidal behaviors (Baller & Richardson, 2002; Clarke et al., 2008; Dohrenwend, 2000; Morrison & Downey, 2000). Regarding acculturation, it is essential to consider that as individuals and communities become more "Americanized," they may let go of shared belief systems, rituals, and social networks that promote integration into their ethnic/racial community, which in turn may increase the risk for suicide (Wadsworth & Kubrin, 2007; Walker, 2007).

Recommendations for Prevention and Intervention Programs

For all racial/ethnic, spiritual/religious, and LGBT groups, the development of suicide prevention and intervention programs must include training mental health professionals in recognizing and responding to warning signs, as well as providing information on within-group intrapersonal, social and situational, and cultural and environmental suicide risk and protective factors. In addition, culturally sensitive prevention and intervention programs should involve collaborators and consultants from members and leaders of racial/ethnic, spiritual/religious, and LGBT communities at all phases of development (inception, implementation, and research and evaluation) (Clarke et al., 2008; May, Serna, Hurt, & DeBruyn, 2005; Suicide Prevention Resource Center, 2008).

AFRICAN AMERICAN

African Americans have the highest levels of public and private spirituality/religiousness. Therefore, with regard to suicide prevention and intervention programs, it is recommended that African American churches be included. The advantages for developing such intervention programs are numerous: African American churches have had a strong history of helping community members, regardless of church membership; they may help shape religious and cultural norms about mental health and help-seeking; they are accessible to community members; programs can be held in more family friendly contexts; and programs could occur in a setting for which one does not have to overcome a history of distrust or a history of cultural insensitivity (Molock, Matlin, Barksdale, Puri, & Lyles, 2008). It is important to bear in mind that there are potential barriers to be addressed when engaging with churches in terms of suicide prevention and intervention. Most notable among these potential barriers are that clergy may be less likely to notice suicide risk than other professionals and may make fewer mental health referrals, as well as the fact that that there is stigma in some church communities with regard to both mental health services and suicide (Goldston et al., 2008). Some of these obstacles may be overcome through gatekeeper training for clergy and other significant lay people within the church community (Molock et al., 2007).

Consistent with other prevention programs designed specifically for African American youth, prevention and intervention programs should incorporate a focus on bolstering ethnic identity (Goldston et al., 2008). In addition, given the link between interpersonal violence and suicide, existing interpersonal violence prevention and intervention programs should include a suicide component (Davis et al., 2009; Willis et al., 2003). Finally, given the link between psychiatric comorbidity and substance use among African Americans, more culturally sensitive mental health and substance use prevention and intervention programs should be developed.

HISPANIC/LATINO

As with other racial/ethnic minorities compared to non-Hispanic Whites, Hispanics/Latinos are less likely to receive mental health treatment, and when they do, they are less likely to adhere to treatment recommendations (Kataoka, Stien, Lieberman, & Wong, 2003; Unützer et al., 2003). Latino youth are less likely to be viewed as suicidal and to receive appropriate crisis intervention services than are adolescents from other demographic backgrounds (Kataoka et al., 2003). When Latino youth do seek out attention for their psychological distress, it is typically with informal sources, including family and peers. Thus, it is helpful if prevention and intervention programs for Latinos are conducted in the community and inclusive of family members and other persons in the individual's social support network.

Another challenge that must be considered when developing prevention and intervention programs is that of language. There is a dearth of Spanish-speaking providers, and while the use of interpreters is a common mechanism to address this challenge, it decreases the individual's understanding of treatment recommendations and inhibits the development of warm rapport between the provider and individual (Julliard et al., 2008). Further, prevention and intervention programs should consider an individual's cultural values, which may vary with level of acculturation (Añez, Silva, Paris, & Bedregal, 2008). Three Hispanic/Latino cultural

values that impact treatment engagement and adherence include *personalismo* (the importance of fostering warm personal relationship), *respecto* (mutual respect), and *confianza* (intimacy and trust in personal relationships); these values need to be taken into account in developing and implementing programs (Añez et al., 2008). Finally, it is recommended that existing evidence-based treatments (cognitive-behavioral, interpersonal, and dialectical behavioral therapies) be modified to increase engagement and treatment adherence for Hispanic/Latinos (Miranda et al., 2005); this may be done by providing an array of options, including individual, family, and group interventions to address suicidality at the individual level (Santisteban & Mena, 2009).

ASIAN AMERICAN/PACIFIC ISLANDER

There is a paucity of prevention and intervention research related to AA/PI individuals (Harachi, Catalano, Kim, & Choi, 2001). Suicidal risk is often under-recognized in the AA/PI population, a problem that is confounded by the low rates of mental health service utilization in this population. Furthermore, AA/PI youth often are more reluctant to share their suicidal thoughts than are their White peers (Morrison & Downey, 2000). Concerns about shame or loss of face are prevalent in this community and may influence both suicide risk and the likelihood of disclosure (Goldston et al., 2008). Prevention and intervention efforts need to be designed and implemented in a fashion that is sensitive to barriers to accessing care in this population, including the finding that AA/PI individuals often tend to be "hidden ideators" and focus more on their physical than their psychological pain (Goldston et al., 2008), as well as the shame-proneness that is so prevalent.

Suicide prevention and intervention programs for AA/PIs should consider different ethnic AA/PI groups separately, as suicide rates often differ by group (Leong et al., 2007). In general, programs should consider acculturation and intergenerational family conflicts (Lau et al., 2002). Given the high value placed on interdependence within the culture, it is advisable to include family members in the treatment (Goldston et al., 2008). Similar to language barriers seen in the Hispanic/Latino population, language barriers also exist for the AA/PI population, where there are even fewer interpreters. Thus, prevention and intervention programs will be most effective if bilingual providers are available and appropriately trained in suicide prevention. For youth, prevention and intervention programs should consider the risk for AA/PI students transitioning from middle school to high school (Nishimura et al., 2005) and from high school to college (Choi et al., 2009; Chung, 2003; Kisch et al., 2005; Leong et al., 2007). For adolescents, programs should address the relationship of alcohol use and suicide, as well as cultural factors, and should be implemented earlier than the ninth grade (Nishimura et al., 2005). For youth of college age, romantic relationships and bolstering support networks with on-campus Asian student associations should be considered (Choi et al., 2009; Chung, 2003).

NATIVE AMERICAN/ALASKA NATIVE

There are relatively few prevention and intervention programs aimed at reducing suicidality among NA/AN adults. For NA/ANs, it is recommended that suicide prevention and intervention programs consider community-based approaches and incorporate culturally specific knowledge and traditions. Given the cultural variability across NA groups, programs must take into account the unique aspects of each tribe.

However, for NA/AN youth, nine prevention programs have been identified that are evidence based (Middlebrook et al., 2001), some of which have promising outcome data with regard to reducing rates of suicide attempts (May et al., 2005). With regard to youth, programs will serve the community well that work with at-risk parents in order to reduce suicidal behavior in their children, develop youth community and recreation centers, and increase access to youth-specific mental health programs in schools and youth centers (Middlebrook et al., 2001). Given that the strongest association with a history of attempted suicide for both male and female NA/AN adolescents is having a friend attempt or complete suicide, routine screening of NA/AN youth for exposure to suicidal behavior and subsequent mental health responses (i.e., depression, posttraumatic stress disorder) should be considered so that appropriate treatment strategies can be implemented (Borowsky et al., 1999; Middlebrook et al., 2001). Finally, given that NA/AN youth who attempt suicide also engage in a variety of, and greater number of, health risk behaviors, suicide prevention programs should be incorporated into other health risk behavior prevention programs (May et al., 2005; Shaughnessy et al., 2004).

SPIRITUALITY/RELIGION

To be truly culturally competent, mental health professionals must address the spiritual/religious beliefs of their clients and their families and appropriately incorporate these beliefs into prevention and treatment programs (Walsh, 2008). Research has shown that spirituality/religion incorporated into treatment can reduce problems (Cowger, 1994), yet mental health professionals typically are not trained in the area of spirituality/religion and rarely address spirituality/religion during the helping process (Hodges & Williams, 2002). To address this deficiency, education and training regarding the role of spirituality/religion should be included at the graduate level. This training should provide skill acquisition with regard to integrating a client's beliefs in a supportive and reaffirming manner, while at the same time being mindful not to assume that their client's beliefs are reflective of group norms (Hodges & Williams, 2002). Incorporation of spiritual/religious concepts has been shown to enrich the client–professional relationship; this is best facilitated when a professional uses active listening, poses specific questions to identify the spiritual and emotional needs of the client, and makes appropriate referrals when necessary to sensitive religious leaders (Hodges & Williams, 2002; Kliewer, 2004). Furthermore, whenever spiritual/religious beliefs are incorporated into treatment, appropriate roles should be maintained and mental health professionals should be careful not to take on the role of spiritual/religious advisor. In addition, it is imperative that mental health professionals not impose their personal spiritual/religious beliefs on the client, especially when the mental health professional shares the client's spiritual/religious tradition.

LESBIAN, GAY, BISEXUAL, AND TRANSGENDER

The LGBT population is at higher risk for suicidal ideation, attempts, and completions than their heterosexual counterparts. LGBT individuals may be unwilling to identify as LGBT until late adolescence or early adulthood, after emotional damage has occurred (King et al., 2008), making access to intervention and prevention programs challenging. Nevertheless, prevention and intervention programs that follow individuals throughout their education, career training, and start of relationships and families would benefit the LGBT community (King et al., 2008). In order to reduce the risk of LGBT suicide, programs should focus on building family support. Further, supporting the development of Parents, Families, and Friends of Lesbians and Gays (PFLAG) groups, LGBT youth groups, family agencies that provide culturally sensitive services to LGBT youth, and gay–straight alliances may reduce the risk for suicide and operate as protective factors (Suicide Prevention Resource Center, 2008). Other programs may consider prevention and intervention around the time that individuals are considering disclosing their LBGT identity to family members. Given that this age range varies widely, and that LGBT people often become aware of their orientation at very young ages, special prevention efforts should be directed to younger adolescents and their parents (Suicide Prevention Resource Center, 2008). Finally, given that LGBT youth often first confide their problems to peers, peer education and training programs may be effective in reducing the risk for suicide in LGBT populations (Suicide Prevention Resource Center, 2008).

Recommendations for Future Research

To develop effective, evidence-based, and culturally competent prevention and intervention programs, it is valuable to have a comprehensive understanding of the intrapersonal, social and situational, and cultural and environmental risk and protective factors for various racial/ethnic, spiritual/religious, and LGBT populations. As this chapter has shown, the science is incomplete regarding protective and risk factors for certain racial/ethnic groups, various spiritual/religious denominations, and the LGBT population. Future research needs to be conducted toward this end. Specifically, it would enhance our understanding if such research focused on culture-specific triggers or precipitants, the ways in which risk and protective factors are influenced by cultural context, and the ways in which the characteristics of suicidal behaviors vary across contexts (Goldston et al., 2008).

Among AA/PIs, for example, there is limited research investigating intrapersonal, social and situational, and cultural and environmental protective factors among both adults and youth. Similarly, among the NA/AN population, there is a dearth of scientific investigation identifying intrapersonal, social and situational, and cultural and environmental risk and protective factors among adults and cultural and environmental protective factors among youth. Regarding spirituality/religion, while there are few studies examining spirituality/religion and suicide in general, research investigating this relationship among the Islamic, Buddhist, and Hindu faiths is particularly limited.

With regard to the LGBT population, the current demographic data (e.g., number of people living in the United States who identify as LGBT) provided by the US Census Bureau, and related suicide prevalence rates are insufficient and misleading. Future research needs to better address complexities regarding defining sexual orientation (King et al., 2008). In addition, there is limited research investigating suicidal thoughts, behaviors, and completions within the transgender population. It is also noteworthy that this chapter did not discuss suicidal behavior within the transgender community; it is recommended that future research include this group of individuals.

Prevention and intervention programs will be more effective at reducing suicidality if they are able to identify the risk and protective factors associated with suicide for various groups, and then use this information to decrease risk factors and bolster the protective factors. In addition, such programs should be mindful of help-seeking behavior and barriers to accessing services and be designed to address these considerations (Goldston et al., 2008). These interventions should be designed and implemented in a fashion that takes into account such factors as acculturation and enculturation (i.e., the process by which a person learns the requirements of the culture by which he or she is surrounded), the role of the family, collectivism and individualism, religion and spirituality, and cultural mistrust and stigma (Goldston et al., 2008). By doing so, the cultural relevance of the programs will be assured.

Acknowledgments

This research was funded by a grant from the National Institute of Mental Health entitled "Group interventions for abused suicidal Black women" awarded to Nadine J. Kaslow.

References

Alegria, M., Mulvaney-Day, N. E., Torres, M., Polo, A., Cao, Z., & Canino, G. (2007). Prevalence of psychiatric disorders across Latino subgroups in the United States. *American Journal of Public Health, 97*, 68–75.

American Psychiatric Association. (2003). Practice guideline for the assessment and treatment of patients with suicidal behaviors. *American Journal of Psychiatry, 160*(Suppl.), 1–60.

Añez, L., Silva, M., Paris, M., & Bedregal, L. (2008). Engaging Latinos through the integration of cultural values and motivational interviewing principles. *Professional Psychology: Research and Practice, 39*, 153–159.

Anglin, D., Gabriel, K. O. S., & Kaslow, N. J. (2005). Suicide acceptability and religious well-being: A comparative analysis in African American suicide attempters and nonattempters. *Journal of Psychology and Theology, 33*, 140–150.

Aubert, P., Daigle, M. S., & Daigle, J. (2004). Cultural traits and immigration: Hostility and suicidality in Chinese Canadian students. *Transcultural Psychiatry, 41*, 514–532.

Baller, R. D., & Richardson, K. K. (2002). Social integration, imitation, and the geographic patterning of suicide. *American Sociological Review, 67*, 873–888.

Balsam, K. F., Huang, B., Fieland, K. C., Simoni, J. M., & Walters, K. L. (2004). Culture, trauma, and wellness: A comparison of heterosexual and lesbian, gay, bisexual, and two-spirit Native Americans. *Cultural Diversity and Ethnic Minority Psychology, 10,* 287–301.

Bartels, S. J., Coakley, E., Oxman, T. E., Constantino, G., Oslin, D., Chen, H., . . . Sanchez, H. (2002). Suicide and death ideation in older primary care patients with depression, anxiety, and at-risk alcohol abuse. *American Journal of Geriatric Psychiatry, 10,* 417–427.

Bontempo, D. E., & D'Aguelli, A. R. (2002). Effects of at-school victimization and sexual orientation on lesbian, gay, or bisexual youth's health risk behavior. *Journal of Adolescent Health, 30,* 364–374.

Borowsky, I. W., Resnick, M. D., Ireland, M., & Blum, R. W. (1999). Suicide attempts among American Indian and Alaska Native youth: Risk and protective factors. *Archives of Pediatric and Adolescent Medicine, 153,* 573–580.

Botempo, D. E., & D'Augelli, A. R. (2002). Effects of at-school victimization and sexual orientation on lesbian, gay, or bisexual youth's health risk behavior. *Journal of Adolescent Health, 30,* 364–374.

Bradford, J., Ryan, C., & Rothblum, E. D. (1994). National lesbian health care survey: Implications for mental health care. *Journal of Consulting and Clinical Psychology, 62,* 228–242.

Brener, N. D., Hassan, S. S., & Barrios, L. C. (1999). Suicidal ideation among college students in the United States. *Journal of Consulting and Clinical Psychology, 67,* 1004–1008.

Burr, J. A., Hartman, J. T., & Matteson, D. W. (1999). Black suicide in U.S. metropolitan areas: An examination of the racial inequality and social integration-regulation hypotheses. *Social Forces, 77,* 1049–1081.

Canino, G., & Roberts, R. C. (2001). Suicidal behavior among Latino youth. *Suicide and Life-Threatening Behavior, 31,* 122–131.

Carrico, A. W., Johnson, M. O., Morin, S. F., Robert, R. H., Charlebois, E. D., Steward, W. T., . . . NIMH Healthy Living Project Team. (2007). Correlates of suicidal ideation among HIV-positive persons. *AIDS, 21,* 1199–1203.

Centers for Disease Control and Prevention. (1998). Suicide among black youths—United States, 1980-1995. *Morbidity and Mortality Weekly Report, 47,* 193–196.

Centers for Disease Control and Prevention. (2004). Youth risk behavior surveillance—United States, 2003. *Morbidity and Mortality Weekly Report, 53,* 1–96.

Centers for Disease Control and Prevention. (2009). Alcohol and suicide among racial/ethnic populations—17 states, 2005-2006. *Morbidity and Mortality Weekly Report, 58,* 637–641.

Chance, S. E., Kaslow, N. J., Summerville, M. B., & Wood, K. (1998). Suicidal behavior in African American individuals: Current status and future directions. *Cultural Diversity and Mental Health, 4,* 19–37.

Chatters, L. M. (2000). Religion and health: Public health research and practice. *Annual Review of Public Health, 21,* 335–367.

Choi, J. L., Rogers, J. R., & Werth, J. L., Jr. (2009). Suicide risk assessment with Asian American college students: A culturally informed perspective. *Counseling Psychologist, 37,* 186–218.

Chung, I. W. (2003). Examining suicidal behavior of Asian American female college students: Implications for practice. *Journal of College Student Psychotherapy, 18,* 31–47.

Clarke, D. E., Colantonio, A., Rhodes, A. E., & Escobar, M. (2008). Pathways to suicidality across ethnic groups in Canadian adults: The possible role of social stress. *Psychological Medicine, 38,* 419–431.

Clements-Nolle, K., Marx, R., & Katz, M. (2006). Attempted suicide among transgender persons: The influence of gender-based discrimination and victimization. *Journal of Homosexuality, 51,* 53–70.

Cochran, S. D., Mays, V. M., Alegria, M., Ortega, A. N., & Takeuchi, D. (2007). Mental health and substance use disorders among Latino and Asian American, gay, and bisexual adults. *Journal of Consulting and Clinical Psychology, 75,* 785–794.

Cochran, S. D., Mays, V. M., & Sullivan, J. G. (2003). Prevalence of mental disorders, psychological distress, and mental health services use among lesbian, gay, and bisexual adults in the United States. *Journal of Counseling and Clinical Psychology, 71,* 53–61.

Cohen-Kettenis, P. T. (2004). Transsexualism. In W. E. Craighead & C. B. Nemeroff (Eds.), *The concise Corsini encyclopedia of psychology and behavioral science* (3rd ed., pp. 1000–1001). Hoboken, NJ: Wiley.

Colucci, E., & Martin, G. (2008). Religion and spirituality along the suicidal path. *Suicide and Life-Threatening Behavior, 38,* 229–244.

Compton, M. T., Thompson, M. P., & Kaslow, N. J. (2005). Social environment factors associated with suicide attempt among low-income African Americans: The protective role of family relationships and social support. *Social Psychiatry and Psychiatric Epidemiology, 40,* 175–185.

Cook, J. M., Pearson, J. L., Thompson, R. A., Black, B. S., & Rabins, P. V. (2002). Suicidality in older African Americans: Findings from the EPOCH study. *American Journal of Geriatric Psychiatry, 10,* 437–446.

Cowger, C. D. (1994). Assessing client strengths: Clinical assessments for client empowerment. *Social Work and Christianity, 39,* 262–268.

Cuellar, J., & Curry, T. (2007). The prevalence and comorbidity between delinquency, drug abuse, suicide attempts, physical and sexual abuse, and self-mutilation among delinquent Hispanic females. *Hispanic Journal of Behavioral Science, 29,* 68–82.

D'Augelli, A. R., Grossman, A. H., Salter, N. P., Vasey, J. J., Starks, M. T., & Sinclair, K. O. (2005). Predicting the suicide attempts of lesbian, gay, and bisexual youth. *Suicide and Life-Threatening Behavior, 36,* 646–660.

Dash, M., Jackson, J., & Rasor, S. (1997). *Hidden wholeness: An African-American spirituality for individuals and communities.* Cleveland, OH: United Church Press.

Davis, S. P., Arnette, N. C., Bethea, K. I., Graves, K. N., Rhodes, M. N., Harp, S. E., . . . Kaslow, N. J. (2009). The Grady Nia Project: A culturally competent intervention for low-income, abused and suicidal African American women. *Professional Psychology: Research and Practice, 40,* 141–147.

Dervic, K., Oquendo, M. A., Grunebaum, M. F., Ellis, S., Burke, A. K., & Mann, J. J. (2004). Religious affiliation and suicide attempt. *American Journal of Psychiatry, 161,* 2303–2308.

Diaz, R. M., Ayala, G., Bein, E., Henne, J., & Marin, B. V. (2001). The impact of homophobia, poverty, and racisms on the mental health of gay and bisexual Latino men: Findings from 3 US cities. *American Journal of Public Health, 91,* 6.

Dohrenwend, B. P. (2000). The role of adversity and stress in psychopathology: Some evidence and its implications for theory and research. *Journal of Health and Social Behavior*, *41*, 1–19.

Eisenberg, M. E., & Resnick, M. R. (2006). Suicidality among gay, lesbian and bisexual youth: The role of protective factors. *Journal of Adolescent Health*, *39*, 662–668.

Epstein, J. A., & Spirito, A. (2009). Risk factors for suicidality among a nationally representative sample of high school students. *Suicide and Life-Threatening Behavior*, *39*, 241–251.

Eshun, S. (2003). Sociocultural determinants of suicide ideation: A comparison between American and Ghanaian college samples. *Suicide and Life-Threatening Behavior*, *33*, 165–171.

Exline, J. J., Yali, A. M., & Sanderson, W. C. (2000). Guilt, discord, and alienation: The role of religious strain in depression and suicidality. *Journal of Clinical Psychology*, *56*, 1481–1496.

Fergusson, D. M., Horwood, L. J., & Beautrais, A. L. (2009). Is sexual orientation related to mental health problems and suicidality in young people? *Archives of General Psychiatry*, *56*, 876–880.

Fitzpatrick, K. K., Euton, S. J., Jones, J. N., & Schmidt, N. B. (2005). Gender role, sexual orientation, and suicide risk. *Journal of Affective Disorders*, *87*, 35–42.

Fortuna, L., Perez, D., Canino, G., Sribney, W., & Alegria, M. (2007). Prevalence and correlates of lifetime suicidal ideation and suicide attempts among Latino subgroups in the United States. *Journal of Clinical Psychology*, *68*, 572–581.

Freedenthal, S., & Stiffman, A. R. (2004). Suicidal behavior in urban American Indian adolescents: A comparison with reservation youth in a southwestern state. *Suicide and Life-Threatening Behavior*, *34*, 160–171.

Garcia, C., Skay, C., Sieving, R., Naughton, S., & Bearinger, L. H. (2008). Family and racial factors associated with suicide and emotional distress among Latino students. *Journal of School Health*, *78*, 487–495.

Garcia-Preto, N. (2005). Latino families. In M. McGoldrick, J. Giordano, & N. Garcia-Preto (Eds.), *Ethnicity and family therapy* (3rd ed., pp. 153–165). New York, NY: Guilford Press.

Garlow, S. J., Purselle, D., & Heninger, M. (2005). Ethnic differences in patterns of suicide across the life cycle. *American Journal of Psychiatry*, *162*, 319–323.

Garroutte, E. M., Goldberg, J., Beals, J., Herrell, R., Manson, S. M., & AI-SUPERPFP Team. (2003). Spirituality and attempted suicide among American Indians. *Social Science and Medicine*, *56*, 1571–1579.

Gay and Lesbian Medical Association and LGBT Health Experts. (2001). *Healthy People 2010 companion document for lesbian, gay, bisexual, and transgender (LGBT) health*. San Francisco, CA: Gay and Lesbian Medical Association.

Gearing, R. E., & Lizardi, D. (2009). Religion and suicide. *Journal of Religious Health*, *48*, 332–341.

Gibbs, J. (1997). African-American suicide: A cultural paradox. *Suicide and Life-Threatening Behavior*, *27*, 68–79.

Goldsmith, S. K., Pellmar, T. C., Kleinman, A. M., & Bunney, W. E. (Eds.). (2002). *Reducing suicide: A national imperative*. Washington, DC: National Academy Press.

Goldston, D. B., Molock, S. D., Whitbeck, L. B., Murakami, J. L., Zayas, L. H., & Hall, G. C. N. (2008). Cultural considerations in adolescent suicide prevention and psychosocial treatment. *American Psychologist*, *63*, 14–31.

Greening, L., & Stoppelbein, L. (2002). Religiosity, attributional style, and social support as psychosocial buffers for African American and white adolescents' perceived risk for suicide. *Suicide and Life Threatening Behavior*, *32*, 404–417.

Grossman, A. H., & D'Augelli, A. R. (2007). Transgender youth and life-threatening behaviors. *Suicide and Life-Threatening Behavior*, *37*, 527–537.

Grossman, D. C., Milligam, C., & Deyo, R. A. (1991). Risk factors for suicide attempts among Navajo adolescents. *American Journal of Public Health*, *81*, 870–974.

Harachi, T., Catalano, R. F., Kim, S., & Choi, Y. (2001). Etiology and prevention of substance use among Asian-American youth. *Prevention Science*, *2*, 57–65.

Harris, T. L., & Molock, S. D. (2000). Cultural orientation, family cohesion and family support in suicide ideation and depression among African American college students. *Suicide and Life Threatening Behavior*, *30*, 341–353.

Hodges, D. R., & Williams, T. R. (2002). Assessing African American spirituality with spiritual ecomaps. *Families in Society: The Journal of Contemporary Human Services*, *83*, 585–595.

Hovey, J. D., & King, C. A. (1996). Acculturative stress, depression, and suicidal ideation among immigrant and second-generation Latino adolescents. *Journal of the American Academy of Child and Adolescent Psychiatry*, *35*, 1183–1192.

Ialongo, N., Koenig-McNaught, A. L., Wagner, B. M., Pearson, J. L., McCreary, B. K., Poduska, J., & Kellam, S. (2004). African American children's reports of depressed mood, hopelessness, and suicidal ideation and later suicide attempts. *Suicide and Life Threatening Behavior*, *34*, 395–407.

Jesdale, B., & Zierler, S. (2002). Enactment of gay rights laws in U.S. States and trends in adolescent suicide: An investigation of non-Hispanic white boys. *Journal of the Gay Lesbian Medical Association*, *6*, 61–69.

Joe, S., Baser, R. E., Breeden, G., Neighbors, H. W., & Jackson, J. S. (2006). Prevalence of and risk factors for lifetime suicide attempts among Blacks in the United States. *Journal of the American Medical Association*, *296*, 2112–2123.

Joe, S., & Kaplan, M. S. (2002). Firearm-related suicide among young African American males. *Psychiatric Services*, *53*, 332–334.

Joe, S., & Marcus, S. C. (2003). Trends by race and gender in suicide attempts among U.S. adolescents, 1991-2001. *Psychiatric Services*, *54*, 454.

Johnson, C. V., & Hayes, J. A. (2003). Troubled spirits: Prevalence and predictors of religious and spiritual concerns among university students and counseling center clients. *Journal of Clinical Psychology*, *56*, 1481–1496.

Julliard, K., Vivar, J., Delgado, C., Cruz, E., Kabak, J., & Sabers, H. (2008). What Latina patients don't tell their doctors: A qualitative study. *Annals of Family Medicine*, *6*, 543–549.

Kaestner, R., Pearson, J., Keene, D., & Geronimus, A. (2009). Stress, allostatic load, and health of Mexican immigrants. *Social Science Quarterly*, *90*, 1089–1111.

Kamal, Z., & Lowenthal, K. M. (2002). Suicide beliefs and behavior among young Muslims and Hindus in the UK. *Mental Health, Religion, and Culture*, *5*, 111–118.

Kaslow, N. J., Price, A., Wyckoff, S., Bender, M., Sherry, A., Young, S.,…Bethea, K. (2004). Person factors associated with suicidal behavior among African American men and women. *Cultural Diversity and Ethnic Minority Psychology*, *10*, 5–22.

Kaslow, N. J., Sherry, A., Bethea, K., Wyckoff, S., Compton, M., Bender, M.,…Parker, R. (2005). Social risk and protective factors for suicide attempts in low income African American men and women. *Suicide and Life Threatening Behavior*, *35*, 400–412.

Kaslow, N. J., Thompson, M., Brooks, A., & Twomey, H. (2000). Ratings of family functioning of suicidal and nonsuicidal African American women. *Journal of Family Psychology, 14,* 585–599.

Kaslow, N. J., Thompson, M., Meadows, L., Chance, S., Puett, R., Hollins, L.,...Kellermann, A. (2000). Risk factors for suicide attempts among African American women. *Depression and Anxiety, 12,* 13–20.

Kaslow, N. J., Thompson, M., Meadows, L., Jacobs, D., Chance, S., Gibb, B.,...Phillips, K. (1998). Factors that mediate and moderate the link between partner abuse and suicidal behavior in African American women. *Journal of Consulting and Clinical Psychology, 66,* 533–540.

Kaslow, N. J., Thompson, M. P., Okun, A., Price, A., Young, S., Bender, M.,...Parker, R. (2002). Risk and protective factors for suicidal behavior in abused African American women. *Journal of Consulting and Clinical Psychology, 70,* 311–319.

Kataoka, S., Stien, B., Lieberman, R., & Wong, M. (2003). Suicide prevention in schools: Are we reaching minority youths? *Psychiatric Services, 54,* 1444.

Kenegay, G. (2005). Transgender health: Findings from two needs assessment studies in Philadelphia. *Health and Social Work, 30,* 19–26.

Kennedy, M. A., Parhar, K. K., Samra, J., & Gorzalka, B. (2005). Suicide ideation in different generations of immigrants. *Canadian Journal of Psychiatry, 50,* 353–356.

Keown, D. (1996). Buddhism and suicide: The case of Channa. *Journal of Buddhist Ethics, 3,* 8.

Keown, D. (1998). Suicide, assisted suicide and euthanasia: A Buddhist perspective. *Journal of Law and Religion, 13,* 385–406.

Kidd, S. A., Henrich, C. C., Brookmeyer, K. A., Davidson, L., King, R. A., & Shahar, G. (2006). The social context of adolescent suicide attempts: Interactive effects of parent, peer, and school social relations. *Suicide and Life-Threatening Behavior, 36,* 386–395.

King, M., Semlyen, J., Tai, S., Killaspy, H., Osborn, D., Popelyuk, D., & Nazareth, I. (2008). A systematic review of mental disorder, suicide, and deliberate self harm in lesbian, gay and bisexual people. *BMC Psychiatry, 8,* 70.

Kisch, J., Leino, E. V., & Silverman, M. M. (2005). Aspects of suicidal behavior, depression, and treatment in college students: Results from the spring 2000 National College Health Assessment Survey. *Suicide and Life-Threatening Behavior, 35,* 3–13.

Kitts, R. L. (2005). Gay adolescents and suicide: Understanding the association. *Adolescence, 40,* 621–628.

Kliewer, S. (2004). Allowing spirituality into the healing process. *Journal of Family Practice, 53,* 616–624.

Koenig, H. G. (2009). Research on religion, spirituality, and mental health: A review. *Canadian Journal of Psychiatry, 54,* 283–291.

Koenig, H. G., Larson, D. B. (2001). Religion and mental health: Evidence for an association. *International Review of Psychiatry, 13,* 67–78.

Krishnan, S., Hilbert, J., & VanLeeuwen, D. (2001). Domestic violence and help-seeking behaviors among rural women: Results from a shelter-based study. *Family and Community Health, 24,* 28–38.

Kubrin, C., Wadsworth, T., & DiPietro, S. (2006). Deindustrialization, disadvantage, and suicide among young Black males. *Social Forces, 84,* 1559–1579.

Kulkin, H., Chauvin, E., & Percle, G. (2000). Suicide among gay and lesbian adolescents and young adults: A review of the literature. *Journal of Homosexuality, 40,* 1–29.

Lau, A. S., Jernewall, N. M., Zane, N., & Myers, H. F. (2002). Correlates of suicidal behaviors among Asian American outpatient youths. *Cultural Diversity and Ethnic Minority Psychology, 8,* 199–213.

Leach, M. M. (2006). *Cultural diversity and suicide: Ethnic, religious, gender, and sexual orientation perspectives.* Binghamton, NY: Haworth Press.

Leong, F. T. L., & Leach, M. M. (Eds.). (2008). *Suicide among racial and ethnic minority groups: Theory, research, and practice.* New York, NY: Routledge.

Leong, F. T. L., Leach, M. M., Yeh, C., & Chou, E. (2007). Suicide among Asian Americans: What do we know? What do we need to know? *Death Studies, 31,* 417–434.

Lesbon, M. (2002). Suicide among homosexual youth. *Journal of Homosexuality, 42,* 107–117.

Lester, D. (1994). Differences in the epidemiology of suicide in Asian Americans by nation of origin. *Omega: Journal of Death and Dying, 29,* 89–93.

Lester, D. (2006). Suicide and Islam. *Archives of Suicide Research, 10,* 77–97.

Locke, T., & Newcomb, M. (2005). Psychosocial predictors and correlates of suicidality in teenage Latino males. *Hispanic Journal of Behavioral Sciences, 27,* 319–336.

Marion, M. S., & Range, L. M. (2003). African American college women's suicide buffers. *Suicide and Life Threatening Behavior, 33,* 33–43.

May, P. A., Serna, P., Hurt, L., & DeBruyn, L. M. (2005). Outcome evaluations of a public health approach to suicide prevention in an American Indian tribal nation. *American Journal of Public Health, 95,* 1238–1244.

Mays, V., & Cochran, S. (2001). Mental health correlates of perceived discrimination among lesbian, gay and bisexual adults in the United States. *American Journal of Public Health, 91,* 1869–1876.

McBee-Strayer, S., & Rogers, J. R. (2002). Lesbian, gay, and bisexual suicidal behavior: Testing a constructivist model. *Suicide and Life-Threatening Behavior, 32,* 2727–2283.

McDaniel, J. S., Purcell, D., & D'Augelli, A. R. (2001). The relationship between sexual orientation and risk for suicide: Research findings and future directions for research and prevention. *Suicide and Life-Threatening Behavior, 31*(Suppl.), 84–105.

McKenzie, K., Serfaty, M., & Crawford, M. (2003). Suicide in ethnic minority groups. *British Journal of Psychiatry, 183,* 100–101.

Meadows, L. A., Kaslow, N. J., Thompson, M. P., & Jurkovic, G. J. (2005). Protective factors against suicide attempt risk among African American women experiencing intimate partner violence. *American Journal of Community Psychology, 36,* 109–121.

Merchant, C., Kramer, A., Joe, S., Venkataraman, S., & King, C. A. (2009). Predictors of multiple suicide attempts among suicidal Black adolescents. *Suicide and Life-Threatening Behavior, 39,* 115–124.

Middlebrook, D. L., LeMaster, P. L., Beals, J., Novins, D. K., & Manson, S. M. (2001). Suicide prevention in American Indian and Alaska Native communities: A critical review of programs. *Suicide and Life-Threatening Behavior, 31,* 132–149.

Miranda, J., Bernal, G., Lau, A., Kohn, L., Hwang, W., & LaFromboise, T. (2005). State of the science on psychosocial intervention for ethnic minorities. *Annual Review Clinical Psychology, 1*, 113–142.

Molock, S. D., Barksdale, C., Matlin, S., Puri, R., Cammack, N., & Spann, M. (2007). Qualitative study of suicidality and help-seeking behavior in African American adolescents. *American Journal of Community Psychology, 40*, 52–63.

Molock, S. D., Matlin, S., Barksdale, C., Puri, R., & Lyles, J. (2008). Developing suicide prevention programs for African American youth in African American churches. *Suicide and Life-Threatening Behavior, 38*, 323–333.

Molock, S. D., Puri, R., Matlin, S., & Barksdale, C. (2006). Relationship between religious coping and suicidal behavior among African American adolescents. *Journal of Black Psychology, 32*, 366–389.

Morrison, L. L., & Downey, D. L. (2000). Racial differences in self-disclosure of suicidal ideation and reasons for living: Implications for training. *Cultural Diversity and Ethnic Minority Psychology, 6*, 372–386.

Newlin, K., Knafl, K., & Melkus, G. D. (2002). African-American spirituality: A concept analysis. *Advances in Nursing Science, 25*(5), 57–70.

Nisbet, P. A. (1996). Protective factors for suicidal Black females. *Suicide and Life-Threatening Behavior, 26*, 325–341.

Nishimura, S. T., Goebert, D. A., Ramisetty-Mikler, S., & Caetano, R. (2005). Adolescent alcohol use and suicide indicators among adolescents in Hawaii. *Cultural Diversity and Ethnic Minority Psychology, 11*, 309–320.

Noh, E. (2007). Asian American women and suicide: Problems of responsibility and healing. *Women and Therapy, 30*, 87–107.

O'Donnell, L., O'Donnell, C., Wardlaw, D. M., & Stueve, A. (2004). Risk and resiliency factors influencing suicidality among urban African American and Latino youth. *American Journal of Community Psychology, 33*, 37–49.

Paproski, D. L. (1997). Healing experiences of British Columbia First Nations women: Moving beyond suicidal ideation and intention. *Canadian Journal of Community Mental Health, 16*, 69–89.

Paul, J., Cantania, J., Pollack, L., Moskowitz, J., Canchoi, J., & Mills, T. (2002). Suicide attempts among gay and bisexual men: Lifetime prevalence and antecedents. *American Journal of Public Health, 92*, 1338–1345.

Peña, J., Wyman, P., Brown, C., Matthieu, M., Olivares, T., & Hartel, D. (2008). Immigration generation status and its association with suicide attempts, substance use and depressive symptoms among Latino adolescents in the USA. *Prevention Science, 9*, 299–310.

Pew Forum on Religion & Public Life. (2008). *U.S. religious landscape survey: Religious affiliation—diverse and dynamics.* Washington, DC: Pew Research Center.

Price, J. H., Dake, J. A., & Kucharewski, R. (2001). Assets as predictors of suicide attempts in African American inner-city youths. *American Journal of Health Behaviors, 25*, 367–375.

Ragin, D. F., Pilotti, M., Madry, L., Sage, R. E., Bingham, L. E., & Primm, B. J. (2002). Intergenerational substance abuse and domestic violence as familial risk factors for lifetime attempted suicide among battered women. *Journal of Interpersonal Violence, 17*, 1027–1045.

Range, L. M., Leach, M. M., McIntyre, D., Posey-Deters, P. B., Marion, M. S., Kovac, S. H., ... Vigil, J. (1999). Multicultural perspectives on suicide. *Agression and Violent Behavior, 4*, 413–430.

Reviere, S. L., Farber, E., Twomey, H., Okun, A., Jackson, E., Zanville, H., & Kaslow, N. J. (2007). Intimate partner violence and suicidality in low-income African American women: A multi-method assessment of coping factors. *Violence Against Women, 13*, 1113–1129.

Russell, S. T., & Joyner, K. (2001). Adolescent sexual orientation and suicide risk: Evidence from a national study. *American Journal of Public Health, 91*, 1276–1281.

Ryan, C., Huebner, D., Diaz, R., & Sanchez, J. (2009). Family rejection as a predictor of negative health outcomes in White and Latino lesbian, gay and bisexual young adults. *Journal of the American Academy of Pediatrics, 123*, 346–352.

Saewye, E., Skay, C., Hynds, P., Pettingell, S., Bearinger, L., & Resnick, M. (2007). Suicidal ideation and attempts in North American school-based surveys: Are bisexual youth at increasing risk? *Journal of LGBT Health Research, 3*, 25–36.

Sandfort, T., Melendez, R., & Diaz, R. (2007). Gender nonconformity, homophobia, and mental distress in Latino gay and bisexual men. *Journal of Sex Research, 44*, 181–189.

Santisteban, D., & Mena, M. (2009). Culturally informed and flexible family-based treatment for adolescents: A tailored and integrative treatment for Hispanic youth. *Family Process, 48*, 253–260.

Shaughnessy, L., Doshi, S. R., & Jones, S. E. (2004). Attempted suicide and associated health risk behaviors among Native American high school students. *Journal of School Health, 75*, 177–182.

Silenzio, V. M. B., Pena, J. B., Duberstein, P. R., Cerel, J., & Knox, K. L. (2007). Sexual orientation and risk factors for suicidal ideation and suicide attempts among adolescents and young adults. *American Journal of Public Health, 97*, 2017–2019.

Smokowski, P. R., & Bacallao, M. L. (2006). Acculturation, internalizing mental health symptoms, and self-esteem: Cultural experiences of Latino adolescents in North Carolina. *Child Psychiatry Human Development, 37*, 273–292.

Stack, S., & Wasserman, I. (1995). The effect of marriage, family, and religious ties on African American suicide ideology. *Journal of Marriage and the Family, 57*, 215–222.

Suicide Prevention Resource Center. (2008). *Suicide risk and prevention for lesbian, gay, bisexual, and transgender youth.* Newton, MA: Education Development Center.

Thompson, M., Kaslow, N. J., Short, L., & Wyckoff, S. (2002). The mediating roles of perceived social support and resources in the self-efficacy-suicide attempts relation among African American abused women. *Journal of Consulting and Clinical Psychology, 70*, 942–949.

Thompson, M. P., Kaslow, N. J., Bradshaw, D., & Kingree, J. B. (2000). Childhood maltreatment, PTSD, and suicidal behavior among African American females. *Journal of Interpersonal Violence, 15*, 3–15.

Thompson, M. P., Kaslow, N. J., & Kingree, J. B. (2002). Risk factors for suicide attempts among African American women experiencing recent intimate partner violence. *Violence and Victims, 17*, 283–295.

Thompson, M. P., Kaslow, N. J., Kingree, J. B., Puett, R., Thompson, N. J., & Meadows, L. (1999). Partner abuse and posttraumatic stress disorder as risk factors for suicide attempts in a sample of low-income, inner-city women. *Journal of Traumatic Stress, 12*, 59–72.

Thompson, M. P., Kaslow, N. J., Kingree, J. B., Rashid, A., Puett, R., Jacobs, D., & Matthews, A. (2000). Partner violence, social support, and distress among inner-city African American women. *American Journal of Community Psychology, 28*, 127–143.

Tillman, K. H., & Weiss, U. K. (2009). Nativity status and depressive symptoms among Hispanic young adults: The role of stress exposure. *Social Science Quarterly*, *90*, 1229–1250.

Twomey, H., Kaslow, N. J., & Croft, S. (2000). Childhood maltreatment, object relations, and suicidal behavior in women. *Psychoanalytic Psychology*, *17*, 313–335.

US Census Bureau. (2008). *An older and more diverse nation by midcentury*. Retrieved November 2013, from http://www.census.gov/newsroom/releases/archives/population/cb08-123.html.

US Census Bureau (2011a). *American Fact Finder*. Retrieved November 2013 from http://www.census.gov/people/.

US Census Bureau (2011b). *Native North American Languages Spoken at Home in the United States and Puerto Rico: 2006–2010*. Retrieved from http://www.census.gov/prod/2011pubs/acsbr10-10.pdf

Unützer, J., Katon, W., Callahan, C., Williams, J., Hunkeler, E., & Harpole, L. (2003). Depression treatment in a sample of 1,801 depressed older adults in primary care. *American Geriatric Society*, *51*, 505–510.

Utsey, S. O., Hook, J. N., & Stanard, P. (2007). A re-examination of cultural factors that mitigate risk and promote resilience in relation to African American suicide: A review of the literature and recommendations for future research. *Death Studies*, *31*, 399–416.

Vandecreek, L., & Mottram, K. (2008). The religious life during suicide bereavement: A description. *Death Studies*, *33*, 741–761.

Vanderwerker, L. C., Chen, J. H., Charpentier, P., Paulk, M. E., Michalski, M., & Prigerson, H. G. (2007). Differences in risk factors for suicidality between African American and White patients vulnerable to suicide. *Suicide and Life-Threatening Behavior*, *37*, 1–9.

Ventegodt, S., & Merrick, J. (2005). Suicide from a holistic point of view. *Scientific World Journal*, *5*, 759–766.

Wadsworth, T., & Kubrin, C. E. (2007). Hispanic suicide in the U.S. metropolitan areas: Examining the effects of immigration, assimilation, affluence, and disadvantage. *American Journal of Sociology*, *112*, 1848–1885.

Walker, R. L. (2007). Acculturation and acculturative stress as indicators for suicide risk among African Americans. *American Journal of Orthopsychiatry*, *77*, 386–391.

Walker, R. L., Lester, D., & Joe, S. (2006). Lay theories of suicide: An examination of culturally relevant suicide beliefs and attributions among African Americans and European Americans. *Journal of Black Psychology*, *32*, 320–334.

Walker, R. L., Utsey, S. O., Bolden, M. A., & Williams, O. (2005). Do sociocultural factors predict suicidality among persons of African descent living in the U.S. *Archives of Suicide Research*, *9*, 203–217.

Walsh, F. (Ed.). (2008). *Spiritual resources in family therapy* (2nd ed.). New York, NY: Guilford Press.

Willis, L. A., Coombs, D. W., Cockerham, W. C., & Frison, S. L. (2002). Ready to die: A postmodern interpretation of the increase of African-American adolescent male suicide. *Social Science and Medicine*, *55*, 907–920.

Willis, L. A., Coombs, D. W., Drentea, P., & Cockerham, W. C. (2003). Uncovering the mystery: Factors of African American suicide. *Suicide and Life Threatening Behavior*, *33*, 412–429.

Wissow, L. S., Walkup, J., Barlow, A., Reid, R., & Kane, S. (2001). Cluster and regional influences on suicide in a Southwestern American Indian tribe. *Social Science and Medicine*, *53*, 1115–1124.

Yeh, M., McCabe, K. M., Hough, R. L., Dupuis, D., & Hazen, A. (2003). Racial/ethnic differences in parental endorsement of barriers to mental health services for youth. *Mental Health Services Research*, *5*, 65–77.

Zayas, L. H., Bright, C. L., Alvarez-Sanchez, T., & Cabassa, L. J. (2009). Acculturation, familism and mother–daughter relations among suicidal and non-suicidal adolescent Latinas. *Journal of Primary Prevention*, *30*, 351–369.

Zayas, L. H., Lester, R. L., Cabassa, L. J., & Fortuna, L. R. (2005). Why do so many Latina teens attempt suicide? A conceptual model for research. *American Journal of Orthopsychiatry*, *75*, 275–287.

Comprehensive Theories of Suicidal Behaviors

Edward A. Selby, Thomas E. Joiner, Jr., *and* Jessica D. Ribeiro

Abstract

Suicide is a harmful, frightening, and often misunderstood behavior. This is because it can seem paradoxical, seeming to go against basic human motivations of self-preservation and avoidance of pain. In order to understand this behavior, a comprehensive understanding of the various theories of and motivations for this behavior is necessary. The following chapter will review theories of suicide ranging from biological and psychodynamic theories to cognitive and interpersonal theories. This will be followed by a brief review and comparison to theories and models of nonsuicidal self-injury. All theories will be evaluated regarding their key postulates, empirical evidence supporting the theory, and shortcomings of the theory.

Key Words: suicide, self-injury, psychache, hopelessness, interpersonal psychological, affect regulation, escape theory, experiential avoidance, emotional cascades

Death by suicide, which claims the lives of approximately 30,000 individuals in the United States each year (Kochanek & Hudson, 1995), has been a mysterious behavior to humans because it seems so paradoxical. Although most people fear and desire to avoid death, there are others who desire it, and even some who purposely inflict their own death. Life is difficult at times, but what could make it so unbearable that death would seem to be the best solution? It is only within the last few decades that we have begun to have a better understanding of suicidal behavior, identifying not only strong potential causes for suicide but also identifying individuals who may be more likely or capable of suicide. As will be seen, theories of suicide range from those involving biological causes, to societal structures that promote suicidal behavior, to internal conflicts that drive a desire for death.

Obtaining a full understanding of suicidal behavior requires distinguishing between factors that lead to suicidal self-injury and those leading to nonsuicidal self-injury. Nonsuicidal self-injury (NSSI) refers to intentionally inflicting damage to one's own body tissue without suicidal intent. This definition includes a wide array of behaviors: cutting, burning, scratching, pinching, and hitting oneself, and in the current context refers to NSSI in individuals without developmental disorders. Although NSSI is a diagnostic criterion for borderline personality disorder (BPD; *DSM-IV*, APA, 1994), it also is a behavior that can be found in the absence of a BPD diagnosis and is prevalent in approximately 4% of adults in the United States (Briere & Gil, 1998; Klonsky, Oltmanns, & Turkheimer, 2003). There have also been suggestions that there may be a distinct NSSI disorder (Selby, Bender, Gordon, Nock, & Joiner, 2012), although findings for such a potential diagnosis are still preliminary. NSSI appears to be more prevalent in young adults and adolescents; estimates among adolescents range from 14% (Ross & Heath, 2002) to 46.5% (Lloyd-Richardson, Perrine, Dierker, &

Kelly, 2007) who report having engaged in NSSI at least once. Given the prevalence of NSSI, and the findings that it is often present in individuals who are not diagnosed with BPD and have a range of other Axis I disorders (Klonsky, 2007), understanding the current theoretical basis and motivations for this behavior is crucial to understanding and treating this behavior.

Overview

This chapter will explore theories of suicide, presented first, followed by theories of NSSI, in relation to suicide. The major theories of suicide that will be discussed include biological theories of suicide, psychodynamic theories of suicide, Durkheim's sociological theory (1897), Beck and colleague's hopelessness theory (1985, 1990), Shneidman's psychache theory (1996), Baumeister's escape theory (1990), Linehan's emotion dysfunction theory (1993), and Joiner's interpersonal-psychological theory (2005). An overview of these theories is presented in Table 15.1. We will explore the basic postulates of these theories, current evidence in support of the theories, and strengths and weaknesses of each theory. As will be seen, many of the theories of suicide have similar postulates, but each has unique aspects that contribute to understanding the various forms of and motivations for suicide.

The second section of the chapter will compare and contrast these theories in relation to the

Table 15.1 Theories of Suicide

Suicide Theories	Basic Postulates
Biological theories	Suicide may result from an interaction between genetic biological predispositions (neurotransmitter dysfunction) and life stressors, the combination of which may increase suicide risk.
Sociological theory: Durkheim (1987)	Suicide is the result of either high or low *social regulation* of individuals, or either high or low *moral integration*. This results in four primary types of motivations for suicide: egoistic—low social regulation (loneliness); altruistic—high social regulation (suicide to benefit society); anomic—low moral regulation (societal disengagement); fatalistic—high moral regulation (societal oppression).
Hopelessness theory: Beck and colleagues (1985, 1990)	Suicide is the result of overwhelming feelings of *hopelessness*—that no matter what one does, his or her life will not improve. These feelings of hopelessness are the primary driving force of suicidal behavior.
Psychache theory: Shneidman (1996)	Suicide is the result of intense psychological pain, referred to as *psychache*. Psychache is the result of a deficit in a variety of basic human needs; it is so painful that death by suicide is seemingly the only way to end the pain. This theory also has a lethality component—as options for reducing psychache decrease, the likelihood that an individual will engage in suicidal behavior increases, with a low probability of survival.
Escape theory: Baumeister (1990)	Escape theory suggests that suicide is a form of *escape from aversive self-awareness* and describes the process involved in leading up to suicide. The process involves six steps: (1) falling short of standards, (2) attributions to the self, (3) high self-awareness, (4) negative affect, (5) cognitive deconstruction, and (6) consequences of deconstruction (suicide).
Emotion dysregulation theory: Linehan (1993)	Suicide is the result of *emotion dysregulation*. Suicidal individuals experience intense, hypersensitive, and prolonged negative emotional experience due to criticizing and invalidating environments. Dysregulated behaviors are used as a way of distracting from negative emotion, such as self-injury, and suicide is the ultimate way to extinguish negative affect.
Interpersonal-psychological theory: Joiner (2005)	Suicide is the result of an interaction between three components: (1) feelings that one does not have connection with others (*thwarted belongingness*), (2) thoughts and feelings that one is a burden on those around them (*perceived burdensomeness*), and (3) a greatly diminished fear of pain and death due to repetitive experience with, and habituation to, painful and fear-invoking life events (*the acquired capability to enact lethal self-injury*).

functions and theories of NSSI. Theories of NSSI that will be discussed include biological theories, psychodynamic models, social functions, the antidissociation hypothesis, the feeling generation hypothesis, the antisuicide hypothesis, affect regulation theories, the Experiential Avoidance Model (Chapman, Gratz, & Brown, 2006), and the Emotional Cascade Model (Selby, Anestis, & Joiner, 2008). Although there is a wide array of theories of NSSI, the reasons people engage in NSSI appear to be just as broad. Each theory/model will be presented in terms of theoretical postulates, current evidence in support of the theory, and questions that remain unanswered by the theory. An overview of these theories is presented in Table 15.2.

Theories of Suicide

BIOLOGICAL THEORIES OF SUICIDE

The major approach of biological theories to understanding suicide is that there appears to be an inherited, physiological risk component to suicide, sometimes referred to as a diathesis. This biological diathesis, according to biological theories, is then aggravated through environmental factors referred to as stress. It is the combination of a diathesis and stress that may result in suicidal behavior (Mann, 2003; Mann, Waternaux, Haas, & Malone, 1999). Potential candidates for the biological diatheses suggested in suicidal behaviors are the dysregulation of the serotinergic system and problematic functioning in the ventromedial prefrontal cortex (Caspi et al., 2003; Mann, 2003; Oquendo & Mann, 2000). Specifically, the polymorphisms of the serotonin transporter gene (5HTT), which involves reuptake of serotonin from the synaptic cleft, have been linked to family history of suicidal behavior (Joiner, Johnson, & Soderstrom, 2002). Inherited impulsivity also has been suggested as a diathesis that may be linked to suicidal behavior (Mann et al., 1999), one which may make an individual more likely to act on suicidal ideation when under stress. Thus, the diathesis-stress view of suicide may be able to

Table 15.2 Theories/Functional Models of Nonsuicidal Self-Injury (NSSI)

NSSI Theory	Description
Biological theories	NSSI causes endorphins to be released, which then results in pleasant feelings that are rewarding.
Social functions	NSSI is a viewed as a way of manipulating others, communicating emotional experience, and/or avoiding unpleasant activities.
Psychodynamic theories (Carroll et al., 1980)	NSSI is a viewed as a method of confirming boundaries between the self and others by generating scars.
Antisuicide Model (see Suyemoto, 1998) Affect regulation theories: Nock & Prinstein (2004) Self-punishment hypothesis (see Klonsky, 2007)	NSSI is used as a compromise with suicidal desire; by destroying bodily tissue one satisfies a desire to destroy his/her self without actually doing so. NSSI is used as a way of decreasing negative affect and/or increasing positive affect. NSSI is used as a way of expressing anger at and punishing oneself.
Antidissociation theory (Gunderson, 1984; Simpson, 1975)	NSSI is used as a method of "shocking" oneself out of a dissociative state.
Feeling generation theory	NSSI is used as a way of generating positive feelings due to an overall deficit of positive emotion.
Experiential Avoidance Model: Chapman et al. (2006)	NSSI serves as a method of avoiding negative emotion. By engaging in NSSI, negative emotion is avoided and is thus negatively reinforcing. Over time, this reinforcement results in NSSI becoming a conditioned response to negative emotion.
Emotional Cascade Model: Selby et al. (2008)	Emotional cascades, arising from intense rumination and negative emotion about an upsetting problem, cause NSSI because self-injury provides a potent form of distraction that inhibits rumination. Interfering with rumination results in subsequent emotional relief.

explain who is at an increased risk for death by suicide (those with the diathesis) and why those with the diathesis may engage in suicidal behavior (e.g., following a stressor such as abuse; Gibb, McGeary, Beevers, & Miller, 2006). Although the diathesis-stress view receives some support, it lacks support in that common diatheses, such as serotonin dysfunction, is fairly common in individuals with depression (Caspi et al., 2003), yet data suggest that only between 2% and 6% of those with depression will eventually die by suicide (Bostwick & Pankratz, 2000). Therefore, although many individuals may have biological diatheses, and many of those individuals may also experience various forms of stress, only a select group goes on to complete suicide.

A biological theory of suicide that also integrates societal aspects has been proposed by DeCatanzaro (1995). One of the problems with integrating suicidal behavior and inherited biological dysfunction is explaining how these genetic traits remain through natural selection. It is the nature of animals to behave in ways that promote self-preservation, and doing so allows them to pass their traits onto offspring through survival and reproduction. Suicide is a case that appears to go against this self-preservation nature. DeCatanzaro attempts to reconcile this conflict by proposing that when individuals perceive that they are a burden on family members with similar genetic makeup in such a way that those family members have a reduced probability of survival and reproduction, then suicide may be a manner of promoting the passing on of one's genes. There is some support for this theory in that there is a strong relationship between feelings of perceived burdensomeness toward one's family and suicidal ideation (Brown, Dahlen, Mills, Rick, & Biblarz, 1999; De Catanzaro, 1995). However, testing an evolutionary theory such as this can be difficult, so this potential evolutionary role of suicide requires further exploration.

Currently, biological theories of suicide are able to identify potential predispositions to suicide, such as neurotransmitter dysfunction, yet there is currently little understanding of how these predispositions may result in increased suicidal behavior or how environmental factors may trigger these predispositions. Although informative, biological theories of suicide also appear to lack some specificity in predicting suicidal behavior due to the problem that both the inherited and environmental components are somewhat common (e.g., serotonin system dysfunction and life stressors), yet suicide remains far

less common. Biological approaches to understanding suicide may provide important information on who may be at higher risk for suicide, but more research is needed to establish more refined predictions of suicidal behavior.

SOCIOLOGICAL THEORY OF SUICIDE

One of the first comprehensive theories of death by suicide was proposed in 1897 by Emile Durkheim. In his book *Le Suicide*, Durkheim proposed that social forces are the primary cause of suicide. He suggested that suicide is a result of disturbed regulation of the individual by society, and that there are two primary societal forces that have the most influence on suicide: social integration and moral regulation. By social integration, Durkheim refers to the degree to which the individual is integrated into society in terms of bonds with others and society as a whole. Moral integration, on the other hand, involves the degree to which society regulates the beliefs and behaviors of individuals through mechanisms such as societal norms and the legal system. Durkheim proposes that there are four types of death by suicide, each of which results from either extreme on one of the two factors: egoistic, altruistic, anomic, and fatalistic.

The first form of suicide that Durkheim proposes is egoistic. Egoistic suicide arises from deficits in social integration, in which the individual feels like he or she lacks a connection with something greater than himself or herself. These individuals may feel that they are an outcast of society or that they have nothing that binds them to society. It is because of the low social integration that these individuals feel that their lives are not worth much to society at large.

On the other end of the social integration spectrum is altruistic suicide, in which the individual is too integrated into society. These individuals feel that society would benefit from their deaths. Such persons may feel that they can contribute to the greater good of society through sacrificing themselves. One potential type of altruistic suicide might be suicide missions, such as the kamikaze pilots in World War II, who may have felt that their deaths were aiding their country. Another modern example may be suicide bombers, who are willing to sacrifice their lives for religious or political reasons.

While egoistic and altruistic suicides each involve one extreme or the other of social integration, a third form of suicide, anomic, is caused specifically by a deficit in moral regulation. Anomic suicide occurs when society fails to instill a sense of meaning and provide aspirations for individuals. Anomic suicides, in Durkheim's view, would be more common during times of economic disturbances, which reduce individual ability to identify or achieve goals. An example of an anomic suicide may be one where, during an economic depression, an individual dies by suicide because he or she believes that there is neither a potentially positive outcome nor means for achieving one. Fatalistic suicide, a fourth form, in contrast to anomic suicide, occurs when the moral regulation of a society is extreme. This form of suicide, according to Durkheim, would take place in an overly oppressive society that controls most aspects of individual life, and suicide is essentially a release from living such a dismal existence. Although fatalistic suicide seems less rare in Western/industrialized societies, one example of fatalistic suicide may be when a prisoner dies by suicide rather than continuing existence within the prison system.

Durkheim's sociological theory of suicide made an important contribution to the current understanding of death by suicide in that it was the first real theory to specifically identify types of suicide and ascribe reasons for them. This theory also is unique in that most theories of suicide are focused on the level of the individual, whereas Durkheim's theory is focused on the societal level. This focus is advantageous in that it can provide potential explanations for shifts in suicide rates over time and associate these shifts with important societal factors. Durkheim's theory created a foundation for subsequent theories of suicide, most of which to this day integrate his ideas in one way or another.

Despite its positive contributions, however, Durkheim's theory does have shortcomings in its interpretation of death by suicide. Because his theory neglects variables at the individual level, its major shortcoming is that it does not explain why everyone in society does not die by suicide when the societal conditions for suicide are high (e.g., why does not everyone die by suicide during economic downtimes?). Because all people should be influenced by these societal processes, when the conditions are right according to Durkheim's theory, everyone should have at least some suicidal ideation. Yet this is not the case, meaning that there must be at least some individual factors that serve to moderate these societal conditions that would otherwise result in death by suicide.

PSYCHODYNAMIC THEORIES OF SUICIDE

Psychodynamic theories of suicide have attempted to address the internal and unconscious conflicts that individuals experience within themselves and address how these factors contribute to suicide. One psychodynamic theory of suicide proposed by Menninger (1938) suggested that deaths by suicide involve one of the three following motives: a desire to be killed resulting from self-blame, a desire to kill others, or a desire to die as a way of escaping pain. This theoretical approach to suicide is supported by findings that self-blame predicts suicide (Brevard, Lester, & Yang, 1990), that suicidality and violence potential are highly correlated (Apter et al., 1990), and that thoughts and feelings of revenge are important risk/contributing factors for suicidality (Rudd et al., 2006; Selby, Anestis, & Joiner, 2007). Few theories of suicide address the link between aggression and suicide, and Menninger's (1938) theory actually makes the desire to kill others a distinct motive for suicide, which may help in understanding the phenomenon of murder-suicide. This theory is unclear, however, about how individuals respond to these motivations. For example, take the desire to kill others, does someone with this motive kill himself or herself to avoid killing those others, or does he or she kill the other person(s) and then himself or herself?

Another psychodynamic theory by Hendin (1991) suggests that suicide involves both conscious and unconscious attachment to death. That is, some who die by suicide may feel that suicide is a form of rebirth, while others may believe that suicide is a form of self-punishment. Thus, death is viewed as a way of resolving conflicts within one's current life. One unique aspect of this theory is that it takes into account an individual's views on death, including the potential that death may be a positive experience (in a liberating sense) or possibly a form of redemption. This theory lacks predictive power, however, as it is not clear how people may develop these attachments to death, nor does it address who, among those who develop these feelings about death, will actually die by suicide.

ESCAPE THEORY OF SUICIDAL BEHAVIOR

Baumeister's (1990) escape theory of suicide is a social-psychological theory that focuses on how individuals come to attempt suicide. Baumeister's escape theory is an elaboration of Baechler's (1980) escape theory of suicide, which defines suicide as "any behavior that seeks and finds the solution to an existential problem by making an attempt on the life of the subject" (Baechler, 1980, p. 74). Baechler's original contention was that suicide was seen as one way of solving a life problem. In this view, suicide was not an end per se; rather, suicide was seen as a means to an end (Baechler, 1980). Finding Baechler's original theory insufficiently explicated and overly rationalistic, Baumeister expanded on the theory, proposing a succession of six key steps that ultimately beget suicide attempts. According to Baumeister (1990), the process will only lead to a suicide attempt if each step brings about a particular outcome. The six steps are as follows: (1) falling short of standards, (2) attributions to the self, (3) high self-awareness, (4) negative affect, (5) cognitive deconstruction, and (6) consequences of deconstruction.

The first step requires that current circumstances fall well below an individual's standards. This can result from unrealistically high expectations, recent negative life events, or a combination of the two. According to the theory, the crucial element that initiates the suicidal process is the magnitude of the discrepancy between expected and actual outcomes or circumstances. If the discrepancy between expected and actual outcomes is large and negative, the likelihood of a suicide attempt increases; conversely, if the discrepancy is small, the likelihood of a suicide attempt considerably decreases.

The second step of the escape theory concerns how the negative outcomes are interpreted. Specifically, according to the theory, failures and disappointments should only lead to a suicide attempt if an individual makes internal attributions about the current circumstances, which foster low self-esteem as well as a sense of inadequacy and/or worthlessness. Further, the negative self-attributions are taken to be stable and likely predictive of future disappointments. Insofar as an individual can make external attributions about the disappointing circumstances, according to the theory, motivations to attempt suicide should not arise.

In step three, escape theory suggests than an individual will develop a heightened sense of self-awareness, which stems directly from falling short of standards and negative self-attributions. More specifically, an individual will become acutely aware of how he or she measures up, with respect to self-standards and others' standards. Often seeing himself or herself as falling short of expectations, the individual's self-perception will be colored by feelings of inadequacy, incompetence, or guilt. Next, step four of the escape theory holds that, as a consequence of an individual's heightened self-awareness and feelings of inadequacy, he or she will develop an aversive and acute negative affect, largely colored by feelings of depression and anxiety.

Insofar as an individual finds the negative affective state aversive, he or she will attempt to escape it. To do so, given that the negative affect develops in response to feelings of inadequacy and increased self-awareness, the individual may try to stop feeling the negative emotions, making the negative self-attributions, and/or being as self-aware. Specifically, the individual will withdraw into a numb state of "cognitive deconstruction," which is the fifth stage of the suicide cycle. Cognitive deconstruction involves a subjective shift to less meaningful, less integrative forms of thought and awareness. The state is characterized by constrained perspective of time focused on the present, concreteness, lack of integrative thought, and an interest in immediate—as opposed to long-term—goals.

Lastly, step six of escape theory holds that cognitive deconstruction results in four consequences that are particularly pertinent to suicidality, namely, disinhibition, passivity, lack of emotion, and irrational thought. Disinhibition, as a consequence of cognitive deconstruction, refers to the diminished ability to inhibit immediate impulses. In the absence of certain inhibitions, an individual will be more likely to engage in unrestrained or impulsive behavior, especially suicidal behavior. Passivity, a second consequence of deconstruction, reflects the suicidal individual's general attitude toward his or her present condition. According to the theory, adopting a passive attitude allows an individual to identify more as a victim than an active agent in taking his or her own life. Third, cognitive deconstruction is associated with attenuated emotion. Lack of affect is taken to be a key feature of cognitive deconstruction because, presumably, it is a sign of low-level thinking. Importantly, the theory posits that the individual's affect is not absent, per se; rather, affect is willfully subdued by the individual as a means of escaping negative feelings and emotions. Lastly, suicidal individuals are vulnerable to irrational thinking, which is hypothesized to be another means of preventing meaningful thought. Taken together, disinhibition is viewed as particularly salient as it acts to weaken the crucial inhibitions that protect individuals against suicidal behavior.

To date, at least to our knowledge, the empirical evidence for Baumeister's escape theory of suicide, as a whole, is somewhat sparse. Indeed, the literature examining the causal chain proposed by the theory remains largely theoretical; however, there has been some research examining the predictions of the model. For instance, although not direct empirical tests of the theory, the results of several studies in college students (O'Conner & O'Conner, 2003; Tassava & Rudderman, 1999) and clinical outpatients (Dean & Range, 1999; Hunter & O'Conner, 2003) have provided evidence consistent with the theory. One potential reason for the lack of research on the theory, and a potential drawback of the theory, is that there are numerous steps involved leading up to suicide, making it difficult to test the theory as a whole and identify which individuals are in which stage, thus decreasing its effectiveness in risk assessment. Still, Baumeister's escape theory provides an intriguing evaluation of the processes that may lead up to suicidal behavior.

HOPELESSNESS THEORY OF SUICIDE

One of the first modern theories of suicide was proposed by Beck and colleagues (1985, 1990), who suggested that overwhelming thoughts and feelings of hopelessness were what caused people to develop suicidal ideation and eventually die by suicide. Suicidal ideation, they suggested, is a function of hopeless cognitions about the unchangeable negativity of one's situation, such that no matter what one does, the negative situation will never change. In the hopelessness theory, suicidal individuals may think things such as "No matter what I do, I will always be a failure," and these thoughts may contribute to suicidal ideation. The hopelessness view of suicide is similar to Durkheim's anomic suicide, in that when things in one's life become difficult (e.g., economic troubles), suicidal individuals are likely to feel powerless and thus hopeless.

In addition to the role of hopeless cognitions in suicidality, Beck (1996) later added the concept of *modal processing* to provide further understanding of psychological disorders and suicidality. In modal processing, the role of individual personality is integrated into suicidal behavior through five cognitive schema modes: (1) the cognitive system, (2) the affective system, (3) the motivational and behavioral system, (4) the physiological system, and (5) the conscious control system. Rudd, Joiner, and Rajab (2001) further elaborated on these modal systems as they apply to suicidal behavior. The cognitive system contains suicidal thoughts and beliefs, the behavioral system involves behaviors that promote suicidality (e.g., planning and preparation for suicide), the affective system involves negative affect (e.g., sadness and depression), and the physiological system involves suicidal-related physiological arousal. The modal processing approach implies that when one of these schema modes is activated, the effects will spread to the other schemas and

activate them as well. So, as an individual begins to develop hopeless cognitions, he or she also will begin to experience depressed affect, physiological changes, and importantly, he or she will begin to behave in ways that propagate suicidal ideation and cause the individual to progress to more suicidal behavior.

There are a number of studies indicating that hopelessness is a risk factor for suicide attempts and completion. For example, one longitudinal study found that psychiatric patients who score high on a measure of hopelessness were subsequently more than four times as likely to die by suicide as those who initially scored low on the hopelessness scale (Brown, Beck, Steer, & Grisham, 2000). Another study with a similar longitudinal approach found the relationship between hopelessness and death by suicide to be even higher, with high scores on hopelessness resulting in an 11 times more likely chance of death by suicide over the next 13 years (Kuo, Gallo, & Eaton, 2004). Further, hopelessness also has been found to predict future suicidal behavior in both children and adolescents (Huth-Bocks, Kerr, Ivey, Kramer, & King, 2007; Nock & Kazdin, 2002). These findings indicate that hopelessness is an important predictor of future suicidal behavior.

Despite the impressive power of hopelessness in predicting future death by suicide, the hopelessness theory of suicide does not fully account for all aspects of suicide. The most important shortcoming of the theory is that many people feel hopeless but ultimately do not die by suicide. Take terminal illness, for example. Not all individuals in these hopeless situations die by suicide and many may even find a way to come to terms with their situation, even if it is a hopeless one. There also is evidence that people vary in their levels of hopelessness (Young et al., 1996), begging the question of how much hopelessness is needed for suicide to occur. Thus, although hopelessness may help explain why some people desire death by suicide, it may not explain why some people with high levels of hopelessness will die by suicide, while others will not. Future research may increase the specificity of the hopelessness theory of suicide by identification of specific facets of hopelessness more related to suicide than others (e.g., hopeless feelings about a career versus hopeless feelings about being perpetually alone).

PSYCHACHE THEORY OF SUICIDE

One view of suicide, proposed by Edwin Shneidman (1996, p. 4), is that "In almost every case, suicide is caused by pain, a certain kind of pain—psychological pain, which I call *psychache*. Furthermore, this psychache stems from thwarted or distorted psychological needs." Many people who have experienced an episode of severe depression express that that state was indeed very painful. Shneidman reasoned that for some people, the psychache becomes so great that death by suicide is the only way to relieve the pain. Shneidman (1998) also proposed that there is an extensive list of basic human needs, such as affiliation with other people, and that seven of these needs must have a deficit in order for an individual to experience psychache.

Shneidman (1985) extended his theory to include the postulate that the lethal potential of psychache increases as the options open to an individual experiencing psychache decrease. Essentially, as an individual runs out of options for reducing his or her psychache, his or her desire for suicide grows stronger, resulting in more severe suicide attempts and a smaller probability of survival. This lethality component of psychache is what separates mild suicidal behavior from lethal suicidal behavior, in that someone who has psychache at lower levels may make a suicide attempt, but this attempt will have a much higher probability of survival and may have the possibility of bringing help to the individual. Thus, Schneidman argues that it is the severity of psychache that constitutes the degree of an individual's suicidal desire and risk.

Although Shneidman's psychache theory makes a number of important contributions to the theoretical understanding of suicidal behavior, it also has some drawbacks. One important limitation to the theory is that there is no clear mechanism through which one develops the lethality necessary for serious suicidal behavior. Psychache theory is unclear in regard to the point at which an individual crosses the threshold for having lethal levels of psychache, or why this happens, other than that he or she begins to run out of options for improving his or her situation. Also, Shneidman's list of required basic needs, seven of which must be in deficit to experience psychache, is a large list with many combinations of potential factors that contribute to suicidal desire. This large list of things that contribute to feeling psychache results in specificity and prediction problems with the theory, and there is little empirical evidence to support the requirement of needing precisely seven deficits in these needs for suicidal ideation. With more research, specific types of emotional pain that could be classified as psychache may be identified, as well as the unique factors that result in the experience of psychache.

EMOTION DYSREGULATION THEORY OF SUICIDE

Linehan (1993) has proposed a theory of suicide that, although aimed more specifically at individuals with borderline personality disorder (BPD), still has important implications for understanding suicide in general. Linehan (1993) proposed that emotion dysregulation is a major causal factor of dysregulated behavior, especially suicidal behavior. She suggests that individuals with BPD have biological vulnerabilities that instill an emotional vulnerability such that they experience (1) emotions as extremely intense, (2) an increase in sensitivity to upsetting stimuli, and (3) a slow return to emotional baseline when upset. Dysregulated behaviors, such as self-injury, are then used as methods of distraction from negative emotional states.

Importantly, Linehan also proposes that BPD individuals experience environmental factors that interact with this emotion dysregulation, primarily emotional invalidation. Emotional invalidation refers to pervasive criticizing, or trivializing of the communication of internal experiences, as well as repeated punishment of appropriate emotional expression. This is often coupled with intermittent reinforcement of extreme emotional displays. This emotional invalidation from others may start in childhood and carry on into adulthood, and a perception of childhood emotional invalidation has been linked to dysfunction within current romantic relationships in individuals with features of BPD (Selby, Braithwaite, Joiner, & Fincham, 2008).

Furthermore, Linehan extended her theory and proposes that suicidal behavior is a result of the interaction between emotional invalidation and emotion dysregulation. The emotional states generated by this emotional vulnerability and the invalidation of others are extremely intense and aversive, such that extreme behaviors are sought out as desperate attempts to manage this negative affect. Linehan further suggests that death by suicide may be the ultimate way to alter one's affective state (1993, p. 60), and that suicide attempts may be the most desperate way of trying to extinguish this intense negative affect. Similar to Schneidman's psychache theory, the pain of these emotional states is so intense that death seems like a reasonable way to reduce the emotional state—permanently.

There are a variety of studies that have found support for Linehan's model, although much of this support is indirect. Based on her theory, Linehan formulated dialectical behavior therapy (DBT; Linehan, 1993), a therapy which specifically targets suicidal and self-injurious behavior in individuals with BPD by developing skills for coping with emotion dysregulation and facilitating adaptive interpersonal strategies. There are a number of studies that support the efficacy of DBT, especially with regard to reducing self-injurious and suicidal behaviors (Koons et al., 2001; Linehan, Armstrong, Suarez, Allmon, & Heard, 1991; Linehan 1999, 2002; Vernheul et al., 2003). The most recent randomized controlled trial of DBT found that treatment with DBT was superior to treatment by community experts in reducing suicide attempts and the use of emergency mental health services for suicidal ideation (Linehan et al., 2006). Despite this clinical evidence for the Emotion Dysregulation Model of suicide, there are few studies that specifically link emotion dysregulation to suicidal behavior. One study found that an interaction between the tendency to imagine violence and revenge when upset and experiencing symptoms of depression significantly predicted suicidal ideation, indicating that individuals experiencing suicidal symptoms may have maladaptive ways of regulating positive affect (Selby, Anestis, & Joiner, 2007).

The emotion dysregulation theory of suicide is novel in that it links the emotional states of suicidal individuals to behavior in a way that explains why suicide attempts may inhibit negative emotional states. Yet there are some aspects of suicidal behavior that are difficult to understand in the context of this model. Importantly, emotion dysregulation is a common phenomenon in psychological disorders with over half of the Axis I disorders and all of the Axis II personality disorders involving emotion dysregulation in some form (Gross & Levenson, 1997). Yet, despite the frequent experience of emotion dysregulation for many individuals, only a small percentage of those with psychological disorders die by suicide. The emotion dysregulation theory also is unclear in explaining what distinguishes severe suicide attempts from mild suicide attempts, other than the severity of emotion dysregulation.

INTERPERSONAL-PSYCHOLOGICAL THEORY OF SUICIDE

The interpersonal-psychological theory of suicidal behavior (Joiner, 2005) holds that an individual will only engage in serious suicidal behavior if he or she has both the desire to die by suicide and the *capability* to act on that desire. Joiner's (2005) model underscores the crucial difference between suicidal ideation and suicidal behavior, which some theories of suicide neglect to do. The theory extends

beyond solely addressing the question of who *wants* to die by suicide, to the question of who *can* die by suicide. As such, the theory is distinct from many other theories of suicide in that it has the potential to make more specific predictions about suicidal behavior, not solely suicidal ideation.

The interpersonal-psychological theory (see Fig. 15.1) points to two key interpersonal states that are associated with the desire for death by suicide: the experience of feeling alienated from valued social groups, such as peers and family (i.e., *thwarted belongingness*), and the perception that the self is so incompetent that one's presence is a liability to others (i.e., *perceived burdensomeness*). According to the theory, the needs to belong and make meaningful contributions to one's social circle are vital aspects of human nature. By thwarting those needs, individuals are at heightened risk of developing the desire for suicide. More specifically, the theory holds that experiencing both states—thwarted belongingness and perceived burdensomeness—concurrently is most likely to lead to the desire of death by suicide.

Moreover, according to the theory, the desire alone is not sufficient for a lethal suicide attempt. Indeed, should an individual develop the desire for suicide, in order to act on that desire, he or she must develop the capability to do so. Joiner (2005) argues that death by suicide is not an easy undertaking—in part because humans are inherently driven by strong self-preservation motives. Engaging in suicidal behavior clashes with these intrinsic motivations. As such, an individual must "work up" to being able to engage in lethal self-injury by repeatedly engaging in behaviors that clash with drives for self-preservation. This, according to the theory, will instill in the individual the ability to engage in lethal self-injury and is referred to as the *acquired capability* for suicide.

The basis for this proposition rests primarily on the principles of Solomon and Corbit's opponent process theory. Opponent process theory, broadly described, holds that with repeated exposure to an affective stimulus, the reaction to that stimulus shifts over time such that the original response to the stimulus is weakened and the opposing response is strengthened (Solomon & Corbit, 1974). Placed in the context of the interpersonal-psychological theory, Joiner (2005) argues that the capability for death by suicide is acquired via repeated exposure to painful and provocative experiences. Repeated exposure to painful and provocative experiences results in habituation, which, consequently, leads to a higher tolerance for pain and a sense of fearlessness

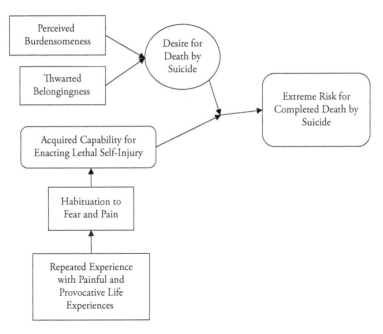

Figure 15.1 The interpersonal-psychological theory of suicide.

about death. Importantly, the acquired capability is conceptualized as existing on a continuum, accumulating over time with repeated exposure to salient experiences and potentiated by the nature of those experiences, such that the more painful or provocative an experience is, the more risk it will confer.

Taken together, the interpersonal-psychological theory puts forth four key hypotheses. First, the theory proposes that two interpersonal states—thwarted belongingness and perceived burdensomeness—act as proximal, causal risk factors for the desire for death by suicide. Second, the theory proposes that the desire for suicide is most likely to develop if an individual experiences both proposed interpersonal states simultaneously. Third, the ability to act on the desire for death by suicide is acquired via repeated exposure to painful and provocative experiences. Lastly, serious suicidal behavior will only occur in the presence of all three constructs—thwarted belongingness, perceived burdensomeness, and the acquired capability for lethal self-injury. To date, the interpersonal-psychological theory has undergone 20 direct empirical tests, the results of which are summarized next.

The first prediction of the theory is that perceived burdensomeness and thwarted belongingness are proximal, causal factors that increase the likelihood of suicidal desire. Several studies have investigated the roles of the two interpersonal states as such. With respect to perceived burdensomeness—the

misperception that one's death is worth more than one's life—four studies have been conducted examining its relation to suicidal desire. Consistent with the prediction that perceived burdensomeness is a risk factor for suicidal desire, Van Orden, Witte, Gordon, Bender, and Joiner (2008) found that perceived burdensomeness significantly predicted increased levels of suicidal ideation, over and above age, gender, and depressive symptoms, in a representative sample of undergraduates. Evidence for this prediction also can be taken from a study conducted by Joiner, Pettit, and colleagues (2002), wherein raters were trained to evaluate suicide notes on three dimensions: perceived burdensomeness, hopelessness, and generalized emotional pain. Perceived burdensomeness was found to be the best predictor—as compared to hopelessness and generalized emotional pain—of suicide attempter versus suicide completer such that as levels of perceived burdensomeness increased, the severity of suicidal symptoms was found to increase as well. In the same study, perceived burdensomeness also was found to predict lethality of suicide method, whereas hopelessness and emotional pain were not.

Direct evidence to date also has been in line with the hypothesis that thwarted belongingness serves as a proximal cause of the desire for suicide. For instance, a study conducted by Conner et al. (2007) to examine the relationship between prior suicide attempt and levels of belongingness in a sample of methadone maintenance patients indicated that individuals who reported greater belongingness decreased their odds of having a past suicide attempt by approximately 6%. Interestingly, the relationship did not hold for accidental overdoses—a result which speaks to the specificity of the prediction. Furthermore, Joiner, Hollar, and Van Orden (2006) also have found evidence for the critical "buffering" role of events that foster feelings of belongingness, which are associated with lower suicide rates.

The second prediction of the theory—that the interaction of low feelings of belonging and the perception of being a burden to others will lead to the desire for death by suicide—has been examined in two direct tests. The first study, conducted by Van Orden and colleagues (2008), examined the effects of the interaction of perceived burdensomeness and thwarted belongingness on suicidal ideation, as measured by the Beck Suicide Scale (Beck & Steer, 1991), in a diverse sample of undergraduates. Individuals who reported high levels of perceived burdensomeness and thwarted belonging were found to have the highest levels of suicidal ideation, after controlling for age, gender, and level of depression. The second study examining this prediction examined the relationship between perceived family support (belongingness), feelings of mattering (burdensomeness), and suicidal desire in a heterogeneous community sample of young adults (Joiner et al., 2009). Results from this study further substantiated the prediction. Results indicated that the suicidal desire was most severe in individuals who reported both low family support and low feelings of mattering. This relationship held even after controlling for 6-month and lifetime histories of depression.

The third main prediction of the theory holds that the capacity to engage in lethal self-injury is primarily acquired through repeated exposure and habituation to painful and provocative experiences. A corollary of this prediction is that the most direct means of acquiring the capability for death by suicide is via previous suicide attempts; however, other less direct pathways—via other fear-inducing, risky behaviors or exposure to physical violence—also are viable means of increasing the ability to engage in lethal self-injury. For instance, in line with this prediction Van Orden and colleagues (2008) assessed the relationship between past suicide attempts and the acquired capability to inflict lethal self-injury in a sample of clinical outpatients. The capability to inflict lethal self-injury was measured by the Acquired Capability Scale, a self-report measure that assesses fearlessness about lethal self-injury and the

perception of one's ability to tolerate self-inflicted pain (Van Orden et al., 2008). Findings supported the theory's hypothesis in that individuals who reported the highest levels of acquired capability were the most likely to have a history of multiple past attempts.

In addition to past suicide attempts serving as a vehicle of increasing the likelihood of engaging in future self-injury, as alluded to earlier, the theory holds that there are other viable pathways of acquiring the capability to engage in lethal self-injury. For example, in a study conducted by Nock, Joiner, Gordon, Lloyd-Richardson, and Prinstein (2006), adolescents who reported longer histories of non-suicidal self-injury (NSSI) and engagement in multiple methods of NSSI were found to have the highest rates of past suicide attempts. Furthermore, the same study found that individuals with a history of engaging in NSSI and reports of no pain during NSSI were approximately two times more likely to have attempted suicide in the past compared to those reporting an experience of pain during NSSI. More recently, Gordon & colleagues (2010) provided further evidence for the role of habituation and opponent processes in engaging in self-injurious behaviors. Investigators found that individuals who reported a history of self-injurious behaviors were significantly more likely to feel relief, and the absence of fear, following an episode of self-injury.

Lastly, the theory proposes a three-way interaction of perceived burdensomeness, thwarted belongingness, and the acquired capability to engage in lethal self-injury, such that individuals who evidence high levels of perceived burdensomeness, low feelings of belongingness, and have developed the capacity to engage in self-injury will be more likely to die by suicide. Joiner and colleagues (2009) examined this prediction in a large sample of suicidal young adults. In this study, family support, feelings of mattering, and a history of past suicide attempts were used as proxies for perceived burdensomeness, belongingness, and the acquired capability to engage in lethal self-injury, respectively. Evidence was in line with the prediction that the intersection of these three constructs would be particularly dangerous: Individuals who reported highest levels of perceived burden and lowest levels of belongingness were much more likely to attempt suicide, in the presence of the acquired capability to do so. Importantly, this relationship held even after taking into account levels of depression, hopelessness, and borderline personality disorder features, all of which have been documented as powerful risk factors for suicide attempts.

Although there are a number of empirical studies that provide evidence in support of the interpersonal-psychological theory of suicide, the theory is not perfect. One drawback concerns how much acquired capability is needed to enact a lethal suicide attempt. Is it only people at the highest levels of acquired capability, or can those with moderate levels still attempt suicide? Furthermore, how do drugs and alcohol interact with acquired capability; do they lower the threshold needed for suicide? Despite these unanswered questions, the interpersonal-psychological theory provides a valuable framework for understanding suicide and assessing suicide risk. Additional research on this theory is likely to provide additional useful information.

SUMMARY OF SUICIDE THEORIES

As can be seen from the various theories of suicide that have been discussed, the most common theoretical reason for suicide is deep emotional pain. The view of what causes this emotional pain changes somewhat according to each theory, whether it is hopelessness, aversive self-awareness, psychache, emotion dysregulation, or perceived burdensomeness and thwarted belongingness. Indeed, some of the theories have intriguing components that make them quite distinct from the others. Suicide is a devastating phenomenon that can have many forms and motivations. As theories of suicide have developed over the years, they have provided more parsimonious explanations of suicidal behavior that can help in understanding the different motivations for suicide. Ideally, as theories of suicide continue to be explored and developed, the theories will identify key targets for treatment of suicidality that will contribute to saving lives.

Theories of Nonsuicidal Self-Injury

Nonsuicidal self-injury (NSSI), as mentioned at the beginning of the chapter, involves the purposeful destruction of bodily tissue without suicidal intention. This is a behavior that is difficult to understand because it appears to be so paradoxical, especially when many people who report engaging in NSSI claim to hurt themselves to "feel better." Most people desire to avoid pain or will endure it if necessary for a desirable outcome (e.g., surgery); but to purposely inflict pain on and injure oneself, and in doing so derive a pleasurable feeling, would appear to go against human nature. Each of the

major theories of NSSI will be compared to theories of suicide in order to highlight theoretical common ground and important differences between the two forms of behavior.

Psychophysiological Theories of Nonsuicidal Self-Injury

Some theories posit a biological function of mood regulation (or attempting to feel better) during NSSI, primarily involving the release of endorphins. Endorphins are endogenous opioids that are released in response to tissue damage and have the function of natural painkillers while simultaneously inducing feelings of euphoria (Hawkes, 1992; Willer, Dehen, & Cambier, 1981). The opioid hypothesis of NSSI suggests that the influences of endorphins may cause the mood-regulating effects of NSSI (Favazza & Conterio, 1988; Richardson & Zaleski, 1986), which are discussed in more detail later in the chapter. This hypothesis has not been supported, however, by empirical findings that naloxone (an opiate antagonist similar to naltrexone) did not diminish improvements in affect following the performance of a self-injury proxy (Russ, Roth, Kakuma, Harrison, & Hull, 1994).

Even though the opioid hypothesis has hit some empirical roadblocks, there still appears to be a physiological basis to NSSI that may be illuminated by animal models. For example, some research findings suggest that the dopamine neurotransmitter pathway may be involved in NSSI. Many drugs have been found to stimulate the dopamine system, and it is thought that this effect on the brain is what makes many substances addictive (Volkow, Fowler, Wang, Swanson, & Telang, 2007); this same reasoning has been applied to self-injury in that NSSI may alter the dopamine system in such a way that NSSI becomes addictive (Sivam, 1995). For example, the monoamine inhibitor pemoline has been found to induce self-injury in rats (King, Au, & Poland, 1995), and it is thought to do so because it may result in blocking dopamine reuptake, thus increasing synaptic levels of dopamine. However, self-injury does not appear to present until approximately 24–48 hours after pemoline injection, suggesting that glutamate-mediated neuroplasticity may be involved in the self-injurious behavior that the rats develop (Muehlmann & Devine, 2008).

One important aspect that is shared by biological theories of both NSSI and suicide is that the biological pathways to behavior in both theoretical approaches focus on predispositions to future behavior. For example, both approaches suggest that NSSI and suicide can result from dysregulated levels of neurotransmitters (dopamine and serotonin). Thus, they have important implications for identification of individuals at higher risk for these behaviors, and they may be useful for identifying those in need of preventative interventions. Although these biological theories are important for understanding who may be at higher risk for future NSSI or suicidal behavior, these theories have some difficulty differentiating who will engage in one versus the other behavior. For these theories to be more useful in the future understanding of suicide and self-injury, more specific mechanisms linking biological dysfunction to observable behavior are needed.

Social Theories of Nonsuicidal Self-Injury

NSSI has a long history of being considered to have social functions. It has often been considered a way that the individual uses to manipulate others or influence the surrounding environment (Chowanec, Josephson, Coleman, & Davis, 1991; Podovall, 1969). Other, less stigmatizing views of NSSI suggest that it may be a way of communicating intense internal pain, be a cry for help, be a means of avoiding abandonment, or be an attempt to be taken more seriously by others (Allen, 1995). Alternatively, other theories have viewed NSSI as a response to negative interpersonal interactions, such as criticism from a loved one, or other actions that invalidate the individual's emotions (Linehan, 1993).

In a study on the functions of NSSI, Nock and Prinstein (2004) examined four hypothesized functions of NSSI, all of which were supported by empirical evidence. Two of these referred to automatic reinforcement, meaning how NSSI functioned to influence internal states. These functions are often referred to as affect-regulating functions and will be discussed in more detail shortly. The other two major functions that Nock and Prinstein (2004) proposed pertained to social reinforcement. The first social function they proposed, automatic positive reinforcement, refers to the use of NSSI as a method of obtaining desired social outcomes from others. These outcomes refer to attention or care from another person who may not provide this attention otherwise. The second social function proposed by Nock and Prinstein (2004) is automatic negative reinforcement. This refers to an individual's use of NSSI to avoid certain social outcomes. Social functions of NSSI have been supported by a number of additional studies (Briere

& Gil, 1998; Brown, Comtois, & Linehan, 2002; Herpertz, 1995; Laye-Gindhu & Schonert-Reichl, 2005). Yet, despite the role that social reasons play in NSSI, they do not appear to represent the most commonly endorsed motivation for NSSI.

Social theories of NSSI and social theories of suicide are very different. Perhaps the most stark difference between the two is that social theories of NSSI tend to view the behavior as manipulative in some way (soliciting a desired response from someone), while social theories of suicide view suicide as the result of unbearable social conditions (Durkheim, 1897) or as a loss of connections with others (Joiner, 2005). Although suicide attempts can be attempts at manipulation for some individuals, as an individual's suicidal intent and preparation increase, the more likely it is that the individual will attempt to hide his or her suicidality from others. As an important example, as suicidal ideation increases, many individuals will completely withdraw from friends, family, or society (Van Orden et al., 2006). Yet it is important to note that the social functions of NSSI may not be entirely to manipulate others, but for many the behavior may serve as a way to connect with others who self-injure. For example, there is evidence that online NSSI communities exist, where individuals who self-injure interact and socialize, often encouraging and normalizing NSSI (Whitlock, Powers, & Eckenrode, 2006). Thus, although the bulk of research does not indicate social functions as the sole driving force behind NSSI and suicide, the social aspects of these behaviors remain an important part of understanding the psychopathology underlying these behaviors.

Psychodynamic Theories of Nonsuicidal Self-Injury

Psychodynamic theories have had a broad range of views on the nature and function of NSSI (often referred to as self-mutilation in these theories). The Sexual Model of NSSI suggests that self-injurious behaviors serve as a means of sexual gratification, sexual punishment, or for attempts to avoid sexual feelings (see Suyemoto, 1998). In the Sexual Model view, NSSI can serve to be a pleasurable experience that is unconsciously gratifying. Yet simultaneously it also can be a way to punish oneself for sexual desire, and self-injury to the genital area may be a way of attempting to destroy this desire (Daldin, 1988; Friedman, Glasser, Laufer, Laufer, & Wohl, 1972; Woods, 1988).

Other psychodynamic theories do not view sexual desire as a major motive for NSSI. Object relations views of NSSI suggest that individuals who self-injure have difficulty separating internal representations of self from others (Carroll, Schaffer, Spensley, & Abramowitz, 1980). Because of this difficulty in separating views of themselves from views of others, when they feel negativity toward someone they are close to, they also feel that same negative perception about themselves. Thus, NSSI, in objection relations theory, provides one way for self-injuring individuals to distinguish their identity from others, for example, through carving their skin and producing scars. Skin, in this view, is the most basic barrier between the individual and his or her environment, and by producing scars on the skin the individual affirms his or her personal identity and autonomy.

Another theoretical model of NSSI that is often classified as having psychodynamic roots is the Antisuicide Model of NSSI. In this model, NSSI is viewed as a compromise to suicide attempts. The reasoning is that through self-injury the individual is able to satisfy self-destructive impulses and desires without actually dying (Firestone & Seiden, 1990; Himber, 1994). Although the Antisuicide Model of NSSI makes intuitive sense, few studies have examined this function of NSSI, and few of those studies have found much empirical support for the model. In a sample of individuals with BPD, those in the sample rated "to prevent me from acting on suicidal feelings" as the seventh most common reason for NSSI (Shearer, 1994). Likewise, two other studies found that less than 50% of inpatient or nonclinical adolescents reported engaging in NSSI to "stop suicidal ideation or attempts" (Nixon, Cloutier, & Aggarwal, 2002) or "it stopped me from killing myself" (Laye-Gindhu & Schonert-Reichl, 2005), respectively.

The psychodynamic theories of NSSI provide an interesting contrast to the psychodynamic theories of suicide. While psychodynamic theories of NSSI focus on NSSI primarily as a way of establishing and confirming self-identity, or serving as a compromise with suicidal desires, the psychodynamic theories of suicide focus on suicide as a means of escape from suffering or as a way of punishing oneself. One thing that psychodynamic theories of suicide and NSSI both have in common is that although they can provide explanations for these behaviors, unfortunately they lack predictive ability for determining who will engage in these behaviors. This means that the concepts from these theories are not currently helpful in suicide risk assessment situations. This potentially may be due to the lack of research on

these theories in the assessment of future suicidal behavior and NSSI.

Affect Regulation Theories of Nonsuicidal Self-Injury

Although many theories have been proposed for why people engage in NSSI, perhaps the most common theme and bulk of empirical evidence support the function of affect regulation (see Klonsky, 2007). In addition to her emotion dysregulation theory of suicide, Linehan (1993) also proposed that self-injury is a way of reducing negative affect by shifting attention away from emotional stimuli. Along these lines, Brown, Comtois, and Linehan (2002) found support for the affect-regulating properties of NSSI in a sample of inpatients diagnosed with BPD. In this study they examined self-reported reasons for engaging in NSSI and suicidal behavior and found that the most common reasons patients reported for engaging in NSSI were to distract themselves from negative affect, to generate feelings, and to punish themselves, whereas the reason most often reported for engaging in suicidal behavior was to make others better off.

Further evidence for the affect-regulating effects of NSSI comes from a similar study with non-BPD individuals who engaged in NSSI. Nock and Prinstein (2004) examined the functional aspects of NSSI in a group of adolescent inpatients and found that one of the most common reasons for engaging in NSSI was to reduce negative emotional experience (other reasons included feeling generation and social reinforcement). Nock and Prinstein (2005) replicated these results. Additional studies have indicated that self-reported reasons for engaging in NSSI involve tension release (Herpertz, 1995), decreasing feelings of rage (Osuch, Noll, & Putnam, 1999), distraction from painful feelings (Briere & Gil, 1998), and to "control my mind when it is racing" (in a nonclinical sample; Favazza & Conterio, 1989). So, although there may be various reasons for engaging in NSSI, many of these reasons have the common theme of decreasing negative emotions. There are four specific theories involving the affect regulation motivation for NSSI that require further discussion: (1) Self-Punishment Model, (2) Antidissociation Model, (3) Feeling-Generation Model, and (4) Experiential Avoidance Model.

The self-punishment theory of NSSI (see Klonsky, 2007) suggests that NSSI provides a way for an individual to display anger against himself or herself and inflict self-punishment for wrongdoing. Self-punishment appears to be a common reason that individuals who engage in NSSI report as motivation for self-injury across various studies (Bennun, 1983; Brown, Comtois, & Linehan, 2002; Klonsky, 2007). It has been suggested that NSSI is a way of continuing the criticism and invalidation from others (Linehan, 1993), with the individual thinking that he or she deserves to be derogated and punished due to the constant negative feedback from those around him or her. Other researchers also have suggested that NSSI is a way of expressing anger at oneself (Bennun, 1983; Soloff, Lis, Kelly, Cornelius, & Ulrich, 1994).

The Antidissociation Model of NSSI suggests that those individuals who self-injure do so in response to states of dissociation or depersonalization. Dissociation is an experience in which the individual feels as though he or she is outside of his or her body, feels like everything is unreal, or feels numbness or nothing at all. Dissociative states have been considered to be commonly associated with self-injurious behavior (Suyemoto, 1998). It has been suggested that dissociation is a response to extreme emotional states and that physical pain or the sight of blood may shock the person's system and inhibit the dissociative state (Gunderson, 1984; Himber, 1994; Simpson, 1975).

Evidence supporting the antidissociation function of NSSI is mixed, with some findings supporting the model (Armey & Crowther, 2008; Brown et al., 2002; Favazza & Conterio, 1989; Herpertz, 1995) and other studies failing to support this model (Laye-Gindhu & Schonert-Reichl, 2005; Nock & Prinstein, 2004). One possible explanation for such mixed findings is that dissociation is actually an extreme form of negative emotion and participants have difficulty describing the experience as either dissociation or negative emotion. Such an extreme experience of negative emotion may result in difficulty concentrating and focusing on anything, which may have similar qualities as dissociation (Selby & Joiner, 2009).

The feeling generation hypothesis is similar to the antidissociation hypothesis, except that rather than using NSSI as a method of inhibiting dissociation, NSSI is used as a way to generate positive feelings or sometimes to generate any feeling at all. Recent research has identified that commonly reported reasons for engaging in NSSI involve feeling generation (Brown et al., 2002) as well as automatic positive reinforcement (Nock & Prinstein, 2004). Other studies have also supported the feeling generation hypothesis (Brown et al., 2002; Laye-Gindhu & Schonert-Reichl, 2005; Osuch et al., 1999;

Penn, Esposito, Schaeffer, Fritz, & Spirito, 2003; Shearer, 1994). Yet there also is evidence that does not support the feeling generation hypothesis. One study found that only 7% of the sample endorsed "to produce feelings and a sense of being real when I feel numb and 'out of touch'" (Shearer, 1994). Another study found that only 7% of a sample of self-injurers reported using NSSI "for excitement" (Nixon et al., 2002).

The Experiential Avoidance Model of NSSI (Chapman, Gratz, & Brown, 2006) capitalizes on the affect regulation evidence that research has implicated as a major function of NSSI. In this model, the authors not only provide a compelling functional assessment of NSSI, but they also suggest how repetitive use of NSSI can result in a conditioned behavioral response that propagates NSSI. The term *experiential avoidance* refers to any behavior that is used as a method of avoiding or escaping from an unwanted internal experience (Hayes, Wilson, Gifford, Follette, & Strosahl, 1996). Internal experiences that individuals desire to avoid may include thoughts, feelings, and bodily sensations that they find uncomfortable. Avoidance behaviors then work through negative reinforcement, where the behavior removes the unwanted internal experience and the behavior is likely to increase in frequency because the reward for the behavior is the removal of an aversive stimulus.

The Experiential Avoidance Model (EAM; see Fig. 15.2) posits that that when individuals experience emotion dysregulation and negative affect, they respond by engaging in NSSI as a way of escaping the negative affect they are experiencing. The EAM suggests that NSSI helps to avoid negative emotion through mechanisms such as physiological changes, distraction, and self-punishment. By avoiding negative emotion, NSSI becomes rewarding, much in the same way that avoiding an anxiety-provoking situation, such as asking an intimidating boss for a raise, may be rewarding in that the anxiety of the situation is removed. The authors go one step further, however, and suggest that as NSSI is used to avoid negative emotional states, NSSI becomes a conditioned first response to any sign of negative emotion, resulting in heavy use of NSSI to avoid any negative emotion at all. NSSI may be promoted as a behavioral response to negative emotion because the negative effects of NSSI may become habituated with repeated experience.

The EAM finds some of its strongest support in the research on thought suppression, negative emotion, and NSSI. Thought suppression refers

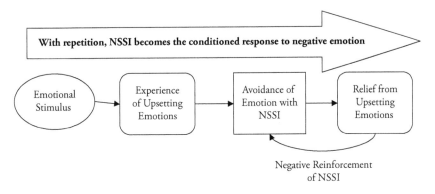

Figure 15.2 The Experiential Avoidance Model of nonsuicidal self-injury (NSSI).

to a deliberate attempt to reduce the frequency or intensity of unpleasant cognitions, in other words, trying not to think about something. Recent meta-analyses suggest that deliberate attempts to suppress specific thoughts may actually have a paradoxical "rebound" effect where the frequency of the unwanted thought increases following efforts to suppress it (Abramowitz, Tolin, & Street, 2001; Wenzlaff & Wegner, 2000). A tendency to engage in thought suppression has been linked to a variety of negative psychological consequences in general (Purdon, 1999; Wegner, Schneider, Carter, & White, 1987).

There also is evidence that thought suppression may be involved in NSSI. For example, Cheavens et al. (2005) examined the role of thought suppression in BPD and found that thought suppression fully mediated the relationship between negative affect intensity/reactivity and BPD features, which includes self-injury. In a similar study Rosenthal and colleagues (2005) replicated this finding. Najmi, Wegner, and Nock (2007) conducted a study examining the role of thought suppression in NSSI. In this study they found that thought suppression is associated with the presence and frequency of NSSI and that thought suppression mediated the relationship between emotional reactivity and the frequency of engaging in NSSI. They suggest that when individuals who engage in NSSI attempt to suppress negative emotional thoughts, the result is an increase in the frequency of these thoughts, and that this intense affective state triggers NSSI.

Affect regulation theories of NSSI have many similarities with theories of suicide. The most obvious example is the Emotion Dysregulation Model of suicide (Linehan, 1993), which suggests that both suicide and NSSI are extreme ways to regulate difficult emotional experiences. Other suicide theories that have this emotion regulation component include psychache theory (Shneidman, 1996), hopelessness theory (Beck, Steer, Kovacs, & Garrison, 1985), and the interpersonal-psychological theory (Joiner, 2005). As has been mentioned, emotion regulation is common to many theories of NSSI as well. This commonality between theories for both behaviors also serves as a drawback, however, because the theories lack specificity. Affect regulation theories are good at explaining why people may engage in these behaviors, and they have some predictive validity for determining who will engage in these behaviors, but they are not particularly useful at distinguishing who will self-injure versus attempt suicide when upset. This may be where the interpersonal-psychological theory of suicide (Joiner, 2005) is particularly useful, as this theory takes into account the affect regulation motivations for suicide, but it also distinguishes who has the ability to engage in a lethal suicide attempt through the acquired capability component. Future research on affect regulation theories of suicide and NSSI should attempt to distinguish the role of affect regulation in these two types of behavior.

The Emotional Cascade Model of Nonsuicidal Self-Injury

Although a number of affect regulation theories of NSSI have generated advances in the understanding of NSSI, most remain unclear as to why NSSI may be used to avoid negative affect when there are other, less painful and intimidating ways to avoid emotional experience, for example, taking a cold shower. One recent affect regulation theory of NSSI, the Emotional Cascade Model (Selby, Anestis, & Joiner, 2008; Selby & Joiner, 2009), may delineate an important mechanism explaining why NSSI may be used, rather than other behaviors, in a way that is consistent with other affect regulation models.

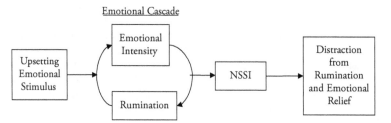

Emotional Cascade

Figure 15.3 The Emotional Cascade Model of nonsuicidal self-injury (NSSI).

In the Emotional Cascade Model (see Fig. 15.3), the authors propose that rumination on negative affect results in an extremely intense state of negative emotion, and that NSSI serves as a potent distracter from rumination. Rumination is a cognitive process whereby an individual constantly and repetitively thinks about the causes and consequences of problems, as well as how he or she feels about those problems, in a way that is unproductive (Nolen-Hoeksema, 1991). Importantly, rumination has been found to amplify negative affect (Moberly & Watkins, 2008). The Emotional Cascade Model suggests that in order to distract from intense rumination, and the associated increasing negative affect, some individuals will engage in a dysregulated behavior that provides potent physical sensations to focus on, such as pain or the sight of blood in NSSI. Thus, by focusing on the physical sensations of the behavior, the individual is able to distract from rumination and negative emotion.

Although the Emotional Cascade Model is relatively new, there is some empirical evidence to support it. Multiple studies have found that rumination is associated with NSSI (Armey & Crowther, 2008; Hilt, Cha, & Nolen-Hoeksema, 2008; Selby, Connell, & Joiner, 2010). Furthermore, one study examined the relationship between emotional cascades and NSSI in individuals with BPD. This study found that a latent variable of emotional cascades (composed of various measures of rumination) significantly predicted NSSI, as well as suicide attempts, even when controlling for depression and additional Cluster B personality disorders (Selby, Anestis, Bender, & Joiner, 2009). Another recent study using experience sampling, where people complete multiple assessments of emotions and thoughts on a daily basis, found that emotional cascades at one momentary assessment predicted the occurrence of various dysregulated behaviors, including NSSI, at the subsequent momentary assessment (Selby & Joiner, 2013). Using these same data, Selby and colleagues (2013) found that

emotional cascades, as indicated by high variability in rumination about the past and sadness, predicted more frequent NSSI reported over the 2-week assessment period.

The findings on thought suppression (discussed earlier) provide further support for the role of rumination and emotional cascade in BPD, and in fact rumination and thought suppression appear to form a positive feedback loop together. Erber and Wegner (1996) have suggested that rumination is a result of thought suppression, caused by the rebound effects of thought suppression. This hypothesis is support by a study in which Najmi, Wegner, and Nock (2007) showed that thought suppression appears to increase self-injurious and suicidal thoughts, and thus it may increase the frequency of NSSI. On the other hand, Martin and Tesser (1996) have suggested that thought suppression not only results from rumination but is an active attempt to inhibit a ruminative response. Although no studies to our knowledge have provided evidence for the causal link between rumination and thought suppression, Erskine, Kvavilashvili, and Kornbrot (2007) recently showed that thought suppression was predicted by rumination—which suggests that if rumination is present, thought suppression is likely to be present as well. Although more evidence is needed to clarify the relationship between rumination and thought suppression, it seems possible that an individual who is ruminating may attempt to suppress those thoughts and in doing so increase rumination. Likewise, even if thought suppression comes immediately after an emotional stimulus, the result may be more rumination and more negative affect.

As with all models of NSSI, the Emotional Cascade Model also has some limitations. For example, NSSI is less common in adulthood than adolescence (Briere & Gil, 1998; Ross & Heath, 2003), indicating that some self-injurers may later discontinue the behavior. Yet if individuals who self-injure experience emotional cascades stop self-injuring as they get older, how is it that they are coping more adaptively with emotional cascades? Do they ruminate less with age? There is also the question of why some people may choose NSSI as their particular method for coping with emotional cascades, rather than something like binging on food or alcohol. In a recent study conducted by Selby, Connell, and Joiner (2010), the authors suggested that combining the emotional cascade theory and the interpersonal-psychological theory of suicide may be useful for understanding who self-injures to regulate negative emotion rather than using other behaviors. The authors found that there was an interaction between trait rumination levels and a measure of acquired capability which predicted frequency of NSSI over the previous year, indicating that those who have a high tendency to ruminate and have a high level of acquired capability are more likely to self-injure, perhaps because they are less afraid to use pain as a method of emotion regulation.

When compared to theories of suicide, the Emotional Cascade Model differs in its approach to negative emotion by viewing the emotional states that preceded NSSI as intense, yet temporary. In contrast, the affect regulation components of suicide theories involve a much more general and prevalent difficulty with negative emotion, which permeates most of the individual's life. Although emotional cascades may be involved in the suicide attempts of some individuals, behaviors such as NSSI are more likely to be predicted by emotional cascades because NSSI is an effective method for relieving an emotionally distressing state, at least temporarily. Suicide, on the other hand, is usually not an impulsive behavior or response to a single distressing event (Witte et al., 2008), but rather suicide attempts are the end trajectory of numerous distressing events, planning and preparation, and building up the courage to carry out the attempt (Joiner, 2005). Thus, emotional cascades are neither necessary nor are they sufficient for a lethal suicide attempt. More research is needed, however, to distinguish the extent of the role of emotional cascades in suicide and suicide attempts.

Overall Comparison of Nonsuicidal Self-Injury Theories to Theories of Suicide

The main common ground between theories of suicide and NSSI is a focus on dealing with painful emotional states. Most theories for each type of behavior have some component involving escape from negative emotions. But an important difference is that the negative emotion involved in theories of suicide appears to be a much more pervasive, stable, and constant experience than the negative affect involved in theories of NSSI, which is usually a temporary state. Future research on theories of suicide and NSSI should attempt to further address the differences in negative affect between the two behaviors and determine whether they are qualitatively different, or if the main theoretical difference is the constant prevalence of that negative affect in suicide. Theories of both suicide and NSSI also need to explore mechanisms that distinguish who will engage in one behavior versus the other. Finally, many people experience negative emotion in various forms, yet suicidal and nonsuicidal self-injurious behaviors occur among only a small subset of people. Future research should attempt to identify additional factors that may interact with negative emotion, such as the acquired capability, which may be useful in distinguishing who among those experiencing negative emotion will go on to engage in these self-injurious behaviors.

Conclusion: Theories of Suicidal Behavior

Theories of suicide and NSSI are vastly important. Not only do they help us formulate an understanding of why people would engage in these taboo and frightening behaviors, but they also serve as a guide for future research that will illuminate the causes of, and treatments for, these behaviors. Although each theory has its strengths and weaknesses, each of them contributes to a larger understanding of suicidal behavior. As theories are refined through empirical evidence, we may one day have a full understanding of suicide and self-injury.

Challenges and Future Directions

Although theories of suicidal behavior have made important progress in understanding both suicide and NSSI, there are still a number of limitations to these theories that have yet to be addressed. Perhaps the biggest limitation to these theories is a general lack of experimental evidence supporting the causal role of the proposed mechanisms leading to these behaviors (i.e., psychache, hopelessness, negative emotion, emotional cascades, etc.). Currently, most of the support for these theories is correlational or longitudinal. Unfortunately, the very nature of these behaviors makes it difficult to test them experimentally due to both practical and ethical considerations. For example, how does one specifically test whether hopelessness causes suicide attempts? Even if this could be done, it would be unethical to attempt to elicit suicide attempts.

However, ways exist to test these behaviors through proxies (e.g., assessing pain tolerance as a proxy for NSSI), and future work on the theories should attempt to obtain experimental evidence using practical and ethical proxies for suicide and NSSI.

A second major challenge facing theories of suicide and NSSI is to increase the specificity and sensitivity of these theories. Currently, most of the theories of suicide and NSSI propose mechanisms that are relevant to a large number of people (i.e. feelings of hopelessness or difficulty regulating negative emotion), yet the majority of individuals experiencing these problems do not attempt suicide, die by suicide, or engage in NSSI. If a theory of suicide cannot distinguish between someone who is depressed but not at risk for a suicide attempt from another individual who is depressed and at high risk, then it lacks practical utility. Future studies should attempt to identify specific mechanisms and risk factors that, when combined with current theories, generate more accurate predictions about who is at the highest risk for suicide and NSSI.

Acknowledgments

Support for this chapter was provided, in part, by National Institute of Mental Health grant F31MH081396 to Edward A. Selby, under the sponsorship of Thomas E. Joiner, Jr. The content is solely the responsibility of the authors and does not necessarily represent the official views of the National Institute of Mental Health or the National Institutes of Health.

References

Abramowitz, J. S., Tolin, D. F., & Street, G. P. (2001). Paradoxical effects of thought suppression: A meta-analysis of controlled studies. *Clinical Psychology Review, 21*, 683–703.

Allen, C. (1995). Helping with deliberate self-harm: Some practical guidelines. *Journal of Mental Health, 4*, 243–250.

American Psychiatric Association. (1994). *Diagnostic and statistical manual of mental disorders* (4th ed.). Washington, DC: American Psychiatric Association.

Apter, A., Van Praag, H. M., Plutchik, R., Sevy, S., Korn, M., & Brown, S.L. (1990). Interrelationships among anxiety, aggression, impulsivity, and mood: A serotonergically linked cluster? *Psychiatry Research, 32*, 191–199.

Armey, M. F., & Crowther, J. H. (2008). A comparison of linear versus non-linear models of aversive self-awareness, dissociation, and non-suicidal self-injury among young adults. *Journal of Consulting and Clinical Psychology, 76*, 9–14.

Baechler, J. (1980). A strategic theory. *Suicide and Life-Threatening Behavior, 10*, 70–99.

Baumeister, R. F. (1990). Suicide as escape from self. *Psychological Review, 97*, 90–113.

Beck, A. T. (1996). Beyond belief: A theory of modes, personality, and psychopathology. In P. M. Salkovskis (Ed.), *Frontiers of cognitive therapy* (pp. 1–25). New York, NY: Guilford Press.

Beck, A. T., Brown, G., Berchick, R. J., & Stewart, B. L. (1990). Relationship between hopelessness and ultimate suicide: A replication with psychiatric outpatients. *American Journal of Psychiatry, 147*, 190–195.

Beck, A. T., & Steer, R. A. (1991). *Manual for Beck Scale for Suicide Ideation.* San Antonio, TX: Psychological Corporation.

Beck, A. T., & Steer, R. A. (1993). *Beck Scale for Suicide Ideation.* San Antonio, TX: Psychological Corporation.

Beck, A.T., Steer, R., Kovacs, M., & Garrison, B. (1985). Hopelessness and eventual suicide: A 10-year prospective study of patients hospitalized with suicidal ideation. *American Journal of Psychiatry, 142*, 559–563.

Bennun, I. (1983). Depression and hostility in self-mutilation. *Suicide and Life-Threatening Behaviors, 13*, 71–84.

Bostwick, J. M., & Pankratz, V. S. (2000). Affective disorders and suicide risk: A reexamination. *American Journal of Psychiatry, 157*, 1925–1932.

Brevard, A., Lester, D., & Yang, B. (1990). A comparison of suicide notes written by suicide completers and suicide attempters. *Crisis, 11*, 7–11.

Briere, J., & Gil, E. (1998). Self-mutilation in clinical and general population samples: Prevalence, correlates, and functions. *American Journal of Orthopsychiatry, 68*, 609–620.

Brown, G. K., Beck, A. T., Steer, R. A., & Grisham, J. R. (2000). Risk factors for suicide in psychiatric outpatients: A 20-year prospective study. *Journal of Consulting and Clinical Psychology, 68*, 371–377.

Brown, M. Z., Comtois, K. A., & Linehan, M. M. (2002). Reasons for suicide attempts and nonsuicidal self-injury in women with borderline personality disorder. *Journal of Abnormal Psychology, 111*, 198–202.

Brown, R. M., Dahlen, E., Mills, C., Rick, J., & Biblarz, A. (1999). Evaluation of an evolutionary model of self-preservation and self-destruction. *Suicide and Life-Threatening Behavior, 29*, 58–71.

Carroll, J., Schaffer, C., Spensley, J., & Abramowitz, S. I. (1980). Family experiences of self-mutilating patients. *American Journal of Psychiatry, 137*, 852–853.

Caspi, A., Sugden, K., Moffitt, T. E., Taylor, A., Craig, I. W., Harrington, H.,…Poulton, R. (2003). Influence of life stress on depression: Moderation by a polymorphism in the 5-HTT gene. *Science, 301*, 386–389.

Chapman, A. L., Gratz, K. L., & Brown, M. Z. (2006). Solving the puzzle of deliberate self-harm: The experiential avoidance model. *Behaviour Research and Therapy, 44*, 371–394.

Cheavens, J., Rosenthal, M. Z., Nowak, J. A., Daughters, S. B., Kosson, D. S., Lynch, T. R., & Lejuez, C. W. (2005). Testing the role of emotional avoidance in the development of borderline personality disorder. *Behaviour Research and Therapy, 43*, 257–268.

Chowanec, G. D., Josephson, A. M., Coleman, C., & Davis, H. (1991). Self-harming behavior in incarcerated male delinquent adolescents. *Journal of the American Academy of Child and Adolescent Psychiatry, 30*, 202–207.

Conner, K., Britton, P., Sworts, L., & Joiner, T. E. (2007). Suicide attempts among individuals with opiate dependence: The critical role of felt belonging. *Addictive Behaviors, 32*, 1395–1404.

Daldin, H. J. (1988). Psychological factors differentiating self-mutilating behavior in adolescence. *Journal of Child Psychotherapy, 14*, 61–66.

Dean, P. J., & Range, L. M. (1999). Testing the escape theory of suicide in an outpatient clinical population. *Cognitive Therapy and Research, 23*, 561–572.

deCatanzaro, D. (1995). Reproductive status, family interactions, and suicidal ideation: Surveys of the general public and high-risk groups. *Ethology and Sociobiology, 16*, 385–394.

Durkheim, E. (1897). *Le Suicide: Etude de socologie.* Paris, France: F. Alcan.

Erber, R., & Wegner, D. M. (1996). Ruminations on the rebound. In R. S. Wyer, Jr. (Ed.), *Ruminative thoughts. Advances in social cognition* (pp. 73–79). Mahwah, NJ: Erlbaum.

Erskine, J. A. K., Kvavilashvili, L., & Kornbrot, D. E. (2007). The predictors of thought suppression in young and old adults: Effects of rumination, anxiety, and other variables. *Personality and Individual Differences, 42*, 1047–1057.

Favazza, A. R., & Conterio, K. (1988). The plight of chronic self-mutilators. *Community Mental Health Journal, 24*, 22–30.

Favazza, A. R., & Conterio, K. (1989). Female habitual self-mutilators. *Acta Psychiatrica Scandinavica, 79*, 283–289.

Firestone, R. W., & Seiden, R. H. (1990). Suicide and the continuum of self-destructive behavior. *Journal of American College Health, 38*, 207–213.

Friedman, M., Glasser, M., Laufer, E., Laufer, M., & Wohl, M. (1972). Attempted suicide and self-mutilation in adolescence: Some observations from a psychoanalytic research project. *British Journal of Psychoanalysis, 53*, 179–183.

Gibb, B. E., McGeary, J. E., Beevers, C. G., & Miller, I. W. (2006). Serotonin transporter (5-HTTLPR) genotype, childhood abuse, and suicide attempts in adult psychiatric inpatients. *Suicide and Life-Threatening Behavior, 35*, 687–693.

Gordon, K. H., Selby, E. A., Anestis, M. D., Bender, T. W., Witte, T. K., Braithwaite, S.,...& Joiner Jr, T. E. (2010). The reinforcing properties of repeated deliberate self-harm. *Archives of Suicide Research, 14*, 329–341.

Gross, J. J., & Levenson, R. W. (1997). Hiding feelings: The acute effects of inhibiting positive and negative emotions. *Journal of Abnormal Psychology, 106*, 95–103.

Gunderson, J. G. (1984). *Borderline personality disorder.* Washington, DC: American Psychiatric Press.

Hawkes, C. H. (1992). Endorphins: The basis of pleasure? *Journal of Neurology, Neurosurgery, and Psychiatry, 55*, 247–250.

Hayes, S. C., Wilson, K. G., Gifford, E. V., Follette, V. M., & Strosahl, K. (1996). Experiential avoidance and behavioral disorders: A functional dimensional approach to diagnosis and treatment. *Journal of Consulting and Clinical Psychology, 64*, 1152–1168.

Hendin, H. (1991). Psychodynamics of suicide, with particular reference to the young. *American Journal of Psychiatry, 148*, 1150–1158.

Herpertz, S. (1995). Self-injurious behavior: Psychopathological and nosological characteristics in subtypes of self-injurers. *Acta Psychiatrica Scandinavica, 91*, 57–68.

Hilt, L. M., Cha, C. B., & Nolen-Hoeksema, S. (2008). Nonsuicidal self-injury in young adolescent girls: Moderators of the distress-function relationship. *Journal of Consulting and Clinical Psychology, 76*, 63–71.

Himber, J. (1994). Blood rituals: Self-cutting in female psychiatric inpatients. *Psychotherapy, 31*, 620–631.

Hunter, E., & O'Connor, R. C. (2003). Hopelessness and future thinking in parasuicide: The role of perfectionism. *British Journal of Clinical Psychology, 42*, 355–365.

Huth-Bocks, A. C., Kerr, D. C. R., Ivey, A. Z., Kramer, A. C., & King, C. A. (2007). Assessment of psychiatrically hospitalized suicidal adolescents: Self-report instruments as predictors of suicidal thoughts and behaviors. *Journal of the American Academy of Child and Adolescent Psychiatry, 46,* 387–395.

Joiner, T. E. (2005). *Why people die by suicide.* Cambridge, MA: Harvard University Press.

Joiner, T. E., Hollar, D., & Van Orden, K. A. (2006). On Buckeyes, Gators, Super Bowl Sunday, and the Miracle on Ice: "Pulling together" is associated with lower suicide rates. *Journal of Social and Clinical Psychology, 25*, 179–195.

Joiner, T. E., Johnson, F., & Soderstrom, K. (2002). Association between serotonin transporter gene polymorphism and family history of attempted and completed suicide. *Suicide and Life-Threatening Behavior, 32*, 329–332.

Joiner, T. E., Pettit, J. W., Walker, R. L., Voelz, Z. R., Cruz, J., Rudd, M. D., & Lester, D. (2002). Perceived burdensomeness and suicidality: Two studies on the suicide notes of those attempting and those completing suicide. *Journal of Social and Clinical Psychology, 21*, 531–545.

Joiner, T. E., Van Orden, K. A., Witte, T. K., Selby, E. A., Ribeiro, J. D., Lewis, R., & Rudd, M. D. (2009). Main predictions of the interpersonal-psychological theory of suicidal behavior: Empirical tests in two samples of young adults. *Journal of Abnormal Psychology, 118*, 634–646.

King, B. H., Au, D., & Poland, R. E. (1995). Pretreatment with MK-801 inhibits pemoline-induced self-biting behavior in prepubertal rats. *Developmental Neuroscience, 17*, 47–52.

Klonsky, E. D. (2007). The functions of deliberate self-injury: A review of the evidence. *Clinical Psychology Review, 27*, 226–239.

Klonsky, E. D., Oltmanns, T. F., & Turkheimer, E. (2003). Deliberate self-harm in a nonclinical population: Prevalence and psychological correlates. *American Journal of Psychiatry, 160*, 1501–1508.

Kochanek, K. D., & Hudson, B. L. (1995). *Advance report of final mortality statistics, 1992. Monthly vital statistics report* (Vol. *43*, No. 6, Suppl.). Hyattsville, MD: National Center for Health Statistics.

Koons, C. R., Robins, C. J., Tweed, J. L., Lynch, C. R., Gonzalez, A. M., Morse, J. Q.,...Bastian, L. A. (2001). Efficacy of dialectical behavior therapy in women veterans with borderline personality disorder. *Behavior Therapy, 32*, 371–390.

Kuo, W., Gallo, J. J., & Eaton, W. W. (2004). Hopelessness, depression, substance disorder, and suicidality. *Social Psychiatry and Psychiatric Epidemiology, 39*, 497–501.

Laye-Gindhu, A., & Schonert-Reichl, K. A. (2005). Nonsuicidal self-harm among community adolescents: Understanding the "whats" and "whys" of self-harm. *Journal of Youth and Adolescence, 34*, 447–457.

Linehan, M. M. (1993). *Cognitive-behavioral treatment of borderline personality disorder.* New York, NY: Guilford Press.

Linehan, M. M., Armstrong, H. E., Suarez, A., Allmon, D., & Heard, H. L. (1991). Cognitive-behavioral treatment of chronically parasuicidal borderline patients. *Archives of General Psychiatry, 48*, 1060–1064.

Linehan, M. M., Comtois, K. A., Murray, A. M., Brown, M. Z., Gallop, R. J., Heard, H. L.,...Lindenboim, N. (2006). Two-year randomized controlled trial and follow-up of dialectical behavior therapy vs therapy by experts for suicidal behaviors and borderline personality disorder. *Archives of General Psychiatry, 63*, 757–766.

Linehan, M. M., Dimeff, L.A., Reynolds, S.K., Comtois, K., Shaw-Welch, S., Heagerty, P., & Kivlahan, D. R. (2002). Dialectical behavior therapy versus comprehensive validation plus 12-step for the treatment of opioid dependent women meeting criteria for borderline personality disorder. *Drug and Alcohol Dependence, 67*, 13–26.

Linehan, M. M., Schmidt, H., III, Dimeff, L. A, Craft, J. C., Kanter, J., & Comtois, K. A. (1999). Dialectical behavior therapy for patients with borderline personality disorder and drug-dependence. *American Journal on Addictions, 8*, 279–292.

Lloyd-Richardson, E. E., Perrine, N., Dierker, L., & Kelley, M. (2007). Characteristics and functions of non-suicidal self-injury in a community sample of adolescents. *Psychological Medicine, 37*, 1183–1192.

Mann, J. J. (2003). Neurobiology of suicidal behaviour. *Nature Reviews Neuroscience, 4*, 819–828.

Mann, J. J., Waternaux, C., Haas, G. L., & Malone, K. M. (1999). Toward a clinical model of suicidal behavior in psychiatric patients. *American Journal of Psychiatry, 156*, 181–189.

Martin, L. L., & Tesser, A. (1996). Some ruminative thoughts. In R. S. Wyer, Jr. (Ed.), *Ruminative thoughts. Advances in social cognition* (pp. 73–79). Mahwah, NJ: Erlbaum.

Menninger, K. A. (1938). *Man against himself*. New York, NY: Harcourt, Brace.

Moberly, N. J., & Watkins, E. R. (2008). Ruminative self-focus and negative affect: An experience sampling study. *Journal of Abnormal Psychology, 117*, 314–323.

Muehlmann, A. M., & Devine, D. P. (2008). Glutamate-mediated neuroplasticity in an animal model of self-injurious behavior. *Behavioural Brain Research, 189*, 32–40.

Najmi, S., Wegner, D. M., & Nock, M. K. (2007). Thought suppression and self-injurious thoughts and behaviors. *Behaviour Research and Therapy, 45*, 1957–1965.

Nixon, M. K., Cloutier, P. F., & Aggarwal, S. (2002). Affect regulation and addictive aspects of repetitive self-injury in hospitalized adolescents. *Journal of the American Academy of Child and Adolescent Psychiatry, 41*, 1333–1341.

Nock, M. K., Joiner, T. E., Gordon, K. H., Lloyd-Richardson, E., & Prinstein, M. J. (2006). Non-suicidal self-injury among adolescents: Diagnostic correlates and relation to suicide attempts. *Psychiatry Research, 144*, 65–72.

Nock, M. K., & Kazdin, A. E. (2002). Examination of affective, cognitive, and behavioral factors and suicide-related outcomes in children and young adolescents. *Journal of Clinical Child and Adolescent Psychology, 31*, 48–58.

Nock, M. K., & Prinstein, M. J. (2004). A functional approach to the assessment of self-mutilation. *Journal of Consulting and Clinical Psychology, 72*, 885–890.

Nock, M. K., & Prinstein, M. J. (2005). Contextual features and behavioral functions of self-mutilation among adolescents. *Journal of Abnormal Psychology, 114*, 140–146.

Nolen-Hoeksema, S. (1991). Responses to depression and their effects on the duration of depressive episodes. *Journal of Abnormal Psychology, 100*, 555–561.

O'Connor, R. C., & O'Connor, D. B. (2003). Predicting hopelessness and psychological distress: The role of perfectionism and coping. *Journal of Counseling Psychology, 50*, 362–372.

Osuch, E. A., Noll, J. G., & Putnam, F. W. (1999). The motivations for self-injury in psychiatric patients. *Psychiatry, 62*, 334–346.

Oquendo, M. A., & Mann, J. J. (2000). The biology of impulsivity and suicidality. *Psychiatric Clinics of North America, 23*, 11–25.

Penn, J. V., Esposito, C. L., Schaeffer, L. E., Fritz, G. K., & Spirito, A. (2003). Suicide attempts and self-mutilative behavior in a juvenile correctional facility. *Journal of the American Academy of Child and Adolescent Psychiatry, 42*, 762–769.

Podovall, E. M. (1969). Self-mutilation within a hospital setting: A study of identity and social compliance. *British Journal of Medical Psychology, 42*, 213–221.

Purdon, C. (1999). Thought suppression and psychopathology. *Behaviour Research and Therapy, 37*, 1029–1054.

Richardson, J. S., & Zaleski, W. A. (1986). Endogenous opiates and self-mutilation. *American Journal of Psychiatry, 140*, 867–872.

Rosenthal, M. Z., Cheavens, J. S., Lejuez, C. W., & Lynch, T. R. (2005). Thought suppression mediates the relationship between negative affect and borderline personality disorder symptoms. *Behaviour Research and Therapy, 43*, 1173–1185.

Ross, S., & Heath, N. (2002). A study of the frequency of self-mutilation in a community sample of adolescents. *Journal of Youth and Adolescence, 31*(1), 67–77.

Ross, S., & Heath, N. L. (2003). Two models of adolescent self-mutilation. *Suicide and Life-Threatening Behavior, 33*, 277–287.

Rudd, M. D., Berman, A. L., Joiner, T. E., Nock, M. K., Silverman, M. M., Mandrusiak, M.,…Witte, T. (2006). Warning signs for suicide: Theory, research, and clinical applications. *Suicide and Life-Threatening Behavior, 36*, 255–262.

Rudd, M. D., Joiner, T. E., & Rajab, M. H. (2001). Treating suicidal behavior: An effective, time-limited approach. In *Treatment manuals for practitioners* (pp. 15–42). New York, NY: Guilford Press.

Russ, M. J., Roth, S. D., Kakuma, T., Harrison, K., & Hull, J. W. (1994). Pain perception in self-injurious borderline patients: Naloxone effects. *Biological Psychiatry, 35*, 207–209.

Selby, E. A., Anestis, M. D., Bender, T. W., & Joiner, T. E. (2009). An exploration of the Emotional Cascade Model in borderline personality disorder. *Journal of Abnormal Psychology, 118*, 375–387.

Selby, E. A., Anestis, M. D., & Joiner, T. E. (2007). Daydreaming about death: Violent daydreaming as a form of emotion dysregulation in suicidality. *Behavior Modification, 31*, 867–879.

Selby, E. A., Anestis, M. D., & Joiner, T. E. (2008). Understanding the relationship between emotional and behavioral dysregulation: Emotional cascades. *Behaviour Research and Therapy, 46*, 593–611.

Selby, E. A., Bender, T. W., Gordon, K. H., Nock, M. K., & Joiner, T. E. (2012). Non-suicidal self-injury (NSSI) disorder: A preliminary study. *Personality Disorders: Theory, Research, and Treatment, 3*, 167–17.

Selby, E. A., Braithwaite, S. R., Joiner, T. E., & Fincham, F. D. (2008). Features of borderline personality disorder, perceived childhood emotional invalidation, and dysfunction within current romantic relationships. *Journal of Family Psychology, 22*, 885–893.

Selby, E. A., Connell, L. D., & Joiner, T. E. (2010). The pernicious blend of rumination and fearlessness in non-suicidal self-injury. *Cognitive Therapy and Research, 34*, 421–428.

Selby, E. A., Franklin, J., Carson-Wong, A., & Rizvi, S. L. (2013). Emotional Cascades and Self-Injury: Investigating Instability of Rumination and Negative Emotion. *Journal of Clinical Psychology, 69*, 1213–1227.

Selby, E. A., & Joiner, T. E. (2009). Cascades of emotion: The emergence of borderline personality disorder from emotional and behavioral dysregulation. *Review of General Psychology*, *13*, 219–229.

Selby, E. A., & Joiner, T. E. (2013). Emotional cascades as prospective predictors of dysregulated behaviors in borderline personality disorder. *Personality Disorders: Theory, Research, and Treatment*, *4*, 168–174.

Shearer, S. L. (1994). Phenomenology of self-injury among inpatient women with borderline personality disorder. *Journal of Nervous and Mental Disease*, *182*, 524–526.

Shneidman, E. S. (1985). *Definition of suicide*. New York, NY: Wiley-Blackwell.

Shneidman, E. S. (1996). *The suicidal mind*. Oxford, UK: Oxford University Press.

Shneidman, E. S. (1998). Further reflections on suicide and psychache. *Suicide and Life-Threatening Behavior*, *28*, 245–250.

Simpson, M. A. (1975). The phenomenology of self-mutilation in a general hospital setting. *Canadian Psychiatric Association Journal*, *20*, 429–434.

Sivam, S. P. (1995). GBR-12909-induced self-injurious behavior: Role of dopamine. *Brain Research*, *690*, 259–263.

Soloff, P. H., Lis, J. A., Kelly, T., Cornelius, J., & Ulrich, R. (1994). Self-mutilation and suicidal behavior in borderline personality disorder. *Journal of Personality Disorders*, *8*, 257–267.

Solomon, R. L., & Corbit, J. D. (1974). An opponent-process theory of motivation. *Psychological Review*, *81*, 119–145.

Suyemoto, K. L. (1998). The functions of self-mutilation. *Clinical Psychology Review*, *18*, 531–554.

Tassava, S. H., & Ruderman, A. J. (1999). Application of escape theory to binge eating and suicidality in college women. *Journal of Social and Clinical Psychology*, *18*, 450–466.

Van Orden, K. A., Joiner, T. E., Hollar, D., Rudd, M. D., Mandrusiak, M., & Silverman, M. M. (2006). A test of the effectiveness of a list of suicide warning signs for the public. *Suicide and Life-Threatening Behavior*, *36*, 272–287.

Van Orden, K. A., Witte, T. K., Gordon, K. H., Bender, T. W., & Joiner, T. E. (2008). Suicidal desire and the capability for suicide: Tests of the interpersonal-psychological theory of suicidal behavior among adults. *Journal of Consulting and Clinical Psychology*, *76*, 72–83.

Vernheul, R., van den Bosch, L. M. C., Koeter, M. W. J., de Ridder, M. A. J., Stijnen, T., & van den Brink, W. (2003). Dialectical behaviour therapy for women with borderline personality disorder: 12-month, randomised clinical trial in The Netherlands. *British Journal of Psychiatry*, *182*, 135–140.

Volkow, N. D., Fowler, J. S., Wang, G., Swanson, J. M., & Telang, F. (2007). Dopamine in drug abuse and addiction. *Archives of Neurology*, *64*, 1575–1579.

Wegner, D. M., Schneider, D. J., Carter, S. R., & White, T. L. (1987). Paradoxical effects of thought suppression. *Journal of Personality and Social Psychology*, *53*, 5–13.

Wenzlaff, R. M., & Wegner, D. M. (2000). Thought suppression. *Annual Review of Psychology*, *51*, 59–91.

Whitlock, J. L., Powers, J. L., & Eckenrode, J. (2006). The virtual cutting edge: The internet and adolescent self-injury. *Developmental Psychology*, *42*, 407–417.

Willer, J. D., Dehen, H., & Cambier, J. (1981). Stress induced analgesia in humans. *Science*, *212*, 680–691.

Witte, T. K., Merrill, K. A., Stellrect, N. E., Bernert, R. A., Hollar, D. L., Schatschneider, C., & Joiner, T. E., Jr. (2008). "Impulsive" youth suicide attempters are not necessarily all that impulsive. *Journal of Affective Disorders*, *107*, 107–116.

Woods, J. (1988). Layers of meaning in self-cutting. *Journal of Child Psychotherapy*, *14*, 51–60.

Young, M. A., Fogg, L. F., Scheftner, W., Fawcett, J., Akiskal, H., & Maser, J. (1996). Stable trait components of hopelessness: Baseline and sensitivity to depression. *Journal of Abnormal Psychology*, *105*, 155–165.

Comprehensive Theoretical Models of Nonsuicidal Self-Injury

Colleen M. Jacobson *and* Kristen Batejan

Abstract

During the past several years, interest in nonsuicidal self-injury (NSSI) has grown considerably, thus sparking increased theorizing and research into the etiological roots of this perplexing yet relatively common behavior. The current chapter provides an overview of the main theoretical explanations for NSSI, with a more detailed description of those with an adequate amount of empirical support. While the majority of the theories (e.g., psychodynamic, interpersonal, affect regulation, cognitive, biological) have received at least some empirical support, the affect regulation and interpersonally based theories seem to have the largest amount of empirical grounding. Specifically, research indicates that the majority of people who self-injure do so to relieve unwanted negative feelings, while a large minority also engages in NSSI in order to elicit an interpersonal response. Highlighting the need for a comprehensive model of NSSI, this chapter concludes with the presentation of an integrated theory of the etiology of NSSI, which incorporates various distal and proximal risk factors.

Key Words: nonsuicidal self-injury, etiology, development, affect regulation, social reinforcement, function

Engagement in nonsuicidal self-injury (NSSI) has become a significant public health problem as lifetime rates among adolescents and young adults reach over 20%. Specifically, data from self-report surveys indicate a lifetime prevalence rate of up to 23% for high school students and recent college-based surveys identify lifetime rates of NSSI ranging from 17% to 38% with 12-month prevalence rates falling around 7% (Gratz, Conrad, & Roemer, 2002; Whitlock, Eckenrode, & Silverman, 2006). Further, evidence suggests that the rates of self-cutting are increasing in recent years. For example, incidence of self-cutting presenting to the hospital increased by 300% from 1990 to 2000 (Olfson, Gameroff, Marcus, Greenberg, & Shaffer, 2005). Due to the relatively high prevalence of self-injurious behaviors, NSSI has received a notable amount of attention from clinicians, theorists, and researchers over the past several years.

A sizeable portion of this attention has focused on gaining insight into why people engage in such a perplexing behavior as self-injury. What experiences, predispositions, and psychological states lead people to purposefully hurt themselves? Initially, one may be inclined to turn to theories of suicide and suicidal behaviors for answers to this puzzling question. However, although similar in that both behaviors involve purposeful physical harm to oneself and that there is a large degree of overlap between those who engage in suicidal behaviors and those who engage in NSSI, NSSI and suicidal behaviors differ in important ways (see Chapter 15 for a review of theoretical models of suicide). Most notably, acts of suicidal behavior are primarily motivated by a desire to die while, by definition, acts of NSSI are motivated by goals other than death. Thus, an independent area of research focusing specifically on the etiology of NSSI has developed. Several theories ranging from psychodynamic explanations to behavioral explanations to biological explanations of NSSI exist. Although many of the theories have at least a small amount of empirical support, the affect regulation and interpersonal models of NSSI have received the most attention and, thus, the most empirical support. The current chapter will provide an overview of the main theoretical explanations for NSSI, with a more detailed description of those with greater amounts of empirical support.

The majority of NSSI theories presently in the literature are limited in that they address a single aspect of a phenomenon that is likely multidetermined. Although comprehensive theories are lacking, nearly all researchers and clinicians in the field of NSSI would likely agree that the etiology of NSSI is varied and complex, as with most psychiatric disorders and maladaptive behaviors. Thus, an adequate theory will account for both distal and proximal biological, psychological, and social factors leading to NSSI and explain the translational relationships among each component. After reviewing each independent theory, this chapter will conclude with the presentation of an integrated etiological model of NSSI.

Psychodynamic Models of Nonsuicidal Self-Injury

The earliest etiological theories of self-injury are grounded in psychoanalytic and psychodynamic philosophy and include themes of conflict between the life and death drives, aggression, and sexual impulses. Menninger published one of the original pieces to address self-injury in 1938. Menninger, as well as others, noted the difference between acts of self-injury and suicidal acts, commenting that acts of self-injury are not intended to end in death (Firestone & Seiden, 1990; Himber, 1994; Menninger, 1938). Rather, people engage in self-injury as a compromise between competing life and death drives, such that engagement in self-injury stops them from complete destruction or suicide. Although an intriguing idea, there is little empirical research to support this theory.

The sexual impulse theory of self-injury suggests that people engage in self-injury for a combination of sexually related motives: to gain control over one's sexual impulses, to destroy or purify one's body due to unwanted or dirty sexual impulses, and as a negative reaction to menarche (Daldin, 1988; Doctors, 1981; Rosenthal, Rinzler, Wallsh, & Klausner, 1972; Simpson, 1975). Although there is little direct empirical evidence to support the sexual

impulse theory of NSSI, Suyemoto (1998) cites indirect supporting evidence. She suggests that the fact that engagement in NSSI rarely occurs prior to puberty, the high rates of sexual abuse among people who engage in NSSI and the high rates of sexual dysfunction among self-injurers point to a connection between self-injury and sexuality.

The final psychodynamic theory of self-injury suggests that people engage in self-injury as a means of carrying out aggressive impulses toward oneself (Bennum, 1984; Erlich, 1978). Theorists purport that people engage in self-injury in order to atone for unacceptable desires, behaviors, feelings, and thoughts (Lane, 2002). The self-aggression theory has received some empirical support. For example, findings from two independent studies of adolescents who engage in self-injury found that a large minority reported doing so to punish themselves (Nock & Prinstein, 2004; Ross & Heath, 2003). Further, another study involving adolescents found that over 50% reported engaging in self-injury because of negative feelings toward themselves (Laye-Gindhu & Schonert-Reichl, 2005). Conversely, research among adults who self-injure tends to indicate that only a small minority do so as a means of self-punishment (Briere & Gil, 1998; Osuch, Noll, & Putnam, 1999).

Interpersonal Models of Nonsuicidal Self-Injury

Once seen as a manipulative behavior or as a means of influencing others (Favazza, 1989; Klonsky, 2007; Ross & McKay, 1979), more recent research has shown that there are other interpersonal functions to NSSI such as a way to cry for help, avoid abandonment, be taken seriously, affect people's behavior, elicit attention, and elicit reinforcing responses (Klonsky, 2007). Favazza (1989) believes that instead of NSSI being a manipulative behavior, it may serve as a genuine cry for help. This behavior begins a cycle in which an individual feels badly, which leads to engagement in NSSI, which leads to increased attention from others. The attention provides some soothing, which in turn causes the individual to use NSSI to enact others to help soothe his or her pain again.

Boundaries Model

Although originally a concept from psychodynamic literature, the boundaries model can be included in the interpersonal framework, as the basis of this theory consists of the relationship between the self and the other. The boundaries model states that the individual using NSSI does so in an effort to create a distinction between the self and the other (Suyemoto, 1998; Suyemoto & MacDonald, 1995). The act of NSSI (e.g., cutting or burning the skin) may help differentiate the self from the world. Theorists suggest that an individual who uses self-injury to create boundaries from others has trouble establishing a sense of himself or herself as an individual or as someone who is unique (Suyemoto, 1998; Suyemoto & MacDonald, 1995). Because there is no clear boundary between the self and someone else, a loss, actual or perceived, may be experienced as a loss of self. Therefore, an act of NSSI such as cutting, and then in turn bleeding, may help the individual acknowledge a feeling of reality.

The boundaries model is rooted in object relations theory. People who engage in NSSI, it has been theorized, had faulty attachments to their primary caregivers, typically their mothers, and therefore cannot attain stability for their object representations; their boundaries have blurred between themselves and their parents. Although intriguing, there is no empirical support for the boundaries model of self-injury.

The need to create an identity, or boundary from someone else, can lead to the identification of the individual as a self-injurer who is solely defined by his or her symptoms or behaviors. This identification may help the individual feel unique, which causes him or her to embrace his or her identity as someone who engages in NSSI. Therefore, an identity as a "cutter" helps differentiate the self from the other (Favazza, 1998; Podovoll, 1969; Suyemoto, 1998; Suyemoto & MacDonald, 1995). It seems that individuals who embrace this identity hold a sense of pride, as it is evident that there is something different about them (Favazza, 1989); they are no longer confused about their identity.

Communications Theory

A growing body of research has examined the degree to which people engage in self-injury as a means of communication with others. In a four-function model of NSSI, Nock and Prinstein (2004, 2005) identified two interpersonal functions: social-negative reinforcement (SNR) and social-positive reinforcement (SPR) using the Functional Assessment of Self-Mutilation (FASM; Lloyd, Kelley, & Hope, 1997). SNR is when an individual uses NSSI to avoid or escape from an interpersonal demand, whereas SPR refers to when NSSI assists the person in gaining attention from others or access to materials (Nock & Prinstein, 2004, 2005). Adolescent psychiatric inpatients tended to report more reasons based on automatic-negative reinforcement and automatic-positive reinforcement (both reviewed later) than social-negative reinforcement and social-positive reinforcement (Nock & Prinstein, 2004). Only 15.3% of the adolescents reported "to get a reaction from someone" as a reason to self-injure. Interestingly, younger age and ethnic minority status were significantly associated with SNR and SPR (Nock & Prinstein, 2005). Also, social-perfectionism was found to be related to SNR and SPR; the authors hypothesized that possible reasons may include attempting to get assistance or remove perceived expectations from others. Nixon and colleagues (2002) studied hospitalized adolescents and found that 11% of girls endorsed the reason "get care or attention from others" for NSSI, while no boys endorsed this reason.

Socially related reinforcers for NSSI appear to be more common among community samples of adolescents than inpatient groups of self-injurers. In a community sample of adolescents, Lloyd-Richardson and colleagues (2007) found that self-injurers endorsed both social-reinforcement items (19%–31%) as frequently as intrapersonal automatic-reinforcement items (22%–28%). One of the most commonly endorsed reasons for NSSI was "to try to get a reaction from someone, even if it's negative." In another community adolescent sample, interpersonal reasons for NSSI were not endorsed as frequently as affect regulation reasons; however, a large minority of participants indicated that they self-injured for socially related reasons: 41% said they wanted to be noticed, 39% said they were angry at someone, and 30% said they wanted others to see how desperate they were (Laye-Gindhu & Schonert-Reichl, 2005). Klonsky and Olino (2008) worked with a college population and determined that individuals who endorsed the most socially reinforcing functions also were found to use more NSSI methods, had an earlier onset of NSSI, and displayed more anxiety.

In a sample of adult self-injurers, most of whom experienced childhood sexual abuse, interpersonal reasons for NSSI were commonly endorsed and included "get attention or ask for help" (40% endorsed), "feel closer to someone" (10% endorsed), and "get therapist's attention" (16% endorsed) (Briere & Gil, 1998). Also of interest, 56% of this sample expressed anger at others before the act of NSSI while only 2% felt anger at others after the act. Finally, Himber (1994) interviewed a small sample of female psychiatric inpatients and found the most common interpersonal reasons for engaging in NSSI were a cry for help or communicating how much pain one was in. It seems that these individuals had trouble asking for help, so instead they showed (by cutting) that they needed help. These women also experienced shame resulting from the self-injury, especially from the reaction of others. Thus, while a reason to self-injure may be to reach out for help to someone, it also can produce feelings of guilt and shame.

Social Learning Theory/Social Modeling and Contagion Effect

Social learning theory can help explain why individuals begin using self-injury (Suyemoto, 1998). One explanation is that children may learn at a young age that injuries are associated with increased care and later they may attempt to self-care through self-injury. Also, adolescents may witness others getting attention or help from NSSI and mimic the behavior to experience the same benefits (Suyemoto, 1998). In an early study of self-injury, results indicated that one of the reasons adolescent patients were engaging in NSSI was social status among peers (Offer & Barglow, 1960). If an adolescent takes on the role as a "cutter" and other adolescents view this person as someone to look up to, this may evoke strong feelings and copy-cat cases (Favazza, 1989). Self-injury also can become a competitive behavior among peers where they compare severity of injuries and number of wounds (Simpson, 1980). This type of behavior can lead to contagions.

Nonsuicidal self-injury among adolescents appears to be a behavior strongly affected by peer influence (Prinstein, Guerry, Browne, & Rancourt, 2009; Walsh & Rosen, 1985). In an inpatient adolescent sample, 11.9% said they had learned of NSSI from seeing others engage in it (Nixon, Cloutier, & Aggarwal, 2002). Further, adolescents may be copying others because it creates a bond with that person. They may then be able to communicate their feelings to each other because of their shared experiences (Rosen & Walsh, 1989). In an inpatient sample of adolescents, Walsh and Rosen (1985) found that adolescents were triggering the behavior among others in the program, as new cases of self-injury emerged in patients who had never previously hurt themselves. Further, in an adolescent inpatient setting, 82.1% of the adolescents who had self-injured reported that they had a friend who engaged in the behavior as well (Nock & Prinstein, 2005).

Interestingly, it seems that boys may be more susceptible than girls to engage in NSSI in order to feel part of a group. In an adolescent community sample, 15% of boys endorsed the reason "it helped me join a group" while no girls endorsed this reason (Laye-Gindhu & Schonert-Reichl, 2005). This same reason (belonging to a group) also was endorsed among 16.7% of male inpatient psychiatric patients, and again, no females listed this reason (Nixon et al., 2002).

Environmental Interpersonal Correlates/Risk Factors

There have been numerous studies, both examining clinical and community samples, attempting to identify specific risk factors and correlates of nonsuicidal self-injury. The focus of this section will discuss correlates and risk factors of an interpersonal nature. In the research, it is apparent that those who self-injure have been exposed to or experienced interpersonal distress.

Primary distal interpersonal risk factors, often determined through retrospective reporting, include sexual abuse, physical abuse, and emotional maltreatment (Briere & Gil, 1998; Glassman, Weierich, Hooley, Deliberto, & Nock, 2007; Gratz, 2003, 2006; Gratz et al., 2002; Prinstein et al., 2009). In a female college sample, 53.3% of self-injurers reported some form of abuse (12% physical; 20% sexual; 44% emotional) experienced as a child (Whitlock et al., 2006). In another college sample, childhood sexual abuse was the only predictor (among many possible risk factors) of NSSI (Gratz et al., 2002; Gratz, 2003) among females; while childhood separation was the biggest predictor of NSSI among males (Gratz et al., 2002). Weierich and Nock (2008) found that NSSI was significantly associated with childhood sexual abuse, but not physical or emotional abuse. Out of the adolescents who had experienced childhood sexual abuse, 89% had self-injured. Even though it was not found to be significantly associated to NSSI, it is interesting that 59% of those who had suffered from physical and emotional abuse went on to self-injure.

Other interpersonal risk factors have been established such as childhood separation and loss (Gratz, 2003), pathological/dysfunctional family relationships (Carroll, Schaffer, Spensley, & Abramowitz, 1981; Crowell et al., 2008; Gratz, 2006), parent–child discord, and disrupted bonding (Gratz, 2006). Additionally, individuals growing up in invalidating environments where communication of emotions and feelings is ignored, punished, or trivialized may be at risk for NSSI (Gratz, 2006). There are other types of detrimental interpersonal experiences associated with adolescent NSSI, such as expressed emotion (EE) in the family (Wedig & Nock, 2007) and an insecure attachment with a parent (Gratz, 2003; Prinstein et al., 2009; Yates, 2004). High expressed emotion is an expression of critical or hostile and emotionally overinvolved remarks or attitudes. In the Wedig and Nock (2007) study, parental EE, more specifically parental criticism, was positively associated with adolescent NSSI. In the Yates, Tracy, and Luthar (2008) study, perceived parental criticism predicted NSSI in a sample of adolescent girls and boys. Further, the feeling of alienation toward one's parents decreased the likelihood that youth would rely on others during times of distress and increased the acts of NSSI. Finally, among a community sample, scores on early maladaptive schema subscales of a maladaptive schema scale related to difficulties with interpersonal relationships (Mistrust/Abuse, Emotional Deprivation, and Social Isolation/Alienation) were higher among self-injurers than a control group (Castille et al., 2007).

Theory and clinical opinion have long contended that NSSI occurs in the immediate aftermath of distressful interpersonal events. A good deal of empirical evidence is now available to support this claim, identifying loneliness, rejection, loss, or interpersonal conflict with family, peer, or romantic partner as proximal interpersonal risk factors for NSSI (Gratz, 2003; Himber, 1994; Prinstein et al., 2009; Yip, 2005). For example, among 54 patients admitted to an inpatient unit with a history of repeated self-injury, the large majority (83%) recalled frustrating external, interpersonal events occurring prior to self-injury (56% experienced rejection; 12% experienced separation) (Herpertz, 1995). Another study found that rates of NSSI increased significantly within the time period immediately preceding anticipated loss (of a residential therapist) among 32 adolescents in a residential treatment program (Rosen, Walsh, & Rode, 1990). Conversely, rates of other behaviors such as running away and aggressive acts did not increase. In general, Simpson and Porter (1981) found individuals who self-injured had inadequate interpersonal relationships. It appears they did not have a strong support system to provide them comfort or help, which then led to a strong feeling of disappointment in others. Finally, there is some evidence to suggest that engagement in NSSI may be an effective way of affecting the dynamics of an interpersonal relationship. In a longitudinal study of NSSI in adolescents, parental relationship quality was found to be significantly poorer among adolescents who engaged in NSSI than adolescents who did not engage in NSSI (Hilt, Nock, Lloyd-Richardson, & Prinstein, 2008). However, among the self-injurers parental relationship quality, specifically relationships with the father, had increased at 9-month follow-up, suggesting that fathers may be influenced by situational factors, such as a child's engagement in NSSI.

Affect Regulation Model of Nonsuicidal Self-Injury

Several theorists and researchers have proposed that NSSI is engaged in as a method of affect regulation; the affect regulation hypothesis has received the greatest amount of empirical support which is reviewed next. Specifically, prior work suggests that engagement in NSSI may act to regulate affect by either (1) removing or decreasing negative feelings or (2) initiating desired feelings in the face of an absence of feelings. In addition, several studies indicate that people who engage in NSSI experience chronically elevated negative affect and report higher levels of other characteristics that are linked to affect regulation.

Affect Regulation Theories

The affect regulation theory of NSSI fits nicely into the biosocial theory of borderline personality disorder (BPD) proposed by Marsha Linehan (1993). Linehan's theory may be quite relevant to NSSI in general, as the large majority (up to 80%) of people with BPD report engaging in self-injurious behaviors. However, it is important to note that not all self-injurers meet criteria for BPD. The biosocial theory hypothesizes that people with BPD have high emotional reactivity to stimuli and that they return to their baseline levels of emotional arousal more slowly than those who do not have BPD. Therefore, patients with BPD are often left feeling emotionally overwhelmed and many find relief in emotion regulation behaviors such as engagement in NSSI.

Although the biosocial theory of BPD was not initially developed to be specific to NSSI, Chapman, Gratz, and Brown (2005) proposed the Experiential Avoidance Model (EAM) of NSSI, which also hypothesizes that NSSI is engaged in for affect regulation reasons. The EAM is based on the assumption that NSSI is a negatively reinforced behavior engaged in to reduce unwanted negative affect or arousal. The model contends that a person engages in self-injury following a sequence of events. First, a stimulus is experienced that elicits a strong, negative emotional response, which paired with difficulties regulating emotions when aroused and poor distress tolerance (two characteristics proposed to be associated with BPD according to Linehan) leads to a desire to avoid the negative emotion. Engagement in NSSI follows to provide temporary relief from the negative feelings. The authors propose that after engaging in NSSI several times, the behavior becomes an automatic, conditioned response to emotional arousal. There is a good deal of evidence (reviewed next) to support the theory that NSSI is often engaged in to stop negative feelings, as suggested by this model. However, as is evident throughout the rest of this chapter, such an explanation is somewhat simplistic: It does not explain why some people choose NSSI to regulate negative affect, while others choose different behaviors to do so.

Nock and Prinstein (2004) conceptualized engagement in NSSI through a behavioral learning theory perspective and identified four distinct yet related mechanisms that may act to reinforce engagement in NSSI. NSSI may work to regulate emotions through two types of automatic (i.e., internal) reinforcement: (1) negative reinforcement, such that negative feeling states are decreased, and (2) positive reinforcement, such that desired feeling states (e.g., self-punishment, "real" feelings, relief) are increased. As described in the previous section, Nock and Prinstein (2004) also hypothesized that NSSI may be reinforced through social, or interpersonally mediated, reinforcement mechanisms; these will not be reviewed again here.

Empirical Support for the Affect Regulation Theory of Nonsuicidal Self-Injury

The affect regulation theory of NSSI has received a significant amount of empirical support from studies conducted by various investigators using several different methodologies. The methodologies employed are largely self-report and retrospective in nature. For example, a number of studies present participants with a list of possible reasons for engaging in NSSI and ask the participants to endorse those that apply to them. Other studies request that patients describe their feelings following an episode of NSSI. Another set of studies asks participants to indicate their feelings immediately prior to and then following engagement in NSSI with the goal of determining which feeling states are changed by the

self-injury. Excitingly, two recent studies employed a novel methodology, ecological momentary assessment, in order to assess feeling states prior to and following self-injury in real time, thus eliminating recall bias.

A relatively large body of research has addressed the etiology of NSSI by assessing the function of, or reasons for, engaging in the behavior by asking patients to indicate why they self-injure based on a given list of potential reasons. Automatic, negative reinforcement typically receives the most support, although there also are a significant number of people who report engaging in NSSI because it increases desired feelings. In Favazza and Conterio's (1989) landmark study of 240 women with a history of NSSI, 65% reported engaging in NSSI to "feel relaxed," 58% to "feel less depressed," and 55% to "feel real again." Similarly, in another early study of adults with a history of repeated self-injury, the most commonly endorsed motivation for self-injury was for tension release (78%; Herpertz, 1995). Over three-quarters of another sample (small college student survey) reported engaging in NSSI to relieve unwanted feelings (Gratz, 2000).

Results of studies that have assessed reasons for self-injury among adolescent populations are surprisingly similar to the adult studies. A large portion of adolescents who engage in NSSI report doing so in order to "release unbearable tension" (Nixon et al., 2002), "stop bad feelings" (Lloyd-Richardson, Perrine, Dierker, & Kelley, 2007; Nock & Prinstein, 2004), to regulate affect (Kumar, Pepe, & Steer, 2004), and to "reduce emotional pain" and "get frustrations out" (Ross & Heath, 2003). Further, two independent studies demonstrated that engagement in NSSI for reasons linked to emotion regulation, as opposed to other reasons such as for positive reinforcement, is associated with increased rates of overall psychopathology and suicidal behaviors (Konsky & Olino, 2008; Nock & Prinstein, 2005).

Studies examining self-reported reasons for engaging in self-injury find some evidence, although usually less than negative automatic reinforcement, for the automatic positive reinforcement function of self-injury. In several studies, a relatively large minority of subjects will report that they engage in self-injury to "feel real again," "to bring on feelings when none exist," or "to feel something even if it is pain" (Lloyd-Richardson et al., 2007; Nock & Prinstein, 2004). Further, research has found that adolescents who engage in NSSI report higher levels of dissociation than their non-self-injuring peers (Zlotnick, Shea, Pearlstein, Costello, & Begin,

1996; Zoroglu et al., 2003). Thus, those who experience dissociative or unreal states are more likely at risk for self-injury because the self-injury elicits a more desirable state.

When asked to describe their feelings immediately following an episode of NSSI, the majority of people will report experiencing some type of positive emotional mood shift such as relief (Nixon et al., 2002), although some also experience an increase in negative feelings, especially after the immediate relief has subsided. Among a sample of 42 self-injuring adolescents, 92% reported feeling relief following self-injury (Nixon et al., 2002). Additionally, in a study of 240 women with a history of NSSI, 66% reported feeling better immediately following engagement in self-injury, while only 21% said they felt worse (Favazza & Conterio, 1989). Among a sample of 64 high school students who reported engagement in NSSI, the prototypical pattern was for negative affect to increase just prior to self-injury and decrease after self-injury (Laye-Gindhu & Schonert-Reichl, 2005). In addition, positive feelings, mainly relief, increased following self-injury. Further, among 93 adults with a recent history of self-injury, feelings of anger at others, anger at self, and fear were reduced and feelings of relief and shame were increased (Briere & Gil, 1998). Overall, the large majority (77%) of participants reported a decrease in negative affect, while only 13% of participants reported an increase in negative affect.

A handful of studies suggest that although NSSI may be reinforcing in the short term, it can lead to unwanted, negative feelings in the long term. In the Favazza and Conterio (1989) study referenced earlier, the majority of people said they felt better immediately following NSSI. However, 50% reported feeling worse a few days after the self-injury. Similarly, in the study of 42 adolescents referenced earlier, feelings following self-injury were varied and ambivalent (Nixon et al., 2002). Although 92% of the sample reported feeling relief, 64.3% also reported feeling shame, 59.5% felt guilt, and 50% felt disappointment. Finally, among a community sample of adolescents reporting self-injury, in addition to feelings of relief, negative feelings, such as guilt and shame, also increased subsequent to self-injury (Laye-Gindhu et al., 2005). These findings indicate a mixture in the consequences of self-injury.

Two recent studies have employed "real-time" ecological momentary assessment to examine the precipitants and antecedents of engagement in NSSI. Although this type of real-time analysis relies on self-report, it is a significant improvement to the most commonly used methodology of retrospective questioning, which is subject to recall bias. First, Muehlenkamp and colleagues (2009) conducted a study of 30 women with a diagnosis of bulimia nervosa, many of whom had a history of engagement in NSSI. The women carried a palm pilot with them 24 hours/day over a 2-week period and recorded their feeling states prior to and immediately following engagement in NSSI. Nineteen of the 30 women engaged in NSSI during the study period. Consistent with previous research, elevated feelings of negative affect (which included a combination of several negative feelings) preceded NSSI. Interestingly, contrary to previous research, levels of positive affect increased following NSSI, while levels of negative affect remained unchanged.

Nock and colleagues (2009) conducted an EMA study of 30 adolescents and young adults who reported experiencing thoughts of NSSI within the 2 weeks prior to the study. The participants carried palm pilots for 2 weeks and were instructed to record their thoughts and feelings prior to and following any episode of NSSI. Overall there were 106 episodes, engaged in by 87% of the participants, during the 2-week trial. The most commonly reported feelings occurring prior to engagement in NSSI were feeling rejected, anger toward oneself/self-hatred, feeling numb, and anger toward others, while feelings of depression and sadness were not elevated. Participants also were asked to indicate reasons why they engaged in NSSI immediately following each episode. The most commonly endorsed reasons were related to intrapersonal negative reinforcement (65% of episodes), followed by intrapersonal positive reinforcement (25%), while a small minority of participants endorsed reasons related to interpersonal reinforcement. Thus, among this small group of adolescents and young adults, interpersonally related precipitants (rejection and anger toward others) commonly led to engagement in NSSI while intrapersonally mediated consequences tended to reinforce the behaviors (thus promoting repeated NSSI). The results of these two EMA studies, while limited in generalizability due to very small sample sizes, provide invaluable information regarding the etiology of self-injury.

Affect-Linked Correlates of Nonsuicidal Self-Injury

A relatively large body of research suggests that people who engage in NSSI experience higher levels of negative affect in general (e.g., depression, anxiety, hostility, anger, negative self-esteem) than their non-self-injuring peers (Andover, Pepper, Ryabchenko, Orrico, & Gibb, 2005; Garrison et al., 1993; Gratz & Roemer, 2004; Laye-Gindhu & Schonert-Reichl, 2005; Ross & Heath, 2003). Additionally, rates of various psychiatric disorders, such as depressive disorders, anxiety disorders, post-traumatic stress disorder, eating disorder symptomatology, substance use disorders, and BPD, marked by high negative affect are elevated among self-injurers (Andover et al., 2005; Jacobson, Muehlenkamp, Miller, & Turner, 2008; Klonsky, Oltmanns, & Turkheimer, 2003; Nock, Joiner, Gordon, Lloyd-Richardson, & Prinstein, 2006; Ross & Heath, 2002). As mentioned earlier, the biosocial theory of BPD (Linehan, 1993) theorizes that people with BPD experience their emotions more intensely than those who do not have BPD and are slower to have their emotions return to a baseline level. Engagement in NSSI is very common among people with BPD, and it is possible that the two share a common etiology. Recent empirical research does support the hypothesis that people who self-injure have higher levels of emotional reactivity than those who do not self-injure. Heightened emotional reactivity may increase the intensity of negative emotions that are felt by self-injurers to unbearable levels and engagement in NSSI may act to lessen the intensity of the emotions. Specifically, in one study of adolescents, higher levels of emotional reactivity were associated with engagement in NSSI (Nock & Mendes, 2008; Nock, Wedig, Holmberg, & Hooley, 2008) and emotional reactivity mediated the relationship between psychopathology and NSSI, such that the effect of psychopathology on engagement in NSSI was significantly weakened when emotional reactivity was controlled for. Relatedly, higher levels of self-criticism have been linked to NSSI, with self-criticism fully mediating the relationship between sexual abuse and NSSI (Glassman et al., 2007).

Constructs related to having difficulty experiencing and expressing one's emotions also may play a role in the development of self-injury. One theory suggests that people engage in self-injury as a direct consequence of an inability or unwillingness to express their feelings verbally (McLane, 1996). Empirical research supports this theory. For example, several independent studies have assessed the association between emotional inexpression (i.e., alexithymia, emotional inexpressivity, and avoidant coping) and engagement in nonsuicidal self-injury (Andover, Pepper, & Gibb, 2006; Gratz, 2006;

Zlotnick et al., 1996; Zlotnick, Woldsdorf, Johnson, & Spirito, 2003), with each study identifying a significant, independent relationship between the two. Relatedly, one study of male college students found that those who engaged in self-injury scored higher on a scale of emotional nonacceptance than those who did not (Gratz & Roemer, 2004).

Taken together, the findings related to emotion reactivity and emotional inexpressivity suggest that people who engage in NSSI may experience emotions more strongly internally and be less comfortable verbally expressing their emotions to others. Future research should address whether the combination of these two risk factors (high emotion reactivity and high inexpressivity) is particularly noxious in terms of risk for NSSI.

Cognitive Models of Nonsuicidal Self-Injury

There is a small body of evidence to suggest that some people may engage in NSSI for cognitive reasons, specifically to stop or suppress unwanted thoughts. For example, in the seminal Favazza and Conterio (1989) study, 72% of the 240 self-injuring women reported engaging in self-injury to control their minds when racing. Similarly, among a group of adolescents, higher levels of thought suppression (tendency to try to suppress unwelcome thoughts) were associated with an increased likelihood of engaging in NSSI and greater frequency of NSSI. In addition, thought suppression mediated the relationship between emotional reactivity and NSSI (Najmi, Wegner, & Nock, 2007). Finally, among a study of incarcerated women, female prisoners who engaged in NSSI reported higher levels of thought suppression than those who did not engage in NSSI (Chapman, Gratz, & Brown, 2005). Because thoughts and emotions are inextricably related, the evidence to support the cognitive role of self-injury also provides indirect support for the emotion regulation role as the unwanted thoughts likely lead to unwanted emotions (Chapman et al., 2005).

Biologically Based Models of Nonsuicidal Self-Injury

The majority of research that has addressed the biology/pathophysiology of self-injury has been conducted among women with BPD, and in the majority of cases, suicidal and nonsuicidal self-injury are not differentiated. Despite these shortcomings, research suggests several biologically mediated pathways to engagement in NSSI. This section will review some of the main findings regarding the biological underpinnings of NSSI; please see Sher and Stanley (2008) as well as Chapters 11 and 13 for more comprehensive reviews.

There is growing evidence that there is some genetic predisposition for engaging in NSSI. NSSI is a common symptom of a genetic disorder, that is, Lesch-Nylan syndrome (Pellicer, Buendia-Roldan, & Pallares-Trujillo, 1998), and animals engage in NSSI, thus suggesting a genetic etiology (Iglauer et al., 1995). More recent research indicates that the T allele of GN3 is a nonspecific risk factor for engagement in NSSI (Joyce et al., 2006).

Several studies suggest that endogenous opioids play a role in NSSI (Casner, Weinheimer, & Gulatieri, 1996; Coid, Allolio, & Rees, 1983; Kempermen et al., 1997). Specifically, altered endogenous opioid levels have been identified in people who engage in NSSI (Coid et al., 1983; Sandman, Hetrick, Taylor, & Chicz-DeMet, 1997), additionally, those who engage in NSSI report altered pain sensitivity (usually in the form of not experiencing pain when self-injuring; Kemperman et al., 1997; Russ, Campbell, Kakuma, Harrison, & Zanine, 1999), and some respond to opioid antagonists (Casner et al., 1996; Kars, Broekema, Glaudemans-van Glederen, Verhoeven, & Van Ree, 1990). Further evidence for a role of endogenous opioids is found among nonhuman primates, as monkeys who self-injure prefer to bite themselves in body areas where acupressure-induced analgesia is experienced (Marinus, Chase, & Novak, 2000). It is possible that opioid deficiency could result from experiencing chronic and severe abuse during childhood or that the two interact with one another (Sher & Stanley, 2009).

Studies have concluded that people and monkeys who engage in NSSI have altered serotonergic function, specifically reduced serotonergic neurotransmission (New et al., 1997; Simeon et al., 1992; Tiefenbacher, Novak, Lutz, & Meyer, 2005). Some research also implicates the dopamine system in NSSI behavior (Breese, Criswell, & Muehller, 1990; Lloyd et al., 1981; Okamura, Murakami, Yokoyama, Nakamura, & Ibata, 1997). Finally, a body of research suggests that people who engage in NSSI have amygdala hyperactivity compared to those who do not engage in such behaviors (Donegan et al., 2003; Herpertz et al., 2001). While in its early stages, research examining a potential biological etiology of NSSI is intriguing and likely to greatly expand as interest in NSSI continues to grow.

Conclusions and Integrative Model of Nonsuicidal Self-Injury

During the past several years, interest in NSSI has grown considerably, sparking increased theorizing and research into the etiological roots of this perplexing yet relatively common behavior. As has been clarified earlier, several independent theories of NSSI, spanning from psychodynamic to cognitive to biological bases, have been purported, each with varying amounts of empirical support. Overall, the affect regulation model of NSSI has received the most research attention; and that research has yielded promising results. The interpersonally based models of NSSI, especially those focusing on the communication and social modeling aspects of self-injury, are also quite compelling. However, none of these theories are able to fully account for engagement in repeated NSSI alone. Rather, each theory accounts for a piece of the complex puzzle of risk factors and circumstances that lead to engagement in NSSI.

Recently, Nock (2009) proposed one of the first fully integrative etiological models of NSSI in which both distal and proximal risk factors of various sorts (ranging from biological predisposition to environmental risks to limited intrapersonal and interpersonal coping mechanisms to stress response to NSSI-specific vulnerability factors) are included. Here we describe Nock's model in some detail, while suggesting some additions/modifications we feel would improve the already impressive model. Figure 16.1 presents the adapted version of Nock's model. Note that the additions we have added to the original model are in bold, while the original model appears in plain text.

The integrated model of NSSI posits that distal risk factors such as a genetic predisposition for strong emotional reactivity, high levels of familial criticism and hostility, and experiencing abuse and/or maltreatment during childhood interact with one another, leaving one at an elevated risk for both interpersonal and intrapersonal vulnerability factors for engaging in NSSI. Note that we added a bidirectional arrow going from childhood abuse to biological factors, as experiencing prolonged abuse during childhood can alter one's biological mechanisms, including neurotransmitter function, thus increasing risk for intrapersonal vulnerability factors for engagement in NSSI. Similarly, high emotional reactivity in a child can increase risk for being a victim of maltreatment.

The intrapersonal, more proximal risk factors for NSSI include high aversive emotions, poor distress

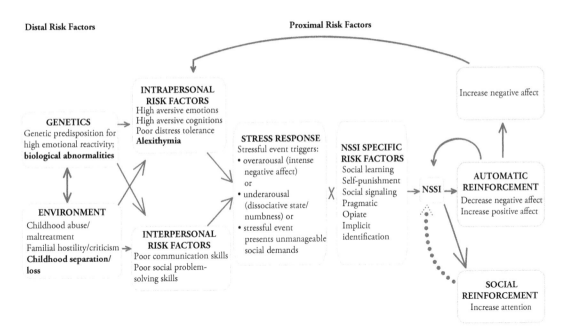

Figure 16.1 Integrated model of nonsuicidal self-injury (NSSI). (Figure adapted from Nock, 2009.)

tolerance, and discomfort with strong feelings or expressing those feelings verbally (i.e., alexithymia). The interpersonal proximal risk factors for NSSI include poor communication skills and poor social problem-solving skills. These underlying vulnerability factors interact with stressful events, such as an interpersonal loss and interpersonal disputes, which trigger underarousal (i.e., dissociation or numbness) or overarousal (i.e., extremely intense negative affect) and/or leave one feeling unable to manage social demands.

Nock then goes on to present six NSSI-specific vulnerability factors, all of which have been described earlier in this chapter, which may explain why only certain people with the previously described combination of risk factors go on to engage in NSSI, while others may choose different ways to regulate emotions and/or solve interpersonal problems. The social learning hypothesis suggests that people are influenced to engage in NSSI by watching their peers engage in the behavior; there is some research to support this hypothesis (Nock & Prinstein, 2005). The self-punishment hypothesis suggests that self-deprecation may encourage NSSI as a form of self-directed abuse and may be one pathway through which abuse during childhood leads to later engagement in NSSI (Glassman et al., 2007). This hypothesis has received a fair amount of empirical support (Laye-Gindhu & Schonert-Reichl, 2005; Nock & Prinstein, 2004; Ross & Heath, 2003). The social signaling hypothesis suggests that people

use NSSI when less intense strategies of communication, such as speaking, have been ineffective at eliciting a desired response in the past. The pragmatic hypothesis suggests that people engage in NSSI because it is effective and easy to execute in many settings. The opiate hypothesis suggests that certain people experience no or little pain during self-injury; these people are not deterred by the pain that most people would experience if they were to cut themselves. Finally, the implicit identification hypothesis suggests that people begin to identify with being a "cutter" or self-injurer and therefore immediately choose that behavior when feeling overwhelmed or stressed. It is likely a combination of several of these NSSI-specific risk factors that lead a subgroup of people to self-injure.

Finally, rather than ending the integrated model of NSSI with engagement in NSSI, we felt it was important to further highlight the reinforcing and maintaining mechanisms operant in repeated NSSI. As reviewed earlier and highlighted in Figure 16.1, engagement in NSSI may be reinforced through two routes: automatic reinforcement (through increasing positive emotions or decreasing negative emotions) or social reinforcement (by increasing attention from others). By definition, a behavior increases in frequency when it is reinforced; therefore, if a person experiences either type of reinforcement, she or he is at risk for engaging in the behavior again. Further, some empirical research suggests that experiencing automatic reinforcement is associated with more severe psychopathology and a greater likelihood of making a suicide attempt (Klonsky & Olino, 2008; Nock & Prinstein, 2005), likely leaving those who experience automatic reinforcement to be at greater risk for engaging in NSSI on a chronic basis. Therefore, in Figure 16.1, note that while there is an arrow going from automatic reinforcement back to NSSI, the arrow going from social reinforcement to NSSI is dotted, indicating that it may be the weaker of the two connections. Finally, although research suggests that NSSI brings immediate relief, such behaviors have been found to commonly lead to an increase in negative feelings, such as shame and disappointment in oneself in the long run. This increase in negative feelings also then leaves people at increased risk for repeated engagement in NSSI, as it loops back to high levels of negative affect.

In summary, research indicates that NSSI is a behavior resulting from the combination of several risk factors and environmental circumstances. At this point, the majority of work that has addressed the etiological roots of NSSI has focused on one specific mechanism at a time. The challenge for future researchers is to empirically test more complex, integrated theories of NSSI, such as those proposed by Nock (2009) and in this chapter. Only with a comprehensive theory based in empirical findings can we further tailor our prevention and treatment efforts of NSSI.

References

Andover, M. A., Pepper C. M., & Gibb, B. E. (2006). Self-mutilation and coping strategies in a college sample. *Suicide and Life Threatening Behavior, 37*, 238–243.

Andover, M. S., Pepper, C. M., Ryabchenko, K. A., Orrico, E. G., & Gibb, B. E. (2005). Self-mutilation and symptoms of depression, anxiety, and borderline personality disorder. *Suicide and Life Threatening Behavior, 35*, 581–591.

Bennum, I. (1984). Psychological models of self-mutilation. *Suicide and Life Threatening Behavior, 14*, 166–186.

Breese, G. R., Criswell, H. E., & Muehller, R. A. (1990). Evidence that lack of brain dopamine during development can increase the susceptibility for aggression and self-injurious behave by influencing DI-dopamine receptor function. *Progress in Neuro-Psychopharmacology & Biological Psychiatry, 14*(Suppl.), 65–80.

Briere, J., & Gil, E. (1998). Self-mutilation in clinical and general population samples: Prevalence, correlates, and functions. *American Journal of Orthopsychiatry, 68*, 609–620.

Carroll, J., Schaffer, C. B., Spensley, J., & Abramowitz, S. I. (1981). Family antecedents of adult self-mutilators. *International Journal of Family Psychiatry, 2*, 147–161.

Casner, J. A., Weinheimer, B., & Gulatieri, C. T. (1996). Naltrexone and self-injurious behavior: A retrospective population study. *Journal of Clinical Psychopharmacology, 16*, 389–394.

Castille, K., Prout, M., Marczyk, G., Shmidheiser, M., Yoder, S., & Howlett, B. (2007). The early maladaptive schemas of self-mutilators: Implications for therapy. *Journal of Cognitive Psychotherapy, 21*, 58–71.

Chapman, A. L., Gratz, K. L., & Brown, M. Z. (2005). Solving the puzzle of deliberate self-harm: The experiential avoidance model. *Behaviour Research and Therapy, 44*, 371–394.

Coid, J., Allolio, B., & Rees, L. H. (1983). Raised plasma met-enkephalin in patients who habitually mutilate themselves. *Lancet, 2*, 545–546.

Crowell, S. E., Beauchaine, T. P., McCauley, E., Smith, C. J., Vasilev, C. A., & Stevens, A. L. (2008). Parent-child interactions, peripheral serotonin, and self-inflicted injury in adolescents. *Journal of Consulting and Clinical Psychology, 76*, 15–21.

Daldin, H. J. (1988). A contribution to the understanding of self-mutilating behavior in adolescence. *Journal of Child Psychotherapy, 14*, 61–66.

Doctors, S. (1981). The symptom of delicate self-cutting in adolescent females: A developmental view. In S. C. Feinstein, J. G. Looney, A. Z. Schwartzberg, & A. D. Sorosky (Eds.), *Adolescent psychiatry* (pp. 443–460). Chicago, IL: University of Chicago Press.

Donegan, N. H., Sanislow, C. A., Blumberg, H. P., Fulbright, R. K., Lacadie, C., Skudlarski, P.,...Wexler, B. E. (2003). Amygdala hyperactivity in borderline personality disorder: Implications for emotional dysregulation. *Biological Psychiatry, 54*, 1284–1293.

Erlich, H. S. (1978). Adolescent suicide: Maternal longing and cognitive development. *Psychoanalytic Study of the Child, 33*, 261–278.

Favazza, A. R. (1989). Why patients mutilate themselves. *Hospital and Community Psychiatry, 40*, 137–145.

Favazza, A. R. (1998). The coming of age of self-mutilation. *Journal of Nervous and Mental Disease, 186*, 259–268.

Favazza, A. R., & Conterio, K. (1989). Female habitual self-mutilators. *Acta Psychiatrica Scandinavica, 79*, 283–289.

Firestone, R. W., & Seiden, R. H. (1990). Suicide and the continuum of self-destructive behavior. *Journal of American College Health, 38*, 207–213.

Garrison, C. A., Cheryl, L. A., McKeown, R. E., Cuffe, S. P., Jackson, K. L., & Waller, J. L. (1993). Nonsuicidal physically self-damaging acts in adolescents. *Journal of Child and Family Studies, 2*, 339–352.

Glassman, L. H., Weierich, M. R., Hooley, J. M., Deliberto, T. L., & Nock, M. K. (2007). Child maltreatment, non-suicidal self-injury, and the mediating role of self-criticism. *Behaviour Research and Therapy, 45*, 2483–2490.

Gratz, K. L. (2000). The measurement, functions, and etiology of deliberate self-harm. Unpublished master's thesis, University of Massachusetts Boston.

Gratz, K. L. (2003). Risk factors for and functions of deliberate self-harm: An empirical and conceptual review. *Clinical Psychology, 10*, 192–205.

Gratz, K. L. (2006). Risk factors for deliberate self-harm among female college students: The role and interaction of childhood maltreatment, emotional inexpressivity, and affect intensity/reactivity. *American Journal of Orthopsychiatry, 76*, 238–250.

Gratz, K. L., Conrad, S. D., & Roemer, L. (2002). Risk factors for deliberate self-harm among college students. *American Journal of Orthopsychiatry, 72*, 128–140.

Gratz, K. L., & Roemer, L. (2004). Multidimensional assessment of emotional regulation and dysregulation: Development, factor structure, and initial validation of the Difficulties in Emotion Regulation Scale. *Journal of Psychopathology and Behavioral Assessment, 26*, 41–54.

Herpertz, S. (1995). Self-injurious behavior: Psychopathological and nosological characteristics in subtypes of self-injurers. *Acta Psychiatrica Scandinavica, 91*, 57–68.

Herpertz, S.C., Dietrich, T. M., Wenning, B., Krings, T., Erberich, S. G., Willmes, K., ... Sass, H. (2001). Evidence of abnormal amygdala functioning in borderline personality disorder: A functional MRI study. *Biological Psychiatry, 50*, 292–298.

Hilt, L. M., Nock, M. K., Lloyd-Richardson, E. E., & Prinstein, M. J. (2008). Longitudinal study of nonsuicidal self-injury among young adolescents, rates, correlates, and preliminary test of an interpersonal model. *Journal of Early Adolescence, 28*, 455–469.

Himber, J. (1994). Blood rituals: Self-cutting in female psychiatric inpatients. *Psychotherapy, 31*, 620–631.

Iglauer, F., Beig, C., Dimigen, J., Gerold, S., Gocht, A., Seeburg, A., ... Willmann, F. (1995). Hereditary compulsive self-mutilating behaviour in laboratory rabbits. *Lab Animal, 29*, 385–393.

Jacobson, C. M., Muehlenkamp, J. J., Miller, A. L., & Turner, E. B. (2008). Psychiatric impairment among adolescents engaging in different types of deliberate self-harm. *Journal of Clinical Child and Adolescent Psychology, 37*, 363–375.

Joyce, P. R., McKenzie, J. M., Mulder, R. T., Luty, S. E., Sullivan, P. F., ... Kennedy, M. A. (2006). Genetic, developmental and personality correlates of self-mutilation in depressed patients. *Australian and New Zealand Journal of Psychiatry, 40*, 225–229.

Kars, H., Broekema, W., Glaudemans-van Glederen, I., Verhoeven, W. M., & Van Ree, J. M. (1990). Naltrexone attenuates self-injurious behavior in mentally-retarded subjects. *Biologcical Psychiatry, 27*, 741–746.

Kemperman, I., Russ, M. J., Clark, W. C., kakuma, T., Zanine, E., & Harrison, K. (1997). Pain assessment in self-injurious patients with borderline personality disorder using signal detection theory. *Psychiatry Research, 70*, 175–183.

Klonsky, E. D. (2007). The functions of deliberate self-injury: A review of the evidence. *Clinical Psychology Review, 27*, 226–239.

Klonsky, E. D., & Olino, T. M. (2008). Identifying clinically distinct subgroups of self-injurers among young adults: A latent class analysis. *Journal of Consulting and Clinical Psychology, 76*, 22–27.

Klonsky, E. D., Oltmanns, T. F., & Turkheimer, E. (2003). Deliberate self-harm in a nonclinical population: Prevalence and psychological correlates. *American Journal of Psychiatry, 160*, 1501–1508.

Kumar, G., Pepe, D., & Steer, R. A. (2004). Adolescent psychiatric inpatients' self-reported reasons for cutting themselves. *Journal of Nervous and Mental Disease, 192*, 830–836.

Lane, R. C. (2002). Anorexia, masochism, self-mutilation, and autoerotism: The spider mother. *Psychoanalytic Review, 89*, 101–123.

Laye-Gindhu, A., & Schonert-Reichl, K. A. (2005). Nonsuicidal self-harm among community adolescents: Understanding the "whats" and "whys" of self-harm. *Journal of Youth and Adolescence, 34*, 447–457.

Linehan, M. (1993). *Cognitive-behavioral treatment for borderline personality disorder*. New York, NY: Guilford Press.

Lloyd, K. G., Hornykiewicz, O., Davidson, L., Shannak, K., Farley, I., Goldstein, M., ... Fox, I. H. (1981). Biochemical evidence of dysfunction of brain neurotransmitters in the Lesch-Nyhan syndrome. *New England Journal of Medicine, 305*, 1106–1111.

Lloyd, E. E., Kelley, M. L., & Hope, T. (1997, April). *Self-mutilation in a community sample of adolescents: Descriptive characteristics and provisional prevalence rates*. Poster session presented at the Annual Meeting of the Society for Behavioral Medicine, New Orleans, LA.

Lloyd-Richardson, E. E., Perrine, N., Dierker, L., & Kelley, M. L. (2007). Characteristics and functions of non-suicidal self-injury in a community sample of adolescents. *Psychological Medicine, 37*, 1183–1192.

McLane, J. (1996). The voice on the skin: Self-mutilation and Merleau-Ponty's theory of language. *Hypatia, 11*, 107–121.

Marinus, L. M., Chase, W. K., & Novak, M. A. (2000). Self-biting behavior in rhesus macaques is preferentially directed to body areas associated with acupuncture analgesia. *American Journal of Primatology, 51*, 71–72.

Menninger, K. (1938). *Man against himself*. New York, NY: Harcourt, Brace.

Muehlenkamp, J. J., Engel, S. G., Wadeson, A., Crosby, R. D., Wonderlich, S. A., Simonich, H., & Mitchell, J. E. (2009) Emotional states preceding and following acts of non-suicidal self-injury in bulimia nervosa patients. *Behaviour Research and Therapy, 47*(1), 83–87.

Najmi, S., Wegner, D. M., & Nock, M. (2007). Thought suppression and self-injurious thoughts and behaviors. *Behaviour Research and Therapy, 45*, 1957–1965.

New, A. S., Trestmen, R. L., Mitropoulou, V., Benishay, D. S., Coccaro, E., Silverman, J., & Siever, L. J. (1997). Serotonergic function and self-injurious behavior in personality disorder patients. *Psychiatry Research, 69*, 17–26.

Nixon, M. K., Cloutier, P. F., & Aggarwal, S. (2002). Affect regulation and addictive aspects of repetitive self-injury in hospitalized adolescents. *Journal of the American Academy of Child and Adolescent Psychiatry, 41*, 1333–1341.

Nock, M. K. (2009). Why do people hurt themselves? New insights into the nature and functions of self-injury. *Current Directions in Psychological Science, 18*, 78–83.

Nock, M., Joiner, T. E., Gordon, K. H., Lloyd-Richardson, E., & Prinstein, M. J. (2006). Non-suicidal self-injury among adolescents: Diagnostic correlates and relation to suicide attempts. *Psychiatry Research, 144*, 65–72.

Nock, M. K., & Mendes, W. B. (2008). Physiological arousal, distress tolerance, and social problem solving deficits among adolescent self-injurers. *Journal of Consulting and Clinical Psychology, 76*, 28–38.

Nock, M. K., & Prinstein, M. J. (2004). A functional approach to the assessment of self-mutilative behavior. *Journal of Consulting and Clinical Psychology, 72*, 885–890.

Nock, M. K., & Prinstein, M. J. (2005). Contextual features and behavioral functions of self-mutilation among adolescents. *Journal of Abnormal Psychology, 114*, 140–146.

Nock, M. K., Prinstein, M. J., & Sterba, S. (2009). Revealing the form and function of self-injurious thoughts and behaviors: A real-time ecological assessment study among adolescents and young adults. *Journal of Abnormal Psychology, 118*, 816–827.

Nock, M. K., Wedig, M. M., & Holmberg, E. B., & Hooley, J. M. (2008). The Emotion Reactivity Scale: Development, evaluation, and relation to self-injurious thoughts and behaviors. *Behavior Therapy, 39*, 107–116.

Offer, D., & Barglow, P. (1960). Adolescent and young adult self-mutilation incidents in a general psychiatric hospital. *Archives of General Psychiatry, 3,* 194–204.

Okamura, H., Murakami, T., Yokoyama, C., Nakamura, T., & Ibata, Y. (1997). Self-injurious behavior and dopaminergic neuron system in neonatal 6-hydroxy-dopamine-lesioned rat: 2. Intracerebral microinjection of dopamine agonists and antagonists. *Journal of Pharmacology and Experimental Therapeutics, 280,* 1031–1037.

Olfson, M., Gameroff, M. J., Marcus, S. C., Greenberg, T., & Shaffer, D. (2005). Emergency treatment of young people following deliberate self-harm. *Archives of General Psychiatry, 62,* 1122–1128.

Osuch, E. A., Noll, J. G., & Putnam, F. W. (1999). The motivations for self-injury in psychiatric inpatients. *Psychiatry, 62,* 334–345.

Pellicer, F., Buendia-Roldan, I., & Pallares-Trujillo, V. C. (1998). Self-mutilation in the Lesch-Nyhan syndrome: A corporal consciousness problem?—A new hypothesis. *Medical Hypotheses, 50,* 43–47.

Podovoll, E. M. (1969). Self-mutilation within a hospital setting: A study of identity and social compliance. *British Journal of Medical Psychology, 42,* 213–221.

Prinstein, M. J., Guerry, J. D., Browne, C. B., & Rancourt, D. (2009). Interpersonal models of nonsuicidal self-injury. In M. K. Nock (Ed.), *Understanding nonsuicidal self-injury: Origins, assessment, and treatment* (pp. 79–98). Washington, DC: American Psychological Association.

Rosen, P. M., & Walsh, B. W. (1989). Patterns of contagion in self-mutilation epidemics. *American Journal of Psychiatry, 146,* 656–658.

Rosen, P. M., Walsh, B. W., & Rode, S. A. (1990). Interpersonal loss and self-mutilation. *Suicide and Life-Threatening Behavior, 20,* 177–184.

Rosenthal, R. J., Rinzler, C., Wallsh, R., & Klausner, E. (1972). Wrist-cutting syndrome: The meaning of a gesture. *American Journal of Psychiatry, 128,* 47–52.

Ross, S. & Heath, N. (2002). A study of the frequency of self-mutilation in a community sample of adolescents. *Journal of Youth and Adolescence, 31,* 67–77.

Ross, S. & Heath, N. (2003). Two models of adolescent self-mutilation. *Suicide and Life Threatening Behavior, 33,* 277–287.

Ross, R. R., & McKay, H. B. (1979). *Self-mutilation.* Lexington, MA: DC Heath.

Russ, M. J., Campbell, S. S., Kakuma, T., Harrison, K., & Zanine, E. (1999). EEG theta activity and pain insensitivity in self-injurious borderline patients. *Psychiatry Research, 89,* 201–214.

Sandman, C. A., Hetrick, W. P., Taylor, D. V., & Chicz-DeMet, A. (1997). Dissociation of POMC peptides after self-injury predicts responses to centrally acting opiate blockers. *American Journal on Mental Retardation, 102,* 182–199.

Sher, L. & Stanley, B. (2008). Biological models of non-suicidal self-injury. In M. K. Nock (Ed.), *Understanding nonsuicidal self-injury: Origins, assessment, and treatment* (pp. 99–116). Washington, DC: American Psychological Association.

Sher, L. & Stanley, B. H. (2009). The role of endogenous opioids in the pathophysiology of self-injurious and suicidal behavior. *Archives of Suicide Research, 12,* 299–308.

Simeon, D., Stanley, B., Frances, A., Mann, J. J., Winchel, R., & Stanley, M. (1992). Self-mutilation in personality disorders: Psychological and biological correlates. *American Journal of Psychiatry, 149,* 221–226.

Simpson, M. A. (1975). The phenomenology of self-mutilation in a general hospital setting. *Canadian Psychiatric Association Journal, 20,* 429–434.

Simpson, M. A. (1980). Self-mutilation as indirect self-destructive behavior. In N. L. Farberow (Ed.), *The many faces of suicide: Indirect self-destructive behavior* (pp. 257–283). New York, NY: McGraw-Hill.

Simpson, C. A., & Porter, G. L. (1981). Self-mutilation in children and adolescents. *Bulletin of the Menninger Clinic, 45,* 428–438.

Suyemoto, K. L. (1998). The functions of self-mutilation. *Clinical Psychology Review, 18,* 531–554.

Suyemoto, K. L., & MacDonald, M. L. (1995). Self-cutting in female adolescents. *Psychotherapy, 32,* 162–171.

Tiefenbacher, S., Novak, M. A., Lutz, C. K., & Meyer, J. S., (2005). The physiology and neurochemistry of self-injurious behavior: A nonhuman primate model. *Frontiers in Bioscience, 10,* 1–11.

Walsh, B. W., & Rosen, P. (1985). Self-mutilation and contagion: An empirical test. *American Journal of Psychiatry, 142,* 119–120.

Wedig, M. W., & Nock, M. K. (2007). Parental expressed emotion and adolescent self-injury. *Journal of the American Academy of Child and Adolescent Psychiatry, 46,* 1171–1178.

Weierich, M. R., & Nock, M. K. (2008). Posttraumatic stress symptoms mediate the relation between childhood sexual abuse and nonsuicidal self-injury. *Journal of Consulting and Clinical Psychology, 76,* 39–44.

Whitlock, J., Eckenrode, J., & Silverman, D. (2006). Self-injurious behaviors in a college population. *Pediatrics, 117,* 1939–1948.

Yates, T. M. (2004). The developmental psychopathology of self-injurious behavior: Compensatory regulation in posttraumatic adaptation. *Clinical Psychology Review, 24,* 35–74.

Yates, T. M., Tracy, A. J., & Luthar, S. S. (2008). Nonsuicidal self-injury among "privileged" youths: Longitudinal and cross-sectional approaches to developmental process. *Journal of Consulting and Clinical Psychology, 76,* 52–62.

Yip, K. (2005). A multi-dimensional perspective of adolescents' self-cutting. *Child and Adolescent Mental Health, 10,* 80–86.

Zlotnick, C., Shea, M. T., Pearlstein, T. S. E., Costello, E., & Begin, A. (1996). The relationship between dissociative symptoms, alexithymia, impulsivity, sexual abuse, and self-mutilation. *Comprehensive Psychiatry, 37,* 12–16.

Zlotnick, C., Woldsdorf, B. A., Johnson, B., & Spirito, A. (2003). Impaired self-regulation and suicidal behavior among adolescent and young adult psychiatric inpatients. *Archives of Suicide Research, 7,* 149–157.

Zoroglu, S. S., Tuzun, U., Sar, V., Tutkin, H., Savas, H. A., Ozturk, M. A.,...Kora, M. E. (2003). Suicide attempt and self-mutilation among Turkish high school students in relation with abuse, neglect, and dissociation. *Psychiatry and Clinical Neurosciences, 57,* 119–126.

PART 4

Assessment

CHAPTER

17

Core Competencies, Warning Signs, and a Framework for Suicide Risk Assessment in Clinical Practice

M. David Rudd

Abstract

Suicide risk assessment is one of the most challenging tasks in day-to-day clinical practice. Bolstered by an emerging empirical foundation, the last two decades have witnessed the emergence of core competencies in suicide risk assessment, along with the recognition of the importance of warning signs in formulating imminent risk. This chapter offers a risk assessment framework guided by identified core competencies. It also integrates multiple domains for assessment, including the risk framework to acknowledge the critical role played by warning signs in differentiating both acute and chronic risk for suicidal individuals. The framework provided is simple, straightforward, and practical, providing detailed questions to guide the assessment process.

Key Words: suicide risk assessment, competencies, warning signs, suicide risk framework, acute and chronic suicide risk

Assessing suicide risk is consistently among the most anxiety-provoking challenges in clinical practice (Rudd, 2006). Paradoxically, suicidality is also the most frequently encountered emergency in clinical practice and, arguably, unavoidable for mental health clinicians (Buzan & Weissberg, 1992; Rudd, 2006). It is estimated that approximately one-quarter of mental health practitioners will lose a patient to suicide over the course of their career, with the numbers for psychiatrists reaching as high as one-half (Chemtob, Hamada, Bauer, Torigoe, & Kinney, 1988; McAdams & Foster, 2000; Pope & Tabachnick, 1993).

As a result of this high rate of occurrence and related clinical importance, core competencies and practice guidelines for assessing and managing suicide risk have emerged over the course of the past decade (Rudd, Cukrowicz, & Bryan, 2008). More specifically, the American Psychiatric Association (2003) published practice guidelines that have clear implications for day-to-day practice, cutting across all domains, including assessment, clinical management,

treatment, and supervision of trainees. More recently, the Suicide Prevention Resource Center (SPRC, 2006) published core competencies for the assessment and management of suicide risk. Both inform and help guide day-to-day practice, cutting across all domains of clinical functioning, and likely have had profound influence on the standard of care across multiple clinical settings. The last decade has also witnessed the emergence of suicide warning signs as an important clinical construct. Similarly, a number of clinical management techniques have garnered empirical support and proven useful in practice (e.g., commitment to treatment statement and crisis response or safety planning), and "common elements" of effective treatments for suicidality have been identified, all with clear implications for immediate clinical management when suicide risk is recognized.

As the empirical foundation for suicide risk assessment and clinical management grows, it is essential for clinicians to recognize, understand, and integrate into practice new constructs, guidelines, clinical management techniques, and competencies as they emerge. This chapter provides a general framework for suicide risk assessment; one that integrates identified core competencies and suicide warning signs. Several clinical management strategies are also discussed, along with the common elements of empirically supported treatments for suicidal behavior. Immediate clinical management decisions following a suicide risk evaluation ideally should be driven by an empirical foundation, that is, clinical tools proven to work.

Core Competencies as a Foundation to Assessment

The core competencies in suicide risk assessment and management target seven identifiable clinical domains: (a) attitudes and approach, (b) understanding suicide, (c) collecting accurate assessment information, (d) formulating risk, (e) developing a treatment plan, (f) the clinical management of care, and (g) understanding legal and regulatory issues related to suicidality (SPRC, 2006). There are a total of 24 competencies across the seven domains. Although arguably limited to date, there is an emerging empirical foundation for core competencies in suicidality. What is important to recognize is that these identified core competencies provide the foundation or "entry-level" skills necessary for clinical work with suicidal patients. In short, effective assessment and clinical management require not just a recognition and understanding of the seven domains, but competency across all.

The core competency model essentially argues that you cannot isolate any one domain, but rather that all seven are connected in an intricate and interdependent fashion. In short, conducting an assessment and formulating suicide risk requires a broad skill set and expansive knowledge base. The point to be made is that the general assessment framework provided herein can be somewhat misleading, potentially implying that all requisite knowledge and skills are summarized in this chapter, an assumption that would be profoundly wrong. A keen awareness and understanding of the core competencies in suicide risk assessment and management is essential to effective clinical practice (SPRC, 2006).

A General Assessment Framework

Joiner et al. (1999) offered a general framework for suicide risk assessment that included seven domains: (a) previous suicidal behavior, (b) the nature of current suicidal thinking and behaviors, (c) precipitant stressors, (d) general psychiatric symptoms,

(e) the presence of hopelessness, (f) impulsivity and self-control, and (g) protective factors. As illustrated in Table 17.1, it is recommended that an additional category be added targeting suicide warning signs (Rudd, Berman et al., 2006), recognizing their significant role in the emergence of imminent risk. Table 17.2 translates these domains to a structured risk assessment form that can be applied directly to day-to-day clinical practice.

Although widely utilized in public health campaigns, suicide warning signs have not been routinely integrated into the risk assessment framework, despite their link to imminent risk. It is important to recognize the difference between warning signs and risk factors. Hendin et al. (2001) defined a suicide risk factor as the presence of any factor empirically demonstrated to correlate with suicidality, regardless of timeframe. In contrast, warning signs have a number of distinctive features, with perhaps the most critical being timeframe. Warning signs imply near-term risk, whereas risk factors address risk over much longer periods of time, ranging from a year to a lifetime (Rudd, Berman et al., 2006). The following definition has been offered: "A suicide warning sign is the earliest detectable sign that indicates heightened risk for suicide in the near term (i.e., within minutes, hours, or days). A warning sign refers to some feature of the developing outcome of interest (suicide) rather than to a distinct construct (e.g., risk factor) that predicts or may be causally related to suicide" (Rudd, Berman et al., 2006, p. 258). Given the relationship of the warning signs construct to the nature of imminent risk, it is essential to integrate these elements into any risk assessment framework.

Joiner et al. (1999) argued that the most critical domain for any assessment is suicidal thinking and related behaviors. I would certainly agree, with one caveat. Suicide warning signs need to be considered of comparable importance, organized accordingly and disproportionately weighted in the eventual risk formulation. Over the last several decades compelling data have emerged in the literature indicating that three distinct groups need to be differentiated during the assessment process: suicide ideators, suicide attempters, and multiple attempters (cf. Rudd, Joiner, & Rajab, 2004). A multiple suicide attempter is defined as anyone who has made two or more genuine suicide attempts (i.e., there is evidence of intent to die). Evidence indicates that multiple attempters are characterized by persistently elevated psychiatric symptomatology, chronic suicidal thoughts with variable intent, greater diagnostic comorbidity (both Axis I and II), and elevated

Table 17.1 Risk Assessment Domains

I: Predisposition to suicidal behavior
- History of psychiatric diagnoses (increased risk with recurrent disorders, comorbidity, and chronicity), including major depressive disorder, bipolar disorder, schizophrenia, substance abuse, and personality disorders such as borderline personality disorder.
- History of suicidal behavior (increased risk with previous attempts, high lethality, and chronic disturbance). Those having made multiple attempts (i.e., two or more) are considered at chronic risk.
- Recent discharge from inpatient psychiatric treatment (increased risk within first year of release). Risk is highest during the first month post discharge, with a particular elevation of risk during the first week.
- Same-sex sexual orientation (increased risk among homosexual men).
- Male gender.
- History of abuse (sexual, physical or emotional).

II: Identifiable precipitants or stressors (*most can be conceptualized as losses*)
- financial
- interpersonal relationship(s) and relationship instability (loss of social support)
- professional, identity
- acute or chronic health problems (can be loss of independence, autonomy, or function)

III: Symptomatic presentation (have patient rate severity on 1–10 scale)
- Depressive symptoms—e.g., anhedonia, low self-esteem, sadness, dyssomnia, fatigue (increased risk when combined with anxiety and substance abuse).
- Bipolar disorder (increased risk early in course of disorder).
- Anxiety (increased risk with trait anxiety and acute agitation).
- Schizophrenia (increased risk following active phases).
- Borderline and antisocial personality features.

IV: Presence of hopelessness (have patient rate severity on 1–10 scale)
- Severity of hopelessness.
- Duration of hopelessness.

V: The nature of suicidal thinking and behaviors
- Current ideation: frequency, intensity, and duration.
- Presence of suicidal plan (increased risk with specificity).
- Availability of means (multiple methods).
- Lethality of means (including both medical and perceived lethality).
- Active suicidal behaviors (including preparation and rehearsal behaviors).
- Suicide intent (subjective and objective markers).

VI. Previous suicide attempts (and nonsuicidal self-injury)
- Frequency of suicide attempts and nonsuicidal self-injury.
- Perceived lethality and outcome.
- Opportunity for rescue and help seeking.
- Preparatory behaviors (including rehearsal).
- Reaction to previous attempts (feelings about survival and lessons learned).

VII: Presence of suicide warning signs (organize in a single section, including items from other domains).
- Active suicidal thinking.
- Preparation and rehearsal behavior.
- Hopelessness.
- Anger.
- Recklessness, impulsivity, dramatic mood changes.
- Anxiety and agitation.
- Feeling trapped.
- No reasons for living, no purpose in life.
- Increased alcohol or substance abuse

VIII: Impulsivity and self-control (have patient rate on 1–10 scale)
- Subjective self-control.
- Objective control (e.g., substance abuse, impulsive behaviors, aggression).

Table 17.1 Continued

IX: Protective factors
- Presence of social support. Support needs to be both present and accessible. Make sure the relationships are healthy.
- Problem-solving skills and history of coping skills.
- Active participation in treatment.
- Presence of hopefulness.
- Children present in the home.
- Pregnancy.
- Religious commitment.
- Life satisfaction. Have the patient rate life satisfaction on a scale of 1–10. Life satisfaction should correspond with the patient's stated reasons for living and dying.
- Intact reality testing.
- Fear of social disapproval.
- Fear of suicide or death. This suggests that the patient has not yet habituated to the idea of death, a very good sign.

---

risk for a subsequent attempt, particularly in the first year following an index attempt. As a result, risk assessment for multiple attempters is different in that "chronic" risk is acknowledged, clarified, and targeted in immediate clinical management and treatment. Chronic risk is best conceptualized as heightened vulnerability (and probability) for future suicidal crises or episodes. As indicated in Table 17.2, chronic risk is indicated on the assessment form, along with space for a brief summary of risk indicators (e.g., recurrent Axis I diagnoses, the presence of an Axis II diagnosis, a history of unresolved trauma or abuse, multiple suicide attempts).

The Nature of Current Suicidal Symptoms and Behaviors

The core of any assessment for suicide risk is a careful and thorough assessment of suicidal thinking and behavior, with a particular focus on an accurate understanding of suicide intent. It is important to recognize that intent is very much fluid in nature, with suicide warning signs providing observable markers consistent with potential elevations in intent to die. The presence or absence of suicidal thinking is not particularly useful in formulating risk; it is the nature of the suicidal thinking, the specificity, duration, and related features that help the clinician gauge intent to die.

I would encourage clinicians to adopt a standard approach to exploring suicidal thinking. Figure 17.1 illustrates a simple six-step sequence, with specific questions to clarify the nature and severity of his or her suicidal thinking/behavior and ultimately gauge intent using both the patient's subjective statements and objective markers (i.e., observable behavior) (Rudd, 2012). The flowchart is organized in a hierarchical manner, with the goal of reducing anxiety, apprehension, and associated resistance by

transitioning from past episodes back to the current crisis after the initial screening question(s). As illustrated, the initial question is: *Have you had thoughts about suicide, thoughts of killing yourself?* The importance of unambiguous language cannot be overstated. I would discourage clinicians from using any phrasing other than the two guiding themes just noted. They leave no room for misunderstanding.

When exploring suicidal thinking, three constructs are particularly important to remember: suicidal thoughts, morbid ruminations, and nonsuicidal self-injury. Differentiating between active suicidal thoughts, morbid ruminations, and nonsuicidal self-injury is an essential clinical task in the risk assessment process. Although there is certainly overlap across the three constructs, the underlying motivation or intent is different for each. Morbid ruminations (thoughts about death, dying, and not wanting to be alive but *without* active thoughts of killing oneself), suicidal thoughts (thoughts of killing oneself), and nonsuicidal self-injury (underlying motivation is emotion regulation or for a reason other than death) are distinct and convey remarkably different levels of risk. Suicidal thinking is differentiated by an active desire to kill oneself (e.g., Rudd, 2006). Morbid ruminations have previously been referred to as passive suicidal thoughts, noting their routine occurrence in cases of clinical depression (cf. Maris, Berman, Maltsberger, & Yufit, 1992). It is often necessary for the clinician to provide the patient definitions of each, with improved understanding actually facilitating broader emotion regulation efforts and serving as a clinical intervention. Ultimately, though, clarification early in the assessment process helps improve subsequent efforts to monitor risk over time.

As noted earlier, it is not unusual for suicidal patients to also engage in repetitive nonsuicidal

Table 17.2 Standard Suicide Risk Assessment Preprinted Form

A comprehensive suicidality assessment was conducted due to: (check one about the nature of the referral)
___ Referral source identified suicidal symptoms or risk factors.
___ Patient reported suicidal thoughts/feelings on intake paperwork/assessment tools *(please attach a copy of the assessment instrument with applicable items circled)*.
___ Patient reported suicidal thoughts/feelings during the intake interview.
___ Recent event already occurred (circle appropriate: suicide attempt, suicide threat).
___ Other:
In the following sections, circle Y for "yes" and N for "no" and provide accompanying details.

Describe the therapeutic alliance/relationship at the end of the initial session:
Poor-------------Routine-------------Good
If Poor, please indicate problems observed:
_____

Precipitants to Consider:
Y N Significant loss. Describe: _____
Y N Interpersonal isolation. Describe: _____
Y N Relationship problems. Describe: _____
Y N Health problems. Describe: _____
Y N Legal problems. Describe: _____
Y N Other problems. Describe: _____

Nature of Suicidal Thinking:
Y N Suicide Ideation:
• Frequency: Never   Rarely   Sometimes   Frequently   Always
• Intensity: Brief and fleeting   Focused deliberation   Intense rumination
         Other: _____
• Duration (i.e. "Average Day"): ____ Seconds ____ Minutes ____Hours
Y N Current Intent
• Subjective reports (Provide quote): _____
• Objective signs (behaviors): _____
Y N Suicide plan:
• When_____
• Where_____
• How_____ Y N Access to means
Y N Suicide Preparation _____
Y N Suicide Rehearsal _____
Y N Reasons for Dying:_____
Y N Reasons for Living: _____
Y N Evidence of emergence of capability to die by suicide? _____

History of Suicidal Behavior, Nonsuicidal Self-Injury
Y N History of Suicidality
• Ideation_____
• Single Attempt _____
• Multiple Attempts _____
Y N History of Nonsuicidal Self-Injury (no intent to die)
Type: _____
Frequency:_____
Duration: _____

Symptom Severity:
Depression: Rating (1–10)_____
Anxiety: Rating (1–10)_____
Anger: Rating (1–10)_____

(continued)

Table 17.2 Continued

Agitation: Rating (1–10)_____
Onset of symptom clusters:_____
Duration of symptom clusters:_____

Hopelessness:
Rating (1–10)_____
Onset:_____
Duration:_____

Perceived Burdensomeness:
Rating (1–10)_____
Onset:_____
Duration:_____

Sleep Disturbance:
Rating of severity: (1–10)_____
Initial, middle or terminal insomnia (circle)
Nightmares? Yes or No

Impulsivity/Self-Control:
Y N Impulsivity
• Subjective reports: _____
• Objective signs: _____
Y N Substance abuse Describe: _____

Warning Signs Present?
Y N Active suicidal thinking
Y N Active suicidal behavior
Y N Severe anxiety
Y N Agitation
Y N Feeling trapped
Y N Anger, Rage
Y N Recklessness
Y N Dramatic mood changes
Y N No reason for living, purpose in life
Y N Increased alcohol or substance use
Y N Hopelessness
Y N Social withdrawal

Additional Factor to Consider:
Y N Homicidal ideation Describe: _____
Summarize the Presence of Protective Factors:

Recent hospital discharge for suicidality? Y N
How long ago was the discharge? _____
Additional risk factors: (check all that apply)
_____ Age over 60   _____Male   _____Previous Axis I or II psychiatric diagnosis
_____ History of family suicide
_____ History of physical, emotional or sexual abuse   ___ Access to firearms

Mental Status (WNL=Within Normal Limits):
Alertness: alert.....drowsy....lethargic.....stuporous......other:
Oriented to: person place time reason for evaluation
Mood: euthymic, elevated, dysphoric, agitated, angry,
Affect: flat, blunted, constricted, appropriate, labile
Thought continuity: clear and coherent, goal-directed, tangential, circumstantial, other:
Thought content: WNL, obsessions, delusions, ideas of reference, bizarreness, morbidity, other:

Table 17.2 Continued

Abstraction: WNL, notably concrete, other:
Speech: WNL, rapid, slow, slurred, impoverished, incoherent, other:
Memory: grossly intact, other:
Reality testing: WNL, other:
Notable behavioral observations:

Rating of Acute Risk (circle appropriate category from distillation of above factors and warning signs)
None-----Mild-----Moderate-----High

Presence/Absence of Chronic Risk (circle appropriate category)
Absent
Present
If present, summarize markers of chronic risk:

DSM-IV-R Diagnosis:
Axis I:
Axis II:
Axis III:
Axis IV:
Axis V:
P: At the current time, outpatient care **can/cannot** provide sufficient safety and stability.
Intervention plan for safety is:
1.
2.
3.
4.
Patient agrees to this plan: Y N
Patient was provided a written **crisis response plan**: Y N
Patient was provided a commitment to treatment statement: Y N

---

self-injury, particularly those with chronic suicidal behavior (Nock, 2009). Although these episodes can co-occur, differentiating them is important for an accurate understanding of current risk. As stated in Figure 17.1, morbid ruminations convey lower risk. However, patients can quickly transition from morbid to suicidal thoughts, something that is not uncommon for those with a history of previous attempts, particularly multiple attempters. The clinician can help the patient understand the difference, using the transition from morbid to suicidal thinking as an easily recognized sign that needs to be openly shared and can be integrated into a subsequent safety or crisis management plan (Wenzel, Brown, & Beck, 2008).

When documenting suicidal thoughts, direct quotes from the patient are best. Examples of questions clinicians might ask include "Can you tell me exactly what you've been thinking?" and "What are the thoughts that go through your head?" Direct quotes can provide useful insights into understanding and gauging intent. Intent has both subjective (a patient's stated intent) and objective (the patient's demonstrated intent) elements (cf. Rudd, 2006). The specificity of suicidal thinking is one marker of intent, with greater detail and specificity suggesting greater intent. As a general rule, greater specificity is characterized by greater duration and, ultimately, greater intent to die. Specificity is captured in the how, when, where, and why of the suicidal crisis. Greater specificity often translates to longer duration of the thoughts and associated behavior (e.g., preparation and rehearsal). As Rudd (2012) noted, additional markers of objective intent include the following:

• Preparation behavior (e.g., letter writing, redoing one's will or insurance, accessing a method, researching methods on the Internet)
• Rehearsal behavior (actually getting one's method out and "practicing" or preparing for suicide)
• Stated reasons for living and reasons for dying (the simple numeric difference conveys evidence of intent)

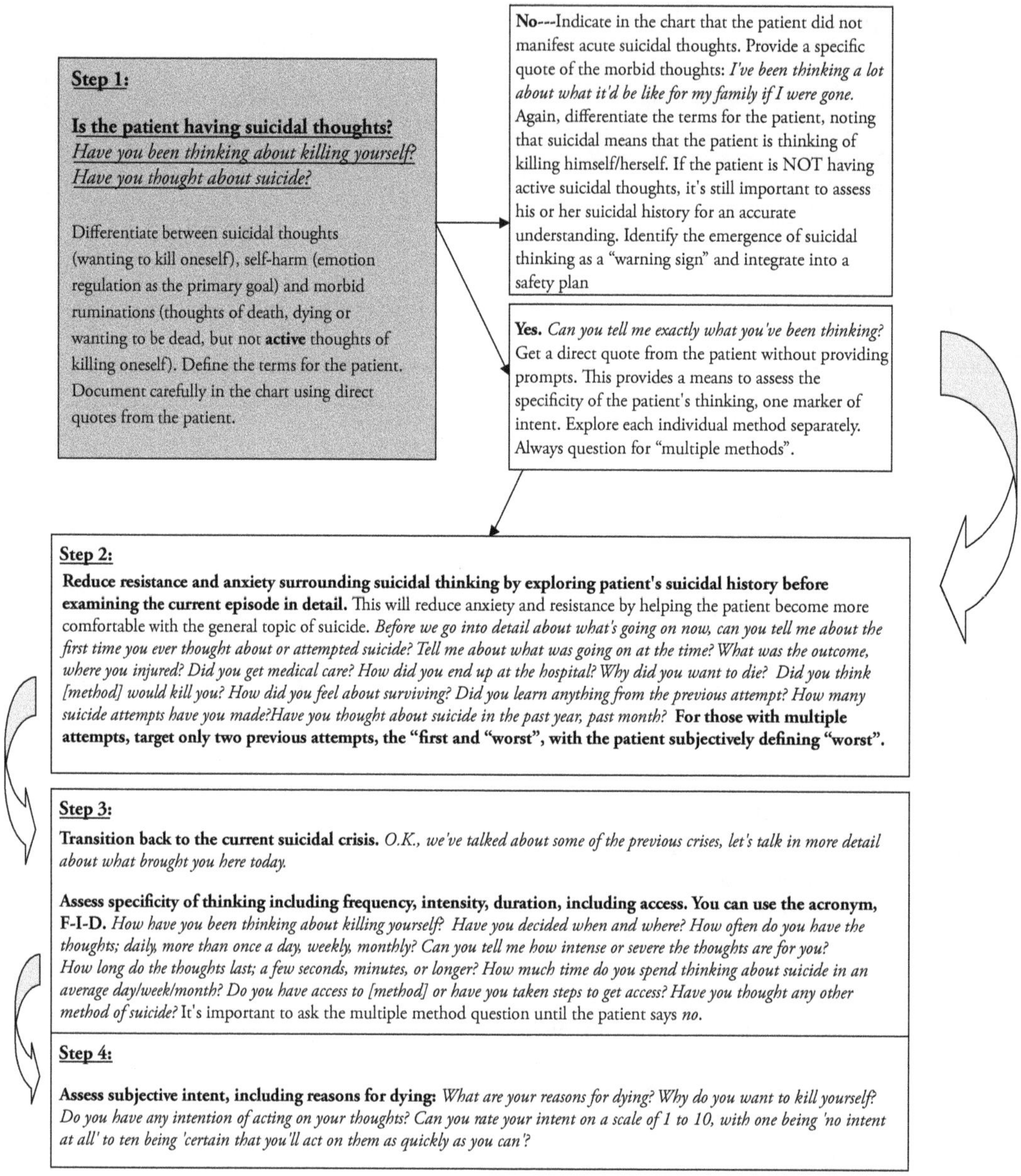

Step 1:

Is the patient having suicidal thoughts?
Have you been thinking about killing yourself?
Have you thought about suicide?

Differentiate between suicidal thoughts (wanting to kill oneself), self-harm (emotion regulation as the primary goal) and morbid ruminations (thoughts of death, dying or wanting to be dead, but not **active** thoughts of killing oneself). Define the terms for the patient. Document carefully in the chart using direct quotes from the patient.

No---Indicate in the chart that the patient did not manifest acute suicidal thoughts. Provide a specific quote of the morbid thoughts: *I've been thinking a lot about what it'd be like for my family if I were gone.* Again, differentiate the terms for the patient, noting that suicidal means that the patient is thinking of killing himself/herself. If the patient is NOT having active suicidal thoughts, it's still important to assess his or her suicidal history for an accurate understanding. Identify the emergence of suicidal thinking as a "warning sign" and integrate into a safety plan

Yes. *Can you tell me exactly what you've been thinking?* Get a direct quote from the patient without providing prompts. This provides a means to assess the specificity of the patient's thinking, one marker of intent. Explore each individual method separately. Always question for "multiple methods".

Step 2:
Reduce resistance and anxiety surrounding suicidal thinking by exploring patient's suicidal history before examining the current episode in detail. This will reduce anxiety and resistance by helping the patient become more comfortable with the general topic of suicide. *Before we go into detail about what's going on now, can you tell me about the first time you ever thought about or attempted suicide? Tell me about what was going on at the time? What was the outcome, where you injured? Did you get medical care? How did you end up at the hospital? Why did you want to die? Did you think [method] would kill you? How did you feel about surviving? Did you learn anything from the previous attempt? How many suicide attempts have you made? Have you thought about suicide in the past year, past month?* **For those with multiple attempts, target only two previous attempts, the "first and "worst", with the patient subjectively defining "worst".**

Step 3:
Transition back to the current suicidal crisis. *O.K., we've talked about some of the previous crises, let's talk in more detail about what brought you here today.*

Assess specificity of thinking including frequency, intensity, duration, including access. You can use the acronym, F-I-D. *How have you been thinking about killing yourself? Have you decided when and where? How often do you have the thoughts; daily, more than once a day, weekly, monthly? Can you tell me how intense or severe the thoughts are for you? How long do the thoughts last; a few seconds, minutes, or longer? How much time do you spend thinking about suicide in an average day/week/month? Do you have access to [method] or have you taken steps to get access? Have you thought any other method of suicide?* It's important to ask the multiple method question until the patient says *no.*

Step 4:
Assess subjective intent, including reasons for dying: *What are your reasons for dying? Why do you want to kill yourself? Do you have any intention of acting on your thoughts? Can you rate your intent on a scale of 1 to 10, with one being 'no intent at all' to ten being 'certain that you'll act on them as quickly as you can'?*

Figure 17.1. A hierarchical approach to exploring suicidal thoughts and intent. (Modified from Rudd, 2006 and Rudd, 2012.)

• Perceived lethality of previous suicide attempts (*Did you think [method] would kill you?)*
• Any efforts to prevent discovery or rescue in previous suicide attempts
• His or her emotional reaction to previous attempts (How did you feel about surviving? Did you learn anything about yourself from the attempt?)

Reasons for living and reasons for dying provide an interesting, practical, and useful way of understanding the patient's ambivalence and associated intent to die. In short, the clinician can gauge manifest intent by simply reviewing the number of stated reasons in response to each question. The assessment form in Table 17.2 has a space for identified reasons to be listed. The simple numeric difference between each (subtracting reasons for dying from reasons for living) can be used as a simple method to attach a numeric value to the patient's ambivalence. As Joiner (2005) has discussed, the patient's capacity to suicide builds with exposure, including nonsuicidal self-injury, multiple attempts, and preparation and rehearsal behaviors. It is important for the clinician to recognize that when there is mounting evidence of objective intent, the patient has progressed from "thinking" about suicide to actively implementing a suicide plan (e.g., engaging in preparation and rehearsal), providing clear evidence of not only greater intent but heightened risk. It is also important for the clinician to recognize that the patient's emotional reaction to previous attempts can help identify what I have called persistent or "residual" intent to die (e.g., answers such as "I learned that next time I need to use a gun") (Rudd, 2006). Residual intent is characteristic of multiple suicide attempters, that is, those at chronic risk for suicide. Table 17.2 provides an assessment form for organizing each relevant data point as it is collected from the patient.

As illustrated in Figure 17.1, it is recommended that previous suicide attempts be explored before the current crisis. The primary rationale is to reduce anxiety and any related resistance. Thoughtful examination of all past suicide attempts will likely take multiple sessions if the patient has an extensive history. Current risk, however, can be understood with good accuracy by exploring the "first" and "worst" of the attempts (Joiner, Steer, Brown, Beck, & Rudd, 2003), with the patient identifying "worst" subjectively. Rudd (2006) has recommended the use of an "extended evaluation" for those with chronic suicidal problems. When examining specific suicide attempts, I would encourage clinicians to consider the contextual factors (the acronym P-M-O-R is helpful for recall) illustrated in Table 17.3 (Rudd, 2012). Despite the lack of a specific formulaic approach, the questions provided in Table 17.3 provide considerable information to inform and formulate an estimate of objective suicide intent.

As indicated in Figure 17.1, after the exploration of a patient's suicidal history (either in full or abbreviated fashion) is accomplished, you can transition back to the current crisis. Following is a series of questions that provide for such a transition (Rudd, 2012):

• Can you tell me about the first time you ever thought about suicide [or attempted suicide]?
• Have you thought about or attempted suicide in the past year?
• Have you thought about or attempted suicide in the past few months?
• Now let's talk in more detail about the suicidal thoughts [or attempt] that brought you here today.

Once you have transitioned to the current episode, you need to assess the *specificity* of the patient's thinking. This includes the frequency, intensity, and duration of thoughts, along with questions about when and where, along with access to the stated method(s). As has been mentioned before, one indicator of intent is the specificity of the patient's thinking. Using the patient's own words (i.e., quoting him or her directly about suicidal thoughts) conveys that you will, and are, listening. It is also important to emphasize the need to question about multiple methods since patients will sometimes withhold their accessible method until questioned

Table 17.3 Contextual Factors of Past Attempts

• **P**recipitant? What triggered the crisis according to the patient? *What triggered your thinking about suicide/attempt? What was going on in your life at the time you made the suicide attempt?*
• **M**otivation for the attempt? Did he or she want to die? *What were your reasons for wanting to die? Did you want to die when you [method]?* What did they actually do? *Please tell me exactly what you did.* What was the patient's perception of lethality? *Did you think [method] would kill you?*
• **O**utcome? Was there any associated injury? If so, was medical care required? If required, did the patient follow-through and get recommended medical care? *Were you injured by the suicide attempt? Did you receive medical care? Why did you choose not to get medical care when it was recommended?* How did the patient end up accessing care? Was it initiated by the patient? Was it by random chance? *How did you get to the hospital? Did you call someone?* Did the patient take active steps to prevent discovery or rescue? *Did you take steps to try and prevent your discovery or rescue when you made the suicide attempt? Did you time the attempt or otherwise make it difficult for someone to find you?*
• **R**eaction? What was the patient's emotional reaction to surviving the suicide attempt? *How do you feel about surviving? Did you learn anything helpful about yourself [or others] from the previous attempt?*

Source: From Rudd (2012).

more thoroughly. Details about a patient's suicidal thinking can be captured with the following questions (Rudd, 2012):

- How are you thinking about killing yourself?
- Do you have access to [method]?
- Have you made arrangements or planned to get access to [method]?
- Have you thought about any other way to kill yourself? Ask this question until the patient says that no other methods have been considered.
- How often do you think about killing yourself? Once a day, more than once a day, once a week, monthly?
- You said you think about suicide every day. How many times a day?
- When you have these thoughts, how long do they last? A few seconds, minutes, or longer?
- On average how much time [day, week, or month] do you spend thinking about suicide?
- What exactly do you think about [or do] for that [period of time]?
- When you have these thoughts, how intense or severe are they? Can you rate them on a scale of 1 to 10, with one being "not severe at all" to 10 being "so severe that I will act on them."
- Have you thought about when you would kill yourself?
- Have you thought about where you would kill yourself?
- Have you thought about taking steps or timing your attempt to prevent anyone from finding or stopping you?
- Have you prepared for your death?
- Have you rehearsed or practiced your suicide?
- Do you have any intention of acting on your thoughts? Can you rate your intent on a scale of 1 to 10, with one being "no intent at all" to ten being "certain that you'll act on them as quickly as you can"?

A detailed assessment of suicidal thinking is important for a number of reasons, but in particular it is important for the clinician to recognize that the simple presence or absence of suicidal thinking is not a particularly good indicator of escalating risk. This is particularly true for multiple attempters and those experiencing chronic ideation. Fleeting, nonspecific suicidal thoughts with no associated intent (subjective or objective) are not unexpected and are not evidence of risk escalation beyond the individual's chronic baseline level. It is important to recognize that a patient could continue to experience suicidal thoughts on a daily basis but actually be making considerable progress, with no evidence of significant risk if the duration (and associated specificity) of the thoughts reduced from, say, several hours a day to less than a few minutes. Reduced duration frequently translates to reduced specificity, less severity, and lower intent, along with lower risk. This frequently parallels a drop in other symptom constellations as well.

It is important for all clinicians to recognize that such a detailed and specific assessment of suicidal thinking does not result in increased dysphoria, but rather it can actually reduce acute risk (cf. Gould et al., 2003). Such detailed questioning helps set the tone and expectations for all subsequent clinical interactions with the patient. It provides an implicit sanction, approval, and reinforcement for the patient to be honest and specific with the clinician. Detailed questioning is an intervention that facilitates a good therapeutic alliance. Most important, though, such an approach provides the details necessary to make accurate risk assessment decisions. An accurate understanding of suicide risk starts with a thorough and detailed understanding of the patient's suicidal thinking.

General Symptomatic Presentation, the Presence of Hopelessness, and Recognition of Warning Signs

The presence of Axis I and II symptoms are naturally a part of the general assessment framework (see Tables 17.1 and 17.2). Diagnostic comorbidity is a particular concern with suicidal individuals, with the co-occurrence of mood and anxiety disorders getting much of the attention (e.g., Joiner, 2005). Hopelessness has long been among the strongest risk factors for suicide and suicide attempts (Beck, Steer, Beck, & Newman, 1993). As is indicated in Table 17.2, it is recommended that clinicians actually go beyond the issue of Axis I diagnosis and ask patients to rate the severity of their anxiety, depressive symptoms, and hopelessness on a 1–10 scale. This provides an easy way to monitor variations in symptom severity from session to session and independent of diagnosis. Given the emergence of sleep disturbance as both an essential symptom (one that cuts across a range of Axis I diagnoses) in monitoring suicide risk and a potential warning sign, it is strongly recommended that clinicians assess sleep disturbance as part of any general assessment and also continue to monitor each and every session using a simple 1–10 rating scale (Ribeiro et al., 2012). It is important to mention that nightmares have been demonstrated to have particular potency for those struggling with posttraumatic stress disorder, including war veterans (Ribeiro et al., 2012). As with sleep disturbance, there are emerging data supporting the use of perceived burdensomeness (feeling that one is a burden on loved ones and they would be better off if the patient were dead) as an essential symptom in the suicide constellation (Joiner, 2005). An argument will soon be made in the empirical literature to include perceived burdensomeness as a warning sign for suicide, with the construct potentially representing a unique form of hopelessness.

A number of warning signs are included in the psychiatric symptom section of the assessment form in Table 17.2. All of those listed fall within the cluster of those formally recognized as suicide warning signs, including anger, agitation, a lack of purpose and meaning in life, and feeling trapped (Rudd, Berman et al., 2006). Simple rating scales are again recommended for monitoring purposes. Additional warning signs of active suicidal thoughts and associated preparation or rehearsal behaviors are included in the section covering the specific characteristics of suicidal thinking. As illustrated in Table 17.2, all of the warning signs are clustered in a separate section so the clinician can make a separate and distinctive assessment of the presence or absence of identifiable warning signs. The presence of warning signs has been linked to the emergence of imminent risk, a factor that will certainly impact risk formulation and subsequent clinical management.

The implications of general symptom severity and the presence or absence of warning signs for suicide risk vary depending on attempt history (e.g., a single attempter relative to a multiple attempter) and the presence of current suicidal thinking and markers of intent. As mentioned previously, it is critical to recognize that multiple attempters evidence chronic risk and that moderate (or above) acute risk can emerge even in the presence of less intense general psychiatric symptoms. Additionally, the presence of active warning signs for multiple attempters will most likely translate to at least moderate-risk but more likely a high-risk designation (see Table 17.2 and Joiner, Walker, Rudd, & Jobes, 1999).

The Question of Impulsivity

Consistent with the warning sign of "recklessness," an impulsive behavioral style warrants recognition and exploration in the process of conducting a suicide risk assessment. As illustrated in Table 17.2, it is recommended that the clinician consider both subjective statements from the

patient regarding impulsivity, along with observable behavioral markers of impulsivity (primarily evidence of aggressive behavior). It is also important to note that substance abuse is included in the impulsivity section, in recognition of the significant disinhibiting role of substance abuse and dependence. Overall, a patient with a pattern of emotion dysregulation (e.g., multiple attempters), coupled with an impulsive history and active suicidality, should be considered at heightened risk. It is worth mention that many, if not most, multiple attempters will exhibit periods of emotion dysregulation and impulsivity since both have been connected in clinical research (Joiner, 2005).

The Role of Protective Factors

There are a range of protective factors that need to be considered when assessing suicide risk, some with profound influence on subsequent risk formulation and clinical decision making. Arguably most important is accessible and available social support (Fridell, Johnsson, & Traskman-Bendz, 1996). Person-centered variables such as demonstrated problem-solving ability and emotional self-control also serve a prominent protective function (Rudd et al., 1996). Naturally, the ability to establish and maintain the therapeutic alliance is an essential protective factor (Michel & Jobes, 2010). Table 17.1 includes several other protective factors that have empirical support but are far more limited in nature (Rudd, 2006). From a risk formulation perspective, it is critical for clinicians to recognize that the management of high-risk suicidal patients does not necessarily have to occur in an inpatient setting, but if a decision is made to provide care in an outpatient setting, adequate protective factors need to be in place.

During the assessment interview, protective factors can be captured with the following questions (Rudd, 2012):

• Even though you've had a very difficult time, something has kept you going. What are your reasons for living?
• Are you hopeful about the future? Can you rate your hopefulness on a 1–10 scale (with 1 being hopeless and 10 being hopeful for the future)?
• What would need to happen to help you be more hopeful about the future?
• In the past, what has kept you going in difficult times like this?
• Who do you rely on during difficult times?
• Has treatment been effective for you in the past?

Some General Thoughts About Formulating Risk

As is illustrated in Table 17.2, a simple continuum of risk is recommended, one that ranges from mild to moderate to high. The existing empirical foundation simply does not support more complex and precise distinctions. As a general rule, as symptom severity and complexity increase, so do suicide intent, the emergence of warning signs, and the presence of associated suicidal behaviors (e.g., preparation, rehearsal, or attempts). Mild risk is characterized by mild psychiatric symptoms and suicidal thinking with no associated intent or behaviors. There certainly are other elements, but these are paramount. Moderate risk emerges as symptoms escalate, warning signs start to emerge, and there is evidence of subjective (but not objective) intent. Once there is objective evidence of suicide intent (i.e., preparation and rehearsal) it is more likely that a high-risk designation will be used. High risk is characterized by four essential elements, including serious psychiatric symptoms, the presence of active intent (subjective or objective), the presence of warning signs, and limited protective factors. As should be evident, the differentiation across categories is a function of two primary elements: active intent (manifest either subjectively or objectively) and the presence of warning signs. Overall, symptom severity will increase across the three risk categories, but not always. It is important to point out that a designation of high risk does not mean mandatory hospitalization. When adequate protective factors are in place and active intent is minimized by removal of access to weapons and the presence of an acceptable crisis response or safety plan, outpatient management is certainly possible and used with great frequency.

Common Elements of Treatments That Work to Guide the Assessment and Management Process

In reviewing the treatment protocols for the handful of interventions found effective for suicidality, a cluster of "common elements" (i.e., techniques, clinical management strategies, and targeted interventions) emerge and provide the empirical foundation for the immediate clinical management of patients at risk for suicide (Rudd, Trotter, & Williams, 2008). Following is a summary of identified common elements of treatments that work. The list can arguably be described as "six things that can save lives in clinical practice with suicidal patients." The reason these elements are included is because these six things can inform the assessment process, allowing the clinician to lay a solid foundation for ongoing care.

AN EASY-TO-UNDERSTAND MODEL OF SUICIDALITY

All of the treatments have clearly articulated, well-defined, and understandable theoretical models that are embedded in empirical research. The models are simple, straightforward, and easily understood by the patient. The theoretical models also have common elements, as might be expected for cognitive-behavioral-therapy-oriented treatments. They all identify cognitions, emotional processing, and associated behavioral responses as critical to understanding motivation to die, associated distress (and symptoms), and ultimately changing the suicidal process. As noted next, effective models explain suicidality as the function of poor skill development secondary to developmental issues and related trauma. Patients find the models easy to understand, distilling them down to thoughts, feelings, and behaviors that are associated with suicide risk and hopelessness. The ability to diagram the relationship for the patient may well facilitate understanding, the collaborative nature of care, and eventual compliance. All of this starts during the initial assessment process and can easily be offered as a general summation at the end of the session. For example, one way of introducing this summation could be: "Let's talk about how we might explain why you tried to kill yourself and what we would do in treatment to target the problems."

A FOCUS ON TREATMENT COMPLIANCE

Effective treatments target treatment compliance in a specific and consistent fashion. More specifically, all had specific interventions and techniques that targeted poor compliance and motivation for treatment. When a patient was disengaged, noncompliant, and not participating in care, that very dynamic became the primary focus of treatment. Treatment is only effective if the patient is active, involved, and invested. It is clear from effective treatments that compliance with care needs to be a central and primary focus, with clear plans about "what to do" if noncompliance emerges. Just as suicidal behavior needs to be a primary target, motivation and investment in care are important. When motivation, investment, and involvement drop, they need to become a primary treatment target until effectively resolved. Often times, noncompliance is simply a function of inadequate skills on the part of the patient. From an assessment perspective, noncompliance can be viewed as evidence of hopelessness and related intent to die.

TARGETING IDENTIFIABLE SKILLS

Consistent with easy-to-understand clinical models of suicidality driving the treatment process, effective treatments target identifiable skill sets (e.g., emotion regulation, anger management, problem solving, interpersonal relationships, cognitive distortions). In these treatments, patients understood what was "wrong" and "what to do about it" in order to reduce suicidal thinking and behaviors. Patients also had the opportunity to practice and build skill sets over time, with a long-term goal of skill generalization. The issue of poor coping skills is certainly a focal point during the assessment process.

PATIENTS TAKE PERSONAL RESPONSIBILITY FOR TREATMENT

Consistent with each of the aforementioned points, effective treatments emphasize self-reliance, self-awareness, self-control, and issues of personal responsibility. Effective treatments are clear in the goal that if patients developed appropriate skills, the distress and upset tied to early events would diminish, as would associated suicidal urges. Consistent with this goal, patients assumed a considerable degree of personal responsibility for their care, including crisis management and individual safety (i.e., means restriction). Again, this is consistent with the issue of improved compliance and motivation for care. Although there are a range of models available for facilitating compliance and crisis management, clinicians should consider use of the "commitment to treatment agreement" (CTA) and the crisis response plan (CRP) (Rudd, Mandrusiak, & Joiner, 2006). An effective assessment will hopefully lead to the patient being willing to make a commitment to treatment agreement, one that includes a crisis response plan.

GUARANTEEING EASY ACCESS TO CRISIS AND EMERGENCY SERVICES

Effective treatments emphasize the importance of crisis management and access to available emergency services during and after treatment, with a clear plan of action being identified. Additionally, effective treatments more often than not dedicate time to practicing the skill sets necessary to effective crisis management, with patients learning to identify what characterizes a "crisis or emergency," using a "safety" or "crisis management plan," and learning to use these services in judicious and appropriate fashion. Every assessment for suicide risk should end with the delineation of a crisis response or safety plan.

MAKING THINGS EASY BY WRITING

Effective treatments consistently document what happens in treatment, from the initial model of suicidality, to the commitment to treatment agreement, to the crisis response plan, along with session-by-session notes. Suicidal patients are highly distressed and, more often than not, function at nonoptimal levels, all of which impairs cognitive processing. An easy and effective solution is to make frequent and ready use of writing in treatment. The process of documenting a treatment journal for patients can start at the initial assessment, providing a clear and understandable model for the patient to understand his or her suicidality, along with a commitment to a treatment agreement and crisis response plan.

Concluding Thoughts

There is little debate that the assessment and management of suicide risk are at the top of the list of clinical challenges. The use of a consistent and empirically supported approach, however, not only reduces clinician anxiety and apprehension but also leads to improved clinical effectiveness. This chapter includes a general framework for the assessment process, one informed by common elements of treatments that work as well as identified core competencies, and one that includes suicide warning signs. A simple mild, moderate, and high designation is recommended. At the heart of risk formulation is an accurate understanding of suicide intent and recognition of observable warning signs. Although there is not a precise and formulaic approach available, some broad guidelines for decision making are offered.

References

American Psychiatric Association. (2003). *Practice guideline for the assessment and treatment of patients with suicidal behaviors*. Arlington, VA: Author.

Beck, A. T., Steer, R. A., Beck, J. S., & Newman, C. F. (1993). Hopelessness, depression, suicidal ideation, and clinical diagnosis of depression. *Suicide and Life Threatening Behavior*, *23*, 139–145.

Buzan, R. D., & Weissberg, M. P. (1992). Suicide: Risk factors and prevention in medical practice. *Annual Review of Medicine*, *43*, 37–46.

Chemtob, C., Hamada, R., Bauer, G., Torigoe, R., & Kinney, B. (1988). Patient suicide: Frequency and impact on psychologists. *Professional Psychology: Research and Practice*, *19*, 416–420.

Fridell, E., Johnsson, O. A., & Traskman-Bendz, L. (1996). A 5-year follow-up study of suicide attempts. *Acta Psychiatrica Scandinavica, 93*, 151–157.

Gould, M. S., Greenberg, T., Velting, D. M., & Shaffer, D. (2003). Youth suicide risk and preventive interventions: A review of the past 10 years. *Journal of the American Academy of Child and Adolescent Psychiatry, 42*, 386–405.

Hendin, H., Maltsberger, J. T., Lipschitz, A., Haas, A. P., & Kyle, J. (2001). Recognizing and responding to a suicide crisis. *Suicide and Life Threatening Behavior, 31*, 115–128.

Joiner, T. E. (2005). *Why people die by suicide.* Cambridge, MA: Harvard University Press.

Joiner, T. E., Steer, R. A., Brown, G., Beck, A. T., & Rudd, M. D. (2003). Worst point suicidal plans: A dimension of suicidality predictive of past suicide attempts and eventual death by suicide. *Behavior Research and Therapy, 41*, 1469–1480.

Joiner, T., Walker, R., Rudd, M., & Jobes, D. (1999). Scientizing and routinizing the assessment of suicidality in outpatient practice. *Professional Psychology: Research and Practice, 30*(5), 447–454.

Maris, R. W., Berman, A. L., Maltsberger, J. T., & Yufit, R. (1992). *Assessment and prediction of suicide.* NewYork, NY: Gulford Press.

McAdams, C. R., & Foster, V. A. (2000). Client suicide: Its frequency and impact on counselors. *Journal of Mental Health Counseling, 22*, 107–121.

Michel, K., & Jobes, D. A. (2010). *Building a therapeutic relationship with the suicidal patient.* Washington, DC: American Psychological Association.

Nock, M. K. (2009). *Understanding non-suicidal self-injury: Origins, assessment and treatment.* Washington, DC: American Psychological Association.

Pope, K., & Tabachnick, B. (1993). Therapists' anger, hate, fear, and sexual feelings: National survey of therapist responses, client characteristics, critical events, formal complaints, and training. *Professional Psychology: Research and Practice, 24*, 142–152.

Ribeiro, J. D., Pease, J. L., Gutierrez, P. M., Silva, C., Bernert, R. A., Rudd, M. D., & Joiner, T. E. (2012). Sleep problems outperform depression and hopelessness as cross-sectional and longitudinal predictors of suicidal ideation and behavior in young adults in the military. *Journal of Affective Disorders, 136*(3), 743–750.

Rudd, M. D. (2006). *Assessment and management of suicide risk.* Sarasota, FL: Professional Resource Press.

Rudd, M. D. (2012). The clinical risk assessment interview. In R. Simon & R. E. Hales (Eds.), *The APP textbook of suicide assessment and management* (2nd ed., pp. 57–74). Washington, DC: American Psychiatric Publishing.

Rudd, M. D., Berman, L., Joiner, T. E., Nock, M. K, Silverman, M., Mandrusiak, M., ... Witte, B. S. (2006). Warning signs for suicide: Theory, research, and clinical application. *Suicide and Life-Threatening Behavior, 36*(3), 255.

Rudd, M. D., Cukrowicz, K. C., & Bryan, C. J. (2008). Core competencies in suicide risk assessment and management: Implications for supervision. *Training and Education in Professional Psychology, 2*, 219–228.

Rudd, M.D., Joiner, T.E., & Rajab, M.H. (1996). The relationships between suicide ideators, attempters, and multiple attempters in a young adults sample. *Journal of Abnormal Psychology, 105*(4), 541–550.

Rudd, M. D., Joiner, T. E., & Rajab, M. H. (2004). *Treating suicidal behavior: An effective time limited approach* (2nd ed.). New York, NY: Guilford Press.

Rudd, M. D., Mandrusiak, M., & Joiner, T. E. (2006). The case against no-suicide contracts: The Commitment to Treatment statement as an alternative for clinical practice. *Journal of Clinical Psychology, 62*(2), 243–251.

Rudd, M. D., Trotter, D., & Williams, B. (2008). Psychological treatments for suicidal behavior: What are the common elements of treatments that work? In D. Wasserman (Ed.), *Oxford textbook of suicidology* (pp. 427–438). Oxford, UK: Oxford University Press.

Suicide Prevention Resource Center. (2006). *Core competencies in the assessment and management of suicidality.* Newton, MA: Author.

Wenzel, A., Brown, G., & Beck, A. T. (2008). *Cognitive therapy for suicidal patients: Scientific and clinical applications.* Washington, DC: American Psychological Association.

Assessment of Nonsuicidal Self-Injury

E. David Klonsky *and* Stephen P. Lewis

Abstract

This chapter provides guidance regarding the assessment of nonsuicidal self-injury (NSSI). Assessors are encouraged to enhance rapport through "respectful curiosity" and a "low-key, dispassionate demeanor." The assessment should cover several aspects of NSSI, including personal history of NSSI (e.g., methods, frequency, medical severity), social history of NSSI (e.g., roles of peers, family members), the contextual features (e.g., environmental, cognitive, affective, biological factors), concomitant risky behaviors (e.g., substance use), the functions of NSSI (e.g., affect regulation, other intrapersonal and social functions), and suicide risk. When feasible, assessors should utilize valid instruments to aid in the assessment of NSSI. Valid omnibus measures include the Suicide Attempt Self-Injury Interview (SASII; Linehan, Comtois, Brown, Heard, & Wagner, 2006) and the Self-Injurious Thoughts and Behaviors Interview (SITBI; Nock, Joiner, Gordon, Lloyd-Richardson, & Prinstein, 2006). Valid functional measures include the Functional Assessment of Self-Mutilation (FASM; Lloyd-Richardson, Kelley, & Hope, 1997) and the Inventory of Statements About Self-Injury (ISAS; Klonsky & Glenn, 2009).

Key Words: nonsuicidal self-injury, self-harm, assessment, measurement, interview, case formulation, risk assessment

Accurate and comprehensive assessment is critical in both empirical and clinical domains. For researchers, an accurate description of the behavior of interest plays a central role in the advancement of theory and ensures consistency in terms used, thus serving as a guide for future empirical endeavors. Clinically, a thorough assessment is the vehicle through which one develops a working case formulation, which is essential for informing diagnostic and treatment decision making. In this chapter, we discuss, and offer recommendations about, the assessment of nonsuicidal self-injury (NSSI). Specifically, we address the art of interacting with individuals who engage in NSSI, highlight features and attributes involved in the onset and maintenance of NSSI, and provide an extensive review of extant NSSI assessment measures.

The information presented in this chapter should be useful for a wide audience, including, but not limited to, researchers, treatment professionals, and clinicians in training.

A Preliminary Comment

For many, NSSI is a counterintuitive behavior. In the course of everyday life people go to great lengths to avoid pain and injury. This instinct is evidenced by thriving markets for ibuprofen, novocaine, helmets, "slippery when wet" signs, and countless other products and services meant to prevent and alleviate pain and injury. Unfortunately, people often react judgmentally toward behaviors that are contrary to avoiding injury and thus difficult to understand. Stigma against, and misunderstanding about, NSSI is not uncommon and may render people who self-injure the target of strong reactions such as shock, disgust, or blame. People who injure themselves are often judged to be manipulative, severely impaired, unreasonable, or assigned one of many other negative attributions. However, extensive research has revealed that NSSI typically serves practical functions such as the quick and efficient alleviation of overwhelming negative emotions (Klonsky, 2007), and it can be performed by intelligent and high-functioning people (Whitlock, Eckenrode, & Silverman, 2006). Therefore, accurate assessment of NSSI requires, and deserves, an open and nonjudgmental mind as much as methods of the highest reliability and validity.

Limits of Confidentiality

A tricky issue that emerges when assessing for NSSI is when should an individual's level of risk be considered a reason to breach confidentiality? Although confidentiality can be broken when the assessor believes that a client is at imminent and serious risk to himself or herself, determining the level of risk for someone who self-injures is difficult. As discussed later in this chapter, NSSI is distinct from suicide. However, both behaviors involve an element of risk to self, and research suggests that having a history of self-injury increases the risk for suicide (e.g., Muehlenkamp & Gutierrez, 2007). Consequently, the assessor or therapist may have trouble determining when breaking confidentiality is necessary to keep a client safe. There also may be concern that breaking confidentiality, especially when unwarranted, might harm rapport and therapeutic alliance.

Of course, when assessing for NSSI, it is important, at the outset, to inform individuals of *all* limits of confidentiality and, in this regard, to be aware of state or provincial laws to which this might relate (e.g., age of consent). Making these limits clear from the beginning of the assessment process can go a long way when working with an individual who self-injures and when working through instances in which breaking confidentiality may be necessary. In addition to ascertaining one's level of current suicidality, there are several other factors to take into account that may help in determining whether breaking confidentiality is warranted. These include, but are certainly not limited to, the age of the client (which, may be especially relevant when working with a young person and his or her family); the degree of injury typically and most recently incurred by the individual; the preference of the individual being assessed; and determining

the role of important others in the assessment and treatment process (e.g., how a parent can help keep a young person safe and support a young person toward wellness). Should confidentiality have to be broken, it is helpful for the person being assessed to play an active role in discussions about this process. Indeed, the issue of confidentiality may be particularly relevant when working with adolescents, as parents often voice concern over their child and want to know about behaviors that may threaten their safety. Miller, Rathus, and Linehan (2007) provide an excellent set of guidelines that can help therapists working with young people who engage in NSSI to navigate these tricky issues.

The Importance of Good Rapport

Establishing a strong and collaborative rapport with individuals who self-injure is conducive to (a) gathering important information that informs the case formulation and (b) effectively managing the behavior. Many who self-injure are cognizant that an act of NSSI can evoke varying reactions from those in their lives; unfortunately, many of these reactions are negative. As such, it is not uncommon for individuals who self-injure to be concerned that the mental health professional conducting the assessment will also react negatively and that they will be left feeling misunderstood, invalidated, and stigmatized. Therefore, it is important for the individual conducting the assessment to be aware of, and manage, his or her own reactions when working with an individual who self-injures. This will be critical to developing and maintaining a strong rapport and collaborative alliance with the individual being assessed. In the absence of good rapport, one may be reticent to disclose, or may even alter, information about one's NSSI. For example, our clinical experience has illustrated that individuals who self-injure may minimize the frequency or severity of the behavior or offer socially acceptable reasons for their NSSI, which may not entirely reflect their true reasons for the behavior.

Dr. Barry Walsh, a noted researcher and treatment expert in the field of NSSI, has highlighted the importance of good rapport when working with individuals who engage in NSSI. Specifically, Dr. Walsh (2012) discusses the importance of using a "low-key, dispassionate demeanor" (p. 84) when working with an individual who engages in NSSI—in both assessment and treatment contexts. Other approaches may be problematic. For example, an interview style that suggests negative feelings (e.g., disappointment, disapproval) about

NSSI on the part of the assessor, or one that conveys a heightened interest in the behavior, may be disconcerting to the individual being assessed. It is also important for the individual conducting the assessment to not offer excessive expressions of support as it may be perceived as pardoning or even encouraging NSSI. A calm, low-key, yet compassionate approach represents a useful middle ground when facilitating rapport. Related to this, a tone that conveys a "respectful curiosity" (Kettlewell, 1999) is recommended. In this approach, the assessor conveys a genuine interest in understanding an individual's history and experience of NSSI, while maintaining a nonjudgmental, deferential demeanor—a view that is detailed by Walsh (2012, 2007).

Domains of Interest
History of Nonsuicidal Self-Injury

An early but necessary step in assessing NSSI involves collecting information about one's history of the behavior. Among some of the key variables to consider are the method(s) of NSSI used by the individual (e.g., cutting, burning, scratching, hitting), the frequency of the behavior, where on the body the injury/injuries occur (e.g., arms, shoulders, thighs, stomach), the age of onset, and the timing of the most recent episode. In line with this, it is important to determine the medical severity of the injuries, including the degree of bleeding and laceration or bruising (if any), how frequently one's injuries required home care (e.g., bandages, attention), whether (and, if so, how frequently) professional medical treatment has been needed (e.g., stitches, burn treatment), how often the individual sought help from emergency services (regardless of wound severity), and how often NSSI has caused more tissue damage than initially intended. Alongside these factors, the duration and number of wounds occurring within an episode of NSSI also should be assessed. Finally, it also will be important to delineate the nature and severity of "typical" instances of NSSI, "recent" instances, and the most "severe" instance.

In addition to gathering information about the individual's personal history of NSSI, it is also important to elicit whether important others in the life of the individual also have engaged in NSSI. This includes a family and social history of the behavior. In most clinical assessments, asking about one's family history regarding the variable of interest is a critical part of understanding one's current and future risk for that outcome. For example, it is

widely recognized that having a family history of suicide confers a higher risk for death by suicide. Understanding one's family history of NSSI and of suicide may therefore be helpful in formulating a case and enhancing the quality and comprehensiveness of the risk assessment.

Furthermore, it also may be useful to understand one's social history of NSSI. Doing so may shed light on the contexts in which self-injury occurs (as described later) but also may enhance the understanding of what contributes to NSSI. There is now sufficient evidence to suggest that NSSI sometimes occurs as a product of peer influence. This may be particularly relevant when working with adolescents. A growing set of reports from youth inpatient settings have indicated that rates of NSSI can increase by virtue of having even one young person in that setting who engages in NSSI (e.g., Ghaziuddin, Tsa, Naylor, & Ghaziudddin, 1992; Rosen & Walsh, 1989; Taiminen, Kallio-Soukainen, Nokso-Kovisto, Kaljonen, & Helenius, 1998). Social contagion for NSSI also has been reported in school settings (e.g., Hawton, Rodham, & Evans, 2006; Walsh, 2012), although future research is needed to better understand this phenomenon in schools and other non-inpatient settings. Peer influence on NSSI also may be exacerbated via the Internet, where it is widely and actively discussed (Lewis, Heath, Michal, & Duggan, 2012). These discussions involve the normalization of NSSI as well as youth sharing methods of NSSI with one another (Lewis et al., 2012; Whitlock, Powers, & Eckenrode, 2006; Whitlock, Purgington & Gershkovich, 2009). Risks including NSSI normalization and reinforcement are also salient concerns on popular video-sharing Web sites, such as YouTube, in which graphic NSSI imagery is presented in videos with informational or melancholic/hopeless messages that are frequently and favorably viewed (Lewis, Heath, St. Denis, & Noble, 2011). Given the Internet's ubiquity and accessibility, further investigation is needed to understand its benefits and risks in relation to NSSI. To address potentially problematic online NSSI activity, please consult a review by Lewis and colleagues (2012), who offer guidelines in this regard. In addition, identifying whether NSSI occurs with others (or has been influenced by others) is an important step in assessment— particularly when working with youth. Prinstein and colleagues (2009) provide an excellent review of interpersonal models of NSSI and discuss the aspect of a self-injury contagion within the framework of peer influence and health risk behaviors.

Context

Contextual factors involved in NSSI represent another important consideration in the assessment of NSSI. These include environmental, cognitive, affective, and biological variables—all of which can enhance the understanding of what is involved in the genesis, sustenance, and desistance of NSSI.

ENVIRONMENT

An infinite number of environmental factors can be involved in NSSI—and all may play varying temporal roles before, during, and after the behavior occurs. Indeed, life events and situations related to friends, family, significant others, work, and school can all relate to NSSI in varying but important ways. For example, NSSI may occur pursuant to poor or unsatisfactory academic performance or an interpersonal dispute with a family member, close friend, or romantic partner. Acts of NSSI also can be enacted alone and kept from others, or performed with others (e.g., with two or more friends in a school bathroom), and reactions from others following an act of NSSI can be either favorable or unfavorable. Given the variance in environmental factors across episodes of NSSI, it is critical to understand how NSSI operates at the individual level.

COGNITIONS

Similar to environmental factors, cognitions are infinite in number and occur before, during, and after NSSI. Understanding the types of thoughts associated with NSSI is key for understanding why an individual self-injures. Examples of thoughts experienced by those who self-injure come from Walsh (2006) and may include "only cutting will do the job" (p. 102), "this is too much to bear" (p. 102), "I deserve this pain" (p. 103), "cutting myself relieves distress better than anything else" (p. 103), "he's going to break up with me again...life sucks.... I might as well hurt myself because what's the use?" (p. 103), and "I'm all alone; I have no friends" (p. 114). The thoughts one has about NSSI influence the likelihood that the behavior will continue. As such, assessing aspects of NSSI-related thoughts, such as their content (e.g., distorted nature, prominent themes such as hopelessness, helplessness, or self-deprecation), frequency, and degree of conviction (i.e., how much the individual believes the thought to be true) will be important for assessment

and may be especially salient when developing a plan for intervention (Walsh, 2012).

In addition to identifying which thoughts occur in the context of NSSI, it also may be useful to identify thoughts about the behavior itself. According to social-cognitive models of self-harm, which includes NSSI as well as acts not typically considered NSSI (e.g., overdosing), one's attitudes toward the behavior may predict the intent to harm oneself in the future (O'Connor & Armitage, 2003; O'Connor, Armitage, & Gray, 2006). Specifically, more favorable attitudes toward self-harm (e.g., viewing it as useful or helpful) have been found to be associated with a stronger intent to engage in harming oneself again in the future (O'Connor & Armitage, 2003; O'Connor et al., 2006) and may predict future suicidality (thoughts and behavior) (O'Connor et al., 2006). More recent findings, from other research examining NSSI in young adults, suggest that individuals with a history of self-harm endorse favorable attitudes toward NSSI (including cutting, hitting, and burning) and toward overdosing with the intent to die. Findings further indicate that more favorable attitudes toward all of these behaviors predict the intent to engage in future self-harm (Lewis, Rosenrot, & Santor, 2011).

Styles of thinking also have been implicated in NSSI (Selby, Anestis, & Joiner, 2008). It has been proposed that higher degrees of ruminative thought pertaining to one's negative emotional experiences amplify the degree of negative affect, which, in turn, may lead to NSSI as a means of reducing the negative affect. Although this nascent area requires further research, it may be useful, in some cases, to assess an individual's type of thinking style (e.g., rumination) in tandem with other aspects of cognition in the context of NSSI. Doing so may lead to a greater understanding of what contributes to NSSI and why, for some, it is repeated over time.

AFFECT

Individual affective experiences (i.e., emotions or feelings) occurring prior to, during, or after engaging in NSSI represent another important domain to assess. Consistent with current conceptualizations of NSSI as a means by which to avoid or assuage the experience of negative affect (e.g., Chapman, Gratz, & Brown, 2006), elucidating one's emotions at these different points in time is critical to properly manage NSSI. Additionally, identifying these feelings is a vital part of understanding the motives one has for NSSI (Klonsky, 2007). Among some of the primary emotions to assess are anger (self- and other-directed), anxiety/stress, sadness/ low mood, frustration, guilt, shame, disgust, emptiness (including emotional numbness), hopelessness, and loneliness. Typically, at least some of these will occur in the context of NSSI. Some emotional experiences, such as shame and guilt, can both precede and follow NSSI. In accord with this latter point, it is important to determine the emotions one feels after NSSI (e.g., feelings of calmness, relief, or satisfaction), which may help the assessor to understand why the behavior is repeated or "works" for the individual engaging in NSSI. Finally, some individuals feel suicidal before or after engaging in self-injury. Therefore, it is incumbent on the person conducting the assessment to determine the degree of association between NSSI and risk for suicide.

A final note regarding the assessment of affect in the context of NSSI merits discussion. Specifically, in addition to identifying the content of one's emotional experience (that is, the type of emotions experienced by the individual self-injuring), it also is important to understand one's emotional or affective style—that is, the frequency, intensity, and reactivity of emotions. Reasons for this come from advances in the study of NSSI, which underscore the role of affect dysregulation in the NSSI behavior (e.g., Chapman et al., 2006). Various features of emotion that pertain to how one manages negative affect have been implicated in NSSI. For instance, emotional reactivity, or one's sensitivity to, and experienced intensity and persistence of, negative emotion, has been found to associate with self-injurious thoughts and behavior (Nock, Wedig, Holmberg, & Hooley, 2008); related to this, individuals who self-injure report spending more time and effort suppressing negative emotions in their daily lives (Najmi, Wegner, & Nock, 2007). Individuals with a history of NSSI wish to escape stressful tasks sooner than individuals with no such history, which further suggests a difficulty in either regulating or experiencing negative emotions (Nock & Mendes, 2008). As discussed earlier, the experience of intense negative affect in conjunction with rumination about these affective experiences also may be important to understand when assessing NSSI (Selby et al., 2008)—a sentiment endorsed by other prominent researchers in the field (e.g., Nock, 2009). In short, understanding one's difficulty with regulating his or her moods may be important for understanding the functions NSSI serves for an individual and for forming an effective treatment plan (e.g., developing more adaptive affect regulation strategies).

BIOLOGICAL FACTORS

Biological and physiological factors also play a role in NSSI. These may include changes in one's biochemistry that may result from engaging in specific actions, ingesting certain substances, or the presence of medical conditions. A key consideration is the role of substance use/abuse in the context of NSSI. In some cases, it may be that the substances (including alcohol, marijuana, heroin, cocaine) are used to lower one's inhibitions, rendering NSSI more likely to occur. In others, it may be that substances are used to dampen the pain associated with NSSI, which, in turn, exacerbates the risk for more severe injuries (e.g., greater tissue damage). If the individual is self-injuring and using substances, it will be important to determine the functions provided by each (i.e., NSSI and substance use may or may not occur in similar contexts, and they may or may not have similar motivations). Although substance use/abuse is an important consideration in the context of a thorough NSSI assessment, there are other relevant biological factors to assess as well. These include insomnia, fatigue, illness, thyroid abnormalities, and premenstrual syndrome, all of which may increase one's vulnerability to stress and thereby elevate the risk for NSSI.

Functions

Identifying the functions of NSSI, which are also known as motives or reasons for the behavior, is an essential part of understanding why people self-injure. As described earlier, contextual factors involved in NSSI can shed light on these functions. The import of contextual variables notwithstanding, it is useful to directly assess functions as well. A review of the literature suggests two general functions for NSSI, those that are (1) automatic or intrapersonal, and those that are (2) social or interpersonal (Klonsky & Glenn, 2009; Nock & Prinstein, 2004, 2005). Intrapersonal functions pertain to reinforcement by oneself (e.g., NSSI performed to assuage negative affect), whereas social functions pertain to reinforcement by others (e.g., NSSI performed to influence and/or elicit desired behaviors from others).

Although NSSI functions can be broadly conceptualized as either intrapersonal or social, subsumed under each general category are a number of more discrete functions, which warrant assessment (Klonsky, 2007; Klonsky & Glenn, 2009). Among some of the more common intrapersonal functions are affect regulation (i.e., alleviating acute negative affect or emotional intensity), self-punishment (i.e., directing anger or punishment at oneself), antidissociation (i.e., interrupting periods of depersonalization or dissociation such as feeling unreal or numb), and antisuicide (i.e., avoiding or coping with suicidal thoughts). Among some of the more common social functions are interpersonal influence (i.e., shaping others' behavior), peer bonding (i.e., developing or strengthening attachments with friends), and autonomy (i.e., asserting one's independence from others). From a clinical perspective, the accurate assessment of these functions can be crucial when developing a case formulation and treatment plan. Additionally, it also may be important to determine which motives were achieved in terms of yielding an a priori desired outcome (e.g., to reduce tension). For example, if NSSI was performed to reduce acute negative affect, NSSI is more likely to be performed again if this aim was achieved (Klonsky, 2009; Lewis & Santor, 2010). We provide a summary of measures used to assess NSSI functions later in the chapter.

Concomitant Maladaptive Behavior

In line with understanding whether an individual is using substances at the time of NSSI, assessing for the occurrence of other behaviors may be useful for a few reasons. First, it is often the case that NSSI occurs alongside other risky behaviors, such as alcohol and drug abuse (e.g., Hilt, Nock, Lloyd-Richardson, & Prinstein, 2008) and other acts, such as disordered eating behaviors (e.g., Solano, Fernandez-Aranda, Aitken, Lopez, & Vallejo, 2005; Ross, Heath, & Toste, 2009), among others. Knowing what other behaviors occur (in addition to NSSI) can add valuable information to the assessment and corresponding case formulation. Second, it has been suggested that individuals engage in various behaviors, including NSSI and those listed earlier, for similar purposes (Chapman et al., 2006; Selby et al., 2008); the overlap between these behaviors and their underlying function has been highlighted as an important area for future study (Nock, 2009). If several of these behaviors are used to serve similar functions, this would indicate a similar underlying mechanism across these behaviors and further suggest that treatment for each can be implemented in parallel. Alternatively, differences in functions for these types of behaviors would highlight the need for future research and unique treatment approaches to address individual behaviors. Therefore, although it is still unclear how these behaviors relate and how they may be distinct, the assessor may find it useful to understand both whether the individual is engaging in other behaviors and whether these acts are serving similar or different functions.

Suicidality

The relation between self-injury and suicide is complex. On the one hand, NSSI and attempted suicide are distinct behaviors. The fundamental differences between the two lie in the intent and medical severity of the acts. In contrast to NSSI, suicide attempts are performed with intent to die and typically lead to more severe bodily damage. On the other hand, NSSI and suicidality are not completely unrelated. Many individuals who engage in NSSI report having suicidal thoughts and may be at risk for suicide over time. Recent research suggests that people with histories of NSSI are at increased risk for both having and acting upon suicidal thoughts (Klonsky, May, & Glenn, 2013).

In this way, assessment of suicide is a vital piece of any assessment of self-injury. Results from recent research also highlight aspects of NSSI that may help guide clinical decision making and further elucidate one's risk for suicide. Features of NSSI that may indicate elevated suicide risk include having a longer standing history of NSSI, NSSI using multiple methods, a lack of experienced pain at the time of NSSI, and greater endorsement of intrapersonal functions for NSSI (Klonsky & Glenn, 2009; Nock et al., 2006). One's social context during NSSI is also important to understanding suicide risk. Specifically, those who self-injure in isolation report more suicidal thinking, plans, and attempts compared to those who occasionally or frequently self-injure in the presence of others (e.g., friends) (Glenn & Klonsky, 2009). Other variables that predict suicidality among those who self-injure include depression, hopelessness, and impulsivity (Dougherty et al., 2009). Collectively, these points accentuate the need for a suicide risk assessment alongside an assessment for NSSI, as well as assessment of NSSI-specific features that indicate an elevated suicide risk.

Other Domains of Interest

In addition to the aforementioned research, recent research findings have highlighted a number of other factors that might be important assessment considerations. One such variable is the degree of pain experienced during NSSI. Specifically, individuals who experience lower levels of pain when they self-injure have been found to be at a greater risk for inflicting more severe tissue damage and for attempting suicide (Nock, Joiner, Gordon, Lloyd-Richardson, & Prinstein, 2006). Additionally, it may be important to determine the interval of time between the urge to self-injure and the act of NSSI. Indeed, some people may engage in NSSI almost immediately following the urge to injure, whereas others may wait hours (Klonsky & Olino, 2008). Assessing the time that typically elapses between self-injurious urge and act may be particularly relevant in treatment contexts. Longer durations between NSSI urges and acts may indicate more of an opportunity for individuals to implement strategies that can help to avoid and guard against engagement in NSSI (Klonsky & Glenn, 2008).

Finally, since there are many methods used by individuals to self-injure, it is useful to assess the types of implement(s) or tool(s) used (e.g., scissors, pocket knife). It is also important to determine the accessibility of these implements preceding acts of NSSI as some tools might be more readily and routinely available, which might increase the likelihood of NSSI occurring in certain contexts. Some individuals use the same implement during each episode (e.g., razor blade kept on the second shelf of the medicine cabinet). Others use a variety of tools, and this may depend on what is accessible in the moment (e.g., paper clip, glass shard, razor blade, scissors, fingernail, kitchen knife). Thus, understanding (1) what tools are used and (2) how accessible these tools are may be particularly useful in terms of reducing one's access to the means of NSSI, which in turn may help to reduce the frequency or occurrence of the behavior (Klonsky & Glenn, 2008). Sometimes treatment might involve having clients take the practical step of removing their access to the implement of choice. However, this will often depend on the readiness of the client and the nature of his or her NSSI (e.g., method, frequency, level, and type of impulsivity).

Assessment Instruments

Although there is general agreement regarding the importance of assessing the domains described earlier, finding standardized methods for conducting the assessment is less straightforward. Only a handful of NSSI measures have been developed and their psychometric properties are not as well established as those for measures of suicidality. Next we describe four types of instruments: omnibus, functional, behavioral, and brief/screening measures. Please refer to Table 18.1 for a summary of each instrument's psychometric properties; the content assessed by each measure is summarized in Table 18.2.

Omnibus Measures

Omnibus instruments assess several NSSI domains, rendering them more comprehensive compared to other measures. Next, we describe two omnibus instruments that stand out due to their breadth and strong psychometric properties.

The first instrument we discuss is the Suicide Attempt Self-Injury Interview (SASII; Linehan, Comtois, Brown, Heard, & Wagner, 2006), a 31-item instrument, which, unlike most NSSI measures, adopts an interview format. The SASII assesses all intentional, nonfatal acts that result in injury to the self, and it clearly delineates those acts with suicidal intent from those without suicidal intent. Moreover, its assessment of NSSI is very thorough. Specifically, within each episode of self-injury assessed, the SASII assesses an expansive list of important areas related to NSSI, including context, frequency, lethality, topography, intent, outcome expectations, resulting physical condition, medical treatment received, antecedent events, planning/preparation, contextual and behavioral factors, and functional outcomes.

An obvious advantage of the SASII is the rich information it yields about each act of NSSI. This strength, however, can make the SASII time consuming when assessing a respondent with a long-standing and extensive history of NSSI. Therefore, a short form of the SASII also exists as does a computerized scoring version. When developed, the SASII was tested in the assessment of psychiatric inpatients, individuals admitted to emergency rooms, and females diagnosed with borderline personality disorder (BPD) (Linehan et al., 2006); this latter group represents the population in which the SASII has been primarily used (Brown, Comtois, & Linehan, 2002; Koons et al., 2001; Linehan, Armstrong, Suarez, Allmon, & Heard, 1991; Linehan, Heard, & Armstrong, 1993). Overall, the measure has excellent interrater reliability and good validity (Linehan et al., 2006). The scale is intended to evaluate past behavior only and is not meant to predict future behavior or to assess level of risk.

The second measure we discuss and highly recommend is the Self-Injurious Thoughts and Behaviors Interview (SITBI; Nock et al., 2007). The SITBI is a 169-item instrument (with a 72-item short-form version), which also adopts a structured interview format and measures the topography,

Table 18.1 Psychometric Properties of Instruments for Assessing Nonsuicidal Self-Injury

Instrument	Internal Consistency	Interrater Reliability	Test-Retest Reliability	Construct Validity	Highly Recommended
Omnibus Measures					
SASII	G	E	E	G	X
SITBI	NA	E	A	G	X
SBQ	G	NA	A	G	
SHBQ	G	NA	A	G	
Functional Measures					
FASM	A	NA	U	A	
ISAS	G	NA	G	G	
SIQ	G	NA	U	A	
SIMS	G	NA	U	A	
SHRQ	G	NA	U	A	
Behavioral Measures					
DSHI	G	NA	G	G	
SHI	A	NA	U	A	
Brief Measures					
SNAP Items	NA	NA	U	A	
TSI Item	NA	NA	U	A	

SASII, Suicide Attempt Self-Injury Interview; G, good; E, excellent; A, adequate; SITBI, Self-Injurious Thoughts and Behaviors Interview; NA, not applicable; U, unavailable; SBQ, Suicidal Behaviors Questionnaire; SHBQ, Self-Harm Behavior Questionnaire; FASM, Functional Assessment of Self-Mutilation; ISAS, Inventory of Statements About Self-Harm; SIQ, Self-Injury Questionnaire; SIMS, Self-Injury Motivation Scale; SHRQ, Self-Harm Reasons Questionnaire; DSHI, Deliberate Self-Harm Inventory; SHI, Self-Harm Inventory; SNAP, Schedule for Nonadaptive and Adaptive Personality; TSI, Trauma Symptom Inventory.

frequency, and presence of suicide plans, ideation, gestures, and attempts as well as thoughts and episodes of NSSI. The SITBI defines NSSI as any act of deliberate self-harm engaged in without suicidal intent, and similar to the SASII, the instrument has distinct and detailed modules to comprehensively assess these acts. In this regard, the SITBI assesses NSSI methods, age of onset, frequency, functions, severity, precipitants, concurrent consumption of drugs or alcohol, medical treatment, social influences, impulsivity, and the respondent's intent for, or estimated likelihood of, future occurrence of NSSI. The SITBI is time efficient, taking between 3 and 15 minutes to complete, and can be administered by well-trained and well-supervised bachelor's-level personnel. Unique to the SITBI is that it has both a standard version and a parent-report

version, which is useful when working with young people. Currently, the SITBI is being used in a variety of clinical and research settings, but it only has been evaluated on a single sample of adolescents and young adults to date; as such, it requires additional examination among a wider range of populations. Based on the initial study, interrater reliability was excellent, and test-retest reliability was good to excellent depending on the domain assessed. Additionally, the SITBI demonstrated construct validity via convergence between it and extant measures assessing NSSI and suicidality.

The aforementioned two measures adopt an interview format to assess a wide range of NSSI domains; however, there are two other important omnibus measures that adopt a questionnaire format. The first is the Suicidal Behaviors Questionnaire (SBQ)

Table 18.2 Scope of Instruments for Assessing Nonsuicidal Self-Injury (NSSI)

Instrument	Type	No. Items	History	Methods	Frequency	Lethality	Intent/ Functions	History of Suicidality
Omnibus Measures								
SASII	I	31	X	X	X	X	X	X
SITBI	I	169	X	X	X	X	X	X
SBQ	S	90	X	X	X			X
SHBQ	S	32	X	X	X	X		X
Functional Measures								
FASM	S	22	X	X	X	X	X	
ISAS	S	39	X	X	X		X	
SIQ	S	30	X	X	X	X	X	X
SIMS	S	35					X	
SHRQ*	S	21	X	X	X		X	
Behavioral Measures								
DSHI	S	17	X	X	X	X		
SHI	S	22	X	X	X	X		
Brief Measures								
SNAP items	S	2	X					X
TSI item	S	1	X		X			

SASII, Suicide Attempt Self-Injury Interview; I, (structured) interview; S, self-report; SITBI, Self-Injurious Thoughts and Behaviors Interview; SBQ, Suicidal Behaviors Questionnaire; SR, self-report; SHBQ, Self-Harm Behavior Questionnaire; FASM, Functional Assessment of Self-Mutilation; ISAS, Inventory of Statements About Self-Harm; SIQ, Self-Injury Questionnaire; SIMS, Self-Injury Motivation Scale; SHRQ, Self-Harm Reasons Questionnaire (* = revised SHRQ); DSHI, Deliberate Self-Harm Inventory; SHI, Self-Harm Inventory; SNAP, Schedule for Nonadaptive and Adaptive Personality, 375 items in the total measure; TSI, Trauma Symptom Inventory, 100 items in the total measure.

(Linehan, 1981). The SBQ is comprised of 90 items that assess one's self-report of past and predicted future instances of NSSI (defined as intentional self-harm with no intent to die), as well as past and future suicidal ideation, attempts, and gestures. In addition to assessing the method, frequency, and intent of each act of NSSI, the SBQ includes 55 items that measure one's understood reasons for his or her self-injury. In this way, the SBQ provides an excellent assessment of the functional uses of NSSI. Among hospital populations, the SBQ has demonstrated reliability and validity (Linehan, Camper, Chiles, Strosahl, & Shearin, 1987; Linehan, Chiles, Egan, Devine, & Laffaw, 1986). Although the SBQ was developed as an extensive self-report questionnaire, there are also two shorter versions (Cole, 1988; Linehan, 1996) and one interview version (SBI; Ivanoff & Jang, 1991). These alternative

versions have been used among psychiatric outpatients, university students, nonclinical populations, and inmate populations (Addis & Linehan, 1989; Cotton, Peters, & Range, 1995; Ivanoff & Jang, 1991; Sabo, Gunderson, Najavits, Chauncey, & Kisiel, 1995).

The second omnibus questionnaire is the Self-Harm Behavior Questionnaire (SHBQ; Gutierrez, Osman, Barrois, & Kopper, 2001), which has 32 self-report items examining suicidal behaviors, ideation, attempts, and gestures, as well as risk-taking behaviors and NSSI. In the SHBQ, NSSI is defined as intentional self-harm lacking suicidal intent (i.e., "nonlethal suicide-related behavior," p. 477), but it is considered primarily as an antecedent and predictor of future suicidality (i.e., ideation and behavior). Several relevant NSSI domains are assessed within the NSSI module of the

SHBQ, including method, frequency, age of onset, most recent occurrence, lethality, and medical outcome of self-injury. The SHBQ has good interrater reliability, internal consistency, and convergent validity with other measures of suicide-related behaviors, and it has been translated into German (Fliege et al., 2006); it has also recently been validated in a sample of ethnically diverse adolescents in which it retained its factor structure and had good internal consistency and convergent validity (Muehlenkamp, Cowles, & Gutierrez, 2010).

Functional Measures

As noted earlier, understanding why people self-injure is a critical component of assessment. To date, several measures have been developed that assess the motives for, or functions of, NSSI.

One commonly used measure is the Functional Assessment of Self-Mutilation (FASM; Lloyd-Richardson, Kelley, & Hope, 1997), which defines NSSI as deliberate damage to body tissue that is not suicidal in its intent, assesses the presence of NSSI behaviors such as cutting/carving, burning, scraping skin to draw blood, hitting self on purpose, and pulling out hair, as well as the frequency of the behavior, age of onset, and history of NSSI. The FASM also assesses functions of self-injury using 22 possible reasons for the behavior (e.g., "To stop bad feelings," "To punish yourself," "To feel relaxed," "To be like someone you respect"), followed by free-response space that is provided for respondents to report unlisted reasons. Reasons from this measure can be conceptualized using a four-factor model comprised of the following: automatic (i.e., intrapersonal) negative reinforcement, automatic (i.e., intrapersonal) positive reinforcement, social-negative reinforcement, and social-positive reinforcement (Lloyd-Richardson, Perrine, Dierker, & Kelley, 2007; Nock & Prinstein, 2004, 2005). The FASM has adequate internal consistency (Lloyd-Richardson et al., 1997) and has been utilized in nonclinical samples (Lloyd-Richardson et al., 1997), clinical samples (Guertin, Lloyd-Richardson, Spirito, Donaldson, & Boergers, 2001), incarcerated youth (Penn, Esposito, Schaeffer, Fritz, & Spirito, 2003), and adolescents (Lloyd-Richardson et al., 2007; Nock & Prinstein, 2004, 2005). Two limitations of the FASM regard the automatic-negative scale and should be noted. First, this scale includes only two items, even though automatic-negative functions are endorsed more frequently than other types of functions (Klonsky, 2007; Nock & Prinstein,

2004). Second, in a recent study, one of these two items was moved to the automatic-positive scale in part due to unacceptably low internal consistency reliability (Nock et al., 2007). Thus, there is some concern about whether the FASM provides reliable, valid, and comprehensive measurement of the most commonly reported functions for NSSI.

A more recent measure is the Inventory of Statements About Self-Harm (ISAS) (Glenn & Klonsky, 2007; Klonsky & Glenn, 2009; Klonsky & Olino, 2008), which was developed to provide as comprehensive as possible a measure of NSSI motives. The measure assesses each of the functions identified in an extensive review of the literature (Klonsky, 2007; e.g., affect regulation, self-punishment, interpersonal influence) plus several others (e.g., peer bonding). Three items are used to assess each individual function on the ISAS. Thus, respondents rate how well items complete the standard phrase: "When I harm myself, I am...." Examples of items and functions assessed are "calming myself down" (affect regulation), "punishing myself" (self-punishment), "seeking care or help from others" (interpersonal influence), and "fitting in with others" (peer bonding). Participants rate how much they endorse each item using a three-point scale comprised of the following responses: "very relevant," "somewhat relevant," or "not relevant." The questionnaire takes approximately 8 minutes for most participants to complete.

An exploratory factor analysis with promax rotation in a large nonclinical sample of self-injurers indicated two superordinate factors, which were congruent with other research examining NSSI motives (Nock & Prinstein, 2004). The first factor (eigenvalue = 5.9) encompassed functions related to social reinforcement (i.e., interpersonal influence, peer bonding, sensation seeking, and interpersonal boundaries). The second factor (eigenvalue = 1.6) encompassed functions related to intrapersonal reinforcement (i.e., affect regulation, self-punishment, antisuicide, antidissociation). These were the only two factors with eigenvalues greater than one and use of thee scree plot also suggested retaining two factors. The two factors displayed excellent internal consistency and correlated in expected ways with key clinical variables, suggesting good construct validity (Glenn & Klonsky, 2007; Klonsky & Glenn, 2009). Subsequent studies have provided further support for the psychometric properties and clinical utility of the ISAS in a variety of populations and languages (e.g., Bildik, Somer, Kabukcu Basay, Basay, & Ozbaran, 2013; Glenn & Klonsky,

2011; Kortge, Meade, & Tennant, 2013; Lindholm, Bjarehed, & Lundh, 2011). Given the comprehensiveness and robust psychometric properties of the ISAS, we recommend its use when a thorough assessment of NSSI motivations is desired.

Another scale, the Self-Injury Questionnaire (SIQ; Santa Mina et al., 2006), has 30 self-report items designed to assess a wide range of underlying motives for self-injury that are both suicidal and nonsuicidal in nature. The SIQ uses four subscales to assess intentions for each method of self-injury. These subscales are "body alterations, indirect self-harm, failure to care for self, and overt self-injury" (p. 222). Instances of self-injury are further measured in terms of frequency, type and function, and their relation to childhood maltreatment. The SIQ has demonstrated strong internal consistency and good construct validity and was developed using a nonclinical population.

The Self-Injury Motivation Scale (SIMS) (Osuch, Noll, & Putnam, 1999) is comprised of 35 self-report items, each tapping different motives for NSSI. Results from a factor analysis indicated six motivation factors. Of these, four were more easily interpretable. These included modulating affect (e.g., "to decrease feelings of rage"), inflicting self-punishment (e.g., "to remind myself that I deserve to be hurt or punished"), influencing others (e.g., "to seek support or caring from others"), and self-stimulation (e.g., "to experience a 'high' that feels like a drug high"). The other two factors were less interpretable and were named by the authors as desolation and magical control. Overall, the SIMS demonstrated good reliability and validity in its original study sample of 99 adult patients. It has since been used in a sample of adolescents who engaged in self-cutting, with similarly strong psychometric properties (Kumar, Pepe, & Steer, 2004).

The final measure we will discuss is the Self-Harm Reasons Questionnaire (SHRQ; Lewis & Santor, 2008). The SHRQ is a brief measure that assesses the history and methods of, as well as the reasons for, self-harm (defined as any intentional act engaged in to cause injury to the self). The measure consists of 15 items assessing reasons for self-harm (e.g., "I wanted to get rid of my anxiety"), to which respondents indicate their level of endorsement on a seven-point scale from "strongly agree" to "strongly disagree." Exploratory factor analysis (using promax rotation) for the SHRQ has suggested a five-factor solution, which accounts for 80% of scale variance. Resulting subscales include tension management (e.g., "I wanted to get rid of anxiety"), negative

mood management (e.g., "I wanted to get rid of sadness or depression"), trauma management (e.g., "I wanted to stop overwhelming flashbacks, memories, or nightmares"), interpersonal communication (e.g., "I wanted to get back at someone"), self-hate (e.g., "I wanted to punish myself"), and the distal goal subscale (e.g., "I wanted to regain control").

Recently, the SHRQ has been revised to attend to a difficult-to-interpret factor (i.e., the distal goal subscale) and to include additional items based on literature published since the pilot test of the original SHRQ (e.g., Klonsky, 2007). Similar to the original version, the revised version also assesses frequency of behavior. In total, the revised version consists of 21 items that take on a similar format as the original SHRQ to assess reasons for self-harm (i.e., "I wanted to…") and use the same response scheme. Factor analytic results (again using promax rotation) have supported a five-factor model that is slightly different than the original measure, although findings from the revised version are consistent with extant literature (e.g., Klonsky, 2007; Nock & Prinstein, 2004, 2005) and all subscales are easily interpretable. The factors for the revised version accounted for 67% of total item variance and resultant subscales include antidepression and suicide subscale (e.g., "I wanted to reduce my sadness or depression"), interpersonal communication subscale (e.g., "I wanted to get help for an emotional or psychological difficulty"), antidissociation subscale (e.g., "I wanted to stop feeling detached from the people or things around me"), self-hate subscale (e.g., "I wanted to punish myself"), and antitension subscale (e.g., "I wanted to reduce my anxiety"). All subscales have alpha coefficients in the moderate to high range. Validity for the measure is currently being investigated, but scales from the SHRQ (original and revised versions) correlate with clinical symptoms as expected, suggesting some construct validity for the measure. The original SHRQ and the revised version were examined using university students (original) and young adults recruited online (revised); the measure is presently being translated into Icelandic and is being tested in larger, more diverse samples.

Behavioral Measures

The next type of assessment instruments discussed are behavioral measures that primarily assess one's history of NSSI behaviors (without additional detail, such as an assessment of functions). These measures are most useful when assessing one's history of self-injury in terms of methods used and

NSSI frequency. Some of the measures described earlier include brief behavioral assessments that can be used on their own, including the FASM and ISAS. Additional behavioral measures are described next.

One behavioral measure warranting discussion is Kim Gratz's Deliberate Self-Harm Inventory (DSHI) (Gratz, 2001), which is comprised of 17 items that assess one's self-report of various behavioral domains regarding NSSI. For this measure, NSSI is defined as "deliberate, direct destruction or alteration of body tissue without conscious suicidal intent, but resulting in injury severe enough for tissue damage to occur" (p. 253). In all, the DSHI assesses 16 specific nonsuicidal self-injurious behaviors (and one "other" category specified by respondent) for history, age of onset, frequency, and severity, and it includes commonly occurring behaviors like skin cutting, skin carving, and intentional bruising. Presently, two newer versions of the DSHI are being developed in order to assess NSSI over time. The original version of the DSHI was developed using a population of college students (Gratz, 2001) and has shown good psychometric properties (including high internal consistency, adequate convergent, construct, and discriminant validity, and adequate test-retest reliability over a maximum period of 4 weeks). The measure also has been translated into a German version (Fliege et al., 2006), which also has shown good internal consistency and high test-retest reliability. A Swedish version, which was slightly modified, also has been developed (Lundh, Karim, & Quilisch, 2007), although its psychometric properties have not yet been reported.

The second behavioral measure we will discuss is the Self-Harm Inventory (SHI; Sansone, Wiederman, & Sansone, 1998), which is made up of 22 items that use a dichotomous (yes/no) response scheme to assess individuals' self-reports of self-harm (defined as intentionally self-destructive behaviors). A possible limitation of the measure is that it does not assess intent to die, which makes it difficult to disentangle suicide-related self-injury from NSSI. Strengths of the measure include its assessment of history, frequency, and method of commonly occurring self-injurious behaviors. Examples of these questions are as follows: "Have you ever, intentionally, or on purpose: Cut yourself on purpose?/ Burned yourself on purpose?/ Set yourself up in a relationship to be rejected?" These questions are then followed by a single open-ended response, which allows respondents to provide information about forms of self-injury not captured by the previous 22 items. Another strength of the SHI is that it was developed for use in clinical (Sansone, Fine, & Nunn, 1994; Sansone, Gage, & Wiederman, 1998; Sansone, Sansone, & Morris, 1996) and nonclinical (Sansone, Wiederman, & Sansone, 1998; Sansone, Wiederman, Sansone, & Touchet, 1998; Wiederman, Sansone, & Sansone, 1998) populations; similar to the DSHI, the SHI also has been translated into German and Dutch versions. The measure has been shown to have adequate convergent validity with measures of depression (Sansone, Wiederman, Sansone, & Touchet, 1998), BPD (Sansone, Gage, et al., 1998), and history of childhood abuse (Sansone, Wiederman, & Sansone, 1996).

Brief Measures

Finally, we discuss measures of NSSI that are brief in nature and thus only include a single item or a few items to assess NSSI. These measures may be most useful when conducting a brief assessment, screening for NSSI, or when examining NSSI in the context of other factors as described next. One such measure is the Schedule for Nonadaptive and Adaptive Personality (SNAP; Clark, 1996). The SNAP is a clinically validated 375-item self-report questionnaire that was developed to assess trait dimensions in personality pathology. Within these items are two that ask about NSSI (i.e., "When I get very tense, hurting myself physically somehow calms me down," "I have hurt myself on purpose several times"). Due to its brief nature, neither item provides a distinction between suicidal and nonsuicidal acts, although there is good evidence to suggest that these items are endorsed by individuals who deny attempted suicide (Klonsky et al., 2003).

The second brief measure is the Trauma Symptom Inventory (TSI; Briere, 1995). Although there are 100 items on this self-report questionnaire, the measure includes a single item that asks respondents to indicate the frequency with which they engaged in "intentionally hurting yourself [e.g., by scratching, cutting, or burning] even though you weren't trying to commit suicide." Overall, the TSI has demonstrated reliability and validity in clinical samples, although psychometric properties of the single NSSI item were not reported. The TSI was originally developed to assess specific symptoms of trauma, and as such, it may offer particular utility to those clinicians and researchers seeking to clarify relations between a history of childhood trauma (e.g., abuse) and NSSI.

Summary

In both research and clinical contexts, an accurate and comprehensive assessment of NSSI is paramount. When working with an individual who has self-injured, and in order to enhance rapport, questions and discussions about NSSI should be communicated using a "respectful curiosity" and in a "low-key, dispassionate demeanor." Key components of the assessment should illuminate several NSSI-related foci, including a discussion of limits to confidentiality, one's personal history of NSSI (including methods, frequency, age of onset, most recent episode, and medical severity), one's social history of NSSI, the context in which NSSI occurs (including environmental, cognitive, affective, and biological factors), concomitant risky behaviors, the functions of, or reasons for, NSSI (which entails both intrapersonal and social functions), and an assessment for suicide risk. To date, relatively few instruments of NSSI have been developed and tested for psychometric properties. Two psychometrically sound and comprehensive-in-scope options are the Suicide Attempt Self-Injury Interview (SASII; Linehan et al., 2006) and the Self-Injurious Thoughts and Behaviors Interview (SITBI) (Nock et al., 2006). When assessing functions of NSSI, both the Functional Assessment of Self-Mutilation (FASM) and Inventory of Statements About Self-Injury (ISAS) (Glenn & Klonsky, 2007; Klonsky & Glenn, 2009; Klonsky & Olino, 2008) have good psychometric properties, although the latter includes more comprehensive coverage of NSSI motivations. Although several measures have been developed and tested, the field would benefit from the continued development of new, and validation of both new and existing, NSSI instruments.

Clinical Recommendations

To establish a strong and collaborative rapport while assessing NSSI, we recommend that the clinician clearly outline all limits of confidentiality from the outset and maintain a nonjudgmental, dispassionate demeanor while conveying "respectful curiosity" about an individual's history and experience of NSSI. This will be conducive to accurately assessing important domains of interest regarding NSSI, which should include the individual's personal, family, and social history of NSSI; methods; environments; thoughts and aspects of cognitions; emotions (including content and style); biological factors; concomitant maladaptive behaviors (e.g., substance and alcohol use, disordered eating); and functions associated with NSSI. It also is advised that risk for suicide be assessed in tandem with the inquiring about NSSI. To assist in the assessment of NSSI, we recommend use of valid assessment measures (described in this chapter) when feasible.

Research Recommendations

Future research should work to develop new or refine current measures with the goal of distinguishing more clearly NSSI from suicidal self-injury. This also will benefit clinicians who use these measures when working with patients. It also is recommended that future measures capture and measure aspects of NSSI in terms of changes over time (i.e., to better understand the NSSI trajectory and to account for changes resulting from therapy). Finally, many of the existing assessment measures have only been tested in a single or a handful of populations. In order to understand the generalizability of these measures and to identify where more circumscribed measures for specific populations might be needed, future research should examine these instruments within a broader spectrum of populations.

References

Addis, M., & Linehan, M. M. (1989, November). *Predicting suicidal behavior: Psychometric properties of the Suicidal Behaviors Questionnaire.* Poster session presented at the Annual Meeting of the Association for the Advancement of Behavior Therapy, Washington, DC.

Bildik, T., Somer, O., Kabukcu Basay, B., Basay, O., & Ozbaran, B. (2013). The validity and reliability of the Turkish version of the inventory of statements about self-injury. *Turkish Journal of Psychiatry, 24*, 49–57.

Briere, J. (1995). *Trauma symptom inventory (TSI) professional manual.* Odessa, FL: Psychological Assessment Resources.

Brown, M. Z., Comtois, K. A., & Linehan, M. M. (2002). Reasons for suicide attempts and nonsuicidal self-injury in women with borderline personality disorder. *Journal of Abnormal Psychology, 111*, 198–202.

Chapman, A. L., Gratz, K. L., & Brown, M. (2006). Solving the puzzle of deliberate self-harm: The experiential avoidance model. *Behaviour Research and Therapy, 44*, 371–394.

Clark, L. A. (1996). *Schedule for adaptive and nonadaptive personality: Manual for administration, scoring, and interpretation.* Minneapolis: University of Minnesota Press.

Cole, D. A. (1988). Hopelessness, social desirability, depression, and parasuicide in two college student samples. *Journal of Consulting and Clinical Psychology, 56*, 131–136.

Cotton C. R., Peters, D. K., & Range, L. M. (1995). Psychometric properties of the suicidal behaviors questionnaire. *Death Studies, 19*, 391–397.

Dougherty, D. M., Mathias, C. W., Marsh-Richard, D. M., Prevette, K. N., Dawes, M. A., Hatzis, E. S.,...Nouvion, S. O. (2009). Impulsivity and clinical symptoms among adolescents with non-suicidal self-injury with or without attempted suicide. *Psychiatry Research, 169*, 22–27.

Fliege, H., Kocalevent, R., Walter, O. B., Beck, S., Gratz, K. L., Gutierrez, P. M., & Klapp, B. F. (2006). Three assessment tools for deliberate self-harm and suicide behavior: Evaluation and psychopathological correlates. *Journal of Psychosomatic Research, 61*, 113–121.

Ghaziuddin, M., Tsai, L. Y., Naylor, M. W., & Ghaziuddin, N. (1992). Mood disorder in a group of self-cutting adolescents. *Acta Paedopsychiatrica: International Journal of Child & Adolescent Psychiatry, 55*,103–105.

Glenn, C. G., & Klonsky, E. D. (2011). One-year test-retest reliability of the inventory of statements about self-injury (ISAS). *Assessment, 18*, 375–378.

Gratz, K. L. (2001). Measurement of deliberate self-harm: Preliminary data on the deliberate self-harm inventory. *Journal of Psychopathology and Behavioral Assessment, 23*, 253–263.

Guertin, T., Lloyd-Richardson, E., Spirito, A., Donaldson, D., & Boergers, J. (2001). Self-mutilative behavior in adolescents who attempt suicide by overdose. *Journal of the American Academy of Child and Adolescent Psychiatry, 40*, 1062–1069.

Gutierrez, P. M, Osman, A., Barrois, F. X., & Kopper, B. A. (2001). Development and initial validation of the self-harm behavior questionnaire. *Journal of Personality Assessment, 77*, 475–490.

Hawton, K., Rodham, K., & Evans, E. (2006). *By their own young hand: Deliberate self-harm and suicidal ideas in adolescents.* London, UK: Jessica Kingsley.

Hilt, L. M., Nock, M. K., Lloyd-Richardson, E. E., & Prinstein, M. J. (2008). Longitudinal study of non-suicidal self-injury among young adolescents: Rates, correlates, and preliminary test of an interpersonal model. *Journal of Early Adolescence, 28*, 455–469.

Ivanoff, A., & Jang, S. J. (1991). The role of hopelessness and social desirability in predicting suicidal behavior: A study of prison inmates. *Journal of Consulting and Clinical Psychology, 59*, 394–399.

Kettlewell, C. (1999). *Skin game: A cutter's memoir.* New York, NY: St. Martin's Press.

Klonsky, E. D., May, A.M., & Glenn, C.R. (2013). The relationship between nonsuicidal self-injury and attempted suicide: Converging evidence from four samples. *Journal of Abnormal Psychology, 122*, 231–237.

Klonsky, E. D. (2007). The functions of deliberate self-injury: A review of the evidence. *Clinical Psychology Review, 27*, 226–239.

Klonsky, E. D. (2009). The functions of self-injury in young adults who cut themselves: Clarifying the evidence for affect-regulation. *Psychiatry Research, 166*, 260–268.

Klonsky, E. D., & Glenn, C. R. (2008). Resisting urges to self-injure. *Behavioural and Cognitive Psychotherapy, 36*, 211–220.

Klonsky, E. D., & Glenn, C. R. (2009). Assessing the functions of non-suicidal self-injury: Psychometric properties of the inventory of statements about self-injury (ISAS). *Journal of Psychopathology and Behavioral Assessment, 31*, 215–219.

Klonsky, E. D., & Olino, T. M. (2008). Identifying clinically distinct subgroups of self-injurers: A latent class analysis. *Journal of Consulting and Clinical Psychology, 76*, 22–27.

Klonsky, E. D., Oltmanns, T. F., & Turkheimer, E. (2003). Deliberate self-harm in a non-clinical population: Prevalence and psychological correlates. *American Journal of Psychiatry, 160*, 1501–1508.

Koons, C. R., Robins, C. I., Tweed, J. L., Lynch, T. R., Gonzalez, A. M., Morse, J. Q., ... Bastian, L. A. (2001). Efficacy of dialectical behavior therapy in women veterans with borderline personality disorder. *Behavior Therapy, 32*, 371–390.

Kortge, R., Meade, T., & Tennant, A. (2013). Intrapersonal and interpersonal functions of deliberate self-harm (DSH): A psychometric examination of the Inventory of Statements About Self-injury (ISAS) scale. *Behaviour Change, 30*, 24–35.

Kumar, G., Pepe, D., & Steer, R. A. (2004). Adolescent psychiatric inpatients' self-reported reasons for cutting themselves. *Journal of Nervous and Mental Disease, 192*, 830–836.

Lewis, S. P., Heath, N. L., Michal, N. J., & Duggan, J. M. (2012). Non-suicidal self-injury, youth, and the Internet: What mental health professionals need to know. *Child and Adolescent Psychiatry and Mental Health, 6*, 13.

Lewis, S. P., Heath, N. L., St. Denis, J. M. & Noble, R. (2011). The scope of non-suicidal self-injury on YouTube. *Pediatrics, 127*, e552–557.

Lewis, S. P., Rosenrot, S. A., & Santor, D. A. (2011). An integrated model of self-harm: Identifying predictors of intent. *Canadian Journal of Behavioural Sciences, 43*, 20–29.

Lewis, S. P., & Santor, D. A. (2008). Development and validation of the self-harm reasons questionnaire. *Suicide and Life-threatening Behavior, 38*, 104–115.

Lewis, S. P., & Santor, D. A. (2010). Motives for self-harm: Motive achievement and prediction of future intent. *Journal of Nervous and Mental Disease, 198*, 362–369.

Lindholm, T., Bjarehed, J., & Lundh, L. G. (2011). Functions of nonsuicidal self-injury among young women in residential care: A pilot study with the Swedish version of the inventory of statements about self-injury. *Cognitive Behaviour Therapy, 40*, 183–189.

Linehan, M. M. (1981). *Suicide behaviors questionnaire.* University of Washington, Seattle.

Linehan M. M. (1996). *Suicidal behaviors questionnaire (SBQ).* Department of Psychology, University of Washington, Seattle.

Linehan, M. M., Armstrong, H. E., Suarez, A., Allmon, D., & Heard, H. L. (1991). Cognitive-behavioral treatment of chronically parasuicidal borderline patients. *Archives of General Psychiatry, 48*, 1060–1064.

Linehan, M. M., Camper, P., Chiles, J. A., Strosahl, K., & Shearin, E. (1987). Interpersonal problem solving and parasuicide. *Cognitive Therapy and Research, 11*, 1–12.

Linehan, M. M., Chiles, J. A., Egan, K. J., Devine, R. H., & Laffaw, J. A. (1986). Presenting problems of parasuicides versus suicide ideators and nonsuicidal psychiatric patients. *Journal of Consulting and Clinical Psychology, 54*, 880–881.

Linehan, M. M., Comtois, K. A., Brown, M. Z., Heard, H. L., & Wagner, A. (2006). Suicide attempt self-injury interview (SASII): Development, reliability, and validity of a scale to assess suicide attempts and intentional self-injury. *Psychological Assessment, 18*, 302–312.

Linehan, M. M., Heard, H. L., & Armstrong, H. E. (1993). Naturalistic follow-up of a behavioral treatment for chronically parasuicidal borderline patients. *Archives of General Psychiatry, 50*, 971–974.

Lloyd-Richardson, E. E., Kelley, M. L., & Hope, T. (1997, April). *Self-mutilation in a community sample of adolescents: Descriptive characteristics and provisional prevalence rates.* Poster session presented at the Annual Meeting of the Society for Behavioral Medicine, New Orleans, LA.

Lloyd-Richardson, E. E., Perrine, N., Dierker, L., & Kelley, M. L. (2007). Characteristics and functions of non-suicidal self-injury in a community sample of adolescents. *Psychological Medicine, 37*, 1183–1192.

Lundh, L. G., Karim, J., & Quilisch, E. (2007). Deliberate self-harm in 15-year-old adolescents: A pilot study with a modified version of the deliberate self-harm inventory. *Scandinavian Journal of Psychology, 48*, 33–41.

Miller, A. L, Rathus, J. H., & Linehan, M. M. (2007). *Dialectical behavior therapy with suicidal adolescents*. New York, NY: Guilford Press.

Muehlenkamp J. J., & Gutierrez, P. M. (2007). Risk for suicide attempts among adolescents who engage in non-suicidal self-injury. *Archives of Suicide Research, 11*, 68–82.

Muehlenkamp, J. J., Cowles, M. L., & Gutierrez, P. M. (2010). Validity of the self-harm behaviors questionnaire with diverse adolescents. *Journal of Psychopathology and Behavioral Assessment, 32*, 236–245.

Najmi, S., Wegner, D. M., & Nock, M. K. (2007). Thought suppression and self-injurious thoughts and behaviors. *Behaviour Research and Therapy, 45*, 1957–1965.

Nock, M. K. (2009). Why do people hurt themselves? New insights into the nature and functions of self-injury. *Current Directions in Psychological Science, 18*, 78–83.

Nock, M. K., Holmberg, E. B., Photos, V. I., & Michel, B. D. (2007). The self-injurious thoughts and behaviors interview: Development, reliability, and validity in an adolescent sample measure. *Psychological Assessment, 19*, 309–317.

Nock, M. K., Joiner, T. E., Gordon, K. H., Lloyd-Richardson, E., & Prinstein, M. J. (2006). Non-suicidal self-injury among adolescents: Diagnostic correlates and relation to suicide attempts. *Psychiatry Research, 144*, 65–72.

Nock, M. K., & Mendes, W. B. (2008). Physiological arousal, distress tolerance, and social problem solving deficits among adolescent self-injurers. *Journal of Consulting and Clinical Psychology, 76, 28–38.

Nock, M. K., & Prinstein, M. J. (2004). A functional approach to the assessment of self-mutilative behavior. *Journal of Consulting and Clinical Psychology, 72*, 885–890.

Nock, M. K., & Prinstein, M. J. (2005). Contextual features and behavioral functions of self-mutilation among adolescents. *Journal of Abnormal Psychology, 114*, 140–146.

Nock, M. K., Wedig, M. M., Holmberg, E. B., & Hooley, J. M. (2008). The Emotion Reactivity Scale: Development, evaluation, and relation to self-injurious thoughts and behaviors. *Behavior Therapy, 39*, 107–116.

O'Connor, R. C., & Armitage, C. J. (2003). Theory of planned behavior and parasuicide: An exploratory study. *Current Psychology, 22, 247–256*

O'Connor, R. C., Armitage, C. J., & Gray, L. (2006). The role of clinical and social cognitive variables in parasuicide. *British Journal of Clinical Psychology, 45*, 465–481.

Osuch, E. A., Noll, J. G., & Putnam, F. W. (1999). The motivations for self-injury in psychiatric patients. *Psychiatry, 62*, 334–346.

Penn, J. V., Esposito, C. L., Schaeffer, L. E., Fritz, G. K., & Spirito, A. (2003). Suicide attempts and self-mutilative behavior in a juvenile correctional facility. *Journal of the Academy of Child and Adolescent Psychiatry, 42*, 762–769.

Prinstein, M. J., Guerry, J. D., Browne, C. B., & Rancourt, D. (2009). Interpersonal models of nonsuicidal self-injury. In M. K. Nock (Ed.), *Non-suicidal self-injury: Current science and practice (pp. 79–98)*. Washington, DC: American Psychological Association.

Rosen, P. M., & Walsh, B. W. (1989). Patterns of contagion in self-mutilation epidemics. *American Journal of Psychiatry, 149*, 656–658.

Ross, S., Heath, N. L., & Toste, J. R. (2009). Non-suicidal self-injury and eating pathology in high school students. *American Journal of Orthopsychiatry, 79*, 83–92

Sabo, A. N., Gunderson, J. G., Najavits, L. M., Chauncey, D., & Kisiel, C. (1995). Changes in self-destructiveness of borderline patients in psychotherapy. *Journal of Nervous Mental Disorders, 183*, 370–376.

Sansone, R. A., Fine, M. A., & Nunn, J. L. (1994). A comparison of borderline personality symptomatology and self-destructive behavior in women with eating, substance abuse, and both eating and substance abuse disorders. *Journal of Personality Disorders, 8*, 219–228.

Sansone, R. A., Gage, M. D., & Wiederman, M. W. (1998). Investigation of borderline personality disorder among non-psychotic, involuntarily hospitalized clients. *Journal of Mental Health Counseling, 20*,133–140.

Sansone, R. A., Sansone, L. A., & Morris, D. (1996). Prevalence of borderline personality symptoms in two groups of obese subjects. *American Journal of Psychiatry, 153*, 117–118.

Sansone, R. A., Wiederman, M. W., & Sansone, L. A. (1996). The relationship between borderline personality symptomatology and healthcare utilization among women in an HMO setting. *Journal of Managed Care, 2*, 515–518.

Sansone, R. A., Wiederman, M. W., & Sansone, L. A. (1998). The Self-Harm Inventory: Development of a scale for identifying self-destructive behaviors and borderline personality disorder. *Journal of Clinical Psychology, 54*, 973–983.

Sansone, R. A., Wiederman, M. W., Sansone, L. A., & Touchet, B. (1998). An investigation of primary care patients on extended treatment with SSRI's. *American Journal of Managed Care, 4*, 1721–1723.

Santa Mina, E. E., Gallop, R., Links, P., Heslegrave, R., Pringle, D., Wekerle, C., & Grewal, P. (2006). The self-injury questionnaire: Evaluation of the psychometric properties in a clinical population. *Journal of Psychiatric and Mental Health Nursing, 13*, 221–227.

Selby, E. A., Anestis, M. D., & Joiner, T. E. (2008). Understanding the relationship between emotional and behavioral dysregulation: Emotional cascades. *Behavior Research and Therapy, 6*, 593–611.

Solano, R., Fernandez-Aranda, F., Aitken, A., López, C., & Vallejo, J. (2005). Self-injurious behaviour in people with eating disorders. *European Eating Disorders Review, 13*, 3–10.

Taiminen, T. J., Kallio-Soukainen, K., Nokso-Kovisto, H., Kaljonen, A., & Helenius, H. (1998). Contagion of deliberate self-harm among adolescent inpatients. *Journal of the American Academy of Child and Adolescent Psychiatry, 37*(2), 211–217.

Walsh, B. (2012). *Treating self-injury: A practical guide (2nd ed.)*. New York, NY: Guilford Press.

Walsh, B. (2007). Clinical assessment of self-injury: A practical guide. *Journal of Clinical Psychology, 63*, 1057–1068.

Whitlock, J. L., Eckenrode, J. E., & Silverman, D. (2006). The epidemiology of self-injurious behavior in a college population. *Pediatrics, 117*, 1939–1948.

Whitlock, J. L., Powers, J. P., & Eckenrode, J. E. (2006). The virtual cutting edge: Adolescent self-injury and the Internet [Special issue]. *Developmental Psychology, 42*, 407–417.

Whitlock. J., Purginton, A., & Gershkovich, M. (2009). Media, the internet, and nonsuicidal self-injury. In M. K. Nock (Ed.), *Non-suicidal self-injury: Current science and practice* (pp. 139–155). Washington, DC: American Psychological Association.

Wiederman, M. W., Sansone, R. A., & Sansone, L. A. (1998). History of trauma and attempted suicide among women in a primary care setting. *Violence and Victims, 13*, 3–9.

PART 5

Prevention and Intervention

Prevention of Suicidal Behaviors

José Manoel Bertolote

Abstract

This chapter presents a brief historical perspective of the concept of suicide from its origins to its current-day status as a major public health problem. In view of its magnitude and possibilities for prevention, this chapter also reviews its etiology, in terms of both risk and protective factors. Public health strategies are presented and discussed, as well as suicide prevention programs and initiatives outside the public health framework. Strategies and interventions that have demonstrated their efficacy/ effectiveness are highlighted. Other interventions that are less effective (including those potentially harmful) also are presented and discussed with special attention paid to youth suicidal behavior. Finally, I recommend efforts for improving existing information and creating new ones (particularly related to suicide attempts) especially in low- and middle-income countries.

Key Words: suicidal behavior, suicide, suicide attempts, suicide prevention, risk and protective factors, suicide prevention strategies, suicide prevention programs, youth, public health

Throughout the ages suicide has evolved from a primarily theological interest to a worldwide phenomenon capturing the attention of several other branches of knowledge and science. Shortly after the reference to the behavior for the first time with a Greek neologism—*autofonos*—in 1643 (in an otherwise Latin text by Thomas Browne), the word was translated into English in a 1645 edition as "suicide." Suicide over time was perceived as a distinct phenomenon: In the first half of the 19th century, suicide was considered a sign of a mental disorder (Esquirol, 1838; Pinel, 1809); at the end of the 19th century, Durkheim (1987) considered it a paradigm of social phenomena; Freud (1920/1961), at the beginning of the 20th century, perceived it as a psychological issue; and, Camus (1942), later in the same century, saw it as a philosophical problem. More recently, however, in view of the growing impact suicide mortality has had on overall mortality, public health proponents have started to

pay attention to this complex phenomenon, with emphasis on its prevention (De Leo, Bertolote, & Lester, 2002; World Health Organization [WHO], 1998).

Although suicide might seem a simple concept, in reality it is quite broad and comprehensive, covering several shades. This in part has led different authors to propose several qualifications to the original expression (e.g., suicide *attempt, completed* suicide) and to other self-injurious behaviors (e.g., self-harm, suicidal behavior, self-injury, self-destructive behavior) (Shneidman, 1984). In view of its behavioral nature rather than a specific nosographic condition, in this chapter the expression "suicidal behaviors" will be used to cover different forms of suicidalism, including suicidal ideation, suicide plans, suicide attempts, and deaths resulting from a suicide attempt (completed suicide) as per the definition put forward by the World Health Organization. Suicide is the act of deliberately killing oneself or, more specifically, an act deliberately initiated and performed by the person concerned in the full knowledge, or expectation, of its fatal outcome (WHO, 1998).

This chapter has been written from a public health perspective and therefore takes into account contributions and knowledge from several areas, including medicine and psychology, as well as other areas of social science.

Magnitude of the Problem

Suicide mortality has progressively increased to claim now more than 850,000 lives every year (Bertolote & Fleischmann, 2009). Overall, suicide death predominates in males over females in a proportion of about 3 to 1, although suicide attempts tend to predominate in females over males. An exception to this universal rule is seen in China, where suicide mortality rates for the age group 24–34 years predominate in females (Phillips, 2002). It should be noted, however, that there is a worldwide trend toward a reduction in both those gaps (Bertolote & Fleischmann, 2009).

Unlike gender, age differences in rates of suicide are not as apparent. Although worldwide suicide mortality rates have for ages predominated among older people (current peak: males aged 75 years and more), in many countries, the picture has dramatically changed, and the peak age for suicide mortality is no longer found among the oldest. In Japan, for instance, the highest suicide rates are observed among men aged 55–64 years, and in New Zealand, among men aged 25–34 years (World Health Organization, 2010).

A clear indication of the sociocultural nature of suicidal behavior is given by the comparison of suicide mortality rates across religions. In addition to the overall impact religion has on mental health (Gartner, Larson, & Allen, 1991; Wasserman, 2009), Bertolote and Fleischmann (2002) demonstrated a strong correlation between national suicide mortality rates and religious denominations: The lowest rates were found in Muslim countries, followed by Roman Catholics, Protestants, and Buddhists; atheistic countries had the highest suicide mortality rates.

Methods employed for committing suicide are another indication of the cultural variation observed in this area. Whereas in most Western countries hanging and shooting are the most frequently employed methods, in many Asian countries (e.g., China, Vietnam, India, Sri Lanka, Pakistan and several Pacific Islands) pesticide ingestion is the most frequently employed method (Bertolote, Fleischmann, Butchart, & Besbelli, 2006; Eddleston et al., 2006; Gunnel et al., 2007; Khan, 2009; Phillips et al., 2002; Wasserman et al., 2008). One explanation for this preference is availability of means: The majority of classes of pesticides used for suicide in Asia have been banned by international treaties—a ban implemented in Western countries but largely ignored elsewhere (Bertolote et al., 2006).

Most of what is known about suicide mortality comes from two sources. Data on age, sex, and method employed are reported on a yearly basis by some member states of the World Health Organization (WHO). The WHO processes that information and regularly posts it on its Web site (http://www.who.int/mental_health/suicide). Some of this information also may be posted on national Web sites on vital statistics. More detailed information usually comes from specific research published in scientific journals and books, as well as being presented at scientific conferences and congresses.

Although the information available on the WHO Web site covers prevalence rates and characteristics of suicide in 120 member states (out of the 194 total member states) representing more than 80% of the global population, additional information usually comes from countries where research is supported. The information obtained from psychological autopsy studies comes from a handful of countries: 80% of deaths from suicide carefully scrutinized come from countries that together represent less than 5% of the world's population. China and India alone contribute approximately 25% of all deaths from suicide (nearly 225,000 deaths every year) but only have published results from studies of 788 cases of suicides (Gururaj et al., 2004; Phillips et al., 2002; Vijayakumar, 2003). On the other hand, Denmark, with less than 0.1% of the world's population, is responsible for publications covering 24% of all cases of suicide in which psychiatric diagnosis was ascertained.

Given that most of what is known about risk and protective factors derives from these types of studies, one should be very conservative when drawing generalizations from them.

Unlike suicide mortality data, there is no systematic national data collection on suicide attempts. One study—the WHO-EURO multisite study—has collected data on suicide attempts in over 30 countries. Results have indicated that the rate of suicide attempts can be 10–30 times greater than that of completed suicide (Schmidtke et al., 1996).

If generalized to the world population, this would indicate that 9–25 million suicide attempts take place every year.

Nature of the Problem

There are several conceptualizations of suicide—each one reflecting more or less the area from which it stems. Public mental health experts consider suicide as a behavioral process that starts with vague considerations about death and dying (suicidal ideation), which may become fixed (persistent or fluctuating), may evolve into the elaboration of a plan (suicide plan), and may end up in a suicidal act. From an outcome perspective, the suicidal act can be a suicide attempt (when the perpetrator survives) or a completed suicide (when death ensues). The human-ecological model developed by WHO (shown in Fig. 19.1) highlights that this process always takes place in an environment with both cultural and physical elements that, to a great extent, shape the behavior and explain the huge differences observed in suicide rates and methods employed to attempt to or to kill oneself across place and time.

Contemporary suicidologists consider suicide, according to a stress-vulnerability model, as a complex interplay of sociocultural factors, traumatic life experiences, psychiatric history, personality traits, and genetic vulnerability (Mann, Waterneaux, Haas, & Malone, 1999; Wasserman, Sokolowski, Wasserman, & Rujescu, 2009). All these factors can be understood as risk or protective factors, depending on the circumstances, as will be seen ahead.

Etiology of Suicide

As seen before, knowledge of the etiology of and risk factors for suicide is crucial for the establishment of effective prevention programs, irrespective of the conceptual model preferred. Nonetheless, suicide is a complex, multifactorial, multidetermined behavior that does not have one single, individualized etiology. In this case, one can identify an intricate array of risk and protective factors that interplay, and it is not easy to single out or measure the relative weight of each of them. For purposes of clarity, these factors will be discussed separately, and risk factors will be further subdivided into predisposing and precipitating factors.

It should be said, however, that many risk factors so far identified as being implicated in suicidal behavior are not modifiable (as we shall see) and, as such, their knowledge may not be very relevant in intervention programs, but their importance nevertheless remains for the purposes of designing preventive programs.

Risk Factors

The identification and analysis of risk factors (and, more recently, of protective factors) has been a major concern of suicidology and suicidologists since the 19th century. Many books, chapters, and papers have been written on the subject, and a large proportion of the research related to suicide revolves around risk factors. Therefore, the list of factors that have been suggested, proposed, investigated, or demonstrated to be associated with suicidal behaviors is almost endless. Many have been found to be significantly associated with some form of suicidal behavior; however, most studies have investigated one or a few factors in isolation, frequently failing to control for other factors that might have a protective role, thus biasing the observed results.

It is important to make a temporal distinction between risk factors that have a distal relation with the suicidal act that can be understood as predisposing factors (genetic and personality constitution) and risk factors that have a proximal relation to the suicidal act (i.e., precipitating factors), which intervene shortly before that act (hence, usually and mistakenly considered "the cause" of suicide).

From a practical viewpoint, the WHO has identified a few risk factors that, alone or in combination,

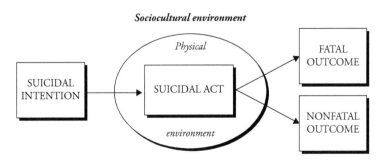

Figure 19.1. Suicide: WHO Ecological Model. (From World Health Organization, 1998.)

increase risk of suicidal behaviors (WHO, 2000; see Table 19.1).

Gender and age, although frequently included in lists of risk factors for suicide, are not seen in Table 19.1 due to their bimodal risk pattern; that is, while completed suicide is more frequent among men, suicide attempts are seen more frequently among women. Similarly, completed suicide more frequently occurs among the elderly, while suicide attempts occur more frequently among youth.

For preventive purposes, though, it should be noted that, as Foster and Wu (2002) have indicated, many of these risk factors—such as age, gender, ethnicity, and losses (affective and material)—are fixed (Forster & Wu, 2002) and thus cannot be modified and are not amenable to any specific individual intervention. Therefore, the potential usefulness of their knowledge lies in designing suicide prevention programs for other people carrying those risks, aiming at obviating or attenuating their negative impact before they exert their effects.

Protective Factors

As indicated before, there is considerably less interest in and research on protective factors than there is on risk factors. Nevertheless, there is ample room to believe that an important amount of difference found between suicidal and nonsuicidal subjects could be explained by protective factors not adequately explored or statistically controlled. The list of potential protective factors can be extensive (see Table 19.2; adapted from Wasserman, 2001).

It should be said that most of these proposed protective factors have not been formally evaluated or tested. A few, however, have been clinically tested and proved to be specific protective factors against suicidal ideation and attempts, for example, the so-called emotional intelligence (EI; Cha & Nock, 2009), responsibility for family (Chan et al., 2008), and moral and religious objections to suicide (Lizardi et al., 2008). These studies, nevertheless, were conducted with relatively small samples and are eagerly waiting for replication in other settings, with larger samples.

A quick comparison of the contents of Tables 19.1 and 19.2 shows that assessing the presence or absence of these factors, particularly in retrospective studies (as are most of the studies on suicide mortality, particularly the ones employing psychological autopsy approaches), is much easier and straightforward in the case of risk factors than of protective factors. The evaluation of the latter usually needs active participation of the subject, whereas most of the former can be assessed by secondhand informants, or even preexisting data banks.

At any rate, as it will be seen in the next sections, programs and strategies aiming at the prevention of suicidal behavior have relied more often on eliminating or blocking risk factors rather than on enhancing protective factors. It is not absurd to think that programs and strategies based on the promotion and reinforcement of protective factors might achieve better results than the ones obtained so far.

Table 19.1 Factors Usually Seen in Persons at Risk of Suicidal Behaviors

Predisposing Factors (distal in relation to the suicidal act)		Precipitating Factors (proximal in relation to the suicidal act)
Sociodemographic and Individual Factors	Environmental Factors	Recent Life Stressors
• Previous suicide attempt(s) • Psychiatric disorders (generally depression, alcoholism, schizophrenia, and personality disorders) • Physical illness (terminal, painful, shameful, or debilitating illness, AIDS) • Family history of suicide, alcoholism, and/or other psychiatric disorders • Divorced, widowed, or single status • Living alone (socially isolated) • Unemployed or retired • Bereavement or sexual abuse in childhood • Recent discharge from a psychiatric hospital or ward	• Easy access to means of attempting/ committing suicide	• Marital separation • Bereavement • Family disturbances • Change in occupational or financial status • Rejection by a significant person • Shame and fear of being found guilty

Table 19.2 Factors Considered to Be Protective in Relation to Suicidal Behaviors

Cognitive Style and Personality	Family Patterns	Cultural and Social Factors	Environmental Factors
• A sense of personal value • Confidence in oneself • Seeking help when in difficulty • Seeking advice when facing important choices • Openness to others' experiences and solutions • Openness to learning • Ability to communicate	• Good family relationships • Support from family • Devoted and consistent parenting	• Adherence to positive values, norms, and traditions • Good relations with friends, colleagues, and neighbors • Support from relevant people • Non-drug-using friends • Social integration through work, church activities, sports, clubs, etc. • A sense of purpose in life	• Good diet • Good sleep • Sunlight • Physical exercise • Non-drug, non-smoking environment

Models of Prevention
Levels of Prevention

In the early 1960s, Leavell and Clark (1965) proposed, as part of their Community Health program, a model of prevention that became widely accepted and had a long-lasting influence on the field up until now. Applying what was considered effective for infectious diseases to the prevention of chronic degenerative diseases, they defined three levels of prevention (primary, secondary, and tertiary) that *grosso modo* replaced what was known as health promotion and specific protection, early identification and treatment, and rehabilitation, respectively.

Primary prevention encompasses activities related to both general health promotion and specific protection against specific diseases (e.g., immunization), aiming at preventing the occurrence of the disease.

Secondary prevention is the early detection and intervention (e.g., treatment) for the purposes of deterring and reversing a disease condition, thus avoiding resulting incapacities or death.

Tertiary prevention refers to measures taken to restore an individual to his or her optimum functioning once a disease or disability has stabilized or to avoid premature death.

Knowing the etiology of the target disease is fundamental to the application of Leavell and Clark's preventive model. Although primarily created for medical diseases, this model can be applied to psychopathology and clinical behaviors, such as suicide. Once the etiology and natural history of the target condition are known, one can establish the progression of the disease—with four periods, namely, prepathological, prodromic, pathological, and recovery—on which key moments are defined in order to implement primary, secondary, or tertiary prevention.

For example, it is very different to prevent the emergence of suicidal ideation, the creation of suicide plans, or engagement in suicide attempts because the *locus* of intervention is (1) the intrapsychic space of the concerned individual, (2) both the internal and the cultural environments, and (3) mostly the physical environment.

To makes things more complex, results from a recent WHO multisite intervention study conducted in nine countries (Bertolote et al., 2005; see Fig. 19.2) has evidenced that although the sequence of ideation → planning → attempt almost inevitably follows that order, however, the proportional difference between both ideation and planning, on the one hand, and plans and attempts, on the other hand, varies enormously from place to place.

Moreover, there seems to be no correlation between suicidal ideation, on the one hand, and deaths from suicide, on the other hand, as shown in Figure 19.3, with combined data from Bertolote, Fleischmann, De Leo, and Wasserman (2009) and Weissman et al. (1999).

In brief, all things considered, Leavell and Clark's (1965) model has several shortcomings in its application to the prevention of suicidal behaviors, which facilitated the generalized adoption of another conceptual model, discussed next.

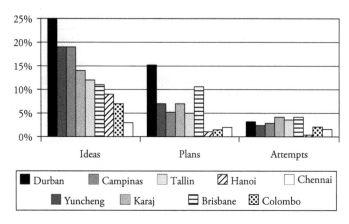

Figure 19.2. Suicidal ideation, plans, and attempts in World Health Organization SUPRE-MISS sites.

Risk Population-Based Prevention

In 1987 Gordon put forward another conceptual model for preventive actions, made popular by Mrazek and Hoggarty (1994), this time taking into account risk factors and population coverage rather than the natural history of the disease. As such, its main advantage over Leavell and Clark's (1965) model resides in its functionality with conditions whose etiology is unknown. In other words, it is more appropriate for behavioral problems, such as the case with suicide. Those authors categorized preventive interventions as universal, selective and indicated, according to the risk that individuals have of developing a particular problem.

Universal prevention refers to actions directed toward the whole population, irrespective of its degree of risk, and aims at delaying or impeding the appearance of a specific problem, such as drinking or suicide attempts. Because the whole population is involved, there is no selection of participants and the team does not need any specialization in health matters, rather a specific training. A good example is the observance of a Suicide Prevention Day, during which the population is made aware of suicide as a problem, and how to face it.

Selective prevention targets subgroups of the general population known to carry a given risk of a specific problem, and it aims to delay or impede the appearance of its consequences by detecting and minimizing the effects of risk factors. Applied to suicide prevention programs, selective prevention targeting individuals with mental disorders known to be strongly associated with suicide (such as depression, alcohol misuse, and schizophrenia) may be effective in reducing the occurrence of these behaviors. There is an active search for participants, once their vulnerability is known. The prevention team must be trained to deal with an array of issues that go beyond health matters only, and which involve sociocultural and economic issues, family relations, adolescence, old age, and behavioral disorders, in general, all of which may relate to risks of engaging in suicidal behavior.

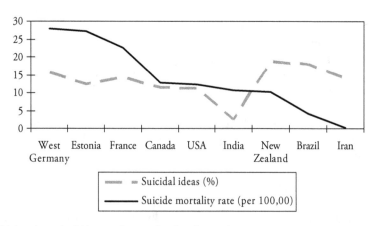

Figure 19.3. Suicidal thoughts and suicide mortality rates in selected countries.

Indicated prevention targets individuals with a clear risk or manifestations of the problem. In this way, participants are actively recruited and prevention aims to stop the behavior that has already started. A program targeting people who attempted suicide is a good example of indicated prevention.

Table 19.3 outlines interventions by level of coverage, according to Mrazek and Hoggarty's (1994) model, as applied to suicidal behaviors.

Suicide Prevention Programs and Initiatives

Although a serious concern for national and international authorities, the prevention of suicidal behavior was seen only at the end of the 20th century. However, individual efforts, usually inspired by humanitarian, philanthropic, or religious principles, can be tracked back to the very beginning of the 20th century. In fact, the first documented programs aimed at preventing suicide were initiated in 1906 in both New York (National Save-A-Life League) and London (Suicide Prevention Department of the Salvation Army) (Bertolote, 2004).

The first suicide prevention programs were not empirically validated. Now, however, prevention programs based on empirical findings have begun to emerge in order to decrease the cost and increase the effectiveness of these programs. Recently, agencies, such as the WHO, have placed much more scrutiny on the cost-effectiveness of suicide prevention programs.

Reflecting those recent concerns, in the last 20 years several authors have carefully scrutinized numerous specific suicide prevention programs. Gunnel and Frankel (1994) examined existing evidence from research (1975 1994) on ways to reduce the incidence of suicide. They found that out of 19 intervention programs for suicide only 2 were randomized controlled studies. For some of the other studies, the main objective was unclear from the outset (e.g., whether the outcome of interest was the reduction of mortality from suicide or any suicidal behavior).

Other serious limitations found were related to the small number of subjects included in the studies that did not provide enough statistical power (one should not forget that despite the impressive number of cases of suicides attempted and completed, on an aggregate level, a death from suicide is a rare event), the short period of follow-up, and the imprecise description of what exactly were the operating elements of the interventions.

More recently, Crawford, Thomas, Khan, and Kulinskaia (2007) conducted a meta-analysis of systematic reviews on the efficacy of psychosocial interventions following self-harm and, to a large extent, confirmed most of the previous criticisms presented 10 years earlier by Gunnel and Frankel (1994).

In an interesting discussion that followed the publication of Crawford et al.'s (2007) paper, Rudd (2007) argued that these types of interventions are not amenable to meta-analysis and that serious methodological limitations prevent us from drawing definite conclusions on the real impact of those interventions. He also warned about the dangers of misinforming the public with imprecise data.

In brief, traditional suicide prevention initiatives antedate the era of evidence-based practice and systematic evaluation, with many current suicide prevention programs and initiatives still following those initial traditions. Methodologists do not always find good material for analysis in programs that were not conceived with evaluation in mind. This is not the appropriate space to discuss these methodological questions, but it should be remembered that things have started to change; there is a great variety of programs already conceived according to sound scientific and methodological principles.

Table 19.3 Examples of Effective Prevention Programs for Suicidal Behaviors by Coverage

Level of Coverage	Target	Intervention
Universal	• The whole population	• Limitation of access to toxic substances
Selective	• Individuals with low to moderate risk of suicidal behaviors	• Treatment of people with mental disorders (including substance use disorders)
Indicated	• Individuals with a clear, high risk of suicidal behaviors	• Close therapeutic follow-up of people with bipolar disorders or with recurrent psychotic episodes • Close (psychosocial) follow-up of previous attempters

Strategies for Suicide Prevention

The emergence of prevention programs for suicidal behavior in the public health arena can be tracked back to a seminal document jointly produced by the WHO and the Economic and Social Council (ECOSOC) of the United Nations (UN), titled *Prevention of Suicide: Guidelines for the Formulation and Implementation of National Strategies* issued in 1996 (United Nations, 1996). It considered suicide prevention to be "multifactorial, multidetermined and transactional in its origin, and to develop cumulative through identifiable, but complex, pathways or trajectories." It served as the basis for the development of national strategies for the prevention of suicidal behavior in several countries, including Finland, Norway, Sweden, New Zealand, Australia, the United Kingdom, The Netherlands, Estonia, France, the United States, and Brazil.

The novelty and importance of that document was two-fold. On the one hand, it was the first time that authoritative and respected international organizations acknowledged that suicidal behaviors were indeed major social and economic problems affecting several nations, which is a strong political statement. On the other hand, on a more technical side, it put forward detailed guidelines indicating (1) organizing principles; (2) relevant policy areas; (3) objectives; (4) steps in the formulation of a strategy; (5) its implementation, review, and appraisal; (6) gathering international support; and (7) publication and dissemination.

A few years later, following a decision from the 39th World Health Assembly, the WHO launched its Suicide Prevention Programme (SUPRE), based on expert opinion, and best practices from members of the WHO International Panel of Experts on Suicide Prevention. Based on the limited evidence available at the time, three basic strategies were considered effective for the prevention of suicidal behaviors: (1) treatment of mental disorders; (2) restriction of access to methods used in suicidal behaviors (guns, gases, poisons, and other toxic substances); and (3) responsible media reporting (WHO, 1998).

Admittedly, the original UN/WHO document was based on limited research. More recently, however, there have been a few reviews of those strategies, further to empirical evaluations of some of the elements indicated in that document, as well as others identified or suggested afterward. Some of these reviews were done at the national level and some on a more international level.

On an international level, experts—some of whom were part of the original group that produced the WHO/UN document discussed earlier—from 15 countries met in Salzburg, Austria, in August 2004 to review efficacy of suicide prevention interventions. They confirmed the relevance of the areas previously proposed by WHO-SUPRE for the prevention of suicidal behaviors (i.e., treatment of mental disorders, restriction of access to methods, and responsible media reporting) and added another two areas, namely, education and awareness programs for the general public and professionals, and screening methods for high-risk persons (Mann et al., 2005).

As an example of a review at the national level, Beautrais et al. (2007) examined the literature and reviewed strategies for suicide prevention in New Zealand.

A summary of the evaluations conducted by the WHO/UN, reported by Mann et al. (2005) and Beautrais et al. (2007), using a typology based on an evidence hierarchy for classifying suicide prevention initiatives put forward in the latter paper, is shown in Table 19.4. The grading of the evidence, proposed by Beautrais et al. (2007), is as follows:

• Initiatives for which *strong evidence* of effectiveness exists: Initiatives that showed consistent evidence of program efficacy, though randomized trial designs.

• Initiatives that appear *promising*: Programs that showed some effectiveness, although not yet sufficient or consistent enough to classify them as strong.

• Initiatives for which no evidence of effectiveness exists but which *may be beneficial* in suicide prevention: Initiatives that span a range of macrosocial, mental health, family support, and related programs that encourage positive health and well-being, but for which no direct evidence of suicide-specific program effectiveness exists.

• Initiatives for which evidence of harmful effects exist: Initiatives in relation to which concerns have been raised regarding their safety, giving rise to the belief that they may risk increasing (rather than decreasing) rates of suicidal behaviors.

From Table 19.4, it can be concluded that in relation to the prevention of suicidal behaviors there are more promises than accomplishments. Although those programs have already saved thousands of lives, one cannot but agree with Beautrais et al.'s (2007) apt remark (2007) that there is not

Table 19.4 Strength of the Evidence of Effectiveness of Diverse Initiatives for the Prevention of Suicidal Behaviors

Strong Evidence	Promising	Potentially Beneficial	Harmful
• Restriction of access to suicide methods • Gatekeeper education	• Pharmacotherapy for mental illness • Psychotherapy and psychosocial interventions for mental illness • Providing support after suicide attempts • Responsible media coverage of suicide • Training for general medical practitioners • School-based competency promoting and skill enhancing programs • Screening for depression and suicide risk • Crisis centers and crisis counseling • Support for family and friends bereaved by suicide	• Improving control of alcohol • Community-based mental health services and support services • Support for families facing stress and difficulty • General public awareness and education	• School-based programs that focus on raising awareness about suicide • Public health messages about suicide and media coverage of suicide issues • No-harm and no-suicide contracts • Recovered or repressed memory therapies

much strong evidence for the efficacy of most suicide prevention initiatives, usually not evaluated, in spite of strong claims about their effectiveness.

Taking into account previous experiences and the available evidence in the scientific literature, in 2000 WHO launched a multisite international study (SUPRE-MISS), involving eight countries (Brazil, China, Estonia, India, Iran, South Africa, Sri Lanka, and Vietnam), in five of which a randomized controlled trial was conducted to evaluate treatment strategies for suicide attempters treated in emergency care settings. Results of this large and complex study indicated ambiguous results concerning the reduction of repetition of suicide attempts: decrease in China, India, and Sri Lanka, but an increase in Brazil and Iran (Fleischmann & Bertolote, 2008); however, it found a clear reduction in overall mortality and in mortality specifically from suicide in all sites (Bertolote et al., in press).

Prevention of Suicidal Behaviors Among Youth

As indicated earlier, in the last 50 years there has been a shift in the peak age of suicidal behaviors toward younger ages. In the developed world suicide is among the three leading causes of death for people aged 15–25 years (Bertolote & Fleischmann, 2009). This has led many authorities to take action, and, in many countries, initiatives related to suicide have mainly been geared toward young people.

Two systematic reviews of suicide prevention programs directed at youth (Guo & Harstall, 2002; Ploeg et al., 1996) confirmed that the presence of mental disorders and comorbid psychiatric diseases

characterize children and adolescents with the highest risk factors for suicidal behavior. Although risk factors for completed suicide and attempted suicide in this age group are not entirely the same, there is still a considerable overlap.

Regarding the efficacy/effectiveness of suicide prevention programs for this age group, Guo and Harstall (2002) echo the conclusions of Gunnel and Frankel (1994), Mann et al. (2005), and Beautrais et al. (2007) on similar programs aimed at adults and older people: For most programs, study designs testing their efficacy have serious methodological flaws that prevent a thorough analysis; a major limitation is that many samples are too small to provide sufficient statistical power.

More recently, there has been a controversy concerning the role of antidepressant medication (particularly the selective serotonin reuptake inhibitors, or SSRIs) in eliciting suicidal ideation in adolescents (Brent, 2009; Bridge et al., 2007). As a result, in some countries, a warning box ("black box") has been included on the packages of those drugs. An immediate consequence of this action was the reduction in the number of prescription antidepressants prescribed to adolescents (Libby et al., 2007). Some professionals and specialists now are worried that this restraint may cause more harm than benefit (Beautrais et al., 2007; Brent, 2004).

Guo and Harstall's (2002) review pointed out the potential harmful effects of educational programs—a quite popular strategy, as well as the limited generalizibility of the results of the few studies that demonstrated efficacy (given their restricted geographical origin). This should not be construed as a statement that suicide prevention programs for youth "don't work." Perhaps we are not yet in the stage of launching massive suicide prevention programs for youth, but there is room for hope, as smaller scale programs already have demonstrated efficacy (Brent, 2009; Malone & Yap, 2009; Spirito & Esposito-Smythers, 2009).

Conclusion

The magnitude and nature of suicidal behavior clearly pose this problem as a major public health issue in most countries, irrespective of their level of development or income.

Over the years, experience and experimentation already have indicated a few fruitful avenues for action and another few dangers to be avoided. Control of access to method of suicide and education/awareness of gatekeepers are among those interventions that have systematically demonstrated their effectiveness in reducing suicide mortality (WHO, 1998). Next, appropriate treatment (pharmacological, psychological, and psychosocial) of people with mental disorders (mainly depression, alcoholism, and schizophrenia) already has proved its efficacy/effectiveness in decreasing suicidal behaviors (Baldessarini et al., 2006; Tiihonen, Lönnkvist, et al., 2006; Tiihonen, Wahlbeck, et al., 2006; Wasserman, Värnik, & Eklund, 1994).

Despite the specific efficacy of isolated interventions, all of them acquire their full potential when integrated in and coordinated by a national or regional strategy. After all, suicidal behavior now clearly is perceived as "everybody's business." Several international bodies now include suicide prevention in their agenda, and an array of countries now formally adopt and are implementing sound, evidence-based suicide prevention strategies and programs.

Nevertheless, most of the accumulated knowledge about suicidal behaviors comes from only a few countries, most of which Western, industrialized countries, and there is a pressing need of concerted efforts to bridge this gap, thus benefiting all in need.

Future Directions

1. Efforts should be directed toward improving the quality of information related to suicidal behaviors. The number of countries reporting on suicide mortality should increase, and national/regional registries on suicide attempts should be established.

2. Psychological autopsy studies are a major source of information on suicide and should be conducted more often, particularly in low- and middle-income countries from which little is known, particularly on risk and protective factors. Local suicide prevention programs should be based on local risk and protective factors, and not on those identified elsewhere.

3. Research on protective factors also is needed.

References

Baldessarini, R. J., Tondo, L., Davis, P., Pompili, M., Goodwin, F. K., & Hennen, J. (2006). Decreased risk of suicides and attempts during long-term lithium treatment: A meta analytic review. *Bipolar Disorders, 8,* 625–639.

Browne, T. (1643). *Religio Medici.* Retrieved November 10, 2013, from http://penelope.uchicago.edu/relmed1645.pdf.

Beautrais, A., Fergusson, D., Coggan, C., Collings, C., Doughty, C., Ellis, P., ... Surgenor, L. (2007). Effective strategies for suicide prevention in New Zealand: A review of the evidence. *New Zealand Medical Journal, 120,* U2459.

Bertolote, J. M. (2004). Suicide prevention: At what level does it work? *World Psychiatry, 3,* 147–151.

Bertolote, J. M., & Fleischmann, A. (2002). A global perspective in the epidemiology of suicide. *Suicidologi, 7,* 6–8.

Bertolote, J. M., & Fleischmann, A. (2009). A global perspective on the magnitude of suicide mortality. In D. Wasserman & C. Wasserman (Eds.), *Oxford textbook of suicide and suicide prevention* (pp. 91–98). Oxford, UK: Oxford University Press.

Bertolote, J. M., Fleischmann, A., Butchart, A., & Besbelli, N. (2006). Suicide, suicide attempts and pesticides: A major hidden public health problem. *Bulletin of the World Health Organization, 84,* 260.

Bertolote, J. M., Fleischmann, A., De Leo, D., Bolhari, J. Botega, N., De Silva, D., ... Wasserman, D. (2005). Suicide attempts, plans, and ideation in culturally diverse sites. *Psychological Medicine, 35,* 1457–1465.

Bertolote, J. M., Fleischmann, A., De Leo, D., Phillips, M., Botega, N., Vijayakumar, L., et al. (2010). Repetition of suicide attempts: Data from five culturally different low- and middle-income countries emergency care settings participating in the SUPRE-MISS study. *Crisis, 31,* 194–201.

Bertolote, J. M., Fleischmann, A., De Leo, D., & Wasserman, D. (2005). Suicide attempts, plans and ideation in culturally diverse sites: The WHO SUPRE-MISS community survey. *Psychological Medicine, 35,* 1457–1465.

Bertolote, J. M., Fleischmann, A., De Leo, D., & Wasserman, D. (2009). Suicidal thoughts, suicide plans and attempts in the general population on different continents. In D. Wasserman & C. Wasserman (Eds.), *Oxford textbook of suicide and suicide prevention* (pp. 99–104). Oxford, UK: Oxford University Press.

Bertolote, J. M., Fleischmann, A., Eddleston, M., & Gunnel D. (2006). Deaths from pesticide poisoning: A global response. *British Journal of Psychiatry, 189,* 201–203.

Brent, D. (2009). Effective treatments for suicidal youth. In D. Wasserman & C. Wasserman (Eds.), *Oxford textbook of suicide and suicide prevention* (pp. 668–676). Oxford, UK: Oxford University Press.

Brent, D. A. (2004). Antidepressant and pediatric depression: The risk of doing nothing. *New England Journal of Medicine, 351,* 1598–1601.

Bridge, J., Iyengar, S., Salary, C. B., Barbe, R. P., Birmaher, B., Pincus, H.,...Brent, D. A. (2007). Clinical responses and risk for reported suicidal ideation and suicide attempts in pediatric antidepressant treatment: A meta-analysis of randomized controlled trials. *Journal of the American Medical Association, 297*, 1683–1696.

Camus, A. (1942). *Le mythe de Sisyphe*. Paris, France: Gallimard.

Cha, C. B., & Nock, M. K. (2009). Emotional intelligence is a protective factor for suicidal behavior. *Journal of the American Academy of Child and Adolescent Psychiatry, 48*, 422–430.

Chan, W. S. C., Law, C. K., Liu, K. Y., Wong, P. W. C., & Yip, P. S. F. (2008). Suicidality in Chinese adolescents in Honk Kong: The role of family and cultural influences. *Social Psychiatry and Psychiatric Epidemiology, 44*, 278–284.

Crawford, M. J., Thomas, O., Khan, N., & Kulinskaia, E. (2007). Psychosocial interventions following self-harm: Systematic review of their efficacy in preventing suicide. *British Journal of Psychiatry, 190*, 11–17.

De Leo, D., Bertolote, J. M., & Lester, D. (2002). Self-directed violence. In E. G. Krug, L. L. Dahlberg, J. A. Mercy, A. B. Zwi, & R. Lozano (Eds.), *World report on health and violence* (pp. 183–212). Geneva, Switzerland: World Health Organization.

Durkheim, E. (1897). *Le suicide: Etude de sociologie*. Paris, France: Alcan.

Eddleston, M., Karunaratne, A., Weerakoon, M., Kumarasinghe, S., Rajapakshe, M., Sheriff, M.,...Gunnell, D. (2006). Choice of poison for intentional self-poisoning in rural Sri Lanka. *Clinical Toxicology, 44*, 283–286.

Esquirol, E. (1838). *Des maladies mentales: Considerées sous les rapports médical, higiénique et médico-legal*. Paris, France: J. B. Baillière.

Fleischmann, A., & Bertolote, J. M. (2008). Effectiveness of brief intervention and contact for suicide attempters: A randomized controlled trial in five countries. *Bulletin of the World Health Organization, 86*, 703–709.

Forster, P., & Wu, L. (2002). Assessment and treatment of the suicidal patient in an emergency setting. In M. H. Allen (Ed.), *Emergency psychiatry* (pp. 75–113). Washington, DC: American Psychiatric Publishing.

Freud, S. (1961). *Beyond the principle of pleasure* (J. Strachey, Trans.). New York, NY/London, UK: Norton (original work published 1920).

Gartner, J., Larson, D. B., & Allen, G. D. (1991). Religious commitment and mental health: A review of the empirical literature. *Journal of Psychology and Theology, 19*, 6–25.

Gordon, R. (1987). An operational classification of disease prevention. In J. A. Steinberg & M. M. Silverman (Eds.), *Preventing mental disorders* (pp. 20–26). Rockville, MD: US Department of Health and Human Services.

Gunnel, D., Eddleston, M. Phillips, M., & Konradsen, F. (2007). Worldwide patterns of fatal pesticide self-poisoning. *BMC Public Health, 7*, 357.

Gunnel, D., & Frankel, S. (1994). Prevention of suicide: Aspirations and evidence. *British Medical Journal, 308*, 1227–1233.

Guo, B., & Harstall, C. (2002). *Efficacy of suicide prevention programs for children and youth* (HTA 26: Series A Health Technology Assessment). Calgary, AB: Alberta Heritage Foundation for Medical Research.

Gururaj, G., Isaac, M. K., Subbakrishna, D. K., & Ranjani, R. (2004). Risk factors for completed suicides: A case-control study from Bangalore, India. *International Journal of Injury Control and Safety Promotion, 11*, 183–191.

Khan, M. M. (2009). Suicide prevention in Pakistan. In D. Wasserman & C. Wasserman (Eds.), *Oxford textbook of suicide and suicide prevention* (pp. 3–7). Oxford, UK: Oxford University Press.

Leavell, H. R., & Clark, E. G. (1965). *Preventive medicine for the doctor in his community: An epidemiological approach* (3rd ed.). New York, NY: McGraw Hill.

Libby, A., Brent, D. A., Morrato, E. H., Orton, H. D., Allen, R., & Valuck, R. J. (2007). Decline in treatment of pediatric depression after FDA advisory on risk of suicidality with SSRIs. *American Journal of Psychiatry, 164*, 884–891.

Lizardi, D., Dervic, K., Grunebaum, M. F., Burke, A. K., Mann, J. J., & Oquendo, M. A. (2008). The role of moral objections to suicide in the assessment of suicidal patients. *Journal of Psychiatric Research, 42*, 815–821.

Malone, K., & Yap, S. Y. (2009). Innovative psychosocial rehabilitation of suicidal young people. In D. Wasserman & C. Wasserman (Eds.), *Oxford textbook of suicide and suicide prevention* (pp. 685–690). Oxford, UK: Oxford University Press.

Mann, J. J, Apter, A., Bertolote, J. M., Beautrais, A., Currier, D., Haas, A.,...Hendin, H. (2005). Suicide prevention strategies: A systematic review. *Journal of the American Medical Association, 294*, 2064–2074.

Mann, J. J., Waterneaux, C., Haas, G., & Malone, K., (1999). Toward a clinical model of suicidal behavior in psychiatric patients. *American Journal of Psychiatry, 156*, 181–189.

Mrazek, P. J., & Haggerty, R. J. (Eds.). (1994). *Reducing risks for mental disorders: Frontiers for preventive intervention research. Committee on Prevention of Mental Disorders*. Washington, DC: Institute of Medicine.

Phillips, M. R. (2002). Suicide rates in China. *Lancet, 359*, 2274.

Phillips, M., Yang, Z., Zhang, Y., Wang, L., Ji, H., & Zhou, M. (2002). Risk factors for suicide in China: A national case-control psychological autopsy study. *Lancet, 30*, 1728–1736.

Pinel, P. (1809). *Traité médico-philosophique sur l'aliénation mentale*. Paris, France: J. A. Brosson.

Ploeg, J., Ciliska, D., Dobbins, M., Hayward, S., Thomas, H., & Underwood, J. (1996). A systematic overview of adolescent suicide prevention programs. *Canadian Journal of Public Health, 87*, 319–24.

Rudd, M. D. (2007). Inaccurate conclusions based on limited data. Electronic letter to the *British Journal of Psychiatry*, May 02, 2007. Retrieved November 10, 2013 from http://bjp.rcpsych.org/content/190/1/11.1/reply last.

Schmidtke, A., Bille-Brahe, U., De Leo, D. Kerkhof, A., Bjerke, T., Crepet, P.,...Sampaio-Faria, J. G. (1996). Attempted suicide in Europe: Rate trends ad sociodemographic characteristics of suicide attempter during the period 1989–1992. Results of the WHO/EURO Multicentre Study on Parasuicide. *Acta Psychiatrica Scandinavica, 93*, 327–338.

Shneidman, E. S. (1984) Suicide prevention. In R. Corsini (Ed.), *Encyclopedia of psychology* (Vol. 3, pp. 383). New York, NY: Wiley.

Spirito, A., & Esposito-Smythers, C. (2009). Individual therapy techniques with suicidal adolescents. In D. Wasserman & C. Wasserman (Eds.), *Oxford textbook of suicide and suicide prevention* (pp. 678–683). Oxford, UK: Oxford University Press.

Tiihonen, J., Lönnkvist, J., Wahlbeck, K., Klaukka, T., Tanskanen, A., & Haukka, J. (2006). Antidepressants and the risk of suicide, attempted suicide and overall mortality in a nationwide cohort. *Archives of General Psychiatry, 63*, 1358–1367.

Tiihonen, J., Wahlbeck, K., Lönnkvist, J., Klaukka, T., Ioannidis, J. P., Volavka, J., & Haukka, J. (2006). Effectiveness of antipsychotic treatments in a nationwide cohort of patients in community care after first hospitalization due to schizophrenia and schizoaffective disorders: Observational follow-up study. *British Medical Journal, 333*, 224–227.

United Nations. (1996). *Prevention of suicide: Guidelines for the formulation and implementation of national strategies.* New York, NY: United Nations.

Vijayakumar, L. (2003). Psychosocial risk factors for suicide in India. In L. Vijayakumar (Ed.), *Suicide prevention: Meeting the challenge together* (pp.149–162). Hyderabad, India: Orient Longman.

Wasserman, C. (2009). Suicide: Considering religion and culture. In D. Wasserman & C. Wasserman (Eds.), *Oxford textbook of suicide and suicide prevention* (pp. 3–7). Oxford, UK: Oxford University Press.

Wasserman, D. (2001). Negative life events (loses, changes, traumas and narcissistic injury) and suicide. In D. Wasserman (Ed.), *Suicide, an unnecessary death* (pp. 111–118). London, UK: Martin Dunitz.

Wasserman, D., Sokolowski, M., Wasserman, J., & Rujescu, D. (2009). Neurobiology and the genetics of suicide. In D. Wasserman & C. Wasserman (Eds.), *Oxford textbook of suicide and suicide prevention* (pp. 165–182). Oxford, UK: Oxford University Press.

Wasserman, D., Than, H. T., Minh, D. P., Goldstein, M., Nordenskiold, A., & Wasserman, C. (2008). Suicidal process, suicidal communication and psychosocial situation of young suicide attempters in a rural Vietnamese community. *World Psychiatry, 7*, 47–53.

Wassermann, D., Värnik,, A. & Eklund, G. (1994). Male suicides and alcohol consumption in the former USSR. *Acta Psychiatrica Scandinavica, 89*, 306–313.

Weissman, M. M., Bland, R. C., Canino, G. J., Greenwald, S., Hwu, H. G., Joyce, P. R.,…Yeh, E. K. (1999). Prevalence of suicide ideation and suicide attempts in nine countries. *Psychological Medicine, 29*, 9–17.

World Health Organization (1998). *Primary prevention of mental, neurological and psychosocial disorders.* Geneva, Switzerland: Author.

World Health Organization. (2000). *Preventing suicide: A resource for general physicians.* Geneva, Switzerland: Author.

World Health Organization. (2010). *Mental Health: Country reports and charts.* Retrieved August 2013, from http://www.who.int/mental_health/prevention/suicide/country_reports/en/index.html.

Psychological Treatment of Suicidal Behaviors

Erin F. Ward-Ciesielski *and* Marsha M. Linehan

Abstract

To date, there have been only 46 randomized, controlled trials (RCTs) of treatments designed specifically to target suicidal behaviors. Of these trials, only a fraction of them have been shown to effectively reduce these target behaviors. Additionally, the RCTs are further limited by several significant methodological flaws, including the lack of consistent operational definitions, small sample sizes, and exclusion of high-risk individuals. This chapter discusses these limitations and the ways in which they impact the interpretation of specific RCTs evaluating interventions for suicidal behaviors. The different interventions that have been evaluated are organized based on their central components (e.g., inpatient treatment, pharmacotherapy, caring letters) and the strengths, weaknesses, and results of each trial are discussed. Finally, overall recommendations are provided for both researchers in the field of treatment development and evaluation and for providers who are seeking effective strategies to deal with suicidal behaviors in treatment.

Key Words: blind assessment, inclusion criteria, intervention research, methodology, randomized controlled trial, standards of care, suicide treatment

As discussed in other chapters in this volume, suicide is a very low base-rate phenomenon. As such, it is nearly impossible to predict future suicide with the statistical models presently available. Even models that can make true-positive indications have rates of false-positive determinations that are well above a level that would give us confidence in their clinical utility (e.g., Goldstein, Black, Nasrallah, & Winokur, 1991; Hughes, 1995). This leaves us at a sizeable disadvantage when we begin to consider implementing treatment programs for individuals deemed to be at high risk for suicide. Despite our best calculations, we will overestimate risk for the vast majority of individuals who will never take their own lives. Further, for each of those correctly identified, we know that there are countless others who will be falsely labeled as low risk.

This is our task and our burden as suicide intervention researchers. We must develop and evaluate programs across all levels of suicidality. We must expand prevention efforts to decrease suicide risk across all individuals as well as intervention strategies to reduce risk when suicidal thoughts or behaviors emerge. Finally, we must attend to postintervention issues following the death of an individual by suicide.

This chapter will address the middle component of this triad: intervention. We will review the available empirically supported psychological and biological treatments. Throughout this discussion we will provide recommendations both for clinicians treating suicidal clients and for suicide intervention researchers. We aim to present a thorough and accurate summary of the randomized intervention trials available to date—complete with relevant clinical suggestions—while also providing recommendations for research still needed in order to move the field forward toward developing more effective treatments for suicidal behaviors.

Limitations and Weaknesses

Before beginning a discussion of the literature, it is important to note that the field of suicide intervention research is rife with significant weaknesses that impede empirical progress. Some weaknesses make it necessary to repeat study conditions in order to ensure that results remain or become significant with larger sample sizes. Others force us to question the very assumptions on which treatment providers base their clinical judgment. We discuss these at length in the following section. The specific limitations to be addressed are (1) the relative shortage of randomized controlled trials, (2) the lack of empirical definitions, (3) the infrequent use of validated measures, (4) the almost complete absence of assessment reliability evaluation within studies, (5) the frequent absence of blind assessment, and (6) the frequent exclusion of the highest risk suicidal clients.

The single most important weakness in the area of suicide intervention is the astounding lack of rigorous clinical trials to develop and evaluate treatments. We are focusing this discussion only on randomized clinical trials (RCTs) of treatments that target suicidal behaviors, with minor exceptions. The importance of randomization in treatment trials cannot be overemphasized. Without the random assignment of subjects to treatment conditions, it cannot be assumed that changes that occur during or after the implementation of the intervention are actually the result of that intervention. Results obtained can only be thought of as correlation (Linehan, 1997). While 46 RCTs have specifically targeted suicidal behavior (RCTs are denoted with an asterisk in the references), this number is disparagingly small considering that suicide was the tenth leading cause of death in the United States in 2010 (Centers for Disease Control and Prevention, 2012).

The paucity of studies in this area is even more obvious when compared to the numbers of RCTs listed in the Cochrane Central Register of Controlled Trials (2014). For example, in contrast to the 60 trials listed for suicide (including suicide data from some trials that did not specifically target suicide), there are 547 trials for liver disease (ranked as the 12th leading cause of death), 1,197 for hypertension (ranked 13th), and 68 for Parkinson's disease (ranked 14th). Interestingly, there are 670 trials listed for AIDS, a cause that is not listed in the top 15 causes of death. When compared to

clinical trials for depression (1,306 trials), schizophrenia (243 trials), bipolar disorder (81 trials), and anxiety disorders (259 trials), the number of clinical trials focusing on reduction of suicidal behavior is amazingly low.

In addition to the lack of research studies in this area, many of the studies that have been conducted are of limited utility. Of those RCTs targeting the reduction of suicidal behaviors, most employ small sample sizes and, as a result, are underpowered. Most do not explicitly define the behaviors they are targeting. The majority do not use outcome measures that have adequate psychometric properties. Many exclude individuals with diagnosed mental disorders in need of treatment or individuals with high suicide risk. These factors make it difficult to interpret nonsignificant findings because a significant effect of an intervention may have been present with an appropriately large sample size, a more accurately defined treatment target, a psychometrically sound measure, or a more severe clinical population.

There are many reasons these particular weaknesses necessitate critique. Perhaps the weakness with the broadest and most detrimental implications for the field as a whole is the lack of operational definitions. It is impossible to have a cohesive and productive field of study without first developing rigorous operational definitions for the classes of behaviors being evaluated (O'Carroll, Berman, Mosciicki, Tanney, & Silverman, 1996). Even more basic is a consistent terminology for the behaviors to be defined. During the last several decades, the field of suicide intervention research has seen the use of terms such as nonsuicidal self-injury, intentional self-harm, suicide attempt, parasuicide, suicidal ideation, and self-injurious thoughts all to represent components of the larger category of suicidal behaviors. Further adding to the frustration caused by the litany of terms, only a handful of research teams define the way in which they are using any one of the terms. We are thus left with results that are less meaningful and generalizable. It is clear that the provision of definitions is infrequent with only 21 (45%) of the 46 RCTs targeting suicidal behaviors including any sort of operational definition of the class of behavior they are targeting in their treatments and measuring as outcome. Further, within these 21 trials, even the definitions themselves are inconsistent. Throughout our discussion of the research literature on interventions for suicidal individuals, we will include the definitions provided by researchers when they are available. Additionally, we will note when trials did not include operational definitions.

Owing to this wide range of labels, we are limited in our ability to compare some research studies by the terms that researchers themselves have used. At times it is difficult to determine whether one study's "suicide attempt" is the same behavior as another study's "parasuicide" when these terms have not been defined. In some cases, these two words might have been used interchangeably; however, far more frequently there are differences in the two ranging from subtle, nuanced variations to downright conflicting definitions. Ideally, the field will choose terms, operationally define them, and use them consistently throughout subsequent research programs. This will further facilitate a process of redefinition and clarification that we cannot hope to move toward until we can be clear what we are talking about in the present.

Once we recognize that suicide treatment researchers have yet to form a clear and consistent language from which to work, the next weakness bearing serious consideration is the state of outcome measures that are used in treatment studies. Namely, there is a relative absence of measures of suicidal behaviors that have adequate psychometric properties. Although there are psychometrically sound measures of suicide attempts and nonsuicidal self-injury like the Suicide Attempt and Self-Injury Interview (SASII; Linehan, Comtois, Brown, Heard, & Wagner, 2006), and the Self-Injurious Thoughts and Behaviors Interview (Nock, Holmberg, Photos, & Michel, 2007) as well as measures of suicidal ideation like the Beck Scale for Suicide Ideation (BSI; Beck, Steer, & Ranieri, 1988) and the Suicidal Behaviors Questionnaire (SBQ; Addis & Linehan, 1989; Osman et al., 2001), these measures are rarely used in suicide intervention studies. In fact, only a fraction of the RCTs (9 of 46; 20%) targeting suicidal behaviors used a measure that has been published and demonstrated adequate reliability and validity.

Instead of using these available measures to evaluate outcome, many studies develop idiosyncratic measures (e.g., Hawton, et al., 1981), use items from measures that have been previously criticized for their clinical utility (e.g., Bagby, Ryder, Schuller, & Marshall, 2004) and reliability, or simply do not report which outcome measures they used at all (e.g., Montgomery, Roy, & Montgomery, 1981; Torhorst, Moller, Kurz, Schmid-Bode, & Lauter, 1988; Verkes et al., 1997). Additionally, some research teams develop new measures, whether formally or informally, that have a similar purpose to those already available (e.g., Cedereke, Monti, & Ojehagan, 2002; Guthrie et al., 2001). Although in many instances this might be necessary, we have no idea of the validity of these outcome reports until the psychometric analyses on validity and reliability are completed. Unfortunately, this process is distressingly rare within the field of suicide intervention research. In effect, we are left with a handful of empirically grounded measures and a large number of measures that are useless without the appropriate evaluation. Additionally, other researchers who wish to replicate findings using the same outcome instruments are left with the burden of evaluating these measures before they can be used with confidence.

Further, even when psychometrically sound measures are used in studies, the reliability of assessments within individual studies is not evaluated with any consistency. Most of the RCTs discussed in this chapter did not report the context of their assessments. Of those that did, a fundamental tenet of clinical trials methodology—namely, blind assessment—was reported in only 12 (26%) of the RCTs. Only with the use of blind assessment can we be sure that the results obtained were not the inadvertent result of an assessor's bias based on knowledge about the treatment condition assigned (e.g., Kazdin, 1977; Rosenthal, 1966).

A final weakness, excluding participants at a high risk for suicide from studies, has arguably crippled the field of suicide intervention research as much as any other limitation. First, in most clinical trials of what are now viewed as evidence-based treatments (EBTs) for mental disorders, individuals viewed by the investigators to be at risk for suicide are commonly excluded. Not only are they excluded, but operational definitions and reliability data on the measures they used for exclusion are rarely included. Thus, although these treatments may have been shown effective for major depression (e.g., cognitive therapy, behavioral activation), panic disorder (e.g., exposure), and other mental disorders, at present we cannot confidently implement them with a suicidal individual with the same diagnosis. Research evaluating whether these same EBTs are efficacious for a higher risk treatment population has yet to be done. Suicidal individuals are similar to pregnant women in that they are not only commonly excluded from clinical trials but the ethical costs of not learning how to treat these individuals is rarely discussed.

Perhaps even more immobilizing is the fact that even intervention studies targeting suicidal behaviors routinely exclude those at the highest risk for death by suicide (e.g., those with multiple suicide attempts, drug dependence diagnoses, depression, or other co-occurring mental health diagnoses). Unfortunately, this means that much of the research involving treatment of individuals with co-occurring disorders and suicidal behavior has yet to be done. Encouragingly, this trend appears to be improving in more recent studies. A decade ago, Linehan (1997) commented on the fact that trials that included the highest risk individuals had yielded a more consistently significant impact on decreasing suicidal behaviors. Currently, those at highest risk are being included more frequently, and there does not appear to be a difference in results obtained by studies that did and did not exclude high-risk individuals.

As with virtually all other treatments for mental disorders or medical illnesses, no treatment can completely eliminate the risk of the disorder or illness. The same is true of suicide. Although many interventions have been shown to reduce specific suicidal behaviors, no intervention has demonstrated effectiveness at *eliminating* the risk of death by suicide. This is another burden our field must bear. There is, without a doubt, much work to be done in this area.

Standards of Care

There are two models by which the treatment of suicidal behaviors can be approached. The first is to view suicidal behaviors as symptoms of a mental disorder. This more traditional approach leads to treating the disorder itself and stems from the belief that suicidal behaviors will decrease as a result. For example, there are evidence-based treatments (EBTs) for depression. Suicidal behavior is popularly associated with depression and has been found to be more common among individuals with depression than in nondepressed controls (e.g., Oquendo, Lizardi, Greenwald, Weissman, & Mann, 2004). Thus, in this model, suicidal behavior is viewed as a symptom of depression and, therefore, is expected to decrease when depression is treated. In other words, depression is the disorder believed to cause suicidal behaviors and these behaviors are indirectly targeted by directly targeting the disorder.

The second model of treatment for suicidal behavior conceptualizes suicidal behavior as disordered behavior that may be a result of any number of environmental and individual characteristics, including but not limited to mental disorders (Linehan, 1981). Rather than relying on EBTs that have been shown effective for other mental disorders, this newer model leads to the development and evaluation of EBTs that treat suicidal behaviors

specifically. That is, suicidal behavior is viewed as the disordered behavior to be treated directly, rather than the symptom of another mental disorder.

Interestingly, we have very little empirical evidence supporting either one of these models. As described earlier, there are a disproportionately small number of RCTs that include suicidal behaviors as a primary outcome. Perhaps even more interestingly, there are no RCTs reporting that treating the disorder (e.g., depression) reduces the risk of death by suicide. Although suicidal behaviors are frequently reported as secondary outcomes in RCTs of treatments for depression, we do not have evidence that treating depression (or any other disorder) reduces the risk of death by suicide (Linehan, 1997).

At present, the model of treating the disorder to reduce the suicide risk is the most prominent standard of care. It can best be evaluated by looking at pharmacological trials. Countless RCTs have been conducted in order to evaluate the effectiveness of various pharmacological treatments for specific mental disorders. Many of these trials also have included measures of suicidal behavior as secondary outcomes to the primary ones related to the specific disorders of interest. Rigorous meta-analyses have been conducted based on these trials in order to determine the effect of these medications on suicidal outcomes.

Beasley and colleagues (1992) conducted one such meta-analysis of 17 brief clinical trials that compared fluoxetine with (1) a tricyclic antidepressant, (2) a placebo, or (3) both. In total, these 17 trials included 3,065 subjects. Beasley et al. (1992), interested in the potentially detrimental effects of antidepressants on suicidality, looked at emergence of suicidal ideation, worsening of suicidal ideation, and improvement of suicidal ideation in their meta-analysis. They found a trend in which emergence of suicidal ideation was less in the fluoxetine groups than the placebo groups and that suicidal ideation improved significantly more with fluoxetine than with placebo. These results seem to provide promising evidence for the use of fluoxetine in individuals who are diagnosed with major depression and also report suicidal ideation.

However, of particular importance for this discussion is the percentage of actual suicidal acts (i.e., completed suicide and suicide attempts) in each condition of each study. As the vast majority of the trials included in this meta-analysis excluded individuals at high risk for suicide, it is not surprising that suicidal acts occurred infrequently. Even so, the numbers of suicidal acts relative to the number of subjects in each of the three conditions were not significantly different (fluoxetine 0.3%, tricyclic antidepressants 0.4%, placebo 0.2%). This suggests that while suicidal ideation may emerge, increase, or improve during brief antidepressant treatment, the actual number of suicidal behaviors in which subjects engage is not significantly impacted by the treatment of major depressive disorder.

In a recent update of the previously mentioned meta-analysis, Beasley and colleagues (2007) compared 18 RCTs in which fluoxetine was compared to a placebo control for the treatment of major depression. This analysis included a total of 3,751 subjects. Again, across all 18 studies, there was an unsurprisingly infrequent occurrence of suicidal acts. As was found in the previous meta-analysis, the percentage of suicidal acts relative to the number of subjects in each condition was not significantly different (fluoxetine 0.2%, placebo 0.2%). Also similar to the previous meta-analysis, Beasley et al. (2007) found that there were significant differences between incidents of worsening, improving, and resolving suicidal ideation between subjects in the fluoxetine and placebo conditions, but this again failed to impact the incidence of suicidal acts, which further supports the stance that treating the disorder is not sufficient.

Finally, Khan and colleagues (2000) looked at the antidepressant trials in an FDA sample of 19,639 subjects. In the comparison of investigational antidepressants, active comparators, and placebo control conditions, the rates of suicide attempts and completed suicides were not significantly different between groups (investigational 0.8%, comparator 0.7%, placebo 0.4%). One year later, Khan and colleagues (2001) also investigated the antipsychotic trials in an FDA sample of 10,118 subjects. As in the previous meta-analysis, they found that the rates of suicide attempts and completed suicides were not significantly different between those assigned to new antipsychotics (5.0% and 0.7%), established antipsychotics (5.7% and 0.9%), and placebo (3.3% and 1.8%) conditions.

Although these results allowed Khan et al. (2000, 2001) to make the point that individuals randomly assigned to placebo conditions are not at increased risk for suicidal behaviors, it simultaneously provides further evidence that individuals in active antidepressant and antipsychotic conditions are not at *reduced risk* either. Based on consistent evidence from these pharmacological treatment study meta-analyses, it appears that treating the disorder directly does not decrease the risk of suicide.

Although there is no evidence supporting the first model of treating the disorder to reduce suicide, the second model is growing in empirical support. Thus, we will focus our discussion of psychological and pharmacological interventions on those studies that take this second model into consideration. The RCTs that we will discuss in greater detail in this chapter are chosen because suicidal behaviors are the primary treatment outcomes.

Intervention Research
Pharmacotherapy

There have been five pharmacotherapy trials that have specifically targeted suicidal individuals, the majority of which were conducted almost 30 years ago. Four of these trials (Draper & Hirsch, 1979; Montgomery et al., 1979; Montgomery, Roy, & Montgomery, 1981; Verkes, Hengeveld, van der Mast, Fekkes, & van Kempen, 1998) selected individuals who had a history of suicidal behavior prior to the index event that brought them into the hospital for enrollment. The fifth (Meltzer et al., 2003) only required that subjects be at high risk of suicide (which might include previous suicidal behavior but did not require it) in order to be included in the study.

Three of the four trials requiring individuals to have engaged in suicidal behaviors involved antidepressant treatments as the experimental condition. Draper and Hirsch (1979; Hirsch, Walsh, & Draper, 1983) randomly assigned individuals who were admitted to the hospital following parasuicide ("a non-fatal act of deliberate self-injury which simulates a suicidal act but does not lead to death," p. 189S) to one of three pharmacological conditions: an antidepressant (mianserin or nomifensine) or a placebo. High-risk subjects (those already in psychiatric treatment) were excluded from this trial. Neither antidepressant condition, when compared to the placebo, yielded significantly different percentages of subjects engaging in parasuicide during the 12-week follow-up period. This study had a total sample of 114 subjects, leaving uncertainty about whether there was a large enough sample to detect a significant effect of either of the antidepressants.

Montgomery et al. (1981) also randomized subjects to antidepressant and placebo control conditions using mianserin as the experimental treatment. Subjects included in this trial were required to have two previously documented acts of deliberate self-harm (undefined) in addition to the suicide attempt for which they were hospitalized at the time of enrollment in the study. As such, high-risk subjects were not excluded from the trial. However, similar to Draper and Hirsch (1979), they did not find a significant difference in the percentage of subjects who attempted suicide between the two conditions during the 24 weeks of the study.

Third, Verkes et al. (1997, 1998) recruited subjects who had been admitted to the emergency room following a suicide attempt (undefined) and randomized them to receive paroxetine or placebo in addition to supportive psychotherapy. They recruited a moderately sized sample (91 subjects in total); however, high-risk subjects (those with an Axis I disorder) were excluded from participation. At the 8-month follow-up, there was no significant difference between conditions on rates of subsequent suicide attempts.

The fourth trial that recruited individuals with previous suicidal behaviors was conducted by Montgomery and colleagues (1981) and compared flupenthixol (an antipsychotic medication) to a placebo control condition for personality disorder (namely, borderline and histrionic personality disorder) patients admitted to the hospital after their third suicidal act (undefined). In this trial, Montgomery and colleagues found a significant difference in the number of subjects attempting suicide between the two conditions, with 3 subjects in the experimental condition compared to 12 in the control attempting suicide during the 24-week trial.

As was the case with the pharmacological trial conducted by Draper and Hirsch (1979), the results of the two trials conducted by Montgomery and colleagues (1979, 1981, 1982) must be interpreted with caution. None of the three trials provided operational definitions for the specific behaviors they were considering to be suicide attempts or suicidal acts. In addition, Montgomery and colleagues' studies have not been replicated in the over 25 years since they were conducted, and only one of their studies (1981, 1983) employed blind assessment.

Finally, and much more recently, Meltzer and colleagues (2003) investigated the impact of clozapine on schizophrenics at high risk for suicide. High risk was defined as having either (1) a history of suicide attempts or inpatient hospitalization to prevent suicidal behavior in the past 3 years, (2) moderate to severe current suicidal ideation with depressed symptoms, or (3) command hallucinations for self-harm within 1 week of study enrollment. There was a significantly greater number of suicide attempts ("actions committed by a patient, either with willful intent or as a response to internal compulsions or disordered thinking, that put him or her

at high risk for death," p. 84) in subjects receiving clozapine compared to those in the control condition who received olanzapine (6.9% compared to 11.2%).

The major weakness of this trial is that without a placebo condition we do not know whether clozapine reduced suicidal behaviors or olanzapine inhibited the reduction of suicidal behaviors in the control condition. Strengths of this trial include the inclusion of high-risk individuals and blind assessment throughout the course of the trial. Taken with the results from the other four pharmacotherapy trials as well as the many trials evaluating antidepressant medications for suicidal behaviors, the data do not appear to strongly support that pharmacotherapy itself is likely to be a sufficient treatment for suicidal behavior. Although the results of the Meltzer trial are promising, the percent differences between the two conditions are small compared with the larger differences reported in the psychological trials discussed next. However, as the data currently stand, replication with the addition of a placebo condition is needed, and further investigation with more severe clinical samples is certainly warranted in this area.

Hospitalization

Next we consider behavioral trials targeting suicidal individuals. For many clinicians, inpatient hospitalization is considered the standard of care for individuals deemed to be at high risk for imminent suicide. However, the outcomes from trials evaluating this intervention have less than encouraging results. First, two trials have compared brief inpatient hospitalization to treatment as usual outside the inpatient unit (Van der Sande et al., 1997; Waterhouse & Platt, 1990). Waterhouse and Platt (1990) randomized subjects to inpatient admission (median length of admission, 17 hours) or discharge home following parasuicide ("a non-fatal act in which an individual deliberately ingests a substance in excess of any prescribed or generally recognized therapeutic dosage," p. 237). Subjects were excluded, however, if they were considered to be at a high risk for suicide. Not surprisingly then, there was not a significant difference between the frequency of hospital readmission during the 16-week follow-up period.

Van der Sande and colleagues (1997) also evaluated the effect of brief inpatient admission compared to treatment as usual on subsequent suicide attempts ("act[s] with non-fatal outcome[s], in which an individual deliberately initiates a non-habitual behavior that, without intervention from others, will cause self-harm, or deliberately ingests a substance in excess of the prescribed or generally recognized therapeutic dosage, and which is aimed at realizing changes which the subject desires via the actual or expected physical consequences," p. 36). In this case, treatment as usual involved referral to routine clinical services. In addition to the brief inpatient admission, subjects in the experimental condition also received brief outpatient, problem-oriented counseling and 24-hour emergency access to counseling staff. However, high-risk subjects (those with habitual self-mutilation, habitual excessive drug and alcohol use, and those requiring psychiatric hospitalization) were excluded from the trial and Van der Sande et al. (1997) did not find a significant difference in the number of suicide attempts during the 12-month follow-up. Somewhat disconcertingly, they found a trend wherein the high-risk subjects (those who had a score of at least four on the Risk of Repetition Scale; Buglass & Horton, 1974) in the experimental condition had more suicide attempts than high-risk subjects discharged home.

Types of Inpatient Treatment

Neither of the aforementioned trials involved specific interventions while the subjects were on the inpatient unit. Instead, they compared treatment as usual on the inpatient unit to treatment as usual outside inpatient admission. Conversely, two other trials (Liberman & Eckman, 1981; Patsiokas & Clum, 1985) compared variations of inpatient treatments that an individual could receive. Liberman and Eckman (1981) selected a small sample (24 subjects in total) of multiple suicide attempters (undefined) who were admitted to the inpatient unit following a suicide attempt. These subjects were randomized to receive behavior therapy or insight-oriented therapy during their 10-day admission. High-risk individuals were included in this study; however, in comparing the number of suicide attempts 2 years after the inpatient treatment, there were no significant differences between the two conditions.

Patsiokas and Clum (1985) also selected a small sample of patients admitted to the inpatient unit for suicide attempts (undefined). These subjects were randomly assigned to receive (1) cognitive therapy, (2) problem-solving skills training, or (3) nondirective, reflective psychotherapy, each of which was conducted in ten 1-hour sessions over the course of 3 weeks. Similar to the findings of Liberman and Eckman (1981), Patsiokas and Clum (1985) found no differences between the three conditions on self-reported suicidal ideation or intent.

Taken in concert, these four trials of inpatient interventions for suicidal individuals raise serious questions about the efficacy of hospitalizing individuals who present with suicidal behaviors. This issue is particularly important since not only can we hospitalize suicidal individuals involuntarily in every US state but also because there is compelling evidence that individuals with prior inpatient treatment are at high risk for suicide both immediately following hospitalization and in the long term (Combs & Romm, 2007; Kallert, Glockner, & Schutwohl, 2008). Although it is comforting to believe that these high postdischarge rates are caused by patient characteristics predating hospitalization, we must also consider the possibility that hospitalization of suicidal individuals is actually iatrogenic. Based on the data, at this point we cannot say that inpatient treatment keeps suicidal individuals alive for even 5 extra minutes, nor can we say that it reduces suicidality more than control conditions.

Removing Suicidality as a Condition for Emergency Treatment

Another approach to intervening when individuals are suicidal is the "green card" intervention, which provides subjects with cards that allow them access to a treatment facility or provider without the requirement that they be suicidal to do so. Three trials have evaluated this green card method (Cotgrove, Zirinsky, Black, & Weston, 1995; Evans, Morgan, Hayward, & Gunnell, 1999; Evans, Evans, Morgan, Hayward, & Gunnell, 2005; Morgan, Jones, & Owen, 1993). Morgan and colleagues (1993) selected patients admitted to a general hospital after an episode of deliberate self-harm (DSH: undefined). These subjects were randomized to receive either (a) treatment as usual plus a green card that offered rapid, easy access to on-call psychiatry residents and encouragement to access this resource or (b) treatment as usual only. Treatment as usual in this trial consisted of a referral to the primary health care team or to an inpatient unit. While they did not find a significant difference in the number of subjects who engaged in repeated DSH, when they included in the analyses DSH as well as serious threats, the condition that received the green cards had significantly fewer episodes than the control condition (4.95% compared to 13.51%).

Cotgrove and colleagues (1995) offered a randomized subset of young adolescent subjects admitted to the study hospitals for a suicide attempt ("all acts of deliberate self-poisoning and deliberate self-injury," p. 570) green cards that permitted rapid, "no questions asked" hospital admission if requested. Despite being compared to treatment as usual involving standard treatment from the clinic or child psychiatry and including high-risk individuals, the experimental condition did not have significantly different numbers of suicide attempts during the 1-year follow-up.

Thirdly, Evans, Morgan and colleagues (1999) recruited adults who were admitted to an inpatient unit following parasuicide (undefined). Subjects in both conditions received usual care while the experimental condition also received the option of 24-hour crisis telephone consultation for up to 6 months. While post-hoc analyses revealed that there were significantly fewer instances of repetition of parasuicide for the group of subjects in the experimental condition who were enrolled following their first parasuicidal act when compared to the control condition, there were no significant differences in repetition between the group of subjects who were enrolled following repeated parasuicidal behaviors, nor was there a difference in the rate of repeated hospitalization due to parasuicide at the 12-month follow-up.

While these results are inconsistent, Morgan and colleagues (1993) used a larger sample size and, as a result, may have been more able to detect differences between the experimental and control conditions than Cotgrove and colleagues (1995). The fact that the green card condition did yield a significantly lower frequency of deliberate self-injury and serious threats of self-injury seems to suggest that making it easier for individuals to ask for help *before* becoming suicidal is a promising intervention. It certainly bears consideration that these trials, especially that of Morgan et al. (1993), should be replicated with the addition of blind assessment to ensure that the results are consistent.

Continuity of Care

Yet another approach to treatment for suicidal individuals rests on the assumption that, when possible, patients should continue to see the same provider regardless of whether they are in inpatient or outpatient care. That is, if a patient first starts receiving treatment on an inpatient unit, he or she should continue to meet with the same provider when he or she is discharged on an outpatient basis. Two trials have evaluated this approach (Bennewith et al., 2002; Torhorst et al., 1987 in Möller, 1989). Torhorst and colleagues (1987) recruited subjects

admitted to the hospital for a suicide attempt (undefined) by intoxication. These subjects were randomized to continued care with the inpatient therapist in an outpatient setting or referral to a suicide prevention center and follow-up with a new outpatient therapist. Although there was not a significant difference between the groups in the number of deaths by suicide, contrary to predictions, deaths by suicide plus suicide attempts were significantly *more* frequent in the continuity of care group compared to the control (18% vs. 5%).

In another trial evaluating continuity of care compared to usual care (i.e., noncontinuous care), Bennewith and colleagues (2002) gathered a large sample of subjects with an episode of deliberate self-harm (DSH: "hospital's medical notes confirmed that the act had been deliberate and not fatal, had been done in the knowledge that it was potentially harmful, and, in the case of drug overdose, that the amount of drug taken was excessive," p. 1255). The subjects in the experimental condition were monitored for new acts of DSH. The first new episode of DSH registered by the research staff prompted a letter to be sent to the subject's general practitioner informing the practitioner of the incident and providing him or her with a letter that could be forwarded to the subject inviting the subject to make an appointment for consultation. Additionally, these general practitioners were sent guidelines for the management of DSH. Subjects in the control condition received usual care. While subjects in the experimental condition contacted their general practitioners more frequently following an episode of DSH, they did not have a lower frequency of DSH episodes than those in the control condition.

These two trials evaluated the notion that continuity of care is an important component of treatment for suicidal individuals in different ways. While Torhorst and colleagues (1987) evaluated the question directly, Bennewith and colleagues (2002) also provided data for the potential benefit of allowing general practitioners to be in control of contacting their clients rather than implementing an intervention controlled by research staff. However, neither of these trials provided positive support for the necessity of continuity of care across treatment modalities. This is especially compelling because Bennewith and colleagues (2002) included high-risk subjects and maintained blind assessment throughout the trial. Researchers who believe in the notion of continuity of care, despite this evidence, are encouraged to replicate these trials and develop new ways to test this hypothesis.

Caring Letters

A further research question in the field of suicide intervention research is whether brief contact following suicidal behavior has a significant impact on subsequent suicidal behavior. Five studies have addressed this question (Carter, Clover, Whyte, Dawson, & D'Este, 2005, 2007; Fleischmann et al., 2008; Litman & Wold, 1976; Motto, 1976; Motto & Bostrum, 2001; Vaiva et al., 2006) using various specific methods.

In his original study of a brief contact intervention, Motto (1976; Motto & Bostrum, 2001) selected subjects who refused to follow up on referrals they received to outpatient treatment following inpatient hospitalization for depression or suicidal behaviors (undefined). A randomized half of these individuals received a standard letter at intermittent time intervals over the course of 4 years. The letters were nondemanding in nature and simply stated that "It has been some time since you were at the hospital and we hope things are going well for you. If you wish to drop us a note we would be glad to hear from you" (p. 224). The letters were signed by the person who conducted the individual's assessment while he or she was hospitalized. At the 2-year follow-up time point, the number of suicides in the group of subjects who received the caring letters was half the number of suicides in the no-contact group.

A second study conducted 30 years after the original (Carter et al., 2005, 2007) found similar results. Carter and colleagues selected subjects who presented to a toxicology unit with deliberate self-poisoning (undefined). These subjects were randomized and, in addition to treatment as usual, half received a postcard intermittently during the 12 months following their discharge. The occurrence of incidents of deliberate self-poisoning at 12 months and admissions for self-poisoning during 24-month follow-up were not significantly different between the group receiving the postcards and the group that did not. However, the cumulative number of repeated episodes of hospital-treated deliberate self-poisoning at 12 months was significantly less for the postcard receivers than for the other group. This is an important finding because the postcards were only mailed during the first 12 months.

Owing to the consistent findings of these studies, the inclusion of high-risk subjects in both, and the minimal resources that such an intervention would require, it seems imperative that the implementation of brief, caring letters as an addition to the standard of care for high-risk individuals be considered. Nondemanding personal follow-up following suicidal behavior is the only intervention that has been shown to decrease the probability of death by suicide. It is possible that one reason the letters that Motto sent were so effective is because they were signed by a person who had prolonged contact with the subject (i.e., a provider who conducted an assessment over multiple hours). This contact may have facilitated a sense of connection between the subject and assessor, which then made the letters more meaningful and personal. Another possible explanation of observed effectiveness is that the letters or postcards in each study were nondemanding in nature. The subject was not required to respond; however, if he or she did choose to do so, a follow-up letter was sent based on that response. This intervention could be easily implemented in any inpatient, outpatient, or primary care setting, where individuals identified as at risk of suicide were then sent a nondemanding letter signed by an important person (e.g., assessor, psychiatric resident, clinic director) at interval for a period of time.

Caring Phone Calls

Other methods of reaching out to high-risk individuals have been evaluated as well. Litman and Wold (1976) first tested the use of an alternative method of outreach when they contacted subjects at high risk for suicide who had called a crisis line with weekly phone calls made by volunteers to maintain a continuing relationship with the subject. Subjects in this experimental condition, when compared to individuals who had usual crisis services available to them when they initiated the phone contact themselves, were not different on any suicidal behaviors, including death by suicide. Notably, the results of this study are inconsistent with the two discussed earlier, perhaps because of the prolonged nature of the contact. Additionally, the phone calls put a demand on the subjects that was not present in the letters and postcards sent by the two other research teams.

More recently, two additional caring outreach studies have been conducted using phone calls (Fleishmann et al., 2008; Vaiva et al., 2006) to contact suicide attempters (undefined) at designated time intervals following their attempt. Fleishman and colleagues (2008) found a significant difference in the number of deaths by suicide between the group who received the repeated phone contact and the group who did not over the 18 months of the study. Individuals assigned to the phone contact condition made significantly fewer suicide attempts. Additionally, Vaiva and colleagues (2006) found that significantly fewer suicide attempts were made by individuals in the group of subjects who received telephone contact 1 month following their suicide attempts when compared to those who received no contact. However, when the other condition (telephone contact 3 months post attempt) was compared to the no-contact condition, there was no difference in the number of subsequent suicide attempts.

The specific methods of these two more recent trials may be responsible for their somewhat inconsistent results. Fleishman et al. (2008) contacted subjects multiple times during the course of the 18-month study, which is more analogous to Motto's original design (1976) that found a similar significant discrepancy in the number of deaths by suicide between the experimental and control groups. However, another potential reason for the inconsistent results obtained with telephone contact in these three studies is that this method of outreach may be considered fundamentally different than the letters or postcards sent in the studies described earlier. Namely, phone calls present a more demanding situation for subjects wherein a response is expected in the form of answering the phone and carrying on a conversation. The caring letters, on the other hand, do not require the subject to do anything unless he or she chooses to respond.

Brief Problem-Focused Interventions

In addition to these brief contact interventions, there are several trials that can be categorized as brief, problem-focused interventions for suicidal individuals. These interventions include various outpatient interventions that typically include a limited number of sessions of cognitive-behavioral therapy (e.g., Brown et al., 2005; Evans, Tyrer, et al., 1999). Unfortunately, albeit somewhat predictably, these trials also yield inconsistent findings related to their effectiveness at treating specific suicidal behaviors.

To date, three trials have evaluated manual-assisted cognitive-behavioral therapy (MACT; Evans, Tyrer, et al., 1999; Tyrer et al., 2003; Weinberg, Gunderson, Hennen, & Cutter, 2006). Each of the studies, however, has defined its sample, target behaviors, and intervention slightly differently. To begin, Evans, Tyrer and colleagues (1999) recruited patients seen after an episode of deliberate self-harm (DSH: undefined) who also had a previous history of DSH in the past year and had a disturbance in the flamboyant personality cluster (antisocial, histrionic,

and borderline personality disorders). Subjects were randomly assigned to the MACT condition or treatment as usual. The MACT condition included between two and six sessions of structured, cognitively oriented, problem-focused therapy based on a brief manual. Perhaps because the sample size was so small (32 subjects total), there was no significant difference between experimental and control conditions in the number of subjects who engaged in a suicidal act during the 4–6 months following treatment.

Tyrer and colleagues (2003) also recruited subjects following a repeated episode of parasuicide or deliberate self-harm (undefined). While Evans, Tyrer, et al. (1999) included high-risk individuals, Tyrer and colleagues did not; however, they did use a much larger sample size (239 subjects in the experimental condition and 241 in the control). In this trial, subjects randomly assigned to the experimental condition received a booklet including information based on cognitive-behavioral therapy principles and were offered up to seven treatment sessions with a MACT-trained therapist. Similar to Evans, Tyrer, and colleagues (1999), Tyrer et al. (2003) did not find a significant difference between the numbers of subjects who engaged in deliberate self-harm across the two conditions. Additionally, there was no difference in the number of deaths by suicide between the conditions.

Finally, Weinberg and colleagues (2006) randomized women with a borderline personality disorder diagnosis and a history of repeated DSH ("intentional self-inflicted injury without intent to die," p. 482) to receive treatment as usual with or without the addition of MACT sessions. Individuals assigned to the MACT condition had significantly fewer acts of DSH than those assigned to the control condition (mean frequency, 1.98 compared to 6.69, respectively). However, there was no significant difference between treatment conditions in terms of the amount of time to repeated DSH or suicidal ideation.

One potential explanation for the nonsignificant findings in the first two trials may be that subjects were given the option of not attending offered sessions. Those subjects in the Evans and colleagues' trial (Evans, Tyrer, et al., 1999) only attended an average of 2.7 out of 6 possible sessions. In the third trial by Weinberg et al. (2006), all subjects in the experimental condition completed the full six sessions of the intervention. This may suggest the importance of in-person meetings to make the intervention optimally effective. Additionally, Weinberg and colleagues (2006) excluded subjects with prior suicide attempts ("intentional act of self-inflicted injury that involves intent to die," p. 482) while the other two MACT trials included these subjects. This made for a less severe sample, and it is possible that the greater homogeneity of these subjects made it less difficult to detect significant differences.

Three other trials have evaluated brief problem-solving or skills training interventions (Donaldson et al., 2005; Hawton et al., 1987; McLeavey, Daly, Ludgate, & Murray, 1994). Hawton and colleagues (1987) randomly assigned subjects admitted to the emergency room for deliberate self-poisoning (undefined) to receive brief, problem-oriented counseling in the clinic or a referral. This brief intervention, however, failed to yield frequencies of repeated deliberate self-poisoning or deaths by suicide that were significantly different between the two conditions.

McLeavey and colleagues (1994) took Hawton et al.'s intervention one step further and compared problem-oriented counseling to brief interpersonal problem-solving skills training with a group of subjects admitted to the hospital following an episode of intentional self-poisoning (undefined). There was not a significant difference between the two conditions on subsequent self-poisoning. However, consistent with much of the suicide intervention literature, McLeavey and colleagues used a very small sample size and excluded subjects at high risk for suicide. This may account for some of their difficulty in detecting a significant effect of the intervention.

While McLeavey (1994) and Hawton (1987) targeted adult populations, Donaldson (2005) selected adolescents in the emergency room or inpatient unit following a suicide attempt ("any intentional, nonfatal self-injury, regardless of medical lethality, if intent to die is indicated" p. 114). The experimental condition received skills-based treatment that included problem-solving training and affect management by way of cognitive and behavioral strategies (e.g., cognitive modification, relaxation, homework). This intervention was compared to Brent and Kolko's (1991) Supportive Relationship Treatment, which did not include any problem-solving skills training or homework. The experimental condition receiving skills-based treatment did not yield a significantly lower frequency of suicide attempts during the 6-month follow-up when compared to the supportive relationship treatment control.

Other research teams have similarly developed brief outpatient interventions (Brown et al., 2005; Salkovskis, Atha, & Storer, 1990). Salkovskis and colleagues (1990) provided treatment as usual with and without the addition of a brief (five-session) cognitive-behavioral problem-solving intervention. They recruited patients admitted to an emergency room with repeated suicide attempts (undefined), who had taken antidepressants as part of an overdose, and who scored at least a four on Buglass and Horton's (1974) scale to predict repeated suicidal behavior. They found that there were significantly fewer repeated suicide attempts at 6 months in the experimental group compared to the control condition (0% compared to 37.5%, respectively). However, the cumulative number of suicide attempts during the 18-month follow-up was not significantly different between the groups. As is common with these trials, the sample size used in this study was small, with only 20 subjects in total.

Brown and colleagues (2005) recruited high-risk subjects who had made a suicide attempt ("a potentially self-injurious behavior with a nonfatal outcome for which there is evidence, either explicit or implicit, that the individual intended to kill himself or herself," p. 564) in the previous 48 hours. All subjects received treatment as usual in addition to intensive case management. Subjects in the experimental condition also were offered 10 sessions of cognitive-behavioral therapy. This intervention included specific suicide prevention strategies and skills training to identify thoughts and suicidal beliefs and develop adaptive coping behaviors. During the 18-month follow-up, subjects in the experimental condition made significantly fewer suicide attempts than those in the control condition (24.1% compared to 41.6%, respectively). Unfortunately, the absence of blind assessment reduces somewhat the certainty that we can place on these results.

While it is somewhat arbitrary to collapse these varied studies into a category of brief, problem-focused interventions, they all appear to have in common a time-limited, strategic approach to treating specific suicidal behaviors. Additionally, many of these studies have nonsignificant results and appear to have no more influence on subsequent suicidal behaviors than control conditions. However, there are promising results within these interventions. Brown and colleagues (2005), Salkovskis and colleagues (1990), and Weinberg and colleagues (2006) have all found significant intervention effects on subsequent suicidal behaviors. Even more inspiring is the fact that both Brown and Salkovskis included high-risk individuals in their trials and were able to significantly reduce suicide attempts beyond the level of the control condition. These studies certainly deserve consideration for replication and validation, especially considering that neither Brown nor Salkovskis employed assessors who were blind to the treatment condition of subjects. Further, the other studies may not need to be disregarded completely. Instead, their nonsignificant findings may be the result of insufficient power or less severe clinical populations. More investigation would undoubtedly be a valuable addition to the field.

Intensive Problem-Focused Treatment

Taking intervention one step further, many research teams have evaluated interventions that involve intensive problem-focused treatment with the addition of an outreach component (e.g., Hawton et al., 1981; Welu, 1977). Some of these interventions include 24-hour phone access for subjects in crisis (e.g., Chowdhury, Hicks, & Kreitman, 1973), while others incorporate home visits into their protocol (e.g., Van Heeringen et al., 1995).

Although home sessions are not common in mental health practices, there is some evidence that providing home visits as part of an intervention protocol may be effective (e.g., Harrington et al., 1998; Welu, 1977). Welu (1977) provided home visits and weekly contact by a mental health worker in addition to treatment as usual for patients brought into the emergency room following a suicide attempt ("any non-fatal act of self-damage inflicted with self-destructive intention, however vague or ambiguous," p. 19). The mental health workers monitored the subjects while also providing therapy, crisis intervention, or family therapy as needed. As a result of this intervention, Welu found that subjects in the experimental condition made significantly fewer suicide attempts than those in the control condition (4.8% compared to 15.8%, respectively). Fortunately, Welu (1977) included high-risk individuals and also recruited a relatively sizeable sample (119 subjects in total). Both of these facts make his results more promising for future replication.

Four additional trials evaluated home-based interventions (Gibbons, Butler, Urwin, & Gibbons, 1978; Guthrie et al., 2001; Harrington et al., 1998; Hawton et al., 1981). Gibbons and colleagues (1978) randomized subjects who had been hospitalized for deliberate self-poisoning ("the deliberate taking of a pharmacologically active substance in more than the prescribed dose or the usual consumption," p. 112). Subjects received treatment as usual or task-centered casework provided by case workers in the subjects' homes. At the 1-year follow-up assessment, the experimental condition did not have fewer self-reported incidents of self-poisoning, nor fewer documented hospitalization readmissions due to self-poisoning when compared to the control condition.

Hawton and colleagues (1981) also recruited subjects who had been admitted to the emergency room following deliberate self-poisoning ("intentional self-administration of more than the prescribed or recommended dose of any drugs whether or not there was evidence that the act was intended to cause self-harm," p. 172). When comparing brief, problem-oriented counseling provided in the home combined with phone access to hospital staff as needed to weekly problem-oriented counseling on an outpatient basis, they did not find a significant difference in the frequency of repeated episodes of deliberate self-poisoning.

Similar to Hawton and colleagues (1981), Harrington and colleagues (1998) evaluated a brief, manualized, home-based family therapy. Subjects were 16 years or younger and had received a diagnosis of deliberate self-harm (DSH: undefined). Compared to treatment as usual, there was not a significant difference between the numbers of subjects who engaged in DSH during the 6-month follow-up period.

Finally, Guthrie and colleagues (2001) randomized subjects who presented at the emergency room following deliberate self-poisoning to receive treatment as usual or interpersonal psychodynamic therapy (IPT) for four sessions. These four sessions were provided to the subject in-home. At the follow-up 6 months following the intervention, the numbers of subjects who had engaged in repeated episodes of self-harm were significantly fewer in the experimental condition that received four in-home sessions of IPT than the control condition that was referred to their general practitioner (9% compared to 28%, respectively). Taken together, these inconsistent results present an area for further evaluation. Each of the trials included relatively large sample sizes; however, only Welu (1977) and Guthrie et al. (2001) included high-risk individuals. Perhaps it would be possible to detect a difference in a more severe clinical population. Additionally, only Hawton et al. (1981) and Gibbons et al. (1978) employed blind assessment across their trials. This may cast doubt upon the two trials with significant results that did not adhere to this gold standard. Replication with more rigorous assessment procedures is indicated.

Another pair of clinical trials has evaluated the use of home visits for subjects who are not compliant with treatment (Chowdhury et al., 1973; Van Heeringen et al., 1995). In the early 1970s, Chowdhury and colleagues (1973) recruited patients with a history of parasuicide ("any deliberate act of self-poisoning or self-injury which resulted in the patient being referred to the hospital," p. 70) who were admitted to the poison center for a parasuicidal act. In addition to treatment as usual, subjects in the experimental condition received home visits following nonattendance in their usual outpatient treatment and 24-hour emergency service availability. Despite this attempt at catching clients who were not compliant with their outpatient treatment, researchers did not find a significant difference in the recurrence of parasuicide between the two conditions.

Similarly, Van Heeringen and colleagues (1995) visited experimental condition subjects in their homes following missed attendance at scheduled outpatient sessions. All subjects were patients who had been referred to the emergency room following a suicide attempt ("includes deliberate self-poisoning [the deliberate ingestion of more than the prescribed amount of medical substances, or ingestion of substances never intended for human consumption, irrespective of whether harm was intended] and deliberate self-injury [any intentional self-inflicted injury, irrespective of the apparent purpose of the act]," p. 964). While the numbers of deaths by suicide were not significantly different between the two conditions, the researchers saw a trend in which the incidence of repeated suicidal behavior was lower in the experimental condition than the control (10.7% compared to 17.4%, respectively).

Intensive Treatment Plus Outreach

Three final trials of interventions including an outreach component also incorporate tapering or staggering the frequency of treatment (Allard, Marshall, & Plante, 1992; Termansen & Bywater, 1975; Wood, Trainor, Rothwell, Moore, & Harrington, 2001). First, Termansen and Bywater (1975) randomized patients who had been admitted to the emergency room following a suicide attempt ("any act of self-injury, regardless of its seriousness, which was motivated by self-destructive tendencies," p. 29) into one of three conditions: in person follow-up, phone contact follow-up, or no follow-up. Subjects in the two follow-up conditions initially received daily contact, which was tapered to as infrequent as every other week over the course of 12 weeks. Although high-risk subjects were included, the differences between the numbers of repeated suicide attempts between the two follow-up conditions and between the phone contact condition and the control were not significant. However, subjects in the face-to-face follow-up condition made significantly fewer suicide attempts than subjects in the no follow-up control condition (6.1% compared to 21.9%, respectively).

Similarly, Allard and colleagues (1992) recruited suicide attempters who were admitted to the emergency room (suicide attempt: "any life-threatening behavior, with a real or professed intention of causing one's own death, not resulting in death," p. 307). High-risk subjects were not excluded from the study. Once they met inclusion criteria, subjects were then randomized to receive treatment as usual or intensive weekly meetings with mental health workers that were gradually tapered off to monthly meetings. At follow-up, there were no significant differences between experimental and control conditions in the rates of suicide attempts or suicides. However, the frequencies of both suicide and of suicide attempts were *higher* in the experimental treatment than in the control treatment, suggesting that the absence of significant findings favoring the experimental treatment was not due to a small sample size.

Finally, Wood and colleagues (2001) evaluated an intervention for adolescents referred for deliberate self-harm (DSH: "any intentional self-inflicted injury, irrespective of the apparent purpose of the act," p. 1247). The intervention that the control condition received consisted of six acute group sessions in conjunction with long-term group sessions combining cognitive-behavioral therapy and psychodynamic group psychotherapy strategies and a median two and a half individual sessions. They found a significantly lower mean number of acts of DSH in the experimental when compared to the control condition (means: 0.6 and 1.8, respectively) in addition to significantly fewer subjects engaging in multiple acts of DSH (6% compared to 32%, respectively). High-risk subjects (those ruled too suicidal for ambulatory care) were excluded from this study; however, Wood and colleagues did keep assessors blind to the treatment condition to which subjects were assigned.

Dialectical Behavior Therapy

To date, the intervention with the most empirical support for the reduction of suicidal behaviors is dialectical behavior therapy (DBT; Linehan, 1993). DBT has four RCTs demonstrating its efficacy at treating suicidal behaviors (Koons et al., 2001; Linehan et al., 1991, 2006; Linehan, Heard, & Armstrong, 1993; Verheul et al., 2003). DBT is a principle- and protocol-based, manualized treatment that was developed specifically for suicidal, difficult-to-treat clients. It has since been consistently shown to be an effective intervention for suicidal and other extreme behaviors. In addition to weekly individual therapy and phone consultation to patients, DBT includes skills training in four primary areas of deficit: mindfulness, emotion regulation, distress tolerance, and interpersonal effectiveness.

In the first RCT of DBT, Linehan and colleagues (1991) recruited women meeting criteria for borderline personality disorder who had a history of parasuicide ("any intentional, acute self-injurious behavior with or without suicidal intent, including both suicide attempts and self-mutilative behaviors," p. 1060) and a recent incident within the 2 months prior to enrollment in the trial. These subjects were randomized to receive DBT for 1 year or treatment as usual, referral to outpatient treatment. Subjects in the DBT condition had fewer episodes of self-inflicted injury (i.e., suicide attempts and self-inflicted injury combined) at the end of the treatment year (63.6% compared to 95.5%, respectively). Additionally, this difference between conditions was maintained during another year of posttreatment follow-up (26.3% compared to 60%).

These compelling results were replicated 15 years later when Linehan and colleagues (2006) again recruited borderline women with a history of suicidal behavior ("intentional, non-fatal, self-injurious acts committed with or without intent to die," p. 757) in the 8 weeks prior to referral and at least one other intentional self-injury in the preceding year. Subjects in the experimental condition again received DBT while those in the control condition received treatment by expert nonbehavioral therapists in the community. The number of subjects who attempted suicide was significantly lower in the DBT treatment condition than in the control (23.1% compared to 46%, respectively).

Koons and colleagues (2001) provided further support for DBT in their randomized trial with female borderline veterans. They found that subjects in the DBT condition had greater decreases in intentional self-harm (including suicide attempts) at the follow-up assessment compared to the treatment as usual control condition (10% compared to 20%, respectively). Finally, Verheul and colleagues (2003) found that borderline women who received DBT engaged in significantly fewer self-mutilating behaviors during 1 year of treatment than subjects who were assigned to clinical management as a control condition (35% compared to 57%, respectively).

Taken in concert, these four studies provide the strongest empirical support of any intervention targeting suicidal behaviors to date. DBT has three more randomized trials than any other intervention we have discussed. While Koons et al. (2001) and Verheul et al. (2003) did not specifically select subjects with a history of suicidal behavior, women with borderline personality disorder have been selected in these studies because they represent a group with staggering suicide rates compared to other populations. Because DBT was developed for this difficult population, it is the most compelling intervention and one that should be implemented with complex suicidal patients. The inclusion of the highest risk suicidal patients makes it all the more important that this treatment be considered when severe suicidality is present. Additionally, its efficacy with suicidal patients who do not meet the criteria for borderline personality disorder should be evaluated. Finally, while the results obtained from these studies are consistent, larger sample sizes may provide even more support for the use of this treatment with suicidal populations.

When we look at the four studies of DBT in conjunction with the other eight described earlier, we can see clearly that in 8 of the 12 clinical trials of intensive treatment and/or outreach interventions, there have been significant reductions in suicidal behaviors compared to control conditions. Seven of these interventions have been effective at reducing suicidal behaviors, leaving psychological interventions at the forefront of empirically supported treatments for reducing death by suicide.

Research and Practical Recommendations

Perhaps the most important and consistent point that can be taken from this review is that individuals trained to directly treat suicidal behaviors are having the greatest impact across many different types of interventions. This should be the new standard of care unless new data discount this model. The current standard of care that posits suicidal behavior as a symptom of a mental disorder has no empirical support, while numerous interventions that treat the suicidal behaviors directly show promise, if not persuasive evidence. In areas where only one study exists or where multiple studies are poorly constructed or inconsistent, replication should be made a priority.

There are several major clinical recommendations that can be drawn from this review. First, there is no question that providers should employ outreach strategies as a standard component of any intervention in addition to maintaining availability to their patients. This may involve providing phone consultation to patients throughout the course of treatment or meeting with the patient in his or her own home to promote compliance and attachment to the provider or intervention. It also may involve sending nondemanding letters to patients following the completion of an intervention regimen. The mode is not as important as the principle: namely, facilitating connection and attachment between provider and patient. Of equal importance is the tenet that the outreach and availability on the part of the provider should not be contingent on the patient's displays of suicidality. Instead, these strategies should be employed consistently throughout the intervention so that they do not inadvertently reinforce increases in suicidal behavior.

Second, successful treatments for suicidal individuals incorporate procedures for crisis management. To enact this in clinical settings requires that providers generate a plan with a suicidal patient prior to a crisis situation and enact that plan in the event of a crisis. This plan might include the use of skills for coping with the crisis or tolerating the intensity of the crisis. It also might include accessing available resources such as social support or phone contact with the provider. Of most significance is the process of planning ahead and following the designated plan during a crisis in which it will be most difficult for the patient to generate alternative ways of coping spontaneously.

Finally, it is critical that providers teach suicidal patients alternative ways to cope with stressful and difficult situations. In thinking of suicidal behaviors as attempts to cope with unbearable circumstances, the role of the provider is to teach, model, and practice new ways of managing these circumstances. The inconsistent findings of the trials of manual-assisted cognitive-behavioral therapy (MACT; Evans, Tyrer, et al., 1999; Tyrer et al., 2003; Weinberg et al., 2006) suggest that simply providing patients with an explanation of the new skills is insufficient.

Instead, modeling and practice are needed in order to replace the suicidal behaviors with more adaptive ways of coping with current and future crisis situations.

In addition to these clinical recommendations, there are several research suggestions to be drawn from this review. It is difficult to draw clear and concise conclusions from many of the studies because their weaknesses are so pervasive and cast doubt upon nearly every trial. Subsequent studies of interventions for suicidal individuals must make every effort to maintain a rigorous empirical standard. For example, blind assessment to prevent experimenter bias is crucial. Without it, results simply cannot be trusted and further replication will be necessary. Additionally, target outcomes must be defined, and validated measures of those outcomes must be employed.

Obviously, replication is needed for most, if not all, of the trials presented in this chapter. Trials with much larger sample sizes are required for the most promising treatments. All too frequently research teams attempt to generate new interventions rather than further improving upon those with preliminary empirical support. For instance, further variations of the trials of nondemanding caring outreach with other populations would provide support for the implementation of such a procedure across mental or medical health services.

Arguably, the most important new research study that should be conducted in this field is one in which depressed and suicidal individuals are randomly assigned to receive (1) a treatment targeting depression exclusively, (2) a treatment targeting suicide exclusively, or (3) a treatment targeting both depression and suicide. This study should rigorously attempt to answer the question of whether it is sufficient to treat suicidal behaviors indirectly or if directly targeting these problematic behaviors is required. As it has been so frequently assumed that treatment of the mental disorder will result in a decrease in suicidal behaviors, it will be imperative that this question be addressed intentionally.

As the research currently stands, it also is indisputably clear that DBT (Linehan, 1993) is the treatment of choice for suicidal individuals who have complex presentations and are difficult to treat. Of utmost value, however, would be a study in which suicidal individuals without borderline personality disorder were treated with DBT. It is yet to be determined whether DBT would maintain its successful outcomes in other diagnostic populations and to conduct such research could drastically expand the applicability of the treatment.

Further, hospitalization for suicidal individuals continues to be a standard treatment decision. Because some trials evaluating this practice have not been replicated in decades, a rigorous evaluation of inpatient hospitalization following suicidal behaviors is needed. In the event that such a replication yields results which indicate that inpatient hospitalization is ineffective at reducing suicidal behaviors and long-term suicide risk, this intervention should, at best, be considered no more reliable than a control intervention. If results similar to those found by Van der Sande and colleagues (1997) indicate that individuals in the hospital are at an increased risk, this intervention should be eliminated or only employed on a voluntary and consented basis.

References

Addis, M., & Linehan, M. M. (1989, November). *Predicting suicidal behavior: Psychometric properties of the suicidal behaviors questionnaire.* Poster session presented at the Annual Meeting of the Association for the Advancement Behavior Therapy, Washington, DC.

*Allard, R., Marshall, M., & Plante, M. (1992). Intensive follow-up does not decrease the risk of repeated suicide attempts. *Suicide and Life-Threatening Behavior, 22,* 303–314.

Bagby, R. M., Ryder, A. G., Schuller, D. R., & Marshall, M. B. (2004). The Hamilton Depression Rating Scale: Has the gold standard become a lead weight? *American Journal of Psychiatry, 161,* 2163–2177.

Beasley, C. M., Ball, S. G., Nilsson, M. E., Polzer, J., Tauscher-Wisniewski, S., Plewes, J., & Acharya, N. (2007). Fluoxetine and adult suicidality revisited: An updated meta-analysis using expanded data sources from placebo-controlled trials. *Journal of Clinical Psychopharmacology, 27,* 682–686.

Beasley, C. M., Dornseif, B. E., Bosomworth, J. C., Sayler, M. E., Rampey, A. H., Heiligenstein, J. H.,...Masica, D. N. (1992). Fluoxetine and suicide: A meta-analysis of controlled trials of treatment for depression. *International Clinical Psychopharmacology, 6*(Suppl. 6), 35–57.

*Bennewith, O., Stocks, N., Gunnell, D., Peters, T. J., Evans, M. O., & Sharp, D. J., (2002). General practice based intervention to prevent repeat episodes of deliberate self-harm: Cluster randomized controlled trial. *British Medical Journal, 324,* 1254–1261.

Brent, D. A., & Kolko, D. J. (1991). *Supportive relationship treatment manual.* Pittsburgh, PA: University of Pittsburgh/WPIC, Department of Psychiatry.

*Brown, G. K., Ten Have, T., Henriques, G. R., Xie, S. X., Hollander, J. E., & Beck, A. T. (2005). Cognitive therapy for the prevention of suicide attempts: A randomized controlled trial. *Journal of the American Medical Association, 294,* 563–570.

Buglass, D., & Horton, J. (1974). A scale for predicting subsequent suicidal behavior. *British Journal of Psychiatry, 124,* 573–578.

*Carter, G. L., Clover, K., Whyte, I. M., Dawson, A. H., & D'Este, C. (2005). Postcards from the EDge project: Randomised controlled trial of an intervention using postcards to reduce repetition of hospital treated deliberate self poisoning. *British Medical Journal, 331,* 805–809.

Carter, G. L., Clover, K., Whyte, I. M., Dawson, A. H., & D'Este, C. (2007). Postcards from the EDge: 24-month outcomes of a randomised controlled trial for hospital-treated self-poisoning. *British Journal of Psychiatry, 191,* 548–553.

*Cedereke, M., Monti, K., & Ojehagan, A. (2002). Telephone contact with patients in the year after a suicide attempt: Does it affect treatment adherence and outcome? A randomized controlled study. *European Psychiatry, 17,* 82–91.

Centers for Disease Control and Prevention. (2012). Deaths: Final data for 2010. *National Vital Statistics Report, 60,* 4.

*Chowdhury, N., Hicks, R. C., & Kreitman, N. (1973). Evaluation of an after-care service for parasuicide (attempted suicide) patients. *Social Psychiatry, 8,* 67–81.

Cochrane central register of controlled trials. Retrieved March 2014, from http://onlinelibrary.wiley.com/cochranelibrary/search

Combs, H., & Romm, S. (2007). Psychiatric inpatient suicide: A literature review. *Primary Psychiatry, 14,* 67–74.

*Cotgrove, A., Zirinsky, L., Black, D., & Weston, D. (1995). Secondary prevention of attempted suicide in adolescence. *Journal of Adolescence, 18,* 569–577.

*Donaldson, D., Spirito, A., & Esposito-Smythers, C. (2005). Treatment for adolescents following a suicide attempt: Results of a pilot trial. *Journal of the American Academy of Child and Adolescent Psychiatry, 44,* 113–120.

*Evans, J., Evans, M., Morgan, H. G., Hayward, A., & Gunnell, D. (2005). Crisis card following self-harm: 12-month follow-up of a randomized controlled trial. *British Journal of Psychiatry, 187,* 186–187.

*Evans, K., Tyrer, P., Catalan, J., Schmidt, U., Davidson, K., Dent, J.,...Thompson, S. (1999). Manual-assisted cognitive-behaviour therapy (MACT): A randomized controlled trial of a brief intervention with bibliotherapy in the treatment of recurrent deliberate self-harm. *Psychological Medicine, 29,* 19–25.

*Evans, M. O., Morgan, H. G., Hayward, A., & Gunnell, D. J. (1999). Crisis telephone consultation for deliberate self-harm patients: Effects on repetition. *British Journal of Psychiatry, 175,* 23–27.

*Fleischmann, A., Bertolote, J. M., Wasserman, D., De Leo, D., Bolhari, J., Botega, N. J.,...Thanh, H. T. (2008). Effectiveness of a brief intervention and contact for suicide attempters: A randomized controlled trial in five countries. *Bulletin of the World Health Organization, 86,* 703–709.

*Gibbons, J. S., Butler, P., Urwin, P., & Gibbons, J. L. (1978). Evaluation of a social work service for self-poisoning patients. *British Journal of Psychiatry, 133,* 111–118.

Goldstein, R. B., Black, D. W., Nasrallah, A., & Winokur, G. (1991). The prediction of suicide: Sensitivity, specificity, and predictive value of a multivariate model applied to suicide among affective disorders. *Archives of General Psychiatry, 48,* 418–422.

*Guthrie, E., Kapur, N., Mackway-Jones, K., Chew-Graham, C., Moorey, J., Mendel, E.,...Tomenson, B. (2001). Randomised controlled trial of brief psychological intervention after deliberate self poisoning. *British Medical Journal, 323,* 1–5.

*Harrington, R., Kerfoot, M., Dyer, E., McNiven, F., Gill, J., Harrington, V.,...Byford, S. (1998). Randomized trial of a

home-based family intervention for children who have deliberately poisoned themselves. *Journal of the American Academy of Child and Adolescent Psychiatry, 37,* 512–518.

*Hawton, K., Bancroft, J., Catalan, J., Kingston, B., Stedeford, A., & Welch, N. (1981). Domiciliary and out-patient treatment of self-poisoning patients by medical and non-medical staff. *Psychological Medicine, 11,* 169–177.

*Hawton, K., McKeown, S., Day, A., Martin, P., O'Connor, M., & Yule, J. (1987). Evaluation of outpatient counseling compared with general practitioner care following overdoses. *Psychological Medicine, 17,* 751–761.

Hirsch, S. R., Walsh, C., & Draper, R. (1983). The concept and efficacy of the treatment of parasuicide. *British Journal of Clinical Pharmacology, 15,* 189S–194S.

Hughes, D. H. (1995). Can the clinician predict suicide? *Psychiatric Services, 46,* 449–451.

Kallert, T. W., Glockner, M., & Schutzwohl, M. (2008). Involuntary vs. voluntary hospital admission: A systematic literature review on outcome diversity. *European Archives of Psychiatry and Clinical Neuroscience, 258,* 195–209.

Kazdin, A. E. (1977). Artifact, bias, and complexity of assessment: The ABCs of reliability. *Journal of Applied Behavior Analysis, 10,* 141–150.

Khan, A., Khan, S. R., Leventhal, R. M., & Brown, W. A., (2001). Symptom reduction and suicide risk among patients treated with placebo in antipsychotic clinical trials: An analysis of the Food and Drug Administration database. *American Journal of Psychiatry, 158,* 1449–1454.

Khan, A., Warner, H. A., & Brown, W. A. (2000). Symptom reduction and suicide risk in patients treated with placebo in antidepressant clinical trial: An analysis of the Food and Drug Administration database. *Archives of General Psychiatry, 57,* 311–317.

*Koons, C. R., Robins, C. J., Tweed, J. L., Lynch, T. R., Gonzalez, A. M., Morse, J. Q.,...Bastian, L. A. (2001). Efficacy of dialectical behavior therapy in women veterans with borderline personality disorder. *Behavior Therapy, 32,* 371–390.

*Liberman, R. P., & Eckman, T. (1981). Behavior therapy vs. insight-oriented therapy for repeated suicide attempters. *Archives of General Psychiatry, 38,* 1126–1130.

Linehan, M. M. (1981). A social-behavioral analysis of suicide and parasuicide: Implications for clinical assessment and treatment. In H. Glazer & J. F. Clarkin (Eds.), *Depression: Behavioral and directive intervention strategies* (pp. 229–294). New York, NY: Garland STMP Press.

Linehan, M. M. (1993). *Cognitive behavioral treatment of borderline personality disorder.* New York, NY: Guilford Press.

Linehan, M. M. (1997). Behavioral treatments of suicidal behaviors: Definitional obfuscation and treatment outcomes. In D. M. Stoff & J. J. Mann (Eds.), *Neurobiology of suicide: From the bench to the clinic* (pp. 302–328). New York, NY: Annals of the New York Academy of Sciences.

*Linehan, M. M., Armstrong, H. E., Suarez, A., Allmon, D., & Heard, H. L. (1991). Cognitive-behavioral treatment of chronically parasuicidal borderline patients. *Archives of General Psychiatry, 48,* 1060–1064.

Linehan, M. M., Comtois, K. A., Brown, M. Z., Heard, H. L., & Wagner, A. (2006). Suicide attempt self-injury interview (SASII): Development, reliability, and validity of a scale to assess suicide attempts and intentional self-injury. *Psychological Assessment, 18,* 303–312.

*Linehan, M. M., Comtois, K. A., Murray, A. M., Brown, M. Z., Gallop, R. J., Heard, H. L.,...Lindenboim, N. (2006).

Two-year randomized controlled trial and follow-up of dialectical behavior therapy vs. therapy by experts for suicidal behaviors and borderline personality disorder. *Archives of General Psychiatry, 63,* 757–766.

Linehan, M. M., Heard, H. L., & Armstrong, H. E. (1993). Naturalistic follow-up of a behavioral treatment for chronically parasuicidal borderline patients. *Archives of General Psychiatry, 50,* 971–974.

*Litman, R. E., & Wold, C. I. (1976). Beyond crisis intervention. In E. Schneidman (Ed.), *iSuicidology: Understanding and responding* (pp. 143–156). Madison, CT: International Universities Press.

*McLeavey, B. C., Daly, R. J., Ludgate, J. W., & Murray, C. M. (1994). Interpersonal problem-solving skills training in the treatment of self-poisoning patients. *Suicide and Life-Threatening Behavior, 24,* 382–394.

*Meltzer, H. Y., Alphs, L., Green, A. I., Altamura, A. C., Anand, R., Bertoldi, A.,...International Suicide Prevention Trial Study Group. (2003). Clozapine treatment for suicidality in schizophrenia: International Suicide Prevention Trial (InterSePT). *Archives of General Psychiatry, 60,* 82–91.

*Möller, H. J. (1989). Efficacy of different strategies of aftercare for patients who have attempted suicide. *Journal of the Royal Society of Medicine, 82,* 643–647.

*Montgomery, D., Roy, D., & Montgomery, S. (1981). Mianserin in prophylaxis of suicidal behavior: A double blind placebo controlled trial. In *Dépression et Suicide, Proceedings of the 11th Congress of the International Association for Suicide Prevention* (pp. 786–790). Paris, France: International Association for Suicide Prevention.

Montgomery, S. A., & Asberg, M. (1979). A new depression scale designed to be sensitive to change. *British Journal of Psychiatry, 134,* 382–389.

Montgomery, S. A., & Montgomery, D. (1982). Pharmacological prevention of suicidal behavior. *Journal of Affective Disorders, 4,* 291–298.

*Montgomery, S. A., Montgomery, D. B., Jayanthi-Rani, S., Roy, P. H., Shaw, P. J., & McAuley, R. (1979). Maintenance therapy in repeat suicidal behavior: A placebo controlled trial. In *Proceedings of the 10th International Conference for Suicide Prevention and Crisis Intervention* (pp. 227–229). Ottawa, ON: International Association for Suicide Prevention.

*Morgan, H. G., Jones, E. M., & Owen, J. H. (1993). Secondary prevention of non-fatal deliberate self-harm: The green card study. *British Journal of Psychiatry, 163,* 111–112.

*Motto, J. A. (1976). Suicide prevention for high-risk persons who refuse treatment. *Suicide and Life-Threatening Behavior, 6,* 223–230.

Motto, J. A., & Bostrom, A. G. (2001). A randomized controlled trial of postcrisis suicide prevention. *Psychiatric Services, 52,* 828–833.

Nock, M. K., Holmberg, E. B., Photos, V. I., & Michel, B. D. (2007). The self-injurious thoughts and behaviors interview: Development, reliability, and validity in an adolescent sample. *Psychological Assessment, 19,* 309–317.

O'Carroll, P. W., Berman, A. L., Maris, R. W., Moscicki, E. K., Tanney, B. L., & Silverman, M. M. (1996). Beyond the tower of Babel: A nomenclature for suicidology. *Suicide and Life-Threatening Behavior, 26,* 237–252.

Oquendo, M. A., Lizardi, D., Greenwald, S., Weissman, M. M., & Mann, J. J. (2004). Rates of lifetime suicide attempt and rates of lifetime major depression in different ethnic groups in the United States. *Acta Psychiatrica Scandanavia, 110,* 446–451.

Osman, A., Bagge, C. L., Gutierrez, P. M., Konick, L. C., Kopper, B. A., & Barrios, F. X. (2001). The Suicidal Behaviors Questionnaire-Revised (SBQ-R): Validation with clinical and nonclinical samples. *Assessment, 8,* 443–454.

*Patsiokas, A. T., & Clum, G. A. (1985). Effects of psychotherapeutic strategies in the treatment of suicide attempters. *Psychotherapy, 22,* 281–290.

Rosenthal, R. (1966). *Experimenter effects in behavioral research.* New York, NY: Appleton-Century-Crofts.

*Rudd, M. D., Rajab, M. H., Orman, D. T., Stulman, D. A., Joiner, T., & Dixon, W. (1996). Effectiveness of an outpatient intervention targeting suicidal young adults: Preliminary results. *Journal of Consulting and Clinical Psychology, 64,* 179–190.

*Salkovskis, P. M., Atha, C., & Storer, D. (1990). Cognitive-behavioural problem solving in the treatment of patients who repeatedly attempt suicide: A controlled trial. *British Journal of Psychiatry, 157,* 871–876.

*Termansen, P. E., & Bywater, C. (1975). S.A.F.E.R.: A follow-up service for attempted suicide in Vancouver. *Canadian Psychiatric Association Journal, 20,* 29–33.

*Torhorst, A., Möller, H. J, Burk, F., Kurz, A., Wachtler, C., & Lauter, H. (1987). The psychiatric management of parasuicide patients: A controlled clinical study comparing different strategies of outpatient treatment. *Crisis, 8,* 53–61.

*Torhorst, A., Möller, H. J., Kurz, A., Schmid-Bode, K. W., & Lauter, H. (1988). Comparing a 3-month and a 12-month-outpatient aftercare program for parasuicide repeaters. In H. J. Möller, A. Schmidtke, & R. Welz (Eds.), *Current issues of suicidology* (pp. 419–424). Berlin, Germany: Springer-Verlag.

*Tyrer, P., Thompson, S., Schmidt, U., Jones, V., Knapp, M., Davidson, K.,...Wessely, S. (2003). Randomized controlled trial of brief cognitive behaviour therapy versus treatment as usual in recurrent deliberate self-harm: The POPMACT study. *Psychological Medicine, 33,* 969–976.

*Vaiva, G., Ducrocq, F., Meyer, P., Mathieu, D., Philippe, A., Libersa, C., & Goudemand, M. (2006). Effects of telephone contact on further suicide attempts in patients discharged from an emergency department: Randomised controlled study. *British Medical Journal, 332,* 1241–1245.

*van der Sande, R., van Rooijen, L., Buskens, E., Allart, E., Hawton, K., van der Graaf, Y., & van Engeland, H. (1997). Intensive in-patient and community intervention versus routine care after attempted suicide: A randomized controlled intervention study. *British Journal of Psychiatry, 171,* 35–41.

*van Heeringen, C., Jannes, S., Buylaert, W., Henderick, H., de Bacquer, D., & van Remoortel, J. (1995). The management of non-compliance with referral to out-patient after-care among attempted suicide patients: A controlled intervention study. *Psychological Medicine, 25,* 963–970.

*Verheul, R., van den Bosch, L. M. C., Koeter, M. W. J., de Ridder, M. A. J., Stijnen, T., & van den Brink, W. (2003). Dialectical behaviour therapy for women with borderline personality disorder: 12-month, randomized clinical trial in The Netherlands. *British Journal of Psychiatry, 182,* 135–140.

*Verkes, R. J., Fekkes, D., Zwinderman, A. H., Hengeveld, M. W., Van der Mast, R. C., Tuyl, J. P.,...van Kempen, G. M. (1997). Platelet serotonin and [3H]paroxetine binding correlate with recurrence of suicidal behavior. *Psychopharmacology, 132,* 89–94.

*Verkes, R. J., Hengeveld, M. W., van der Mast, R. C., Fekkes, D., & van Kempen, G. M. J. (1998). Mood correlates with blood serotonin, but not with glucose measures in patients with recurrent suicidal behavior. *Psychiatry Research, 80,* 239–248.

*Waterhouse, J., & Platt, S. (1990). General hospital admission in the management of parasuicide: A randomized controlled trial. *British Journal of Psychiatry, 156,* 236–242.

*Weinberg, I., Gunderson, J. G., Hennen, H., & Cutter, C. J., Jr. (2006). Manual assisted cognitive treatment for deliberate self-harm in borderline personality disorder patients. *Journal of Personality Disorders, 20,* 482–492.

*Welu, T. C. (1977). A follow-up program for suicide attempters: Evaluation of effectiveness. *Suicide and Life-Threatening Behavior, 7,* 17–30.

*Wood, A., Trainor, G., Rothwell, J., Moore, A., & Harrington, R. (2001). Randomized trial of group therapy for repeated deliberate self-harm in adolescents. *Journal of the American Academy of Child and Adolescent Psychiatry, 40,* 1246–1253.

*Asterisks within the reference section indicate randomized, controlled trials of treatments targeting suicidal behaviors.

The Pharmacologic Treatment of Suicidal Patients

Jan Fawcett *and* Katie A. Busch

Abstract

Although suicide occurs most commonly in mood disorders, it is also seen across the diagnostic spectrum of psychiatric disorders. Suicide has not been found to be predictable in an individual, but certain variables reviewed in this chapter have been found to be risk factors for suicide. Most difficult is the clinical recognition of acute risk factors for suicide in time for therapeutic intervention. Pharmacologic treatments have been found for patients at long-term risk as well as acute risk for suicide. Lithium carbonate as well as antidepressants, given for at least 6 months, reduce long-term suicide risk. New-generation antipsychotic medications with anxiolytic and impulsivity-reducing properties, such as quetiapine and olanzapine, may be useful in the reduction of these acute risk factors for suicide. Data aiding the clinician in the recognition of acute suicide risk as well as treatments for the prevention of suicide are needed.

Key Words: suicide, suicide attempt, agitation, anxiety, impulsivity, major loss, suicide rehearsal, treatment resistance, acute versus chronic risk

Those who have elected to devote their careers to preventing suicide have chosen a most difficult professional undertaking. First, it is not currently possible to predict with certainty which individuals are going to take their lives at any particular point in time (Clark, Young, Scheftner, Fawcett, & Fogg, 1987; MacKinon & Farberow, 1976; Pokorny, 1993). Second, it has been shown that up to 78% of patients who take their lives deny any suicidal intent before doing so, and about 50% of patients die on their first attempt (Isometsa & Lonnqvist, 1998; Busch, Fawcett, & Jacobs, 2003). Although the overall ratio of suicide attempts to deaths is 30:1, the ratio has been found to be 3:1 for patients with bipolar disorder, which probably also applies to major depression (Baldessarini, Pompili, & Tondo, 2006; Baldessarini, 2004).

If suicide is not predictable in any one individual, then it is a corollary that one can never be sure that he or she has been successful with any particular therapeutic intervention in preventing suicide. However, if all of one's efforts fail to prevent a suicide, that failure is very evident. The clinician may even be rewarded for his or her efforts by being sued by a bereaved significant other of the patient. Yet, if one chooses to treat patients who are significantly ill with psychiatric disorders, then there is no way to avoid entering this arena.

What makes this quest even more difficult is the lack of data available to help a clinician foresee the likelihood of suicide, especially at a particular point in time. Current risk factors for suicide include suicidal ideation (Kessler, Borges, & Walters, 1999); prior suicide attempts (Coryell & Young, 2005); prior high-intent attempts (Suominen, Isometsa, Ostamo, & Lonnqvist, 2004); hopelessness (Holma et al., 2010); severity, duration, and recurrence of depression (Courtet, 2010; Holma et al., 2010; Sinclair, Hariss, Baldwin, & King, 2005); a recent major loss (Peteet, Maytal, & Rokni, 2010; Szanto et al., 2006, Szanto, Prigerson, Houck, Ehrenpreis & Reynolds, 1997); comorbid severe anxiety (Busch, 2003; Fawcett et al., 1990; Pfeiffer, Ganoczy, Ilgen, Zivin, & Valenstein, 2009; Stordal, Morken, Mykletun, Neckelmann, Dahl 2008); alcohol and/or drug abuse (Dumais et al., 2005; Fawcett et al., 1990; Flensborg-Madsen et al., 2009); a history of impulsive aggression (Dumais et al., 2005; Nock et al., 2009; Zhang et al., 2010); being a White male over 65 years old (Centers for Disease Control and Prevention, 2007); living alone (Baraclough & Pallis, 1975; Crawford, Kuforii, & Ghosh, 2010); having a family history of suicide in a first-degree or second-degree relative (Baldessarini & Hennen, 2004; Brent, 2010; Roy, 1983); recent discharge from a psychiatric hospital (Goldacre, Seagroat, & Hawton, 1993, Kan, 2007); a chronically painful medical condition (Ilgen et al., 2010; Lofman, Rasanen, & Hakko, 2011; Scott et al., 2010); and the year after a diagnosis of cancer (Ahn et al., 2010; Fang et al., 2010; Meltzer et al., 2003). These have been established in the literature in various combinations and have been shown to indicate a high degree of risk for suicide over 10 years of follow-up.

However, these risk factors, or some combination of them, do not allow the clinician to foresee who is likely to make a serious suicide attempt in the next few hours, days, or weeks. This latter determination is the most difficult task of the clinician, to foresee an immediate risk and attempt a therapeutic intervention. Further, a task that is more richly supported by data, but which is often not recognized by the treating clinician, is the recognition of the presence of a combination of the risk factors enumerated earlier (chronic high-risk factors for suicide) and the administration of treatments that will lower the likelihood of the development of an acute high-risk suicidal state. Over the past 20 years evidence that severe anxiety may be both an acute suicide risk factor that is treatment modifiable as well as a chronic suicide risk factor has been increasing. This will be discussed next.

This chapter will discuss the risk factors that might be targeted in therapeutic attempts to reduce both chronic and acute suicide risk, as well as modifiable symptoms that have a possibility of reducing acute suicide risk if treated in the appropriate clinical context. Consideration will be given to known possible mechanisms underlying suicidal behavior that are targeted for pharmacologic treatment. Later in the chapter, we will summarize pharmacologic approaches to the treatment of both acute and chronic high suicide risk traits or symptoms and finally a summary of approaches to the treatment of patients with certain modifiable symptoms and vulnerabilities to certain life events that often precipitate high suicide risk.

The reader is cautioned, however, that currently there are no FDA-approved treatments for suicidal states with the possible exception of closaril (Clozapine) for the treatment of suicide risk in patients with schizophrenia (Meltzer et al., 2003). There is a considerable body of data supporting the long term antisuicide effect of lithium treatment, which will be reviewed. The other treatment approaches mentioned can be shown to reduce symptom or trait targets associated with increased chronic or acute suicide risk. It is important to note that the ethical considerations for testing the anti-suicide effects of a medication are significant and render the usual gold standard study of the efficacy of a medication, a random assignment, placebo controlled, double blind study (RCT) useless. Any study of antisuicide effects of a medication to reduce suicidal behavior thus far has been done by comparing one active medication against another (Meltzer et al., 2003).

It must of course be kept in mind that the decision to act to end one's life can be reached in many different ways and there are doubtlessly many pathways to suicide. The use of appropriate medications at the right time in the most effective manner may well contribute significantly to lowering both chronic and acute risk, but these medications must be administered as an effective component of an overall therapeutic context offering support, availability, and flexibility to have a likelihood of success. We know, for instance, that adherence to a medication regimen varies widely and is most likely to vary in a life crisis, when the patient is in great psychic pain, desperate, hopeless, and unable to conceive of a better future. There can be nothing mechanical or rigid about efforts to reduce suicide risk using pharmacologic agents; the effort must be continually adaptive to the patient's response and changing clinical situation. Such treatment should occur in a context of empathy and appropriate psychotherapeutic interventions.

Behavioral Variables That Lead to Suicidal Behavior

Suicide traditionally has been associated with aspects of severe depression, including thoughts of hopelessness, helplessness, worthlessness, uselessness, self-criticism, and even self-hatred. Additionally, depressed individuals may feel that others would be better off if they were out of the picture, and they may have strong wishes to escape the psychic pain created by this condition. Hopelessness often reaching delusional proportions may limit patient adherence to any treatment. Efforts to maintain hope in the face of patients' negative expectations are essential to the success of any treatment. Although suicide also occurs with lower frequency across a spectrum of patients with other diagnoses, such as eating disorders, schizophrenia, alcohol and substance abuse, anxiety disorders, and personality disorders, there is evidence that comorbid depressive features are present as a factor in many of these instances and these disorders are also associated with suicide (Harris & Baraclough, 1997).

Over the past two decades, it has become increasingly evident that clinical anxiety, by itself and especially when comorbid with both unipolar major depression and bipolar depression, is a particularly strong risk factor for suicide (Busch et al., 2003; Fawcett et al., 1990; Nock et al., 2009; Pfeiffer et al., 2009; Simon, Hunkeler, Fireman, Lee, & Savarino 2007; Stordal et al., 2008). Both epidemiological and clinical studies have increasingly shown that the presence of clinical anxiety (which is frequently present in mood disorders) is a risk factor for poor therapeutic response (Fava et al., 2006) and for an increased risk of suicidal behavior (Sareen, Houlahan, Cox, & Asmundson, 2005; Simon, Zalta, et al., 2007). One of these studies found that elevations in the severity of comorbid psychic anxiety/agitation, severe insomnia, and panic attacks indicate a higher acute risk for immediate suicide (Fawcett et al., 1990).

Another behavioral trait that has been associated with suicide and suicide attempts is aggressive impulsivity, which is frequently associated with alcohol and substance dependence or abuse disorders, Cluster B personality disorders, and bipolar mixed states (Nock et al., 2009). One study has linked the level of manifest impulsivity to levels of anxiety (Nock et al., 2009).

Psychosis also has been considered a risk factor for suicide, but studies have been divided, with some studies failing to show a direct relationship in both mood disorders and schizophrenia (Black, Winokur, & Nasrallah, 1988; Fawcett et al., 1990). It is reported that patients with schizophrenia have a significant incidence of suicide, but studies of risk factors point more to depressed mood than to positive psychotic symptoms, such as auditory or visual hallucinations, delusions, or thought disorder, as the causes (Large, Smith, Sharma, Nielsson, & Singh, 2011).

Chronic High Suicide Risk and Acute (Imminent) High Suicide Risk

A major issue that has not received adequate attention in suicide prevention is the assessment of chronic high suicide risk versus the assessment and treatment of acute or imminent suicide risk. A prospective study of suicide in 954 patients with major affective disorders, 85% of which had been inducted into the study while hospitalized and followed as outpatients (increasing the risk of suicide), showed that 13 patients committed suicide in the first year of follow-up, while a total of 34 patients died by suicide over a 10-year follow-up period. The baseline ratings on the Schedule for Affective Disorders and Schizophrenia (SADS), current form (SADS-C), which measures symptom severity, revealed that comparisons of symptom severity of the 13 individuals who completed suicide with the rest of the patients being followed showed no difference between the suicide completion and comparison group in severity of suicidal ideation, recent or past suicide attempts, or severity of hopelessness. These factors were significantly higher when a comparison was made between the 34 individuals who completed suicide, which occurred by the 10-year follow-up, with the comparison group.

This outcome demonstrates a difference in "predictor factors" for suicide between short-term suicide completers and long-term suicide completers. The short-term suicide completers were significantly higher on severity of psychic anxiety, panic attacks, global insomnia, and recent onset of alcohol abuse. This study, one of the first to investigate suicide prospectively with standard behavioral measures, also was the first to investigate the amount of time to suicide from a baseline measurement period. The implication was that "standard" suicide prediction factors did not effectively identify patients who committed suicide from a larger comparison group over a 1-year period (Fawcett et al., 1990). Further, this prospective study found that severe anxiety symptoms and severe insomnia were indicators of acute suicide risk.

Severe Psychic Anxiety or Comorbid Anxiety Disorders as Risk Factors for Suicide

Subsequent to the study showing severe psychic anxiety as an acute risk factor for suicide described earlier (Fawcett et al., 1990), a study of the records of 76 inpatients who committed suicide in the hospital or within a few days of absconding or being discharged was performed. The study found that 79% of patients showed evidence of severe anxiety and/or agitation in the week prior to their suicide and that 76% of these patients denied suicidal intent in their most recent communication with nursing staff (Busch et al., 2003). Twenty-six percent of these patients had made no suicide agreements or "contracts" with staff, as recorded in their charts. Other studies have shown clearly that neither a denial of suicidal intent nor a no-suicide contract is a deterrent to suicide. Further, such declarations are insufficient information to base a suicide risk assessment on without a careful clinical evaluation (Busch et al., 2003). Another study of 100 consecutive patients admitted to the hospital from the emergency service for suicide attempts found that 80% of patients interviewed within a month of their attempt noted the presence of severe anxiety measured by the SADS-C psychic anxiety ratings (Hall, Platt, & Hall, 1999).

In the past 10 years, a number of publications of both epidemiologic data and clinical findings have shown that the presence of severe anxiety or comorbid anxiety disorders is associated with an increased risk of suicide or suicide attempts. Epidemiologic studies have shown that a higher preoccupation with suicide or occurrence of suicide attempts is associated with anxiety disorders, particularly posttraumatic stress disorder (Sareen, Cox, et al., 2005), or depression comorbid with anxiety disorders (Bolton, Paqura, Enns, Grant, & Sareen, 2010). One large epidemiologic study of over 16,000 suicides in Norway studied monthly ratings of anxiety and depression as a part of a larger health outcomes study and found a $r = .76$ correlation between severity of anxiety/depression and the time of suicide occurrence (Stordal et al., 2008). Clinical studies, such as STAR*D for unipolar depression (Fava et al., 2004, 2006) and STEP-BD for bipolar disorder (Simon, Zalta, et al., 2007), have found the co-occurrence of more severe anxiety to be associated with poor clinical outcome as well as increased levels of suicidal ideation or suicide attempts, respectively. Coryell has published data showing that baseline anxiety severity ratings with the SADS-C show a stepwise relationship to the amount of time spent in a depressive episode over a 16- to 20-year follow-up period in bipolar patients (Coryell et al., 2009) and has recently found a similar correlation between anxiety and amount of time

in depression over a 16- to 20-year follow-up in the entire mood disorder group, including major depression (personal communication). A study of combined managed care databases of patients with bipolar disorder found that the presence of a comorbid anxiety disorder diagnosis showed an increase rate of suicide (HR = 1.81) and suicide attempts (HR = 1.4), while a comorbid diagnosis of substance dependence showed only an increase in suicide attempts (HR = 2.53), but not suicide (Simon, Hunkeler, et al., 2007). A recent study of 114 outpatients with bipolar disorder found a positive relationship between anxiety severity and impulsivity levels (Taylor et al., 2008). A very important study of 887,859 Veterans Administration patients with depression has recently reported an elevated odds ratio for suicide (1.25–1.27) for patients diagnosed with comorbid anxiety disorder not otherwise specified, generalized anxiety disorder,, and panic disorder, but not other anxiety disorders such as posttraumatic stress disorder, social phobia, and obsessive-compulsive disorder. The odds ratio for suicide was also elevated for any patient who received benzodiazepine or buspirone for anxiety (excluding those given at night for sleep), OR = 1.71, and show an even greater elevation of odds ratio for suicide in patients receiving high doses of these medications, OR = 2.26, indicating that severity of anxiety may play a larger role than anxiety disorder diagnosis. The finding also raises the question of whether benzodiazepines are effective in treating significantly severe anxiety in mood disorder patients or whether they might have an adverse effect on outcome with respect to suicide (Pfeiffer et al., 2009).

Taken together, the studies reviewed earlier show an association between suicidal attempts and suicide with comorbid anxiety disorders and particularly measures of anxiety severity. There is a trend in these data for relationships existing between severity of psychic anxiety and acute risk of suicide and between the presence of comorbid disorders and an elevated chronic risk for suicide.

Impulsivity as a Risk Factor for Suicide

A number of studies have found a relationship between the trait of impulsivity and both suicide and aggression (Nock et al., 2009). Increased levels of impulsivity and aggression have been found in alcohol and drug abuse, Cluster B personality disorders, attention-deficit/hyperactivity disorder, and bipolar mixed states (Swann et al., 2005). All of these disorders are commonly comorbid with mood disorders.

It is not yet clear whether impulsive behavior can be shown to increase prior to suicidal behavior, acting as an acute clinical predictor. Swann has shown that high impulsivity ratings on the Barrett scale are associated with more severe suicide attempts in bipolar patients (Swann et al., 2005). The aforementioned finding of a relationship between anxiety severity and level of impulsivity (Nock et al., 2009) raises the possibility that impulsivity, as a trait, may show an increase in response to stress and anxiety, prior to suicidal behavior. Therefore, impulsivity may be a clinical target for assessment of acute risk and for treatment.

A recent report from the World Health Organization World Mental Health survey of suicidal behavior and mental disorders from face-to-face interviews from 108,664 responders from 21 countries found that while depression leads to suicidal ideation, it does not by itself usefully predict which individuals with suicidal ideation will attempt suicide, although the presence of disorders characterized by anxiety/agitation and problems with impulse control increases the likelihood that people will act on such thoughts (Nock et al., 2009). This model suggests a possibility that treatment that can modify or reduce anxiety/agitation and impulsiveness may be useful in reducing acute suicide risk.

Psychosis as a Risk Factor for Suicide

The data for psychosis as a risk factor for suicide are mixed. Some studies find a correlation and some fail to find a correlation of psychosis with suicide (Black et al., 1988). Psychosis is a measure of illness severity and may indicate the presence of other severity symptoms such as severe anxiety and agitation, which as noted earlier, are risk factors for suicidal behavior. Antipsychotic medications are widely used to treat severe agitation in psychotic patients (Zimbroff, 2003) as well as psychosis alone.

Mechanisms Whereby Medications May Modify Risk Factors for Suicide
Serotonin Metabolism, Depression, and Impulsivity

The serotonin system in the brain is involved with a wide array of behaviors. There is evidence that disorders of serotonin metabolism are involved with clinical depression, clinical anxiety, and the trait of impulsivity, all of which are behavioral states implicated in suicidal behavior (Mann et al., 2005). Two classes of medications that modify serotonin metabolism in the brain have been shown to affect suicidal behavior.

Antidepressant medications (ADMs), particularly those that increase the availability of serotonin in the postsynaptic cleft such as tricyclic antidepressants (TCAs), monoamine oxidase inhibitors (MAOIs), and especially specific serotonin reuptake inhibitors (SSRIs), have been show to affect suicidal behavior. ADMs are effective to varying degrees in treating clinical depression, tending to show greater effect in more severe cases (Fournier et al., 2010). SSRIs have been most studied and have been shown to reduce suicidal ideation (Beasley et al., 2007), but a meta-analysis of FDA studies for approval of effect and safety has not shown a reduction in suicide over the typical 8–12 week duration of the RCT studies compared to placebo (Khan, Khan, Kolts, & Brown, 2003). In a 40- to 44-year follow-up study of 200 patients formerly hospitalized with major depression and 220 patients formerly hospitalized with bipolar disorder (i.e., a sample at high risk for suicide by virtue of being post hospitalization), researchers found that antidepressant treatment, often combined with lithium or antipsychotic medication, if given for a minimum of 6 months, results in a significant decrease in suicide rates (Angst, Angst, Gerber-Werder, & Gamma, 2005). This indicates that ADM reduces the long-term risk of suicide if the patient is maintained for at least 6 months on medication. Since SSRI medications are approved by the FDA as efficacious in treating both major depression and a range of anxiety disorders, and have become first-line treatments for these disorders, one might presume that long-term treatment of depressive and anxiety symptoms and prevention of their recurrence is a mechanism whereby ADMs can reduce suicide risk.

Further, recent studies have shown a decline in suicides in various countries to be correlated with the frequency of use of antidepressants, and one study has shown an increase in suicides when ADM use declined (Gibbons et al., 2007). The data suggest that SSRI and ADM medications in general may reduce suicide when given over a period of time (e.g., 6 months) and that SSRIs also may reduce impulsiveness when given over time. The overall indication is that antidepressant medications may be useful in decreasing the long-term risk of suicide when they are clinically effective in the patient being treated.

The story has become more complex as findings emerged showing an increase in "suicidality" (i.e., suicide thoughts, threats, attempts) in children, adolescents, and young adults up to age 25 years with SSRI treatment occurring in large RCT studies compared with placebo treatment (4% vs. 2% incidence of suicidality, p <.01). This study did not show any suicides in this group, but it did show an increase in the rate of suicidal behavior (Hammad, Laughren, & Racoosin, 2006). Many studies have been published for and against this issue. The studies finding this effect have primarily been RCT studies for regulatory agencies like the FDA in this country (Hammad et al., 2006), while studies finding no such effect have primarily been large treatment managed care databases. One such study by Simon and Savarino (2007) showed a tendency for suicide attempts to be highest in the month before the onset of treatment; lower, but elevated in the first month of treatment with ADM; and then declining each subsequent month. These results suggest that patients being treated had an initial high risk for suicidal behavior that declined over time. The only case report study this author could find reporting high-risk suicidal behavior was one in which three depressed patients developed severe anxiety and agitation, severe enough to think that "death would be a relief," after receiving an increase in fluoxetine dosage (Prozac, an SSRI) (Rothschild & Locke, 1991). These patients made serious suicide attempts (e.g., jumping from a four-story building) but survived and re-experienced similar feelings when rechallenged with fluoxetine. The state was successfully treated by dose reduction or propanolol, a medication that blocks beta-adrenergic receptors for norepinephrine, which often is secreted through the system in elevated amounts during attacks of anxiety. These findings demonstrate that some patients develop worsening or increased anxiety and agitation, perhaps secondary to akathisia, a condition thought to be secondary to increased serotonin function, which induces physical restlessness and anxiety. Akathisia produces an intense motor restlessness accompanied by anxiety, in the case of SSRI, presumably secondary to a rapid increase of serotonin function in the central nervous system.

Thus, we have evidence of the potential of ADM to cause symptoms of worsening or increased suicidal behavior, most frequently in patients 24 years or under, when first exposed to an SSRI or after a dosage increase. We have correlative evidence of a reduction in suicides over time associated with the use of SSRI medications and a general trend to a decrease in suicidal ideations compared to placebo treatment. Although we have no evidence to support a decrease in suicides at 8–12 weeks of treatment with SSRIs, we do have a study showing a decrease in suicides among a high-risk group of patients maintained on ADM, and other medications, over a 6-month period (Angst et al., 2005). One could summarize this information by concluding that a small minority of patients may get worse or experience anxiety/agitation and suicidal thoughts, although the majority may show a decrease in suicidal ideation but no evidence of reduced suicides in 8–12 weeks of treatment, and there is evidence to support that maintenance SSRI and other ADM with added other medications in many instances for at least 6 months shows a 2.5 reduction in suicide and correlative findings that increased utilization of SSRIs is related to a significant decrease in suicides. It is important to be aware of the difference between suicidal behavior (i.e., suicidal thoughts, threats, attempts) and suicide (i.e., in which death occurs). Clearly, ADMs have demonstrated a long-term capacity to reduce suicide. However, the findings of a small increase in suicidal behavior in the child- to 25-year age range suggest that ADMs should be used with care, informed consent, education of the patient and parents, and careful follow-up as indicated by the FDA Black Box Warning issued for ADM medications. Moreover, although ADMs may reduce long-term suicide risk, at present there is no evidence that they will reduce imminent suicide risk. There also is evidence showing that response to ADM is such that up to 70% of people may experience remission with four different courses of treatment, leaving 30% with no full response (33% with one course, 63% with two courses) over 2 years (Rush et al., 2009). Clearly, although helpful, ADMs and SSRIs leave much yet to be accomplished in the treatment of suicidal behavior.

There are a considerable number of studies showing that lithium carbonate reduces suicide and suicide attempts by about 80% over 18 months of follow-up in both bipolar and unipolar depression, based on comparisons with patients not treated with lithium (Baldessarini, Pompili, & Tondo, 2006). Although clinicians often worry about the danger of overdoses with lithium or problems with side effects, data continue to show a consistent reduction in suicides. One study even showed a reduction of suicidal behavior in bipolar patients who had not achieved a full response to lithium therapy, suggesting that the antisuicide effect may be independent of the effect on other symptoms of bipolar disorder (Muller-Oerlinghausen, Felber, Berghofer, Lauterbach, & Ahrens, 2005). There also are studies suggesting that lithium may reduce aggression and impulsivity (Sheard, Marini, Bridges, & Wagner,

1976). This would be consistent with an effect of enhancing serotonin function.

Studies suggest that the therapeutic effect of lithium may be based on the effect of lithium to enhance serotonin function (de Montigny, Cournoyer, Morissette, Langlois, & Caille, 1983). An increase in serotonin function would be expected over time to reduce impulsivity (which is associated with decreased serotonin function).

Effects of Antipsychotic Medications on Suicidal Behavior

Both the typical antipsychotic medications such as haloperidol, thioridazine, or perphenezine and the new-generation antipsychotics (NGAs) have proven useful in the treatment of severe agitation, especially when given by intramuscular injection, if such a form is available (Zimbroff, 2003). The NGAs may be useful in the treatment of anxiety and even depression, especially the more sedative ones such as quetiapine (Seroquel) and olanzapine (Zyprexa). This class of medications has recently shown a capacity for antidepressant effects, either alone or in combination with antidepressant medications (Baker et al., 2003; Hirschfeld, Weisler, Raines, & Macfadden, 2006; McIntyre et al., 2009). The typical antipsychotics primarily act by blocking dopamine receptors, and the NGAs have this effect in addition to acting as antagonists of serotonin receptors (e.g., 5 HT2a), which may result in decreased anxiety (Ereshefsky, 1999).

With this wide spectrum of action, sedative NGAs are particularly useful in acutely treating severe anxiety and agitated states that present in mood disorders, schizophrenic disorders, personality disorders, and even severe anxiety disorders such as posttraumatic stress disorder. These medications require careful medical monitoring of blood sugar and serum lipids when used long term or for over three months. Studies have documented the effect of quetiapine (Seroquel) in significantly reducing anxiety in bipolar I and II depressed patients (Vieta, Calabrese, Goikolea, Raines, & Macfadden, 2007) and olanzapine (Zyprexa) in reducing suicidal ideation when administered as an augmentation to other mood stabilizers in patients with bipolar mixed states (Houston et al., 2006).

The Effect of Antianxiety Medications on Suicidal Behavior

Based on the associations between severe anxiety and suicidal behavior, especially when comorbid with depression, it is clinically evident, despite the lack of controlled studies, that medications effective in reducing the severity of anxiety symptoms may be able to modify a major risk factor for suicide in patients with depression. Although studies have shown that the benzodiazepine clonazepam can hasten the effect of fluoxetine by reducing anxiety and ameliorating sleep disturbance (Londborg, Smith, Glaudin, & Painter, 2000), there is some evidence that short-acting benzodiazepines (e.g. alprazolam) may disinhibit patients with borderline personality disorder (Cordry & Gardner, 1988). More recent evidence has shown an association of increased rates of suicide in depressed patients receiving benzodiazepines for anxiety in a dose-related fashion (Pfeiffer et al., 2009), and an additional study has cautioned against the use of benzodiazepines in depressed anxious patients, finding that they show no evidence of reducing suicide risk and contending that they may increase risk by causing disinhibition (Youssef & Rich, 2008). These studies do not differentiate specific benzodiazepines or separate them by onset of action or duration of action. Finally, a study of elderly patients reported a four-fold increase in suicide in patients taking sedatives and hypnotics (Carlsten & Waern, 2009). More slowly absorbed, longer acting benzodiazepines such as clonazepam have been used to treat anxiety in depressed patients with some benefit (Londborg et al., 2000). Shorter acting benzodiazepines have been used, but evidence that these medications may increase disinhibition in patients with borderline personality disorder (Cordry & Gardner, 1988), and the recent studies showing an increase in rates of suicide in anxious depressed patients reviewed earlier (Pfeiffer et al., 2009), suggest that these agents should be used with great caution in depressed suicidal patients.

More recently the NGAs have proven very useful in reducing severe anxiety and agitation as noted earlier. Studies have shown that the NGA quetiapine (Seroquel) has a capacity to reduce anxiety in bipolar patients (Hirschfeld et al., 2006) and when added to antidepressants in unipolar depressed patients (Dannlowski et al., 2008; McIntyre, Gendron, & McIntyre, 2007). Further, the NGA olanzapine (Zyprexa) has been shown to reduce suicidal ideation in agitated bipolar patients in a mixed state (Houston et al., 2006).

The Treatment of Suicidal Patients

Suicide is very difficult to prevent. First, assessing suicide risk can be difficult, as patient denials of intent cannot be relied on without a careful assessment of their clinical state. A second layer of difficulty for the clinician is added by the patient's right to refuse treatment. Although antidepressant medications may reduce suicide risk long term if the patient is responsive to them and if the treatment is continued, a significant proportion of patients with acute suicidal risk states do not experience a reduction of suicide risk either in the first 2 months of treatment or longer term because of lack of response, intolerance of side effects, lack of adherence to regularly taking the medication, and recurrence of symptoms. Also, about a third of severely depressed patients are treatment resistant, failing initial attempts at treatment while in an acute high-risk suicidal state. Moreover, a considerable proportion (30%–60%) may experience a relapse of depression and a suicidal state despite an initial response to medication. Many of these patients are at high chronic risk based on prior suicidal behavior, and after relapse, are at a high acute risk for suicide. The risk of lifetime death from suicide has been estimated to range from 4% to 15% for depressed patients, depending on whether the patient is an outpatient, has been hospitalized for suicide risk resulting in a much higher risk. An important factor in long-term suicide risk depends on the presence of having made or rehearsed prior suicide attempts, and on whether the patient's illness is responsive to pharmacologic treatment.

In chronic high suicide risk patients who respond to ADMs, keeping the patient on a maintenance treatment while in remission has been shown to reduce depressive recurrence and suicide risk (Angst et al., 2005). Additionally, patients with recurrent depression and high chronic suicide risk can achieve a reduction of suicide risk by a maintenance course of lithium as an augmentation. The treatment of comorbid anxiety states with either long-acting slowly absorbed benzodiazepines, such as clonazepam, or NGAs may reduce suicide risk, although no studies have demonstrated this outcome as of yet.

The treatment of acute high-risk suicidal states is very difficult. If the patient who is not legally committable will accept hospitalization, this is the best option, and if the patient manifests severe anxiety/ agitation it should be aggressively treated. If the patient refuses hospitalization and does not demonstrate sufficient evidence of high suicide risk to be involuntarily hospitalized, which is not uncommon, keeping in close contact daily by phone can be lifesaving. In situations such as this, mobilizing family or friends to stay with the patient day and night can also be important. In the case of severe anxiety/ agitation, one of the more sedating NGAs such as

quetiapine (Seroquel) or olanzapine (Zyprexa) can be used in adequate doses to give the patient relief, while keeping in close contact through the crisis and trying to persuade the patient to accept hospitalization. It is possible to get the patient through an acute suicidal crisis, but it requires that the clinician recognize the risk and initiate an intervention that involves supportive others and treats the source of the patient's psychic pain, until the patient is stabilized. Patients who do not evidence distress, and who have planned a suicide while denying any intent, exercise their inherent rights to refuse treatment and may not be saved. Fortunately, in many cases, suicide can be prevented in both the short term and in the long term. The medications described earlier are not perfect for the task, but they can be used successfully as an important, sometimes crucial aspect of a lifesaving intervention.

Future Directions

As momentous as it is, suicide is a rare event. At the present time there is no evidence to suggest that it is predictable in any individual case that clinicians deal with, despite various statistical findings in groups of suicides. There have been attempts to better predict suicides using various measures, such as evidence of adrenal hyper function measured initially by corticosteroid excretion (Bunney & Fawcett, 1965) and by nonsuppression of adrenal function by dexamethasone, a potent, artificial adrenal steroid (Coryell & Schlesser, 2007). There also have been studies relating suicide to low cholesterol levels, suggesting that this might be a peripheral trait marker for impulsivity (Fawcett, Busch, Jacobs, Kravitz, & Fogg, 1997), and low cerebrospinal (CSF) levels of 5HIAA (5- hydroxy-indole-acetic acid), which has been shown to correlate with high rates of impulsive suicide (Linnoila et al., 1983). The question is whether it is possible to find a biological or psychological measure that will identify immediate or acute suicide risk. Recent studies of implicit cognition in suicidal patients may add another dimension to more accurate acute suicide risk assessment. Although it is possible to predict a high risk for suicide over time in those who have previously attempted suicide (Coryell & Young, 2005), what clinicians really need is information to help determine acute or immediate risk for a serious suicide attempt. Recent studies on implicit cognition may lead to a useful tool that will enhance risk assessment (Nock et al., 2010).

Then there is the question of whether psychological measures might be developed to alert the clinician to acute suicide risk. Many current scales, such as the SIS developed by Beck and colleagues (Beck, Kovacs, & Weissman, 1979), depend on information about previous attempts, which, although strong predictors of future attempts, only apply to 38% of males and 62% of females (Isometsa & Lonnqvist, 1998). Studies have shown that a significant proportion of decisions to commit suicide are made impulsively, about 10 minutes prior to the attempt (Deisenhammer et al., 2009). Of course, many of these people may have debated the subject in their mind before the sudden decision. In addition, any findings that purport to determine an immediate high suicide state need to be useful in the clinical situation. This limits reliance on sophisticated scanners, isotope labeled ligands, and computerized testing algorithms, which, although possibly producing information of heuristic value to the clinician, are currently not capable of assessing acute suicide risk.

This results in a focus on the long-term prevention of suicide. At this point lithium use as a deterrent to suicide is limited in the United States. Research efforts could look for new pharmacologic agents that address comorbid anxiety and impulsivity, as well as the depression underlying suicide more effectively, so that long-term treatment would have an enhanced effect in deterring suicide, and pharmacologic antidepressant treatment would be more effective.

Another real possibility is that combinations of new medications and cognitive-behavioral treatments could be developed to reduce suicide risk in those determined to be at high chronic risk. This can be accomplished by addressing high-risk traits and biological vulnerability to depression pharmacologically, while dealing with issues such as anxiety and depression responses to life stress with cognitive-behavioral techniques that promote the learning of coping skills.

It is these authors' belief that any solution leading to a reduction of suicide risk will depend on pharmacologic treatments that can address the elements promoting suicide, in synchrony with cognitive and behavioral learning that enhances coping with life's "slings and arrows" in people who have had the misfortune to inherit or to be taught (through various levels of traumatic experience) to develop low self-esteem, poor coping skills, and poor control of affective responses. Instead of studies comparing the efficacy of medications to various psychotherapies, it is time for a synthesis—for research aimed at developing synergy between biological-pharmacologic and learning-based therapies such as cognitive restructuring and behavioral therapies tailored to the needs of individual patients. Once this synergy is achieved, we then need people to be highly trained and readily available to share these therapeutic inputs with those patients who desperately need help—before they give up on conscious life. There is much to be done in order to reduce the terrible loss of human potential and consciousness resulting from suicide.

References

Ahn, E., Shin, D. W., Cho, S. I., Park, S., Won, Y. J., & Yun, Y. H. (2010). Suicide rates and risk factors among Korean cancer patients, 1993-2005. *Cancer Epidemiology, Biomarkers and Prevention, 19*(8), 2097–2105.

Angst, J., Angst, F., Gerber-Werder, R., & Gamma, A. (2005). Suicide in 406 mood-disorder patients with and without long-term medication: A 40 to 44 years' follow-up. *Archives of Suicide Research,.9*(3), 279–300.

Baker, R. W., Tohen, M., Fawcett, J., Risser, R. C., Schuh, L. M., Brown, E., ...Tollerson GD. (2003). Acute dysphoric mania: Treatment response to Olanzapine versus placebo. *Journal of Clinical Psychopharmacology, 23*(2), 132–137.

Baldessarini, R. J., & Hennen, J. (2004). Genetics of suicide: An overview. *Harvard Review of Psychiatry, 12*(1), 1–13.

Baldessarini, R. J., Pompili, M., & Tondo, L. (2006). Suicide in bipolar disorder: Risks and management. *CNS Spectrum, 11*(6), 466–471.

Baraclough, B. M., & Pallis, D. J. (1975). Depression followed by suicide: A comparison of depressed suicides compared with living depressives. *Psychological Medicine, 5*(1), 55–61.

Beasley, C. M., Jr., Ball, S. G., Nilsson, M. E., Polzer, J., Tauscher-Wisniewski, S., Plewes, J., & Acharya, N. (2007). Fluoxetine and adult suicidality revisited: An updated meta-analysis using expanded data sources from placebo-controlled trials. *Journal of Clinical Psychopharmacology, 27*(6), 682–686.

Beck, A. T., Kovacs, M., & Weissman, A. (1979). Assessment of suicidal intention: The scale for suicide ideation. *Journal of Consulting and Clinical Psychology, 47*(2), 343–352.

Black, D. W., Winokur, G., & Nasrallah, A. (1988). Effect of psychosis on suicide risk in 1593 patients with unipolar and bipolar affective disorders. *American Journal of Psychiatry, 145*(7), 849–852.

Bolton, J. M., Paqura, J., Enns, M. W., Grant, B., & Sareen, J. (2010). A population-based longitudinal study of risk factors for suicide attempts in major depressive disorder. *Journal of Psychiatric Research, 44*(13), 817–826.

Brent, D. (2010). What family studies teach us about suicidal behavior: Implications for research, treatment, prevention. *European Psychiatry, 25*(5), 260–263

Bunney, W. E. Jr., & Fawcett, J. A. (1965). Possibility of a biochemical test for suicidal potential: An analysis of endocrine findings prior to three suicides. *Archives of General Psychiatry, 13*, 232–239.

Busch, K. A., Fawcett, J., & Jacobs, D. (2003). Clinical correlates of inpatient suicide. *Journal of Clinical Psychiatry, 64*(1), 14–19.

Carlsten, A., & Waern, M. (2009). Are sedatives and hypnotics associated with increased suicide risk of suicide in the elderly? *BMC Geriatrics, 9*, 20.

Centers for Disease Control and Prevention. (2007). *National Center for Injury Prevention and Control, Web based statistics query and reporting system (WISQARS)*. Retrieved August 2013, from http://www.cdc.gov/injury/wisqars/index.html.

Clark, D. C., Young, M. A., Scheftner, W. A., Fawcett, J., & Fogg, L. (1987). A field test of Motto's risk estimator for suicide. *American Journal of Psychiatry, 144*(7), 923–926.

Cordry, R. W., & Gardner, D. L. (1988). Pharmacotherapy of borderline personality disorder. Alprazolam, carbamazepine, Trifluoperazine and tranylcypromine. *Archives of General Psychiatry, 45*(2), 111–119.

Coryell, W., & Schlesser, M. (2007). Combined biological tests for suicide prediction. *Psychiatry Research, 150*(2), 187–191.

Coryell, W., Solomon, D. A., Fiedorowicz, J. G., Endicott, J., Schettler, P. J., & Judd, L. L. (2009). Anxiety and outcome in bipolar disorder. *American Journal of Psychiatry, 166*(11), 1238–1243.

Coryell, W., & Young, E. A. (2005). Clinical predictors of suicide in primary major depressive disorder. *Journal of Clinical Psychiatry, 66*(4), 412–417.

Courtet, P. (2010). Suicidal risk in recurrent depression. *L'Encephale, 36*(Suppl. 5), S127–131.

Crawford, M. J., Kuforii, B., & Ghosh, P. (2010). The impact of social context on socio-demographic risk factors for suicide: A synthesis of data from case control studies. *Journal of Epidemiology and Community Health, 64*(6), 530–534.

Dannlowski, U., Baune, B. T., Bockermann, I., Domschke, K., Evers, S., Arolt, B., ... Rothermundt, M. (2008). Adjunctive antidepressant treatment with quetiapine in agitated depression: Positive effects on symptom reduction, psychopathology and remission rates. *Human Psychopharmacology, 23*(7), 587–593.

Deisenhammer, E. A., Ing, C. M., Strauss, R., Kemmler, G., Hinterhuber, H., & Weiss, E. M. (2009). The duration of the suicidal process: How much time is left for intervention between consideration and accomplishment of a suicide attempt? *Journal of Clinical Psychiatry, 70*(1), 19–24.

de Montigny, C., Cournoyer, G., Morissette, R., Langois, R., & Caille, G. (1983). Lithium carbonate addition in tricyclics antidepressant-resistant unipolar depression. Correlations with the neurobiologic actions of tricyclics antidepressant drugs and lithium ion on the serotonin system. *Archives of General Psychiatry, 40*(12), 1327–1334.

Dumais, A., Lesage, A. D., Alda, M., Rouleau, G., Dumont, M., Chawky, N., ... Turecki, G. (2005). Risk factors for suicide completion in major depression: A case control study of impulsive and aggressive behaviors in men. *American Journal of Psychiatry, 162*(11), 116–124.

Ereshefsky, L. (1999). Pharmacologic and pharmacokinetic considerations in choosing an antipsychotic. *Journal of Clinical Psychiatry, 60*(Suppl. 10), 20–30.

Fava, M., Alpert, J. E., Carmin, C. N., Wisniewski, S. R., Trivedi, M. H., Biggs, M. M., ... Rush, A. J. (2004). Clinical correlates and symptom patterns or anxious depression among patients with major depressive disorder in STAR*D. *Psychological Medicine, 34*(7), 1299–1308.

Fava, M., Rush, A. J., Alpert, J. E., Carmin, C. N., Balasubramani, G. K., Wisniewski, S. R., ... Shores-Wilson, K. (2006). What clinical and symptom features and comorbid disorders characterize outpatients with anxious major depressive disorder: A replication and extension. *Canadian Journal of Psychiatry, 51*(13), 823–835.

Fawcett, J., Busch, K. A., Jacobs, D., Kravits, H. M., & Fogg, L. (1997). Suicide: A four-pathway clinical-biochemical model. *Annals of the New York Academy of Sciences, 836*, 288–301.

Fawcett, J., Scheftner, W. A., Fogg, L., Clark, D. C., Young, M. A., Hedeker, D., & Gibbons, R. (1990). Time-related predictors of suicide in major affective disorder. *American Journal of Psychiatry, 147*(9), 1189–1194.

Flensborg-Madsen, T., Knop, J., Mortensen, E. L., Becker, U., Sher, L., & Gronbaek, M. (2009). Alcohol use disorders increase the risk of completed suicide- irrespective of other psychiatric disorders. A longitudinal cohort study, *Psychiatry Research, 167*(1–2), 123–130.

Fang, F., Keating, N. L., Mucci, L. A., Adami, H., Stamfer, M. J., Valdimarsdottir, U., & Fall, K. (2010). Immediate risk of suicide and cardiovascular death after a prostate cancer diagnosis: Cohort study in the United States. *Journal of the National Cancer Institute, 102*(5), 307–314.

Fournier, J. C., DeRubeis, R. J., Hollon, S. D., Dimidjian, S., Amsterdam, J. D., Shelton, R. C., & Fawcett, J. (2010). Antidepressant drug effects and depression severity: a patient-level meta-analysis. *Journal of the American Medical Association, 303*(1), 47–53.

Gibbons, R. D., Brown, C. H., Hur, K., Marcus, S. M., Bhaumik, D. K., Erkens, H. A., ... Mann, J. J. (2007). Early evidence on the effects of regulators' suicidality warnings on SSRI prescriptions and suicide in children and adolescents. *American Journal of Psychiatry, 164*(9), 1356–1363.

Goldacre, M., Seagroat, V., & Hawton, K. (1993). Suicide after discharge from psychiatric inpatient care. *Lancet, 342*(8866), 283–286.

Hall, R. C., Platt, D. E., & Hall, R. C. (1999). Suicide risk assessment: A review of risk factors for suicide in 100 outpatients who make severe suicide attempts. *Psychosomatics, 40*(1), 18–27.

Hammad, T. A., Laughren, T., & Racoosin, J. (2006). Suicidality in pediatric patients treated with antidepressant drugs. *Archives of General Psychiatry, 63*(3), 332–339.

Harris, E. C., & Baraclough, B. (1997). Suicide as an outcome for mental disorders. A meta-analysis. *British Journal of Psychiatry, 170*, 205–228.

Hirschfeld, R. M., Weisler, R. H., Raines, S. R., & Macfadden, W. (2006). Quetiapine in the treatment of anxiety in patients with bipolar I or II depression: A secondary analysis from a randomized, double-blind, placebo-controlled study. *Journal of Clinical Psychiatry, 67*(3), 355–362.

Holma, K. M., Melartin, T. K., Haukka, J., Holma, I. A., Sokero, T. P., & Isometsa, E. T. (2010). Incidence and predictors of suicide attempts in DSM-IV major depressive disorder: A five year prospective study. *American Journal of Psychiatry, 167*(7), 801–808.

Houston, J. P., Ahl, J., Meyers, A. L., Kaiser, C. J., Tohen, M., & Baldesserini, R. J. (2006). Reduced suicidal ideation in bipolar I disorder mixed-episode patients in a placebo-controlled trial of Olanzapine combined with lithium or divalproex. *Journal of Clinical Psychiatry, 67*(8), 1246–1252.

Ilgen, M. A., Zivin, K., Austin, K. L., Bohnert, A. S., Czyz, E. K., Valenstein, M., & Kilbourn, A. M. (2010). Severe pain predicts greater likelihood of subsequent suicide. *Suicide and Life-Threatening Behaviour, 40*(6), 597–608.

Isometsa, E. T., & Lonnqvist, J. K. (1998). Suicide attempts preceding completed suicide. *British Journal of Psychiatry, 173*, 531–535.

Kan, C. K., Ho, T. P., Dong, J. Y., & Dunn, E. L. (2007). Risk factors for suicide in the immediate post-discharge period. *Social Psychiatry and Psychiatric Epidemiology, 42*(3), 208–214.

Kessler, R. C., Borges, G., & Walters, E. E. (1999). Prevalence of risk factors for lifetime suicide attempts in the National Comorbidity Survey. *Archives of General Psychiatry, 56*(7), 617–626.

Khan, A., Khan, S., Kolts, R., & Brown, W. A. (2003). Suicide rates in clinical trials of SSRIs, other antidepressants, and placebo: Analysis of FDA reports. *American Journal of Psychiatry, 160*(40), 790–792.

Large, M., Smith, G., Sharma, S., Nielsson, O., & Singh, S. P. (2011). Systematic review and meta-analysis of the clinical factors associated with the suicide of psychiatric in-patients. *Acta Psychiatrica Scandinavica, 124*(1), 18–29.

Linnoila, M., Virkkunen, M., Scheinin, M., Nuutilo, A., Rimon, R., & Goodwin, F. K. (1983). Low cerebrospinal fluid 5-hydroxyindoleacetic acid concentration differentiates impulsive from nonimpulsive violent behavior. *Life Sciences, 33*(26), 2609–2614.

Lofman, S., Rasanen, P., & Hakko, H. (2011). Suicide among persons with back pain: A population-based study of 2310 suicide victims in Northern Finland. *Spine, 36*(7), 541–548.

Londborg, P. D., Smith, W. T., Glaudin, V., & Painter, J. R. (2000). Short-term cotherapy with clonazepam and fluoxetine: Anxiety, sleep disturbance and core symptoms of depression. *Journal of Affective Disorders, 61*(1-2), 73–79.

MacKinnon, D. R., & Farberow, N. L. (1976). An assessment of the utility of suicide prediction. *Suicide and Life-Threatening Behavior, 6*(2), 86–91.

Mann, J. J., Bortinger, J., Oquendo, M. A., Currier, D., Li, S., & Brent, D. S. (2005). Family history of suicidal behavior and mood disorders in probands with mood disorders. *American Journal of Psychiatry, 162*(9), 1672–1679.

McIntyre, A., Gendron, A., & McIntyre, A. (2007). Quetiapine adjunct to selective serotonin reuptake inhibitors or venlafaxine in patients with major depression, comorbid anxiety, and residual depressive symptoms: A randomized, placebo-controlled pilot study. *Depression and Anxiety, 24*(7), 487–494.

McIntyre, R. S., Muzina, D. J., Adams, A., Lourenco, M. T. C., Law, C. W. Y, Soczynska, J. K., ...Kennedy, S. H. (2009). Quetiapine XR efficacy and tolerability as monotherapy and as adjunctive treatment to conventional antidepressants in the acute and maintenance treatment of major depressive disorder: A review of registration trials. *Expert Opinion in Pharmacotherapy, 10*(18), 3061–3075.

Meltzer, H. Y., Alphs, L., Green, A. I., Altamura, C., Anand, R., Bertoldi, A., ...Potkin, S. (2003). Clozapine treatment for suicidality in schizophrenia: International Suicide Prevention Trial (InterSePT). *Archives of General Psychiatry, 60*(1), 82–91.

Muller-Oerlinghausen, B., Felber, W., Berghofer, A., Lauterbach, E., & Ahrens, B. (2005). The impact of lithium long-term medication on suicidal behavior and mortality of bipolar patients. *Archives of Suicide Research, 9*(3), 307–319.

Nock, M. K., Hwang, I., Sampson, N., Kessler, R. C., Angermeyer, M., Beautrais, A., ...Williams, D. R. (2009). Cross-national analysis of the associations among mental disorders and suicidal behavior: Findings from the WHO world mental health surveys. *PLoS Medicine, 6*(8), 1–17.

Nock, M. K., Park, J. M., Finn, C. T., Delbirto, T. L., Dour, H. J., & Banaji, M. R. (2010). Measuring the suicidal mind: Implicit cognition predicts suicidal behavior. *Psychological Sciences, 21*(4), 511–517.

Peteet, J. R., Maytal, G., & Rokni, K. (2010). Inimaginable loss: Contingent suicidal ideation in family members of oncology patients. *Psychosomatics, 51*(2), 166–170.

Pfeiffer, P. N., Ganoczy, D., Ilgen, M., Zivin, K., & Valenstein, M. (2009). Comorbid anxiety as a suicide risk factor among depressed veterens. *Depression and Anxiety, 26*(8), 752–757.

Pokorny, A. D. (1993). Suicide prediction revisited. *Suicide and Life-Threatening Behaviour, 23*(1), 1–10.

Rothschild, A. J., & Locke, C. A. (1991). Reexposure to fluoxetine after suicide attempts by three patients: The role of akathisia. *Journal of Clinical Psychiatry, 52*(12), 491–493.

Roy, A. (1983). Family history of suicide. *Archives of General Psychiatry, 40*(9), 971–974.

Rush, A. J., Warden, D., Wisniewski, S. R., Fava, M., Trivedi, M. H., Gaynes, B. N., & Nierenberg, A. A. (2009). STAR*D: Revising conventional wisdom. *CNS Drugs, 23*(8), 627–647.

Sareen, J., Cox, B. J., Afifi, T. O., de Graff, R., Asmundson, G. J. G., ten Have, M., & Stein, M. B. (2005). Anxiety disorders and risk for suicidal ideatuion and suicide attempts: A population-based longitudinal study of adults. *Archives of General Psychiatry, 62*(11), 1249–1257.

Sareen, J., Houlahan, T., Cox, B. J., & Asmundson, G. J. G. (2005). Anxiety disorders associated with suicidal ideation and suicide attempts in the National Co-Morbidity Survey. *Journal of Nervous and Mental Disease, 193*(7), 450–454.

Scott, K. M., Hwang, I., Chiu, W. T., Kessler, R. C., Sampson, N. A., Angermeyer, M., ...Nock, M. K. (2010). Chronic physical conditions and their association with first onset of suicidal behavior in the world mental health surveys. *Psychosomatic Medicine, 72*(7), 712–719.

Sheard, M. H., Marini, J. L., Bridges, C. L., & Wagner, E. (1976). The effect of lithium on impulsive-aggressive behavior in man. *American Journal of Psychiatry, 133*(12), 1409–1413.

Simon, G. E., Hunkeler, E., Fireman, B., Lee, J. Y., & Savarino, J. (2007). Risk of suicide attempt and suicide death in patients treated for bipolar disorder. *Bipolar Disorder, 9*(5), 526–530.

Simon, G. E., & Savarino, J. (2007). Suicide attempts among patients starting depression treatment with medications or psychotherapy. *American Journal of Psychiatry, 164*(7), 989–991.

Simon, N. M., Zalta, A. K., Otto, M. W., Ostacher, M. J., Fischmann, D., Chow, C. W., ...Pollack, M. H. (2007). The association of co-morbid anxiety disorders with suicide attempts and suicidal ideation in outpatients with bipolar disorder. *Journal of Psychiatric Research, 41*(3–4), 255–264.

Sinclair, J. M., Harriss, L., Baldwin, D. S., & King, E. A. (2005). Suicide in depressive disorders: A retrospective case-control study of 127 suicides. *Journal of Affective Disorders, 87*(1), 107–113.

Stordal, E., Morken, G., Mykletun, A., Neckelmann, D., & Dahl, A. A. (2008). Monthly variation in prevalence rates of comorbid depression and anxiety in the general population at 63-65 degrees North: The HUNT study. *Journal of Affective Disorders, 106*(3), 273–278.

Suominen, K., Isometsa, E., Ostamo, A., & Lonnqvist, J. (2004). Level of suicidal intent predicts overall mortality and suicide after attempted suicide: A 12-year follow-up study. *BMC Psychiatry, 4*, 11.

Swann, A. C., Dougherty, D. M., Pazzaglia, P. J., Pham, M., Steinberg, J. L., & Moeller, F. G. (2005). Increased impulsivity associated with severity of suicide attempt history in patients with bipolar disorder. *American Journal of Psychiatry, 162*(9), 1680–1687.

Szanto, K., Prigerson, H., Houck, P., Ehrenpreis, L., & Reynolds, C. F. (1997). Suicidal ideation in elderly bereaved: The role of complicated grief. *Suicide and Life-Threatening Behaviour, 27*(2), 194–207.

Szanto, K., Shear, M. K., Houck, P. R., Reynolds, C. F., Frank, E., Caroff, K., & Russell, S. (2006). Indirect self-destructive behavior and overt suicidality in patients with complicated grief. *Journal of Clinical Psychiatry, 67*(2), 233–239.

Taylor, C. T., Hirshfeld-Becker, D. R., Ostacher, M. J., Chow, C. W., LeBeau, R. T., Pollack, M. H., … Simon, N. M. (2008). Anxiety is associated with impulsivity in bipolar disorder. *Journal of Anxiety Disorders, 22*(5), 868–876.

Vieta, E., Calabrese, J. R., Goikolea, J. M., Raines, S., & Macfadden, W. (2007). Quetiapine monotherapy in the treatment of patients with bipolar I or II depression and a rapid-cycling disease course: A randomized, double-blind, placebo-controlled study. *Bipolar Disorder, 9*(4), 413–425.

Youssef, N. A., & Rich, C. L. (2008). Does acute treatment with sedative/hypnotics for anxiety in depressed patients affect suicide risk? A literature review. *Annals of Clinical Psychiatry, 20*(3), 157–169.

Zhang, J., Wieczorek, W., Conwell, Y., Tu, X. M., Wu, B. Y. W., Xiao, S., & Jia, C. (2010). Characteristics of young rural Chinese suicides: A psychological autopsy study. *Psychological Medicine, 40*(4), 581–589.

Zimbroff, D. L. (2003). Management of acute psychosis: from emergency to stabilization. *CNS Spectrum, 8*(11 Suppl. 2), 10–15.

Prevention of Nonsuicidal Self-Injury

Nancy L. Heath, Jessica R. Toste, *and* Shannon-Dell MacPhee

Abstract

One of the least addressed issues in the field of nonsuicidal self-injury (NSSI) is prevention. In the absence of existing empirically validated prevention programs, the present chapter reviews best practice guidelines for creating preventive interventions. Evidence-based recommendations for school-based prevention programs are described, including issues pertaining to program development, program to population matching, and program implementation. Finally, the recommendations are interpreted with reference to the NSSI literature to propose tentative guidelines for the creation of preventive interventions for NSSI.

Key Words: prevention, nonsuicidal self-injury, adolescents, school based, best practice

The study of nonsuicidal self-injury (NSSI) has developed substantially over the last two decades. Research exploring prevalence, correlates, risk factors, function, and even suggestions regarding treatment have emerged; however, as a newly developing field, many unanswered questions remain. One of the least addressed issues in the field of NSSI is effective approaches for prevention of this behavior. In one of the only papers addressing prevention of NSSI, Whitlock and Knox (2009) observe that although there is growing information concerning the risk factors for NSSI, there have been no primary prevention programs for NSSI based on this knowledge. However, despite the lack of research or discussion of prevention of NSSI in the literature, mental health professionals, school personnel, and practitioners in the community seek guidance on prevention of NSSI in youth. Schools perceive NSSI as a growing problem (Best, 2006; Heath, Toste, & Beettam, 2006), and inquiries often center on prevention. In the absence of any empirically validated prevention programs for NSSI, how are we to proceed? As the field moves toward the development

of prevention programs, it is imperative that the extensive knowledge from the field of prevention science directs our efforts. Thus, the present chapter provides a guideline for the development of effective prevention programs for NSSI; current knowledge related to NSSI behaviors is integrated within best practice guidelines drawn from the field of prevention science.

In order to explore possibilities for prevention of NSSI, it is essential to define *prevention*. Historically, in the early 1900s prevention was the domain of public health and medicine and was dominated by the medical model with an exclusive focus on physical health (Gullotta & Bloom, 2003). In the middle of the 20th century a more complex prevention focus emerged that combined perspectives from psychiatry and epidemiology to form a new psychiatric definition (Caplan, 1964). This definition was the first to suggest targeting populations for prevention efforts, as well as proposing levels of preventive intervention (primary, secondary, and tertiary).

However, in the 1970s a new movement in prevention developed. It was a rejection of both the medical and psychiatric definitions, which were criticized as being pathology or problem centered. The President Jimmy Carter Commission on Mental Health (1978) formed a Task Force on Primary Prevention, which in turn generated a definition of *primary prevention in mental health* that took a strength-based focus. The definition emphasized the importance of capacity building within target populations, rather than rehabilitation or therapy with individuals (Bloom & Gullotta, 2003). Thus, current definitions of *prevention* are characterized by levels of prevention consistent with Caplan's (1964) early work, in addition to retaining the strength-based focus.

Three dimensions of prevention address the problem at different points in time: (a) *primary* prevention aims to stop the problem before it occurs, (b) *secondary* prevention focuses on delaying the onset of the problem, and (c) *tertiary* prevention seeks to reduce the impact of the problem after it has occurred. These three levels originally delineated by Caplan (1964) have been interpreted differently by various authors. In a comprehensive examination of youth-based prevention programs, Durlak (1997) identified the three levels or targeted populations as being related to the risk status of the participants. Primary prevention is an intervention with the normative population that seeks to avert future occurrence of the problem behavior. Secondary prevention (or selective prevention) targets groups of individuals perceived to be at some risk of the problem behavior and aims to alter the course of development to avoid the emergence of the behavior. Tertiary prevention is undertaken once the behavior has occurred and aims to minimize the negative effects of the behavior. Tertiary prevention is better understood as early intervention (Durlak, 1997) and therefore will not be discussed within the context of this chapter. The focus of the present chapter is to evaluate strategies that may contribute to the reduction in NSSI behaviors among the youth population.

Prevention and Nonsuicidal Self-Injury

Self-injury is not a new phenomenon within clinical settings. However, research related to NSSI among community samples of adolescents has emerged only over the past two decades. There have been numerous reports that NSSI has increased during this period (Nock, 2009), although it is unclear if this is truly an increase of occurrence or an apparent increase resulting from awareness and reporting

of the behavior. Regardless, NSSI has become a significant health concern in North America, with 14% to 20% of the community-based, nonclinical adolescent population reporting engaging in this behavior (Heath, Schaub, Holly, & Nixon, 2009; Lloyd-Richardson, Perrine, Dierker, & Kelley, 2007; Muehlenkamp & Gutierrez, 2007; Ross & Heath, 2002) with some studies finding rates as high as 39% (e.g., Lloyd, 1997). These rates are a cause of great concern for professionals working with adolescents in hospital, community, and school settings. Adolescents generally report a resistance to seeking help for NSSI (Heath, Baxter, Toste, & McLouth, 2010). Although NSSI differs from a suicide attempt, current research suggests that when adolescents engage in this behavior over longer periods of time, with higher frequency, and with multiple methods (e.g., cutting, burning, scratching, punching), they are at higher risk for making a suicide attempt (Miller, Muehlenkamp, & Jacobson, 2009). As such, issues related to prevention of this behavior are of particular interest to researchers and health professionals.

Adolescents who engage in NSSI most commonly report an age of onset ranging from 12 to 14 years (see Rodham & Hawton, 2009 for review), and there is some early evidence that the onset of the behavior is even younger for some (Heath et al., 2010). Thus, prevention efforts should occur during this crucial period of early adolescence—specifically, the upper elementary and middle schools years. The high rates of NSSI during these years, coupled with the number of hours students spend at school, make the school settings an ideal environment for the implementation of prevention programs.

Although there is a dearth of evidence-based prevention programs for NSSI, efficacy of prevention programs for mental health issues and other negative outcomes has been demonstrated (Durlak & Wells, 1997; Greenberg, 2004; Greenberg et al., 2003). Both broad-based and targeted prevention programs have been shown to substantially reduce problem behaviors and symptoms, as well as build protective factors (Greenberg, Domitrovich, & Bumbarger, 2001). Therefore, the goal of creating an effective prevention program in the area of NSSI for delivery through the schools is feasible and has precedent (e.g., Nation et al., 2003; Reddy, Newman, De Thomas, & Chun, 2008). The field of prevention science has served to inform many of the most effective school-based prevention programs (Durlak, 1997; Greenberg et al., 2003). Drawing upon this body of literature, it is possible to provide best practice guidelines for the development of a prevention program for NSSI.

Best Practice Guidelines for School-Based Prevention

In developing a school-based primary prevention program, the first step is to select the target group. A universal or population-based approach targets all members of a specific population (e.g., all students in a particular school). Another approach focuses on a high-risk group that is not yet exhibiting any difficulties. This approach is referred to as a selective preventive intervention. The final strategy particularly relevant to school-based programs is to focus on those students undergoing a significant transition (e.g., transition to middle school). The foundation of the transition approach is that certain life tasks or developmental milestones are particularly difficult and stressful and are associated with negative effects (Durlak, 1997). Both the selective and transition approaches are examples of secondary prevention. Research and knowledge in the field of the problem behavior should inform the decision of who will be selected as the target group for prevention efforts.

Following the selection of the target group, the next decision must address the level of intervention. One can intervene at the individual level with youth and/or with different elements of the environment. Many primary prevention programs focus exclusively on the individual level; however, ecological theory supports the need to intervene at the environmental level with family, peers, school, community, and sometimes the physical environment (e.g., restricting access to means for suicide prevention). When selecting the level of intervention, it is also important to consider the likelihood of participation of each group. It is a waste of valuable resources to attempt to intervene with the community if it is apparent that the community will be resistant to the intervention.

Stemming from results of extensive meta-analyses related to universal and selective primary prevention, it is possible to outline specific recommendations for the development and implementation of future preventive intervention programs (Durlak, 1997; Durlak & Wells, 1997; Graczyk, Domitrovich, & Zins, 2002; Greenberg et al., 2003; Hage et al., 2007; Nation et al., 2003; Weissberg, Kumpfer, & Seligman, 2003; Weisz, Sandler, Durlak, & Anton, 2005). In the following sections, drawing on this extensive literature, guidelines are summarized with brief descriptions. The first section focuses on program development considerations, and the following section centers on issues relevant to the program to population match. The final section refers to issues concerning implementation of the prevention program.

Program Development

1. *Empirically Driven.* A fundamental tenet in developing a preventive program is that it has a sound theoretical and empirical base. This overarching premise applies to all of the decisions and guidelines that follow. This necessitates a review of the evidence in the field of interest and drawing from those findings to decide the selected group believed to be the most at risk for developing the problem behavior or the developmental stage associated with the highest risk. In addition, research establishing the factors that contribute to the development of the problem behavior direct the choice of content in the intervention.

2. *Strength Based.* A critical concern is that every prevention effort must be two-fold, both working to reduce risk, while enhancing protective factors. Although these two are inextricably intertwined, a conscious focus on capacity building is beneficial. Too often prevention programs exclusively target the reduction of risk factors, decreasing the potential effectiveness of the program. Including a strength-based focus that seeks to build competencies known to be protective is an essential feature of effective prevention programs.

3. *Breadth.* Multilevel interventions have been found to be more effective than individual or single-level preventive interventions. Although the more levels addressed the more powerful the intervention, an advantage exists simply in having two levels rather than one. With limited resources it may be impossible to extend the intervention to every level; however, a thoughtful and evidence-based selection of the most important levels should be undertaken with a minimum of two levels being the goal. Furthermore, with youth, the involvement of parents has reliably been found to be a particularly powerful addition to prevention in an array of areas. Additionally, interventions that cross domains (e.g., psychological, academic, physical) demonstrate more change than those that limit themselves to a single domain. Consistent with an ecological framework, interventions addressing change in the academic realm have, when evaluated, frequently documented benefits in the psychological domain. Specifically, Durlak

(1997) posited that a program should never be limited to a single domain, whenever resources make an ecological approach feasible.

4. *Sufficient Dosage*. It is important that the prevention intervention be of sufficient intensity and duration that it has an effect. Ideally, the dosage, or program intensity, is matched to the potential risk experienced by the participants. The greater the need or deficits of the youth, the greater the dosage required. Dosage may vary as a function of preventive intervention quality (type of contact or intervention) and/or quantity (time or duration). In addition, booster or follow-up sessions are needed to maintain and reinforce gains (Nation et al., 2003). Evaluations of existing programs are needed to determine what constitutes a "sufficient" dosage for a particular group and target behavior.

5. *Enhance Support*. In prevention research with children and adolescents, it is evident that the opportunity to develop a strong positive relationship with a significant other is a powerful protective factor across many areas of risk (Ainsworth & Bowlby, 1991; NICHD-ECCRN, 2002, 2004; Nickolite & Doll, 2008). This positive relationship may be attained through the improvement of the parent–child relationship or with significant others, including peers, teachers, or community members. In general, working to ensure the development of a strong relationship with at least one adult is helpful.

6. *Maximize Participation*. One of the greatest challenges to effective prevention is lack of participation or engagement. Although recruitment and retention will always remain a substantial hurdle in prevention programs, the use of a collaborative approach in the development of the program has been found to increase participation. Following identification of the target group and levels of intervention, a collaborative approach would include information sharing and consultation with chosen representatives from each group (e.g., parents, teachers, youth) in the actual development of the program.

7. *Incorporates Evaluation*. In planning a preventive intervention it is essential to incorporate mechanisms for evaluation. The evaluation is needed for the continual improvement and response to possible arising difficulties and for the documentation of the program fidelity and effectiveness. Effective programs are never static and are designed to be refined in response to the regular feedback provided by systematic evaluation.

Furthermore, documentation of the effectiveness is vital to obtain and maintain system support and thus contributes to the sustainability of the program.

8. *Sustainable*. In designing a preventive intervention the demands must be matched to the available resources to be sure that the program is sustainable over the long term. In addition to considerations of dosage or intensity, all programs benefit from a long-term design. This long-term perspective can include multiple time points and follow-up sessions (e.g., "boosters"), as well as participation of new groups of participants over time as the program is increasingly refined.

Program to Population Match

1. *Culturally Sensitive*. Nation and colleagues (2003) observe that the "relevance of prevention programs to the participants appears to be a primary concern in producing positive outcomes" (p. 453). Relevance may be a product of many different dimensions of the program, including, cultural and/or community beliefs and norms. Developing a prevention program that is culturally appropriate must go beyond superficial changes of language/images or information to an awareness of differing perspectives or values that will alter the receptiveness of the community to the program. It is also essential to recognize that communities which may be geographic, institutional, affiliative, or virtual communicate and share beliefs, values, and norms that must be addressed. Examples of this may be found in certain groups in adolescence (e.g., certain social cliques like "emos" or "goths") who share an identity and communicate their beliefs and norms concerning a variety of behaviors, including self-injury. Meaningful collaboration in the development stage with stakeholders will increase the probability that the program will be socioculturally relevant.

2. *Context Specific*. In developing a prevention program one must match the program to the context on a more practical and theoretical level. Practically, there are constraints in the school environment around the amount of available time and space that must be considered. On a more theoretical level, schools perceive their mandate to be primarily instructional or academic and may resist interventions seen as too far removed from this goal. Preventive interventions carried out in the schools need to be sensitive to the school's perspective and match

activities to be as consistent as possible with the context.

3. *Developmentally Appropriate.* Programs should be developmentally appropriate on both the superficial task demands as well as on a deeper level. Although almost all programs take into account reading, attention or developmentally appropriate interests, programs should consider developmental stages that may predispose youth to be more or less receptive to particular interventions. For example, in middle childhood children are still very open to enhancing the parent–child relationship through open communication; however, by adolescence a program that targets parent–youth communication would have to consider the natural and healthy move toward independence and privacy.

4. *Timing Sensitive.* In discussing the choice of a "selective preventive" approach, it was noted that it is of critical importance to focus on key developmental or transition periods known to be central to the development of the target behavior. This matching the timing of the program to fit the developmental trajectory of the behavior permits a more efficient use of resources and enhances the effectiveness of the intervention. However, selection of the appropriate time period is dependent on knowing enough about the developmental trajectory of the target behavior.

Program Implementation

1. *Staff Training.* The training of staff delivering the intervention is an obvious core factor in effective programming. Training should extend beyond rote training of implementation to include underlying principles and goals of each step to permit staff to respond flexibly to unanticipated events without threatening the integrity of the intervention.

2. *Fidelity of Program.* Lack of intervention fidelity is one of the most common underlying causes of poor outcome (Durlak, 1998). Staff training must highlight the importance of ensuring the fidelity of the intervention. Repeated evaluations and monitoring of intervention delivery should be completed.

3. *Collaborative.* As noted earlier, collaboration with stakeholders is needed in the development of the prevention program; however, collaboration is equally important in the implementation of the program.

4. *Flexibility.* Prior to initiating implementation of the program, a hierarchy of all the elements in the program should be created, clearly identifying which are the critical elements and which may be more subject to change. This provides an additional tool in ensuring the flexibility needed to individualize the program while identifying key aspects for program fidelity.

Ineffective Prevention Approaches

The editors of the *Encyclopedia of Prevention* made the decision to format the description of prevention efforts in each area with a section on strategies that have been shown *not* to work, arguing that dispelling common myths and frequently used ineffective strategies is also important in developing prevention in a particular field (Gullotta & Bloom, 2003). Thus, with regard to strategies that prevention science indicates are not effective, some cautions may be offered. First, overwhelmingly it is apparent that providing information only, or single-time "school assemblies" or information sheets, to individuals at risk is demonstrably ineffective. Although iatrogenic effects have not been found in either suicide or NSSI as a result of this information-sharing strategy (Kalafat, 2003; Muehlenkamp, Walsh, & McDade, 2009), neither have any benefits been revealed. Durlak (1997) notes that school-based prevention in particular is subject to engaging in information only "prevention" programs for a variety of reasons unrelated to effective prevention planning and that this is a poor use of limited resources.

A second clearly noneffective and potentially harmful approach to prevention specific to the area of NSSI is the use of explicit materials and "artistic" explorations of NSSI. Personal stories describing the NSSI, video projects, and explicit visual images may all serve as "triggers" resulting in increased incidents of NSSI. Occasionally, school personnel will present graphic video images or movies about NSSI to youth in the belief that this will serve to "scare them out of trying it." Unfortunately, too often this results in an increase rather than a decrease in the emergence of the behavior, although this has only been documented anecdotally (Lieberman, Toste, & Heath, 2009).

In summary, guidelines for effective preventive interventions drawn from prevention psychology combined with known noneffective strategies may be applied to the future development of a school-based prevention program for NSSI. In the following pages the specific application of these guidelines to the prevention of NSSI is explored based on the literature in the field of NSSI.

Existing Prevention Programs for Nonsuicidal Self-Injury

There currently exist few programs that focus on the prevention of self-harming behaviors, and only one such program that targets NSSI within schools. Some limited research has assessed prevention of NSSI in the community. One study was found that explored self-harm among adults. Morgan, Jones, and Owen (1993) describe an approach that is proposed as "secondary prevention;" this study investigated the effect of offering rapid, easy access to on-call mental health professionals to patients (mean age of 27.4 years) who had been admitted to the hospital after an episode of deliberate self-harm. One year follow-up data indicated a significant reduction in deliberate self-harm. However, it is unclear whether it was the availability of help that resulted in the reduction of behaviors or whether this was a cessation of the behavior after early episodes, as this has been shown to be common among young adults who "try" using self-harm as a coping strategy (Walsh, 2006). Further, this strategy does not serve to prevent the occurrence of NSSI or target populations who may be at risk for engaging in this behavior. Therefore, this study would be more accurately understood as a tertiary prevention or early intervention strategy for NSSI.

A more promising approach for school-based prevention was employed by Klingman and Hochdorf (1993) in their evaluation of a cognitive-oriented program aimed to reduce distress and self-harming behaviors among junior high school students. This program was implemented in groups of approximately 18 students, by school mental health professionals (e.g., school counselors or psychologists), over a period of 12 weeks with one 50-minute session per week. The first phase of the program focused on psychoeducation and the conceptual understanding of distress and responses to distress, including the role that cognitions and emotions play in maintaining distress. During the second phase, skill acquisition, students were guided through a series of exercises that modeled adaptive coping skills. This also included education related to help-seeking behavior, identifying suicide warning signs, and guidelines for responding to peers who are at high risk for engaging in self-destructive behaviors. The final phase of the program included home assignments that focused on rehearsing and applying newly acquired skills (e.g., modification of irrational thinking or negative self-talk). Postintervention results indicate positive effects on knowledge, awareness, attitudes, and awareness of distress coping skills but no indication that the target behavior (i.e., self-destructive behavior) was affected at all. This study demonstrates promise in school-based programs and offers some early evidence that targeting underlying difficulties is central to prevention. However, Klingman and Hochdorf (1993) focused on the broader construct of self-harm, which includes a wide array of self-destructive behaviors. As a result, it is impossible to generalize these results to NSSI prevention.

Although these studies have implemented strategies, there is a need for the development, implementation, and evaluation of comprehensive school-based programs aimed at the prevention of NSSI. To the knowledge of the authors, there is only one program that identifies itself as a prevention program for NSSI. The Signs of Self-Injury (SOSI) program was created by Screening for Mental Health, Inc. (Jacobs, Walsh, McDade, & Pigeon, 2009) as an expansion of the widely used school-based suicide prevention program, Signs of Suicide (SOS; Aseltine & De Martino, 2004). This program involves psychoeducation provided to school personnel, focusing on warning signs and response to student disclosure of NSSI, as well as guidelines for developing school policy. This information is shared through written materials and short videos, including vignettes of responding to student disclosure with the suggested guidelines. The program also includes a student component, which is implemented by school personnel in one class session of approximately 50 minutes. This session includes the sharing of basic information about NSSI, a series of video vignettes that inform students about how they can respond to peers who engage in NSSI and discussion questions to be used to facilitate conversation. Following the ACT® model of the SOS program, the vignettes teach students to Acknowledge the signs, Care for the person by showing desire to help, and Tell a trusted adult.

A preliminary evaluation of the SOSI program was conducted as a pilot study in five high schools (Muehlenkamp et al., 2009). Four schools targeted special education classes for students with emotional and behavioral difficulties, while the fifth implemented the program with all students during health class. The goals of this pilot study were to examine possible iatrogenic effects, as well as changes in students' knowledge, help-seeking attitudes, and help-seeking behaviors related to NSSI. Students completed a survey before the SOSI program and then again approximately 5 weeks postimplementation. The SOSI program was deemed to not have iatrogenic effects, as self-reported rates of NSSI thoughts and acts did not increase from pre- to postimplementation. In addition, students' knowledge of NSSI and adaptive attitudes increased from pre- to postimplementation; specifically in that they reported less discomfort and avoidance related to peers who engage in NSSI. Students also reported that they felt better able to help a friend who was self-injuring. However, there were no changes in reported help-seeking behaviors for self or peers.

Although initial evaluation of the SOSI program has shown some promise for enhancing student awareness and understanding of NSSI, it is unclear whether implementation of this program will actually result in increased help-seeking by students who engage in NSSI or, ultimately, a decrease in rates of NSSI. Additional research is necessary to further understand the possible change in student behavior, as well as a more in-depth examination of iatrogenic effects that may result from group discussions related to NSSI. Furthermore, the focus of the SOSI program is to provide school personnel and students with information and guidelines for responding to incidents of NSSI. As such, this program is a tertiary prevention program, intervening when the behavior has occurred to minimize further difficulties rather than a primary or secondary prevention program with the intent of averting NSSI before it occurs.

In light of the fact that there are no existing programs for the prevention of NSSI per se, it could be argued that broader mental health preventive interventions could be applied. However, the mental health programs currently in use have not targeted NSSI and, as such, it is unclear how NSSI may be influenced by implementation of these programs. In the future, mental health promotion programs should include variables relevant to NSSI in their intervention and outcome evaluation. In summary, there is an absence of empirically validated prevention programs specifically in the area of NSSI, and we cannot rely on mental health promotion programs as they do not directly address NSSI or associated factors. Therefore, the development of a strong empirically based preventive intervention is needed.

Application of Best Practice Guidelines: Nonsuicidal Self-Injury in the Schools
Identifying Contributing Factors

With reference to the aforementioned guidelines, one of the first and most critical steps in planning a prevention program is to identify central contributing factors to the occurrence of the target behavior, namely NSSI. Although the field of NSSI is relatively young, making the definitive identification of contributing factors impossible, it may be possible to suggest some probable correlates through the review of early research findings in the areas of risk factors, function, and treatment. A full review of these areas is beyond the scope of this chapter and has been undertaken elsewhere in this volume (see also Chapter 11 and Chapter 23). However, next is a brief summary of the findings as they pertain to selecting correlates for targeting in prevention programs. Current evidence would suggest that prevention programs for NSSI should target contributing factors such as emotion dysregulation, communication, and self-derogation (Klonsky, 2007; Klonsky & Glenn, 2009; Muehlenkamp, 2006; Nock, 2008).

EMOTION DYSREGULATION

Individuals who engage in NSSI frequently report that the behavior serves to reduce overwhelming negative emotions (Favazza & Conterio, 1989; Nock & Prinstein, 2004). Further, among young adults, it has been consistently found that those who engage in NSSI report significantly higher levels of emotion dysregulation than those who do not engage in the behavior (Gratz & Roemer, 2004; Heath, Toste, Nedecheva, & Charlebois, 2008). Treatment approaches for NSSI, such as dialectical behavior therapy (DBT) consistently emphasize techniques associated with emotion regulation, distress tolerance, and mindfulness skills (Gratz & Chapman, 2009; Hollander, 2008). As such, there is clear evidence to support emotion dysregulation as an underlying factor contributing to the development of NSSI.

COMMUNICATION

Although emotion dysregulation has been widely supported in the research literature as a core feature of NSSI, current evidence suggests that social factors may also play a role in this behavior for a number of individuals, particularly adolescents (Heath, Ross, Toste, Charlebois, & Nedecheva, 2009; Hilt, Nock, Lloyd-Richardson, & Prinstein, 2008). Nock (2008) presents an elaborated social theory of NSSI and reviews evidence to suggest that NSSI is maintained by social reinforcement from peers or family. It is argued that NSSI serves as a form of communication to others when alternative less extreme forms of communication are perceived as being ineffective.

The understanding of communication difficulties as a possible contributing factor to the occurrence of NSSI has been supported in the literature investigating self-reported functions of this behavior (e.g., Heath, Ross, et al., 2009; Lloyd-Richardson, Nock, & Prinstein, 2009; Lloyd-Richardson et al., 2007). In addition, empirically supported treatment approaches for NSSI invariably include training in effective communication (Gratz & Chapman, 2009; Hollander, 2008; Walsh, 2006).

SELF-DEROGATION

There is some early evidence to suggest that individuals who engage in NSSI report higher levels of self-derogation as compared to those who do not self-injure (Herpertz, Sass, & Favazza, 1997; Klonsky, Oltmanns, & Turkheimer, 2003). When considering self-reported functions of NSSI, self-punishment and self-directed anger are often cited by young adults (Klonsky, 2007; Nock & Prinstein, 2004). Taken together, these findings suggest that working to change negative self-talk, in conjunction with focus on emotion regulation and communication, may be an important consideration in NSSI prevention. These three factors have relatively strong support for their association with NSSI and, as such, should serve as the empirical foundation for preventive interventions for this behavior.

Developing a Preventive Intervention for Nonsuicidal Self-Injury

Thus far, the present chapter has reviewed prevention science guidelines for the development and implementation of a prevention program in youth, attempted to identify evidence-based contributing factors to be targeted in NSSI, and reviewed relevant prevention programs for NSSI and mental health. The next step in the process is to apply the guidelines and knowledge concerning contributing factors to delineate a possible framework for future prevention programs in NSSI. Thus, the following recommendations culled from prevention science are applied in a preliminary outline of a prevention program specifically for NSSI.

DEVELOPMENT STAGE

In developing preventive intervention programs for NSSI at this time, two possible approaches seem to have potential. The first is to undertake a universal curriculum-based approach in the early grades that incorporates a focus on developing emotional intelligence and skill building in the areas of emotion competence. The need to broaden the mission of the schools to include an emotion and coping component has been recognized (e.g., Greenberg, 2004). There are programs that provide guidance on incorporating an emotion-coping element into the curriculum using a universal prevention approach (e.g., Lantieri, 2008). However, although this approach seems likely to be beneficial in prevention of NSSI, there is absolutely no evidence indicating that these programs actually affect NSSI.

A second more modest approach would be to plan a selective intervention focused on the time period just before the documented common onset of NSSI, thus around the age of 12 years or just before transition to middle or high school. For instance, a preventive intervention consistent with the literature might focus on all fifth-grade students, preparing them for the transition to middle school, and include training sessions that highlight competencies in multiple domains of stress management, emotion dysregulation, effective communication, and challenging negative self-talk. In addition, it would be important to involve parent, peers, and teachers in skill building or education regarding how to support children, friends, and students in healthy emotion regulation and coping through validation and support (Hollander, 2008). Finally, providing information to parents, peers, and school personnel on warning signs that a youth is struggling and how to respond may also be recommended, although the focus should not be limited to NSSI but rather to a broader index of emotional well-being. The program should span at least a full year, preferably two, and have regular follow-ups and booster sessions in the following years. At this time there is no way of predicting how much contact or time is needed to really effect change in this area and thus recommendations regarding dosage cannot be offered. Treatment programs have reported change within a fairly limited time frame (e.g., Miller, Rathus, & Linehan, 2006), but this cannot be assumed to apply in the prevention program. While a longer time perspective is recommended in prevention programs and the need for sustainability is important, in the absence of any empirically validated prevention programs in this area the initial efforts need to be modest with evaluations built in and then decisions made regarding the continuity of the program. Nevertheless, the plans for extending the program beyond the initial stage need to be established at the program development and planning stage.

To enhance participation, collaboration with the school's administration is needed to highlight how the goals of the program are relevant to their own perceived mandate, the potential benefits for the school, and the possibility of incorporating some elements of particular interest or concern to the school into the program. Similarly, meeting with and establishing a collaborative program team that has representatives from the student body, teachers, parents, and school administration in the early stages of the development allows for continuous collaboration.

PROGRAM TO POPULATION MATCH

Developing a preventive intervention that is well matched to the target group in the area of NSSI has specific challenges. Beyond the standard considerations of culture and local community norms, NSSI is a unique phenomenon whereby an online or virtual community of self-injury exists that is highly cohesive, active, and accessible for youth while remaining completely hidden to others in the youth's life (Whitlock & Knox, 2009). Many of these communities, while ostensibly encouraging recovery, actually serve to encourage initiation and maintenance, and normalize the behavior as an acceptable and effective "coping strategy." Similarly, outside specific chat rooms or Web sites dedicated to self-injury, in youth culture online at YouTube (http://www.youtube.com) there are an array of videos of youth who self-injure, again ostensibly to discourage youth from beginning, but creating exposure of all youth to NSSI in a dramatic and youth-appealing manner. It is strongly recommended that any practitioners planning on developing a program for NSSI familiarize themselves with this youth culture perspective on NSSI (Whitlock, Lader, & Conterio, 2007).

As noted earlier, a school-based prevention program must be negotiated within the framework of the school schedule constraints. Targeting the whole grade requires that a time be set aside for the program each week over a period of weeks or months. Although there may be resistance to the idea of losing time from academics to more socioemotional factors, most schools are beginning to recognize the need and benefit of expanding the educational mandate to include social-emotional competence and well-being (Greenberg et al., 2003). Nevertheless, collaborating with the school to incorporate the program into the curriculum is imperative. Added-on programs (e.g., lunchtime, after school) are not recommended.

Offering the program as the youth are entering puberty and transitioning to middle/high school has the advantage that students are struggling with many developmental stressors and may be particularly receptive to guidance framed as coping with stress.

PROGRAM IMPLEMENTATION

Guidelines for the implementation of a prevention program as noted earlier include effective staff training, monitoring and documenting the program fidelity, and building in some flexibility. However, issues that may arise specifically in dealing with NSSI prevention are (a) the need for additional staff training as many practitioners feel a level of discomfort with NSSI; (b) training around suicide and NSSI overlap and guidelines for continuous monitoring for suicide risk; and (c) the uncertainty in establishing a clear hierarchy of critical contributing factors in the absence of an empirical body of literature.

In contrast to many of the problem behaviors targeted in school-based prevention programs (e.g., substance abuse, conduct disorder), NSSI elicits a level of discomfort among many practitioners that may interfere with service delivery (Best, 2006; Heath et al., 2006). Preventive interventions for NSSI should center on issues related to overall well-being and coping, with NSSI being one example of a maladaptive coping strategy used by youth. Nevertheless, it is probable that incidents of NSSI will be revealed through such discussions, even though the focus is not directly on this behavior. Therefore, staff training has to explicitly explore personal feelings of discomfort and disgust with the behavior.

As the research reviewed in Chapter 3 reveals, although NSSI is a distinct and separate behavior from suicidal attempts, there is a relationship between the two, such that youth who engage in NSSI are at greater risk for suicide ideation and attempts. Therefore, staff training and program implementation must include a procedure for the continuous monitoring of possible suicide risk.

Finally, the recommendation to create a hierarchy of critical contributing factors and associated elements in the prevention program to permit flexibility in the delivery of the prevention program can only be tentative at this time. The field of NSSI is only newly emerging and lacking in definitive information concerning contributing factors. Under these circumstances it is impossible to narrow the focus beyond overall emotional coping to more specific factors.

Conclusion

At this time there are no empirically validated prevention programs in the area of NSSI. Prevention science provides evidence-based guidelines for developing prevention programs that should be used in the future development of prevention programs in the area. The most significant challenge in developing a preventive intervention for NSSI is the relative dearth of evidence concerning the contributing factors to the development of NSSI. In the absence of longitudinal studies, only correlates of NSSI are identified and the developmental trajectory unknown. Currently, prevention program areas in the field should be developed with reference to prevention psychology best practice guidelines as summarized in this chapter. However, as knowledge progresses in the field concerning contributing factors to the development of NSSI, prevention interventions will evolve. In essence, the development of prevention in NSSI is at best tentative and at worst premature. Therefore, it is imperative that every preventive intervention incorporates a rigorous evaluation.

Future Directions

The study of the prevention of NSSI is in its infancy and future directions abound. However, the following questions may serve as a starting point in moving forward in the study of prevention of NSSI:

What factors are the most significant in the development of NSSI? As stated in the present chapter, for prevention programs to be developed, the field of NSSI must advance in order to establish understanding of the factors contributing to the development of NSSI. Currently, without longitudinal studies examining the emergence of NSSI, there is no definitive evidence on essential contributing factors, only correlates that are hypothesized to be contributing factors. Furthermore, future research is needed to explore the most salient factors in the development of NSSI through the relative comparison of multiple factors, rather than isolated studies of one variable.

Are these contributing factors subject to change? Following the documentation of important contributing factors, it is necessary to determine whether the identified factors are responsive to intervention and which interventions are most effective. This will necessitate numerous well-considered and planned preventive interventions with precise evaluations of outcome.

Do existing mental health promotion programs with their broad approach affect the emergence of NSSI? An alternative future direction is to incorporate measures of NSSI and associated difficulties into existing mental health promotion outcome evaluations. If existing programs in the area of mental health are changing the course of NSSI, then a further examination to reveal which of the multitude of elements in the programs are responsible for the change would be helpful in our understanding of prevention of NSSI.

References

Ainsworth, M. S., & Bowlby, J. (1991). An ethnological approach to personality development. *American Psychologist*, *46*, 333–341.

Aseltine, R. H., & DeMartino, R. (2004). An outcome evaluation of the SOS suicide prevention program. *American Journal of Public Health*, *94*, 446–451.

Best, R. (2006). Deliberate self-harm in adolescence: A challenge for schools. *British Journal of Guidance and Counselling*, *34*, 161–175.

Caplan, G. (1964). *The principles of preventive psychiatry*. New York, NY: Basic Books.

Durlak, J. A. (1997). *Successful prevention programs for children and adolescents*. New York, NY: Plenum Press.

Durlak, J. A. (1998). Why program implementation is important. *Journal of Prevention and Intervention in the Community*, *17*, 5–18.

Durlak, J. A., & Wells, A. M. (1997). Primary prevention mental health programs for children and adolescents: A meta-analytic review. *American Journal of Community Psychology*, *25*, 115–152.

Favazza, A. R., & Conterio, K. (1989). Female habitual self-mutilators. *Acta Psychiatrica Scandinavica*, *79*, 283–289.

Graczyk, P. A., Domitrovich, C. E., & Zins, J. E. (2002). Facilitating the implementation of evidence-based prevention and mental health promotion efforts in schools. In M. D Weist, S. W. Evans, & N. A. Lever (Eds.), *Handbook of school mental health* (pp. 301–318). New York, NY: Springer.

Gratz, K. L., & Chapman, A. L. (2009). *Freedom from self-harm: Overcoming self-injury with skills from DBT and other treatments*. Oakland, CA: New Harbinger.

Gratz, K., & Roemer, L. (2004). Multidimensional assessment of emotional regulation and dysregulation: Development, factor structure, and initial validation of the Difficulties in Emotion Regulation Scale. *Journal of Psychopathology and Behavioral Assessment*, *26*, 41–54.

Greenberg, M. T. (2004). Current and future challenges in school-based prevention: The researcher perspective. *Prevention Science*, *5*, 5–13.

Greenberg, M. T., Weissberg, R. P., O'Brien, M. U., Zins, J. E., Fredericks, L., Resnik, H., & Elias, M. J. (2003). Enhancing school-based prevention and youth development through coordinated social, emotional, and academic learning. *American Psychologist*, *58*, 466–474.

Gullotta, T. P., & Bloom, M. (2003). *Encyclopedia of primary prevention and health promotion*. New York, NY: Kluwer Academic/ Plenum.

Hage, S. M., Romano, J. L., Conyne, R. K., Kenny, M., Matthews, C., Schwartz, J. P., & Waldo, M. (2007). Best practice guidelines on prevention practice, research, training, and social advocacy for psychologists. *Counseling Psychologist*, *35*, 493–566.

Heath, N. L., Baxter, A. L., Toste, J. R., & McLouth, R. (2010). Adolescents' willingness to access school-based support for non-suicidal self-injury. *Canadian Journal of School Psychology*, *25*(3), 260–276.

Heath, N. L., Ross, S., Toste, J. R., Charlebois, A., & Nedecheva, T. (2009). Retrospective analysis of social factors and non-suicidal self-injury among young adults. *Canadian Journal of Behavioural Science, 41*, 180–186.

Heath, N. L., Schaub, K., Holly, S., & Nixon, M. K. (2009). Self-injury today: Review of population and clinical studies in adolescents. In M. K. Nixon & N. L. Heath (Eds.), *Self-injury in youth: The essential guide to assessment and intervention* (pp. 9–27). New York, NY: Routledge.

Heath, N. L., Toste, J. R., & Beettam, E. L. (2006). "I am not well-equipped": High school teachers' perceptions of self-injury. *Canadian Journal of School Psychology, 21*, 73–92.

Heath, N. L., Toste, J. R., Nedecheva, T., & Charlebois, A. (2008). An examination of non-suicidal self-injury in college students. *Journal of Mental Health Counseling, 30*, 137–156.

Herpertz, S., Sass, H., & Favazza, A. R. (1997). Impulsivity in self-mutilative behavior: Psychometric and biological findings. *Journal of Psychiatric Research, 31*, 451–465.

Hilt, L. M., Nock, M. K., Lloyd-Richardson, E. E., & Prinstein, M. J. (2008). Longitudinal study of nonsuicidal self-injury among young adolescents. *Journal of Early Adolescence, 28*, 455–469.

Hollander, M. (2008). *Helping teens who cut: Understanding and ending self-injury.* New York, NY: Guilford Press.

Jacobs, D., Walsh, B. W., McDade, M., & Pigeon, S. (2009). *Signs of self-injury prevention manual.* Wellesley Hills, MA: Screening for Mental Health.

Kalafat, J. (2003). Suicide, adolescence. In T. P. Gullota & M. Bloom (Eds.), *Encyclopedia of primary prevention and health promotion* (pp. 1099–1105). New York, NY: Kluwer Academic/Plenum.

Klingman, A., & Hochdorf, Z. (1993). Coping with distress and self harm: The impact of a primary prevention program among adolescents. *Journal of Adolescence, 16*, 121–140.

Klonsky, E. D. (2007). The functions of deliberate self-injury: A review of the empirical evidence. *Clinical Psychology Review, 27*, 226–239.

Klonsky, E. D., & Glenn, C. R. (2009). Psychosocial risk and protective factors. In M. K. Nixon & N. L. Heath (Eds.), *Self-injury in youth: The essential guide to assessment and intervention* (pp.45–58). New York, NY: Routledge.

Klonsky, E. D., Oltmanns, T. F., & Turkheimer, E. (2003). Deliberate self-harm in a nonclinical population: Prevalence and psychological correlates. *American Journal of Psychiatry, 160*, 1501–1508.

Lantieri, L. (2008). *Building emotional intelligence: Techniques to cultivate inner strength in children.* Boulder, CO: Sounds True.

Lieberman, R., Toste, J. R., & Heath, N. L. (2009). Nonsuicidal self-injury in the schools: Prevention and intervention. In M. K. Nixon & N. L. Heath (Eds.), *Self-injury in youth: The essential guide to assessment and intervention* (pp. 195–215). New York, NY: Routledge.

Lloyd, E. E. (1997). Self-mutilation in a community sample of adolescents. *Dissertation Abstracts International: Section B: The Sciences and Engineering, 58*, 5127.

Lloyd-Richardson, E. E. (2008). Adolescent nonsuicidal self-injury: Who is doing it and why? *Journal Developmental and Behavioral Pediatrics, 29*, 216–218.

Lloyd-Richardson, E. E., Nock, M. K., & Prinstein, M. J. (2009). Functions of adolescent nonsuicidal self-injury. In M. K. Nixon & N. L. Heath (Eds.), *Self-injury in youth: The essential guide to assessment and intervention* (pp. 29–41). New York, NY: Routledge.

Lloyd-Richardson, E. E., Perrine, N., Dierker, L., & Kelley, M. L. (2007). Characteristics and functions of non-suicidal self-injury in a community sample of adolescents. *Psychological Medicine, 37*, 1183–1192.

Miller, A. L., Muehlenkamp, J. J., & Jacobson, C. M. (2009). Special issues in treating adolescent nonsuicidal self-injury. In M. K. Nock (Ed.), *Understanding nonsuicidal self-injury: Origins, assessment, and treatment* (pp. 251–270). Washington, DC: American Psychological Association.

Miller, A. L., Rathus, J. H., & Linehan, M. M. (2006). *Dialectical behavior therapy with suicidal adolescents.* New York, NY: Guilford Press.

Morgan, H. G., Jones, E. M., & Owen, J. H. (1993). Secondary prevention of non-fatal deliberate self-harm: The green card study. *British Journal of Psychiatry, 163*, 111–112.

Muehlenkamp, J. J. (2006). Empirically supported treatments and general therapy guidelines for non-suicidal self-injury. *Journal of Mental Health Counseling, 28*, 166–185.

Muehlenkamp, J. J., & Gutierrez, P. M. (2007). Risk for suicide attempts among adolescents who engage in nonsuicidal self-injury. *Archives of Suicide Research, 11*, 69–82.

Muehlenkamp, J. J., Walsh, B. W., & McDade, M. (2009). Preventing non-suicidal self-injury in adolescents: The signs of self-injury program. *Journal of Youth and Adolescence, 39*, 306–314.

NICHD-ECCRN. (2002). The relation of global first grade classroom environment to structural classroom features and teacher and student behaviors. *Elementary School Journal, 102*, 367–387.

NICHD-ECCRN. (2004). Multiple pathways to early academic achievement. *Harvard Educational Review, 74*, 1–29.

Nickolite, A., & Doll, B. (2008). Resilience applied to school: Strengthening classroom environments for learning. *Canadian Journal of School Psychology, 23*, 94–113.

Nock, M. K. (2008). Actions speak louder than words: An elaborated theoretical model of the social functions of self-injury and other harmful behaviors. *Applied and Preventive Psychology, 12*, 159–168.

Nock, M. K. (Ed.). (2009). *Understanding nonsuicidal self-injury: Origins, assessment, and treatment.* Washington, DC: American Psychological Association.

Nock, M. K., & Prinstein, M. J. (2004). A functional approach to the assessment of self-mutilative behavior. *Journal of Consulting and Clinical Psychology, 72*, 885–890.

Nation, M., Crusto, C., Wandersman, A., Kumpfer, K. L., Seybolt, D., Morrissey-Kane, E., & Davino, K. (2003). What works in prevention: Principles of effective prevention programs. *American Psychologist, 58*, 449–456.

Reddy, L. A., Newman, E., De Thomas, C. A., & Chun, V. (2008). Effectiveness of school-based prevention and intervention programs for children and adolescents with emotional disturbance: A meta-analysis. *Journal of School Psychology, 47*, 77–99.

Rodham, K., & Hawton, K. (2009). Epidemiology and phenomenology of nonsuicidal self-injury. In M. K. Nock (Ed.), *Understanding nonsuicidal self-injury: Origins, assessment, and treatment* (pp. 37–62). Washington, DC: American Psychological Association.

Ross, S., & Heath, N. L. (2002). A study of the frequency of self-mutilation in a community sample of adolescents. *Journal of Youth and Adolescence, 31*, 67–77.

Walsh, B. W. (2006). *Treating self-injury: A practical guide.* New York, NY: Guilford Press.

Weissberg, R. P., Kumpfer, K. L., & Seligman, M. E. P. (2003). Prevention that works for children and youth: An introduction. *American Psychologist, 58,* 425–432.

Weisz, J. R., Sandler, I. N., Durlak, J. A., & Anton, B. S. (2005). Promoting and protecting and youth mental health through evidence-based prevention and treatment. *American Psychologist, 60,* 628–648.

Whitlock, J., Lader, W., & Conterio, K. (2007). The internet and self-injury: What psychotherapists should know. *Journal of Clinical Psychology, 63,* 1135–1143.

Whitlock, J., & Knox, K. L. (2009). Intervention and prevention in the community. In M. K. Nixon & N. L. Heath (Eds.), *Self-injury in youth: The essential guide to assessment and intervention* (pp.173–194). New York, NY: Routledge.

Psychological Treatments for Nonsuicidal Self-Injury

Barbara Stanley, Virginia Fineran, *and* Beth Brodsky

Abstract

There are few psychological treatments for nonsuicidal self-injury (NSSI) that meet the standards of empirically supported psychosocial interventions. Most studies have investigated the outcome of self-injurious behavior as a whole, whether or not suicidal intent was present. This chapter describes existing behavioral and cognitive treatments (i.e., dialectical behavior therapy, cognitive therapy, cognitive-behavioral therapy) that have empirical support for the treatment of NSSI in psychiatric populations, in which NSSI most commonly occurs, as well as in special populations (e.g., among those with autism and trichotillomania). Directions for future research also are discussed.

Key Words: treatment, non-suicidal self-injury, NSSI, behavioral and cognitive treatments, Dialectical Behavior Therapy, Cognitive Therapy, Cognitive-Behavior Therapy

Nonsuicidal self-injury (NSSI) has emerged as a phenomenon increasingly attracting attention from clinicians and researchers in the field. NSSI had previously been contextualized as an aspect of specific disorders such as borderline personality disorder (BPD) or been grouped together with suicide attempts and other acts of self-harm regardless of suicidal intent. However, NSSI more recently has been explored and defined as a behavior with characteristics unique from suicide attempts in that it is intentionally self-destructive behavior performed *without* intent to die. Similarly, the emphasis also has shifted from categorizing NSSI as a symptom of a specific psychiatric diagnosis toward viewing NSSI as a distinct behavior to target and treat regardless of diagnosis.

Unfortunately, there is no "gold standard" treatment for this phenomenon, and empirical support for the psychological treatment of NSSI is scarce. For the most part, any treatment for NSSI is subsumed under treatments for suicidal and parasuicidal behavior, which may or may not include NSSI. More often than not, the research studies that include analyses of parasuicidal behaviors fail to differentiate between self-injurious acts that are performed with or without the intent to die. Although there is some empirical support for treatments for suicidal individuals, their applicability to NSSI is mostly unknown. Because NSSI does not necessarily occur within the context of suicidal ideation, the same treatments may not be effective for the individuals who engage in NSSI primarily. With the reported rise of NSSI particularly in adolescent populations, the importance of identifying treatments specifically addressing NSSI is becoming increasingly apparent.

Basic survey research in nonclinical populations has been conducted to determine how people engaging in NSSI avert these urges and behaviors. Klonsky and Glenn (2008) published the results of a survey they conducted to determine the prevalence of NSSI in an undergraduate population and the tactics used to resist engaging in self-injurious behavior. Of the more than 2,700 college students,

39 had a history of NSSI with a mean of 17 NSSI acts over their lifetime. Subjects reported the most frequently used, though not necessarily most helpful, methods to resist urges to self-injure were "keeping busy" and "being around friends." The most effective methods of resisting the urge to engage in NSSI were "playing sports or exercising" and "removing means/instrument."

As with any treatment development, an understanding of the etiology of and reasons underlying the behavior is necessary. Shearer (1994) reports that the most frequently reported function of NSSI among an inpatient BPD sample are as follows: in order to feel concrete pain instead of overwhelming emotional pain (59%), followed by self-punishment (49%), the reduction of anxiety and feelings of despair (39%), to feel in control (22%), to express anger (22%), to feel something when feeling numb or out of touch (20%), to seek help from others (17%), and to keep bad memories away (15%). In addition, the functions of self-injury are very much affected by the cognitions that accompany the emotional experience. Individuals who self-injure often hold fixed beliefs, what Linehan (1993) refers to as myths, and what Beck (1995) labels dysfunctional cognitions that support the function of the self-injury. Thus, most treatment that targets the reduction of NSSI addresses emotional distress, cognitive distortions, and behavioral dyscontrol related to nonsuicidal, deliberate self-harm urges and behaviors. We review here the treatment approaches that have some empirical support while underscoring the fact that much empirical work remains to be conducted in the development of empirically supported treatment for NSSI.

Dialectical Behavior Therapy

Dialectical behavior therapy (DBT) is a treatment that was developed to treat individuals with BPD. One criterion for the diagnosis of BPD is "recurrent suicidal behavior, gestures, or threats, or self-mutilating behavior" (American Psychiatric Association, 1994), and many clients demonstrating NSSI also meet diagnostic criteria for BPD (Chapman, Specht, & Cellucci, 2005; Nock, Joiner, Gordon, Lloyd-Richardson, & Prinstein, 2006).

DBT is a manualized treatment that combines elements of behavioral, cognitive, and supportive psychotherapies. The treatment typically lasts 12 months and is comprised of both individual sessions (1 hour a week) and group sessions (2.5 hours a week). Individual therapy utilizes directive, problem-oriented techniques such as behavioral

skills training, contingency management, cognitive modification, and exposure to emotional cues. Furthermore, these directive techniques are balanced with supportive techniques such as reflection, empathy, validation, and acceptance. During individual therapy, a hierarchy of behavioral goals is set up, and then each behavior is targeted for change according to the hierarchy. Foremost among the behaviors targeted are suicidal and self-injurious behaviors, followed by therapy interfering behaviors and behaviors that disrupt quality of life. The approach of DBT is to teach patients how to problem solve and manage emotional trauma rather than performing direct crisis intervention. Group sessions have a psychoeducational format and provide behavioral skills training in three areas: (1) interpersonal skills, (2) distress tolerance/reality acceptance skills, and (3) emotion regulation skills.

Much of the DBT research measures reduction of any type of self-injurious behavior, without distinguishing between suicidal and nonsuicidal self-injury. Linehan et al. (1991) developed DBT and investigated its efficacy in treating parasuicidal behavior in individuals diagnosed with BPD. Parasuicidal behavior, as defined by Linehan et al. (1991), consists of any intentional, acute, self-injurious behavior with or without suicidal intent, including both suicide attempts and self-mutilative behaviors. In the original efficacy study, 44 subjects were included in the outpatient trial, with 22 in the experimental DBT group and 22 in the treatment as usual (TAU) control group. The subjects were all females aged 18 to 45 years with a diagnosis of BPD and had at least two parasuicide episodes in the 5 years before enrollment, one of which occurred in the 2 months before enrollment. Those with a comorbid diagnosis of schizophrenia, bipolar disorder, substance dependence, or mental retardation were excluded. Participants agreed to terminate other individual psychotherapy if assigned to DBT.

Compared to the TAU group, the DBT group experienced a significant reduction in frequency and medical risk of parasuicidal behavior at each assessment point during treatment (pre–4 month, 4–8 month, 8–12 month, year total). Furthermore, more patients stayed in therapy in the DBT group than the TAU group by the 4–8 month assessment point; the attrition rate for the DBT group was very low at 16.7%. And lastly, in comparison with the TAU group, those in the DBT group spent significantly fewer days in psychiatric inpatient hospitalization both during the pre–4 month period and during the entire year. However, there were no significant differences in improvement between DBT and TAU in levels of depression, hopelessness, suicidal ideation, and reasons for living.

In a follow-up study, Linehan evaluated whether the beneficial effects of DBT were maintained 1 year after the completion of therapy (Linehan, Heard, & Armstrong, 1993). The subjects who completed DBT had fewer acts of parasuicide as well as fewer medically treated acts, and they also reported less anger and better social adjustment at the 1-year follow-up assessment point than those who had been in the TAU group. In another study that included 111 women who were randomized to either 1 year of DBT or 1 year of "community treatment by experts," DBT was found to be superior in preventing suicide attempts (Linehan et al., 2006).

Stanley et al. (2007) evaluated the efficacy of a brief version of DBT in reducing NSSI urges and behavior in an open outpatient trial treating 20 subjects meeting criteria for BPD. The DBT was condensed to a 6-month treatment targeting suicidal behavior and ideation, including NSSI behavior. Urges to self-injure, number of self-injury episodes, suicide ideation, and subjective distress were assessed at baseline and after completing 6 months of treatment. By the end of treatment, the subjects showed improvements in all four of these variables, demonstrating significantly fewer self-injury urges and episodes as well as less suicidal ideation and subjective distress than what they had reported at baseline. Further exploration including a comparison group and a follow-up to establish the maintenance of the treatment effects would be needed to make a more compelling case for the efficacy of brief DBT in treating NSSI.

Bohus and colleagues (2004) tested a 3-month inpatient DBT treatment program for individuals diagnosed with BPD, to determine the overall effectiveness of inpatient DBT in reducing BPD symptoms and lowering the frequency of "self-mutilating acts." Of the 60 subjects who agreed to participate in the study, 31 received DBT while 19 were put on a waitlist receiving TAU while waiting to receive DBT, and 20 subjects dropped out. All participants were female and had either one suicide attempt or at least two NSSI acts within the last 2 years. Overall, 68% of the entire sample engaged in "self-mutilating" behavior at the pretreatment stage. Those receiving outpatient DBT or DBT after discharge from the inpatient unit were excluded from the study, as well as anyone diagnosed with bipolar I disorder or schizophrenia. In addition to standard DBT treatment (i.e., weekly sessions each of individual therapy, group skills training, peer group meetings and team consultation, and a weekly 1-hour group session of mindfulness group), there was 1.5 hours of individual body-oriented therapy. Psychoeducation classes were used to elaborate on the bio-behavioral or biosocial theory of BPD and to present current research in the area. The mindfulness group was an expansion of the standard DBT Mindfulness module with a focus on "sitting practice," and the body-oriented therapy was utilized psychomotor interaction and exercises to improve the "body concepts." The waitlist group had some form of outside mental health care, with 12 being hospitalized in non-DBT inpatient units at least once (with an average of 44 treatment days), and 14 receiving outpatient care (6.1 sessions on average). Both the DBT and waitlist group had a high percentage of participants on psychotropic medications, 74% and 79%, respectively.

Of the 68% who were self-injuring at pretreatment, 62% of the DBT group abstained from NSSI at 1 month postassessment. In contrast, only 31% of the waitlist group was not self-injuring at the same assessment point. Although not a randomized controlled trial, these findings suggest that a DBT-based intensive, multicomponent treatment is more effective than standard psychiatric care in addressing self-injurious behavior.

Cognitive Therapy

Cognitive therapy (CT) places an emphasis on altering dysfunctional "core" beliefs and changing problematic behaviors. The core beliefs are challenged through Socratic questioning and behavioral experiments. The treatment is collaborative, with the patient and therapist working together during each session to set goals, prioritize, and follow an agenda. Participants meet for 50 minutes weekly for 50 weeks with their therapist, with the option of an additional 12 sessions as needed over the course of 1 year. An open clinical trial (Brown, Newman, Charlesworth, Crits-Christoph, & Beck, 2004) was conducted to determine the effectiveness of CT for BPD. Of the 34 individuals who participated in the study (28 women), 66% had engaged in parasuicidal behavior within 2 months of beginning the study, and 88% had engaged in self-harm over a lifetime. Of the 29 individuals who completed the year of CT, 34% (10 individuals) reported at least one self-injury behavior within the last 6 months of treatment. Furthermore, of the 24 subjects who completed the follow-up assessment 18 months after the baseline, the rate drops to 22% (5 subjects) who engaged in self-injury since the termination assessment.

Cognitive-Behavioral Therapy

In 2008, Slee and colleagues investigated the effectiveness of a short, manualized cognitive-behavioral therapy (CBT) in treating individuals who had recently engaged in "self-harm," defined as any self-injury or self-poisoning (overdose) with or without the intent to die (Slee, Garnefski, van der Leeden, Arensman, & Spinhoven, 2008). The CBT intervention was based on a cognitive-behavioral model of maintenance factors of self-harm, targeting a change in suicidal and negative thinking and problem-solving deficits by developing cognitive and behavioral skills for coping with situations that trigger self-harm. The sessions focused on identifying and modifying mechanisms that maintained self-harm. The first step of the treatment was to assess the most recent episode of self-harm, including its circumstances, motives, reasons, cognitions, emotions, and behaviors before and during the episode. The next step involved the therapist and patient jointly addressing how emotional, cognitive, and behavioral factors, such as dysfunctional cognitions, emotion regulation difficulties, and poor problem solving, play a part in the maintenance of the patient's self-harming behavior. Lastly, relapse prevention was addressed toward the end of treatment.

Potential participants were screened through the Leiden University Medical Centre and the Rivierduinen mental health center, and 82 subjects completed the study. In the experimental condition, 40 subjects received 12 weekly or as-needed in case of crisis sessions of CBT in addition to the treatment they were already receiving (CBT on top of TAU), and in the control condition, 42 subjects received TAU. Participants were aged 15 to 35 years and were excluded if diagnosed with any severe psychiatric disorder requiring intensive inpatient treatment.

Assessments were conducted at baseline, 3 months, 6 months, and 9 months after baseline. Compared to the TAU-only group, the CBT and TAU combined group at the 9-month assessment point had fewer self-harm episodes within the past 3 months. Additionally, in comparison with the TAU group, the CBT and TAU combined group showed significant improvements in levels of depression, anxiety, self-esteem, suicide cognition, perceived burdens, helplessness, poor distress tolerance, unlovability, and problem solving by the 9-month assessment point, and for some outcome measures, as early as the 3-month and 6-month assessment points.

The two groups received comparable levels of care in terms of psychotherapy sessions, psychotropic medications, and psychiatric hospitalizations, but the specific types of psychotherapy, medications, and techniques were not recorded for the TAU condition, so an in-depth comparison between the two conditions is not possible. In addition, since the experimental condition was not isolated to CBT, the beneficial effects of the treatment cannot be attributed to the cognitive-behavioral component of the treatment.

Manual Assisted Cognitive Treatment

Weinberg and colleagues (2006) conducted a study examining the efficacy of a treatment called manual assisted cognitive treatment (MACT), a short-term individual therapy developed in 2004 that incorporates elements of DBT, CBT, and bibliotherapy. The study aimed to reduce "deliberate self-harm" (DSH) in individuals with BPD and is one of the few existing studies that used NSSI as a distinct primary outcome measure. Thirty subjects were included in the study, with half in the experimental condition and the other half in the control condition. Fifteen subjects received six sessions of MACT on top of their existing treatment (MACT and TAU combined), and 15 subjects received TAU. Participants were females aged 18–40 years with a diagnosis of BPD and a history of repetitive deliberate self-harm and at least one episode during the month before enrollment. Those with comorbid psychotic disorders, bipolar I disorder, substance dependence, elevated suicide risk, a history of suicide attempts, or a history of only one DSH episode were excluded from the study. Each of the six sessions in MACT was structured around a chapter of a booklet that covers various DBT and CBT components such as functional analysis of DSH episodes, emotion regulation strategies, problem-solving strategies, management of negative thinking, and relapse prevention strategies.

Compared to the TAU-only group, the MACT and TAU combined group significantly decreased in DSH frequency immediately posttreatment and sustained the improvements at the 6-month follow-up assessment point. In addition, the DSH episodes in the MACT and TAU combined group were significantly less severe than those in the TAU group at the 6-month follow-up. At posttreatment and 6-month follow-up, there were no significant differences between the two groups in suicidal ideation and time to repetition of DSH.

Because the experimental condition was not an exclusive investigation of MACT but MACT as an adjunctive therapy to TAU, we cannot attribute the improvements solely to the MACT portion of the combined therapy. Furthermore, individuals with a history of suicide attempts were excluded from the trial, so the beneficial effects of this combined MACT and TAU cannot be generalized to individuals who both self-injure and attempt suicide (Weinberg, Gunderson, Hennen, & Cutter, 2006).

Cognitive Analytic Therapy

Chanen and colleagues (2008) analyzed the effectiveness of cognitive analytic therapy (CAT) versus good clinical care (GCC) in reducing parasuicidal behavior in a group of 78 adolescents with BPD characteristics. CAT is a brief therapy, typically 16 sessions, which, as the name implies, is an integration of cognitive and analytic therapies (Ryle, 2004). It was created for use within the confines of the National Health Service in the United Kingdom and is described as being active, integrated, and focused (Ryle, 2004). The emphasis is placed on identifying and revising the "procedures" that maintain the patient's problems. From the CAT perspective, these "procedures" mainly happen unconsciously, yet through discovery they are linked to repeated problem behaviors. CAT aims to identify and revise such procedures, thus altering the behavior (Ryle, 2004).

Ryle (2004) describes the use of a "psychotherapy file" to help patients identify typical common problem procedures (described as Traps, Dilemmas, and Snags) as they are associated with a particular mood. At the fourth session, the therapist and the patient collaborate on a Reformulation that the therapist has developed. The Reformulation includes an overview of the client's life; his or her struggles, strengths, and weaknesses in coping with problems; and lastly, a list of Target Problem Procedures to be worked on. From this point forward, sessions are largely unstructured but focused on discussing material in terms of the Target Problem Procedures. Ultimately, it is not presumed that the patient will have completed their goals by the end of therapy (16 sessions), but that they will have the tools to continue working toward changing their "faulty procedures" (Ryle, 2004).

In the study conducted by Chanen and colleagues (2008), parasuicide was monitored and categorized as daily, weekly, monthly, or none. About 75% of the CAT group and 68% of the GCC group were engaging in parasuicidal behavior at baseline. After completing 1 year of treatment, 69% of the CAT group and 67% of the GCC group were no longer engaging in any parasuicidal behavior at the 24-month follow-up assessment point. GCC is a treatment developed specifically for the study. It is described by the authors as a "simple, problem-solving model for all participants, with additional modules determined by the co-occurring problems" (Chanen et al., p. 479). Subjects in both treatments had access to case management, psychiatry services, activity groups, and the same inpatient standard care. There was no meaningful or substantial difference between the two treatments in their respective rates of change over time for BPD total scores and for frequency of parasuicidal behavior.

Behavioral Activation and Acceptance Commitment Therapy

Lynch and Cozza (2009) suggest behavioral activation therapy for depression (BATD; Lejuez, Hopko, LePage, Hopko, & McNeil, 2002) as an intervention that may be useful in treating those engaging in NSSI. BATD has several commonalities with DBT, mainly validation and behavioral activation through contingency management. Just as in DBT, increased activity is viewed as a necessary component in decreasing NSSI. A significant difference, however, is that BATD does not focus on skills acquisition but instead focuses on increasing rewarding and healthy behaviors, which will in turn increase positive affect. By increasing positive experiences, the client develops a life worth living (Hopko, Lejuez, Ruggiero, & Eifert, 2003).

Acceptance commitment therapy (ACT; Hayes, Strosahl, & Wilson, 1999) is another intervention that is being adapted for use with those engaging in NSSI. As the name implies, the focus of the therapy is to acknowledge and then accept one's internal experiences, including emotions, thoughts, and sensations. In theory, verbal interactions cause behavioral repertoires (e.g., NSSI) that may generate psychological difficulties. Thus, the main targets in sessions are behaviors that interfere with the client's life and the internal reactions to those behaviors. This intervention is similar to DBT in that it explicitly targets identification and acceptance of emotions. However, DBT balances acceptance with change interventions, whereas in ACT there is less focus on change with more emphasis on unconditional acceptance.

Other Cognitive Treatment Approaches

Newman (2009) describes a cognitive therapeutic approach specifically targeting NSSI whose strategies stem from methods that were developed for suicidal individuals. According to Newman (2009), cognitive therapists conceptualize NSSI as a failed attempt at self-help, which is reinforced by the environment's response and by one's internal response (Newman, 2009). The goal of CT for NSSI is therefore to have clients help themselves more skillfully by teaching healthier alternatives to deal with emotional upheaval, to develop delay strategies, and to develop a life with more hope and self-fulfillment.

The first step is to identify dysfunctional beliefs. Assessments such as the Functional Assessment of Self-Mutilation (FASM; Lloyd, Kelley, & Hope, 1997) have been developed for use at the beginning of treatment to assist the therapist in generating hypotheses about the client's faulty beliefs (Newman, 2009).When the work begins in therapy, the client's beliefs regarding NSSI are directly addressed. The therapist offers empathy, validation, and candor about the seriousness of NSSI. The next step is to highlight the all-or-nothing thinking that may lead an individual to believe that NSSI is the *only* way to alleviate anger or emotional suffering. The therapist works with the client to examine any evidence to the contrary, such as when the client did not engage in NSSI and was able to get through an emotionally difficult period (Newman, 2009). Rational responses that are generated by the client and therapist can be put on flashcards for use in difficult situations. Berk and colleagues (2004) suggest this method with the idea that it is extremely difficult for clients to generate alternative solutions when they are emotionally vulnerable and more susceptible to NSSI. If clients can at look at the flashcards, they will at least provide themselves with a reminder, and possibly a trigger, to find a more skillful coping strategy as an alternative to NSSI.

Clients will most likely hold fast to their maladaptive beliefs. To overcome this, therapists can acknowledge that even slight adjustments in their thinking and behaviors may be sufficient. For instance, introducing the client to behaviors that are less painful and cause little or no damage, such as the *ice cube method, which instructs clients to squeeze ice in their hand(s) while in distress* (Layden et al., 1993; Linehan, 1993), will be an easier transition than insisting on no self-harm. Furthermore, a strong push for change, by contradicting the client's beliefs, will most likely come across as invalidating. From this stage, a move toward symbolic gestures of self-harm can be encouraged (e.g., drawing on oneself with an erasable red marker; Haines, Williams, Brian, & Wilson, 1995). Over time, clients will be able to consider healthier alternatives to NSSI (Newman, 2009).

For those clients who believe that NSSI serves as a means of self-punishment, *rehabilitative self-punishment* may be an effective tool for therapists. This strategy works by eliciting behaviors from the client that are considered to be healthy and productive by society's standards yet are found to be quite difficult and aversive to the client. Examples may include increasing exercise, running errands, or doing household chores (Newman, 2009). After the list is generated, it is posited to the client that any of these aversive situations could replace NSSI as a means of self-punishment. Understanding that this idea may be quickly rejected by the client, the therapist is encouraged to start a discussion about how the client decides how the chosen mean of self-punishment is decided upon and why (Newman, 2009). The thoughts around this can then be challenged to elicit further discussion and solution building.

Because those who engage in NSSI are notably engaging in faulty problem solving, possibly as a result of faulty communication styles, another part of CT for NSSI is improving communication and problem-solving skills (Newman, 2009). The therapist can work on these skills through role-playing exercises, simulated letter writing, journaling, and offering direct feedback (Newman, 2009). In addition, the therapist can help the client to develop a crisis plan as a problem-solving skill. The crisis plan should be readily available to the client and should operate as the go-to as soon as there is an urge to self-harm (Newman, 2009).

Open Access to Emergency Treatment

Another potentially effective strategy is providing open access to emergency treatment to those at risk. A randomized controlled trial of 212 deliberate self-harm (NSSI and suicidal behavior) patients tested the "Green Card" (GC) approach (Morgan, Jones, & Owen, 1993). After being admitted to the hospital for deliberate self-harm, patients were randomized to the experimental condition (Green Card) as an add-on to TAU or TAU alone. In the Green Card condition, patients were literally given a green card that contained information for patients on whom to contact in the event they were feeling the urge to self-harm. The Green Card also encouraged the patient to seek help at an early stage, prior to deliberate self-harm occurring, either by attending the Accident and Emergency Department or by telephone. In addition, the Green Card included an "on-demand crisis admission" whereby the subject could be hospitalized immediately if this were necessary (Morgan, Jones, & Owen, 1993). Thus, the Green Card was intended to be viewed as a life-line for patients (Morgan, Jones, & Owen, 1993). Three weeks after the initial hospital visit the patient was sent a second Green Card as a reminder. Additionally, the patient's general practitioner was notified that the patient had the Green Card for use. Those in the TAU group were either referred back to their primary health care team or to a psychiatric inpatient unit.

One year following the initial visit, 15 patients made contact referring to the Green Card (prior to a DSH incident) and the Green Card group had a total of 144 inpatient days compared to 379 days in the TAU group, leading Morgan et al. (1993) to speculate that the offer of a lifeline may be sufficient to reduce self-harm. This study, while promising, has limited value in relation to treatment of NSSI because overdoses were the primary means of deliberated self-harm (97%) and, thus, efficacy for cutting, burning, and self-hitting is unknown.

Treatments of Nonsuicidal Self-Injury in Special Populations
Autism Spectrum Disorders and Intellectual and Developmental Disabilities

Compared to the rate of self-injury in the general population, the prevalence of self-injury is significantly higher in individuals with autism spectrum disorders, severe mental retardation, or intellectual or developmental disabilities (Dominick, Davis, Lainhart, Tager-Flusberg, & Folstein, 2007; Kurtz et al., 2003; Oliver, Murphy, & Corbett, 1987). In those with autism, the research has found prevalence of self-injury to range broadly from 20% to 71%, depending on the age and intellectual levels of the samples (Dominick et al., 2007). More specifically, a few studies have found that those with both autism and mental retardation have higher levels of self-injury than those with autism alone (Bartak & Rutter, 1976; Poustka & Lisch, 1993).

In a review conducted by Matson and LoVullo (2008), different methods of self-injury were revealed, some of which include head hitting, banging against other objects, biting, scratching, hair pulling, and eye gouging. Most investigations of self-injury and its treatment within those with learning disabilities have been case studies. Because of the highly specific

and individualized behaviors of these individuals and responses of the caretakers, it is often difficult to implement an identical, systematic procedure when treating these individuals. The overwhelming trend that emerges in the treatment literature for this population is behavior therapy; often included is an applied behavioral analysis or a functional analysis of the behavior, which is tied to the idea that the self-injury is a learned behavior within this group. Oftentimes these individuals have deficits in communication ability, which results in using alternative means to attract the attention of caretakers to fulfill their needs, which may include self-injurious behavior (Iwata et al., 1994; Matson & LoVullo, 2008).

Matson and LoVullo (2008) noted that physical restraints, positive and negative reinforcement, communication training, replacement behaviors, extinction, play therapy, and functional assessment were the most common interventions. Treatments incorporating functional analysis attempt to identify the functional characteristics of self-injurious behavior, and though both the external environment and individuals' internal environment are important, the current treatment model targets the external cues surrounding the behavior as those are substantially easier to identify (Davies, Howlin, Bernal, & Warren, 1998). Iwata et al. (1994) argue that self-injury is a learned behavior that has been acquired through the individual's history of social and physical interactions with the environment, such as the reaction or attention from caretakers gained. They conclude that by analyzing the conditions that produce and maintain self-injury, this behavior can be treated and prevented. Because self-injury attracts the attention of caretakers and elicits eye contact, physical or emotional reassurance, provision of desired object or activities, and other reinforcement, this self-destructive behavior is maintained. However, by training the caretakers to refrain from using these positive reinforcers in response to a self-injury episode or antecedents leading up to an episode, this behavior can be extinguished. Similarly, using positive reinforcement when the individuals engage in a desired behavior, such as communicating or gesturing toward their desires, or other functionally equivalent replacement behaviors would help these individuals lessen their self-injury.

Trichotillomania

Another area of research that may be related to NSSI is that focused on trichotillomania. Characterized by compulsive hair pulling or picking, sometimes to the point of tissue damage at the site of pulling, and because of the resulting reduction in anxiety or tension, trichotillomania is sometimes included in the spectrum of NSSI. Similar to the research on treatments for NSSI, there is a lack of studies in the literature for treatments targeting trichotillomania, especially empirically supported psychosocial interventions. Of the few existing studies, most support the use of some kind of behavioral or cognitive-behavioral therapy in treatment. Habit-reversal therapy (HRT) and the combination of HRT with acceptance and commitment therapy (ACT) seem to be the most effective of the treatments currently studied (Bloch et al., 2007; Chamberlain, Odlaug, Boulougouris, Fineberg, & Grant, 2009; Flessner, Busch, Heideman, & Woods, 2008).

The major components of HRT include awareness training (recognizing situations leading up to the episode), competing response training (using other methods such as fist clenching), relaxation training, prevention training, habit interruption, and social support (Chamberlain et al., 2009). Woods, Wetterneck, and Flessner (2006) argue that another variable, experiential avoidance, may be a component of the phenomenon, whereby individuals have excessively negative evaluations of their hair-pulling behavior, are very unwilling to experience these private events, and make extensive efforts to control or escape these desires and behaviors. Thus, ACT can be employed to target the experiential avoidance by promoting acceptance of these private feelings and urges to help these individuals toward their goals instead of focusing on emotion control strategies. Coupled with psychoeducation and habit reversal training, the authors label this combination therapy "Acceptance-Enhanced Behavior Therapy" and have demonstrated its efficacy in decreasing hair-pulling behavior after 12 weeks of treatment (Flessner et al., 2008; Woods et al., 2006).

Common Elements Across Treatment Approaches

The phenomenon of NSSI is not unidimensional. Instead, it is a symptom that arises in various clinical populations and is driven by different mechanisms and motivations. However, there are commonalities among the various treatment approaches that can be applied to targeting NSSI more generally across populations.

For example, the functional analysis and subsequent attempts at behavioral modification that are so heavily supported in the ASD, DD, and ID populations are techniques central to the DBT and CBT that treat NSSI in personality disordered and depressed and anxious patients. These combination-behavior therapies aim to identify the antecedents leading up to the behavior and the types of internal and external consequences that reinforce the behavior. These therapies target the NSSI behavior by addressing and finding substitutes for the reinforcing cues and by managing contingencies.

Similarly, the components of HRT used to treat trichotillomania involve methods that could be incorporated into treating NSSI generally. For example, the key elements of HRT involve a type of functional analysis (recognizing situations leading up to the behavior) and coming up with alternative ways to cope such as using other methods that are not physically dangerous. ACT techniques are comparable to the acceptance and validation concepts of DBT, whereby the individuals engaging in NSSI are encouraged to accept the thoughts and feelings that they experience as opposed to placing harsh, excessive negative judgments on themselves for having these thoughts and feelings.

Directions for Treatment Research

Despite promising advances in the field, there is limited empirical evidence for the efficacy of psychological treatments in decreasing NSSI. Randomized clinical trials of psychosocial interventions need to distinguish between suicidal behavior and nonsuicidal self-injurious behavior as outcome measures. Future research in psychopharmacological interventions for NSSI should compare the efficacy of these biological and pharmacological treatments with the efficacy of the various psychosocial treatments, as well as the efficacy of combined psychopharmacological and psychosocial interventions.

Unfortunately, most of the existing research fails to follow up and explore whether these promising treatment effects are maintained, or when they do follow up with the studies, the treatment effects seem to drop off (Muehlenkamp, 2006). Further prospective and longitudinal investigations are necessary to arrive at significant conclusions regarding the lasting beneficial effects of treatment. It is also necessary and important to determine which aspects of the treatments used to treat parasuicidal behavior, performed with and without suicidal intent, would work specifically for NSSI.

References

American Psychiatric Association. (1994). *Diagnostic and statistical manual of mental disorders* (4th ed.). Washington, DC: Author.

Bartak, L., & Rutter, M. (1976). Differences between mentally retarded and normally intelligent autistic children. *Journal of Autism and Childhood Schizophrenia, 6,* 109–120.

Beck, J. S. (1995). *Cognitive therapy: Basic and beyond.* New York, NY: Guilford Press.

Berk, M. S., Henriques, G. R., Warman, D. M., Brown, G. K., & Beck, A. T. (2004). A cognitive therapy intervention for suicide attempters: An overview of the treatment and case examples. *Cognitive and Behavioral Practice, 11,* 265–277.

Bloch, M. H., Landeros-Weisenberger, A., Dombrowski, P., Kelmendi, B., Wegner, R., Nudel, J.,...Coric, V. (2007). Systematic review: Pharmacological and behavioral treatment for trichotillomania. *Biological Psychiatry, 62*(8), 839–846.

Bohus, M., Haaf, B., Simms, T., Limberger, M. F., Schmahl, C., Unckel, C.,...Linehan, M. M. (2004). Effectiveness of inpatient dialectical behavioral therapy for borderline personality disorder: A controlled trial. *Behaviour Research and Therapy, 42*(5), 487–499.

Brown, G. K., Newman, C. F., Charlesworth, S. E., Crits-Christoph, P., & Beck, A. T. (2004). An open clinical trial of cognitive therapy for borderline personality disorder. *Journal of Personality Disorders, 18*(3), 257–271.

Chamberlain, S. R., Odlaug, B. L., Boulougouris, V., Fineberg, N. A., & Grant, J. E. (2009). Trichotillomania: Neurobiology and treatment. *Neuroscience and Biobehavioral Reviews, 33*(6), 831–842.

Chanen, A. M., Jackson, H. J., McCutcheon, L. K., Jovev, M., Dudgeon, P., Yuen, H. P.,...McGorry, P. D. (2008). Early intervention for adolescents with borderline personality disorder using cognitive analytic therapy: Randomised controlled trial. *British Journal of Psychiatry, 193*(6), 477–484.

Chapman, A. L., Specht, M. W., & Cellucci, A. J. (2005). Borderline personality disorder and deliberate self-harm: Does experiential avoidance play a role? *Suicide and Life Threatening Behavior, 35,* 388–399.

Davies, M., Howlin, P., Bernal, J., & Warren, S. (1998). Treating severe self-injury in a community setting: Constraints on assessment and intervention. *Child Psychology and Psychiatry Review, 3,* 26–32.

Dominick, K. C., Davis, N. O., Lainhart, J., Tager-Flusberg, H., & Folstein, S. (2007). Atypical behaviors in children with autism and children with a history of language impairment. *Research in Developmental Disabilities, 28*(2), 145–162.

Flessner, C. A., Busch, A. M., Heideman, P. W., & Woods, D. W. (2008). Acceptance-enhanced behavior therapy (AEBT) for trichotillomania and chronic skin picking: Exploring the effects of component sequencing. *Behavior Modification, 32*(5), 579–594.

Haines, J., Williams, C. L., Brian, K. L., & Wilson, G. V. (1995), The psychophysiology of self-mutilation. *Journal of Abnormal Psychology, 104,* 471–489.

Hayes, S. C., Strosahl, K., & Wilson, K. G. (1999). *Acceptance and commitment therapy: An experiential approach to behavior change.* New York, NY: Guilford Press.

Hopko, D. R., Lejuez, C. W., Ruggiero, K. J., & Eifert, G. H. (2003). Contemporary behavioral activation treatments for depression: Procedures, principles, and progress. *Clinical Psychology Review, 23,* 699–717.

Iwata, B. A., Pace, G. M., Dorsey, M. F., Zarcone, J. R., Vollmer, T. R., Smith, R. G.,...Mazalesk. (1994). The functions of self-injurious behavior: an experimental-epidemiological analysis. *Journal of Applied Behavior Analysis, 27*(2), 215–240.

Klonsky, E. D., & Glenn, C. R. (2008). Resisting urges to self-injure. *Behavioural and Cognitive Psychotherapy, 36*(2), 211–220.

Kurtz, P. F., Chin, M. D., Huete, J. M., Tarbox, R. S. F., O'Connor, J. T., Paclawskyj, T. R., & Rush, K. S. (2003). Functional analysis and treatment of self-injurious behavior in young children: A summary of 30 cases. *Journal of Applied Behavior Analysis, 36*(2), 205–219.

Layden, M., Newman, C. F., Freeman, A., & Morse, S. B. (1993). *Cognitive therapy of borderline personality disorder.* NJ: Allyn & Bacon, Longwood Division, Needham Heights, MA.

Lejuez, C. W., Hopko, D. R., LePage, J. P., Hopko, S. D., & McNeil, D. W. (2002). A brief behavioral activation treatment for depression. *Cognitive and Behavioral Practice, 8,* 164–175.

Linehan, M. M., Armstrong, H. E., Suarez, A., Allmon, D., & Heard, H. L. (1991). Cognitive-behavioral treatment of chronically parasuicidal borderline patients. *Archives of General Psychiatry, 48,* 1060–1064.

Linehan, M. M., Comtois, K. A., Murray, A. M., Brown, M. Z., Galllop, R. J., Heard, H. L.,...Lindenboim, N. (2006). Two-year randomized controlled trial and follow-up of dialectical behavior therapy vs. therapy by experts for suicidal behaviors and borderline personality disorder. *Archives of General Psychiatry, 63,* 757–766.

Linehan, M. M., Heard, H. L., & Armstrong, H. E. (1993). Naturalistic follow-up of a behavioral treatment for chronically parasuicidal borderline patients. *Archives of General Psychiatry, 50,* 971–974.

Lloyd, E., Kelley, M. L., & Hope, T. (April 1997). *Self-mutilation in a community sample of adolescents: Descriptive characteristics and provisional prevalence rates.* Paper presented at the Annual Meeting of the Society for Behavioral Medicine, New Orleans, LA.

Lynch, T. R., & Cozza, C. (2009). Behavior therapy for nonsuicidal self-injury. In M. K. Nock (Ed.), *Understanding nonsuicidal self-injury* (pp. 221–250). Washington, DC: American Psychological Association.

Matson, J. L., & LoVullo, S. V. (2008). A review of behavioral treatments for self-injurious behaviors of persons with autism spectrum disorders. *Behavior Modification, 32*(1), 61–76.

Morgan, H. G., Jones, E. M., & Owen, J. H. (1993). Secondary prevention of nonfatal deliberate self-harm: The green card study. *British Journal of Psychiatry, 163,* 111–112.

Muehlenkamp, J. J. (2006). Empirically supported treatments and general therapy guidelines for non-suicidal self-injury. *Journal of Mental Health Counseling, 28,* 166–185.

Newman, C. F. (2009). Cognitive therapy for nonsuicidal self-injury. In M. K. Nock (Ed.), *Understanding nonsuicidal self-injury* (pp. 201–209). Washington, DC: American Psychological Association.

Nock, M. K., Joiner, T. E., Gordon, K., Lloyd-Richardson, E., & Prinstein, M. J. (2006). Non-suicidal self-injury among adolescents: Diagnostic correlates and relation to suicide attempts. *Psychiatry Research, 144,* 65–72.

Oliver, C., Murphy, G. H., & Corbett, J. A. (1987). Self-injurious behaviour in people with mental handicap: A total population study. *Journal of Mental Deficiency Research, 31*(Pt, 2), 147–162.

Poustka, F., & Lisch, S. (1993). Autistic behaviour domains and their relation to self-injurious behaviour. *Acta Paedopsychiatrica, 56*(2), 69–73

Ryle, A. (2004). The contribution of cognitive analytic therapy to the treatment of borderline personality disorder. *Journal of Personality Disorders, 18*(1), 3–35.

Shearer, S. L. (1994). Phenomenology of self-injury among inpatient women with borderline personality disorder. *Journal of Mental Disorder, 182*(9), 524–526.

Slee, N., Garnefski, N., van der Leeden, R., Arensman, E., & Spinhoven, P. (2008). Cognitive-behavioural intervention for self-harm: Randomised controlled trial. *British Journal of Psychiatry, 192*(3), 202–211.

Stanley, B., Brodsky, B., Nelson, J., & Dulit, R. (2007). Brief dialectical behavior therapy (DBT-B) for suicidal behavior and non-suicidal self injury. *Archives of Suicide Research, 11*(4), 337–341.

Weinberg, I., Gunderson, J. G., Hennen, J., & Cutter, C. J. (2006). Manual assisted cognitive treatment for deliberate self-harm in borderline personality disorder patients. *Journal of Personality Disorders, 20*(5), 482–492.

Woods, D. W., Wetterneck, C. T., & Flessner, C. A. (2006). A controlled evaluation of acceptance and commitment therapy plus habit reversal for trichotillomania. *Behaviour Research and Therapy, 44*(5), 639–656.

Pharmacologic Treatment of Nonsuicidal Self-Injury

Paul L. Plener *and* Gerhard Libal

Abstract

Among different treatment modalities for nonsuicidal self-injury (NSSI), the practitioner might consider adding a psychopharmacologic agent. This chapter reviews studies dealing with the pharmacologic treatment of NSSI and intends to inform the clinician about when such a treatment trial might be warranted and which substances should be considered. The evidence for psychopharmacological treatment options for NSSI is extremely limited. Medication should only be used in combination with psychotherapeutic treatment and not as a monotherapy, and it should be administered only by clinicians with an expertise in psychopharmacological treatment.

Key Words: nonsuicidal self-injury, psychopharmacology, suicidality, atypical antipsychotics, SSRI

Nonsuicidal self-injury (NSSI), understood as the deliberate destruction of one's own body tissue without conscious suicidal intent, is a debilitating condition that poses a threat to patients, their relatives, and clinicians. NSSI is deemed socially unacceptable, repetitive, and leads to minor or moderate harm (Lloyd-Richardson, Perrine, Dierker, & Kelley, 2007). It has been demonstrated that psychotherapeutic approaches can help to end NSSI (Bohus & Schmahl, 2007; Katz, Cox, Gunasekara, & Miller, 2004); however, in some cases, it might be justified to add a further treatment component: psychotropic medication. This chapter aims to present studies dealing with the psychopharmacological treatment of NSSI or related conditions, which should help the reader to develop an understanding about when psychopharmacological interventions might be warranted and also when they are not. In addition to presenting a rationale for psychopharmacological treatment based on a neurobiological understanding of NSSI, we will highlight the obstacles and future directions of research in this field.

What Is Self-Injury?

One of the main obstacles in searching for evidence of psychopharmacological treatment of NSSI is that NSSI has so far not been defined as a syndrome by itself (Muehlenkamp, 2005) and has therefore not appeared in classification systems such as the *Diagnostic and Statistical Manual of Mental Disorders*, fourth edition (*DSM-IV*; American Psychiatric Association, 1994) or the *International Classification of Diseases*, tenth edition (*ICD-10*, World Health Organization, 2010), except from being mentioned as symptom of borderline personality disorder (BPD). This leads to the fact that NSSI was hardly used as an outcome measure in studies so far, limiting our knowledge about the effectiveness of interventions even in groups often displaying NSSI (such as studies done in BPD populations). However, in the *DSM-5* NSSI is represented as a disorder in section three, which means that further research is required before it might be accepted as a formal disorder. Nevertheless, in *DSM-5* NSSI is viewed as a diagnostic entity which might encourage further studies. Recently NSSI has also been reported as a side effect in medication trials (such as, e.g., in Asarnow et al., 2011 and Wilkinson, Kelvin, Roberts, Dubicka, & Goodyer, 2011). In general, there is limited knowledge about the psychopharmacology of NSSI, but there is a growing body of literature about treating self-injury in individuals with neurodevelopmental disorders (NDDs) (Sandman, 2009), such as pervasive developmental disorders (PDDs), autism spectrum disorders, mental retardation, or genetically inherited syndromes (e.g., Lesch-Nyhan-syndrome, Cornelia de Lange syndrome). In trying to categorize different forms of "self-mutilation," Favazza (1992) suggested to differentiate between stereotypic and major forms (mostly in NDDs and in psychotic disorders) as well as moderate forms (referring to the more moderate harm of the body). The latter can be found in high prevalence both in community (e.g., Muehlenkamp, Claes, Havertape, & Plener, 2012) and clinical (Nixon, Cloutier, & Aggarwal, 2002) samples. Despite the fact that these moderate "self-mutilations" (which best resemble the newly defined condition of NSSI) are often found in the context of psychiatric disorders, there have also been reports about the occurrence of NSSI in adolescents without severe psychopathological problems (Stanford & Jones, 2009). Following the approach for the NSSI syndrome in *DSM-5*, we will limit this chapter on "normally" developed individuals, thus excluding NDD populations. Readers who are interested in this specific population are advised to look at the already existing excellent reviews on self-injury in this population (e.g., Parikh, Kolevzon, & Hollander, 2008; Sandman, 2009; Scahill & Koenig, 1999). This separation is also necessary in the light of seemingly different effectiveness of certain agents within these subgroups, as for example the use of the opioid antagonists naloxone and naltrexone hydrochloride is a well-known strategy showing good results in several studies and reviews in patients with NDD (Sandman 1990, 1991; Sandman et al., 1993; Symons, Thompson, & Rodriguez, 2004; Thompson, Hackenberg, Cerutti, Baker, & Axtell, 1994), whereas the results from studies in BPD populations are rather mixed. Although the 2009 British NICE guidelines on BPD (http://www.nice.org.uk/nicemedia/live/12125/43045/43045.pdf) state that "there is no evidence that drugs reduce the rates of self-harm and/or suicide attempts," most research with regard to NSSI in "normally" developing individuals has been done in BPD populations. We will present data from those studies, in which

NSSI or comparable constructs have been used as outcome variables. Furthermore we also included recent studies, mostly conducted in adolescents with depression, reporting on NSSI as a side effect of antidepressant treatment.

Why and When to Consider Psychopharmacological Treatment

To date, there is no drug worldwide, which is approved to specifically treat NSSI. Every psychopharmacological intervention to address NSSI is "off label," meaning that drug regulation agencies such as the Federal Drug Administration (FDA) or the European Medicines Agency (EMA) have not granted an approval for any drug to specifically address this condition. This is crucial to keep in mind and to discuss with patients when considering psychopharmacological treatment. In some countries there are specific procedures for administering off-label drugs and clinicians have to be aware of this fact when getting an informed consent for treatment. The off-label nature of all prescriptions in the field of NSSI underlines the necessity to base psychopharmacological treatment on knowledge of the recent literature as well as on a thorough assessment (Harper, 2012). Furthermore, we strongly recommend that psychopharmacological treatment attempts in this context should only be made by medical professionals with an expertise in psychopharmacology (such as, e.g., psychiatrists).

When considering a psychopharmacological treatment approach, it is necessary to understand the rationale behind this approach to be able to inform the patient accordingly. All psychotropic medications work via influencing neurotransmitters in the brain. Sometimes there can be dysbalances, caused by genetic vulnerability, life events, or the interplay of both (epigenetic), which affect the neurobiology of the brain and consequently sometimes can result in psychiatric disorders and suffering. There are different strategies to address psychiatric disorders, most prominent among them being psychotherapy. However, often there is a need for supporting psychotherapeutical treatment approaches through medication because the level of suffering or damage is intolerable or is an acute threat to the patient's life or health, or the disorder is severe, thus not allowing progress in psychotherapy. In these cases psychopharmacological treatment can help the patient, but it has to be kept in mind that it still needs to be understood as support and not as sole therapy. Given the limited evidence in the psychopharmacological treatment of NSSI, psychiatric treatment should not be reduced to the administration of psychotropic drugs without accompanying psychotherapy. At its best, psychopharmacological treatment can help to create an opportunity for new learning experiences provided through psychotherapy (Libal & Plener, 2008). It is advisable to keep up psychopharmacological support for a stabilizing phase after the patient improves, but generally, the duration of treatment should be guided by the rule: "as short as possible but as long as necessary."

Summing up the aforementioned points, when treating NSSI, clinicians should do the following:

• Be aware of the off-label nature.
• Always combine psychopharmacological treatment with psychotherapeutical treatment.
• Administer medication as long as necessary to reach a satisfying level of functioning.

Review of Psychopharmacological Interventions

Building on recent selective reviews (Bloom & Holly, 2011; Harper, 2012; Plener, Libal, & Nixon, 2009; Sandman, 2009) and one systematic (Plener, Libal, Fegert, & Kölch, 2013) review of psychopharmacological treatment of NSSI, we aim to describe the best available evidence for a psychopharmacological treatment strategy. Building on a neurobiological framework, we categorize by classes of psychotropic agents. For more information, refer to Chapter 11 in this volume. This somehow reductionist approach underestimates the complexity of neurobiological systems and psychopharmacological agents, as most of them address more than one system of neurotransmitters. We will close this chapter by providing clinical recommendations.

Antidepressants

This group includes both tricyclic antidepressants (TCAs) and selective serotonin reuptake inhibitors (SSRIs). The rationale for looking into antidepressants to influence NSSI stems from a broad range of studies, reporting a dysfunction in serotonergic neurotransmission (Pies & Popli, 1995; Roberts, 2003; Russ, 1992; Winchel & Stanley, 1991, for review, see Groschwitz & Plener, 2012). Serotonergic neurotransmission is influenced by both TCAs and SSRIs (the latter being more "selective" for targeting only the serotonin neurotransmission), as they provide an improved signal transmission through an inhibition of serotonin reuptake from the synaptic cleft to the presynaptic neuron. SSRIs have been recommended

for the treatment of NSSI (Pies & Popli, 1995; Roberts, 2003) and it has been reported, that out of 225 patients with personality disorders receiving psychopharmacological treatment, 4% received an antidepressant to treat their self-harm (Crawford et al., 2011). However, results from studies in BPD populations remain mixed. Whereas Verkes et al. (1998) described a reduction of suicide attempts in a double-blind placebo controlled study of paroxetine ($n = 91$), Simpson et al. (2004) were unable to show differences between a group taking fluoxetine and a group taking placebo as an "add-on" to dialectical behavior therapy. Unfortunately, NSSI was not addressed specifically in the study of Simpson et al. (2004), whereas Markovitz et al. (1991) reported a reduction of NSSI in 10 out of 12 patients with BPD after an open-label trial of fluoxetine. These rather mixed findings are also represented in the Cochrane review by Hawton et al. (2009), who came to the conclusion that the pooled odds ratios for studies of antidepressants versus placebo did not show sufficient evidence for the reduction of deliberate self-harm (including NSSI), a view also supported by the Cochrane Review on Pharmacological Interventions for BPD (Stoffers et al., 2010).

The black box warning of the FDA in 2004, issued after reports about suicidality as a possible adverse event during SSRI treatment of adolescents and young adults (Brent, 2004; Isacsson et al., 2005; Whittington et al., 2004), also resulted in a closer look on NSSI as a possible adverse event during SSRI treatment in this patient group. Even before the FDA warning, there had been reports about NSSI after SSRI administration (Donovan et al., 2000; Teicher et al., 1993) and consequently NSSI was assessed as a side effect in recent trials. In the Adolescent Depression Antidepressant and Psychotherapy Trial (ADAPT), effectiveness of SSRI therapy in combination with psychotherapy (CBT) or routine care was assessed over 28 weeks in 208 adolescents with moderate to major depression. The number of participants injuring themselves decreased in both treatment groups (SSRI + routine care: from 23 to 9, SSRI + CBT: from 30 to 12) regardless of the accompanying psychosocial intervention (Goodyer et al., 2007; Wilkinson et al., 2011). In the Treatment of SSRI-Resistant Depression in Adolescents (TORDIA) study, which studied the switching of treatment regimes in treatment-resistant depressed adolescents ($n = 334$, of which 38% had a history of NSSI), 31 participants injured themselves, counting up to 50 NSSI events in the first 12 weeks (Brent et al., 2009) and

57 events in 37 individuals in 24 weeks (Asarnow et al., 2011). Higher rates of NSSI were reported in patients who also received benzodiazepines (4 out of 10), a relationship that remained stable after controlling for a prior history of NSSI (Brent et al., 2009). As Asarnow et al. (2011) pointed out, the recovery of depression was slower in participants with a history of NSSI. One needs to keep in mind that although suicidality and/or NSSI might emerge as adverse events, this is no reason to refrain from treating depression. In conclusion, recommendations for using SSRIs as a first-line treatment for NSSI (e.g., Smith, 2005) are not backed by a substantial body of literature, and SSRIs cannot be recommended as a first-line choice for the treatment of NSSI. However, the use of SSRIs might be necessary in treating depression. This is in line with recommendations for treating BPD, derived from the Cochrane review (Lieb, Völlm, Rücker, Timmer, & Stoffers, 2010). SSRIs have to be considered as a first-line approach in the psychopharmacological treatment of depression in adolescents (with TCAs lacking evidence for such an effect in this age group). Concerns about suicidality or NSSI as possible adverse events have been raised and, although the data coming from recent trials such as ADAPT or TORDIA do not show an alarming signal with regard to NSSI as a side effect, the clinician is advised to be cautious and supervise the patient very carefully when administering antidepressants in NSSI. Therefore, monitoring patients at least once a week within the first 4 weeks is recommended. In severe cases we advise monitoring more frequently.

Antipsychotics

The class of drugs labeled "antipsychotics" is named after its primary use in psychotic disorders/schizophrenia. Although all antipsychotics act via blocking dopamine receptors, most of them also interact with other neurotransmitter systems (e.g., influence on serotonin or histamine receptors). There are older "conventional" antipsychotics (e.g., haloperidol, flupenthixol) and newer "atypical" antipsychotics (AAs) (e.g., olanzapine, clozapine, risperidone, quetiapine, ziprasidone [and even newer developments such as] aripiprazole, paliperidone, iloperidone, asenapine, and lurasidone). AAs have also come into focus for the treatment of bipolar disorders and BPD within the last years. It was reported that AAs seem to be effective in BPD patients with "psychotic, impulsive and suicidal complaints" (Grootens & Verkes, 2005), and Abraham and

Calabrese (2008) pointed out in their review of the psychopharmacological treatment of BPD that olanzapin "emerges as an effective and the most studied pharmacological agent for the short-term management of borderline personality disorder" (p. 27). They reported that in five trials 100 patients were randomized to olanzapine treatment with overall positive findings. However, NSSI was only used in a few studies as an outcome measure, and a lot of studies are only on case-report level, such as Chengappa et al. (1999) reporting a reduction of NSSI in patients with BPD under clozapine (n = 7) and Hilger et al. (2003) reporting reduction of NSSI in BPD patients under quetiapine (n = 2). Under controlled conditions results are often not that promising. Schulz et al. (2008) reported a greater decrease on the suicidal/ self-injury item of the Zanarini rating scale for BPD in the placebo group (n = 159) than in patients treated with olanzapine (n = 155) in a double-blind, placebo-controlled trial. In addition, there was one report of self-mutilation as an adverse effect in the olanzapine group. Larger decreases of NSSI in the placebo group than in the olanzapine group were also reported from a double-blind, placebo-controlled trial (n = 24, all BPD) by Linehan et al. (2008), whereby both groups received additional dialectical behavior therapy. Nickel et al. (2006, 2007) reported a reduction of NSSI under aripiprazole from a double-blind, placebo-controlled trial of 52 patients with BPD (follow-up: 18 months). In the aripiprazole group (n = 26) the rate of patients injuring themselves was reduced from seven to two after 8 weeks, whereas in the placebo group (n = 26) the rate increased from five to seven after 8 weeks (Nickel et al., 2006). After 18 months four patients in the aripiprazole group showed NSSI, compared to eleven patients in the placebo group (Nickel, Loew, & Pedrosa, 2007). These findings are also represented in the Cochrane review on pharmacological interventions in BPD as the only positive finding regarding the effectiveness of an atypical antipsychotic for treating self-injury in BPD (Stoffers et al., 2010). Ingenhoven and Duivenvoorden (2011) stated in their meta-analysis on the use of antipsychotics in BPD that these class of drugs seem to be efficient in treating anger but show only small effects on cognitive perceptual symptoms and mood lability and no effect on treating impulsive behavioral dyscontrol, depressed mood, and anxiety. In another meta-analysis, the small effects of AAs on affective dysregulation were confirmed and low effects were also described for AAs in treating impulsive behavioral dyscontrol (Vita, De Peri, & Sacchetti, 2011). Based on their Cochrane review, Lieb et al. (2010) reported positive results of antipsychotics on affective dysregulation and impulsive behavioral dyscontrol, as well as positive findings for AAs on cognitive perceptual symptoms.

In adolescents reduction of NSSI was reported after administration of quetiapine (n = 2) (Good, 2006) and under ziprasidone (n = 8) (Libal, Plener, Ludolph, & Fegert, 2005). Although AAs seem to have a more benign side effect profile with regard to producing extrapyramidal motoric symptoms (e.g., tremor, rigor, dyskinesias), they share the risk of other adverse events such as weight gain and developing glucose tolerance (Correll, 2007; Kumra et al., 2008), and it has been reported that children show an even higher risk for developing metabolic adverse events than adults (for discussion, see Vitiello et al., 2009).Given the limited evidence of effectiveness and the high number of possible severe adverse events, the use of AAs needs to be restricted to severe cases of NSSI.

Mood Stabilizers

The name "mood stabilizer" is used as an umbrella term for drugs, having the shared potential to stabilize dysregulated emotions. This class contains—among others—anticonvulsants, originally used for treating epilepsy. Examples of psychotropic agents include valproate, carbamazepin, and lithium.

Most evidence for the use of mood stabilizers in reducing NSSI stems from case reports. Cordás et al. (2006) reported reduction of NSSI after treatment with oxcarbazepine in bulimia (n = 2), whereas Bellino et al. (2005) did not find changes in "parasuicidal behavior" in patients with BPD (n = 17) using the same substance. Reduction of NSSI in BPD under topiramate was reported by Cassano et al. (2001) (n = 1). Lithium is commonly used in the treatment of bipolar disorder (Burgess, 2001; Cipriani, Pretty, Hawton, & Geddes, 2005) and has shown ample evidence of an antisuicidal property (Lewitzka, Bauer, Felber, & Müller-Oerlinghausen, 2013). Masters (2008) reported a rapid decrease in self-injury in adolescents after lithium administration but unfortunately did not report numbers to estimate the effect. So far, given the lack of evidence for treatment of NSSI, lithium cannot be recommended for this use; furthermore, there is a potential for drug overdose ending fatally, which has to be kept in mind, when administering lithium to a vulnerable patient population.

Antihypertensive Agents

The suggested use of antihypertensive agents (alpha-agonists) is focused on influencing acute states of inner tension leading to urges to self-injure (Sandman, 2009). In a pilot study of 14 women with BPD, these urges to self-injure were reduced by clonidine; however, outcome on actual NSSI was not reported (Philipsen et al., 2004).

Opioid Antagonists

Among the neurotransmitters that are discussed for initiating and maintain NSSI, endogenous opiates play a prominent role (Groschwitz & Plener, 2012; Osuch & Payne, 2009; Sandman, 2009; Sher & Stanley, 2009) and there has been evidence for their involvement in NSSI both neurobiologically, by differing levels of endogenous opiates in the liquor cerebrospinalis (Stanley et al., 2010), and by the clinical notion of sometimes addictive properties of NSSI in subgroups of repetitive self-injurers (Nixon et al., 2002; Plener et al., 2013). The idea of administering agents to block opioid receptors (opiate antagonists such as naloxone and naltrexone hydrochloride) with the aim of stopping reinforcing properties of NSSI seems interesting and has been studied intensely, especially in NDD populations. However, studies in NDD and "normally" developed populations seem to paint a different picture. Whereas thorough reviews of opioid antagonist treatment in NDD reported good effects in reducing NSSI (Sandman, 1990, 1991; Symons et al., 2004), the evidence for an effect in other populations is much weaker and stems from studies on case-report level. A reduction of NSSI under treatment with opioid antagonists has been reported from Roth et al. (1996) (n = 7), Sonne et al. (1996) (4 out of 5), McGee (1997) (n = 1), Griengl et al. (2001) (n = 1), and Agarwal et al. (2011) (n = 1); all of the reported patients were adults. Therefore, it has to be assumed that, although the evidence for opioid antagonist treatment in NDD population is rather good, evidence for the use in "normally" developed patients, such as, for example, patients with BPD, is at the moment rather weak. Treatment trials might be warranted in severe cases, but there is no sufficient evidence to suggest opioid antagonists in general for treating NSSI.

Benzodiazepines

Psychotropic agents with the potential for relieving anxiety and sedation have been considered as interesting medications to treat NSSI. Among them, mostly benzodiazepines (e.g., diazepam, lorazepam, alprazolam) have been studied. Apart from one report ($n = 3$) of midazolam's effectiveness against NSSI in mentally retarded patients (Bond, Mandos, & Kurtz, 1989), findings are mostly negative or even point in the direction of an increase of NSSI. Whereas Rothschild et al. (2000) reported no difference concerning NSSI acts between alprazolam (1.9%), clonazepam (1.8%), and no benzodiazepine (2.9%) from a retrospective chart review ($n = 323$), worsening of NSSI under alprazolam was reported in patients with BPD (Cowdry & Gardner, 1988). As mentioned before, data from the TORDIA study (Brent et al., 2009) point toward a worsening of NSSI in adolescents receiving benzodiazepines (together with an antidepressant); however, due to the small number of patients receiving this combination, these findings have to be interpreted with caution. These data support recommendations (e.g., Smith, 2005) that benzodiazepines should be used with caution in NSSI patients and—considering their addictive potentials—should be limited to short-term interventions (Libal & Plener, 2008).

Other Agents

As lower levels of omega-3 fatty acids in the blood have been reported from self-harming patients (Garland et al., 2007), the potential of eicosapentaenoic acid and decosahexaenoic acid in treating NSSI has been examined. However, in a randomized controlled trial ($n = 49$), no differences were observed for NSSI between the group receiving omega-3 fatty acids and those receiving placebo (Hallahan et al., 2007). In a case report, the glutamate antagonist riluzole (normally used in the treatment of amyotrophic lateral sclerosis) has been found to be effective, reducing NSSI in two cases of patients with BPD (Pittenger, Krystal, & Coric, 2005).

Ethical Considerations

The administration of psychopharmacological treatment in NSSI poses an ethical dilemma on the clinician, as a choice needs to be made between nontreatment (at least nonpsychopharmacological treatment), which may result in severe bodily damage with potential for lasting disabilities, and treatment, which is based on very little evidence from studies in this field and has the potential of (sometimes severe) adverse events. It is important to be transparent about these issues when informing the patient about possible treatment alternatives. This

ethical dilemma can (hopefully) be solved through more research in this field in the future, at least by providing a better evidence base for clinical decisions, while adverse events will still be needed to be considered. Until now the only way to deal with this issue seems to personalize every treatment decision regarding psychopharmacological therapy for NSSI. To date, there is no agreed-upon general solution, except for the recommendation that treatment needs to be individualized targeting either co-occurring Axis I disorders or mental states that worsen NSSI.

Recommendations

Due to the fact that NSSI is seldom used as an outcome measure, the literature regarding recommendations for the psychopharmacological treatment of NSSI is limited. In a review of psychopharmacological treatment approaches for NSSI (Plener et al., 2009), we compared the existing studies based on the evidence to a model proposed by Harbour and Miller (2001). They proposed a four-level model with several submodules, ranging from the lowest level 4 (opinion of an expert) to the highest level 1++ (high-quality meta-analysis, systematic review of randomized controlled trials). The majority of published trials for adults had a level of evidence between 2 and 3, whereas studies among adolescents showed levels between 3 and 4 (Plener et al., 2009). Nevertheless, despite low levels of evidence, psychopharmacological treatment can become necessary for severely impaired individuals (Mercer, Douglass, & Links, 2009; Nose, Cipriani, Biancosino, Grassi, & Barbui, 2006), and it is the clinicians' responsibility to base this choice on the best available evidence.

In their recommendations for clinical practice, Harper (2006, 2012) and Villalba and Harrington (2000) point out that a thorough diagnostic evaluation of the patient's NSSI is the first step when considering the use of a psychopharmacological component. This includes paying attention to the recent life circumstances, the character of the recent NSSI event(s), the context in which it happens, and any associated clinical symptoms (Harper, 2006). Additionally, the evaluation should assess the functional motivation for NSSI (Nitkowski & Petermann, 2009). Katz and Fotti (2005) proposed a treatment approach for emotionally dysregulated behaviors that seems to fit well for NSSI. In this approach, Axis I disorders in patients with NSSI (such as, e.g., depression or anxiety) ought to be treated according to national guidelines. In a second step, symptom clusters associated with NSSI (e.g., irritability, inner tension, anger) are the main target of the psychopharmacological intervention, and the psychotropic agent is chosen accordingly.

The evidence for psychotropic agents directly targeting NSSI is very limited and stems from case reports. Whereas in NDD populations opioid antagonists have been shown to be successful, the case for the use of opioid antagonists to reduce NSSI in "normally" developing patients is built on few reports and not on controlled trial. The NICE guidelines for the treatment of BPD (Stoffers et al., 2010) therefore recommend abstaining from directly trying to treat self-injury. In situations where it is necessary to control a strong urge to self-injure, there might be a need for "pro re nata" medication to sedate the patient, using low-potency conventional antipsychotics. If possible, benzodiazepines should be avoided in the treatment of NSSI.

For our recommendations, see Box 24.1.

Conclusion

Despite rising numbers of publications concerning NSSI, data or recommendations about the psychopharmacological treatment of this condition are scarcely available. This scarcity may be due to several factors, including the following:

1. A consensus on "what NSSI really is" (e.g., which behaviors to include, underlying intentions, exclusion criteria) has been missing so far. Due to the inclusion of NSSI in section three of the upcoming *DSM-5*, classificatory issues are settled and NSSI can be looked at as a clearly defined outcome criteria in future studies.

2. So far, NSSI still is perceived as a behavior or as a symptom of BPD, but not as a formal disorder. Therefore, funding for studying psychopharmacological treatment of NSSI was hard to obtain in the past but presumably will be easier in the future.

3. The understanding of the neurobiology of NSSI is thus far "in its extreme infancy" (Osuch & Payne, 2009). Despite a growing body of literature on the neurobiology of BPD, on suicidology, and on PDDs, the understanding of NSSI itself is poor and often highly speculative. A rationale for psychopharmacological treatment needs to be built on an understanding of the neurobiological processes it aims to influence. As there currently is only limited knowledge of the neurobiological processes associated with NSSI, finding new ways of influencing neurobiological states remains experimental and is often not driven by neurobiologically based hypotheses.

Future Directions

There are several fields for future research to establish a basis for psychopharmacological treatment:

1. A widely agreed-upon-consensus on the classification of NSSI and instruments for valid assessment of NSSI.

2. Based on such a consensus, work on the issue of differentiating NSSI from BPD, suicidal behavior, and PDD needs to be performed. Although it is clear that any of the aforementioned conditions can be present together with NSSI, it is crucial to develop an understanding of NSSI as a

---

Box 24.1 Recommendations for the Psychopharmacological Treatment of Nonsuicidal Self-Injury

We therefore recommend the following:

1. Every psychopharmacological intervention needs to be based on thorough patient information and (in case of adolescent patients) information of the patient's caregivers. The clinician should inform about the off-label use of medication if applicable.

2. Underlying Axis I disorders should be treated according to national guidelines.

3. If no Axis I disorder is present, but psychopharmacological aid is needed in the treatment process, symptom clusters should be targeted.

For states of inner tension, impulse control deficits, or affective lability, an AA or a mood-stabilizing agent should be considered.

For depressive symptomatology, bulimic symptoms, obsessive-compulsive disorder, and anxiety, the use of selective serotonin reuptake inhibitors (SSRIs) is recommended. However, the risk for developing suicidal ideation or nonsuicidal self-injury as a reaction to SSRIs should be kept in mind, especially in adolescents and young adults.

behavior separated from the broader constructs, as well as the overlaps between these constructs.

3. Research on the neurobiology of NSSI should focus on individuals who engage in self-injury without wanting to die and who do not fulfil criteria for BPD, and it should differentiate between individuals who are and who are not developmentally delayed.

4. Well-designed and independently funded treatment intervention studies are needed. These studies should comprise both randomized double-blind, placebo-controlled studies as well as studies with a naturalistic design, showing effectiveness and efficiency in populations relevant for clinical practice, including "high-risk" individuals (e.g., people with suicidal ideation).

References

Abraham, P. F., & Calabrese, J. R. (2008). Evidenced-based pharmacologic treatment of borderline personality disorder: A shift from SSRIs to anticonvulsants and atypical antipsychotics? *Journal of Affective Disorders, 111*, 21–30.

Agarwal, L. J., Berger, C. E., & Gill, L. (2011). Naltrexone for severe self-harm behavior: A case report. *American Journal of Psychiatry, 168*, 437–438.

American Psychiatric Association. (1994). *Diagnostic and statistical manual of mental disorders* (4th edition). Washington, DC: Author.

Asarnow, J. R., Porta, G., Spirito, A., Emslie, G., Clarke, G., Wagner, K. D., ... Keller, M. (2011). Suicide attempts and nonsuicidal self-injury in the treatment of resistant depression in adolescents: Findings from the TORDIA Trial. *Journal of the American Academy of Child and Adolescent Psychiatry, 50*, 772–781.

Bellino, S., Paradiso, E., & Bogetto, F. (2005). Oxcarbazepine in the treatment of borderline personality disorder: A pilot study. *Journal of Clinical Psychiatry, 66*, 1111–1115.

Bloom, C. M., & Holly, S. (2011). Toward new avenues in the treatment of nonsuicidal self-injury. *Journal of Pharmacy Practice, 24*, 472–477.

Bohus, M. J., & Schmahl, C. G. (2007). Psychopathologie und Therapie der Borderline-Persönlichkeitsstörung. *Nervenarzt, 78*, 1069–1081.

Bond, W. S., Mandos, L. A., & Kurtz, M. B. (1989). Midazolam for aggressivity and violence in three mentally retarded patients. *American Journal of Psychiatry, 146*, 925–926.

Brent, D. A. (2004). Antidepressants and pediatric depression - The risk of doing nothing. *New England Journal of Medicine, 351*, 1598–1601.

Brent, D. A., Emslie, G. J., Clarke, G. N., Asarnow, J., Spirito, A., Ritz, L., ... Keller, M. B. (2009). Predictors of spontaneous and systematically assessed suicidal adverse events in the treatment of SSRI-resistant depression in adolescents (TORDIA) study. *American Journal of Psychiatry, 166*, 418–426.

Burgess, S., Geddes, J. Hawton, K., Townsend, E., Jamison, K., & Goodwin, G. (2001). Lithium for maintenance treatment of mood disorders. *Cochrane Database of Systematic Reviews, 3*, CD003013.

Cassano, P., Lattanzi, L., Pini, S., Dell'Osso, L., Battistini, G., & Cassano, G. B. (2001). Topiramate for self-mutilation in a patient with borderline personality disorder. *Bipolar Disorders, 3*, 161.

Chengappa, K. N. R., Ebeling, T., Kang, J. S., Levine, J., & Parepally, H. (1999). Clozapine reduces severe self-mutilation and aggression in psychotic patients with borderline personality disorder. *Journal of Clinical Psychiatry, 60*, 477–484.

Cipriani, A., Pretty, H., Hawton, K., & Geddes, J. R. (2005). Lithium in the prevention of suicidal behaviour and all-cause mortality in patients with mood disorders: A systematic review of randomized trials. *American Journal of Psychiatry, 162*, 1805–1819.

Cordàs, T. A., Tavares, H., Calderoni, D. M., Stump, G. V., & Ribeiro, R. B. (2006). Oxacarbazepine for self-mutilating bulimic patients. *International Journal of Neuropsychopharmacology, 9*, 769–771.

Correll, C. U. (2007). Weight gain and metabolic effects of mood stabilizers and antipsychotics in pediatric bipolar disorder: A systematic review and pooled analysis of short term trials. *Journal of the American Academy of Child and Adolescent Psychiatry, 46*, 687–700.

Cowdry, R. W., & Gardner, D. L. (1988). Pharmacotherapy for borderline personality disorder. *Archives of General Psychiatry, 45*, 111–119.

Crawford, M. J., Kakad, S., Rendel, C., Mansour, N. A., Crugel, M., Liu, K. W., ... Barnes, T. R. E. (2011). Medication prescribed to people with personality disorder: The influence of patient factors and treatment setting. *Acta Psychiatrica Scandinavica, 124*, 396–402.

Donovan, S., Clayton, A., Beeharry, M., Jones, S., Kirk, C., Waters, K., ... Madeley, R. (2000). Deliberate self-harm following antidepressant drugs. *British Journal of Psychiatry, 177*, 551–556.

Favazza, A. R. (1992). Repetitive self-mutilation. *Psychiatric Annals, 22*, 60–63.

Garland, M. R., Hallahan, B., McNamara, M., Carney, P. A., Grimes, H., Hibbeln, J. R., ... Conroy, R. M. (2007). Lipids and essential fatty acids in patients presenting with self-harm. *British Journal of Psychiatry, 190*, 112–117.

Good, C. R. (2006). Adjunctive Quetiapine targets self-harm behaviors in adolescent females with major depressive disorder. *Journal of Child and Adolescent Psychopharmacology, 16*, 235–236.

Goodyer, I., Dubicka, B., Wilkinson, P., Kelvin, R., Roberts, C., Byford, S., ... Harrington, R. (2007). Selective serotonin reuptake inhibitors (SSRIs) and routine specialist care with and without cognitive behaviour therapy in adolescents with major depression: Randomised controlled trial. *British Medical Journal, 335*, 142–150.

Griengl, H., Sendera, A., & Dantendorfer, K. (2001). Naltrexone as a treatment of self-injurious behavior-a case report. *Acta Psychiatrica Scandinavica, 103*, 234–236.

Grootens, K. P., & Verkes, R. J. (2005). Emerging evidence for the use of atypical antipsychotics in borderline personality disorder. *Pharmacopsychiatry, 38*, 20–23.

Groschwitz, R. C., & Plener, P. L. (2012). The neurobiology of non-suicidal self-injury (NSSI): A review. *Suicidology Online, 3*, 24–32.

Hallahan, B., Hibbeln, J. R., Davis, J. M., & Garland, M. R. (2007). Omega-3 fatty acid supplementation in patients with recurrent self-harm. *British Journal of Psychiatry, 190*, 118–122.

Harbour, R., & Miller, J. (2001). A new system for grading recommendations in evidence based guidelines. *British Medical Journal*, *323*, 334–336.

Harper, G. (2006). Psychopharmacological treatment. In B. W. Walsh (Ed.), *Treating self-injury. A practical guide* (pp. 212–220). New York, NY and London, UK: Guilford Press.

Harper, G. (2012) Psychopharmacological treatment. In B. W. Walsh (Ed.), *Treating self-injury. A practical guide* (2nd ed., pp. 195–203). New York, NY and London, UK: Guilford Press.

Hawton, K., Townsend, E., Arensmann, E., Gunnel, D., Hazell, P., House, A., & van Heeringen, K. (2009). Psychosocial and pharmacological treatments for deliberate self harm. *Cochrane Database of Systematic Reviews*, *4*, CD001764. doi: 10.1002/14651858.CD001764.

Hilger, E., Barnas, C., & Kasper, S. (2003). Quetiapine in the treatment of borderline personality disorder. *World Journal Biological Psychiatry*, *4*, 42–44.

Ingenhoven, T. J. M., & Duivenvoorden, H. J. (2011). Differential effectiveness of antipsychotics in borderline personality disorder: Meta-analyses of placebo-controlled, randomized clinical trials on symptomatic outcome domains. *Journal of Clinical Psychopharmacology*, *31*, 489–496.

Isacsson, J., Holmgren, P., & Ahlner, J. (2005). Selective serotonin reuptake inhibitor antidepressants and the risk of suicide: A controlled forensic database study of 14,857 suicides. *Acta Psychiatrica Scandinavica*, *111*, 286–290.

Katz, L. Y., Cox, B. J., Gunasekara, S., & Miller, A. L. (2004). Feasibility of dialectical behavior therapy for suicidal adolescent inpatients. *Journal of the American Academy of Child and Adolescent Psychiatry*, *43*, 276–282.

Katz, L. Y., & Fotti, S. (2005). The role of behavioral analysis in the pharmacotherapy of emotionally-dysregulated problem behaviors. *Child and Adolescent Psychopharmacology News*, *10*, 1–5.

Kumra, S., Oberstar, J. V., Sikich, L., Findling, R. L., McClellan, J. M., Vinogradov, S., & Schulz, S. C. (2008). Efficacy and tolerability of second-generation antipsychotics in children and adolescents with schizophrenia. *Schizophrenia Bulletin*, *34*, 60–71.

Lewitzka, U., Bauer, M., Felber, W., & Müller-Oerlinghausen, B. (2013). Anti-suicidal effect of lithium: Current state of research and its clinical implications for the long-term treatment of affective disorders. *Nervenarzt*, *84*, 294–306.

Libal, G., & Plener, P. L., (2008). Pharmakologische Therapie des selbstverletzenden Verhaltens im Jugendalter. In R. Brunner & F. Resch (Eds.), *Borderline-Störungen und selbstverletzendes Verhalten bei Jugendlichen* (pp. 165–195). Göttingen, Germany: Vandenhoeck & Ruprecht.

Libal, G., Plener, P. L., Ludolph, A. G., & Fegert, J. M. (2005). Ziprasidone as a weight-neutral treatment alternative in the treatment of self-injurious behavior in adolescent females. *Child and Adolescent Psychopharmacology News*, *10*, 1–6.

Lieb, K., Völlm, B., Rücker, G., Timmer, A., & Stoffers, J. M. (2010). Pharmacotherapy for borderline personality disorder: Cochrane Systematic Review of Randomised Trials. *British Journal of Psychiatry*, *196*, 4–12.

Linehan, M. M., McDavid, J. D., Brown, M. Z., Sayrs, J. H., & Gallop, R. J. (2008). Olanzapine plus dialectical behaviour therapy for women with high irritability who meet criteria for borderline personality disorder: A double-blind, placebo-controlled pilot study. *Journal of Clinical Psychiatry*, *69*, 999–1005.

Lloyd-Richardson, E. E., Perrine, N., Dierker, L., & Kelley, M. L. (2007). Characteristics and functions of non-suicidal self-injury in a community sample of adolescents. *Psychological Medicine*, *37*, 1183–1192.

Markovitz, P. J., Calabrese, J. R., Schulz, C., & Meltzer, H. Y. (1991). Fluoxetine in the treatment of borderline and schizotypal personality disorders. *American Journal of Psychiatry*, *18*, 1064–1067.

Masters, K. J. (2008). Anti-suicidal and self-harm properties of lithium carbonate. *CNS Spectrums*, *13*, 109–110.

McGee, M. D. (1997). Cessation of self-mutilation in a patient with borderline personality disorder treated with naltrexone. *Journal of Clinical Psychiatry*, *58*, 32–33.

Mercer, D., Douglass, A. B., & Links, P. S. (2009) Meta-analyses of mood stabilizers, antidepressants and antipsychotics in the treatment of borderline personality disorder: Effectiveness for depression and anger symptoms. *Journal of Personality Disorders*, *23*, 156–174.

Muehlenkamp, J. J. (2005). Self-injurious behavior as a separate clinical syndrome. *American Journal of Orthopsychiatry*, *75*, 324–333.

Muehlenkamp, J. J., Claes, L., Havertape, L., & Plener, P. L. (2012). International prevalence of adolescent non-suicidal self-injury and deliberate self-harm. *Child and Adolescent Psychiatry and Mental Health*, *6*, 10.

Nickel, M. K., Loew, T. H., & Pedrosa, G. F. (2007). Aripiprazole in treatment of borderline patients, part II: An 18-month follow-up. *Psychopharmacology*, *191*, 1023–1026.

Nickel, M. K., Muehlbacher, M., Nickel, K., Kettler, C., Gil, F. P., Bachler, E.,... Kaplan, P. (2006). Aripiprazole in the treatment of patients with borderline personality disorder: A double-blind, placebo-controlled study. *American Journal of Psychiatry*, *163*, 833–838.

Nitkowski, D., & Petermann, F. (2009). Behavioural analysis of self-injurious behaviour. *Nervenheilkunde*, *28*, 227–231.

Nixon, M. K., Cloutier, P. F., & Aggarwal, S. (2002). Affect regulation and addictive aspects of repetitive self- injury in hospitalized adolescents. *Journal of the American Academy of Child and Adolescent Psychiatry*, *41*, 1333–1341.

Nose, M., Cipriani, A., Biancosino, B., Grassi, L., & Barbui, C. (2006). Efficacy of pharmacotherapy against core traits of borderline personality disorder: Meta-analysis of randomized controlled trials. *International Clinical Psychopharmacology*, *21*, 345–353.

Osuch, E. A., & Payne, G. W. (2009). Neurobiological perspectives on self-injury. In M. K. Nixon & N. L. Heath (Eds.), *Self-injury in youth* (pp. 79–111). New York, NY and London, UK: Routledge.

Parikh, M. S., Kolevzon, A., & Hollander, E. (2008). Psychopharmacology of aggression in children and adolescents with autism: A critical review of efficacy and tolerability. *Journal of Child and Adolescent Psychopharmacology*, *18*, 157–178.

Philipsen, A., Richter, H., Schmahl, C., Peters, J., Rusch, N., Bohus, M., & Lieb, K. (2004). Clonidine in acute aversive inner tension and self-injurious behavior in female patients with borderline personality disorder. *Journal of Clinical Psychiatry*, *65*, 1414–1419.

Pies, R. W., & Popli, A. P. (1995). Self-injurious behavior: Pathophysiology and implications for treatment. *Journal of Clinical Psychiatry*, *56*, 580–588

Pittenger, C., Krystal, J. H., & Coric, V. (2005). Initial evidence of the beneficial effects of glutamate-modulating agents in the treatment of self-injurious behavior associated with borderline personality disorder. *Journal of Clinical Psychiatry*, *66*, 1492–1493.

Plener, P. L., Libal, G., & Nixon, M. K. (2009). Use of medication in the treatment of nonsuicidal self-injury in youth. In M. K. Nixon & N. L. Heath (Eds.), *Self-injury in youth* (pp. 275–309). New York, NY and London, UK: Routledge.

Plener, P. L., Libal, G., Fegert, J. M., & Kölch, M. G. (2013). Psychopharmacological treatment of non-suicidal self-injury. *Nervenheilkunde, 32*, 38–41.

Roberts, N. (2003). Adolescent self-mutilatory behavior: Psychopharmacological treatment. *Child and Adolescent Psychopharmacology News, 8*, 10–12.

Roth, A. S., Ostroff, R. B., & Hoffman, E. R. (1996). Naltrexone as a treatment for repetitive self-injurious behaviour: An open–label trial. *Journal of Clinical Psychiatry, 57*, 233–237.

Rothschild, A. J., Shindul-Rothschild, J. A., Viguera, A., Murray, M., & Brewster, S. (2000). Comparison of the frequency of behavioural disinhibition on alprazolam, clonazepam, or no benzodiazepine in hospitalized psychiatric patients. *Journal of Clinical Psychopharmacology, 20*, 7–11.

Russ, M. J. (1992). Self injurious behavior in patients with borderline personality disorder: Biological perspectives. *Journal of Personality Disorders, 6*, 64–81.

Sandman, C. A. (1990/91). The opiate hypothesis in autism and self-injury. *Journal of Child and Adolescent Psychopharmacology, 1*, 193–199.

Sandman, C. A. (2009). Psychopharmacologic treatment of nonsuicidal self-injury. In M. K. Nock (Ed.), *Understanding nonsuicidal self-injury. Origins, assessment, and treatment* (pp. 291–323). Washington, DC: American Psychological Association.

Sandman, C. A., Hetrick, W. P., Taylor, D. V., Barron, J. L., Touchette, P., Lott, I., ... Martinazzi, V. (1993). Naltrexone reduces self-injury and improves learning. *Experimental and Clinical Psychopharmacology, 1*, 242–258.

Scahill, L., & Koenig, K. (1999). Pharmacotherapy in children and adolescents with pervasive developmental disorders. *Journal of Child and Adolescent Psychiatric Nursing, 12*, 41–43.

Schulz, S. C., Zanarini, M. C., Bateman, A., Bohus, M., Detke, H. C., Trzaskoma, Q., ... Corya, S. (2008). Olanzapine for the treatment of boderline personality disorder: Variable dose 12-week randomised double-blind placebo-controlled study. *British Journal of Psychiatry, 193*, 485–492.

Sher, L., & Stanley, B. (2009). Biological models of nonsuicidal self-injury. In M. K. Nock (Ed.), *Understanding nonsuicidal self-injury. Origins, assessment, and treatment* (pp. 99–117). Washington, DC: American Psychological Association.

Simpson, E. B., Yen, S., Costello, E., Rosen, K., Begin, A., Pistorello, J., & Pearlstein, T. (2004). Combined dialectical behavior therapy and fluoxetine in the treatment of borderline personality disorder. *Journal of Clinical Psychiatry, 65*, 379–85.

Smith, B. D. (2005). Self-mutilation and pharmacotherapy. *Psychiatry, 2*, 29–37.

Sonne, S., Rubey, R., Brady, K., Malcolm, R., & Morris, T. (1996). Naltrexone treatment of self-injurious thoughts and behaviours. *Journal of Nervous and Mental Disease, 184*, 192–195.

Stanford, S., & Jones, M. P. (2009). Psychological subtyping finds pathological, impulsive, and 'normal' groups among

adolescents who self-harm. *Journal of Child Psychology and Psychiatry, 50*, 807–815.

Stanley, B., Sher, L., Wilson, S., Ekman, R., Huang, Y., & Mann, J.J. (2010). Non-suicidal self-injurious behavior, endogenous opioids and monoamine neurotransmitters. *Journal of Affective Disorders, 124*, 134–140.

Stoffers, J., Völlm, B.A., Rücker, G., Timmer, A., Huband, N., & Lieb, K. (2010) Pharmacological interventions for borderline personality disorder. *Cochrane Database of Systematic Reviews, 6*, CD005653. doi: 10.1002/14651858.CD005653.pub2.

Symons, F. J., Thompson, A., & Rodriguez, M. C. (2004). Self-injurious behaviour and the efficacy of naltrexone treatment: A quantitative synthesis. *Mental Retardation and Developmental Disabilities Research Reviews, 10*, 193–200.

Teicher, M. H., Glod, C. A., & Cole, J. O. (1993). Antidepressant drugs and the emergence of suicidal tendencies. *Drug Safety, 8*, 186–212.

Thompson, T., Hackenberg, T., Cerutti, D., Baker, D., & Axtell, S. (1994). Opioid antagonist effects on self-injury in adults with mental retardation: Response from and location as determinants of medication effects. *American Journal of Mental Retardation, 99*, 85–102.

Verkes, R. J., Van der Mast, R. C., Hengeveld, M. W., Tuyl, J. P., Zwinderman, A. H., & Van Kempen, G. M. (1998). Reduction by paroxetine of suicidal behavior in patients with repeated suicide attempts but not major depression. *American Journal of Psychiatry, 155*, 543–547.

Villalba, R., & Harrington, C. J. (2000). Repetitive self-injurious behavior: A neuropsychiatric perspective and review of pharmacologic treatments. *Seminars in Clinical Neuropsychiatry, 5*, 215–226.

Vita, A., De Peri, L., & Sacchetti, E. (2011). Antipsychotics, antidepressants, anticonvulsants, and placebo on the symptom dimensions of borderline personality disorder: A meta-analysis of randomized controlled and open-label trials. *Journal of Clinical Psychopharmacology, 31*, 613–624.

Vitiello, B., Correll, C., van Zwieten-Boot, B., Zuddas, A., Parellada, M., & Arango, C. (2009). Antipsychotics in children and adolescents: Increasing use, evidence for efficacy and safety concerns. *European Neuropsychopharmacology, 19*, 629–635.

Whittington, C. J., Kendall, T., Fonagy, P., Cottrell, D., Cotgrove, A., & Boddington, E. (2004). Selective serotonin reuptake inhibitors in childhood depression: Systematic review of published versus unpublished data. *Lancet, 36*, 1341–1345.

Wilkinson, P., Kelvin, R., Roberts, C., Dubicka, B., & Goodyer, I. (2011). Clinical and psychosocial predictors of suicide attempts and nonsuicidal self-injury in the Adolescent Depression Antidepressants and Psychotherapy Trial (ADAPT). *American Journal of Psychiatry, 168*, 495–501.

Winchel, M. W., & Stanley, M. (1991). Self-injurious behavior: A review of the behavior and biology of self-mutilation. *American Journal of Psychiatry, 148*, 306–317.

World Health Organisation. (2010). *ICD-10: International statistical classification of diseases and related health problems 10th revision.* Retrieved August 2013, from http://apps.who.int/classifications/apps/icd/icd10online/.

PART 6

Special Issues

Overlap Between Suicidal Behavior and Interpersonal Violence

Marc Hillbrand

Abstract

Suicidal behavior and interpersonal violence coexist in individuals to an extent that considerably exceeds chance covariation. Grasping the nature of this overlap enriches our understanding of suicidal behavior and that of interpersonal violence. The most extreme form of this overlap consists of homicide-suicide and the related concepts of mass murder, suicide bombing, and victim-precipitated homicide. The present chapter describes these phenomena and offers an overview of milder forms of coexisting suicidal behavior and interpersonal violence, organized by topical area: prospective studies, externalizing behaviors, neuropsychological factors, substance use disorders, trauma, protective factors, and exposure to violence. An overview of theoretical models follows. Implications of this body of knowledge for our understanding of suicidal behavior and suggestions for future inquiries conclude the chapter.

Key Words: suicide, homicide, aggression, comorbidity, violence, self-injury

Psychopathological conditions are best understood not in isolation as distinct entities but in the context of the complex nexus of etiological factors in which they exist. To explain conduct disorder, for instance, it is necessary to grasp the context of familial coercion from which it emerges and the developmental process that leads to adult antisociality (Odgers et al., 2008). Among psychopathological conditions, the pattern of comorbidity that is associated with the highest mortality is seen in individuals who engage in deliberate efforts to cause physical harm to self (suicidal behavior, self-injury) as well as harm to others (interpersonal violence). The present chapter examines this phenomenon with an emphasis on elucidating what the overlap between the two forms of aggression suggests about suicidal behavior.

Self-harm and interpersonal violence are two forms of aggression, that is, behaviors intended to injure someone physically or psychologically (Berkowitz, 1993). Self-harm or aggression against self (AAS) is the deliberate attempt to inflict physical injury to self (suicidal behavior, self-injury). Interpersonal violence or aggression against others (AAO) is the deliberate attempt to cause physical injury to other(s). The evidence for overlap between AAS and AAO comes from various fields of inquiry but falls in two general areas: extreme forms of comorbid AAS and AAO (e.g., homicide-suicide), and milder forms of comorbid AAS with AAO (e.g., a mildly conduct disordered youth is hospitalized after a suicide attempt; a chronic spouse batterer becomes suicidal once incarcerated).

Extreme Forms of Comorbid Aggression Against Self and Aggression Against Others in Adults

Homicide-suicide (HS) is defined as a homicide or a series of homicides followed by the perpetrator's suicide. It is a phenomenon that is much less well understood than homicide or suicide due in part to its low incidence and, until recently, due to the lack of an adequate national surveillance system (Hillbrand, 2001; Marzuk, Tardiff, & Hirsch, 1992). The recently launched National Violent Death Reporting System will soon yield accurate incidence rates for HS (Powell et al., 2006). Until those data are available, the best incidence estimate of HS is .03% each year of all US deaths (Marzuk et al., 1992). Incidence estimates of HS in other countries are remarkably similar to the US estimate and fall between .02% and .05% (Coid, 1983; Milroy, 1993). This stands in stark contrast to the dramatic differences in homicide rates across the globe, with countries such as the United States having a homicide rate more than 25 times greater than countries like Austria (Fingerhut & Kleinman, 1990). This suggests that homicide-suicide rates are largely independent of homicide rates. A remarkable manifestation of this phenomenon is the fact that countries with low rates of violence have among homicides a much higher proportion of homicide-suicides than countries with high rates of violence. The homicide rate in the United Kingdom is less than 1 per 100,000; in parts of the United Kingdom up to 33% of homicides are followed by suicides (Milroy, 1993).

The similar worldwide prevalence of homicide-suicide points to the possible role of genetic factors. In general, the greater the biological component of a disorder, the smaller the variability in worldwide prevalence. Conditions with a smaller genetic component (e.g., bulimia nervosa) show wider variability than conditions with a greater genetic component (e.g., schizophrenia). For instance, the World Health Organization World Mental Health Surveys Consortium (2004) reported the 12-month prevalence of selected mental disorders. The United States, the country with the highest rate of impulse control disorder, a disorder with a relatively low genetic component (Hollander & Rosen, 2000), had prevalence 70 times greater than in Nigeria, the country with the lowest prevalence. In contrast to this 70-fold difference, the magnitude of the discrepancy between the country with the highest and the lowest prevalence of any disorder was 6-fold for anxiety disorders and 12-fold for mood disorders, two disorders with heavy genetic loadings (Craddock & Jones, 1999; Hettema, Neale, & Kendler, 2000). Biological factors are thus likely to play a significant role in homicide-suicide, as is true in suicide (Arango, Huang, Underwood, & Mann, 2003).

It is likely that depression, a disorder with a significant biological component and present in many perpetrators of homicide-suicide (Marzuk et al., 1992), may contribute to this relative invariance. The same is true of suicide. For instance, the US homicide rate is eight times that of the United Kingdom, but the US suicide rate is only 40% higher than the UK rate (Brock & Griffiths, 2003; Buda & Tsuang, 1990). By contrast, clinical characteristics associated with homicide vary widely as a function of sociocultural differences (Daly & Wilson, 1988; Maris, 1992).

Suicides and suicide attempts run in families beyond the influence of mood disorders. Offspring of depressed suicide attempters are six times more likely to attempt suicide than offspring of depressed non-attempters (Brent et al., 2002a). Twin studies show that between 15% and 45% of the variance of suicidal behavior can be attributed to genetic influences (Mann, Bortinger, Oquendo, Currier, Li, & Brent, 2005; Mann, Brent, & Arango, 2001). Suicide rates among first-degree relatives of individuals who attempted or completed suicide are higher than comparison groups, even when the influence of psychiatric comorbidities is statistically controlled (Brent, Bridge, Johnson, & Connolly, 1996). This heritability of suicidal behaviors exceeds what is attributable to the inheritability of mood disorders, which are strongly linked to suicide (Roy, Segal, Centerwall, & Robinette, 1991). Future research will shed light on the inheritability of comorbid AAO-AAS.

Several phenomena that are related to (completed) homicide-suicide are attempted homicide-suicide, mass murder, suicide bombing, and victim-precipitated homicide (e.g., "suicide by cop"). A brief description of these variants of homicide-suicide follows. For a more extensive review, see Hillbrand (2001).

In attempted homicide-suicide, events outside the control of the aggressor interfere with completion of the acts. The following vignettes are recent news events that exemplify this.

• A man in his thirties, distraught over a romantic breakup, decides to kill his ex-partner and then himself. He documents this intent in a detailed suicide note. On his way to her house, a teenager speaks to him disrespectfully. Enraged, he shoots and kills the teen. Alerted by witnesses, the police arrest him on the way to his ex-lover's house.

• A young man in his twenties becomes delusionally convinced that his father has molested him. He disembowels the father and then slashes his own throat. The father survives due to prompt medical attention.

These cases illustrate the fact that it is possible for individuals to have the intent and the ability to kill self and other(s), but one or more of the intended victims sometimes survive due to factors outside the control of the individual intent on homicide-suicide. For instance, in the second vignette, the mother was a nurse and succeeded in performing first aid before the prompt arrival of emergency personnel. Similarly, a man with lifelong schizophrenia who had planned a patricide-suicide killed his father but survived a highly lethal drug overdose. Completed homicide-suicides are so rare that it may be advisable to study them jointly with attempted homicide-suicides. Attempted homicide-suicides are probably more common, but their incidence has never been studied and remains unknown. The challenge, however, lies in identifying among all attempted and completed homicides those where suicidal intent and ability to follow through were present, and among all attempted and competed suicides those where homicidal intent and ability to follow through were present.

A majority of homicide-suicides involve two deaths (the "perpetrator" and his or her victim), but some involve many more (Marzuk et al., 1992). A phenomenon that overlaps with homicide-suicide has been dubbed "mass murder." It is the willful injuring of five or more persons of whom three or more are killed by a single offender in a single incident (Dietz, 1986). Suicide is a common conclusion of these killing sprees, occurring in about half of mass murders (Dietz, 1986; Hempel, Meloy, & Richards, 1999). Hempel et al. (1999) describe the typical mass murderer as a loner with chronic extreme anger, paranoid ideation, and depressed mood.

A distinct variant of homicide-suicide involves what is often labeled suicide bombing or politically motivated mass killings (Hiss & Kahana, 1988). They range from rare mass killings like the 9/11/01 attacks on the World Trade Centers or the crash of Egypt Air 990, in which hundreds or thousands of lives are taken, to much more common incidents in which a single terrorist straps himself or herself with explosives that are later detonated, usually in crowded enemy areas, and typically but not always causing the death of the perpetrator (Taylor & Ryan, 1988). Much of the knowledge about suicide bombing comes from interviews of unsuccessful bombers (Merrari, 2008). Although these phenomena meet the definitions of homicide-suicide and of mass murder, they are distinct in that there appears to be not real suicide intent, rather a placid acknowledgment that political success can only be obtained through self-sacrifice.

The phenomenon of victim-precipitated homicide, or more commonly, "suicide by cop," was first described by Wolfgang (1959). In these incidents, individuals use lethal force or the semblance of it against law enforcement officers with the apparent intent to cause police to kill them (Van Zandt, 1993). Preincident suicide notes or statements later reveal the perpetrator's suicidal intent (Kennedy, Homant, & Hupp, 1998). The recent increase of such justifiable homicides by law enforcement personnel in which victims appeared to have a suicidal motive has resulted in the fact that many police officers now receive training on how to manage these situations as safely as possible (Parent, 1998; Van Zandt, 1993).

Homicide-suicide is not a new phenomenon; historical examples abound. In these and many similar historical events, a nexus of complex psychological, political, religious, and other social factors interacted to determine the deadly outcome. The first-century warriors of Masada completed mass suicide after they killed their less zealous coreligionists. The followers of the charismatic preacher Jim Jones also completed mass suicide after killing US Congressman Ryan, his four companions, and presumably also some of their less committed followers (Hazani, 1993). In 1984, Sikh militants took over the Golden Temple of Amritsar and took numerous Indian hostages. They then triggered the Indian security forces to storm the sanctuary by savagely killing their hostages in plain view of the soldiers, causing the death of all the Sikhs (Hazani, 1993).

Extreme Forms of Comorbid Aggression Against Self and Aggression Against Others in Youth

US schools have gradually become safer in recent years as measured by the total number of violent incidents. This trend is attributable to a variety of preventive measures, including school personnel education, violence-prevention curricula, enhanced security, and law enforcement activities such as federally coordinated efforts to combat gang-related violence. In spite of this positive development, some recent incidents of school violence such as the 1999 Columbine High School and 2002 Erfurt Gymnasium massacres have shocked the world. These incidents typically involve a small number of youths who harbor long-standing grudges against various peer groups and against school personnel. They are morbidly fascinated by violence and weapons. Lax supervision by their parents makes access and accumulation of weapons possible. Victimization through bullying is often of etiological relevance, as is the hopelessness, despair, and suicidal intent of the would-be killer or killers.

Though the incidence of school-based violent deaths is low (.068 per 100,000; Anderson et al., 2001), the incidence of these violent deaths is increasing and their impact is potent on the public at large. An analysis of 220 such events revealed that most killers (54%) gave warnings of their violent intent, showed signs of suicidal behavior (odds ratio = 7.0), and tended to have been bullied (odds ratio = 2.6; Anderson et al., 2001).

Some scholars and social commentators have argued for a law enforcement approach to the problem of school violence. They have favored interventions such as school uniforms, metal detectors, drug-sniffing dogs, and so on (Vossekuil, Fein, Reddy, & Modzeleski, 2004). An examination of the time line of the Columbine shootings illustrates the futility of this approach (Hillbrand, 2006).

11:14: The first and most powerful bomb that Klebold and Harris smuggled into the school fails to explode.

11:19: Klebold and Harris kill two students outside the school.

11:23: The first 911 call is placed.

11:26: The first police cruiser arrives.

11:27: Klebold and Harris enter the library and start shooting at students there.

11:35: Twelve students are dead.

11:46: The second bomb they had smuggled into the school explodes partially.

11:47: Their third bomb explodes partially.

12:06: The first SWAT team enters the school.

12:08: Klebold and Harris commit suicide.

2:30: The SWAT teams begin freeing students in hiding.

4:30: Law enforcement officials declare the school under control.

Following the killings, a controversy emerged about the appropriateness and promptness of the Jefferson County Sheriff's Department's handling of the case. The Sheriff's Office issued a report on May 15, 2000, documenting in great detail what occurred during the 311-minute-long ordeal. It states that officers could not have saved lives if they had responded more quickly. A group of parents of victims challenged this assertion, and six families sued the Sheriff's Department.

The evidence overwhelmingly supports the Sheriff's Office report's conclusion. Columbine High School, unlike most US schools, had a uniformed and armed Sheriff's deputy permanently assigned to it. Deputy Neil Gardner was on duty that day, wearing the yellow shirt identifying him as a community resource officer. He was cruising around the school in his patrol car. He received a first radio call at 11:20: "Female down in parking lot." He drove his cruiser to the parking lot to investigate. He arrived at the scene of the first shooting and stepped out of his car. He saw Eric Harris shooting at students near the west doors of the school. Harris turned his attention away from the students and aimed his rifle at Deputy Gardner, who was particularly visible in his bright yellow shirt. He fired 10 shots. Gardner, leaning over the top of his cruiser 60 yards away, could clearly see Harris's rifle and returned fire. He fired four shots. Harris's weapon jammed. He ran into the building while Gardner radioed for help. It was 11:26 a.m. Within a minute, Sheriff's deputies arrived, having received the first 911 call at 11:23. By 11:35, 16 minutes after Harris and Klebold fired the first shoots, 12 students were dead. It took 5 more hours before the deputies regained control of the situation.

It is difficult to imagine how the Sheriff's deputies could have responded more promptly. Klebold and Harris kept diaries and various other revealing documents on their computers that make psychological autopsies possible. In these, they clearly documented their joint determination to kill, and to kill as many people as possible. They did not expect to survive the assault. Only chance prevented a much higher death toll. Of the three bombs that they smuggled into the school, one failed to explode and the other two exploded only partially. Their plan was to blow up the cafeteria and kill everyone in it. The bomb was set up to explode at 11:14 a.m., a time when the cafeteria was usually very crowded. That morning, there were 488 people in the cafeteria. No prompter response by police could have prevented the carnage this bomb was scheduled to cause.

The implications from these events are clear. Law enforcement approaches cannot be the sole solution to the problem of school violence. Most of what mental health professionals currently do constitutes tertiary prevention, namely treating the traumatized survivors of events such as the Columbine massacre. The Columbine time line illustrates the futility of much current thinking, which constitutes secondary prevention: more metal detectors, more officers, and so on. A primary prevention approach of education of parents, school personnel, violence prevention curricula, bullying detection programs, and other preventive efforts appears much more promising.

Nonlethal Comorbid Aggression Against Self and Aggression Against Others

Evidence for the covariation of AAS and AAO comes from a wide variety of studies. An exhaustive review of this literature falls beyond the scope of this chapter. The reader is referred to Hillbrand (2001) for an earlier review. An overview of the correlational studies that document the comorbidity of AAS and AAO follows, organized by topical area: prospective studies, externalizing behaviors, neuropsychological factors, substance use disorders, trauma, protective factors, and exposure to violence.

Prospective Studies

There have been only two prospective tests of the hypothesis that AAO predicts AAS. Angst and Clayton (1998) followed a cohort of army recruits and noted that aggression predicted subsequent suicide. Oquendo (2004) enrolled 308 mood-disordered individuals (major depressive disorder and bipolar disorder) in a study of the treatment of depression. Aggression was measured using the Barratt's Impulsivity Scale, the Buss-Durkee Hostility Inventory, and the Brown-Goodwin Lifetime Aggression Scale. Aggression thus measured proved to be a significant predictor of suicide attempt during the 2-year follow-up period.

In an enlightening test of the hypothesis that AAO predicts AAS, Conner et al. (2001) used a retrospective case control design and a national representative sample to examine data from the National Mortality Followback Survey. They interviewed next of kin of 753 suicide decedents and compared them to accident victims. Overall, suicide decedents were 2.5 times more likely than accident victims to have been violent "sometimes" or "frequently." Those without alcohol misuse were four times more likely to have

been violent "sometimes" or "frequently." The link between suicide and violence was also particularly strong among women and among the young (ages 20–34 years). The authors report several noteworthy interactions in the postdiction of suicide, namely between violence and alcohol misuse and between violence and gender: Violent individuals without alcohol misuse were 12 times more likely to commit suicide than nonviolent individuals without alcohol misuse, and violent women were eight times more likely to commit suicide than nonviolent women. Conner's study has important implications: The link between AAO and AAS cannot be simply attributed to the effects of alcohol use disorders; rather, there may exist a group of alcohol abusers prone to severe impulsivity manifesting in heightened vulnerability to suicidal and homicidal urges.

Externalizing Disorders

One psychiatric diagnosis associated with suicidal behavior is conduct disorder, a disorder that has interpersonal violence as a diagnostic criteria. For example, Beautrais (2002) found that youth (under age 25 years) who committed suicide were four times as likely to have engaged in lifetime antisocial behavior as nonsuicidal individuals. Flannery, Singer, and Webster (2001) described a sample of 349 male and 135 female adolescents who reported attacking someone with a knife or shooting at someone within the past year and matched controls. These violent adolescents reported higher levels of exposure to violence and victimization; the violent female adolescents also had significantly higher levels of suicidal behavior. Among incarcerated women, suicidal behavior is associated with antisocial deviance (Verona, Hicks, & Patrick, 2005). Negative life events, including violent and nonviolent crime, predict suicidal behavior in personality disordered individuals (Yen et al., 2005). Individuals who attempted suicide were more likely than individuals who made a suicidal gesture to exhibit impulsive and aggressive symptoms (Nock & Kessler, 2006). Externalizing disorders are thus characterized by extensive overlap between AAS and AAO.

The same is true among individuals with schizophrenia spectrum disorders. Individuals with schizophrenia who committed suicide were six times more likely to have engaged in aggressive behavior against others than comparison group members (De Hert, McKenzie, & Peuskens,

2001). Apter et al. (1991) found differential patterns of association between violent and nonviolent psychiatric patients: Among nonviolent patients suicidal behavior was associated with sadness (but not with anger), whereas violent suicidal behavior was associated with anger but not with sadness. This finding highlights the importance of exploring the factors that increase and those that mitigate suicide risk in individuals who present primarily with externalizing problems (delinquency, violence, substance use disorders) as they may differ from risk and protective factors for individuals who present primarily with internalizing disorders.

The comorbidity between internalizing and externalizing disorders (Weiss, Jackson, & Susser, 1997) renders this exploration even more challenging. Verona, Sachs-Ericsson, and Joiner (2004) found, for instance, that in a large community sample (n = 4,745), individuals diagnosed with an antisocial personality disorder had nearly a three-fold increased rate of suicide attempts. Most remarkably, they found that the link between suicidal behavior and externalizing disorders is independent of internalizing disorders and independent of the comorbidity between internalizing and externalizing disorders. The link between suicidal behavior and comorbid internalizing and externalizing disorders was even stronger in women than in men. This suggests the possibility that suicidal behaviors in women with externalizing symptoms may be the function of the combination of emotional instability (such as depression or anxiety) and behavioral dyscontrol (represented by acting-out behaviors).

It is conceivable that the pattern of comorbidity among suicidal behavior, internalizing disorders, and externalizing disorders may differ across ethnic groups. Castle et al. (2004), for instance, examined data from the National Mortality Followback Survey and discovered a differential pattern linking suicide and antisocial behavior in Caucasians and African Americans: In both groups, antisocial behavior conferred risk, but whereas the link was linear among Caucasians, it was nonlinear among African Americans. This illustrates the importance of studying patterns of covariance in ethnically diverse samples, as they may differ.

Neuropsychological Abnormalities

Several hypothetical models of brain impairment have been considered to potentially contribute to AAS and AAO. Prominent among these is the model implicating executive dysfunction and the orbitofrontal system, involved in decision making. Orbitofrontal lesions have been shown to be associated with high-risk behavior and disadvantageous decision making (Bechara et al., 1989; Damasio, Grabowski, Frank, Galaburda, & Damasio, 1994; Eslinger & Damasio, 1985). Jollant et al. (2004) enrolled 69 individuals who had made a significant suicide attempt in a study of decision-making processes using the Iowa Gambling Task. They reported that individuals with suicidal histories performed considerably worse on the decision-making task (i.e., made more disadvantageous choice) and had greater lifetime aggression scores. These findings suggest the possibility of a specific brain anomaly involving primarily the ventral orbitofrontal region and the amygdala as a biological substrate for AAO and AAS. Though this was only an initial study that awaits replication, research in this field appears promising.

Substance Use Disorders

Numerous studies of substance users have reported covariation among substance use, AAS, and AAO. Roy (2001) found a link between suicidal behavior and hostility measured with the Foulds Hostility and Direction of Hostility questionnaire in a sample of 214 cocaine-dependent individuals. From the study by Conner et al. (2001), it appears unlikely that the comorbidity of AAS and AAO is attributable to the effects of substance use (e.g., disinhibition).

Trauma

Trauma is often found in the histories of suicidal individuals and those of violent individuals (Reviere, Battle, Farber, & Kaslow, 2003). Brodsky et al. (2001), for example, found that in a sample of depressed individuals, those who had been abused were more likely to have attempted suicide and had higher impulsivity and aggression scores. Similarly, Oquendo et al. (2003) found that individuals with posttraumatic stress disorder and major depressive disorder had higher suicidal behavior *and* lifetime aggression than those with posttraumatic stress disorder without major depressive disorder. A number of developmental trajectories have been hypothesized to explain the comorbidity between abuse, suicidal behavior, and violence. One possibility is that trauma history may be linked to generalized impulsivity that manifests itself in greater propensity to respond with either AAS or AAO under stress. Alternatively, a trauma history may be a fertile environmental breeding ground for both AAO and AAS independent of generalized impulsivity. The Brodsky et al. study, showing that abuse and suicidal behavior are associated even when impulsivity and aggression are controlled, makes this alternative hypothesis more likely.

Another possibility is that victimization, suicidal behavior, and violence are all expressions of a genetic predisposition: Victimization may have, for instance, been at the hands of a relative possessing the same genetic predisposition to aggression. Brent et al. (2002) showed that the offspring of suicide attempters with siblings concordant for suicidal behavior had higher rates of sexual victimization, a higher risk of suicide attempt, and higher lifetime impulsive aggression than did offspring of nonsuicidal probands. Remarkably, impulsive aggression was also the most powerful predictor of early age at first suicide attempt.

There is also some support for this genetic predisposition from the primate literature. For instance, although rhesus monkeys raised without maternal presence show lifelong patterns of greater aggression compared to animals raised with a maternal presence (an environmental effect), their cerebrospinal fluid levels of monoamine metabolites show significant heritability (a genetic effect) (Higley et al., 1993). Additionally, the countervailing effect of protective factors (availability of supportive parent(s) and peers) appears to influence the coexistence of trauma, AAO, and AAS. Romans et al. (1995) found that among abused children, a positive adult presence in the posttraumatic phase diminished the likelihood of later suicidal behavior.

Several studies have investigated the comorbidity of depression and childhood sexual victimization. They have revealed that this comorbidity is associated with earlier onset of depression (but not more severe depression) and higher rates of parental conflict, domestic violence, suicidal behavior, self-injury, and borderline personality disorder (Bowen, 2000; Elliott, Browne, & Kilcoyne, 1995; Gladstone, Parker, Wilhelm, Mitchell, & Austin, 1999). Gladstone et al. (2004) presented data that suggest that another correlate of comorbid depression and childhood sexual abuse, at least among women, is interpersonal victimization. In a sample of 126 consecutively admitted women in a mood disorder unit (base rate of sexual victimization = 29%), those who had been sexually victimized were four times as likely to have been physically abused as a child; as adults, they were six times more likely to have experienced sexual victimization, three times more likely to have experienced interpersonal violence, and twice as likely to have engaged in a suicide attempt. Path analysis revealed that interpersonal victimization was associated with emotional abuse and neglect (including perception of maternal indifference) through a mediating link of higher personality dysfunction scores. In other words, growing up in a family where conflicts are severe and frequent and in which the father was physically and sexually abusive and the mother was experienced as indifferent and neglectful heightens the risk of adult depression, suicidal behavior, and interpersonal victimization. The association among these behaviors appears to relate to personality dysfunction.

Protective Factors

Most of the literature on the comorbidity of AAS and AAO has thus far focused on various risk factors. It appears likely that factors such as healthy socialization, social support, and feeling that life has a meaning will be shown to protect against the risk of co-occurring AAS and AAO, as has been shown to be the case for AAS and AAO that occur in isolation (Plutchik & van Praag, 1989, 1990, 1994). An empirical study documenting a protective effect is that by Dervic et al. (2004). Spirituality appears to protect individuals from comorbid AAO/AAS. In a study of 351 individuals who were treated as inpatients for a mood disorder (80% major depressive disorder, 20% bipolar disorder), those describing themselves as religiously affiliated had lower rates of lifetime suicide attempts, lower lifetime aggression, and reported more reasons for living. Moral objections to suicide appear to mediate the link between spirituality and suicidal behavior.

Exposure to Violence

A number of studies have suggested that mere witnessing of violence may increase vulnerability to suicide, at least among females. In a sample of 3,735 community youths, Flannery, Singer, and Wester (2001) observed that violent adolescent males and females were more likely to have been exposed to violent victimization. Further, violent adolescent females (but not males) were also more depressed and suicidal than nonviolent peers. Similarly, Marzuk et al. (2002) showed that whereas New York City policemen had slightly lower rates of suicide than the general population, policewomen were four times more likely to die by suicide than those in the general population.

Theoretical Models

The various conceptual models that explain the comorbidity of AAS and AAO all articulate the phenomenon within a biopsychosocial framework. They either emphasize biological over psychological factors (Coccaro, 1995) or psychological factors over biological factors (Beck, 1999; Hillbrand, 2001; Plutchik & van Praag, 1990; Shaffer, 1974). Among the primarily psychological models, some stress developmental factors (Shaffer, 1974), and others stress dynamic factors (Beck, 1999; Hillbrand, 2001; Plutchik & van Praag, 1990).

Coccaro has formulated a biological model of comorbid AAS-AAO (Coccaro et al., 1989). Labeled the serotonin-aggression hypothesis, it has been described as the most replicated finding of the entire field of biological psychiatry (Coccaro, 1995). According to this hypothesis, regulation of aggressive behavior is compromised by a dysfunction of the serotonergic system. Coccaro proposes that dysregulated inhibitory processes increase sensitivity to stimuli that elicit aggression and diminish sensitivity to cues that signal punishment. Diminished brain serotonergic activity is hypothesized to disinhibit the expression of aggression. Proxy measures of central serotonergic activity typically are used in these studies because brain serotonin cannot easily be measured. They include the primary serotonin metabolite 5-hydroxyindoleacetic acid (5-HIAA), platelet serotonin, whole blood serotonin, and endocrine responses to drug challenges with drugs such as fenfluramine. Most of the tests of the serotonin hypothesis of aggression (e.g., Brown et al., 1979) report a negative correlation between serotonin indices and measures of interpersonal violence and suicidal behavior. This model predicts the selective serotonin reuptake inhibitors (SSRIs) to be the drugs of choice for coexisting aggression against others and against self, an untested prediction. The model makes no prediction with regard to the object of aggression (self or others). Support for this model is considerable, coming from correlational as well as experimental studies of rodents, nonhuman primates, and humans (for reviews, see Brown, Botsis, & van Praag, 1994; Coccaro, 1995; Hillbrand, 2001; Moffitt et al., 1998).

There is a rich literature on the various developmental trajectories that lead to adult AAO (Odgers et al., 2008) and those leading to AAS (Buda & Tsuang, 1990; Leenars, 1991; Stillion & McDowell, 1989). A developmental path leading to comorbid AAS-AAO has been proposed by Shaffer (1974). The suicidal youths he described were characterized by depression as well as violence against others, quick temper, impulsivity, alcohol and drug abuse, and interpersonal difficulties. Future research is needed to determine whether this is the typical pathway leading to coexisting aggression against self and against others.

Dynamic models that explain the comorbidity of AAS and AAO include those of Plutchik and van Praag (1990, 1994), Hillbrand (2001), and Beck (2004). Dynamic approaches examine how various factors influence aggressive behavior. A number of dynamic conceptual frameworks have been developed to explain the coexistence of AAS and AAO. Plutchik and van Praag (1989, 1994) have proposed a two-stage model of countervailing forces. According to this model, aggressive impulses are activated by losses, threats, challenges, and status changes. Whether this activation results in an overt aggressive response is then a function of factors that increase the probability of aggressive behavior (amplifiers) and factors that diminish the likelihood of aggressive behavior (attenuators). Amplifiers include distrust, access to weapons, and a tolerant attitude toward the expression of aggression. Attenuators include timidity, close family ties, appeasement from others. The first stage of the model describes the complex interaction of amplifiers and attenuators that determines the probability of aggressive behavior. The second stage determines the object of the aggression, namely self (suicide, self-injury) or other (interpersonal violence). Factors such as hopelessness, depression, and other psychiatric symptoms increase the probability that the aggression will be directed toward the self. By contrast, factors such as impulsivity, conduct disorder, and psychopathy increase the probability that the aggression will be directed toward others. Individuals possessing both sets of factors (e.g., hopelessness *and* impulsivity) would be at an increased risk of co-occurring aggression against self and against others. Empirical tests of the theory are limited, and Plutchik and van Praag (1990) have refined their theory over time and as a result of studying numerous clinical samples.

Their theory has considerable conceptual appeal. It is least specific, however, with regard to object choice (aggression against self vs. others).

Hillbrand (1992, 1995, 2001) has suggested that AAS and AAO coexist as manifestations of severe behavioral dyscontrol as a function of shared risk factors and shared protective factors. Both forms of aggression share biological, psychological, and social risk factors, as well as protective factors. Biological factors include serotonergic abnormality (Coccaro, 1995) and low serum cholesterol (Hillbrand & Spitz, 1999). Psychological factors include modeling, negative affect, depression, and its components hopelessness and despair, negative as well as positive reinforcement, command hallucinations, impulsivity, substance abuse, and anger (Berkowitz, 1993; Favazza, 1989; Hillbrand, 1995; Plutchik & van Praag, 1990). Social factors include exposure to media reports of violence or suicide, access to firearms, poor social supports, and unemployment (Buda & Tsuang, 1990), as well as cultural factors, though these have received little empirical attention. Victim availability, mood fluctuations, modeling effects, and use of the defense mechanism of projection contribute to object choice (self or other). In support of this theory, Hillbrand has described clinical samples (forensic psychiatric patients) in which the most interpersonally violent individuals were also the most self-destructive ones (Hillbrand, 1992, 1995). This may, however, only be true of forensic psychiatric patients (Nicholls, Brink, Desmarais, Webster, & Martin, 2006).

Beck (1999) has argued that anger, hostility, and violence are the expressions of the same type of cognitive distortions that account for the genesis of depression and suicidal behavior, including the egocentric bias, automatic thoughts, catastrophizing, dichotomous thinking, personalization, and various other attributional biases. He suggests that loss and fear lead to distress and to a change in focus from the self to the "offender," the person perceived to be causing the distress. This in turn leads to feelings of anger and the resultant mobilization for attack. Interpersonal losses, fears, and threats activate thoughts and later feelings that set the stage for aggression. If the focus switches to the "offender," externally directed aggression results; without this switch of focus, self-directed aggression is more likely. Beck does not elaborate on this switch of focus. It is consistent with his thinking to view cognitive faults as determining whether the switch occurs. Although (regrettably) the object of little empirical testing, Beck's model appears promising. Its main contribution is the description that the same cognitive distortions that play a prominent causative role in suicidal behavior exert a similar effect in violence against others.

Conclusion

The overlap between AAS and AAO has clinical and policy implications. The epistemological framework one uses to consider this phenomenon influences how one thinks about it. Dodge (2008) has listed a number of conceptualizations that the general public commonly uses to make sense of violence and that are not helpful: the violent individual as superpredator, as afflicted by a chronic illness, as needing to be quarantined, and so on. By contrast, using the public health ideas of disease prevention within a preventive system of care yields solutions such as injury prevention and public education. For example, Kapusta and colleagues (2007) have shown that changing gun laws in the direction of greater restriction of access has a beneficial impact on homicide rates as well as suicide rates.

The plethora of studies that document the overlap between AAS and AAO highlight the necessity to educate clinicians and researchers that their work needs to be informed by the nature of this pattern of comorbidity. Many clinicians approach risk assessment by focusing on either suicidal behavior or interpersonal violence, when in fact assessing both concurrently is warranted (Hillbrand, 2001; Kleespies, 2009; Kleespies, Deleppo, Gallagher, & Niles, 1999). There is an emerging sense of the need for concurrent assessment in a number of systemic approaches to clinical risk management. For instance, Peter Gutierrez and his colleagues developed a consultation model for suicide prevention in the Veterans Affairs system (Gutierrez et al., 2009). In this sophisticated approach to assessing and managing the suicide risk in veterans, assessment of risk of interpersonal violence (e.g., anger management and impulsivity) figures prominently.

Of all medications tested for their antisuicidal effect, only lithium therapy has shown a clear antisuicidal benefit (Cipriani, Pretty, Hawton, & Geddes, 2005). Lithium also has demonstrated antiaggressive effects (Moeller, Barratt, Dougherty, Schmitz, & Swann, 2001; Sheard, Marini, Bridges, & Wagner, 1976). Future research will hopefully reveal whether these effects extend to comorbid aggression against self and against others.

Many fundamental questions about the overlap between AAS and AAO remain unanswered. Future research should explore whether suicidal individuals who also engage in interpersonal violence differ in any systematic way from suicidal individuals who do not engage in interpersonal violence. Identifying such presumptive factors may point to potential treatment targets. Conversely, it should explore whether violent individuals who are also suicidal differ in any systematic way from violent individuals who are not suicidal.

Commonly given reasons for engaging in AAS as well as AAO relate to emotional regulation, namely counteracting negative affect associated with shame, anger, and so on and creating positive affect, for example, relief from numbness (Prinstein, 2008). Future research should thus also attempt to identify the factors that determine object choice (self or other) in individuals who engage in AAS and AAO. One way to frame this question is within Beck's model. It has two components. Once an individual has experienced loss and fear that cause distress, is there indeed a switch in focus from the self to the "offender"? If so, what factors facilitate the switch in focus from the self to the "offender," and which operate in the opposite direction? It would also be desirable to determine whether, among currently suicidal individuals, comorbid AAO constitutes a risk factor for future suicidal behavior, and whether among violent individuals, comorbid AAS increases the risk of future violence. From the perspective of treatment, it would be good to know whether treating the cognitive distortions that fuel suicidal thinking of individuals with comorbid AAS and AAO decreases their future risk of violence.

References

Anderson, M., Kaufman, J., Simon, T., Barrios, L., Paulozzi, L., Ryan, G.,...School-Associated Violent Deaths Study Group. (2001). School-associated violent deaths in the United States, 1994–1999. *Journal of the American Medical Association, 286*, 2695–2702.

Angst, J., & Clayton, P. J. (1998). Personality, smoking and suicide: A prospective study. *Journal of Affective Disorders, 51*, 55–62.

Apter, A., Kotler, M., Sevy, S., Plutchik, R., Brown, S. L., Foster, H.,...van Praag, H. M. (1991). Correlates of risk of suicide in violent and nonviolent psychiatric patients. *American Journal of Psychiatry, 148*, 883–887.

Arango, V., Huang, Y. Y., Underwood, M. D., & Mann, J. J. (2003). Genetics of the serotonergic system in suicidal behavior. *Journal of Psychiatric Research, 37*, 375–386.

Beautrais, A. (2002). Suicide and serious suicide attempts in youth: A multiple-group comparison study. *American Journal of Psychiatry, 160*, 1093–1099.

Bechara, A., Damasio, A. R., Damasio, H., & Anderson, S. W. (1994). Insensitivity to future consequences following damage to human prefrontal cortex. *Cognition, 50*, 7–15.

Beck, A.T. (1999). *Prisoners of hate: The cognitive basis of anger, hostility, and violence.* New York, NY: Harper Collins.

Berkowitz, N. (1993). *Aggression: Its causes, consequences, and control.* New York, NY: McGraw-Hill.

Bowen, K. (2000). Child abuse and domestic violence in families of children seen for suspected sexual abuse. *Clinical Pediatrics, 39*, 33–40.

Brent, D. A., Bridge, J., Johnson, B. A., & Connolly, J. (1996). Suicidal behavior runs in families: A controlled family study of adolescent suicide victims. *Archives of General Psychiatry, 53*, 1145–1152.

Brent, D. A., Oquendo, M., Birmaher, B., Greenhill, L., Kolko, D., Stanley, B.,...Mann, J. J. (2002a). Peripubertal suicide attempts in offspring of suicide attempters with siblings concordant for suicidal behavior. *American Journal of Psychiatry, 160*, 1486–1493.

Brent, D. A., Oquendo, M., Birmaher, B., Greenhill, L., Kolko, D., Stanley, B.,...Mann, J. J. (2002b). Familial pathways to early-onset suicide attempt: Risk for suicidal behavior in offspring of mood-disordered suicide attempters. *Archives of General Psychiatry, 59*, 801–807.

Brock, A., & Griffiths, C. (2003). Trends in suicide by method in England and Wales, 1979 to 2001. *Health Statistics Quarterly, 20*, 7–18.

Brodsky, B. S., Oquendo, M., Ellis, S. P., Haas, G. L., Malone, K. M., & Mann, J. J. (2001). The relationship of childhood abuse to impulsivity and suicidal behavior in adults with major depression. *American Journal of Psychiatry, 158*, 1871–1877.

Brown, S. L., Botsis, A., & van Praag, H. M. (1994). Serotonin and aggression. In M. Hillbrand & N. J. Pallone (Eds.), *The psychobiology of aggression* (pp. 27–40). Binghamton, NY: Haworth Press.

Buda, M., & Tsuang, M. T. (1990). The epidemiology of suicide: Implications for clinical practice. In S. J. Blumenthal, & D. J. Kupfer (Eds.), *Suicide over the life cycle* (pp. 17–37). Washington, DC: American Psychiatric Press.

Castle, K., Duberstein, P. R., Meldrum, S., Conner, K. R., & Conwell, Y. (2004). Risk factors for suicide in blacks and whites: An analysis of data from the 1993 national mortality followback survey. *American Journal of Psychiatry, 161*, 452–458.

Cipriani, A., Pretty, H., Hawton, K., & Geddes, J. R. (2005). Lithium in the prevention of suicidal behavior and all-cause mortality in patients with mood disorders: A systematic review of randomized trials. *American Journal of Psychiatry, 162*, 1805–1819.

Coccaro, E. F. (1995, January-February). The biology of aggression. *Scientific American*, pp. 38–47.

Coccaro, E. F., Siever, L. J., Klar, H. M., Maurer, G., Cochrane, K., Cooper, T. B.,...Davis, K. L. (1989). Serotonergic studies in patients with affective and personality disorders. *Archives of General Psychiatry, 46,* 587–599.

Coid, J. (1983). The epidemiology of abnormal homicide and murder followed by suicide. *Psychological Medicine, 13,* 855–860.

Conner, K. R., Cox, C., Duberstein, P. R., Tian, L., Nisbet, P. A., & Conwell, Y. (2001). Violence, alcohol, and completed suicide: A case-control study. *American Journal of Psychiatry, 158,* 1701–1705.

Conner, K. R., Duberstein, P. R., & Conwell, Y. (2000). Domestic violence, separation, and suicide in young men with early onset alcoholism: Re-analyses of Murphy's data. *Suicide and Life-Threatening Behavior, 30,* 354–359.

Craddock, N., & Jones, I. (1999). Genetics of bipolar disorder. *Journal of Medical Genetics, 36,* 585–594.

Daly, M., & Wilson, M. (1988). *Homicide.* New York, NY: Aldine DeGruyter.

Damasio, H., Grabowski, T., Frank, R., Galaburda, A. M., & Damasio, A. R. (1994). The return of Phineas Gage: Clues about the brain from the skull of a famous patient. *Science, 264,* 1102–1105.

De Hert, M., McKenzie, K., & Peuskens, J. (2001). Risk factors in suicide in young people suffering from schizophrenia: A long-term follow-up study. *Schizophrenia Research, 47,* 127–134.

Dervic, K., Oquendo, M. A., Grunebaum, M. F., Ellis, S., Burke, A. K., & Mann, J. J. (2004). Religious affiliation and suicide attempt. *American Journal of Psychiatry, 161,* 2303–2308.

Dietz, P. E. (1986). Mass, serial and sensational homicides. *Bulletin of the New York Academy of Medicine, 62,* 477–491.

Dodge, K. A. (2008). Framing public policy and prevention of chronic violence in American youths. *American Psychologist, 63,* 573–590.

Elliott, M., Browne, K., & Kilcoyne, J. (1995). Child sexual abuse prevention: What offenders tell us. *Child Abuse and Neglect, 19,* 579–594.

Eslinger, P. J., & Damasio, A. R. (1985). Severe disturbance of higher cognition after bilateral frontal lobe ablation: Patient EVR. *Neurology, 35,* 1731–1741.

Favazza, A. (1989). Why patients mutilate themselves. *Hospital and Community Psychiatry, 40,* 137–145.

Fingerhut, L. A., & Kleinman, J. C. (1990). International and interstate comparisons of homicide among young males. *Journal of the American Medical Association, 263,* 3292–3295.

Flannery, D. J., Singer, M. I., & Wester, K. (2001). Violence exposure, psychological trauma, and suicide risk in a community sample of dangerously violent adolescents. *Journal of the American Academy of Child and Adolescent Psychiatry, 40,* 435–442.

Gladstone, G., Parker, G., Wilhelm, K., Mitchell, P., & Austin, M. P. (1999). Characteristics of depressed patients who report childhood sexual abuse. *American Journal of Psychiatry, 156,* 431–437.

Goldston, D. B., Daniel, S. S., Erkanli, A., Reboussin, B. A., Mayfield, A., Frazier, P. H., & Treadway, S. L. (2009). Psychiatric diagnoses as contemporary risk factors for suicide attempts among adolescents and young adults: Developmental changes. *Journal of Consulting and Clinical Psychology, 77,* 281–290.

Gutierrez, P. M., Brenner, L. A., Olson-Madden, J. H., Breshears, R. E., Homaifar, B. Y., Betthauser, L. M.,...Adler, L. E. (2009). Consultation as a means of veteran suicide prevention. *Professional Psychology: Research and Practice, 40,* 586–592.

Hazani, M. (1993). Sacrificial immortality: Towards a theory of suicidal terrorism and related phenomena. *Psychoanalytic Study of Society, 19,* 441–442.

Hempel, A. G., Meloy, J. R., & Richards, T.C. (1999). Offender and offense characteristics of a nonrandom sample of mass murderers. *Journal of the American Academy of Psychiatry and Law, 27,* 213–225.

Hettema, J. M., Neale, M. C., & Kendler, K. S. (2001). A review and meta-analysis of the genetic epidemiology of anxiety disorders. *American Journal of Psychiatry, 158,* 1568–1578.

Higley, J. D., Thompson, W. W., Champoux, M., Goldman, D., Hasert, M. F., Kraemer, G. W.,...Linnoila, M. (1993). Paternal and maternal genetic and environmental contributions to cerebrospinal fluid monoamine metabolites in rhesus monkeys. *Archives of General Psychiatry, 50,* 615–623.

Hillbrand, M. (1992). Self-directed and other-directed aggressive behavior in a forensic sample. *Suicide and Life-Threatening Behavior, 22,* 333–340.

Hillbrand, M. (1995). Aggression against self and aggression against others in violent psychiatric patients. *Journal of Consulting and Clinical Psychology, 63,* 668–671.

Hillbrand, M. (2001). Homicide-suicide and other forms of co-occurring aggression against self and against others. *Professional Psychology: Research and Practice, 32,* 626–635.

Hillbrand, M. (2006). Adolescent homicide-suicide. *Forensische Psychiatrie und Psychotherapie Werkstattschriften, 3,* 3–16.

Hillbrand, M., & Spitz, R. T. (1999). Cholesterol and aggression. *Aggression and Violent Behavior, 4,* 359–370.

Hiss, J., & Kahana, T. (1988). Suicide bombers in Israel. *American Journal of Forensic Medicine and Pathology, 19,* 63–66.

Hollander, E., & Rosen, J. (2000). Impulsivity. *Journal of Psychopharmacology, 14,* 39–44.

Johnson, B. A., Brent, D. A., Bridge, J., & Connolly, J. (1998). The familial aggregation of adolescent suicide attempts. *Acta Psychiatrica Scandinavica, 97,* 18–24.

Jollant, F., Bellivier, F., Leboyer, M., Astruc, B., Torres, S., Verdier, R.,...Courtier, P. (2005). Impaired decision making in suicide attempters. *American Journal of Psychiatry, 162,* 304–310.

Kapusta, N. D., Etzersdorfer, E., Krall, C., & Sonneck, G. (2007). Firearm legislation reform in the European Union: Impact on firearm availability, firearm suicide, and homicide rates in Austria. *British Journal of Psychiatry, 191,* 253–257.

Kennedy, D. B., Homant, R. J., & Hupp, R. T. (1998). Suicide by cop. *Federal Bureau of Investigation Law Enforcement Bulletin, 67,* 21–27.

Kleespies, P. M. (2009). *Behavioral emergencies: An evidence-based resource for evaluating and managing risk of suicide, violence, and victimization.* Washington, DC: American Psychological Association Press.

Kleespies, P. M., Deleppo, J. D., Gallagher, P. L., & Niles, B. L. (1999). Managing suicidal emergencies: Recommendations for the practitioner. *Professional Psychology: Research and Practice, 30,* 454–463.

Leenars, A. A. (1991). *Life span perspectives of suicide.* New York, NY: Plenum.

Mann, J. J., Bortinger, J., Oquendo, M. A., Currier, D., Li, S., & Brent, D. A. (2005). Family history of suicidal behavior and mood disorders in probands with mood disorders. *American Journal of Psychiatry, 162,* 1672–1679.

Mann, J. J., Brent, D. A., & Arango, V. (2001). The neurobiology and genetics of suicide and attempted suicide: A focus on the serotonergic system. *Neuropsychopharmacology, 24,* 467–477.

Maris, R. W. (1992). Overview of the study of suicide assessment and prediction. In R. W. Maris (Ed.), *Assessment and prediction of suicide* (pp. 3–22). New York, NY: Guilford Press.

Marzuk, P. M., Nock, M. K., Leon, A. C., Portera, L., & Tardiff, K. (2002). Suicide among New York City police officers, 1977–1996. *American Journal of Psychiatry, 159,* 2069–2071.

Marzuk, P. M., Tardiff, K., & Hirsch, C. S. (1992). The epidemiology of murder-suicide. *Journal of the American Medical Association, 267,* 3179–3183.

Merrari, A. (2008, August). *The psychology of suicide terrorism.* Paper presented at the Annual Convention of the American Psychological Association, Boston, MA.

Milroy, C. M. (1993). Homicide followed by suicide (dyadic death) in Yorkshire and Humberside. *Medical Science and Law, 33,* 167–171.

Moeller, F. G., Barratt, E. S., Dougherty, D. M., Schmitz, J. M., & Swann, A. C. (2001). Psychiatric aspects of impulsivity. *American Journal of Psychiatry, 158,* 1783–1793.

Moffitt, T. E., Brammer, G. L., Caspi, A., Fawcett, J. P., Raleigh, M., Yuwiler, A., & Silva, P. (1998). Whole blood serotonin relates to violence in an epidemiological study. *Biological Psychiatry, 43,* 446–457.

Nicholls, T. L., Brink, J., Desmarais, S. L., Webster, C. D., & Martin, M. L. (2006). The Short-Term Assessment of Risk and Treatability (START): A prospective validation study in a forensic psychiatric sample. *Assessment, 13,* 313–327.

Nock, M. K., & Kessler, R. C. (2006). Prevalence of and risk factors for suicide attempts versus suicide gestures: Analysis of the National Comorbidity Survey. *Journal of Abnormal Psychology, 115,* 616–623

Odgers, C. L., Moffitt, T. E., Broadbent, J. M., Dickson, N., Hancox, R. J., Harrington, H., ... Caspi, A. (2008). Female and male antisocial trajectories: From childhood origins to adult outcomes. *Development and Psychopathology, 20,* 673–716.

Oquendo, M. A., Friend, J. M., Halbertstam, B., Brodsky, B. S., Burke, A. K., Grunebaum, M. F., ... Mann, J. J. (2003). Association of comorbid posttraumatic stress disorder and major depression with greater risk for suicidal behavior. *American Journal of Psychiatry, 160,* 580–582.

Oquendo, M. A., Galfalvy, H., Russo, S., Ellis, S. P., Grunebaum, M. F., Burke, A., & Mann, J. J. (2004). Prospective study of clinical predictors of suicidal acts after a major depressive episode in patients with major depressive disorder or bipolar disorder. *American Journal of Psychiatry, 161,* 1433–1441.

Parent, R. B. (1998). Suicide by cop: Victim-precipitated homicide. *Police Chief, 65,* 111–114.

Plutchik, R., & van Praag, H. M. (1989). The measurement of suicidality, aggressivity and impulsivity. *Progress in Neuro-Psychopharmacology and Biological Psychiatry, 13,* 23–34.

Plutchik, R., & van Praag, H. M. (1990). Psychosocial correlates of suicide and violence risk. In H. M. van Praag, R. Plutchik, & A. Apter (Eds.), *Violence and suicidality: Perspectives in clinical and psychobiological research* (pp. 37–65). New York, NY: Brunner/Mazel.

Plutchik, M., & van Praag, H. M. (1994). Suicide risk: Amplifiers and attenuators. In M. Hillbrand & N. J. Pallone (Eds.), *The psychobiology of aggression* (pp. 173–186). Binghamton, NY: Haworth Press.

Powell, V., Barber, C. W., Hedegaard, H., Hempstead, K., Hull-Jilly, D., Shen, X., ... Weis, M. A. (2006). Using NVDRS data for suicide prevention: Promising practices in seven states. *Injury Prevention, 12,* ii28–ii32.

Prinstein, M. J. (2008). Introduction to the special section on suicide and nonsuicidal self-injury: A review of unique challenges and important directions for self-injury science. *Journal of Consulting and Clinical Psychology, 76,* 1–8.

Reviere, S. L., Battle, J., Farber, E. W., & Kaslow, N. J. (2003). Psychotic-spectrum symptoms, trauma, and posttraumatic stress disorder among suicidal inner-city women. *Psychiatric Services, 54,* 1290–1292.

Romans, S. E., Martin, J. L., Anderson, J. C., O'Shea, M. L., & Mullen, P. E. (1995). Factors that mediate between child sexual abuse and adult psychological outcome. *Psychological Medicine, 25,* 127–142.

Roy, A. (2001). Characteristics of cocaine-dependent patients who attempt suicide. *American Journal of Psychiatry, 158,* 1215–1219.

Roy, A., Segal, N. L., Centerwall, B. S., & Robinette, C. D. (1991). Suicide in twins. *Archives of General Psychiatry, 48,* 29–32.

Shaffer, D. (1974). Suicide in childhood and adolescence. *Journal of Child Psychology and Psychiatry, 15,* 275–291.

Sheard, M. H., Marini, J. L., Bridges, C. I., & Wagner, E. (1976). The effect of lithium on impulsive aggressive behavior in man. *American Journal of Psychiatry, 133,* 1409–1413

Stillion, J. M., & McDowell, E. E. (1989). *Suicide across the life span.* Bristol, PA: Tayor & Francis.

Taylor, M., & Ryan, H. (1988). Fanaticism, political suicide and terrorism. *Terrorism, 11,* 91–111.

Van Zandt, C. R. (1993). Suicide by cop. *Police Chief, 7,* 24–30.

Verona, E., Hicks, B. M., & Patrick, C. J. (2005). Psychopathy and suicidality in female offenders: Mediating influences of personality and abuse. *Journal of Consulting and Clinical Psychology, 73,* 1065–1073.

Verona, E., Sachs-Ericsson, N., & Joiner, T. E. (2004). Suicide attempts associated with externalizing psychopathology in an epidemiological sample. *American Journal of Psychiatry, 161,* 444–451.

Vossekuil, B., Fein, R. A., Reddy, M., & Modzeleski, W. (2004). *The final report and findings of the Safe School Initiative: Implications for the prevention of school attacks in the United States.* Retrieved August 2013, from http://www2.ed.gov/admins/lead/safety/preventingattacksreport.pdf. Washington, DC: Government Printing Office.

Weiss, B., Dodge, K. A., & Bates, J. E. (1992). Some consequences of early harsh discipline: Child aggression and a maladaptive social information processing style. *Child Development, 63,* 1321–1335.

World Health Organization World Mental Health Survey Consortium. (2004). Prevalence, severity, and unmet need for treatment of mental disorders in the World Health Organization World Mental Health Surveys. *Journal of the American Medical Association, 291*, 2581–2590.

Wolfgang, M. (1959). Suicide by means of victim-precipitated homicide. *Journal of Clinical and Experimental Psychopathology, 20*, 335–349.

Yen, S., Pagano, M. E., Shea, M. T., Grilo, C. M., Gunderson, J. G., Skodol, A. E.,... Zanarini, M. C. (2005). Recent life events preceding suicide attempts in a personality disorder sample: Findings from the collaborative longitudinal personality disorders study. *Journal of Consulting and Clinical Psychology, 73*, 99–105.

Suicide Terrorism

Ellen Townsend

Abstract

Here the key characteristics of suicide terrorists are discussed. The discussion mainly focuses on the results of empirical studies that have examined suicide terrorism with human participants who have been involved with suicide attacking in some way. The characteristics of suicide terrorists are compared with those of suicidal behavior more generally. Suicide terrorists are very different from those engaging in other suicidal behaviors and are unlikely to be suicidal. Based on these data, I suggest that it is currently not possible to identify those at risk of becoming a suicide attacker. Finally, I discuss some concrete ways in which to move forward with research on suicide terrorism, including the use of specific theories from social psychology (self-determination theory and the theory of planned behavior) and suicidology (cry of pain theory), as well as specific research techniques (e.g., the psychological autopsy).

Key Words: suicide terrorism, suicide bombing, suicide attacks, risk factors, psychology

In a sense, a discussion of suicide terrorism is somewhat out of place in a handbook on suicide. As Grimland et al. (2006) put it (p.116), "Suicide bombing looks like suicide, but in important aspects it is incomparable with suicide." Elsewhere I have argued that we should not even consider suicide terrorists to be a subgroup of the suicide population (Townsend, 2007). Nonetheless, it is possible that the methods used by suicidologists could be extremely useful in examining suicide bombing behavior in order to further our understanding of the factors that coalesce to produce a person who is willing to kill himself or herself in order to kill and maim others. It also is important to highlight the numerous ways in which suicide terrorism appears to differ from other suicide acts.

In this chapter I shall review current theoretical and empirical work on suicide terrorism/suicide bombing. This will not be an exhaustive review, as other authors have already provided comprehensive and insightful reviews of this work (e.g., Grimland,

Apter & Kerkoff, 2006; Post et al., 2009; Silke, 2003). Here, I focus on the issues that seem most pertinent in relation to the potential suicidality of the act of suicide terrorism. In the main I draw upon empirical studies that have attempted to examine suicide terrorist behavior. I examine what characterizes individuals who commit such acts. I then extend my previously published argument that suicide terrorists cannot, on the basis of current evidence, be considered to be suicidal (Townsend, 2007). Next, I discuss whether there are currently any effective methods for identifying those at risk. Finally, I outline important directions for future research.

Most of the scant evidence pertaining to suicide terrorism is concerned with acts carried out in Palestine or by Islamic fundamentalists around the world. Hence, the focus of this chapter is on this type of suicide attack (though there is likely to be some overlap with other types of suicide terrorism). Moreover, this focus is justified given that the attention of scholars around the globe has understandably turned to uncovering the psychology of Islamic fundamentalist groups (Post et al., 2009; Victoroff, 2005).

What Characterizes Suicide Terrorists? Theoretical and Empirical Perspectives

There are few empirical studies of suicide terrorism. This is perhaps understandable, given the practical difficulties involved with studying the behavior of such individuals. To my knowledge (at the time of writing), there are just seven published empirical studies that examine suicide terrorism in a direct way with human participants involved with suicide terrorist activity (Araj, 2008; Berko, 2007; Fields, Elbedour, & Hein, 2002; Hassan, 2001; Meloy, 2004; Post, Sprinzak, & Denny, 2003; Schbley, 2003). Only four of these seven studies appear in peer-reviewed journals (Araj, 2008; Meloy, 2004; Post et al., 2003; Schbley, 2003). A brief description of each of these empirical studies follows. Where available, precise information is given about the number of participants in each study, as well as their age/gender.

Araj (2008). Here 88 interviews (lasting on average for more than 90 minutes) were conducted in 2006. Forty-five interviewees were senior leaders of influential Palestinian political organizations. Interviews of close relatives and friends to 43 suicide bombers were conducted (suicide bombers were randomly selected from a pool of 173 suicide bombings that had taken place between 2000 and 2005). At least four close relatives of each of the 43 suicide bombers were interviewed.

Berko (2007). This researcher interviewed failed suicide bombers in prison over a number of years as part of her PhD thesis. She recounts the experiences of a number of would-be male and female suicide bombers. She also interviewed individuals who dispatched suicide bombers.

Meloy (2004). In this case study, information about Mohamed Atta (a 9/11/2001 suicide attacker) was presented. Data gathered from family and friends were used. The paper also included information about physical evidence surrounding the act, archival data from public and private records, and indirect assessment of personality using the Revised NEO Personality Inventory (Costa & McCrae, 2002).

Schbley (2003). Here 15 religious terrorists were interviewed and 341 potential suicide terrorists, recruited opportunistically from Hizbullah

members attending a parade on the Day of Jerusalem (December 14, 2001), answered a questionnaire.

Post, Sprinzak, and Denny (2003). In this study, 35 incarcerated Middle Eastern terrorists (21 from Islamic Jihad and Hizbullah, 14 secular terrorists from Fatah) took part in a semistructured interview.

Fields, Elbour, and Hein (2002). First, over 1,000 children and adolescents aged 6–16 years from Northern Ireland, Israel, the West Bank, Gaza, Lebanon, and South Africa were recruited over a 25-year period. These recruits completed psychometric tests on personality and violence (among other variables such as the Thematic Apperception Test), which were then used to develop a protocol for postmortem interviews with the families and friends of suicide terrorists. Secondly, interviews were conducted with families and friends of Palestinian suicide terrorists who carried out their attacks between 1993 and 1996. The terrorists were all male and aged 19–25 years at death. Nine control subjects were selected by asking the families of the dead terrorists to nominate friends possessing a similar background and characteristics to their dead relative. Four family members and two male friends of each suicide terrorist and control were interviewed. The postmortem evaluation included assessment of personality type, psychological state, and life experiences. Measures included Coopersmith's scale of self-esteem and the Achenbach Child Behavior Checklist.

Hassan (2001). Nearly 250 people in militant Palestinian camps in Gaza were interviewed. The sample included suicide terrorist volunteers who were unable to complete their mission, families of dead suicide terrorists, and the men who trained the terrorists. Interviews were conducted between 1996 and 1999. Participants ranged in age from 18 to 38 years.

In the sections that follow empirical evidence and current theoretical perspectives are interwoven in order to elucidate what characterizes the suicide bomber/suicide terrorist. As noted earlier, the factors focused on here are those that may have the most potential overlap with other suicides.

Motivations for Suicide Terrorism

It is probably not possible to describe a "typical" suicide terrorist (Silke, 2003). However, it does seem that suicide cells (groups who organize and carry out suicide attacks) generally prey on young, unattached men (Atran, 2003; Merari, 2005) and that these young men have deeply held religious beliefs in common (Hassan, 2001).

RELIGIOUS BELIEFS

It has been suggested that religious beliefs are absolutely crucial in understanding motivations for suicide attacks (Orbach, 2004; Salib, 2003). It is important to note here that Islam forbids suicide—it is simply not permitted under any situation (Abdel-Khalek, 2004; Taylor & Ryan, 1988). A terrorist interviewed in one empirical study became extremely angry when the interviewer posed a question about suicide saying, "This is not suicide. Suicide is selfish; it is weak. This is *istishad* [martyrdom or self-sacrifice in the service of Allah]" (Post et al., 2003, p. 179).

Hassan (2001) interviewed nearly 250 individuals from various militant Palestinian camps in Gaza between 1996 and 1999, and concluded that these suicide terrorists are extremely religious. Moreover, they consider their actions to be sanctioned by Islam. One Muslim psychologist rejects the idea that suicide terrorism involves suicide entirely. Instead, the act is viewed as one of martyrdom, based on the Islamic principles of Jihad (holy war), which is considered as legal behavior (Abdel-Khalek, 2004). Research on suicide terrorist groups suggests that members are indoctrinated into believing in their own immortality—they are completely convinced of this (Hassan, 2001; Orbach, 2004). They also believe that the paradise into which they will ascend manifests itself as an actual corporal presence. Such belief in gaining entrance to such an afterlife is supported by evidence from an interview with a 27-year-old man selected for a suicide attack. When asked how he felt about being selected, he replied, "by pressing the detonator, you can immediately open the door to paradise—it is the shortest path to heaven" (Hassan, 2001, ¶6). Moreover, Hassan's interview with an Imam affiliated with Hamas resonates with these beliefs. The Imam said:

> ...the first drop of blood shed by a martyr during jihad washes away his sins instantaneously. On the Day of Resurrection, he can intercede for seventy of his nearest and dearest to enter heaven; and he will have at his disposal seventy-two houris, the beautiful virgins of Paradise. (Hassan, 2001, ¶25)

More evidence supporting the importance of religious beliefs comes from postmortem interviews with the families and friends of deceased suicide terrorists. In one study, eight of the nine terrorists were described by their significant others as being very religious (Fields et al., 2002). Further, Berko (2007) notes that her research underlines the important role that religion plays in preparing a suicide bomber for an attack. On the basis of a content analysis of texts about suicide terrorism, Kimhi and Even (2004) suggest that a religious prototype of suicide terrorism exists. And, worryingly, it is thought that religious fundamentalist suicide terrorists may pose the greatest danger to society (Post et al., 2003).

Such findings clearly highlight the role of religious beliefs in suicide terrorism. However, others claim that not all Islamic suicide terrorism is religiously motivated and that political forces are more important in the development of suicide terrorism (Araj, 2008; Merari, 1998, 2005; Pape, 2003, 2005; Sprinzak, 2000). Of course, a range of motivations for suicide terrorism exist, and these have been discussed by Moghadam (2003), who proposed a two-phase model of suicide terrorism encompassing individual and organizational goals.

VENGEANCE

Another motivation that may be prominent in determining the willingness of certain individuals to act as suicide terrorists is vengeance, namely, "getting back" at someone (Beck, 2002; Moghadam, 2003; Rosenberger, 2003), especially at those in power/authority (Pape, 2003). Rosenberger (2003) argues that the idea of vengeance in suicide terrorism is crucial to understanding the suicide attacker, and Abdel-Khalek (2004) suggests that vengeance is a central feature of martyrdom in relation to the "Palestinian cause."

Moreover, personal revenge is a common motivation for a suicide mission (Fields et al., 2002; Kushner, 1996; Moghadam, 2003). It appears that terrorists are likely to have had a relative or close friend who they believe has been wronged, or even killed, by the "perceived enemy," and so they join terrorist organizations in an extremely vengeful frame of mind (Kushner, 1996). Fields et al. (2002) report that five of the nine suicide terrorists in their case-controlled postmortem study had been injured as a result of the *intifada* in Gaza. Eight of these participants had been imprisoned and tortured during this time, and five the terrorists' families were purported to have been beaten and humiliated by soldiers. Seven families of the deceased suicide terrorists felt that a key motivation for the terrorist had been a direct response to the perceived injustices perpetrated by Israeli occupation.

Araj's (2008) interviewees appeared to agree that most instances of suicide terrorism are a direct response to harsh state repression and that such attacks represent an attempt to obtain revenge for acts carried out by Israelis. One bomber's suicide note began:

> Who does not feel outrage and is not eager for revenge when participating in funerals for fallen martyrs, especially collective funerals in Nablus.... I marched in their funerals, chanted with the angry crowds, deeply eager for revenge but didn't know how. (p. 297)

The Secretary-General of the Palestinian People's Party, Bussam al-Salhee, suggests that the killing of Israeli civilians via suicide bombing was a direct response to the deaths of Palestinian civilians (Araj, 2008).

MURDEROUS INTENT

Suicide terrorists are murderers: Their own suicide act deliberately takes the life of another, or many others. The primary intention of the act carried out is murder (in order to elicit terror), rather than suicide. Indeed, suicide in this instance can actually be viewed as a "by-product" of the attack (B. C. B. Park, personal communication, November 2, 2005). Indeed, in most suicides there is an absence of murderous intent and this factor separates suicide terrorists from others who take their own life. I have previously discussed the fact that while other kinds of murder-suicide do occur, these types of suicides differ significantly from other suicides on a number of dimensions (see Townsend, 2007).

Key Psychological Factors

The message that recurs repeatedly in the writings of researchers and theorists in relation to the psychology of suicide bombing is that there *is no* specific psychology. Indeed, what appears to characterize a suicide bomber is his or her normality (Silke, 2003). Moreover, it has been suggested that attempts to psychologically profile suicide bombers have not been successful (Grimland, Apter, & Kerkof, 2006). However, it is important to stress—in line with Victoroff's assertion (2005)—that the research suggesting that it is impossible to use individual factors to identify those at risk of becoming a terrorist is based on research which is methodologically inadequate in important respects (e.g., small sample sizes, lack of control groups, lack of hypothesis testing) (Jones, 2008). Therefore, it is necessary to explore a range of variables that may be relevant to characterizing the suicide bomber in psychological terms.

HOPE

It has been suggested that, owing to their strong belief in their cause and the rewards believed to be awaiting them in heaven, suicide terrorists goes to their death feeling hopeful rather than hopeless. They strongly believe that their death will bring about certain gains, such as achieving entrance to an afterlife, being an inspiration to others and thus advancing their cause, and delivering others from suffering (Hassan, 2001; Williams, 1997). Atran (2003, p. 1537) claims that suicide terrorists do not demonstrate hopelessness or a sense of "nothing to lose." Indeed, in a postmortem study of suicide bombers, interviews with family members revealed that they believed that the bomber was unafraid of death, owing to the fact that he expected to gain entrance to paradise following his martyrdom act (Fields et al., 2002).

AGGRESSION AND ANGER

Anger and aggression seem to be important factors in suicide attacks (Atran, 2003). The available research suggests that the majority of suicide terrorists are likely to have been skillfully manipulated into feeling the way they do largely as a result of intragroup and intergroup processes fueled by religious beliefs (Atran, 2003; Beck, 2002; Hassan, 2001; Post et al., 2003; Salib, 2003). Additionally, suicide terrorists may feel angry because of the perceived state repression they have experienced (Araj, 2008).

MENTAL ILLNESS

Many researchers have suggested that suicide terrorists are generally not suffering with mental illness (e.g., Atran, 2003; Post et al., 2009; Silke, 2003). In fact, Atran (2003) suggests that suicide terrorists are "nonpathological" and that, rather, the problem faced by researchers is to determine why so many of these individuals are recruited in order to carry out the wishes of suicide terrorist organizations. Whether the incidence of mental illness in suicide terrorists is higher than in the general population is currently not known (Lamberg, 1997). However, current knowledge suggests that suicide terrorists do not carry out their terrorist acts as a result of mental illness (Bond, 2004; Colvard, 2002; Gordon, 2002; Hassan, 2001; Merari, 2005; Williams, 1997).

GROUP PROCESSES, INDOCTRINATION, AND COLLECTIVISM

The resolution to "act" as a suicide attacker is not decided upon or planned in isolation (Atran, 2003;

Burdman, 2003; Moghadam, 2003; Rosenberger, 2003; Volkan, 2002). Instead, such terrorists are carefully groomed and coached into carrying out the attack. Atran (2003, p. 1536) suggests that "No instances of religious or political suicide terrorism stem from lone actions of cowering or unstable bombers." Given that the decision to operationalize a suicide terrorist is almost always made by others (Poland, 2002), it is likely that a good proportion of the variance in suicide terrorist behavior is explained by group and collectivist processes (Colvard, 2002; Post et al., 2009).

Atran (2003) claims that suicide attacks are driven by a "sense of obligation" in response to authority, rather than by an individual's murderous intent per se. He draws a comparison with Milgram's famous obedience to authority experiments in which, given the right circumstances, ordinary individuals obey orders and perform actions that are detrimental to others (Milgram, 1974). Could it be that the murderous intent discussed earlier does not exist at the level of the individual, but rather in relation to those in authority organizing the suicide attacks (Merari, 1998, 2005; Rosenberger, 2003)? Rosenberger (2003) argues that "The leaders, in fact, are murdering their suicide bombers pure and simple" (p. 17). This sentiment resonates with the findings from Berko's (2007) interview study in which failed suicide bombers and the leaders of suicide cells were interviewed. It was clear in a number of cases that the potential suicide bomber did not want to carry out the act but had been forced to do it by his or her dispatchers. However, it is extremely doubtful that any indoctrination experienced by a suicide attacker means that the attacker lacks murderous intent altogether.

Peer influence is highlighted as a key reason for joining a terrorist group. Interviews with 35 incarcerated Middle Eastern terrorists revealed that they perceived that everybody else was joining up so they felt they should join, too (Post et al., 2003). Atran (2003, p. 1537) suggests that "loyalty to [an] intimate cohort of peers, which recruiting organizations often promote through religious communion," is key to understanding suicide terrorism. A charismatic leader devises meticulous plans, which are often carried out in groups or cells of about three to six individuals, and carefully leads the attacker to their death (Atran, 2003; Poland, 2002). The individual is carefully selected and prepared for suicide attacks, and in some cases extreme coercive measures are used (Post et al., 2003; Silke, 2003).

Crucially, group and individual processes interact in order to produce a suicide attacker. An individual selected for a suicide terrorism mission is commonly subjected to a process of indoctrination to strengthen the motivation for carrying out the attack and to prevent this motivation from waning. Typically, the process of indoctrination takes place in a number of stages—with each stage relying on particular cognitive, emotional, and social psychological processes. Certain specific personal characteristics may increase the likelihood of an individual's susceptibility to these processes, including religious or political values that resonate strongly with the indoctrinating organization (Baron, 2000). For example, in suicide terrorism, indoctrination may be driven by religious beliefs (e.g., the reward of martyrs in the afterlife) or nationalist themes (e.g., the humiliation of Palestine by Israel) (Merari, 2005). A member of Hamas has explained the "preparation" of a suicide terrorist as follows (Hassan, 2001):

> We focus his attention on Paradise, on being in the presence of Allah, on meeting the Prophet Muhammad, on interceding for his loved ones so that they, too, can be saved from the agonies of Hell, on the houris and on fighting the Israeli occupation and removing it. (¶30)

Two "assistants" stay with the potential suicide terrorist at all times in the week before an attack and they report any wavering or doubts to a senior member of the group who may be called in to provide inspiration and support (Hassan, 2001). However, Silke (2003) notes that it is "increasingly recognized that it is a mistake to view suicide bombers as brainwashed pawns" (p. 94). Disturbingly, there appears to be a surfeit of would-be recruits to suicide cells who are clamoring at the doors of those who dispatch suicide attackers to get involved (Hassan, 2001). Having said this, Berko's (2007) interviews suggest that there also are a good number of suicide bombers who are being forced into carrying out the act.

In interviews, would-be terrorists have described how their membership of the terrorist group importantly combined their personal identity with the collective identity and goals of the group (Post et al., 2003). Volkan (2002) suggests that vulnerabilities in a person's identity may permit the imposition of a wider group identity. It has been suggested that suicide attackers may suffer from low self-esteem, which increases vulnerability in relation to powerful peer influences and reactions to those in authority (Israeli, 1997). However, in a roughly case-controlled postmortem interview study of a small group of suicide terrorists, no evidence of lowered self-esteem was uncovered (Fields et al., 2002). Post et al. (2003) note, on the basis of interviews with incarcerated terrorists, that the would-be bombers were unable to differentiate their own goals from the goals of the group. They suggest that "An overarching sense of the collective consumes the individual" (p. 176).

To summarize, the available evidence suggests that an appreciation of the group processes in indoctrinating organizations is crucial in the understanding of suicide terrorism (Atran, 2003; Merari, 1998, 2005; Moghadam, 2003; Schbley, 2003). Some authors have argued that these processes are likely to be more important in determining suicide attacks than religious beliefs (e.g., Merari, 1998, 2005). However, a psychometric study administered opportunistically to over 300 potential suicide terrorists (members of Hizbullah attending a parade to celebrate the Day of Jerusalem) demonstrated that respondents who were high school educated, had the highest level of religious training, and the highest levels of religiosity were most willing to become suicide attackers (Schbley, 2003).

ALTRUISM

Some authors have suggested that suicide terrorists should be considered as a type of "altruistic suicide" (suicide based on sacrificing oneself for the good of others) (Leenaars & Wenckstern, 2004; Stack, 2004). It is perhaps plausible to suggest that a number of suicide bombers go to their death in order to emancipate their homeland (Araj, 2008) or to prevent shame and stigma from blighting their family because of their perceived immoral behavior (Berko, 2007).

PERSONALITY TRAITS

Is it possible that there are certain personality traits which may help to seed the foundations of suicide terrorism? Lachkar's (2002) theory outlines the personality characteristics of suicide terrorists based on a psychoanalytic approach in which the role of parenting—particularly in relation to the terrorist's relationship with his or her father is viewed as critical. Dysfunctional parenting is thought to contribute to the development of borderline-type personality traits in the suicide attacker. She argues that this leads to suicide cells developing gang-like group dynamics, such that the terrorist cell becomes enmeshed with the terrorist's sense of identity. These claims are not, however, backed up with empirical

evidence, though this claim is supported by the work of Post et al. (2003), who report that membership of terrorist groups for 35 incarcerated Middle Eastern terrorists involved the perceived fusion of an individual's identity with the group identity.

Thus, a possible risk factor for acting as a suicide terrorist exists at the level of individual personality. However, some insist that there is no such thing as a suicide terrorist personality type and claim that suicide terrorists come from a variety of backgrounds with diverse personalities (Hassan, 2001; Schbley, 2003; Silke, 2003; Victoroff, 2005). However, as noted earlier, it is possible that certain personal characteristics may lead certain individuals to be more susceptible to indoctrination techniques than others (Baron, 2000).

Are Suicide Terrorists Really Suicidal?

Having discussed the empirical and theoretical perspectives concerning some of the key characteristics of suicide terrorism, it is necessary now to determine whether suicide terrorists are, in fact, suicidal. In the sections that follow, the issues which have emerged repeatedly in the suicide terrorism literature (discussed earlier) are discussed in relation to existing empirical knowledge about, and theoretical perspectives on, suicidal behavior.

Comparing Motivations for Suicide/ Suicide Terrorism

Diverse reasons are given for suicidal behavior, including difficulties with finances, relationships, employment, mental health, drugs, and alcohol, to name but a few. Indeed, it is virtually impossible to describe a "typical suicide" generally. The following sections demonstrate that the motivations for suicide terrorists in killing themselves are not usually found in the general suicide population.

RELIGION

Religion is a key factor in motivating and maintaining many suicide terrorist attackers. However, research demonstrates that religious beliefs (Dervic et al., 2004; Nonnemaker, McNeely, & Blum, 2003) and religious attendance (Rasic et al., 2009) may actually protect against suicidal behavior. Depressed inpatients who report no religious affiliation have more lifetime suicide attempts than those who report having a religious affiliation (Dervic et al., 2004). Data from the National Longitudinal Study of Adolescent Health in the USA demonstrated that private religiosity (measured by frequency of prayer and the perceived importance of religion) was associated with a significantly lower probability of having had suicidal thoughts or having engaged in suicidal behavior (Nonnemaker et al., 2003). Further, attending religious services has been shown to protect against suicide attempts—even when the effects of social support are accounted for (Rasic et al., 2009). So while protective against suicide in the general population, strong religious beliefs may actually be a significant risk factor in becoming a suicide terrorist (as discussed earlier).

VENGEANCE

The explanations of suicidal individuals for their behaviors rarely relate to vengeance or coercion. Rather, the reasons most commonly chosen by individuals who are suicidal relate to loss of control and escape (Bancroft et al., 1979). Vengeance, though not common, is found to be a motivator for some completed suicides. For example, some data support the notion of revenge via suicide by women suffering abuse (Counts, 1987; Meng, 2002). However, it is important to note that this sort of "revenge suicide" does not involve physical harm to others as part of the suicide act.

A crucial point to make about the potential motivational differences between terrorist suicides and other suicides is that there is a strong instrumental element to the motive of the suicide terrorist. After all, the real goal of suicide terrorism is to create terror (Pape, 2003), with the ultimate aim of effecting religious or political change, which is certainly not the case with suicides in general. So, to summarize, the motives of suicide terrorists appear to be very different compared to other suicides, which concurs with the latest writings of at least one expert on political terrorism (see Pape, 2005).

MURDEROUS INTENT

It is possible that the subgroup of the suicide population which could be thought of as most closely related to suicide terrorists is homicide-suicides. These suicides are exceptionally rare. Indeed, it has been reported that of the 600,000 deaths which occur in England and Wales each year, an average of 60 occur as homicide-suicides (Barraclough & Harris, 2002). Consider this figure in the context of the number of suicides in 2002 (N = 4,751) (National Statistics, 2012) and the rarity of these acts becomes apparent—accounting for 1.3% of all suicides. The rate of homicide-suicides in the United States appears to be very similar, accounting for around 1.5% of all suicides (Marzuk, Tardiff, & Hirsch, 1992).

However, even within this subgroup of suicides a clear difference exists between homicide-suicides and suicide terrorists. The majority of homicide-suicide cases involve one victim and one suspect and, in around 90% of incidents, it is a family member who is the victim, most commonly the female partners of male suspects (Barraclough and Harris, 2002; Berman, 1979; Chan, Beh, & Broadhust, 2003; Marzuk et al., 1992). Alternatively, suicide terrorist attacks involve many victims and one suspect, where the victims are unknown to the killer. Moreover, most homicide-suicide acts involve enmeshment and vengeance between the victim and the perpetrator (Berman, 1979). However, for the suicide terrorist, it is likely that enmeshment occurs with his or her peer group (Lachkar, 2002), not with the victims of the attack. The temporal spacing of the acts of homicide and suicide is another significant difference between many homicide suicides and suicide attacks. In suicide terrorism the acts are simultaneous, whereas homicide-suicide has been defined as "a person [who] has committed a homicide and subsequently commits suicide within one week of the homicide" (Marzuk et al., 1992, p. 3179). However, this is not the only definition of homicide-suicide, as other researchers do not apply the 1 week criterion when defining homicide-suicide (e.g., Berman, 1979). Nonetheless, exploring homicide-suicides as the closest relative to suicide terrorists from the "general suicide population" demonstrates that there are large and important differences between key characteristics of the two types of behavior, and between the victims of these acts.

In addition, there is little evidence to suggest the existence of suicidal intent in most suicide terrorists. Atran (2003) has suggested that suicidal symptoms are completely absent in suicide terrorists. Indeed, suicidal intent is actively and categorically denied by those involved in carrying out such attacks (Post et al., 2003; Schbley, 2003). Perhaps unsurprising given that the suicide terrorist's act ensures an afterlife which manifests itself as a real physical presence, and that suicide is forbidden in Islam (Abdel-Khalek, 2004). Moreover, participants feelings about suicide in the interview studies quoted earlier allude to the vilification of suicide and complete denial of suicidality in these bombers (Hassan, 2001; Post et al., 2003).

Comparing the Psychology of Suicide Terrorists to Other Suicides

It has been suggested that suicide terrorists may be psychologically similar to other suicides owing to their desire to remove themselves from an intolerable situation "due to unmet emotional needs" (Leenaars & Wenckstern, 2004, p. 134). Leading suicidologists suggest that suicidal acts must fundamentally be understood as behaviors "aimed at obtaining relief from an unbearable mental state" (Michel, 2000, p. 666). For example, Shneidman (e.g., 1996) claims that suicide is caused by psychological pain, which he terms "psychache." However, in the following sections it becomes clear that the knowledge we have about the psychology of suicide terrorists does not resonate with what is known about other suicides.

HOPE

Earlier it was suggested that suicide terrorists go to their death feeling hopeful rather than hopeless. However, in the literature there is mixed opinion on this issue. Salib (2003) claims that anger and hopelessness may be primary motivations for the suicide terrorist. So do such terrorists exhibit the common features of important psychological models of suicidal behavior, such as the "cry of pain" theory (Williams, 1997; Williams & Pollock, 2000)? According to Williams, suicidal acts are the cries of pain from individuals who are defeated in some important aspect of their lives and feel trapped in that situation, devoid of hope of escape or rescue. Moreover, hopelessness is a key risk factor in suicidal behavior (Brown et al., 2000). Indeed, Williams (1997) has argued that because of the riches perceived to be awarded to them in the afterlife, suicide terrorists may be different from other suicides in this respect, dying with hope and positive feelings about the future. So although an initial motivation to become a suicide attacker may be anger and hopelessness (Salib, 2003), it seems that suicide attackers may commit the act with more positive feelings than others who kill themselves (Williams, 1997).

AGGRESSION AND ANGER

As noted earlier, anger and aggression certainly seem to be important factors in suicide attacks (Atran, 2003), but some research suggests that the majority of suicide terrorists are likely to have been induced to feel the way they do owing to intragroup and intergroup processes, which are driven by religious beliefs (Atran, 2003; Beck 2002; Hassan, 2001; Post et al., 2003; Salib, 2003), or as a response to perceived harsh state repression (Araj, 2008). In contrast, anger in other suicides seems to be strongly driven by biological mechanisms involving the serotonin system (Giegling, Hartmann, Möller, & Rujescu (2006) and is exacerbated by interacting personality, social, and psychological factors (Mann, Waternaux, Haas, & Malone, 1999; Williams, 1997). Suicides that involve violent methods have an impulsive component that is biologically mediated by the serotonin system (Bertolote, Fleischmann, & Wasserman, 2005; Träskman, Åsberg, Bertilsson, & Sjostrand, 1981). Interestingly, the impulsive element of such violent suicidal acts seems to be lacking in suicide attacks, where it seems that careful plans are made. Moreover, although anger may to some extent drive an individual toward the path of suicide terrorism (if, say, the individual wishes to avenge the death or mistreatment of a loved one by a perceived enemy), it is unlikely that she or he goes to his or her death feeling such a negative emotion (given the rewards awaiting him or her in the afterlife) (Hassan, 2001; Post et al., 2003).

MENTAL ILLNESS

One possible point of psychological commonality worth considering is the prevalence of mental illness in suicide terrorists and other suicides. Diagnosable mental illness is known to be a significant and serious problem in both attempted (Haw, Hawton, Houston, & Townsend, 2001) and completed suicides (Arsenault-Lapierre, Kim, & Turecki, 2004; Bertolote et al., 2005; Cavanagh, Carson, Sharpe, & Lawrie, 2003; Lonnqvist, 2000). Depression, in particular, is a problem in both completed and attempted suicides. Interestingly, however, this does not seem to feature in suicide terrorism. In Berko's (2007) study a dispatcher of suicide attackers was reported to have said that he wanted "sad guys" (p. 7) to carry out suicide attacks. However, the meaning of "sad" here was not akin to misery or depression; rather, it was that he wanted "those who were social nonentities and had no status but who might get recognition by dying" (p. 7). Williams (1997) has written on the key differences between suicide attackers and other people who complete suicide. In relation to depression he notes the following:

> Most people who commit suicide are depressed when they do so; they see death as the end to their suffering. One of two feelings usually predominates in the mind of the person who is suicidal in this depressive sense, both stemming from hopelessness. The first is that they have been abandoned by everyone; the second that they are a burden to everyone, especially to those they love. Contrast this with the martyr. They see hope and believe in a cause. (p. 111)

This postulation certainly resonates very strongly with findings from a number of the empirical studies described in the present chapter (e.g., Hassan, 2001; Post et al., 2003), suggesting that suicide attackers are not mentally ill. Having said this, on the basis of current empirical evidence we do not know whether mental illness is a significant risk factor for suicide terrorism. Rigorous psychological autopsy studies of individuals who die in suicide attacks would provide useful information on this point.

GROUP PROCESSES AND INDOCTRINATION

It is likely that a major difference between suicide terrorists and other suicides is whether the decision to act is made at the level of the individual or at the level of the group (and directed by group leaders). The fact is that group processes described earlier in this chapter are entirely absent in most other cases of suicide. Most people who take their own life somehow arrive at the decision to die on their own and then proceed to die alone. In addition, the degree of planning observed in suicide attackers is not evident in most other suicides. Indeed, Stengel (1964) once noted, "Carefully planned acts of suicide are as rare as carefully planned acts of homicide" (p. 74). It is true that there are some examples of suicides which involve group (e.g., cult suicides) and dyadic processes (e.g., suicide pacts), but these are extremely rare. An additional fundamental difference between these suicide acts and suicide attacks is that innocent victims (who have not "signed up" to die) are not killed as part of the suicidal behavior. Therefore, group processes appear to provide yet another important dimension on which suicide terrorists and other suicides differ. However, the examination of group processes and how these interact with individual differences will be a crucial direction for future research in understanding suicide terrorism.

ALTRUISM

There is a distinct lack of empirical evidence relating to altruistic suicide. Leenars and Wenckstern (2004) have highlighted the paucity of evidence and identified just one paper—a qualitative study (Park, 2004) addressing this issue. Park's evidence (two martyrdom notes) was used to support the claim that these kinds of notes were the same as other suicide notes (Leenaars & Wenckstern, 2004). However, the "martyrdom notes" were actually those of "self-immolators"—individuals who burned themselves to death as a protest but without harming others (B. C. P. Park, personal communication, November 2, 2005). This, therefore, is insufficient evidence on which to base the claim that suicide terrorists should be considered the same as other suicides, altruistic or otherwise. Park's (2004) study suggests that *self-immolators* may fit the model of an altruistic suicide, but it is not appropriate to extend these findings to the case of suicide terrorists who kill both themselves and others. Indeed, a vital omission from both of the notes analyzed by Leenaars and Wenckstern (2004) was the intent of the self-immolators to take the lives of others at the same time as taking their own life. This is in direct contrast to suicide terrorists who are known to cite this as a reason for them acting as an attacker in another form of "martyrdom note"—the preact video (also known as video testaments (Atran, 2003). Furthermore, self-immolation is rarely considered a terrorist act, since the act is not intended to cause terror, but rather to elicit sympathy and understanding from a target audience (Niebuhr, 1960).

It also has been suggested that suicide terrorists may possess elements of "fatalistic type" suicide in that the persons carrying out these acts are subject to political totalitarianism (Pedahzur, Perliger, & Weinberg, 2003). However, this claim is based on the concepts of altruistic and fatalistic suicide from Durkheim's typology using data gathered from reports from the Israeli newspaper "Ha'aretz." Such data (as the authors themselves acknowledge) could be censored and biased according to the viewpoint of the editor or the writer of the articles. As such, it is probable that the results of this study are unlikely to accurately reflect the cases they report on.

It is important to emphasize that classic examples of altruistic suicide do not involve the death of others in the altruistic act (with the exception, perhaps, of the Japanese Kamikaze pilots). If we accept that suicide terrorists may possibly belong to a new category of altruistic suicide, it is very unlikely that altruism will be the sole cause for the behavior. Even a cursory review of the suicide literature reveals that suicide is a truly multifaceted problem. Characterized as a "multidimensional malaise" (Leenaars, 1996), suicide involves a complex interaction and sequencing of events, each having social, biological, and psychological influences. No one thing causes suicide (e.g., O'Carroll, 1993), meaning that altruism is unlikely to be the only factor contributing to a so-called altruistic suicide. Certainly, a number of authors claim that the actions of terrorists are stimulated by a wide set of motives (Moghadam, 2003; Salib, 2003; Silke, 2003).

PERSONALITY

Personality disorder appears to be diagnosable in nearly half of all suicide attempters. Haw et al. (2001) interviewed a representative sample of suicide attempters who had been admitted to a general hospital following their attempt. They found that the most common disorders in their sample were anxious, anankastic, and paranoid as measured by the Personality Assessment Schedule (Tyrer, Alexander, & Ferguson, 1988). Evidence is currently lacking as to whether suicide terrorists have a diagnosable personality disorder.

Can We Conclude That Suicide Attackers Are Suicidal?

The available evidence demonstrates that suicide terrorism is very different from other suicidal behavior. Perhaps it is more useful to consider suicide terrorism as a dimension of terrorist behavior and the suicide terrorist as belonging to a subgroup of the terrorist population. It appears that there are few, if any, factors that are truly common to both suicide terrorists and other suicides. Indeed, on the basis of current evidence I suggest that it is not even possible to conclude that suicide terrorists can be considered as a type of altruistic suicide—I am not alone in suggesting this (e.g., Abdel-Khalek, 2004). Perhaps the suicide terrorist could be considered an atypical variant of the category of altruistic suicide (Leenaars & Wenckstern, 2004) or as a new type of "fatalistic-altruistic" suicide (Pedahzur et al., 2003), but the data that support these claims are potentially misleading in important ways and lack strong empirical evidence to support them. (The notion of altruistic suicide would require adjustment to permit a distinction to be made between those who harm others and those who do not.)

Some have questioned whether suicide terrorists should be viewed as cases of suicide at all (Israeli, 1997; Spencer, 2002). Indeed, those involved in carrying out such acts deny that what they are doing involves suicide (Araj, 2008; Post et al., 2003; Schbley, 2003). Instead, such acts are viewed as a form of martyrdom (Abdel-Khalek, 2004; Kushner, 1996; Post et al., 2003; Schbley, 2003), which appear to be largely driven by religious beliefs, social pressure, and group processes (Atran, 2003; Gordon, 2002; Moghadam, 2003; Post et al., 2009). Suicide terrorists do not appear to be truly suicidal in the way that suicidal behavior is usually defined and understood (but see Lankford, 2010).

Significant differences seem to exist between suicide terrorists and other suicides in terms of key factors known to underpin suicide generally. Indeed, even the characteristics of the closest related subgroup, which is probably that of the homicide-suicide, differ markedly with what (little) is known about suicide terrorist behavior. A key feature of the suicide terrorism process that is absent in the general suicide population (with the exception of a small number of mass suicides and suicide pacts) is the coercive processes used by those in authority. However, it is important to note that methodologically sound empirical studies of suicide terrorism are lacking (Townsend, 2007). Robust, theory-driven empirical studies are now desperately needed and must be developed in methodologically sound ways.

Can We Effectively Identify Those at Risk of Becoming a Suicide Terrorist?

Why are some individuals more likely than others to become influenced sufficiently to be willing to die as suicide attackers? Four issues emerge as crucial in the discussion of suicide terrorism here. First is the possibility that individual differences in personality and psychology may be important—especially in relation to how the individual reacts in a group setting and his or her susceptibility to coercion which may result from this. Second is the role strong religious beliefs play in the wish to act as a suicide terrorist. Religion seems to operate at a number of levels, from leading an individual to feel vindicated in carrying out an attack to ensuring that the individuals stays on the path to martyrdom once he or she has chosen it. Third, it also is clear that group processes operate to attract and sustain suicide bombing behavior. Moreover, it is highly likely that these three factors may interact in the development of a suicide attacker. Finally, it has been shown here that suicide attackers are extremely unlikely to be suicidal, so it may not be useful to focus on risk factors that are traditionally associated with suicidal behavior.

Unfortunately, data are currently insufficient to make strong predictions about who may be at risk of becoming a suicide attacker. This makes the job of designing and implementing interventions to prevent such attacks very difficult indeed. Robust evidence, reported in a systematic and transparent manner, is now urgently required. Hence, in the final section of this chapter, I concentrate on potentially useful directions for research in this domain.

Conclusions and Directions for Future Research
Research at a Societal/Group Level

Given the complexity of the phenomenon of suicide terrorism, it is clear that a multidisciplinary approach is required in order to elucidate the key factors which lead to a suicide attack (Post et al., 2009). Some have argued that societal-level or group-level interventions would be more useful than individual ones (Berko 2007; Grimland et al., 2006; Post et al., 2009). For example, it may be useful to work with the media to try to downplay the impact of acts of suicide terrorism (Grimland et al., 2006). Moreover, the role of the media in maintaining outgroup hostility as well as in highlighting the impact of suicide attacks must be explored. Currently, the media may serve to promote both recruitment to suicide cells and copycat terrorist behavior. The influence of media portrayals on suicidal behavior has led to the development of media guidelines to help prevent contagion effects. Similar guidelines may now be required for handling media reports of suicide attacks.

Another societal-level strand of research that may be useful is early interventions in schools and nurseries to downplay the glorification (Grimland et al., 2006) and glamorization of charismatic leaders (Post, 2009) and heroic martyrs (Berko, 2007). Other potentially important societal-/group-level questions include how individuals might resist coercion and indoctrination, and where they can turn if they feel they are being coerced. As shall be noted later, empathy may be a key construct to understand here, as this seems to be associated with resistance to coercion (Jones, 2009). Finally, mechanisms for leaving the group and downplaying the glamour of the group also are important issues to consider (Post et al., 2009).

It is clear then that social psychology will have a crucial role in furthering the understanding of the group processes which culminate in terrorist attacks, and it may ultimately contribute to the prevention of future attacks. There is a reasonable knowledge base that relates to the factors underpinning hostility between groups in terms of the influences on intergroup bias (Hewstone, Rubin, & Willis, 2002; Reed & Aquino, 2003; Tzeng & Jackson, 1994) and determining what can be done about such biases and conflict between groups (Beck, 2002; Hewstone et al., 2002). But we now need specific research on ingroup/outgroup hostility and other group processes (such as coercion) that influence the development of suicide attacks. Green

and Seher (2003) recently highlighted the fact that the academic literatures on prejudice and ethnic conflict have developed in isolation from each other and that an integrated research synthesis in this area is now needed.

A highly relevant series of experiments have demonstrated that individuals who feel supported and loved by others are more accepting of people who do not belong to their own group (Mikulincer & Shaver, 2001). This, the authors suggest, also highlights an important role for attachment theory in understanding reactions toward outgroups. In this series of studies, a priming paradigm was used to activate a sense of a "secure base" in Jewish students. Results demonstrated that this sense of a "secure base" diminishes negative reactions to members of salient outgroups (e.g., Arabs and ultra-Orthodox Jews).

Research at the Level of the Individual

It is important to note that the call to focus on antisuicide terrorist interventions at the level of groups and society is based on very little low-quality empirical evidence (Victoroff, 2005). Moreover, there are vital individual-level psychological factors that may underpin some of the group processes discussed earlier. For example, the potential importance of coercive strategies on would-be suicide bombers was discussed earlier in this chapter. A crucial point to take away from the Milgram paradigm is that there is always a group of individuals who are resistant to coercion, and proximity to the victim (e.g., ability to hear screaming) appears to be an important factor in this (Jones, 2009). Therefore, a useful strategy for future work would be to examine the role of empathy—specifically the capacity to empathize with a perceived enemy. Empathy has been defined as "an affective response that stems from the apprehension or comprehension of another's emotional state or condition and is similar to what the other person is feeling or would be expected to feel" (Eisenberg, 2000, p. 671).

The lack of empathy for the "perceived enemy" would contribute to what Berko (2007) refers to as the suicide terrorists' complete dehumanization of Jewish people. Imprisoned terrorists that she interviewed admitted that they had not even considered Jewish people to be human until they met them in prison. Bandura, Barbaranelli, Caprara, and Pastorelli (1996) note that the perception of another person as a human being fosters empathy owing to perceived similarity. To cast a person or persons as "subhuman" renders them incapable of feeling and unable to have the normal range of fears and hopes that characterizes the human condition. Indeed, experimental studies have demonstrated that dehumanized individuals are treated ruthlessly compared to humanized ones by individuals who would otherwise be thought of as caring (Bandura, Underwood, & Fromson, 1975). Bandura (2004) has written specifically on moral disengagement as applied to terrorists, and he points to the importance of the dehumanization of the enemy. He argues that, in order to instill the facility to murder innocent people, intensive psychological instruction in moral disengagement is required. Cognitive restructuring is the mechanism that underpins the redefinition of the morality of killing in the mind of a suicide attacker. Moral justification is viewed as sanction for violent means.

Interestingly, experimental evidence suggests that feeling empathy for a member of a stigmatized group, such as convicted murderers, people with AIDS, or homeless people, can actually significantly improve attitudes toward that group (Batson, Polycarpou, Harmon-Jones, & Imhoff, 1997). As the authors of this paper note, changing attitudes to stigmatized groups is extremely difficult and cognitive approaches (i.e., where positive information is provided about the group in question) do not seem to have fared very well in achieving this change in attitude. However, Batson and colleagues used an empathy-based affective approach where feelings toward a member of the stigmatized group were induced using vignettes. It is possible that such a strategy may be useful in improving attitudes toward a perceived enemy who is necessarily a member of a highly stigmatized group in the mind of a terrorist. Such an approach may be most useful if implemented in schools in the areas commonly used by those involved in the recruitment of suicide attackers.

Specific Research Methods and Theories

There are a number of specific research techniques and theoretical approaches that may prove to be particularly useful in the pursuit of some of the research agenda set out earlier. These, along with specific methodological considerations for future studies, are discussed in the paragraphs that follow.

THE PSYCHOLOGICAL AUTOPSY METHOD

I have previously suggested that researchers wishing to understand the behavior of suicide terrorists could profit from adopting commonly used methods in suicidology (Townsend, 2007). The psychological autopsy method, for example, has been used very effectively to increase our understanding of the psychological, social, medical, and psychiatric risk factors associated with suicide. The aim of this technique is to produce as comprehensive an account as possible in order to form a view as to why suicide terrorists took their own life. The technique combines interviews closest to the deceased and an in-depth examination of evidence from existing sources such as medical notes, criminal records, and social work reports. On the basis of these data a picture is built up of the deceased's physical and mental health, their personality, social supports, and so on. It is currently the technique that is most direct in trying to assess the relationship between certain risk factors and death by suicide (Cavanagh et al., 2003).

A study of young people who died by suicide demonstrated that over 50% had expressed suicidal thoughts within the year before death and over 40% had made clear statements of intent within a month before death (Houston, Hawton, & Shepperd, 2001). Research such as this has emphasized the importance of listening seriously to, and providing adequate support for, those who disclose suicidal feelings, plans, and ideas. A systematic review of psychological autopsy studies has revealed mental disorders to be the variable most strongly associated with suicide (Cavanagh et al., 2003). In this study the median proportion of cases with detectable mental disorder was very high indeed, at 91%.

The psychological autopsy technique could be an effective tool in the study of what drives the behavior of suicide terrorists. However, it is possible that there may be significant pragmatic and cultural barriers to carrying out this type of research with this population. For example, it is likely that medical records will be difficult to access and that those close to the suicide attacker may be unwilling to be interviewed. Having said this, Hassan (2001) demonstrated that members of militant camps are extremely willing to be interviewed about suicide terrorists. This, therefore, is a technique that may yield important insights into the mind of the suicide terrorist and help to identify those at risk of acting as suicide attackers.

Meloy's (2004) in-depth case analysis of Mohammed Atta (a September 11, 2001 suicide attacker) represents an important development in this direction, though future studies would need to investigate a number of cases and compare them with a suitable control group (e.g., nonsuicidal terrorists or another group who had died by violent means). Also, Araj (2008) conducted interviews with friends and family of 43 suicide attackers. In addition, Fields et al. (2002) have used what they term "postmortem interviews" with a group of Palestinian suicide terrorists which involved interviews with families and friends of suicide terrorists. They also recruited a control group of males roughly the same age and background as the terrorists. Researchers wanting to adopt the psychological autopsy method to study suicide terrorists should heed the recommendations of Hawton et al. (1998).

CONTEMPORARY THEORIES IN SOCIAL PSYCHOLOGY: SELF-DETERMINATION THEORY AND THE THEORY OF PLANNED BEHAVIOR

The discussion of the characteristics of suicide terrorists leads me to conclude that two contemporary theories proposed by social psychologists have the potential to be particularly useful in the future study of suicide attackers. These are self-determination theory (SDT; Deci & Ryan, 2000) and the theory of planned behavior (TPB; Ajzen, 1991).

In SDT a distinction is made between different types of motivation. Intrinsic motivation refers to doing something because it is interesting and enjoyable, whereas extrinsically motivated behaviors are done because they lead to some separate outcome (Deci & Ryan, 2000). Moreover, they propose a taxonomy of human motivations in which there are a number of different forms of extrinsic motivation that vary according to their perceived locus of causality. The most externally driven extrinsic motivation is called "external regulation." Externally regulated behaviors are thought to be performed to satisfy an external demand or reward. It seems plausible that the expected rewards awaiting the would-be suicide attacker in the afterlife constitute their behavior as being significantly externally regulated. However, another type of extrinsic motivation, "introjected regulation," also is relevant to suicide attackers. Introjection involves regulation in order to avoid negative emotions such as guilt or anxiety, or to enhance feelings of pride and self-worth. As noted earlier, suicide dispatchers are known to seek out individuals with depressed self-worth and recruit them to martyrdom on the basis that this will enhance their status (Berko, 2007). SDT may, therefore, provide a very useful theoretical framework within which to examine the motivation of suicide attackers. Studies adopting an SDT framework can use either experimental methods in the laboratory or survey-based instruments in the field in order to measure motivation (Ryan & Deci, 2000).

Ryan and Deci (2000) suggest that the main reason that individuals are likely to carry out extrinsically motivated behaviors is that they resonate with the values of significant others. It may, therefore, be important to examine SDT in relation to other contemporary social psychological theories such as the theory of planned behavior (Ajzen, 1991), which examines the links between attitudes and behaviors and takes into account factors such as moral norms and subjective norms. Subjective norms, as applied to the suicide bomber, would reflect the beliefs of the people the terrorist cares about, and how such people would view their suicide attacking behavior. TPB has been applied in many domains, and there is evidence documenting the application of this theory in various contexts (e.g., Armitage & Conner, 2001). Recently TPB has been shown to be a useful theoretical framework in the understanding of suicidal behavior (O'Connor & Armitage, 2006), and it also may be helpful in understanding suicide terrorism.

CONTEMPORARY THEORIES OF SUICIDAL BEHAVIOR

I have concluded that suicide attackers are different from other suicide attempters on the basis of existing data in relation to these two groups. However, a more robust approach would be to compare these two groups directly in an empirical study. Such a study should be theoretically driven by contemporary theories of suicidal behavior such as the cry of pain theory (Williams, 1997; Williams & Pollock, 2000). Researchers have developed items to measure the key components of this model such as perceived "defeat" and "escape" (O'Connor, 2003). Using such measures with a group of would-be suicide attackers, such as those interviewed in some of the studies described here (e.g., Berko, 2007; Hassan, 2001; Post et al., 2003), would give an accurate indication of the similarity between suicide attackers and other suicide attempters.

METHODOLOGICAL CONSIDERATIONS FOR FUTURE STUDIES

As stressed earlier, it is important that future studies of suicide terrorism adopt a theoretical approach. It also is extremely important that future studies use robust methods to collect data on suicide attackers (whether using a retrospective technique like the psychological autopsy or a prospective study with failed or would-be suicide attackers). Sampling techniques should be fully described, as should response rates for the suicide attacker group, as well as any control group that is being compared to the suicide terrorist group. Standardized questionnaires, with robust validity and reliability, should be used where possible in order to permit sensible comparisons between studies. Measures of self-presentation and social desirability should be taken in order to examine the influence of these factors in questionnaire responding. Data collection procedures should be reported fully and accurately, and results sections should include details of participants and descriptive statistics for the major measures.

Acknowledgments

I am grateful to Drs. Scott Campbell, Ben Park, and Martin Hagger for their advice.

References

Abdel-Khalek, A. (2004). Neither altruistic suicide, nor terrorism but martyrdom: A Muslim perspective. *Archives of Suicide Research, 8*, 99–113.

Ajzen, I. (1991). The theory of planned behaviour. *Organizational Behaviour and Human Decision Processes, 50*, 179–211.

Araj, B. (2008). Harsh state repression as a cause of suicide bombing: The case of the Palestinian-Israeli conflict. *Studies in Conflict and Terrorism, 31*, 284–303.

Armitage, C. J., & Conner, M. (2001). Efficacy of the theory of planned behavior: A meta-analytic review. *British Journal of Social Psychology, 40*, 471–499.

Arsenault-Lapierre, G., Kim, C., & Turecki, G. (2004). Psychiatric diagnoses in 3275 suicides: A meta-analysis. *BMC Psychiatry, 4*(37) 1–11.

Atran, S. (2003). Genesis of suicide terrorism. *Science, 299*, 1534–1539.

Bancroft, J., Hawton, K., Simkin, S., Kingston, B., Cumming, C., & Whitwell, D. (1979). The reasons people give for taking overdoses. *British Journal of Medical Psychology, 52*, 353–365.

Bandura, A. (2004). The role of selective moral engagement in terrorism and counterterrorism. In F. M. Mogahaddam & A. J. Marsella (Eds.), *Understanding terrorism: Psychological roots, consequences and interventions* (pp. 121–150). Washington, DC: American Psychological Association.

Bandura, A., Barbaranelli, C., Caprara, G. V., & Pastorelli, C. (1996). Mechanisms of moral disengagement in the exercise of moral agency. *Journal of Personality and Social Psychology, 71*, 364–374.

Bandura, A., Underwood, B., & Fromson, M. E. (1975). Disinhibition of aggression through diffusion of responsibility and dehumanization of victims. *Journal of Research in Personality, 9*, 253–269.

Baron, R. S., (2000). Arousal, capacity and intense indoctrination. *Personality and Social Psychology Review, 4*, 238–254.

Barraclough, B., & Harris, C. (2002). Suicide preceded by murder: The epidemiology of homicide-suicide in England and Wales 1988-92. *Psychological Medicine, 32*, 577–584.

Batson, C. B., Polycarpou, M. R., Harmon-Jones, E., & Imhoff, H. J. (1997). Empathy and attitudes: Can feeling for a member of a stigmatized group improve feelings toward the group? *Journal of Personality and Social Psychology, 72*, 105–118.

Beck, A. T. (2002). Prisoners of hate. *Behavior Research and Therapy, 40*, 209–216.

Berko, A. (2007) *The path to paradise: The inner world of suicide bombers and their dispatchers.* Westport, CT, Praeger Security International. VA: Potomac Books.

Berman, A. L. (1979). Dyadic death: Murder-suicide. *Suicide and Life-Threatening Behavior, 9*, 15–23.

Bertolote, J. M., Fleischmann, A., & Wasserman, D. (2005). Suicide and mental disorders: Do we know enough? *British Journal of Psychiatry, 183*, 382–383.

Bond, M. (2004). The making of a suicide bomber. *New Scientist, 182*, 34–37.

Burdman, D. (2003). Education, indoctrination and incitement: Palestinian children on their way to martyrdom. *Terrorism and Political Violence, 15*, 96–123.

Cavanagh, J. T. O., Carson, A. J., Sharpe, M., & Lawrie, S. M. (2003). Psychological autopsy studies of suicide: A systematic review. *Psychological Medicine, 33*, 395–405.

Chan, C. Y., Beh, S. L., & Broadhust, R. G. (2003). Homicide-suicide in Hong Kong, 1989-1998. *Forensic Science International, 137*, 165–171.

Colvard, K. (2002). Commentary: The psychology of terrorists. *BMJ, 324*, 359.

Costa, P., & McRae, R. (2002). *NEO PI-R professional manual.* Lutz, Fl.: Psychological Assessment Resources.

Counts, D. A. (1987). Female suicide and wife abuse: A cross-cultural perspective. *Suicide and Life-Threatening-Behavior, 17*, 194–204.

Deci, E. L., & Ryan, R. M. (2000) The "what" and "why" of goal pursuits: Human needs and the self-determination of behavior. *Psychological Inquiry, 11*, 227–268

Dervic, K., Oquendo, M. A., Grunebaum, M. F., Ellis, S., Burke, A. K., & Mann, J. J. (2004). Religious affiliation and suicide attempt. *American Journal of Psychiatry, 161*, 2303–2308.

Eisenberg, N. (2000). Emotion, regulation, and moral development. *Annual Review of Psychology, 51*, 665–697.

Fields, R. M., Elbedour, S., & Hein, A. F. (2002). The Palestinian suicide bomber. In C. E. Stout (Ed.), *The psychology of terrorism: Clinical aspects and responses* (pp. 193–223). Westport, CT: Prager.

Giegling, I., Hartmann, A. M., Möller, H-J., & Rujescu, D. (2006). Anger- and aggression-related traits are associated with polymorphisms in the 5-HT-2A gene. *Journal of Affective Disorders, 96*, 75–81.

Gordon, H. (2002). The 'suicide' bomber: Is it a psychiatric phenomenon? *Psychiatric Bulletin, 26*, 285–287.

Green, D. P., & Seher, R. L. (2003). What role does prejudice play in ethnic conflict? *Annual Review of Political Science, 6*, 509–31.

Grimland, M., Apter, A., & Kerkof, A. (2006). The phenomenon of suicide bombing: A review of psychological and non-psychological factors. *Crisis, 27*, 107–118.

Hassan, N. (2001, November 19). An arsenal of believers: Talking to the 'human bombs'. *New Yorker.*

Haw, C., Hawton, K., Houston, K., & Townsend, E. (2001). Psychiatric and personality disorders in deliberate self-harm patients. *British Journal of Psychiatry; 178*, 48–54.

Hawton, K., Appleby, L., Platt, S., Foster, T., Cooper, J., Malmberg, A., & Simkin, S. (1998). The psychological autopsy approach to studying suicide: A review of methodological issues. *Journal of Affective Disorders, 50,* 269–276.

Hewstone, M., Rubin, M., & Willis, H. (2002). Intergroup bias. *Annual Review of Psychology, 53,* 575–604.

Houston, K., Hawton, K., & Shepperd, R. (2001). Suicide in young people aged 15-24: A psychological autopsy study. *Journal of Affective Disorders, 63,* 159–170.

Israeli, R. (1997). Islamikaze and their significance. *Terrorism and Political Violence, 9,* 96–121.

Jones, J. (2008). *Blood that cries out from the earth: The psychology of religious terrorism.* New York, NY: Oxford University Press.

Kimhi, S., & Even, S. (2004). Who are the Palestinian suicide bombers? *Terrorism and Political Violence, 16,* 815–840.

Kushner, H. W. (1996). Suicide bombers: Business as usual. *Studies in Conflict and Terrorism, 19,* 329–337.

Lachkar, J. (2002). The psychological make-up of a suicide bomber. *Journal of Psychohistory, 29,* 349–367.

Lamberg, L. (1997). Psychiatrist explores apocalyptic violence in Heaven's Gate and Alum Shinrikyo cults. *Journal of the American Medical Association, 278,* 191–193.

Lankford, A. (2010). Do suicide terrorists exhibit clinically suicidal risk factors? A review of initial evidence and a call for future research. *Aggression and Violent Behavior, 15,* 334–340.

Leenaars, A. (1996). Suicide: A multidimensional malaise. *Suicide and Life-Threatening Behavior, 26,* 221–236.

Leenaars, A., & Wenckstern, S. (2004). Altruistic suicides: Are they the same or different from other suicides? *Archives of Suicide Research, 8,* 131–136.

Lonnqvist, J. K. (2000). Psychiatric aspects of suicidal behavior: Depression. In K. Hawton & K. van Heeringen (Eds.), *The international handbook of suicide and attempted suicide* (pp. 107–120). Chichester, UK: Wiley.

Mann, J. J., Waternaux, C., Haas, G. L., & Malone, K. M. (1999). Toward a clinical model of suicidal behavior in psychiatric patients. *American Journal of Psychiatry, 156,* 181–189.

Marzuk, P. M., Tardiff, K., & Hirsch, C. S. (1992). The epidemiology of murder-suicide. *Journal of the American Medical Association, 267,* 3179–3183.

Meloy, J. R. (2004). Indirect personality assessment of the violent true believer. *Journal of Personality Assessment, 82,* 138–146.

Meng, L. (2002). Rebellion and revenge: The meaning of suicide in rural China. *International Journal of Social Welfare, 11,* 300–309.

Merari, A. (1998). The readiness to kill and die: Suicidal terrorism in the Middle East. In W. Reich (Ed.), *Origins of terrorism: Psychologies, ideologies, theologies, states of mind.* (pp. 192–207). Washington, DC: Woodrow Wilson Center Press.

Merari, A. (2005). Suicide terrorism. In R. I. Yufit & D. Lester (Eds.), *Assessment, treatment and prevention of suicidal behavior* (pp. 431–453). New York, NY: Wiley.

Michel, K. (2000). Suicide prevention and primary care. In K. Hawton & K. van Heeringen (Eds.), *The international handbook of suicide and attempted suicide* (pp. 661–674). Chichester, UK: Wiley.

Milgram, S. (1974). *Obedience to authority.* New York, NY: Harper Row.

Mikulincer, M., & Shaver, P. R. (2001). Attachment theory and intergroup bias: Evidence that priming the secure base schema attenuates negative reactions to out-groups. *Journal of Personality and Social Psychology, 81,* 97–115.

Moghadam, A. (2003). Palestinian suicide terrorism in the second intifada: Motivations and organizational aspects. *Studies in Conflict and Terrorism, 26,* 65–92.

National Statistics. (2012). *Suicides, England and Wales, 2000-2003.* Retrieved November 2013, from http://www.ons.gov.uk/ons/taxonomy/index.html?nscl=Suicide+Rates#tab-data-tables.

Niebuhr, R. (1960). *Moral man and immoral society.* New York, NY: Scribner.

Nonnemaker, J. M., McNeely, C. A., & Blum, W. R. (2003). Public and private domains of religiosity and adolescent health risk behaviors: Evidence from the National Longitudinal Study of Adolescent Health. *Social Science and Medicine, 57,* 2049–2054.

O'Carroll, P. (1993). Suicide causation: Pies, paths and pointless polemics. *Suicide and Life-Threatening Behavior, 23,* 27–36.

O'Connor, R. (2003). Suicidal behavior as a cry of pain: Test of a psychological model. *Archives of Suicide Research, 7,* 297–308.

O'Connor, R., & Armitage, C. (2006). Theory of planned behavior and parasuicide: An exploratory study. *Current Psychology, 3,* 196–205.

Orbach, I. (2004). Terror suicide: How is it possible? *Archives of Suicide Research, 8,* 115–130.

Pape, R. A. (2003). The strategic logic of suicide terrorism. *American Political Science Review, 97,* 343–361.

Pape, R. A. (2005). *Dying to win: The strategic logic of suicide terrorism.* New York, NY: Random House.

Park, B. C. B. (2004). Sociopolitical contexts of self-immolations in Vietnam and South Korea. *Archives of Suicide Research, 8,* 81–97.

Pedahzur, A., Perliger, A., & Weinberg, L. (2003). Altruism and fatalism: The characteristics of Palestinian suicide terrorists. *Deviant Behavior, 24,* 405–423.

Poland, J. M. (2002). Suicide bombers: A global problem. *Humboldt Journal of Social Relations, 27,* 100–135.

Post, J. M., Sprinzak, E., & Denny, L. M. (2003). The terrorists in their own words: Interviews with 35 incarcerated middle eastern terrorists. *Terrorism and Political Violence, 15,* 171–184

Post, J. M., Ali, F., Henderson, S. W., Shanfield, S., Victoroff, J., & Weine, S. (2009). The psychology of suicide terrorism. *Psychiatry, 72,* 13–31.

Rasic, D. T., Shay-Lee, B., Elias, B., Katz, L. Y., Enns, M., & Sareen, J. (2009). Spirituality, religion and suicidal behaviour in a nationally representative sample. *Journal of Affective Disorders, 114,* 32–40.

Reed, A., II, & Aquino, K. F. (2003). Moral identity and expanding circle of moral regard toward out-groups. *Journal of Personality and Social Psychology, 84,* 1270–1286.

Rosenberger, J. (2003). Discerning the behavior of the suicide bomber: The role of vengeance. *Journal of Religion and Health, 42,* 13–20.

Ryan, R. M. & Deci, E. L (2000). Intrinsic and extrinsic motivations: Classic definitions and new directions. *Contemporary Educational Psychology, 25,* 54–67.

Salib, E. (2003). Suicide terrorism: A case of folie à plusieurs? *British Journal of Psychiatry, 182,* 475–476.

Schbley, A. (2003). Defining religious terrorism: A causal anthropological profile. *Studies in Conflict and Terrorism, 26,* 105–134.

Shneidman, E. S. (1996). *The suicidal mind.* Oxford, UK: Oxford University Press.

Silke, A. (2003). The psychology of suicidal terrorism. In A. Silke (Ed.), *Terrorists, victims and society: Psychological perspectives on terrorism and its consequences* (pp. 93–108). Chichester, UK: Wiley.

Spencer, J. S. (2002). The suicide bomber—is it a psychiatric phenomenon? *Psychiatric Bulletin, 26*, 436.

Sprinzak, E. (2000). Rational fanatics. *Foreign Policy, 120*, 66–73.

Stack, S. (2004). Emile Durkheim and altruistic suicide. *Archives of Suicide Research, 8*, 9–22.

Stengel, E. (1964). *Suicide and attempted suicide.* Oxford, UK: Penguin.

Taylor, M., & Ryan, H. (1988). Fanaticism, political suicide and terrorism. *Terrorism, 11*, 91–111.

Townsend, E. (2007). Suicide terrorists: Are they suicidal? *Suicide and Life-Threatening Behavior, 37*(1), 35–49.

Träskman, L., Åsberg, M., Bertilsson, L., & Sjostrand, L. (1981). Monoamine metabolites in CSF and suicidal behavior. *Archives of General Psychiatry, 38*, 631–636.

Tyrer, P., Alexander, J., & Ferguson, B. (1988) Personality Assessment Schedule (PAS). In P. Tyrer (Ed.), *Personality disorder: Diagnosis, management and course* (pp. 140–167). London, UK: Butterworth/Wright.

Tzeng, O. C. S., & Jackson, J. W. (1994). Effects of contact, conflict, and social identity on interethnic group hostilities. *International Journal of Intercultural Relations, 18*, 259–276.

Victoroff, J. (2005). The mind of the terrorist: A review and critique of psychological approaches. *Journal of Conflict Resolution, 49*, 3–42.

Volkan, V. (2002). September 11 and societal regression. *Group Analysis, 35*, 456–483.

Williams, J. M. G. (1997). *Suicide and attempted suicide.* London, UK: Penguin.

Williams, J. M. G., & Pollock, L. (2000). The psychology of suicidal behavior. In K. Hawton & K. van Heeringen (Eds.), *The international handbook of suicide and attempted suicide* (pp. 79–94). Chichester, UK: Wiley.

Physician-Assisted Suicide and Euthanasia

Agnes van der Heide

Abstract

Dying is often the end of a protracted disease process that involves a more or less gradual deterioration of the quality of life. Terminally ill people often foresee their own death, and having some sense of control over the dying process is important for many of them. Some consider physician assistance in suicide or euthanasia as a last resort for a dignified death. Several countries have legalized such assistance in dying, sometimes after a period of heated debate. One of the most important arguments in this debate states that it is wrong to allow physician assistance in dying because the negative consequences outweigh potential benefits. To date, extensive research has not yielded clear evidence that legalization of physician assistance in dying has resulted in a slippery slope, that is, in a tendency to provide assistance in dying to vulnerable or incompetent patient groups.

Key Words: end-of-life care, palliative care, euthanasia, physician-assisted suicide, death and dying, health law

End-of-life decision making is an essential part of modern medical practice. Pathways toward a good death and the acceptability of different forms of physician assistance in dying are topics of debate in many countries. Several countries or states have legalized physician-assisted suicide or euthanasia, including the Netherlands, Belgium, Luxemburg, Switzerland, and the states of Oregon and Washington in the United States. The Netherlands has the most long-standing and explicit history of debating, allowing, and regulating physician assistance in dying. An important feature of the 30-year process that resulted in the legalization of physician-assisted suicide and euthanasia in this country was that it was supported by large-scale empirical scientific research, which gave valid and reliable insights into the occurrence and impact of end-of-life decision-making practices. Recently, a few countries have followed with comparable studies.

This chapter starts with a short overview of the altered role of health care in death and dying. Awareness of the increasing medical impact on the process and timing of dying is important in order to understand and appreciate current debates and practices surrounding assistance in suicide and euthanasia. Subsequently, the debate and process that ultimately resulted in the enforcement of the Dutch euthanasia law will be discussed, followed by some comments on similar but often more complicated processes in several other countries. The results of the studies of practices of end-of-life decision making that supported this legalization process are then summarized to provide a comprehensive basis for understanding the most important arguments against legalization of physician-assisted suicide and euthanasia. This chapter is concluded with some general comments on the pros and cons of legalization of physician-assisted suicide and euthanasia.

Death and Dying in Modern Health Care

At the beginning of the 20th century, dying was regarded in most cases as a natural and inevitable event, with a limited role for medicine and health care. Most people died from infectious diseases and the duration of the terminal disease process was usually limited. Since then, a shift has occurred in the causes of death: Infectious diseases have to a great extent been replaced by degenerative and human-made diseases, such as cardiovascular disease, cancer, and accidents (Field & Cassel, 1997; Lynn & Adamson, 2003; Nusselder, van der Velden, van Sonsbeek, Lenior, & van den Bos, 1996; Parker & Thorslund, 2007; Wolleswinkel-van den Bosch, Looman, van Poppel, & Mackenbach, 1997). In modern times, the majority of people dying of disease pass away after a more or less protracted period of chronic disease, in which their condition and quality of life gradually deteriorate.

At the same time, life expectancy has increased substantially, mainly due to healthier diets and better hygiene. In 2010, the average life expectancy in the Netherlands was 79 years for men and 83 years for women, and they are predicted to further increase to reach 84 years for men and 87 years for women at the middle of the 21st century (van Duin & Garssen, 2010). Together with the temporary postwar rise in birth rates, the increased life expectancy has resulted in the aging of the population in all developed countries. In the year 2040, the number of people aged 65 years or over is expected to have doubled as compared to the number in the year 2000, and within the age group of 65 years or older the percentage of people aged 80 years plus is expected to increase to 40% (van Duin & Garssen, 2010), a pattern that holds for most Western countries. Due to these developments, elderly people account for a significant majority of decedents, and they consume a large part of health care expenditures.

The epidemiological shift in causes of death and the aging of the population have contributed to the development of the end of life as a new focus of health care. Curing disease and preventing death are the traditional goals of health care, and death was, until recently, primarily regarded as a defeat of medicine. It is now increasingly recognized that medical care also can contribute importantly to patients' well-being when curing disease or postponing death are no longer possible. Improving the quality of life for patients and their families facing life-threatening illness, through the prevention and relief of pain and other physical, psychosocial, and spiritual problems, is the key goal of palliative care at the end of life, as stated by the World Health Organization (WHO; Sepúlveda, Marlin, Yoshida, & Ullrich, 2002).

The growing involvement of medicine with dying has substantially altered the nature and place of death in society. Death has become more and more of a medical event and health care is attributed much responsibility for the quality and timing of the dying process. Research has shown that much is to be gained in end-of-life care. One of the most important studies in this area has been the Study to Understand Prognosis and Preferences for Outcomes and Risks of Treatment (SUPPORT), in which about 9,000 terminally ill patients and their relatives were followed for several months (Covinsky et al., 2000; Knaus et al., 1995). One of the main findings of this study was that the dying process often suffers from less than optimal communication between caregivers and terminally ill patients, and that patients do not appreciate the applied medical interventions in many cases. Despite important advances in pain and symptom management at the end of life, many dying patients experience pain and other physical and mental problems (Lynn et al., 1997; Teunissen et al., 2007; Tolle, Tilden, Hickman, & Rosenfeld, 2000). Cardio-pulmonary resuscitation, mechanical ventilation, and even nasal-gastric feeding tubes are life saving for some, but for others they prolong dying and can result in great suffering for patients and their families. Advance care planning is often advocated as a means to enhance end-of-life care, but advance care directives have been shown to be rather ineffective (Castillo et al., 2011; de Boer, Hertogh, Dröes, Jonker, & Eefsting, 2010). It seems to be difficult for patients as well as professional caregivers to anticipate the moment of dying and the preceding terminal phase of the disease, and to discuss possible aims of and choices in medical care before the end moment is there.

The growing awareness of the importance and shortcomings of current end-of-life care is intertwined with the growing involvement of patients in medical decision making that also extends to end-of-life care: People increasingly wish to have some control over their last phase of life. The appreciation of patient autonomy and self-determination is a cornerstone for modern end-of-life care, in addition to the relief of suffering and improvement of the quality of life. The SUPPORT study has convincingly shown that patients' preferences in end-of-life care also relate to treatment choices that concern the balance between quality and quantity of life. Focusing on quality of life often involves making medical decisions that also affect the expected time of death. A series of Dutch studies on end-of-life decision-making practices has been the first to show that decisions regarding terminal disease, in many cases, involve considerations about the appropriateness of applying potentially life-prolonging treatment, and that the relief of suffering prior to death is often considered to have a potential of hastening death (Onwuteaka-Philipsen et al., 2003; van der Heide et al., 2007; van der Maas et al., 1997; van der Maas, van Delden, Pijnenborg, & Looman, 1991). The acknowledgment that not all patients want to live to the bitter end, even if their pain and suffering can be controlled, has in some countries resulted in laws that under specific conditions permit active physician assistance in dying.

Regulation of Physician-Assisted Suicide and Euthanasia
The Netherlands

The debate about physician-assisted suicide and euthanasia in the Netherlands was triggered in 1973 by the so-called Postma case (Weyers, 2004). In this case, a physician helped her dying mother to end her own life following repeated and explicit requests for euthanasia. While the court upheld that the physician had committed a murder, the physician eventually received a short, suspended sentence. In its verdict, the court offered an opening for regulating physician assistance in dying by acknowledging that a physician does not always have to keep a severely suffering patient alive against his or her will. As the first public test case, the Postma case broke social taboos in a country with strong Christian traditions. It also reflected the growing awareness among many young medical professionals of the limits of medical care and the importance of patients' self-determination.

During the 1980s, the debate in the Netherlands regarding physician-assisted suicide and euthanasia progressed and formalized. In 1980, the national Committee of Attorneys General took a formal interest in physicians' end-of-life decisions. To achieve uniformity in the legal policy concerning assistance in dying by physicians, it decided that it would review every case of euthanasia to decide whether the attending physician would be legally prosecuted. In 1982, the government assigned a committee of experts to study and give advice on the permissibility and possibilities of regulating

assistance in dying by physicians. The committee issued its report in 1985 and established the definitions of physician-assisted suicide and euthanasia that have been used in the Netherlands ever since: Assisting in suicide is supplying or prescribing lethal drugs with the aim of enabling a person to end his or her own life; euthanasia is the administration of lethal drugs with the aim of ending the life of a person upon his or her explicit request. The committee proposed criteria for "due care" that had to be met in every case to avoid legal prosecution (State Commission on Euthanasia, 1985). These criteria had to be further developed through case law.

An important euthanasia case was the "Schoonheim case," which occurred in 1984 (Weyers, 2004). It was the first euthanasia case that was evaluated by the Dutch Supreme Court. In this case, euthanasia was performed on the explicit request of a 95-year-old patient who suffered unbearably from a combination of deteriorating eyesight, hearing, and speech, as well as being bedridden; the patient exhibited general decline and loss of dignity. The Court concluded that the physician had acted in a situation of "necessity," that is, the physician had been confronted with a conflict of duties: the duty to relieve unbearable suffering and the duty to do no harm. The defense of necessity was approved and the physician was dismissed from prosecution. Later on, in the "Chabot-case" (1994), where a Dutch psychiatrist ended the life of a woman suffering from depression, the Supreme Court added that suffering due to psychological problems also can be unbearable and may result in a situation of necessity. In the "Brongersma case" (2002), this was further specified in the sense that suffering should originate from a medically classifiable disease, from either a somatic or psychiatric origin. Brongersma was an 86-year-old male, who mainly suffered from loneliness and relatively minor health problems due to his high age. He was assisted in suicide by his general practitioner, who was prosecuted but not punished.

The Royal Dutch Medical Association was highly influential in the process that resulted in the legalization of physician-assisted suicide and euthanasia in the Netherlands. In the 1980s it already took an official supportive position regarding the legalization of physician-assisted suicide and euthanasia, and called for the elimination of barriers for physicians who were willing to report and account for their life-ending acts. They rephrased the due care criteria obtained from case law into medical-professional requirements that had to be met when assisting in suicide or performing euthanasia. These criteria state that before deciding to comply with a request for euthanasia or physician assistance in suicide, the physician has to assess that (1) the patient's request is voluntary and well considered, (2) the patient's suffering is unbearable and hopeless, (3) the patient is adequately informed about his situation and prospects, and (4) there are no reasonable alternatives to relieve the suffering. Further, (5) another, independent physician should be consulted and (6) the termination of life should be performed with due medical care and attention (de Haan, 2002). A distinct feature of the due care criteria is that they are purposely formulated in an open manner, the idea being that further content will be given to these criteria in the review procedures and case law.

Since the start of the debate on physician-assisted suicide and euthanasia, some physicians have been willing to have their cases reviewed, but their number was very limited until the mid-1980s. The Royal Dutch Medical Association considered formal societal control of the practice of euthanasia and physician assistance in suicide to be of extreme importance and encouraged physicians to report their cases. In 1985, the Ministry of Justice explicitly declared that, as a general rule, physicians who had complied with the due care criteria for physician-assisted suicide or euthanasia that had been developed in case law would not be prosecuted. In 1993, the Ministry of Justice proclaimed a formal notification and review procedure, to harmonize regional prosecution policies and eliminate practices that were perceived as hampering the physicians' willingness to report, such as policemen interrogating relatives shortly after a patient had died of euthanasia. This notification procedure entailed that the physician performing euthanasia must inform the local medical examiner about his or her act through filling out an extensive questionnaire. Subsequently, the medical examiner informed the public prosecutor, who decided whether the physician had adhered to the due care criteria and would be prosecuted. As a next step, in 1998, the government established a system of multidisciplinary review. All cases were, from that time forward, first reviewed by one of five regional review committees, each consisting of a lawyer, a physician, and an ethicist. The committees advise the public prosecutor about whether the due care requirements had been fulfilled, and the public prosecutor subsequently decided about prosecution. This reporting procedure was widely endorsed by physicians.

In 1994, an important change occurred in the composition of the national Dutch government: The Christian Democratic Party, which had been the majority party within all governing coalitions for decades, was excluded, and a government of liberals and social democrats came into power for 7 years. In 2001, this government proposed a law that defined the circumstances in which physicians would not be prosecuted for providing their patients with lethal drugs. The criteria for due care that had been formulated by the Royal Dutch Medical Association and the multidisciplinary review system were important elements of the proposed law. Parliament agreed, and on April 1, 2002, the Dutch Termination of Life on Request and Assisted Suicide (Review Procedures) Act came into force. It regulated the ending of life by a physician at the request of a patient who was suffering unbearably without hope of relief. The law includes a special ground for exemption from criminal liability in the Criminal Code for physicians who terminate life on request or assist in a patient's suicide, which means that such physicians can no longer be prosecuted, provided they satisfy the statutory due care criteria and notify death by nonnatural causes to the appropriate regional euthanasia review committee. The main aim of the law is to bring matters into the open, to apply uniform criteria in assessing every case in which a doctor assists in suicide or terminates life, and to ensure that maximum care is exercised in such cases. An important feature of the law is that physicians are not obliged to comply with a request for assistance in suicide or euthanasia. Further, neither physicians nor nurses can ever be censured for failing to comply with requests for physician-assisted suicide or euthanasia. The basic principle underlying physicians' and nurses' ability to refuse such a request is that patients have no absolute right to assistance in dying and doctors have no absolute duty to provide such assistance. The Act was the first to legalize euthanasia worldwide, but in fact it predominantly regulated existing practice. The only major change was that, under the Act, the review committees need to forward to the public prosecutor only those cases in which they judge that the due care criteria have *not* been met. Further, the Act specifies age limits for underage patients: Physician assistance in suicide and euthanasia are permitted for competent children aged 16 to 18 years, provided that the parents are involved in the decision making, and for competent children aged 12–16 years, provided that the parents agree with the decision.

Under the law, physician-assisted suicide and euthanasia are subject to the similar criteria for due care. Further, the law allows only physicians to be involved in these practices. A very important feature of the Dutch regulation is the definition that is used to demarcate the practice of physician-assisted suicide and euthanasia, in which the explicit request of the patient is central. Ending someone's life in the absence of an explicit request is illegal and not considered as a form of euthanasia. The definitions do not include the withdrawal or withholding of (potentially) life-prolonging treatments, nor the alleviation of pain or other symptoms with medication that may hasten death as an unintended but acknowledged side effect. Both these practices are considered to be part of normal medical practice and are subject to regular professional and legal regulations.

Other Countries

Physician-assisted suicide and euthanasia are legally regulated in a few other countries or states. For instance, Oregon's voters approved assisted suicide in 1994, which resulted in the Death with Dignity Act (ODDA) that legalized physician-assisted suicide for terminally ill individuals (Charatan, 1994). In 2008, residents of the state of Washington voted 58% to 42% to accept the Washington Death with Dignity Act, which is comparable to the Oregon law (Dyer, 2008). Both acts permit physicians to provide assistance in suicide by prescribing a lethal dose of medication for adults with an illness expected to lead to death within 6 months. Such patients may self-administer this medication in order to end their life. The attending physician and an independent consulting physician must determine that the patient is competent and has made a voluntary and informed decision. Assistance in suicide is not allowed for patients "suffering from a psychiatric or psychological disorder or depression causing impaired judgment." Physicians have to account for their act with the state authorities by reporting all prescriptions for lethal medications and filling in a compliance form that checks whether they complied with the criteria; surveillance is aimed at evaluating the overall effect of the Act (Steinbrook, 2008).

Switzerland does not have a law that specifically regulates physician assistance in dying; however, since the early 19th century, the Swiss Penal Code has allowed assistance in suicide provided that the person seeking assistance has decisional capacity and the person assisting is not motivated by reasons of self-interest (Bosshard, 2008). There is no specification of medical or procedural preconditions, except that opening the tap of the drip or tube that contains the lethal medication must always be carried out by the person wanting to die, which must be attested to by a witness. Assistance in suicide is mostly provided by right-to-die organizations, who are obliged to account for their practices before the legal authorities. Since no official notification system or review procedure exists in Switzerland, data on the frequency and practice of physician-assisted suicide are limited.

The Belgian parliament approved a law on euthanasia in 2002 (Griffiths, Weyers, & Adams, 2008). Physician-assisted suicide is not included in the Belgian law that only regulates euthanasia, under a definition that is similar to the Dutch definition. The Belgian law does not regulate euthanasia for minors. A physician can only proceed when he or she knows the patient well enough to be able to assess whether the request for euthanasia is voluntary and well considered, whether the patient's medical situation is without prospect of improvement, and whether the individual's suffering is unbearable. The Belgian euthanasia law was voted in after only 3 years of debate in parliament by the Federal Advisory Committee on Bioethics. Furthermore, in contrast to the situation in the Netherlands, no medical association supported the process in Belgium. The monitoring system in Belgium is largely comparable to the Dutch monitoring system, although less transparent: Belgian procedures are primarily anonymous, whereas the Dutch are not.

In 2009, Luxembourg was the third European country to legalize euthanasia (Watson, 2009). The Luxembourg law follows the Belgian experience and stipulates that physician-assisted suicide and euthanasia are allowed as long as physicians first consult a colleague to ensure that the patient has a terminal illness, is in a "grave and incurable condition," and has repeatedly asked for assistance in dying. Within 8 days of helping a patient to end his or her life, the doctor must fill out a questionnaire and submit it to a national committee of nine members, who will verify whether the various procedures were correctly followed.

Societal Background of the Legalization of Physician Assistance in Dying

Opinion polls show that some form of accepting and regulating euthanasia and physician assistance in suicide is increasingly supported by the general population in most Western countries (Cohen et al., 2006a). Public acceptance of physician-assisted suicide and euthanasia in the Netherlands is extremely high: In 1966, nearly 50% of the general population was found to consider euthanasia acceptable, and this percentage increased to 90% in 1998. The medical profession is less supportive than the general public in most countries. However, the notification and review procedures are widely endorsed by Dutch physicians: In 2005, about 80% of all cases of physician-assisted suicide and euthanasia were found to have been reported. Most unreported cases seemed to involve the use of drugs with a doubtful lethal potential, such as opioids for terminally ill patients, which may be considered to be part of a gray area between assistance in dying and regular relief of suffering (Rietjens et al., 2007). The Netherlands is thus the only country where, after a 30-year period of extensive but rather placid debates in the political, medical, and societal arenas and ample efforts to develop careful procedures for public review and accountability, the legalization process was widely supported by medical professionals, the general public, and national politics.

In most other countries and states, the issue of accepting or legalizing physician assistance in dying has provoked heated debates within the medical profession as well as in the political arena, with an often passionate opposition of the Christian church and Christian political parties. The laws in Belgium and Luxembourg were passed by a small majority of the votes in parliament. The Washington Death with Dignity Act was accepted by a 58% to 42% majority of its residents. Several attempts have been made to denounce the lawfulness of the Oregon Death with Dignity Act. The Australian Rights of the Terminally Ill Act, which was passed in 1995 in the Northern Territory as the world's first euthanasia legislation, was overturned in 1997 by Australia's Federal Parliament, after four patients had died under the Act.

The increased inclination among the general population to accept physician-assisted suicide and euthanasia is often considered to be the result of changes in modern society, such as individualization, diminished taboos concerning death, and an increased recognition that prolonging life should not always be the preferred focus of medical treatment. On a worldwide scale, attitudes toward euthanasia have been found to be related to the extent to which cultures have a traditional-religious versus a secular-rational orientation (Cohen et al., 2006b; Inglehart & Welzel, 2011). Within a traditional-religious-oriented culture, people tend to appreciate religion, family, and deference to authority as important values and to reject divorce, abortion, suicide, and euthanasia. Societies with secular-rational values have the opposite preferences on all of these topics. Within Western Europe, southern countries with a Catholic tradition tend to have a traditional-religious orientation, whereas in central and northern countries secular-rational values prevail. Another cultural axis, with a similar geographical pattern, involves a polarization between materialist and postmaterialist values. The unprecedented wealth in advanced societies has resulted in a shift from materialist values of economic and physical security toward postmaterialist values of subjective well-being, self-expression, and quality of life. Self-expression values give high priority to participation in decision making in economic and political life, and presumably in medical issues as well.

Several explorative studies have suggested that cultural differences between countries have a major impact on decision making in many fields of health care (Payer, 1996). Cultural values may at least partly determine professional opinions on what is defined as appropriate medical treatment for patients with life-threatening diseases. Cultural diversity also is likely to be related to public attitudes toward end-of-life care. Adequate relief of symptoms, psychosocial completion, and having a sense of control have been found as important characteristics of an optimal quality of the end of life in different countries (Rietjens, van der Heide, Onwuteaka-Philipsen, van der Maas, & van der Wal, 2006). The translation, however, of these common perspectives into preferences concerning end-of-life care is likely to be influenced by culturally based factors, such attitudes concerning the balance of quantity versus quality of life, an open versus a concealed approach of impending death, and autonomy versus paternalism.

It is noteworthy that the Netherlands has a history in which candor is highly valued (Rietjens, van der Maas, Onwuteaka-Philipsen, van Delden, & van der Heide, 2009), resulting in an open climate in which new views and ideas are generally welcomed and freely discussed. In Dutch political culture, there is a general conviction that it is better to guide and monitor social developments than to try to stop them, which has resulted in the well-known tradition of socio-legally regulating controversial practices, such as abortion, drug use, and assisted dying. The Dutch culture of openness and guidance also translates into a high frequency of explicit discussions of end-of-life decision making between physicians and patients and their families, higher than in some other European countries (van der Heide et al., 2003).

Other contextual factors that have to be taken into account in understanding differences in the acceptance and regulation of end-of-life decisions between countries concern the health care system. Currently, many efforts are undertaken to develop international comparative quality indicators for end-of-life care. It is very difficult to establish feasible, reliable, and valid indicators, and comparing the quality of end-of-life care between countries seems a bridge too far for the time being. However, the standards of health care are comparable between most industrialized countries, and it is unlikely that the quality of end-of-life care has an important role in explaining the variance in end-of-life decision making. Several other aspects of the organisation of health care are more likely to affect end-of-life decision making. The Dutch health care system has several important attributes that shaped a context of safeguards in which the legalization of euthanasia could take place. Social policies in the Netherlands have given broad support for equity in sharing financial burdens. As a result, virtually everyone is covered by health insurance and health care is freely accessible and affordable to all. Also, the general structure of the Dutch health care system is quite unique. The Dutch general practitioner is the pivot of primary care in the Netherlands and, as a result, end-of-life care is in many instances provided at home; 44% of the people who die of cancer or another chronic disease die at home (van der Velden, Francke, Hingstman, & Willems, 2009). Almost all inhabitants in the Netherlands have a general practitioner with whom they often have a long-standing and personal relationship This relationship enables general practitioners to carefully judge and understand their patients' situation and whether a request for assistance in dying is really voluntary, well considered, and based upon unbearable and hopeless suffering, which are the main criteria of due care for euthanasia or physician-assisted suicide. Cohen et al. (2007) found in their analysis of four countries that euthanasia and physician assistance in suicide are in general mostly provided at home.

Further, in some countries, such as the United Kingdom, end-of-life care is to a large extent organized as a separate branch in health care, with specialized institutions, caregivers, and supplies. In countries such as the Netherlands, end-of-life care is seen as an integral part of all health care sectors where patients die. Quality of end-of-life care is predominantly secured by providing physicians with the opportunity to consult expert teams or individual consultants. In addition, many general hospitals, larger nursing homes, and residential care homes have units for terminal or palliative care. It is unclear whether the organization of end-of-life care as a separate specialty has an impact on end-of-life decision-making practices. Within palliative care it is widely acknowledged that continued aggressive care is not beneficial for all patients with advanced disease. However, active hastening of death is often seen as challenging the core values of palliative care. Studies on the association between levels of palliative care training of individual physicians and their end-of-life practices had ambiguous results: It has been found that physicians highly skilled in palliative care tend to make more end-of-life decisions (Emanuel et al., 2000), but the reverse also has been suggested to be true (Löfmark et al, 2008).

The Practice of End-of-Life Decision Making
Research

Internationally comparable data on end-of-life decision-making practices are rather scarce. The broadly accepted notion within palliative care that continued "aggressive" interventions may not always be beneficial to the patient has not yet been translated in end-of-life decision making as a broadly accepted field of research. This is probably due to the sensitive nature of the issue: Conscious abandonment of the paradigmatic medical goal of postponing death is not easily empirically addressed without evoking debate about what is "right" and what is "wrong."

However, an important and unique feature of the process of legalizing physician-assisted suicide and euthanasia in the Netherlands was that it went hand in hand with a series of four nationwide studies of end-of-life decision-making practices. Before 1990, estimates of the frequency and characteristics of euthanasia, physician-assisted suicide, and other end-of-life decisions widely varied. At that time, the government decided that further policy concerning the legalization of euthanasia should await the findings of a committee appointed to scientifically study the frequency and characteristics of physicians' life-ending practices in the Netherlands. In 1990, this committee, the "Remmelink Committee," asked a research group, supervised by professor Paul J. van der Maas, to conduct a nationwide study on this issue (van der Maas et al., 1991). The 1990 study was replicated in 1995, 2001, and 2005 (Onwuteaka-Philipsen et al., 2003; van der Heide et al., 2007; van der Maas et al., 1997). Each study year, thousands of physicians provided information in written questionnaires and personal interviews. To enhance the cooperation of physicians, doctors who participated in the studies were held immune from prosecution. This series of studies has provided reliable and valid insights in Dutch trends and developments in the practice of end-of-life decision making.

The Dutch studies were aimed at understanding the practice of medical end-of-life decision making from a number of perspectives. It was considered important to know (a) what a physician actually does or omits to do; (b) what his or her intention in doing so is; (c) what the (most likely) effect of the act is; (d) how the patient is involved in making the decision about the act; and (e) whether the patient is competent, that is, able to assess the situation and to make a decision about it adequately. The key questions in all studies that underlie the classification of end-of-life decisions are shown in Box 27.1. An affirmative answer to the last question resulted in classifying an act as euthanasia when the drug

was administered by the physician at the explicit request of the patient, and as physician-assisted suicide when the patient had taken the drug himself or herself. A prominent aspect of the key questions is that terms such as "euthanasia" or "physician-assisted suicide" are not used in the questionnaire. This was especially important in the first study in 1990, a time at which these terms were not clearly defined and could have widely varying connotations and interpretations among physicians.

The Dutch questions and classification system were used in several studies in other countries, too, such as Australia (1996), Belgium (1998), and the United Kingdom (2006, 2008). The 2001 study in the Netherlands was conducted in conjunction with the EURELD project that, using identical study designs, simultaneously studied end-of-life practices in six different European countries: Belgium, Denmark, Italy, the Netherlands, Sweden, and Switzerland (van der Heide et al., 2003). Other well-known studies on end-of-life decision-making practices mainly concern intensive care units (ICUs), such as the ETHICUS study, a comparative study conducted in 1999/2000 in 37 ICUs in 17 European countries (Sprung et al., 2003). Insights into the practice of physician-assisted suicide in Oregon are mainly based on physicians' reports to the Oregon State Public Health Division.

Practice of Physician-Assisted Suicide and Euthanasia

In 1990, 1.7% of all deaths in the Netherlands were the result of euthanasia, as compared with 2.4% in 1995 and 2.6% in 2001 (see Table 27.1). This increasing trend reversed in 2005, when the percentage was 1.7% again, or approximately 2,300 cases annually. The number of patients who had explicitly asked their physician for assistance in suicide or euthanasia was substantially larger than the number of actual cases in all study years: The number of requests was 9,700 in 2001 and 8,400 in 2005, which means that about one-third of all requests are complied with. Despite a preference of the Royal Dutch Medical Association for physician assistance in suicide, it was much less common than euthanasia in all study years; the 2005 study found an annual number of about 100 cases of physician-assisted suicide. Possible explanations for the frequent choice of euthanasia over physician-assisted suicide are that physicians want to control the act and process of ending life. Assistance in suicide rather often involves unforeseen difficulties, such as a longer

---

Box 27.1 Key Questions to Classify End-of-Life Decisions

Concerning this patient:
Did you withhold or withdraw medical treatment

- while taking into account the possibility or certainty that this would hasten the patient's death, or
- with the explicit intention of hastening the patient's death?

Did you intensify the alleviation of pain and symptoms

- while taking into account the possibility or certainty that this would hasten the patient's death, or
- partly with the intention of hastening the patient's death?

Was death the result of the administration, supply, or prescription of drugs with the explicit intention of hastening the patient's death?

Table 27.1 Frequency of Euthanasia and Other End-of-Life Practices in the Netherlands, in 1990, 1995, 2001, and 2005

	1990	1995	2001	2005
No. of Studied Cases	5,197	5,146	5,617	9,965
	(%)	(%)	(%)	(%)
Euthanasia	1.7	2.4	2.6	1.7
Physician- assisted suicide	0.2	0.2	0.2	0.1
Ending of life without explicit patient request	0.8	0.7	0.7	0.4
Alleviation of symptoms with hastening of death as a likely side effect	19	19	20	25
Refraining from life-prolonging treatment	18	20	20	16

than expected time to death or failure to induce a continued coma (Groenewoud et al., 2000). Euthanasia also is preferred when patients are physically too weak or otherwise unable to swallow the oral barbiturate mixture that is typically used in assistance in suicide. The decline in the frequency of physician-assisted suicide and euthanasia in the period from 2000 to 2005 has been suggested to be the result of an increased use of other last-resort options to relieve unbearable suffering at the end of life, such as continuous deep sedation. Table 27.1 further shows that the frequency of ending life without an explicit patient request was significantly smaller than the frequency of euthanasia and decreased from 0.8% of all deaths, or approximately 1,000 cases, in 1990 to 0.4%, or approximately 550 cases, in 2005.

The rates of physician-assisted suicide and euthanasia in the Netherlands are clearly higher than the rates that were found elsewhere (see Table 27.2). The Australian study was conducted during the short period in which euthanasia was legally allowed in the state of Northern Territory, which may explain the relatively high euthanasia rate in that study. Based upon physicians' reports to the Oregon State Public Health Division, the frequency of physician-assisted suicide in the state of Oregon is estimated at about 0.25% of all deaths (http://public.health.oregon.gov/ProviderPartnerResources/EvaluationResearch/DeathwithDignityAct/Documents/year15.pdf).

In all studied countries, euthanasia and physician assistance in suicide are mainly provided at the request of patients with cancer who die under the age of 80. Their estimated life expectancy is usually

Table 27.2 Most Important Decision Concerning the End of Life, as Percentage of All Deaths

	NL	NL	BE	CH	DK	SW	IT	AU	UK
	2005				2001 (EURELD study)			1996	2006
Euthanasia plus physician-assisted suicide	1.8	2.8	0.3	0.6	0.1	0.0	0.0	1.8	0.2
Ending of life without explicit patient request	0.4	0.6	1.5	0.4	0.7	0.2	0.1	3.5	0.3
Intensified alleviation of symptoms	25	20	22	22	26	21	19	31	33
Limiting life-prolonging treatment	16	20	15	28	14	14	4	29	30
Total	43	44	38	51	41	36	23	65	64

NL, Netherlands; BE, Belgium; CH, Switzerland; DK, Denmark; SW, Sweden; AU, Australia; UK, United Kingdom.
Sources: NL 2005 (van der Heide et al., 2007); EURELD study 2001 (van der Heide et al., 2003); AU 1996 (Kuhse, Singer, Baume, Clark, & Rickard, 1997); UK 2006 (Seale, 2006).

limited to 1 month or less. In the Netherlands, over 80% of all cases of euthanasia and physician assistance in suicide are performed by general practitioners, at the patient's home. In Belgium and Oregon, physician assistance in dying is also often provided in hospitals by clinical specialists.

Typical reasons why patients ask their physician to provide assistance in dying include the absence of any prospect of improvement, loss of dignity, and suffering from severe symptoms. Severe pain is a reason in a minority of all cases and virtually never comes up as the sole reason to ask for physician assistance in dying. Cognitive decline, such as in Alzheimer's disease, are rare reasons, but review committees have approved cases in which envisaged cognitive decline due to an established diagnosis of early dementia was the primary cause of suffering.

Physician assistance in dying in the absence of an explicit patient request is rare in most countries studied, but the rates are relatively high in Belgium and Australia (see Table 27.2). This practice mostly involves the use of opioids in patients with an estimated life expectancy of less than 1 week, who rather often have cancer and who have become incompetent in the terminal stage of their disease. The ETHICUS study asked physicians whether they had actively shortened the dying process in patients who died at intensive care units (ICUs). Physicians reported to have done so in 0–19% of all deaths within ICUs in the various countries (Sprung et al., 2003).

Other End-of-Life Decisions

Assistance in suicide and euthanasia represents only a small fraction of physicians' involvement in hastening death or refraining from prolonging life. Intensified alleviation of symptoms with opioids in dosages that have "shortening of life" as an expected side effect is a much more common practice in all studied countries. It was most frequently found in Australia and the United Kingdom (see Table 27.2). The EURELD study also yielded comparative data about the use of continuous, deep sedation at the end of life, which is suggested to have potential life-shortening effects in some cases. Continuous deep sedation was most common in Belgium (8.2%) and Italy (8.5%; Miccinesi et al., 2006). Most other studies found higher rates, from 15% of deaths to more than 60%, but these studies often involved specialized end-of-life settings and broader definitions, so that higher frequencies are to be expected (Chiu, Hu, Lue, Cheng, & Chen, 2001; Fainsinger et al., 2000; Müller-Busch,

Andres, & Jehser, 2003; Sykes & Thorns, 2003). Intensive alleviation of symptoms with opioids or sedatives is typically used for patients with a very limited life expectancy, who are approaching death while suffering from severe symptoms, such as pain, dyspnea, or anxiety. Cancer patients also are overrepresented in this group. Patients dying in hospitals and patients dying at home more often receive opioids or sedatives as compared to patients dying in nursing homes.

End-of-life care also often includes decisions to withhold or withdraw potentially life-prolonging treatment because prolonging life is not considered in the best interest of the patient because of the side effects or other burdens of such treatment. Wide variations between and within countries and between care settings have been found for the practice of withdrawing and withholding potentially life-prolonging treatment and for the proportions of deaths that are preceded by do-not-resuscitate (DNR) orders (van Delden et al., 2006). Decisions to limit life-prolonging treatment are rare in Italy; more common in Denmark, Sweden, Belgium, and the Netherlands; and they are rather frequently made in Switzerland, Australia, and the United Kingdom (see Table 27.2). In the EURELD study, a DNR order had preceded death in about half of all cases in Switzerland, the Netherlands, and Sweden; in about 40% in Belgium and Denmark; and in a quarter of all deceased patients in Italy (van Delden et al., 2006). Limitation of treatment more often than other decisions involves elderly patients. Further, these decisions are often made earlier in the disease process and involve more shortening of life than intensive alleviation of symptoms. Decisions to refrain from potentially life-prolonging treatment and DNR agreements are most often made by clinical specialists and nursing home physicians. Death at an ICU is even more frequently preceded by treatment limitations. The ETHICUS study found that 73% of all deceased patients in ICUs had limitations of treatment. Percentages of deceased ICU patients for whom life-sustaining treatment had been withheld varied between 16% and 70% per country; for withdrawing treatment, the range was 5%–69% (Sprung et al., 2003).

Characteristics of the Decision Making

Large variations between countries have been found for the extent to which physicians consider the patients for whom they make end-of-life decisions competent and able to participate in the decision-making process. In the EURELD study, Dutch and Swiss physicians reported that only one-third of their deceased patients had been competent, and such rates were even lower in Denmark, Belgium, Sweden, and especially Italy, where only 9% were considered competent. Further, the rates at which physicians had discussed their decisions with competent patients were rather low in Sweden (38%) and Italy (42%), but much higher in Switzerland (78%) and the Netherlands (92%; van der Heide et al., 2003). These figures were comparable but somewhat less outspoken for discussing decisions with family in cases of incompetent patients. It is remarkable that high frequencies of end-of-life decisions seem to be associated with high levels of patient involvement in the decision making. A decision-making model in which self-determination of the patient plays an important role may involve higher rates of end-of-life decisions than a more paternalistic model. This hypothesis is in accordance with the frequently reported disapproval of patients of continued aggressive care at the end of life and with the finding that the dying process typically involves less than optimal communication between caregivers and terminally ill patients (Hofmann et al., 1997; Teno et al., 1997).

Reporting of Physician-Assisted Suicide and Euthanasia

Table 27.3 shows that in the Netherlands the reporting rates of cases of physician-assisted suicide and euthanasia have substantially increased after 1990. In 1990, 18% of all cases were reported to the public prosecutor. This percentage increased to 41% in 1995, 2 years after the government's proclaim of a uniform notification procedure. The installment of multidisciplinary review committees in 1998 was followed by a further increase to 54% in 2001, and the enforcement of the euthanasia act in 2002 resulted in a reporting rate of 80% in 2005.

An extensive evaluation of the euthanasia law in the Netherlands in 2005 revealed that a majority of Dutch physicians were of the opinion that the law improved their legal certainty and contributed to the carefulness of life-terminating acts. The main aims of the law, that is, providing legal certainty, transparency, and public control, and contributing to improvement of the quality of life-terminating acts of physicians, while recognizing the importance of the basic medical value of protection of life, were found to have been achieved. Nonreporting mainly concerns cases of euthanasia. Failure to report cases was initially predominantly related to physicians' reluctance to a judicial inquiry or fear for legal prosecution. In 2005, many physicians who had not reported their act(s) stated that they had not perceived it as euthanasia or ending the patient's life. Fear for legal prosecution was rarely mentioned. Not perceiving acts that fulfill the definition of euthanasia, that is, providing lethal medication upon the patient's request, predominantly concerns cases in which physicians used opioids instead of drugs with a more obvious lethal potential, such as neuromuscular relaxants.

The evaluation of reported cases in the Netherlands shows that physicians almost always adhere to the due care requirements when they assist in suicide or perform euthanasia. Review committees rarely identify problems in their review of reported cases. The verdict of noncompliance is given in less than 10 cases per year, and such a verdict has, until 2008, not resulted in legal prosecution.

It is unknown to what extent physicians are willing to report and account for their life-ending practices in other countries with legal systems that allow euthanasia or physician-assisted suicide. Belgium's Euthanasia Committee, which reviews all reported cases and publishes a report every 2 years, has stated that the procedure is working well. The most recent statistics show that Belgium had 429 cases of physician-assisted suicide in 2006. Of these, 340 occurred in the northern Dutch-speaking part of the country and 89 in the southern Francophone region.

Table 27.3 Reported Cases of Physician-Assisted Suicide and Euthanasia in 1990, 1995, 2001, and 2005

	1990	1995	2001	2005
Total estimated number of physician-assisted suicide and euthanasia	2,700	3,600	3,800	2,425
Reported number of physician-assisted suicide and euthanasia	486	1,466	2,054	1,933
Reporting rate	*18%*	*41%*	*54%*	*80%*

Hastening of death by physicians is rare under Oregon's Death with Dignity Act. Between 1998 and 2007, physicians reported a total of 541 prescriptions for lethal doses of medication; 341 people died as a result of taking the medications. The group of patients who died after ingesting a lethal dose of medication had a median age of 69 years, almost all were White and relatively well educated, and the group consisted of slightly more men than women, according to data collected by the Oregon Department of Human Services. About 86% were enrolled in hospice programs, and 82% had terminal cancers (Hedberg, Hopkins, Leman, & Kohn, 2009).

Legalizing Physician-Assisted Suicide or Euthanasia—The Debate
Arguments for Physician-Assisted Suicide or Euthanasia

The main arguments that underlie the societal experiments of allowing and regulating physician-assisted suicide or euthanasia relate to well-being and autonomy. All systems that allow physician assistance in dying have in some way included the notion that physician assistance in dying is only acceptable as a last resort intervention to address the absence of well-being and end severe suffering. The Dutch law is rather explicit and states that the physician has to be convinced that the patient's suffering is unbearable and without prospect of relief. A basic argument to allow assistance in dying is thus medical necessity: The medical goal of avoiding or ending unbearable suffering cannot be achieved in any other way that is acceptable to the patient. Other systems also give the physician an important role in judging whether the patient's situation warrants assistance in dying. The Oregon law, for example, states that the patient must be diagnosed by two physicians as having a terminal illness, defined as 6 months or less to live. The patient's own opinion on his or her situation and prospects is seen as a necessary, but insufficient, prerequisite.

The inclusion of the argument of well-being in current law sets limits on the reach of the argument of autonomy. This argument refers to the interest persons have in living their own lives according to their own conceptions of a good life and to the right of self-determination that ensures that persons, assuming they meet certain criteria for competency, are left free to act on these conceptions. If a person comes to the conclusion that continuing life is worse than no life at all and, after due consideration, asks a physician to end his or her life,

systems that allow assistance in dying in principle give physicians the opportunity to comply with such a request. However, physicians always need justification for their acts other than patient preferences. As a result, physician assistance in dying is not seen as a patient right. Medical values play a substantial role in end-of-life decision making, and whether physician-assisted death is justifiable is largely a matter of medical discretion in current legal systems (van Delden, 1999).

An additional argument to legalize physician assistance in dying is the lack of a moral difference between active assistance in dying and end-of-life practices that are more generally considered permissible, such as refraining from life-supporting treatment if the continuation of life is not considered to be in the best interest of the patient. Many deaths nowadays are preceded by medical decisions that are likely to shorten life or hasten death. In this view, physician-assisted suicide and euthanasia are practices at one end of a continuum of medical acts that have a major impact on the time and quality of dying. Further, physician assistance in dying has been shown to occur in many countries, regardless of legal regulations. A lack of legal regulation may result in illegal practices or negligence of due care criteria. Evidence of this hypothesis is limited, but an exploration among physicians and nurses who worked in AIDS care in Australia and California provided some insight in the potential drawbacks of an "underground" practice of physician-assisted suicide and euthanasia, such as "botched attempts," ending of life without consent, and lack of accountability (Magnusson, 2002). Proponents of legal regulation hold the view that it is better to guide and monitor life-ending practices than to forbid them.

Arguments Against Physician-Assisted Suicide or Euthanasia

Arguments against physician-assisted suicide or euthanasia are either principled or nonprincipled (Kopelman & De Ville, 2001). Principled arguments concern the wrongness of providing assistance in dying per se. Principled arguments cannot be contested with empirical data on the effects or shortcomings of tolerating or legally regulating this practice. Nonprincipled arguments do not take the stance that providing assistance in dying is essentially wrong in all circumstances. Those who defend nonprincipled arguments state that physician assistance in dying may have benefits for individual patients, but that it is nevertheless wrong to provide such assistance or tolerate this practice because the negative consequences outweigh these possible benefits. Another nonprincipled argument states that the defense of necessity, that is, the argument that physician assistance in dying is the only possible way of ending a patient's suffering, is flawed in the large majority of cases, due to the availability of acceptable alternatives. Nonprincipled arguments are mostly empirical in nature and should therefore take into account empirical data.

PRINCIPLED ARGUMENTS

Defenders of principled arguments against physician-assisted suicide and euthanasia hold the view that no person should have the right to deliberately end his or her own or someone else's life. The point of view is based on the belief that life belongs to God or that intended hastening of death is against human nature and a degradation of humanity. This argument also is used to counter autonomy and self-determination as values that plead in favor of allowing physician assistance in dying. Asking for physician assistance in dying is against God's will or against the human nature and such a request can therefore not be well considered by definition.

Principled arguments against physician-assisted suicide and euthanasia have been discussed for centuries, but secularization and individualization within Western societies have confined their impact in current debates. Opinion polls, such as the European Values Study, have found a significant decrease of nonacceptance of euthanasia among the general public in many western European countries during the last two decades (Cohen et al., 2006a). Further, life stances of physicians in six European countries were found to have a limited impact on their end-of-life decision-making practices (Cohen et al., 2008.). Another development that limits the impact of principled arguments against physician-assisted suicide and euthanasia is that they not only concern the active ending of life but also relate to decisions about whether to use medical interventions to prolong life, which are nowadays inevitable in many cases of patients with terminal diseases. Advances in medicine have greatly increased the possibilities to postpone death. At the end of the 1960s, however, an internationally shared feeling emerged that medicine's propensity to prolong life goes too far in some cases. The response to this notion differed among countries. Some countries, such as the United States, focused on nontreatment decisions, while others, such as the Netherlands, mainly discussed euthanasia. It is

noteworthy that the Netherlands was certainly not the first country to debate euthanasia. In the middle of the 19th century, euthanasia was discussed in England, Germany, and the United States, but not in the Netherlands. In fact, the first proposal to legalize euthanasia was made in 1906 in the state of Ohio (Emanuel, 1994).

NONPRINCIPLED ARGUMENTS

Current debates about the acceptability of physician assistance in dying mainly focus on nonprincipled arguments. The most important nonprincipled arguments concern the possible negative impact of allowing physician assistance in dying on the quality and availability of end-of-life care, the risk of a "slippery slope," and possible problems with assessing whether the legal criteria of due care are met. Evidence from empirical studies can be helpful to carefully assess the validity and reach of these arguments.

ADEQUATE PALLIATIVE CARE MAKES
ASSISTANCE IN DYING REDUNDANT

An important nonprincipled argument against physician-assisted suicide is that palliative care offers alternatives to relieve severe suffering in most, if not all cases. Modern palliative care offers many interventions to adequately treat pain, dyspnea, or other symptoms that are common in patients with advanced diseases. However, pain is a reason to ask for assistance in dying in only a minority of cases, and it is rarely the sole reason. The absence of any prospect of improvement for patients who are at the end stage of a lethal disease and who are suffering from a general deterioration, loss of physical functions, and extreme tiredness or dependence much more frequently underlies requests for euthanasia or assistance in suicide. Alleviation of such more general or existential aspects of suffering is difficult. The Dutch legal system addresses concerns about the presence of less far-reaching alternatives to alleviate suffering by requiring that physicians together with the patient come to the conclusion that no "reasonable" alternatives were available to improve the patient's situation. It is, however, to date somewhat unclear what "reasonable" means in this context. An evaluation of the reported cases of physician-assisted suicide and euthanasia in the Netherlands in 2005 has shown that physicians had, in about 20% of all cases, reported that alternative treatments, such as increasing pain medication or sedation, were available, but that patients had refused these alternatives in the large majority of cases. Physicians thus seem to give much weight to patients' preferences concerning possible alternatives, just like the review committees who generally approved these cases. Thus, in practice the confining impact of the medical framework on the reach of the patient's self-determination within the legal system for physician-assisted suicide and euthanasia does not fully extend to the availability of alternative treatment options.

The argument that palliative care offers sufficient alternative ways of relieving suffering at the end of life also is used in a broader sense. It is often stated that findings in many studies of patients with advanced diseases (e.g., metastasized cancer), frequently suffering from pain and other symptoms, should be seen as the result of inadequate treatment. A widely present lack of knowledge concerning adequate pain treatment and misunderstandings about the side effects of opioid treatment, among medical professionals as well as patients, is supposed to stand in the way of adequate end-of-life care. Efforts of the medical profession should be focused on education and research that help to improve treatment of severe symptoms such as pain, instead of considering hastening death as a way to address suffering at the end of life. The European Association for Palliative Care has expressed concerns that legalization of euthanasia or physician-assisted suicide may involve underdevelopment or devaluation of palliative care (Materstvedt et al., 2003). In contrast, several commentators have suggested that the legalization of physician-assisted death has contributed to substantial improvements in palliative care. In Oregon, this relates to the appropriate training of physicians, the communication of a patient's wishes regarding life-sustaining treatment, pain management, rates of referral to hospice programs, and the percentage of deaths occurring at home (Okie, 2005). An analysis of the process of legalization of euthanasia in Belgium and the contemporary development of palliative care also suggested that these areas of medical practice can be mutually reinforcing (Bernheim et al., 2008). The Netherlands was, in the past, often criticized for its presumed lack of palliative care. The existence of only a few hospices, for example, was interpreted as proof of the poor quality of end-of-life care. Much of this criticism was based on a misunderstanding of the Dutch health care system, where most palliative care is provided at home or in a nursing home, but it is true that palliative care was relatively underexposed in the beginning of the euthanasia debate (van Delden & Battin, 2008). In the last two decades, however, much effort has been put forth to improve the quality and accessibility of end-of-life care.

SLIPPERY SLOPE

A second type of argument against physician-assisted suicide and euthanasia is the "slippery slope" argument. According to this argument, allowing physician assistance in dying in specified circumstances, that is, for competent patients who make a well-considered and voluntary request, will inevitably lead to its expansion to vulnerable groups. Letting go the absolute prohibition of physicians' engagement in active ending of life is expected to result in physicians' inclination to more easily choose ending of life as a way to resolve suffering for patients who cannot speak for themselves, such as comatose patients, persons who are incompetent due to dementia or mental diseases, or infants. Further, "normalization" of the practice of ending life involves a degradation of the worth of human life. As such, proponents of this belief fear it will contribute to a conscious or unconscious feeling of redundancy or inferiority among elderly people, people with chronic diseases, or people with physical disabilities, who will, as a result, more easily tend to ask for physician assistance in dying.

The first point to be noted concerning this issue is the stability of the practice of physician-assisted suicide and euthanasia that can be seen in most jurisdictions. In the Netherlands, the incidence of physician-assisted suicide has remained virtually unaltered over the years, whereas there has been a slight increase in the incidence of euthanasia between 1990 and 2001 (van der Heide et al., 2007). This increase mainly involved patients from groups in which the rates of physician-assisted dying were already highest, that is, patients with incurable malignancies, severe symptoms, and a limited life expectancy. In 2005, the euthanasia rate had decreased again to the level of 1990, which suggests that the enforcement of the euthanasia law in 2002 did not have a major impact in terms of starting off a "slippery slope."

Battin and colleagues have more thoroughly examined data from Oregon and the Netherlands to assess this concern (Battin, van der Heide, Ganzini, van der Wal, & Onwuteaka-Philipsen, 2007). Without providing conclusive proof about the impact on all vulnerable patients, their analysis showed that people in Oregon or the Netherlands who died with a physician's assistance were most likely to be members of groups enjoying comparative social, economic, educational, professional, and other privileges. In both jurisdictions a smaller percentage of older people received assistance in dying than of younger patients, and gender ratios were slightly higher for males over time. In Oregon, assistance was not more common among the uninsured. In the Netherlands, recipients of assistance in dying were likely to be of equal or higher educational status. Inferential data further suggest that recipients of physician assistance in dying were less likely than the background population to be poor, to have a physical disability alone without concomitant serious or terminal illness, to be a mature minor, or to be a member of a racial minority. Whether low rates of physician-assisted dying among vulnerable persons reflect a protective effect of safeguards or unequal access to assistance is unclear.

AUTONOMY AND WELL-BEING

The most substantial criteria of due care relate to the two main arguments for allowing physician assistance in dying: the argument of autonomy and the argument of well-being. Reflecting the autonomy principle, patients have to be well informed of their situation, prospects, and feasible alternatives, and they have to be capable of making a well-considered and voluntary request. Further, patients must be diagnosed as having 6 months or less to live (Oregon) or as suffering unbearably without any hope of relief (Netherlands), which relates to the principle of well-being. Assessing whether these criteria of due care are met in individual cases of patients who request their physician to assist in dying can be difficult, which is seen as evidence of the impossibility of carefully providing and controlling assistance in dying.

Some commentators claim that a wish for assistance in dying is in itself proof of the incompetency of the person involved. The nonprincipled version of this argument states that requests for assistance in dying have a high risk of being influenced by a depressive mood or other causes of (temporary or partial) incompetency. This risk is recognized by jurisdictions that allow physician assistance in dying, as all of them include safeguards. The Oregon law requires physicians to refer patients for a mental health evaluation if they believe that the patient's request may be influenced by a mental disorder. Approximately 20% of requests for physician assistance in dying in Oregon have been estimated to come from depressed patients, but none progressed to actual assistance. None of 292 patients who died under the Oregon Act until 2006 had a mental illness influencing their decision, though there have been three disputed cases among the 9-year total of 456 who received prescriptions. Because not all patients who requested assistance were specifically evaluated by mental health professionals and because many cases of depression are missed in primary care, it is possible that some depressed patients received lethal prescriptions (Battin et al., 2007). If a patient in the Netherlands has a psychological illness, the attending physician should consult two independent specialists, at least one of whom must be a psychiatrist, and they must personally examine and interview the patient. Physician assistance in dying is very rarely provided to patients with mental illnesses. About two-thirds of explicit requests for assistance in dying are not granted. In 1995 it was found that in about one-third of all requests that were not granted, physicians gave the presence of psychiatric illness as at least one reason for not complying. Depression was mentioned as the predominant symptom in patients who died by physician-assisted suicide or euthanasia in 3% of all cases. The review committees' annual report about the year 2008 describes two cases of patients with psychiatric illnesses that were both finally approved. The review committees' judgment follows the Chabot judgment from 1994, where a psychiatrist was convicted of assisting the suicide of a patient whose suffering was psychological. No penalty was imposed, but in upholding the conviction, the Supreme Court stated that, if the cause of suffering was psychological, the court must exercise the utmost caution in establishing whether the circumstances constituted force majeure. In April 1995, the Medical Disciplinary Tribunal came to the same conclusion as the Supreme Court and the psychiatrist was reprimanded.

Evaluation of the patient's prognosis (i.e., prospects and degree of suffering) has been found to be the most difficult aspect of considering requests for assistance in dying for physicians (Buiting et al., 2008). It is difficult to ascertain whether a person who requests physician assistance in dying fulfills the criterion of having a life expectancy of 6 months or less, as is done in Oregon. When considering this argument, it should be noted that the prediction of an individual person's life expectancy becomes more accurate when death approaches, and that physician assistance in dying is typically provided to patients with cancer that is incurable according to current medical insights, who have an estimated life expectancy of 1 month at most. Cases of patients with a longer prognosis are rare. Interestingly, the Dutch law does not include life expectancy as a criterion. Instead, it states that the physician has to be convinced that the patient is suffering unbearably without any prospect of relief. Whether or not suffering is unbearable is, in principle, is to be judged by the patient and determined by his or her physical and mental resources and personality. The physician is required to add some objectification to this subjective judgment, by assessing whether he or she feels that the patient's evaluation of suffering is conceivable.

It seems obvious that absolute certainty about the patient's competence, prognosis, and degree of suffering in all cases is impossible. Jurisdictions have included due care criteria that relate to these concerns, and obligatory consultation of an independent medical expert in the criteria of due care also is meant to be a safeguard that maximizes certainty about the patient's situation. Whether or not the lack of absolute certainty justifies prohibition of assistance in dying in all cases is a matter of principled judgment.

PHYSICIAN ROLE

A final pair of arguments against legalization of physician assistance in dying concerns the role of the physician. The first of these two arguments is that physicians are essentially trained to protect the lives of their patients, in terms of quality and quantity, and being engaged in the ending of life is, by some, found to be at conflict with these primary responsibilities. Whereas this conflict may be relevant for physicians who oppose assistance in dying, it is obviously not troubling physicians who feel that providing such assistance can be an important contribution to the quality of the dying trajectory of some patients. Further, in the Netherlands, where physician assistance in dying is broadly accepted by the general public, no signs have been observed that physicians' involvement in euthanasia or suicide poses a threat to the physician–patient relationship.

A second argument against physician assistance in dying that relates to the role of the physician is that persons with a wish to die can stop eating and drinking until they pass away. Physician involvement is thus redundant, except for the usual medical care in the dying phase. Several case histories of competent persons who deliberately hastened their death by voluntary refusal of food and fluids while receiving care either at home or in a hospice have been reported. A study in the Netherlands found an annual frequency of dying by voluntary cessation of eating and drinking of 2.1% (Chabot & Goedhart, 2009). Fifty percent of such deaths were preceded by a request for physician assistance in dying that had been turned down. Research in Oregon has shown that hospice nurses generally rate the quality of dying by voluntary refusal of food and fluids as "good" (Harvath et al., 2004). In the Dutch study, caregivers judged the dying process in about 75% of such cases as "a dignified death" (Chabot & Goedhart, 2009).

Concluding Remarks

It is unlikely that the debate about the acceptability of physician assistance in suicide and euthanasia will ever be fully resolved. The practice of physician assistance in dying has been studied rather extensively in several countries. Quantitative studies, as well as anecdotal information and case histories, have shown the existence of a probably small-scale, underground practice of physician-assisted dying in several countries where such practice is illegal. News reports regularly describe judicial inquiries of suspected cases in different countries. Physicians from all over the developed world have, sometimes anonymously and sometimes openly, given details about their experiences. Regulatory systems requiring doctors to report cases to the judicial authorities, while guaranteeing that such reporting will not lead to prosecution if the physician complies with a set of guidelines for careful practice, should be seen as social experiments to assess whether this practice can be kept within agreed borders and publicly controlled.

Important common elements in many of the reported case histories are that the doctors involved seem to be devoted professionals with a deeply felt respect for patient autonomy, doctors who are committed to providing their patients with optimal end-of-life care. For these doctors, providing assistance in dying is the result of the desire to contribute to a good death for their patients. However, choosing to engage in the practice of physician-assisted dying involves a number of practical and other hazards, especially where it is illegal. The arrangements necessary to keep these practices hidden in order to avoid legal consequences include using inappropriate drugs and giving sublethal doses, sometimes by inappropriate routes of administration, for example, to avoid injection holes. Further, patient records or death certificates are falsified, and wrongful or incomplete information about the patient's health status and dying process is often given to nurses, pharmacists, or other caregivers. Relatives, and sometimes the patients themselves, may be involved in the conspiracy, either by helping to create unsuspicious circumstances or by administering the drugs. Being unable to openly discuss all relevant issues surrounding the dying process may negatively affect the patient's state of mind and complicate the process of mourning and coming to terms with the occasion for the bereaved relatives and caregivers.

Another threat is that secrecy prevents the development of an accepted standard for prudent practice. This makes it difficult, even for devoted doctors who try to maintain high ethical standards, to define the limits of acceptability. Case reports often concern doctors who have chosen to assist in the dying of a close relative, friend, or colleague, although personal involvement of doctors with their patients is considered a reason not to engage in the medical care of such people in general, and especially in end-of-life decision making. Further, an illegal status of active assistance in dying also may obscure the critical role of an explicit and voluntary patient request. One of the most important ethical justifications for doctors to engage in a practice that seems to contrast so sharply with the typical goals of medical care is respect for patients' autonomous wishes about their own end of life. But in countries where it is illegal, assistance in dying without an explicit patient request has been found to occur even more frequently than assistance in dying at the explicit request of patients.

Experiences with regulating physician assistance in dying in the Netherlands and Oregon have shown that a regulatory system based upon the idea of being simultaneously tolerant in individual cases and sufficiently protective of human life in general has been rather effective. The reporting of cases of physician assistance in dying rarely leads to judicial consequence, and the large majority of cases are reported, at least in the Netherlands. However, legalization also involves difficult and ongoing questions about the conditions for accepting the practice. All legal systems that allow assistance in dying have, for example, interpreted the issue as being part of medical practice. However, the request is not only made in order to bring an end to severe physical suffering; it also may partly or even predominantly originate from psychosocial or existential problems, and in many cases the exact origin may not be identifiable. Legalization of physician-assisted dying therefore inevitably involves further discussion of the medical borders of this practice. Should physician-assisted dying be allowed for types of suffering that do not originate from medical diseases per se, such as being tired of life at a very advanced age? Further, whether assistance in dying should exclusively be given by physicians, especially when existential elements of suffering predominate, can be questioned. When society asks doctors to act upon existential judgments they are not trained to make, the result is not only an extra emotional burden for them but also is a threat to the credibility of the moral and legal framework for the acceptance of physician assistance in dying and, consequently, a decrease in societal support.

Modern Western health care and public health seem to involve a certain level of public demand for physician assistance in dying, both in countries where it is legal and where it is illegal. This demand makes discussion of this issue inevitable and necessary. A regulatory system allowing physician assistance in dying offers better guarantees for the quality of medical care and for patient involvement than does illegality. However, legalization inevitably provokes difficult questions about the limits of the involvement of doctors in their patients' problems. Whether accepting and legalizing physician assistance in dying should, in the end, be positively weighed is obviously not only, and perhaps not primarily, an empirical but also a judicial and ethical question. It is clear that none of the current legal systems can serve as the final blueprint or can be the end of the discussion. On the contrary, legalization should above all be considered as the starting point for further societal and scientific debate on the role of doctors in achieving the aim of providing as many patients as possible with a good quality of dying.

References

Battin, M. P., van der Heide, A., Ganzini, L., van der Wal, G., & Onwuteaka-Philipsen, B. D. (2007). Legal physician-assisted dying in Oregon and the Netherlands: Evidence concerning the impact on patients in "vulnerable" groups. *Journal of Medical Ethics, 33*, 591–597.

Bernheim, J. L., Deschepper, R., Distelmans, W., Mullie, A., Bilsen, J., & Deliens, L. (2008).Development of palliative care and legalisation of euthanasia: Antagonism or synergy? *British Medical Journal, 336*(7649), 864–867.

Bosshard, G. Switzerland. In J. Griffiths, H. Weyers, & M. Adams (Eds.). (2008). *Euthanasia and law in Europe* (pp. 463–482). Oxford, UK: Hart.

Buiting, H. M., Gevers, J. K., Rietjens, J. A., Onwuteaka-Philipsen, B. D., van der Maas, P. J., van der Heide, A., & van Delden, J. J. (2008). Dutch criteria of due care for physician-assisted dying in medical practice: a physician perspective. *Journal of Medical Ethics, 34*(9), e12.

Castillo, L. S., Williams, B. A., Hooper, S. M., Sabatino, C. P., Weithorn, L. A., & Sudore, R. L. (2011). Lost in translation: The unintended consequences of advance directive law on clinical care. *Annals of Internal Medicine, 154*(2), 121–128.

Chabot, B. E., & Goedhart A. (2009). A survey of self-directed dying attended by proxies in the Dutch population. *Social Science and Medicine, 68*, 1745–1751.

Charatan, F. B. (1994). Oregon's voters approve assisted suicide measure. *British Medical Journal, 309*(6966), 1391.

Chiu, T. Y., Hu, W. Y., Lue, B. H., Cheng, S. Y., & Chen, C. Y. (2001). Sedation for refractory symptoms of terminal cancer patients in Taiwan. *Journal of Pain Symptom Management, 21*, 467–472.

Cohen, J., Bilsen, J., Fischer, S., Löfmark, R., Norup, M., van der Heide, A., . . . Deliens, L. (2007). End-of-life decision-making in Belgium, Denmark, Sweden and Switzerland: does place of death make a difference? *J Epidemiol Community Health, 61*(12), 1062–1068.

Cohen, J., Marcoux, I., Bilsen, J., Deboosere, P., van der Wal, G., & Deliens, L. (2006a). Trends in acceptance of euthanasia among the general public in 12 European countries (1981-1999). *European Journal of Public Health, 16*(6), 663–669.

Cohen, J., Marcoux, I., Bilsen, J., Deboosere, P., van der Wal, G., & Deliens, L. (2006b). European public acceptance of euthanasia: Socio-demographic and cultural factors associated with the acceptance of euthanasia in 33 European countries. *Social Science and Medicine, 63*, 743–756.

Cohen, J., van Delden, J., Mortier, F., Löfmark, R., Norup, M., Cartwright, C., . . . Eureld Consortium. (2008). Influence of physicians' life stances on attitudes to end-of-life decisions and actual end-of-life decision-making in six countries. *Journal of Medical Ethics, 34*(4), 247–253.

Covinsky, K. E., Fuller, J. D., Yaffe, K., Johnston, C. B., Hamel, M. B., Lynn, J., . . . Phillips, R. S. (2000). Communication and decision making in seriously ill patients: findings of the SUPPORT project. The Study to Understand Prognosis and Preferences for Outcomes and Risks of Treatments. *Journal of the American Geriatric Society, 48*(5 Suppl.), S187–193.

de Boer, M. E., Hertog, C. M., Dröes, R. M., Jonker, C., & Eefsting, J. A. (2010). Advance directives in dementia: Issues of validity and effectiveness. *International Psychogeriatrics, 22*(2), 201–208.

de Haan, J. (2002). The new Dutch law on euthanasia. *Medical Law Review, 10*(1), 57–75.

Dyer, C. (2008). Washington follows Oregon to legalise physician assisted suicide. *British Medical Journal, 337*, a2480.

Emanuel, E. J. (1994). The history of euthanasia debates in the United States and Britain. *Annals of Internal Medicine, 121*(10), 793–802.

Emanuel, E. J., Fairclough, D., Clarridge, B. C., Blum, D., Bruera, E., Penley, W. C., . . . Mayer, R. J. (2000). Attitudes and practices of U.S. oncologists regarding euthanasia and physician-assisted suicide. *Annals of Internal Medicine, 133*, 527–532.

Fainsinger, R. L., Waller, A., Bercovici, M., Bengtson, K., Landman, W., Hosking, M., . . . deMoissac, D. (2000). A multicentre international study of sedation for uncontrolled symptoms in terminally ill patients. *Palliative Medicine, 14*, 257–265.

Field, M. J., & Cassel, C. K. (Eds.). (1997). *Approaching death: Improving care at the end of life*. Washington, DC: Institute of Medicine, Committee on Care at the End of Life, National Academy Press.

Griffiths, J., Weyers, H., & Adams, M. (Eds.). (2008). *Euthanasia and law in Europe*. Oxford, UK: Hart.

Groenewoud, J. H., van der Heide, A., Onwuteaka-Philipsen, B. D., Willems, D. L., van der Maas, P. J., & van der Wal, G. (2000). Clinical problems with the performance of euthanasia and physician-assisted suicide in The Netherlands. *New England Journal of Medicine, 342*, 551–556.

Harvath, T. A., Miller, L. L., Goy, E., Jackson, A., Delorit, M., & Ganzini, L. (2004). Voluntary refusal of food and fluids: Attitudes of Oregon hospice nurses and social workers. *International Journal of Palliative Nursing, 10*(5), 236–41.

Hedberg, K., Hopkins, D., Leman, R., & Kohn, M. (2009). The 10-year experience of Oregon's Death with Dignity Act: 1998-2007. *Journal of Clinical Ethics, 20*(2), 124–132.

Hofmann, J. C., Wenger, N. S., Davis, R. B., Teno, J., Connors, A. F., Jr., Desbiens, N., . . . Phillips, R.S. (1997). Patient preferences for communication with physicians about end-of-life decisions. *Annals of Internal Medicine, 127*, 1–12.

Oregon Health Authority Public Health. Death with Dignity Act Annual Reports. Year 15. Retrieved February 2014, from http://public.health.oregon.gov/ProviderPartnerResources/EvaluationResearch/DeathwithDignityAct/Pages/ar-index.aspx.

Inglehart, R., & Welzel, C. (2011). *The WVS cultural map of the world*. Retrieved September 2011, from http://www.worldvaluessurvey.org/wvs/articles/folder_published/article_base_54.

Knaus, W. A., Harrell, F. E., Jr., Lynn, J., Goldman, L., Phillips, R. S., Connors, A. F., Jr., . . . Wagner, D. P. (1995). The SUPPORT prognostic model. Objective estimates of survival for seriously ill hospitalized adults. Study to Understand Prognosis and Preferences for Outcomes and Risks of Treatments. *Annals of Internal Medicine, 122*, 191–203.

Kopelman, L. M., & De Ville, K. A. (2001). The contemporary debate over physician-assisted suicide. In L. M. Kopelman & K. A. De Ville (Eds.), *Physician-assisted suicide. What are the issues?* (pp. 1–25). Dordrecht, The Netherlands: Kluwer Academic.

Kuhse, H., Singer, P., Baume, P., Clark, M., & Rickard, M. (1997). End-of-life decisions in Australian medical practice. *Medical Journal of Australia, 166*, 191–6.

Löfmark, R., Nilstun, T., Cartwright, C., Fischer, S., van der Heide, A., Mortier, F., . . . EURELD Consortium. (2008). Physicians' experiences with end-of-life decision-making: Survey in 6 European countries and Australia. *BMC Medicine, 6*, 4.

Lynn, J., & Adamson, D. M. (2003). *Living well at the end of life. Adapting health care to serious chronic illness in old age.* [Rand Health White Paper WP 137]. Santa Monica, CA: Rand.

Lynn, J., Teno, J. M., Phillips, R. S., Wu, A. W., Desbiens, N., Harrold, J., . . . Connors, A. F., Jr. (1997). Perceptions by family members of the dying experience of older and seriously ill patients. *Annals of Internal Medicine, 126*, 97–106.

Magnusson, R. S. (2002). *Angels of death. Exploring the euthanasia underground*. Australia, Victoria: Melbourne University Press.

Materstvedt, L. J., Clark, D., Ellershaw, J., Førde, R., Gravgaard, A. M., Müller-Busch, H. C., . . . EAPC Ethics Task Force. (2003). Euthanasia and physician-assisted suicide: A view from an EAPC Ethics Task Force. *Palliat Med, 17*(2), 97–101.

Miccinesi, G., Rietjens, J. A., Deliens, L., Paci, E., Bosshard, G., Nilstun, T., Norup, M., . . . EURELD Consortium. (2006). Continuous deep sedation: Physicians' experiences in six

European countries. *Journal of Pain Symptom Management,* *31*, 122–129.

Müller-Busch, H. C., Andres, I., & Jehser, T. (2003). Sedation in palliative care—a critical analysis of 7 years experience. *BMC Palliative Care, 2,* 2.

Nusselder, W. J., van der Velden, K., van Sonsbeek, J. L., Lenior, M. E., & van den Bos, G. A. (1996). The elimination of selected chronic diseases in a population: The compression and expansion of morbidity. *American Journal of Public Health, 86,* 187–194.

Okie, S. (2005). Physician-assisted suicide—Oregon and beyond. *New England Journal of Medicine, 352*(16), 1627–1630.

Onwuteaka-Philipsen, B. D., van der Heide, A., Koper, D., Keij-Deerenberg, I., Rietjens, J. A., Rurup, M. L., ...van der Maas, P. J. (2003). Euthanasia and other end-of-life decisions in the Netherlands in 1990, 1995, and 2001. *Lancet, 362*(9381), 395–399.

Parker, M. G., & Thorslund, M. (2007). Health trends in the elderly population: Getting better and getting worse. *Gerontologist, 47,* 150–158.

Payer, L. (1996). *Medicine and culture.* New York, NY: Holt.

Rietjens, J. A., Bilsen, J., Fischer, S., van der Heide, A., van der Maas, P. J., Miccinessi, G., ...van der Wal, G. (2007). Using drugs to end life without an explicit request of the patient. *Death Studies, 31*(3), 205–221.

Rietjens, J. A., van der Heide, A., Onwuteaka-Philipsen, B. D., van der Maas, P. J., & van der Wal, G. (2006). Preferences of the Dutch general public for a good death and associations with attitudes towards end-of-life decision-making. *Palliative Medicine, 20,* 685–692.

Rietjens, J. A. C., van der Maas, P. J., Onwuteaka-Philipsen, B. D., van Delden, J. M. M., & van der Heide, A. (2009). Two decades of research on euthanasia from the Netherlands. What have we learnt and what questions remain? *Bioethical Inquiry, 6,* 271–283.

Seale, C. (2006). National survey of end-of-life decisions made by UK medical practitioners. *Palliative Medicine, 20,* 3–10.

Sepúlveda, C., Marlin, A., Yoshida, T., & Ullrich, A. (2002). Palliative care: The World Health Organization's global perspective. *Journal of Pain Symptom Management, 24*(2):91–96.

Sprung, C. L., Cohen, S. L., Sjokvist, P., Baras, M., Bulow, H. H., Hovilehto, S., ...Ethicus Study Group. (2003). End-of-life practices in European intensive care units: The Ethicus Study. *Journal of the American Medical Association, 290,* 790–797.

State Commission on Euthanasia. (1985). *Rapport van de Staatscommissie Euthanasie.* Den Haag, The Netherlands: Staatsuitgeverij.

Steinbrook, R. (2008). Physician-assisted death—from Oregon to Washington State. *New England Journal of Medicine, 359*(24), 2513–2515.

Sykes, N., & Thorns, A. (2003). Sedative use in the last week of life and the implications for end-of-life decision making. *Archives of Internal Medicine, 163*(3), 341–344.

Teno, J., Lynn, J., Wenger, N., Phillips, R. S., Murphy, D. P., Connors, A. F., Jr, ...Knaus, W. A. (1997). Advance directives for seriously ill hospitalized patients: Effectiveness with the patient self-determination act and the SUPPORT intervention. *Journal of the American Geriatric Society, 45,* 500–507.

Teunissen, S. C., Wesker, W., Kruitwagen, C., de Haes, H. C., Voest, E. E., & de Graeff, A. (2007). Symptom prevalence in patients with incurable cancer: A systematic review. *Journal of Pain Symptom Management, 34,* 94–104.

Tolle, S. W., Tilden, V. P., Hickman, S. E., & Rosenfeld, A. G. (2000). Family reports of pain in dying hospitalized patients. *Western Journal of Medicine, 172,* 374–377.

van Delden, J. J. M. (1999). Slippery slopes in flat countries—a response. *Journal of Medical Ethics, 25,* 22–24.

van Delden, J. J. M., & Battin M. P. (2008). Euthanasia: Not just for rich countries. In R. Green & A. Donovan (Eds.), *Global bioethics* (pp. 243–261). Oxford, UK: Oxford University Press.

van Delden, J. J. M., Lofmark, R., Deliens, L., Bosshard, G., Norup, M., Cecioni, R., & van der Heide, A. (2006) Do-not-resuscitate decisions in six European countries. *Critical Care Medicine, 34,* 1886–1890

van der Heide, A., Deliens, L., Faisst, K., Nilstun, T., Norup, M., Paci, E., van der Wal, G., & van der Maas, P. J. (2003). End-of-life decision-making in six European countries: Descriptive study. *Lancet, 362,* 345–350.

van der Heide, A., Onwuteaka-Philipsen, B. D., Rurup, M. L., Buiting, H. M., van Delden, J. J., Hanssen-de Wolf, J. E., ...van der Wal G. (2007). End-of-life practices in the Netherlands under the Euthanasia Act. *New England Journal of Medicine, 356*(19), 1957–65.

van der Maas, P. J., van Delden, J. J., Pijnenborg, L., & Looman, C. W. (1991). Euthanasia and other medical decisions concerning the end of life. *Lancet, 338*(8768), 669–674.

van der Maas, P. J., van der Wal, G., Haverkate, I., de Graaff, C. L., Kester, J. G., Onwuteaka-Philipsen, B. D., ...Willems, D. L. (1996). Euthanasia, physician-assisted suicide, and other medical practices involving the end of life in the Netherlands, 1990-1995. *New England Journal of Medicine, 335*(22), 1699–1705.

van der Velden, L. F., Francke, A. L., Hingstman, L., & Willems D. L. (2009). Dying from cancer or other chronic diseases in the Netherlands: Ten-year trends derived from death certificate data. *BMC Palliative Care, 8,* 4.

van Duin, C., & Garssen, J. (2010). *Bevolkingsprognose 2010-2060: Sterkere vergrijzing, langere levensduur.* Nederland, Den Haag: Centraal Bureau voor de Statistiek.

Watson, R. (2009). Luxembourg is to allow euthanasia from 1 April. *British Medical Journal, 338,* b1248.

Weyers, H. (2004). *Euthanasie: Het process van rechtsverandering.* Amsterdam, The Netherlands: Amsterdam University Press.

Wolleswinkel-van den Bosch, J. H., Looman, C. W., van Poppel, F. W., & Mackenbach, J. P. (1997). Cause-specific mortality trends in The Netherlands, 1875-1992: A formal analysis of the epidemiologic transition. *International Journal of Epidemiology, 26,* 772–781.

CHAPTER
28

Survivors of Suicide

Holly Parker

Abstract

Every year, tens of thousands of individuals in the United States lose a loved one to suicide. As a result of their loss, people bereaved by suicide (i.e., survivors of suicide) are susceptible to a wide range of psychosocial challenges that can impair one's quality of life. Importantly, suicide survivors themselves appear to be at an increased risk of dying by suicide. Despite the potential difficulties and risks for survivors, very little is known about suicide bereavement. Thus, the aim of this chapter is to delineate the current state of the literature in this field and provide suggestions for future research. Primary topics addressed in this chapter include psychosocial sequelae of suicide bereavement across adult loved ones, practitioners, adolescents, and children; whether suicide bereavement is distinct from other types of loss; coping with loss; cross-cultural considerations; and current and innovative treatment approaches.

Key Words: suicide, bereavement, psychosocial, survivors, coping, treatment, empirical, review

Suicide is a widespread problem. According to the National Center for Health Statistics, over 30,000 people die by suicide each year. In 2010, the latest year for which we have mortality statistics, there were 38,364 suicides. Although these statistics attest to the prevalence of suicide, they do not reflect the full impact of suicide by considering those left behind in its wake. The reality is that people who have lost a loved one to suicide are not alone in the United States. Although there are no official statistics on the impact of suicide, it has been estimated that for every individual who dies by suicide, six people are impacted (Shneidman, 1973). More recent attempts to empirically assess the number affected was quite close to this estimate, slightly over five individuals, although there was some variation around this number depending on the type of loss (Berman, 2011). Thus, if we assume that six individuals are impacted by each suicide and consider the loved ones of each of the 38,364 individuals who died by suicide in 2010 (and a presumably similar number of suicides in subsequent years), then approximately 230,184 individuals will be left behind to grieve a loved one's suicide each year. This staggering number translates into 630 individuals every day and roughly one person every 2 minutes.

Despite the large number of people who lose a loved one to suicide each year, also known as "survivors of suicide," investigators have primarily focused on suicidal behavior, risk factors for suicide, and psychopathological conditions associated with suicide, such as depression. Because suicide has been the focus of research, rather than loss from suicide, the experience of survivors of suicide is a less explored area in the literature by far. For example, a search of PsychINFO, a research engine for psychology articles from 1872 to 2013, generated 36,566 citations for "suicide," but only 550 citations for "survivors of suicide."

Unfortunately, as the dearth of research in this field indicates, we know very little about the experience of suicide bereavement and factors that may influence its course, such as social support, stigma, age, culture, relationship to the deceased, and coping processes. Moreover, our knowledge of treatment options for individuals bereaved by suicide also is limited. Yet it would seem quite important to examine loss to suicide in greater detail, as it is a special kind of death that can elicit a variety of emotions from people, such as sadness, shock, disgust, anger, curiosity, and compassion, because the act of killing oneself seems so contrary to the imperative of all animals to survive. Importantly, it also presents the survivors with the difficult process of reconciling feelings associated with the loss of their loved one with their feelings about the loved one's decision to end his or her own life.

The large numbers of individuals who are impacted by suicide and the extensive suffering involved are reflective of the importance from both a human interest and public health perspective of enhancing our knowledge base of the experiences, coping abilities, resources, challenges, and treatment options for people in the aftermath of suicide. Thus, the aim of this chapter is to illustrate the current knowledge base in suicide bereavement, to highlight gaps in our understanding, and to suggest future directions in research.

Caveats in the Suicide Bereavement Literature

Given that our empirical knowledge of the field of suicide bereavement is still in its infancy, there are certain challenges inherent to summarizing what we know in a new, emerging area, as a number of researchers in this field have observed (Ellenbogen & Gratton, 2001). Arguably, some of these difficulties are part of conducting research, particularly in suicide bereavement (and bereavement more generally); fortunately, other challenges can be remedied through changes in the methods used to examine our research questions.

First, most studies of suicide bereavement rely on cross-sectional data from survivors, rather than prospective, longitudinal designs. Second, many studies do not employ a comparison group, and those that do may not select appropriate groups, such as comparing suicide survivors with nonbereaved controls only. Third, sample sizes are generally small, which may mask significant group differences through insufficient statistical power. Fourth, sampling methods vary widely across studies, with some studies drawing from medical examiners' records, others recruiting from community or undergraduate samples, and others pulling from survivors who

are in treatment. In addition, a fifth challenge is a high rate of refusal among survivors to participate in research, which is likely a function (understandably) of their reluctance to volunteer for studies at a time when they are facing a myriad of emotional and logistical life stressors that often accompany bereavement. It has been estimated that most studies obtain a response rate of 60% to 70% (i.e., Ellenbogen & Gratton, 2001). Moreover, among those who do participate, the demographic characteristics represented are skewed, with a majority of participants being Caucasian women from middle- to upper-class socioeconomic backgrounds. As a result, the external validity of the findings from such studies is in doubt. Conceptually driven challenges in the field are that the theoretical basis of research questions and the operational definitions of concepts have not always been clearly illustrated. Unfortunately, these issues compromise the advancement of our understanding of underlying processes and mechanisms in suicide bereavement.

There are other methodological challenges as well. Some studies attempt to assess grief without a measure specifically designed for grief, replacing it with other measures of distress, such as the Beck Depression Inventory (BDI). Moreover, the majority of studies on suicide bereavement do not control for potential confounding variables, such as the quality of the relationship to the deceased. This undermines our ability to clarify how the experience of losing someone to suicide influences survivors' reactions, grief trajectories, or treatment responses. Finally, some researchers have argued that studies employing quantitative analyses also should incorporate qualitative analyses of bereavement, as this would help us to determine whether there are categorically specific features of suicide bereavement (Ellenbogen & Gratton, 2001). The aforementioned challenges in the literature notwithstanding, what have we learned about suicide bereavement?

Suicide Bereavement as a Traumatic Stressor

Without question, losing a loved one is one of the most difficult experiences an individual can bear (Holmes & Rahe, 1967). The loss that accompanies a loved one's death can be excruciating, leaving some relatives and friends with chronic grief, depression, and posttraumatic stress disorder (PTSD).

The experience of losing a loved one to suicide almost certainly qualifies as a traumatic stressor. It is outside the realm of normal human experience, it is shocking, and it often involves witnessing the death of a love one. It can involve considerable guilt, which predicts the development of PTSD above and beyond other predictors of posttraumatic stress (e.g., McNally, 2003, p. 85). Kaltman and Bonanno (2003) noted that the violent nature of the death places people who lose a loved one to suicide at risk for PTSD, which also can increase the severity of the grief course.

There is some evidence to suggest that there is a stronger association between suicide bereavement and PTSD among those who were directly exposed to the suicide (i.e., witnessing it, hearing it, being in close proximity when it occurred, finding the body) relative to those who learned of the suicide through other means (e.g., being informed by the police or loved ones; discovering evidence of a loved one's suicide via a newspaper article). Individuals who experienced direct exposure to the suicide (as defined earlier) reported more re-experiencing PTSD symptoms than those who were not directly exposed (Parker, 2004). Survivors who were directly exposed also reported more avoidance symptoms compared to those who learned of the suicide through relatives or friends. In contrast, there appears to be no difference in avoidance symptoms between direct exposure and learning of the suicide from the police, or through discovery of evidence that a loved one died by suicide (Parker, 2004). Research estimates of the percentage of suicide survivors who will actually witness their loved one's suicide is wide, ranging from approximately 4% to 23.7% (if being present over the phone is considered, which is consistent with the notion of "direct exposure") (McDowell, Rothberg, & Koshes, 1994).

In addition to determining aspects of the suicide event itself that may be associated with the development of PTSD, it also will be important to expand our understanding of contextual relationship factors that may increase the likelihood of PTSD. For example, preliminary research suggests that individuals who lived with the deceased were more likely to report both re-experiencing and avoidance symptoms compared to those who did not live with the deceased (Parker, 2004).

Beyond factors associated with the suicide and the survivor's relationship with the deceased, we also must consider individual differences among survivors that may increase the risk for PTSD. One likely example is education. In one study, suicide survivors with a high school education were more likely to report re-experiencing symptoms of PTSD relative to those who completed some college, who graduated from college, or who earned a graduate degree (Parker, 2004).

Another important, plausible individual differences factor associated with PTSD among survivors of suicide is blame. Research strongly suggests that different types of blame affect psychological adjustment after the loss of a loved one and other highly stressful events, but the question of how blame impacts emotional health has produced mixed findings. Some researchers have found that blame toward others for a traumatic event can be helpful in coping, because it deflects feelings of responsibility and guilt, a risk factor for PTSD, and protects one's self-esteem (Miller & Porter, 1983). Alternatively, other researchers argue that blame toward others after a traumatic event leads people to feel that the event and the world are out of their control, which can undermine healthy emotional adjustment (Janoff-Bulman, 1992). As of the writing of this chapter, there exists sparse empirical research on blame and suicide bereavement, particularly with regard to posttraumatic stress.

Preliminary data that exist on blame and PTSD among survivors of suicide suggest, strikingly, that people who blame the deceased experience the lowest PTSD symptom severity, as well as the mildest avoidance and arousal symptoms relative to those who blame third parties (that is, someone other than oneself or the deceased) and those who do not blame anyone (Parker & McNally, 2006). However, the contrast in symptom severity appeared greatest between people who blamed the deceased and those who exclusively blamed others. This seems counterintuitive, particularly in light of research suggesting that the expression of positive emotion after the loss of a loved one is associated with better emotional outcomes compared to the expression of negative emotions (Bonanno & Keltner, 1997). This pattern is, however, consistent with Janoff-Bulmann's (1992) theory that blame toward others makes an event more traumatogenic by undermining one's assumptions that the world is a safe, fair, predictable place in which negative events do not occur randomly. The suicide of a loved one is a different type of loss because the loved one was the cause of his or her own death. If others caused it or are to blame, then this violates the assumption that the world is just, fair, and predictable, thereby making the event more traumatogenic. In contrast, blame directed toward the deceased places order back into the trauma because the loved one "made his or her own decision."

We are at the beginning of our understanding of how a loved one's suicide, the relationship with the loved one, and individual differences within the survivor contribute to the development of PTSD. As of this writing, research designs in this area have largely been cross-sectional. Although this provides a valuable "snap shot" of the associations between PTSD and suicide bereavement, this does not elucidate predictors of PTSD or how such predictors may interact with each other.

Thus, research that incorporates a prospective, longitudinal design is needed to advance our knowledge of what predicts PTSD after a loved one's suicide, as well as protective factors that decrease the probability of developing PTSD and facilitate recovery. It is reasonable to assume that there will be substantial overlap between risk and protective factors for PTSD after a loved one's suicide and after other traumatic events (e.g., motor vehicle accident, combat). Assuming this is accurate, then predictors of PTSD in the context of other types of trauma, such as preexisting mental health issues (e.g., van der Velden & Wittmann, 2008), poor social support (e.g., Iversen et al., 2008), anxiety sensitivity (e.g., Hensley & Varela, 2008), psychological processes at the time of the trauma (e.g., Ozer, Best, Lipsey, & Weiss, 2008), depression and acute stress (Birmes, Daubisse, & Brunet, 2008), and even cigarette smoking shortly after the trauma (van der Velden, Kleber, & Koenen, 2008), should be examined in future research. However, given the phenomenological discrepancies between losing a loved one to suicide and being involved in a motor vehicle accident, there are likely to be predictors that are specific to suicide bereavement (e.g., blame toward the deceased) that remain to be examined.

Arguably, this issue is made more complex by recent evidence that PTSD symptoms among individuals experiencing bereavement may cluster into a different set of factors compared with PTSD symptoms following other types of trauma. These bereavement-related PTSD factors are (1) re-experiencing, (2) avoidance, (3) dysphoria, and (4) hyperarousal (Boelen, van den Hout, & van den Bout, 2008). Subsequent research should examine the validity of this factor structure in suicide bereavement, the risk and protective variables associated with these symptoms, and whether response to treatment is different from PTSD following other types of trauma.

Grief

The suicide of a loved one is, fundamentally, the death of a loved one that brings with it the experience of grief (i.e., emotional suffering in response to

the loss) during a period of bereavement (i.e., the period of time after a loss when one grieves). Before discussing grief in the context of suicide bereavement, it is worth clarifying some important concepts in the grief literature more broadly.

First, what does it mean to grieve "normally" versus "abnormally?" Many researchers agree that certain symptoms often appear in people grieving the loss of a loved one and are not indicative of abnormal grief or mental illness. For instance, after a loved one's death, many people experience numbness or disbelief. It also is common for people to have intense feelings of loss, physiological arousal, and strong desires to see the person again. As people realize that the loss of the loved one is permanent, it is not unusual to experience feelings of despair, which may be accompanied by decreased interest in people and activities enjoyed prior to the loss. With time, most individuals notice that the pain of their grief lessens and that they can begin to rebuild their lives without their loved one (Stroebe & Stroebe, 1987). Generally, at 6 months after the loss of a loved one, the majority of bereaved individuals will be able to accept the loss and will begin the process of re-engaging in meaningful relationships, satisfying work experiences, and pleasurable leisure activities. They will have largely maintained their sense of self-worth and will not experience notable difficulties in functioning after this period of time (Zhang, El-Jawahri, & Prigerson, 2006).

In contrast, a number of psychologists have observed a pattern of pathological grief that occurs among approximately 10% to 15% of people who have lost a loved one (Bonanno & Kaltman, 2001), although there has been some uncertainty about what it means to pathologically grieve. Researchers have recently examined a pattern of grief known as complicated grief disorder (CGD), which is marked by a set of symptom criteria that persists for more than 6 months after the loss of a loved one. It includes the following symptoms: (a) daily yearning for the loved one over the past month that is experienced as upsetting or that interferes with functioning; and (b) four symptoms over the last month that are experienced as extreme, such as difficulty trusting people, problems accepting the death, extreme anger or bitterness about the loss, numbness, problems engaging in relationships, believing that life is meaningless or empty without the loved one, and feeling agitated since the loss (Zhang, El-Jawahri, & Prigerson, 2006). Researchers have argued that CGD warrants consideration as a distinct, valid psychiatric disorder that should be included in the fifth edition of the *Diagnostic and Statistical Manual for Mental Disorders* (Lichtenthal, Cruess, & Prigerson, 2004).

Part of the rationale for conceptualizing this grief pattern as a separate psychiatric disorder is that the experience, clinical course, and outcomes of CGD are different from what one would see in the case of PTSD, major depressive disorder, or adjustment disorder. For example, CGD is marked by emotional distress due to separation from the deceased loved one, which is not present in PTSD. Moreover, it has been argued that the development of PTSD is associated with the severity of the traumatic event and feelings of terror or helplessness, whereas the relationship to the lost loved one is associated with the intensity of grief (Lichtenthal et al., 2004). Thus far, research has supported the distinctiveness of CGD symptoms from symptoms of PTSD and depression in predicting difficulties adjusting to the death of a loved one, as well as cardiovascular reactivity when discussing the deceased (Bonanno et al., 2007). For example, CGD appears to predict low mood and low self-esteem, insomnia, and difficulty in functioning, and it has been linked to changes in smoking and nutritional patterns, cancer and heart conditions, and even influenza (Mitchell, Kim, Prigerson, & Mortimer-Stephens, 2004).

The distinction between PTSD and CGD may become less clear in the case of a violent death such as suicide (as opposed to illness, a nonviolent death) because an individual is likely to experience intense horror or helplessness associated with the death. These intense feelings are particularly likely if the individual witnessed the death or found the body. This does not mean that a valid distinction between PTSD and CGD does not remain. In the case of suicide, an individual may experience comorbid PTSD and CGD.

However, it also is possible that with a violent death such as suicide, symptoms of CGD may not validly predict adjustment above and beyond what can be accounted for by PTSD symptoms (Bonanno et al., 2007). Therefore, additional research should be done to examine the development, course, and treatment of the validity of CGD, posttraumatic stress, and depression in the case of suicide.

At this time, one study has examined factors associated with the occurrence of CGD solely among suicide survivors. Its findings indicated that close relatives (i.e., spouses, parents, children) of a suicide victim exhibited an increased rate of CGD compared to distant relatives (Mitchell et al., 2004). This may reflect the increased level of attachment among close relatives as opposed to more distant relatives, as other research on grief has found that the strength of an individual's attachment to his or her deceased loved one influences the level of grief beyond the type of relationship lost (e.g., parent, spouse, sibling) (Reed & Greenwald, 1991). However, subsequent research with a combined sample of suicide and accident survivors found that kinship relation played some role in survivors' grief intensity (Reed, 1998). Additional research needs to clarify the relative influence of kinship and the attachment bond on the emotional sequelae of suicide bereavement.

Although research indicates that CGD symptoms, as opposed to depressive symptoms, do not ameliorate in response to therapy or antidepressants (Glass, 2005), prospective studies have raised some questions about the symptom discrepancy between CGD and chronic prebereavement depression (Bonanno et al., 2007). This is an important issue to explore in any bereaved population, but the elevated prevalence of depression among suicide victims and their family members (compared to the general population) makes this a particularly critical issue to clarify among survivors of suicide. In other words, research will need to determine the extent to which CGD and depression are discrepant, and whether the pattern of symptom discrepancy among suicide survivors is similar relative to those experiencing other types of loss.

What do we know about CGD, apart from ways in which it is distinct from depression and PTSD? Some theorists propose that CGD develops in reaction to the stress of an individual's inability to accept a life of active engagement and bonding with others without the loved one present (Shear et al., 2007). In turn, such theorists maintain that difficulty with accepting the loss is reflected in alternating extremes of extended preoccupation with the deceased (e.g., looking at pictures or visiting the cemetery for hours), as well as efforts to avoid any thoughts or reminders of the deceased (Shear et al., 2007). In either case, avoidance is viewed as a critical aspect of CGD. More specifically, a bereaved individual who is preoccupied with the deceased essentially avoids accepting the loss by refusing to engage in the daunting process of re-establishing daily routines and developing meaningful new relationships without that person. Similarly, an individual's avoidance of reminders of the deceased represents an attempt to engage in daily tasks and participate in other relationships without facing the difficult task of experiencing painful emotions associated with the loss.

Theorists also have viewed CGD from a cognitive-behavioral perspective that emphasizes the role of three kinds of cognitive responses to the loss that sustain grief and increase its intensity (Boelen, 2006). The first response in this model is that the bereaved individual does not effectively accept the loss and incorporate it into his or her life narrative (e.g., continuing to review the events leading up to the suicide and imagining how the outcome could have been different). The second cognitive response is one in which the bereaved individual reacts negatively to his or her own grief experience. This may come in the form of negative core beliefs about the loss (e.g., "Life will never be enjoyable again") or about certain grief reactions (e.g., "It isn't normal to feel this way"). The third proposed response is characterized by avoidance, which can be cognitive or behavioral, and can reflect anxiety or depression (e.g., avoidance of people or situations that were once enjoyed, rumination to avoid feelings and acceptance of loss). Currently, it is unknown whether suicide survivors who are likely to develop CGD are just more prone to engage in these three types of cognitive processes (i.e., cognitive processes acting as an indicator of CGD), or whether these processes facilitate CGD (i.e., cognitive processes acting as precipitating or maintaining factors of CGD). Yet another untested possibility is that some other variable (or set of variables) mediates the relationship between this set of cognitive processes and CGD.

These questions remain to be explored and understood, but they have important implications for the types of interventions clinicians would use with survivors. One potential treatment based on this cognitive-behavioral framework could be focused on (a) helping clients re-engage in previously avoided activities; (b) exploring and gently challenging negative beliefs about oneself, others, and the world; and (c) promoting a greater understanding and acceptance that the deceased is no longer around (Boelen, 2006).

More recently, the term "complicated grief" was changed to "prolonged grief disorder" (PGD), which is comprised of more recent diagnostic criteria (Goldsmith, Morrison, Vanderwerker, & Prigerson, 2008). Like CGD, PGD is characterized by a pattern in which the bereaved individual deeply misses the deceased, finds it quite challenging to accept that the deceased will not be a presence in his or her life anymore, and experiences difficulty functioning in his or her daily life (Goldsmith et al., 2008). Longitudinal research also suggests that PGD is not the same condition as anxiety or depression; rather it actually seems to predict depression, as well as other physical and psychological health difficulties such as hypertension and thoughts of suicide (Goldsmith et al., 2008). Thus, another benefit of its detection is that it will enable mental health providers to identify suicide survivors in need of support who do not suffer from a mood or anxiety disorder (Boelen & Prigerson, 2007).

Moreover, given PGD's predictive validity for health problems and suicidal ideation, research will be needed on individual difference factors in the development of PGD among those bereaved by suicide. For instance, recent research has found that African Americans were more likely than Caucasians to meet criteria for PGD, as were people who lost loved ones suddenly (Goldsmith et al., 2008). The comparative differences between African Americans and Caucasians are not well understood and remain to be replicated and extended to suicide survivors in other ethnic and cultural groups.

The question of what factors predict PGD is an important issue to explore because it will connect grief intervention directly to suicide prevention. To the best of this author's knowledge, although there are no available data on what outcomes PGD (as opposed to CGD) predicts among survivors of suicide, the results from one study provided the first and only strong link between CGD and thoughts of suicide among suicide survivors (Mitchell, Kim, Prigerson, & Mortimer, 2005). Suicide survivors who developed CGD were 9.68 times more likely to think about ending their lives compared to those without CGD even after risk factors were controlled for in the analyses (Mitchell et al., 2005). The next task is to determine whether similar results would emerge for PGD.

Relief

The loss of a loved one to suicide, like many forms of loss, can engender a variety of emotions and reactions. Arguably, one potential reaction to a loved one's suicide that survivors have difficulty discussing is that of relief. The topic of relief brings about the following questions: (a) how many survivors experience this feeling, and (b) why does it occur?

To date, there is no empirical data on the proportion of suicide survivors who report experiencing relief after their loved one's death. Yet it is likely that the relatively taboo nature of relief after a suicide would cause any statistics to be underestimates of the actual number, even if such data existed.

However, we have good reason to hypothesize that relief is a common reaction.

First, research suggests that the experience of living with a suicide victim who struggled with substantial emotional pain and difficulty is a stressful one for family members (Jordan, 2001). For example, according to one study, 65.3% of a sample of women whose husbands died by suicide had been abused in the marriage, typically in the form of verbal abuse (Constantino, Sekula, Lebish, & Buehner, 2002). Consequently, surviving family members may experience reduced stress levels after the loved one's passing (Jordan, 2001).

Another factor that may be associated with stress reduction and relief after a family member's suicide is whether the death was expected to occur (Jordan, 2001). To consider some examples, family members who are aware that their loved one wishes to die may fearfully wonder when that moment will come. Depending on the circumstances, they may conduct an informal "suicide watch" in which various family members take turns monitoring the loved one. They may closely guard against saying anything that would upset the loved one, or anxiously wonder whether they will find their loved one's body when they return home. Arguably, these are exhausting living conditions, and even though a suicide completion means the survivors' feared outcomes ultimately occurred, relief might come with an end to the anxious anticipation and constant monitoring.

We have very little knowledge of relief in suicide bereavement, and there are a wide variety of questions whose answers will help to advance the field. For instance, it is important to know whether relief reduces the likelihood of developing PTSD, depression, a CGD reaction (e.g., prolonged grief disorder), or suicidality. If relief is protective against these outcomes, are there any conditions in which relief would constitute a risk factor? What situational and individual difference factors predict who will experience relief and who will not? How might relief differ among child versus adult survivors, or cross-culturally? How might it interact with one's physical health after the loss?

Although the aforementioned issues explore those reactions that adult suicide survivors may experience, they do not address (1) what suicide bereavement looks like among children and adolescents, and (2) whether suicide bereavement is quantitatively or qualitatively different from other kinds of loss, and if so, how it is different. It is these comparative questions to which we now turn.

Child and Adolescent Survivors of Suicide

Perhaps the most fundamental question to ask is whether, and how, children and adolescents are impacted by the loss of a loved one to suicide. From a qualitative perspective, investigators in one study (Demi & Howell, 1991) identified salient themes from interviews with individuals who lost a parent or sibling when they were children or young adults. These themes were divided into aspects of emotional pain, namely experiencing, hiding, and healing. Examples of emotional pain included blaming, low self-esteem, stigmatization, anger, and loneliness. Instances of hiding pain included coping strategies such as trying to deny emotions, avoiding reminders of the deceased, or thoughts about dying, engaging in addictive behavior, and keeping the suicide a secret. Healing the pain comprised activities such as seeking psychotherapy and talking about emotions and experiences with others or by oneself (e.g., journaling). A more recent similar qualitative investigation with adolescent suicide survivors identified four themes: making sense of the loss, guilt, unsafe coping, and ways of interacting with friends (Bartik, Maple, Edwards, & Kiernan, 2013). Although it is unclear whether the data in either study are externally valid and represent the experiences of most young survivors of suicide, they provide useful directions for research on the phenomenology of suicide bereavement among youth, and how they may influence subsequent psychosocial functioning, the grief course, and suicide risk.

Researchers have studied child and adolescent adjustment from a quantitative perspective as well. A cross-sectional study compared psychological functioning among child and adolescent suicide survivors aged 5–14 years who lost a close family member (i.e., sibling, parent) with data from a "normal" community sample of children and adolescents. The results indicated that suicide survivors exhibited more difficulties in adjusting to school. They also experienced a higher prevalence of psychological symptoms (Pfeffer et al., 1997). Specifically, 25% of the suicide survivors exhibited symptoms of major depressive disorder that were serious enough to warrant clinical attention, and 31% of the bereaved families reported having at least one child who had thoughts of suicide. Moreover, 40% of these suicide survivors exhibited PTSD symptoms with severity in the moderate range.

Additional analyses revealed that the psychological symptoms of the surviving parent, as well as recent stressors in the child or adolescent's life, significantly predicted difficulty in school adjustment and psychological symptoms (Pfeffer et al., 1997). Although analyses of the surviving parents' psychological symptoms indicated greater severity compared to a standard community sample, their symptoms were less severe relative to a sample of individuals receiving outpatient treatment. Given that the surviving parents' symptom severity fell between that of a community sample and an outpatient sample, it is possible that the symptom severity of child and adolescent survivors follows a similar pattern, but this remains to be tested.

It also is unknown how attachment patterns between children and the surviving parents affect children's psychosocial outcomes, and whether some parental psychological symptoms constitute a greater risk factor for poor child adjustment than do others. In addition, it is unclear whether the psychological symptoms in the surviving parent were long-standing and chronic, whether they developed in response to the stress of living with the suicide victim, or whether they developed during bereavement. These questions should be examined, as knowledge of the temporal nature of parental symptoms will impact immediate family postvention efforts and longer term family assessment and intervention. To the extent that the surviving parents' symptoms developed through a stressful home environment prior to the death, future research will need to clarify whether the surviving parent's psychological symptoms directly predict child adjustment, or whether the severity of the suicide victim's psychological symptoms acts as a mediator between these two variables.

Importantly, there is reason to believe that a similar pattern of school and psychosocial difficulties among child suicide survivors occurs cross-culturally (e.g., Sethi & Bhargava, 2003); however, the literature on adjustment among children bereaved by suicide is quite sparse. Thus, research on the aforementioned questions should be replicated in other cultural contexts.

Although this study (Pfeffer et al., 1997) took an important step in identifying outcomes of children and adolescent suicide survivors, relative to "average" children in the community, it did not inform whether the experiences of the survivors represented children and adolescents in bereavement generally or suicide in particular. Other research comparing psychosocial functioning across children who lost a parent or sibling to suicide versus those who experienced different forms of loss suggests that child suicide survivors experience relatively more shame and

stigma (Wright, 1999). Further, such children also received less accurate information about the death and were exposed to family members who spoke more negatively about the deceased. Moreover, child suicide survivors were more likely to receive treatment for major depression and to identify depression as a shared trait with the deceased. Despite these different experiences, Wright (1999) concluded that the process of adjusting and recovering across child suicide bereavement and other forms of loss shares more commonalities than differences.

In contrast, other research has failed to find evidence that child and adolescent suicide survivors are at increased risk for depression after a close family member's suicide. A longitudinal study of the siblings and parents of adolescent suicide victims indicated that although siblings experienced more grief compared to a control group, they were not more likely to develop major depression or PTSD (although the mothers of adolescent suicide victims were more likely to develop PTSD) (Brent, Moritz, Bridge, Perper, & Cannobio, 1996). Thus, more research is greatly needed on the development of CGD and PGD, PTSD, major depression, and risk for suicide among children and adolescents following a close family member's suicide. From a positive psychological perspective, it also will be important to determine conditions under which children and adolescents are not only at a decreased risk for these issues but are also more likely to experience growth, personal strengths, and thriving.

What can the literature tell us about a child's home environment prior to a suicide victim's death? To date, there is no prospective, longitudinal research to examine a child's home environment with a suicidal member to determine its impact on the child before and after death. Although comparatively biased, retrospective data provide the best means of addressing this question, but like most domains of the suicide bereavement literature, empirical knowledge is limited. As of this writing, research indicates that family members who die by suicide experienced more psychological symptoms compared to individuals who died by other means. Specifically, there appears to be less stability in the families of suicide victims, with lower quality relationships between parents who died by suicide and their children relative to relationships with parents who did not die by suicide (Cerel, Fristad, Weller, & Weller, 2000). According to the observations of surviving parents, psychological and social stressors of child suicide survivors were significantly less within 1 month after the loss compared to the stress level of children who lost a family member to other means (Cerel et al., 2000). It is likely that the experience of living with the deceased contributed to this finding, as there were no group differences between children bereaved through suicide versus other forms of death in the surviving parent–child relationship or the types of social support children received across suicide and other losses.

How do adolescents adjust to a peer's suicide? In one longitudinal study, peers of suicide victims were compared on their emotional adjustment to demographically matched adolescents in the community who were not exposed to suicide. They were assessed several months after the death (the median time was 7 months), again at 12 to 18 months after the initial meeting, and once more 3 years after the first assessment (Bridge, 2002). The results indicated that the participants were at risk for developing major depression 1 month after the suicide, but not beyond this time period. The predictors of major depression included having a family history of depression or attention-deficit/hyperactivity disorder (ADHD), having spoken to the deceased within 1 day before the death, and feeling responsible for the suicide. Moreover, a family history of depression interacted with perceived responsibility for the death to increase the probability that survivors would develop major depression. Finally, adolescents who abused alcohol were more likely to befriend someone who would eventually commit suicide, which itself increased the likelihood of developing major depression (Bridge, 2002).

A subsequent longitudinal study examined predictors of adjustment among adolescents who lost a friend to suicide by separately addressing CGD, PTSD, and major depression (Melhem et al., 2004). The survivors were assessed at 6 months, 12–18 months, and 3 years after the suicide. Predictors of major depression included female gender, a family history of major depression, a close friendship with the deceased, contact within 24 hours of death, conflict with family members or peers, and perceived accountability for the death. CGD predictors included a personal history of having major depression and a family history of anxiety, and PTSD risk was associated with financial stress and being at the location where the suicide occurred.

The literature is mixed on whether adolescents are at increased risk for suicide following a peer's suicide. Some research suggests that adolescents who were exposed to a peer's suicide are at heightened risk, and that this risk occurs regardless of whether the adolescent was a close friend of the deceased (Brent et al., 1989) or a more distant acquaintance (e.g., Gould, Shaffer, & Kleinman, 1988). In contrast, other research has failed to find a relationship between exposure to a peer's suicide and subsequent suicide risk (e.g., Brent et al., 1996; Watkins & Guitierrez, 2003).

Additional research is needed to determine whether exposure to a peer's suicide increases the likelihood of various degrees of suicidality, ranging from general thoughts of death and suicide, to developing a plan and active attempts. There also is much to be learned about the factors and conditions that predict an increased risk of suicide for the survivor versus those that are protective. Such analyses should seek to replicate and expand upon current research by considering the predictive role of adjustment-related variables such as coping behavior, social support, stigmatization, and the use of postvention and treatment programs on the development of CGD, major depression, and post-traumatic stress after a peer's suicide.

Mental Health Professionals as Suicide Survivors

When someone dies by suicide, it is usually anticipated that individuals representing a range of relationships with the deceased will experience bereavement. This includes spouses and significant others, parents, siblings, close family members, and close friends. This range is often a limited one and omits other kinds of relationships, such as the therapeutic relationship between a clinician and the suicide victim. The situation is an unfortunate one, in part because therapists, like the client's family members and close friends, can experience a client's suicide as traumatic. In the wake of a client's suicide, therapists also may experience symptoms of PTSD, depression, or dysphoria (Sakinofsky, 2007). In addition to these emotional reactions, a clinician may be penalized at their place of work or made to contend with lawsuits. The issue of a client's suicide is not a remote one for practitioners. For instance, it is estimated that approximately 30% of psychiatrists in training will lose a client to suicide, and this figure increases to 50% over the course of a psychiatrist's career (Sakinofsky, 2007). Given the relatively limited public acknowledgement of suicide bereavement among mental health professionals, it is probably not surprising that this issue has received literally no attention in the literature.

Clinicians in one study reported experiencing a variety of emotions upon learning of their client's suicide, such as anger, shame, guilt, grief, shock, betrayal, self-doubt, and fear of being blamed (Hendin, Lipschitz, Maltsberger, Haas, & Wynecoop, 2000). Most of the therapists sampled (21 out of the 26) reported that they would have made at least one important change in their approach to the client's treatment in light of the suicide. These changes primarily involved hospitalizing the client, altering the client's medication, and speaking with the client's former therapists. Despite fears of being held at fault, the majority of the therapists met with their deceased client's family members and did not encounter blame or criticism from them.

In contrast, there appear to have been some professional ramifications at the individual level. For example, some of the clinicians were more cautious about working with clients who endorsed suicidality. There also were consequences at a larger institutional level. Although most of the therapists said they felt supported by fellow clinicians, they also reported that the institutions where they worked were generally unhelpful. Specifically, they reported either being blamed or receiving what felt like empty consolation about their inability to prevent the suicide.

To address these challenges, Hendin et al. (2000) suggested that a separate, neutral group, unconnected to the clinician or the clinician's institution, should conduct all case reviews of a client's suicide. There also have been calls for clinical supervisors to provide a caring, nonjudgmental environment to student therapists who lose a client to suicide, and for colleagues to actively support fellow clinicians who experience this type of loss. Psychologists also have noted the importance of writing a detailed account of what transpired in relation to the suicide, in case such an account is required in court or at the psychologist's workplace (Sakinofsky, 2007).

These are excellent recommendations, and it would be valuable to assess therapists' emotional and professional outcomes as a result of these changes. Independently of whether the aforementioned recommendations are implemented, additional research should address factors associated with the development of PTSD, major depression, and CGD among therapists after a client's suicide, as well as other outcomes such as psychosocial functioning, social support, stigmatization, therapist "burnout," clinical effectiveness with other clients, rumination about counterfactuals to "un-do" the suicide, and potential suicidality of the clinician. In addition to assessing adjustment challenges, research also will need to determine conditions that

promote resilience and growth across personal and professional functioning among therapists following a client's suicide.

Suicide Bereavement Versus Other Types of Bereavement

Do survivors of suicide experience bereavement differently than individuals who have lost loved ones through other forms of death? Some researchers have found that losing a loved one to suicide is no different, or at least no worse, than losing a loved one in other ways. In one study, individuals who lost a spouse to natural death or chronic illness had similar rates of PTSD as those who lost a loved one through sudden death, such as suicide or accident (Zisook, Chentsova-Dutton, & Shucter, 1998). A comparison of survivors of suicide, illness, and accidents revealed that accident survivors showed the poorest outcome, with increased psychiatric symptoms after 1 year, whereas survivors of suicide and illness improved. In contrast, both survivors of suicide and illness experienced more difficulties forming new social relationships and more difficulty accepting the loss of their spouses. Suicide survivors felt more abandoned by the deceased compared to the other groups, and also felt the most shame, but their shame decreased after the initial assessment (Grad & Zavasnik, 1999).

In his review of the literature comparing survivors of suicide and other types of death, McIntosh (1993) concluded that suicide survivors are more similar to other survivors and that if there are any differences, they are minimal 2 years after the loss. Research comparing adjustment and psychosocial functioning across students in an introductory psychology class who had lost loved ones to suicide, accident, or natural death found evidence of few differences across the different types of loss. Specifically, there was no difference in survivors' reports of talking with others about the loss, ability to put the death out of their minds, tendency to ruminate, feelings of guilt, or present level of grief (McIntosh & Kelly, 1992). The survivors across the three types of loss also did not differ in their reported family relationships or quantity of friends both prior to and after the death occurred. Notably, survivors of suicide differed from survivors of accidents and natural death in three ways. First, they were more likely to blame others for the death. Second, they were more likely to report that their family members had been blamed. Third, they were more likely to believe that they could have stopped the death from happening (McIntosh & Kelly, 1992).

Other researchers have maintained that survivors of suicide experience a more severe grief course compared to those who lost a loved one through nonviolent death (e.g., chronic illness), but that this discrepancy does not hold with violent deaths (i.e., accidents or homicide). A study comparing psychological outcomes among parents who lost a child to suicide, accidents, or sudden infant death syndrome (SIDS) found that accident and suicide survivors suffered greater emotional distress compared to those who lost children to SIDS, but emotional distress did not differ across those bereaved by accident and suicide (Dyregrov, Nordanger, & Dyregrov, 2003). A longitudinal study showed that individuals who lost a loved one through violent death (i.e., suicide, accident, homicide) experienced more symptoms of depression and PTSD over time than did participants who lost a loved one through natural death, and the experience of having PTSD intensified the grief course (Kaltman & Bonanno, 2003). In an investigation of parental bereavement after the violent death of a child, researchers found that death by suicide did not lead to more distress and less acceptance than did death by accident or homicide (Murphy, Johnson, Wu, Fan, & Lohan, 2003b). Notably, one study found a greater association between PTSD and loss of a child through homicide than through suicide (Murphy, Johnson, Chung, & Beaton, 2003a), although additional research is needed to more fully understand the relationship between different types of violent loss and PTSD symptoms.

Yet other investigators have argued that the experience of losing a loved one to suicide is different from losing a loved one to other forms of death. In his review of the literature, Jordan (2001) argued that even though suicide bereavement shares many similarities with other kinds of bereavement, certain types of experiences or "themes" are specific to suicide bereavement and set it apart from bereavement following other types of death.

Jordan noted that in the wake of a suicide, survivors often feel more rejected and more anger toward the deceased. In one study, survivors of suicide felt more abandoned and ashamed than did survivors of accidents or illness after an initial assessment, but these differences disappeared over time (Grad & Zavasnik, 1999). In other research comparing suicide survivors to people who lost loved ones to sudden deaths, survivors of suicide felt less separation anxiety but more rejection (Reed, 1998).

Similarly, a comparison of parents who lost sons through suicide or accidents was conducted at 6 and 9 months after the death (Seguin, Lesage, & Kiely, 1995). Suicide survivors at 6 months exhibited higher levels of depression compared to accident survivors, but the groups were similar at 9 months. However, suicide survivors had experienced more loss in their lives overall, as well as a higher incidence of significant life events after the death. It is possible that these differences stemmed from higher levels of shame among suicide survivors, but we cannot verify this due to the cross-sectional nature of the study.

One distinction between suicide survivors and those who lost loved ones through other deaths may be in meaning making, as the literature indicates that suicide survivors experience particular difficulty when attempting to make sense of their loss (Jordan, 2001). This is not to say that survivors of other types of death find it easy to make sense of their tragedy. Certainly, homicide and accident survivors may struggle with meaning reconstruction during bereavement. Losing a loved one at the hand of an aggressor, in a car accident, or in a plane crash is often overwhelming and confusing. However, the loss of a loved one to suicide is arguably confounding in a distinct way from other forms of death because, as opposed to the context of an accident or homicide, the victim purposefully caused his or her own demise. Survivors of suicide must struggle with the knowledge that their loved ones made the choice to end their lives, leaving the survivors behind (in several cases to find their bodies). Accordingly, some research has indicated that suicide survivors experience a greater need to find an explanation for the death (Barrett & Scott, 1989).

Jordan (2001) also argued that suicide survivors experience more guilt and shame than do other types of survivors. Indeed, a comparison of individuals who lost a loved one to suicide versus natural death revealed that suicide survivors had higher scores on subscales of the Grief Experience Questionnaire (GEQ) that measured stigmatization and shame, as well as rejection and "unique reactions" (i.e., a set of experiences proposed to be unique to survivors of suicide, such as feeling that the loved one was trying to get revenge by committing suicide) (Harwood, Hawton, Hope, & Jacoby, 2002). Reed and Greenwald (1991) found that although people who lost a loved one to suicide experienced less emotional distress and shock compared to people who lost a loved one to an accident, those grieving a suicide death experienced more guilt, shame, and feelings of rejection.

As Jordan (2001) and others have observed, there are some important qualitative differences between survivors of suicide and survivors of other types of death (e.g., difficulties with meaning making, shame, guilt, blame, rejection, anger). Interestingly, the kinds of qualitative differences may depend upon the relationship lost. For example, spouses of suicide victims may be more likely to experience guilt and feelings of rejection, shame, and stigma compared to survivors of other losses, whereas shame and stigma in particular may be more prevalent among parents and small children of suicide victims (Harwood et al., 2002).

Some research has indicated that suicide survivors, compared to people who lost loved ones to other deaths, experience more severe grief overall (in addition to greater feelings of rejection, shame, and responsibility) (Barrett & Scott, 1989); however, the evidence for this claim is mixed. Other research has suggested that although suicide survivors share similar levels of general grief as those bereaved through other types of death, they experience specific grief reactions more intensely, such as feelings of rejection and the "unique reactions" noted earlier (Barrett & Scott, 1990).

Moreover, Barrett and Scott (1990) argued that survivors of suicide experience four different sets of grief reactions. The first set of reactions constitutes those that would commonly occur after losing a loved one (e.g., physical symptoms, anger). The second set involves reactions that occur in the context of a death that is not "natural" and is seen as preventable (e.g., feeling abandoned, stigma, shame). The third set of reactions results from losing a loved one to an unexpected, sudden death (e.g., feeling responsibility or blame, searching for meaning). The fourth set of reactions is specific to traumatic loss through suicide (e.g., feeling rejected by the suicide victim, believing the deceased died to take revenge, hiding how the loved one died).

Hawton and Simkin (2003) noted that reported instances of more intense grief experiences among survivors of suicide relative to those who lost loved ones through other deaths occurred because researchers did not control for the impact of losing a loved one overall (that is, irrespective of loss). When the emotional impact of loss itself was controlled, research did not support the claim that suicide bereavement is *quantitatively* more severe than are other types of loss.

However, in line with the research discussed earlier, the literature supports the existence of qualitative features (i.e., themes) that make suicide bereavement distinct (e.g., Hawton & Simkin, 2003; Sakinofsky, 2007). Specifically, survivors of suicide appear to be more likely to experience feelings of being rejected by the deceased, shame, stigmatization, and guilt. As bereaved individuals try to understand their loss, they may engage in self-blame and experience feelings of guilt if they believe that they did not do enough to prevent the death, or if they perceive themselves as acting as a catalyst in some way (Hawton & Simkin, 2003).

Accordingly, survivors of suicide (representing kinships or friendships) may be at a greater risk for developing major depression or PTSD than are other bereaved individuals (Sakinofsky, 2007). A study that compared adjustment at 3 months post loss among those who lost loved ones to suicide with those bereaved by "natural" deaths indicated that survivors of suicide reported poorer physical and psychological health. They also expressed a greater need to meet with a mental health provider, a difference that remained when other factors were controlled, such as demographic differences, neuroticism, and how much participants anticipated the death (de Groot, de Keijser, & Neeleman, 2006).

However, the research on adjustment following loss to suicide has been inconsistent. Other researchers have argued that the literature does not support a distinction between suicide and different forms of loss in emotional adjustment variables such depression and anxiety, PTSD, suicidal acts, and overall mental health. Levels of general grief appear similar as well, although this similarity may break down with measures designed to assess reactions commonly associated with suicide bereavement. Accordingly, suicide bereavement has been associated with higher levels of stigma, efforts to hide the cause of death, blaming, shame, and feelings of rejection among suicide survivors compared to those bereaved by other deaths (Sveen & Walby, 2007).

Overall, what can we conclude about distinctions between individuals who lost loved ones to suicide versus other modes of death? On balance, the literature seems to suggest that the similarities across bereavement groups outweigh the differences, and it may be that the distinction in health and psychosocial functioning outcomes exists between violent, sudden death and nonviolent, expected death (Sakinofsky, 2007). Yet we should exercise caution even in this conclusion, as it is likely that there remain certain qualitatively different experiences (i.e., themes) that set suicide bereavement apart from other losses, even other traumatic ones, such as difficulty with meaning making, self-blame, guilt, shame, stigma, and distance from social supports (Sakinofsky, 2007).

Future research should continue to examine the existence of experiences that are specific to suicide bereavement (i.e., themes), ideally with larger samples; there are a number of questions to be addressed in this area. For example, is suicide bereavement "truly" different from other losses, in particular, bereavement experiences, and will we be able to identify them reliably? To the extent that these themes mark distinctions between suicide bereavement and other deaths, research will need to address the boundaries of these thematic differences. More specifically, in what contexts are survivors of suicide likely to struggle with meaning making, self-blame, stigma, and social isolation, and when are they likely to experience a sense of clarity and closure, self-compassion, and a sense of being supported and validated by others? Are some of these experiences or themes more detrimental in their physical and emotional impact than are others? Does the inverse of some of these themes (e.g., self-compassion instead of self-blame) generate physical and psychological resilience, personal growth, and well-being, or are they mere markers or resilience and thriving? Are different coping styles or therapeutic interventions more helpful in some themes versus others?

Yet the question of how these themes (e.g., meaning making, self-blame, stigma, social isolation) or any other variable influences adjustment in suicide bereavement must not be examined in a vacuum. Our accuracy and depth of understanding of adjustment in suicide bereavement can only be achieved by considering the larger context in which these themes exist. Arguably, the larger context will be composed of individual differences factors (e.g., personality, family history), cognitive factors (e.g., attention, perception, memory, executive functioning), physical factors (e.g., health behaviors, chronic pain or illness, nutrition), and social factors (e.g., number of individuals present, stereotypes, heuristics, closeness of social supports, relationship to deceased). Thus, the field of suicide bereavement would strongly benefit from the integration of research in clinical, cognitive, behavioral medicine/health psychology, and social psychological science. Such integration will allow investigators to determine how the situational context interacts with the aforementioned themes (e.g., meaning making, self-blame, stigma, social isolation) to influence physical and psychosocial adjustment to suicide bereavement. Given that this relationship may be bidirectional, research might in turn address how physical and psychosocial adjustment influences the situational context, themes of suicide bereavement, and their interaction.

Stigma and Social Support

When one considers that (1) unfortunately, stigma remains associated with suicide in most cultures, and (2) a person's social world influences his or her well-being, it becomes clear how important it is to learn more about the extent to which stigma following a suicide becomes attached to the survivors.

How do people perceive individuals who have lost loved ones to suicide? To date, there has been very little research on peoples' perceptions of individuals bereaved by suicide. The literature that exists has almost always involved undergraduate students, which constrains the generalizability of the results by restricting the range of variables such as age, education, and income, to name a few. Moreover, the studies have yielded mixed results. In light of these challenges, the findings should be interpreted as valuable, initial explorations of social perceptions of suicide survivors upon which future investigators can build. The general paradigm employed in this research involves asking participants to rate written descriptions of bereaved people that are identical except for the type of loss they experienced.

In one study, some undergraduate students read about a situation in which their best friend's mother passed away, and others read about the mother of an acquaintance who passed away. Across both situations, the deaths involved leukemia, a car accident, or suicide (Walcott, 1993). The results indicated that across all types of death, participants who imagined that their best friend's mother died reported that they would be more comfortable supporting their friend, and expressed a greater interest in helping. This provides some evidence for the notion that suicide survivors are as likely as people grieving other losses to receive social support (Walcott, 1993). Notably, this relationship held for friends only. In the case of acquaintances, female participants were more likely to help an acquaintance only if they reported positive, nonstigmatizing attitudes regarding suicide. Thus, the extent to which suicide survivors can receive social support from friends outside of their closest social sphere is dependent upon the views toward suicide that their acquaintances hold.

How do people perceive bereaved individuals they do not know? Undergraduate students in another study read case descriptions of individuals who lost a loved one to suicide, an accident, or a disease. These case descriptions contained examples of typical grief reactions that people commonly experience. The participants' task was to evaluate the individual in each case based on their level of functioning, likability, responsibility for the death, psychosocial impairment, and the seriousness of their grief experiences. Interestingly, there seemed to be an interaction between the gender of the bereaved individual and the type of death. Overall, participants rated bereaved men more negatively. However, this changed when suicide bereavement was considered, in which case female survivors of suicide were rated as having poorer social functioning than their male counterparts. Moreover, participants believed that friends of women suicide survivors were less likely to mention the death to them than they were to male suicide survivors. These results suggest that social perceptions may make it more difficult for women who have lost a loved one to suicide to interact with individuals in their communities, their extended social networks (i.e., acquaintances), and possibly even their close friends (Thornton, Whittemore, & Robertson, 1989). Granted, an important assumption in the aforementioned data (Thornton et al., 1989) is that female suicide survivors are actually viewed by people in their social network as having more difficulty functioning socially, and that their friends are less likely to ask them about the loss. Yet when we consider that the study addressed public perceptions of suicide survivors, it is reasonable to assume that people who lose loved ones to suicide will encounter these unfavorable perceptions and reluctance from friends to talk with them. Future research will be needed to replicate this study, ideally with a community sample representing a wider range of age, education, and income level (variables on which the college sample is restricted) to ensure external validity. To the extent that these findings are valid, the hypothesized relationship between social functioning of female suicide survivors and their friends' willingness to initiate discussions about the suicide merits investigation. It will allow investigators to examine the nature of the relationship, why it is specific to women, and whether the reverse of the proposed relationship is true. That is, for an unknown reason, do female suicide survivors experience more difficulty functioning socially after the death, which deters friends from asking about the loss?

Moreover, a fuller understanding of the relationship between survivors' demographic characteristics, social functioning, and social support is needed

to help psychologists anticipate the kinds of social challenges they may encounter in bereavement, and how these challenges either influence or are influenced by the social context (e.g., large gatherings, dating) and the emotional sequelae of suicide bereavement (grief, depression, PTSD, suicidality, chronic illness).

In addition to the suicide survivor's demographic characteristics, evidence suggests that the type of loss and the demographic characteristics of the deceased influence social perceptions of the survivor. In the aforementioned study with undergraduates who rated case histories (Thornton et al., 1989), individuals who lost loved ones through suicide appeared to have more stigma (i.e., negative social attitudes about a characteristic or quality) associated with them and their loss compared to those who lost loved ones to illness (e.g., greater perceptions of emotional disturbance among suicide survivors).

Similarly, other research representing a community sample of raters with a wider age range similarly found that individuals who died by suicide and the survivors of suicide were perceived as more emotionally disturbed and as more responsible for the death of their loved ones compared to families bereaved through heart attack or homicide (Tyler, 1990). Moreover, the community sample of raters perceived those who lost loved ones to suicide as being less likable than were those who lost loved ones to heart attacks or homicide (Tyler, 1990). This suggests that the community participants were more explicit in their endorsements of stigmatizing attitudes, a disconcerting finding given that these are the kinds of individuals, rather than undergraduate students, who suicide survivors are likely to encounter. Overall, these findings indicated that relative to people grieving other deaths, suicide survivors encounter stigmatizing societal perceptions that not only was the deceased emotionally disturbed, but he or she also was personally blameworthy for the deceased's death, especially when the deceased was a child.

These results are relatively consistent with other literature suggesting that society assigns more stigma and blame to suicide bereavement than it does to death by natural causes. Suicide survivors are socially viewed as having been neglectful toward the deceased and any psychological difficulties they were struggling with at the time of their death. In turn, the stigma that survivors encounter at the social or interpersonal levels only exacerbates the stress and difficulty of an already painful, stressful loss (Cvinar, 2005). Jordan (2001) argued that stigma is conveyed to suicide survivors through overt behavior as well as though more subtle means, including the hesitancy that people experience in how to be supportive.

Research also indicates that suicide survivors are acutely aware of negative societal perceptions of suicide and suicide survivors. Relative to individuals bereaved by other kinds of death, suicide survivors reported greater stigma, as well as more blame and shame (Sveen & Walby, 2007; Wright, 1999). Jordan (2001) noted that although there are no differences across bereavement groups in the level of perceived social support from a quantitative perspective, there are important qualitative distinctions in their social experiences. First, there is some evidence to suggest that people bereaved by accidents experience more positive interactions with others compared to suicide survivors. Second, people grieving a natural death appear to receive more emotional support compared to suicide survivors. Third, suicide survivors were more likely to report experiencing demands that they recover from their loss. Fourth, suicide survivors were more likely to believe that other suicide survivors were the only ones who could understand what they were feeling and experiencing (Jordan, 2001).

Other research suggests that suicide survivors experience similar levels of stigma as individuals bereaved by other deaths; yet even then, suicide bereavement is among those losses associated with higher levels of stigma. For example, relative to people who lost a loved one to natural death, survivors of suicide and accidents were more likely to be blamed, and they experienced more feelings of stigma, shame, and embarrassment. Suicide and accident survivors similarly noticed others gossiping about their loss, but suicide survivors were more likely to feel that their friends could not understand how they felt (McIntosh & Kelly, 1992). Despite suicide survivors' beliefs that their friends could not understand them, they talked with good friends about their loss to a similar degree as accident survivors.

Although research has not been entirely consistent on whether suicide survivors experience greater stigma, the bulk of the literature suggests that they do. Jordan (2001) argued that suicide survivors are emotionally impacted by stigma and incorporate it into their self-concept. In turn, these negative self-perceptions are likely to influence how survivors interact with other people. For instance, research suggests that suicide survivors find it difficult to socially interact and talk about

their loved one's suicide with others (Jordan, 2001; McMenamy, Jordan, & Mitchell, 2008). When survivors encounter social stigma (irrespective of whether it is real or imagined), or they experience shame, they are more likely to disengage from their social circles (Sakinofsky, 2007). In addition, they are more likely to feel a need to hide the cause of their loved one's death (Sveen & Walby, 2007). Notably, these findings appear to be at odds with the finding that suicide survivors were willing to talk with good friends despite doubts that they could be understood (McIntosh & Kelly, 1992), but it is difficult to determine whether a discrepancy actually exists. It is possible that suicide survivors find it difficult to talk with acquaintances and strangers, but not with good friends. Research is needed to address this question.

Thus, social stigma against suicide survivors appears to undermine social support, increase isolation, and negatively influence survivors' self-concepts. Through stigma's damaging impact on social support, stigma also may exert a negative influence on psychological adjustment to bereavement by exacerbating symptoms of grief, depression, or PTSD. Although perceived social support among parents who lost a child to suicide was not predictive of PTSD at the time of the study, it did predict PTSD 5 years later (Murphy et al., 2003a). Similarly, other research indicates that social support may alleviate feelings of rejection, depression, and separation anxiety (Reed, 1998), and it may promote resilience and protection against major depression, PTSD, and CGD (Vanderwerker & Prigerson, 2004).

Overall, stigma arguably undermines social support, which in turn influences the type and severity of reactions that suicide survivors will experience. In light of this, it is essential to address social stigma toward suicide survivors. This might be done through public service announcements and outreach programs that dispel harmful myths about suicide survivors, normalize grief reactions, and offer advice on how to provide support. Moreover, research should move beyond investigating explicit beliefs about suicide survivors to include studies of the implicit attitudes that people are not aware of but that heavily influence behavior. In this vein, the Implicit Associations Test (IAT; Greenwald, McGhee, & Schwartz, 1998) is a promising tool to measure these subtle biases against suicide survivors, the conditions under which these biases change, and the extent to which suicide survivors themselves hold these biases. Another way to address the detrimental impact of social stigma is to incorporate interventions that either reduce survivors' feelings of stigmatization or stigma's harmful impact. Toward this end, clinical researchers have been emphasizing the importance of addressing stigmatization through assessment or treatment (e.g., Cerel & Campbell, 2008; Pfeffer, Jiang, Kakuma, Hwang, & Metsch, 2002).

Beyond stigma's negative psychosocial impact, the influence of social stigma on suicide survivors' physical health is unknown, yet it is quite likely that a strong relationship between stigma and physical health exists. Literature on the relationship between physical health and emotional stress provides strong grounds to hypothesize that suicide survivors are vulnerable to reduced immunity and chronic illness (e.g., Connor, 2008). Suicide survivors also may be vulnerable to chronic pain, but the literature supporting this is less clear. Specifically, some research suggests that people with depressed mood exhibit reduced pain tolerance (e.g., Willoughby, Hailey, Mulkana, & Rowe, 2002). In contrast, other research suggests that social exclusion (as in the case of stigma) is associated with emotional numbness, and increased thresholds and tolerance of physical pain (DeWall & Baumeister, 2006).

The value of research efforts on physical health amongst suicide survivors cannot be emphasized strongly enough. A quite possible hypothesis (which this writer believes but cannot empirically support as of this writing) is that physical health reciprocally influences the emotional sequelae of suicide bereavement, such as the type and severity of grief reactions, PTSD, depression, and post-traumatic growth. Thus, research efforts on the health of suicide survivors should examine the potentially bidirectional relationship between physical health and emotional adjustment, and how this relationship interacts with psychosocial variables such as stigma, social support, and perceived rejection.

In addition to research efforts to understand the role of stigma and social support in the psychological, social, and physical health sequelae of suicide bereavement, another avenue of research to consider is the impact of more intimate social connections. Do suicide survivors who are grieving their loss experience more or less intimacy in their close relationships? There is very little research on this question, but existing evidence suggests that elevated grief is associated with reduced intimacy (e.g., Maycock, 1998). However, this does not mean that suicide survivors who are grieving the loss of a loved one will lose their intimacy in close relationships. Research shows that suicide survivors with a secure attachment style are more likely to use coping styles that enable them to manage their grief and enjoy higher levels of intimacy (Maycock, 1998). Additional research is needed on the relationship between attachment style and intimacy, and how these factors interact with the emotional, physical, and social outcomes of suicide bereavement. Although additional research on suicide survivors' intimacy is needed, we can tentatively say that suicide survivors may maintain, and perhaps increase, intimacy in the wake of their loss. This finding also is indicative of the important influence of coping styles on survivors' grief.

Coping

There has been very little research on coping strategies among survivors of suicide and how these strategies may ameliorate the psychological, physical, and social sequelae of suicide bereavement. Given that suicide bereavement appears to involve qualitatively different kinds of experiences from other types of loss, knowledge of helpful coping strategies for other populations may not be informative for suicide survivors, although this statement itself is a question waiting to be tested.

To the best of this author's knowledge, there is no prospective, longitudinal research directly examining coping strategies that predict positive versus negative psychological, physical, and social outcomes among survivors of suicide. However, cross-sectional research among suicide survivors has begun to address coping strategies that may be associated with healthy outcomes. Specifically, one such coping strategy has been referred to in the literature as a "repressive coping style" (Parker & McNally, 2008).

Some psychologists have described repressive coping as a defensive style in which people attempt to avoid acknowledging that they are upset or are experiencing negative emotions; they also avoid information that challenges their self-concept of being imperturbable (e.g., Weinberger, 1990). In the wake of trauma, such as a serious heart attack, repressive coping predicted lower levels of PTSD beyond sociodemographic variables, acute stress disorder, variables associated with heart attack severity, and the patient's estimated severity of the attack (Ginzburg, Solomon, & Bleich, 2002).

Repressive coping may also be emotionally beneficial after a loved one's suicide (Parker & McNally, 2008). In one study, "repressors" bereaved by suicide exhibited less depression, less of a desire to suppress intrusive thoughts, and fewer somatic symptoms and general grief reactions. Thus, they appeared to experience a more mild grief course for some of the most common bereavement symptoms, suggesting that they were more able to cope with the general stress of bereavement compared to people who did not exhibit this coping style (i.e., "nonrepressors"). They appeared to use healthier coping styles, such as productive, solution-focused strategies (e.g., making a plan for how to cope with the suicide, focusing on each step in that plan), rather than the escape and avoidance strategies that nonrepressors reported (e.g., alcohol and drug use, sleeping, eating). It is possible that suicide survivors who used a repressive coping style reported healthier coping strategies and fewer psychological symptoms because they were being defensive and minimizing the severity of their experiences, as repressors are hypothesized to do. However, the repressors in this study did not fit that conceptualization. They did not deny that the suicide had occurred, nor did they minimize the emotional pain it caused. Instead, they participated in an emotionally demanding study when the suicide was significantly more recent for them than it was for survivors who were nonrepressors. This research suggests that repressors may be more accurately classified as people who use a coping style characterized by a positive reinterpretation of most situations, and that they are not chronically avoiding negative information (Parker & McNally, 2008). Notably, the traditional notion of repressive coping in the literature did not map onto the suicide survivors who met the operational definition of the term, but this research is early in its development and any conclusions reached are tentative. Future studies will need to replicate and expand upon these findings to determine what construct the operational definition is measuring among suicide survivors, and whether suicide survivors who fit this construct actually experience more resilient bereavement outcomes.

In addition to research on repressive coping, studies are greatly needed on other coping approaches that predict healthy physical and psychosocial adjustment following a loved one's suicide, as well as those that predict negative outcomes. Research also will need to go beyond this initial question by addressing how individual characteristics (e.g., personality, family history) interact with coping approaches. Ideally, this will eventually help psychologists to ascertain coping styles that best "match" a particular individual.

There also are a number of examples of coping approaches that are likely to promote physical and psychosocial resilience that should be investigated further in suicide bereavement. They include self-care activities such as exercise, getting sufficient sleep (as opposed to too little or too much), eating well, accepting one's emotions, maintaining or increasing enjoyable and soothing activities, maintaining reasonable work hours, talking with other suicide survivors (e.g., those who are further along in their bereavement process), taking social risks by actively reaching out to one's support network, planful problem-focused coping, positively reappraising one's situation (e.g., noticing how one has grown through adversity), creating a gratitude journal, engaging in meditation or other mindfulness practices (e.g., yoga), and incorporating humor into one's life. As is apparent from the list of strategies just listed, the topic of coping among survivors of suicide is a valuable area of study that remains relatively unexplored.

Some coping strategies are likely to decrease well-being during suicide bereavement and warrant further study. One example is "ruminative coping," which involves repetitively focusing on one's emotional upset, the reasons for being distressed, thoughts and worries about the past and future, and the meaning behind the loved one's passing. Although it appears that this approach would overwhelm the bereaved with painful emotions, it does not involve any problem solving and actually serves as an avoidance strategy that prevents an individual from fully adjusting to the reality of the loved one's loss (Stroebe et al., 2007).

Interventions

A potentially helpful coping strategy not mentioned earlier involves seeking support from mental health professionals. Who is likely to seek treatment? Research indicates that individuals who seek mental health services are not representative of the larger population of suicide survivors, and there are few minority groups that seek services after a loved one's suicide (Campbell, 1997). In addition to the question of who seeks mental health services during suicide bereavement, it also is important to ask who needs services. Research suggests that for most bereaved individuals, grief dissipates with time on its own. Accordingly, those most in need of treatment are those with CGD (or prolonged grief disorder) (Zhang et al., 2006).

Given that suicide survivors' sudden, violent loss increases the likelihood of traumatic grief, which in turn places them at a significantly elevated risk for PTSD symptoms and suicidality (see Regehr & Sussman, 2004), it follows that they are a bereavement group likely to be in great need of mental health services, and clinical research on effective interventions is warranted. Despite the large number of treatment programs addressing suicide bereavement, the clinical efficacy of most of them has not been empirically examined (Sakinofsky, 2007). Unfortunately, among those who have been investigated, their clinical efficacy has not been supported (Bonanno, 2006), and in some cases participants' grief symptoms became more severe (Neimeyer, 2000). Given the risk of providing treatments that are unhelpful or worsen symptoms, it is critical to be aware of treatment options that are likely to alleviate suicide survivors' suffering, promote resilience, and enhance quality of life.

Clearly, before suicide survivors can start a treatment program, they need to find it. The standard approach of many treatment programs has relied on "passive postvention," a model in which information about the program is advertised in venues such as local newspapers, flyers, or in funeral home booklets. Typically, suicide survivors are required to find this information on their own (Cerel & Campbell, 2008).

In contrast, "active postvention" is a new outreach model in which trained suicide survivors and staff from crisis centers arrive at the scene of the suicide to provide support, information, and service referrals (Cerel & Campbell, 2008). Cross-sectional research suggests that suicide survivors who receive active postvention are more likely to seek treatment earlier than are those who receive passive postvention. Active postvention recipients also were more likely to participate in support groups for suicide survivors. A complication of these findings is that active postvention recipients also were more likely to have a loved one who used a violent method of suicide. Thus, a prospective replication is needed, as the cross-sectional nature of the study makes it impossible to know whether the active postvention approach or the violence of the loss accounts for these group differences (Cerel & Campbell, 2008).

Assuming that suicide survivors in need of treatment manage to locate it, what kinds of treatment can they expect to receive? Most interventions have traditionally envisioned the need for "grief work" in which the bereaved persons must fully explore and express their negative and positive emotions (with a special emphasis on negative emotions) regarding the deceased, the loss, and themselves. The goal in

this approach is for bereaved individuals to achieve emotional separation from the lost loved one and reengage with their lives. According to this conceptualization, if "grief work" is not attained, then the bereaved person is likely to experience CGD reactions (Regehr & Sussman, 2004).

Importantly, empirical research has not supported the model upon which most bereavement interventions have been based. Longitudinal studies suggest that individuals who do not engage in grief work are not at risk of developing delayed grief reactions or CGD (Bonanno & Field, 2001). Moreover, grief work is not more beneficial than engaging in avoidance (which has not been shown to be helpful) (Archer, 1999; Regehr & Sussman, 2004). More recent treatment approaches to grief have involved a more flexible, "dual-process" approach that builds upon the assumption that it is normal for bereaved individuals to alternate between denial of the loss and recurrent intrusive thoughts about it, and that CGD is more likely to develop when people try to control this natural process (Shear et al., 2007).

Which interventions are most efficacious for survivors of suicide? The majority of the existing treatment literature addresses bereavement generally, rather than suicide bereavement specifically. Nevertheless, by virtue of addressing bereavement, these interventions are likely to have at least some applicability to the suicide survivor population; however, future research will need to examine the efficacy of these interventions for suicide bereavement specifically.

In a randomized controlled, 16-session clinical trial, researchers compared complicated grief therapy (CGT) with interpersonal psychotherapy (IPT). CGT provides information about typical grief reactions, encourages bereaved individuals to identify and pursue personally valued goals, and relies on the "dual-process" approach described earlier to help clients learn to adjust to their loved one's death and re-engage in their lives. A foundation of CGT is that CGD is traumatic. Accordingly, CGT also requires clients to engage in imaginary conversations with the deceased and to describe the loved one's death, which enables clients to habituate to the traumatic distress associated with thoughts of the deceased and the death (Shear, Frank, Houck, & Reynolds, 2005; Zhang et al., 2006). IPT also includes an emphasis on motivating participants to re-engage in their lives, but it differs in its focus on helping the client process both the positive and negative aspects of his or her relationship with the deceased.

The results indicated that CGT and IPT both reduced CGD reactions; however, the proportion of individuals who showed dramatic (i.e., 20-point reductions) on a measure of CGD was significantly higher among those treated with CGT. This contrast was greater among individuals who lost loved ones through violent death; 56% showed substantial reductions in grief symptoms, compared to only 13% with IPT. In contrast, more people who lost a child showed substantial reductions in CGD symptoms with IPT compared to CGT (Shear et al., 2005).

Another 16-session randomized controlled clinical trial for CGD compared IPT with a combination therapy of IPT and CGT, across Caucasian and African Americans. The results indicated that there was no difference in grief symptoms across ethnicity, and that the treatments were equally efficacious in reducing CGD symptoms. However, the researchers did not differentiate between violent and nonviolent death (Cruz et al., 2007). Although these results need to be replicated, they suggest that CGT may be a better treatment option for people who lost a loved one through a violent suicide than IPT (Sakinofsky, 2007). Research also is needed on which of these treatment options would be preferable for parents who lost a child through violent suicide, as well as for individuals who lost loved ones through nonviolent suicide. Although Caucasians and African Americans appeared to respond similarly to grief interventions (Cruz et al., 2007), this finding appears to be inconsistent with research cited earlier finding that African Americans were at an increased risk for developing prolonged grief disorder (Goldsmith et al., 2008). It may be that groups differing in risk for PGD will not necessarily differ in their response to grief interventions, but this issue should be investigated more fully.

Researchers also have examined the potential utility of cognitive-behavioral therapy (CBT) in the treatment of CGD. The primary goal of CBT in CGD would be to identify and change problematic core beliefs and behaviors to promote healthy emotional adjustment to the loss, but researchers have been unsure of how to develop a grief intervention that fulfills this aim until recently (Boelen, 2006). A 12-session comparison of CBT (i.e., six sessions of cognitive restructuring and six sessions of exposure therapy) and supportive counseling for CGD indicated that although CBT resulted in lower grief scores and psychological distress compared to supportive counseling, exposure therapy was more efficacious than cognitive restructuring

(Boelen, de Keijser, van den Hout, & van den Bout, 2007). Unfortunately, CBT may not be efficacious for CGD among survivors of suicide. Results from a randomized controlled trial comparing CBT to treatment as usual indicated that participants who received CBT did not exhibit a significant decrease in symptoms of CGD, depression, or suicidal thoughts, although it did lower dysfunctional grief symptoms and survivors' beliefs that they were blameworthy (de Groot et al., 2007).

Future Directions for Practice and Research

Additional research is needed to determine whether CBT treatments will be helpful in reducing reactions associated with complicated and traumatic grief (including prolonged grief disorder), as well as psychological distress among suicide survivors. Thus, a potentially fruitful line of inquiry will be to determine whether empirically supported treatments for posttraumatic stress, depression, and emotion regulation difficulties can be adjusted and successfully applied to alleviate the grief symptoms and psychological suffering associated with suicide bereavement. Examples of such potentially helpful treatment approaches include cognitive processing therapy, dialectical behavior therapy, acceptance and commitment therapy, and seeking safety (for individuals facing co-occurring CGD and substance abuse). An additional possible treatment intervention would be one that incorporates positive psychological approaches. This is an intriguing area of research, as positive psychology has not been sufficiently integrated into our treatment approaches for grief, despite research suggesting that the expression of positive emotions is prospectively associated with a mild grief course among bereaved individuals (Bonanno & Keltner, 1997). Future studies will need to clarify which positive psychological interventions are efficacious in alleviating grief and emotional distress, as well as whether these interventions can stand on their own or need to be integrated into other approaches.

More recent treatment research for CGD has incorporated technological innovations such as the Internet and virtual reality, which tend to use a cognitive-behavioral approach. Clinical research on Internet-based interventions appears to support their efficacy. Results from a 5-week intervention indicated that participants who received the treatment exhibited less mental distress, avoidance, and intrusive thoughts compared to participants on a wait list; these gains were maintained 3 months and

1.5 years later (Wagner, Knaevelsrud, & Maercker, 2006; Wagner & Maercker, 2007). Another study found that the intervention increased participants' posttraumatic growth but had no impact on optimism (Wagner, Knaevelsrud, & Maercker, 2007).

An example of such an approach is EMMA's World, an eight-session, CBT-based, virtual reality program that helps bereaved individuals process and convey both negative and positive emotions (Botella, Osma, Palacios, Guillen, & Banos, 2008). Clients receive psychoeducation about bereavement, learn breathing exercises to manage physical stress, and engage in cognitive restructuring and exposure. Early results suggest that virtual reality approaches such as EMMA's World may be efficacious in reducing general CGD symptoms. Although virtual reality approaches have yet to be applied to CGD for suicide bereavement, they hold great promise as a viable treatment option and constitute an exciting avenue of future clinical research.

As of this writing, the efficacy of psychotropic medication for symptoms of CGD, traumatic grief, and PGD is unknown, although some evidence suggests that a combined treatment of IPT and nortriptyline is efficacious in decreasing depression during bereavement (see Zhang et al., 2006). There have been studies on potentially efficacious group-based interventions for suicide survivors, but most of them did not involve a randomized, controlled clinical trial (e.g., Constantino & Bricker, 1996; Constantino, Sekula, & Rubenstein, 2001; Pfeffer, Jiang, Kakuma, Hwang, & Metsch, 2002).

Importantly, additional research is needed that compares suicide survivors of different ethnic and cultural groups across the aforementioned treatment modalities. However, these treatments may not match the grief experiences of individuals in various cultural and ethnic groups. For instance, research has indicated that suicide survivors in Hong Kong perceive suicide as a "bad death" and are more likely to rely on family members rather than treatment providers to discuss their feelings (Wong, Chan, & Beh, 2007). As a result, a large majority of suicide survivors noticed an increase in family intimacy and connectedness, rather than the decrease associated with grief reported in other studies (Maycock, 1998). Moreover, their experience of relief was different from that of Western suicide survivors, as they tended to feel relieved for the deceased, rather than for themselves (Wong et al., 2007). Unfortunately, it is currently unknown how grief interventions may need to be modified to maximize efficacy among different cultural and ethnic

groups. Thus, this is an area in urgent need of study, as suicide survivors whose grief experiences do not fit currently available treatments will lack help if needed.

All of the aforementioned approaches merit further, rigorous investigation. As this chapter illustrates, suicide bereavement presents survivors with unique challenges that heighten their susceptibility to adjustment difficulties following the loss, including increased risk for suicide. Given these challenges, it is critical to advance our understanding of the physical and psychosocial sequelae of suicide bereavement in order to understand how stigma, social support, and coping behavior influence adjustment across different ethnicities and cultures, and to determine the most efficacious, effective, and culturally sensitive types of outreach and treatment interventions. Hopefully, as our knowledge of these issues develops, we will be in a better position to alleviate suicide survivors' suffering; promote growth, mastery, and resilience; and enhance their quality of life.

References

Archer, J. (1999). *The nature of grief: The evolution and psychology of reactions to loss*. London, UK: Routledge.

Barrett, T. W., & Scott, T. B. (1989). Development of the grief experience questionnaire. *Suicide and Life-Threatening Behavior, 19*, 201–215.

Barrett, T. W., & Scott, T. B. (1990). Suicide bereavement and recovery patterns compared with nonsuicide bereavement patterns. *Suicide and Life-Threatening Behavior, 20*, 1–15.

Bartik, W., Maple, M., Edwards, H., & Kiernan, M. (2013). Adolescent survivors after suicide: Australian young people's bereavement narratives. *Crisis, 34*, 211–217.

Berman, A. L. (2011). Estimating the population of survivors of suicide: Seeking an evidence base. *Suicide and Life-Threatening Behavior, 41*, 110–116.

Birmes, P. J., Daubisse, L., & Brunet, A. (2008). Predictors of enduring PTSD after an industrial disaster. *Psychiatric Services, 59*, 116.

Boelen, P. A. (2006). Cognitive-behavioral therapy for complicated grief: Theoretical underpinnings and case descriptions. *Journal of Loss and Trauma, 11*, 1–30.

Boelen, P. A., de Kijser, J., van den Hout, M. A., & van den Bout, J. (2007). Treatment of complicated grief: A comparison between cognitive-behavioral therapy and supportive counseling. *Journal of Consulting and Clinical Psychology, 75*, 277–284.

Boelen, P. A., & Prigerson, H. G. (2007). The influence of symptoms of prolonged grief disorder, depression, and anxiety on quality of life among bereaved adults: A prospective study. *European Archives of Psychiatry in Clinical Neuroscience, 257*, 444–452.

Boelen, P. A., van den Hout, M. A., & van den Bout, J. (2008). The factor structure of posttraumatic stress disorder symptoms among bereaved individuals: A confirmatory factor analysis study. *Journal of Anxiety Disorders, 22*, 1377–1383.

Bonanno, G. A. (2006). Is complicated grief a valid construct? *Clinical Psychology: Science and Practice, 13*, 129–134.

Bonanno, G. A., & Field, N. P. (2001). Examining the delayed grief hypothesis across 5 years of bereavement. *American Behavioral Scientist, 44*, 798–816.

Bonanno, G. A., & Kaltman, S. (2001). The varieties of grief experience. *Clinical Psychology Review, 21*, 705–734.

Bonanno, G. A., & Keltner, D. (1997). Facial expressions of emotion and the course of conjugal bereavement. *Journal of Abnormal Psychology, 106*, 126–137.

Bonanno, G. A., Neria, Y., Mancini, A., Coifman, K. G., Litz, B., & Insel, B. (2007). Is there more to complicated grief than depression and posttraumatic stress disorder? A test of incremental validity. *Journal of Abnormal Psychology, 116*, 342–351.

Botella, C., Osma, J., Palacios, A. G., Guillen, V., & Banos, R. (2008). Treatment of complicated grief using virtual reality: A case report. *Death Studies, 32*, 674–692.

Brent, D. A., Kerr, M. M., Goldstein, C., Bozigar, J., Wartella, M., & Allan, M. J. (1989). An outbreak of suicide and suicidal behavior in a high school. *Journal of the American Academy of Child and Adolescent Psychiatry, 35*, 646–653.

Brent, D. A., Moritz, G., Bridge, J., Perper, J., & Cannobio, R. (1996). The impact of adolescent suicide on siblings and parents: A longitudinal follow-up. *Suicide and Life-Threatening Behavior, 26*, 253–259.

Bridge, J. A. (2002). Major depressive disorder among youth exposed to a friend's suicide. *Dissertation Abstracts International, 62*(9-B), 3966.

Campbell, F. R. (1997). Changing the legacy of suicide. *Suicide and Life-Threatening Behavior, 27*, 329–338.

Cerel, J., & Campbell, F. R. (2008). Suicide survivors seeking mental health services: A preliminary examination of the role of an active postvention model. *Suicide and Life-Threatening Behavior, 38*, 30–34.

Cerel, J., Fristad, M. A., Weller, E. B., & Weller, R. A. (2000). Suicide bereaved children and adolescents: II. Parental and family functioning. *Journal of the American Academy of Child Psychiatry, 39*, 437–444.

Connor, T. J. (2008). Don't stress out your immune system—just relax. *Brain, Behavior, and Immunity, 22*, 1128–1129.

Constantino, R. E., & Bricker, P. L. (1996). Nursing postvention for spousal survivors of suicide. *Issues in Mental Health Nursing, 17*, 131–152.

Constantino, R. E., Sekula, L. K., Lebish, J., & Buehner, E. (2002). Depression and behavioral manifestations of depression in female survivors of the suicide of their significant other and female survivors of abuse. *Journal of the American Psychiatric Nurses Association, 8*, 27–32.

Constantino, R. E., Sekula, L. K., & Rubinstein, E. N. (2001). Group intervention for widowed survivors of suicide. *Suicide and Life-Threatening Behavior, 31*, 428–441.

Cruz, M., Scott, J., Houck, P., Reynolds, C. F., III, Frank, E., & Shear, M. K. (2007). Clinical presentation and treatment outcome of African Americans with complicated grief. *Psychiatric Services, 58*, 7000–702.

Cvinar, J. G. (2005). Do suicide survivors suffer social stigma: A review of the literature. *Perspectives in Psychiatric Care, 41*, 14–21.

de Groot, M. H., de Keijser, J., & Neeleman, J. (2006). Grief shortly after suicide and natural death: A comparative study among spouses and first-degree relatives. *Suicide and Life-Threatening Behavior, 36*, 418–431.

de Groot, M., de Keijser, J., Neeleman, H., Kerkhof, A., Nolen, W., & Burger, H. (2007). Cognitive behavior therapy to prevent complicated grief among relatives and spouses bereaved by suicide: Cluster randomized controlled trial. *British Medical Journal, 334*, 994.

Demi, A. S., & Howell, C. (1991). Hiding and healing: Resolving the suicide of a parent or sibling. *Archives of Psychiatric Nursing, 5*, 350–356.

DeWall, C. N., & Baumeister, R. F. (2006). Alone but feeling no pain: Effects of social exclusion on physical pain tolerance and pain threshold, affective forecasting, and interpersonal empathy. *Journal of Personality and Social Psychology, 91*, 1–15.

Dyregrov, K., Nordanger, D., & Dyregrov, A. (2003). Predictors of psychosocial distress after suicide, SIDS, and accidents. *Death Studies, 27*, 143–165.

Ellenbogen, S., & Gratton, F. (2001). Do they suffer more? Reflections on research comparing suicide survivors to other survivors. *Suicide and Life-Threatening Behavior, 31*, 83–90.

Ginzburg, K., Solomon, Z., & Bleich, A. (2002). Repressive coping style, acute stress disorder, and posttraumatic stress disorder after myocardial infarction. *Psychosomatic Medicine, 64*, 748–757.

Glass, R. M. (2005). Is grief a disease? Sometimes. *Journal of the American Medical Association, 293*, 2658–2660.

Goldsmith, B., Morrison, R. S., Vanderwerker, L. C., & Prigerson, H. G. (2008). Elevated rates of prolonged grief disorder in African Americans. *Death Studies, 32*, 352–365.

Gould, M. S., Shaffer, D., & Kleinman, M. (1988). The impact of suicide in television movies: Replication and commentary. *Suicide and Life-Threatening Behavior, 18*, 90–99.

Grad, O. T., & Zavasnik, A. (1999). Phenomenology of bereavement process after suicide, traffic accident, and terminal illness (in spouses). *Archives of Suicide Research, 5*, 157–172.

Greenwald, A. G., McGhee, D. E., & Schwartz, J. K. L. (1998). Measuring individual differences in implicit cognition: The implicit association test. *Journal of Personality and Social Psychology, 74*, 1464–1480.

Harwood, D., Hawton, K., Hope, T., & Jacoby, R. (2002). The grief experiences and needs of bereaved relatives and friends of older people dying through suicide: A descriptive and case-control study. *Journal of Affective Disorders, 72*, 185–194.

Hawton, K., & Simkin, S. (2003). Helping people bereaved by suicide. *British Medical Journal, 327*, 177–178.

Hendin, H., Lipschitz, A., Maltsberger, J. T., Haas, A. P., & Wynecoop, S. (2000). Therapists' reactions to patients' suicides. *American Journal of Psychiatry, 157*, 2022–2027.

Hensley, L., & Varela, R. E. (2008). PTSD symptoms and somatic complaints following Hurricane Katrina: The roles of trait anxiety and anxiety sensitivity. *Journal of Clinical Child and Adolescent Psychology, 37*, 542–552.

Holmes, T. H. & Rahe, R. H. (1967). The social adjustment rating scale. *Journal of Psychosomatic Research, 11*, 213–218.

Iversen, A. C., Fear, N. T., Ehlers, A., Hughes, J. H., Hull, L., Earnshaw, M., …Hotopf, M. (2008). Risk factor for post-traumatic stress disorder among UK armed forces personnel. *Psychological Medicine, 38*, 511–522.

Janoff-Bulman, R. (1992). *Shattered assumptions*. New York, NY: Free Press.

Jordan, J. R. (2001). Is suicide bereavement different? A reassessment of the literature. *Suicide and Life Threatening Behavior, 31*, 91–102.

Kaltman, S., & Bonanno, G. A. (2003). Trauma and bereavement: Examining the impact of sudden and violent deaths. *Journal of Anxiety Disorders, 17,* 131–147.

Lichtenthal, W. G., Cruess, D. G., & Prigerson, H. G. (2004). A case for establishing complicated grief as a distinct mental disorder in DSM-V. *Clinical Psychology Review, 24,* 637–662.

Maycock, K. E. B. (1998). *A study of the impact of suicide on grief and intimacy.* Retrieved from ProQuest Information and Learning. (AAM9810468).

McDowell, C. P., Rothberg, J. M., & Koshes, R. J. (1994). Witnessed suicides. *Suicide and Life-Threatening Behavior, 24,* 213–223.

McIntosh, J. L. (1993). Control group studies of suicide survivors: A review and critique. *Suicide and Life-Threatening Behavior, 23,* 146–161.

McIntosh, J. L., & Kelly, L. D. (1992). Survivors' reactions: Suicide vs. other causes. *Crisis, 13,* 82–93.

McMenamy, J. M., Jordan, J. R., & Mitchell, A. M. (2008). What do suicide survivors tell us they need? Results of a pilot study. *Suicide and Life-Threatening Behavior, 38,* 375–389.

McNally, R. J. (2003). *Remembering trauma.* Cambridge, MA: Belknap Press of Harvard University Press.

Melhem, N. M., Day, N., Shear, M. K., Day, R., Reynolds, C. F., III, & Brent, D. (2004). Predictors of complicated grief among adolescents exposed to a peer's suicide. *Journal of Loss and Trauma, 9,* 21–34.

Miller, D. T., & Porter, C. A. (1983). Self-blame in victims of violence. *Journal of Social Issues, 39,* 139–152.

Mitchell, A. M., Kim, Y., Prigerson, H. G., & Mortimer, M. K. (2005). Complicated grief and suicidal ideation in adult survivors of suicide. *Suicide and Life-Threatening Behavior, 35,* 498–506.

Mitchell, A. M., Kim, Y., Prigerson, H. G., & Mortimer-Stephens, M. (2004). Complicated grief in survivors of suicide. *Crisis, 25,* 12–18.

Murphy, S. A., Johnson, L. C., Chung, I., & Beaton, R. D. (2003a). The prevalence of PTSD following the violent death of a child and predictors of change 5 years later. *Journal of Traumatic Stress, 16,* 17–25.

Murphy, S. A., Johnson, L. C., Wu, L., Fan, J. J., & Lohan, J. (2003b). Bereaved parents' outcomes 4 to 60 months after their children's death by accident, suicide, or homicide: A comparative study demonstrating differences. *Death Studies, 27,* 39–61.

Neimeyer, R. A. (2000). Searching for the meaning of meaning: Grief therapy and the process of reconstruction. *Death Studies, 24,* 541–558.

Ozer, E. J., Best, S. R., Lipsey, T. L., & Weiss, D. S. (2008). Predictors of posttraumatic stress disorder and symptoms in adults: A meta-analysis. *Psychological Trauma: Theory, Research, Practice, and Policy, 5,* 3–36.

Parker, H. A. (2004, May 11). *Repressive coping in people who have lost loved ones to suicide.* Dissertation defense, Harvard University, Cambridge, MA.

Parker, H. A., & McNally, R. J. (2006, April). *Blame and coping in people who have lost loved ones to suicide.* Poster session presented at the Annual Meeting of the American Association of Suicidology, Bloomfield, CO.

Parker, H. A., & McNally, R. J. (2008). Repressive coping, emotional adjustment, and cognition in people who have lost loved ones to suicide. *Suicide and Life-Threatening Behavior, 38,* 676–687.

Pfeffer, C. R., Jiang, H., Kakuma, T., Hwang, J., & Metsch, M. (2002). Group intervention for children bereaved by the suicide of a relative. *Journal of the American Academy of Child and Adolescent Psychiatry, 41,* 505–513.

Pfeffer, C. R., Martins, P., Mann, J., Sunkenberg, M., Ice, A., Damore, J. P., …Jiang, H. (1997). Child survivors of suicide: Psychosocial characteristics. *Journal of the American Academy of Child and Adolescent Psychiatry, 36,* 65–74.

Reed, M. D. (1998). Predicting grief symptomatology among the suddenly bereaved. *Suicide and Life-Threatening Behavior, 28,* 285–301.

Reed, M. D., & Greenwald, J. Y. (1991). Survivor-victim status, attachment, and sudden death bereavement. *Suicide and Life-Threatening Behavior, 21,* 385–401.

Regehr, C., & Sussman, T. (2004). Intersections between grief and trauma: Toward an empirically based model for treating traumatic grief. *Brief Treatment and Crisis Intervention, 4,* 289–309.

Sakinofsky, I. (2007). The aftermath of suicide: Managing survivors' bereavement. *Canadian Journal of Psychiatry, 52,* 129–136.

Seguin, M., Lesage, A., & Kiely, M. C. (1995). Parental bereavement after suicide and accident: A comparative study. *Suicide and Life-Threatening Behavior, 25,* 489–498.

Sethi, S., & Bhargava, S. C. (2003). Child and adolescent survivors of suicide. *Crisis, 24,* 4–6.

Shear, K., Frank, E., Houck, P., & Reynolds, C. F. (2005). Treatment of complicated grief: A randomized controlled trial. *Journal of the American Medical Association, 293,* 2601–2608.

Shear, K., Monk, T., Houck, P., Melhem, N., Frank, E., Reynolds, C., & Sillowash, R. (2007). An attachment-based model of complicated grief including the role of avoidance. *European Archives of Psychiatry in Clinical Neuroscience, 257,* 453–461.

Shneidman, E. S. (1973). *On the nature of suicide.* San Francisco, CA: Jossey-Bass.

Stroebe, M., Boelen, P. A., van den Hout, M., Stroebe, W., Salemink, E., & van den Bout, J. (2007). Ruminative coping as avoidance: A reinterpretation of its function in adjustment to bereavement. *European Archives of Psychiatry in Clinical Neuroscience, 257,* 462–472.

Stroebe, W., & Stroebe, M. (1987). *Bereavement and health: The psychological and physical consequences of partner loss.* Cambridge, MA: Cambridge University Press.

Sveen, C., & Walby, F. A. (2007). Suicide survivors' mental health and grief reactions: A systematic review of controlled studies. *Suicide and Life Threatening Behavior, 38,* 13–29.

Thornton, G., Whittemore, K. D., & Robertson, D. U. (1989). Evaluation of people bereaved by suicide. *Death Studies, 13,* 119–126.

Tyler, M. G. (1990). *Social perceptions of survivor families: A study of community reaction toward survivors of suicidal, homicidal, and natural deaths.* Retrieved from ProQuest Information and Learning. (1990-55678-001).

van der Velden, P. G., Kleber, R. J., & Koenen, K. C. (2008). Smoking predicts posttraumatic stress symptoms among rescue workers: A prospective study of ambulance personnel involved in the Enschede fireworks disaster. *Drug and Alcohol Dependence, 94,* 267–271.

van der Velden, P. G., & Wittman, L. (2008). The independent predictive value of peritraumatic dissociation for PTSD symptomatology after type I trauma: A systematic review of prospective studies. *Clinical Psychology Review, 28,* 1009–1020.

Vanderwerker, L. C., & Prigerson, H. G. (2004). Social support and technological connectedness as protective factors in bereavement. *Journal of Loss and Trauma, 9,* 45–57.

Wagner, B., Knaevelsrud, C., & Maercker, A. (2006). Internet-based cognitive-behavioral therapy for complicated grief: A randomized controlled trial. *Death Studies, 30,* 429–453.

Wagner, B., Knaevelsrud, C., & Maercker, A. (2007). Post-traumatic growth and optimism as outcomes of an internet-based intervention for complicated grief. *Cognitive Behavior Therapy, 36,* 156–161.

Wagner, B., & Maercker, A. (2007). A 1.5 year follow-up of an internet-based intervention for complicated grief. *Journal of Traumatic Stress, 20,* 625–629.

Walcott, A. M. (1993). *Social support of the grieving process for survivors of suicide.* Retrieved from ProQuest Information and Learning. (1994-72160-001).

Watkins, R. L., & Gutierrez, P. M. (2003). The relationship between exposure to adolescent suicide and subsequent suicide risk. *Suicide and Life-Threatening Behavior, 33,* 21–32.

Weinberger, D. A. (1990). The construct validity of the repressive coping style. In J. L. Singer (Ed.), *Repression and dissociation* (pp. 337–386). Chicago, IL: University of Chicago Press.

Willoughby, S. G., Hailey, B. J., Mulkana, S., & Rowe, J. (2002). The effect of laboratory-induced depressed mood state on responses to pain. *Behavioral Medicine, 28,* 23–31.

Wong, P. W. C., Chan, W. S. C., & Beh, P. S. L. (2007). What can we do to help and understand survivors of suicide in Hong Kong? *Crisis, 28,* 183–189.

Wright, T. R. (1999). *The impact of suicide during childhood on the mourning process and psychosocial functioning of child and sibling survivors.* Retrieved from ProQuest Information and Learning. (AAM9911076).

Zhang, B., El-Jawahri, A., & Prigerson, H. G. (2006). Update on bereavement research: Evidence-based guidelines for the diagnosis and treatment of complicated bereavement. *Journal of Palliative Medicine, 9,* 1188–1203.

Zisook, S., Chentsova-Dutton, Y., & Shucter, S. R. (1998). PTSD following bereavement. *Annals of Clinical Psychiatry, 10,* 157–163.

Conclusion to the Handbook

Matthew K. Nock

Abstract

This conclusion provides some closing thoughts on the impressive new advances presented in the different chapters of this volume. However, it also presents a reminder that there remains to be a great deal that we do not understand about suicide and self-injury, and as a result there are major limitations in our ability to predict and prevent these challenging problems.

Key Words: suicide, self-injury, self-harm

Self-injurious behaviors have perplexed philosophers, scientists, clinicians, and the general population for thousands of years. Fortunately, recent research has brought significant advances in our understanding of the occurrence, etiology, assessment, and treatment of suicidal and nonsuicidal self-injury. This volume summarized such advances, drawing from a wide array of theoretical perspectives and scientific approaches.

Each chapter in this book reported on the most exciting recent advances in the field and proposed important directions for future work in each area. The authors have done an amazing job making these points, and so I will not reiterate them here. Instead, I want to conclude this handbook by thanking the authors for writing such thoughtful and thorough chapters; thanking all of the researchers and clinicians who produced the work summarized in this

volume; and thanking you, the reader, for your interest in this topic and your efforts toward helping to solve some of the great challenges that exist in this area of study.

Although this book highlights the great strides that have been made in understanding suicidal and nonsuicidal self-injury, it is important to keep in mind that we still have a very long way to go. There are many things about these behaviors that we do not yet understand. We lack an accurate means of predicting these behaviors and an effective method of preventing them. These facts are humbling, but they also are motivating. Although there is a long road ahead, the continued, persistent efforts of scientists, clinicians, educators, family members, and others will no doubt continue to improve our understanding of self-injurious behaviors and ultimately lead to the prevention of these devastating problems.

INDEX

Page numbers followed by *b*, *f*, or *t* indicate boxes, figures, or tables, respectively.

CPSIA information can be obtained
at www.ICGtesting.com
Printed in the USA
BVHW091058181218
535491BV00004B/16/P